GUNTHER SCHULLER

GUNTHER SCHULLER

A LIFE IN PURSUIT OF MUSIC AND BEAUTY

WITH AN INTRODUCTION BY JOAN SHELLEY RUBIN

GUNTHER SCHULLER

 UNIVERSITY OF ROCHESTER PRESS

The University of Rochester Press gratefully acknowledges the National Endowment for the Arts; the Howard Hanson Institute for American Music at the Eastman School of Music, University of Rochester; and David Scudder for their generous support of this publication.

First published 2011

University of Rochester Press
668 Mt. Hope Avenue, Rochester, NY 14620, USA
www.urpress.com
and Boydell & Brewer Limited
PO Box 9, Woodbridge, Suffolk IP12 3DF, UK
www.boydellandbrewer.com

ISBN-13: 978-1-58046-342-3

This work is a memoir. The experiences and conversations recounted here are the result of the author's recollection and are rendered as a subjective accounting of events that occurred in his life. His perceptions and opinions are entirely his own and do not represent those of the publisher or sponsors.

Library of Congress Cataloging-in-Publication Data

Schuller, Gunther.
   Gunther Schuller : a life in pursuit of music and beauty / Gunther Schuller.
     p. cm.
   Includes bibliographical references and index.
   ISBN 978-1-58046-342-3 (hardcover : alk. paper) 1. Schuller, Gunther. 2. Composers—United States—Biography. I. Title.
   ML410.S385A3   2011
   780.92—dc23
   [B]

2011028317

A catalogue record for this title is available from the British Library.

This publication is printed on acid-free paper.
Printed in the United States of America

In memory of my beloved Marjorie

CONTENTS

Photographs follow p. 256.

INTRODUCTION

The Musician as Mediator

NEAR THE BEGINNING of his landmark study *Early Jazz* (1968), Gunther Schuller describes a chord pattern called "fours" that jazz musicians sometimes introduce into the conventional thirty-two bar song form. After noting that the pattern can give rise to intriguing sounds when the improvisers play different parts of the whole structure as the piece progresses, he remarks, "The 'bridge' produces especially interesting combinations." It is tempting to apply Schuller's characterization of a musical device to the man himself. In the course of the career that this rich memoir documents, Schuller bridged Europe and the United States, whites and African-Americans, classical and popular musical traditions, professionals and the general public; his account of his emotional life reveals a simultaneous attraction to the physical and the spiritual, the natural environment and the urban scene. With particular reference to his efforts as a composer and critic, the bridges amount to what cultural historians characterize as acts of mediation—negotiations between artistic production and audiences that, in Schuller's hands, have resulted in "especially interesting combinations."

Among the dualities marking his personal life, the most obvious, perhaps, is Schuller's combination of European heritage and American identity. Born in 1925 in New York City to German immigrants and schooled abroad in the early 1930s, Schuller nevertheless found in American places like the Adirondacks and New York City sources of beauty, wonder, and inspiration. His affirmation of American democracy, moreover, has always been more than an ideological position; it has been integral to his conduct as a person. His capacity to link the Old and New Worlds has made him a true cosmopolitan, able to sustain a wealth of international friendships and an appreciation for the dignity of every individual.

Schuller's sensibility likewise reveals a second, more subtle conjunction: between spiritual transcendence and intense physicality. Recalling a journey to one of his favorite American locales, Lake Placid, he writes, "The trip became even more exhilarating on the final leg," as the train passed through forests "bathed in the bright early morning sunlight." The "pure clean mountain air, the intoxicating pine fragrance" (as well as the lack of sleep!) heightened his receptivity to feelings that, he avers, would otherwise have escaped him. There are Emersonian overtones in that passage: it evokes the author of *Nature* "standing on the bare ground," his "head bathed by the blithe air," who touches a higher plane. Yet as a musician and an athlete, Schuller also delighted in physical energy and sensuality. He most fully conveys his melding of the spiritual and the physical in a romantic portrayal of his beloved wife Margie before and after their marriage in 1948. Against the constraints of provincial propriety (Marjorie Black was from Fargo, North Dakota), the values of self-expression (in sex as well as art) ultimately won out, producing an enduring union of heart and mind, body and soul.

To consider Gunther Schuller's musical tastes and activities is to discover "especially interesting combinations" in abundance. Within the realm of classical music, Schuller has spanned the two schools that dominated composition during the first half of the twentieth century: neoclassicism and twelve-tone experimentation. As a composer he gravitated to the twelve-tone method (modifying Schoenberg's rules to suit his own preferences).

Yet he earned accolades as "an important up-and-coming talent" from the tonal neoclassicists—such figures as Aaron Copland, William Schuman, and Roy Harris—who made up
the American musical "establishment" in the postwar period. Schuller himself has best delin-
eated his position vis à vis the tonal and atonal camps: he occupies a middle ground between
the "professional avant-gardists" who have regarded him as too tethered to tradition and the
audiences and critics who have found him "too modern." Both, Schuller insists, are "misjudgments," but he acknowledges a constant "pull" between "the most valuable of the past
and the most substantial and prescient of the present." The result has been "a harmonious
equilibrium" that bespeaks his creativity and integrity. Meanwhile, as a performer and a listener, Schuller has embraced the entire history of Western music, with a special fondness for
the canonical works of the eighteenth and nineteenth centuries.

But the most salient features of Schuller's bridging activities in the field of music are the
multiple connections he forged between the classical repertory and jazz. These connections
took several forms. First, his characteristic open-mindedness led him to explore jazz on a personal level even though he was classically trained. During his years in Cincinnati and, later, in
New York City, as well as on tour with the Metropolitan Opera Orchestra, he reveled in the
jazz scene, especially as swing gave way to bebop. Schuller's recovery of underrated musical
groups who would ultimately enrich the lives of their audiences and contribute to the development of jazz styles, but who happened—Schuller says in some cases inexplicably—not to make
it big, will be of particular interest to historians.

Schuller's reminiscences about his heady participation in the jazz scene reprise the theme
of his Americanness, jazz being, as he writes, "our country's one and only homegrown quintessentially American music." They also yield insight into the way in which Schuller's career
has yoked together African-American culture and, at the time, the distinctly separate space
of white Americans. Schuller's determination, as a historian and critic, to affirm the African-
American origins of jazz rhythms underpins his writings such as *Early Jazz*. But his physical
presence as a white person in largely black clubs—as well as the warmth he experienced and
the relationships he formed with African-Americans—is evident in the pages of this memoir.
Although whites and blacks alike had joined to form a huge consumer demand for jazz by the
late 1940s, this was still the era of segregated public accommodations for bands on tour. Schuller, true to his democratic ideals, would have none of it. He notes with pride that, thanks to his
participation in the last session of what became Miles Davis's *Birth of the Cool*, Davis, who was
often meeting with Schuller, may have been the first black musician to set foot in the locker
room of the Metropolitan Opera House.

In addition, Schuller acted as a kind of informal impresario for his African-American colleagues, while benefiting in return from the entrée they provided him into jazz's inner circle.
The most important of these collaborations was with John Lewis, the eventual founder of the
Modern Jazz Quartet, whom Schuller met in 1948. Lewis's classical background and Schuller's knowledge of evolving jazz modes informed a deep friendship based on mutual respect
and shared intellectual excitement. Schuller introduced Lewis to white instrumentalists in the
New York Philharmonic, some of whom would subsequently perform Lewis's music; Lewis
enabled Schuller to meet such luminaries as Ben Webster, Lester Young, Dizzy Gillespie, and
J. J. Johnson.

The personal (and racial) dimension of Schuller's negotiation between classical music and
jazz coexisted, moreover, with Schuller's efforts as a composer to fuse the two musical styles.
In the mid-1940s, he undertook to enlarge the symphony orchestra "pops" repertory—centered at that time around Gershwin songs and "light classics"—by arranging jazz numbers for
symphonic players. The Duke Ellington and Count Basie tunes he adapted for the Cincinnati Orchestra made headlines for bringing together musical forms that some concert-goers

thought "absolutely antithetical." Schuller also arranged Lewis's compositions for ensembles that mixed jazz and classical musicians.

Schuller's endeavor to bridge, compositionally, classical music and jazz culminated in the 1950s with the emergence of a new genre that Schuller in 1957 dubbed the "Third Stream." Together with Lewis, whose Modern Jazz Quartet became identified with the Third Stream movement, Schuller promoted a sound that merged tonality and atonality, composition and improvisation, string instruments with the winds and brass conventionally associated with jazz ensembles. Lewis's insistence on performing in formal dress and in concert halls (as opposed to clubs and bars) was part of the Third Stream aura; so was his commitment to what Schuller calls "a highly refined artistic expression" consisting of "lucidity," proportion, and moderation. Schuller himself wrote numerous examples of Third Stream music in these years, including *Transformation*, performed at the Brandeis University Creative Arts Festival that Schuller organized in 1957 to showcase music balancing classical and jazz elements. The piece, he observes, combined twelve-tone harmonic structures with improvisatory sections. Schuller continued to champion Third Stream composition in the later phase of his career, setting up a Third Stream Department (and a degree program in jazz studies) after he assumed the presidency of the New England Conservatory of Music in 1967.

In those activities as entrepreneur and composer, Schuller has exemplified the figure of the cultural mediator, setting the terms on which audiences encounter forms of artistic expression. Mediators influence the meanings that cultural artifacts of all sorts accrue as they pass from authors, artists, or composers to readers, viewers, and listeners. Historians of American print culture have been especially enterprising in tracing both readily visible and less obvious forms of mediation: for example, the role of seventeenth-century printers and booksellers in casting Puritan ministers as authors within a literary marketplace; the effect of copyright restrictions on the assembling of anthologies; the interventions of editors, publishers, book club judges, advertisers, prize committees, librarians, and teachers in getting certain books—understood in certain ways—into the hands of readers. Schuller has performed an analogous function in the realm of music.

To go further, acts of mediation often serve (at least temporarily) to establish the position of an artist or a particular work in the scheme that scholars have called cultural hierarchy. Mediators help to rank a book or a piece of music as high, middlebrow, or popular culture; they make judgments, implicitly or explicitly, about whether, within those categories, works are good or bad. They aid in deciding what constitutes art and what is "mere" entertainment, what has the prospect of surviving over time and what is likely to be ephemeral. Debates about the so-called canon of Western literature have made clear the provisional nature of such hierarchical arrangements and exposed the biases that inflect them. We now understand that Matthew Arnold's definition of culture as "the best that has been thought and said in the world" is all well and good, but that definitions of "the best" have been different at different historical moments, and that critics and other mediators have had a hand in shifting standards—for instance, championing modernism over sentimentality, making Shakespeare widely accessible through cheap print, or promoting the inclusion of women as canonical authors. These interventions have affected ordinary people's notions of the artistic and the classical no less than the syllabi or discographies of academics.

Most accounts of cultural mediators in twentieth-century America have focused on figures who sought to bring high culture to a wide public, and whose projects can therefore be seen as moving in a downward direction from a coterie audience to a middlebrow one. Henry Seidel Canby, the chair of the Book-of-the-Month-Club Board of Judges, is a case in point: Canby (whose son, the classical music critic and radio commentator Edward Tatnall Canby, appears in Schuller's memoir) wanted to educate the "average intelligent reader" about the attributes of good books and to help him or her take the measure of new fiction in the context of literary traditions. Some of the ventures Schuller mentions in this memoir resemble that version of mediation. In 1957, he created a weekly radio program for the New York City station WBAI called "The Scope of Jazz." Together with co-host Nat Hentoff, as well as distinguished guests, Schuller provided "explanatory and critical commentary" on the entire history of the genre. Two years later, he started a classical radio show, "Contemporary Music in Evolution," on which he strove to identify the signal features of a given piece and to explore the steps by which modern atonality developed from nineteenth-century tonal works. The responses from listeners that Schuller quotes with justifiable pride confirm the way in which the program operated to demystify and make accessible for its audience music that might otherwise have remained locked up in the tower, so to speak, of high culture. "I am so grateful to you," people told him, "because you opened my mind and ears," or "you really helped me to understand this modern music, and that it isn't just a bunch of meaningless noises."

Yet especially for cultural historians one of the great contributions of Schuller's autobiography is that it provides an example of mediations working in the other direction: that is, toward the elevation of popular entertainment into high art. The word "serious" is central to Schuller's critical vocabulary. Jazz, he is careful to argue, grew—Schuller might say "progressed"— over the course of the twentieth century from a genre usually dismissed as lowbrow to a form that equaled classical music in seriousness. (It is thus an excellent reminder of the fluidity of cultural hierarchy.) In particular, Schuller notes the movement in the late 1940s away from big bands toward chamber ensembles, and the corresponding shift from jazz as dance and vocal music to instrumental compositions meant to be "enjoyed and valued" as creative works.

Musicologists are still identifying the multiple sources of that transformation, but institutions that mediated the reception of performances and recordings are at the heart of the story—and, thus, so is Schuller. The appearance of the Modern Jazz Quartet on a concert stage was inextricably bound to its undanceable, intellectual sound, but Schuller's interventions in promoting John Lewis as an artist helped to advance the idea that jazz belonged in Carnegie Hall. Similarly, Schuller's involvement as associate editor of the *Jazz Review* meant that he had a hand in conferring on jazz the same high culture cachet that the "little magazine" bestowed on modernist poetry in the 1910s, and that periodicals such as the *Paris Review* perpetuated in the postwar period. Schuller's installation of academic jazz studies at the New England Conservatory likewise furthered the revaluation of the genre from a people's music (one pejoratively associated with African-Americans, at that) to serious art. Even the Third Stream concept, although intended to be neither jazz nor classical but, rather, an amalgam of both, can be seen as raising the status of jazz within the cultural hierarchy by bringing it into proximity with art music.

Although beyond the chronological range of this memoir, Schuller's introduction to *Early Jazz* provides perhaps the best summary of his double role as a mediator. On the one hand, he observes that, in writing the book, he imagined his reader as a "friend" interested in such questions as "What makes jazz work?" and "Why do so many people find jazz exciting?" On the other hand, that effort to make the music comprehensible to a non-musician is less important to Schuller's purpose than his desire to address musicians, especially those with classical training; the volume is in no sense a popularization. His objective, he declares, is to take jazz "seriously" rather than to approach it as an "amateur" or to lapse into the "enthusiasm" of previous writers on the subject. In consequence, the book requires readers to decipher musical notation and to grapple with the author's sophisticated analyses of jazz pieces as texts—and as art.

To speak about Schuller as a mediator, a builder of bridges, or—to use his own word—an exemplar of "equilibrium"—is not at all to suggest that his reminiscences are bereft of strong opinions. On the contrary, the pages that follow contain Schuller's pithy judgments about a host of performers, composers, and conductors. He depicts the behavior of Arturo Toscanini, Leopold Stokowski, and Fritz Reiner as ranging from tyrannical to sadistic, the opera singer Risë Stevens as given to vocal exaggeration. By the same token, in chapter 8 alone, Schuller offers unstinting praise for such stars of the Metropolitan Opera's 1948–49 season as Lauritz Melchior and Ljuba Welitsch, lauds the talents of the Hungarian-born cellist Janos Starker, and voices his admiration for the unjustly forgotten musicians of the NBC Symphony. Taken together, Schuller's assessments are an invaluable critical guide to the larger part of the American musical universe in the 1940s and 1950s. But they are also notable for revealing Schuller's generosity of spirit. For example, Schuller readily acknowledges that, for all his abuse of the orchestra, Reiner exerted a "mesmerizing power" that elicited the musicians' best sound. As he asserts in the preface to this book, Schuller also firmly believes that American life is poorer for the disappearance of the many cultural opportunities of which he and Margie availed themselves in their New York days. As a result, he has taken pains to incorporate into his reminiscences a snapshot of the city's "artistic Golden Age." Some readers may disagree that New York in 2011 is tarnished in comparison to sixty or seventy years ago, but they will have to deal with Schuller's instructive documentation of the earlier period in order to win that argument.

A Life in Pursuit of Music and Beauty records as well the joys and tribulations of the professional musician: the challenges of conducting, the uncertainties of dependence on freelance gigs for income, the hardships and adventures of life on the road, the various strategies instrumentalists employ to adjust pitches, the struggles of singers as their voices wane. As part of the story of a working musician, Schuller describes his remarkable ability to transcribe complex works from recordings. He also enunciates his conviction that, to survive, a piece of music requires preservation by means of paper, vinyl, or, now, digitized format—all of which he has labored to produce. And he confesses his devotion to his "first love," composing. The passages in *A Life in Pursuit of Music and Beauty* that deal with those matters testify, over and over, to Schuller's realization of the goal to which he dedicated himself on his exhilarating trip to the Adirondacks in 1945: his formative decision to make music "not just a profession or a business" but, rather, "a way of life."

In the broadest terms, Schuller's career assists us in constructing a dynamic model of how a culture works: an appropriate conclusion, given Schuller's own dynamic personality. But perhaps it is even more appropriate to end not by revisiting the lofty rhetoric of mediation and hierarchy but by returning to the ground of Schuller's own discipline: that is, to his music itself. In 1959, thanks to an agreement worked out by John Lewis, Atlantic Records recorded Schuller's *Conversations* for two quartets: one string ensemble and one jazz group (in this instance, the Modern Jazz Quartet, for which Schuller had written the piece). It was the first of Schuller's Third Stream compositions to be recorded. According to Schuller, "*Conversations* is all about how two separate worlds of music, initially opposed to each other, gradually find various ways of coming together, of conversing with each other and learning from each other." One might say that *Conversations*, released at the point when Schuller concludes this first volume of his memoirs, captures in music the themes not just of "Third Stream" but of his entire professional and personal history. We are fortunate that *Gunther Schuller: A Life in Pursuit of Music and Beauty* extends the conversation to include a new audience of readers, who will find that Schuller's chronicle of "especially interesting combinations" has much to teach them about music, American culture, and the achievements of a life shaped by extraordinary talent, unusual dedication, and unbridled passion.

Joan Shelley Rubin
University of Rochester

PREFACE

I HAD MANY GOALS in writing this autobiography. Obviously, one was to document the incredibly fortunate, exciting life in music (and its sister arts) that I have been privileged to live thus far. And although much of the narrative is inevitably about my life and career, it is also very much a documentation of the artistic, cultural, social, and political environment in which I have labored these past three-quarters of a century, both in America and Europe. I have also intended this book to be informative and educative, not only as a reminder of so much of the past that is now unremembered and ignored, but also in regard to the multiple areas of music to which I have devoted my life. I can't expect even the most musically oriented reader to be conversant with the six or seven musical careers I have pursued simultaneously for most of my life. I felt a need to both reminisce and explain.

The reality is that most people know me only in one or at most two branches of music, and even then probably only superficially. Many people know me only as a jazz historian or in my work as a composer and performer in jazz a half century ago, in collaboration with so many legendary jazz musicians, from Dizzy Gillespie, Miles Davis, and John Lewis, to Ornette Coleman and Eric Dolphy, Charles Mingus and Gil Evans, and dozens of other great figures in that field. Many others know nothing about my life in jazz and know me only as a classical composer of advanced contemporary music—either admiringly or disapprovingly. Still others know me only as a conductor and as a writer on conducting as an interpretive, re-creative performance art.

Some remember me as a horn player, one who had the great fortune to work with hundreds of the most famous conductors of the past, from Toscanini and Reiner and Monteux to Stokowski and Mitropoulos. A few know me primarily as an educator, as president of the New England Conservatory (for ten years) and as artistic director of the Boston Symphony's Tanglewood Music Center (twenty-two years). Some know me only as the person who brought back ragtime and traveled the world with the New England Ragtime Ensemble. Finally, still others know me—and want to know me only—as "Mr. Third Stream," the person who fostered the creative fusion of jazz and classical music, bringing those two musical worlds together. There are also my careers as a music publisher and a record producer, activities that have occupied me a great deal during the last thirty-five years but are perhaps the least known aspect of my multiple involvements with music.

To serve my diversely interested readership well I have sought as one of my central goals to write very informatively about these various areas of music. If I brought up a particular musical activity in which I was importantly engaged I felt I had to go into some detail as to what that was, and what it meant for me, and why it is important for readers to know about that particular musical endeavor. I extend this informative approach to nonmusical arenas such as film, the visual arts, and literature, which have all been profoundly influential on me and are vital interests of mine.

Last but certainly not least, this book is an encomium to the love of my life, my dear wife and greatest supporter (as well as severest critic), Marjorie, who passed away nineteen years ago, and without whose support and devotion I could never have accomplished the many things I have been able to achieve.

This is not your typical autobiography, which basically recounts the personal history and major achievements of the individual in question. Naturally, much of this book is about me and my early life and career. It is simultaneously a history of American culture, and in particular of American music in the last seventy-five years, and—rather uncommon—of both classical music and jazz. Of course, it is not a comprehensive history in the ordinary sense, such as a proper music historian or musicologist would undertake. This blend of memoir and history was inevitable, since I have been so broadly and deeply engaged in almost all aspects of our culture (not just music) and in its evolution in the mid-twentieth century. How and why will all become even clearer in volume two of this narrative.

In a way, the real hero in this autobiography is New York City—that is, the New York City of the late 1930s into the early 1960s—which I call in my narrative the cultural paradise of the world. That New York does not exist anymore. New York is still the musical capital of the world, in the sense that performers, artists, and musical organizations of any kind have to be seen at some time (or preferable permanently) as a major presence there. But the city has changed dramatically. The wide-ranging and rich cultural ambiance that I feasted on in my formative years has vanished. What has replaced it is largely now imported, whereas in those midcentury years it was essentially indigenous, home grown, and, most important, further enriched by an enormous influx of refugees from Hitler's Nazi-dominated Europe, whether in music (Stravinsky and Schoenberg) or literature (Thomas Mann and Vladimir Nabokov), the visual arts (Pablo Picasso, Marc Chagall, Walter Gropius) or the sciences (Albert Einstein and Edward Teller), and especially in Hollywood films (Fritz Lang and Billy Wilder).

So much of who I became and what I have been able to achieve would in all likelihood never have happened except for my being born in that particular New York and into a musical family, and as a consequence of the connections and relationships available there. Since so much of what I write about is long forgotten and obsolete, I took full liberty—and great pleasure—in vividly remembering and reminding the reader, in the narrative and notes, of the unbelievably rich life that was there for the living in that artistic Golden Age of New York City.

Culturally we have gained much in recent decades, but we have also lost a lot. I wish I could bring back some of what we lost.

Chapter One

CHILDHOOD

I FELT THAT I HAD never before seen such an intensely radiant yet translucent green. It was overwhelming and incomprehensible: how could there be something so beautiful, so magical, so mystical—and yet so common, so universal. Maybe it was its very universality, its omnipresence, that made it so unique—a vivid, pellucid green that seemed to burn into my very soul.

Or was it the bright, clear sky blue that set off the sunlit green and made it so luminescent? The leaves trembling in a gentle breeze, boundless in their variety of shape and size, were gathered in my gaze into a vast thousand-piece mosaic, the impenetrable sky blinking through the shifting, swaying foliage. The whole scene seemed unfathomable, inexpressible in its utter beauty and transcendent perfection.

Tears welled in my eyes. I was seized by an uncontainable excitement—experiencing something so perfect and so emotionally overwhelming! In that epiphanal moment I glimpsed, perhaps for the first time, the innate complexity—and simplicity—of nature. Suddenly I understood how music and creating music, communicating through music, resonated with that same complexity and simplicity, that same potential for perfection and beauty.

Lying there in the warm, fragrant grass, gazing up at the crown of that elm tree and through its foliage to the sky beyond, lost in reverie, I had for a few moments forgotten that I was not alone. By my side lay the woman I loved, the love of my life, as enthralled as I was by the ineffable beauty of the scene. The warmth of her body, untouched, radiated toward me, the scent of her hair close by, her feelings intertwined with mine, bound together in a metaphysical communion that I could savor but only dimly comprehend.

It was a brilliant, cloudless summer day back in 1947; we were lying on the banks of the Ten Mile River, a small stream that flows through a tiny village with the Indian name Webatuck, 120 miles north of New York City. Our toes almost touching the water, gazing upward at that tree, breathing in the serene beauty enveloping us, we were in a trancelike high, the intensity of which I—and Marjorie—had never before experienced. Neither of us spoke for a long time. I think we couldn't. We were both caught in a dreamlike, spellbinding moment that we could feel but probably never fully express in words.

In that timeless, warm, tranquil moment, I think I felt in one powerful revelation what life—living, *being*—was all about; or at least what life in its most sublime moments could be. My heart was full, bursting with love of living, drifting in some never-before-experienced wordless ecstasy. It all came together in that heady moment: nature, music, love, and sex— united in some inexplicable symbiotic allness.

In retrospect, sixty-four years later, I recall this instant as one of the several defining moments in my life when an event occurred or a person came into my life that helped to shape me, deepen me, extend and broaden my emotional and intellectual horizons. I know that such moments enter our lives only rarely, unexpectedly, unpredictably, and that when they do—when they capture us—they tend to transform us. I also know—and somehow knew even then, sixty-four years ago—that one had better be ready to receive these benefactions, to be open and receptive, allowing that sudden new illumination to shine in. I know that such unveilings stir us in our primal expressive realms, the intellectual and the emotional. That is where the mind and heart meet in something we call love: love of a person, an idea, beauty, nature—something we are compelled to respond to and meld into our lives, into our deepest essence, our innermost persona.

I was twenty-one years old then, a long time ago. But it is an experience—a tiny, momentary blip on life's screen, that I have not only never forgotten but am still deeply stirred by in the vividness of its memory. It is emblazoned in my mind, one of many, many events in my life that cumulatively made me what I eventually became, what I am now. And I like to think that it is that same union of mind and heart that resides in my music, inspires and infuses it, and that motivates and challenges me as a composer, conductor, and performer.

But even beyond those personal strivings, it was Marjorie, my late wife, who was the central inspiring force that magnetized and augmented my life's work. When I was younger I didn't always realize or fully appreciate this fact—and it *is* a fact, not a mere feeling or opinion. I always knew that my love for her was so deep as to be indissoluble, irreducible, inextinguishable, something that was beyond both rescission and rational explanation. It just was. And it was so from the very beginning when we first met in 1943, when I was still seventeen and she had just turned nineteen.

But the true fullness of my love for her did not strike me until her death, when I realized that everything—absolutely everything—I had ever undertaken in my life was always first and foremost *for her*, a silent offering, a gift to her, to make her happy and, if possible, in some way to fulfill her life. I realize now that all this was done as some kind of recompense for the fact that she had devoted her whole life to me, helping and encouraging me (not necessarily uncritically) in my life's chosen work. If my life's accomplishments may some day be considered really worthy, then I know in my heart of hearts that they could not have been achieved without her support, her care, and her love.

Whether it was my composing, my performing (as a horn player or a conductor), my teaching and writing, my speaking out on tough issues: all of it was, perhaps more unconsciously than consciously, dedicated to her, in what I see now in retrospect as a wondrously reciprocal relationship.

But to return to that pastoral scene by the brook,[1] it was unquestionably one of those moments in life that shapes and forms, and in which my love for Margie and the miracles of nature harmonized into a wondrously intimate mutualism. Much of that summer of 1947 was spent in idyllic Webatuck, where my parents in 1945 had bought twenty-five cedar-wooded acres on a hilltop overlooking the Ten Mile River Valley, only a few miles from the New York-Connecticut border. My father, a violinist and member of the New York Philharmonic, had acquired the land with the intention of building a small summer home there. The initial plan was to build a simple cabin or bungalow, mostly for summer weekends. But my mother, who was a very talented designer and protoarchitect (she had gone to art and design school for three years in Germany), persuaded my father to consider more ambitious plans, which resulted some five years later in adding a very handsome and comfortable year-round residence—two conjoined houses—as fit for Christmas holidays as for summer vacations.

My father loved this area of New York State. I think it reminded him, with its rolling hills, forests, babbling brooks and streams, and tiny farm villages, of some of the places in Germany that he had known in his youth—places like the Black Forest, the Odenwald, or the Erz Mountains in his native Saxony. I think my father would have preferred something further north, perhaps in the Adirondacks, where there were lots of pine forests and, of course, higher mountains. My father loved pines, and didn't care all that much for the thousands of cedars and oaks that bedecked the hills in and around Webatuck.

But then reality and pragmatism won out over far-reaching dreams: Webatuck was only a short two-hour drive from New York City, which allowed my father quite often to drive directly to the Philharmonic's summer concerts in the evening and come back to Webatuck shortly after midnight. This worked well, especially if there was no rehearsal the next morning. Moreover,

Lewisohn Stadium, the summer home of the Philharmonic, was located on the campus of City College in the upper reaches of Manhattan, near 155th Street. Thus my father, in the summers on the way into the city, could avoid going all the way down to Carnegie Hall, the orchestra's winter home.

For my parents, longtime city dwellers, apartment habitués in crowded Queens, their twenty-five-acre estate was a kind of paradise, as it was for my wife and me and eventually our children, Edwin and George. To be able to elude the city's humid heat and summer crowds was appropriate recompense for the years of confinement in New York City. To escape to land that had first been settled and farmed by the Dutch in the 1600s, and to have, in addition, the luxury of owning an entire 500-foot-high hill, with a 270-degree view on three sides, was beyond my parents' wildest dreams.[2] And so it was inevitable that whatever edifice would ultimately be built, it would definitely sit on top of the hill, leaving all the lower woodlands pristine and untouched. There was only one slight hitch: the top of the hill was solid rock with only a thin layer of soil (which partially explains the dense cedar forest). After weeks of razing trees and blasting away layers of rock in order to put down a solid foundation, and drilling to a depth of ninety feet for a water supply, and several years of building and construction, a beautiful dwelling eventually graced our hilltop Eden.

When I was five or six, I learned from my mother that I was born in Lenox Hill Hospital, at Sixty-Eighth Street and Lexington Avenue,[3] and that I was a beautiful, big, nine-pound-plus baby. Many years later I was told that my birth had been a very painful one for my mother, and that I was delivered November 22, 1925, at two fifteen a.m. (according to the birth certificate). That, I found out, was thought to be of considerable significance—at least to some people—since it meant that I was born on the cusp between Scorpio and Sagittarius. Around the same time I learned—I don't recall exactly when, except that it was when I was already studying music—that November 22 was St. Cecilia's day, named for the patron saint of music. Two other interesting facts about my birthday and my birth emerged still later in my life, one of them coming to light—to my considerable embarrassment—when I was already in my forties. I cannot now, thirty-some years later, understand how I was so slow-witted for so many years not to realize that my parents *had* to get married because of me. They were married on May 12, 1925, and I was born six months later. I knew their wedding date very well, but I had never done that little bit of obvious arithmetic, and so it wasn't until one of my cousins, surprised at my stupidity, pulled me aside at a family gathering in the 1970s, and in a whisper pointed out this bit of personal history.

Other information regarding my birth date emerged when, in later years, I was voraciously devouring all manner of music encyclopedias—MacMillan's, Thompson's, Slonimsky's, Grove's, the German *Musik in Geschichte und Gegenwart* (Music in the Past and Present), and various jazz reference books—and discovered that musicians much more famous than I, also associated with St. Cecilia's Day (through birth or death), were Wilhelm Friedemann Bach, Benjamin Britten, the great cellist Emanuel Feuermann, Henry Purcell,[4] Josquin des Près, Joaquin Rodrigo, Arthur Sullivan, Hoagy Carmichael, and coincidentally even Scott Joplin, a fact that I only learned in the early 1970s when I was heavily involved in the revival of ragtime music. I presumed that these great musicians had all been blessed by Saint Cecilia, and that perhaps—if I worked hard—someday I too might deserve her saintly patronage.

I've also often wondered, realizing that another eighteen million babies were born on my birth date somewhere on this globe, who they were, what they did, how many led totally anonymous lives, but also how many in one way or another, though uncelebrated, contributed importantly to society, to their community, to human history.

Nineteen twenty-five was probably no more remarkable than any other year during that post–World War I decade, but some notable and, in retrospect, memorable events did occur.

In music alone, a number of important premieres took place: Ravel's fairy tale opera *L'Enfant et les sortilèges*, Berg's *Wozzeck* (after 137 rehearsals!), Berg also completed his beautiful *Chamber Concerto*, the twenty-five-year-old Aaron Copland had two important first performances, his *Organ Concerto* and his *Music for the Theatre* (one of Copland's first pieces to use jazz elements), Arthur Honegger's *Concertino for Piano and Orchestra* (also with jazz influences), Busoni's opera *Doktor Faust*, Varèse's *Intégrales*, Gershwin's *Piano Concerto*, and the highly experimental *Preludio a Cristobal Colon* by Mexican composer Julián Carrillo, employing quarter, sixth, and eighth tones (which to my knowledge have never been played correctly, at least in a live performance). Duke Ellington created his first compositions, aided and abetted by trumpeter Bubber Miley and clarinetist Barney Bigard.

In the other arts, things were equally lively. Four of my favorite twentieth-century literary classics were written or published in 1925: Franz Kafka's *Der Prozess* (*The Trial*),[5] Theodore Dreiser's *An American Tragedy*, F. Scott Fitzgerald's *The Great Gatsby*, and Sinclair Lewis's *Arrowsmith*. Of almost equal significance is the birth in 1925 of the *New Yorker* magazine (one year after the founding of *Time* magazine).

The mid-twenties were unarguably a great period in films. In 1925 alone America produced Chaplin's *The Goldrush*, Harold Lloyd's *The Freshman*, King Vidor's *The Big Parade* (to list just three); the Soviet Union gave us Eisenstein's *Battleship Potemkin*, Germany had G. W. Pabst's *Die freudlose Gasse* (*The Joyless Street*); and, above all, late December 1924 saw the premiere of one of the half dozen greatest films of all time: Erich von Stroheim's *Greed*, brutally mutilated and truncated by the MGM studio bosses, nonetheless surviving as an unforgettable masterpiece (and most recently partially restored). Other cinematic masterpieces of the midtwenties were: in Germany, F. W. Murnau's and Emil Jannings's *The Last Laugh* (1924), Fritz Lang's *Metropolis* (1924) and *Die Nibelungen* (1926), Murnau's *Faust* (1926); in France, René Clair's *Entracte* (1924), with accompanying music by Erik Satie and the artistic involvement of Marcel Duchamp and Man Ray, Fernand Léger's *Le Ballet méchanique* (with music by the American "enfant terrible" of music, George Antheil); and in Russia there was Pudovkin's *Mother* (1926).

I mention these cinematic achievements with particular fervor and nostalgia because they and dozens of other outstanding films of the 1920s and 1930s became an all-consuming passion in my young adult years. I spent untold hours—two or three almost every afternoon for about ten years—at the Museum of Modern Art film showings. Great films related significantly to me as a composer, for films seemed to me so much like music, like symphonies or operas, with thematic developments and variations, primary and secondary subjects, expositions, codas (dénouement); both were narrative forms, occurring and of necessity experienced in time, although the one, music, is abstract and nonspecific, the other, cinema, generally chronicles particular identifiable events.

Between 1924 and 1926 important achievements and developments in the visual arts would include Picasso's *Three Dancers* (1925) and his shift toward abstraction; Joan Miró embarked on his surrealistic period with his *Catalan Landscape*; Walter Gropius's Bauhaus moved from Weimar to Dessau, and there began to exert a major influence in the world of architecture, along with Le Corbusier's publication of *Towards a New Architecture*.

In literature Thomas Mann had just published *The Magic Mountain* (1924), ten years after he started writing his magnum opus; Mary Webb wrote her *Precious Bane* in 1924; that same year Eugene O'Neill premiered *All God's Chillun Got Wings*, starring Paul Robeson; and in 1926 A. A. Milne brought us the inspired and delightful *Winnie the Pooh*, which, alas, born into a German-speaking family, I never was given to read, but on which, happily, my two children cut their literary teeth.

Other fields—science, technology, politics, daily life—were no less productive and creative. It was in 1925 that Werner Heisenberg and Niels Bohr developed the theory of quantum mechanics, and several other scientists (James Franck, Gustav Hertz, Wolfgang Pauli) worked on various aspects of atomic theory. A year after Henry Ford built his ten millionth car, Walter Chrysler founded the Chrysler Corporation, turning Detroit into the automobile capital of the world. Kodak invented the first 16mm movie film. The first plans to build the George Washington Bridge, spanning the Hudson River from upper Manhattan to New Jersey, were laid. Air travel developed after World War I into a potential major industry, and the German airline Lufthansa was founded in 1926 (I flew on it as a one-and-a-half-year-old baby one year later).

In politics and governmental affairs, events both good and bad occurred. Lenin and Woodrow Wilson died in 1924; Italian Fascists elected Mussolini, and all other political parties in Italy were dissolved or banned. The aging German general and chief of the army, Paul Hindenburg, became president of Germany, but Hitler, just out of jail, reorganized his Nazi Party and in 1925 published the first volume of *Mein Kampf*. A year later he organized the youth movement called *Hitlerjugend*, and Goebbels was appointed Nazi *Gauleiter* (district leader) of Berlin. Stalin rose to power in the Soviet Union and had his archrival, Leon Trotsky, banished from Moscow, leading eventually to Trotsky's expulsion from the Communist Party and exile to Mexico. Gustav Stresemann, chancellor of Germany (and one of Hitler's predecessors), won the 1926 Nobel Peace Prize.

In America, New York's Governor Al Smith repealed Prohibition in his state. But in the South, John T. Scopes, a schoolteacher, was indicted and tried in Tennessee for teaching the theory of evolution. Defended by Clarence Darrow, and prosecuted by William Jennings Bryan, Scopes was convicted but then acquitted on a technicality.

Gene Tunney outboxed Jack Dempsey and gained the world heavyweight title. The Charleston practically overnight became the nation's most popular dance in 1925; and the comedian Will Rogers was at the absolute zenith of his career. Playing mah-jongg, now enjoying renewed popularity, became a worldwide craze, especially in Europe—a craze that I would be caught up in a decade later in my school years in Germany.

Whether and how these heady, frenetic times into which I was born affected my childhood and my life must remain open to question and conjecture. But if the social, economic, political environment in which one is formed has a direct (and indirect) impact on one's life, then I am, for better or worse, like millions of other Americans, a product of that incredible between-the-two-great-wars era. But what is interesting, and somewhat unusual, is that I tasted both the affluence of America in the twenties and the poverty, as well as the political and social tensions in Europe in the thirties. Born in America, I knew nothing of the turmoil in postwar Europe of the 1920s; growing up in Germany in the thirties I missed the isolationism and Great Depression of the United States. My parents emigrated from Germany to the United States in 1923, undoubtedly because of the absolute hopelessness of the German postwar situation. Unemployment had by then struck 45 percent of the population, a staggering statistic, and inflation was completely out of control: a moldy loaf of bread could cost *four million* marks. Germans had been immigrating to the New World by the tens of thousands annually ever since the political uprisings of the late 1840s, and in 1923 more than ever America was still considered the land of unlimited opportunities (*Das Land der unbegrenzten Möglichkeiten*).

My father was born in Saxony in a small town called Burgstädt, located halfway between Leipzig and Chemnitz, while my mother came from the Rhineland city of Krefeld. They met in the United States, not in Germany, by sheer chance under somewhat unusual circumstances. The site for this encounter was New Haven, Connecticut. Why there? Well, among the more pertinent explanations is the fact that my mother, though German, was not born in Germany but in New Haven. Her father, who had established several steel and tool-and-dye factories in Germany and Belgium, around the turn of the century got the idea of trying his luck in America by starting a factory there. He settled on New Haven to build his American empire, and it was during the three years that he tried to make his mark in the American steel industry that my mother was born (in 1903). When his steel enterprise failed after four or five years, he took his young family back to Germany.[6]

When my mother decided to leave Germany at age twenty-one, she must have thought it best to return to the only place in the States that she knew, and that was New Haven. Having been raised on classical music at home, it was perhaps also inevitable that she would go to the run-out concerts of the New York Philharmonic, which it gave in Yale University's Woolsey Hall several times a year.

My father, also wanting to try his fortune in the New World, got a job playing in the orchestra of the newly founded German Wagner Opera Company, conducted by one of Wagner's (allegedly) illegitimate sons, Ernst Knoch, just as the whole company was about to embark on a six-week American tour. When the tour ended my father, enamored with America, especially New York City, decided to stay and auditioned for and joined the New York Philharmonic.[7] At one of the concerts in New Haven in late 1924, during the intermission, my father wandered out into the foyer of Woolsey Hall, probably looking for female companionship, when his eye lit upon a young attractive girl, reading the program notes, who turned out—wonder of wonders—to speak German and to be, in fact, German.

The first few years with the New York Philharmonic must have been very exciting for my father, for when Josef Stransky left his post as music director of the orchestra in 1923 after a relatively successful eleven-year tenure, three great conductors presided over the Philharmonic: Willem Mengelberg, Wilhelm Furtwängler (1925–27), and Arturo Toscanini. (Toscanini eventually outmaneuvered Mengelberg to become the orchestra's music director in 1930–36.) It was in the midtwenties that some pretty important musical events took place in New York. The Philharmonic first performed Stravinsky's *Rite of Spring*, conducted by none other than Furtwängler (a work one does not normally associate with that conductor). The Philharmonic also participated in what one might consider the first sound film, namely, *Don Juan*, with John Barrymore and Mary Astor, which was presented in August 1926 with a specially composed synchronized recorded score (mostly by one William Axt—not Richard Strauss's *Don Juan*, by the way) on $33^1/_3$ RPM discs and featuring not only the Philharmonic but also Giovanni Martinelli and the Metropolitan Opera chorus, violinists Mischa Elman and Efrem Zimbalist, and conducted by Henry Hadley. The whole affair was a huge success, which a year later led to the development and introduction of sound-on-film (not sound-on-disc) in the famous *The Jazz Singer*, as well as in Fox's Movietone News films and Warner Brothers' *Lights of New York* (1928).

My father recalled that during the later Stransky years, the Philharmonic had become somewhat undisciplined, rather lackadaisical about many musical and performance matters. The fault apparently lay largely with Stransky. As the successor to Gustav Mahler in 1911, Stransky initially carried forward Mahler's high standards and disciplined approach, and had within two years of his arrival not only increased the number of concerts annually by about a third but had also arranged for the orchestra to make its first (widely heralded) recordings. Yet in his later years he had become, as much of the press put it at the time, and as many of the Philharmonic's top subscribers saw it, "rather slovenly" in his direction of the orchestra. As a result of this perception, Stransky was relieved of his duties and the three conductors were engaged to bring the orchestra back to its former illustrious status.

A lot of work had to be done. As just one example, when Mengelberg was engaged as guest conductor, he spent the entire first half of his first rehearsal with the orchestra, so my father recalled, on getting the Philharmonic to play a proper, correct, dramatic *fp*, that is, an immediate dynamic reduction from *f* to *p*, with the emphasis on *immediate*, not the lazy, gradual *diminuendo* that might last two or three beats. According to my father the Philharmonic retained from that moment on a near-perfect *fp* for over a decade (through the Toscanini years), and in general a very high level of musical discipline, much of it initiated and enforced by Mengelberg in his first few weeks with the orchestra. Of course, there were also complaints about Mengelberg, especially in the orchestra: that he was too demanding, that he talked too much, lectured the musicians repetitiously. But in the end he achieved his goal of making the orchestra the best trained in America, so that, as Winthrop Sargeant, the critic and writer who played violin in the Philharmonic in those years reported, "by the time Mengelberg had thoroughly rehearsed a maneuver, the Philharmonic could carry it out automatically by itself." The fruits of these efforts can be heard to this day in Mengelberg's and the Philharmonic's superb 1928 recording of Strauss's *Ein Heldenleben*, one of the greatest performances and recordings of all time.

My father also told me often how awestruck the orchestra was by Toscanini in the 1925–26 season, the most fearsome and temperamental disciplinarian among the conductors of the time, but a genius who also electrified the orchestra with his passion for perfection, his sheer relentless energy and tremendous knowledge of the music.

My father—Arthur was his given name—in many ways lived a privileged and relatively uncomplicated life, seemingly never becoming actively or even peripherally involved with the great issues and sociopolitical imbroglios of the time, troubles and misfortunes somehow always gliding harmlessly by him. Even as a teenager, in the midst of World War I, when most Germans, especially as the war progressed, were experiencing increasing financial hardships and extreme food shortages, my father seems to have lived the life of Reilly. He was fourteen and a student at the Musikhochschule in Leipzig—taking violin and viola lessons with Hans Sitt, studying theory and composition with Max Reger—when the war broke out; this was when he made his professional debut as a violinist, hired as an extra in the famous Gewandhaus Orchestra in Bruckner's Seventh Symphony with the great Arthur Nikisch conducting, and by age sixteen he was already making a career as concertmaster in half a dozen spa orchestras in various parts of Germany. Orchestral ranks had become rather depleted by 1916, when thousands of German musicians were drafted, sent to the front—many of them never to return. As a result there were frequent openings in most orchestras, especially in the resident orchestras at the numerous spas and resorts that dotted the German landscape in the early part of the century.

We must remember that this was the era when every little hotel, restaurant, and café had live music: not just a pianist, but at least a piano trio or quintet. The spa orchestras, usually with forty to fifty players, were maintained at a very high level, particularly during the war, because that is where many of the generals and other elite of the German army and navy would spend their often quite extended furloughs and vacations. These orchestras had to be kept at top quality in order to provide a proper cultural entertainment for the vacationing military brass. My father was befriended by many of these rich, influential celebrities and war heroes, frequently invited to dine with them; more crucially, he was protected by several of them from being drafted into the army. One general in particular, very influential in the upper echelons of the military and a great music lover, not only managed to keep my father retained at his favorite spa—so that he could hear him play his favorite Mozart and Spohr violin concertos—but, when he was returned to the front, he also recommended my father to several of his colleagues who were about to have furloughs, in effect getting him successive jobs as concertmaster in other spa orchestras. In this way my father played in half a dozen different orchestras between 1916 and 1918, always as concertmaster.

Young and handsome, my father evidently had no shortage of girlfriends, many of them farmers' daughters who supplied my father with butter, eggs, bread, vegetables, and other staples in the final years of the war when food was severely rationed and hard to come by.

After the war my father auditioned for and joined a number of excellent orchestras, including in 1919 the orchestra in Mannheim, where he was principal viola under the already famous Wilhelm Furtwängler. My father received a beautiful letter of recommendation from the legendary maestro when he left for the concertmaster position in Plauen (in Saxony, near the Bavarian border), a letter he proudly showed me many, many times. He also played for a while with the Pfalz (Palatinate) Orchestra, which was at times conducted by the youngest son of Johann Strauss Sr., Eduard Strauss.

Most of these orchestras, as is still the custom in Germany and most European countries today, served as both symphony and opera orchestras, and included a good dose of operetta and lighter musical fare in their repertoire. In that way my father became acquainted very quickly with an immense amount of music, not only the standard eighteenth- and nineteenth-century symphonic repertory, but also the moderns of the time ranging from Richard Strauss, Schreker, Reger, and Pfitzner, to Lehar and Kalman, and everything in between. One should not assume from this pattern of flitting about from orchestra to orchestra that my father was fired from any of these positions. No, it was rather that he, an inveterate traveler with an insatiable *wanderlust*, periodically pulled up stakes, seeking new places, new people, conquering, as it were, new territories.

These peregrinations stopped, of course, once my father settled down in America, spending the next forty-two years with the New York Philharmonic and in extra freelance work with a host of other orchestras, ranging from theatre orchestras like the Roxy and Capitol on Broadway to many of the famous radio-based orchestras (Firestone, Bell Telephone, Cadillac, and so on).

In the summers he would quite often take vacations in Europe, working his way across the Atlantic by playing the violin—as *Stehgeiger*—or playing in one of the several small café orchestras that all the great ocean liners of the time had on board. Although he wasn't paid any salary, for him this was heaven on earth: traveling and playing music, his two major passions. What could be more wonderful!

In all these ways he was very fortunate, being always fully employed and never seriously affected by the two major economic upheavals of our time, the Wall Street crash and the deprivations of the Great Depression of the 1930s.

As for my mother, when some years ago I became interested in my parental ancestry, genealogical research revealed that my mother's direct forebears came more or less from France. I say "more or less" because the provinces of Alsace and Lorraine have for centuries been alternately German and French as a result of perennial wars, political maneuverings, and land transfers engineered by state systems, kings, emperors, dukes, and other royalty, always with no concern for the people that lived in those lands. The results of these back and forth political swings and cross-acculturations are fascinating to behold, as expressed, for example, in the superb cuisine for which those provinces are known: a remarkable mixture of German and French culinary styles (several of the world's best four or five star restaurants are located in that region). These Franco-German cultural mergings are also expressed in the art of those provinces, its architecture (its many extraordinary cathedrals, monasteries, and churches), reflected even in the rich language Alsacians and Lorrainians speak—a heavy patois of German with a French accent (or vice versa).

From that side of my family tree my mother inherited the excitable temperament and quick mind of the French, and the strict discipline and work ethos (and energy) of the Germans. Her forebears immigrated northward, first to the mountainous region of the Eifel, southwest of Cologne, and thence still further toward the Cologne region itself. Nearby Krefeld, my mother's birthplace, has been an industrially and culturally rich city ever since the mid-nineteenth century, known primarily for its weaving and textile industry, but also its fine museums and art galleries. For us musicians the name Krefeld has always had a special resonance because the first performance of Mahler's Third Symphony took place there in 1903.

On my father's side, I have traced our genealogy back to the eighteenth century, when certain Schullers were known to be farmers and small town merchants in southwestern Saxony. But I am convinced, even if I cannot in any way prove it, that we Schullers go all the way back to what is now Romania, specifically the longtime German-speaking province of Siebenbürgen (Transylvania) at the southern edge of the Carpathian Mountains—also known, by the way, as Dracula country. My surmise regarding my Eastern European ancestry is based on the historical fact that in that region (Transylvania) the name Schuller is exceedingly common; there is even a hilly forest range called *Schuller*. I also base it on the actual existence in the fifteenth century of a great architect named (guess what?) Günther Schuller, which is exactly my name as written on my birth certificate, *umlaut* and all. That earlier Schuller was renowned in all of southeastern Europe for his architectural achievements, not only for the beautiful church he built in the city of Kluj (in its German appellation, Klausenburg) in the 1450s but also for his many splendid governmental and official buildings scattered throughout that region. Not that my parents ever heard of that fifteenth-century architect at the time of my birth, but I believe, for whatever it's worth, that it must be more than a mere coincidence of name designation that links me to that earlier Schuller.[8] If I only could prove it—or disprove it.

The connection between Transylvania and Germany's province of Saxony is not fictitious. History shows that, after this previously Roman-dominated region was overrun in the third century AD by a wildly divergent assemblage of "barbarian" clans and tribes (Huns, Goths, Lombards, Kumans), but ultimately driven out in the twelfth century by the Hungarian King Ladislaus I, Transylvania was repopulated and recultivated by Saxons from Flanders and the lower Rhineland, turning it in effect into a German province. The Saxons stayed on, even after the invasions by the Mongols in the thirteenth century and the Turks and Ottomans several hundred years later, right to the present time—although considerable numbers of them escaped, migrating back to Germany during the Ottoman domination. That's how I believe my ancestors became "proper" Germans and how I stem from a Transylvanian background.

My mother's maiden name was Elsie Bernartz, the family name probably a Germanized mutation of the French Bernard. I believe that it is from her family's French background that she inherited what is often referred to as a "French temperament": volatile, explosive, easily given to sudden violent outbursts. For she was a strict, at times even cruel, disciplinarian, not only with her children but also in her own life. Blessed with unbounded energy and a tremendous intellectual drive—she had a sharp, fast mind—she worked extra hard every day of her life, not only as a mother and wife but also on herself, as it were, relentlessly trying to salvage in various private artistic endeavors whatever was preservable from her artistic ambitions, and what, I am sure, she had envisioned as a life in the arts, most likely as a painter or designer.

As fate will sometimes deal us crucial, life-changing blows, or confront us with unforeseeable interventions, so my mother suffered and experienced a few of these in her formative years. In that sense, even her decision to leave Germany, where she probably would have had a career in the arts—the renowned German painter, sculptor, and lithographer Käthe Kollwitz had expressed a keen interest in my mother's youthful work—and her emigration to America, her marriage to my father, becoming a wife and mother and more or less ending whatever artistic career ambitions she had held—all these were decisive in changing the course of her life.

But much more momentous—and downright cruel—was an event that really shook and demoralized her totally. When the ship that brought her to America docked at the Chelsea Piers in mid-Manhattan, where all the great ocean liners were berthed between 1907 and the 1960s, the net that carried her big steamer trunk and several suitcases partially filled with hundreds of her drawings, paintings, sketchings, and designs—her entire accumulated art work—broke and fell into the Hudson River, never to be retrieved. It broke her heart, and I'm sure it took her a long, long time to recover from this calamity—perhaps she never recovered.

She had already experienced her share of hardship by then. Her relatively happy childhood in Krefeld, and for some years in Flanders, was suddenly shattered in August 1914 when her father, in Belgium at the time, was unceremoniously arrested within a few days after the outbreak of World War I, allegedly as a German spy, and incarcerated for the duration of the war. (The quick arrest and imprisonment of my grandfather was, I'm sure, largely motivated by the fact that he, as a German national and manufacturer of heavy machinery and military weapons, was seen as a partner in Kaiser Wilhelm's alarming prewar arms build up.) Somehow his wife (my grandmother Cleophile), and the six children were allowed to return to Krefeld. But there, with no father and no income for the family, they really fell on hard, hard times, even when Cleo, who had never been obliged to do an honest day's work, began to take in work as a seamstress. The normal deprivations of wartime were hard enough, but for the huge family of seven to endure these without a father and any financial subsistence for the duration of the war was an unusually cruel burden to bear. My mother, eleven years old when her father disappeared out of her life and the eldest of six children, now that her mother was working all day to make a little money to put some food on the table, had to take over the supervision of her younger siblings, three sisters and two brothers. She became a surrogate parent, deprived of any semblance of a normal childhood. Standing in lines for hours for a half a loaf of bread or to buy a few potatoes (which would often be partially rotten, glassy, a sickening greenish color, putrid smelling), just to help the family to somehow subsist—this was her daily life.

I know these were terrible times for my mother, an extended period of desperate survival and terrible deprivations, although she never talked much about those years. What a contrast to my father's untroubled life! It made my mother stronger, tougher—even harder—and much of that toughness and hardness I had to endure later in my own childhood. Having experienced those grim times and having through sheer tenacity and the basic instinct for survival pulled through, my mother had little patience for laziness of any kind, any lack of discipline, any disobedience (apparent or real), any activity that was less than purposeful and determined. As cruel as she sometimes was to me, both physically and verbally, I know that she meant well and that it was the only way she knew how to deal with my more than occasional rebelliousness.

Rhinelanders, especially Colognese, are a proud, landbound, self-sufficient, independent lot, who don't have much of a taste for national (Teutonic) pride, an attitude that has, however, nothing to do with parochialism or provincialism. Their playfully subversive, roguishly anti-authoritarian way of life finds its ultimate rebellious release in the annual and by now famous excesses of Mardi Gras in Cologne (*Fasching* in German). The north Rhinelanders' gusto for frolicsome insubordination has another interesting side, the development over millennia of a kind of enlightened tolerance and frisky defiance of hidebound bureaucratic authority, whether it was the Romans two thousand years ago or the French during the Napoleonic era.

In addition, Cologne has long been the cultural center for modern art and music in Germany, a situation of which its citizenry is justly proud. It possesses a culturally innovative consciousness that dates from at least the eleventh century—when the north Rhine region became a center of early medieval ecclesiastical architecture, followed two centuries later by the great Gothic cathedral architecture that flourished along the Rhine, and the ensuing veritable deluge of superior Gothic and early Renaissance paintings, diptychs, and triptychs, all housed in the city's two great museums. This breakthrough spirit has been honed and sharpened over many centuries, as can be seen in Cologne's outstanding museums and art galleries, which, along with its remarkable radio and television complex, the WDR (West German Radio), have always supported and nurtured the Rhinelanders' love of the avant-garde.

This has generated nowadays a vigorous rivalry between Berlin, the new capitol of Germany, and Cologne, only a few miles north of Germany's former capital of Bonn. The *Kölners* blithely disregard what they consider Berlin's second-rate, conservative cultural ambitions, brashly believing that the central artistic axis of Europe travels from London via Amsterdam through Cologne and—with a respectful bow to Paris in the west—on to Munich, Milan, and Rome, leaving Berlin dangling on some far-off eastern periphery. And that feisty, independent, innovative Rhenish spirit I began to see and recognize, as I matured, in my mother, who grew up virtually within the shadow of the Cologne Cathedral; as a young girl she breathed in the special self-confident air of a city located only 125 miles from the French border, a city that has always preferred looking westward toward France (Gaul) and Belgium (Flanders), rather than east (Prussia).

My mother's artistic interests and creative talents, so hopelessly thwarted by the disastrous loss of all her early art work, nonetheless expressed themselves in a variety of ways throughout her life, as in—herewith just a few samplings—her meticulously detailed, absolutely professional architectural designs (for the Webatuck home), her later decades-long fashioning of thousands of costume dolls (which she privately sold all over the world), her fine collections of china and silver. As a result of her artistic decorative sense, my parents' apartments, no matter how many times they moved, were always elegantly, tastefully furnished. My mother loved the modern (often Scandinavian) furniture designs; their bedroom was an almost museumlike work of art in itself, with its sleek, molded, blonde bureaus, chaises, and master bed.

I was also always fascinated by the masterly fashion with which she would place various objects, whether an Italian Murano vase, a uniquely molded cigarette case, a floral decoration, a Tiffany lamp, or even some simple trinket—all were set in just the right place. Some of the childhood toys she was able to bring with her from Europe had their pride of place in a beautiful living room glass cabinet, including the tiny, beautifully decorated Dutch wooden shoes she had worn in Flanders, next to them—even more exotic—a pair of old-style Chinese shoes with which young girls' feet were bound and stunted, sent to her by her cousin Peter Kutt, who emigrated to Tsingtao, China, in the 1920s.

By comparison with my mother's temperament, my father was easygoing and mild mannered. When my mother sent me to bed without dinner for some infraction of her strict code of behavior, my father would later sneak food into my room. When my mother had beaten me into submission, my father would find some way to soothe my wounds, whether physical or psychological. He was a gentle man, and soft, and had a tendency not to get involved in any controversy, any disputes, at home. Right or wrong, my parents' converse temperaments combined to create a disciplinary balance and guiding equilibrium in me over the years, not to mention that I spent nearly seven years away from home at school in Germany and at St. Thomas Choir School in New York.

When my brother Edgar and I were tiny tots my father would help get us to bed most nights (when he was free from the Philharmonic) and tell us stories, often bedtime stories that he invented. I was too young to be able to remember now, some seventy years later, any details, and how long he kept this imaginative storytelling up, but it seems to me it was almost two years. These stories were built around one central character with a German name, Pubs (American: Poops), which in German means fart. Edgar and I—he was about three, I was six— hardly knew what a fart was, although we vaguely knew it was something generally unmentionable. But our father's Poops was a gentle, kindly character, more akin to Winnie the Pooh (which my father did *not* know), or a kind of Till Eulenspiegel, or Robin Hood, who roamed— actually floated—around the world doing good deeds and fighting bad guys, robbing the rich to give to the poor. In my childish imagination Poops looked something like Mr. Potato Head does today. Each of my father's Poops episodes lasted at most ten minutes. They made Edgar and me laugh and giggle, with no thoughts, of course, of falling asleep. In retrospect I marvel at my father's inventive imagination.

I also remember from that time that for some years my brother and I slept together in the same bed and that, as Edgar dozed off into Morpheus's arms, I would slip my forefinger into one of his tiny warm curled hands—our touching way of quietly bonding each night.

Most of what I received in the way of punishment I surely deserved. I was often fresh, surly, insolent, temperamental (like my mother), and always eager to push my behavior to some outer edge. My brother Edgar was more docile, more like my father, and consequently usually escaped my mother's wrath, even when he too misbehaved. This made me pretty jealous, with the result that as time passed and I got smarter and cleverer, I also learned—to my later shame—how to pass the blame for some of my own bad behavior and youthful stupidities onto Edgar. Of course, my parents usually caught me out in these diversionary tactics; the backlash was that they then sometimes blamed me for Edgar's occasional naughtiness. But generally my brother and I got along very well—no serious sibling rivalries—until our early teen years when we did have some terrible fights.[9] Mostly we tended to stick together against my parents when the occasion arose, mostly, I am sure, at my instigation.

Perhaps the most ill advised, incredibly stupid—indeed quite dangerous—misdeed I ever committed occurred in 1934, when I was eight and had just returned home from Germany during a summer vacation. One evening my parents had gone to a Philharmonic concert, leaving us two boys alone (my parents didn't believe much in babysitters). I have no idea what possessed me to do this, but soon after they left I started a little fire on the windowsill of our sixth-floor apartment kitchen window. Mind you, directly on the sill itself. We had, of course, opened the window, and pretty soon, to my horror, I saw that the fire, fanned by the breeze coming through the window, was burning into the sill, making a noticeable charred indentation. In considerable panic—thank God there were no curtains on that window—Edgar and I doused the flames with water from the nearby sink and tried to figure out how to hide what I had perpetrated, to somehow cover up my ridiculous misadventure before our parents got home.

As stupid as we had just been, we suddenly became pretty ingenious, although in the end we learned that crime doesn't pay. Somehow I knew that somewhere in the apartment, in a closet, there was a pail of near-white beige paint, exactly the color of the windowsill. I knew that I couldn't deal with the half-inch indentation, but naively thought that painting it over might hide it, at least for that night. In my hurry, I splashed some paint onto the floor and, worse yet, onto my fingers and hands. I spent the next hour trying to scrape the paint off my fingers with the rough steel wool my mother used to clean pots and pans. The paint was tough, and I scraped my fingers nearly bloody, a pain I can vividly recall to this day. We managed to get to bed, feigning sleep, just minutes before my parents came back home.

Our whole subterfuge didn't work, of course, because the smell of the paint and of burnt wood immediately gave our stupid prank away. To my eternal shame, frightened to death at my mother's impending wrath, I tried meekly to blame the whole thing on my little brother, five years old. She didn't buy it, and I received one of the most extensive beatings of my entire life, until my father, afraid that she might kill me, came to my rescue. I was in the doghouse for weeks and the episode spoiled my entire vacation at home.

Premonition

The room is full. A concert is about to begin, and the place is abuzz with the excited voices of seventy children. The occasion is the monthly musical evening, organized by the school's faculty. Eight children are to perform that night: a pianist, a violinist (accompanied by one of the teachers), and six other boys and girls playing a variety of recorders; one piece for a quartet of two soprano recorders, alto, and tenor, the other (involving me) a series of duet variations for alto and baritone recorder on a German folksong.

The audience of children, age six to twelve, is seated on the floor, all huddled together, legs crossed in lotus fashion. At one end of the room, in high-back, richly ornamented wood-carved chairs built into the wall and raised a foot or two above the floor, sit stern-faced faculty. In their position high above the small sea of children they dominate the room. They are both audience and judge, whose critical ears and penetrating scrutiny we young performers are expected to satisfy. Especially forbidding, certainly to me, is Herr Kieschke, the elderly head of the faculty and, as fate would have it, my teacher on the baritone recorder.

Long before the day of the concert, I had been approaching the evening with a distinct sense of foreboding. For I didn't like Herr Kieschke; nor did I like the baritone recorder or, for that matter, any of the family of recorders. I don't recall how I got inveigled to play that preposterous instrument, almost as tall as I was, with its hooty, dry, unsensual sound and its, to me, silly metal bocal. At least the other kids who played recorders got to blow directly into their instruments. I can only conjecture that I may have been chosen to play the baritone recorder because I was tall for my age. I certainly don't recall having any great interest in the instrument, not even in music in general, nor, as far as I can recall, having any talent for it.

Herr Kieschke was not a musician. He taught a variety of subjects—arithmetic, geography, Latin, among others—and played music (and the recorder) as a hobby. He was very tall and lean—in one of those strange recollections by which we can retroactively associate experiences separated by many years, I am certain that he looked a lot like Furtwängler—but with a wan face, an unusually long neck and partly balding head, a typical German professorial intellectual that I in later years judged to have spent too many years in classrooms and musty dim-lit libraries. As everyone knows, a sixty-year-old man looks inordinately ancient and forbidding to a nine-year-old, and Herr Kieschke's generally humorless demeanor certainly did not endear him to me.

An area of about 140 square feet had been cleared for us performers as a kind of ministage; before us a sea of faces, our audience of peers, and behind us, the faculty. I and my fellow students were third in the program, and thus had to await our turn to perform outside in the hallway, all the while getting more and more nervous. As the first two pieces finished, I remember so vividly, even to this day, the sinking feeling in my stomach when I entered the room. I felt that I was being led to the gallows, to my ultimate doom.

The performance did not go well. I was terrified to play before what seemed to me an immense audience, a faceless mass of bodies that, I was certain, was there specifically to see me fail. With each successive phrase, my breathing became slower—and shorter. Something—I knew not what—was constricting my lungs, my chest. The blood was racing around in my head at a furious pace. I tried to struggle on, but after what seemed like an eternity I broke down, crying, sobbing, groveling in the most abject failure I had ever experienced in my young life.

I left the room in disgrace. It took me a long, long time to get over my deep embarrassment, my hurt pride. Herr Kieschke barely talked to me for weeks.

*   *   *   *   *

I didn't know then—and still don't know today—exactly what made me fall apart so completely. I suspect that I had not practiced or prepared myself enough, and perhaps was simply rebelling against Herr Kieschke's not-so-benign tutelage. More likely it was an enormous case of stage fright, having never before appeared or performed in public.

Stage fright can be totally debilitating; it certainly was so for me that evening. It drains one's physical and mental strength, leaving one with a feeling of total impotence and helplessness.

What is so odd about it is that we do not know precisely what causes it, what fears bring it on, and how those fears immobilize one's breathing and becloud one's mind. The most that I can recall from very occasional moments of stage fright that I experienced later as a professional horn player—strangely never as a conductor—is that it involved some indefinable, reasonless fear of failure, of letting someone or oneself down. It is a virtually unpreventable and uncontrollable condition, the only countervailing resource one can apply is to have brought one's performance skills, one's craft—whether as a musician, an actor, a dancer—to such a high level that, even at one's most weakened (and frightened) level, one can still function at least adequately, professionally—or better.

Given my embarrassingly inauspicious musical debut as a nine-year-old, it seems rather remarkable (and inexplicable to me), that not too many years later, at age sixteen, I was able to embark on and maintain a highly successful musical career that embraced many disciplines in the field, including performing as a professional horn player in some of the world's highest and most demanding professional artistic ranks.

How did this happen? How *could* this happen? I continue to ponder those questions as I write these words, almost three-quarters of a century later. And, of course, I don't really know the answers, certainly not fully, unequivocally, objectively. To cover these mysteries of life we invent words such as "destiny," "fate," or phrases such as "in God's hands"—convenient, and I suppose, useful linguistic contrivances, which we invoke when we stand before the unexplainable. We know more now—or presume to know more—than in the past. In an era of genetic discoveries and DNA mapping we apparently know at least that we humans develop primarily out of a confluence or interaction of genetics and environmental factors, external conditions and influences that can range from socioeconomic, behavioral, and physical, to astrological, intellectual, and educational. Even with all that we must include the element of chance—events or situations that we can neither predict, nor control, nor explain.

How fascinating it is to contemplate that in the entire existence of human beings over the last, say, twenty thousand years, as a result of these numberless interlocking, overlapping, crossbreeding influences, no two humans have ever had identical personalities, identical characteristics, capabilities, interests, and talents. It is even more mind-boggling to consider how complex these interacting causalities are when one realizes that there have been in that span of time some 650 generations of millions and (more recently, billions) of people, living and reproducing on this planet at any given time. Even one billion multiplied by 650 makes 650 billion; that is to say, 650 billion genetic crossbreedings and cross-fertilizations, not one like any other.

What this means, coming back to the fields of music and hereditary influences, is that the genes that generate a disposition for musical talent can help to produce ten generations of musicians, as in the case of the Bach family, or conversely can lie dormant and unproductive for centuries, only to suddenly, unexpectedly, reappear once again. Nor do these developments necessarily occur in direct genealogical lineages. The sudden appearance of everything from blond hair and hammertoes and tall lanky bodies to musical or scientific talent—and a whole range of other hereditary possibilities—can descend from a second cousin five generations back. In short, the genetically induced variables are infinite in number and completely unpredictable.

In my case, there seems to have been a fairly clear genetic disposition for me to become a musician. As it is, I represent the fourth generation of musicians on my father's side. His father and his grandfather were both professional musicians, the leading town musicians (*Stadtmusiker*) in several provincial towns in Saxony, Germany. They were violinists and pianists, conductors of their local orchestras or choral groups—the so-called *Stadtpfeifer*—and were also the major (sometimes only) music teachers in the town, teaching privately and in the schools. My two sons, both excellent jazz musicians, are thus the fifth generation of musicians, and who knows what their offspring—if any—will turn out to be.

On my mother's side, despite a fair amount of genealogical research, there is no evidence, going back some three or four generations, of any professional musical activity. Yet my mother was remarkably musically sensitive and knowledgeable. Much of that knowledge may have come simply from being married to a professional working in the major musical center of the world (New York), quite naturally going to hundreds of concerts of the New York Philharmonic. She surprised me with the sharpness of her keen musical ear for intonation, for balances, and for timbral details. My mother played the piano well enough to play simple pieces and accompany the family in Christmas carols and other little holiday songfests.

And yet, though one might want to conclude that on the face of such hereditary evidence, especially on my father's side, I was destined to become a musician, genetic laws do not necessarily function that way at all. Overwhelming historical evidence shows that in innumerable cases a significant history of artistic talent, or any kind of skill in a given family—scientific, medical, legal, athletic, dramatic, etc.—does not insure that the next offspring will be similarly gifted. Had my disastrous musical debut in Germany been considered reliable evidence, the conclusion would obviously have been that I had absolutely no musical talent.

But only two years later, I was discovered to have a beautiful soprano voice, near-perfect intonation in singing, and a remarkable ability to sight-read almost any kind of music, including even atonal, dissonant music of considerable intervallic and linear complexity. I have no idea whatsoever how—and even when—I acquired those skills. All I can remember is that shortly after my eleventh birthday I suddenly had a strong, virtually irrepressible urge to get involved with music, indeed primarily to compose music.

It was then that my parents told me that as a five- or six-year-old I would sit in the bathtub playing with my plastic or rubber ducks, singing most of Wagner's *Tannhäuser* Overture— the original 1845 version—even down to imitating most of the instrumental sonorities of the piece: clarinets, horns, cellos, etc. I don't recall what I did with the famous skipping thirty-second note string passages in the climatic moments of the Overture; I must have sung the much easier trombone parts. (Oh, for the availability of tape recording in 1931!) So there must have been some musical talent brewing in me even then.

And I did retain some degree of interest in music during the years I was in school in Germany. I remember how, in our singing of Bach chorales every morning, I relished particularly those wondrously perfect vocal lines and the beautiful harmonies they produced. I'm sure I didn't know *why* I appreciated the beauty of those melodies, or what exactly made Bach's voice-leadings so perfect, so well-balanced, so perfectly functioning, both linearly (melodically) and vertically (harmonically). I just remember the thrill of discovery, that special sense of youthful wonderment, and the gradual realization that there is such a thing in the world as artistic, creative, aesthetic perfection.

Be all that as it may, environment and chance, seen in retrospect, played a clearly discernible role in my development toward becoming a musician, revealing how very much genetics and environment can and often do intersect. Whatever musical seeds were sown in me from my parental heritage, the fact is that a sequence of events and experiences that, at first glance, would appear to be unrelated nevertheless coalesced into a pattern that ultimately—and rather quickly as such things go—culminated in my turning to music as my life's work.

The absolutely first memory I have of anything in my early childhood is so unusual, so anomalous, so bizarre, that I cannot in retrospect be absolutely certain that I actually witnessed it, that it wasn't something I dreamt. It was the birth of my brother Edgar in 1928—yes, the actual birth in my parents' bedroom. I cannot explain why this took place in our home in Jackson Heights, Queens, rather than in a hospital; how it was that, inconceivable as it may seem, I was allowed as a not quite three-year-old child to witness such a scene.

The scene—with all its frantic commotion, my mother's cries of pain, my first sight (I assume) of blood—is so vivid in my memory that I am convinced it could not be a mere dream. Apart from two or three typical recurring childhood nightmares that we all seem to have, the thousands of dreams I have had in my long life have all quickly evaporated, their specific details and content lost forever. Even the memory of typical, normal childhood nightmares is bedimmed to the vaguest of generalities.[10] By contrast, the scene of my brother's birth is still clearly etched in my mind's eye, embedded in my consciousness as precisely as if it were a thrice-familiar photograph: who was in the room (my father was not) and what part of the room—a woman whom I had not seen before (presumably a midwife)—the dark-brown iron bedstead, a large picture on the wall over my mother's head, even the patterned, beige wallpaper. Somehow I never asked my parents about this matter, and they are now dead; so is my Aunt Lydia, whom I remember clearly being in the room. But recently, my brother confirmed that it was as I remember; I was indeed present in the room, he having been told as much by our parents.

That is the only strangely frightening scene I can remember of my very early childhood. For the rest, I seem to have led a rather uneventful existence, playing for hours on end with my extensive collection of toys. I remember particularly a wooden wagon on which the front wheels could turn left and right—very important to a three-year-old—but to which I was particularly attracted because it was painted a strong deep blue and vivid orange. I remember being told that these were the official colors of the city of New York, displayed foremost on the city's flags. It was the first inkling I have of my lifelong fascination with colors, including, of course, orchestral colors, timbres, sonorities—as reflected vividly in my own music.

There was one episode in my young life, however, that can only be described as very unusual, perhaps even unique. Because my father's work with the New York Philharmonic was limited to the twenty-eight weeks of the winter season and another eight weeks in the summer, he frequently made trips in the late summer, early fall to Germany. I think for some years after his arrival in the United States in 1923 he considered the possibility of returning some day to his homeland. He had had outstanding successes there as a young violinist, playing—from his fourteenth year on—with about a dozen different orchestras, most often as concertmaster and concerto soloist. In the New York Philharmonic he was at first hired to fill a position in the viola section, two years later moving only to the third stand of the second violins.[11] And so the temptation was always present to return to the old country and try a solo career there. There was also the desire to visit relatives in Germany, both on his side (in Saxony) and on my mother's (in the Rhineland). Thus there developed a pattern of traveling to Europe almost every year, continuing well into the late 1930s.

During some of these yearly overseas trips I was left in the care of family friends in Queens, while on other occasions I was taken along. My first trip abroad was in 1927 when I was only a one-and-a-half-year-old baby, an unusual thing for my parents to do, certainly in those early days, a trip about which, of course, I remember nothing. But what was unusual—and even maybe daring—was that my parents took me on a plane flight from Vienna to Prague on the one-year-old Lufthansa airline. Such an undertaking was so unheard of and, as it turned out, so absolutely unprecedented, that baby Gunther's picture appeared in dozens of German and Austrian newspapers as the youngest child ever to fly on a European commercial airline. Thus I made a bit of Guinness Book history as a one-and-a-half-year-old.

From that trip there also exists a photo of me—used in later years to amuse guests and embarrass me—sitting on the potty in Burgstädt, my father's hometown, while (according to my Aunt Lydia) I was trying to sing the melody of the first waltz from Johann Strauss's *Roses of the South* and waving my hands as if conducting.

I had the usual boy's fascination with toy building blocks,[12] cars, and trucks, particularly dump trucks, which I pushed endlessly around my room, accompanied by my very loud "brrrmmmmm" motor noises. I was really in heaven sometime in 1929 when the open field and wooded area at the end of our street in Jackson Heights, Queens was suddenly cleared and developed for housing; those big ol' wonderful Mack trucks came charging by every thirty seconds or so. That was also the time when I received my first tricycle, and I remember trying constantly to find the more dangerous and daringly difficult dirt mounds and ruts near the edge of the excavations over which to ride, with, of course, many a painful spill, scraped knees, and bloody shins—all much to the annoyance of my mother. She naturally had to clean me up several times a day, accompanied by overly enthusiastic spankings, which, however, never persuaded me to change my ways.

In all these boyish activities I seem to have developed from the very beginning a strong penchant for pushing things to the edge, a certain daring, an incurable devil-may-care attitude. Some of it was show-offy, some if it was testing how far I could go, and how much I could get away with, some of it was sheer stubbornness. I am sure this exasperated my mother, rather short-tempered herself and impatient with my constant rebelliousness. I suppose the best way to describe me was as a somewhat unruly, temperamental, and headstrong child.

Into those early years—before my parents temporarily exiled me to a school in Germany in early 1932—also fall the fascinating summer weekend excursions, initiated by my father, to a whole string of abandoned farmsteads and estates just a few miles east of where we lived in Queens. It is impossible to imagine now, seventy years later, given the housing and population explosion that befell western Long Island in the mid-1930s and after the war—we all remember the sudden eruption of Levittown—that Queens (or more precisely Long Island City, which encompassed a dozen or so separate neighborhoods, such as Sunnyside, Woodside, Jackson Heights, Astoria, Flushing, and later Rego Park, Kew Gardens, and Forest Hills), ended just west of Elmhurst and (further south) Jamaica. Immediately beyond those Long Island City townships there were hundreds of deserted potato and vegetable farms and orchards, as well as former grand estates, now abandoned and vacant, in most cases due to the great number of sudden bankruptcies in the aftermath of the stock market crash of 1928. My father, indefatigably seeking out new places and sights, knew all these secret hideouts. As vivid in my mind's eye as if I had visited there last week, I can see me playing with my little brother during these weekend excursions, crawling around the half-fallen-down barns and farmhouses, exploring abandoned dried-up wells and rusting farm machinery, climbing ancient gnarled trees, picking apples and pears from unattended orchards—some of these pursuits rather dangerous. I'm surprised in retrospect that my parents let us roam around so freely. One of my favorite pastimes was building long dirt roads in some of the sandier areas—my miniature version of the highways and parkways that were beginning to be built in and around New York—smoothing out and leveling these super highways with an empty Maxwell House coffee can.

My fascination was much stimulated by our occasional visits to some of the abandoned luxury estates, many of which had immaculately paved private asphalt roads in the middle of the property, perhaps one or two miles long, now leading nowhere in particular, but still lined with stately colonnades of trees—like some lost, empty landscape in a 1920s French surrealist film. We would drive up and down these abandoned roads, just for the sheer pleasure of driving unchallenged on some former millionaire's private property.

Of course, we didn't head just eastward toward the farmlands beyond Queens, but also, especially on holidays, westward into town. Town meant Manhattan with its brand new skyscrapers, the Chrysler Building (1929) and the even taller Empire State Building (1931). And then there was beautiful Fifth Avenue; and it really was *beautiful* back then—elegant, clean, relatively uncrowded, no hot dog stands or sidewalk vendors selling cheap watches and silly trinkets. Window shopping for Edgar and me was like visiting some magical fantasyland. On one of those trips to Manhattan across the Queensboro Bridge my parents took us to see

St. Patrick's Cathedral and, a few blocks further north, St. Thomas Episcopal Church, at Fifty-Third Street and Fifth Avenue. Its eighty-foot altar and beautiful stained glass windows were an awesome and inspiring sight. Little did I realize that not too many years later I would be lifting my soprano voice to the glory of God every Sunday for three years, right under that magnificent altar.

One of my more memorable childhood adventures took place in the summer of 1931, when again I was taken along on a brief vacation in Germany, primarily to visit with our relatives. (I suspect another purpose of the trip was to check out a certain private school in Germany to which I was sent a year later.) My father, the inveterate traveler, took all of us on several hiking trips, mostly in the beautiful Erzgebirge (Iron Ore Mountains), a two-hour drive southwest of my father's hometown. But for me, the high point of these excursions lay in the other direction, southeast, to climb the Schneekoppe (Snowcap) Mountain, at nearly four thousand feet the highest mountain in that entire east German region, located just inside what was then the border between Czechoslovakia and Germany (but is now a part of Poland and called Snêzka). A symmetrically cone-shaped mountain, Schneekoppe—looking very much like Japan's Mount Fuji—is not a real mountaineer's climb but rather, with its gently rising slopes and well-tended paths, a good eight-hour hike (up and back down), at times over more strenuous, rougher terrain and a few large boulder fields.

Little five-and-a-half-year-old Gunther was the undisputed hero of the day, for—wanting as usual to show off—he made it to the peak all alone a whole hour and a half before the rest of the troop, which consisted of not only my parents but also my two aunts, Lydia and Ilse (then in their early thirties and late twenties, respectively), and two other relatives of my father. My speed climb was, I suspect, one of many exercises in declaring my independence; I was determined to show that I didn't need anyone's help, and that I was stronger, faster, and therefore better than anyone. In my small puerile mind, that evening was a colossal triumph for me, and I can even now, eighty years later, recall the feelings of pride, of achievement, the ego-satisfying approbation of my elders, especially Aunt Lydia, who never stopped gushing about what a brave child little Gunther was.

With matured hindsight, I realize now that my boyish achievement that day was in large part attributable to two characteristics I inherited, I am convinced, from my mother: a strong goal-oriented drive and an unusually high level of physical energy. Most of what I have been able to achieve in my adult life and musical career can be accounted for by those twin qualities, plus a strong sense of discipline and joy in work, qualities that were strengthened and nurtured in the two superb schools I was privileged to attend in the next eight years.

In the fall of 1931, shortly before my sixth birthday, I entered elementary school in Sunnyside, Queens, where my parents had moved into a big new apartment house on Forty-Eighth Street. My father's frequent summer trips to Germany had the unfortunate side effect of the family having to move to new homes almost every year. We pretty much covered the entire area of western Queens, various neighborhoods near the Queensboro Bridge that provided relatively easy access either by car or subway to midtown Manhattan and my father's main place of work, Carnegie Hall. I don't remember much of that half year in public school except that our classes seemed to consist primarily of finger painting, drawing circles, and consuming considerable quantities of cookies and milk. I was just passing time there because my parents had already decided to send their unruly, hard-to-manage child to a school in Germany, to get some real discipline and a "good German education."

In January, my parents put me, rather unceremoniously, almost as if they were glad to get rid of me for a while, on the SS *Europa*, one of the newest and finest of the new Hapag-Lloyd Steamship Company's ocean liners. The transatlantic crossing took a whole week in those days, with stops in Cork, Ireland, and Cherbourg, France, before landing at the German North Sea port of Bremerhaven. There I was met by my relatives from Krefeld, my grandmother Cleophile and my Aunt Louise (we called her Lulu), who then escorted me to my new school in Gebesee, a little town of two thousand inhabitants about fifty miles north of Erfurt, smack in the geographical center of Germany.

To send a six-year-old boy unaccompanied across the Atlantic was, to say the least, highly unusual, not to say heartless and cruel—and certainly not allowable nowadays, perhaps even punishable by law. A stewardess was put in charge of me and instructed to keep a sharp eye on this rather unmanageable kid. But she did not possess the authority of parents, and consequently, after a day or so of homesickness, I began to gain complete run of the ship. Although I was booked in third class far down in the hull of the ship, I soon found a way to cross over to the upper decks of second and first class, where, I was told later, I evidently became everyone's darling little boy!

My aunt and grandmother were told by the stewardess that I passionately loved cooked red cabbage, to the point that I demanded it every day, and that, because I loved smoked eel even more—a North German delicacy that the Hamburg- and Bremen-based Hapag Lloyd ships featured regularly—I refused to wash my hands for three days lest they lose the wonderful smell of smoked eel.

I arrived at my new school in mid-January in the dead of winter. I could hardly have anticipated that I had landed in a young boy's paradise. The Gebesee school (called in German *Internat*), a private school that catered regularly to foreign children but usually of German extraction, was one of a consortium of seven schools scattered throughout Germany. My parents had heard about the schools from my mother's cousin, Peter Kutt, who had gone to the one in Haubinda, a tiny hamlet near the central German Vogelsberg mountain range. My parents had vacillated in choosing between Gebesee and the school in Spiekeroog, on one of the small islands off the northwestern coast of Germany, very near the Dutch border. The latter was closest to my mother's relatives in the northern Rhineland; the former was located in Thuringia in the geographic center of Germany and thus nearer to my father's relatives in the neighboring province of Saxony. It seems my father and Gebesee won out.

The seven international schools had been founded in the midtwenties by a German educator named Hermann Lietz, well known for his educational philosophy based on a thoroughly comprehensive, wide-ranging, and challenging curriculum, combined with very strict discipline, and coed. Gebesee took children from first through sixth grade; other schools, like Haubinda, served children age nine through fourteen. In two other schools in the consortium, students were prepared, as in an American high school, for advancing to university. Although sometimes compared to the famous Waldorf or Rudolf Steiner schools, the comparison was not quite germane, since the curricula of the Lietz schools were free of any of those competitors' anthropomorphic and quasi-religious overtones.

Why a boy's paradise? Imagine a school located within the expansive four-acre grounds of a real late eighteenth-century castle, encircled by a fortress wall six feet thick, the main entrance of which had a huge two-foot-thick wooden gate, replete with drawbridge, iron gratings, embrasures and all. The castle grounds encompassed not only a large chestnut tree-lined courtyard—in earlier times probably a parade ground—surrounded by six two-story dormitory and classroom buildings, but also barns and stables for horses, cattle, sheep, and hogs, as well as a beautiful park and formal gardens dotted with fountains and goldfish ponds. The park, graced by one of the most beautiful two-hundred-year-old red beech trees I've ever seen, overlooked the town's old mill and millpond just outside the castle grounds. And beyond the formal gardens lay our special paradise, an extensive higher-lying wooded area where we kids could build tree houses and underground caves, the latter replete with tiny sleeping bunks and fireplaces.

The centerpiece of the entire complex was the great *Schloss* building, in classic late eighteenth-century style, four stories high, turrets at either end, and a grand, wide portal entrance that one crossed through into a smaller formal rose garden and a spacious circular driveway.

The seventy-odd students in the school were divided into six "families" of about twelve kids each, co-ed and headed by a "father" and a "mother." The youngest families were at first housed in the courtyard buildings, four kids to a room, from which one eventually graduated to the dorms in the main *Schloss*. When I arrived in January 1932, I was entered into second grade at midterm, and assigned to a family whose titular "parents" were a married teacher couple, a Herr und Frau Herrmann Finck, whom we little kids called "Buchfink" (the German word for wood finch)—evidently, if I recall correctly, with their blessing. This was a fine arrangement for a six year old because one had not only the guidance and support of two surrogate parents but also a sense of belonging to a special group.

It was in this group that I met my first best boyhood friend, a Brazilian named Jürgen Paschen, from Belem in northern Brazil.

Scholastically the school was at an incredibly high level. Imagine a curriculum where, in the second grade, along with reading, writing, and arithmetic, we were taught beginning French and Latin. That same year I remember our geography teacher acquainting us with the then relatively new discoveries of the tectonic plates that covered the globe, and the equally new theories of how Africa and South America had separated thirty million years ago, how Australia had drifted apart from Asia, and how there had been a tropical land named Gondwana that had later turned into ice-bound Antarctica. Pretty heady stuff for a six year old whose favorite subject was geography!

Other subjects we were required to take were shop, at least for one year, where we learned the basics of carpentry and made little tables, three- or four-legged stools, small wooden sculptures, and the like; art, drawing, and sketching, not only with crayons but also paint and water colors, classes in which I discovered that I had a real talent. Most of what I drew and painted there is lost, probably left in Gebesee after my precipitous departure from Germany in 1936, but a few examples of my work have survived. I remember especially a series of seven pictures based on the well-known children's tale *Why the Sky Fell*, which fascinated me and inspired my visual imagination.

In another class we were taught weaving, crocheting, embroidery, and needlepoint—yes, even the boys. I still have an embroidery depicting three birds, two sitting on separate branches, a third one, a woodpecker, pecking away at a tree bark. I also still have a small multicolored, cross-stitched purse with a rather modern abstract design.

We were also introduced to the basics of farming and animal breeding, right within our own castle walls. It was a pretty large farm complex, consisting of at least six or seven buildings. We were allowed to watch everything: the milking of cows, grooming of horses, feeding of chickens. A favorite attraction was the big pigpen, with its snorting inhabitants and cute little piglets, all of them wallowing in the mud. The geese were allowed to wander around freely. I thought they were cute until one day a gander bit me hard in the leg and taught me how nasty geese can be.

But what I loved most—nonfarmers and city folk will laugh and find this weird and bizarre—were the mixture of odors in the farm complex, not only the hay barns but also the compost heaps and manure bins, wonderfully pungent earthy smells. The only unpleasant experience I can recall occurred when one of my classes was taken to a cowshed, where we were shown how cows were killed: by stunning them, hitting them hard on the skull with a huge wooden hammer. I nearly threw up at the sight, it was so awful, and I am mighty glad in retrospect that they didn't show us how the cows were butchered.

We were each given our own little plot of land, where we were encouraged to grow flowers as well as to tend and harvest vegetables. As one of only two or three Americans in the school at the time, I grew American corn, which I had my parents send me, and which I later ate and shared with my best friends, having learned that the corn grown in Germany was not the fine edible kind we have in America, but a tasteless mealy corn used only as cattle feed.

The school also offered a very active sports program, everything from *Fussball* (soccer), both forms of hockey, swimming, ping-pong, skiing in the winter (down hill and cross-country), and a German version of baseball called *Schlagball*.

Bicycling was extracurricular, but we boys organized our own bicycling tournaments that included racing, jumping (over earthen mounds, akin to ski jumping), riding as long as possible on only the back wheel, and, of course, skidding in whatever fantastic and daring gyrations we could invent. I was quite good at most of these sports, but especially at any sort of daredevil bicycling. My most celebrated and audacious—now I think crazy—stunt involved riding at full speed through a nearby densely wooded area (about a mile from the castle) on a very steep slope, which at about a ninety-degree angle dropped approximately a hundred feet straight down to a river. Any wrong move in navigating between the density of trees—there was no bicycle path as such, nor any underbrush to break your fall—and you would either crash into trees or slip and fall down the slope, especially after a rain, when the smooth clayish ground was still muddy and slippery. Absolutely crazy!

Although the high scholastic standards of the school and the strict discipline imposed by the teachers required us to concentrate much time and effort on our studies, I don't recall any of these educational demands being excessively onerous. Indeed, we seemed to have plenty of time for play and games, in both structured (as in the official sports programs) and free leisure periods. In that regard, the extensive grounds within the castle walls provided seemingly endless opportunities to play a great variety of hide and seek games, cops and robbers, cowboys and Indians, as well as to build tree houses and excavate underground caves. The fairly extensive wooded area at one end of the castle grounds offered everything from interesting trees to climb to dense bush and underbrush areas, as well as hazelnut trees, which we raided regularly. I remember in particular realizing that all the trees and bushes diffused different scents, nature's subtlest perfumes, especially in springtime and—even more especially—after rainfalls.

In this extensive wooded haven it was easy to hide and play our boyish war games. Much of this was inspired by and often carried out in exact scenarios taken from the books of Karl May, a nineteenth-century German author who wrote more than a dozen fictional tales and sagas about life on the American frontier, books that we all read with great relish.[13] Just as American kids grew up on Westerns and "cowboys and Indians" serialized movies, German boys lived, dreamed, ate, and slept sequel after sequel of Karl May's thrillers, identifying with their special heroes, particularly favorite characters like the great Indian chief Winnetou and his white trapper friend, Old Shatterhand. To boys in Germany in the 1930s Old Shatterhand was as great a hero as the Lone Ranger was to American kids.

My fascination with Karl May's stories continued well into my early teen years, for I recall that when I was about thirteen and had begun writing music, I had the grand idea of composing an opera based on one of May's books that had as one of the more fascinating fictional characters a German music professor who had gone to the New World after the 1848 German uprisings to bring "the great German music culture" to the "barbarian" American West. But I never got past a dozen pages of the libretto and the beginnings of an overture, one of many soon-aborted composition projects of my very early teen years.

Once in a while we were taken in groups of ten or twelve to Gebesee's local movie house. We saw some of the early Nazi films (*Hitlerjunge Quex, Horst Wessel*), but young—and innocent—as we were, we saw these mostly as exciting adventure stories rather than political propaganda films. Somehow we were spared the most malignant anti-Semitic racist films of slightly later vintage. What we kids really loved were the nonpolitical films like *M*, Fritz Lang's 1931 masterpiece (*M* stands for murderer), and *Emil und die Detektive* (1931), directed by Gerd Lamprecht. It is in those films that I first saw my all-time favorite villains: the doleful, pathetic, bulging-eyed Peter Lorre (in *M*), and the truly evil, sinister, lecherous Fritz Rasp (in *Emil*). The latter film really excited us kids, because in it the villain is stalked and eventually captured not by the police, but by a gaggle of streetwise teenage boys, with whom we, of course, identified—and who, I found out years later, were not professional child actors but untrained children off the streets of Berlin.

I was pretty quick on my feet, a very good runner, and, of course, always absolutely determined to win any game or sport, whether I was hiding or seeking, or whether I was the bad guy or the good guy. I was a scrappy little fighter with a quick, unrestrainable temper that led me to take on older, bigger kids, almost always to my immediate regret. I was more than once beaten up pretty badly, but like the proverbial little wire terrier always ready to harass and attack the bigger bulldog, I seemed unable to resist the temptation to see if I could wrestle down an older boy. One in particular was the frequent target of my ire and, I realize now, my jealousy. He was a year ahead of me, a handsome, well-built, smart-looking kid, whom I really detested. He seemed impossibly arrogant and cocky, always reveling in his good looks and expensive clothes, obviously feeling superior to the rest of us kids. Why? Because his father—I believe his name was Fiedler—was a much-celebrated flying ace hero in World War I, a member of Richthofen's legendary fighter squadron. I never did beat Fiedler, as best as I can recall, but I felt proud, even with a bloodied nose, that I had had the courage to take him on, and basked in the praise and encouragement I received from many of the kids my age or younger who also loathed Fiedler.

Many of our tree houses were fairly elaborate affairs, some with two tiny rooms, equipped with elaborate twirled rope ladder systems, and all made of logs or discarded wood planks left over from previous tree houses or provided for just this purpose by the school's staff carpenters and handymen. The big thrill for me was to climb up into the tree house with a friend—like Jürgen—and spend the whole afternoon there in heavenly isolation, dreaming up adventure stories (including Wild West tales), or trading from our extensive collections of marbles, stamps, tin soldiers, or miniature warships.

But I found the cave dwellings we built into the ground even more fascinating. They were usually half underground, often dug out of the side of an earth mound, with a wooden or thatched roof overhead, held up at the corners by sturdy logs or tree trunks. The best part was the small fireplace some of us built into one wall, where we would roast potatoes (in the fall) or bake candies, cookies, and various other goodies. The fire hazard was probably considered minimal, since we usually built the fireplace into the rather damp clay soil and, of course, away from the wood ceiling. These little huts were small enough and open-ended on one side so that at the slightest sign of danger we could have scrambled out into the open in a matter of seconds.

We kids were allowed outside the castle grounds for a few hours in the late afternoon after classes. We might go swimming in the Unstrut, a nearby river, or ride our bikes in the surrounding countryside, hike in the nearby woods, or wander through neighboring farmers' orchards, picking the delicious cherries or wild strawberries—or, as became more and more my habit, head for a tiny little candy and cookie shop, half a block from the castle's main gate, where for a few pennies I would buy not candies but a slice of pumpernickel spread with mustard. Delicious!

Considerable time was spent on sports, including skiing and ice-skating. The terrain in and around Gebesee, mostly flat farmland, was not suitable for skiing, not even cross-country. So we were taken every winter for one whole week to Oberhof in the Thüringer Wald, a mountain range less than a day's travel south of Gebesee. Oberhof was already then a major ski center; it had many downhill trails, ski lifts (the rope kind), slalom slopes, ski jumps, and wonderful extensive cross-country trails. In the three winters that I was taken to Oberhof—1933, 1934, 1935—I learned to become quite a good skier, at least for my age.[14] I often went off on my own—slalom practicing or cross-country skiing. I especially loved that, reveling in the scenery, the snow-covered pines, the occasional long-range views of some distant valley or neighboring mountain, the pregnant silence of the woods, that wonderful acoustic isolation in heavy snow, the only sound the crunching noise of my skis on the packed snow.

Ski equipment was extremely primitive in those days, even for professional skiers: the plainest, flat, all-wooden skis, ordinary laced leather boots, the simplest snap-on bindings that in my case seemed always to slip off or break, making me mad as hell. How many times I lay there alone on some lonely slope, frustrated, alternately cursing and crying—with rarely anyone to witness my plight.

Ice-skating was another big winter sport for me in Gebesee. There were a number of ponds in the immediate neighborhood of the *Schloss*, not only the millpond directly adjacent to the castle wall, but several larger ponds further outlying, leftover arms of the Unstrut, a few kilometers north of Gebesee. I had never skated at home in Queens, but in Germany, as in Holland and other northern European countries, everyone ice-skated. So I learned to skate, and by my second winter in Germany got pretty good at it, trying—always the little show-off—to master all kinds of daring stunts, jumps, weird twists and turns, rather than simply skating endlessly around the perimeter of the pond. Eventually I paid a price for my swaggering ways. One day I stumbled on a fallen tree branch that had become half frozen in the ice, fell precipitously and landed hard on my chin, opening a gash that required some seventeen stitches and that left a scar and welt that I still bear.

Being rather wild and reckless as a child, I also naturally became accident prone, and left Germany in 1936 with quite a number of serious scars. One of the worst accidents I inflicted on myself occurred when playing in the school's big courtyard, near a little excavation that had just been uncovered (probably some work on a sewer or an underground pipe), climbing around on a large sawhorse. I fell off and, sliding all the way down one side, my leg got caught on a large rusty hook, which ripped open a two-inch gash in my left shin. Very painful! What amazes me in retrospect is that I never seem to have learned from my various misadventures to moderate my behavior. And there was one really big accident yet to come!

It was in Gebesee that I also learned to swim. I still recall the occasion with a considerable twinge, for the initiation to swimming in the school was seen as a sort of baptism or rite of passage, during which you established your manhood. The ceremony was swift and uncomplicated. You were unceremoniously thrown into the ice-cold water, left to fend for yourself—no harness to hold you afloat, no one to assist or guide you, just the sports teacher yelling at you from the pond's bank, telling you to paddle with your arms and legs. It was advice which in any case I could not hear because I was wildly and noisily thrashing about in the water, fighting for my life. It was so cold—this obviously was not in the summer—that my heart and my breathing nearly stopped when I hit the water. Cruel as this initiation exercise was, it did make you learn how to swim in a remarkable hurry; it was a matter of survival.

Almost as frustrating, and cruel, was the annual maypole-climbing contest—frustrating because the pole was smeared with slippery grease, and no matter how hard I tried clinging to the pole with my hands, feet, and knees, I could never reach the top of the pole. My failure was especially frustrating and embarrassing because, as usual, I was hoping to impress my girlfriend of the time, and was really infuriated when my nemesis, wise-ass Fiedler, succeeded in reaching the top of the pole, receiving the adulation of the crowd.

By contrast, the pond or lake where I learned to ice-skate was the scene of one of my happiest childhood undertakings. In the carpentry and shop class, I had built with my friend Jürgen a small replica of a sort of Polynesian outrigger sailboat. We had made it as authentic in detail as we could, about two-and-a-half-feet long, with masts about twelve inches high. To our relief the boat did not capsize when we launched it; in fact it floated beautifully, indeed I would say regally, proudly—to the considerable approbation of our fellow students and my favorite teacher, Robert Schneider. The pond at that time of year was populated by hundreds of baby tadpoles. Thinking that our Kontiki should be manned by sailors, we fished a bunch of tadpoles from the water and put them on our ship. To our delight most of them did not jump ship, but stayed aboard, evidently enjoying the sun, and cruising around the pond as the current and a gentle breeze in the sails wafted our little naval masterpiece along.

But the fondest memories I still carry with me from my schooldays in Germany are of the wonderful hiking trips, usually lasting an entire week, that we were all taken on every year in the spring and the fall. One trip took us to the Kyffhäuser mountain range, with its major tourist attraction, the famous Kyffhäuser Monument, built during the German Empire in the late nineteenth century, which depicts William I and the Holy Roman Emperor Frederick Barbarossa, a charismatic leader who died in 1190 during the Third Crusade.[15] On another more extensive tour, after taking a train to Treffurt on the river Werra, we hiked northwestward along the Werra all the way to Hannover-Münden, where the Werra flows into the Weser, passing through many beautiful old medieval river towns like Eschwege, Schwebda, and Witzenhausen. We were constantly exploring ancient castles and cloisters, and climbing some of the many one-thousand- to two-thousand-foot mountains, not high by American Rockies standards, but for us little kids (many of us were city dwellers) marvelously exciting adventures. What made these hiking trips so wonderful was that, true to this day, Germany has the greatest and most extensive hiking trails and beautifully tended walking paths in all of Europe, through impeccably kept forests and peaceful valleys, past hundreds of old farmsteads, over mountain peaks and along river gorges, with a never-ending variety of scenic sights.

Another year, on another trip in the same west German region, we were taken on a long hiking tour along the Weser River, from the ancient cities of Höxter and Corvey all the way to the town of Hameln, famous for the legend of the Pied Piper of Hamelin. These trips, quite apart from their educational value, were occasions to get to know our fellow students; at school we were generally segregated into different age groups and "families" and classes. On our trips we generally stayed in wonderfully kept youth hostels, a big thing in Germany because of the great love in that country for hiking, especially in the 1920s and 1930s, when hardly any Germans owned cars, and when there were thousands of hiking clubs. In the evenings in the hostels, we kids always had a few hours of leisure time, and I know that many a youthful romance was inaugurated on such occasions. I know that my first amorous feelings and sexual stirrings date from that time, feelings directed primarily at a girl one year older than I, whose name I remember only as Melitta.

But our biggest and longest hiking trip was one that covered practically the entire length of the Thüringer Wald, the mountain range running diagonally across central Germany from northwest to southwest, about one hundred kilometers (thirty-five miles) long. Its highest mountain is the Inselsberg (Island Mountain), some three thousand feet high, rather bare near the top, with a wonderful youth hostel and sports camp where we stayed for two nights. We traversed the whole range, always over well-marked climbing trails and beautifully kept walking paths and roads, touching upon many towns and hamlets—from Ruhla through Schmalkalden, Zella-Mehlis, Suhl, Ober-Weissbach (another great mountain camp), to Lauscha and Neustadt—everywhere mind- and eye-opening sights and experiences. One of these, in Lauscha, took on a special meaning for me a few years later. In that town there was the greatest concentration of glass blowers in all of Germany, comparable only with Murano in Venice. We visited not only the glass blowing plants but also several of the town's glass museums, with their exhibits of great art works, some of them hundreds of years old, ranging from vases and dishes through all manner of glass sculptures and miniature animals to artificial glass eyes. Little did I know that one of these items would soon accompany me for the rest of my life.

Among the many stimulating experiences I encountered in my years in Germany, the annual Fasching festivities stand out as very special. Fasching is the German equivalent of the Mardi Gras of New Orleans or Rio de Janeiro. Immediately before the Lenten season for several days (and nights!) all normal work and conventional behavior are totally suspended, especially in the Catholic regions of Germany. In Gebesee as well, it was an occasion for unbridled revelry. Everybody was dressed in outrageously exotic costumes, and black or sequined masks were donned to hide one's identity, thus permitting unrestrained licentiousness and whatever moral laxity might strike one's mind. I was too young to fully comprehend what was going on, and surely too innocent to participate in any libertine or risqué behavior. But I certainly remember well the undertow of libidinous, sensual feelings that mysteriously overtook me.

During the five years I was in school in Germany I spent most of my vacations, including the long summer holidays, more or less alternating with my relatives in Krefeld and Burg-städt; in the former town with my grandmother Cleophile and aunt Lulu, in the latter town with grandmother Alma and aunt Ilse. These were especially happy times for me. In Burgstädt there were the frequent visits to the beautiful Wettinhain Park with its Taurastein, a 120-foot tower from which one could see in a 360-degree panoramic view the entire region with its rolling hillsides, fields, forests, and many small villages, sometimes separated only by a mile or two, each with its pretty church spire. The other big attraction, perhaps my favorite excursion goal, was the Rochsburg, a well-preserved eighteenth-century castle perched on top of a steep hill, picturesquely encircled on three sides by the valley of the river Mulde. In the fall the hill was a riot of colors, almost equal, I think, to the famous yearly foliage displays in New England. From Burgstädt to the Rochsburg was a good one-and-a-half-hour hike, on easy walking paths through beautifully kept fields and pastures, woods cleared of all underbrush (typical in Germany), alongside brooks and streams, down a steep dark ravine to the Mulde River below the castle, and thence across a hanging bridge and all the way up again to the ramparts of the castle. There on a sunlit terrace we quenched our thirst with lemonade or Weissbier, a tasty, foamy, minimally alcoholic refresher, served in big bowl-like glasses.

At my Burgstädt grandmother's, my time was divided between watching her and my aunt at work, and roaming through the many atlases, some dating back to the 1850s, that my father and his father had accumulated over the years. My grandmother, in her sixties at the time, had lost all of her teeth, and like most elderly Germans did not bother with dentures. I remember watching in amazement and curiosity how every morning, sitting by the kitchen window, she would dunk big chunks of hard dry bread into her hot tea, softening up the bread so that she could munch it down—all the while gazing out the window at the several gooseberry bushes and cherry trees in the little yard in the back of the house.

Both she and her daughter (my aunt Ilse) worked at home, sewing beautiful, delicate, colorful appliqués onto batches of plain unadorned gloves and blouses, which were delivered to them once a week. This work took great patience and subtle skill. I marveled at the control and accuracy with which they applied the decorations and petite floral designs, never seeming to make a mistake. I watched them for hours on end, and I'm sure that at a very early age I gained a deep sensitivity for detail from watching them at work.

Even more untold hours were spent poring over those atlases and touring maps, constantly making endless imaginary journeys to all the far-flung corners of the globe. That is where I first spotted Iceland (with its volcanoes and glaciers), Greenland, Tierra del Fuego (the southern tip of South America), Point Barrow (in Alaska, the northernmost point on the North American continent), Spitzbergen (Svalbard), Fiji, Rora Tonga in the middle of the Pacific, and Novosibirsk—all of which I have by now managed to visit, fulfilling many of my boyhood dreams. How lucky I have been!

My endless atlas explorations were experienced against a background of the equally interminable practicing of scales and interval exercises by the indefatigable Herr Naumann, a pianist and the town's main piano teacher. He lived in the apartment house next door on the same floor level as my grandmother. I remember being amazed (and annoyed) that the house walls were so paper thin that we could hear every boring note he ever played (he seemed never to play in any dynamic less than *forte*). On the other hand I was impressed by his stamina and his evident desire to keep ahead of his students by maintaining his technique at tip-top level. Sadly, we never heard him play any real music.

I also did a lot of reading, mostly German romantic novels, like the very moving lyric love story *Ekkehard*, by Josef Scheffel, but also lots of Grimm fairy tales: *Hänsel und Gretel*, *Schneewittchen* (*Snow White*), *Der Fischermann und syn Fru* (*The Fisherman and His Wife*), mostly delightful stories with the expected happy endings. But the one story that wasn't so happy, and that haunted me for weeks and months because it was so impossibly sad and tragic, was *Das klagende Lied* (*The Plaintive Song*). It tells a tragic tale of murder and atonement—and of a flute. The flute made of a slain knight's bone can yield only songs of lament and anguish. It takes its revenge on the killer, the murdered knight's own brother, now a king, when he, at the grand festive wedding to his young queen, asks to play the flute. As it intones its mournful lament, the castle—like Klingsor's castle in *Parsifal*—disintegrates. The entire court, the murderer king and his queen, expire in a terrible holocaust.

Hardly a happy children's fairy tale, it induced weeks of terrible nightmares. Some years later, however, in my late teens, I often thought about using *The Plaintive Song* for an opera; but even then I could never bring myself to do it. I didn't know at the time that Gustav Mahler's first large orchestral work, composed at age nineteen—and submitted in a competition to a jury headed by Brahms (which rejected the work)—was based on *Das klagende Lied*.[16] Perhaps it was the resultant poor reputation that discouraged conductors from programming the work. It seems to have received only three performances in Europe in the next sixty or so years. The first American performance occurred only in 1970, by the New Haven Symphony Orchestra, conducted by Frank Brief.

In the winter vacations in Burgstädt the big thing was, of course, the shopping, the preparations and decorations for Christmas, the highlight of which, for me at any rate, was not *Heiliger Abend* (Christmas Eve), although that was pretty exciting—that's when presents are exchanged and Santa Claus appears in the flesh—but rather going to the bakery down the street on December 23 to watch the town's baker make our special *Stollen*, the famous German Christmas cake. Believe me, dear reader, since you have undoubtedly heard of or perhaps have even tasted imported Dresden or Lübeck *Stollen*, there is nothing like the *Stollen* made by the town baker in Burgstädt—true to this day.[17] The Herr Bäckermeister would let me watch the whole operation, from the preparation and kneading of the dough, through the baking in the huge clay oven, to the final butter and sugar coating, as masterfully done as any great painter.

It was also in Burgstädt that I experienced—not once, but quite a few times—some of my earliest erotic sensations. These occurred when I noticed that when my beautiful aunt Ilse, then in her midtwenties, sat down, she lifted the back of her skirt, letting it hang over the back of her chair, thus sitting on her silk panties. As I am not a sexologist or a behavioral scientist, I cannot say whether my sexual arousal could be considered normal, common, or odd and aberrational (or none of the above). All I know is that these voluptuous feelings were real and irresistible. I must assume that such early pleasurable, carnal stirrings were the tiny tremorous forerunners of my lifelong adoration of women's lingerie.

But in Krefeld my vacations were—inexplicably—concerned with entirely different preoccupations. There I seem to have spent the majority of my time drawing and painting with watercolors, crayons, or colored pencil. My subjects were mostly flowers, blossoms and leaves, inspired, I'm sure, by the lovely garden my grandmother Cleophile and aunt Lulu maintained in back of their house, and their *Schrebergarten*.[18] Compared to the meager gooseberry bushes in the Burgstädt backyard, in Krefeld the dozen luscious gladiolas, giant dahlias, nasturtiums, and asters, along with prettily blooming vegetables, such as gourds and cucumbers, kept me constantly captivated and busy all summer, analyzing, dissecting, and replicating nature's floral bounty. I eventually graduated to more minuscule nature subjects, particularly different grasses and wheats, their intricate subtle structuring fascinating me enormously. Alas, none of these several hundred drawings survived, presumably they were left behind at my precipitous departure from Germany in late 1936.

My summers in Krefeld were thus relatively calm and stationary. But there was one great exception, whereby I threw my relatives into a complete state of panic. My fascination with maps and geography did not abate just because I was doing a lot of drawing. Indeed by the summer of 1936—I was still ten—I had memorized virtually the entire street design, street car routes and all, of not only Krefeld but also its outlying suburbs, including Ürdingen, a smaller town about three miles east of Krefeld on the west bank of the Rhine, where there was one of the relatively few Rhine bridges north of Cologne. I knew that Ürdingen also had a small marina where sailboats were moored.

I don't know what possessed me, but one fine summer day I stopped drawing, and while Cleo and Lulu were out shopping, and with only a few *Pfennige* in my pocket and a detailed street map in my hand, I wandered off toward Ürdingen, determined to see that bridge and those sailboats. I don't recall feeling particularly cooped up at my grandmother's, happily immersed as I was in my floral designs. But there must have arisen in me a sudden streak of Schullerian independence reaching out for some tangible sense of freedom, combined with an urgent need to satisfy my fascination with geographic exploration—even if only on a tiny scale; for Ürdingen and the Rhine were only some three miles from our house on the Oberdiessemerstrasse.

I knew exactly where I was going, and more or less as the crow flies headed straight for my intended targets, never for a moment giving any thought to the concerns my sudden absence would evoke in my grandmother and aunt Lulu, whose responsibility it was to keep a firm eye on the occasionally overadventurous little Gunther.

I made it to Ürdingen and the bridge, along endless trolley tracks and under several train viaducts, through heavy noonday traffic, not without some fascinated window-shopping. Occasionally, elder folks would look at me curiously; German ten year olds did not wander around alone without parents or older relatives.

My triumphant escape and blithe unconcern, the relish I felt at my unfettered freedom, suddenly came to an abrupt end when, just as I was reaching the sailboat marina, I was accosted by two policemen, who with some annoyance let me know that they had been looking for me all afternoon. Their annoyance was *their* problem; for my part I was proud—defiantly so—that I could have so easily eluded the entire Krefelder police force. On the other hand, one has to be impressed with the fact that after only five or six hours they found me in Ürdingen, east of Krefeld, not west, south, or north, directions which ostensibly would have been equally enticing to a boy with a driving *wanderlust*. Soon Lulu arrived, in hysterics, of course, crying with tears of joy, happy to find the little tike safe and sound. Bless her, she never bawled me out as we went home on the streetcar. Grandmother Cleo, with her French hot temper, wasn't so benignly inclined, and unleashed a torrent of near-expletives, which finally made me realize that I had really perpetrated a colossal and thoughtless foolishness.

Such episodes, as exciting as they may have seemed to me at the time, pale in comparison to one particularly riveting experience that Providence sent my way. As the reader may have gathered by now, for a young boy my life was certainly full of all sorts of excitements and adventures, what with traveling alone across the Atlantic to Germany at age six, various exciting vacation trips in America and Europe with my parents, climbing mountains, waterfalls, hiking in deep forests, the stimulating educational experiences in Gebesee, and—somewhat less pleasant—the various major hospitalizing experiences I incurred there. But nothing would match the extraordinary circumstances that permitted me to witness a major shipwreck in a massive, violent mid-Atlantic storm and the heroic rescue of the sinking ship's crew. It was an experience indelibly etched in my mind, which I recall almost as vividly as if it were yesterday.

In mid-December of 1934 I was returning to America from Germany for a Christmas vacation at home. My mother had again done some mountain climbing and skiing in the Bavarian Alps, after which she picked me up in Gebesee, whence we both traveled to Bremerhaven and embarked for New York on the *Europa*, the same ship on which I had been sent to Germany almost three years earlier. During the second day after leaving Cherbourg in France, heading westward, the sea became stormier by the hour as the winds hit near hurricane dimensions. The twenty-five-thousand-ton *Europa* was tossing about wildly in the increasingly mountainous waves, and I noticed that the outer decks had emptied out, as most passengers, evidently seasick, were in their cabins. It was quite frightening for me—a nine-year-old boy—to witness this exhibition of nature's awesome power, as the ship slowly fought its way through the howling winds and heavy seas, nothing in sight other than the turbulent ocean and dark, driving, tattered clouds.

What happened next was even more dramatic. As my mother and I were later able to piece things together, a Norwegian trawler named *Sisto* had radioed an SOS around one a.m. (on the eighteenth of December). The *Sisto*, its rudder damaged, was in serious trouble, taking on considerable quantities of water. By midday a British tanker named *Mobiloil* had reached the *Sisto*, and was pumping oil on the surrounding water to somewhat calm the seas, a standard rescue procedure. But a few hours later the *Mobiloil*, planning to rescue the Norwegian crew with its lifeboats, discovered that the seas were much too heavy to attempt such a rescue. In such a storm a lifeboat couldn't really navigate properly, or, worse, could easily be smashed to bits against the hull of the sinking ship.

But then, a new SOS from the troubled *Sisto*, stating that it was starting to take on water seriously, caused five or six other ships, including our *Europa*, to change their courses and head for the *Sisto*. The German Hapag-Lloyd steamship *New York* (the sister ship of the *Europa*), on its way eastward, bringing passengers from America to Europe for the Christmas holidays, happened to be nearest to the *Sisto* and was delegated to take over the rescue operation. Word got around quickly on board that there was a nearby ship in real trouble and that the *Europa* was changing course to help with the rescue.

I remember my bitter disappointment when all passengers were instructed to leave the upper open decks and stay inside below. Needless to say, this imminent rescue operation was something I didn't want to miss. Still, my mother and I went down to our D deck cabin, hoping to watch things from there. But then, imagine my annoyance when our steward began to close off our cabin's two portholes with their outer iron covers. So we headed upstairs again, for fortunately the big windows in the dining rooms, lounges, and library could not be similarly sealed off. But even so our outside view was considerably impaired, since on the ship's upper levels such communal rooms are, of course, encircled by the outer decks, and everywhere the windows were either steamed up or blurred by the spray of the penetrating, driving rain. Sitting there, peering out at the impenetrable darkness, even during daylight hours, I can recall our huge ship trembling in all corners, especially when the propellers, due to the ship's extreme alternating upward and downward motions—diving precipitously into the mountainous waves and then immediately riding up to the next peak—were freely, and pointlessly, whirling in the air.

It was all so exciting. I couldn't think of eating or sleeping, even though my mother, as night fell, tried to get me to do both. No way! The *Europa* reached the rescue scene in the evening when it was already pitch-dark and we could hardly see anything. But I remember screaming with excitement at my mother and other passengers, all of us with our noses glued to the windows, when for a second or two I saw a faint reddish light bobbing up and down in the darkness. It was the *Sisto*. Sometime later, the whole scene was suddenly lit up. It turned out that in the about-to-begin rescue effort led by the *New York*, the *Europa*'s role was to illuminate the area with its gigantic searchlights. Now we could see not only the *Sisto*, lurching from side to side, up and down, heavy swells constantly breaking over its deck, but also some of the other ships that had meanwhile arrived at the scene. Three ships—I read later that they were the *Mobiloil*, the British *Aurania*, and the German *Gerolstein*—had maneuvered themselves abreast in a line windward of the *Sisto*, to help break the fierce winds with their sizable hulls and thus to somewhat calm the sea. All the ships were also pumping more oil on the waters.

Expecting the *New York* to quickly send several lifeboats over to the *Sisto*, we were all astonished that, for what seemed an interminable time, we saw no movement of any kind; nothing was happening. What could be wrong? We learned later that a lifeboat rescue was deemed *absolutely* impossible by the Norwegians, and that they suggested waiting until dawn, hoping for the heavy weather to abate.

But the weather did not abate. Instead it got worse. Around midnight it began to snow and hail. Then suddenly we saw, against all expectations, a large lifeboat being lowered from the *New York*'s upper decks. As it descended it slammed several times against the ship's hull, bouncing around wildly in the drenching squall.

From time to time we could see in the *Europa*'s eerie illumination the half-sunk *Sisto*, a cluster of men apparently lashed to the ship's bridge house. We also could see that the *Sisto*'s cargo consisted of timber, huge stacks of logs that surprisingly had not been pitched overboard.

With mounting excitement we saw the *New York*'s lifeboat draw fairly close to the *Sisto*, and we wondered how they would get the Norwegians off their sinking ship. It was obviously a dangerous undertaking under any circumstances, but to attempt this in a seventy-mile-an-hour snow- and hailstorm seemed to some of us watching to border on lunacy.

But it wasn't long before we could see the German sailors' ingenious solution for rescuing the Norwegians. Suddenly several ropes appeared, hanging in midair between the Germans' lifeboat and the *Sisto*, taut enough on the one hand to stabilize the lifeboat and to keep it from dancing, careening, tossing wildly about; on the other hand slack enough to allow the Norwegian sailors to jump overboard while hanging on to the towline. One by one they lept into the ocean, the German sailors helping to pull them toward the *New York*. Since the *Sisto* was a low-lying freighter and already half sunk, the jump into the hellish waters was basically not that far. Most of the Norwegians jumped when the waves below were at their highest, but a few of them seemed to hesitate at the most favorable moment, and so found themselves leaping thirty to forty feet into a huge abyss, clinging desperately to the towline as their ship was tossed upward at the same time that the wave below dropped away. That these sailors, who had spent most of the last twenty-four hours out on deck in the icy-cold, fierce, piercing winds, humongous waves endlessly washing over their ship, still had the presence of mind and strength to assist in their own rescue seems to me almost miraculous.

Finally, somewhere around three or four a.m., both the Norwegians and their German res-cuers had all been hauled up onto the rope ladders of the *New York* on the ship's lee side, and to safety through its main landing portal.

During the rest of our voyage, many details of the rescue operation came to light as the *Europa*'s crew supplied us with almost hourly bulletins. We read with astonishment that the deliverance of the *Sisto*'s crew—the ship did sink several hours later—was considered the most remarkable undertaking of its kind in modern nautical history, in part because it involved the greatest (and apparently unprecedented) cooperative assemblage of ships in a single rescue operation: some six or seven ships. We learned that more than six thousand people—passen-gers and ship's crews—watched the entire action, and that many women on the various passen-ger ships had fainted watching it or had become hysterical. Obviously I had much to talk—and brag—about with my father and brother and friends when I got home.

The next summer (1935) I was not invited back home. Instead my father came to Germany, and after visiting his folks in Burgstädt he took me with him on a two-week vacation, traveling and sightseeing, hiking around central Germany, from the beautiful Harz Mountains down to northern Bavaria and the Pfalz (palatinate), where he had played in that region's official sym-phony orchestra. I don't remember much about the various places we visited, but I do recall rather clearly one wonderful evening in Bad Wildungen, another one of Germany's numerous spa resorts, where together we heard a beautiful performance of Mozart's Violin Concerto in D Major, played superbly, so my father said—and he was a tough critic—by the local concertmaster.

I also recall a considerably less edifying experience—it is amazing what one remembers from one's youthful past (or for that matter, *doesn't* remember)—when we went rowboating in a huge reservoir known as the Eder Talsperre (Eder Dam) near the resort of Waldeck; the new dam and reservoir had been completed some six months earlier. We rowed around the lake for most of the day in perfect summer weather, surrounded by the beautiful mountains and forests that encompassed the reservoir, eventually picnicking somewhere for lunch. In late afternoon both of us suddenly felt a call of nature (no. 2), and finding ourselves alone in the middle of this vast lake, nearly a mile from any shoreline, we rowed to a tiny nearby island and relieved ourselves in this magnificent wilderness paradise. That instant represented a strangely intimate and wonderful moment in my life, in my relationship to my much beloved father, all alone there, just the two of us, doing something as universal and as natural as human life can offer, which humans had been doing for countless thousands of years.

In fact, that whole trip with my father that summer is one of the happiest memories I have of my entire childhood, certainly not because of that episode, but because there is nothing quite like the relationship, the bonding, between a son and father when they are alone together on an extended trip or visit. Away from all earthly cares—or so it seemed to me—and away from home, randomly roaming around the countryside, seeing so many beautiful places, I think it was the closest that my father and I ever were to each other.

In the summer of 1936, it was evidently my mother's turn to take me and my brother Edgar on a little vacation trip. We traveled generally by train and on this occasion covered a region in Germany around the Harz Mountains, roughly fifty-five miles northwest of Erfurt, a region dotted with many of Germany's best preserved medieval towns and cities (Gotha, Blankenberg, Wernigerode), clustered around the Harz mountain range. I was particularly struck by the beauty and original decorative design of the so-called *Fachwerk* houses—every-where in the towns and on the farms—an architectural style in which the inner structure is made visible through elaborate square-timber beaming and cross-patterning. In their con-stant individualized variants I thought—and told my mother—that all these houses were works of art. She approved.

We visited many of the medieval churches and little chapels that dot the region, each one also a work of art, created mostly—I began to realize—not by internationally famous architects and artists, but by humble local artisans and craftsmen. This was a revelatory experience for me.

The highlight of the trip was a three-day stay in Gandersheim, where we were lodged in a picturesque pension just outside of town, called *Waldschlösschen*, as its name implies a small castlelike edifice with turrets and multiple terraces at the edge of a beautiful wood of oak and pine. Virtually alone there—we saw only two other couples—Edgar and I had the run of the place and its extensive gardens, a veritable horticultural paradise. The terraces were all opulently lined with flowers of all kinds, not only the usual geraniums but also violets, yellow and orange nasturtiums, asters, gladiolas, and so forth. The only trouble with this wealth of flowers was that they attracted swarms of bees and wasps. That might not have been a problem, except that these insects, happily feeding on the richness of pollen and nectar, were also enamored of the succulent strawberry jams we were served every morning as we breakfasted on the terrace. The three of us had to spend an inordinate amount of time fending off the hordes of insects, a struggle that the bees and wasps won after two days. On our third day we managed to enjoy our freshly crisp buttered rolls and jam in relative peace—in the pension's indoor restaurant.

But the most vivid memory of our Gandersheim sojourn is related to my mother taking me—we left Edgar at the pension with our hosts—to the town's *Stiftskirche* (cathedral), a beautiful, well-preserved, late-Gothic church that, even more important to me, housed the manuscripts, poems, compositions, and other ecclesiastical incunabula of Roswitha von Gandersheim, a twelfth-century nun, a contemporary of the now more famous Hildegard von Bingen. I was fascinated by her impeccably composed manuscripts, many of them with beautiful illuminations. It was my first encounter with such religious manuscripts, and I must say I'm proud that they made such an indelible impression on me at age ten, that they have remained vividly etched in my memory all these many years. It was perhaps the nicest gift my mother ever passed on to me.

In the 1930s my mother spent some time almost every year visiting friends in southern Bavaria, in a little village near Garmisch-Partenkirchen named Grainau (old German for "green pastures"), mountain climbing in the summer (or fall), skiing in the winter. When she had gone there originally in 1931 to go mountain climbing, she had found very pleasant accommodations at a typical Bavarian *Gasthaus*, the Pension Maurus. As she returned to Grainau year after year, the Mauruses (whom I eventually met when Margie and I began our frequent, nearly annual trips to Europe in the 1950s) became, more than mere innkeeper hosts, very close friends. Indeed, the Mauruses took to Elsie, an attractive, young, energetic German American—moreover from the wealthy United States—like a daughter, the daughter they could never have. She was family. Over the years my mother became a seasoned expert mountaineer, gradually scaling all the major peaks of the German and Austrian Alps from the Zugspitze (Germany's highest mountain, 9,721 feet) to the Gross Glockner (Austria's highest at 12,461 feet). In fact, she climbed the Zugspitze four or five times, from different approaches and directions.

But there are aspects of these yearly Bavarian visits that puzzle me, and that suggest a cloudier side. My mother obviously left her husband to fend for himself in New York, alone and busy with the Philharmonic's Lewisohn Stadium seasons. And I have to wonder whether he concurred with her continual absences. Also, what happened with little Edgar? With me at school in Germany, my father certainly could not have taken care of him all by himself.

It is also a bit peculiar that my mother visited me only twice in the three-and-a-half years I was in Germany, once on the occasion of the vacation trip in 1936, the other on one of my Burgstädt winter vacations. Of the latter I retain only the most unpleasant memories. In my grandmother's apartment there was only one small guest room, a tiny claustrophobic attic room with a single bed (and a very low ceiling), where I usually slept when I was in Burgstädt on vacation. This meant that on my mother's Burgstädt visit she and I had to sleep in the same bed, a very narrow one at that, not suitable for two people, with only one (typical German) bedcover, a so-called *Bettdecke*—not a good situation to begin with. What made matters worse was that I had contracted a horrendous itchy throat cold, and although I tried valiantly—oh, did I try!—to suppress every oncoming cough, it was a mostly futile effort. I held my breath as long as I could, but inevitably, of course, another irrepressible cough would explode forth. Instead of trying to get me some throat lozenges or some hot milk with honey (a popular German cold remedy), she uncontrollably unleashed torrents of whispered screams at me and beat me several times. It was one of the most miserable, frightening, nightmarish nights of my entire life. She beat me like one would beat a disobedient dog, clearly unable in her irrational fury to comprehend that I could not control my coughing, that I was not coughing expressly to annoy her.

But back to my mother's Bavarian visits. I became aware many years later that, sad to say, my parents' marriage was not what one would call a happy one. I mention this because after witnessing one too many of their regular, endless screaming bouts, which often came precariously close to physical violence, I remember resolutely vowing in my midteen years that when I married I would not let such volcanic eruptions destroy my marriage. Not that I really knew what the remedy was, but I vaguely understood that unforgiving, prideful, standoff confrontation was not the answer, that one or the other side would have to give in. My father, basically a very calm, easygoing sort, tried often enough to ignore his wife's quick-tempered, stubbornly nagging outbursts. But when finally he could no longer stand her out-of-control diatribes, the elemental force and violence of *his* reactions were truly frightening, truly cataclysmic—more fearsome than the worst summer thunder-and-lightening storm. And like a summer storm, it usually cleared the air. But each such encounter left ever-deeper, unhealing wounds and hardening scars on both of my parents.

Although they remained together until the end, this endless battling and the frequent separations led to more troubles later on. For I am convinced that while my mother was away on her Bavarian jaunts, my father—handsome, desirable, financially secure and successful through the Depression years, a good catch for any predatory female—probably could not resist certain attractive temptations that came his way. My mother, for her part, developed a gigantic crush on one of her mountain climbing companions, Peter Strauss, a married man from Garmisch, a handsome, strapping, virile young fellow who was considered one of the most skillful mountaineers and champion skiers in the region. I am certain their quiet, well-hidden affair never became physical, and, when interrupted for more than ten years by World War II, cooled to a close family friendship with Peter and his wife, Karina. Years later, on my own trips and vacations in Germany and Europe with Margie—and even our young son, Edwin, still a baby—we frequently visited Garmisch, staying with the Strausses, and in Grainau with the Mauruses.

It was in my last year and a half at Gebesee that I experienced what I suppose were my first real love pangs, inspired by and directed toward Melitta. I can't imagine that at nine or ten these feelings could be called real love, but whatever they were, it sure was exciting; not sexually, of course, but emotionally, psychically. Melitta was well-built, almost stocky, very strong, a tomboyish type, rather good in sports (especially as a batter in *Schlagball*), with a handsome face and blondish hair that she wore in two long heavy braids. That much I can remember clearly. Our relationship, rather than a loving one, was mostly a sort of competitive, teasing one. We found some way to nag each other nearly every day, particularly on school outings such as our field and hiking trips, when all of us girls and boys were thrown together, especially in the evenings. Also at those wonderful annual harvests; when, for example, all the potatoes had been gathered up, we were taken out to the fields in early evening, fires were started, and we'd dig up the potatoes overlooked by the pickers and roast them. Oh, were they delicious! At such times there was lots of romancing and teasing. Melitta was my favorite target, as I was hers. Her favorite gibe was to relentlessly dare me to do some ridiculous or slightly dangerous thing, and I, of course, unable to resist the temptation, unhesitatingly felt compelled to meet her challenges head on. My pride, my independence—my manhood—were at stake: I couldn't let a mere girl triumph in these testing (hormonal?) skirmishes. I made a fool of myself often enough, rather than admitting defeat. She was devilishly clever in egging me on toward some hopelessly stupid enticement.

She was tough! My tauntings of her were gentler, less confrontational, subtler, mostly more frivolous, more bantering, and more designed to lure her into admiring and liking me. These games that we played remind me in retrospect of what I learned many, many years later from countless nature programs about the playful, harmless antics of exuberant bear cubs or territorial rivalries of young lioness adults, so endemic and ubiquitous in the animal kingdom.

My play with Melitta and my stay in Gebesee came to a rather abrupt termination in 1936. In that year things were beginning to happen that dramatically affected the character, spirit, mood, and activities—even the curriculum—of the school. It began one day with the sudden intrusion of the Nazi's *Hitlerjugend*, although the school, attended mostly by foreign children of German background, had been declared off-limits to any attempts at politicization and the imposition of Nazi ideologies. But, as we all now know, Hitler never respected any agreements or treaties. He and his adjutant, Baldur von Schirach, one day decided to implant the *Hitlerjugend* in all the internats and special schools and colleges in Germany.

It all happened very suddenly. One day we kids were given the brown *Hitlerjugend* uniforms to wear, and told that we would have to engage in a certain amount of training and parading, read National Socialist literature, and see Nazi propaganda movies about young brownshirted heroes like Alfred Strateger and Horst Wessel.

I was too young (only ten) and had led too much of a sheltered life in the school the previous four years—it had been amazingly free from any political infiltration—to understand the full implication and impact that this new order would have on me and the school. But I dimly sensed that there was something drastically wrong here. By the way, girls were also drafted into something called *Bund Deutscher Mädchen* (League of German Girls). The next thing I knew a big, burly, tough looking, sadistic Nazi officer was put in charge of us boys, and we had to suddenly do all kinds of marching (to nowhere in particular, just marching for the heck of it), exercises (push-ups, calisthenics, long distance running and trotting, etc.), and an inordinate amount of saluting and standing at the strictest iron-backed attention—with lots of *Sieg Heil*-ing!—while our commander harangued us with his speechifying, to make us into better Germans.

While this nonsense was relatively tolerable, the viciousness of our *Kommandant* was not. I bore the full brunt of this man's brutality one morning, when, according to him, the knot of my brown tie was not properly tied and symmetrically shaped. He took a heavy leather belt with thick iron buckles at its ends and beat the crap out of me, as the saying goes. I was black and blue all over for days. A few days later I was told that he had been reprimanded for his out-of-control behavior by the headmaster of the school, Herr Preuss; but I don't recall that this had much of an effect on this Nazi brute, because at various times random beatings, not just me but also some of the other boys, continued.

I wrote to my parents about these matters, and I know they became somewhat alarmed. But at a distance of three thousand miles I think they also did not (and really could not) realize the full extent and implication of what was happening to the school, and probably felt that this was just some temporary aberration, and that things couldn't really be that bad or get worse. This paralleled pretty much the thinking of most of the world as it watched Hitler's rapid rise to absolute dictatorial power, his strutting arrogance, his uncanny ability to mesmerize the German population with his insane speeches and harangues, and the ruthlessness with which he managed bit by bit to abrogate and defy pacts, treaties, and international agreements that had to do with decency, morality, and civilized human behavior and values.

As I say, I was too young and politically naïve to fully understand what was going on, but I recall being frightened in some vague, creepy way, at the same time quite impressed by the films of the Nazi's massive and impeccably staged rallies (in Nuremberg and at the 1936 Berlin Olympics, among others), which we kids were now obliged to watch. I also remember being somewhat amazed—and disturbed—by noting that German women in general, both young and old, were particularly taken with Hitler's whole persona and behavior. Even in my own family—my aunts, my grandmothers, and their female friends—I could see their faces shine with an adoring blissfulness, an inner glow in their eyes, whenever they heard the Führer on the radio or talked about him. The whole female population of Germany was in love with this madman.

While things were becoming creepily eerie for me and many of my school comrades, an even more dramatic event was to precipitously terminate my stay at the Gebesee school.

The first Advent Sunday in Germany is a very big pre-Christmas holiday. It is like Thanksgiving in America. Children are showered with presents from their parents and family, and so it was also with the kids in my school "family." I had by now graduated from the Finck family to an older one, headed by Robert Schneider, my favorite teacher. Everyone, including all the foreign kids, had received one or two packages—except me. Advent for my parents in America was not such a big deal, and so they hadn't sent me anything. As was customary, Schneider and the kids organized a grand unveiling of all the parcels for late that Sunday morning, around eleven o'clock. We twelve boys and girls gathered in the dormitory around one of the beds, and one by one each kid opened his or her gift package, everybody else looking on eagerly, peering over the bedstead to see what was going to emerge from those packages.

I was standing next to my friend Jürgen as he started to open a huge bundle that had been sent to him from Brazil. Unlike most of the packages, which were wrapped with string or rope, Jürgen's was wound with wire, actually soldered together at the wire ends. With his big Swiss army knife Jürgen tried to cut the wire, but it wouldn't give. Pushing harder, with me and the other kids all leaning forward to see what wondrous exotic things would soon be revealed, the wire suddenly snapped. In a split second I suddenly couldn't see anything and felt some fluid running down my face and body—a river of blood. For a few seconds I had no idea what had happened, but then I realized in horror that Jürgen's knife, on the rebound from the wire that wouldn't cut at first, had gone into my head. But amazingly I had felt nothing, only that streams of blood began to gush from somewhere around my eyes.

I staggered toward the door—I don't know why—with the kids screaming in my ears. Herr Schneider took me down to the infirmary two floors below—no elevators in the Schloss—where our school nurse tried, I suppose, to stop the bleeding, which was more or less impossible. I passed out from the loss of blood, and the next thing I can recall I was lying in an ambulance, on my way to the nearest hospital. That was in Erfurt, more than an hour away by car.

Of the ensuing operation—a gruesome business, as it turned into two successive operations—I remember almost everything, being awake virtually throughout. What had happened was that Jürgen's knife had cut through the side of my right eye, penetrating further in, and had stopped (so I was later told) one or two millimeters from my brain. I would surely have been dead had it gone in any further. The operation having to take place so close to my brain, I could not be given any ether, the only anesthetic in those days. We are talking about 1936, and German medical practice, especially in a hospital in a small city like Erfurt, was not exactly state of the art or comparable with what was available at the time in America.

Anyone who might be squeamish to read about the almost medieval operation that I endured is encouraged to skip the next two paragraphs. I recall being strapped very tightly to the operating table with about six heavy, black, four-inch-wide leather straps, from my toes to my chin and head. Furthermore, two nurses stood on either side of me—four in all—also holding and pressing me down, obviously all this to keep me from moving. The operation having to take place within millimeters of my brain, if I were to twitch or move abruptly, a slip of the surgeon's knife would have instantly killed me. I can feel as if it were yesterday: the doctor poking around in my eye with his instruments. The pain was excruciating, and my screams and wails still echo in my mind. The doctors were trying to save my eye, and were attempting to sew and stitch it back together. I could feel each stitch and the suture being pulled through. I am surprised I didn't faint—or perhaps I did for a while.

When the doctors saw what they had wrought, they determined that it looked too horrible, and decided instead to remove my eye entirely. I imagine that I looked like a Cyclops or some Hollywood Frankenstein monster. So, more cutting, more stitching, more impossible pain, all the while the valiant nurses hanging on for dear life—mine, literally.

Eventually it was over, and I was sent to a recovery room, where I remained for over a week, and where, suddenly one day, my mother appeared (with my brother in tow).[19] Can you imagine what she and my father had gone through in that first week of December? The school authorities had, of course, advised my parents of what had transpired. My mother took the first ship to Germany, but in those days a transatlantic crossing took at least seven days, and, of course, there was as yet no transatlantic commercial air travel.

A week or so later we traveled back to New York, me with an artificial glass eye in my head. Who could have predicted that what I had seen in Lauscha only months before would be something I would from then on have to wear for the rest of my life.

We arrived home just before Christmas: a reunion both happy and sad.

Chapter Two

BOYHOOD

To be is to do.

—Socrates

IT WAS ONLY A LITTLE TOY GLOCKENSPIEL, but, curiously, it inspired me to do something that I had never contemplated, even in my wildest daydreams, namely, to compose some music. On a scale of one to ten (a Stradivarius being a ten and my father's early nineteenth-century Klotz violin a solid eight), Edgar's toy glockenspiel was a minus one. It wasn't a real glockenspiel; it produced a tinny, clinky-clanky, resonantless sound. But somehow—weirdly—I became drawn to it as my eight-year-old brother kept banging away endlessly at the thing. Our parents had given Edgar the toy for Christmas, and as we sang German carols on Christmas Eve, they tried to get him to play along on the glockenspiel. But this turned out to be a bad idea; between Edgar's wrong notes (he tried, but—well) and his instrument's bad intonation, any reverent feeling for a holy or silent night was pretty much dispelled.

But only a few days later—I remember it was before the New Year—something possessed me, not to play the glockenspiel but to *compose* for it. I cannot imagine what prompted this odd desire. It is true that right after returning from Germany in early December I had begun to show some interest in music by fooling around on my father's piano. I had no idea what I was doing, but I was fascinated by the strange sounds I was producing haphazardly; they were mostly dissonances, but occasionally I landed by accident on some pure major triad. It wasn't long before my father decided to give me lessons in the hope that I would learn to play the piano properly instead of banging aimlessly around on it—which had begun to annoy him. He started teaching me from a German manual he himself had worked from as a boy. It consisted primarily of elementary finger exercises and scales, and, later, short little pieces in simple four-part harmonic progressions. It seems that I did rather well and even enjoyed practicing. But I recall that my father sometimes got annoyed at my always wanting to use fingerings other than those prescribed in the manual.

Around the same time, I noticed a flute lying in a glass vitrine in our living room, along with a beautiful Meissen porcelain tea set (I was told it had belonged to Arthur's grandparents), some small vases (from Lauscha), and various other ornaments and knickknacks. It was the wooden flute that Arthur had played as a teenager in his father's Burgstädt orchestra, and which he had brought with him from Germany in 1923. When I asked him if I could play it, he said yes, of course, pleased that his old flute would find some use again. Both of my parents were surprised at my sudden interest in music, for which I had previously shown no inclination at all.

I discovered that I liked playing the flute even more than the piano. It had such a gentle, friendly sound. I made good progress rather quickly. What is notable is that, at this early stage of my involvement with music, I was already a very good sight reader. I have no idea how and why I had acquired this particular ability. My father was quite astounded.

I had never had any thoughts of composing music. Some might regard my thumping around on the piano as some primitive form of composing, an embryonic urge to make something up. In any case, that stupid glockenspiel of Edgar's did something to me, as I suddenly con-ceived the idea of composing a piece, not for it—even I knew that that idea would be dead on arrival—but for my family; in other words, a piece for my father (violin), my mother (piano), my brother (glockenspiel), and me (flute). I knew I had to keep the music very simple, not only for me and my mother—she played mostly German folksongs and hymns by ear, rather than reading music—but obviously for my little brother. Keeping it simple was no problem, since my paltry creative impulses couldn't have produced anything other than some infantile twaddle, but also because Edgar's glockenspiel had only twelve notes. What I wrote was mostly whole notes and half notes, interspersed occasionally with quarter or eighth notes, no more than thirty measures long. I know this to be the case because those snippets of manuscript have survived—despite dozens of moves over the years through all the various neighborhoods of Queens and Manhattan, and later to Boston—perhaps awaiting some future musicologist's urtext edition of Gunther Schuller's opus minus one.

We played the little piece on New Year's Eve after rehearsing it a couple of times. I don't know whether Edgar played all the right notes; it wouldn't have made much difference, because the relatively few notes I gave him to play weren't that important to begin with. Some family friends as well as my two uncles, Alex and Rudi, were in attendance, and everyone said encouraging things. What else were they going to say? But I was pleased with the whole experience. Something had clicked into place inside me, and soon I was filling a music notebook my mother gave me with lots of little black notes.

I find it strange in retrospect that I was taking piano lessons from my father but studying the flute and composing all on my own. My piano lessons were going reasonably well. I really loved that old piano manual, partly because I found in its latter pages, interspersed between the technical exercises, short little pieces, miniature compositions, graded in increasing stages of difficulty, matching one's advancing technical capabilities. Those pieces were my first real composing inspirations; they showed me something about elementary musical form and such basic ideas as having to make a beginning, with a theme or melody, and then an ending.

I loved one of the pieces in that book so much—I remember that it was in C minor and had a sort of Spanish flavor—that I copied it out more or less verbatim, and then proudly presented it to my father as my own composition. He, who knew every note in that book, immediately caught on to my silly subterfuge. (I wonder how I could have been so naïve as to think that I could fool my father.) actually, I was not so intent on deceiving him as I was deeply in love with that piece and wanting to impress him with it, to show him how I had gained some degree of composition control. To Arthur's great credit, he didn't scold me, but in his gentle way made me understand that I should never try that trick again—a lesson well learned.

It was actually a fairly harmless affair and not all that unusual. Because, in truth, we all, no matter in what endeavors, learn initially by imitation, whether it is, in infancy, something as elemental as learning to walk, or to talk, or later, at a more advanced stage, to learn to skate or ride a bicycle. Even in my young adulthood I was sometimes so deeply in love with a certain piece of music that I absolutely had to incorporate parts of it in my own music, almost to the point of plagiarism. And I am sure that this is true of other composers or creative artists in any field (painting, literature, etc.).

In early January, a mere three weeks after returning from Germany, I returned to my old public school in Woodside, Queens, which I had briefly attended as a six-year-old. This was a difficult time for me because I had forgotten virtually all my English during my four and a half years in Germany. My mother told me later that I knew only three words when I returned: yes, no, and vegetable, which I pronounced vegetéb'l. Although I could more or less understand the teachers' English, I had considerable trouble reading textbooks, and had even more problems writing assignments, exams, and papers. My language handicap also isolated me from the other kids in school. Most of them taunted me for my thick German accent, but a few of the class bullies also enjoyed pushing me around, beating me up, and calling me a *Kraut* and a Nazi. I was beaten up quite a bit, out in the schoolyard or on the way to school. Those kids could tell that I was a serious student—one strike against me—and therefore assumed that I was a sissy. It certainly didn't help matters that my mother made me dress in short pants (yikes), and made me wear a wool cap and gloves. (I quickly learned to hide those in my briefcase, but there was nothing I could do about the short pants.) I fought back as best I could, but when three tough kids are beating up on you, there isn't much you can do. However, there was one thing I did manage to do: I would not give them the satisfaction of seeing me cry.

I turned increasingly to my musical studies, flute, piano, and—gropingly—composing. It was around this time that my father tried me out on the violin, but it became clear rather quickly that I had no talent for it whatsoever, because I had virtually no operational independence of my two hands—a condition that makes violin playing impossible, but which, ironically, became instrumental in permitting me to be an excellent professional horn player only a few years later. (Since there is nothing French about the French horn, as it is always called, and as there also isn't anything English about the so-called English horn—both are misnomers—I will henceforth refer to my chosen instrument only as a horn.) The lack of independence of the hands also surfaced as a problem in my piano studies. I never had problems playing chords—and I *loved* playing them—but anything contrapuntal, with two hands moving at different speeds and in different directions, gave me great problems. It was very discouraging and frustrating. On the flute I had no such problems. First of all, the flute can only play one note at a time. Second, fingering on a flute is logically sequential, and limited to activating only seven keys or finger holes, as opposed to the contrary motion of two hands and ten fingers, which is so often required in piano playing.

Luckily, within a few months of my return to America my English started to come back exponentially. The fact is that once one has learned a language as a mother tongue it can be recaptured rather quickly. I took to reading dictionaries—I mean literally *reading*, not just looking up an occasional word—and saw my linguistic proficiency expanded by leaps and bounds. My greatest joy and fascination came a bit later, when my aunt Lydia gave me a book of synonyms for my twelfth birthday. (I still have it.) I spent hours poring over this volume, spellbound by the endless richness of the English language, relishing the subtle distinctions between synonomically related words. In this way I quickly acquired a rather substantial vocabulary, including gobs of quadrosyllabic words, with which I used to astound my parents.[1] Again the little show-off!

It was also my aunt Lydia who presented me with one of the most inspiring, practical, and educationally important presents I ever received in my young years. For Christmas 1938 she gave me the just published, up-to-date, 2,089-page *MacMillan Encyclopedia of Music and Musicians*, which I devoured in the succeeding weeks and months, literally reading it like a novel from cover to cover. In those years I had a terrific memory and an insatiable desire to learn, to study. As a consequence of reading and constantly perusing that encyclopedia, I made gigantic leaps in my knowledge of music and its history. More important, it raised my curiosity level about everything related to music by many factors.

It was around this time that my parents discovered I had a fine soprano voice, and that I could carry a tune with perfect intonation. (Was that attributable to my singing those Bach chorales every morning for about four-and-a-half years in Gebesee?)

It happened so often in the course of my long life that seemingly unconnected strands of events suddenly came together, in effect determining the next phase of my development as a musician and as a person, as for example when in the fall of 1937 a chain of events and coincidences culminated in my being accepted by the famous St. Thomas Choir School, associated with St. Thomas Episcopal Church in New York, at the time *the* preeminent English-style choir school in America, founded and led by T. Tertius Noble.

John Barbirolli was then music director of the New York Philharmonic, having just succeeded Arturo Toscanini. My father, sitting virtually under Barbirolli's nose at the front desk of the second violins, in time came to know the conductor personally. One day, in a casual conversation during a rehearsal intermission, Barbirolli, who had somehow heard of young Gunther's interest in music, inquired about his progress. Arthur mentioned that I had a beautiful soprano voice, and read music fluently, whereupon Barbirolli, who knew Dr. Noble and his superb reputation as a choir master, organist, and composer—Barbirolli performed several of Noble's compositions with the Philharmonic during those years—recommended that I audition for acceptance to the famed Choir School. Before I knew what was happening, my father took me to a small private recording studio, where I cut a ten-inch acetate disk, singing both parts of the opening duet scene from Humperdinck's *Hänsel und Gretel*. (This is possible since in that scene Hänsel and Gretel, in teasing alternating banter, never sing together). The disk was sent to Dr. Noble for a preliminary screening, after which I was invited to a live audition. I remember virtually nothing about it except that I had to sing the fearsome "Rejoice, Rejoice" from Handel's *Messiah*. I must have sung it quite well and confidently, because by the next September I was enrolled at St. Thomas. The school was then located at 121–23 West Fifth-Fifth Street, halfway between St. Thomas Church and Carnegie Hall.

In retrospect, this quite unpredictable turn of events looms large in my development—personally, musically, intellectually. Not only did I receive my first formal training there in music theory and harmony, from Dr. Noble himself, but the school was also known for its remarkably high scholastic standards. And although I later became a high school dropout (at age sixteen), I know with absolute certainty that whatever I am as a person of some intellectual capacity, of strong unshakable moral values, an uncommon sense of discipline, and the ability to work hard and enjoy it, I owe largely to the superb education I received at St. Thomas, as well as what had been acquired earlier at the private school in Germany.

My father frequently took me with my mother to New York Philharmonic concerts. Sitting way up in the top balcony in Carnegie Hall, I could almost physically feel the music floating upward toward me. I can vividly recall the instinctive pleasure I had in hearing and trying to absorb all the wondrous sounds emanating from that stage. One particular incident stands out as leading me in the direction of pursuing dual careers in composing and playing an instrument.

Sitting up there in Carnegie's vast upper reaches, I was attracted one day to a very special sight, some 360 feet below: a shiny, glittering object, glistening in the reflecting stage lights of Carnegie Hall. It was a golden flute—so much more beautiful than my father's old wooden flute. The owner of that golden flute was John Amans, the Philharmonic's Dutch-born principal flutist, whom Willem Mengelberg had brought to America during his short tenure as interim musical director of the Philharmonic in the 1920s. That brightly gleaming instrument fascinated me, especially as it moved gently back and forth with the occasional head movements of Amans. (The orchestra was playing Wagner's *Parsifal*, and Amans was nodding his head, hoping to keep the other two flutes rhythmically together in those triplet rhythms that occur in the opera's Prelude.) What made it visually so irresistible was that the flute was made of gold; it radiated a burnished glow that the silver flutes I had occasionally seen from afar never produced.

I had never seen a golden flute before. Nor, as it turns out, had anyone else. The story is that in 1936 Georges Barrère, a famous French flutist and frequent soloist in America—the Rampal of his day—had ordered a flute to be built for him made of platinum. The occasion was much celebrated in the press and musical circles. It also prompted Barrère to ask his friend Edgard Varèse to write a solo flute piece for him. That piece is the famous *Density 21.5*, so named for the metallurgical properties of platinum, and is arguably next to Debussy's *Syrinx* the most famous and most often performed composition for unaccompanied flute. In response to Barrère's new platinum flute, Amans had the first gold flute constructed. Seeing it glisten in the refracted light that Friday afternoon, I knew that that was the instrument I wanted to concentrate on, not the piano. As childish as that may sound, the annals of music performance are filled with countless tales of young boys (and lately girls) becoming wind or brass instrumentalists, mesmerized by the shiny brass of a cornet or a trombone, the odd-looking upward protuberance of a bassoon, or the bulky shape of a tuba or double bass.

Of course my father couldn't get me a golden flute. He couldn't have afforded one, even if there had been one to buy, because that first golden flute was the only one made for many, many years. Since wooden flutes had gone out of favor in the last half century, replaced by the new, more brilliant sounding silver instruments beginning to be built in the 1890s, my father got me a silver flute. It was a rather cheap and poor instrument that he acquired for forty-five dollars from the Philharmonic's piccolo player, Mortimer Rapfogel, who would also be my flute teacher. I am sure both men saw the transaction as a good deal: my father got a flute for very little money, and Rapfogel got rid of a practically worthless instrument. In any case, that's how I officially became a performer—through this curious chain of circumstances, initiated by Barrère's platinum flute and abetted by my father's presence in the New York Philharmonic. None of this would have happened had I been born and raised in some hinterland town.

I was pretty much in heaven at St. Thomas. Everything was consistently challenging and nurturing for whatever latent talents, musical and intellectual, I possessed. Our primary duties as students were to provide the music for the various services at St. Thomas Church (the premier high Episcopal diocese on the East Coast), particularly on Sundays. The all-male choir consisted of forty boy sopranos and four each of male altos, tenors, and basses. During my three years as a chorister at St. Thomas I had the good fortune to sing all the great celebrated choral and oratorio masterpieces, some of them several times. These ranged from Handel's *Messiah*, Haydn's *Creation*, and the Brahms *Requiem*, to Bach's *St. Matthew Passion*, works by Palestrina and Heinrich Isaac, and even some of the French repertory, for example, sections of César Franck's *Les Béatitudes*.

The three men's sections each had outstanding soloists: John Sahlbeck (alto); Robert Betts (tenor), who was already known to me as one of the soloists in Stokowski's 1932 recording of Schönberg's *Gurrelieder*; and Robert Crawford, who was famous for having composed (in 1938) the official air force song. I also fondly remember one of our bass singers, Albion Adams, a tall, imposing, kindly gentleman with a dark-rich basso voice. Although we boys generally had little contact with the twelve adult singers in our choir—rehearsals and services left little time for socializing—Adams more than the other adult choristers befriended us boys. I remember particularly that he was always encouraging me in my musical studies.

T. Tertius Noble was organist and director of the choir, but he was also a fine composer of dozens of church anthems, *Nunc dimittises* and *Te Deums*, as well as a number of orchestral works, two of which Barbirolli performed with the New York Philharmonic. When I arrived at the school, Dr. Noble, then a youthful seventy, was a highly esteemed musician, and I consider myself most fortunate to have come under his tutelage, not only as one of the boys and an occasional soloist in his choir but also as his private student in basic harmony, theory, and counterpoint. As fate would have it, Dr. Noble turned out to be my one and only "proper" music teacher, and I couldn't have had a better one. Although a strict disciplinarian in matters of musical training, he was also a kindly, benevolent man, a true English gentleman, a bit crusty and distant at times, but straight as an arrow. He was the center of our school's little musical and educational universe.

Strict discipline also governed all other activities at school, from personal matters, dress code, and table manners, to classroom and study etiquette. All this was managed in a healthy, balanced way, which gave us a remarkably solid foundation in life's values and in mature, intelligent, ethical behavior, as well as an abiding respect for one's fellow human beings. These matters were treated with the utmost seriousness, and were considered to be primary and essential in our training and growth as young men—for that is how we were regarded. Since such matters were taken care of, each of us could devote our talents and energies to our personal, intellectual, emotional, and spiritual development.

Dr. Noble's academic counterpart was Mr. Benham, the school's headmaster and overall director, seconded by Mrs. Atwater, the school's housemother, an elderly "dragon" of a lady—or so we all regarded her—who brooked no nonsense from any of us. We knew these were two people to be respected and feared. You didn't mess with them because you knew you couldn't get away with anything. Having already been in their respective positions for several decades, they knew every trick, every smartass little subterfuge that teenage boys will trot out in their feeble attempts at rebellion. They had seen and heard it all. But we boys didn't realize that. We thought we could outsmart the ancient Mrs. Atwater. But, oh no, that was not in the cards.

To their credit, Mr. Benham and Mrs. Atwater played no favorites. They treated all of us democratically. If one of us veered out of line, we got what we deserved. Some of the more rebellious types, myself included, would from time to time test their disciplinary resolve; it was a game we felt we had to play. Dear old Mrs. Atwater always—yes, always—came out on top. As much as I hated her at times, I know now that she taught me some important lessons, and helped me channel my natural creative and physical energies into more maturely productive directions. During my third year at St. Thomas she actually mellowed toward me. She used to let me come to her living quarters on the first floor to practice my flute and piano. Her apartment was the only place in the building that had a piano, and I remember really charming her, almost to the point of tears, by playing certain movements of Schumann's *Kinderscenen*, especially "Träumerei."

Mr. Benham was a bit tougher to win over. That didn't happen until I had actually left St. Thomas. I don't think he ever liked me or saw any of my talents until years later, when I was already a well-known and successful musician playing principal horn at the Metropolitan Opera. In the early 1950s he invited me to play the Brahms Horn Trio at one of the monthly musicales he organized at his home in Amenia, a little town about 120 miles north of New York City. This was at a time when I was helping my parents build our Webatuck homestead, just fifteen miles south of Amenia. At school, given the distance between his exalted position as headmaster of St. Thomas and myself, I had never realized that Mr. Benham had a soft heart for classical music.

There was hidden behind his rosy-cheeked, genial-looking exterior a man of stern, unswayable temperament. When he became irritated with someone or something, he would turn beet red. He brooked neither disrespect nor silliness, and he could be a very effective disciplinarian. One time I was late for breakfast by about forty-five seconds, after bounding down four flights of stairs two or three steps at a time. When I arrived at the dining hall not fully dressed, with my shirttail hanging out of my pants and my hair unkempt, he severely reprimanded me, embarrassing me in front of all the other kids. When I impudently sassed him back, he gave me a monumental full-handed slap on my right cheek, which staggered me and spun me around at least 240 degrees. My face burned all day, as much from embarrassment as from the sting of his mighty blow. That was the last time I sassed *him* back!

Disciplined deportment was expected from us at all times, and extended into all areas of conduct. Having to be on time, properly dressed, with your shoes shined, hands and fingernails clean—a bit of a problem for me, always working with smudgy mimeograph stencils and inking rollers in the *Ioneer* office (the school's newspaper)—all that didn't bother me very much. It was nothing more than what my parents had expected of me for many years. I didn't see it as punishment. Indeed, I knew that disciplined behavior taught me about manners and what Mr. Benham called "civilized behavior." Interestingly enough, it also taught me about the significance of and concern for detail—a matter that has stood me in good stead as a musician, composer, and conductor, where attention to detail is everything. As Mies van der Rohe put it so wisely, "God is in the details." (Unfortunately some wag corrupted that profound and beautiful truism into the nonsensical "The devil is in the details," which perversion, alas, has become the only version ever heard.)

A powerful if annoying lesson in appreciating detail—a lesson we learned *every* morning before breakfast—was that we boys were responsible for picking up by hand every speck, every piece of lint or dirt, from our dormitory's carpets. We were the vacuum cleaners who kept the dorms neat and clean, and many of the kids griped incessantly about this infliction. We also had to make our own beds according to very specific and demanding instructions. Exactly how you arranged the sheets, blankets, and pillow on the mattress was strictly prescribed and measurable in millimeters. The trickiest part of this routine was to see how perfectly you could line up the folds at the four corners of the bed. Near the end of the half-hour period between the first morning bell and the three-minute warning bell to assemble for breakfast, there was a bed inspection, much feared because any bed showing infractions was noted in a system of demerits. Furthermore, your slippers, pajamas, and various night table accoutrements had to be neatly placed according to precise instructions—not always easy when one of your fellow dorm inmates had hidden your slippers, tied your pajamas in knots, or indulged in other irritating pranks.

Some younger readers may think me rather odd, if not downright weird, but these and other similar disciplinary experiences taught me a certain stoic humility and a great sensibility for the tiny things in life, for minutiae and detail. These lessons I have applied all of my adult life, not only in composing and notating my music, and surely in conducting, but also in such diverse quotidian matters as, say, weeding meticulously in my garden and my gravel parking place, or keeping an impeccably clean kitchen.

The teachers at St. Thomas were terrific: brilliant, dedicated, consistently and persistently intent on enriching our young, still immature minds. I think they knew that the art of teaching consists of learning how to teach yourself, not being satisfied to stuff your brain full of this or that standard information. They *inspired* you to study and work hard. One was also further motivated to excel by the biweekly awarding of so-called first and second honors.

My favorite teacher was Ralston Coles, who taught history and French; the most intelligent, razor-sharp mind of the lot. Yet I had mixed feelings about him. On the one hand I admired him for his polymathic brilliance, for his encyclopedic mind and his verbal articulateness. (My best and most admired school friend, Richard Verdery, who himself was an intellectual wizard and verbal virtuoso, always said about Coles that "he detested any words that are not lengthy," that he "delighted in sesquipedalian adjectives.") On the other hand, I was quite leary of Coles's withering sarcasm, especially when it fell on me. I also had a real aversion to his extremely conservative political and social views, which he would enunciate with great relish and lucidity in defiant and always sharply delivered pronouncements. I think of him as a gifted right-wing intellectual, a William Buckley or George Will, whose mind and intelligence and beautiful language you had to admire, even as you disagreed with what he was saying. In retrospect I find it astonishing—and puzzling—that he was never reprimanded by Mr. Benham or the rest of the (more liberal) faculty for venting his vehemently antiprogressive—I believe, subtly anti-Semitic—views on his youthful, impressionable young charges. In the end I learned to discriminate between the two Coleses, admiring the brilliance of the mind while very wary of the politics and social ethics. It may have also been one of my earliest experiences in learning that you didn't have to hate someone with whom you disagreed on some issues.

The school's overall schedule was intelligently laid out, reflecting a fine balance and wide range of academic studies, a strong, vigorous sports program, and music and vocal training, including the mandatory weekly choir rehearsals. During the week we lived and studied in the school, a five-story brownstone at 121–23 West Fifty-Fifth Street, with eight dormitory rooms on the fifth floor, five kids to a room. On Sundays, following the four o'clock afternoon vesper service, we went home, returning to the school the next day, Monday, at seven p.m. In 1938, my second year at St. Thomas, a sizable annex building extending all the way through to Fifty-Sixth Street was added. It housed new and larger classrooms than those in the Fifty-Fifth Street building, and a huge, well-equipped gymnasium with a spacious stage at one end, where chamber music concerts and plays could be performed.

In the fall and spring our sports—mostly soccer, football, and baseball—moved outdoors to the southern end of Central Park, about five blocks away. I particularly loved to play soccer, having played it regularly in Germany, and was often voted captain of our team. With my very deft footwork I was considered the champion dribbler in the school. The new gymnasium made it possible for us to train not only in all sorts of calisthenics and physical exercise but also in basketball, a sport much less known in the thirties and forties than it is nowadays.

Initially, I cottoned much less to American baseball, softball actually, so close and yet in important ways so different from the German *Schlagball*. But infected with some of my fellow students' enthusiasm for baseball, I soon became fascinated with the complexities and psychological aspects of the game—much to the dismay of my parents, who, like most Germans, thought baseball was just a stupid game played by culturally illiterate people.

In my last year at St. Thomas I became the leading pitcher of our team. But a few weeks into the short season, one fine day late in the fall, my pitching career came to an abrupt end when a well-hit ball struck me smack on my forehead, just half an inch away from my artificial eye. Had the ball hit me in the eye, the glass would have shattered, and if its fine shards had lacerated or penetrated my brain behind the eye cavity, I probably would have died instantly. I and my teachers felt it was too risky for me to continue playing baseball. And so, just as I was beginning to enjoy my new starring role, I reluctantly gave up the game and retreated to the relative safety of my musical studies.

We didn't play football, but it seemed nevertheless to be everyone's favorite sport, eliciting in every boy fanatic partisanship on behalf of his home team. So recently returned from Europe, where American football was unknown, or ridiculed, I really didn't at first understand and appreciate the technical and psychological intricacies of the game. I listened in puzzled wonderment to most of the other boys' excited shouts and catcalls, yeahs and boos, that greeted the official reading every Monday evening of the previous weekend's football scores and game highlights. Naturally baseball scores and statistics were also followed with passionate interest. In the late thirties, when the best teams for several years were St. Louis, Detroit, and Cleveland, my baseball heroes were Hank Greenberg, Stan Musial, Red Schoendienst, Whitey Ford, Bob Feller, Bob Boudreau, and later Joe DiMaggio and Ted Williams, but especially the first three. Beyond their obvious talent, there was a certain grace and dignity in their manner and bearing. I remember getting all caught up in the 1938 World Series between Cleveland and Detroit, and the inevitable royal battle between Feller and Greenberg.

I was never given to homesickness. Life at St. Thomas was too interesting, exciting, and varied in its educational and musical challenges to sit around unhappily missing my parents. But there was, especially in my first year at the school, a strange longing for the outside world, a fascination and curiosity about all the myriad human activities that I sensed were being played out there, beyond Fifty-Fifth Street. There were also feelings of loneliness and isolation, being cooped up in the school for six days every week, emotions that I recall now, more than seventy years later, with some affection and a poignant sense of nostalgia. These feelings were triggered only in my very early days at the school, especially at night, by hearing the constant honking of car horns and the muffled murmurings on the street below. I wanted to be immersed in the city's bustling energy, to be with people heading home from the theatre, from concerts, from restaurants, or ambling down Sixth Avenue or taking a late-night stroll in nearby Central Park. (Yes, in those days you *could* take long walks in Central Park, even at night, and cars were allowed to freely honk their horns.)

An even stranger beckoning from the outside world—one that I was never able to account for—was a constantly blinking light from a nearby building that I saw every night for many months. I could see it from my fifth-floor window when lying in bed. It kept me mesmerized and awake sometimes for hours. The light came from one window high up in a medical building on the northeast corner of Fifty-Seventh Street and Sixth Avenue. Very strange and mysterious! Who or what was signaling, and to whom? Was it some German spy—in the years just before the war—sending secret messages over the rooftops of midtown Manhattan to some other west side high-rise? It was like the incessant, strangely menacing, ominous off-and-on blinking light on the billboard outside Gatsby's house in the film version of Scott Fitzgerald's *The Great Gatsby*.

The only unpleasant experiences I can recall from my first year at St. Thomas were the hazings to which all freshmen were subjected by the seniors. I understood right away that hazing, essentially the bullying and torturing of freshmen by older seniors, was a long-established and unassailable tradition that teachers and administrators tolerated, even sanctioned, and certainly never interfered with. Soon after my arrival at St. Thomas I was subjected to the typical taunting, browbeating, and physical abuse that little gangs of seniors would inflict upon us younger kids. But sometimes their imagination would lead them far beyond ordinary hazing traditions; one day, in an afternoon free period while I was practicing my flute in the dorm, I was suddenly accosted by four or five seniors who stripped me half naked, exposed my genitals, and began rubbing a particularly acidic toothpaste onto my penis, causing a painful burning sensation that lasted all night and most of the next day. The seniors thought this behavior was hilarious fun. But for us powerless victims it was annoying at the least, painful at worst, and in any case terribly humiliating. But we knew we had to suffer it; we understood, without having to be told, that we could not squeal on our tormentors. It wouldn't have done any good. The teachers would have denied that anything like that went on in their school.

My rapidly advancing language skills, my high grades in English, and my talent in drawing and design soon garnered me a position as an editor of the weekly school paper, the *Ioneer* (get it? Eye and ear). I soon advanced to coeditor in chief. My editorial partner was the brilliant, tall, lanky Richard Verdery. He was really the brains behind the paper during my years at St. Thomas. He made most of the important editorial and writing decisions, while I did most of the physical work of putting the eight-page sheet together, including the layout and the artwork, using drawing and design skills acquired in my art classes in Germany. The *Ioneer* was typed up by Richard each week, and then the fifty or so copies were laboriously hand-cranked and collated on the school's mimeograph machine. My hands would be ink-stained for hours after the final press run, much to the dismay of Mrs. Atwater, whose main mission in life was to instill supreme and absolute cleanliness in her boys. The paper, created and entirely run by the students, dealt with three essential areas of school activities: school news, chronicling various special events during a given week; music news, a program listing of the two Sunday services at St. Thomas Church; and sports news, an account of the important weekly sports activities within and outside the school. (Our regular sports rivals were teams from schools such as

Grace, Collegiate, St. John the Divine, Barnard, and occasionally other prep schools in New Jersey and Connecticut.) The *Ioneer* was assembled by associate editors and supervised by the editor in chief and a faculty advisor.

My work as art editor consisted of supervising the basic layout of each issue, usually designing and drawing the cover, and determining the sequence of the special features. The cover drawing had to be stenciled with a special instrument into a blue mimeograph sheet, through which ink was then pressed onto final printout copies. This meant that your drawing onto the mimeograph sheets had to be done *perfectly*. Errors could not be corrected because any corrections would show through on the printout. Over the two years I was art editor, also doubling as music editor, I designed and drew at least a dozen front covers and quite a few extra drawings for the inside pages that included Halloween, Christmas, and Thanksgiving subjects, portraits of Lincoln and Washington, a representation of Columbus's landing in the Caribbean, a detailed drawing of an early American 1820s locomotive, a depiction of the Trylon and Perisphere at New York's 1939 World's Fair, and generic depictions of the beautiful main entrance of our Fifty-Fifth Street brownstone building and the facade of the new Fifty-Sixth Street gymnasium building. I say "generic" because when I took over as art editor, I thought it might be practical to design one basic cover (such as the school's handsome main entrance) and run it for several months—like a restaurant retaining a certain basic menu for a period of time—rather than inventing a new cover each week. But I was overruled by the faculty advisor and instructed to return to a constantly changing cover subject ("like *Time* magazine," he said).

In my last year at St. Thomas (1939–40), when I was promoted to coeditor with Dick Verdery, I was expected to write some of the feature articles that were the heart and soul of the *Ioneer*. All in all I wrote a dozen or more articles, everything from minibiographies of Thomas Edison and Victor Hugo to articles on the sinking of the battleship Maine in 1898 (which precipitated the Spanish American War), an article on swing as the latest development in jazz, and an article—kind of prophetic, as readers will learn—on why eight to ten hours of sleep was not really necessary. But perhaps my best youthful literary effort for the *Ioneer* was an article on Christmas in Germany. I single this out only because it was written a year *before* I joined the *Ioneer* staff and only a year *after* I had returned to America from Germany, when—I remind the reader—I had retained relatively little of my English. I loved just about everything about German yuletide traditions: the way Christmas trees were decorated, the carol singing in the villages, the Passion plays in Oberammergau, the famous Christmas cakes (*Stollen*) from Dresden and sweetcakes (*Pfeffernüsse*) from Nuremberg, the tree ornaments and glassblowing industry in Lauscha, Germany's biggest toy museum in Sonneberg, the giving of gifts on Christmas Eve rather than on December 25. And I wrote it in perfect, eloquent English.

But the best writer during my three years at St. Thomas was Dick Verdery. He had a real flair—nurtured by Mr. Coles—for beautiful and imaginative, creative language. He authored a brilliant series of articles on the school's five masters—the faculty—in a gently satirical, sardonic, yet somehow very respectful tone. Dick's subjects ranged from serious contemplations on the value and meaning of education, a trenchant comparison between Caesar and Hitler, a dissertation on Seward's Folly (the U.S. acquisition of Alaska), to an account of a summer hiking trip in Wyoming's Tetons and a hilarious recital of his trying to get up in the morning.

It is hard for me to describe how many happy hours I spent in that dark, dank basement room that was our *Ioneer* office, feeling that Richard and I were accomplishing something very special and important. There were also the anxieties of those stressful final hours before meeting the paper's weekly Friday evening deadline. Good experience, though—a terrific lesson in work discipline, attention to detail, and keeping things on schedule!

At St. Thomas we were taught a great deal about American democratic processes in an effective, hands-on, pragmatic way. The two upper classes were called eighth and ninth forms, rather than grades, and constituted nearly half the student body of forty boys. They were organized into and were obliged to serve in either at least one of a dozen semiannually rotating committees or as proctors in charge of various extracurricular educational school activities. The most popular committees were entertainment and game room, followed by the library committee. Other positions were postman (in charge of the mail room) and church line (overseeing our processions to and from church, from Fifty-Fifth to Fifty-Third Street and Fifth Avenue, and within the church). All these committees were overseen by the school council—a kind of parliament—made up of the prefects, one from each of the respective classes, and three or four representatives. All these committees and the council were presided over by the council president, a position I was honored to hold for one semester.

Between the excellent class presentations by the teachers and our copious homework assignments, we were kept on a very challenging educational tether. No one was allowed to lag behind; remedial tutoring was immediately arranged. Languages—French, Latin, and, of course, impeccable English—were especially stressed, for which I am eternally grateful. The linguistic foundation I received in Latin, both in Germany and at St. Thomas, and the additional training in French (combined with my fluent mother-tongue German) has stood me in good stead all through my professional career in music, especially in the last forty years as a guest conductor of many European orchestras.

I particularly appreciated the superb selection of literature we were urged to read at St. Thomas, both in English classes and on our own time. And not just typical boy's reading matter, such as Dickens's novels (*David Copperfield* and *Tale of Two Cities*), Mark Twain's *Huckleberry Finn*, Stevenson's *Treasure Island*, and Fennimore Cooper's tales of the French and Indian wars (*The Last of the Mohicans* and *The Deerslayer*), but also lofty essays by Addison and Steele (from the famous eighteenth-century English literary journal *The Spectator*), the writings of Voltaire, and, above all, the essays of Emerson ("Self-Reliance," "Intellect," and "Nature").

I shall never forget the thrill of reading Emerson's "Self-Reliance." It inspired me then and there to live my life by its ethical, moral, and spiritual philosophy. I admired its tough-minded social and humanist precepts, which embodied such principles as independence, individualism (in the sense of self-reliance), and absolute integrity and honesty. They galvanized my mind and heart, and brought me, after several rereadings, to a much more nuanced intellectual level.

Nor were the visual arts neglected at St. Thomas. On numerous occasions we were taken to New York's major museums: the Metropolitan Museum and, quite often, the Museum of Modern Art, which happened to be directly adjacent to St. Thomas Church, on Fifty-Third Street. It was at the Metropolitan that I saw my first Botticellis, Vermeers, El Grecos, Fra Angelicos, Donatellos, and Titians. My already highly developed sense of color and fascination with textures was especially enriched by the Titians and Tintorettos. I remember being absolutely mesmerized by the exquisite detail and perfect play of light and shade in the magnificent brocade robes and folds of the garments in Titian's portraits of famous men, or the luminous greens and oranges that he loved and used so effectively. It was my first inkling of how a painting, even a mere portrait, could have emotional expressivity. In later years, as I learned more about developments in painting and sculpture, I began to see and appreciate what a remarkably decisive innovator Titian had been, especially as his technique became at once more complex and free, and thus even more expressive. Tintoretto, an admirer (and briefly a student) of Titian, impressed me immediately, probably not so much for the intrinsic qualities of his work—the dramatic use of light and shadow, mysterious dark corners, and almost abstractly unearthly scenes—as for the fact that he reminded me a lot of El Greco, at that time already my favorite Renaissance painter. I assumed that Tintoretto had been influenced by El Greco, but I didn't know when I was thirteen that it was quite the opposite: El Greco's use of light and shade shows the direct influence of Tintoretto.

Another powerful enrichment of my imagination and emotional sensibility took place when I had my first serious cinematic experiences. My parents didn't go much to the movies, and I can recall being taken to them only a few times, most memorably to see *Trader Horn* (1931), which scared me half to death. (Naturally, I didn't see any American films during my four-and-a-half years in Germany, and, of course, I totally discount the Nazi propaganda films we were forced to see in Gebesee.) At St. Thomas we were taken to such very good films as John Ford's masterful *The Hurricane* (1937), with its spectacularly realized tropical storm, Richard Thorpe's *Adventures of Huckleberry Finn* (1939), and Walt Disney's *Snow White and the Seven Dwarfs*, which we saw in 1938 in its premiere at Rockefeller Center's Radio City Music Hall.[2] From these early cinematic encounters, I eventually graduated to Walt Disney's and Leopold Stokowski's *Fantasia* (1940). That film masterpiece truly changed my life, particularly its Stravinsky *Rite of Spring* sequence, which, as far as I can remember, was the first time I heard that remarkable music. It completely bowled me over. I knew then and there that I had to be a composer.

At the time I didn't know that *Fantasia* presented a severely abridged version of *Le Sacre du printemps*. I learned later that Stravinsky hated it, and was evidently hoping to sue Disney to prevent it from using the *Fantasia* footage. Apparently Stravinsky, who was almost as avaricious as Richard Strauss (or for that matter any Hollywood producer), objected strenuously—and understandably—to his music being mutilated and his failure to receive royalties from *Fantasia*. But even given Stravinsky's arguably justifiable objections, artistic and financial, I hope he appreciated that hundreds—perhaps thousands—of musicians were turned onto *The Rite of Spring* (and by implication lots of other modern music) through *Fantasia*, musicians who might otherwise never have heard the work, or at least not until many years later. It was Disney's cinematic masterpiece that prompted many young musicians to declare *Le Sacre* the unqualified masterpiece of twentieth-century music, and to, like me, become serious composers because of it. We, of course, all found out years later that the Disney production offered a dismembered and incomplete rendition of *Le Sacre*. But it didn't really matter. It was the power of the music, the startling originality and perfection of its craftsmanship, that reached out to us. We knew that this was "our" music.

Another film that I recall with the fondest memories is Frank Capra's visionary *Lost Horizon* (1937). I don't think I could as an eleven year old have fully understood the film's allegorical fantasy about a utopia (Shangri-La), where all men were noble and decent, and where evil (specifically, corrupt businessmen and fascist dictators) would be conquered by good men and the power of pure love. But I certainly was impressed by the quasi-ancient, quasi-authentic, quasi-Tibetan music Dimitri Tiomkin wrote for the film, especially in the so-called torch-light procession sequence. I was haunted by it for weeks, and as a fledgling composer I was mightily tempted to write some such mystical, mysterious music. Of course I didn't have the skill or the imagination to do anything of the kind, but it was my first vague inkling of a deep, abiding interest in ethnic music—even pseudo indigenous—what is now often called "world music" by the record companies. I was also very impressed—in fact awed and frightened—by one scene, the death of the (seemingly three-hundred-year-old) High Lama, acted so persuasively by Sam Jaffe behind his layers upon layers of wrinkly makeup. I recall that many years later, seeing John Huston's *Asphalt Jungle* by chance on television, I instantly recognized the actor walking away from the camera in his initial entrance, seen only from the back, as Sam Jaffe. He was that distinctive and instantly identifiable. He was a remarkably good and underappreciated character actor.

Later, after I had left St. Thomas in 1940, my parents would occasionally take Edgar and me to see German film comedies in Manhattan's Yorkville, the German section of the city, at the Eighty-Sixth Street Casino Theatre. Those films often featured Heinz Rühmann or Hans

Moser (funny men in Berlin's prewar UFA studios). They were fluffy, often entertaining, non-propagandistic movies that the Nazis were turning out in great numbers to keep the folks at home entertained and diverted from Hitler's preparations for conquering the world. A visit across the street from the Casino Theatre to the famous Café Geiger *Konditorei*, famous for its luscious Viennese pastries and Sachertorte, was always included when in Yorkville, as was a shopping spree at Schaller and Weber, for years the best purveyor of German sausages and meats and other European delicatessen. It makes my mouth water just to think of their incredibly tasty *Leberkäs*!

I do remember seeing some weightier film fare now and then, most notably a sequence in an otherwise forgettable film, *Die Grosse Liebe* (*The Great Love*), starring the remarkable deep- and dark-voiced mezzo-soprano—and beauty—Zarah Leander, singing intensely movingly the famous "Che Faro" aria from Gluck's opera *Orpheus and Eurydice*. I was reduced to tears and haunted by that music and Leander's singing for a long time. Another affecting experience was a romantic, melancholy film called *Fiakerlied*, starring the elegant and extraordinarily handsome Viennese actor Paul Hörbiger—Vienna's answer to France's Maurice Chevalier—in a teary-eyed tale about the gradual professional and psychological degradation of a Viennese fiacre coachman around the turn of the century, partly modeled (although in a different social milieu) on Sternberg's famous *Blue Angel* (1928). It was also at the Eighty-Sixth Street Casino that I first saw a person drown, in this case in a crime thriller in which the murderer (the actor Oskar Sima) is trapped in a snake-infested swamp and sinks down to his death in quicksand. The moment he disappears was shown in an incredible, sharp close-up.

But my most important film experience of that time—I was still at St. Thomas—was seeing *Rasputin*, a great French film directed by Marcel L'Herbier, starring the inimitable Harry Baur, a superb French actor of the 1930s. I had by that time already read quite a bit about the Russian mystic, sybarite monk who dominated the czar's, and much of the country's, political life until he was assassinated by members of the royal Yusupov family. Seeing *Rasputin* inspired me to resolve to some day very soon write an opera on *Rasputin*—which I never did. But *Rasputin* was the first film that made me realize (I was thirteen at the time) that cinema in the hands of great actors and film directors could be much more than entertainment spectacles. It could be truly great art, as sublime as the greatest musical and literary works.

What was somewhat unusual about my seeing *Rasputin* was that it was hardly typical movie fare for a thirteen-year-old lad to see and, above all, that I was allowed to go there by myself. One of my teachers, knowing of my interest in Rasputin, alerted me to the film's showing just up the street from school at the Fifty-Fifth Street Cinema. I am amazed that my parents did not object to my seeing this movie—it is, after all, a film about a dissolute, alcoholic, womanizing monk—and alone at that. I must have seen *Rasputin* on a late Monday afternoon, just prior to returning that evening to school. In any case, this event was the real starting point for my life-long obsession with the art of the cinema.

Back at St. Thomas, Mr. Benham and the faculty, intent on providing educative, enriching experiences for their young flock, took us on various excursions to places such as the Hayden Planetarium, an all-day outing to West Point and the famous Storm King Highway (which follows the west bank of the Hudson River through the highlands to wind around the steep slopes of Storm King Mountain near its north end, with panoramic views of the river and surrounding mountains), three visits to the 1939 New York World's Fair (we also sang in several concerts there), a specially arranged tour of New York's famous Waldorf Astoria hotel, a visit to the Empire State Building, and New York's major museums.

The trip to West Point was quite a special occasion for me. I remember particularly the spectacular fall colors of the surrounding mountainous scenery, and being quite taken with the view of the twisting, gorgelike, S-shaped narrowing of the Hudson River below the

Academy. We went on a grand tour of West Point's extensive grounds, nestled in the hills on the west side of the Hudson, and heard a detailed account of the Academy's century-and-a-half-old tradition in the military history of our country. But what really impressed itself on my youthful mind was the almost comical, unnaturally rigid behavior of the cadets. To me and my friend Dick Verdery there seemed to be a strange incompatibility between the magnificent, huge, Gothic-style mess hall, with its beautiful stained glass windows—as beautiful as those in St. Thomas Church—and its occupants: several thousand stiff-backed, grey-uniformed, regimented young men, having lunch and looking like so many faceless statuary ciphers. It was an oddly incongruous sight, and it made me wonder about any and all regimented behavior and its place in our world. The final highpoint of the visit was a brief concert in the late afternoon in West Point's chapel, given by a fine group of cadets who sang several of Dr. Noble's beautiful four-part *a cappella* men's choruses. That set me off composing a string of *Te Deums* and anthems with biblical texts.

A few of us who were especially interested in music were taken to Carnegie Hall for concerts of the National Orchestral Association, with Leon Barzin conducting, as well as to the New York Philharmonic's famous children's concerts, and occasionally even to some of its regular subscription concerts. I especially remember one conducted by Georges Enesco, the great Romanian violinist and composer, and another with John Barbirolli and one of my heroes, Emanuel Feuermann, the great cellist, as soloist in Schubert's *Arpeggione* Sonata (as turned into a cello concerto with orchestra by Gaspar Cassado). I know it was one of those epiphanal moments of discovery, in this case my discovery of the cello as one of my all-time favorite instruments.

The Philharmonic's children's concerts were very special for me, since they represented during those St. Thomas years my only regular musical education in orchestral or symphonic repertory. During the week I was busy with classes and other school activities, and therefore unable to listen to New York's classical music stations, WQXR and WNYC. Radio in those days—long before transistors and small, lightweight radios—were bulky cabinet-size affairs, for which there was no room in the dorms. My only radio time was limited to the twenty or so hours at home between Sunday evening and Monday afternoon. Ernest Schelling was director-conductor of the children's concerts, and consistently programmed only the finest, historically most important music. His concerts hardly ever made concessions to the tempting notion that children should be served lighter, more entertaining fare. In the 1938–39 season's six concerts, Schelling put together, for example, an all-Wagner program, a concert devoted entirely to the music of Mendelssohn, another featuring the harp and its literature exclusively (with Carlos Salzedo as soloist), as well as a program of Christmas music from different countries—all in all offering an amazingly wide range of music, from Gregorian Chant and Bach to Beethoven and Berlioz and Richard Strauss. Most important, we were asked to write brief essays in response to half a dozen questions relating to each concert. I remember enjoying writing those little three-sentence essays, presumably my first rudimentary attempts to write something intelligent about a musical experience. I usually added little pencil drawings. For the Wagner program, I drew a picture of a tuba and a pretty accurate portrait of Wagner (Wagner invented the tuba).

In 1939 I must have sent in one of my compositions to the annual children's concerts competition, vying for one of the prizes given each year for the best young person's composition. I know this only from the fact that I have in my memorabilia from that time a five-by-three photograph of Schelling, baton in hand, on the back of which he had written: "Try again next year!" I did so, by the way, but by that time Schelling had died, and Rudolf Ganz had taken over the children's concerts.

On quite another educational track, in my second year at St. Thomas I discovered the Bible, which in turn led to one of the strangest episodes in my long life. Although my father was nominally a Lutheran and my mother a Catholic, my parents were not churchgoing. I don't recall any Bible readings as a child, even in school in Germany. But gradually at St. Thomas, in weekly church services and the singing of anthems and hymns, based mostly on New Testament texts, and in hearing weekly sermons by Dr. Roelif Brooks, I became increasingly fascinated with the Bible, not so much as a religious text, but as an outstanding historical document and, in the King James version, a wondrously beautiful specimen of the English language. As a result, one day I decided to do something I believe very few people have ever undertaken: I decided to read the Bible from cover to cover. And I actually did so, even though it took me many months. I even made myself read the thirty pages of genealogy in Chronicles I and II, the endless recounting of "Zabad begat Ephlal, and Ephlal begat Obed, and Obed begat John, and John begat Azariah, and Azariah begat Abadiah" (I love that word "begat"). When asked what impulse drove me to engage in these reading marathons, I would suggest that it was just an insatiable curiosity and a desire to know all there is to know. I had an innate longing to constantly nurture my intellectual and emotional needs.

The reading of the Bible coincided with my seeing Cecil B. DeMille's *King of Kings* around Easter in the spring of 1938. This combined cinematic and literary immersion in matters religious and biblical kindled in me some sudden impassioned desire to emulate Jesus Christ. It was a religious conversion of sorts, an overwhelming experience—I suppose of the kind that struck St. Paul on the road to Damascus—that I found absolutely impossible to resist. When I think back to that time now, I cannot imagine what possessed me, what twist of fate inspired me to suddenly engage in this strange behavior, making me believe and feel that I was wearing some kind of godly halo. It wasn't just DeMille's movie that drove me to this odd idea; by a curious coincidence I was also reading Dickens's *David Copperfield*, and I remember identifying deeply with the hero's total, selfless devotion to his friend Steerforth. I don't think it was self-centered arrogance on my part as much as it was a childish pretentiousness, sentimental in the extreme, brought on by a chance conflux of feelings—mingling DeMilles's simpleminded, overromanticized version of Christ's life with *David Copperfield* and my reading of the Bible— that collated into some strange zealous emotional amalgam. As juvenile as my fantasizing may have been, it had bizarre consequences that were serious and complex—and, to me, most mystifying. To wit, among the boys at the school there were twin brothers—I'll call them Billy and Johnny—one class ahead of mine, with whom I had developed a casual friendship. I did not at first realize that they were both very religiously inclined. (In their adult years both became ordained ministers.) Evidently, although I cannot be sure of their actual motivation, they were captivated by my pretend Christlike demeanor, and, as far-fetched as it may seem, sneaked into my dormitory room one night to masturbate me.

Surprise and consternation can hardly describe my feelings. I had no idea what was going on. Nothing like that had ever occurred in my life before. I was sexually so innocent—in my family one never talked about such matters—that I had neither heard of masturbation nor had any awareness that there was something called homosexuality. I was, of course, awakened by the boys' uxorious administerings, not knowing what to do or even what to feel. I knew only that I (or we) mustn't make any noise, lest we wake the other kids in the dorm. I vaguely sensed that, if discovered, there would be the direst consequences: abject embarrassment, unimaginable punishments, and very likely expulsion from the school. My mind was in turmoil, torn between fear and an extraordinary, never-before-experienced pleasure. It couldn't have been long before I reached orgasm, a delicious sensation that momentarily benumbed my mind. I had never felt anything so exciting, so powerful, so overwhelming, so beautiful. And yet I dimly knew that something "sinful" had occurred. In a flash the two boys disappeared, sneaking back to their adjacent dorm, leaving me utterly bewildered, emotionally drained, my mind befogged—and with sperm all over my loins.

In retrospect, I am amazed at the brothers' incredible daring, and I wonder whether they knew clearly what they were doing, and what they were risking. I know now what I didn't know then, that the sexual urge can drive you to do almost anything, impelled by a blind-to-danger, mind-numbing compulsion. I also wonder whether they had their little midnight adventures with other boys as well. Fortunately, to my great relief, no one else was aware of what had transpired. I remember feeling guilty for a long time, continually in fear that I would still be found out. I couldn't face the brothers for weeks and did my best to avoid them. When—incredibly—a few weeks later they attempted to repeat their night visit, I instinctively recoiled, rolling over on my stomach. They quickly rushed back to their room.

I didn't tell anybody what had happened. I didn't feel I could confide in anyone. Eventually I confronted Billy and Johnny, telling them firmly to leave me alone, and that I was terribly upset by what had happened. Weeks later they apologized profusely and, oddly enough, we remained rather good friends—platonic, to be sure. I held no grudge against them, vaguely realizing that they were simply different, not evil, not even sinful or depraved. I still feel that way today.

My pious playacting episode, trying to impersonate Jesus, was short lived. I can't really account for it. I suppose that somewhere, sometime in our childhood, we all veer off into some fantasy or romance. Such anomalies don't usually last very long, and—for all I know—manage to enrich us in some unfathomable way.

Things returned to normal for me, which meant hard work at school, studying and singing, and, above all, growing musically. My studies with Dr. Noble progressed very well, as the steady flow of theory and counterpoint exercises allowed me to advance gradually to more and more actual composing. This led to dozens of choral anthems, offertories, *Te Deums*, and the like, all based on New Testament texts. Many of those compositions were left unperformed, and in some cases unfinished; I didn't yet have the technique to form and develop the pieces properly, to their logical conclusion. But it was good practice. I gradually realized that you can learn a lot from your mistakes: from what you don't yet know. I published two of these early anthems some forty-five years later, discovering to my surprise—after having let them gather dust on shelves for decades—that they weren't all that bad, actually rather precocious and remarkably chromatic and full textured.

In my studies with Dr. Noble he had me concentrate on theory and counterpoint (in all species), at first mainly four-part writing and voice leading, and later fugal and canonic techniques. He was very strict with me, and figuratively rapped my knuckles many a time when I allowed parallel or hidden fifths (and octaves) to creep into my harmony exercises. I still have my manuscript notebooks from those years, filled with these studies, adorned in the margins with Dr. Noble's corrections. I was probably not the most obedient student, for I was continually experimenting with expanding my harmonic vocabulary, although I surely did not yet have the syntactical skills to control these chromatic explorations. Dr. Noble had to pull me back many times to safer, more basic regions.

In this connection I remember that by my second year of singing in the choir I was getting bored with certain harmonically very conventional pieces, such as Vaughan Williams's Mass in G Minor or some of Charles Villiers Stanford's, Hubert Parry's, and John Stainer's anthems, which seemed to me hopelessly bland. I called them "white-note" pieces. When we were handed a new piece, I could tell at a glance whether I'd like it or not by scanning the pages to see if it had lots of accidentals. If it was devoid of these, I knew it was one of those white-note compositions, and that it would be boring. Conversely, I got very excited when, occasionally, we were given highly chromatic pieces, even mildly atonal ones. I much preferred the more harmonically modern anthems and services of Philip

James (1890–1975)—whom I had met through Dr. Noble, and who always encouraged me in my composing efforts—especially his beautiful, poignant *By the Waters of Babylon* and *The Lord is My Shepherd*. I really loved these pieces, and if I had at this long distance to say which more or less modern music of the time I admired most at the Choir School it was Philip James's music. Alas, he is now virtually forgotten. I also enjoyed some pieces by Alfred Whitehead (1887–1974); Clarence Dickinson (1873–1969), one of the most successful church music composers of the time; David McKinley Williams (1887–1978), longtime organist of St. Bartholomew's on Park Avenue in New York; and George Oldroyd (1886–1951), a fine English composer of sacred music. Incidentally, the piece I believe we sang most often—besides Bach's very popular *O Light of Life* (from *Christus der ist mein Leben*)—was Leopold Stokowski's rather beautiful *Benedicite*, composed in 1907, when he too was organist at St. Bartholomew's Church.

The first rehearsal each week for the weekend services took place on Wednesday evenings in the basement choir room of St. Thomas Church. That is where my ability to sight-read anything, even highly chromatic or atonal works—most notably in several of Seth Bingham's and Philip James's compositions—often resulted in my being the only boy left singing after some ten or fifteen bars. By the end of the week, of course, the other boys had learned their parts very well.

Our weekly treks to the church for rehearsals and Sunday services had extramusical dimensions. It was one of the relatively few times we were either permitted or required to go outside of our Fifty-Fifth Street dormitory building. We would march in double formation to the rehearsal, either down Fifty-Fifth or Fifty-Fourth Street, toward Fifth Avenue. Both streets were lined with some of the finest, most expensive restaurants in midtown Manhattan, and although we could hardly be considered gourmets or connoisseurs of Continental cuisine, we did walk those streets with feelings of envy at this glamorous outside world. My absolute favorite was a combination apartment house and restaurant that, intriguingly for my young inquiring mind, had an entrance on 17 West Fifty-Fourth Street *and* 24 West Fifty-Fifth Street. What I really loved about the building was its unusual, elegantly modern, curved, rounded contours, and its beautiful beige-colored bricks. Curved forms in architecture were unheard of in the late 1930s. I never tired of peering through the big bay windows of the restaurant at the candlelit tables, the white tablecloths, the glistening wine and water glasses, the splendidly dressed diners. To my young unworldly mind it all represented the height of elegance, wealth, and good living. Then, on these few blocks along Fifth Avenue, there were some of the city's fanciest stores and most beautiful window displays: Tiffany, Cartier, Elizabeth Arden (with its famous bright-red door). They've been overshadowed by the Guccis, Gaps, and Vuittons of our times, not to mention the mobile hotdog stands and cheap jewelry hawkers. Instead of the immaculately clean Fifth Avenue I knew, its sidewalks are now littered with cigarette butts, candy wrappers, chewing gum, and other detritus of our modern civilization. I'm grateful that I can remember those cleaner, happier times.

Of all the beautiful church services in which I was privileged to participate, those that stand out in my memory as special and extraordinarily moving experiences were the annual Christmas and Easter services. What made the Easter services especially uplifting was that almost all of St. Thomas's mighty eighty-foot altar was on that occasion adorned with thousands of Easter lilies, donated by the church's wealthy and devoted parishioners; the flowers' intoxicating scents perfumed the entire choir area. But the most impressive church service of all for me was the annual Christmas candlelight service. It was truly magical, as the lights dimmed and the congregation sat in hushed silence. The only illumination came from the candles held by our choir and the church's ushers; we treaded quietly in a slow devotional procession all around the immense cathedral, all the while softly, movingly, singing carols.

I count the greatest musical experiences in my three years at St. Thomas those occasions when our choir was invited to perform Bach's *St. Matthew Passion* with the New York Philharmonic, and a year later, the Brahms *Requiem* with the NBC Symphony Orchestra, both times with Bruno Walter conducting. I had sung these extraordinary works already several times, since performances of both the *Messiah* and *Requiem* were a perennial tradition at St. Thomas, but always accompanied by the organ. To experience these great works with orchestra was truly revelatory, just at a time when I was becoming increasingly fascinated by instruments, their tone qualities and timbres, and their expressive characteristics. What a thrill it was—as luck would have it—to be seated during the *Requiem* right next to the tuba—that work being one of the rare times that Brahms actually used a tuba, an instrument I saw as an overgrown kin to my horn.

Although we were involved only in the opening movement of Bach's *St. Matthew Passion*, in which a boy's choir intones a chorale superimposed on a magnificent 12/8 double chorus, we sat on stage throughout the entire performance, and I was enthralled by all the sounds 360 degrees around me. We were seated in the middle of the stage, the huge chorus behind us, the orchestra and soloists in front of us, fanning out both to our left and right—my father sat up front on the first desk of the second violins. Though I was too young, too inexperienced to fully appreciate and understand from a technical point of view this deeply moving, profoundly spiritual and mystical music, I can recall and feel to this day the goose pimples that overcame me. And goose pimples don't lie! You can't fake them. They just come upon you, when the beauty and depth of the experience overwhelms you.

But even greater fortune was mine when halfway through my second year Dr. Noble asked me to become the page turner for his weekly—or his students' occasional—Sunday five p.m. organ recitals. I was so proud to have been chosen for this special honor. And educationally it was one of the most wonderful gifts Dr. Noble could have bestowed on me. By the time I left St. Thomas a year and a half later, I had become acquainted with—and had on my own seriously studied—an immense cross-section of the organ literature by both major established composers and lesser known moderns. Dr. Noble, at age seventy-one, was remarkably wide-ranging and adventurous in his recital repertory; his selections extended from Bach, Handel, and other baroque composers all the way to modern Americans such as Leo Sowerby, Philip James, and Seth Bingham. During those nearly fifty recitals in which I assisted him at St. Thomas's great Aeolian-Skinner organ, I discovered everything from Bach's peerless organ works and the sonatas of Mendelssohn, César Franck, and Hindemith, to the turn-of-the-century French modernists: Vierne, Widor, Dupré, Duruflé—even the young Olivier Messiaen.[3] There was also music from the new Dutch and Belgian organ school, composers such as Flor Peeters, Marius Flothuis, and Paul de Maleingreau.[4] I was particularly affected by Messiaen's unique harmonic language, his unusual, often barless rhythmic notation, and his music's mesmerizing sacred and spiritual nature.

It was during these years of being so deeply steeped in the organ literature that I became aware of the huge, seemingly unbridgeable gulf between organists and the rest of the music world. Organists are more or less ostracized from the greater musical society, a situation not of their choosing, to be sure. Worse yet, the great majority of orchestra musicians, singers, pianists, and so on, are totally and rather arrogantly unaware of the greatness of the vast organ literature; they are even largely ignorant of Bach's hundreds of incomparable organ works.

As much as I learned from Dr. Noble's lessons and from my page turning at his organ recitals, I believe the greatest gift he bestowed upon me was his suggestions for reading and study materials that he thought I might find interesting. Perhaps the most influential book he gave me to read was his friend and colleague Arthur Eaglefield Hull's work on early twentieth-century modern music entitled *Modern Harmony*. This wonderful manual, containing several hundred music examples amplifying the text, acquainted me with a huge swath of contemporary music in one fell swoop. This included samplings from Schönberg (*Erwartung* and *Five Orchestra Pieces* Op. 16), Ravel (*Gaspard de la nuit*), Strauss (*Elektra*), Scriabin (*Prometheus*), Delius (*Sea Drift*), Szymanowski (*King Roger*), and many other composers working in a highly chromatic or atonal language. I devoured and practically memorized that book. Those who know my music well know that it has from the very beginnings shown a propensity for strong, rich harmonies. I think this was inborn in me, but I also believe that the last sentence in Hull's text confirmed for me the righteousness of my penchant for harmonic enrichment as a central element in my developing musical language. It was a sentence I remembered and carried with me for decades: "Of the five senses of music—melody, harmony, form, rhythm, tone color—it is harmony, more than any other which takes us nearest to the edge of the infinite."

Hull's other books, monographs on Scriabin and Johann Sebastian Bach, were once widely read; all reached multiple editions but are now, alas, quite forgotten. That's a shame, because few writers on music are as knowledgeable, as passionately involved with their subjects, and yet as balanced and equitable in their views as Hull amazingly was. When I first studied his book I was astonished at the breadth and depth of his knowledge, the sheer wisdom of his commentaries, which are never musicologically ponderous or convoluted or ideologically biased. The range of musical subjects and illustrations extends from Kuhnau's *Bible Sonatas* of 1670 to the most advanced of the early twentieth-century moderns, touching in between on interesting but obscure composers such as Blanche Selva, Auguste Sérieyx, and the eighteenth-century English composer William Shield.

Dr. Noble recommended many books to me over the years, including particularly fascinating ones on the lives and music of Gesualdo, Delius, Grieg, and Beethoven. Along with such biographical and analytical literature, my most consistent studies focused on three major books on orchestration: Berlioz's 1844 *Treatise on Instrumentation*, Rimsky-Korsakoff's *Principles of Orchestration*, and Cecil Forsyth's *Orchestration* (1914). Within months I had those three tomes virtually memorized because I was *so* passionately fascinated with this subject. Around this time, as I became so enamored of the organ—for good reason called the "king of instruments"—I began to transcribe some of the symphonic works I was studying (such as Bruckner and Mahler symphonies, Sibelius tone poems, even some of the more complex late Scriabin piano works) for organ. Although much of this was left unfinished, it definitely was an amazingly enriching learning experience.

At that time in America—indeed until the 1960s—hardly anyone cared about or played baroque or the so-called tracker organs. Aeolian-Skinners and a few Cavaillé-Colls reigned supreme. I loved the organ at St. Thomas (modified several times since my years there), not knowing that there *was* any other type or style, because it made—as Dr. Noble often put it— "such a magnificent noise." It was a great thrill to hear his playing of Bach (or Handel or Franck) fill the vast cathedral-like spaces of St. Thomas Church. Having by nature a special love for low- and middle-register sounds and instruments, I would encounter the ultimate acoustic sensation when, in the exiting procession at the end of the four p.m. Sunday service, we choristers passed right under the organ's magnificent thirty-two-foot pipes, and literally felt the slowly throbbing vibrations physically in our bodies and under our feet—an incredible ear-expanding experience!

I recall one particular musical event that fascinated me and touched me so very deeply that it still lingers in my memory more than seventy years later. It was in 1938, when my father took me to Town Hall (in midtown Manhattan) to hear a concert by the Dresdner *Kreuzchor* from Germany on one of their annual American tours. I think my father was especially interested in this famous group, since Dresden, one of Germany's great music centers, was only forty miles from his hometown of Burgstädt, and because the Dresdner *Kreuzchor* was the

German counterpart to the St. Thomas Church Choir in New York. And I'm sure he wanted me to hear our competitors from abroad. The *Kreuzchor*, founded in the 1600s, was known as one of the most superbly trained all-male choirs, consisting of about forty boy sopranos and altos. It rivaled in quality (or perhaps even excelled) the equally famous Vienna Boys' Choir. This particular *Kreuzchor* concert featured, along with works by Bach, Schütz, and Hans Leo Hassler, several pieces by contemporary German composers, including a remarkable *a cappella* work by Günther Raphael (1903–60), *Christus, der Sohn Gottes* (*Christ, Son of God*). The work was based on the episode related in three of the New Testament Gospels (Matthew, John, and Mark) in which Christ walks on water in the Sea of Galilee. The text ends with the words "Thou art truly the Son of God." I liked the piece very much, especially for its strong chromaticism, which reminded me of Max Reger's best music. Raphael uncannily—and quite graphically—depicted the waves in gently undulating figures; the wind, and even a storm, in wildly rising and falling gestures and agitated disturbing rhythms. It showed me, as a young fledgling composer—even more than any Strauss tone poem—what power music potentially possesses to express and represent not just moods and emotions but at times even certain concrete physical situations, especially when there is a verbal text or narrative involved. The piece made such a deep impression on me (also on my father), that half a century later, in 1987, after surfacing occasionally as a lingering irrepressible memory, it inspired me to compose a work on the same New Testament scenario. The work, called *Thou Art The Son of God*, is scored for full SATB chorus and chamber ensemble.

All the while I was steadily adding to my growing record collection of 78s. I still have and cherish them all, many of them superb recordings, even technically, that have never been surpassed or reissued on LP or CD. Major transformative experiences in my life in those teen years were my acquisition in 1940 of Scriabin's *Poem of Ecstasy* and *Prometheus*, both sumptuously recorded by Stokowski and the Philadelphia Orchestra in 1933, as well as Beecham's several volumes of 1930s recordings of the works of Frederick Delius. Both of these composers took up Wagner's late (on the verge of atonality) chromaticism, each developing from it their own distinctive, personal harmonic language—which in turn became, along with certain variants thereof by composers such as Stravinsky (early Stravinsky, that is), Szymanowski, Ravel, Debussy, Ibert, and Milhaud, the linguistic platform upon which I began to build my own style. Schönberg, Berg, and Webern were at the time not yet a significant influence on my composing because hardly any of their works had been recorded up to 1940; nor were they ever played in concerts, with the few rare exceptions of early tonal Schönberg, such as his *Verklärte Nacht* String Sextet.

Arthur Eaglefield Hull's *Modern Harmony* had made me aware of Scriabin's late work, and now, through Stokowski's recordings, his music took hold of me in a way that I had never yet experienced. It is almost impossible to describe. To this day I don't fully understand what happened to me, and *still* happens to me, when I hear pieces like *Prometheus* (or Delius's *Sea Drift*, based on Walt Whitman's famous poem). It is something beyond any intellectual or analytical understanding. Something mystical, something overpoweringly physiological, takes over my mind and body, giving me goose bumps, or bringing tears to my eyes—feelings and manifestations that are automatic, totally reflexive, and can in no way be resisted.[5] When these supernormal sensations take over, I feel like I am melting, as if some spiritual force has penetrated my psyche and my body.

I have pondered this experiential phenomenon for decades without ever being able to fully understand it. Could it be that certain specific chromatic or bitonal harmonies, to which I automatically react in the way described, produce some empathetic emotional vibrations or pulsations somewhere in me? I know that most conventional harmonies, say, ninth or seventh chords, triads, half-diminished chords, all wonderful chords connoting quite diverse expressive characteristics, do not affect me in the same way. I find them beautiful, but they do not affect me physically, psychologically. This leads me to assume that there is something special about the acoustic, intervallic, vibrational content of certain highly chromatic harmonies that provoke in me the reactions I have described. I wonder whether these harmonies produce similar reactions in others? Also, are there other types of harmonies that affect other people similarly, but which happen not to affect me in the same way? What is the interconnection between certain acoustic phenomena and certain specific physiological and biological reactions.

Around the same time that I acquired the *Poem of Ecstasy* and *Prometheus* albums, I discovered a whole series of Scriabin piano solo recordings, comprising virtually his entire late oeuvre, on an obscure label called Paraclete (headquartered in New Haven). There seems to have been in the late 1930s and early 1940s an almost secret (occult?) society of Scriabin devotees, some of them pianists, all virtually unknown, who embarked on a project to record *all* of Scriabin's voluminous piano works, although the project, as far as I know, was never completed. The pianists included Samuel Yaffe, Yolande Bolotine, and Ida Krehm. I bought all of their recordings at the Gramophone Record Shop, and all his works from about the Op. 53 Fifth Sonata on in printed scores. I feverishly plowed through this mountain of music, gorging myself at the same time on the Paraclete recordings. These were not great imaginative performances, but at minimum they were soberly representative of the music. I didn't care if they failed to be at the highest interpretational levels, it was so thrilling to hear those remarkable harmonies in acoustic reality. Most of this music was quite beyond my limited pianistic abilities, especially at Scriabin's designated tempos. I could only stumble through the music in slow motion, linger at will on some delicious, sensuous harmony. But to actually *hear* the music on recordings was an incredibly voluptuous experience for my young ears and mind. I soon became drawn into a veritable vortex of harmonic delirium, which was beyond my capacity to comprehend or to resist. Ultimately, I became so obsessed with Scriabin's late music, especially the Op. 65 Etudes, the last five Sonatas, the Op. 74 Preludes (his last work), and, of course, the orchestral symphonies and tone poems, that I decided that I must learn to play—somehow, my insufficient technique notwithstanding—the complete solo piano part of *Prometheus*.

My parents became really alarmed at this turn of events; they thought I had become emotionally unhinged, and tried to bring me back to reality. But I was so possessed by the mesmerizing force of this music that I was unreachable for a while, trapped in some almost out-of-body experience, orbiting helplessly in some vertiginous musical outer space. This strange, overwhelming, and almost hallucinatory state of affairs lasted nearly two months, by the end of which I *did* learn to play almost the entire *Prometheus* piano part. Days and days of struggling four or five hours at a time went by as I was enveloped in some wondrous Scriabinesque acoustic and harmonic haze. A few of the *trés animé* and *prestissimo* episodes were clearly beyond my nontechnique, but I could and did play those passages at a slower tempo.

It is interesting to note that the word Paraclete, the name of the New Haven record company, means "holy spirit." Scriabin did in fact belong to a group of theosophist mystics in Brussels who followed Hinduism and believed in hypnotism and reincarnation. I am not given to occultism, and I don't think I could ever be hypnotized or could place much credence in supernatural powers. But I guess I came close to such a state of mind, transfixed by this remarkable unique music. It was certainly a cathartic experience, and Scriabin's linguistic legacy endures in the harmonic fabric of my music to this day, deeply embedded in my personal atonal twelve-tone language but certainly discernible by a pair of very discerning ears.

Soon after my return home from Germany in 1936, I found myself developing considerable interest in something called jazz. For many readers, who know that I have spent half of my professional life in the world of jazz, that may seem like an odd statement. And it is even strange coming from someone born in America. But the fact is that in my entire childhood I had virtually no exposure to jazz. The only music I heard in my parent's home was classical music.[6] I certainly never heard any jazz in Hitler's Germany, such music was *verboten*. Even after I returned to America, I had relatively little chance to hear any jazz. At St. Thomas I was busy all day in classes, with sports in the afternoon, homework, and studies in the evening. There were no radios in the entire school, except in Mrs. Atwater's living room, and she would not have allowed any jazz to penetrate her inner sanctum. The only time I would have been able to hear jazz would have been in the twenty-two-hour period from seven p.m. on Sunday to five p.m. on Monday, when at home—and, of course, in the summers, when there was no school.

I don't remember when I actually became aware of jazz as a distinct musical genre, and whose music it was that first caught my attention. It might have been the Benny Goodman, Tommy Dorsey, or Glenn Miller bands. From the late 1930s through the war years, jazz was *the* popular music of the United States. It was the height of the big band era, particularly the music called swing. It was played in thousands of ballrooms and hotels and clubs, by the great bands that roamed the land—Goodman, Shaw, Dorsey, Ellington, and Basie. And the four network stations (WEAF, WOR, WJZ, WCBS) broadcast fifteen minutes of jazz every night at eleven fifteen, right after the fifteen-minute nightly newscast. But if I had been listening to music on the radio during those twenty-two weekend hours, it would only have been to classical music on WQXR.

In the summers I probably did listen once in a while to WNEW's very popular program *Make Believe Ballroom* and, on one of the big network stations, to a Saturday night program called *Hit Parade*. And to the extent that I had occasionally tuned in to some of those late-night jazz broadcasts, I probably hadn't listened very attentively because I was very likely occupied reading a book, composing, or studying some score.

In any case, sometime in the early summer of 1939 I had one of those epiphanal experiences—such as my discovery of Scriabin's music—that turned out to be transformative and that crucially affected the future course of my life. The occasion was my hearing the music of Duke Ellington on a radio broadcast from the Cotton Club at Forty-Ninth Street and Broadway.[7] It's hard for me to believe that I hadn't encountered Ellington's music before that. It is more likely that in my casual listening to jazz—as opposed to my serious involvement with classical music—I just hadn't paid any particular attention. It is also the case that programs such as *Make Believe Ballroom* tended (as the name implies) to feature the more popular dance band type of jazz, rather than the hard swinging music of black orchestras such as Basie, Ellington, and Lunceford.

In any event, on that particular eleven-fifteen Ellington broadcast my ears caught sounds the likes of which I had never before heard. There was something about all those strange sonorities and that special rhythmic feeling that I knew I hadn't ever come across in any classical music, not even in any modern twentieth-century music such as Stravinsky's or Milhaud's. But what particularly caught my ear was a passage that sounded as if it was being played by two bass clarinets. That *really* impressed me; I didn't know that jazz bands would have *any* bass clarinet, let alone two. (Harry Carney, the orchestra's baritone saxophone, had been doubling on bass clarinet since the early 1930s.) That sound of two bass clarinets playing together was one of my favorite instrumental sounds in the world. I had heard it for the first time in Stravinsky's *The Rite of Spring*, where it occurs very prominently in the section called "Rondes printaniers" ("Spring Rounds"); two bass clarinets repeatedly play a stepwise ascending figure in the low register in parallel fifths. It is a most amazing unearthly sound (unfortunately not sufficiently brought out in many recordings and performances). To hear that in a jazz orchestra,[8] along with all the other remarkable sounds—the beautiful harmonies that I already knew from the music of Ravel and Delius, the incredible orchestral blends, the strange array of muted sounds in the brass, the infectious rhythms—that was really a startling musical experience.

Although my parents had little use for jazz, for me it was at that moment immediately clear that in the hands of a master like Ellington jazz was as great and important a music as any classical music. At the highest levels of creativity both musics were equal in quality. I knew then that sooner or later I would have to become actively involved with jazz, but *without* abandoning classical music.

I was so smitten with Ellington's music that the next day I declared to my father: "You know, Dad, that music I heard last night, by Ellington? Well, that music is as great as any classical music, any Mozart or Beethoven or Dvořák: beautiful melodies, beautiful harmonies, incredible instrumentation. It's perfect, just as perfect. It's just different in style and feeling." My poor father nearly had a heart attack. For days he was worried about me—maybe about my sanity. But over time he relaxed when he saw that I was not going to abandon classical music.

In expressing an equal and passionate interest in both jazz and classical music, and in beginning to think of pursuing a double career in both areas, I was forging new ground. Even though it was something I wasn't able to realize until years later, I was absolutely certain that for now, as a listener, it was the only path I would henceforth follow. While I did not say so directly to my parents, the implication they gathered from my sudden interest in jazz—my seemingly intractable notion that Beethoven's and Ellington's music were qualitatively equal—really puzzled and disturbed them. Still, since I seemed as devoted as ever to my horn and composing, they tolerated my obsession—my aberration, as they thought of it—hoping that it was a mere caprice, and that it would soon pass and be forgotten. Little did they know!

In due course I began to devote my musical energies equally to both musics, shuttling back and forth between them. How I did that, and how easily and naturally it came to me, I cannot explain. All I knew is that those things that I heard in great classical music, that is, memorable melodies or themes, striking harmonies, interesting captivating rhythms, a fascinating variety of sonorities and timbres, stated in clear forms and structures—not to mention technical mastery—I also heard in the best of jazz. And that was more than enough for me.

Incidentally, it was my discovery of Ellington that led me, at age thirteen, to think of starting to collect jazz records, although I was not able to pursue that particular ambition until a year later. Being cooped up at St. Thomas in one building for six days a week more or less eliminated any chance of shopping, let alone browsing in record stores.

In my third year at St. Thomas (1939–40) I was chosen to sing some of the soprano solos in the great oratorios, which were part of our standard repertory. Among them were *In Verdure Clad* from Haydn's *Creation*, the heavenly soprano solo in the Brahms *Requiem*, and several arias and recitatives in Handel's *Messiah*. I always wanted to sing the *Messiah*'s famous "Rejoice, Rejoice" soprano aria as a solo. It was one of Dr. Noble's favorites and a required audition piece for admission to the choir school. But he always had all forty boys sing it in unison, quite a virtuoso tour de force, and evidently a long-standing tradition in English choir schools. These assignments were shared with a boy named Joseph Bush, who had a wonderfully rich, mature voice, often using a touch of vibrato—rare with boy sopranos. Needless to say, my solo outings at St. Thomas made my parents very proud of me. And to my great relief, I did not get nervous, let alone break down, as I had years earlier trying to perform in public in Gebesee.

One of the most important events that year at St. Thomas, 1939–40, was my public debut as a composer. I had written a short one-movement piece for string quartet, which Dr. Noble and my father thought worthy of a public performance, and which was then played by my father and three of his Philharmonic colleagues at a special concert held in the school's new gymnasium auditorium. My father copied out the parts for me because my handwriting was still pretty bad. I was so nervous and excited—the blood racing around wildly in my brain—that I didn't remember anything about the concert or even what I thought of my piece, except, vaguely, the applause at the end. In succeeding weeks I did realize that some of the four-part writing was a bit clumsy, its continuity rather short-breathed, and that my string writing was somewhat less than idiomatic. But as I said earlier, it's amazing how much you can learn from your mistakes. It was in the end a great learning experience.

Perhaps even more important for my later career was taking up the horn in 1942, the instrument with which I would make my living in music for twenty-one years. I had begun to complain to my father that I was getting rather bored with the flute. His Philharmonic colleague and friend, Robert Schulze, fourth horn of the orchestra and one of the two major horn teachers in New York, suggested that I try the horn to see if I might like it better than the flute. Schulze was a longtime member of a remarkable horn section that graced the New York Philharmonic from the mid-1920s to the early 1940s. It was headed by Bruno Jänicke, filled out by his two brothers-in-law, Adolf and Robert Schulze, second and fourth horn, respectively, and an Italian named Luigi Ricci, who had joined the Philharmonic in 1917 at age eighteen. Jänicke was in his prime, at the time one of the very few truly great *artists* on the horn, along with Anton Horner (another German immigrant, principal horn of the Philadelphia Orchestra). With Jänicke you never thought of someone playing a *horn*, let alone the infamous difficulties associated with the instrument. It was just the most beautiful music making: elegant, pure-toned, refined, sensitively and intelligently blending with the instruments around him, and richly expressive in the solos (as in Brahms symphonies, for example). He was my absolute idol. His sound—never too fat, never too thin—and his impeccably tasteful style of playing, singing gloriously on his instrument, became my model. Unfortunately Jänicke never took any students; he passed applicants on to his protégé and brother-in-law, Robert Schulze, on the faculty of the Manhattan School of Music.

In due course Herr Schulze came over to our house with an Alexander horn,[9] and a large cigar box full of mouthpieces. We had all assembled in the kitchen, my parents and Edgar, in eager attendance. Schulze told me to "stand over there, by the wall," about ten, fifteen feet away. Moving his head back and forth, he studied my face, my lips for a few minutes—like a doctor examining a patient. Satisfied with what he had seen, he fished around in the cigar box—it must have contained about fifty mouthpieces—and suddenly, with a triumphant smile, he shouted, "Ich hab's (I have it)." He now fitted the mouthpiece into the horn and asked me to purse my lips. With no further instructions he told me to blow into the horn. I said something like: "What do you mean? Show me." "Ah, just blow. You know what to do." I gingerly placed the mouthpiece on my pursed lips, not really knowing what I was doing, and blew into the mouthpiece. What came out of the horn, to everyone's surprise, especially mine, was not some horrendous bleating or flatulent noise, but a rather beautiful pure middle F, a fifth below middle C. "You see, I didn't have to show you. You knew exactly what to do." Everyone applauded. I was ecstatic. Schulze declared me an absolutely natural talent for the horn. I think he was right, for only two years later, at age sixteen, I entered the ranks of professional horn players in New York.

I did not give up the flute right away, and played both instruments for almost two more years. Later, in public high school, I played flute and piccolo in the band in the mornings at seven a.m., and horn in the school's orchestra in the afternoon after regular classes. But I eventually abandoned the flute because I realized every afternoon that I would ruin my flute embouchure by playing the horn, and every morning that I would ruin my horn embouchure by playing the flute. Something had to give, and it was the flute.

At first I had very few horn lessons, being still full time at St. Thomas, and only once in a while able to sneak in a lesson with Mr. Schulze. And at St. Thomas I couldn't practice the horn much, it being a fairly loud and strongly projecting instrument. Regardless of where I might practice, I would be heard everywhere, disturbing everyone in the building—even if I practiced in the basement in the *Ioneer* office. But once I left St. Thomas, Mr. Schulze enrolled me at the Manhattan School of Music on New York's Upper East Side on 105th Street, not as a full-time student, but primarily to take horn lessons with him.

It wasn't all hard work and discipline at St. Thomas. We were often treated very generously, especially on such occasions when the choir—or sometimes just the forty boys—was invited to provide music for receptions, weddings, and other kinds of formal functions. One time we were invited to a gigantic brunch party that Elizabeth Arden was giving for all of her employees. It took place in her huge factory in Woodside, Queens, quite near to where I lived. We boys were allowed, indeed urged, to mingle with the guests and staff. I shall never forget my astonishment at seeing two immense thirty-foot-long tables along two sides of a gymnasium-sized room, completely laden with food—every kind of fruit, cheese, meat, cake, pie, and drink. Henry the Eighth's famous banquets could not have been more sumptuous. We were not kept segregated behind the scene as hired help, but were heartily invited to partake of this incredible feast. Later, when we left the premises, we were each given gifts—various cosmetics (soap, perfumes, lotions, all exquisitely wrapped or boxed)—not only for ourselves but also for our relatives. I remember giving my aunt Lydia a twelve-inch-tall, oval-shaped, beribboned doll case, inside of which there was a very big mauve-colored ball of the best and most expensive French soap that money could buy. Aunt Lydia had never in her simple life received such an outrageously expensive gift.

On another occasion, we were driven in limousines to a castlelike mansion on a huge estate in Mount Kisco, a wealthy suburb just north of New York City. There we were invited to sing a number of secular anthems and madrigals at an outdoor garden party, including some quite modern works by the likes of Philip James, Leo Sowerby, and Seth Bingham. I figured out many years later that the occasion was an afternoon reception, given for—or was it by?—Samuel Barber, Gian Carlo Menotti, and Benjamin Britten, who were all either living or visiting there. For me, a fledgling composer, just being in the presence of these famous composers was an awesome experience.

In the summer vacations, my life was increasingly exciting and fulfilling. There was the great World's Fair of 1939 and 1940 at Flushing Meadows, not far from where we lived in Queens, arguably the best all-around world's fair ever created in this country. My parents went often, always taking Edgar and me along. Given my life-long fascination with color, the dozens of multicolored hydraulic fountains, scattered throughout the entire fair grounds, made a tremendous impression on me. They were truly spectacular displays, certainly for that time. Not only were the individual fountains of different sizes and shapes—many of them consisting of half a dozen different multispired fountains rolled into one—but they also changed colors constantly in myriad configurations, patterns, and varied tempos. One of the largest and most spectacular of these water displays was created and designed by Alexander Calder. But most fascinating were the fountains in the large Lagoon of Nations, a spectacular *Son et lumière* show, with at least a hundred different-sized, multicolored fountains, all shooting upward at different speeds and heights, rising and falling in constantly changing patterns, and they were always accompanied by exciting music (such as Jean Sibelius's *Finlandia*, Liszt tone poems, or early Wagner overtures). I had often been mesmerized on my several transatlantic crossings by looking at the vast oceanscapes for hours, and the foaming, cresting waves rushing by. But the constantly moving, shifting fountains at the World's Fair were even more hypnotic. For me they were a symphony of light and color, a ballet of dancing water sculptures that had me riveted to the ground. (Near the Lagoon there was the famous Trylon and Perisphere, the thematic sculptural centerpiece of the fair.)

Speaking of water, there was also the famous Billy Rose Aquacade at that 1939 World's Fair. We visited it several times to watch the water ballets starring the young Esther Williams and Johnny Weissmuller (of *Tarzan* fame) doing their thing, accompanied by a fifty-piece symphony orchestra.

One of the most intoxicating aspects of the fair was the amount of good music to be heard almost everywhere—classical as well as the best of big band swing-era jazz, played over hundreds of loudspeakers stationed all over the fairgrounds. I must also mention the many live concerts, performed by all kinds of orchestras and bands (jazz as well as classical concert bands). Though generally offering the more familiar popular classical fare, it still was a rich musical feast for my eager ears.

Despite the imminence of war in Europe, some sixty countries had a pavilion at the fair. Germany was conspicuous by its absence. I must have visited them all. It was the first time I began to understand the word *exotic*, especially in the Japanese, Turkish, and Peruvian exhibits. I remember being particularly impressed by the Russian Pavilion, which had a replica of an entire Moscow subway station, also an ingenious, gigantic, wall-long map of the Soviet Union in which every important geographic or geological feature was highlighted by precious or semiprecious gems and metals: gold, silver, lapis lazuli (azure blue), turquoise, emerald, opal, aquamarine, garnet, ruby, and topaz (the latter my birthstone). With multicolored lights projected on it in another symphony of light and rhythm, the whole map glittered and glistened.

One of the most popular exhibits at the fair was the General Motors Pavilion, especially its famous Futurama ride created by Norman Bel Geddes, representing a futuristic view of what a 1960 American metropolis would look like. By means of a quarter-mile-long moving ramp equipped with upholstered chairs and individual loudspeakers (delivering an explanatory narration), the visitor was slowly conveyed along a scale model of a modern city replete with skyscrapers, eight-lane highways, off-ramps, bridges, and tunnels, with hundreds if not thousands of cars moving in a maze of varying speeds and in diverse directions. We were told that automobiles in the future would travel as fast as one hundred miles an hour. As seen from above in a birds-eye view, Bel Geddes's prophetic panoramic vision promised unalloyed future happiness, driving in high-speed cars through clean, slum-free cities resplendent with parks and cultural centers; it all seemed to us like fantasyland. Little did we realize then that its seeming irreality would, less than twenty or thirty years later, already be obsolete, replaced by a world of severe traffic gridlock and smoggy, hopelessly overcrowded, congested cities and dying inner cities.

You can imagine that my parents did their best to keep me and my friend Willy Manthey away from the infamous Great White Way, whose seedier attractions, including Gypsy Rose Lee's notorious burlesque show, were the amusement center of the World's Fair. I am sure my parents thought that as thirteen- and fourteen-year-olds we would not be aware of those (allegedly) less elevating but very tempting midway offerings, purposely located by the fair's organizers at its farthest northeastern corner. Little did they know! In the fair's second year Willy and I were able, under some phony pretext, to surreptitiously sneak away to Gypsy Rose Lee's emporium. Not that we, at our age, had any chance of penetrating that citadel of seduction; but we were driven by an irresistible, overwhelming libidinous force to at least stand in awe somewhere near the place. We just *had* to be there, in her presence—or as near as we could get. In retrospect, it all seems rather silly and embarrassing, but there we stood, hearts palpitating, faces blood flushed, our minds exploding from our pitiful erotic imaginings. In fact, innocent and naïve as we were, we hardly even knew what sex was, let alone what lay between a woman's thighs. But we knew there was something damned exciting.

Only a few years later, when I actually saw one of Gypsy Rose Lee's shows—doves, fans, and all—I was incredibly disappointed. It was all tease with hardly any sensual substance, so calculatedly smooth and slick that I felt nothing. It was so bland and squeaky clean that I didn't even feel frustrated. Actually, my youthful fantasies, standing there in front of Gypsy's World's Fair pavilion, were infinitely more thrilling and exciting.

When I nowadays head by taxi from LaGuardia over the Triboro Bridge toward Manhattan, and pass by the famous Hell's Gate Bridge, I'm often reminded how Edgar and I marveled at the turbulence of the water below—at that point a narrowed arm of the East River—and the incredibly long freight trains moving above on the Hell's Gate Bridge. There were sometimes as many as 150 railroad cars snaking their way slowly across the bridge. I remember writing in a little notebook I kept the exact number of freight cars every time we drove by, of course hoping always to see the little caboose at the end.

In that same notebook I also kept track of how many of each make of car we saw on the road, not only Fords, Chevrolets, Studebakers, DeSotos, and Pontiacs, but also—most exciting—foreign cars, or rare automobiles such as the Cord, Duesenberg, and Jaguar. To see a custom-built Cord, the most elegant, sleek, modern automobile on the road—a pretty rare occurrence—was the high point of our lives.

Speaking of filling notebooks, it was at this time that I began to make huge listings of composers' names, tabulating the growing number of performances each got on radio with stick numbering ++++. I wasn't all that interested in how many performances Mozart, Beethoven, and Tchaikovsky got, because I knew that they would top the charts by far. Indeed, I resented how much space they took up in my little pocket notebook. No, I was more interested in how the less popular composers, the underdogs such as Gesualdo, Mossolov, Deems Taylor, Scriabin, Max Reger, Julián Carrillo, and others fared. These were lists not only of what was played on WQXR and WNYC but also what I also heard in concerts—from which the reader can gain an idea of how incredibly rich the classical music fare in New York was in those days.

On one of our 1939 visits to the World's Fair, we made a slight detour to the nearby tiny LaGuardia airport to see the inaugural flight of the new German transatlantic flying boats. For us it was like another World's Fair exhibit, as the big ship splashed down in Flushing Bay and was hauled out of the water onto its dock ramp, the plane's six propellers glistening and shimmering in the bright sunlight. On a revisit the next year, we watched with great pride as the silver Pan Am clippers began *their* overseas service. As I now fly Boston to New York so frequently, I am constantly reminded of the excitement of seeing those huge flying ships; that original LaGuardia terminal—a handsome circular art deco building shaped like a hatbox and featuring remarkable murals by the Mexican painter Diego Rivera—is now the Delta Shuttle terminal, and is still known as the Marine Terminal.

Recalling that brings back a memory of two years earlier—of May 6, 1937, to be exact—when I and my family saw the Hindenburg, the worlds biggest and most famous dirigible, from the roof of our twelve-story apartment building in Woodside, Queens, in its last hour. This giant zeppelin was another Nazi pride-and-joy mechanism, used very effectively as a propaganda instrument to show the world that Hitler's Germany could do anything England and America could do, only bigger and better. The Hindenburg flew right over our house, beginning its initial descent only a few thousand feet over us, so close that we could clearly hear the deep, sonorous, steady hum of its motors. And we could just make out the passengers' faces, peering down through the ship's slanted lounge windows at the thousands of people on rooftops watching *them*. I remember being amazed at the speed with which the Hindenburg flew; it disappeared in a matter of minutes into the distance, bound for Lakehurst, New Jersey—and to its doom.

We barely got back down to our sixth-floor apartment when the news broke on the radio that the Hindenburg had gone up in flames just as it was landing and being anchored to the pylon in Lakehurst. We could not believe our ears, having just thirty minutes earlier witnessed her flying over our house. It is hard to forget the hysterical voice of the radio announcer trying to describe this horrendous disaster that killed thirty-five people. Sixty-two passengers survived by jumping overboard to the ground. That they weren't crushed and buried in the flames of the crumbling falling debris is a miracle. Within days we all saw the whole horrific event again and again in the newsreels shown in movie theatres.

Obbligato

It was during my years at St. Thomas that I realized that I was blessed with a very fast, alert mind, quick to grasp things, quick to respond. My mind and ears, particularly in regard to music, absorbed enormous amounts of information easily and virtually instantly. I discovered that I especially relished comprehending larger concepts and contexts, within which other things occurred, in other words, learning to think conceptually and contextually. It was at St. Thomas that I grew to appreciate and love the world of ideas—a good thing for a composer. I came to the realization that the notion of "idea in music" seemed to be—and still seems to be— alien to musicians, including many composers. Ideas belong in the realm of literature, logic, intellect, but not in music or art—so the argument went. But I thought—and felt—that music without musical ideas is by definition a lesser creation. The opening statement of Beethoven's *Eroica* symphony is a musical *idea*. And its distinctness produces substance, essence. Substantial ideas are indispensable in the creation of great, important music.

It was also around this time that I began to really grasp the concept of democracy, and its inherent absolute social equality. Whether this came to me from reading a lot of Emerson or Rousseau, or some broader educational or instinctual source, I don't remember. What I do know is that I developed a very clear sense that all human beings in the world, whatever their provenance, their position, and, obviously, whatever their race or color—must be regarded as equivalent in human merit and value in the claim to equal rights and equal justice for all. In the *idea* of democracy I saw my fellow human beings as intrinsically equal at birth, that is, before life's vicissitudes and transformations, the inevitable fluctuations of human affairs, could affect that absolutely fundamental equivalence. As I used to put it to my friend Dick Verdery, when we sometimes discussed such matters in our *Ioneer* office: unequivocal equivalence.

I realized, of course, that the world and mankind weren't made in such a way as to bring about absolute social equality in respect to rights and opportunities. But there was no question in my mind that equalness was and must be a fundamental belief and basic tenet of one's life's creed. This led readily to the belief that I was not superior to any other human being—nor, for that matter, was I *inferior*—and that I therefore must regard everyone that I know, that I meet, that I hear about, as equal in quality to me. That is how I learned to treat every new person I met as if they were already my best friend, as if I had known them as trusted companions for years. It was a wonderful and important experience for me as a young adult to learn to sort out the differences between those who were wealthy and had considerable advantages handed to them at birth, and those who had to struggle against all kinds of odds not of their making to achieve *even* minor goals and modest status. My reading of many books by Dickens helped enormously in this sorting-out process, whether it was *Oliver Twist*, *A Tale of Two Cities*, or *David Copperfield*, or my later reading of most of the works of Thomas Hardy.

Even in my late teenage years when I was occasionally a little cocky about my musical accomplishments, or when I would occasionally come off as youthfully overconfident, I never lost sight of those fundamental principles: that I was in no way superior to anyone else, and that I was in fact just one simple, modest creature, out of several billion people, temporarily allowed to reside on this globe.

I saw instinctively that there were people of immense accomplishments who were older, more experienced, and more talented than I, who inspired me as mentors to strive to equal their grand achievements. This had nothing to do with ego-driven competition or a sense of contest, let alone some kind of control. It was simply the realization that I must always strive for whatever higher achievements my talents, such as they might be, would allow me to fulfill. At times I was swaggeringly disapproving of certain mediocre, second-rate conductors that I had to sometimes work with. But such haughty disparagements were specifically expressed within the context of the highest performance and interpretive standards. I can honestly say that when I felt momentarily superior to conductor X or Y, it was a specific sentiment that never translated into a broader personal, ego-based sense of superiority. To believe that one is good and talented must not be allowed to mean that one is thus better than anyone else.

Later, when I started conducting orchestras, I never, never thought that I, being a conductor, was therefore in some way superior to the musicians in the orchestra. I have always regarded orchestra musicians as my equals, as my colleagues, as my professional comrades, all of us in the service of making the best music that we collectively can achieve. I say this because unfortunately most of the famous *maestri* of my youth—the Reiners, the Szells, and a dozen others—*did* actually think they were superior to all of us musicians. The one grand exception to that was Dimitri Mitropoulos.

This sense of absolute equality between myself and my fellow human beings led, quite logically, to my regarding men and women, although distinct genera of our species, intrinsically equal. I thought it ludicrous, as well as offensive, that most men felt that they were superior to women. I regarded every woman I met, including Marjorie, my wife, as inherently equal to me—and by extension equal to and with other men and women.

I must admit that within that concept I did occasionally experience some puzzlement as to certain social customs or matters of etiquette. I wondered, for example, why, if women were truly equal to men, should a gentleman—or I—open a door for a lady; or why should a man be obliged to help seat a woman at a dinner table. I eventually decided that such customs had nothing to do with equality as such, but rather were nice, respectful, friendly acts of behavior and manners. (By the way, on the basis of absolute equality between men and women, why shouldn't women occasionally open the door for men!) I'll undoubtedly be considered old fashioned, but I do really like opening a door for a woman; it makes me feel good. But I don't feel that I *have* to do it.

It was somewhere in my midteen years that I began to realize—although I was perhaps dimly aware of it even before—that we humans, like our fellow animal brethren, have in us something called instincts! (In females these feelings are called a woman's intuition.) I suddenly understood with the clarity of a revelation that instinctual feelings arise from our most inner selves, and that they are almost always good feelings, to be trusted and relied upon. I know that in the thousands of instances in my life where I followed my instincts, I somehow always did the right thing. In those relatively few occasions where I ignored or suppressed my instincts, there was usually hell to pay.

Women's instincts or intuitions are, as far as I (a dilettante psychologist and amateur behavioral scientist) can tell, more highly developed than in males—having been sensitively honed over the millennia, possibly because women are the ultimate preservers of our species. I have often wondered where instincts originate, more precisely, where these feelings are located, where they come from and then flow to our conscious mind. I remember reading a long time ago in a tome on psychology and human behavior that instincts emanate from our navels. Whether this is nonsense or some mysterious truism, I don't know. But I must confess that on many occasions, when I have consciously sought to elicit an instinctual reaction, I have done so by directing my mind to my navel,[10] and in some mystical way it seemed to work. But for all I really know, that feeling may have been a fantasy, a placebo.

The differences between men and women are as prevalent as the similarities and parallels, and in that context it is fascinating to see overlaps and commonalities between certain areas of behavior. For example, men sometimes exhibit certain female traits, whether physical, psychological, or attitudinal—and, of course, vice versa. If, presumably, forty thousand years ago males and females were distinctively differentiated in these respects, then evidently over the millennia, through various forms of crossability, genetic permutation, and reciprocation, the two genders have developed the ability to take on various qualities of their opposites. If that is so, then for me the big question remains as to why men, generally speaking, rely less on instinct and intuitional feelings.

* * * * *

I knew, of course, that a boy's voice changes sometime in the early teen years, and I began to wonder when this particular transformation would come to pass in me. It was a serious issue, since if and when my voice changed, my wonderful life at St. Thomas would come to an abrupt end. But at the end of my third year at St. Thomas (spring 1940) my soprano voice was in fine shape, and thus I was expected to come back for a fourth year. But over the summer my voice did change, and suddenly I was no longer a soprano, but a bass-baritone. This explains why I did not graduate from St. Thomas, and therefore have no certificate or diploma, no official indication that I ever studied there. Since my departure from my school in Germany was also unexpected and abrupt, I have no piece of paper from there either. Thus far, therefore, I was officially illiterate, uneducated.

When my voice broke in mid-1940, my parents, having already sent me to two private schools, decided that this time I should continue my education at a public school. The nearest one turned out to be Jamaica High School in Jamaica, Queens. My parents had recently moved to a new two-story house in what was called Jamaica Estates. It was a brand-new development, part of a prolonged eastward trek of so many New Yorkers to suburbia, culminating after the war in the vast-scaled Levittown.

Jamaica High had a symphony orchestra and a concert band, as did all high schools in those days—not any more, alas. The conductor of the orchestra, Mrs. Hughes, was a wonderful teacher, with a cheerful, friendly disposition, kind and helpful, who supported me a lot in my ongoing music and horn studies. Over the two-plus years I was there, I'm convinced she often picked pieces for the orchestra to perform because they had important horn solos. I'm sure she realized that I was very serious about music and that I might become a professional musician.

The orchestra was not particularly good, nor complete. We had only one oboe and only two violas, and I think there were other lacunae. But we covered for whatever was missing by playing, as necessary, the cued-in parts that high school orchestra parts always contained. The concert band was more fully populated, and there I played the piccolo. But what sticks in my mind about the band is how bad the clarinet section sounded. One reason for that must have been that they all played metal clarinets, probably old army rejects, which inherently make a tinny, wheezing, brittle sound that is most unattractive.

But there was one very talented clarinetist in the school, and I think he and I were the only two at Jamaica High from that time who went on to become professional musicians. His name was Tony Acquaviva, and he was a year older than I. Quite naturally, as the only other really serious musicians in the school, we became the best of friends. Tony ended up in Hollywood in the 1950s, married the singer Joni James, who had a number of hits, but did not seem to have made the big career as a bandleader that he always dreamed about in high school. I wrote one piece for Tony (and myself) in my last year at Jamaica High, a three-movement piece for clarinet, horn, and piano that later came to be called *Romantic Sonata*, and which clearly reveals some of my very early influences (such as Scriabin, Delius, and—even—Howard Hanson).

Tony played jazz primarily. He idolized Artie Shaw, and already had a well-developed bandleader complex. Around the time I came to Jamaica High—the fall of 1940—he had just formed a sixteen-piece jazz band. It was pretty good for a high school group and a strictly extracurricular activity, and I have to believe that a number of the players in his band were a little older and from outside the school. It wasn't long before Tony asked me to join his band. What school bands played in those days were stock arrangements, that is, published arrangements of famous pieces recorded by bands like Dorsey, Shaw, Miller, James, Herman, etc., but somewhat simplified and made technically more accessible to nonprofessional groups. Generally we looked on those stocks, dumbed down by some hack arranger in Broadway's Tin Pan Alley Brill Building, with considerable disdain. We knew that they were intentionally winnowed down, all the juicy harmonies and more interesting rhythmic ideas reduced and simplified for strictly commercial purposes—that is, in order to sell more copies to less sophisticated customers. But many of the better and more ambitious bands, such as Tony's, would buy those stocks and then, by listening to the recordings on which they were based, put all the good stuff back in. Thus it was a relatively inexpensive way of getting hold of a favorite tune or arrangement and then adapting it to your band's particular strengths or limitations.

Tony's library consisted almost entirely of such rehabilitated stocks, and, of course, these had no horn parts. The horn was not to enter the jazz arena for some years to come. But undaunted, and not wishing to just double some third trumpet or second saxophone part, I wrote my own horn parts, judiciously adding more modern spicy notes—flatted fifths, major sevenths, and such—to enhance and enrich the harmonies, quite often putting back some interesting harmonization or voice-leading that some great arranger (such as Eddie Sauter, Andy Gibson, or Sy Oliver) had put into his arrangement in the first place. This was easy and exciting for me to do because by that time, as a composer, I had in my own compositions begun to use bitonal harmonies and chords, such as those I found in the music of Ravel, Debussy, Milhaud—and also, by the way, of Duke Ellington. Tony loved my amendations, although some of the kids in the band thought they were too far out.

Through various connections Tony was soon getting gigs for his band, mostly in upstate New York or on Long Island, including some air checks on small radio stations. In the early forties, radio stations, even (or especially) small local stations, used to program lots of fifteen- or thirty-minute jazz programs, often at midday and, of course, in the evening just before and after prime time. These gigs usually paid very little—a few bucks, perhaps—or occasionally nothing. But we didn't care; we just wanted to play. One of the most memorable of these gigs took place in the late summer of 1941 in Beacon, New York, about fifty miles up the Hudson River. Tony got us passage on one of the big Circle Line Hudson River boats. I remember that three-hour trip particularly well because, in my fifteen-year-old innocence, I expected it to be a picturesque excursion up the river, along the New Jersey Palisades and, on the other side, to pass by the beautiful estates around the Hyde Park area (including President Roosevelt's home)—altogether a somewhat meditative prelude to the evening's music making. Instead, for most of the band, especially the older guys, it turned out to be an occasion for lots of boozing (gin was the intoxicant of choice in those days) and, as organized by Phil, our trombone soloist and oldest, most experienced player in the group, the passing around of a dozen or so little erotic cartoon booklets, very popular in those days. These brief crude fornication episodes involved comic book characters such as Maggie and Jiggs, Dick Tracy, and Superman, and movie stars such as Errol Flynn[11] and Tyrone Power, Hedy Lamarr and Lana Turner. They were put together in such a way that the real action was not revealed except by rapidly flipping the pages sequentially—not too fast, of course—very much like frames flitting by in a film. I caught only a few glimpses of those "dirty" booklets, being too shy to fully participate in this particular pursuit. But it made me aware that there were such things as erotic books and pictures specifically intended to arouse the viewer pruriently. Today it is called pornography, a term I hate for its etymological association with prostitutes, preferring the word "erotic" because sexual arousal belongs to the realm of Eros (the Greek god of love), and because sex comprises the real stuff of life and its constant procreant renewal.

The Beacon gig was divided into two parts. One was a long three-set dance from eight to one a.m., at the then famous and very popular Beacon Inn, high above the city atop the mile-long cable car, with a magnificent view of the entire area: the winding Hudson far below, the Catskills to the northwest. The other part was a fifteen-minute studio broadcast at twelve fifteen p.m. the next day on the local Beacon radio station. The dance went well. Tony was a big success with his Artie Shaw imitations, and I recollect having at least one long solo chorus (memorized, not improvised), that I had incorporated in our arrangement of *Tangerine*, coming in riskily on a high concert E.

But the ensuing night hours turned out to be an absolute nightmare. The Inn's proprietors had, to our dismay, put the *entire* band in one large room, with only four beds and a few extra cots. Can you imagine sixteen mostly half-potted musicians all dumped into this tiny space, hardly anyone wishing or able to sleep? Most of this crew spent much of the night endlessly exchanging stories, dirty jokes, or playing cards, half-naked, the older guys kicking us younger ones out of our beds in the middle of the night (if we had been lucky enough to corral one in the first place). Things didn't calm down until around five or six in the morning. I remember spending most of the night on the hard floor, under someone's bed.

A sad-looking, bleary-eyed bunch of miscreants showed up the next morning at the eleven o'clock prebroadcast rehearsal in downtown Beacon. Tony, who had slept well and dreamt blissfully in the private room he had been given, was shocked and upset when he heard how execrable we sounded. But somehow we pulled ourselves together for the twelve-fifteen show. The only anxious moment—for me anyway—was watching that minute hand on the big studio clock above the control room window heading relentlessly for 12:29 when we still had about nine or ten bars to play. Needless to say, the announcer's thanks to the band and his closing spiel were definitely on the brief side.

At Jamaica High I had one other quite close friend (besides Acquaviva), named Richard Sandifer, with whom I intermittently kept in touch until his death in early 2004. Though not a musician, he was passionately devoted to classical music. He had a fascinating career, primarily as the captain for many years of the merchant marine's SS *President*.

It was around this time, while I was busy with both flute and horn, that I began going back to the piano, fairly seriously this time. This, along with a heavy load of homework, kept me busy more or less around the clock. I loved it. I was growing, not just physically but also intellectually and emotionally, learning, achieving something new and exciting every day. In and out of school I felt my talents being challenged, and thereby focused and channeled into a very rewarding and motivating work ethos.

Even while I was still at St. Thomas I was doing more and more composing, separate from my theory studies with Dr. Noble. In short order I filled several music notebooks and dozens of score pages, turning increasingly from sacred anthems and church services to orchestral works, all characterized by a lot of trial and error. Many of these works were started with great enthusiasm and excitement, but sooner or later (mostly sooner) abandoned. I just didn't have sufficient skill or technique to develop a musical idea into an effective, logically constructed composition. I knew little about form. I usually stumbled forward into some gigantic climax but then recognized that I was creatively stuck, my initial enthusiasm having petered out. Most of the time I didn't have the patience to try to work my way out of the problem. In the meantime, another idea or a beginning for another piece would hit me, usually inspired by something I heard on the radio or in a concert, but that would soon suffer the same fate as the previous abandoned pieces.

In those teen learning-and-studying years I was constantly bombarded with new influences, new inspirations. There was in New York *so* much music to hear, to absorb, to study—on recordings, on the radio, in concerts—that I was simply overwhelmed. I sometimes became quite confused as to which stylistic or linguistic direction to take. That I was seriously searching for *some* direction is attested to by how much and how often I would copy out—in full score—entire movements of symphonies (by Beethoven, Bruckner, or Mahler, for example, or pieces by Ravel and Debussy, or Delius). Or I would make piano reductions of the pieces. Rather than technically, intellectually analyzing the compositions, as one might do in a conservatory composition or theory course, I felt that writing out a full score note by note was an even better approach to learning the great masterpieces of musical literature. It was a terrific way of connecting intimately with every one of those thousands of notes that some great master had written, in effect retracing the steps by which he had composed the piece. I felt I could learn all or most of what I needed to know because I was determined to observe all the important internal relationships and inner workings of a piece of music. This direct, virtually physical contact—not merely aural—with the music itself, with the score, was the more penetrating, more deeply absorbing way to learn and study, as opposed to sitting in a class, having a teacher deliver that knowledge to you, second hand, as it were, through someone else's explications. I realized that I had to go through that learning process by myself, needing to be as intimately in touch with the music as possible, and that meant the score itself.

I don't think that was youthful arrogance; it was rather a sense, a feeling, of independence. I wanted to do things on my own, and as a result I cannot recall ever having the desire to study with a teacher or another composer. I wanted to do what had to be done by myself.

In some ways this slowed down my learning progress because I was still too inexperienced to always fully appreciate and understand what I was seeing, as I copied or transcribed the music. And since this studying was self-directed, I undoubtedly stumbled into some unnecessary detours and bypassed certain important matters that a wise and experienced teacher could have helped me avoid. On the other hand, what I *did* learn at my own tempo really stuck with me, having penetrated more deeply through painstaking self-study rather than knowledge acquired via a secondhand source.

I have often replied, when asked with whom I had studied composition, that I never studied with anybody (except basic theory with Dr. Noble), that I am an autodidact. I go on to say that my real teachers were the great composers themselves, through their scores, and the orchestra—that is to say, playing in orchestras, great orchestras, studying and analyzing the music while playing it, not just hearing the music at a distance, but actually experiencing it physically, feeling the vibration of the music as it coursed through me, coming at me through the floor of the stage or in the sound waves around me. That is a holistic experience that can only occur while playing in an orchestra, assuming one is also listening seriously and fully engaged in the rehearsal or performance process. It cannot be experienced to the same degree sitting in an audience in, say, the twentieth row of an auditorium or the second balcony. One needs to be *in* the orchestra, *inside* the music. I had the good fortune to be so immersed thousands of times, starting in my sixteenth year, when I became a professional horn player, but even before that as I started playing in the Manhattan School of Music orchestra and other student orchestras.

Not all of my early compositional efforts remained unfinished. Among the several pieces I actually completed were a *Chanson triste* for horn and orchestra, a *Variations and Fugue on a Czech Folksong* (very much influenced by Reger and Weinberger), a tone poem called *Night in the Pines*, inspired by Robert Louis Stevenson's evocative account of a night spent in the pine forests of the Languedoc region in southeastern France, and two movements of a projected symphony, which I boldly called Symphony No. 1, as if I knew that I was going to write more than one. I remember that the piece was influenced and inspired by some works of Maurice Duruflé, particularly the Prelude and Scherzo for organ that Dr. Noble had played in one of his recitals.

I submitted that short two-movement symphony in February 1942 to a competition held annually by the New York Philharmonic Young People's Concerts. The winners were: first prize of $200, André Mathieu,[12] with a Concertino for Piano and Orchestra; second prize, split between Allen Sapp[13] and Luise Vosgerchian;[14] and third prize, Dika Newlin.[15] In addition, two other special prizes—$25 each—were given: fourth prize to me, and fifth to Mario di Bonaventura.[16] Only Mathieu's work was performed at the concert, but I was, of course, thrilled to be awarded a prize—any prize, as I was the youngest of all five winners. And it was the first time my name was mentioned as a composer in a major public venue: Carnegie Hall, of all places, the world famous hallowed temple of music.

Rudolf Ganz was at that time conductor of the Philharmonic's Young People's Concerts. When my name was announced to the audience in Carnegie Hall, Ganz, who was Swiss-born and spoke fluent German, and knew that this young honorable mention winner was his close friend Arthur Schuller's son, and therefore certainly knew my family name, nonetheless, to the horror of my mother sitting with me in the first balcony, pronounced my name "Skuller" rather than Schuller (the German "sch" sounded as "sh"). Very embarrassing, and to this day inexplicable to me!

Sometime in early 1940 I realized that I should start a record collection—in both jazz and classical music. It was all well and good to hear recordings played on WQXR or WNYC, or WNEW, but that was such a fleeting experience. I felt that I needed to own recordings so that I could study the music through repeated listenings with a score in hand, which was critical to my growth as a musician and composer. I did not realize until years later that there was also an inherent danger in learning from recordings, especially if *only* from recordings, because the recorded interpretation of a particular work might not be true to the score and the composer's intentions. (I shall return to this subject, for it began increasingly to occupy my mind and eventually, half a century later, led to what I consider one of the most important achievements of my life: my book *The Compleat Conductor*.) I began collecting records assiduously, spending what little pocket money I received from my parents on these precious purchases. I discovered that there was a record store on Fifty-Seventh Street near Carnegie Hall in the basement of Steinway Hall, where, to make my visits even more enticing, a rather attractive and amazingly knowledgeable young lady was the main sales person. We became good friends in time and I owe much to her for alerting me, sometimes a month in advance, to the most exciting new recordings that were about to be released.[17]

By the time I was sixteen, I had amassed a sizable collection of recordings, primarily by the moderns: Ravel, Debussy, Ibert, Milhaud, Scriabin, Stravinsky, Prokofiev, Holst (*The Planets*), Vaughan Williams (*London Symphony*), Hindemith, and Shostakovich (the First and Fifth Symphony). A single 78-disc cost anywhere from fifty cents to a dollar, while three-record albums cost about three dollars. The Steinway Hall shop did not sell jazz records, nor did other record stores such as the Grammophone Shop. Thus I did not acquire any jazz recordings until a bit later, when I discovered a chain of stores along Sixth Avenue that specialized in jazz and even sold used records.

Debussy's and Ravel's music, particularly through their virtually identical chromatic harmonic language, was almost as overpowering an experience and influence as Scriabin's music.

His work was very sparsely represented on recordings and very rarely performed in concerts. *Prometheus* and *Poem of Ecstasy* were for almost two decades the only major recordings of Scriabin's music. The entire oeuvre of Debussy and Ravel was already available on records by the time I became seriously involved with music. It was, in fact, *the* most recorded modern, early twentieth-century music. I'm sure that it comprised almost half of my record collection.

I learned a tremendous amount about all the music I was studying from recordings. But in the process I also learned that a recording may not correspond to what is actually in the score. Let me offer one example of how misleading—and downright wrong—a recording can be. There was one important Debussy orchestral work that had not yet been recorded in the early period of my record collecting, and that was "Sirènes," the third movement of his *Nocturnes*. One day my friend at the Steinway Hall record shop told me that Stokowski had just recorded the entire *Nocturnes* with the Philadelphia Orchestra. When I got home with my new treasure, I skipped over "Nuages" and "Fêtes" and went directly to "Sirènes."[18] I was very excited, bathing in the luxuriant sounds of Debussy's music and the Philadelphia Orchestra's lush sonic palette, when in the middle of the second side ("Sirènes" took up three 78 sides), I was suddenly startled in my quasi-reverie by some awful dissonances that were completely out of place in Debussy's harmonic language. How can that be? I listened again to the offending passage and went a little further, only to discover that the errant harmonies occurred two more times! How could such a thing happen *on a recording?* It was unbelievable. I got out my score of "Sirènes" and saw that the entire Philadelphia horn section had played the right notes but *one bar too early*, and not just once but also in the two repetitions of that four-bar phrase, stretching across twelve measures and some forty-five seconds of music. How can it be that no one—not the horn players, not the recording supervisor in the control room, not Stokowski—heard this gross misrepresentation and tried to stop it from occurring?

I had my father listen to the recording, just to confirm that my ears weren't playing tricks on me. *He* could not believe what he heard, nor explain it. I pondered this strange situation for many days, but finally concluded that it all had to do with Stokowski's personality and podium behavior, later confirmed by someone who was a longtime member of the Philadelphia Orchestra and involved with almost every recording that the orchestra made in the 1920s and 1930s.

There is no question that Leopold Stokowski, the musician, was in many respects a genius, gifted with certain remarkable, I'd say unique, talents, beyond anyone I can think of. But he was also in almost equal measure a severely flawed human being, given far too often to tyrannical, malevolent, perverse behavior, at times of a sadistic nature that was in its dimensions truly incomprehensible. This maleficence was driven by an astonishing combination of willfulness and egotism, of a size and sort quite beyond that of any other conductor I know of. (The closest competitors would be Bernstein and Celibidache.) Part of Stokowski's egotism expressed itself in a penchant for charlatanry, for outrageous pretense. For almost his entire life he affected a phony Polish accent, which presumably was meant to perpetuate the myth he had concocted as a young man that he was of noble Polish birth. He was, in fact, born in London's East End and grew up with a strong Cockney brogue. (Two friends of mine, Jerome Toobin, producer of Stokowski's United Artists recordings, Robert Blake, the recording engineer for those sessions, and I are possibly the only three musicians who ever heard Stoky speak Cockney, his native dialect.) I don't think there was a single orchestra musician in America or Europe who didn't witness or hear about the evil side of Stokowski's personality.

When you went into music you heard about Stokowski's obdurate podium tactics, his immense ego, his recklessly willful way with any composer's music, the preposterous liberties he could take in his interpretations, and his callous ignoring of the printed page. Ironically, this willfulness also expressed itself many times in that he did *not* engage in such strange behavior;

on many occasions he treated people and the music he conducted with the utmost respect and love. It was weird. A real Jekyll and Hyde personality.

You also learned two other things: one, that you never countered Stokowski in response to a criticism or any comment whatsoever, especially if you thought he was wrong, and even if your inclination was to respond in the mildest, most respectful manner. Above all, you never asked Stokowski a question about a wrong or questionable note or rhythm. If he hadn't heard or corrected an error, he would take your question, no matter how well intended, as a deep insult. Stokowski was unwilling to ever admit a mistake. You also learned that Stoky almost never heard wrong notes. It really could be dangerous to work with Stokowski (audiences, music lovers, and record collectors were, of course, completely unaware of the true nature of his podium behavior). But then you also learned that on occasion you could have some incredibly thrilling musical experiences with him.

While pondering how such an incredible mistake could occur on a recording made by such a world famous orchestra and conductor and by the most successful record company in the world, RCA Victor, I remembered something. On Stokowski's mostly wonderful recording of Scriabin's *Poem of Ecstasy* (which I had bought two years earlier) there was also a major wrong-note glitch. A dramatic *fortissimo* passage in the three trombones about two thirds of the way in, which was supposed to be in unison, came out in parallel fourths. In that case the first and second trombone parts had been printed in the wrong clef; a transposed repeat of that same phrase a bit later was correctly printed and correctly played in unison. This would have told any conductor, especially in the context of that particular section of the piece, that the repetition of the passage was correct, and that therefore the first appearance of it had to be corrected. But either Stokowski never heard the error, or the trombonists, fearing that they would lose their jobs, never said a word. Still worse, they were afraid to correct the mistake on their own. Even that was dangerous—although the ultimate irony is that Stokowski might never have heard the difference.[19]

In the case of "Sirènes," the only way that those wrong, ridiculously dissonant, atonal sounds would have been captured on RCA Victor's B 14518 is by way of the following explanation. Recordings are usually made after the scheduled work has been rehearsed, usually four rehearsals, and performed in public at least once. The Philadelphia Orchestra played every week's programs a minimum of three times, and then usually recorded the work the following Monday. What this means—as incredible as it may seem—is that the Philadelphia Orchestra rehearsed "Sirènes" with Stokowski at least three times (perhaps four), played the work in public at least three times in the orchestra's weekend concerts at the Academy of Music, and then recorded it early the next week. How can it be that in those (at minimum) six instances of rehearsing and playing "Sirènes" during that week—I estimate a total of at least two hours each time—no one heard and corrected the errant notes? It was, of course, Stokowski's job to hear them and correct them; and I can't think of any conductor, even some of the worst I played with, who wouldn't have stopped, if not the first time at least by the second or third occurrence, and corrected the error. Not Stokowski.

The answer to this bizarre conundrum is that absolutely no one, neither in the horn section—not even the famous principal horn, Arthur Berv—nor the recording producer-supervisor on the session, dared to say anything, knowing full well that it would almost certainly lead to a precipitous early retirement. I know. That's exactly what happened to me in 1962.

I mentioned earlier that there was someone who confirmed, although somewhat obliquely, that my diagnosis of the "Sirènes" situation was accurate. He said such incidents occurred many times over the years. That was Sylvan Levin, a great musician I admired very much, for many years Stokowski's right-hand man in Philadelphia and also the superb solo pianist on the recording of Scriabin's *Prometheus*. In the 1970s I contacted Levin several times, asking him about some of the weirder aspects of Stokowski's persona. Each time he pleaded the Fifth Amendment. It wasn't until after Stokowski's death—he died in 1977 at age ninety-five—that Sylvan finally felt he could respond to my repeated requests, though even then rather reluctantly. I asked him about Stokowski's apparent inability to correct wrong notes or, as I put it (to give him some latitude in his response), "was it perhaps some strange unwillingness"—knowing full well that it wasn't anything of the sort. Levin waited a long time, and finally, in a very soft voice allowed: "Well, Gunther, you're on the right track."

Sylvan Levin was a gentleman, and was really very hesitant to rat on his admired boss, even posthumously. I felt bad for having pressed him.

In 1938 my parents bought a two-room bungalow on one lot of land in Rocky Point, on the north shore of Long Island, about sixty miles east of New York City and about seven miles east of Port Jefferson. That became our summer vacation spot for the next seven years. Rocky Point proper, a tiny village with a population of about one thousand (in the 1940s), was located on Route 25, two miles inland from the Long Island Sound and the shoreline beach. But greater Rocky Point (including the village of Shoreham), which tripled its population in the summer, extended out to the Sound. That part of Rocky Point was perched high on steep eighty-foot bluffs that stretched eastward almost all the way to Orient Point, the northeastern most tip of Long Island. Rocky Point thus had many miles of beautiful sandy beach, where I, my brother, and my new friends Willy Manthey and his sister Dorian, spent the better part of each day. The Manthey family, also German immigrants, were our immediate neighbors in Rocky Point.

Avid reader that I was, I had the idea of organizing daily reading sessions for the four of us kids. But that quickly evolved—I guess because I was the eldest—into my reading to the other three: Edgar, Willy, and Dorian. Since we all spoke and understood German, it was agreed that I would read from the exciting Karl May adventure stories about the American Wild West that I had first encountered in Gebesee. We covered several of May's books that first summer in Rocky Point.

I also remember regaling all of us, including sometimes our parents, by reading the stories of the great popular operas (*Carmen*, *Salomé*, *The Barber of Seville*, Wagner's *Ring*, etc.), not in high German, but in the Saxon dialect—regarded in Germany as the most distorted, funniest, vulgar sounding of all German dialects. (I had learned to speak it fluently during my vacations in Burgstädt.) These completely twisted, satirized accounts of the operas were so zanily hilarious that I could never read more than a few sentences before we'd all be on the floor, doubled up with laughter, our eyes tearing, our stomachs aching. (Years later many people in America and England would be similarly entertained for decades by Anna Russell's inimitable opera satires, this time in high English, and also, of course, by Victor Borge's brilliantly preposterous and well-informed takeoffs on opera.)

I recall also starting to read *Anthony Adverse* (by Hervey Allen) to my little audience, a vast, sprawling novel of some twelve hundred pages, which had become a *huge* best-seller in America in the mid-1930s. However, its unbelievably slow moving, convoluted plot, and flowery, sometimes dense language began to dampen our collective enthusiasm. But what really brought my reading of that book to an abrupt halt was when I came upon a passage a quarter of the way in, in which the teenage hero has his first sexual encounter. I recall, not without some embarrassed bemusement, that I was so abashed by this poetically disguised but powerful evocation of a passionate night of lovemaking that I felt I couldn't read it to my three younger charges, especially in front of Dorian. Truth be told, I was so aroused that I secretly copied the whole passage out in longhand and—silly as it may seem now—read it over many times in my juvenile fantasizing.

Apart from those reading sessions and helping my mother with various chores in the garden and the house, plus practicing my horn and lots of composing, I was as free as a bird from June through August. It was heaven. And I realized later that those three summers of 1940, 1941, and 1942 were the last truly carefree times I was to enjoy.

I started an iris garden on my own in Rocky Point that became my pride and joy. The big German irises were and still are among my favorite flowers, going back to the days when I had drawn dozens of them during my vacations in Krefeld. As that iris garden grew and expanded, I became utterly fascinated with the endless variety of shapes and sizes and colorations of irises. In their incredible diversity they seemed to me to be a wonderful analogue to the hundreds of musical compositions I had come to love. Eventually I began consulting a number of iris catalogues, seeking out the newest crossbred varieties (always with fanciful new names), and spending quite a bit of my hard-earned money on these special bulbs. Some of them cost as much as five dollars, a lot of money in those days. (You could eat two or three meals for that amount, four or five if you dined at the famous Horn & Hardart automat!)

The village of Rocky Point didn't have much to offer besides a post office, a gas station, a grocery store, and a seed and farm machinery warehouse where the local potato and vegetable farmers bought their supplies. But it also had a roller skating rink—very popular in America in those years. For us kids it was the only entertainment (except for radio shows such as *The Green Hornet* or Orson Welles's *Only the Shadow Knows*). We went skating at least three or four times a week in the evenings, always to the accompaniment of canned organ music recorded by the "Queen of the Roller Rinks," Ethel Smith. For me, skating soon turned from a mildly athletic sport to an exciting social activity, for it easily led to certain inevitable romantic involvements. During that first summer in Rocky Point I fell in love—or so I thought—with several girls, including Dorian, a gentle, quiet, intelligent girl, with whom I had (what we surely thought were) very deep and serious conversations. But I also bounced back and forth between Dorian and a Rocky Point neighbor's daughter, Sally DeRosa, a rambunctious, energetic, flighty tomboy. (She reminded me of Melitta in Gebesee.) Of course, boys love to tease girls, and I remember always teasing Dorian, while Sally was rather good at teasing *me*, in an overt, near-physical, way. Ah, those happy, innocent times!

Willy, a year younger than I, became my closest friend. The Mantheys, immigrants from Swabia, a province in southwest Germany, where an almost incomprehensible but pleasingly rolling dialect is spoken, were longtime friends of my parents, and had also acquired a summer bungalow in Rocky Point. Like my parents, they had come to the United States in the early 1920s; they were simple, nice, friendly people, with very little intellectual or cultural aspirations. Besides their Swabian dialect they spoke a horribly mangled mélange of English and German, which my parents and I, being bilingual, could just about make out. They were unpretentious, modest people who, having forgotten much of their original German, often made fun of their own linguistic foibles. One of their favorite self-deprecating phrases was: "De vay der Deutsch verdirbt iss virklich terrible (the way he ruins German is really terrible)."

Frau Manthey was a docile, warm, cheerful woman, who several times acted as my surrogate mother. I was sent off to the Mantheys several summers when I was very young and my parents went back to Germany to visit their relatives. I can recall my contented feelings being under Frau Manthey's gentle, benign care. She was so different from my own high-strung, temperamental mother.

Willy and I loved bike riding, and we were compelled to do a lot of it every day. For to get from our bungalow homes to either the village—to buy groceries, or head for the roller rink—or the beach, we had to ride a mile or so either way, continually negotiating the town's virtually impassable roads. Because Rocky Point's bungalow community rested almost entirely on the shoreline bluffs—actually very high sand dunes—what roads there were, crudely bull-dozed and unpaved, consisted of thick, heavy sand. With their deep ruts, they were extremely resistant to forward movement. Most of these roads (if one could even call them that) were closed to cars, especially some that had several roller-coaster twenty-degree inclines, which even my parents' brand-new Plymouth could never have negotiated. But Willy and I thrived on the challenges these crude, primordial sand roads presented. Being hearty, good-ol' American boys, we could not let a mere road defeat us, no matter how impassable. Our best fun was when we took our girlfriends along on the back of our bikes, scaring the wits out of them, as we'd swoop or skid wildly down some sandy gorge at thirty miles an hour.

We all spent a lot of time at the beach, a beautiful twenty-mile stretch on Long Island Sound. The broad sandy beach abutted miles of imposing eighty-foot bluffs. We swam and snorkeled, dove off the several good-sized rocks, felicitously placed there near the shore by Mother Nature so that we could show off our diving skills. We also played a lot of volleyball. But our most exciting game was racing each other down the bluffs in giant leaps and jumps and slides.

Life on the beach was not without its perils; crabs or lobsters nipped away at your heels, and there was the dangerously strong pull of the tides and currents. Accident-prone as I seemed to be, one day I swam directly into a broken milk bottle that someone had carelessly thrown into the water. I didn't feel anything—in water one tends not to—until a few minutes later when I got out of the water and saw a two-inch flab of flesh hanging down from my right knee—another addition to my collection of wounds and scars accumulated during the years in Germany.

During those summers at Rocky Point, I got quite involved with various aspects of improving our simple one-and-a-half-room bungalow. Perhaps primitive is a better way to describe our place, for at first it barely had running water except in our kitchen sink and an outdoor shower, which my father absolutely insisted on having. There certainly wasn't any flush toilet, just a wooden outhouse. Eventually my uncle Alex (my mother's younger brother), who was a plumber by trade, excavated and built us a ten-foot-deep cistern. I not only helped excavate the sandy soil, I also later helped seal the well's four walls with hot black tar—not fun on a blistering ninety-degree summer day. I also became my mother's assistant gardener; my job was to weed the vegetable garden, keep our small front lawn cut and watered, tend to the dozens of hostas lining our driveway, and care for the several stately nicotiana plants that had been given to us by the Mantheys.

My other uncle, Rudi, also came out to Rocky Point a few times to help us with various building and gardening chores. Both of my uncles were remarkably talented and handy in a wide variety of skills, including plumbing, gardening, carpentry, and anything electrical or mechanical. They were innately talented, but in addition they had as young men in Germany apprenticed in all those varied vocations. I am witness to the fact that both of them could fix *anything*, and my parents certainly took advantage of their skills. They did a lot of work for us free, or at minimal cost.

What I loved most about my uncles was that they both were great pranksters, zany cutups, always acting silly and telling jokes. Both of them were very good at magic and card tricks, constantly outdoing each other to amuse and entertain us kids. One or the other of them would always greet us with a wind-up buzzer in his hand, or suddenly surprise us wearing a big fake nose or Groucho moustache, or—to my mother's disgust—sneak onto a chair one of us was about to occupy some little gadget that, when you sat on it, made an awful farting noise.

Uncle Alex was very fond of music. He used to read lots of composers' biographies, and had a small but highly selective record collection. It is to him, by the way, that I owe my second encounter with opera. In the summer of 1937 he took me to Verdi's *Il Trovatore* at the old five-thousand-seat Hippodrome at Sixth Avenue and Forty-Fourth Street. I really loved it, but I think I was more impressed by the staging than the music, especially the bluish and reddish lighting used in many of the opera's more dramatic scenes, which gave an aura of mystery and conflict to the proceedings. At age twelve I was probably still more interested in color and visual images than in musical sounds.

Both of my uncles died relatively young, Rudi from cancer, undoubtedly caused by smoking and drinking too much, and Alex had a horrible accident; as he sat on a bench in front of his house in Meridian, Connecticut, a huge piece of steel equipment flew off a passing truck, killing him instantly.

One of my parents' closest and omnipresent family friends was a Dutch violist named Henrik Van Vendeloo, a lively, intelligent, and generous character, who always came to our house bearing presents. One day he brought my parents a big, fat, but somewhat elderly goose. To keep the goose from wandering off, my mother built a wire enclosure at one corner of our Rocky Point lot, near the outhouse. The plan was to eat the goose at some grand festive occasion some months later. The trouble was that when Van Vendeloo and my parents finally got around to killing and cooking the big bird, which had flapped around in its cage for so many months trying to escape, its meat was so tough, so hard and wiry that it was absolutely inedible.

I remember the outhouse as being, apart from its normal functions, the place where an important rite of passage, common in every young person's life, took place: namely, the initiation into cigarette smoking. One early evening while my parents were away shopping, four of us (I and my brother, my friend Willy, and another Rocky Point kid) sneaked behind the outhouse and with shaky hands lit our first cigarettes. I was fourteen, and I recall that after only three puffs my career as a smoker was over. I couldn't stand the taste of burnt tobacco and damn near choked on the smoke—a happy circumstance that guaranteed my being a nonsmoker all my life.

Music was, of course, a big part of my life in those summers at Rocky Point, studying scores, composing, and of course practicing the horn. I also started going more often with my father to the concerts of the New York Philharmonic in their summer season at the Lewisohn Stadium. In that way I heard a great deal of music, much of it new to me. The orchestra had a substantial roster of guest conductors: Artur Rodzinski, Efrem Kurtz, José Iturbi, Vladimir Golschmann, Alexander Smallens, Antonia Brico, and regularly featured such major soloists as Heifetz, Elman, Milstein, Casadesus, Arrau, Rubinstein, Rachmaninov, Piatigorsky, as well as famous singers of the day, such as Helen Traubel, Ezio Pinza, Gladys Swarthout, Mack Harrell. During that time I happened to be in attendance at the Lewisohn Stadium when the eleven-year-old Lorin Maazel made his conducting debut. I was too young and inexperienced to assess how well Maazel did, but I know that many in the Philharmonic thought that he was exceptionally talented, that he conducted with a rare expressiveness and maturity—virtually unknown in someone so young—and with an astounding technical self-assurance.

My most important, indeed crucial, musical experience in the summer of 1942 was the several weeks of intense practicing on the horn that I embarked upon—up to eight hours a day. It is what we musicians call our "woodshedding" stint: a period of totally committed determined practicing that is absolutely necessary in the final stages on the path toward full professional status. For a while earlier that year I had begun to realize that I was coasting along too much on my natural talent for the horn, not really bearing down on some of the still lingering technical problems that beset me from time to time. The sudden awareness that I still had a ways to go as a totally secure and technically reliable horn player—no fluffs, no flipped notes, no coarse, unclean slurs, and full dynamic control in *all* registers—occurred one summer day while listening to a Philharmonic broadcast. What impressed and touched me deeply that Sunday afternoon was a brief four-note phrase near the end of Schubert's "Unfinished" Symphony, played so beautifully that it brought tears to my eyes. I have never heard that phrase played more exquisitely, with such a sweet sound and subtle vibrato. It did something to me. I realized what zeniths of perfection—technical, musical, expressive—a musician can at times achieve. It was one of the most beautiful wake-up calls in my young life.

The conveyor of that message was Weldon Wilber, a remarkable, virtually self-taught, at times somewhat idiosyncratic horn player. Bruno Jänicke had just retired from the Philharmonic, and his replacement, Rudi Puletz, was for some reason not yet available to take over. Wilber had been hired on a temporary basis as a possible addition to the Philharmonic's horn section, which in effect expanded the section by engaging two alternating principal horns. Wilber was hired full time the next season as one of the orchestra's principal horns, having by then left his post as first horn in Cincinnati. (Little did I know in that summer of 1942 that, within a year, *I* would be replacing Wilber in the Cincinnati Symphony.)

I launched into my woodshedding spree with a vengeance. Many a day I put in eight to nine hours of practice, with little breaks every once in awhile. It was tough; but I was motivated, determined. Horn playing is physically very tiring; the lips and surrounding facial muscles were not meant to endure the relentless pressure the horn and mouthpiece exert on the embouchure, on the lips, especially in sustained or loud playing. Building up endurance, in which I was still weak, was one of my primary objectives. Indeed, the endurance to play a five-hour Wagner opera or a Bruckner or Mahler symphony and still maintain full control throughout is one of the skills I had to develop. It's very simple: the lips and the diaphragm are muscles, and they have to be trained and strengthened, just as an athlete has to build up his muscles for greater endurance and control. To keep myself totally committed to this perfection- and endurance-building task, I invented all sorts of little punishments should I not meet a particular practice goal. These punishments included not allowing myself to take a break, or to go swimming, or to play with my friends, or to work in the garden, or even to eat lunch or dinner. Many a hot dinner went cold waiting for me to reach my projected goal; and eating my mother's superb Wiener schnitzel or sauerbraten cold was in itself a fairly severe punishment. But the result of this self-imposed regimen of near-torture was everything I could have hoped for. I built up terrific stamina and security, especially in the high register, often practicing a particular passage dozens of times.

Inevitably, during this phase I did neglect my composing, which I still considered my primary musical calling. But I somehow knew that this intense woodshedding period was absolutely mandatory, and I began to understand that in my life and career as a musician I would always have to divide my time between two complementary antipodes: composing (creating) and performing (recreating).

Of course, I also managed to continue my reading on all kinds of musical subjects. I remember particularly with what passion I devoured David Ewen's *The Book of Modern Composers* (1942). It was chock full of information about twenty-nine twentieth-century composers, ranging from Sibelius, Szymanowski, and Stravinsky to Bartók, Schönberg, and Berg. The latter three were especially interesting to me, since they and their music were hardly known or performed in the United States at that time. In fact, it was rather frustrating to read about all that great music when at the same time the vast majority of works described in the book were not available on recordings, in some cases not even as published scores.

It was also during that summer of 1942 that I heard a performance on the radio, moments of which are still vivid, almost audibly palpable, in my memory. My father had recently bought a state-of-the-art shortwave radio to pick up overseas broadcasts of local European (English, Swedish) news reports of the war, and also to hear what could be heard on German radio. I think my parents were unwilling to rely entirely on the relatively few American war correspondents like William Shirer and Edward R. Murrow. One of the bonuses that greeted us was hearing direct concert broadcasts from the BBC, the Swedish Broadcasting Corporation (with the Stockholm Philharmonic), and, to our amazement, one time direct from Germany *during the height of the war*, the Berlin Philharmonic with Furtwängler conducting. That particular broadcast performance featured a glorious rendition of a work that the Berlin Philharmonic and Furtwängler "owned": Schubert's "Great" C Major Symphony. I was overwhelmed by what I heard, even through the occasionally severe transatlantic static. It was the first time I heard that great orchestra—its remarkable late-1930s recordings were not yet available in the United States until after the war. What immediately stood out for me during that broadcast was the orchestra's incredible, luminous-toned cello section. As good as the New York Philharmonic's cello section, led by Joseph Schuster (formerly principal cellist of the Berlin Philharmonic), was, I felt I had never heard any cello sound as beautiful and unified as that of the Berliners. The high point was that miraculous *pianissimo* cello passage in the symphony's second movement, right after its central *fff* climax and two bars of the most beautiful pregnant silence. That melody is as heavenly as any that Schubert, the supreme melodist, ever wrote.

That I was not exaggerating in my youthful fervor as to the inordinate beauty of that performance was confirmed for me many years later, in fact twice. The first time was in 1954 when I heard in person, in Berlin, the Berlin Philharmonic and Furtwängler perform the same symphony. Again the cello section excelled, outshining every other group in the orchestra, but this time I was compelled to put the superb playing of the nine-man bass section, with its *seven* five-string basses, right up there with the cellos.[20] The second truly indisputable confirmation of my original impression came when, about fifteen years ago, that very same concert that my father and I had heard on our shortwave radio in July 1942 was issued on CD, enabling me to relive that wonderful performance again. There was that glorious cello passage again, as beautiful and luminous as I had remembered it.

Perhaps the most overwhelming musical experience for me in that post–St. Thomas period was an electrifying performance of Strauss's *Sinfonia Domestica* by the New York Philharmonic, conducted by Dimitri Mitropoulos. It was my first encounter with this remarkable man, who later played such an important role in my life. If I recall correctly, that *Domestica* performance was the musical and artistic sensation of the 1941 New York season. I already knew the piece well, in part from the Philadelphia Orchestra recording but also from having studied the work from the score that I found in my father's library. I emphasize the word "electrifying" among the many laudatory encomiums I could apply to Mitropoulos's realization of that most extraordinary work. It literally sparked, sizzled, bristled—shocking in its elemental power, constantly on the edge. It was also an inspiring lesson in how a performance could capture the full drama of a Strauss tone poem and at the same time bring out its modernity, its architectonic design, all its orchestrational ingenuity, qualities that were more or less smoothed over in Ormandy's more polished recorded performance. The Philharmonic musicians were on fire, so to speak. I remember the glow in my father's eyes when he came back from a rehearsal, absolutely dazzled. After nineteen years in the Philharmonic, playing with dozens of different conductors, he was no longer easily dazzled. But Mitropoulos's ability to seemingly know every note in this immense score (including *even the rehearsal numbers*), his ability to reveal all of the music's beauty, power, and drama was something he had encountered only very rarely since the Toscanini era.

My summers in Rocky Point were, of course, also filled with lots of happy times and casual lighthearted fun. At least once a week we'd all camp out at night on the beach, building campfires and roasting marshmallows and green apple wedges between juicy dripping slices of bacon on a spit. I think back with longing and nostalgia to those nighttime feasts and wondrous carefree evenings lying on the beach gazing at the starry firmament above us.

There was one additional special attraction that drew me to the beach. Somewhere in Rocky Point there lived an Italian family with seven or eight children, the older ones a few years my senior. It was the handsomest family I thought I had ever seen, but most especially the older, probably nineteen-year-old, daughter. Always the secret voyeur, I was totally mesmerized by her beauty, unable to take my eyes off her. We had no contact with this family, and I was certainly much too shy to approach her. Besides, I had a feeling that two of her brothers, both of them lifeguards on our beach—tanned to a beautiful dark bronze—kept a watchful, protective eye on the young beauty. Although perfectly proportioned in all respects—indeed as flawless as any Greek goddess statue or Michelangelo figure—I realize now that my eyes and my mind were always drawn first and foremost to her face and legs, a lifelong fascination that is with me to this day. Not that I ignore the other features of the female figure; they certainly come powerfully into play at other times. But since in a well-dressed woman those other features are wholly or partially hidden, from a strictly visual and mental perspective the face and legs take on a physical prominence that is irresistible. Moreover, the face and especially the eyes, as so many poets have reminded us, are indeed the windows to a person's soul; and I wanted to penetrate that soul.

In any case, totally oblivious of me, Maria (I think that was her name) occupied my eyes and my mind those Rocky Point summers, granting me a deep, transcendent but secret pleasure (and education), for which I lovingly thank her after all these years—wherever she may be.

One of my happiest memories of those idyllic summers is of a five-day bicycle trip Willy Manthey and I took. When we asked my parents to let us go on a little vacation all our own, they seemed at first reluctant to grant our wish. But then, suddenly, they came up with a surprising compromise solution—I never quite understood its rationale—namely, that we could do our bicycle trip when they, my parents and my brother Edgar, would have to be in New York City for about a week. (Who knows, maybe they were just glad to get rid of me for a while and not have to take me along to New York.) In any event, they did permit us to make the trip, and even gave us some money to buy food and to pay for shelter, if needed, although our plan was to always overnight in a small tent.

Free at last, we felt like a couple of Huck Finns off on an epic adventure. Eastern Long Island, which is what we had decided to explore, was in those days very beautiful in a quaint sort of way, and dotted with little towns and villages and vast stretches of rich farmland, interspersed with wooded groves and orchards[21] and tree-lined winding roads, most of this the lingering heritage of the early Dutch settlers. Indeed, one of our target sites, which I had detected on a map, was a Dutch Reform church built in 1640—very old for America. It was a well-preserved white wooden church, with a beautifully spired clock tower, and the simplest inner design and modest altar—quite a departure from the celebratory magnificence of St. Thomas's elaborate stone-carved altar. Somehow that tiny simple wooden church was just as awe inspiring in its humble beauty as the grand, splendorous cathedral on Fifth Avenue.

The most enjoyable part of our bike tour was that we had purposely not planned anything specific other than visiting the twin ends of Long Island, Orient Point and Montauk Point. This could easily be accomplished in four or five days, leaving us free to roam and rove leisurely wherever else our fancies took us. In this respect I think I was identifying with my uncles, Alex and Rudi, who were always telling me of their *Wanderjahre* in Germany.[22] I now understood better the widely known German term *Wanderlust*: the strong desire to wander freely, to see something of the big outside world.

We did indeed wander more or less freely wherever our bikes—or our feet—led us, nonetheless keeping a sharp lookout for any special, particularly historic sites that we would spot on our maps. And there were plenty of those, Long Island being one of the earliest and most historic regions in America, settled by the Dutch in the early sixteen hundreds. We found so many old gravesites, some with just a dozen tombstones, their epitaphs often severely weatherworn and barely legible. Equally interesting were the many centuries-old farmsteads, much like those my father had taken me to as a six year old in what is now Rego Park, except that those farms were by then abandoned. I doubt that those old Long Island farmhouses are still standing now; they were undoubtedly bought up by some developer as New York City kept expanding in all directions, but particularly eastward, to the end of the island. All the while our greatest delight was lunching on the banks of some brook or small lake, under a sprawling elm tree, looking up through the verdant foliage to the azure sky, feasting on our favorite cheese, salami, bread—and a bottle of wine. What could be more gratifying!

We left Rocky Point at the crack of dawn that first morning and wended our way eastward, traveling along North Country Road, at that time lined for long stretches with raspberry and blackberry bushes. We passed through Wading River and Wildwood State Park, enjoying a few quick dips in the ocean at various beaches along the way. Skirting Riverhead, the largish town at the mouth of the Peconic River, where it flows into the Great Peconic Bay, we continued eastward all the way to Orient Point. We loved this wild, sparsely inhabited place, consisting almost entirely of sand dunes and small lagoons, where underbrush and tiny twisted pines fought a hard existence against wind and sand. We also watched—with some longing—as the ferry for New London, Connecticut, loaded with cars, trucks, and hikers, arrived and departed northward again, the only occasional excitement on that lonely windswept spit of land.

At Greenport, a little ways back toward Riverhead, we headed south by means of two tiny six-passenger ferries via Shelter Island and Sag Harbor toward the Hamptons and Montauk Point. The two ferries, one on the north side of Shelter Island, the other on the south side, run by two wizened, weather-beaten old codgers (they turned out to be brothers), were so small that there was barely room for ourselves and our two bicycles. On Shelter Island, where we stopped toward evening at a lovely old cottage to fill our canteens with fresh water, the owners invited us to pitch our tent on their lawn. Although Willy wanted to press on until darkness set in, I was so enchanted by their garden, with its rose-covered trellises and flowerbeds filled with dahlias, gladioli, and hollyhock, that I persuaded him to bivouac there for the night.

After a very early breakfast the next morning, which our hosts generously offered us—the only real sit-down meal we had in those five days—we crossed on the second ferry over to Sag Harbor, which I later described in a letter to my parents as "the dirtiest little town we saw on the whole trip. In the old abandoned and rusty whaling factories all the windows were broken, and everywhere we saw nothing but dilapidated, seedy looking shanties. We couldn't believe we were still in America."

From there we passed through long stretches of alternatingly swampy and sandy terrain, toward the main road that leads via the Hamptons and a further twenty miles to Montauk Point, the location of one of the most famous and oldest still-functioning lighthouses in America. On that stretch of Long Island's south shore there are no trees to speak of, only hardened, weathered brush and stunted, contorted pines struggling for existence in the windswept terrain, constantly buffeted by Atlantic storms. We reached Montauk Point on our fourth day, greeted by a beautifully sunny, calm afternoon. Although Montauk Point is usually a much-visited site, there was nobody there that day except one lonely fisherman in a tiny rowboat near the shore, down below us in the mildly churning sea.

Built in the mid-1790s, the lighthouse at Montauk Point had for centuries helped mariners avert the dangerous invisible rock formations stretching out from the Point into the Atlantic. The lighthouse keeper allowed us to climb up to the top of the 108-foot tower, affording us a terrific view of the whole fragmented topography of eastern Long Island. Since it was a bit hazy that morning, we could not quite see Orient Point to the north, but looking west from the top of the lighthouse toward Shelter Island was rather like looking at a gigantic map, but in miniature.

Now it was time to head homeward. We planned to overnight near Amagansett and then take a different route back, via the Hamptons, Shinnecock Hills, and Riverhead, to Rocky Point. In contrast to Sag Harbor, we thought East Hampton was the most beautiful town we visited, not to mention the thrill of seeing the nearby windmills, all of them still in operation. Further on, near Water Mill, we saw quite a different kind of sight: a long snake, winding its way slowly across the highway. Suddenly a car came along and, wouldn't you know it, drove right over the snake. Willy and I knew that snakes have more lives even than cats, and so we were not surprised when the snake just kept on wriggling around. But we *were* surprised when very dark-red blood began to trickle from one end of the snake. We watched another ten minutes or so as it continued to writhe its way across the road, until it disappeared behind some bushes.

Another unexpected sight, of quite a different order, greeted us when we reached the Shinnecock Hills Indian reservation, a few miles further down the road. We had headed there with great anticipation, but to our surprise we didn't see any Indians at all. We saw only African Americans. Ok, we found that pretty interesting too, but still we were rather disappointed not seeing what we had expected to see, Native Americans. We had seen them only in the movies, and even then mostly being killed. Although we wandered around a while, we were too shy to ask anyone what had happened to the Indians. We did finally see one, a young girl, maybe twenty years old, with long, very black hair, sitting on the steps of one of the reservation's two churches. We didn't talk to her either; it seemed awfully awkward to go up to her and ask her why she was the only Indian there.

In Hampton Bays we marveled at the many old Norman-style houses with their grey wooden or grass covered roofs, but the rest of the trip back to Rocky Point was uneventful, unfortunately for many long stretches uphill. By the time we got home late that evening, dead tired, our legs were killing us. Mine were actually numb from the long ride. I figured out that we had ridden over fifty miles on that day, averaging about eight and a half miles per hour. Yet we felt a wonderful mixture of exhaustion and exaltation. Besides the sightseeing aspects of our little jaunt, the trip remains one of the happiest memories of my childhood, as an encounter and experience of utter independence and freedom.

For the most part I was coasting at Jamaica High, easily getting Bs and A-minuses without much studying, casually tossing off the assigned homework. I began to realize that I was not learning anything new and that, as a result of my previous superb schooling, in Germany and at St. Thomas, I was about three years ahead of my schoolmates. I turned in some pretty good book reports on Robert Louis Stevenson's *Travels with a Donkey in the Cevennes* (in the French province of Languedoc, especially the chapter titled "A Night in the Pines"), Washington Irving's *Rip Van Winkle*, a book of short stories by the great Canadian humorist Stephen Leacock, and a detailed verbal analysis of Jean Francois Millet's famous painting, *The Sower*. In French, geography, and math (trigonometry, actually) I did only passably well because I spent most of the time in class composing music, more or less sloughing off my homework assignments, in trigonometry just barely keeping up with the class so that at least I wouldn't fail.

Quite often, considering my father's heavy schedule at the Philharmonic (eight services a week), my parents took Edgar and me on various excursions and little day trips. I remember particularly visits to the New York Botanical Garden in the Bronx (reputed to be the most spectacular one on the East Coast), to the Planetarium, and many forays to Yorkville's fantastic meat and sausage stores, *Konditoreien*, and cafés. One time, on one of my father's free days, we drove all the way across New Jersey to the Poconos in eastern Pennsylvania, an exceptionally beautiful region of the country that has many fascinating historic sights from the revolutionary period, especially the Delaware Water Gap and the villages of Bushkill and Dingmans Ferry. I still see in my mind's eye the Delaware River tranquilly winding its way through fields, farm-lands, and two-hundred-year-old barns and homes. I've wanted many times to revisit this area again but have not yet succeeded in doing so. I remember it as one of my many inspiratory experiences of my youth.

The capper, however, was a most extraordinary sight: as we drove one day from the Holland Tunnel northward on the West Side Highway on our way home, we suddenly saw immense clouds of dark-grey smoke and then a huge capsized ship lying on its side. The police had ringed off the area and we couldn't get very close to the scene, but we found out when we got home that it was the USS *Lafayette* (the former French luxury liner *Normandie*), which, stranded in new York when France fell to the Germans in 1940, had been officially taken over by the U.S. Navy and was being converted into an American troop ship. To see such a naval colossus on its side, half submerged in water, was a sight to behold. For many weeks rumors were flying that the fire was the work of saboteurs. But in the end we learned that a work-man's acetylene torch had ignited some of the ship's life preservers, and, as a result, had started a huge fire, gutting the entire ship and causing it to sink into the relatively shallow Hudson River.

My parents' home was typical of cultivated German upper-middle-class tastes of the 1920s, the years of the Weimar Republic. The furniture was mostly modern abstract, influenced by the 1920s Bauhaus movement—the Bauhaus school of art and architecture was founded by German, Austrian, and Swiss architects and artists such as Walter Gropius, Paul Klee, and Wassily Kandinsky—and new furniture designs coming out of Scandinavia, especially Sweden. My mother, who had excellent taste in these matters, found a wonderfully elegant, blond bed-room set, which I eventually inherited when Margie and I moved to Boston in 1967. Mixed in with such upscale furnishings, there were the typical old-fashioned Biedermeier cabinets, vitrines, and tables, so beloved of nineteenth-century Germans, mostly heirlooms passed on to my parents from their families. But my mother enhanced even these rather ordinary furnish-ings, especially in the kitchen, with all manner of colorful, decorative, painted floral designs, a skill she had acquired in her studies with her Krefeld art teacher, Werner Zimmerman.

But what interested me most in my parents' home, even as a four- or five-year-old, was their rather sizable library, mostly in the living room but also scattered throughout the apartment. Even as a young child I was primarily attracted to the several sets of encyclopedias, most of them in German, such as Meyer's eighteen-volume *Lexikon* and a twelve-volume set of Alfred Brehm's *Tierleben* (*The Life of Animals*). I remember poring over this tome for hours upon hours, not only its voluminous pictures and photographs but also its extensive articles, repre-senting the most advanced late nineteenth-century theories and research in animal behavior, updated every decade or so. I was also drawn irresistibly to the many monographs my parents had collected on such subjects as plant life, ancient history, architecture, German writers and poets (Goethe and Schiller), and the lives of famous composers. It seems that little Gunther was even then trying to be the high-minded intellectual.

Meanwhile, my music studies, as a composer and horn player, were progressing well and rapidly. In the high school orchestra, Mrs. Hughes gave me more and more challenging assignments, and finally, in the fall of 1942, the beautiful horn solos in Leo Delibes' wonder-fully sensuous *Sylvia* ballet music. After leaving St. Thomas School, I had enrolled as a part-time student at the Manhattan School of Music, where Robert Schulze was the horn teacher. Being full time at Jamaica high, I could only take my horn lessons and two theory courses at Manhattan in the late afternoons, harmony and counterpoint in one, sight-reading and dicta-tion in the other. This meant that I had to go to the Manhattan School of Music three times a week, which I did (except for the summer vacation months) from the fall of 1940 to December 1942. It also meant taking a fifteen-minute bus ride plus two subway trains from Kew Gardens,

Queens, to 105th Street on Manhattan's Upper East Side. The roundtrip was cumulatively close to three hours, which I usually spent composing or studying.

My life was filled with so much music making and studying that, in retrospect, I wonder how I managed to keep up with it all. By the fall of 1941, I was not only going to both schools, Jamaica High and the Manhattan School of Music, but I was also being offered all kinds of jobs on the horn (mostly unpaid), everything from Italian street parades in Little Italy, in downtown Manhattan, to playing with various amateur or semiprofessional orchestras. I began to get calls from several small opera companies, among them Salmaggi and LaPuma; both were on the Upper West Side in apartments (perhaps in the Ansonia on Broadway and Seventy-Fourth Street) with forty-foot-wide living rooms and high ceilings, quite suitable for semi-staged operas. Amateurish and qualitatively middling though these enterprises were, they did provide crucial opportunities for young singers and fledgling orchestra musicians like me to learn the operatic repertory. They didn't pay us any money; they couldn't afford to since they charged their audiences little or nothing at the door. But I didn't care; I wanted to play and learn. I also played off and on for a couple of years with an amateur orchestra at the Ninety-Second Street Y led by a so-so conductor named Naom Binder, where I gained valuable experience reading through a lot of basic symphonic repertory. My father and Mr. Schulze urged me to take all these jobs, and often even recommended me. As a result, by the time I was sixteen I knew almost all the standard operatic and symphonic repertory: in opera everything from *Cavalleria rusticana* and *Pagliacci* ("Cav and Pag," as they were called by opera insiders, also "ham and eggs") to, of course, Puccini, early Verdi, and operas such as Flotow's *Martha*, all very popular at the time.

But my main orchestral activity was playing in the Manhattan School of Music orchestra, an excellent group led and trained at that time by a wonderful musician and dear, kindly man, Hugo Kortchák, who was in his sixties then, and who as a youngster had been a friend and even a sometime student of Antonin Dvorák. He must have been a rather good conductor and rehearser, for I remember that the orchestra sounded very good in the concerts: clean, warm, rich, flowing, expressive. I also loved Kortchák's programming because it combined the important standard classics with lesser-known works. All the pieces I played with him in the year and a half I was in the orchestra I love dearly to this day; for me they were like first love. These include Dvorák's Cello Concerto, programmed on my first concert, with Leo Teraspulsky (an advanced student at the school, later principal cellist of the Pittsburgh Symphony) as soloist. It is not only one of Dvorák's three or four finest works, but it also has some of the most gorgeous horn writing, including a magnificent horn trio in the second movement.

I was officially third horn in the MSM orchestra; a somewhat older player, Arthur Holmes—who was to have in a short time a profound affect on my life—played first horn. He was a very good player, actually already a young professional. Arthur took a real liking to me, and helped me a great deal in those early days with lots of valuable advice. Moreover, since he was already getting all kinds of outside work, which caused him to occasionally miss some orchestra rehearsals, he would ask me (with Kortchák's blessing) to move up to first chair. I was in musical heaven, getting to play those absolutely perfect, radiant, lyrical Dvorák horn parts—thanks to Arthur's absences.

Another piece I came to love inordinately under Kortchák's direction, much less known than the Dvorák, was one of Wolf-Ferrari's wonderful intermezzi from the opera *The Secret of Susanna*. The second intermezzo features a brilliant, scintillating flute solo, which was brilliantly played by our orchestra's first flutist, Charlie Ehrenberg. He was a year or two older than I, a major talent, and someone I really looked up to and admired. But oddly enough, Charlie seems not to have had much of a professional career. I saw him only a few times after our MSM days, and then he disappeared from the scene.

Two other major talents who had their early orchestral training in the MSM orchestra were John Clark and Bernie Garfield, bass trombonist and bassoonist, respectively. John was to become my very best friend, and went on to join, successively, three of the major orchestras in New York: the NBC Symphony, the New York Philharmonic, and the Metropolitan Opera Orchestra. Bernie Garfield, longtime principal bassoonist of the Philadelphia Orchestra, succeeding Sol Schoenbach, sat directly in front of me in the MSM orchestra, which allowed me to enjoy his rich tone and fluent, easy technique at close range. It was a talent-laden orchestra at the Manhattan School; there were many other fine, gifted musicians who went on to successful careers in various symphony orchestras, whose names I have, alas, after more than a half a century, forgotten.

On a higher professional level, I suddenly found myself playing with the well-established Tollefsen Trio, headed by two English-born musicians in their late fifties. There were relatively few chamber music ensembles in those days in New York, indeed in the whole country—at least compared to nowadays, when there are dozens of very active string quartets and innumerable chamber groups, playing both traditional and contemporary repertory. The Tollefsens dominated the New York chamber music scene, along with the Budapest Quartet, and the once-a-year visitors, the ProArte, Walden, Perolé, and Roth Quartets. Initially headquartered in Brooklyn, the Tollefsens began to perform regularly in Manhattan's Town Hall in the late 1930s, covering a wide range of major classical chamber music literature. Whenever they programmed Schubert's Octet, Beethoven's Op. 20 Septet, or some of Mozart's *Divertimenti*, they called on me as their horn player. (As best as I can recall, I was never paid for these gigs, nor did I expect to be.)

I began to develop a reputation not only as a very secure and musical horn player, but also one who had a beautiful tone. If I (immodestly) agree with that assessment, it is not to praise myself, but to extol and fondly remember Bruno Jänicke, longtime first horn of the New York Philharmonic, whose beautiful, pristinely pure tone and elegant style were my inspiration.

Soon I was getting calls to play with fully professional orchestras, and more frequently even as first horn. The first of these significant opportunities occurred in the summer of 1942—I was still sixteen—when I was hired (for real money this time!) to play first horn in several of the so-called Naumburg concerts, held regularly every summer in Central Park on the Mall, and supported for decades by the Walter W. Naumburg Family Foundation. For one of those concerts the program included Tchaikovsky's Violin Concerto and Mendelssohn's "Italian" Symphony. Quite near the beginning of the Concerto's second movement the first horn has a series of six repeated half-note middle Ds (and one C), placed on the second beat of each $\frac{3}{4}$ measure. It is a simple, innocent-looking passage of no technical difficulty whatsoever, one that would never make it into the horn excerpt study books. But these exquisitely simple notes can be quite beautiful and moving when played correctly and expressively. I have deeply loved those seven measures of quintessential Tchaikovskian lyricism ever since I first heard them as a young boy. Now here was my first chance to show what I felt about this passage, and to show how the horn should fit into the accompaniment of the solo violin's gorgeous theme. As simple as this passage may seem at first sight, what is interpretationally involved are a number of crucial compositional considerations and feelings. In order of importance, my first criterion was to place those notes not merely precisely rhythmically on the second beat but also with a feeling of "bouncing" off the strings' downbeat—in other words, *really* feeling the pulse, the swing, of the $\frac{3}{4}$ measure. My next considerations were to hold the note exactly two beats, as prescribed, that is, neither hanging over into the next measure nor cutting it short; to sustain it with a certain subtle expressivity, that is, not to let it taper off or lose its singing quality; to fit in dynamically with the prevailing p dynamic, and therefore blend with the other accompanying woodwind colors; and, of course, to play the note with the most beautifully glowing, velvety soft yet rich tone I could muster.

I have to admit that I was very proud and pleased to notice at the first rehearsals quite a number of heads turning toward me, especially in the string section (mostly longtime, hardened veterans of the New York freelance scene), looking admiringly at the new kid on the block. More compliments came later during intermission and after the Mendelssohn symphony, which prominently features the horn in a lead position in some high lying exposed passages in the first movement, and soloistically in the "Trio" of the third movement.

Another important performance opportunity came my way in October 1942 when I was hired to play extra horn with the New York Philharmonic in the second set of American performances (October 14 through 18) of Shostakovich's famous Seventh ("Leningrad") Symphony, with Toscanini conducting.[23] I did have mixed feelings about this particular job offer. As thrilled as I was on the one hand to participate in what clearly promised to be a major musical event, I was on the other hand pretty terrified to work with the famously short-tempered and supercritical Toscanini. My fear was based on years of hearing about the maestro's tyrannical podium behavior, not only from my father but also from many other musicians. His temper tantrums were legendary. I could not forget that during much of my childhood I had seen my father, shaken and white as a ghost, return from Philharmonic rehearsals, again and again, in which Toscanini had for the umpteenth time lost his temper, cussing out the musicians in the foulest Italian, breaking his baton in two, or worse, throwing it into the orchestra, smashing his watch on the floor, yelling, ranting, and screaming at the top of his lungs in never ending tirades.[24]

Some of my father's most fearsome experiences with Toscanini were when he annually programmed one of his favorite war horses, the Prelude to Wagner's *Lohengrin*. The Prelude starts with only four solo violins, two firsts and two seconds, in the very high register of the violin. Toscanini seemed never to be satisfied with how the four musicians (obviously four of the best violinists in the orchestra) played this pristine, sustained, A-major chord. On one occasion Toscanini rehearsed it over and over and over again, ultimately making the musicians more and more nervous, until their bows were shaking so badly that they could hardly play at all. On another occasion my father's left eye was nearly poked out one fine day in 1935 when the maestro's baton whizzed past the right side of his forehead, only an inch or two away from his head.

Toscanini's irrational podium behavior being so well known to all of us musicians, I couldn't help wondering whether I, an obvious teenager novice, would quickly become a target of his uncontrollable wrath. That he was also a remarkable conductor and a formidably talented musician—most of the world saw him as a genius and the superstar god of conductors—did not offer me all that much solace. But all that not withstanding, in I ventured at the appointed time. I couldn't disappoint and embarrass my teacher and my father, nor could I easily ignore the very good money. And I'm happy to report that I survived the whole experience unscathed. Toscanini never looked at me, didn't even seem to know that there *was* a seventh horn; and in general, as I recollect, he behaved remarkably rationally, that is, no great temper tantrums and interminable tirades. I tend to believe, Toscanini not being a great proponent of contemporary music (to put it mildly), that he didn't know or understand Shostakovich's music as well as he did his Wagner, Beethoven, and Debussy, his native Italian and other classical repertory. He seemed less perfection driven, less detail conscious, rather satisfied to let Shostakovich's music take care of itself.

The Shostakovich Seventh has always been a controversial work, often considered of lesser quality and inspiration than, say, his First or Fifth Symphony. Bartók made fun of the Seventh Symphony in his Concerto for Orchestra, and many critics considered the bolerolike march theme of the first movement vulgar and obvious, a cheap trick. It certainly was not history's most elevated thematic inspiration, but I thought—and still do—that the carping critics rather insensately ignored the conditions under which the symphony was written, the months-long siege of Leningrad by the German *Wehrmacht*, as well as Shostakovich's avowed intention to represent in that unsubtle, blatant march music the relentless approach of the crude forces of evil. I remember being impressed and excited by the unabashedly primitive power of the music. (I have felt the same excitement several times years later conducting the work.)

What I also remember about that march music was the big fuss made over the very exposed solo drum part by the Philharmonic's snare drum player, Sam Borodkin, a notorious cutup and show-off in the orchestra, who finally had his comeuppance in the rehearsals and performance of the Shostakovich Seventh. The snare drum initiates the march—alone— much as in Ravel's *Bolero*, starting whisper-soft and building over many minutes to a tremendous climax. Playing very soft is the hardest thing to do on a snare drum, and many in the orchestra who had been embarrassed for years by Borodkin's cocky, clownish, wise guy behavior back there in the percussion section were glad to see Sam sweat it out in Shostakovich's nakedly exposed drum part. For once there was no place for him to hide. The combination of facing both Toscanini and this scary solo humbled Borodkin for the first time in anyone's memory. The trouble was that for days on end the rest of us never heard the end of Borodkin's complaining and bitching about the work, about Toscanini, and the hardships of being a musician. Borodkin was truly rattled and never played the opening of the solo softly enough and securely rhythmic. We were all surprised that Toscanini left him alone—for me, a sixteen-year-old novice, an interesting lesson in orchestral power politics: even Toscanini was a little cowed by the infamous Mr. Borodkin.

With these initial professional successes under my belt, and with good prospects for further employment as a horn player in the offing—if not yet as a composer—it was clear to me that it was time to abandon high school and embark on a career as a horn player, happily with my parents' hearty and proud approval.

I was certainly not neglecting composing and my other musical studies. I was a regular at several of the best record stores (Steinway Hall, the Gramophone, Commodore, and Liberty record shops). It was around this time too that I discovered the great music collections of New York's public libraries. The afternoon subway trip from Jamaica High School to uptown Manhattan took about an hour and a half, and required a change of subway from the Independent line at Fifty-Third Street and Lexington Avenue to the IRT at Fifty-First Street. I took advantage of these subway stopovers by interspersing weekly visits to the nearby Fifty-Eighth Street public lending library. The music division of the much larger Forty-Second Street Library was mainly a reference library where you could study any of its holdings while in the library, but couldn't take most things out to study at home. To assuage my insatiable appetite for music and for learning and studying, I would load up at least once a week with an armful of orchestral and vocal scores—Lieder and song cycles, as well as many four-hand piano reductions of major orchestral works—all of which I devoured voraciously in a few days and returned to the library the next week or two.

The four-hand piano reductions that all major music publishers printed in those days—a practice that has unfortunately been abandoned long ago—were especially valuable to me. I learned a wealth of orchestral literature by playing these four-hand transcriptions—Bruckner and Mahler symphonies, the major works of Debussy and Ravel, Reger's beautiful *Mozart Variations*, Stravinsky's *Rite of Spring*, and many, many other great works. My father, who was a very good pianist, handled the upper part while I, a mediocre pianist technically but a good reader (wrong fingerings notwithstanding), dealt with the lower part and the pedals. These were some of my happiest early musical experiences: father and son making music together.

Another thrilling, important educational experience for me at this time was the series of almost weekly musicales my parents organized at our home and maintained for a couple of years. My father had organized a string quartet with three colleagues—alternately Rudolf Heinz or his best friend, Morris Kreiselman, for second violin, Joseph Vieland, viola, and Tony Pastore, cello—to mostly just read and play through several Beethoven or Mozart quartets on each occasion. The evening would end with my mother serving up some of her best German dishes. These were wonderfully happy hours that fed both soul and stomach. Since I had, as far back as I can remember, an innate love and sensitivity for low-register sounds and instruments, it was inevitable that I would sit at Tony's feet and avidly follow every note of the cello part, the harmonic foundation of the music. Hearing those wondrous quartet masterpieces live and at such close range in the intimacy of our living room was one of the greatest gifts my parents, probably without fully realizing it, ever presented me.

My father was really never my teacher. It was a tacit telepathic understanding between him and me—we never spoke about it—that he thought it best not to be my teacher, and I, conversely, really seemed to want to study on my own. Indeed, except for the early rudimentary lessons with Dr. Noble and my horn lessons with Mr. Schulze, I am self-taught as a composer and all-around musician. But, of course, my father did on occasion offer me some very good advice. He had urged me from the beginning to stay not just with the horn literature but to also study and read through on the piano—whether hamperingly or not didn't matter—all kinds of music, or to play on the horn the great song and Lieder literature. That's how I discovered the entire vocal literature from Schubert and Schumann to Brahms, Hugo Wolf, and Strauss, a vast treasure of incomparable masterpieces, as well as the songs of Debussy, Ravel, Duparc, Grieg, and Delius, and some of the modern German composers such as Joseph Marx, Joseph Haas, and Sigfrid Karg-Elert. In this systematic perusal of the lyric repertory I also came across some unforgettably beautiful songs by Erich Wolff, an Austrian composer nobody ever seems to have heard of, but whose songs—he wrote more than sixty of them—my father and I admired very much, and played through many times, over a period of many, many weeks. (It happened often enough that I had to pay rather heavy fines at the Fifty-Eighth Street library for returning the music months late, but it was well worth it.)

My father also once suggested to me, since the high concert F (on top of the treble staff) was considered among horn players the untrespassable upper limit for the horn—despite the fact that both Schumann and Strauss had written some high As (a third higher) and other higher notes—that I should practice high parts at least a third or a fourth higher. It was advice I certainly took to heart, and which, by the way, came in very handy when we were playing soprano songs, which often went up to high As and B flats, my father playing the piano part and I the vocal part on the horn. He said, quite logically, that if I could safely handle notes *above* high F, then high F would lose the fearsome spell that it had on most of us horn players of the time, and would become just another normal and relatively easy note to play. Terrific advice!

With my constant subway riding from Queens to Manhattan and back, and my regular visits to both the Fifty-Eighth and Forty-Second Street libraries, I was also getting around more and more in mid-Manhattan, sometimes secretly—without my parents' knowledge—venturing forth in various new directions, geographically as well as in search of alternate novel experiences. I was held on a very tight leash by my parents, but that didn't entirely prevent me from squeezing in little excursions from the Forty-Second Street Library, for example, to nearby Times Square—known as "sin street"—where I would gawk guiltily and surreptitiously at the burlesque houses (which mayor LaGuardia later closed near the end of 1942), dreaming and imagining what heavenly feminine allurements awaited inside.

The newsstands at Times Square were laden with girlie and pin-up magazines, a booming industry during the war years, in large part to assuage the frustrated appetites of thousands of sex-starved GIs. The famous pin-ups of Betty Grable and Rita Hayworth were fairly tame compared to what could be found between the covers of magazines like *Beauty Parade*, *Eyeful*, and a dozen others. Compared to today's licentious and totally explicit erotic fare, those magazines will seem quaint and mild—and frustrating—since total nudity was not permitted in those days, and a certain code of decency was observed. But for us hot-blooded youngsters, knowing nothing else, these so-called girlie magazines, featuring endless parades of scantily clad beauties teasingly, sexily attired in revealing lingerie, were real hot stuff. For it turns out that a partially undressed female is generally more enticing and seductive than a totally nude one, allowing of course, for matters of taste and experience.

At the same time that I began collecting girlie magazines, hiding them among my hugely expanding music collection, I began haunting several of the great midtown bookstores and shops, such as the Gotham Book Mart, which purveyed a wide range of American, English, and French literary and film magazines. That's where I first became acquainted with the *Partisan Review*, *Kenyon Review*, *Commentary*, and *Horizon*. I got really hooked on these places and spent considerable amounts of money there, money I really didn't have or should perhaps have spent on music and recordings. But the shop owners were generally kind enough to let me browse for hours, probably a bit mystified—or impressed (I don't know which)—that such a young kid was delving into all this highbrow intellectual literature. I lost count of the many happy hours I spent in these literary havens, my excitement much heightened when I would discover that the man at the next stall or table was Alfred Kazin or Clement Greenberg or Kenneth Patchen.

For the record, I don't see any real discrepancy between, say, concurrently reading *Beauty Parade* and *Partisan Review*. The one fed my aesthetic senses, my life-long apperception of beauty, whatever form that might take, and the other nurtured and nourished my mind, my brain cells. In any case, sexual and intellectual drives are not antithetical to each other; they are two sides of the human condition, seen holistically: the one nutriments for the flesh, the other nutrition for the mind.

Moreover, I can say of my mid-to-late teenage years that there was *nothing*—there still isn't—that I didn't want to know, not just in music but in the entire universe around me. It sounds mad; but it's true. I don't know where that insatiable quest for knowledge came from, except that I somehow knew that, as a high school dropout, it was totally up to me to educate myself as richly as possible.

The reader may now understand how it is that I do not drive a car and have indeed never driven one—with one bizarre exception, which will be related elsewhere. First of all, New York's fabulous subway and bus system makes driving in Manhattan essentially superfluous. Second, parking in most of Manhattan is impossible or extremely costly, and was so fifty and sixty years ago. Third, I was so busy going to two schools and studying hard on my own, learning mountains of music and reading everything I could get my hands on, that it literally left no time to learn to drive. Fourth, being sightless in my right eye and therefore having limited radial vision as well as distorted distance vision, I was not keen on the idea of driving a car. For, in walking on New York's crowded sidewalks, I would sometimes bump into someone on my right side or someone would bump into me. Harmless as that was while walking, the same accidental collision while driving might not be so innocuous.

My total immersion in my studies, musical and otherwise, was also the reason why I didn't particularly chase after girls, as most of my fellow teenagers were doing, their lives centering primarily around girls and cars. I had a few girlfriends, of course, nothing spectacular, rather innocent, platonic relationships. But one girl remains fixed in my memory, actually not so much because of *her*, but because of the occasion on which I last saw her. Eleanor was the daughter of German friends of my parents, a rather plain-looking blonde, whom my parents encouraged me to date because they felt she was a nice, proper, decent girl. She had invited me to a dance party at her house on December 7, 1941, with a half dozen other couples—I wasn't much of a dancer—when our very pleasant party ambiance was suddenly shattered and the dance music on the radio (probably Miller or Dorsey) was interrupted with the news of the Japanese aerial attack on Pearl Harbor.[25] That was the end of the dancing. None of us could understand how, after so many decades of isolationism and immunity from wars and any kind of aggression, our country or some city in it could be so barbarously savaged. It was in so many ways the end of a relatively blissful era, discounting for the moment the Great Depression.

With all my practicing and studying, and hanging out so much at libraries, bookstores, and record shops, I am rather amazed, in retrospect, that I composed any music at all in 1942. But during that spring and summer I declared my love for the music of two composers, Delius and Ravel, who were influential in my development at the time, by composing brief pieces in homage to them. In the work I eventually called *Trois hommages* for horn and piano—a third movement based on Milhaud's bitonal style came along in 1946—each movement paid tribute to these composers by respectfully modeling the pieces after their respective quintessential styles. Juvenilia to be sure, these pieces were nonetheless my way of absorbing those composer's contributions to early twentieth-century music and having the music course through my mind and heart, to in the end free myself from it and have its residue subsumed in whatever personal language I might have the talent to develop.

I really didn't want to write so much for the horn—in order to avert the impression that, as a horn player, I could write solely for the horn. On the other hand, I knew the instrument well and knew how to write idiomatically for it. And since I could play the music myself, that is, without waiting for someone else to perform it, I felt I had little choice. A composer, particularly an unknown teenage composer, needs to hear his or her work in order to learn and advance.

Another horn piece came along in 1942, *Nocturne*, which two years later found its way into my first "major" orchestral work, a Concerto for Horn and Orchestra, as its second (slow) movement. It is a somewhat melancholy, pensively aching lyric piece, idiomatically just the kind of thing the horn, with its romantic heritage, its special beauty of tone and unique capacity to "sing" long expressive lines, can do better than almost any other instrument. Oddly enough, its inspiration came in part from some quasi-oriental exotic music, by composers such as Henry Eichheim and Colin McPhee, that Stokowski had recorded in the late 1930s. The *Nocturne* in its horn and piano version also turned out to be the first piece of mine that was published (in 1945, by Mills Music).

My life was now filled with lots of nonstop learning, studying, growing, and developing as a musician, grasping at ever-higher levels of comprehension and expression. And all of this in New York City, whose incomparable cultural life in those midcentury years I soaked up and fed upon with an unquenchable hunger. The New York of today is, like the whole country and indeed the whole world, a totally different place than it was in the 1940s and 1950s. I know full well that much of what I am I owe in large measure to that cultural, intellectual, aesthetic environment that permeated this unique metropolis. The war and the 1960s eventually changed and destroyed all that, replacing that particular New York, with its lingering old-world charms and more relaxed atmosphere, with a much less forgiving, less human, faster-paced, smarter, snappier, more aggressive New York.

Among the cultural riches that particularly affected my life and my development I have to single out the city's many great radio stations: WQXR, WNYC, WNEW, as well as the four network broadcast stations—WEAF and WJZ, both under the NBC (National Broadcasting Company) umbrella, WOR (Mutual Broadcasting System, MBS), and WCBS (Columbia Broadcasting System, CBS). WQXR is today a shadow of its former self, while WNYC has changed over to a largely talk and news format, although on a very high level, as part of the NPR network.

In those earlier days of WQXR, one of the first FM stations in the country (in 1938), its excellent, impeccably presented programming offered the whole range of high-level classical music all day (six a.m. to one a.m.), limited only by what was available on recordings. In addition, there were programs on WQXR of folk and ethnic music—Pru Devon's weekly hour of South American indigenous popular music, produced entirely from her own vast collection of recordings, was a particular delight and learning experience—as well as lighter musical fare in the late afternoon, hosted by the inimitable Duncan Pirnie, as well as superior news programs and intelligent political commentaries by Quincy Howe and H. V. Kaltenborn. WQXR was also famous for its sonorous-voiced announcers, who in fact were chosen specifically for their particular vocal timbre and resonance, which the station had determined at its founding it would require of its announcers. They were the best; and among them my favorite was Duncan Pirnie, who, with the broad range of programs he hosted, seemed to me to be the aesthetic and intellectual heart and soul of the station. In any case, to me the WQXR announcers' distinctive voices were a vocal parallel to the high-level musical programming the station offered.

WNYC was a little more adventurous and edgy in its programming policies, thanks to the station's music director, Herman Neuman, who went so far as to organize for some fifteen years an annual two-week festival of American contemporary music, where many of us young composers had our debut performances and could actually hear our music performed. Wanting to compete with the network stations, each of which had its own self-sponsored symphony orchestra that it presented as a public service, that is, noncommercial, Neuman, on a minimal budget, formed an orchestra of young freelance musicians that gave a concert on WYNC every Sunday morning and performed a broad-ranging repertory of classical and modern music—an orchestra in which I often played during the mid-to-late forties. It was conducted by the very talented Paul Wolfe, later the longtime music director of the Orlando Philharmonic in Florida.

WNYC also featured especially informative programs on various less-explored areas or aspects of music, such as a prolonged series of weekly programs on medieval, Ars Nova, and early Renaissance music, impeccably hosted by the late Leonard Altman, and the wide-ranging broadcasts of music and commentary by the prodigiously knowledgeable Edward Tatnall Canby. All of WNYC's remarkably well-informed commentators went far beyond the usual run-of-the-mill programming, exploring instead the outer, more esoteric realms of music and music history, very often playing obscure and hard-to-get recordings, which, of course, I greedily ingested.[26] These men, whose work should not be forgotten, were the precursors of our present-day NPR commentators: the Ray Smiths, Jim Svejdas, Verne Windhams, Karl Haases, and the Robert J. Lurtsemas, Ron della Chiesas, and Ellen Kushners, to name just a few.

I have already mentioned the nightly eleven-fifteen p.m. live broadcasts on all the networks, presenting the great jazz orchestras via nationwide hookups. This included, besides broadcasts from New York and Harlem, programs from cities and locations—hotels, ballrooms, and clubs—all over the country. In addition, there were the many short public service programs presenting a wide range of classical music and jazz that were scattered throughout the entire broadcast day. In short, there was never any shortage of good and entertaining music on the radio. Beyond that, there was a wealth of high-level classical music available on the four network radio stations throughout the entire week, especially on NBC and CBS, ranging from the regular Sunday broadcasts of the New York Philharmonic, Toscanini's NBC Symphony, and the Saturday matinees of the Metropolitan Opera, to a great variety of weekly symphonic programs such as the General Motors, Firestone, Bell Telephone, Cadillac, Ford Sunday Evening Hour, and the Longine Sinfonietta series. Those programs were, of course, sponsored by the respective corporations. But one was not bombarded three or four times with loud two-minute commercials of mostly misinformation. Two modest, quiet, noninterruptive, forty-five-second statements, one at the beginning, one at the end of the broadcast, sufficed.

Today's readers, especially if younger than fifty, will not realize (or believe) what an extraordinary amount of first-rate music was available *all the time* on the radio in the late 1930s and early 1940s, a veritable cafeteria of musical offerings that I surely feasted on ravenously. Since most readers may not realize specifically *how* rich and diverse this array of offerings actually was, I feel obliged to list a goodly sampling—although certainly far from all—of what was regularly available.

What is often forgotten, over a half century later, is that besides the well-remembered NBC Symphony with Toscanini, the two other broadcasting systems, CBS and the Mutual Network (WOR), also had their own full-time resident symphony orchestras that gave weekly broadcasts of what was then always referred to as serious music. But even more remarkably, between twenty to thirty other American and foreign orchestras were also *regularly* presented on radio in those years; not just, as might be expected, the country's major symphony orchestras, such as Boston, Chicago, Cleveland, Philadelphia, but even minor, less celebrated orchestras, such as Duluth, Denver, or Syracuse.

The list of foreign, mostly European, orchestras heard on American radio (primarily on NBC, which had a huge trans-Atlantic transmitter and receiver near Rocky Point, Long Island) is astonishing: from England, the BBC and London Symphony Orchestras and the Royal Philharmonic; from the Continent, the Vienna and Berlin Philharmonics, the Leipzig Gewandhaus Orchestra, the Concertgebouw in Amsterdam, as well as orchestras from Finland, Lithuania, Czechoslovakia, and from musical centers such as Turin, Dresden, Oslo, and Copenhagen, even the Moscow Symphony. Add to that opera broadcasts from Bayreuth, Salzburg, and Covent Garden, not to mention the traditional Saturday afternoon broadcasts from the Metropolitan Opera and the Cincinnati Zoo Opera transmissions. (There was even one broadcast from my mother's hometown of Krefeld, Germany—in 1938.) I remember hearing concerts from the Eastman School of Music, and I know there were also broadcasts from the Cincinnati and New England Conservatories and the Curtis Institute of Music. And these were not the occasional one or two broadcasts; the Curtis Institute, for example, offered more than twenty broadcasts annually! In addition, CBS for years broadcast the annual Bach Festivals from Bethlehem, Pennsylvania, and NBC countered with the Carmel Bach Festival in California.

There certainly was no dearth of chamber music on the radio, topped by regular concerts from the Library of Congress, and the fifty or so concerts that CBS broadcast annually featuring trios, quintets, larger ensembles (with Schubert's *Octet* and Beethoven's *Septet*), and, of course, lots of string quartets: fifty-three broadcasts on CBS in 1937 alone; and comparable offerings in other years, well into the forties.

Nor was contemporary music neglected; far from it. The network stations even commissioned works from composers such as Vittorio Giannini, Louis Gruenberg, Howard Hanson, Roy Harris, Walter Piston, Leo Sowerby, and William Grant Still, and also provided world premieres by—to name only a few—Marc Blitzstein, the Mexican composer Carlos Chavez, the Romanian Stan Golestan, Americans such as Bernard Herrmann, Charles Ives, Otto Luening, Burrill Phillips, Quincy Porter, and Bernard Rogers, and European composers such as Francis Poulenc and William Walton.

Even early preclassical music (nowadays, of course, fully represented on recordings) was presented on radio in those days. I remember hearing broadcasts by the American Society of Ancient Instruments, led by Ben Stad, a group that played everything on original instruments, and where I first heard music by composers such as Johann Schein, Samuel Scheidt, and Jan Sweelinck.

If that wasn't enough, there were all kinds of special series programs, such as those directed by Erno Rapee, conductor of the Radio City Music Hall Symphony Orchestra, a very savvy, reliable, and efficient Hungarian-born conductor, who in his regular weekly Sunday concerts presented all seven Sibelius symphonies (in 1937), and all nine Mahler symphonies (in 1941);

or the nearly four hundred (yes, four hundred!) broadcasts annually on NBC—it sounds totally incredulous today—featuring not only many of the symphony orchestras but also special series broadcasts such as *Music of Famous Amateurs* (including works by E. T. A. Hoffmann, Martin Luther, Lorenzo de Medici, Niccolo Machiavelli, Frederick the Great of Prussia, François Villon, John Milton, Samuel Pepys, Henry the Eighth, Friedrich Nietzsche, Jean Jacques Rousseau, Charles I of England, and Marie Antoinette) on CBS; or *Exploring Music*, a series devoted to the performance of neglected masterpieces; or the seventy-two broadcasts that the NBC network offered in one year—I heard several of them—celebrating National Music Week; or (on CBS) the delayed broadcast of the sixteenth International Society of Contemporary Music Festival held in 1938 in London, with premieres of Anton Webern's cantata *Das Augenlicht*, Igor Markevitch's *Le Nouvel age*, string quartets by Karl Amadeus Hartmann and Victor Ullman (killed six years later in the Auschwitz death camp), and Messiaen's *La Nativité du Seigneur*. In those days radio even celebrated the works of recently deceased composers; there were, for example, tribute broadcasts in 1938 (on CBS) to MacDowell, Ravel, and Gershwin.

To look at this vast musical paradise from a per day and per week perspective (involving all four networks stations), on any given Sunday I could hear a morning organ recital (very often by the great E. Power Biggs); the Stradivari Orchestra around noon (a string orchestra with everybody playing Stradivarius instruments); CBS's "Invitation to Music," where Bernard Herrmann and Oliver Daniel (the program's producer) would schedule anything from a Walton Symphony or an obscure symphony by Boccherini to excerpts from Alban Berg's *Wozzeck*; at three p.m. the New York Philharmonic, and then at four p.m. the Coca-Cola Hour with Andre Kostelanetz and soloists of the caliber of Rose Bampton or Gladys Swarthout,[27] followed at five p.m. by the General Motors Hour; Duke Ellington or other great jazz orchestras at seven p.m. on the Blue (Mutual) Network, whose music director was Paul Whiteman, and who was known to blend works by Stravinsky, Roy Harris, David Rose, and Gershwin on a single program. The Cleveland Orchestra came on at nine p.m., the Texaco Hour at nine thirty p.m. (with singers such as James Melton or violinists such as Albert Spalding), Phil Spitalny and his All-Girl Orchestra at ten p.m., and finally a program featuring singers the caliber of Eileen Farrell, Vivian della Chiesa, Nadine Conner, and Dorothy Kirsten at eleven thirty p.m. All that on a single Sunday!

Weekdays were only slightly less plenteous from a musical point of view. On Monday evenings there was the Voice of Firestone, the Telephone Hour, and the Carnation Hour, all on NBC, one after another, where you could expect to hear Heifetz or Kreisler or Pinza or Piatigorsky. On Tuesday mornings there was "Gateways to Music" with Bernard Herrmann, also "Salute to Youth" (I heard one broadcast featuring Stokowski's All-American Youth Orchestra playing Shostakovich). On Wednesday evenings one could hear Morton Gould's Cresta Blanca-sponsored program, and "Great Moments in Music" at ten p.m. (on CBS). On Thursday there was Phil Spitalny in a program called "Music from the New World," featuring early music of the Massachusetts pilgrims or the Pennsylvania Moravians, played on old instruments. Friday evening we had various jazz and dance programs. Saturday evening (on the Blue network) there was the Boston Symphony conducted by Serge Koussevitzky, as well as more late-night jazz programs.

In a way, my special radio favorites among this embarrassment of riches were two superb weekly programs devoted exclusively to popular show-tune music by our great American song writers, Gershwin, Berlin, Porter, Kern, Youmans, Rodgers, Vernon Duke, etc., in superb "symphonic" arrangements by two of the three great pioneers of this genre, Andre Kostelanetz and Morton Gould. (The third was David Rose, out on the West Coast. More of him later.) Kostelanetz's program was sponsored by Coca-Cola and was known as the "Coca-Cola Hour—The Pause That Refreshes." It followed the New York Philharmonic on CBS on

Sunday afternoons. Its fifty-or-so-piece orchestra comprised the absolute crème de la crème of New York musicians, taking the best from all sectors: classical freelancers, seasoned Broadway players, jazz musicians when and as needed (for example, Tommy and Jimmy Dorsey, Will Bradley, Jack Jenny, Bernie Leighton, Johnny Guarnieri, Walter Gross), and occasionally members of the symphony orchestras that the three networks maintained. A typical example of the mix of players Kosty used would be the superb principal trumpet of the CBS Symphony, Harry Freistadt, and sitting right next to him, Charlie Margolis, a veteran jazz trumpeter who worked with numerous bands (such as Goldkette, Whiteman, the Dorsey Brothers, Miller, and Shaw) and who handled the jazz assignments. Mitch Miller, oboist and English horn player extraordinaire, who was very interested in jazz, was another one of Kostelanetz's stalwarts.

Kostelanetz's symphonic arrangements were without fail little gems of perfection—creatively, orchestrationally, stylistically. Most of the arrangements were either made by himself or based on detailed orchestrational instructions from him to a small staff of assistants (very much in the manner of the Renaissance painters' apprentice workshops)—an awesome achievement, when you consider that Kostelanetz had to produce seven or eight numbers every week over a period of four years. In the weekly rehearsals Kostelanetz, ever the most meticulous craftsman, would further refine and finalize the arrangements, experimenting with brand new state-of-the-art recording techniques and wholly unusual, original microphone placements. Part of my great admiration for Kostelanetz's work on the Coca-Cola Hour (and his subsequent commercial recordings of the same arrangements of Gershwin, Kern, Porter, and other Broadway composers' show tunes) derives from the sheer sonic beauty and clarity that he achieved on the radio or in the recording studio. Only Stokowski could rival Kostelanetz in that respect.

One strategy that Kostelanetz employed to achieve such ideal renditions was to supervise the rehearsals up to the final dress rehearsal from the studio's control room, while one of his assistants conducted the orchestra. There, Kosty would adjust and refine and tweak the interpretations (occasionally even revise and rearrange), until he felt that they were perfect. Then *he* would go into the studio and conduct the dress rehearsal and the show.[28]

Morton Gould's program was sponsored by Cresta Blanca Wines, and featured brilliant, sometimes diabolically clever and challenging symphonic arrangements, which were tossed off each week with dazzling virtuosity by his amazing orchestra. His performances were not as slick and clean as Kostelanetz's, but because they were more often adventurous and risk-taking technically, they were, in their own way, more exciting and truly startling.

Among all such serious musical fare, there was one early radio show that particularly stands out in my memory, to a large extent because it contained musical segments that were at once truly inspired and outrageously funny and entertaining. Club Matinee came out of Chicago and was hosted by Garry Moore and Ransom Sherman. Its half-dozen comedy segments often included one that presented the most hilarious and, at the same time, most sophisticated satire on classical music and orchestral playing that I have ever heard. It predated the brilliant BBC series and recordings of the fifties, called "Gerard Hoffnung," by nearly two decades, and was probably influenced to some extent by Spike Jones's genial recordings and appearances on radio in the 1940s. But unlike Spike's jazz and pop small groups, Club Matinee's takeoffs were executed—I use the word advisedly—by a small symphony orchestra. For me, already very knowledgeable in the standard orchestral repertory, the Waterproof Philharmonic's—yes, that was its name—total decimation and dismemberment of world-famous popular classics was so ingeniously conceived and so flawlessly rendered that I and my mother would howl with laughter, rolling on the floor, our stomachs hurting for hours afterward. I don't recall that whoever created these fantastic demolitions of classical music was ever credited on the show, but he—or they, if there were several perpetrators—was definitely a genius. So were the musicians who played in that orchestra. The players' comical distortions, exaggerations, "accidental" squeaks and squawks, execrably bad intonation, always blundering in at the wrong time, made for the most perfectly calculated musical train wrecks. Pieces such as Rossini's William Tell Overture or Liszt's Hungarian Rhapsody in C Minor were so deftly and thoroughly torn to shreds that one sometimes wondered how the underlying composition was still recognizable. But it always was.

In the orchestra's typical routines, the music would break down early on in the performance, and come to a whimpering standstill. But after a few seconds it would retrace its steps, trying this time to avoid a similar smashup and, amazingly, succeeded, only to quickly slam into another musical collision, eventually coming to some horrendously screeching climactic halt. Unquestionably, to truly appreciate the bizarre antics of Club Matinee's Waterproof Philharmonic one had to have some basic knowledge of the music that was being massacred. And in all likelihood some of the humorous absurdities and unpredictable incongruities went over some listeners' heads. But the fact that this program was on the air at all, and for about five years, gives some indication of the relative sophistication of general audiences of those days.

I have never understood why these Club Matinee programs have not been revived in the various old-time radio shows that have from time to time been heard on National Public Radio. It could, of course, be because the programs weren't consistently recorded or preserved, or because of some copyright restrictions or other legalities. Or could it be because the interest in and knowledge of classical music is so low that would-be producers feel there is no potential audience for such programs in the present era, when everything has to be visual? Music—serious music—is an aural art, not a visual one, and therefore requires some ability to receive the information via the ears. Today serious music is in very short supply, especially on radio; it is virtually nonexistent on commercial radio, with a few extremely rare exceptions.

Equally entertaining, and in its own way very enlightening, was the Alec Templeton Hour, during which this gifted pianist would improvise spontaneously in any classical composer's style (or for that matter in a jazz manner), and on any classical theme or pop song that the audience would suggest to him. Templeton, who was blind from birth, was an amazingly gifted pianist and composer, and a great musical satirist. He became nationally famous on radio shows for his satiric spoofs of the classics and his infallible ability to instantly create cogent and concise, stylistically accurate improvisations, not only on famous tunes and melodies but also on any five or six notes named at random by the audience. He memorized all his weekly radio scripts over the nine years he flourished on American radio—an amazing feat. As a composer he is best remembered for his ingeniously clever and witty *Bach Goes to Town*, turned into an immense hit by Benny Goodman's 1939 recording, as well as pieces such as *Mendelssohn Mows 'Em Down, Sousa and Strauss in Reverse*, and *The Shortest Wagnerian Opera*.

There was much more on radio of remarkable musical quality and interest; I have only scratched the surface. What is most extraordinary is that the vast majority of these good music broadcasts were presented as public service programs; many were transferred over to television in the late 1940s, surviving well into the early 1960s—but then abandoned. Can you imagine anything like that today? Even public radio and public television, to which good music, whether jazz or classical or ethnic and vernacular, has been completely relegated—I would say ghettoized—cannot begin to match such a rich and varied rainbow of musical offerings as was regularly offered in the past. How deplorable our radio and television wasteland looks by comparison!

Other fine entertainment was available in plenitude on radio, everything from CBS's Sunday morning twin programs *Invitation to Learning* and *Invitation to Music*, to its new weekly series *You Are There*, in which major events in world history (such as the execution of Marie Antoinette, or the Civil War battle between the Merrimac and the Monitor, or John Wesley Powell's first trip through the Grand Canyon in 1869) were reenacted as if occurring today, and told through the eyes and reports of network radio correspondents. I also remember with great pleasure two splendid music programs of intelligent and analytical musical commentary, one by David Randolph, the other by Edward Tatnall Canby (for whom my brother Edgar became the online producer during that period).

Then, in addition to all that, there was the almost unfathomably wide range of *live* musical offerings in New York, an abundance and profusion of all kinds of classical music and jazz that no single individual could even hope to completely access. Beyond those two categories of music you could also find almost any kind of ethnic, vernacular music, whether it was North African or Near Eastern Arab music in Brooklyn, Greek bouzouki music in lower Manhattan, Hungarian gypsy ensembles on the East Side, Portugese fado, authentic Argentinian tangos, and so on. While I was not yet fully aware of these musical riches at age sixteen, I certainly sought them out later, when I haunted the clubs, meeting halls, restaurants, and other venues where such music was regularly offered. In short, there was no excuse to be musically or culturally illiterate in those days.

What was most striking about the virtually limitless availability on radio of all kinds of music and high-quality cultural offerings—wonderfully balanced with light entertainment fare—is that it was not limited to New York or a few other big cities; it was available to the whole country through the creation of nationwide radio networks. By the mid-1930s farmers in Iowa or housewives in rural Kansas could hear the country's many symphony orchestras and great jazz bands on a weekly basis. The names not just of Toscanini, Walter, Ormandy, Stokowski, Koussevitzky, but also of Howard Barlow, Alfred Wallenstein, Bernard Herrmann, and dozens of other radio orchestra leaders became household names in America's heartland. What initial resistance there was to the diffusion of higher art on radio came initially not from country folks in the hinterlands, but, ironically, from renowned soloists and conductors, who felt that their art should be reserved for the elite, and was not made to cater to the masses. But radio changed those attitudes rather quickly when artists realized that precisely through that medium many millions of people would hear their work, compared to the mere hundreds or thousands that might come to a concert hall.

Even more interesting is the fact that this expanded musical consciousness occurred precisely during the Depression years, in part because whatever tendencies toward ever-greater materialism may have motivated people in the previous decades, such dreams and hopes were quickly dashed in the early 1930s. Bereft not only of the means of material acquisition but even of the ability to maintain the minimum essentials of life, the whole country turned inward, finding an inner, higher self, and by coincidence, through the spectacular spread of radio in the 1930s, discovered musical, cultural, and intellectual enrichments that previously only the wealthy and most educated could procure.

These twin developments account for the fact that the Depression years turned into one of the finest, noblest, most productive eras of artistic creativity this United States ever experienced, most notably in music, literature, and education; and that the proportionate balance between quality, creative music of all kinds and commercial music, produced primarily for quick market success and financial profit, was something like 90 percent (creative) to 10 percent (commercial), as opposed to today's 3 percent creative to 97 percent commercial. Indeed, crass commercialism in the arts, to the extent that it has developed in the last thirty to forty years, hardly existed in those earlier times; it was not as aggressive and omnipresent.

I recall a conversation with a music-loving friend of my father's, a recent refugee from Nazi-occupied Europe, who once asked me—it was around 1942 or 1943—if I realized how lucky we Americans were to find such a staggering array of cultural wealth, in all its diverse manifestations, on the radio, and that we could simply find these cultural riches by turning the dial on our radios—suggesting that we shouldn't take these precious gifts for granted, that we should appreciate our good fortune. He was so right.

Of course, I didn't listen only to music on the radio. There were so many other interesting and informative programs on the airwaves in those days, programs such as *Information, Please*, the best, the most intelligent, literate, and entertaining, quiz show ever on radio or television. Its brilliant host-moderator was Clifton Fadiman. Regular panelists were Franklin Adams and John Kieran, both well-known literary lights, concert pianist and sardonic Hollywood and Broadway wag, Oscar Levant, and other guest panelists such as George S. Kaufman, the two Dorothys—Parker and Thompson—Heywood Broun, Orson Welles, Ben Hecht, and Deems Taylor. Over a period of ten years the program provided an astonishing variety of educative information in a wide range of subjects and fields.

Even some of the more escapist entertainment was generally of a very high order. Especially enticing for us kids were programs such as *Inner Sanctum* (which regularly presented Edgar Allen Poe classics such as *The Telltale Heart* and *The Fall of the House of Usher*, with actors Boris Karloff, Peter Lorre, and Claude Raines), *The Green Hornet*, and *The Lone Ranger*—all shows that were especially captivating for me, since they featured classical music for their themes and bridges.

News broadcasts, too, were of a high quality, presenting straight ahead, hard-core news, not the infotainment shows of today. I particularly admired reporters and commentators such as Edward R. Murrow, Alex Drier, Bob Trout, Charles Collingwood, William Shirer, Douglas Edwards, Eric Sevareid, Howard K. Smith, H. V. Kaltenborn, Quincy Howe, Heywood Hale Broun, and Raymond Gram Swing. Even archconservatives like Fulton Lewis Jr.—alas, one of my father's favorites—were somehow worth listening to because there was a certain intelligence and articulateness that informed their outspoken commentaries.

Radio was rich in other cultural and artistic fare, everything from *The Mercury Theatre on the Air* (later the Campbell Playhouse), featuring the acclaimed New York drama company founded by Orson Welles and John Houseman, to the *Lux Radio Theatre*, a long-running classic radio anthology series of adapted Broadway plays, to such programs as *Invitation to Learning* (on literature), and a plethora of highly entertaining, impressively educational quiz and game-show programs. I remember in particular a whole group of such question-and-answer programs sponsored by the Mars Candy Company. One called *Dr. I. Q., The Mental Banker*, was especially informative and educational. As a young teenager I learned much on that program because one retains new information much more readily when one is young. What educative programming can youngsters find nowadays on television, except on public television?

There was also a tremendous amount of excellent comedy on radio, much of which was eventually transferred to television, leading to such great early TV programs as *Show of Shows* (Edgar Bergen and Charlie McCarthy's amazing long run), *The Red Skelton Hour*, *I Love Lucy*, and still later *The Honeymooners*, to name only a few.

It was in 1941 that I also happen to have heard the late Victor Borge's very first appearance on American radio, on Bing Crosby's Kraft Music Hall. My mother had just read about this hugely talented musician and comedian, billed as "The Unmelancholy Dane," the upcoming program, and the whole story of how Borge (real name Rosenbaum) had fled his native Denmark, then under Nazi occupation. A legend today, Borge was as funny then as he was five or six decades later; I laugh my head off at the same routines as much today as I did half a century ago, particularly his famous "Phonetic Punctuation."

In those glorious radio days, between the networks' public service and self-sponsored programs, the whole range of human creativity and inventiveness was well covered, as it was in the early days of television—that is, until the television corporations abruptly abandoned their public service and educational policies in the early 1960s.

As happy as I was with my well-developing compositional work, my musical studies, and my getting around and being appreciated in the larger musical world, somehow things were not going well at home. For reasons I couldn't fathom, my mother in those years (1940–42) became increasingly quick-tempered and irascible. I don't *really* know what caused her to behave in such an intemperate manner, but I suspect her irritableness was engendered at least in part by an accumulation of various frustrations that stemmed from being unable to pursue and express her artistic talents as much as she would have liked. She must have felt imprisoned in her burdensome and relentless household chores,[29] while her husband was living the glamorous life of a much sought after, top-of-the-line musician.

Their marriage had also become increasingly fractious; the first bloom of romantic and sexual love had long ago faded. To exacerbate my mother's plight and deepen her increasing loneliness, my father had a number of fleeting affairs with various adoring females, to whom the very handsome Arthur Schuller, especially when appearing in glamorous full-dress regalia on stage at Carnegie Hall, must have seemed like quite a catch. (One of these "ladies" had the nerve, some twenty-five years later, to brag to me about her liaison with my father.)

But whatever the cause of my mother's choleric temper, I found myself constantly—and excessively—the recipient of her wrath. I was a real thorn in her side, while my brother seemed to be immune to her outbursts. Her punishments were both physical and psychological. She took to beating me mercilessly, not with her hands, but with various objects—sticks, brooms, and worst of all, a heavy inch-thick club with which she used to stir our laundry in a big kettle or tub. I was black and blue much of the time. Or, as on one occasion in 1940 when I had accidentally broken a beautiful modern-style glass cigarette case that she had bought in Germany, she cruelly—after a severe beating—prevented me from listening to WQXR *for three whole days*, knowing full well that two of my most favorite pieces, Shostakovich's Fifth Symphony and Stravinsky's *Rite of Spring*, were scheduled to be played on those very days. Nothing, including all the beatings in the world, could have hurt me more deeply. I became increasingly terrified and haunted by her anger.

One day, in my frequent perusing of my parent's bookshelves, I found a little volume of poems by the great eighth-century Chinese poet Li Po, translated into exquisite German by the turn-of-the-century poet Klabund (real name, Hans Bethge), published by the famous German Insel-Bücherei Publishers in Wiesbaden. Carrying this book around with me in my various subway rides and Manhattan peregrinations, I lost it one day. I was beside myself with fear, knowing that if my mother learned of the loss, I would receive the beating of my life. I spent the next two or three days frantically looking for a bookstore that carried German books. I had a hunch that in the great city of New York one would be able to find anything—*anything*—sooner or later. And I was right. In midtown Manhattan I discovered Adler's bookstore, which specialized in international literature. They had the Li Po–Klabund volume in stock. That was one of the few times I outfoxed my mother; she never even knew that the little book had been missing for several days.

I eventually figured out how to stop her from beating me. I knew that beating a strapping fourteen- or fifteen-year-old youth was ridiculous, French temper and marriage frustrations or not. One day she came after me—it was in the garden behind our house in Jamaica—and this time I put my arms up like a boxer, protecting my body, determined not to weave and bob, not to crouch to avoid her blows, determined rather to stand my ground, erect and defiant. As the blows rained down on my arms, hurting like hell, I calmly told her: "Go ahead, hit me all you want, it doesn't hurt. You can't hurt me anymore!" She soon gave up, realizing that her sadistic attack had no affect on me, that I was denying her the temper-driven pleasure of inflicting pain on me.

It was sometime after that final beating that I decided I'd had enough. One late spring morning I simply ran away from home, with just the clothes on my back and about five dollars in my pocket. The first day I wandered for hours, striking out eastward toward Hollis along the bicycle paths I had ridden so many times before, not really knowing where I was going. But it was a beautiful sunny day, and after a few hours my blind rage morphed into a more relaxed mood. I inhaled the fragrance of freshly cut grass along the parkways and enjoyed nature all around me. That first night I slept on the grass on a parkway embankment, hidden behind some bushes, gazing up at the stars for a long time and reflecting on my wretched existence.

The second day I wandered around aimlessly, now realizing, especially when I saw some cruising police cars, that I had better steer clear of New York's finest; proud and stubborn as I was, I thought that I could evade them. But by late afternoon it began to dawn on me that I was a runaway and that I would have to be constantly hiding and on the lookout not to be caught. It also dawned on me that this wasn't much fun, and that the game I was playing wasn't really turning out to be as liberating as I had expected. It wasn't many hours later, just before sunset—I was lying on the grass in a little tiny park near Union Turnpike, hungry, my clothes dirty and disheveled, beginning to feel guilty and frightened—when a police car pulled up abruptly, screeching to a halt. My parents had called the Missing Persons Bureau already on the first day, and the police had been searching for me for a day and a half. They called my parents to say that I had been found and told them to come and pick me up. The ride back home with my mother was carried out in stony silence, as I, both furious *and* glad that I had been found, didn't really know what to say.

This time there were no beatings, no yelling remonstrations, no reprisal punishments. Elsie, awash in tears, begged me never to do such a thing again, said that she loved me and that she hoped we would never fight again. It did indeed initiate a long-term truce between us, which held for many years, although one or two strands of filial love had surely been broken. The emotional, psychological wounds she had inflicted on me over many years never quite healed and left a few small scars.

My childhood was beginning to wind down, and within a few weeks I was to receive a call from Antal Dorati's assistant at the Ballet Theatre, a call that would launch me on my first long-term professional engagement as a horn player. I felt I was ready.

Chapter Three

YOUTH

IT WAS IN ONE OF THOSE ENORMOUS apartments that used to be so plentiful on the Upper West Side of Manhattan, especially around Seventy-Second or Eighty-Sixth Street, that I was ushered into a large, richly carpeted living room. It was virtually empty except for some high-backed chairs, tables, and lamps; around the perimeter were large earthen jars with flowers, and at one end a huge baronial fireplace. On the far side of the room stood a seven-foot grand piano, loaded with piles of scores. Oddest of all, and unexpected in a living room, was a large crib at one end, with a sleeping baby inside. For a moment I thought I was in the wrong place, but a maid ushered me to a chair near the piano, indicating that the maestro would be with me right away. That "right away" turned out to be nearly twenty minutes, and the maestro was Antal Dorati.[1]

I was in Dorati's apartment to audition for the position of second horn in the thirty-piece Ballet Theatre touring orchestra. My friend, Arthur Holmes (from the Manhattan School of Music), it turned out, was first horn, and had recommended me to Dorati when the previous second horn player, Lester Solomon, had been drafted into the army. After sitting there awhile, nervously wondering when Dorati was going to appear, I quietly unpacked my horn—eager not to wake the sleeping baby—and after a while got up the courage to investigate what was on the piano's music rack. To my delight I saw the score of Shostakovich's Fifth Symphony, opened to the middle of the first movement, a piece I had loved and studied ever since I had bought Stokowski's wonderful 1937 recording four years earlier.

Just then Dorati walked in, dressed in a beautiful maroon bathrobe. (It *was* around nine in the morning). "Ah," he said, in his high-pitched voice and slight Hungarian accent, "you see what I am studying. Do you like Shostakovich?" Nervously: "Oh yes, I have loved that piece for many years." A bit puzzled, he asked: "Oh, so do you compose?" "Yes, sir." "Good for you!"

As nervous as I was—one almost always is at auditions, and this was my first real big audition—I felt I had already won round one. He seemed to be impressed. "Well, let's see what you can do on the horn." "Maestro, can I please have some newspaper? You know, I don't want to let the water out on your beautiful carpet." "Oh, of course." He went to a nearby table and put a sheaf of newspaper on the floor; it was—appropriately—the music section of the *New York Times*.

Dorati was only in his midthirties at the time, amazingly handsome, with rich curly dark hair. I had already heard some of his recordings made in England in the late thirties, mostly popular ballet music. Most of us young musicians had heard that Dorati was rather short-tempered, often indulging in tantrums in rehearsals and quick to fire musicians precipitously—as were many, many conductors of that era. So I approached this audition with considerable trepidation.

As he rattled off the big famous horn solos he wanted to hear me play—the Tchaikovsky Fifth solo, the *Till Eulenspiegel* calls, the *Siegfried* call, etc.—I pointed hesitatingly to the crib. How could I play an audition on a brass instrument in the same room with a sleeping infant? With an impatient wave of the hand, he said: "Oh, just go ahead; she's used to it. She loves music."

The excerpts went very well. After the obligatory sight-reading of some ballet repertory scheduled for the Ballet Theatre's 1942–43 season (Prokofiev's *Peter and the Wolf* and *Lieutenant Kije*, Stravinsky's *Petroushka*, Chausson's *Poème*, various Offenbach and Tchaikovsky ballet excerpts), I offered to play the two major horn solos from Shostakovich's Fifth Symphony. I took the fourteen-bar phrase in the first movement solo in only two breaths, with none before the high E—a slightly risky but more musical way to play that passage. I could tell that Dorati was impressed. That got him. Two days later I heard from his contractor that I had the job.

I joined the Ballet Theatre orchestra in early January 1943 in St. Louis. I was in a perfect dream world, hearing and playing some of the greatest music ever written, such as Stravinsky's *Petroushka*, Chausson's lovely *Poème* for violin and orchestra, Schönberg's *Verklärte Nacht* (*Transfigured Night*), Rossini and Respighi's *La Boutique fantasque*, *Three Virgins and a Devil*, set to Respighi's *Ancient Airs and Dances* and choreographed by Agnes de Mille, Mahler's *Kindertotenlieder*, Prokofiev's *Peter and the Wolf* (without narration), Tchaikovsky's *Swan Lake*, and several ballets created by the great English choreographer Antony Tudor (*Lilac Garden*, *Pillar of Fire*, *Dark Elegies*). I had heard rumors that Tudor had fashioned a ballet based on Shakespeare's *Romeo and Juliet*, choreographed to half a dozen pieces by Delius. Given my passionate love for Delius's music, I was hoping that I would get to play that ballet on tour. But as it turned out *Romeo and Juliet* wasn't quite ready for the 1942–43 winter tour, and thus the company was saving it for a premiere in New York City in its spring 1943 New York season. (Tudor used Delius's *Over the Hills and Far Away*, *Brigg Fair*, *Walk to the Paradise Garden*, *Eventyr*, and the Prelude to *Irmelin*.)

In the bigger cities, where there was a resident symphony orchestra, our little thirty-piece orchestra was supplemented by members of the local symphony. In St. Louis we played in the huge Municipal Auditorium, and I'll never forget how overwhelmed I was listening to Dorati rehearsing Schönberg's *Verklärte Nacht*—it is for strings only—sitting in the middle of this cavernous empty auditorium, the music floating around and above me in the hall's rich acoustics, enveloping, embracing me with its sensuous, passionate sounds.

The Ballet Theatre's winter-spring tour lasted about three months, starting in mid-January and ending in early April, and encompassed virtually the entire United States and southern Canada. From St. Louis we headed northwest through Wisconsin (St. Cloud, Madison), then from Minnesota to North Dakota (Bismarck), thence westward to Montana (Butte, Billings, Missoula), followed by Seattle, Vancouver, Victoria, eventually down to San Francisco and Los Angeles, thence eastward via Arizona and Texas to the country's midsection, Chicago—twelve days there—thence eastward to upper New York State, finally ending up three months later in Toronto and Montreal.

I marvel now how extraordinarily lucky I was to have been chosen to participate in such an extended tour. Here I was at age seventeen seeing vast parts of the country—in all, some thirty American cities—making $125 a week (a *very* good salary in those days), playing wonderful music at a very high professional level, and making new friends with all sorts of enormously talented people (musicians, dancers), forming in some cases life-long friendships—*and* free, on my own, away from home. Out of my weekly salary I did have to pay for hotels and food; what amounted to a per diem was simply included in the salary. To a twenty-first-century reader $125 a week may sound like a pitiful nothing, but not if one remembers that a good, decent hotel room cost $2 or $3. If you wanted to live more cheaply—and quite a few of the musicians and corps de ballet did—you could get a room for as little as 50¢ or 75¢, in what some of us called derisively "flea bags," even though generally there were no fleas and the rooms were clean. A good dinner could be had for $1 or $2. A cup of coffee was—this is no nostalgic myth—5¢! So even living quite well, perhaps splurging now and then on a fabulous meal or expensive hotel room, I could clear $50 to $75 a week.

Since Ballet Theatre had already been touring in the fall, and orchestra rehearsals had taken place months before I joined the company, I was more or less sight-reading the entire book. With only two new members coming into the orchestra, myself and a fine lady bassoonist (Erika Kubey), the company was definitely not going to put on rehearsals so that the two of us could learn our parts. We were expected—and were chosen accordingly—to fit in immediately with the rest of the orchestra.

I was in my element. I hardly did any true sight-reading, having previously studied almost all the music we were playing, either deeply analytically as a composer or becoming very familiar with it as a record-collecting listener. I knew not only my horn parts virtually by heart but also most of the scores and their orchestration. I was thrilled to find myself playing—in this small touring orchestra—in addition to the second horn parts, all kinds of cued-in third and fourth horn, second bassoon, bass clarinet parts, whatever, cues that Dorati, in arranging, say, *Petroushka* for our thirty-piece orchestra, had already put into our wind parts. The result was that, even with this under-sized orchestra, practically everything Stravinsky had written was ingeniously represented and covered, tucked in somewhere in somebody's part. Dorati, himself a fine composer who had studied with the legendary Leo Weiner and Zoltán Kodály at the Budapest Conservatory, was *very* good at this sort of arranging and transcribing. I did surprise him a few times when, hearing that some small detail of orchestration in the original score was missing in our reduced version, I asked him, if I had rests in my part, to let me fill in a missing third bassoon part or whatever happened to not be covered. He liked that!

I was very disappointed when, in the big cities (like Minneapolis or San Francisco), I could play only my second horn part, since the full instrumentation was fleshed out by hiring musicians from the local symphony orchestras.

My close friend from the Manhattan School of Music, the great bass trombonist John Clark, had joined the Ballet orchestra the previous fall. He sat right behind me, and in the sometimes impossibly small theatre pits in which we often had to play, bunched together like sardines, John had to aim his slide between the legs and spokes of my chair. In a ballet called *Bluebeard* put together by Dorati from various works by Jacques Offenbach,[2] Dorati had created an extended bass trombone solo (not in the original Offenbach), in which, as often as John played this astonishing passage, he never fluffed a note. With his full, clear tone, perfect intonation, and remarkable security, John's big moment was always a highlight of our performances. Bill Schneiderman, our excellent timpanist and percussionist, who often had to play three or four instruments more or less simultaneously, most of the time found himself *outside* the pit, usually in a box nearest to the stage, fully visible to the audience.

I must mention our two excellent trumpet players, Cecil Collins and Freddy Caballero, the latter a Mexican and an exceptionally fine player and wonderful person. As many times as we played *Petroushka* on that tour, they never missed a note in those very demanding trumpet parts, including the difficult, nakedly exposed fanfare exchanges at the very end of *Petroushka*, as the puppet's soul rises slowly to its heavenly rest. (In 1943 such "modernistic" trumpet parts were still considered very scary and nerve-wracking, by no means fully assimilated into the standard repertory, as they are now.)

I can't say that touring at that time, especially in the dead of winter, was all a bed of roses. America was at war, heavily so in 1943; what with wartime shortages and all kinds of related hardships and deprivations, traveling could be a pretty tough slog! All normal or modern trains had been appropriated by the armed forces for the massive troop transports that were a major part of the steadily escalating war effort. We, as insignificant artists, were consigned to ancient train cars with, believe it or not, no modern heating system and only a single wood-burning stove in the center of each car. Obviously only a few people could huddle around the stove at one time. The rest of us had to bundle up in overcoats, sweaters, and shawls, and even then— boys and girls, it didn't matter—snuggled up to each other on the very uncomfortable benches, just to try to keep warm.

St. Cloud and some of the other Wisconsin and Minnesota towns were bad enough in the dead of winter. But when we got to North Dakota, widely known for its frequent forty-below temperatures, even the hardiest, most stoic souls among us began to gripe and groan. On the trip across North Dakota to western Montana, with only one performance stopover in Bismarck, we were unable to leave our train for three days and nights in one of the coldest northern winters in memory. Worse yet, it was so cold that something in our train's steam engine—not diesel— froze up, and our train was forced to sit in the station in Jamestown all night and most of the next morning before we could continue westward. That night in Jamestown was horrible; we were freezing our buns off. We ran out of wood for the stove; all the windows were glazed over with ice and icicles; we couldn't go out to eat anything, to perhaps warm up in the train station, because the train doors and steps were frozen solid and couldn't be opened. We were trapped inside. That initial introduction to North Dakota—a state with which I was to have a long-term relationship in the future—was not exactly the most hospitable.

On the brighter side, traveling across the northern United States was for me, the geography enthusiast, the wanna-be travel adventurer, a wondrous experience—or rather, a whole series of wondrous experiences. Just traveling across mountainous western Montana and across the Rockies, with its many high-elevation passes, sometimes only a few hundred yards behind the snow-plowing engines, we were rewarded with one glorious sight after another. The most spectacular sight of all was when we approached Butte—the train still high up in the mountains—as the pine- and snow-covered forest on our left gave way to a two-thousand-foot drop in altitude, suddenly revealing the town half a mile below and the whole copper mine valley underneath us. Sitting on the left side of the train, its engine throwing off a flurry of sparks from its brakes and wheels, it was a bit scary peering over the side down that huge abyss. It felt like being in a plane that was banking deeply to the left for a landing.

Equally exciting, though in a more contemplative way, was my first sight of Mount Rainier. We were approaching Seattle late in the afternoon, about a half hour before sunset. I had been reading Sherlock Holmes for a few hours, when suddenly by chance, glancing out the window, I saw this huge, almost translucent, glowing, sun-drenched, pinkish-orange, snow-covered rounded massif. It was a breathtaking sight, one that I was compelled to not let out of my sight for the next half hour or so, until it disappeared out of view a few miles before reaching Seattle. I had never before seen any mountain so beautiful; its stocky, broad shape set in a wide flat plain (originally a large inland sea). Mount Rainier can be seen unobstructed for miles from virtually all four compass directions. This huge rock mass, the consequence of a gigantic volcanic eruption about five thousand years ago, when half of Rainier collapsed onto itself, seems to rise out of nowhere: no foothills, no surrounding valleys, simply a huge mound of now inactive volcano thrust upward out of the earth.

It was good to visit Canadian Vancouver and Victoria, both of which were still relatively smallish pioneer towns in the early 1940s. I remember in both places the theatres were small rickety wooden buildings, probably built in the 1870s or 1880s—much like the so-called opera houses of the American West. I don't know how the dancers were able to adjust to the small raked stages, or how we musicians were able to crowd into the tiny pits. (I remember that a few string players were given the night off, for there was no room for them, and, once again, Schneiderman was way off in a gilded box.)

From the northwest we headed south, where in Northern California (near Eureka) I saw my first eucalyptus trees and all kinds of exotic flora that one would never see in the East, and certainly not in such incredible plenitude. All told, we spent nearly two weeks in California, mainly in San Francisco, Los Angeles, and San Diego. In Los Angeles for some reason our little orchestra was not supplemented as in other major cities. A big surprise for me was when Stravinsky, who was living in Los Angeles at the time, suddenly showed up prior to a brief refresher rehearsal of *Petroushka*. We were all thrilled to see the great master, who listened patiently and consulted briefly with Dorati after our rendition, seemingly very pleased with what he had heard. We learned later that Stravinsky thanked Dorati and Anton Dolin profusely for performing *Petroushka* as a ballet, because by the 1930s the work was done almost always as a purely orchestral work (in its suite form) and only rarely performed as a ballet. I must add that Dorati was a terrific *Petroushka* conductor, handling all the meter changes, cross-rhythms, and other complexities—still relatively novel in those years, *Petroushka* was only thirty-two years old in 1943—with consummate ease. He made it so easy for us in the orchestra.

As the only composer in the orchestra (besides Dorati), I was especially thrilled to see Stravinsky, my hero and idol, and after some hesitation, shy as I was, I got up enough nerve to ask him for an autograph. I had the scores of my three favorite Stravinsky works—*Petroushka*, *Sacre du printemps*, and *Symphony of Psalms*—with me at the rehearsal (I wouldn't have been caught dead without those scores!), and asked him to autograph my *Sacre* score, which he did, dating it "February 8/43." It is the only autograph I have ever requested of anyone, and I am very proud to own it.

In Los Angeles John Clark and I roomed together in a hotel very near the Philharmonic Auditorium, where we performed. Two things stand out in my memory. First, John, five years my elder, introduced me to electric shavers, still relatively new at that time, and I immediately bought a Remington (I still use them sixty-eight years later). Second, I dearly loved Dvořák's three symphonies—numbers seven, eight, and nine (*From the New World*)—and his Cello Concerto, the only Dvořák orchestral works available on recordings in those days, and was thus quite surprised to suddenly hear on the radio in our hotel room a harmonically even more advanced late Dvořák work: his *Othello* Overture, in a brand new recording. Some twenty-five years later I would open the concert in my conducting debut with the Boston Symphony Orchestra with Dvořák's *Othello*, a piece the BSO had never played before.

My dear friend, Jean Clark Graney, a member of the Ballet Theatre's corps de ballet in the 1940s—her name then was Jeannie Davidson—reminded me recently that just outside of San Diego, prior to our evening's performance, a small single-engine airplane crashed onto the highway, luckily *between* our two buses, causing the second bus with the orchestra to be delayed for hours. It dawned on us that, had our bus been fifty feet further down the road, we all might have been killed in an instant. And Jeannie remembers that we musicians arrived at the theatre two hours late, shaken and white as ghosts.

I had often heard that the San Diego Zoo was one of the finest and largest in America. I pilgrimaged to the outskirts of town and spent the day there with all kinds of animals I had never even heard of, much less seen before. I took about fifty pictures with my little primitive Kodak camera, especially of the alligators and crocodiles. I had also never seen so many hordes of bell-bottom uniformed sailors, swarming all over town, looking for a good time—San Diego being the ultimate navy town on the West Coast.

From the southwest we headed eastward through Tucson (in those days still a tiny, rough frontier town, with mostly unpaved streets), and through Texas northward via Memphis, Pittsburgh, and Syracuse to Canada, where the tour ended. It was on that trip through Arizona that I saw a desert for the first time, and was fascinated to see so clearly that this was once, many thousands of years ago, an extensive ocean. Not only the sand, but so many of the plants and bushes, except the cacti, reminded me exactly of what one would find only at the bottom of the sea.

In Montreal, Jeannie, by that time a three-year veteran with Ballet Theatre, introduced me and John Clark to a wonderful French restaurant, Aux Delices, where I splurged for several days on fabulous French continental cuisine that was totally new to me. I trace my days as a gourmet, perhaps even a gourmand, to those superb culinary experiences in Montreal.

While good food and drink were plentiful and superior in Montreal, in Toronto we discovered quite the opposite. Toronto is now a sophisticated, multicultural, cosmopolitan metropolis, but in 1943 it was still an insulated, puritanically abstemious place, where eating and—God forbid—*enjoying* great food was considered some sort of sin. The best some of us musicians could find was a Greek restaurant not far from the train station, which became our hangout for the four or five days we performed in Toronto. In those days Greek restaurants were uniformly dubbed "greasy spoons." Our Toronto discovery, however, was of a higher order, and I remember having wonderful meals there for $1.25, *with* dessert (even baklava).

I must digress briefly to pay tribute to a remarkable musician in the orchestra, oboist and English hornist Josef Marx, perhaps the first person I met whom I would call a kind of mentor. Joe, who was seven or eight years older than me, was not only an experienced orchestra and chamber music player, but also a baroque music specialist (forty to fifty years before the early music movement). He had studied oboe with the great Leon Goossens in London, and with Jaap Stotijn, famed principal oboist of Amsterdam's Concertgebouw Orchestra. Joe was also an intellectual, extraordinarily well read, an expert on Freud's and Jung's writings, and a kind of maverick and outspoken no-nonsense critic of whatever was fake or dishonest in the American music business. As such, his feelings didn't blend very easily with the more common "don't make waves" attitude of most musicians.

Joe's independence was, alas, also reflected in his sometimes rather eccentric and erratic oboe playing. His use of a wide vibrato, Leon Goossens style, was not at all acceptable to the American oboe world, which more or less adhered to the Tabuteau (famous principal oboist of the Philadelphia Orchestra) school of playing. Joe was in many ways a square peg in a round hole, except that he really—courageously, defiantly—never *wanted* to fit into the expected round hole. It didn't help that Joe was a stocky, bellied, somewhat gnomelike figure, with slightly bulging eyes (due to a thyroid condition). In the often heartless New York musicians' world, Joe's physical appearance was an easy target for those who didn't appreciate his many talents and just enjoyed making fun of him.

I admired Joe very much, and was happy when he took me under his wing on the Ballet Theatre tour almost from day one, as a kind of second father. When Joe noticed that one of the male dancers, Dick Reed, a flamboyant homosexual, was attempting to put the make on me, Joe educated me—still the innocent—rather quickly about the nature and sexual proclivities of dancers in ballet companies.[3] Joe also helped me indirectly with my horn playing. We often roomed together, and I would watch him practice the oboe, which, oddly enough, he did while lying flat on his back on the floor. He told me that he had learned this from Jaap Stotijn, the purpose being to develop and improve a wind player's breathing capacity by strengthening and expanding the diaphragm and abdominal muscles. I had excellent basic training with my teacher, Mr. Schulze, but Joe Marx was able to meticulously analyze the whole human breathing apparatus from a technical and physiological point of view, which was extremely helpful to me not only as a player but also in later years when I in turn became a horn teacher at various schools and conservatories.

Josef Marx was in some ways my intellectual mentor, suggesting all kinds of great literature for me to delve into: Tolstoy, Proust, Huxley, Shaw, subtly weaning me away from my then favorite, Conan Doyle (*Sherlock Holmes*). The first book I read under Joe's benign tutelage was the great sixteenth-century Italian art historian Georgio Vasari's *The Lives of the Most Excellent Painters and Sculptors* (1550). Between Joe, Richard Reed, and of course my friend John Clark (who urged me to read the novels of Thomas Hardy and D. H. Lawrence)—all of us also constantly sharing and exploring our particular musical enthusiasms—my mind was figuratively exploding with newly gained knowledge, enough for me to feed upon for many years to come.

I must return to our Greek restaurant in Toronto, because it was the locale of one of my most extraordinary exploits. Joe had an odd, sneaky sense of humor, and a major tendency to tease people, not in some silly, childish way, but on a daringly challenging level. He certainly loved teasing *me*—actually an expression of his admiration (as teasing almost always is)—especially since I was always stubbornly rising to his bait, consistently falling for his mischievous provocations, just as I had with Melitta in Germany and Sally DeRosa in Rocky Point.

Having noticed how much I liked ice cream sundaes, Joe, one evening at dinner at the Greek restaurant dared me with a smirky smile on his face, in front of the whole group—there were six of us—"I betcha you can't eat fifteen ice cream sundaes in a row." Even though this occurred *after* I had eaten a full calf's liver dinner, with all the fixings, I felt I had to take Joe up on his challenge. To my amazement and that of my dinner partners I managed to down all fifteen sundaes, which the owner of the restaurant brought over one by one, with ever increasing astonishment. Stubborn cuss that I am, I was not going to let Joe win this bet. But I must admit that by the time I got to the eleventh or twelfth sundae, they began to taste like some horrendous medicine. The reader can probably understand that I had some of the wildest, craziest nightmares that night. I have also never had another ice cream sundae.

I was a hero; mighty Joe had been beaten. The owner and two waiters, who had become our pals, never forgot me. I was often in Toronto in succeeding years, and every time I went to that Greek restaurant (until the ownership changed in the midfifties), I was always joyously greeted and celebrated: "Oh, there he is, the kid who ate all those ice cream sundaes!"

Ballet Theatre was at that time—in the pre-Balanchine era—the finest ballet company in the country, rivaled worldwide only by the Sadler Wells and Royal Ballet in London. Sixty years ago there didn't exist the dozens of professional dance companies that abound in the United States today; nor were there more than a handful of modern dance companies. Our dancers were considered the best in the ballet world, technically and expressively, artistically. André Eglevsky was the company's male superstar, but almost as famous and as good in their own right were Hugh Laing, Igor Youskevich, Nicholas Orloff, and three young American talents, Jerry Robbins, Johnny Kriza, and Michael Kidd, as well as the slightly older (English) Anton Dolin. On the ladies' side, there was the brilliant, sparkling, iridescent Irina Boronova, the dramatic Nora Kaye, and superb dancers such as Sono Osato, Rosella Hightower, Maria Karnilova, and Alicia Markova—a dazzling roster of talents.

With my deep love for things visual, I was mesmerized by the magnificent, truly fantastic décor and scenery of Marc Chagall for the ballet *Aleko* (to the music of Tchaikovsky's Trio in A Minor, arranged by Erno Rapee) as well as—even more startling and controversial—Salvador Dali's designs for *Bacchanale*, set to Wagner's Venusberg music from *Tannhäuser*. But what really set the company apart in my opinion were the several superb ballets created by Antony Tudor, the absolute master of the modern narrative ballet. His sublime *Romeo and Juliet, Lilac Garden* (to Chausson's *Poème*) and *Pillar of Fire* (to Schönberg's *Transfigured Night*) were among the main staples of the company's repertory, ballets whose sheer beauty of choreographic composition, and depth and warmth of expression, have perhaps never been equaled, at least in that romantic-impressionist style.

I look back upon my three months with Ballet Theatre with great nostalgia and as an important transformative experience. There was only one problem, which developed and became quite serious as the tour progressed. That problem was Arthur Holmes. Arthur, my friend and most recent benefactor, as it were—he *did* help me get the Ballet job—happened to be the biggest collector of jokes, mostly dirty, that I have ever encountered. Horn players, even in a busy thirty-piece orchestra, have a fair amount of measures rest, sometimes as much as thirty or fifty bars, as well as lots of shorter (two- and four-bar) rests. Arthur had the uncanny ability to spread a joke across, say, a ten-bar rest, or perhaps a longer pause (depending on the length of the joke and the tempo of the music), *always* arriving at the punch line in the two or three final rest measures. Here we were, like two mischievous boys, ducked down behind our music stands so that Dorati wouldn't see us (not a smart idea to begin with), Arthur whispering his diabolical crudities at me.

I should confess that at home a joke rarely passed over anyone's lips, let alone dirty ones; and one of my serious disabilities is that I am totally incapable of telling and even remembering a joke—any joke. I have absolutely no idea what bred this unusual failing in me, but I am therefore an unfailingly good listener and inveterate enjoyer of jokes. And since I never can remember any, I can enjoy the same joke over and over again—a strange kind of bonus.

I was Arthur's captive. His endless repertory of jokes and limericks had me enthralled and laughing—or, more accurately, constantly suppressing my laughter, so as not to disturb the music. This stifling of guffaws was not so easy, especially when Arthur's punch line almost always came just before my next horn entrance. Somehow I never missed an entrance, although I came darn close a few times. Fearing that this situation was getting out of hand, and noticing Dorati's sometimes puzzled looks in my direction, I asked Arthur to stop telling me jokes during performances because I was sure I was going to get in trouble. But Arthur wouldn't stop. Over and over again: "Have you heard this one?" In desperation I'd say: "Oh yes, I know that one." But he knew I was lying. Off he'd go, launching into more crude ribaldry with a devastating punch line. He was very good at telling his jokes with an absolutely straight face. He was merciless.

I knew I would be caught out sooner or later and miss one of my entrances. You cannot play the horn while laughing; it is a physical impossibility. Eventually—and inevitably—one day in March, Dorati called me to his room, and with considerable annoyance in his voice asked me why I was always laughing. It suddenly dawned on me that Dorati took my laughter as a sign of disrespect—for him and for the music, and a sign of juvenile immaturity. I didn't defend myself or explain what was going on; I just couldn't snitch on Arthur. When he finally stopped his jokes, it was too late. A few days later Dorati told me that he would have to fire me at the end of the tour. In a surprisingly friendly tone, he said something to the effect of: look, you're a very talented fellow, but you have a lot to learn about orchestra behavior, and taking things more seriously. If he only knew how really serious I was. I apologized and left, much humbled, like a scolded dog, with my tail between my legs.

It was not the last time that my life's threads would intertwine with Dorati. I am happy to say that our careers intersected importantly half a dozen more times, even extending, as shall be seen, beyond his death in 1988.

I was bitterly disappointed, not so much for the humiliation of being fired, although that was bad enough, but because I had been eagerly looking forward to playing Ballet Theatre's spring season in New York, where the premiere of Anthony Tudor's *Romeo and Juliet* ballet was scheduled—Delius's works, with their glorious horn parts, being among my most favorite music.[4]

Being fired from my first permanent job rather took the wind out of my sails. Not a good start, I thought. Would it affect my chances to get other jobs? Was my reputation tarnished forever? My parents were, of course, very upset with me. I could never explain to them what had really happened. It was too unbelievable and sounded like a lame excuse, blaming someone else, a tactic I abhor and have tried never to employ in my adult life.

I had hardly settled in at home in Jamaica, trying to start composing, when I got a call from Mimi Caputo, a horn player at the Metropolitan Opera, asking me to join him in an orchestra just then being assembled to perform Gounod's *Romeo and Juliette* on a brief tour with the Hollywood star Jeanette McDonald. I had first met Caputo in 1941 when, as a fledgling fifteen-year-old horn player, I had participated in several Italian parades in downtown New York, making a munificent three dollars playing for about four hours while marching up and down the streets of Little Italy on Catholic religious holidays. I had run into Caputo a few more times since then on various odd jobs, and somehow, perhaps through him, word had gotten around among many of the top Italian-born horn players in New York that I loved opera, that even at my tender age I knew the operas well and could be reliably hired to substitute in opera horn sections.[5] Most of these Italian musicians had come to America in the mid-1920s. There were entire families of Italian-born musicians and horn players in New York—such as Corrado, Ricci, DeBiasi, Rescigno, and Caputo—who were all a vital part of the New York musicians' scene. One of their *capitanos* was Mimi Caputo, third horn at the Metropolitan Opera. As I say, Mimi had taken a real liking to me. I think he was amazed that this young American kid, with a German name, loved Italian opera so much and that he played through the opera vocal scores on the piano—which I did do regularly.

Jeannette McDonald was famous for her leading roles and pretty singing in a dozen or so MGM musicals. But in the early forties she saw her Hollywood career begin to decline, and broke with her studio. In the spring of 1943, at age forty-four, she decided as a sort of last fling to create an opera company as a vehicle to star in. She chose Gounod's *Romeo and Juliette*, excerpts of which she had sung in one of her recent film triumphs, *Rose Marie*. Mimi Caputo, who was going to be principal horn on that tour, recommended me for third horn. I was thrilled not only by this wonderful job opportunity but also to be able to travel and tour again, *and* make some good money.

Jeannette McDonald, who was completely in charge (having funded the enterprise mostly herself), hoped that her tour would lead to an engagement at the Met. She had selected the major cities of eastern Canada for the tour. I was worried that my parents wouldn't let me leave home so soon after my return from a three-month tour. I knew that they were still upset with me for being fired from the ballet orchestra, and wanted to keep me at home for a while, to keep me away from that big, bad outside world. I fought back, of course, arguing that my father had started to play with traveling orchestras when he was just fifteen: "How can you deny me a similar kind of opportunity?" In the end my parents did let me take the job (after some vigorous pleading by Caputo and Mr. Schulze, I found out). I know they also asked Mimi to keep a watchful eye on me and not let me get into any trouble.

That Ms. McDonald was very serious about this *Romeo and Juliette* project is evidenced by the fact that she hired some of the finest singers from the Met: Armand Tokatyan, a reigning lyric tenor of the thirties and forties, the great Ezio Pinza to sing the important although secondary role of Friar Laurence, and the Met's Wilfred Pelletier to conduct—all of them artists who did not come cheaply.

I was very happy, free from home, traveling, seeing the world, playing good music at a high professional level, and making new friends. Lifelong friendships were formed, notably the great harpist Gloria Agostini (who only recently passed away, after an astonishingly successful freelance career in New York); Harry Feigin, a first-rate violinist in the Met orchestra; the Cyprus-born Lebanese composer, Anis Fulcihan; Bill Gibson, later for many years principal trombonist of the Boston Symphony; and Arno Mariotti, a wonderful oboist from the Pittsburgh Symphony. Travel this time was by luxurious trains—no rickety trains or buses for Jeanette's high-class tour. I remember the minute we crossed the border from New York into Montreal how startled I was once again to find how different Canada looked and felt, even just glancing out the window of the train. It was so much cleaner; the fields and pastures and woods were well groomed, the towns and villages neat and picturesque, quite French in style and architecture. I was thrilled to visit again beautiful Montreal and sample its superb French cuisine. Once again I haunted the great bookshops, and on the several free nights we had I went to see some great French films (by Marcel Carné, Julien Duvivier, and Jean Renoir), surprisingly racy and daring with their distinctly erotic undertone—surprising because in that part of Canada the Catholic-controlled Film Board was famous for censoring or expurgating films that it deemed licentious and prurient.

Ontario, with its major cities of Toronto, London, and Windsor, and the capital Ottawa—where we also played—were by contrast quite English in their history and character, entirely different from the province of Quebec. I enjoyed this quiet British atmosphere—although the food was again pretty ordinary. On the other hand, I heard a lot of good jazz in Toronto in the several fine clubs along Yonge Street and at the legendary Casa Loma ballroom.

Jeanette MacDonald did very well, I thought, singing and acting with considerable taste and style, something I hadn't anticipated, given her usual cutesy, frilly cavorting in the MGM movies. I found out during the tour that she had been coached to the nines by Léon Rothier, a great French bass recently retired from the Metropolitan Opera, and that she had studied with Alicia Markova, the great ballerina of the Ballet Theatre (also diligently studying some of Markova's films). All in all, with her flowing red hair and incredibly sparkling eyes, McDonald made quite an impression on me and on many of us in the orchestra. I thought the three-week tour offered excellent performances, garnered good audience attendance, and seemed to be on the whole a fine artistic success. But for Jeanette McDonald it was a disappointment, because her costs in financing the whole venture exceeded the income, and because, in the end, the venture did not lead to the hoped for rejuvenation of her operatic career.

Back home, I returned quickly to my usual rounds of practicing, composing, studying scores, reading, attending Philharmonic concerts at the Lewisohn Stadium—not to mention many happy, carefree days in Rocky Point tending my mother's iris, portulacca, and nicotiana garden. I also had a catch-up lesson with Mr. Schulze, who hadn't heard me play in almost a year. He was more than pleased, and told me that there was nothing more that he could teach me.

It was during this period, on one of my frequent visits to the Liberty Record Shop, that I met a remarkable person and musician. I was browsing, as usual on the lookout for some new recorded treasure, hesitating about buying a recording of Debussy's astounding piano prelude, *La Puerta del vino*—a musical representation of the Wine Gate in the Alhambra in Seville, Spain. The particular recording I was looking at was by a well-known pianist of that time, George Copeland, unfortunately now completely forgotten. A tall, lanky, very distinguished looking man standing near me suddenly said: "That's a very good recording. Don't hesitate to buy it. I know that pianist." We started chatting, exchanging typical record collectors' talk. I learned that the gentleman was Prince George Chavchavadze and, discovering that we had so many likes (and dislikes) in common, within half an hour felt that I had known him all my life. Obviously wealthy and upper class, he was also a pianist—he called himself a quite good amateur—who annually played a solo recital in Town Hall.[6] Chavchavadze, who had left Russia in the mid-1920s, was of the legendary royal first family of the ancient kingdom of Georgia, a country annexed by the Soviet Union in 1921. He now lived alone on a large estate near Princeton, New Jersey. Before we parted company he invited me to visit him and to bring my horn along, so we could play some music together, maybe even Beethoven's Horn Sonata.

By now I was a bit leery of any invitation by a single male, having been accosted several times by one of the orchestra musicians on the McDonald tour, and, of course, remembering some of my earlier encounters on the Ballet Theatre tour. But on a hunch—which turned out to be correct—that George was not a homosexual, at least not the aggressive cruising type, I accepted his invitation. My parents, mightily impressed by the princely status and apparent wealth of my new friend, encouraged me to visit him. I traveled from Queens to southern New Jersey several times that summer, where he wined and dined me liberally; several servants and wait staff practically caught the crumbs that I might drop before they hit the floor. George's two spacious, palatial, forty- to fifty-foot living rooms—one was the designated music room—were filled with marvelous paintings, sculptures (I remember two Giacomettis), several indoor fountains, beautiful antiques, and priceless Flemish tapestries. The place was a museum. I didn't see anything like that again until years later, visiting with Prince von Fürstenberg in his castle in Donaueschingen, Germany, or in Isabella Gardner's home-turned-into-a-museum in Boston.

After lunch George and I retreated to the music room and made some wonderful music together: Beethoven's Horn Sonata, two of Mozart's horn concertos, and one by Haydn. I learned that George was a wonderfully musical, intelligent, sensitive musician, for it was as if we had been playing together for years. His favorite composer was Chopin, and after a while he suggested that we improvise together in the style of Chopin. In a flash he worked up a little Chopinesque four-bar motive, on which we improvised at length, building in effect a ten-minute composition, a rather good one at that, I thought.

On one of my subsequent visits, George, who owned state-of-the-art recording equipment for cutting twelve- or ten-inch acetate discs, recorded a few of our extemporizations. (I am sure that I still have one of them somewhere in my huge record collection.) I wonder how well those improvisations of sixty-eight years ago turned out. I can remember that it was a wonderful, strangely liberating, exhilarating experience, listening sensitively to each other, feeding each other little ideas and building upon them, coordinating on exciting climaxes or calm, reposeful passages.

On another visit George surprised me by introducing me to George Copeland, whom he had invited for lunch and an afternoon of music making. The two pianists played some of Schubert's marvelous four-hand piano duets, and Copeland, at my request, played several of Debussy's preludes for me, including the fabulous *La Puerta del vino*, with its remarkable bitonal theme (hauntingly combining D-flat major and E minor), in its sombre evocation of that ancient gate in Spain's Alhambra. Copeland not only knew Debussy personally but was also, along with Howard Goding (for nearly half a century on the faculty of the piano department of the New England Conservatory), one of the very first to introduce Debussy's piano music to American audiences.

Bruno Jänicke had just retired from the New York Philharmonic, and it occurred to me that this might be the best—perhaps the only—time to try to get a lesson or two with him. After some pleading by my father and Mr. Schulze—for many years the incredibly busy Jänicke had declined to do any teaching, passing supplicants on to his brother-in-law, Robert Schulze—he consented to give me a hearing and suggested that I meet him in the Philharmonic's musicians' lounge in Carnegie Hall. Those were precious moments, to finally be with my revered idol and to receive not only his advice but also, as it turned out, his blessings. My playing was so much modeled after his, in musical, artistic, expressive terms, that I thought he was bound to be pleased. We went through most of the famous horn solo passages and excerpts. He said very little, but once in a while, in his quiet, soft-spoken way, he murmured, "sehr schön, sehr musikalisch (very beautiful, very musical)."

In that lesson I told him that I had copied out, note for note, the entire first horn part of both Debussy's *La Mer* and *Iberia*. To my delight, my second lesson consisted entirely of Jänicke having me play completely through both works, interrupting a few times for a bit of advice, mostly about playing with more line, more inner continuity. At the end he patted me on the shoulder and said in German: "Wonderful, you will go far," and added, "you made me very happy." Mr. Schulze, who had also dropped by, was beaming, looking mighty proud.

A few years ago, I received a letter from Bill Vacchiano, my longtime friend and famous principal trumpet of the New York Philharmonic, in which he reminded me that by chance he had gotten something from his locker in the lounge during that Debussy lesson, and that, listening a few minutes to my playing, he knew that I was ready for the big time.

And perhaps I really was. In the midst of my composing, studying, and record collecting, in the early summer of 1943 I was suddenly asked to audition for three different job openings—in the Philadelphia, Pittsburgh, and Cincinnati orchestras. The respective conductors and auditioners were Eugene Ormandy, Fritz Reiner, and Eugene Goossens, a formidable trio of interrogators.

The audition for Ormandy was held on the big stage of Carnegie Hall. Although I had already played there a few times, it was still an awe-inspiring and intimidating place for me. Because my father and Ormandy were longtime friends, from the days when they had sat next to each other (in 1928) in the violin section of the Roxy Theatre orchestra (on Broadway), Ormandy had invited my father to the audition, an unusual thing to do. That made me a bit more nervous because now I had to prove myself to my father as well as Ormandy, a whole other psychological pressure. But the audition went very well, and Ormandy was quite complimentary. I found out that the opening was for assistant first horn, playing next to Mason Jones, who had just recently joined the Philadelphia Orchestra as principal horn.

My next audition was for Fritz Reiner. For that one I had to travel to Reiner's home in Westport, Connecticut, a two-hour-plus trip involving a bus ride, two subways, a train ride to Westport, and a fifteen-minute walk from the train station to Reiner's summer cottage. Since the audition was set for nine in the morning, it meant I had to leave Jamaica around six thirty. That left no time for me to warm up—a ten- to twenty-minute daily ritual for brass players before any kind of performing, especially in the morning.

When I arrived at Reiner's house, I was met by a maid and, in a virtually exact rerun of the audition for Dorati six months earlier, I was asked to sit down and wait in the living room. No sleeping baby this time.

The reader may not know what all musicians of that era knew only too well, that among the tyrannical, ill-tempered conductors that roamed the earth from the 1920s to the 1960s, Reiner was the most feared of all. On the other hand, Reiner was one of the greatest musicians and baton technicians of all time. He knew his scores as well or better than anyone, down to the most miniscule details of notation. Thus, out of a combination of fear and respect for Reiner's knowledge and his supreme technical skills, one tended to play one's absolute best for him. In fact, you had better, or else you didn't survive. Auditioning for Reiner was one of the most dreaded experiences a musician could encounter. And if you survived his clinical scrutiny, you had a right to feel that you were pretty good.

At last, after about fifteen minutes Reiner appeared, not looking terribly happy. (He rarely did anyway.) Given his normally sour-looking disposition and his genius at intimidating musicians, I don't doubt that he purposely kept me waiting just to test my nerves. With Reiner everything was a test as to who would come out on top. Everything was a confrontation, albeit a quiet, stealthy one. I was about to face one of these Reiner tests. Dear reader, you will recall that I had had no opportunity to warm up for the audition. Without inquiring whether I had or suggesting that I might want to warm up, he scowled at me and in his thick Hungarian accent, and in an annoyed, peremptory tone, told me to play the *Siegfried* Call (from Wagner's opera *Siegfried*), one of the most difficult, most feared, and most celebrated horn solos in the entire orchestral literature. It was certainly so regarded by horn players in those years, and more kindly disposed conductors, knowing of that excerpt's difficulty, would work up to it in an audition, not ask for it at the first crack out of the box. But this was Reiner; that was his way of testing you, to see if and how you would stand up to pressure.

The gods were with me that morning, for I nailed that fearsome solo without a hitch. Not that Reiner would show any approbation or give you any hint that he might have been impressed or pleased. Without any comment, he proceeded to take me through a number of other famous horn passages, had me sight-read some more obscure material (I don't recall what), eventually reaching the final Reiner test, which often became the *coup de grace*—swift elimination—for players who hadn't done their homework quite well enough—even if they had up to that point done reasonably well in the audition.

As I've mentioned earlier, Reiner knew every fly speck in any score that he conducted, *all* the especially difficult passages, difficult technically or difficult to sight-read. These were usually obscure little excerpts, not even of any special importance, tucked away in some hidden corner of a score, and usually not in the first horn part, but, say, in the fourth or sixth horn (as in Wagner's *Ring* operas). One of Reiner's favorite impossible-to-sight-read testing passages occurs in the fourth horn part in Wagner's *Siegfried*, a little bit of Wagnerian playfulness, tossing around a motive from the famous *Ride of the Walkyries* in a variety of different transpositions and registers. The particular variant Reiner picked is notated, unlike 98 percent of all horn parts, *in the bass clef* and, worse yet, in one of the rarest of all transpositions, B natural, sounding a diminished fifth away from the notated pitch. It is an absolute brain twister that no one can sight-read, especially when rattled, nervous, and brain-numbed at an audition.

But I knew something like this was coming, and I was ready for Reiner, Mr. Schulze having warned me about many of Reiner's audition tricks. And in any case I had long ago completely devoured the ten volumes of horn excerpts, published in Germany in the 1920s, that were considered a basic, not-to-be-overlooked part of your study regimen, and that included every obscure excerpt one might ever encounter. I knew the excerpt Reiner asked for cold, and delivered it without a hitch. I knew I had won the contest; I had outjousted him. Not given to compliments, Reiner did at least give me his Edward G. Robinson-Al Capone grin—not a pretty sight—and a mild grunt. But it was something.

For the third audition that summer (with Eugene Goossens) I had to fly to Cincinnati. And it was about as different from Reiner's torturous audition as anything could be, Goossens being the patrician English gentleman who treated you not as an adversary but as a colleague and musical partner. I arrived a bit early for the audition and was asked to make myself comfortable and warm up in an anteroom, next to the stage of Cincinnati's cavernous, acoustically very live Music Hall. As part of my warm up I played through some excerpts that I knew I would be asked to play, and in addition, on the spur of the moment, threw in a fantastically heroic, lengthy passage from one of Strauss's late operas, *Daphne*, premiered in Germany in 1938. That opera had not yet been played in the United States; even in Germany (and Europe) it had received very few performances, undoubtedly because of the war that broke out in 1939. It was therefore still quite unknown in musical circles, but especially in America. But I had heard in my father's record collection (consisting mostly of imported German recordings that he used to buy in Yorkville) the only so-far recorded excerpt from *Daphne*, the opera's final scene. It featured, as always in Strauss's operas, the most amazing, challenging horn writing. I had played that recording often, so that I had it completely memorized and copied into one of my music notebooks. What was especially challenging about this lengthy passage was that it was entirely in the always tricky key of F-sharp major.

At the actual audition, after playing a few of the required excerpts, Goosens suddenly turned to me and said: "By the way, what was that you were playing back there? It was some Strauss, wasn't it?" I told him that indeed it was, but before I could tell him what it was, he interrupted me: "But that can't be. My dear boy, I know all of Strauss's orchestral music." Well, in this case, he didn't. And when I told him that what I had played was an excerpt from the final scene of Strauss's *Daphne*, he was a bit stunned. But I could see that he was also quite impressed; and it could be that I won the audition right then and there.

I may have also impressed him by my offering to play some horn solo excerpts from memory—just like my father had done with Stransky in 1923—specifically from two recordings Goossens and the Cincinnati Symphony had made just a year earlier, and which I had bought the minute they came out, that is, William Walton's Violin Concerto and Louis Gruenberg's Violin Concerto, both superb recordings with Jascha Heifetz as soloist. Goossens could certainly tell from my audition that I was interested in an unusually wide range of music, way beyond merely the standard orchestra horn parts.

As it turned out I had passed all three auditions. That is to say, I received word from the three personnel managers that the job was mine if I wanted it. Because the Philadelphia opening was for assistant horn, the Pittsburgh opening for third horn, but the Cincinnati position for principal (first) horn, the reader can well imagine which offer I accepted. Also, I had immediately formed a wonderful impression of Goossens, not only as a fine conductor whose work I already knew from a great number of excellent recordings—but also as a first-rate composer; I admired very much several of his chamber works and songs. But now I saw him also as a kindly, unpretentious gentleman, apparently so unlike the many standoffish, haughty, domineering conductor types of that era.

It was unusual for a music director to pick a teenage musician to fill a principal chair, particularly with someone who had not yet had any regular or consistent symphonic experience. To take an apparently inexperienced musician was considered risky, and I am eternally grateful to Goossens for having the courage to take a chance with me.

Off I went to Cincinnati in October 1943, still only seventeen years old, taking the place of my much admired Weldon Wilber, who had so inspired me that summer day a year earlier, as well as in his recordings with the Cincinnati Symphony: the Walton Violin Concerto and the Vaughan Williams *London Symphony*.

I count the two years I spent in Cincinnati as among the very happiest, the most stimulating, the most mind- and soul-expanding of my altogether very happy, exciting, rewarding life. I was very young and impressionable when I arrived there. Playing with the excellent Cincinnati Symphony and its world-class conductor, getting deeply involved with jazz, forming new friendships with some remarkable individuals, who in certain cases became important mentors for me, and—above all—meeting my wife-to-be, my adored Marjorie, these were all momentous developments in my artistic and personal growth.

The happy excitement began with my very first concert, for which Goossens had programmed Respighi's *Pines of Rome*, Beethoven's Seventh Symphony, Schönberg's orchestration of Bach's "St. Anne" Prelude and Fugue, as well as a little-known *Overture on Russian Themes* by Balakirev. The program was a horn player's feast, and I often wondered whether Goossens chose the Beethoven, Respighi, and the massive Bach-Schönberg, with its many prominent, highly exposed horn parts, all on the same program, to show off his new youthful horn playing find.

I had a very secure and easy high register on the horn, always the danger zone—the death zone—in horn playing. At least it was regarded so in those days, when we all played what are called double horns, and never resorted to the descant or piccolo horns that are the vogue nowadays whenever any high stratospheric horn parts show up. In my day we even played Bach's first *Brandenburg Concerto* on our big instruments; we didn't know any better. It wasn't until I stopped playing in 1962 that lots of new horn makes, descant horns and eventually triple horns, came into prominence, which certainly made the entire baroque and early classical literature a lot easier and safer to play.

As the reader and any music lover knows, horn players constantly live with the reality that, as far as audiences are concerned, the old bromide applies: If they get the note, nobody hears it; but if they should miss it, the whole world hears it. In any case, the relatively high notes—high concert Es—that occur in the Beethoven Seventh and Respighi's *Pines* were no problem for me. I could play them securely and, if required by the composer, softly, which quite a few horn players by virtue of their particular embouchures or physical set ups could not do so easily. In that first week of rehearsals I saw many of the orchestra players' heads turn admiringly toward me. This was a welcome sign of approval, coming from my new colleagues and peers. But above all I was happy that I could satisfy both the music's and my conductor's highest expectations.

In that season-opening week I also heard the playing of Walter Heermann for the first time, the orchestra's principal cellist. His playing of the short four-bar cello solo in the third movement of the *Pines of Rome* gave me goose bumps. As often as I have heard those four bars since then, live and on recordings, I have never heard them played as beautifully, as soulfully, and with such inner intensity as in Walter's rendition. I knew immediately that this was one musician whom I would have to seek out and get to know well.

As a young composer, still learning, still absorbing, I was feasting on Goossens's wonderfully rich and varied programs. In my two seasons, 1943–45, I had the privilege of playing such important masterpieces as Debussy's *La Mer*, Strauss's *Till Eulenspiegel* and the final scene of *Salomé*, De Falla's *Nights in the Gardens of Spain*, Dukas's *La Peri*, Elgar's marvelous *Falstaff*, along with most of the standard repertory staples of Beethoven, Mozart, Brahms, Tchaikovsky, Rachmaninov, and Wagner. Among other orchestral delicacies, Goossens programmed a number of rarely played Haydn symphonies (including No. 55, *The Schoolmaster*; No. 48, *Maria Theresa*; No. 83, *The Hen*; No. 85, *La Reine de France*), also Jaromir Weinberger's now forgotten but then very popular *Variations on "Under the Spreading Chestnut Tree,"* Dohnanyi's *Variations on a Nursery Tune*, Berlioz's *Harold in Italy*, Mahler's *Lied von der Erde*, Tchaikovsky's *Manfred* Symphony, Bruckner's Fourth Symphony, Walter Piston's wonderfully witty *The Incredible Flutist* (which I already knew well from Arthur Fiedler's excellent late-1930s recording), Shostakovich's Seventh Symphony (the second time for me), Ravel's *Daphnis et Chloe* Suite, and Goossens's own exquisite orchestration of Ravel's *Le Gibet* (from *Gaspard de la nuit*). I recall so many wonderful concerts, in particular an all-Wagner program with the remarkably gifted, then very young Astrid Varnay and the inimitable, unique Lauritz Melchior (whose many great Wagner recordings were already well represented in my record library), also a stunning all-Rachmaninov program with *Isle of the Dead* (my favorite) and the two Rachmaninov "Seconds" (Symphony and Piano Concerto). What a sensual musical orgy that was!

Sixty-plus years later this sort of diverse programming may not seem so unusual. But in the thirties and forties, when the entire known orchestral literature was much more limited, Goossens's programming clearly attested to his catholic tastes and his desire to interest various classes of listeners; it revealed, as *Musical Courier*, a leading weekly music magazine of the time, put it, "Goossens's rare music directorial zeal and resourcefulness."[7] Goossens would cannily bring together in almost every concert the important, the well established and familiar with the novel and lesser known, always in a nicely balanced construction. The program novelty was often not only a new or modern work but just as often some celebrated composer's fine composition that was neglected and rarely or never performed (as with Balakirev's *Overture* and the Bach-Schönberg). Goossens frequently included many early- and middle-period Haydn symphonies (many of them with very scary high horn parts), at a time when other conductors scheduled only a few of the very familiar late "London" Symphonies. For many years after I left the Cincinnati Symphony, I would hear some relatively obscure but superb piece of music and be instantly reminded that, oh yes, I had played that composition with Goossens back in the 1940s. He not only designed fine programs; during the two years that I was with him he also wrote the orchestra's program notes every week, excellent informative annotations by a highly intelligent, vastly experienced composer-conductor, felicitously bringing his insights to the orchestra's patrons.

Our soloists in those two years were superb artists such as Fritz Kreisler (playing the Brahms Violin Concerto), Jascha Heifetz (in the Gruenberg Violin Concerto), Artur Rubinstein, Claudio

Arrau, Jose Iturbi, Zino Francescatti, Marjorie Lawrence, Lauritz Melchior, Ezio Pinza, and Kerstin Thorborg, to name just some of the greatest of that era.

For me, both as a young orchestra player and as a budding composer, getting to play so much great but rarely performed music was not only an invaluable professional experience but also decidedly educational. Even the relatively minor Balakirev *Overture on Russian Themes* taught me two quick lessons. I had always assumed, as did all my fellow musicians, that the popular main theme of Tchaikovsky's Fourth Symphony last movement and the familiar F major 6/4 melody in the final tableau of Stravinsky's *Petroushka* to be original with those two composers. Wrong! Balakirev's piece, based on authentic Russian folk songs, used those two melodies liberally. It taught me an instant lesson that I probably could only have learned in a university ethnomusicology course.

I was thrilled to find out that I had inherited a very fine horn section. My second horn partner, Mathias Kuhn, Hungarian-born and in his midforties, was a most meticulous, fastidious player, who had been brought to Cincinnati by Fritz Reiner in the 1920s. Within the first few rehearsals I saw that he was an ideal second horn; not only did he know how to blend with the first horn but he was eager to do so—not necessarily true of all second horn players, especially those who really want to be first horn. The fourth horn, Hans Lind, a German in his late fifties, was also very conscious of providing a rich bottom for the section. My assistant, Gustav Albrecht, had studied and played in Vienna in the late nineteenth century, working with the almighty Brahms himself. In America he played with the Boston Opera Company and with Sousa's famous band, as well as with the Metropolitan Opera (in 1908) under Toscanini and Mahler—a remarkable career for such a young man. Albrecht came to Cincinnati in 1909, and was principal horn in Cincinnati in Ysaÿe's and Reiner's time. Now, in his midsixties, he was a bit past his prime, and I couldn't always rely on him to relieve me (the basic function of an assistant first horn); but since I was so eager to play every note anyway and had good endurance, I really didn't mind. What concerned me more the first few days was that, as an older player with a long, distinguished professional career, Albrecht might resent me a little; perhaps he wondered who this young, inexperienced whippersnapper thinks he is, and whether I would come up to the established high standards of the section. But I saw quickly that he was a very kindly man and genuinely appreciated my playing, doting on my achievements like a proud father, perhaps even seeing in me a reprise of his own early career. Ours was a relationship of true mutual admiration.

The third horn, Joseph Freni, was a fine player, and we quickly became close friends. But he was drafted in mid-1944, and was replaced in my second season by Hilbert Moses. Hilbert, a young man in his twenties, was largely self-taught and a protégé of Weldon Wilber, although his style of playing was a bit more individualistic, rather on the rough and blustery side. But within a few weeks he had tamed down his playing to fit well with Mat Kuhn and me. We hit it off well—we were both much younger than the rest of the orchestra—and, most significant, he was also very interested in jazz and had a real feel for it at a time when most horn players were barely aware of the *existence* of jazz.

As principal horn of the orchestra I was automatically appointed horn teacher at both the Cincinnati College of Music and the Cincinnati Conservatory.[8] The unusual aspect of my faculty appointment was that at age seventeen, about to turn eighteen, I was younger than any of the students in the two schools. Because of the wartime draft, the male student population was fairly decimated, leaving an abundance of young lady singers, pianists, flutists, and violinists. In a few weeks after my arrival in Cincinnati I became aware that a Gunther fan club had sprung up at the college. Not being impervious to female charms and interests, my awareness of this bevy of silent admirers added another welcome dimension to my newly liberated sense of freedom and unfettered independence.

But perhaps it wasn't quite as unfettered as I at first assumed. Unbeknownst to me, my father, who knew many of the German musicians in the orchestra from the old country, had called a number of them to ask that they keep a watchful eye on me so that I wouldn't fall prey to some avaricious, scheming, husband-hunting female. My father's closest friend in the orchestra was Henry Wohlgemuth (real first name, Helmut), the orchestra's principal trumpet, whom my father had known since 1923, when both (new American immigrants) played in the New York Symphony under Josef Stransky. Henry was a wonderful player with a beautiful, rich, warm, perfectly centered tone, representing the best of the old, late nineteenth-century German school of brass playing. I soon learned that Henry had been particularly singled out by my parents to keep me from going astray. Wohlgemuth, bless him, did not take his assignment all that seriously and, having been quite an oat-sowing rogue himself in his younger years, was not about to stifle my ardent youthful ambitions. Henry and I became very good friends—we always communicated in German—and I learned a lot from him. And I came to greatly admire his remarkably warm, absolutely secure way of playing the trumpet.[9]

Wohlgemuth took me out to dinner a few times in those early weeks after my joining the orchestra. One time, when we were eating at Mecklenberg's, the ultimate German-style beer garden and restaurant, I asked him why so many German immigrants had settled in Cincinnati. He thought it was mostly because of Cincinnati's topography and geographic location, which reminded the nineteenth-century German immigrants of their homeland, especially of their storied Rhineland. As they came along the Ohio River from the east and reached the region around the present Cincinnati, seeing its famous seven hills and the river below snaking its way through steeply sloping hillsides on both the Ohio and Kentucky sides, they really thought they were back home on the Rhine, with its legendary ancient vineyards (dating back to Roman times) and tiny villages clinging to the steep slopes and narrow shorelines. Wohlgemuth told me that if you look up from the Ohio River to the ring of seven hills above or, conversely, look down from them at the river below, it is like viewing any number of fabled sights around Koblenz or the wine region of Rhein-Hessen near Bingen. In truth, having traveled up and down the lower Rhine myself many times in my childhood, and visited a few of the several dozen castles and castle ruins perched on the hilly slopes, driving down from Eden Park toward downtown Cincinnati gave me each time an uncanny sense of déjà vu.

Wohlgemuth had joined the Cincinnati Symphony in 1924, a few years after Fritz Reiner had become music director of the orchestra. I asked him what it was like working for Reiner in those days. I was greeted with a torrent of stories that confirmed every horror tale I had ever heard about Reiner. In summary: "Oh, he was impossible! You lived in fear of your life every day. Listen to this: five of my brass playing colleagues and closest friends from this orchestra are now a long time out of music." He explained that their confidence and spirit were broken by Reiner's constantly haranguing and riding them until they became so nervous that their embouchures began to shake uncontrollably. Eventually, no longer able to play at a professional level, they had to retire from the orchestra or were let go. "Two of those guys are now in sanatoriums with serious mental conditions." After a while Wohlgemuth added: "But, of course, Reiner was a fantastic conductor, and when we weren't nervous wrecks we played like a really great orchestra. He made you play your best; but if you couldn't take the pressure, you were in trouble."

The College of Music—long gone now (there is a parking lot in its place)—was directly adjacent to Music Hall, in fact attached to the building so that one could go from the hall's second balcony through a door common to both buildings to the college's second floor. This door, generally locked from the college side, could—as someone discovered—be opened from the music hall side, a discovery that provided the girls who lived in the college's dormitory free access to the Symphony's concerts—that is, until a group of them were caught sneaking through that secret door. But maybe that door unwittingly played a crucial role in bringing two souls together that otherwise only the stars or destiny itself could have conspired to unite.

It happened in my second week of concerts in Cincinnati. Just as the Saturday night concert was about to begin and Goossens was ready to come on stage, I noticed that one section of the first balcony overlooking the orchestra, very sparsely populated the week before during the first set of concerts, was this time suddenly invaded by a dozen young females. A few minutes later, when the concert had begun, I caught a glimpse of an extraordinarily beautiful girl listening very intently to the music.

I'll never, never forget that moment. It was October 16, 1943, only my second week in Cincinnati. I couldn't take my eyes off her. The last work on the program was, of all pieces, Tchaikovsky's Fifth Symphony, with the famous horn solo in the second movement. It is quite a long exposed passage, one that is bound to attract even the most passive listener's attention. It is preceded by seven bars of the most poignantly inviting introductory music—played by the strings—and it was during those somewhat anxious thirty seconds that I fixed my eyes on that enchanting vision up there in the balcony and played the entire solo to her. Time and again, during the rest of that symphony, I kept thinking that this young lady was somebody I absolutely had to meet. But how?

Beside me there was one other newcomer to the Cincinnati Symphony that season: Sammy Green, the tuba player. Sammy was not only a fine player, and like me an import from New York—a Juilliard student of the great William Bell—but also (as we all quickly learned) the orchestra's comic character, punster, and jokester, with a line of old tried-and-true jokes and quips, which he somehow, with his Jewish sense of humor and well-timed delivery, managed to recycle endlessly. Underneath Sammy's brusque exterior there beat a heart of gold; he was a real sweetheart. His handshake, however, would bring you to your knees.[10]

Sammy and I were roommates in a two-story rooming house on Highland Avenue near the corner of MacMillan, a house owned by an elderly couple. Sammy and I shared the upper floor, reachable through an outside wooden staircase, each of us with one large room and a common bathroom. We were given to understand that no lady visitors would be allowed after dark. There were no kitchen facilities, so we had to fend for ourselves for food, most often at a chili place on the corner or at the YMCA near the Music Hall. Breakfast was disposed of quickly and most rewardingly every working day after a short ride on the Vine Street streetcar, in a tiny hole-in-the-wall cafe near Music Hall that served the *best* sugar buns I have ever had in my entire life.

With Sammy as a roommate and, for the most part, also my steady companion, I was relentlessly subjected to his extensive repertory of puns and jokes, although this time not to the extent of jeopardizing my job as in the Ballet Theatre Arthur Holmes episode. Sammy was a single, late-born child whose father had died young and whose mother was now quite old. I gathered that she and Sammy didn't have much of a relationship, and I think he took the job in Cincinnati mainly to get away from his nagging "Jewish mother" rather than working in New York. The Greens were very poor, so poor that Sammy didn't own and could not even afford to buy a proper full dress and white shirt, which, of course, is what musicians were obliged to wear in concerts—at least in those years. My mother had accompanied me to Cincinnati for my first week there, and so naturally she got to know my new roommate. Within days she came under the spell of Sammy's weird sense of humor and crazy Chaplinesque antics. When she found out that he didn't have full dress clothes for his upcoming first concert with the orchestra, she took pity on him and, on her own initiative, borrowed an ancient tailcoat from Wohlgemuth that he found in his attic. A minor problem was that its tapering skirts turned out to be much too short. But since musicians sit while playing in an orchestra, nobody would be able to see Sammy's curtailed tails. Even worse, instead of a real dress shirt, Sammy had bought himself a piece of white cloth-covered cardboard—all he could afford—that hung around his neck and was supposed to be attached to the upper edge of his tuxedo trousers. But the cardboard also turned out to be too short. Since tuba players play with their instrument on their lap, Sammy thought he could hide the fake shirt behind his tuba, thus also holding the shirt in place. What he hadn't anticipated was that every time he turned a page in his part he had to set his tuba down on the floor—also during long periods of rests, of which there are many in tuba parts—the cardboard shirt, being unattached at the bottom, would curve and roll upward, slapping Sammy in the chin. Talk about a Chaplin gag! Now his undershirt was exposed to the whole audience. Sammy would try to tuck the fake shirt back down, but as soon as he would pick up his tuba for his next entrance, not having three hands—two to pick up the tuba, one to hold down the cardboard shirt—it would snap back up. It was a riot! Breaking up with laughter inwardly, I don't know how some of us near him in the brass section kept playing. Thank God there was no tuba in Beethoven's Seventh Symphony. Sammy finally figured out that in the entire *Pines of Rome*, the last piece on the program, he would not be able to put his tuba down at all. He had Bill Wilkins, third trombone sitting right next to him, turn pages for him.

It was lucky that Goossens didn't see any of this comedy going on. Sammy would have been seriously reprimanded. By the second week he had scrounged up some cash to buy a proper full dress and shirt. (This was in the days before credit cards.)

In the meantime, in the course of the passing weeks I met quite a few of the college's female students (although not the beautiful girl I had spied in the second balcony), mostly singers and pianists, among them Paula Lenchner, a singer who ended up a few years later, like me, at the Metropolitan Opera, and Nell Foster, another soprano associated for many years with the Chicago Lyric Opera. Gradually I became aware that I was becoming a target of some interest for these attractive young ladies, a whole new and unexpected experience for me. I guess—I say this with all modesty—I was considered handsome, talented, presumably amorously unattached, and potentially available. Also, I had quickly become the youthful star of the orchestra, the principal horn being a position that, if well represented, lends itself to a degree of adulation, if nothing else simply because of its exposed prominence in any orchestra and the horn's legendary difficulty. It didn't hurt that the major music critic in Cincinnati (on the *Enquirer*) singled me out quite a few times, praising my playing. I was by far the youngest member of the orchestra, most of the players being in their fifties and sixties, brought to Cincinnati in their late twenties during Reiner's regime. So I really stood out in various ways and became the talk of the town, at least in musical and artistic circles.

After the orchestra's Friday afternoon concerts, it was a long-standing tradition for the college to host a little reception in the students' lounge for the week's soloist, or for Goossens when there was no soloist. It was called the symphony tea. About four weeks into the season, I decided to go to one of these receptions. Artur Rubinstein was the guest of honor that week, having just played Beethoven's G Major Piano Concerto, and the students came out in force to see and chat with the renowned pianist and legendary raconteur. Rubinstein was at his best, obviously turned on by the adulation of so many attractive young ladies, charming them with his Chevalier-like, soft Polish-French accent. (Rubinstein spoke eight languages fluently, but except for his native Polish, all were spoken with a certain French flavor). He even accommodated some of the piano students by discussing how and why he played the Beethoven Concerto's unusual *a cappella* opening the way he did.[11] He even sat down and played that opening passage in three different ways, all very logical and beautiful. I listened with fascination: an early lesson for me in how a given phrase or musical idea could be rendered in *subtly* different yet acceptable ways (emphasis on the word "subtly").

In the meantime I had spotted the beautiful girl in the second balcony amongst those clustered around Rubinstein and the Steinway grand, listening intently to his very interesting interpretational demonstration. I assumed she was a pianist, but found out later that she was also a singer, a soprano, and thus enrolled as a double major at the college. I was much too shy to approach her; that would take working up some courage. But I was very happy just to be able to observe her from a distance—she was so impossibly beautiful, not just pretty. There was something deep and warm and open about her that fascinated me, especially in her eyes.

I have always been a rather private person, even in my public life, keeping my feelings and thoughts to myself. I didn't even tell Sammy about my new-found inamorata. I hadn't even learned her name yet.

Most of us on the college faculty or in the symphony orchestra, as well as many of the students, took lunch in the nearby YMCA dining room, the most reasonably priced eating place in the immediate neighborhood. There were usually enough of us to occupy at least three large round tables, each seating eight people. Not only I but practically every student wanted to sit with Walter Heermann, unquestionably the most popular teacher in the entire college. He and I had immediately become friends, true friends, not just colleagues or acquaintances, even though there was a thirty-eight-year difference in our ages. I really think most of the girl students and young female faculty were in love with Walter, a bachelor widower whose wife had died many years earlier. "Everybody loves Walter Heermann," sung to the main theme of Tchaikovsky's Fourth Symphony last movement (the same tune as in the Balakirev *Overture*),

was practically the college's school song. Walter was a

marvelous teacher who really loved teaching; he was a warm, friendly, positive person, always with a ready, natural smile, constantly entertaining us at meals with stories of his youth in Germany—meeting Brahms as a child, emigrating to America, his years with Stokowski in the 1910s, later with Reiner and, of course, Goossens. Add to that his many stories about the hundreds of great soloists he had worked with over the years, and you had a walking, living, treasure house reflecting the rich cultural history of Cincinnati in the early part of the twentieth century.

Around this same time, I met a young violinist and conducting student of Walter Heermann who was visiting Cincinnati on a week's leave from the navy. Roland Johnson not only became one of my best friends and colleagues but also played a significant role in my young life as a composer by commissioning and premiering one of my earliest orchestral works. He was also responsible for my getting to know the person who is to this day my very closest friend, the composer Robert DiDomenica, who was in the navy with Roland in 1944–46. When Walter, after his Cincinnati stint, became conductor of the Madison (Wisconsin) Symphony and eventually retired, Roland Johnson took his place, continuing to lead that orchestra until the midnineties.

I kept hoping that Marjorie—that was the young beauty's name—would appear at our lunches, but she never did. It turned out that her parents had paid for her food needs as part of the tuition, and thus she always ate in the college's small cafeteria. My determination to find some way to meet her was considerably energized when I learned from her friend and fellow student Paula Lenchner that Margie had shyly confided to her that she would one day like to meet me. That is exactly what happened when I ran into Paula and Marjorie one day at the front entrance of the dorm, around seven in the evening. Paula introduced us, but now that we had finally met we were both so tongue-tied with shyness that we could hardly talk. All I could think of saying was something about "hoping to see you soon again."

I found out years later that Margie had kept a rather detailed account of how we met and how our whole relationship developed and grew into the mutual love that bonded us for life. When she showed me that diary I was astonished to read how truly shy and self-effacing she was at the time, almost bordering on an inferiority complex. She wrote that she couldn't figure out why I "would be much impressed" by her. A few sentences later she commented how "beautifully" I had played the Tchaikovsky Fifth solo—"with such a beautiful tone"—and marveled that I was "only eighteen." The first words in the diary were: "The most tremendous things have happened to me since I've been at this school. They don't seem real—so out of this world. But then I wonder what is for real, for as I write this it seems that nothing is clear. A wonderful person has come into my life and has left a deep imprint on me—almost a wound, which might leave a scar. But I hope that the scar will help me gain more character, more strength—I have met Gunther." And a few pages later: "It is impossible for me to explain in this narrative the deep feeling, emotion, and passion [of] these past months. What the effects of all this will be, I don't know. Maybe it will make me a better singer, able to give more of myself. Then all this suffering will have been worth it."

It was at another one of those postconcert gatherings that I saw Marjorie again, and this time with my heart pounding I found some way—I don't remember exactly how—to approach her. We chatted—inanities probably—but I did find out that she was from Fargo, North Dakota, that her name was Marjorie Black, and that she had come to the Cincinnati College of Music to study voice with Lotte Leonard.[12] Years later, when we were long married, if someone asked her how she ended up at the Cincinnati College of Music, she would always say, half in jest, that it was to find a husband.

I immediately sensed that in some deeply felt way music (not necessarily a career in music) meant everything to her, that it was something without which she could not live her life. Maybe at the time I was reading something of myself into her mind and psyche, but that is what I felt reaching me from her quiet, gentle self. I think I knew then and there that Marjorie was going to be my life's companion, the love of my life—as indeed it turned out.

I was now in a considerable state of emotional agitation, to some extent even distracted from my composing and musical studies. Marjorie was on my mind all the time. But, frustratingly, I managed to see her only rarely, even though as a busy horn teacher at the college I kept expecting to run into her sometime, somewhere, at least in the hallways. I took to wandering around the school, hoping to find the voice and piano studios of her teachers. Of course I soon did, but I still never caught a glimpse of her.

As I turned eighteen in November, a small cloud began to appear on my personal horizon: the draft. It wasn't long before I received my notice to appear at the draft board in early December. That was a whole other and very strange experience. Ordered to arrive at seven in the morning, before I knew it I found myself standing naked in a long line of hundreds of young men, about to face the basic physical examination. There we were, not knowing a soul, all in different shapes and sizes: fat, lean, squat, lanky, tall, slight, small, some torsos covered with thick mats of dark hair, others as bare as a baby's skin. While most of us were too shy or polite to appraise the size of the others' "equipment," there were, I noticed, some more brazen types who were busy investigating their neighbors' endowments.

The lines moved extremely slowly. It took over two hours for me, standing there stark naked, to get to the examining doctors' cubicles. I was declared in good shape physically, but, of course, due notice was taken of my sightless artificial right eye. I was next sent to the psychiatric examination. I don't remember much of the discussion, but I recall saying that I was a musician, with an enormous appetite also for reading, studying literature, painting, sculpture, and architecture. I also mentioned that I couldn't imagine myself shooting or purposely killing another human being, even an animal. (Two leading questions the army psychiatrists always asked were, Do you do any fishing or hunting? Have you ever used a gun?) Having arrived at the draft board at seven a.m., I was finally able to leave around eleven thirty, completely missing that morning's orchestra rehearsal.

It took a few weeks before I learned of my fate. I received a postcard stating that I was declared 4F, thus exempted from military service. No explanation was rendered, although I assumed it was primarily because of the loss of my right eye and my limited sight, especially in terms of distance. I was much relieved. So was Goossens. But I must confess, rather ashamedly, that I had not developed much of a patriotic fervor to serve my country, as so many thousands of American boys had who were drafted or who enlisted. I had lived the last six years of my life so totally submerged and absorbed in music that I had no real sense of the danger to my country presented by our German and Japanese enemies. Nor did I realize that I was somewhat selfishly, single-mindedly pursuing my life in music. In my defense I can say that at least this was not merely a matter of career ambition. Far from it; I was not thinking about my career at all. I just wanted to immerse myself totally and unequivocally in music.

I think the reader can understand why I considered myself fortunate to have evaded the draft; it is a common feeling, although in retrospect I might have been more truly fortunate if I, dead or alive, had been able to serve my country. It is a deeply complex issue on which reasonable minds can have widely differing views. But if war and killing are inherently evil propositions, the question then is: shall conscientious objection alone justify draft evasion, an intrinsic refusal to kill other humans, even declared enemies? Or does it automatically compel you to engage in the killing of your fellow human creatures? Any answer will depend for most people on the *reason* for going to war, its intended goals. Since intelligent people realize that most wars have been initiated or caused by power-hungry, arrogant, ruthless, insensitive despots or religious fanatics of one stripe or another, who have dragged innocent, decent people into the maelstrom of senseless bloodshed and slaughter, they may well wonder why *they* should offer up their lives to ward off the aggressions of such ruthless rulers. It's a real conundrum.

The vast majority of people just want to live their lives in peace and quiet, fulfilling the inborn desires and functions that will further the perpetuation and betterment of the human race. But when barbaric hoodlums like Hitler or Stalin threaten the free world, most people believe that they must react and defend themselves; and defending one's self almost always means killing others—a theme so profoundly and sensitively explored in Jean Renoir's great 1937 film *La Grande illusion* (*The Great Illusion*). It is an inexpressible shame that many millions of fine, good people have to sacrifice their lives to eliminate an opposing threat. The real problem with wars, with mutual mass killings, with ethnic cleansing, is that they all provoke, sooner or later, a retaliatory reaction, which in turn guarantees a counterreaction, evolving inevitably into an endless chain of recriminations and recrudescent vindications, each side eternally blaming the other.

So where does a rational, educated, intelligent person come down on these issues? Should you hold to your conscientious objector position, your vehement and immutable antiwar feelings, no matter what the cause or purpose of the war; or should you, without equivocation, robotlike, line up to offer your life, regardless of the declared intent of the war? In the abstract, from a point of view of pure logic, there is no rational response to such questions, indeed not even the *possibility* of a totally clear, rational answer. In the end, each of us makes a decision out of a gamut of accumulated personal convictions.

Naïve as I was in these matters at first, living in the wondrous cocoon of my self-created musical and artistic isolation, the brutal reality that these questions and issues raise suddenly hit home when a year later Marjorie's brother Edwin was one of the sixteen thousand American boys killed in the Battle of the Bulge in France. He had been a young man of twenty-four, intelligent, brilliant, loving, caring, in the bloom of youth. His life was snuffed out in an instant in one machine gun barrage. Ned (as he was called) was just one of the nearly three hundred thousand young Americans who gave their lives to preserve our freedom and democracy.

Access to the girl students—college women were then called "girls" at least until they were twenty-two or twenty-three, after which they became "ladies"—at the College of Music was made very difficult. They almost all had to live in the dorm, all meals were taken at the college, and they were watched over by a very stern-faced den mother, Marian Quintile, who brooked no nonsense, and whose job it was to discourage any "extracurricular activities" on the part of the young ladies. While they could go out in the evening, curfew was at ten p.m., slightly later on weekends. If you were late getting back to the dorm, the front door was locked, you were met by the housemother, given a severe reprimand, and, as I learned later, after a few such offenses the girl's parents or relatives would be notified. (How different things are today!) I dare say that such firmly restrictive dormitory conditions were precisely what parents of daughters at a college, musical or otherwise, demanded of the institution in those days.

Some of the more adventurous, already amorously active older girls eventually figured out a way to beat the curfew. They would return after an evening out near midnight or even later, when Madame Queen (as the housemother was called behind her back) was usually sound asleep in bed. The girl would climb through a first floor window and sneak upstairs, all of this aided and abetted by one or several of her close friends. I heard also that once in a while some of the less popular boyfriendless (probably frustrated) girls snitched on the curfew breakers, causing a big hullabaloo in the dorm for the guilty ones, but also ostracizing the snitchers to an even lonelier solitary existence.

I finally saw Marjorie a third time at another one of the Friday afternoon postconcert receptions in the student lounge. I happened to be with Paula when Margie walked in. I saw her watching us, and I could tell that she knew we were talking about her. Paula virtually pushed me forward toward her. We chatted a bit, probably more platitudes, but as the reception drew to a close, I finally got up enough nerve to ask her to stay on afterward, wondering whether—and desperately hoping that—she would want to listen with me to a brand-new recording I had just bought earlier that day of Manuel DeFalla's *Nights in the Gardens of Spain*.[13] To my relief and indescribable joy she consented to stay, and I spent a couple of the happiest hours of my young life watching her as we listened to DeFalla's wonderful, quintessentially Spanish music. Tears come to my eyes as I write these words, recalling this most precious memory. She listened very intently, much moved by the rich beauty of the music. To my delight she noted the many horn solos along the way. Watching her I could sense that underneath that modest demeanor there was a certain strength of character, something spiritual that, along with her incomparable beauty, touched me deeply. I realized I was hopelessly in love.

A few days later Paula, our intermediary, told her: "Listen, Gunther is truly fascinated with you. Don't you see *how* he looks at you?" In her diary Margie confessed that she loved my being "fascinated," but added the questioning words, "is it just a woman's vanity?" Was that a little streak of insecurity? And what *were* her feelings? Margie belonged to those long-ago generations when young ladies were taught to be outwardly reserved, circumspect in their behavior, especially in relation to the opposite sex; one was not to immediately divulge the state of one's heart and mind. In those days courtships were extensive and a serious business, a process that was approached with deep respect for each other and with a sense of dignity. Girls were taught to resist the advances of boys, whether physical or emotional—to keep them at bay. Yet I sensed that if I had not yet captured her, I had at least captivated her. We agreed to meet again, the implication being—more often. And so we did, but only in the college lounge, talking or listening to records, she sometimes playing the piano—thus gradually spending more and more time together.

On one such college lounge record listening session, I brought along Handel's *Messiah* in its only complete recording—actually it was only nearly complete, not really the entire three-part *Messiah*—and Beethoven's Fourth Piano Concerto in a remarkable performance by Artur Schnabel and Malcolm Sargent's London Philharmonic. (Except for a Gieseking recording of the Beethoven Concerto, that's all that was available in 1944 of those two great masterpieces. Now there are over sixty recordings of the Beethoven and forty of the complete Messiah.) I brought those particular pieces because Margie was studying several arias from the *Messiah* and had been assigned the Beethoven Concerto by her piano teacher, Herbert Newman. Margie also told me that she was working very hard on both works, adding that though she had previously always been pushed in the direction of the coloratura soprano literature, she really now wanted to be a lyric or, possibly, a dramatic soprano.

One of the most talented piano students at the college, Laverne Gustafson (popularly known as Gussie), played a concerto by Anton Rubinstein—brilliantly, by the way—in a college concert that Margie and I attended together. After the concert I walked Margie to the dorm, and as we parted I must have looked at her with such longing that she noted in her diary how it almost made her "cringe. It was such a penetrating look; I shall never forget it." On the spur of the moment I asked her to go with me to Steve's, a beer and hamburger joint kitty-corner from the college, where most of the college kids congregated most evenings. Margie excused herself, saying she was campussed (curfewed) that evening for some reason. I had the impression that she was glad to have an excuse; perhaps she was a little scared. It would have been the first time for us to have actually gone out in public. I suspect she was thrilled to have been asked.

In the succeeding weeks we weren't able to be with each other at all. She was very busy with her voice and piano lessons, many hours of practice, and classes (theory, history, etc.); and I, of course, had a full schedule at the Symphony with five rehearsals and two performances per week, plus many hours of teaching at both schools. But we did find ways to at least be in the same place—at classes, concerts, and rehearsals, events at which neither of us was actually required to be. For example, Eugene Selhorst, the school's organ teacher and resident connoisseur of new music—who became one of my best friends and mentors, the closest thing to an intellectual on the college faculty—gave a two-hour class every Wednesday night in which he played recordings of contemporary music. It seems that Margie found out that I was a regular at those listening sessions. I began to see her there, watching me. In her diary it says that I watched her "like a hawk." Also, Saturday nights, after the symphony concert, she often went with Nell Foster and Phyllis Cook, her roommate, to Pohlar's, a wonderful German restaurant a few blocks from the college and music hall, hoping to find me there. (I was more likely at a jazz club called the Hangar—more of that later.)

Margie was evidently pursuing *me* more actively. This cat and mouse game went on for weeks. In retrospect, I can't fully explain why we were both so shy, so reticent, so timid, except that that's the way young people were three-quarters of a century ago. But it was also that both she and I, while not traditional loners (far from it), didn't mind being alone a fair amount, spending our time mostly studying and working, rather than sitting around engaged in endless empty chatter, drinking beer—which is what most of the college kids did. Margie and I were instinctively attracted to each other, partly because we were both very devoted to our work and our music. We sensed deep down that life was too short to commit to anything less than total dedication to our primary interests.

As we eventually spent more time together, I learned that she was born in September 1924 (she was thus a year and two months older than I), had grown up in Fargo, North Dakota, at age nine had shown talent for the piano, and a few years later was found to have a beautiful, pure soprano voice. This led to her becoming the choir soloist in Fargo's Presbyterian church and being occasionally asked to sing little recitals around town. When she discovered that she deeply loved music and dreamt of having a life in music, she asked her parents to let her study it more seriously. They acquiesced in her wish, choosing the College of Music in Cincinnati, one of the country's oldest and at the time most distinguished music schools, although on their part not without some trepidation and reluctance; they were disinclined to let their daughter go out into the big bad world alone.

I learned that her father, born in Ripon, Wisconsin, but raised in Parsons, Kansas, learned the hard life of the frontier as a boy and young man in the 1880s, and later made his way northward to Fargo, where he opened a small dry goods store. By the 1920s it had expanded into an extensive multifaceted business, comprising a chain of high-quality clothing stores, ownership of the biggest hotel, real estate, and, later, parking lots. By late 1930, Mr. Black had built Fargo's first skyscraper, a beautiful art deco ten-story office building inspired by New York's Empire State Building.

I learned that the Black family was quite wealthy, the richest family in Fargo by far. Their women's apparel store became legendary in the central northern states, partly because of its clever name—Store Without a Name—but primarily because of its uncompromising high-quality, affordably priced women's clothes. From which I deduced that Marjorie's striking and impeccable taste in clothes was an elemental part of this family tradition and an inbred aesthetic requisite.[14]

I also found out that Margie's father was a strict churchgoing Presbyterian—no smoking, no drinking—a staunch political and fiscal conservative (although I didn't quite know at age eighteen what such terms really meant). I hadn't been to church since my St. Thomas days; neither were my parents churchgoing religionists, so no affinity existed there with Margie's parents. And as for business people, especially highly successful ones, I didn't think they were particularly bad or particularly good; I just sensed with my basically liberal and culturally oriented education that they were a different breed. I did realize very clearly that if and when I got to meet Margie's family, I would have to tone down my New York-influenced mind-set, watch my language, not get too excited about Negroes (as blacks were called then) and jazz and Jews and East Coast intellectuals, and in general play down my libertarian (that is to say, advocacy of free will and of absolute liberty), unequivocally democratic, socially open-minded attitudes. Even my being a professional musician—and a composer—would have to be presented and shaded in such a way as to pass Mr. and Mrs. Black's scrutiny, so that it would appear to be a humble and entirely proper form of employment. Musicians, and artists in general, were not regarded as entirely healthy members of the human family. Mr. Black's political-social orientation could be defined and understood by the fact that he considered the *New York Times* a Communist newspaper.

My intention to behave myself in the presence of Margie's parents was not so much motivated by fear of them or anxiety as to what they might think of me, as it was a sincere feeling that I didn't want to offend them in any way, in the clear recognition that they were entitled to their opinions and attitudes, even if I couldn't agree with them. I realized that there would be no point in arguing with them, since they would be, like most elderly persons, quite set in their ways.

What I perceived with considerable wonderment and delight was that in her outlook on the world and on life, Margie didn't seem to be at all like her parents. She wasn't stern or rigid, politically or socially; on the contrary she was warm and gentle. Her mind didn't seem to be filled with deep-seated biases; it was wide open to new experiences, to new considerations. There was a certain gravity, an emotional centeredness, in her. She was innately curious about the world around her, cautiously thirsting for knowledge, sensing the wonderful diversity of people, of nature, of things cultural, and of the wide world of the imagination. At the same time she seemed quite shy to me, in her modest demeanor, not given to talking much about herself, about her past, about her childhood. It made me increasingly curious about her background and how she became involved with music, there having been no particular interest in music or any real musical talent on both her parents' side for many generations, if ever. Moreover, in those days it was quite unusual to take on a double major in a music school, to pursue serious studies in *two* performance disciplines. It was much more common if a student had an interest in two musical arenas to opt for a program of one major and one minor.

As we gradually got to know each other better and exchanged accounts of our backgrounds, family and otherwise, I learned that Margie had spent her first year in college at a school outside of Chicago called Shimer College—a place she said she basically hated, found boring, and a big waste of time. But she admitted that the wasting of time and lack of hard work on her voice and piano lessons was often of her own doing. That was a bit hard for me to believe; for now, in Cincinnati, to the extent I had been able to observe her, she seemed to be very serious about her music studies, certainly not someone just out to have fun at college. But years later, when Margie showed me some of the letters written to her parents during the Shimer year, I was astonished to constantly read such sentences as: "I haven't done much lately," "there isn't much to write about," "not much out of the ordinary going on in my life out here." But the sentence that I really thought appeared too often was: "had so much fun." Even more devastating was one report to her parents that "in the spring time" she and one of her girlfriends didn't "feel like working or studying at all. The golf course is now green again and simply very beautiful—very inviting."

The girl I saw and met at the Cincinnati College of Music in 1943 had evidently gone through a major transformation in her work ethic and devotion to music studies. And there was even more of a transformation to come in other important respects. One Sunday afternoon, rather than playing records, I told her I really wanted to hear about her musical life before coming to the college. We spent the whole afternoon exchanging reminiscences of our variously developing involvement with music. Ever since her earliest teen years she had wanted to be a singer in opera. As she found herself increasingly involved in singing in public, not only in church services and church dinners, but also womens' clubs, high school PTA meetings, and other social get-togethers, she realized that it made her someone special in the public and social life of Fargo—that town of some forty thousand not being one of the more thriving cultural or musical centers of the world, and certainly not overrun with musical talents. She seemed to be the only one in Fargo among her generation who had ambitions about a life in music. She told me that among her high school girlfriends there wasn't one that listened to classical music; they were only interested in popular dance music, not even the high-quality jazz, say, of Ellington or Goodman or Armstrong.

She told me that her voice teacher, a Mr. Sauvé, thought she was a coloratura soprano, but that she had doubts. She didn't quite trust Mr. Sauvé's judgment—he in fact turned out to be wrong—and thought that she really was a lyric-dramatic soprano, what's called a spinto. Her repertory, based largely on what the ladies in the womens' clubs or the church choir directors in Fargo wanted to hear, consisted of favored songs of that era such as "The Last Rose of Summer," "Indian Love Call," Alexander Alabieff's "The Nightingale," and occasionally pieces such as Verdi's "Caro nome," or the lead voice in the famous quartet from *Rigoletto*.

She mentioned that in recent years her singing had become a little uneven, not entirely reliable. It worried her that quite often in the middle of a song or aria she would momentarily experience some hoarseness, which she thought pointed to some vocal or technical deficiency, but which Mr. Sauvé wasn't able to diagnose. Margie thought that Mme Leonard, her teacher at the College of Music, was now working on that problem, although she wasn't sure that they were making much progress. At that point in our relationship—only six weeks in and still very sporadic—I had not heard Margie sing, except one day after I finally located the studio where she took her lessons and listened for about thirty seconds outside the door. The tiny sample I heard sounded quite lovely, a voice with a warm timbre.

As Margie spoke about wanting a career as a singer more than as a pianist (because, I think, she felt she had more talent and passion for singing), it was clear to me that it wasn't so much the career as it was her deep-felt love for music that had gripped her. This became even clearer to me when she recounted the horrible experience of an audition she had taken in New York in 1942 with the famous Elizabeth Schumann. Although Margie admitted that she was nervous at the audition (her main piece was "Caro nome"), knees shaking and short of breath, her high notes perhaps not her best, she didn't think the great lady had the right to completely, unfeelingly, dismiss her as one who had no talent at all, and was wrongly trained—a pretty crushing all-around condemnation of a young singer's aspirations.[15] It was very dismaying—and puzzling—to hear that my dear, kind, gentle Margie could have been so callously treated by anyone, but above all by one of the great vocal heroes of my early youth. I listened regularly to her many superb 1930s Wagner recordings, often with my other superhero, Lauritz Melchior. However, Schumann's accompanist, a Mrs. Westmoreland, seeing how crushed Margie was by the bluntness of the criticism, not only took her aside to tell her "you really have a lovely quality of voice," but also offered to arrange another audition for her a few days later, with another well-known voice teacher at the Curtis Institute, Mme Giannini Gregory. There, Margie sang the quite difficult aria "Ah, fors e lui" from Verdi's *La Traviata*, and evidently did quite well. This time the verdict was: "Very nice, a lovely voice. You can do something with your voice, if you work hard." Margie was much relieved, but secretly wondered, still somewhat shaken by the other audition experience, whether Mme Gregory *really* meant all that she said.

It was obvious to me that singing, making beautiful music with her voice, meant everything to Margie; in her quiet way it was a deep burning desire. She didn't seem to exhibit the kind of self-satisfied overconfidence, even arrogance, that I had noticed so often among singers, even some students at the college, and I wondered whether Margie lacked a certain necessary self-confidence to make a career, especially in opera. Like most aspiring singers, she had a particular fondness for opera. Her parents, who had from the beginning encouraged her in her love for music and were now generously supporting her musical studies, had in her midteen years often taken her to New York on her father's weeklong buying trips—even taking her temporarily out of high school—where they spent almost every evening at the Metropolitan Opera. They also took Margie to operas in Paris and Berlin in 1936, during the course of a two-month trip to Europe to visit relatives in Ireland and to attend the 1936 Olympics in Germany. (Although Margie was only twelve at the time, she remembered quite vividly Jesse Owens's famous gold medal triumph in the one-hundred- and two-hundred-meter races.)

Near the end of the afternoon I got up enough nerve to ask her, what about boyfriends in Fargo? She said she never had any real boyfriends and that she mostly consorted with the girls in her high school. She did go to some school dances with different boys, but didn't like dancing that "didn't lead to anything." (I was much relieved to hear that, like me, she didn't like dancing.) Anyway, she said, "all that those guys generally wanted to do was smooch"—which she hated.

One day a few weeks before Christmas, when I learned that Margie would be going home to Fargo during the school break, I finally got up enough nerve to ask her to go out on a date with me. Even then I didn't have the gumption to approach her directly. (Oh my, how shy and inhibited we all were in those days!) I sent her my message through Paula Lenchner, and told Paula to be sure to mention that I hoped this would be the first of *many* dates, emphasis on many. My audacious plan came to naught, when, as luck would have it,[16] Paula told me that

Margie had been campussed for two weeks, meaning confined to the dormitory. Our first date had to be postponed to the next calendar year.

I didn't find out until months later that Margie, just prior to being campussed, had finally told her parents about me. "This boy" she had been "admiring from a distance has asked me to go out with him, after the symphony concert Saturday night. He's real nice, a high-type boy, very good looking, plays first horn in the Cincinnati Symphony. He also teaches here at the College and composes music. They say he is *very* talented." I then learned that her parents were immediately very displeased with the news that she admired "this boy," and that I had asked her to go out on, of all things, on a late Saturday night. "How could you? And a musician?" That was the last time Margie mentioned me in letters to her family for over a year.

Her absence that Christmastime in 1943—not finding her anywhere, not being able to search even at a distance for her irresistible deep-brown eyes, unable to contemplate her wonderful statuesque body—she had what in opera is called a healthy, well-filled singers's physique—all this was suddenly unbelievably painful for me. The worst days were just at the time of the New Year.

What tore me apart that weekend was that Goossens had scheduled an all-Rachmaninov program, consisting of *Isle of the Dead*, the Second Piano Concerto, and the Second Symphony. The reader should realize that for some people music and sensual urgings are closely related, potentially symbiotic. For example, in one of our earlier record listening afternoons we had discovered that we both were passionate admirers of Rachmaninov's music, that we both experienced virtual meltdowns at some of Rachmaninov's most ecstatic climaxes, as in the *Isle of the Dead* or the Second Symphony. In my enthusiasm on this point, I think I shocked her when I suggested that, to my mind, Rachmaninov (along with Scriabin) wrote just about the most erotic music one could imagine. I was probably testing her a little to see how she would react to the word erotic. For I was convinced that there were sexual fires burning deep down in her, but that they were buried under many layers of inhibitions, of repressed feelings. (I realized this was also to some extent true of me.)

Between the music and my longing for Margie, I was in a deep fog, a daze, almost the whole week. In the first movement of the Second Symphony there is a lyrical, achingly beautiful, sixteen-bar horn solo, full of longing, accompanied by soft strings. I loved this solo dearly, not only because it is so perfectly written for the horn—there *is* no other orchestral instrument that could match the horn in poignancy of expression for that particular passage—but also because it is one of those relatively rare, sublimely simple passages to which the heart cannot remain irresponsive. The solo is preceded by an eleven-bar rest in the horn part. Instinctively, I looked for Margie in her usual balcony place, as I had during the Tchaikovsky Fifth. But there was only an empty seat. I never looked at the music and played that whole solo to her, to the remembered vision I had spotted there three months earlier.

Such experiences and the powerful feelings associated with them are striking examples of how music and emotions, especially the deep pangs of love and longing, are intricately interrelated. And when they overtake you they can't be suppressed or thwarted. They are real and powerful and can't be artificially induced. That's why, even nineteen years after Margie's passing, hearing certain passages in any number of Rachmaninov pieces or some excerpts from Puccini's *La Bohème* (to mention just two works) can bring me to an overwhelming emotional meltdown.

Something on that order of emotional turmoil overtook me during the weeks that Margie was a thousand miles away in Fargo. Playing all that sensuous Rachmaninov music was at once an emotive high and an emotional torture: Margie and the music fused into one single physiological expression.

Almost worse was that after Margie returned from Fargo, for one reason or another we didn't see each other for almost a week. More agony! When we finally happened to meet, it was quite by chance at a drugstore. She was with Phyllis. It was a bizarre encounter. I wanted to hug her and kiss her, but all I could bring myself to do was to talk with Phyllis—what the hell was I thinking of?—about our most recent symphony concert. My sweet Margie, waiting patiently, listening intently, suddenly apologized for breaking in and spoke only one sentence. She thought that Ruth Posselt—a superb violinist who had recently played with us Goldmark's Violin Concerto and Goossens' *Lyric Poem for Violin and Orchestra*—was a much better violinist than Albert Spalding. (She was absolutely right.)

A few weeks later we met again by chance at Pohlar's. This time I wasn't quite as tongue-tied. Margie had her hair in what was called a Veronica Lake straight hair style. She was stunning! I told her she looked very chic. "Really?," she asked shyly. "Yeah, REALLY!," I replied. She smiled her beautiful smile.

I finally got up enough nerve to ask Margie out on our first real date, actually a double date, since we were chaperoned by Sammy Green and Paula Lenchner. We went to Pohlar's, one of my favorite haunts, and according to Margie that was the first time I put my arm around her. She recalled that she was "surprised," but decided not to let it bother her, "to no longer care what people thought." That evening she mentioned almost casually, inadvertently, that her Sundays were always very lonely. Many years later, when we were already married, she reminded me: "Boy, you sure took care of that, but quick." In fact, it was then that our sporadic record-listening trysts at the College of Music lounge moved gradually to my room on Highland Avenue on Sunday afternoons, daytime female visitations being permitted, if not encouraged, by my very strict, watchful landlords. I had brought some of my most precious 78 albums with me from New York. And with my rather generous salary as principal horn in the orchestra and teaching at the college, I had in a relatively short time in Cincinnati acquired at least a dozen new recordings. (I had found a friendly sales lady in downtown Cincinnati in the record department at Willis's music store. I certainly gave Willis—and a few other music stores—quite a lot of business in the two years I was in Cincinnati.)

Margie, who clearly had come to Cincinnati from a sheltered and musically circumscribed life in Fargo, was naturally a bit overwhelmed by the vast number of new musical experiences she encountered in Cincinnati. I think I overwhelmed her even more with my record collection, which, of course, included a fair amount of lesser-known, even esoteric, musical items. But she was always eager to hear and learn more. Whereas in her previous life she had concentrated primarily on vocal and piano literature, in our weekend listening she became quickly aware of the vast riches of the orchestral repertory.

While my working hours were fully occupied by the symphony and composing and studying, and most of my free waking hours devoted to thoughts of Margie, I somehow had enough time to develop very close friendships outside the orchestra and within it. Outside there was Gussie (Laverne Gustafson), a striking, even flashy blonde at the College of Music who looked more like a Hollywood starlet than a graduate student pianist. As probably the best and most advanced student in the entire school, I was naturally attracted to her, although more in admiration of her stunning pianistic talent than her dazzling good looks—attracted more in the sense of a collegial, platonic friendship. Oddly enough, while Margie seemed to easily gain friends and admirers among the girls at the dorm, Gussie was regarded as somewhat of an outsider, possibly because she didn't live at the dorm and because she was a few years older than most of the other girls. There was about her also a slight air of mystery, subtly fed by rumors among the students that she slept around quite a bit. One rumor even had it that Gussie had an older sugar daddy. I was either too naive in such matters to understand what all that meant, or so busy with my musical preoccupations and my deep feelings for Margie, that I paid little or no attention to these rumors about Gussie. All I saw in her was a terrific musician, very knowledgeable about all music, even jazz, and not just standard piano literature. Gussie and I enjoyed countless musical experiences together, sharing our enthusiasms and youthful insights with each other. A terrific sight reader, she used to get four-hand transcriptions of orchestral music from the Cincinnati public library, and we'd play through these great masterpieces, sometimes for hours, thrilled with living and breathing the music we loved so much.

None of this produced anything like a rivalry or contest between Margie and Gussie—certainly not with me. In retrospect, I am amazed at how absolutely clearly I separated the two relationships, especially given Gussie's physical attractiveness: professional and platonic in the case of Gussie, and deeply personal and intimate in Margie's case. I know it was Margie's quiet, unostentatious beauty, a reflection of her inner beauty, that held me unalterably bound to her.

Another young lady, Nell Foster, a singer, impressed me considerably with her beauty, her talent, her intelligence, and her artistic maturity. She was a friend of Margie's and occasionally the two sang duets together in vocal classes, mostly operatic excerpts such as Puccini's "Tutti I fior?" from *Madama Butterfly* (the so-called Flower Duet) or "Che soave zeffiretto" (the Count-Susanna Duet) from Mozart's *Marriage of Figaro*. Nell was, in addition, remarkably well read and versed in poetry, both reading and writing it.[17]

I also became friends in Cincinnati with three other young ladies: Jean Geis, a fine pianist who made a career as a soloist and teacher in Cleveland, and who still plays recitals and concerts there to this day; Linda Iacobucci, who later became principal harpist with the Cleveland Symphony; and Margie's best friend, Phyllis Cook, a talented pianist who subsequently joined (with her husband, Nick Poscia, a horn player with the Cincinnati Symphony and then for many years with the Cleveland Symphony) the faculty of Miami University in Oxford, Ohio.

All in all, the girls at the College of Music were a wonderful lot. They were quite serious about their music studies; and indeed almost all of them went on to hold fine professional positions in music, as teachers or as leading instrumentalists in their home communities. They were also a fun loving bunch, egged on in all kinds of pranks and mischief (mostly directed at the dorm housemother) by an ingeniously talented foursome called the Terrible Four. Their ringleader was a roguish, spoofing limerick poetess and pianist, Helen Miller, and her immediate sidekick and second in command was Ruth Duning, a talented flutist. (The other two were Linda Iacobucci and Elaine Seager, another fine flutist). They engineered many a clever scheme to outwit Madame Queen in their relentless pursuit of circumventing the plethora of strict dormitory rules.

One of the more inspired escapades the Terrible Four engineered was the "Dumlerization" of the college's hallways. Martin Dumler was not only president of the board of the college but also president of a local paper company—as well as a composer (whose works Goossens occasionally programmed). Dumler's paper company supplied the college with all of its toilet paper—the kids called it the "Dumler paper." When Nan Merriman, a graduate voice student at the college, won the National Federation of Music Clubs competition in 1943 and a $1,000 prize, the Terrible Four, in Merriman's honor, festooned the entire stairway from Merriman's third-floor room all the way down to the first floor with Dumler paper. Another time, they hooked up an alarm clock to a high window in the Odeon, the college's concert hall, set to go off in the middle of a commencement address. Generally, after Symphony concerts, the Terrible Four would gather at Steve's and play excerpts from the concert or pop tunes on a dozen beer bottles.

All the girls at the dorm seemed to be reading *The Rubaiyat of Omar Khayyam*, swooning over its sentimental romanticized rhyming quatrains. (But I think so was the whole country in 1944.) They also all seemed to be in love with Charles Boyer, the improbably handsome

Hollywood heartthrob in those years. A sure sign that we all were a very close-knit group is the fact that Margie and I kept loyally in touch with most of those girls, as they did with one another for many decades, even though we were all scattered around the country. They were very much like family.

It was in Cincinnati that I first became more deeply involved with jazz. Before that I was primarily a listener, a young fan, and a fledgling record collector. But by the time I got to Cincinnati, I was beginning to feel the need to do more with jazz than to just enjoy it as a listener. To tell the truth, it wasn't only some innate desire that made me want to pursue this music in a more active way; it was the *opportunity* to do so in Cincinnati, in a way that my life in New York had never permitted. Until I got to Cincinnati I had never gone to a jazz club, nor had I ever thought of playing jazz on the horn, except for that brief period in high school in Tony Acquaviva's band. That all came later, when I returned to New York in 1945.

The horn in 1943 was just beginning to be used in a mere handful of jazz bands, and even then only sporadically. But just two years later the horn would become much more prevalent in jazz orchestras; and arrangers and band leaders, who all had ignored the horn for many years—considering the standard sixteen-piece instrumentation of choirs of saxophones, trumpets, and trombones, plus a rhythm section, more than sufficient to their purposes—suddenly began to discover the horn and its very special tone color. Before long many bands were sprouting a one- or two-man horn section.

In Cincinnati my greater involvement with jazz took primarily two forms. One was to begin transcribing what I considered to be jazz masterpieces from recordings, especially by Ellington, in full score and in all musical details. As a composer of fully notated music and one who had by then already studied hundreds of the great classical works, I wanted to do the same thing with jazz compositions. There were no published scores of jazz pieces at the time; thus there was no possibility of studying a piece from a visual, analytical point of view. Although I had very good ears and could aurally appreciate and analyze all that was going on in a jazz piece, as a composer I wanted to *see* what that music would look like, written out in full notation, in a full score. (I am pretty sure I was the first one to do such full-score transcriptions. I was eighteen at the time.)

The other manifestation of my intensified interest in jazz was my discovering within a few weeks of my arrival in Cincinnati most of the jazz clubs in town, first and foremost two smaller, more intimate clubs, called the Barn and the Hangar, located in an alley right near Fountain Square, Cincinnati's central hub. (That alley and its clubs are long gone now, displaced by a Westin hotel.) I also visited the Cotton Club in the city's black section, where many of the best and most famous jazz orchestras of the land (Basie, Hampton, Lunceford, etc.) appeared regularly, usually for a whole week. The Hangar became my second home in Cincinnati. I spent untold happy hours there listening to the house trio, a wonderful group of musicians who held forth six nights a week from eight in the evening until the wee hours of the morning, playing in a style very close to that of the great Nat "King" Cole Trio.

At one point I told Margie that I wanted her to hear something very special, and played several pieces from my rapidly growing collection of Ellington recordings, particularly some masterful Ellingtonia from the 1940 to 1942 years, that most outstanding period in the Ellington orchestra's fifty-year existence. I started with *Cotton Tail*, *Moon Mist*, and *C-Jam Blues*, but also the beautiful romantic 1930 "tone poem," *Mood Indigo*. Margie had not heard much Ellington in Fargo, or for that matter any of the great black bands of the time, and was deeply moved by this incredible music. She told me that when she was seventeen, she had wanted to go with a high school friend to a dance at Fargo's Crystal Ballroom, where the Ellington band was appearing. But her parents wouldn't let her go to what they considered an absolute den of iniquity. Fargo was then (and for a long time thereafter) Lawrence Welk and polka territory.[18]

Then Margie told me of a more successful attempt to hear some jazz in Fargo, a year later when she was eighteen, namely, Peggy Lee (née Norma Jean Egstrom). That's when I learned that Peggy Lee was a North Dakotan. Her incomparable 1942 recording with Benny Goodman of "Why Don't You Do Right?" was already one of my absolute favorites, having heard it dozens of times on practically every jukebox in every restaurant on my Ballet Theatre and Jeannette McDonald tours. Born in Jamestown, North Dakota, Peggy Lee had started her career at age eighteen in one of Fargo's very few jazz lounges, in fact in one of George Black's competitor hotels, the Powers.

I was surprised and pleased to realize that Margie was more knowledgeable in musical matters than I had first assumed. I was often amazed at how much music she knew, or at least knew of and was interested in, and not—as with most of her fellow students—just her vocal and piano repertory but also stretching out across the whole range of musical styles. I was even more impressed when I realized that her critical evaluation of performances and compositions, even of brand-new works, was almost always right on target. And when there was an area of music that she was unaware of, it was thrilling to see how quickly and how seriously she would pursue these new-found interests.

Where did she acquire all these good, basic, solid musical instincts? And, even more mysteriously, where and when did she develop such astute critical acumen? Certainly not from her parents or her family background. I never did figure it out. I don't think even Margie knew how and why, nor did she think it was anything special—again her innate modesty. In fact, unbelievably, she would often chastise herself in her diary for knowing so relatively little.

We were now gradually seeing each other much more often, although Margie was sometimes still reticent, claiming that she had to practice harder in both of her majors. I didn't think that that was some kind of excuse, I really believed her; I was hearing from her teachers and some of her girlfriends that she was making great progress in both of her major concentrations.

I had become habituated to going every Friday evening, after my afternoon symphony concert, to a very good downtown restaurant called the Cricket, which served just about the best fried chicken I had ever had. I think Margie got wind of the fact that I spent every Friday evening there, because she also began to appear there quite often, much to my delight—although never alone. Paula or Phyllis were always in tow. On one of those evenings she seemed very tired, and actually shut her eyes many times—she later claimed she did it unconsciously. Somehow that prompted me to tell her that I always wanted to see her asleep, her beautiful face in angelic repose. In her diary Margie wrote that she was "astonished at Gunther's frankness. But I really loved it, even though it was so new to me. He had said it so gently."

Our increasingly idyllic relationship was temporarily suspended when Margie's parents, George and Alice, and her brother Ned came to Cincinnati in early March 1944. Ned had been drafted and was now on his way to Fort Dix, New Jersey, presumably to be sent to Europe after his basic training. Margie had only begun to mention me fairly recently in her almost daily letters home, and then only very gingerly, peripherally. In this she wasn't being devious, she just didn't want to worry them if they heard that their daughter, five hundred miles away, had fallen into the hands of a musician, and worse, one from New York, probably a liberal. When Margie introduced me to them on their second day in Cincinnati, it was not as the boyfriend but as a member of the College of Music faculty and principal horn of the Cincinnati Symphony. They seemed to be quite impressed, although when I was invited to have dinner with them the atmosphere was a bit tense at first. But that was to be expected.

I think that by the end of their visit Margie's parents realized that I was not the wild-eyed, undisciplined, profligate artist, undoubtedly out to seduce their daughter and ruin her life forever, that they had probably imagined me to be. Of course, I was on my best behavior, avoiding all political discussion, although it was hard not to respond to some of Mr. Black's veiled (or sometimes not so veiled) anti-Semitic or anti-Catholic remarks. I could tell that his rantings sometimes caused his wife to wince ever so slightly, occasionally going so far as to say: "Oh, George, don't talk like that!" (Years later, watching *All in The Family* and seeing Edith trying to calm down her ranting husband, I would think back to those early years of getting to know Margie's parents, and the sometimes tense moments that would occur at the dinner table.) I think that ultimately George Black did appreciate that, even if I was a musician, I was at least making a pretty good weekly salary and seemed to dress and behave like a normal human being.

I was quite struck by Ned, who I saw right away was a very intelligent and sensitive young man (he was twenty-four), a generous spirit. I wondered how such a broadminded liberal could have issued from such an extremely conservative parental climate, nor could I understand how such a sensitive, gentle soul could have been drafted into the army. I could not imagine him taking a gun and killing another soldier. I found out that he wrote poetry, played the flute, not only loved classical music but was also very knowledgeable in it, and had quite a substantial record collection. His favorite author was Thomas Carlyle. Apart from some French, Ned spoke very fluent Portugese ("Brazilian" Portugese), having spent two years in Brazil on an international exchange program. I liked him a lot and thought that he was a perfect male counterpart to Margie's empathetic character and spirit.

There was only one fairly awkward moment during the Blacks' visit and that, oddly enough, occurred between Ned and me, with whom I certainly hadn't expected to ignite an argument on our first meeting. It was thus doubly ironic that in response to Ned's fervent statement that for him Tchaikovsky was the greatest nineteenth-century composer of them all—implicitly demeaning Beethoven, Brahms, and Wagner, for example—I felt provoked to contradict him, somehow (stupidly) feeling personally challenged. In all likelihood I indulged myself in some exaggerated rhetoric, haughtily downgrading Tchaikovsky to a minor figure, whose music was all emotion and no intellect, or some such nonsense. Little did I realize then how wrong I was and how nearly right Ned was—if he had at least allowed Beethoven and Brahms into his pantheon. I immediately regretted my overly passionate rebuttal, which, so Margie told me, upset Ned considerably, although he was too polite to show it. It turned out that Ned had also met Gene Selhorst, who had inadvertently dropped some deprecating remarks about Tchaikovsky's music. Ned told Margie "not to listen to these musicians; they don't know what they're talking about."

This episode was all the more unfortunate since it was the last time I—or any of us—saw Ned. He was killed in the Battle of the Bulge in France on April 9, 1944. Margie and I visited his grave in the American cemetery in St. Avold four times in later years. I surely had not wanted to offend this gentle soul, but in my youthful, cocky exuberance I got carried away, subliminally thinking, what does he know? *I* am the professional. *I* know about these things!

I should add—only partially in my defense—that it was very common in those days for musicians in general, but also young composers out to conquer the world in particular, to pooh-pooh Tchaikovsky's music as bombastic, emotionally overwrought, and mindless. I was without realizing it mouthing what most professional orchestra musicians were constantly saying about Tchaikovsky. I do think that this kind of widespread denigration of his music was (and in many quarters still is) to a large extent attributable to the relentless overperforming of his Fourth, Fifth, and Sixth Symphonies, and the *Nutcracker Suite*. If one also considers that most performances of those symphonies, and pieces such as *Marche Slave* and the *1812* and *Romeo and Juliet* overtures, were subjected to overblown, overindulgent inter-pretations, a field day for exhibitionistic conductors, then one can well imagine why, upon hearing and playing such performances a few times too often, many musicians were turned off by Tchaikovsky's music.

As sublime as Tchaikovsky's greatest music is, especially his often-underappreciated ballet music, there is in some of Tchaikovsky's most popular music something shallow, unsubtle, repetitious, that can on repeated hearings lead to tedium. I remember experiencing this even in one of his finest works, the Fifth Symphony, when we played it eight times on a two-week symphony tour. I certainly enjoyed playing that great, most popular work, but I must admit that after playing the piece about six or seven times in a row, some of it didn't stand up so well. Having played many other famous, popular pieces, of which I have never tired, multiple times—I will quickly mention all the Beethoven symphonies, Puccini's *La Bohème* and *Tosca*, and a dozen of Joplin's rags, to name just a few diverse examples—I wonder what it is that causes some Tchaikovsky to wear thin after a while, while the Beethoven Seventh or Joplin's *Sun Flower Slow Drag* never do, no matter how often they are played. I'm not sure I know the full answer to both sides of the question, even now after all these years. I'm still working on it.

Margie admired and adored her brother, although she had seen very little of him recently. And when he returned to the States from Brazil in 1941, she was away at Shimer in Chicago. She knew him mostly through his extensive, beautifully written letters, which ranged over a wide spectrum of subjects, from life in Brazil and its culture (both in its indigenous and Euro-pean-imported manifestations) to his love of music and nineteenth-century English literature, and his fascination with transcendentalism.

Before Ned left Cincinnati he told Margie that she must sing with more conviction. I told her that was good advice, "Ned knows what he's talking about." Not unexpectedly, after Ned's death I detected a heightened drive and energy in Margie's dedication to her studies. Ned had told her in that last visit that she would have to transform the notes into feelings and meanings—to transcend the mere notes. Margie told me she wanted to be worthy of him, and should she become a fine, successful artist, she would want her work in part to immortalize him. It was the first glimpse I caught of her lifelong urge to dedicate her life to others, either in memory or in reality. I certainly became the beneficiary of that desire!

I remember Ned with great affection. And I think of him quite often, because it so happens that I have used in the writing of this book a *Roget's Thesaurus* that originally belonged to Ned and that his mother, my mother-in-law, gave me as a present some years after Ned's death.

In the meantime I had also been developing several more close friendships in the Cincinnati orchestra, the most important and closest of which were Paul Bransky, a talented artist, Reu-ben Segal, a young violinist in the orchestra, and an elderly gentleman in the orchestra's viola section, August Söndlin.

Paul was not only a very gifted painter and designer, he was also exquisitely educated. He was gay. I loved being with him in long discussions at dinner and such, talking about literature and art. He was also extraordinarily knowledgeable in music and loved modern music, par-ticularly Stravinksy and Prokofiev. We became lifelong friends. Reuben was a talented violin-ist, in his late twenties, very smart, vastly knowledgeable not only in music but also in areas such as politics (including politics in music), economics, literature, and history. We became good friends almost immediately, a relationship that eventually blossomed into a happy four-some—Reuben and his beautiful wife Bobbie (Roberta), and Margie and myself—and regular Friday dinners at our favorite downtown restaurant, the Cricket. Imagine combining the cor-dial atmosphere of a French sidewalk brasserie with the relaxed hospitality of a Southern-style restaurant, and you have an idea of the Cricket's friendly ambiance. They served the best fried chicken with sweet potatoes and corn bread this side of heaven, and you could sit there for hours, lingering over coffee and drinks, without being hassled. We spent many happy hours of stimulating, even argumentative discussions at the Cricket, as Reuben and I in our youthful exuberance tried to solve all the world's problems.

I learned a lot from Reuben, who was a very keen observer of human behavior. He was to me in Cincinnati what Josef Marx had been in the Ballet Theatre orchestra. Wearing a perpetual scowl—off-putting for many of his colleagues—his outward appearance very much belied an inner warmth and sensitivity that attracted me to him. Reuben became one of my greatest fans, and throughout his long, checkered, and varied career in different parts of the country, we kept in touch and corresponded regularly until his death in his late eighties in 2001. To the very end of his life he still practiced several hours every day, continued to concertize, constantly explored new music, read indefatigably, wrote little plays and poetry, remaining deeply and happily involved with his varied artistic interests.

My relationship to August Söndlin was of an entirely different sort, so special that I dare call it unique—at least in my life. Söndlin, Paris-born and musically educated in Zurich, studied with the renowned violinist Joseph Joachim in Berlin. He joined the Berlin Philharmonic (under Nikisch) as leader of the second violin section, but in the early 1920s he, like thousands of Germans, left for America. Luckily, he immediately got a job with Reiner in Cincinnati. In Berlin he had played with all the great German conductors of the time: Nikisch, Furtwängler, Muck, and Erich Kleiber. When I met him in 1943, he was in his early sixties (which seemed very ancient to me) and near retirement. He seemed to be pretty much ignored by most of his colleagues, even regarded derisively by some and secretly made fun of. I couldn't understand that, for I immediately saw that Söndlin was someone very special. He was polymathically engaged in all the arts, the one true cultural intellectual in the orchestra, which is, I guess, what earned him the scorn (or was it envy?) of many of his colleagues, who blithely considered him a wooly-headed egghead (a good decade before that term came into common and pejorative use).

Söndlin was a very quiet, contemplative person, who kept to his own thoughts. I remember thinking of the phrase "still water runs deep." But if you were at his house, in his music room filled with hundreds of scores, in his spacious library-living room, his extensive hallway galleries of paintings—the whole place a great treasure trove—you would see him come alive with an almost feverish sensual excitement, as if he were just seeing all his treasures for the first time. He introduced me to and urged me to read Shakespeare's plays, but especially the *Sonnets*, Voltaire's plays and his *Dictionnaire philosophique*, the poetry of Goethe, Schiller, and Rilke, the plays of Büchner and Schnitzler, and much more. I will never forget the moment when, as I was admiring the contents of the endless shelves of books—small ones, large ones, fat, thin, tall, slight ones—he suddenly asked me if I had ever read Shakespeare's *Sonnets*. As I sheepishly admitted that I hadn't, he rose from his recamier and with his face suddenly aglow with happy anticipation, he picked a tiny, slim, six-inch-high, red-covered volume from the shelf and handed it to me with a beatific expression, as if he were handing me the Holy Grail. "You must—you absolutely must—know this poetry. It is so musical. Here—take it." "But it's yours." *"Macht nichts!* I want you to have it." There was something oddly sensuous in the way he was urging me to accept this precious gift.

In the two years I was in Cincinnati, I visited his home often, poring over and savoring the treasures of his library, especially the abundance of art books—some of them privately published and so grand and expensive that I knew I would never be able to own any of them. He was also the one who first introduced me to the paintings of Paul Klee, Kandinsky, and Malevich, artists whose work was eventually to play a significant role in my musical life and career.

In the orchestra our relationship took on an even more personal, intimate note. August Söndlin loved music in a deeply emotional way that I have rarely witnessed among the thousands of orchestra musicians I have known. Those words may seem strange, even shocking, to the reader: What! Doesn't every musician love music? The answer is: Well, yes and no; certainly not in the profound way that Söndlin did. All classical musicians, of course, love music in some general, inexplicit way, and they are especially enthusiastic when as youngsters they first get involved with it, learn to play their instrument, and gradually become acquainted with the great literature they are asked to play. The degree of intellectual and emotional involvement with music will vary greatly among musicians, or may wane, in varying degrees, as their orchestral careers devolve into prolonged bouts with apathy and boredom. There are many reasons and causes for this deterioration of interest in music among classical musicians (very rare among jazz musicians). One cause derives from the generally invariable working conditions in orchestras, including the often inordinate repetitiousness of overfamiliar standard repertory that characterizes the programs of most symphony orchestras. One can well imagine that if a musician has sat in an orchestra for, say, thirty years, and has played the Beethoven or Brahms or Tchaikovsky symphonies and the other repertory "war horses" twenty, thirty times, often conducted indifferently and uninspiringly, that a certain tedium can set in, even with musicians who when they were young would have given their right arm to get to play a Tchaikovsky symphony.

The Cincinnati orchestra was filled with a few such elderly musicians when I got there in 1943. Some were bored with Goossens, having been with him for many years; or some were bored with the repertory, even though, as I have noted earlier, Goossens's programming was never ordinary, was in fact almost always challenging and highly varied. But probably those musicians no longer wanted to be challenged and had stopped caring.

Obbligato

Söndlin was one of those relatively rare musicians who fully retained his love and enthusiasm for music, including rehearsing and practicing. Even rarer, he was someone who actually studied the scores—not just the viola parts—of the music we played.

Permit me a slight digression, a revelation that may shock most readers. The vast majority of orchestra musicians, probably 98 percent, never look at a score, never study a score. These are generally fine musicians, who know their individual parts very well, but whose interest in the music does not extend to the work as a whole. On the face of it that means that orchestra musicians are not interested in finding out what is in a score, how their part fits into the rest of the orchestration (harmonically, melodically, thematically, rhythmically, dynamically), how the composer put the whole piece together, and what a vast amount of vital information is actually notated in a score. To be sure, musicians who are very attentive in rehearsals and have good ears will pick up a certain amount of information about the work. But such genuine attentiveness is relatively rare. More often than not, particularly in much-played repertory that no longer requires undivided attention, the average musician's mind is directed toward playing his or her instrumental part without a mistake, rendering it technically correctly, but not extending to the work per se, to the score and the fullness of what it contains. That knowledge is left to the conductor, whose job it is—such is the general assumption—to teach the work to an orchestra. The fact is that the majority of conductors do not *fully* know or appreciate what is in a score either, and their highly individualized interpretations may deviate significantly from what is in the score. But that doesn't seem to bother most musicians, or many don't care anymore. And the best musicians who do care, who do know what's actually in a score, realize that they have to do what a conductor demands, even if it's wrong. They have no choice.

In my vast experience and lifelong involvement with orchestras—hundreds of them—as a performer (horn player), as a conductor, as a composer, I have sadly noted that the only time most musicians consult a score (or consult with a conductor) is when there seems to be a printed mistake in the part, or to check a phrasing or a bowing or a note—again the concern is only with the individual's part. In my day I knew of only one musician in the Metropolitan Opera orchestra beside myself and two in the New York Philharmonic (one of them was my father) who regularly studied the scores and brought them to rehearsals. The player in the Met was Harry Peers, third trumpet in the orchestra. And now, at age eighty-four, long ago retired from the orchestra, he still listens to all kinds of music (and not just operas) with love and reverence, studies scores, and still adds regularly to his already huge record collection.

Reuben Segal and August Söndlin were interested in the work as a whole, beyond their own violin and viola parts. They wanted to know not only *what* a composer had written, and in detail, but wanted to figure out *why*. Which has been precisely my philosophy of conducting for the last half century: not just *what*, but also *why*. *What* is hard enough and seems to be beyond many conductors' interests and capacities, but *why* is even more important—and much more interesting.

While many in the orchestra thought of Söndlin as a peculiar, slightly dotty old nostalgist who pined for the old days of the Weimar Republic, I didn't see him that way at all. Rather, I saw him as a very wise, very experienced, extraordinarily culturally literate musician whose love for music, whose tastes in music, corresponded entirely with mine. This common ground centered in certain works from around the turn of the twentieth century, such as Mahler's *Das Lied von der Erde* (*The Song of the Earth*). Söndlin seemed to be the only one in the orchestra who fully recognized the greatness of Mahler's music. Even Reuben was dubious about that music's value.

Söndlin and I bonded emotionally in a way and at a depth that I have almost never experienced with any other person—except Marjorie. During rehearsal intermissions we would share our excitement and joy in being privileged to help bring some great music to life. But our most touching moments of shared ecstasies came during concerts, none more transcendent than during our performances of *Das Lied von der Erde*. I first heard that work in Bruno Walter's remarkable Vienna Philharmonic performance, recorded at an actual concert in May 1936, with the great Kerstin Thorborg and Charles Kullman as soloists. I have always considered *Das Lied* Mahler's most inspired and most perfect work, even after I got to know all his symphonies in the late 1940s.[19] *Das Lied*—and the Ninth Symphony (also recorded by Walter in Vienna before World War II)—were not only transformative musical experiences for me in my midteen years, but, as works with the most glorious solo horn parts almost ever written, they also took on an especially personal and central role in my musical development.[20] Söndlin shared my high estimation of Mahler's *Das Lied*; in fact I could see that he was in a hypnotized trance at many moments in this extraordinary work—as was I. I often wondered, with my eyes moistening and my breathing becoming heavy, how in the world I could keep on playing. (It is not easy to play the horn while your eyes are filling with tears and your chest is heaving!)

On stage Söndlin and I sat about fifty feet apart from each other, he at the front edge of stage left, I diagonally across the stage, on risers near the back of stage right. At every special moment during the rehearsals and performances we would look at each other, our eyes sending the music and our emotions across the stage, as if in a blissful tryst. I can only describe what transpired between us as a near-erotic experience. Truly, Söndlin was more than a friend: he was an inspiration, a mentor, and I have never forgotten how much I learned from him and how much he gave of himself.

Most of the Cincinnati musicians—many of them German-born or first-generation Americans—were quite friendly to me, the young newcomer. I'm sure at first they must have wondered whether Goossens had lost his marbles, hiring an inexperienced teenager to fill a position as important as principal horn. But as the weeks passed, I saw that they had become convinced that I could deliver the goods and then some, and seemed in fact to be rather proud of me, in a paternal sort of way.

I'm sure there were a number of Nazi sympathizers among the German immigrants in the orchestra, probably more out of a love for their homeland than any true support and admiration for Hitler. Many German Americans, including my parents, were sometimes quite naïve about what was happening to their fatherland, unwilling or unable to believe all the horror stories that were circulating about the Nazi regime. (The same can be said, by the way, of millions of Americans—and one very gullible Mr. Neville Chamberlain.) But there was one musician in the Cincinnati orchestra who was, in fact, an ardent, fanatic Hitler supporter: Hans Meuser, the orchestra's principal bassoonist. An absolutely unreconstructed and loud, defiant defender of National Socialist ideologies, he was a dumb, ignorant, prejudiced anti-Semite who truly believed that Hitler was bringing Germany back to its former pre–World War I glories (whatever those might have been), and, to boot, was saving the German nation from the Jews! He was one of those types; I knew immediately that there was no point in arguing or discussing the matter with him.

I think that Meuser assumed that with my German background, my youth and (presumedly) political innocence, he would be able to convert me to his Nazi philosophies. At first I politely resisted his overtures, but he was amazingly, brashly persistent. One day, at a party he was giving for some of his best German friends in the orchestra—among which he erroneously counted me (and my obviously Jewish friend, Sammy Green)—he cornered me and started once again belaboring me about all the great things that were happening in Hitler's Germany. This time I exploded, and loudly so that all could hear, told him to shut up with his idiotic drivel and stormed out of the house, with Sammy right behind me.

Meuser's revenge for my public face-off with him was not long in coming. In any exposed passages where horn and bassoon play in unison, as happens often in Brahms and Tchaikovsky, especially the Brahms Second Symphony (which we played often, and on tour), Meuser would play purposely out of tune, at least in rehearsals, hoping to make *me* sound bad. It took me some years to reconcile Meuser's idiotic politics with the fact that he was a remarkably good bassoonist, until I eventually learned that there is not necessarily a correlation between great musical talent and liberal democratic ideals.

A few weeks after the Blacks' visit, near the end of my first season in Cincinnati, Goossens had programmed an all-Wagner concert. That was enough to put me in heaven, but wonder of wonders, that night Margie sat not in her usual faraway balcony seat, but much nearer to the stage, in the first row downstairs in what is called the orchestra. I was aglow with a dual inspiration—from her and from Wagner's glorious music. I told her after the concert how her nearby presence, her eyes always on me, had so inspired me. She subsequently wrote in her diary that she hoped that she "would always be that for Gunther."

One week later the Ballet Theatre came to town, and as had been established by the American Federation of Musicians' Local 1, the oldest and for many years strongest local in the country, any visiting dance group would be accompanied by the full Cincinnati Symphony Orchestra, in effect excluding the thirty-piece touring orchestra. I soon learned that for its three-night stand Ballet Theatre had scheduled Tudor's *Romeo and Juliet*. I was ecstatic, realizing that I would finally be playing Delius's wonderful music, with all its magnificent horn parts, although not entirely without some apprehension. I knew that Antal Dorati would be conducting—he who had just fired me eleven months before.

The first rehearsal for the orchestra that week, on a Tuesday morning, began with Delius's *Over the Hills and Far Away*, which starts with several quite exposed horn solos, accompanied only by strings. I was more than ready. Dorati came onto the stage just a few seconds before the rehearsal was to begin, mumbled a few words of greeting to the orchestra, gave a downbeat, and started conducting, although rather diffidently, I thought. To my surprise, he did not look at me, which normally a conductor would do with such an exposed opening horn solo. As my playing floated through the empty, acoustically very resonant hall, he began to look—rather sleepy-faced—around the stage, trying to figure out where the horn sound was coming from. For some seconds he seemed unable to find me, probably because Goossens had the horn section seated not where American orchestras generally have the horns, but English-style, quite far over on stage right, toward the back. Suddenly he spied me, and in incredulous consternation burst out: "What the hell are *you* doing here. I just fired you on second horn—and here you are playing *first* horn?!" The whole orchestra instantly broke up in laughter, as did Dorati once he recovered from his surprise.

He continued the rehearsal, still shaking his head and constantly gawking at me in disbelief. The reader will, I'm sure, believe me when I say that I played my heart out for him, and, of course, for Delius. As he called for the rehearsal's intermission, he motioned me to come and see him. I told him what had happened with my three auditions the previous summer, and that I had been first horn in Cincinnati since the previous October. The upshot was that he invited me to lunch after the rehearsal at his hotel, the Netherland Plaza, at the time the ritziest hotel in Cincinnati. We had a grand time together, exchanging news about our recent composing activities, he bringing me up to date on Ballet Theatre news and gossip. He also told me that he was going to leave Ballet Theatre and in the fall of 1945 become music director of the Dallas Symphony Orchestra. We parted as friends at the end of the week, and I had the distinct feeling that we would soon, somehow or other, meet again.

From where I sat in the makeshift orchestra pit in front of the stage I could not see much of the ballet—rather frustrating for me since I was such an Antony Tudor fan—but I knew that his choreography and the performance of the entire Ballet Theatre Company, especially the work of the major soloists, had been unanimously praised by the New York critics at the world premiere earlier that year. It was considered one of the greatest triumphs in recent American ballet history. Margie was in attendance, of course, raving to me about the whole event: Tudor's choreography, the dancing, the scenery and the staging, the rapturous romantic atmosphere of the whole evening. I learned then that Margie not only loved ballet but was also very knowledgeable and discerning in what was good or great dancing—or not. It turned out that her parents had taken her to ballet performances ever since she was nine or ten to see touring ballet companies in Fargo.

In retrospect I am astonished at how slow I was in courting Margie. Being inwardly impetuous, but outwardly cautious and shy, it wasn't until the late spring of 1944, in other words near the end of my first season in Cincinnati, that I took her to our first movie together *and* our first dinner, a fabulous doubleheader. (The movie was *Gaslight* with Charles Boyer and Ingrid Bergman.)

Like first love itself, it was an unforgettable evening, its memory etched in my mind and soul forever. I picked her up at the college, presenting her with a huge orchid corsage in the dormitory's parlor, watched over sternly by the housemother and a few of the other girls. I whisked Margie off in a taxi to the downtown Hotel Sinton (long gone now), which was reputed to have one of the city's finest restaurants. It was the perfect ambiance for our first real evening out. A spacious candlelit room, our reserved table for two allowing a glimpse of the nearby Ohio River with its bustling river traffic. But I wasn't really in an actual place; I was in some paradisal Eden, alone with my Eve. I had no sense of any other people in the room (except occasionally our waiter); I was totally under the spell of her rich, quietly sensuous beauty, drinking in her persona, scenting her delicate perfume mixed with the gentle fragrance of the orchid I had given her. There was a palpable warmth coming from her; at least I thought so—not a bodily heat but an inner, radiant glow.

Oh, how I wanted to embrace her, to sink into her beauty. I was in a kind of benign delirium, sensing the heat inside of me, all the while carrying on small talk to cover my inner emotional turmoil. None of this had anything to do with sex. These were not sexual urges that were gripping me, no teenage testosterone outbreak. It was something way beyond that, very deep and mysterious, which I had never experienced before.

We splurged on sirloin steaks, a rich Burgundy wine, strawberry shortcake. I remember eventually calming down enough so that I could carry on a rational conversation. But still, much of that evening was as if I had been enveloped in some wonderful, prolonged Elysian dream. And I felt as if we were already married. We cried a little when I dropped her off at the dorm, and I stayed with her in the little dormitory parlor until I was rather brusquely ushered out by Madame Queen, who effectively prevented me from giving Margie what would have been our first kiss—on the cheek.

I couldn't go home right away. I wandered around in Washington Park, across the street from the college and the music hall, wanting somehow to still be near her, restlessly trying out different park benches, avoiding people, watching and listening to the rippling sounds of the old sculptured fountain in the center of the park—somehow trying to retain, imprison, that beautiful evening in my mind.

Those long hours in the park that night led to a brainstorm. In the balmy, warm spring weather we could spend some of our evenings together there, sitting in the dark, unobserved, real close, maybe even getting to some necking.[21] Instead of hanging out at Steve's, after concerts, we could in the future retire to the relative quiet and isolation of the park. We were both getting desperate to find *some* place where we could really be alone. Margie's dorm, with all of its restrictions and curfews, offered no possibilities. My room on Highland Avenue was certainly not an alternative. And neither Margie nor I liked the idea, much resorted to by young lovers in those days, to head for the darkness of a movie house; we didn't think that that constituted privacy. So we took refuge in Washington Park, spending many evenings—and nights—there, deeply in love. And wonder of wonders, in that time of our growing and exploring relationship, Margie hardly ever resisted me. Her acquiescence was quiet, docilely yielding, as if she wanted to be gently led wherever I wanted to take her—up to a point, of course.

I must not have slept much in those days, a condition that, as most people who know me have learned, eventually became a determined way of life. And why not? I was young, healthy, strong, bursting with energy, and so motivated to live the fullest, most challenging life possible that having eight hours sleep every night was definitely not a priority. Also, it shouldn't be a mystery that musicians are by nature night people. Consider that symphony concerts and opera performances *never* end before ten thirty p.m., and in my fifteen years at the Metropolitan Opera, the shortest opera, Puccini's *Tosca*, finished at five of eleven, while dozens of other standard operas ended closer to eleven thirty or midnight.

That's in classical music. But jazz musicians *really* worked the night shift. In those earlier days ballrooms stayed open until two a.m. and most jazz clubs until four a.m., requiring musicians to keep late hours if they wanted to work. Need I mention the so-called breakfast clubs and jam sessions that would *start* at four a.m. and often go on for another three or four hours— a way of life that most "normal" people considered wrong, unhealthy, even sinful and immoral. Things have changed drastically. Already for several decades, jazz and rock and popular music are most often presented at more decent hours in the format of concerts. Nowadays jazz gigs in clubs and cafes end around midnight, or one a.m. at the latest—though that is considered late by most ordinary working folks, who may have to get up in the early morning hours. But even in classical music, if a musician finishes a concert at, say, ten thirty, he or she has first to get home, perhaps eat a snack, relax and unwind from the concert, all of which usually adds up to not being in bed before one a.m.

Beyond keeping such "abnormal" hours, I learned in my Cincinnati days that I could stay up half the night—or all of it—and still function perfectly well the next day. Needless to say, had I found this to be otherwise, had I found that not getting my eight hours of "beauty sleep" was negatively affecting my playing in the symphony, my mental alertness, my ability to go through the next day fully functioning, I would have immediately changed course. But that never happened. And life was too exciting. There was too much to be done, too much to learn and experience, to not take advantage of all of one's energy and stamina to live the fullest, richest life possible.

Indeed, it was in those days, young as I was and stubbornly defiant of physical laws, that I calculated that if I were to sleep eight hours every night, as my parents (supported by the entire medical profession) insisted I do, I would sleep away one third of my life. I knew that that was something I couldn't possibly do. Not that I didn't *like* sleeping, that my body didn't crave sleep. Indeed, I discovered that if I didn't awaken myself with two alarm clocks and immediate injections of coffee, I would easily sleep ten or twelve, even fourteen hours, at a time. No, I didn't sleep very much in Cincinnati. Between my obligations to the symphony, my evening courting of Margie, or my composing and studying late into the night, I began to live an eighteen- to twenty-hour day, especially when early in my stay in Cincinnati jazz began to enter my life in a very serious way.

The reader may wonder whether I did any serious composing that first year in Cincinnati. Truth be told, not really—at least not at first. But in the spring of 1944 I composed three songs, set to the previously mentioned Li Po–Klabund poems, the first three of a song cycle that many years later (in the seventies) was finally published as *Six Early Songs*. My inspiration for this song cycle was threefold: Margie's beautiful soprano voice, Ravel's superb and, alas, rarely performed song cycle *Histoires naturelles*, and the exquisite, aphoristic thirteen-hundred-year-old poetry of Li Po. Although the songs show the influence on me of the French modern school of Ravel and Debussy, the full cycle is I believe one of the very best compositions of my teen years.

The Symphony season ended in mid-April, but I stayed in town almost two weeks longer, mainly because of Margie—much to the dismay of my parents. I just couldn't tear myself away from her, and she was still busy at school. I, too, was obliged to finish up my teaching schedule at both schools, and did this by giving my students two-hour—and in some cases—three-hour lessons, so that I could make up the lesson hours I owed them. That kept me pretty busy. When I finally left for New York in early May, Margie came with me in the taxi to the train station, and it was then that I kissed her for the first time. It was probably a pretty chaste kiss, but even that, in those days, was a major event in the progression of one's amorous relationship—a special moment in time that we both cherished as a beautiful memory while we were separated in the ensuing weeks. The next day she noted in her diary: "The Brahms Second was on the radio yesterday. When I heard those glorious horn parts, it tore my heart out. Oh, give me strength!" We were both beginning to learn how much pain can come into true love.

Marjorie and I had now known each other for almost nine months, coming ever closer. Now suddenly we were apart for the first time, and that wasn't a casual matter. The only solution to this new predicament was to stay in close contact through letters. And thus began a multidecade correspondence—more than a thousand letters from each of us—necessitated by the constant, never-ending separations that characterized our fifty-year life together. I did so much traveling in my career, especially as a conductor. In later years, once our children were grown and had flown the coop, Margie accompanied me on most of my travels. In the early years, however, when she was still trying to work toward a career as a singer, and then during the years of raising our children, she obviously could be with me only on the rarest of occasions. In our exchange of letters it became painfully clear how much we missed each other. My first letter to her, besides describing my train ride to New York as "the most excruciating sixteen hours of my life thus far," laments that "I couldn't stop thinking of you for a second. I couldn't read, eat, or sleep, and as each minute crept by I thought I would burst with longing for you."

Her response three days later was somewhat more muted. She thanked me for my "most wonderful letter," writing how "*very much*" she missed me. The more reserved tone of her letter may have been prompted by a brief moment of discomfiture between us in those usually awkward last minutes before a train actually pulls out. I had asked her how much she loved me. It wasn't the right thing to ask at such a time, hardly the best timing to allow for a meaningful response, and certainly not the right place—a noisy train station restaurant. Under the circumstances it was a rather strained situation, and I knew in retrospect that I had made her uncomfortable with the question. But then, in a second letter, she declared that my question had in fact touched her deeply. She had not been "embarrassed" or "offended," but simply didn't know *how* to answer, and so quickly. She wasn't sure that she really knew "what true love is," adding, "we must talk about this when we see each other again soon."

It was a beautiful example of her absolute honesty in everything she said and did, a confirmation of what I had already noted many times, that she was not given to light, silly, or, for that matter, evasive answers. She was, like me, tackling a subject head-on, openly—or at least really trying to do so. I loved her so much for that. It was part of a deep sensibility that I had sensed in her almost from the first day I laid eyes on her, even before I really got to know her. I saw it in her eyes.

Another striking example of her candor, her openness, and by extension, *our* truthfulness with each other from the very beginning, was that she told me in one of those early letters about how a certain boy, a soldier named Dan Morton, stationed in nearby Ft. Knox, had asked her to go out with him on a weekend when he was visiting in Cincinnati. At first she demurred, but after more pleading on his part, she finally accepted his invitation. He took her to a theatre to hear Henry Busse's orchestra[22]—of all things—which she thought was awful. No surprise there, since I had been priming her on Ellington, Basie, Herman, and Kenton for months. She thought Dan was "a nice, clean-cut boy, but too narrow-minded and set in his ways. Furthermore, he seems to have lost all his ideals about music—if he had any to start with."

But Dan pursued her further, asking her to be his date during the summer, also wanting Margie to learn to dance so that they could go out dancing. That was really the wrong thing to say, for Margie didn't like dancing. In any case, she found him very unexciting. Then she almost apologized in her letter—so much like her—for talking about him that way, adding that she did so only to let me know that "going out with Dan doesn't mean anything. In fact, going out with him made me miss you all the more."

It wasn't some kind of confessional guilt trip on her part. This kind of integrity and mutual respect for each other was not something we ever discussed or consciously adopted; it simply was an inherent, natural expression of our relationship, right from the start, the memory of which I now cherish all the more deeply. Honesty was fundamental in our relationship, it was an ethical-philosophical tenet we embraced our entire life together—through thick and thin.

I was expected to return to Cincinnati to play in the historic May Festival, founded in 1878 by Theodore Thomas, which took place biannually in those days. (Now it is an annual affair.) That was another musical experience of great import in my young career. Again, Goossens's programming covered a wonderful range of choral and orchestral offerings. Particularly outstanding for me were scenes from Gluck's *Orpheus and Eurydice* (with the great Kerstin Thorborg as Orpheus), Haydn's *The Seasons*, William Walton's *Belshazzar's Feast* (with John Brownlee), Bernard Rogers's wonderfully moving oratorio, *The Passion*,[23] Rossini's *Stabat Mater*, featuring Stella Roman, and the entire second act of Wagner's *Tannhäuser*. What a fantastic weeklong musical feast for a young composer.

In the meantime, another bit of fortuitous luck intervened when, only a few days after I had returned to New York, I got a call from someone at the recently formed New York City Opera on behalf of the company's founder and musical director, Laszlo Halász, asking me to play first horn for a few weeks in May.[24] I found out later that, once again, I had been recommended by Mimi Caputo, and by Halász's fellow Hungarian, Antal Dorati. (It pays to have friends and admirers.)

Laszlo Halász (1905–2001), a quite good conductor who is now much forgotten, was an important figure in New York's musical life in the 1940s. He not only founded the New York City Opera in early 1944 (in the old Mecca Temple on West Fifty-Fifth Street, later named City Center) and was its chief conductor for the first seven years, he also created a company whose artistic policy centered on presenting unfamiliar classics and new modern operas, including operas by American composers, offered at modest prices that people with moderate incomes could afford. The company also made it an abiding commitment to offer opportunities to young American and lesser-known European singers. Halász thought of his opera company as an alternative, an antidote, to the Metropolitan Opera, which almost never presented neglected works from the past by, say, Donizetti, Rossini, Bellini, or Verdi. The Met also had a pretty dismal record in the 1930s and 1940s of offering contemporary operas, especially in the waning years of Edward Johnson's regime at the Met.[25]

I was quite flattered to be asked at age eighteen to take on such a prominent position in a fledgling new enterprise, and darn grateful for my early experiences with opera, especially Italian opera, which repertory I played a lot of with those Upper West Side amateur opera groups such as LaPuma and Salmaggi, with their little scratch orchestras. I began to really appreciate that my father and Mr. Schulze had pushed me into learning the basic opera repertory in that manner. Those experiences stood me in good stead, especially since the new New York City Opera orchestra consisted mostly of seasoned opera veterans who *really* knew the standard repertory, which in turn meant that those operas were done with an absolute minimum of rehearsals.

Halász was very efficient in his rehearsing, having a long history as music director of the opera houses of Budapest, Prague, Vienna, and St. Louis. Opera lovers and musicians, especially brass players, may find it interesting that, of those four scheduled operas that first season, the two for which I really had to be on my toes were *Pagliacci* and *Cavalleria rusticana* and *Pagliacci*, and that was because of the strange horn transpositions Leoncavallo and Mascagni used. Both composers were considerably influenced by Wagner's superchromaticism, considering it the musical style most appropriate for their dramatic verismo conceptions. *Cav* and *Pag* are so successful because that particular musical language and the given dramatic action happen to meld together perfectly, offering in the bargain all the tried-and-true essentials of successful opera: lyricism, passion, haunting melodies, stark drama, plus—in both cases—a new realism expressed with remarkable concision. (They are both short, one-act operas.)

But why did these two composers write their horn parts in transpositions—in E and E flat, rarely in F (the standard)—that are almost always at odds with the underlying tonality, given the fluid chromaticism of the music and the fact that by the 1890s (the premiere dates for both operas) the horn had been a fully chromatic instrument for some sixty years? Transpositions other than F were by then pretty much out of date, and if not used idiomatically could be awkward and cumbrous.[26] In any event, my two-week sojourn with the City Opera was a wonderful learning experience, and in addition provided me with some very welcome extra income.

As far as I knew, I was not going to see Margie again until the next fall, when we both would return to Cincinnati, she to continue her studies at the College of Music, I to fulfill my two-year contract with the Symphony. But she didn't seem to be sure of her plans for the summer. Back in New York, in early May—Margie was still in Cincinnati—I wrote her a passionate letter that she later told me made her cry with joy. I remember that I addressed her as "my beautiful Queen Mab."[27] But sadly, this time there was no response from her; I never found out why. I was afraid to write her again, because such a letter would have to be sent to Fargo, and I didn't want to risk her parents thinking that there was anything serious going on between us. A letter from me would certainly have suggested as much to them. (Oh, how I hated all this secrecy and subterfuge.) I assumed that Margie would be spending the summer in Fargo. But, miracle of miracles, when I returned to Cincinnati in May, there she was. I couldn't believe my eyes, or my good fortune. She had somehow persuaded her parents to let her stay not only for the May Festival but also to attend summer school at the college and continue her work with her voice teacher. What that meant was that we could be together most of the summer, since I was also scheduled to play with the Cincinnati Opera in its summer season. Destiny or the alignment of the stars was definitely on my side.

As it turned out I didn't actually see all that much of Margie during the May Festival period, at least not in any private way, in large part because the orchestra's rehearsal and concert schedule was very intensive. We had daily double rehearsals for an entire week, obviously to prepare so many substantial evening filling works, most of them unfamiliar to the orchestra. Then my parents suddenly showed up the day before the first Festival concert. They had wanted to surprise me. Well they certainly did! (Were they checking up on me?) I was happy to see them, of course, and even happier to introduce Margie to them, and still happier when I saw that they liked her right away.

On one of my last nights in Cincinnati during the May Festival—a free night in the schedule—Walter Heermann asked me to play in a chamber ensemble concert with him on one of the local radio stations. I remember we played among other things a whole group of very popular Percy Grainger pieces such as *Handel in the Strand*, *Shepherd's Hey*, and *Country Gardens*. Margie listened to the broadcast in the control booth, after which we went to Walter's house for a postconcert reception, with lots of Walter's orchestra friends, including his brother Emil and the two Segals. But Margie and I wanted to be alone. We had seen so little of each other. So we excused ourselves and took the streetcar down to the college where, to our surprise, we found the dorm's front parlor empty. We sat there in the evening twilight, in total silence. We didn't want to talk; we just wanted to be together, lost in our own thoughts. It was a strangely wonderful experience; I recall it so vividly. It was as if I could feel inside me what Margie was thinking. When her eyes closed momentarily, I kissed her on the cheek. "It was like a bolt of ecstasy flushing through my whole body," she wrote in her diary. "I had never felt anything like that, and had never been so happy."

After the May Festival I followed my parents back to New York. I was glad to see my brother Edgar (who had just finished his first year in high school) and my Aunt Lydia, who was now working as a live-in lady's maid for an elderly millionairess, a Mrs. Sachs, who lived in the Hotel Pierre on Fifth Avenue, probably the poshest and most expensive hotel in New York. Lydia had two rooms to herself, free of charge, in Mrs. Sachs's huge apartment. Her amazingly light workload, for which she was paid most handsomely, consisted mainly of helping with preparations on those relatively rare occasions when Mrs. Sachs had guests. The meals and all housekeeping services were handled by the hotel's staff. Aunt Lydia was the typical loving maiden aunt—she never married—whose whole mission in life seemed to be to spoil her two young nephews. She invited me many, many times for lunch to her little apartment kitchen, where she would serve up the most incredible cream soups, exotic salads, and sandwiches, brought up by room service from the hotel's renowned kitchen and dining room. It was a remarkable experience for an eleven-year-old kid to be served meals that were prepared for kings and royalty, for millionaires and movie stars, all of whom could afford to pay the magnificent sum of three dollars for a bowl of soup at lunch, when an only slightly less spectacular soup at a coffee shop in those years might cost twenty cents.

Back in New York, I also caught up with old Ballet Theatre friends such as John Clark and Cecil Collins, and had a short refresher lesson with Robert Schulze, who was aglow with pride over his now successful former student. Seeing family and old friends was all lots of fun and heartwarming, but in truth I wanted to get back to Cincinnati to see my Margie. I missed her so; it was heartbreaking.

Walter Heermann had been telling me for some time about a fine little chamber orchestra in Lake Placid, New York, the Lake Placid Sinfonietta, with which he played every summer; it was an ensemble composed of many first-rate, seasoned symphony players, mostly from nearby Rochester, but also from other orchestras such as Cleveland, Buffalo, and Cincinnati. Its conductor was Paul White, a fine composer and conductor, and second-in-command to Howard Hanson at the Eastman School of Music in Rochester. The orchestra was in residence for about three months each summer, performing at the Lake Placid Club. Walter had been after me for weeks to join him there, not so much to play in the little orchestra—it didn't use a horn very much—but to just hang out in beautiful Lake Placid in the midst of the Adirondacks. He told me he was fairly sure I could stay free of charge with Paul White and his family, who occupied a huge rambling cottage in the woods near the club's famous golf course. Walter had for many years opted to avoid Cincinnati in the summers. He told me he preferred the cooler climes of the Adirondacks, as opposed to the oppressive heat and humidity of Cincinnati. (Even before Lake Placid Walter had spent years teaching at the famous Interlochen Summer Music Camp in northern Michigan.) I told him that I'd love to join him in Lake Placid, perhaps in late August and September, but that I had agreed to play the seven-week Cincinnati Opera season until then.

The operas that had been scheduled for the 1944 summer season were *Carmen*, *Tosca*, *Pagliacci*, *Hänsel und Gretel*, *Il Trovatore*, *Samson and Delilah*, *Aida*, *La Bohème*, *Barber of Seville*, and *Martha*. I was happy to return to opera after a year of primarily symphonic repertoire, but especially so because Sir Thomas Beecham, a conductor whose work on records I had admired for years, was going to be conducting *Carmen*, *Aida*, and *Pagliacci*. The conductor for the other operas was Fausto Cleva, musical director of the Zoo Opera, and later longtime resident conductor at the Met, with whom I worked there nearly three hundred times in the Italian and French repertory. The Zoo Opera, under Cleva and stage director Tony Stivanello's leadership, spared no expense in bringing some of the finest singers of the time to Cincinnati. The list of guest stars was most impressive, great artists such as the superb Bidu Sayao (heavenly as Mimi—she tore at your heart in the third and fourth acts of *La Bohème*), Rose Bampton (perhaps the most musical Aida I ever heard in my many years in opera), Kerstin Thorborg (as a very captivating, sensual Delilah), the thirty-one-year-old Licia Albanese (glorious as Violetta and Mimi), and John Brownlee, one of the vocally finest and most intelligent baritones of that era. Also on the roster were the youthful Francesco Valentino, as well as such fine tenors as Raoul Jobin and Charles Kullman, the beautiful svelte-voiced Gladys Swarthout, and, above all, bass Virgilio Lazzari, clearly among the very greatest artist-actors in opera of the whole twentieth century. When he sang Sparafucile in *Rigoletto* or even smaller roles such as Ramfis in *Aida* or the Cardinal in *Tosca*, you had chills up and down your spine, not to mention his hilarious antics as Don Basilio in Rossini's *Barber of Seville*. It was in that summer that I quickly learned what *really* great opera singing was.

Beecham was not only one of the most remarkable conductors of his time, he was also well known for his legendary wit, flair, and colorful personality. He was the son of an English baron and wealthy businessman, from whom he inherited his impressive bearing, not to mention a generous inheritance that offered him a certain financial and artistic and professional independence. Beecham was held in high esteem and great affection by orchestra musicians. Already renowned for his brilliant witticisms, casually sprinkled throughout his rehearsals, he was also greatly admired for his ability to achieve remarkable results with a minimum of rehearsing—always a plus for most musicians in evaluating a conductor. It is true that on occasion performances under his baton could be a bit sloppy, undisciplined. But most of the time, musicians tended to be on their toes and especially concentrated, playing their absolute best. Beecham gave you the impression that he trusted you as a professional and that, of course, you would do your best at all times.

A case in point: about one third of the way through his second *Carmen* rehearsal, Beecham, with a sly glint in his eyes, said something to the effect of: "Gentlemen, you seem to know this music, and I think possibly I do too. Let's meet again tomorrow and have a real go at it with the stage." He let us out almost two hours early. (I'm sure the management wasn't too happy about paying the orchestra for a full three-hour rehearsal when we had played for only about one hour.) We, of course, played our hearts out for him, and the resultant performance (with Raoul Jobin, a wonderful Canadian tenor specializing in French roles, and Lily Djanel as Carmen—they called her the "French spitfire") was brilliant, spirited, lively, and had a certain buoyant spontaneity. A couple of slightly ragged places never seriously marred the overall spirit of a Beecham performance.

Cincinnati summers have always been known for their ninety-degree temperatures and awful humidity. Despite the debilitating heat, Sir Thomas came to the rehearsals every morning in a splendid white suit, replete with vest and white shoes, dressed more like a patrician baron attending the races at Ascot than a musician about to vigorously wave his arms for three hours. Beecham was extremely fond of Coca-Cola, consuming during every rehearsal about four or five bottles of the drink, brought to him one by one by his wife, the pianist Betty Humby. Sweating like a trooper in the sweltering heat, large blotches of perspiration would start to saturate first his jacket and vest, then work their way down with each successive Coca-Cola the entire length of his suit, until even the cuffs of Beecham's trousers were soaking wet. How he could move in that wet suit and function musically so well was beyond our comprehension. Nor could we at first understand how at the next morning's rehearsal he would appear again in an impeccably tailored white suit and go though the whole Coca-Cola soaking once again.

Cleva was about as different a personality and conductor from Beecham as one can possibly imagine. I respected him enormously for his vast knowledge of the opera repertory and his technical skills as a conductor. It was nice to hear that my feelings were reciprocated when, halfway through the season, I heard from one of Cleva's Italian friends in the orchestra that he thought I was the best horn player the Cincinnati Symphony ever had. But I think most of the musicians found it difficult to like the man. He always looked unhappy, dissatisfied, unyieldingly grim. As one of my Cincinnati colleagues put it: "He always looks like he has a pile of shit in his mouth." We always psychologized that, being of very small stature, Cleva probably had a Napoleonic complex (hence his irrational distrustfulness and suspiciousness), and that, believing he was another Toscanini, he therefore felt that he could rant and rave and curse—and did he ever!—like the famous maestro. He also didn't seem to have the gift of laughter. The closest he would come to a smile would be a kind of disgusted sarcastic grimace. In the end—and I do not say this patronizingly, for I mean it sincerely—I felt sorry for him because on the podium he seemed incapable of being pleased or happy or relaxed, of enjoying music making. Off the podium, as I learned years later, he was calm, friendly, much less tense, just a regular family man devoted to wife and children, and quite at ease with other people.

During our performance of *Aida* that summer a curious and hilarious thing happened that, incidentally, made even Cleva laugh. Toward the end of the famous Nile aria in act 3, where Aida bemoans her fate and expresses her foreboding of never again seeing her homeland (Ethiopia), with its "verdant hillsides" and "azure skies," she sings the words "*mai più*" ("never again") on the following pitches: , answered immediately by the oboe on the same notes. Not far from the area where our performances took place there was a pond inhabited by geese and ducks. One night when Rose Bampton came to the *mai più*, suddenly not only the oboe responded but one of the ducks as well, unbelievably echoing not only the exact same pitches but even Verdi's triplet rhythms. The chances of such a coincidence occurring must be one in several millions. The audience, the orchestra, and even Cleva, burst into gales of laughter. It was the only time I ever saw Cleva laugh in more than a decade of working with him, but even so I could see him struggling to restrain himself. No one could keep on playing or singing. That one duck brought the performance to a complete standstill. When everyone had finally regained their composure, we started the third act again—and this time without any antidaeon quacking accompaniment.

My good fortune in being able to play that summer opera season was surpassed only by the fact that Margie, after a couple of weeks at home, had also contrived to return to Cincinnati for most of the summer. Although the official reason was that she was going to continue her studies at the college's summer school, I knew deep down that she had really come back to Cincinnati to be with me. Suffice it to say that we continued in our burgeoning relationship where we had left off in April. But now we had even more time for each other. Margie's summer school schedule was much lighter than in the winter-spring semesters, and in my case the opera schedule was also less intense than the symphony's in the winter season. I pulled out all the recordings of operas that I owned for our daytime listening sessions in my room, among them *Carmen, La Bohème, Rosenkavalier, The Marriage of Figaro*, operas which Margie was studying with Mme Leonard, working on some of their most celebrated soprano arias.

We probably all can remember the music associated with our courtships, especially when first falling in love. Since neither Margie nor I cared much for dancing, our courting music came from the classics, and that summer of 1944 in particular from the world of opera. I doubt that for young people in love who cherish classical music there can be anything more emotionally compelling, more poignantly heart-tugging, than Puccini's many love arias—except possibly some of Rachmaninov's more sensuously passionate music.[28] In that summer of 1944 the music that more than any other gave our love its wings, that bonded us in feelings that transported us to new sentient heights, was Puccini's *La Bohème*. While I was reveling in playing Puccini's most pristine masterpiece several times that summer, Margie was working on the two Mimi arias that are among the most affecting soprano solos in the entire operatic repertory: "Si, mi chiamano Mimi" (act 1), and "Donde lieta usci" (act 3). Even under ordinary circumstances, you must be tone deaf or emotionally dysfunctional if you are not deeply moved by these rapturous expressions of Puccini's genius. But being in love—first love at that—is not an ordinary circumstance. The music and our feelings for each other became intertwined in some wondrous emotional union. Great music can do that; it is one of its special powers. And I cannot think of much music with the capacity to work its way into your very soul the way Puccini's most poignant music can, especially those two arias from *La Bohème*, capturing both the joy of love discovered and the pain of love lost.[29]

Besides *La Bohème* and *Tosca*, there were a number of other works with especially romantic, lyric, expressively prominent horn parts, which we bonded to in such warm personal ways. When those solos came along I would play to her, my eyes making loving contact across the stage to her in the audience—a spiritual experience just short of making actual love.

Margie was still living at the college dorm, a situation that presented a considerable impediment to our love evolving into those more intimate spheres that I certainly craved, but to which Margie was, I felt, not yet ready to surrender. We resorted to spending much time in Washington Park as before, but now also stayed in the zoo park after the opera—Margie came to almost every opera performance. In its wooded areas we would usually find some secluded spot where we could enjoy some privacy.

For the girls at the college dorm staying out late was a real problem. The dorm's curfew had been extended during the summer to twelve midnight because most of the students went to the operas, which generally didn't end until eleven. While a few of the more adventurous girls would manage to sneak into the dorm late by climbing through first floor windows, or having someone with a purloined key open some little-used side door, you couldn't do that regularly. The only real alternative was to stay out all night and reappear in the morning—hopefully not too disheveled—as if one had just gone out for a few minutes for a morning walk or to have a cup of coffee at Steve's.

It is amazing to what lengths love will drive you. For all of her proper, restrictive upbringing, Margie was remarkably courageous, even reckless, in her determination to have us spend as much time together as possible, even if it meant defying the dorm rules and staying out all night. It was kind of crazy to be so driven by our longing for each other that we had to resort to sleepless nights in parks and woods, or occasionally an all-night restaurant, unable even then to fully assuage our hunger for each other. Sometimes, on Sunday afternoons, we would go to Burnet Woods, another large Cincinnati park a short streetcar ride from the college, known popularly as lover's lane. We'd be there for hours, under a tree, really close to each other. Margie on her back, I on my stomach, feeling the warmth of her body, unable to take my eyes off her radiant beauty. We knew that our love was the real thing; it went way beyond mere infatuation or sexual urgings. It was so deep, it was painful in its joy, in its utter happiness. It was almost funny to hear how often we declared that all we wanted to do was to make each other supremely happy.

At one point I told her about the four or five girls I had previously dated before Cincinnati, but how I usually tired of them because they seemed so shallow, so unserious, so calculating in just wanting to capture a boyfriend or a husband. And just in case she had sometimes worried about Gussie, I told her: "I really can't stand her anymore." With all that talent and that flashy attractive exterior, "she is so flirty, so capricious—and so moody." I told Margie that leaving her for someone else could never happen, and that if it did—my diary faithfully documented my exaggerated rhetorical ardor—"I would kill myself." But, of course, it wasn't just hyperbole. I really meant it—though perhaps not the "killing myself" part.

With each passing week it had become ever clearer to us that we were truly meant for each other, that it was already as if we were married—except for the love that we had not yet consummated. I knew very well that I could not press her on that subject, not yet. I think I was more in love with her beauty, her soul, her innocence, than with her body, although some part of me certainly knew how to desire that.

We had so many "beautiful, beautiful nights together," as she put it in her diary. She wrote, "I was carried away quite enough, many a night." She knew that she had made me very happy that summer. She was right, and just by being herself, nothing more, nothing less. In her diary she wrote: "But Gunther did even more than that for me."

At one point Margie's parents suddenly showed up in Cincinnati on their way to New York, but obviously with the intent of checking up on their daughter. Knowing that they didn't particularly approve of me, and were always worried about their daughter living so far away, hanging out with a lot of musicians, we naturally kept the closeness of our relationship hidden from them. Margie knew we could not confide in them; they would never have approved or understood.

For her part Margie hated all this secrecy, this lack of openness—especially toward her parents, whom she loved dearly and to whom she felt she owed so much. The inability to be honest with her parents went against all her principles of behavior, principles that, ironically, had been inculcated in her by but her parents. She absolutely hated lying, dissembling, prevaricating. Deception of any kind was so foreign to her. I know because she never lied to me or hid anything from me.

All her parents were supposed to perceive was that ours was a purely platonic friendship, two musical colleagues, nothing more. What they really thought or imagined was probably something else. Fortunately the subject never came up; all conversation, at least in my presence, was cloaked in stilted politeness and empty platitudes. Margie and I knew that for a few days we would literally not be able to see each other, a frustrating interruption for us. She read the dejection in my face when she told me that her parents had just arrived and that she was going to have lunch with them at the Netherland Plaza. It was so like her to worry about my disconsolateness, not her own. Unbelievably, somehow, she managed to send me a brief note from the Netherland Plaza that same afternoon—I was teaching a few lessons at the college— begging me not to worry and above all not to worry about her. She asked me to look at the situation positively, as a chance during her parents' two- or three-day stay "to get some sleep (ahem)," to get lots of work done "with nothing and no one to interfere." It was so sweet and caring. "You have so much to protect, dear Gunther." The last line read: "This better be all for now. I don't want my folks to get suspicious as to what I'm doing."

Margie suffered for years, never free to be completely open with her parents about many matters (religion, politics, race, social concerns—and, of course, sex, a completely taboo subject that was inherently offensive to them) even long after we were married. In our early years together I really had only a vague idea of how truly narrow-minded and intolerant her parents were, but I was to find out before long the true extent of their intellectual and moral limitations, which led to severe verbal and mental abuse every time she went home to Fargo. How she came to dread those visits, and how often I had to rescue her from the resultant bouts of depression.

We finally worked up enough courage—enough defiance of a world of ridiculous rules and restrictions that was making us hide our love in secret places, in the dark, away from spying eyes—to bring Margie to my place at night. It seemed a ludicrous notion that I could bring Margie to my room on a Sunday afternoon in daylight but not on a Sunday evening after dark, as if sex could occur only at nighttime, and more—that even the thought of premarital sex was a sin.

For us it wasn't even a matter of sexual intercourse—or not. It was more a matter of defying the ridiculous notion that a man and a woman could not meet in their private quarters after sunset. It was preposterous. Was the assumption that, if I brought Margie to my room on Highland Avenue, I would undoubtedly forcibly subdue her? That might have been what Mr. Burns imagined or what Margie's parents thought in their fevered imagination. Her inner beauty, her quiet, centered strength was what captivated me, even to the point of incomprehension of how there could be someone so perfect, so loving, so caring.

It is amazing how ingenious and stealthy we can be when, under duress, we are absolutely resolved to achieve a certain goal. The only access to my room on the top floor of the two-family house I lived in was by a creaky outside wooden staircase at the rear of the house. It was visible from the first-floor living room, which meant that my landlord, the ever watchful Mrs. Burns, could easily spot any unwanted visitors. The best way to bypass such a potential intervention was for us to sneak up to my room after the Burns's had retired to their bedroom on the other side of the house. Initially, the creaky staircase worried us, but of course it also creaked when Sammy and I went up there ourselves. So we discarded that concern and ventured forth. We felt so ridiculous, sneaking up that rickety staircase in our stocking feet, looking like a bunch of thieves about to commit a burglary in a B movie—or a Disney cartoon.

Margie came to my room several times that summer, undetected. In the relaxed privacy of my place we listened to records, we communed with each other about all kinds of weighty subjects—men and women, love and sex, religion, our moral values, our hopes and dreams—just two teenagers in love, exploring the world and each other. Sometimes we just lay on my bed, very close, in silent communion. It was magical.

She later wrote in her diary: "I'll never regret going with Gunther to his room. For I learned so much, I loved so much, I lived so much. It was as if we were married; we could not live much closer—except for one thing, to which I was so glad I never gave in. Not that Gunther ever pressed me on the subject. I knew he would never do anything I didn't want. Even when I thought about having sex, which I hardly knew what that really was—what it *really* entailed—something always held me back. I was always a little afraid—and I don't know exactly why."

It was ironic that having succeeded in smuggling Margie up to my room, it was near the end of the summer that all hell broke loose when Margie was caught one night getting back late to the dorm. She was convinced "some damned fool" had snitched on her, one of the girls who didn't like her and was jealous of her. Margie's transgression was reported to the college president, Fred Smith,[30] who immediately called Margie's parents about her infraction—who in turn called *my* parents. The whole affair, as silly as it was, upset Margie terribly, even more for my sake than hers. Oddly enough, even though her parents didn't think all that well of her going with me, in those early years they never actually scolded her about the matter. I was very touched by a letter Margie wrote me later, in which she rationalized that they knew of her "obstinacy" and must have figured that their daughter "will learn through experience and from my conscience, which is strong because of the fine upbringing I owe to them." Her diary expressed concern mainly for me, fearing that my parents would take it out on me—which, however, they didn't. What *was* annoying was the gossip that began to circulate about the affair among some of the college faculty and students, and in the orchestra. It seemed that the whole world suddenly knew that Margie had broken the twelve o'clock curfew. Unbelievable! "We both, but especially Gunther," so her diary records, "have had to pay for this summer, which proves you have to pay for every bit of happiness you get."

As often as I have cast my thoughts back to that summer of 1944, I felt that of all the many, many happy times I have had in my life, that may just have been the happiest of them all. There was something so pure, so innocent, so profoundly touching about our love, our whole relationship. Perhaps it was just what first love is all about. It is probably also true that, as Margie suggested, one pays a price for such happiness. She did think so, in any case. For by the end of the summer she told me that she was a physical wreck—from all those sleepless nights—and also emotionally drained to her very depths. She wrote so feelingly about this in her diary and also, in a confessional mood, in her letters to me. "The whole summer seemed like a dream; I was in a fog most of the time. When I got home my health was at a breaking point. I was so weakened by Gunther's will; his word was the word of God to me. I idolized him, perhaps more than I actually loved him. I don't know. When the day of parting arrived, I was almost glad to leave. Maybe I had had too much of a life so freely given to pleasure and freedom, but, alas, also to freedom from work. I know I didn't do anything radically wrong—except that I didn't work very hard at my piano. I was too tired most of the time."

Which was true. She had under the circumstances seriously neglected her singing and piano practice. But that is what the fires of first love can do to you. It is a primeval force, one that is fundamental to our human existence and continuity. Again, her diary: "I am now a little ill at the thought of doing nothing but playing around, of drinking, of just fulfilling desires. It worries me; it seems so low. Or is it?" Where the point about drinking came from I have no idea, because we never did any even moderately, let alone seriously.

On our final day together that summer I presented her with a drawing in colored chalk, glazed with a fixative, of short interwoven snatches of the arias from *La Bohème*, and a large red rose superimposed on a collagelike representation of the opera's piano score. I was stunned when she in turn gave me a gift of a most beautiful one-of-a-kind, custom-made, hand-painted Sulka tie in beautiful blues, grays, and aquamarine (my favorite color), a tie that she confessed cost twenty-five dollars, an *enormous* amount for a tie in the 1940s, when ties cost fifty cents or at most a dollar. I wore that tie for over twenty years; its colors never faded, but when one of its edges became frayed we had to retire it from active duty. But I still have it to this day, not wanting to part with a gift that Margie had given me with so much love and devotion.

As I've already indicated, we wrote each other very lengthy letters; no little two-pagers for us. It was our way of keeping in touch as closely as possible, and on all manner of subjects. I must say that for someone who had forgotten every word of English just seven years earlier, I did write some rather beautiful letters. They were at times perhaps a bit too flowery, but the thoughts expressed were pure and genuine. Their verbal shadings were inspired by the emotional high on which I found myself when I was alone in New York or, starting in 1946, on long tours with the Metropolitan Opera, or when Margie was far away in Fargo.

A letter from me in Cincinnati, written five days after the end of the Zoo Opera season, describes in rather emotional tones the "hazy stupor that has seized my mind and brain, ever since I kissed you good-bye—which seems like an eternity ago. I am existing more or less like an automaton, living not for myself—or even you—but merely vegetating, just passing the time away. I discard the empty shell of each bygone day with the satisfaction of having killed another twenty-four hours, and thereby being so much closer to a certain September day, when the precious hours God gives us each day will no longer be an empty shell, but a golden chalice overflowing with the joy and ecstasy of life. That is the happiness I felt all through last year and this summer. Every man must seek among the unceasing flood of faces in his life one that he can call his own, one that represents true companionship, that is forever tender and loving. And that one is you."[31]

The only solace I could find was to spend every evening at the Hangar listening to the wonderful jazz of Will Wilkins's fine Nat Cole-style trio. As word got around at the college that "Gunther was hanging out at the Hangar every night," I found myself inevitably surrounded by lots of company, especially Gussie and Paul Bransky, Ruth Duning, Helen Miller, and other college kids—but no Margie. I heard lots of good music at the Hangar in those five days before heading back to New York.

It was at the Hangar that I had the experience of playing jazz in public for the first time, actually improvising on the horn, sitting in with Will's trio. I asked Will to let me play mostly in medium or slow tempos because the horn is at its best as a singing, lyric instrument. I played a few choruses of blues, then *Body and Soul*, as well as Ellington's *Mood Indigo*, in which I interpolated Barny Bigard's famous second-chorus clarinet solo, which in its low register lies so beautifully on the horn. How did I do? I can't at this late date objectively assess my performance, but I remember that I was rather pleased with myself that at least I didn't disgrace myself—meaning I didn't play too many wrong notes. Also, there was rather generous applause after some of my solos.

But I also remember being a little troubled by the feeling that, in the end, I wasn't really at ease or relaxed while playing. Perhaps that was too much to expect at a first outing, but for some reason I didn't regard it as rewarding an experience as composing was. In improvising there always seemed to be—I sat in a few more times with Will's trio—an uncomfortable pressure of worrying about whether I would play the best next notes, as compared to the relaxed feeling when composing of having more than a split second to think about what those next notes were going to be. Another way of putting it is that I simply couldn't *feel* what I was going to play; I was worrying instead and *thinking* about what comes next. Over time I began to realize that I was not by nature destined to be an improviser, but rather more suited to composing in the traditional sense.

As I became more professionally involved at the highest levels of classical performance, and when at the same time a whole new generation of modern-styled, technically advanced jazz improvisers burst onto the scene—Charlie Parker, Dizzy Gillespie (on instruments that, unlike the horn, had been in the center of developments in jazz for some thirty years)—I gave up any idea of pursuing improvising as one of my musical goals. I knew there was no way I could catch up with Bird and Diz, let alone build on their innovations. I *did* feel that I could do so as a composer.

When I got back to New York, I received a call to play a concert with the New York Philharmonic, to be conducted by Dimitri Mitropoulos, in an all-Mendelssohn program featuring the Third Symphony (the "Scotch" Symphony).[32] I was especially thrilled about this engagement because I had not only heard for some years about Mitropoulos's exciting and adventurous programming in Minneapolis (where he was music director since 1937), but I had already been treated to several overwhelming musical experiences with Mitropoulos when he began to guest conduct the Philharmonic in the 1940–41 season. He electrified New York audiences with stunning performances of Strauss's *Sinfonia domestica*, Prokofiev's Third Piano Concerto, playing both the solo piano part and conducting, Schönberg's *Verklärte nacht*, and, in those days still rarely performed works such as Mahler's First Symphony, Vaughan Williams's powerful, aggressively expressive Fourth Symphony, and Rachmaninov's *Symphonic Dances*. I was particularly taken with how convincingly and persuasively Mitropoulos did unfamiliar new music such as Ernst Krenek's *Variations on "I Wonder as I Wander"* and Carlos Chavez's starkly dramatic Piano Concerto.

Although I was pretty excited about working with Mitropoulos, I was less enamored of the all-Mendelssohn program. Not that I thought Mendelssohn was a lesser composer—far from it—but as a young composer, deeply interested in twentieth-century music and quite aware of Mitropoulos's awesome reputation in the contemporary repertory, I would have preferred that my first personal encounter with him would have been with something like at least a Mahler symphony or a Strauss tone poem. As it turned out my playing with the Philharmonic in that concert taught me an important lesson, namely, that a subtle, refined style of playing an instrument, especially a brass instrument—as I had been taught by my teacher (and Jänicke) and that had been very much lauded and appreciated in Cincinnati—was not necessarily considered appropriate in New York. Since the days of Toscanini's tenure the Philharmonic had somehow gradually developed into the most powerful, and, to put it bluntly, loudest playing orchestra in the country, probably in the world. Subtlety and refinement were not something one associated with the Philharmonic's playing in the 1940s. Furthermore, Mitropoulos's intense, dramatic approach, worlds apart from, say, Toscanini's passionate yet disciplined ways, led to performances that were often painted with *very* broad strokes. Indeed, that was part of what had mesmerized New York audiences.

In my first rehearsal that week I was more or less in a state of shock. The cultivated, balanced style that I so enjoyed with Goossens and the Cincinnati Symphony (and previously with the Ballet Theatre and several other orchestras) didn't seem to work at all in the Philharmonic, especially sitting in its powerhouse brass section. I was sonically swamped, and had to quickly ratchet up my playing to a much more intense, brash, coarser style and louder dynamic levels, to fatten up my tone—especially in the big third horn solo in the "Scotch" Symphony's slow movement. I didn't particularly enjoy the experience, but at the same time I quickly learned a valuable lesson, that as a fully rounded professional musician one had to be prepared to work under a great variety of conditions and a wide range of orchestral styles, whether one agreed with them or not.

After that Philharmonic concert and a few more days in Jamaica, Queens, with my parents, I took off for Lake Placid by train. I had been doing a lot of flying earlier that summer. Three times in a few months, back and forth between Cincinnati and New York (on American Airlines), was a lot in those days when commercial flying was still in its infancy. The most advanced plane was the Douglas DC-3, a small plane seating only twenty-one passengers, but nonetheless quite roomy compared to today's horribly overcrowded, congested planes. The DC-3's fuselage was set at a twenty-degree diagonal angle. You entered in the rear of the plane and walked upward toward your seat or the cockpit. What is long forgotten, except by old-timers like me, is that flying in those days was not only a bit of an adventure but also a really pleasurable experience. The service, the food, was superb and elegant; the comfort of the seats and the legroom were closer to what is now called first or business class. Flight attendants, who were called stewardesses—American Airlines called their stewardesses "long-stemmed roses"—were chosen for their grace and beauty, youth and intelligence; and one really was made to feel at home. A passenger was a valued client, not a piece of steerage, as is mostly the case nowadays.

I was fortunate actually to fly on two American Airlines inaugural flights from LaGuardia to Cincinnati, one in June, the other in October. Passengers were individually escorted by a stewardess to the plane on a long red carpet—this was before the days of jetways—and each of us was given a long-stemmed red rose and served champagne once inside the plane. I really loved flying. It gave me a sense of adventure, and, I must admit, a slightly snobbish feeling of superiority, of wealth, by engaging in something that most people wouldn't quite dare to risk or couldn't afford to do.

At the same time I loved trains and the relative leisure of long train rides. You could read for hours, or you could watch the scenery pass by; you could also take fine meals in the elegant dining cars of the day. Taking a train was not so much about getting somewhere, let alone fast, as it was the trip itself. That was the adventure. The trip from Cincinnati to New York, which I took often, was especially beautiful; we traveled at first along the Ohio River, then through the beautiful, rather wild craggy mountainous terrain of West Virginia, ending up at New York's architecturally beautiful glass and steel Pennsylvania Station.[33]

During my few days at home in Jamaica I started Tom Wolfe's *You Can't Go Home Again*, a book, I quickly found out, I couldn't put down. On my way to Lake Placid up the Hudson River via Albany I consumed its first two hundred pages, almost totally ignoring the beautiful Hudson Valley scenery. It was perfect reading for a young man bursting with boundless energy, full of dreams about engaging in "life's grand battle" to bring more beauty and greater love to a "flawed, imperfect" world. Reading that book made me hope that I could perhaps bring something new, something valuable, to the world, and to embrace it in all its beauty, to draw from it all the life sustenance it could offer. Tom Wolfe made me want to dream, made me want to challenge.

I was so excited heading for the Adirondacks, which I remembered so fondly from the many vacation trips my parents had taken there with Edgar and me over the years, first in 1930 and

1931, and then in the beautiful snowy (but very cold) winter of 1932 for the Olympics in Lake Placid, and again several times after my return from Germany to North Creek, a village near the headwaters of the Hudson River, where my parents rented a log cabin-style motel for short winter vacations.

To get to Lake Placid I had to change trains twice, once in Albany (with a two-hour layover), before catching a night train (headed ultimately for Montreal) to Westport on Lake Champlain, and from there in a local "milk train" at six in the morning via Elizabethtown and Keene to Lake Placid—a cumbersome ten-hour all-night trip that, had I learned to drive a car, I could have managed in four to five hours. (Nowadays one would fly from LaGuardia to Lake Placid in ninety minutes or less.) But I can't remember enjoying a trip and a night of no sleep as much as I did that one to Lake Placid. I was on some kind of fantastic high, induced largely by my entrancement with Tom Wolfe's panoramic, heady subjectivism, which harmonized perfectly with my own buoyant hunger for adventure, for new experiences and new friendships.

I can recall so clearly arriving in Albany around midnight, just wandering through the old nineteenth-century wooden train station and the empty platforms, and reveling in the crystal clear, pristine night air, a brilliant full moon overhead. I had no thoughts of wanting to sleep. What a waste of time, if there was living to be done! In my excited state I felt I was somehow in tune with the universe, vibrating with the spheres, as if some strange electric currents were coursing through my body and my brain. Life was *so* beautiful! I could have stayed in that station all night, enjoying this exhilarating feeling of release, of complete openness to the world around me, the starry night sky above in all its wondrous complexity. It was indeed a magical night; I was half-crazed with happiness. At such times I realized that I would never have to resort to pot or drugs; I was already on an incredible high. Who needs marijuana!

I stayed wide awake on the train from Albany to Westport, enjoying the sights along the route in the bright moonlit night—recognizing and remembering the historic towns I had visited or passed through before—Glens Falls, Lake George, Bolton Landing, Ticonderoga, Crown Point, and beautiful Lake Champlain.

The trip became even more exhilarating on the final leg, as the senescent local train wound its way from Elizabethtown upward toward Lake Placid through the Adirondacks' ancient pine forests bathed in the bright morning sunlight, past little lakes, ponds, and bogs with their beaver dams, the rich essences of pristine nature filling my nostrils. Breathing in the pure clean mountain air, the intoxicating pine fragrance, provided yet another, different high. I was glad the little train moved so slowly, arduously chugging up the constant inclines, enabling me to enjoy this serene unspoiled scene all the longer—no houses, no cars, no people. I hoped the train ride to Lake Placid would take all day. There is something about staying up all night that puts you in a special, almost hallucinatory state in which the mind remains incredibly alert, sensitive—receptive to feelings and sensations that would in other circumstances elude you.

I arrived at the Lake Placid station feeling fresh as a daisy. Walter Heermann picked me up and took me directly to a rehearsal of the orchestra, where I met Paul White, the orchestra's conductor, at whose house I was going to be staying. Before the day was over, I was comfortably ensconced in one of the several large guest rooms in Paul White's extensive cottage, and had met Paul's wife, Josie, and their four daughters: Teeny, Pouny, Louly, and Pooky, ages nineteen, sixteen, thirteen, and ten, respectively.

In Paul White I found someone who became a longtime friend; we were so close that I often thought of him as my second father. Paul was one of those supremely gentle souls, kindly, calm, unpretentious and imperturbable, who went about his daily work with an unflappable serenity. (There must be more than mere coincidence at play that this placid man for years spent his summers in Lake Placid.) A very fine musician, Paul was far too modest about his considerable accomplishments as a composer, conductor, violinist, and teacher at the Eastman School of

Music. Although Paul is now more or less forgotten, in his day he was quite famous as a composer, primarily because of a delightful set of short orchestral pieces, the 1933 *Five Miniatures for Orchestra*, which was played regularly at children's concerts. He was also a beloved teacher, through whose fingers passed countless well-trained young musicians at Eastman who went on to populate our American symphony orchestras.

I was already aware of Paul's many accomplishments as a young man, his studies at the New England Conservatory of Music in its heyday in the 1910s, and his later work with Eugène Ysaÿe and Eugene Goossens. It was fascinating for me to learn that Paul regarded Goossens as important a mentor in his young years as I did now, twenty years later.

Paul's own music would be considered conservative by anyone's terms, even in the context of early twentieth-century music. But it was always well made, everything agreeably in place, orderly, unostentatious—very much like Paul himself. I already knew his *Five Miniatures*, having recently acquired Arthur Fiedler's recording (with the Boston Pops) of these charming and clever musical gems. The concluding *Mosquito Dance* is a little masterpiece. Rudolf Ganz and Ernest Schelling played the *Miniatures* every year at the New York Philharmonic Young People's Concerts. When I first met Paul he had just composed his *Sea Chantey* for harp and strings, and was working on his *Lake Placid Scenes*. We spent many happy, relaxed hours discussing where music was going, he calmly puffing away at his beloved pipe, scratching his head from time to time, while I, more impetuous, eagerly tried to move him along harmonically, beyond his well-mannered seventh and ninth chords. He was surprised at the atonal modernity of my music. He looked especially puzzled when I would sit down at the piano and play Scriabin's famous Mystic Chord, or some of the more complex chordal pile-ups in Schönberg's *Erwartung*. Paul never said an unkind word about anyone, and he certainly would never have openly criticized someone else's music. He was too wise, too mature to do that. Instead of ranting against a "dissonant" Schönberg or a "barbaric" Bartók, as so many did, he would simply admit that he just didn't understand such music, and that in all likelihood this was *his* problem, not Schönberg's or Bartók's.

Another sign of greatness with Paul was that as a conductor he never let his personal judgments or feelings about a piece of music affect his interpretation of it. In the many performances of contemporary music I heard him conduct at Eastman over the years, I was always impressed at how well he knew the scores, how totally dedicated and respectful he was of the work. Two performances in particular stand out in my memory: his realization of Shostakovich's First Symphony with the school orchestra—I don't think I have ever heard it played better—and, on another occasion, Bartók's *Music for Strings, Celesta, and Percussion*.

Paul would never have been called an exciting personality, and he would never have rated very high on the charisma meter (which seems to be the primary means of evaluating a conductor's worth nowadays). Excitement in the White family was provided by Josie, Paul's wife. Fiery, passionate, and emotionally volatile, Josie ran the whole family; she really dominated it. She had been one of Ysaÿe's star pupils, which is how she and Paul met—some would whisper that she was also Ysaÿe's mistress—but gave up any solo career ambitions, presumably to raise a big family. As self-effacing and docile as Paul was, Josie was quite the opposite: vigorously outspoken and fearless, easily given to temperamental, even irrational outbursts. Like my own mother, Josie had too much energy to burn, and it would all boil over in explosive pitch battles, in which Paul, quietly puffing on his pipe—it was his major defensive weapon—would calmly and with unreactive passivity weather the tornado, knowing full well that after every storm sooner or later the sun breaks through again. Josie was one tough lady! But once you won her approval, she was as loyal and generous as can be. Suspicious of me at first—as she evidently was of any newcomer—she soon saw that I was OK and meant no harm, especially to her girls, after which I was fully accepted into the family as the son Paul and Josie never managed to have. (A few years later, when I brought Margie to Rochester on one of my frequent visits, she had to undergo the same critical scrutiny until Josie finally gave her approval that it would be OK for me to marry her.)

The four daughters, with whom over the next four or five years I sort of fell in love one by one—not literally, of course—were as different in personality and character as four people could be. Teeny, the oldest of the four, was incredibly proper, almost saintlike, nunlike, sensitive, highly intelligent—an intellectual. Pouny was more like her mother, given to strong emotional swings, at least as a youngster, that fluctuated between joyous, fun-loving, almost giddy highs, and bouts of cloudy, near-depression lows. Louly was in a way the most balanced, the most normal, of the four girls; she was a happy-go-lucky kid with a sunny disposition who took things in stride, never getting very upset when things went wrong nor overly ecstatic when things went well. Pooky, the youngest, not very developed yet when I first knew her, was a bright, alert child whose nickname could easily have been Perky.

Pouny became my first female horn student. With her I learned for the first time what then was confirmed over and over again in many years of teaching and observing horn players, namely, that women have an inborn physical adeptness for playing the horn. I can't fully explain it, but I think it centers on their embouchures, their lips, their skin's texture, and a certain physical resilience. I offer this information purely as circumstantial anecdotal testimony. Pouny married a horn player, Milan Yanchich, a fine musician and publisher of horn-related music who played in the Rochester Philharmonic for nearly forty years.[34]

It didn't take long for me to feel completely at home at the White's compound as part of the family, so unreservedly was I welcomed as a surrogate son and brother to the girls. In this carefree atmosphere, with no professional commitments or obligations, I found myself turning toward the kind of youthful fun-and-games activities that I had pretty much left behind the previous two or three years. It ranged from hiking, mountain climbing, bike riding, croquet, and volleyball, all the way to the almost daily morning pillow fights, when the four girls would gang up on me, usually leaving several rooms in the cottage littered with thousands of feathers and empty pillowcases—until one day when Josie laid down the law: "No more pillow fights!" We also got tired of stuffing the feathers back into the pillowslips.

Not that my weeks in Lake Placid were all fun and games. I finished *You Can't Go Home Again* in short order and then stormed through *Of Time and the River*, once again mesmerized by Wolfe's conflict between his innate pessimism and what I read as a partly hidden but exhilarating optimism—so unusual (and deceptive?), in that all of his books were written during the Great Depression years. I went to all of Paul White's Sinfonietta concerts, constantly enthralled at the way this tiny band of fine players managed to make the transcriptions and arrangements they were obliged to use sound nonetheless so full and authentic. A lot of this sonorous repleteness was due, I think, to the sensitive, intelligent fill-in work of Carl Lamson, the orchestra's pianist, who was (and had been for many years) Fritz Kreisler's excellent accompanist. Performing mostly rearranged standard orchestral works, originally, of course, devoid of piano parts, it was Lamson's task to cover and flesh out all the parts and harmonies missing in the reduced transcriptions.

Interspersed between the public orchestra concerts were evenings devoted entirely to chamber music. That is how I heard my first live performance of Brahms's glorious Clarinet Quintet (I had grown up on Reginald Kell's and the Busch Quartet's fine recording), played beautifully by Stanley Hasty, the new young principal clarinetist of the Rochester Philharmonic, with Paul White and Walter Heermann playing those heavenly first violin and cello parts. It was during one of those chamber music evenings that I met William Shirer, the famous war correspondent, whom we all knew from his daily reports on the war for CBS radio directly from Berlin, where he was stationed. Bill, who loved music dearly, especially chamber music, had a two-room rustic cabin in Lake Placid Village. One of its rooms was large and spacious enough to accommodate small musical groups such as string quartets and pianoless quintets plus a small invited audience.

I saw Bill often in those Lake Placid summers, not only in 1944 but in 1946 and 1947, and even years later when he had relocated to western Massachusetts, near Tanglewood, after the Lake Placid Club had temporarily abandoned its music programs in the 1960s. Music was paramount in Bill's life, and he knew he would find plenty of fine music in Tanglewood and its environs.

Probably the most interesting and unusual thing I did in those happy weeks in Lake Placid was make a transcription for horn of the solo cello part of Ernest Bloch's masterpiece, *Schelomo*, of which I had recently acquired a superb recording by Emanuel Feuermann with Stokowski and the Philadelphia Orchestra, one of the most radiant and sumptuous recordings of that time. Since *Schelomo*'s cello part rarely went above concert A (on top of the staff), it lent itself perfectly to transference to the horn. I never did anything more with this transcription, hardly even telling anyone (except Walter Heermann) about it. It was something I was driven to do by my love for this remarkable work, just for my own enjoyment and edification. But I did play it one time for a small, rather amazed audience at the club, in an informal setting, with Carl Lamson playing the orchestra part on the piano.

When I got back to New York, I found a beautiful letter from Margie, sent several days earlier. It was full of all kinds of good news: how she was "beginning to recover"—her words— "from that exciting, hectic, sleepless, not-practicing summer in Cincinnati"—and, best of all, that for once things were rather calm and peaceful with her parents.

She had begun serious practice on Liszt's technically very demanding A Major Piano Concerto, which she was scheduled to play at her graduation recital sometime in the spring semester. In one of my letters to her I signed off with: "Don't forget to practice the good Dr. Liszt's diminished chords—in all transpositions." We had often joked about Liszt's overuse of diminished seventh chords, as the newest and quickest ways of getting around difficult modulations. In truth, I really think Liszt wrote more diminished chords than any composer of that time. But they *are* very handy, no question.

My second year in Cincinnati, the 1944–45 season, progressed much as the first year had, with many wonderful musical experiences with Goossens. Most outstanding for me among these were our performances of Dukas's *La Peri*, Mahler's *Lied von der Erde*, Stravinsky's *Chant du rossignol* (*Song of the Nightingale*) Suite and *Dumbarton Oaks* Concerto, Strauss's *Till Eulenspiegel* (my first opportunity to play that famous horn piece), and the Final Scene of *Salomé*, arguably Strauss's ultimate masterpiece. The soloist in the latter work was Marjorie Lawrence, one of the very finest and vocally most thrilling dramatic sopranos of the thirties and forties. Her recording of *Salomé*'s Final Scene, made in Paris (in French) in the midthirties, is still to my mind one of the very greatest realizations of that incredible music.

A very special treat early that season was hearing Fritz Kreisler in the Brahms Violin Concerto. Although at age seventy Kreisler was no longer in his prime, his warm, rich, svelte tone and tastefully expressive playing was a real ear-opener for me. One could only adore his playing. I was very flattered when, after our Friday afternoon performance, he complimented me on how I had played the several little F-major horn solos scattered throughout the Concerto's second movement, some of them echoing the solo violin part. He told me that he didn't like it when horn players played those passages too loudly and with too thick a tone. I had discovered by then that major soloists do not generally consort with or speak to orchestral musicians, let alone compliment them. Thus I especially treasure the memory of that encounter with Kreisler, one of the greats of that era.

Above all, there was the supreme joy of seeing Margie again. In the late fall of 1944 I wrote two more songs of my Li Po–Klabund cycle for her, after which we began rehearsing the songs, in hopes of having the college include them on a student vocal recital—which, alas, never happened.

Because we had spent so much time together during the summer, we agreed to try to restrain our amorous impulses, difficult as that might be. Margie was feeling quite guilty about the summer. Not that she had any regrets about the many happy times we had spent together, but rather, quite rationally, she felt that she owed it to herself as well as her parents, who were paying for her education at the college, to get back to some serious, concentrated work. She was also facing critical year-end recitals in the spring in both of her majors.

We converted our evening activities to attending movies and concerts, both at the college and in Cincinnati's other concert halls, such as the Taft Auditorium and, of course, the Music Hall, where major American and European artists appeared regularly. It is there that we heard and saw dozens of world-famous pianists, violinists, singers, etc., such as Brailovsky, Heifetz, Segovia, Casals—and yes, even Elizabeth Schumann, in a beautiful Lieder recital.[35]

It was a heady time for us, working zealously on our various musical goals. Margie seemed to be especially motivated to commit all of her intellectual and physical energies to her musical development. She was inspired to prove to herself, to her teachers, to her family, and to me, that she had the stuff, the talent, and the industry to reach those levels of achievement that could signal a distinctive career in music.

In mid-December Margie left for a Christmas vacation in Oceanside, California with her parents, staying with her sister Anna Jane and Anna's husband, Bill Schlossman, and their first child, Marjorie Ann.[36] I wrote Margie from Rockford, Illinois (on a brief orchestra tour) within twenty-four hours of her departure. After the concert I was nabbed by about twenty-five giggling girls, asking for my autograph. So I signed my letter to Margie: "With all my love, your Frank Sinatra." (He was our favorite singer at the time, along with Billy Eckstine.)

One of my best faculty friends at the college was the organ teacher, Eugene Selhorst. He had been very impressed that I had sung and studied with T. Tertus Noble, whom Gene admired greatly, and that I was also versant with Messiaen's organ music and much of the modern organ literature. Gene himself played a lot of modern French, Belgian, Dutch, and American organ repertory in his recitals, which I always attended. (I kept in touch with him after my Cincinnati years, and was heartbroken when I heard that he had died of cancer in his early forties.) One day as we met for lunch at our YMCA roundtable, Gene told me about two brand-new recordings in which, he was sure, I would be very interested. One was Messiaen's 1930 *Diptyque* for organ (with the exquisite subtitle *Essai sur la vie terrestre et l'eternité bien heureuses*), a piece I loved so much that I transcribed it one day for my Metropolitan Opera Woodwind Quintet. The other was a recording of Alban Berg's Violin Concerto, with the outstanding violinist Louis Krasner (who had commissioned the work in 1935) as soloist, and Artur Rodzinski conducting the Cleveland Orchestra.

Acquiring that Berg recording and hearing that great music for the first time was a momentous occurrence for me that significantly changed my life. The music of the so-called Second Viennese School was virtually nonexistent on records in those days (with the exception of four early works by Schönberg)—there were none by Berg and Webern. As far as twentieth-century music was concerned, my record collection up to this point was heavily weighted in the direction of French, English, and Russian repertory (Ravel, Debussy, Ibert, Vaughan Williams, Delius, Holst, Shostakovich, Gliére). So the issuance of Berg's Violin Concerto was an almost revolutionary moment in the forty- to fifty-year history of recordings: a (partially) dodecaphonic work finally available to be heard, to be studied, to be enjoyed repeatedly.

While I had been exploring for some time bitonal and polytonal harmonies, and to some extent outright atonal pitch combinations, hearing Berg's music really convinced me that something like his idiom was what I wanted my harmonic and melodic language to be. But what exactly was Berg's language? How did it work? How exactly did Berg intermix his primary twelve-tone material with free atonal but also purely tonal elements? Were they limited to the secondary or background material? Just by listening to the recording I could not quite figure it out.

Naturally I decided to buy a score, but discovered to my great dismay that there was no score of the Berg Concerto to be had, not only in Cincinnati or New York but indeed anywhere in the United States. Wherever I asked why, I could never get a clear explanation. Years later I found out why. Universal Edition in Vienna was the publisher not only of Berg's music but also of the entire Second Viennese School and its various stylistic contemporaries and offspring. When the Nazis marched into Austria in 1938 (in the so-called *Anschluss*), they began as part of their new cultural policies to suppress the artistic achievements not only of Jews but also of many non-Jews whose art they considered (and officially declared) "degenerate." The UE directors knew that the Nazis would do everything to prevent the music of Jewish composers in Austria from being performed, not only by officially censoring it but also by appropriating and destroying the printing plates from which multiple copies of scores and parts are produced. In response to this threat, Alfred Schlee,[37] the head of UE, quickly—and secretly—buried the plates in his garden. As a result no music by Schönberg, Webern, or Berg[38]—or by Schulhoff, Weill, Bartók, and many others—was available in America for many years, including the war years.

When I realized that there wasn't any way I could get a hold of a score that I could study and analyze, I decided to transcribe the music from the recording, at least a big chunk of it. Transcribing the whole twenty-five-minute piece would have taken many, many months, especially the fast- or medium-tempo sections. I was particularly fascinated with the Concerto's requiemlike *Adagio* ending, integrating Bach's beautiful "Ich Habe Genug" chorale into the atonal fabric. And so I settled on transcribing (in addition to a few places in the first movement) the last eight minutes of the work, from the great triple *fff* climax in the second movement to the end of the piece, in effect the last two 78 sides of the recording.

I don't think anyone has ever attempted to transcribe an extended segment of an atonal full-orchestra composition from a recording, in all significant details—pitches and rhythms, of course, but also all inner harmonies and voicings, instrumentation, and dynamics. I didn't have much hope of getting the instrumentation absolutely correct because I didn't even know, nor was there any way I could divine from the recording, what exactly the instrumentation was. Were there two or three flutes? How many clarinets, how many trombones, etc.? I didn't even know that Berg had used a saxophone, something no German or Austrian composer I knew of had ever done, except for Strauss's use in 1901 of three saxophones in his *Sinfonia domestica*. (Only a few French composers occasionally included a saxophone.)[39] All I could do was to write down in a short score—what we call a *particell*—any and all the sounds I could hear on the recording, identifying the individual instruments as much as possible. Although I couldn't tell whether, for example, it was a second flute playing or a first flute, I did know that it *was* a flute, and not a clarinet or a muted trumpet.

Margie, Reuben, and even August Söndlin, to whom I had confided my intentions, all thought I was crazy in thinking that I could transcribe such a complex atonal score. But that only fired me up even more. I plunged in, spending all waking, nonworking hours painstakingly notating everything I could hear on that recording. I was never sure that everything that Berg had written had been perfectly recorded and balanced. I finished the transcription in about three weeks. It was a wild thing to do, totally exhausting for me, but also immensely rewarding. Berg's music was like a narcotic (as Scriabin had been for me a few years earlier), and I was inescapably addicted to it.

When I saw the printed score for the first time a few years after the war, I was pleased to see that I had almost all the pitches and notes and rhythmic durations right. It is quite an achievement, which to tell the truth astounds me in retrospect. Indeed, years later, I thought I had almost dreamt the whole episode. I looked for those old manuscript pages of my transcription, and there, by God, was the proof that I actually had done the transcribing—and quite correctly.

Compared to eight minutes of Berg's music, transcribing Ellington's three-minute compositions for a known, clearly differentiated, small four-choir instrumentation had been more or less a snap. The Berg really challenged all of my faculties to the fullest. But my good ear, the two years of dictation classes at the Manhattan School of Music, and my inherited blend of tenacity and energy carried me to the finish line. Delving deeply into Berg's glorious music, which transcribing naturally forces one to do, confirmed that the general stylistic and linguistic direction I was already pursuing was no longer questionable for me. While the composer in me was eager to pursue and advance the innovations already achieved in the twentieth century—if I had sufficient talent to do so—the performer in me, loving the huge classical repertory accumulated over the previous two hundred years, could not detach himself from those cherished eighteenth- and nineteenth-century masterworks. The creator and the *re*-creator in me, I knew, would always have to remain in a complementary symbiotic relationship: the one never rejecting or ignoring the other. Berg's and Schönberg's music—I didn't know any Webern at the time (neither did anyone else in America)—along with Stravinsky's music of the *Sacre* period, represented a bridge, a continuum, from the most advanced late nineteenth-early twentieth-century past to the present.

Certain professional avant-gardists, especially in Europe, have over the years regarded my music as ideologically hopelessly old fashioned, stuck too much in the past. On the other hand, most audiences and conservative composers and critics consider my music to be too far out, too radical and experimental—or, even worse, intellectual, cerebral. For the former I'm not modern enough; for the latter I'm too modern. Both are misjudgments. You can criticize a given piece of music qualitatively, but you cannot qualitatively measure an individual's *creative concepts*. In any case, there has always been a pull within me between the old and the new, between the most valuable of the past and the most substantial and prescient of the present—a pull that I feel has been resolved in my work into a harmonious equilibrium and a certain linguistic and stylistic integrity.

The Cincinnati Symphony, like many orchestras during those war years, did a fair amount of touring, in our case mostly to other Ohio cities, but also to places like Louisville, Kentucky, Fort Wayne, Indiana, and as far west as Davenport, Iowa. Parkersburg, West Virginia is not exactly one of the great musical centers of the world, but it stands out in my mind as the site of a rather important encounter in my life, an event with all kinds of fascinating consequences, both positive and negative. It was on November 13, 1944, in Parkersburg that I first encountered the remarkable talent of Leonard Bernstein; this initial meeting would develop into a lifelong friendship and professional association.

Nowadays young people's concerts and all kinds of run-out concerts are conducted not by the musical director but by various associate or assistant conductors on the orchestra's staff. It is therefore rather startling to realize that Goossens conducted *all* young people's and tour concerts during his entire thirteen-year tenure at the helm of the Cincinnati Symphony Orchestra—with one exception. Why Goossens did not conduct the two concerts we gave in Parkersburg that particular day on our mini tour I don't know. But suddenly there was Leonard Bernstein conducting both an afternoon young people's concert and a weightier evening concert, a dozen compositions in all, which we had already played a few times on the tour and which had been rehearsed and prepared by Goossens. We had a quick sound-check rehearsal, in which Bernstein spotted a few places in the two programs, especially in Stravinsky's *Firebird* Suite, the work scheduled as the evening concert's closer.

I had already become acquainted with some of Bernstein's earliest compositions, reading about them and studying the cited excerpts in *Modern Music*. I remember being intrigued by his melodic-harmonic language, so different from my own. It reminded me of Copland's late-1930s music, which had certainly been a major influence on Bernstein; but it also struck me as being already incipiently original. There were melodic turns and interval combinations that I had not heard or seen before. I had heard glowing reports of Bernstein's work at Tanglewood, and, of course, the whole world had heard about his sensational debut with the New York Philharmonic on November 14, 1943, substituting on very short notice for the ailing Bruno Walter. Within months Bernstein had guest-conducting engagements with every important orchestra in the United States. His manager, Arthur Judson, saw to that. Thus it is likely that, when Goossens became ill over the weekend before that Monday in Parkersburg, Bernstein, already celebrated for his ability to step in for an indisposed conductor on a minute's notice, was quickly sent off to Parkersburg to fill in for Goossens. It could also be that Goossens, who was, like Bernstein, also under Judson's management, was asked to give up a couple of tour concerts to give the "talented kid" a few more concert engagements.

We were all bowled over by Bernstein's conductorial talent, especially his lightninglike, almost explosive physical energy, his ability to abandon himself totally to the music and yet not lose technical control. All of this was so different from Goossens's more balanced, sedate approach. (Only Hans Meuser, our local big-time anti-Semite, let it be known that Bernstein—Mr. Amber,[40] as he called him—wasn't much more than a "fly-by-night flash in the pan.") What I noticed particularly was the suppleness of Bernstein's hands; it was as if he had ball bearings in his wrists that enabled him to bend, flex, rotate them at will—a remarkable gift that I believe, having observed Lennie conduct hundreds of times over nearly five decades, was unique to him. It permitted him to do things with his hands that I've never seen with anyone else; it enabled him to get away with a variety of unorthodox manual movements, especially his (at times excessive) subdivision of beats that, to my knowledge, no other conductor could manage so successfully.

After our evening concert, the orchestra's manager came to me, saying that Mr. Bernstein wanted to see me. I was surprised, since conductors and orchestra musicians generally didn't consort with each other, except perhaps to be reprimanded for some musical misdemeanor. I thought, my God, what have I done now?! When I stepped into his dressing room, however, he embraced me, not just casually, but warmly. It was the first of many, many Bernstein embraces bestowed upon me. (As the whole world came to know, Lennie had an unrestrainable passion for embracing and kissing.) When I had recovered from this unexpected greeting, he said something like: "You are a wonderful horn player! You are the first one to play the solo in the *Firebird* finale correctly." "What do you mean, correctly?" I was a bit puzzled. "What's to play *in*correctly?" "Well, you played that solo with the right 3/2 feeling, with which Stravinsky notated it. Everybody plays it as if it had been written in 4/2."[41] To get direct, unqualified praise from a conductor is a rarity in the orchestral world, especially of the gushy, all-out variety that Lennie loved to dispense. I was, of course, highly flattered. Little did I realize then that our paths would cross many times and in all kinds of alternately very happy—and very difficult—circumstances.

The other very interesting experience for me on that tour was visiting one of America's less famous but very special art museums, Toledo's Peristyle. It was Söndlin who had told me that some day I must go to that museum, mainly because it had one of the best collections of seventeenth-century Dutch paintings (Hals and Rembrandt), and French art from the fifteen hundreds to the early twentieth century, from Delacroix and Millet through Renoir and Pissaro to Picasso, Matisse, and Derain. This was important for me. I hadn't pursued the visual arts very much since the eye- and mind-opening museum visits during my St. Thomas days. That visit to the Peristyle was a kind of reintroduction to a world that I had neglected for too long. With Söndlin as my guide, I saw all those treasures, and also for the first time some astounding works by painters such as Henri Harpignies and Felix Ziem, artists I had never even heard of. It was one of the first times that I realized that even little known or unheralded artists could produce very great art. It was quite a revelation.

One of the most startling and enlightening musical experiences in my second year in Cincinnati was in connection with our performance of Berlioz's *Harold in Italy*, a four-movement symphony for solo viola and orchestra, a work that I had not heard before that time.[42] Already in our first rehearsal I was bowled over by its highly original and brilliant orchestration, not only striking in its unusual timbral mixtures but also in its virtuosic instrumental writing. (Perhaps I should not have been surprised, for I had read and studied Berlioz's *Treatise on Orchestration* when I was thirteen or fourteen, although I suppose more from the point of view of learning the basics of orchestration, not yet able to fully appreciate Berlioz's daring and adventurous use of instruments in his own scores.) I was surprised and—I admit, at first puzzled—by some of the odd, uncomfortable rhythmic configurations that Berlioz plays around with in *Harold*. (Many of my colleagues just called it inept.)

I'll also never forget how startled I was when I heard, right behind me in the percussion section, a sudden exciting burst of percussive sounds at the beginning of the last movement, produced by crash cymbals and two—yes two—tambourines, a brand-new sound for my ears. But my level of astonishment reached its zenith in the second movement, the "March of the Pilgrims," where Berlioz, among many wizardly instrumental combinations, offers a bit of modernism that is, to my mind and ears, an early embryonic forerunner of atonality. I am referring to Berlioz's close juxtaposition of the pitches C and B, not in conjunct motion, but two octaves apart (as one might hear in a Webern composition), repeatedly interspersed throughout the simple E-major pilgrims' hymn. An insistent middle C ♪, bursting in with interruptive *sfz*s on the pilgrims' evening prayer, resolves equally insistently via a two-octave leap to a high B ♪. When later the pilgrims gradually march off into the distance and their hymn fades into silence, the alternating Cs and Bs linger on—stranded in some musical no-man's land, suspended in time, as it were. Their initial interruptive function is suspended; there is nothing left to interrupt. It is surely one of the most unusual, startlingly modern, abstract musical ideas ever conceived, all the more so since this music was composed only *seven* years after Beethoven's death.[43] (Berlioz's earlier and perhaps even more innovative *Symphonie fantastique* followed only *five* years after his adored master's demise).

As exciting as the music was, hearing what was coming out of Joe Sherman's viola was even more startling. Joe Sherman is not a name that the reader will have ever heard of before, but he is the most extraordinary violist I ever encountered in my long life, even more remarkable than the much more famous William Primrose, the most celebrated violist of that era. Born in New York in 1905, Joe was precociously talented and studied with Leopold Auer, the teacher of many of the greatest violinists of the early twentieth century. When the Cincinnati Orchestra's regular principal viola, Erik Kahlson, was drafted in 1942, Joe was moved up to first chair. As I became more familiar with the musicians in the orchestra, I learned that Joe was an extremely reclusive person, a bachelor who lived alone under the most primitive conditions in a tiny attic room in the YMCA, and that he hardly ever talked to anybody and seemed to have no friends—male or female. But I also heard that he was a genius violist—Söndlin certainly thought so—with a deep, wonderfully dark, true viola tone, and a consummate technique. Indeed, all the string players in the orchestra were in awe of him. Furthermore, I learned that his amazing talents were so admired, even beyond our orchestra, that the most famous soloists of the time, such as Heifetz, Milstein, Elman, and Kreisler, made it a point to visit with Joe and try to get him to play duets with them whenever they were in Cincinnati.

When I made some attempts to meet with Joe or to lunch with him at the YMCA, he didn't really rebuff me, but I could see that he really preferred to be alone; it was very difficult to carry on a conversation with him.

Given all those encomiastic stories about Joe, I still was not prepared for the exquisitely soft, rich, warm sound that floated toward me in that first *Harold in Italy* rehearsal, near the beginning of the piece, and then, a little later, even more astonishingly, the sound Joe got on his open *C* string at the Allegro section. It was something I can never forget. The reader might say, with some justification, how can anyone sound so special on a nonfingered open string? I don't know how either, but I do know that Joe did just that; we all could hear it. It was unearthly, as was his entire Berlioz performance. While we in the orchestra struggled variously with Berlioz's strange and very challenging music, Joe, never uttering a word, never asking any questions, seemed to breeze through the music, making it sound so easy and natural—and so beautiful.

I don't think Joe had any great career ambitions. I think he was, in his introverted, quiet way, content to devote himself totally to music and its great secrets. When Erik Kahlson was released from the navy and, by virtue of his contract, returned to the principal viola chair, Joe quietly went back into the section, once again incognito.

I saw Joe Sherman only once more, many years later—another astonishing experience—but will save that account for later in this narrative.

In addition to my teaching at the college and the conservatory, I often played first horn in Walter Heermann's college orchestra, which gave concerts about once a month. I did it just to help out, and because Walter wanted me to play with him. He was a fine conductor and an excellent orchestra trainer, in a very musical, solid, unflashy, no-nonsense way. It was always a joy to play for him. One time he had me as soloist, actually in two pieces: my own *Nocturne* for horn and piano, an earlier work that I had recently orchestrated (at the suggestion, by the way, of Goossens), as well as a beautiful arrangement by Walter of Tchaikovsky's *Serenade mèlancolique* for violin and orchestra, now featuring the horn as soloist rather than the violin. I recall that both performances went very well—with one exception. That exception was my flipping one high note in the Tchaikovsky in one of the performances. I was so embarrassed, and I can still hear and feel that moment as if it were yesterday. (It is absolutely amazing how we musicians tend to remember every playing mistake we ever made.)

One of my happiest moments with the Cincinnati Symphony came when I found out from Goossens that he had programmed his orchestral transcriptions of "Ondine" and "Le Gibet" from Ravel's *Gaspard de la nuit*, and that RCA Victor had agreed to record the two movements as fillers for one of their upcoming albums. Goossens had previously lent me his personal score of the *Gaspard* transcriptions, and I thought they were superb. I was particularly fascinated by the fact that he had put the repeated B flats, which continue like a thread, a kind of pedal point throughout the entire *Le Gibet* in the muted horns—a perfect choice. Even though at first thought playing four minutes of nothing but the same B flats is not exactly an exciting performance prospect. More than that, to play the same note for four minutes without cracking or flubbing takes tremendous concentration and control. But, as I say, it was the musically perfect choice, not only from the standpoint of timbre and orchestrational color, as a dulcet-toned constant throughout the movement, but also because it left the rest of the winds and strings free—Goossens did not use trumpets and trombones in his transcription—to colorize Ravel's amazing roaming chromatic harmonies in different timbres, the B flats fitting in ingeniously into each of those several hundred chordal aggregates.

I had first seen brief excerpts from *Le Gibet* in Eaglefield Hull's *Modern Harmony* while at St. Thomas, and since then had played through the piece myself dozens of times on the piano, analyzing it and relishing its unique harmonic inventiveness. Now that I was going to play it on the horn, I could hardly contain my excitement. For most of the orchestra players it was just another welcome record date and some extra money. I think most of them had never even heard of *Le Gibet* or had any idea of what a special masterpiece it is. (Orchestra musicians in general tend not to be knowledgeable or interested in piano literature.) The performances and the recording went beautifully, although, sadly, as far as I know, RCA Victor never issued our recording.

Goossens had obtained a recording contract with RCA Victor around 1940, and had already produced a series of superb recordings by the time I arrived in Cincinnati, most notably Vaughan Williams's *London Symphony* and Walton's wonderful Violin Concerto (with Jascha Heifetz as soloist).[44] In 1944 the orchestra made three recordings: Stravinsky's *Chant du rossignol* Symphonic Suite, a Suite from Strauss's *Rosenkavalier* (arranged by Antal Dorati), and excerpts from Grieg's *Peer Gynt*. The first two are superb recordings—Goossens was perfect for these works—and it is a shame that they have never been issued on CD, although they were briefly available on LP on one of RCA Victor's subsidiary labels. In the Stravinsky work, quite apart from fully meeting all the technical and virtuosic challenges of the work, the orchestra played with a rare warmth of feeling, with an emotional involvement and a remarkable sensitivity to Stravinsky's delicate and richly colored instrumentation, particularly in the several flute and solo violin duets played by Alfred Fenboque and Emil Heermann.

But at one of the two Stravinsky sessions I found myself quite suddenly in a most unusual situation. There is a seventeen-bar passage, involving the third trombone and tuba, in a repeated hoquetlike interlocking three-note pattern . For some reason our third trombone player, Bill Wilkins, started having trouble playing his two very exposed notes, even in some of the rehearsals. Worse yet, on the recording date he froze up completely, bringing the session to a complete halt. Wilkins didn't seem to be able to play that succession of two-note bars to save his soul, I think out of sheer nervousness. Understandably Goossens was getting quite upset, worried that the whole session might be jeopardized by Wilkins's inability to deliver the passage. Wanting to save Bill any more embarrassment and agony, and to ward off the cancellation of the rest of the recording session—nobody seemed to know what to do next—I went to Goossens during the five-minute break he had quickly called and offered to play the two notes on my horn. Greatly relieved—he hadn't thought of that as a solution to our dilemma—he immediately agreed. And that is how, believe it or not, the passage was finally recorded. I doubt that anyone would be able to tell what I have related here for the first time.

One crucial factor contributing to the excellence of this recording was the Music Hall's rich, warmly resonant acoustics. As a musician who has played (and conducted) in hundreds of halls and auditoria, ranging from the bone-driest and most discouraging to the aurally clearest, most supportive, and downright inspiring, I can say (and undoubtedly I speak for all musicians) that the acoustic quality of a room makes a *huge* difference as to how well we are able to play, how well we can hear and aurally relate to one another in ensemble situations, how clearly and realistically we can hear the entire range and spectrum of orchestral sound, no matter where we sit on the stage. Cincinnati's Music Hall provided just such clear, warm, supportive acoustics (at least until certain renovations were undertaken some years ago that slightly changed the halls sonic characteristics). I can remember vividly how I could hear everything clearly and in absolute equipollent balance—whether it was the violas fifty feet away, kitty-corner across the stage, or the bass section way over on stage left. (Since bass instruments provide the acoustic foundation for virtually all music, their function is most critical; it is important they be heard unimpededly, and not just by a few neighboring sections but by the entire orchestra—a situation that unfortunately only pertains very rarely.)

In resonant acoustics recording, engineers have to be very careful in their microphone placements and in the type of microphones used so that the resultant recorded sound is not blurred and unclear. The Victor engineers did a magnificent job in catching both Stravinsky's colorful, multitextured orchestration and the Music Hall's warm acoustic ambiance in all its splendor. The music glitters and glistens with an astonishing clarity.

I don't know exactly why they were less successful in our recording of the Strauss-Dorati *Rosenkavalier* Suite.[45] I was on the stage playing those wonderfully demanding horn parts, not in the control room, but my impression is that, whereas Stravinsky's orchestration in *Chant du rossignol* is texturally translucent, and light, graceful, like chamber music, Strauss's orchestration is texturally denser and more intense, couched in that venerable rich-sounding German orchestral tradition. The extra force and dramatic propulsion of Strauss's sound, especially in its up-tempo climactic sections, multiplied the reverberation in the hall to the point where the accumulation of rhythmic activity and the sheer sonic force of the music combined to produce a slightly blurred sound.

Even so, the brilliant playing of the orchestra shines through in full splendor, and it makes me sad that so few music lovers and musicians know how superb our recordings from that time are, and how very good this orchestra was, arguably as good as any in the country. Anyone doubting this should remember that an impressive succession of music directors—Eugene Ysaÿe, Fritz Reiner, and Eugene Goossens—had trained and honed the orchestra to remarkably high performance levels over a period of twenty-five years, blending the best of the German and French orchestral performance traditions.

Since Goossens is now an almost totally forgotten conductor, I feel compelled to say that he was one of the very finest conductors among the many, many I worked with and under whom I was privileged to play. If I were stating this in 1945 I could easily be accused of teenage immaturity, an example of a perhaps forgivable youthful but biased ardor. Yet I write this *now*, after nearly seventy years of every kind of experience with orchestras and conductors.

Goossens's early career as a conductor can only be described as brilliantly spectacular and meteoric. Starting as Beecham's assistant conductor around 1916 at the age of twenty-three, in 1921 he formed his own orchestra in London, presenting a legendary series of concerts in which, among other things, he conducted *from memory* the first performance in Britain of Stravinsky's *Rite of Spring*, this only eight years after its premiere. Goosens worked also in ballet and opera, and in 1923 was invited by George Eastman to become conductor of the Rochester Philharmonic. Goossens also entered the history books by conducting the premiere performance of the supposedly unconductable and unperformable second movement of Ives's Fourth Symphony (in New York in 1927), a work that optionally called for the conductor at several points to conduct in two different tempos and meters simultaneously, a feat that Goossens reportedly accomplished with consummate ease.

For some reason Goossens was never sufficiently appreciated in his American years (1923–46), possibly because it was the era of much more celebrated, charismatic superstar conductors such as Toscanini, Stokowski, and Koussevitzky, all, be it noted, active on the East Coast, not the rural Midwest, where it was perhaps assumed nothing musically outstanding could be happening. People also tended to take Goossens for granted because he did things with such ease and naturalness. He had no sense of self-promotion, and, of course, after his tragic problems with Australian immigration over the alleged, never fully proven, importation of fetishistic sexual materials in 1956, all his engagements were canceled and Goossens's career faded into oblivion.[46] But I can assure the reader that he was a superb conductor in all respects, including an impeccable taste in matters of style, podium behavior, and programming. He combined an unassuming, unexhibitionistic, and modest podium manner with the most rivetingly passionate realizations and interpretations, as not only his (our) recordings of Stravinsky's *Song of the Nightingale* Suite and the *Rosenkavalier* Suite amply demonstrate, but also the earlier ones of Walton and Vaughan Williams as well. So do some recently issued recordings Goossens made shortly before his death in London of Stravinsky's *Rite of Spring* and Scriabin's *Poem of Ecstasy*.

Around this time I suddenly found myself deluged with all sorts of strange inquiries and requests, among them a frantic call from Reuben Lawson (the orchestra's associate conductor) asking if I could immediately make an arrangement for the Cincinnati Pops of a tune called *Swinging the Ingots*, by Deke Moffett, an ephemeral bit of fluff very popular in Cincinnati at the time. As inane as this silly little piece was, it had become a big hit on WLW radio, Cincinnati's powerful station heard all over the country. In fact Lawson predicted that *Swinging the Ingots* was going to become a big nationwide hit (probably thinking of Arthur Fiedler and the Boston Pops' recent humongous hit recording of Jacob Gade's *Jalousie*). He added that there were plans afoot to record several of my arrangements. By then my symphonic arrangements of *Mood Indigo* and *Night and Day* had been performed and had attracted a lot of attention, even, to my surprise, as far away as New York. I was hesitant at first to take on *Swinging the Ingots*, partly because it was by no stretch of the imagination a jazz piece, which all my other arrangements had been. But I finally accepted and wrote the silly thing in a few days, score, parts, and all. Lawson put it on one of our Popular Concert programs—he listed it as Symphonic Swing. And then—nothing happened. *Swinging the Ingots* never became the hit Lawson had hoped for; it died very quietly.

Only a few weeks later I received a message from Artur Rodzinski in New York that he had read about the excellence (and success) of my arrangements, and that he wanted to perform some of them next season with the New York Philharmonic. I thought to myself, what is he thinking? The Philharmonic doesn't play pops arrangements in its Carnegie Hall concerts. I have to think that Rodzinski had no idea what such symphonic jazz arrangements actually were.

Then I also received a telegram from Bruno Zirato, the all-powerful manager of the Philharmonic and Arthur Judson's right-hand man, offering me the first horn position in the Philharmonic, beginning immediately. Evidently Weldon Wilber had just been drafted into the army. I wired back that "unfortunately I couldn't accept this generous offer, because I am presently signed up with a two-year contract in Cincinnati." To Margie I wrote: "Isn't this one hell of a fix?"

My mind was reeling with the excitement of all these sudden developments. Margie didn't believe they were real. Frankly, neither did I; it all sounded too good to be true. And, of course, it was; none of it ever happened. It was a good lesson to learn firsthand.

Undoubtedly the most important musical event during my second season in Cincinnati was my dual professional debut as composer and soloist in my own Horn Concerto, with Eugene Goossens conducting. I had from time to time kept Goossens abreast of my composing activities, and, in fact, had shown him my *Nocturne* for horn and piano. Evidently thinking quite well of it, he had suggested that I should orchestrate it, which I did in due course. As a result of that decision I realized that the *Nocturne* would make a fine second (slow) movement in a three-movement horn Concerto I had been working on most of the fall of 1944. When Goosens saw the score he immediately told me he would try very hard to fit the Concerto into one of his programs, near the end of the season. All the season's programs had been completely set for over a year, and he wasn't sure that he could find a place for my piece. I thought it was remarkable that he would even consider trying to squeeze it in; most conductors would have rejected such an idea out of hand.

I immediately set about copying a set of orchestral parts on the chance that he would be able to program the Concerto. Some time later he told me he had indeed found a place for it. Goossens was very good about programming works by local Cincinnati composers; for early April he had planned to do new compositions by John Hausserman and Ethel Glenn Hier. But since he had also programmed pieces by Smetana, Tchaikovsky, and a Haydn symphony (one of the rarely performed ones, No. 85, *La Reine*), as well as four operatic excerpts with Ezio Pinza as soloist—an already substantial program—he debated with himself whether including my twenty-three-minute Concerto wouldn't make the program too long. He eventually found a compromise, which was to exclude the "Nocturne" second movement, reasoning that, since it had just been premiered by the College of Music orchestra with Walter Heermann and myself as soloist, he (Goossens) would premiere just the two outer movements.

The premiere took place on April 6 and 7, 1945, and was quite a big success, both with the audience and Cincinnati's two critics. One of them, Mary Leighton, said, among other things: "[Schuller] isn't just an initiate playing around with notes. He has a fertile creative gift that even in his early efforts shows direction, logic, and resourcefulness. His music has rhythmic vitality and originality and the same comment goes for his harmonic language. His orchestration is lush and imaginative." She added in closing, "To make it more of a heyday for the youngest member of the orchestra, a lad still in his teens, some balcony-seated bobby-soxers gave [Schuller] an ovation when he came on stage, and orchestra members beamed like proud brothers, sisters, and papas when he finished."[47] Just as important to me was a favorable notice in *Modern Music*, at the time (and for the previous twenty years) the leading magazine on contemporary music in the United States.[48] The reviewer was Robert Tangeman, whose wife Nell had sung the mezzo-soprano part in our performance of *Das Lied von der Erde* just a few weeks earlier, on which occasion I had gotten to know the Tangemans, having been invited to a lunch with them by Goossens.

It goes without saying that that performance constituted a major event in my embryonic career as a composer. But more important than the event was the chance to hear the piece several times, in rehearsals and in two concerts. For only by hearing the work—played correctly and well, one hopes—can a young composer learn and progress. Since we learn as much, or perhaps more, from our mistakes than from our best achievements, it is necessary to hear the music in a professional context and a public performance.

My mother came from New York to attend the performances, and at the postconcert dinner celebration at Pohlar's restaurant she presented me with a beautiful, specially inscribed gold ring commemorating the occasion and the date—a ring I still wear.

A few weeks later a new phase of my career—as a horn player, not as a composer—emerged suddenly when I was asked to audition for the third horn position in the Metropolitan Opera Orchestra. My parents, especially my father, were anxious for me to return home and continue my career in New York, which they saw, quite rightly, as the musical capital of the world. Not that he didn't appreciate the opportunities for growth that Cincinnati, and particularly playing with the Cincinnati Symphony and Goossens, had provided. But it wasn't New York.

Judged by all conventional standards, I certainly was very successful in Cincinnati and was positioned to stay there for a good many more years. But my father had other—or better?—ideas. Toward that end, unbeknownst to me, after hearing about a horn opening at the Met from my former teacher, Robert Schulze (still always with his ears to the ground about job openings), my father asked George Szell, with whom he was working at the time at the New York Philharmonic, to audition me for the Met position. Why George Szell? Because Szell was then the unofficial but de facto music director of the Met, and because Szell greatly admired my father's work in the orchestra, his musical intelligence, his obvious serious, attentive, and fully cooperative attitude in rehearsals and concerts, not to mention his impressive knowledge of the music. Szell agreed to hear me, at which point my father wrote a letter to Goossens asking him to release me from my contract with the orchestra. (Was my father that sure that I would win the audition?) All of this occurred without my knowledge while I was busy copying the parts for my Horn Concerto and otherwise preparing for my solo debut.

I was more than content in Cincinnati and had no thoughts of leaving what had become my second home. I had no desire to interrupt or abort what had clearly been a very success-ful two-year tenure, whether looked at in personal, creative, or professional terms. So I was more than surprised when Goossens approached me one day at a rehearsal, telling me that he had just received a letter from my father asking him to release me so that I could return to New York. Goossens asked me if that was really what I wanted to do. I hardly knew what to say, except to assure him how much I loved being in Cincinnati and working with him. I felt I owed him a lot.

In truth, I was quite upset with my father for what I considered at the time to be his maneu-verings behind my back to interrupt my idyllic existence in Cincinnati. Moreover, when I found out that my dear friend Mimi Caputo, who had been so helpful to me in previous years, was the one being fired at the Met, I had serious qualms about auditioning for that particular position. But it wasn't long before my father and Mr. Schulze talked me out of such feelings of guilt and hesitation. After all, Mimi was going to be leaving in any case, and the position would definitely be open. As I thought about it more and calmed down a bit, I realized that my father was really thinking only of my own future good. And, beyond that, the more I thought about the attractive notion of returning to New York, where everything artistic and cultural worth talking about was happening, I realized I really had no choice but to avail myself of this new professional opportunity. It all depended, of course, on my passing the audition with Szell, for which I had to take a quick one-day round-trip flight to New York. Since there were, as usual, some twenty to thirty horn players vying for the position, and quite a few of them still had to be heard from, it was some time before I would hear of any final decision. In the end I didn't hear officially whether I had passed the audition until the Cincinnati season was over, although Szell had privately let my father know that I had made a very good impression on him and on John Mundy, the Met orchestra's personnel manager. They were especially impressed with my easy, almost nonchalant tossing off of two of the most difficult *Meistersinger* excerpts: a very tricky exposed high-lying third horn passage in the first act, feared by all opera horn players, and the virtuosic first and third horn parts in the boisterous fugal finale of the second act.

I found myself in a sort of mindless limbo during my last weeks in Cincinnati, not knowing whether I would be returning home to New York and leaving Cincinnati and all of my friends there. And what about Margie? I wasn't at all sure that I really wanted to return to New York.

My two years in Cincinnati, filled with such a rich cornucopia of musical and personal expe-riences—and discoveries—ended, alas, on a very confused and unhappy note. We all know that affairs of the heart are generally inscrutable, mostly defying rational explication. It eludes my understanding and remains a big blur in my memory as to how and why an unexpected turn of events intervened in my life and Margie's. I don't really know how it happened that she and I drifted apart, and why I drifted toward Gussie—and whether I or Margie initiated that drifting. What I do know is that during this period I was in some kind of emotional fog, in an uncustomary confusion. I didn't feel the pain of our separation until it was almost too late.

A few snatches of disconnected memories do remain, including a dim recollection of some arguments, some silly fights—our first spats; but I can't remember about what. Recently, quite by chance, I found an ancient envelope from 1945, on the back of which I had scribbled some barely legible diarylike notes that "Margie made me furious," that she was "driving me crazy"—and even more dramatic—"going crazy between Margie and Gussie; probably am already."

Margie, writing in her diary, thought that "we broke up because of things like friends advising both of us, and my extreme inferiority complex, which prevents me from doing enough!! Never have I been so despondent—death would have been a welcome guest!"

Still, I'm pretty sure it was my fault—if there is such a thing as fault in such matters. I was living in a strange mental haze, a sort of psychological holding pattern. Also, deep down I was at odds with myself about the whole issue of leaving my congenial Cincinnati environment, about returning home, and about trading the professional security and personal happiness of my Cincinnati life for the fiercely competitive maelstrom of life in New York. I don't know how much of a rivalry there may have been between Gussie and Margie. I personally didn't sense any; but that may have been my naïveté or my preoccupation with the various musical issues and challenges I was facing at the time. For the year and a half that I had known both young ladies, not only were they friends, but they often went with me, both of them, to all kinds of concerts, movies, and dinners together. I thought that it should have been very clear to Gussie that Margie was my true love, that I was actively courting her, and that my friendship with Gussie was strictly professional and platonic.

Yet it is also the case that I was spending more time with Gussie, much to the dismay of my mother, by the way, who instinctively didn't approve of her. It wasn't that Gussie and I were socializing so much; we were mostly enjoying a lot of music together, at concerts or at the Hangar, or playing four-hand piano transcriptions by the hour. I also remember our going to the 1942 revival of *Porgy and Bess* (which toured throughout the country for three years), a stunningly beautiful performance and production with Todd Duncan, Etta Moten, and the amazing John Bubbles as Sportin' Life.[49] I also remember some dinners with Gussie at Pohlar's or at El Arab (a newly opened Near Eastern restaurant), seeing Ibsen's powerful *Doll's House* together, hearing Rudolf Serkin for the first time, catching the Boyd Raeburn band, and being astounded to hear some of that orchestra's already very modern scores,[51] and their extremely talented musician-singer, David Allyn.

Near the end of the spring semester Margie played the Liszt A Major Piano Concerto at her year-end recital, with Walter Heermann conducting. But oddly enough she didn't do a voice recital (as expected, given her double-major program), for reasons that were never clear to me. I remember her telling me that she wanted to continue studying with Lotte Leonard, and would be going to a summer camp somewhere in Ohio where Leonard was going to be teaching. Beyond that, Margie hoped to be moving to New York after the summer to pursue her studies there.

In retrospect it is still hard for me to comprehend why, after two upbeat years in Cincinnati, I left in such a state of confusion, of diffidence. I had so much to be grateful for to that city, where I truly came into my own, and where, as it turned out, the basic patterns and pathways of my adult life and career were set forth. I was concerned as to the wisdom of leaving all this success and happiness for an uncertain future in New York. I was suddenly very unsure of myself, and wondered in what direction my life was heading.

But maybe my uncertainty was a sense—deep down—that abandoning Margie was the biggest mistake I could possibly have made.

INTERLUDE

———

IT DIDN'T TAKE ME LONG to realize that forsaking Marjorie in my last few weeks in Cincinnati, abandoning her for Gussie, was a colossal stupidity. Soon after I got home to New York, staying with my parents in Jamaica, Queens, I began to see how foolish I had been to allow myself to be enticed away from my true love. Back in New York, I had some time to reflect on my new situation, to ponder why deep down I was in a kind of emotional torpor. For the first time in my life I sat around listless, unfocused, oddly uncertain of myself.

I began to understand that Gussie's musical gifts, so natural and easy, and enticing, hid a certain flashy superficialness, and that, on the other hand, Margie's slower pace of learning, often showing signs of real struggle, rested on a much deeper, richer bedrock of talent. With Gussie talent just gushed forth, seemingly unhindered, while with Margie it had to be coaxed out slowly and deliberately—and patiently. Precociously talented myself, with all things musical coming easily to me, and with a quick, alert mind ready to absorb and grasp whatever knowledge came my way, I must have become a mite disenchanted with Margie's slower pace and momentarily captivated by Gussie's dazzling, easy ways.

My mother, generally not one to interfere with her son's love life—my parents were truly remarkable in that regard—nevertheless one day, with the subtlest of hints, let it be known that she didn't care all that much for Gussie, that she wasn't really the right girl for me, and that she didn't quite trust her. My confused feelings were suddenly up against a mature woman's intuitions. Something clicked into place within me, something I couldn't fully rationalize. But it began to worm its way into my conscience. And suddenly I knew with absolute certainty that in one way or another I had to bring Margie back into my life.

But how? When? I remembered her telling me that she wanted to continue studying with Mme Leonard during the summer. But where? Not at the college's summer school, because I knew that Leonard didn't teach there in the summer. Then it came back to me that she had mentioned a summer institute someplace in Ohio (actually it was Kenyon College). I had no idea what or where Kenyon College was, except that I remember thinking that it had something to do with the *Kenyon Review*, a poetry and literature magazine I had seen in the Gotham Book Mart. I had to get to that college some way or other during the summer—indeed as speedily as possible, before it was too late.

In the meantime, with no employment as a hornist in sight, Mr. Schulze and my father were trying hard to get me some work in New York. Their efforts were soon rewarded when I was suddenly called to play first horn in the New York Philharmonic at the orchestra's Lewisohn Stadium summer season, starting in mid-June. It turned out that Rudi Puletz and Weldon Wilber, the new co-principal horns of the Philharmonic, were both unavailable. (Puletz had to finish out his contract in the Cleveland Orchestra's summer concerts, while Wilbur was drafted.)

This was obviously great news for me; but on the other hand it also worried me no end that the Philharmonic's concerts (from mid-June to mid-August) would conflict directly with Margie's stay at Kenyon, at the time still not knowing exactly when that camp or institute was going to take place. After a quick search in one of my atlases, I saw that Kenyon College was in a little town in northeastern Ohio named Gambier, and subsequently learned—to my great relief—that the institute summer session was scheduled to last for a whole ten weeks, from mid-July to early September, only the first half of which would conflict with my Philharmonic commitments. I also discovered that the institute was in no way connected to Kenyon College, that it was merely renting two or three of its buildings. Even more interesting—and surprising—to me was that the institute was organized and directed by a group of composers and performers associated with Schönberg and the Second Viennese School. Although that was certainly of considerable interest to me as a composer, my primary purpose was to retrieve Margie and put our relationship back on track. Yet I could hardly have anticipated how profoundly those weeks in Gambier later that summer would affect my life and career, especially as a composer.

But now two serious concerns crept into my mind. One was what my parents would think if I told them that I was going to go to some unknown place in Ohio in pursuit of one of my Cincinnati girlfriends. I was much too confused, and shy, to try to reach Margie in Fargo, but by sheer coincidence—and great luck—a letter from Nell Foster arrived one day, informing me that she was going to Kenyon to continue her voice studies with Mme Leonard, and that she had heard from Margie that she was enrolled there, confirming as well that the summer institute was going to run at least until late August.

With those concerns and confusions out of the way, I could now concentrate on my upcoming work with the Philharmonic, and at some leisure figure out a plan for how and when I could get to Gambier, and, more critically, how I could persuade my parents to let me trek westward. They would surely consider it a frivolous quest, when I ought to be seriously preparing for my upcoming engagement at the Metropolitan Opera.

I had left Cincinnati in late April a few days after my last concert. There were a lot of sad and painful farewells with my many friends in the orchestra, and at the college and the conservatory. I was pretty sure that I would never see any of them again. Yet on the train to New York, despite my saddened and rather disordered, self-pitying state of mind, within a few hours of what was going to be a long eighteen-hour overnight trip I was suddenly inspired to start composing. The piece that began to pour out of me, and which I finished five days later in New York, was the Suite for Woodwind Quintet, a work that became one of my most often performed and recorded compositions, much beloved by woodwinders all over the world, especially the second (Blues) movement. I was initially inspired by the uneven clickety-clack rhythms of the train's wheels, which in turn triggered fond memories of Villa-Lobos's *Little Train of Caipira*, a marvelous piece I had played and studied in Cincinnati. The clickety-clackety piece became the third (Toccata) movement of the Quintet, and I remember composing it in one fell swoop on that train, out of my inner ear. (Obviously there was no piano around.) The many asymmetric rhythms and meter changes of the Toccata were really kind of old hat by 1945—well mined by Stravinsky and Bartók and a host of other composers. I thought of the Toccata as a kind of "train piece," happily rattling along the countryside and eventually easing into the next station, resting there, with its engine contentedly hissing and wheezing, rather like the Villa Lobos piece.

The Blues movement, my first serious excursion as a composer into jazz territory, followed the very next day, at home, and by April 30 I had also finished what became the Suite's first movement, the Prelude. The fact that the Blues was written for a woodwind quintet—not exactly an ensemble accepted in jazz circles—sans rhythm section was quite unusual in the 1940s.[1] And to give what most people would have considered an idiomatically ideal trumpet part to the oboe, not even the clarinet, was even more unusual. I didn't give a second thought to the fact—the reality—that woodwind players who could or who wanted to play jazz (or at least play in a jazz style) were as rare as hen's teeth. I just thought I had to try it; and, in truth, it wasn't all that long before the woodwinds—the flute, the oboe, the bassoon—like the horn, were welcomed into the jazz world. I knew instinctively that in the entire history of music it was always composers who drove instrumentalists to extend their techniques, to try out newly invented instruments (such as the clarinet in the late eighteenth century), and to expand their musical horizons. I knew that the vast majority of woodwind players, especially oboists and bassoonists, couldn't play jazz, but I also knew that *one day they would be*—a prediction that has certainly been fulfilled in the last thirty to forty years. And as I think back to the composing of the Blues movement over sixty years ago, I am amazed that intuitively, with my special love of bass instruments—especially the double bass, whether in jazz or in classical music—I put some of the music's bass line (such as a "walking bass") into the horn part rather than the bassoon. That surely was a first!

The Suite's first movement, Prelude, shows the temporary influence of Jacques Ibert and little touches of Francis Poulenc, generated by two wonderful recordings of those composers' works that I had acquired. Let me remind the reader that to one degree or another we all learn by imitation and by studying what our predecessors have created. In my case, as a young, self-taught musician of nineteen with no college, conservatory, or university training, working entirely on my own, whatever came unpredictably, accidentally my way—a recording or a particularly revelatory performance—could have such a strong impact on me that I had to take that music and make it my own, have it course through me, as if it *were* my own. A case in point, relevant to the composing of the Prelude, is that Arthur Fiedler's superb 1938 recording of Ibert's *Divertissement*[2] with the Boston Symphony had made a profound impression on me, traces of which one can hear in my Suite for Woodwind Quintet.

I more or less cloistered myself in those first few weeks back in New York in my own room for days on end, writing a lot of music—and thinking a lot about Margie. My notebooks of that period show that after the Woodwind Quintet, I wrote a harmonically rather advanced arrangement for solo piano of *Body and Soul*, and right after that a very simple arrangement for two horns and piano of a group of popular German folk songs. What prompted that little inconsequential opus, with its simplistic elementary horn parts, was the impulse to write something for me and my brother Edgar to play, with my father at the piano, Edgar having recently also started to play the horn—and amazingly well for a rank beginner.

I then plunged into a one-movement Concerto for jazz harp and orchestra, which I wrote for my friend from the Jeanette McDonald tour, Gloria Agostini. She was now, at age twenty, staff harpist at radio station WOR, playing regularly with Paul Whiteman's resident symphony orchestra. I had high hopes—perhaps naïvely—that Whiteman might program my Concerto with Gloria as soloist, because he had over the years premiered and recorded several works for jazz harp, including a Concerto by Dana Suesse, which had turned into a big, popular success. Jazz played on a harp had recently become a raging success, and Gloria thought we might be able to jump on that bandwagon. But nothing ever happened with the Concerto. I don't know whether Whiteman was ever really interested in the piece, or whether he even looked at the score. When Gloria would occasionally ask Whiteman whether he had, she always got some procrastinating nonresponse. It was very frustrating, and in the end I added it to my growing pile of unperformed and unfinished compositions. I haven't looked at it in many years, but perhaps its never seeing the light of day is just as well, for I suspect that it is filled with a few too many swing band clichés of the time.

This flurry of composing continued unabated, because by early June I was embarked on a cello concerto, intended as a gift for my dear Cincinnati colleague and friend, Walter Heermann. I wrote most of the two-movement Concerto in the first three weeks of June, then left it for over a month (concentrating entirely on my work with the New York Philharmonic), and in another short spurt composed all but the last ten bars at the end of July, and later, one day in September, completed the work. I sent it to Walter in early 1946, just before I heard from him that he and his brother Emil were going to leave the Cincinnati Symphony. Walter had played professionally in orchestras for nearly fifty years, and had also decided to stop playing the cello—just my luck—turning instead to full-time conducting as music director of the Madison, Wisconsin Civic Orchestra. It was clear to me that he would never be able to bring my Concerto to life.

A few years later, in 1948, I showed the work to Ernst Friedlander, the cellist of the Pro Arte String Quartet, in residence (by coincidence) in Madison at the University of Wisconsin. Although Ernst complained initially about the Concerto's tremendous difficulty, he eventually became very excited about the piece, and vowed to find an occasion to premiere it. We worked on the piece together when I happened to be in Madison playing with the Pro Arte Quartet, and Ernst even helped me with a few technical problems in the cadenza. But in the end Ernst's vow was never fulfilled. All his attempts to get a performance of the work came to naught, probably because at the time I was still a totally unknown composer, and cellists would invariably be invited to play the Dvořák or Boccherini cello concertos long before taking a chance on a work by an unknown composer barely out of his teens.

I laid the Cello Concerto on a shelf (along with the Jazz Harp Concerto), where it rested comfortably, gathering dust for more than half a century. A few attempts years later, when I had become well established as a composer, to interest several major cellists in premiering the work were fruitless.[3] I also did a lot of serious practicing on the horn in those early summer weeks to get myself in good shape—"keeping my chops up," as we say—preparing for the eight weeks of Philharmonic concerts at the Lewisohn Stadium. Here I was, only nineteen, playing principal horn with one of the world's greatest orchestras, working with a host of world-famous conductors and soloists, and playing a vast amount of varied literature, mostly in my case for the first time. The standard repertory was hardly given any rehearsal time, since the regular Philharmonic players had all performed such pieces dozens of times and knew the music technically well enough to follow any conductor's good or bad interpretation.[4] Which meant that I was mostly sight-reading, although as a composer and an avid student of the orchestral literature, I was quite familiar with most of what we played. But knowing a piece of music in a general, or for that matter in a theoretical, analytical way, is not the same as really knowing an individual instrumental part. Studying a score is done in private and involves no actual sound, but playing an instrument is quite another matter. In playing with an orchestra like the Philharmonic, note perfection is obviously expected. For me, the even more important challenge was to play my part with the fullest respect for every notational detail, and to reveal its relationship to the larger whole and all other parts. I also knew that all eyes (and ears) would be on me as a newcomer. Worse yet, there were always the watchful eyes and ears of my father, at every rehearsal and every concert, sternly—although sometimes proudly—assessing how his son was doing. I did garner a lot of admiring looks from the players, always welcome when one is relatively little known, an unproven commodity, especially in such passages as the extended solos in the slow movement of Beethoven's Ninth Symphony, the lead horn parts in Rimsky-Korsakov's *Capriccio Espagnole* second movement, or in Liszt's *Les Preludes*, a stadium concerts favorite.

Especially flattering was the admiring praise of the Philharmonic's official first horn, Rudi Puletz, whose place I was taking that summer. Why Rudi was sitting directly behind me in the first rehearsal, not playing, just listening, I can't recall now after more than half a century. But I assume that he had been asked by the orchestra's personnel manager to check up on me, to evaluate whether I had what it takes to play first horn in the Philharmonic. There he was, my senior by some thirty years, the renowned former principal horn of the Cleveland Symphony under Rodzinski, and someone I respected enormously, praising my playing.[5] He was particularly laudatory in regard to a certain slightly awkward, leaping octave passage in the Tchaikovsky Sixth Symphony's first movement, an accompanimental passage in the overall scheme of things, which was often played too loudly and ponderously when it was meant to be light and airy and unobtrusive. Rudi was even more astonished when I showed him that in order to help me achieve the desired lightness, I used an alternate fingering for one of the two pitches, something that had evidently never occurred to him.

One evening, however, my generally high batting average took a bad hit, and my confidence (or was it overconfidence?) was seriously shaken. Rimsky-Korsakov's *Scheherezade* was being performed, without even a brief brush-up rehearsal, a work I had never played before. It is fairly lengthy, and I knew I would have to really be on my toes that evening. Over the past few years I had developed, especially in Cincinnati, the practice of playing all solo passages looking straight at the conductor, not at the music.[6] I did this primarily because I realized that if you play with your eyes glued to the notes on the page, your mind and your ear are not as free to hear and feel the music as when you play from memory, from full aural knowledge of the music.[7] This idea, which seems to be pretty obscure to most musicians, is in fact a very simple one—and true. When you play music, your ear should be totally free and open, so that you participate fully, aurally, in what you are performing. But this cannot take place when you are *reading* the music, that is, when your eyes are occupied with the notes on the page. Why? Because in most human beings the brain, through which all visual and aural activities pass and are processed, cannot serve both functions simultaneously and equivalently. If the visual activity becomes the principal occupant of the brain, the aural will be relegated to a secondary role. And playing music without the most intimate, precise listening and hearing leads easily to a less sensitive, less felt, probably routine rendering.

Since I had a quick, virtually instantaneous memory for music and had heard *Scheherezade* dozens of times, I launched into a prominent five-bar solo in the third movement

with full confidence, only to suddenly commit a terrible and unforgivable gaff. As I played an E flat instead of an E natural, I heard a gasp course through the whole orchestra, and saw a dagger glance that could kill from the conductor, Alexander Smallens (at that time the de facto resident conductor at the stadium concerts), not to mention an agonized look from my father.

There is a saying among musicians, especially wind players, that "you're only as good as your last solo," implying that even if you play, say, one hundred solos very well and then screw up on the next one, you're immediately in the dog house. Hardly anyone seems to remember all your good work up to that point. My father was particularly irritated with me, as if I had let *him* down. Well, I suppose I had. Little did he know that I felt a hundred times worse than he did. Most professional musicians remember their relatively few mistakes forever—and painfully. I still cringe inwardly whenever I think of that *Scheherezade* solo, automatically recalling that stupid mishap.

Incidentally, the moral of that story is not that one shouldn't play from memory—nor that one shouldn't look at the conductor—but rather that one should know one's music better.

Several concerts that summer stand out particularly in my memory, either for their program interest or the high quality of the performances or the conductors. A spate of three concerts with Goossens was a wonderful reminder for me of not only what excellent programming ideas he had, everything from meaty works by Prokofiev (*Lieutenant Kije*), Strauss (*Rosenkavalier*), Brahms and Tchaikovsky symphonies, to "novelties" by William Grant Still and one of Goossens's own works, but also what a good musician he was and how he managed to impress and tame the Philharmonic players, notorious for their tough, often uncooperative behavior.

Two other conductors with whom it was a great pleasure to work were Maurice Abravanel (later to become a close friend and a hardworking partner on the Council of the National Endowment of the Arts), who that summer conducted splendid performances of Ravel's *Daphnis et Chloe*, Mozart's "Linz" Symphony, and Milhaud's brand-new *Suite francaise*; and second,

Leonard Bernstein, in three programs that included a terrific performance of the Shostakovich Fifth, an all-Wagner program, and his own superb ballet, *Fancy Free*. Another fine evening was presented by Robert Stolz (1880–1975), the famous operetta composer, whose music my father and I—both of us big fans of Viennese operettas—loved dearly.[8]

The concerts at the stadium could also produce unexpectedly hilarious moments. On the comical and even absurd side, two incidents stick in my memory. A truly ridiculous moment occurred when, in Beethoven's Fifth, after an already ludicrously erratic (unrehearsed) performance, Smallens conducted two extra bars at the end of the symphony—all by himself. Oh my! The orchestra finished with measure 817, but Smallens evidently felt the need to improve on Beethoven by adding a solo of two measures for himself, mm. 818 and 819. It was hard for us to not break out in howls of laughter. Fortunately the audience's applause covered our suppressed guffaws as we hid behind our music stands. Smallens, instead of looking apologetic, stared at us belligerently, between bows. I guess he thought *we* were wrong. Ah, conductors![9]

The other comical episode occurred when Mayor LaGuardia, a keen music lover (mostly of Italian opera), conducted the orchestra in Sousa's *Stars and Stripes* on a most special occasion. I don't know how it happened, but LaGuardia, instead of giving us a downbeat, stabbed at us with such a vigorous *upbeat*, that we all immediately played, hanging on for dear life. The reader may not realize that it is mighty uncomfortable and very difficult to play about 132 *down*beats for over three minutes against a conductor's *up*beats. LaGuardia smiled happily throughout, blissfully beating his way through the whole march, even as we all were caught up in the boisterous euphoria and jubilation of the occasion. That occasion—that heady moment—was in fact August 10, the day World War II ended, the day the Japanese opened surrender and peace negotiations. Minnie Guggenheimer, the director of the stadium concerts, had managed at the last minute to snare Mayor LaGuardia to give a celebratory speech and to conduct the grand finale of the concert, the mandatory *Stars and Stripes*. In that mood of high spirits and joy, and with LaGuardia leading his battalion of musicians as if charging up San Juan Hill adding another level of unrestrained hilarity, we weren't going to be derailed, even by 132 wrong beats. No way, not on that triumphal day!

In the meantime two of my Cincinnati friends, Nell Foster and Bobbie Segal, who had also enrolled at the Kenyon Summer Institute, wrote me in late July that Margie was already in Kenyon and that I could contact her there. I immediately wrote her, asking her to forgive me for my errant behavior in the last few weeks in Cincinnati, that I was very confused and didn't really understand how it all could have happened. "I am truly sorry if I have hurt you. Please let me come see you in Gambier and make things up to you? I know I have made a terrible mistake."

I didn't know whether Margie would respond, not really knowing how deeply hurt she was. Maybe she wouldn't want anything more to do with me, or would resort to some kind of revenge—although I found that pretty unthinkable, considering what a kind, generous, and forgiving person I had found her to be. All I could do was to hope for the best and wait.

To my great relief she eventually responded and in a most beautiful, magnanimous manner. Her letter gave me hope that I would be able to win her back, and it remains after all these years one of my most treasured possessions. Not that it was a letter of instant forgiveness; she let me know how bewildered and hurt she was, especially by a letter from me that— it seems[10]—I had written her on my last day in Cincinnati. In her gentle, unprovoking way she allowed that she "wasn't too happy with that letter; in fact, I was a bit stunned. I won't say anything more, because that subject has become very irritating." A little later she wrote that because of my letter and the "sad realization that I would soon be leaving Cincinnati for good—a town where I have spent two extremely happy years—it was inevitable that I got *very*,

very drunk." She added, cryptically, "It has been a very interesting experience, and it proved the worth of friendship!"

Wow! That hurt. I felt *really* terrible that I could have hurt her so deeply and not realized it at the time.

Oddly enough, that same letter starts with a huge apology, expressed in very self-deprecating language: "There is no doubt about it! I am some peculiar descendant of the rat family—a procrastinating rat!!! Why I haven't written you is hard to explain; so I shan't try." She wrote that it had taken her "a whole month to recuperate" at home in Fargo after leaving Cincinnati, mostly by reading Romain Rolland's *Jean Christophe* as a distraction.[11] "You can imagine the effect *that* had on me."

The rest of that long, ten-page letter—I saw its very length as a decidedly hopeful sign that a reconciliation could be in the offing—was basically couched in a friendly tone, also telling me of her happiness at Kenyon working and studying with a "fantastic music faculty," attending lectures and classes by such eminent literary lights as Eric Bentley, Gustave Reese, John Crowe Ransom (one of America's most distinguished poets, the founder of the *Kenyon Review* and originator of the so-called New Criticism in literature),[12] as well as famous Lieder and opera coaches such as Fritz Cohen and Frederic Waldman, both on the faculty of the Julliard School. She called Kenyon "a wonderful, wonderful place, a perfect prelude to New York."

One can imagine how relieved I was by the cordial tone of her letter. I immediately wrote her that I was determined to find some way to get to Gambier, sending along not only a bottle of her favorite perfume, Tabu, but also the two Li Po songs that I had just composed earlier that summer. I found out later, although I had suspected as much, that in her letters to her parents she never mentioned my name during that entire summer, or the fact that I might be visiting her. Dear heart, she was definitely on my side—and come to think of it, hers too!

I had to wait an agonizingly long two weeks for Margie's next letter—this time eleven pages—in which she hoped to see me soon. "You know, we'll only be here another two weeks." In the meantime she and Nell Foster had spent a weekend in Cincinnati, visiting with Paul Bransky, going to the Zoo Opera and hearing "a wonderful Tannhäuser" with her favorite baritone, Martial Singher, as Wolfram von Eschenbach (but "unfortunately with a terrible tenor in the lead role"). They also spent a lot of time at the Hangar and at some of their favorite restaurants, and saw Ruth Dunning, Jo-Jo Leeds, Gene Selhorst, and other college friends. After checking in at the Gibson Hotel, both were propositioned (via a bellhop) by, of all people, Mr. Gibson himself, the owner of the hotel—an invitation they politely declined.

I was overjoyed to receive such an upbeat letter from her, though here and there it was still a bit reserved in tone. I convinced myself that I would win her back as long as I could somehow get to Gambier. In the end that turned out to be not all that easy. There was another unexpected hurdle or two to overcome.

Near the end of July, in the middle of the Lewisohn Stadium season, I was invited to substitute with the Philharmonic in the last two of its Sunday afternoon broadcast concerts in Carnegie Hall. Again, as in 1944, when I played in an all-Mendelssohn concert, it was Mitropoulos conducting, but this time I was hired to play assistant first horn, not third. The program was typical of Dimitri's penchant for delving into off-the-beaten-track repertory, in this case Darius Milhaud's brilliant and witty *Le Boeuf sur le toit* (*The Beef on the Roof*), based on Brazilian dance and cabaret tunes, and Ravel's ravishing *Valses nobles et sentimentales*, the latter a work that I had thoroughly studied and knew intimately in both its original piano and later orchestrated version, having first come to love it through Piero Coppola's 1936 recording with the Paris Conservatory Orchestra.

Mitropoulos was in top form. He had the orchestra in the palm of his hands—quite a trick with the Philharmonic, which was hard to impress or to move from its well-settled ways. The Milhaud bristled with a vibrant energy and humor, and in the Ravel waltzes Mitropoulos extracted from the initially resistant orchestra a performance that not only shimmered and glowed with Ravelian elegance but also danced and flowed with a remarkably subtle, sensual swing and rhythmic flexibility. I watched Mitropoulos closely all through the rehearsals, marveling at how persuasively he was able to mold this music and the orchestra, trying to analyze exactly how he accomplished this. It would be remarkable for one pianist, with ten fingers and one mind, to perform Ravel's *Valses nobles* with such expressive and rhythmic elasticity; but to achieve that with eighty-five mostly recalcitrant musicians is quite another matter. How Mitropoulos achieved this quasi-miracle remains somewhat of a mystery, although I do know that a lot of it had to do with his eyes, his body language, and ultimately with the messianic ardor and selfless devotion to the music that he always brought to his work as a conductor.

I have heard Ravel's *Valses nobles* countless times, interpreted by dozens of conductors (in concerts and recordings), and have conducted the work many times myself, and have tried—never quite successfully—to emulate what Mitropoulos achieved on that Sunday afternoon in 1945. I have never heard that work realized so perfectly, so idiomatically. It was a magical experience that is still deeply embedded in my memory. (It was so as well for Margie, who, as I found out a week later, also raved about Mitropoulos's rendering of the Ravel, having heard the concert over the radio in Gambier.)

Those last two weeks of rehearsals and performances were hard work for all of us, playing in two series of concerts simultaneously. Both series ended on August 12, with no work in sight for me until October. But that was okay, because I could now single-mindedly pursue my main objective, getting Margie back. They were days filled with inner tensions. I had to figure out—secretly—how to get out to Gambier, and when, and to plan for what might be a major confrontation with my parents. They surely would want me to come with them and Edgar to Rocky Point, and to concentrate there on preparing for my full-time entry into the world of opera. I knew they rightly considered it an incredible privilege to join the Met orchestra, and thus would consider it irresponsible of me to fritter away my time and energies in chasing after some female friend.

But they surprised me; once again, I had underestimated them. They offered only a token resistance to my intended trip. I must admit that I pretty artfully downplayed the whole bit about chasing after a female by stressing instead that I was really going to Ohio to this summer institute to study with some great composers assembled there, such as Ernst Krenek and Roger Sessions, and that some of my Cincinnati friends were also going to be there. My parents gave me their blessing, if a bit reluctantly, for they surely would have preferred to keep me at home. They hadn't seen much of me for nearly two years, but I think they reasoned that their headstrong son, now nineteen, already making a good living as a full professional, ought perhaps to be allowed to lead his own life free of parental restraints.

About a week and a half after my last Philharmonic concert, with my horn at my side, I headed for Gambier, full of hope, although not really knowing what I might encounter there, and what I would actually be doing there. After a daylong train trip from New York to Gambier, via a layover in Columbus, I arrived at Kenyon College in the evening, just before dark. I was surprised to see the entire campus unoccupied except for three smaller buildings, one of which appeared to be an administration office.

What happened next nearly thwarted my entire enterprise. I presented myself to the gentleman in the office, who I found out later was the composer Fritz Cohen, famous for having written the music for the legendary modern ballet *The Green Table*.[13] I told him my name and why I had pilgrimaged to Gambier. With a rather condescending smile, Cohen allowed that

that was a very noble undertaking, but that there was no way I could stay at the college just to see my girlfriend. "Why not?," I asked with a combination of naïveté and obtuseness. "Because this is a school, and you're not enrolled here; all the students have paid a tuition fee"—none of which had ever occurred to me. "And besides," he added with some irritation, "our dormitory is completely filled. You really have to leave." He was quite determined to turn me out.

I was crestfallen, realizing my amazing stupidity in thinking that I could just sort of waltz into this place and expect to be welcomed with open arms. For a moment the thought flashed through my mind to simply pay for the damn tuition of $400, retroactively, but then I realized I didn't have that kind of money at the ready. It finally dawned on me that this was not a Kenyon College summer session; rather, Cohen and his circle of Schönberg followers had leased the campus for nine weeks to perform and work on the music of the Second Viennese School. Totally embarrassed, but desperate to find a way to stay, I pleaded with Cohen to let me stay *somewhere*—anywhere—at least for the night. I also told him that I was a composer who very much admired Schönberg's and Berg's music, and—after he noticed my horn—that I was already a professional hornist, had spent the last two years as first horn of the Cincinnati Symphony, and was about to join the Metropolitan Opera Orchestra—at which point his ears suddenly perked up.

With that he relented and told me that I could stay for the night, and that in the morning he would see what could be done about letting me stay, but only for a few days. Reiterating that there was no room in the dormitory, no bed available anywhere, he told me I would have to sleep in the basement of an unoccupied building next door, where there were some practice rooms that the college had made available. Happy as a lark, I told him I didn't care where I slept, even if it was outside under a tree. He took me to the basement of the vacant building, and with a flashlight—we couldn't find any light switch—pointed to a mattress (with no sheets) in a corner of a small, cell-like room—a rather grim, uninviting sight. The place was like a dungeon, but I didn't care; I was so elated to be able to stay—anywhere. There wasn't much to do in the dank, cold darkness, and so I just plopped myself down on the mattress with my clothes on. Dead tired, my last thoughts before drifting off to sleep were of Edgar Allan Poe's *The Pit and the Pendulum*, and the hope that no rats would come crawling over me during the night.

At seven the next morning I was suddenly awakened by the sounds of a piano, apparently on the floor directly above me, and someone repeating over and over and over again a rapid hammered *fortissimo* passage that I didn't instantly recognize, but that I suddenly realized was the last three bars of the fourth movement of Schönberg's Op. 19 *Six Little Piano Pieces*. Later that day I found out that the relentlessly practicing pianist was the famous—to me anyway—Edward Steuermann, in some seemingly desperate last-minute practice for a concert of Schönberg, Beethoven, Weber, and Chopin that he was to give in a few days. It was a rude but nonetheless very compelling morning awakening!

Cohen had not invited me to any breakfast, and I had no idea where on this large campus I would find a dining room or a cafeteria. Not wanting to disturb the intrepid mysterious pianist above me, I stumbled around a bit, not really knowing where I was. No one seemed to be up at that early hour, and so I camped myself on the doorstep of Cohen's office. A little before ten, he arrived and for a split second seemed surprised to see me. But then, remembering who I was, he told me that at breakfast he had talked with some of his colleagues, one of whom, Rudolf Kolisch, had suggested that maybe they could use a horn player—they didn't have one, only pianists, composers, a few string players, and lots of singers—and that by participating as a performer, unpaid of course, "this young man could," so to speak, "play for his supper." Evidently Mme Leonard had also put in a good word for me.

I was thrilled beyond words. At lunch in the mess hall I was introduced around to the faculty, some of whom I knew by name and reputation, such as Kolisch and Steuermann, the cellist Nicolai Graudan (former principal cellist of the Berlin Philharmonic) and his wife, Joanna, Marcel Dick, the violist of the Pro Arte Quartet, opera conductor and Juilliard teacher Frederic Waldman, and, of course, Krenek and Sessions (I had read a lot about them in David Ewen's *Modern Composers* and in my several music encyclopedias). Although there seemed to be students at a big table off in one corner of the cafeteria, I saw no sign of Margie or Nell. But I did see my dear friends from Cincinnati, Reuben Segal and his wife Bobbie, as well as Paula Lenchner. I waved to them from a distance, signaling that I would see them sometime later. By chance I ran into Mme Leonard in the afternoon, who told me where the girls' dormitory was, and that I would surely find Margie at dinner that evening.

And so it was that I laid eyes on my true love once again after three long, frustrating months. But then, to my utter dismay, given her friendly, seemingly forgiving letters of the past several weeks, our meeting at the dinner was awkward and tense. Frosty and standoffish, she hardly wanted to look at me; and I, stammering some confused apologies, couldn't seem to reach her. I now understood how deeply hurt she had been. In terror I realized that it wasn't going to be all that easy to win her back. She was evidently determined to make me pay for my heartless behavior. When I asked if we couldn't talk things over, alone, after dinner, she told me that she was going to a dance that evening with one of the students, a tenor.

Wow! That *really* hurt! I was desolate and suddenly jealous, something I had never before experienced. Margie was really having her revenge, and I realized I deserved it. I had broken off the relationship with her and now, arrogantly, thought that I could just amble back into her life, expecting her to welcome me with open arms. Well, not so fast, Gunther!

It got worse. In desperation I snuck around to the building where the dance was being held and caught a glimpse of Margie dancing in the arms of her escort—a lanky, handsome fellow. At this point I really lost it. Oh, the tortures of hell! Back in my cell, I was barely able to make myself do some practicing on the horn, and hardly slept at all that night. I had at last found the light switch for the shadeless single bulb hanging from the ceiling. But somehow the room, with its water-streaked cement walls, looked better in total darkness. The next evening Cohen found me a cot and some blankets, and I was put in the college's (presently unoccupied) male dormitory, all alone.

My frustrated feelings were somewhat assuaged when I was approached the next day by Cohen with some suggestions as to what I might be asked to play during the remaining weeks of the session: the Brahms Horn Trio, Schubert's *Auf dem Strom*, maybe the Beethoven Horn Sonata. The thought of playing the Brahms with Kolisch and Steuermann really buoyed my spirits.

Steuermann's concert that evening was a wonderfully exalting experience. I had never heard any Schönberg piano music played live, and so well, so expressively, so lovingly. But it was also the first time I heard Carl Maria von Weber's Piano Sonata in A Flat Major, and I had never heard Chopin—he did various scherzi and nocturnes—played with so much *harmonic* interest, bringing out all the delicious dissonances in Chopin's music, which are usually suppressed or ignored.

I soon learned that there were concerts of one kind or another at least twice a week, preceded by open rehearsals and by many reading sessions and lecture demonstrations in between. I was told that I had missed some great lectures by Erich Leinsdorf ("The Contemporary Composer and the American Music Market"), Krenek ("How Not To Appreciate Music," a typically witty, provocative Krenek title), English literature professor Eric Bentley ("Are the Muses Really Sisters?"), and Gustave Reese ("The Music of Guillaume Dufay"). During the day there were rehearsals everywhere, and composition or analysis classes given not only by Krenek and Sessions but also by some of the instrumentalists such as Graudan and Kolisch. I was overwhelmed by all this beautiful music making, all at a very high level, and by the tremendous amount of new music presented in those two weeks, much of which I had never heard before. That also included my first hearing of Mahler's Third and Seventh Symphonies, played four-hand by Steuermann and Cohen.

I was in musical heaven, rehearsing and performing the Brahms Horn Trio, attending rehearsals of new compositions by not only Krenek and Sessions but also other atonal and twelve-tone composers, some in their world or American premieres. In a short two weeks I was privileged to learn so much about this controversial musical style and language, so maligned for decades in most artistic circles, but here now performed under the best possible—and least prejudicial—circumstances. It was thrilling to hear this music played so lovingly and intelligently, and so punctiliously rehearsed by masters of the idiom. Those precious days enabled me to hear and see the truth, the beauty, in this music. I could really evaluate and understand the music when played by its best and most devoted practitioners, in an atmosphere where the antagonism voiced against dodecaphonic music was completely absent. I watched the rehearsals, listening to how thoughtfully the musicians took the music apart, down to its innermost components, and then put back together again. I saw how meticulously they observed the subtlest dynamic variances and rhythmic detailings. It was a wonderful lesson in how to prepare a piece of music, of whatever style or idiom, for performance and how to arrive through this unequivocally respectful approach at the truest expression of the music—lessons that I still live by to this day. I also took considerable pleasure in the realization that the way these musicians paid attention to *every* notational detail and nuance, taking nothing for granted, was a happy confirmation of how I myself approached performing and, in fact, the way I was taught by Robert Schulze, Bruno Jänicke, and—through observation—by my father.

It was also my first opportunity to observe how the several related dodecaphonic concepts then already in practice[14] provided a certain inner structural syntactic logic. I also observed and learned that using the twelve-tone concept per se does not—and cannot—guarantee high-quality, well-made music, nor does it guarantee the opposite. But then I already knew that *no* system, method, or concept guarantees the creation of great music. When it occurs, it is the composer, not the system or method or technique, that causes it to be what it is.

When Roger Sessions found out that I was a professional horn player, and after he had heard me play the Brahms Horn Trio, he asked me if I could advise him on some aspects of the horn parts in a composition that he was just working on, his opera *Montezuma*. He had written many horn passages in what is called in horn parlance "hand stopping," a way of muting the sound by pressing the right hand hard into the bell of the horn, producing an edgy, buzzy, distant sound, which Wagner, Strauss, Debussy, and Ravel (among others) had used to great effect. But when I saw that Sessions had used hand stopping (marked with a "+" above the notes) almost always in the middle and lower register and in *f* passages, I advised him that they would be barely audible in the context of a large orchestra, since this type of muting cuts the horn's projection by about 50 percent, especially in the horn's already inherently less projecting middle and low registers. I suggested that it would be much more effective to have most of those passages played with a regular mute, inserted in the bell, even though that sound was less buzzy than hand stopping. "But at least what you wrote will be heard," I told him.

He thanked me profusely, and said he would surely take my advice to heart. I never found out whether he did or not until many, many years later—by which time I had already conducted a number of his works and recorded his beautiful Violin Concerto—when he told me he wanted me to be the conductor for *Montezuma*, which Sarah Caldwell decided to produce with her Boston Opera Company. Roger sent me the score of *Montezuma*, all fourteen pounds of it, and as I began to study the work, I saw that all the "+" marked horn passages were still there. My advice of thirty years earlier had remained unheeded. That didn't upset me particularly, but I was quite disappointed when Sarah, after cancelling and postponing *Montezuma* several times in successive seasons, eventually found the wherewithal to put the opera on and then decided to conduct it herself.

I got to know Krenek quite well in those weeks at Kenyon College. He was an almost legendary figure to me by that time, mostly because of the phenomenal flash success of his 1925 opera *Jonny spielt auf*, which was touted in the late twenties as the first "jazz opera."[15] This had interested me greatly when I first read about the work, but when I found two brief recorded excerpts from the opera for my record collection (one called "Blues"), and after acquiring the piano score, I realized that there was virtually no jazz in the work. Under the circumstances and knowing of the opera's checkered career, I did not bring up the question of its brief flash success. But he and I had many interesting conversations about twelve-tone music, a concept that Krenek had adopted in the mid-1930s. And he told me much about his early days in Vienna, and in Kassel, and his travels as a conductor in Switzerland, Austria, and Italy. A verbal virtuoso, both in German and English, Krenek was a brilliant conversationalist; a sly, subtly sardonic smile played constantly on his lips. I greatly admired his intellect and the acuity of his mind. By contrast, among the girl students (so Nell Foster told me) the talk about Krenek was about his beautiful legs!

I found the two Krenek works performed at Kenyon that summer outstanding. His brand-new Violin Sonata, played superbly by Kolisch and Steuermann, interested me so much that I copied out the entire score into one of my manuscript notebooks. Krenek was experimenting with polyphonic concepts and early Renaissance isometric forms (inspired by the works of Heinrich Isaac), as well as with a "free" notation of vertically uncoordinated bar lines. Just as fascinating was his 1935 song cycle, *Travel Diary from the Austrian Alps*, full of wonderful wit and humor and verbal dexterities, and beautifully sung by Lotte Leonard on that occasion.

It was Nell Foster who ultimately helped to bring Margie and me together. Although Margie at first did her best to avoid me, she gradually became persuaded that I was sincere in my feelings of regret and guilt, that my apologies for having treated her so cavalierly were genuine, and that my love for her was true and absolute. In her quiet, reserved way I could tell that she really cared for me, and I got the sense that she enjoyed seeing in what high regard I was held by the faculty at Kenyon.

She told me that she was becoming rather unhappy with Lotte Leonard; she thought that Leonard's teaching was beginning to ruin her voice. Margie had already participated in two concerts before I got to Kenyon that featured some Mozart arias and Schumann Lieder. When I finally heard her sing, her voice did occasionally sound strained. (Nell expressed the same concerns about Leonard's teaching.) The two concerts in which I heard Margie were an opera workshop with scenes from Mozart's *Magic Flute*, with Margie as Pamina, and in the last week of the session the entire second act of Mozart's *Marriage of Figaro*, in which she was the Countess. The singers were all coached by Leonard and by Frederic Waldman. He and Fritz Cohen led daily musicianship classes, while Cohen's wife, Elsa Kahl, trained the singers in stage deportment, acting and movement, even basic balletic exercises. Margie had had very little of that kind of all-around training in Cincinnati, where she had concentrated only on vocal technique and style. But here, at Kenyon, she was suddenly immersed in all the other aspects of operatic-dramatic training. Under the twin pressures of the very intense weekly class schedule and the high demands of the teachers, Margie made tremendous strides in all these opera-related disciplines. I remember that she was also much helped—and inspired—by Nell Foster, who had an absolutely natural inborn talent for acting.

With all these classes, coachings, rehearsals, and the many weekly concerts and lectures, there was little time for socializing on our part. But I was amazed to discover that in this tumultuous schedule Margie also found time to write her parents several four- or five-page letters every week—letters in which my presence at Kenyon was always concealed.

I didn't realize until some years ago that Margie's letters to her parents were all returned to her by her sister, Anna Jane, after their parents passed away. Reading through all these letters was a touching and very emotional experience. They brought back many wonderful memories, but also revealed in considerable detail how she grew and developed as a musician, and how devoted she was to her parents, especially her mother. In one of those letters I was startled—and pleased—to read that she had hated the dance and ensuing party that second evening after my arrival at Kenyon. She wrote her parents that her date, although a "nice boy who acted like a gentleman," was so bland and boring that it nearly drove her crazy, and how disgusted she was with the party, where most everybody got "slobberingly" drunk, where the girls "were so degraded by drinking that it was a horrible, horrible experience for me" and how that had reminded her of her "despised" Frances Shimer College.

Margie did very well in all her work at Kenyon, although I did detect those signs of vocal-technical problems in her singing. I told her that I would help her find another teacher in New York, and suggested further that it would be a great idea for her to continue her piano studies with Steuermann—if he had room in his very busy teaching schedule. I asked him to give her a little audition, which I attended, and in which she played a Schumann Novelette and a Mozart Sonata. She was a bit rusty, since she had hardly touched the piano in all the weeks at Kenyon, concentrating primarily on her singing. Her playing wasn't technically so secure, but I suspect that her warm tone and highly expressive playing must have impressed Steuermann enough to take her on as a student in the fall.

I was living in a dream world that last week at Kenyon, not only because of all the great music making I became involved with and the many new friends I made there, but above all because Margie and I were finally together again. Our love and our feelings for each other were so intense and so deeply felt, partly I suspect because we both now realized that we had come close to losing each other, perhaps forever. As the Kenyon session came to an end, knowing that we would soon have to part company, we were desperate to spend every possible moment together. But that was very difficult or at times impossible, given that we were both so busy with the summer's final rehearsals and concerts. I was scheduled to play the Brahms Horn Trio with Steuermann and Kolisch a second time, and Schubert's *Auf dem Strom* with Paula. I also attended all the rehearsals and turned pages for the world premieres of Krenek's Violin Sonata and Sessions's brand-new *Duo for Violin and Piano*.

In that last week Mme Leonard gave her final workshop class on Lieder in which Margie sang Mozart's "Ach, Ich fühl's" from *The Magic Flute*, Mahler's heavenly "Ich atmet' einen Lindenduft!," and Schumann's "Im wunderschönen Monat Mai," songs that are deeply embedded in my soul not only because they are the finest and purest demonstrations of what the vast Lieder repertory has to offer but also because of their particularly intimate association with Margie. It is impossible for me to hear those songs without tears coming to my eyes, an indescribably beautiful feeling.

As the final days approached, panic set in: how to fend off or delay the dreaded agony of parting. One answer was to spend our nights together, wandering around in the beautiful countryside around Gambier, away from the campus and other people. We had to be alone, silently communing with ourselves and nature, reveling in the rich silence of the night. As luck would have it, it never rained those final days. We walked for hours, enjoying the balmy early September nights, the warm breezes, marveling—as lovers have since time immemorial—at the crystalline, starry firmament, so unfathomable in its vastness and utter perfection. We stopped occasionally to sit under a chestnut tree or lean against some farmer's haystack, eventually returning to our dorms when the first rays of the sun began to paint the horizon in delicate pigments of blue and orange. It's not clear to me how we kept going with only two or three hours sleep each night. I recall only feeling strangely energized, buoyed, fully alive—occasionally sleepy, but not really tired.

The very last night was completely ours. In our wanderings we found an old farmhouse a mile or so from town, with a little garden and a bench and table in the yard. We just sat there in blissful silence, and dreamed our dreams—also mindful of not wanting to wake up our unseen, sleeping hosts. We hardly spoke more than a dozen words all night. We didn't have to; we were beyond mere words. We were communicating at some secret deeper level, the heady silence matched only by the intensity of our feelings.

At dawn the woman of the house suddenly appeared, surprised to see us sitting there huddled together. I apologized for the intrusion and explained that we were in love and that this was our last night together. A kindly lady, she seemed to get the point and, as she went off to milk the cows, generously invited us to stay as long as we wanted. A half hour later, now joined by her husband, she came back with a huge pitcher of fresh milk, and offered us to drink as much as we'd like. Ravenously hungry, we drank more than our fill. Amazingly rich and creamy, still slightly warm, it was the most wonderful milk we had ever tasted.

Our euphoric last night had to end, of course. As we left that beautiful place, our hosts gave us a beautiful bouquet of asters and dahlias, fresh from their garden. We were moved to tears. For that blissful moment and that whole night the world was beyond perfection. All was goodness and light.

At Kenyon College, after all the goodbyes with so many wonderful people, many of whom became lifelong friends and affected my life and career in crucial ways, we packed our bags, walked a mile or two to the tiny Gambier train station and took a "milk train" to Columbus. We had decided—oh wonder of wonders!—to stay overnight, to celebrate our reunion with a grand dinner, and to finally, finally spend our first night together, our honeymoon in effect. We splurged on the best hotel in town, the Statler (long before the Statlers all became Hiltons), and a fabulous four-course dinner, topped off with wine and cognac. It damn near broke us; neither of us had counted on such a festive occasion. But Margie had some money, actually considerably more than I did—remember, no credit cards in those days—and between the two of us we managed to survive the evening financially, with just enough to get us back home, she to Fargo, I to New York.

Our night of nights was glorious—and indescribable, literally. One cannot—at least I cannot—capture in words the surge of passion, the achingly sublime pain of love, all cast in a dreamlike unreality. And who can adequately describe the intoxicating multiple physical and emotional sensations, the heat and passion of one's first sexual encounter, with its unique release of long accumulated, pent-up energies? All I can say is that our mutual rite of passage was a transcendent event, the initiation of an irreversible commitment to making each other happy, bonding forever in the joys of love and pleasure.

In her diary Margie recorded her impressions of that first full physical consummation of our love in a beautifully simple, single paragraph: "We got separate rooms, but spent the night as we pleased, with nothing and nobody to worry about, no one interfering, just ourselves—a selfless, beautiful way to live."

If at the moment of climax it sometimes seems that for a few seconds life seems to have stopped, as one is suspended in some irreal other world, the calming balm of sleep provides the perfect transition back to reality. But in our case it was a painful and cruel reality; the agonies of parting were upon us once again, each with trains to catch, each facing long hours of travel and sorrowful loneliness. We cried a lot, and with endless kisses promised to cherish and love each other forever, looking forward to the joy of reunion in New York, so many dreadful weeks away.

As I think back to that time—and oh, how often I have done so—that summer of 1945 was a striking example of how chance can impact one's life in the most dramatic, powerful, and unpredictable ways. I'm sure it was when I told Margie that I was leaving Cincinnati to join the Metropolitan Opera Orchestra that she decided in her own mind to follow me to New York. But beyond that, my single-minded pursuit of Margie led in ways that I could never have foreseen to an encounter with an array of the most remarkable musicians who influenced the course of my life in crucial respects as mentors, as lifelong friends and admired colleagues.

Most American composers and musicians at that time were uninterested in the music of the Second Viennese School. If by chance they had been curious about it, they would have discovered that the music and recordings were basically unavailable.[16] But I, by pure chance, stumbled into a tiny enclave of Schönbergians, mostly refugees from Hitler's Europe, where I could objectively examine and evaluate the music, closely observing the work of musicians who were the most expert at performing it, clearly masters of this idiom.

What also figured in the fateful events of that summer of 1945 is the fact that by some intuition I had brought my horn along, when there was no actual need for me to do so. Had I not, Fritz Cohen would surely have insisted on my leaving Kenyon. By letting me stay he gained a good horn player—free of charge—enabling him to schedule works that could otherwise not have been presented. The lesson or moral here is that if fate offers you an unexpected opportunity, you had better be ready to receive its chance gifts. In my case, I seem in almost every such instance to have been ready.

Although I always loved train trips, this one back to New York was at best a mixed blessing. The sudden disruption of the idyllic weeks at Kenyon left me in a complete mental fog. I found myself vacillating between desperately trying to hold on to the happy memories of those last blissful days—and nights—with Margie, and the aching feelings of loneliness, the pain of utter emptiness. Even the wonderful musical experiences at Kenyon, the revelatory encounters with so many great musicians, were mostly pushed into the back of my mind. But it was also the first time that I experienced that strange sweetness, that exquisite redolence, that is embodied in all emotional anguish. There is something strangely poignant and seductive deep inside the pain that draws you in again and again, as the moth is drawn to the flame.

Unable to sleep on the entire eighteen-hour trip, I arrived home dead tired, emotionally and physically exhausted. My parents, to their credit, left me alone to stew in my misery, realizing that it would be no use trying to console me. I think they knew that there wasn't much one could do for a lovesick teenager, that the twin balms of time passing and the resultant convalescence would eventually bring me back. I poked around listlessly, trancelike, for days, trying to do some composing, playing through some of my favorite late Scriabin—which in the end didn't help at all, since Margie had also begun to play and study Scriabin. His sensuous harmonies only evoked more sweet painful memories. Listening to some of my favorite recordings, such as Delius's *Sea Drift*, was an even worse cure, since both Whitman and Delius express the pain of loss and parting with such heartbreaking poignancy.

But eventually reality took over; I realized that I'd better prepare for my new job at the Metropolitan Opera, which was to start in late November with a week of prior preparatory rehearsals.

Still, the time between our parting in Columbus, Ohio and the October opening of the Met season was fraught with much anxiety and worries, mainly about Margie and whether she was really coming to New York. I didn't have the nerve to be in touch with her in the interim. But I did spend some relaxing time in Rocky Point with my parents and Edgar, reading a lot and practicing, taking short bicycle hikes, roller skating in Rocky Point's popular rink, and spending a lot of time at the beach—longingly ogling with my ever roving eye my dark-haired Italian beach beauty, as a kind of surrogate Margie.

Chapter Four

DISCOVERING JAZZ

UP TO THE TIME that I moved to Cincinnati in 1943 to join the orchestra there, my musical interests and studies had been primarily in classical music. I had discovered jazz by then, of course, although rather late compared to the average American youngster. That was a function of my spending four years in Germany, in the relative isolation of a private school in a country—Nazi Germany—where jazz was a forbidden (*verboten*) music from 1933 on. There was absolutely no way I could have heard any jazz during those four and a half years. When I did discover jazz upon my return to the United States and became seriously attracted to it, it was through Duke Ellington's music, which in itself is interesting in that it was the work of the greatest composer in jazz, not its (at the time) more famous and popular white band leaders—Benny Goodman, Tommy Dorsey, Artie Shaw, etc. As great as Ellington's musicians were and as much as they individually contributed to the final realization of Duke's music, it was the basic compositions with all their originality and innovativeness that really caught my attention and provoked my interest. I suppose that was more or less inevitable, given that my involvement with music up to then was entirely on the classical side, where the composition is the prime procreative element.

In any case, that I as an American would eventually discover jazz was inevitable, given that jazz is our country's one and only homegrown, quintessentially American music, and that between the 1920s and 1950s jazz was one of the only two musical genres that played a central role in the lives of Americans.[1] Remarkably, jazz and classical music were at that time equally popular; both were extensively represented on both radio and in live presentations—classical music in concert halls, jazz in ballrooms, dance halls, hotels, and nightclubs—and in size their respective audiences were just about equal.

After my discovery of Ellington's music, and Basie's and Lunceford's and the many great composer-arrangers of the Goodman, Dorsey, Shaw, and Barnet orchestras—Eddie Sauter, Sy Oliver, Fletcher Henderson, Eddie Durham—I knew that jazz would have to become an important part of my musical life. I was hooked. I now began to avidly collect jazz records—in addition to my classical collecting—jazz of all kinds, from early Armstrong and "King" Oliver to the latest offerings of the great dance bands and small groups of the early 1940s (such as the Nat King Cole and the various Benny Goodman trios and quartets)—all representing the heyday of the Swing Era. Collecting both classical and jazz records may not sound so unusual nowadays, but over half a century ago it was mighty unusual and special. The two music genres, though each had its loyal partisans, were considered absolutely antithetical to each other, and were rigidly segregated. (That was not so democratic!)

For me, jazz was a most important music, especially in the hands of its greatest practitioners (i.e., Ellington, Armstrong), equal in quality to the best in classical music. And I kept saying so to anyone who would listen to me. It was a musical language (or idiom) that I had no trouble understanding (intellectually, technically) or feeling (emotionally, expressively)—unlike my parents and virtually all my friends and colleagues in classical music. I was utterly fascinated by the rhythmic language of jazz, so different from classical music, but somehow so natural to me, and so relaxed and so free. How and why thousands of classically trained musicians couldn't feel or replicate it was incomprehensible to me. (My father, a great musician, couldn't understand jazz, and couldn't play the syncopations and rhythms of jazz to save his life.) As a young composer, already quite fluent in putting down my musical ideas in the established notational forms, I was particularly fascinated by the fact that jazz composers and arrangers wrote their music in that same notation, but then it was played and expressed quite differently—freely, loosely, more personally. What was that all about? I had to find out more.

By the time I moved to Cincinnati I had come to the realization that in one way or another I needed to become actively involved in jazz, more than just appreciating it, listening to it on the radio and on records. It wasn't long after my arrival in Cincinnati that I discovered the city's many jazz clubs and began attending them regularly, something I had not been able to do in New York. One of these clubs, called the Hangar, became my favorite hangout because it had in residence six nights a week a terrific piano-guitar-bass trio that specialized in playing the repertory of one of my all-time favorite jazz chamber ensembles, the King Cole Trio. The Trio, formed in 1939, had by 1942 and 1943 amassed a number of tremendous hits on the radio and juke boxes such as *Straighten Up and Fly Right, It's Only a Paper Moon, Sweet Lorraine*. I already had a big collection of Cole Trio recordings, but now hearing that music replicated so beautifully, so perfectly, and so respectfully—and in acoustic reality, close up at a distance of less than fifteen feet—was a whole new, inspiring experience.

I more or less lived at the Hangar, absorbing and learning, gaining ever-deeper insights into how those three musicians combined improvisation and the spontaneous elaboration of ideas with the basic underlying composed, notated songs. The three musicians in the Hangar Trio were Lee Anderson (piano), Johnny Fair (guitar), and Will Wilkins (bass). It is a shame—and unfair—that these fabulous musicians never became well known, never got to make any recordings of their own music and their arrangements of song standards. Nor were they ever mentioned in jazz histories or in, say, Leonard Feather's *Encyclopedia of Jazz*, not even, as far as I know, in the monthly jazz magazines *DownBeat* and *Metronome*. They were just a few of the thousands of fine local musicians in hundreds of American cities who never made it to the big jazz centers like New York or Chicago or Los Angeles. Yet, as I traveled increasingly around the country, especially a few years later on the annual nationwide tours of the Metropolitan Opera, I learned that there were untold numbers of very talented musicians everywhere playing fine jazz, either in bands or trios or quartets, providing superb musical entertainment in their home towns, who were often *as* good as those who achieved fame and recognition in the big musical centers and on recordings.

All three Hangar musicians became my close friends, but especially Will Wilkins, the bass player. I spent many a happy evening with them at the club, but also at their homes, where, as a bonus, I got my first taste of African-American cuisine, which meant Southern cooking—wonderfully varied, and excitingly zesty, spicy fare. The Hangar trio was, of course, not the only live jazz I heard. Before long I had several more epiphanous encounters with live jazz: Ellington and his orchestra, and in Cincinnati's several jazz clubs and dance halls in the black section of town (known as the West End, most notably the Cotton Club), where most of the reigning black orchestras appeared regularly.

The most important encounter was hearing Duke Ellington and his orchestra for the first time live. Ellington was already my jazz idol by the time I came to Cincinnati and I had in my record collection practically every Ellington recording that was available, including the first spate of 1940 reissues of Duke's earliest 1920s masterpieces (such as *Mood Indigo, East St. Louis Toodle-oo, The Mooche, Black and Tan Fantasy*, etc.) That first direct encounter with the Ellington band was truly unforgettable, and it occurred quite suddenly in late October 1943, only a week or so after arriving in Cincinnati. I heard that Ellington was coming to town to perform at a place called Castle Farms, an immense ballroom about fifteen miles outside of Cincinnati. I spent an entire evening there, standing in front of the bandstand, listening and watching all my favorite heroes: Lawrence Brown, Johnny Hodges, Harry Carney, Ray Nance, Rex Stewart, and, of course, Duke. While most people were dancing or having a drink, I stood there riveted, thunderstruck, mesmerized by the beautiful sounds coming from that stage. I don't think I moved all evening, except between sets. It was a whole other experience to hear the orchestra live, close up, in all its sonic splendor, not filtered through microphones and the surface noise of shellac grooves. I heard and understood, probably for the first time, how the spontaneity of expression that great musicians bring to music, even in the fully notated parts of an ensemble arrangement, can enliven and inspire the music.

At first, as I entered the tremendous smoke-filled hall, I couldn't hear any music, which meant, of course, that the band was on one of its intermission breaks. This gave me a chance to become accustomed to the sepulchral darkness and to find my way to the bandstand. There were no lights other than some hazy dark-blue and red fixtures here and there, ostensibly to create a seductive atmosphere. I positioned myself as close as possible to the orchestra to be sure that I could soak up every precious sound. I was so taken with big band jazz in the flesh that I kept a diary of these initial encounters. The following quotes are from that diary and frequently reflect my boundless enthusiasm. As a brass player, my attention was immediately drawn to the seven-man brass section. "The trickiest rhythms were handled with such precision that they seemed to emanate from one player or one instrument. Unbelievable also was the sheer power of the brass. When all seven let go, it was well-nigh impossible to stand as close to the bandstand as I did without having my ears sizzle with the heat from their sonic impact." (A bit of poetic hyperbole there.) I exclaimed: "They must all have iron lips!" Of the trumpets I recognized only Ray Nance and Rex Stewart. "All four played"—meaning held their trumpets—"with only one hand, their left hand, at least *in tutti* work, and with the greatest of ease and nonchalance." That included Rex Stewart, who, I learned later, played most of the time not only with just one hand but also, according to my diary, almost exclusively with just his third finger. Rex had become my favorite Ellington trumpet player ever since I heard his magical, soulful, twelve-bar solo on Ellington's 1940 recording of *Dusk*, with its poignantly expressive half-valve bends and gentle scoops. Stewart was "as amazing in his beautiful melodic conceptions as in his unorthodox way of playing. For Stewart plays everything except his fast runs with his third finger, switching from one valve to another."[2]

I was very impressed with the ensemble work of Ellington's five-man saxophone section, wishing that classical sections (and musicians in general) would balance and blend dynamically and sonorically so perfectly, so automatically, without endless laborious rehearsing. Watching that stellar sax section that night I noted in my diary that Johnny Hodges "never broke a smile (I don't believe he can) throughout the entire evening. But he provided more thrills, almost paradoxically, because of his apparent look of boredom. Yet from this shell [sic] streamed the most sensuously beautiful melodies imaginable. The purity of his tone, his very personalized type of phrasing (especially his ability to bend and glissando notes with just his embouchure— no fingerings) place him among the very greatest."

I could not help but take note also of Harry Carney's central role in the band. This uniquely gifted baritone saxophonist functioned not only as the foundation of the sax section and as a sonorous anchor in Ellington's advanced harmonizations, but also as the most distinctive timbral voice in the entire ensemble. With his special tone color, he very often appeared to be leading the orchestra from the bottom, from the low register—as I put it: "giving the band a terrific lift and richness."

But ultimately Lawrence Brown stood out for me above and beyond everyone else—perhaps because the horn, my instrument, was in so many respects (range, register, tone, lyric expressiveness) like the trombone—noticing especially in *Do Nothing Til You Hear From Me* the "rich exquisite purity of his tone, which," so I wrote, "I am forced to place even above Tommy Dorsey's."

With my love of bass-register instruments I naturally took notice of "Junior" Raglin's remarkable—and seriously underrated—playing. I saw and heard him do pizzicato runs "with incredible speed and clarity, employing two fingers, as violinists are wont to do in the Tchaikovsky Fourth Symphony," a technique that in the early forties was, I believe, still virtually unheard of on the bass.[3] Ellington certainly admired and respected Raglin; he recorded several duet sides with him, as he had done earlier with Blanton. Sadly, illness forced Raglin in 1947 to retire from playing. As good as he was—certainly in my opinion—his achievements were perhaps overshadowed by the revolutionary breakthroughs of his predecessor, Jimmy Blanton. But one should remember that Raglin carried on exactly in Blanton's manner, superbly filling the expanded role the bass played in Ellington's orchestra, as innovated by Blanton.

As for Ellington himself, although I had become aware in recordings of his completely original piano style, so different from Art Tatum, Earl Hines, Teddy Wilson, and Nat Cole, I was not prepared, when hearing him live, for the sheer power and projection of the sound he produced on a piano. The many years that I heard him play I noticed sometimes, say, on a slow night on tour, when the band's playing might have gotten a little diffident, Ellington would energize and animate the whole orchestra with just one powerful, perfectly placed chord. It was like an electric current charging through the orchestra. Hearing Ellington that first time in person, I realized that I had until then never heard any classical pianist play with such a rich depth of tone, and that he had some uncanny touch that, powered by his body and large hands, connected directly through the entire piano mechanics (of keys, levers, and hammers) to the strings, producing a purity and centered fullness of sound and tone that I have heard perhaps only with two or three other pianists, jazz or classical. And as loud or forceful as he might play at times, I never heard him produce, live or on recordings, a harsh, hard, or edgy sound; there was always that fleshy, full, rich tone.

The next time I heard the Ellington orchestra in person was about a year later, on October 28, 1944, again at Castle Farms. This time I took Margie and Gussie along, although rather late in the evening, since my symphony concert that Saturday night went on much longer than usual. Jeanette McDonald, the evening's soloist, was such a success with the audience that she had to sing five encores—with just piano. We in the orchestra had to stay on stage, listening to what I called in my diary "a very tasteless conglomeration of cheap tripe." (I guess I was a tough critic even then.) When we got to Castle Farms, I decided that this time I would find us a table, have some drinks, and sit in relative comfort. But the only available table was so far away from the bandstand, and the noise of the crowd was so overwhelming, that I realized we would hardly be able to hear the music. So we fought our way through the dancing crowd to the bandstand, as close as we could get, standing and listening, transfixed.

It was another remarkable musical experience, this time especially in being able to share my enthusiasm for the band and Ellington with Margie and Gussie. Margie had by now heard her share of great Ellington on my recordings; and Gussie, already interested in jazz for quite a few years, not only knew a lot of Ellington's music as a listener but had also been playing some of his compositions in solo piano versions, as published in several folios of Duke's music that had come out in the late 1930s.

In the first set we heard an astonishing solo by a trumpet player who (I found out later) had joined the orchestra only a month earlier. Lawrence Brown told me his name was William Alonzo Anderson, known best by his nickname, Cat. In my diary I ecstatically wrote that his solo was "one of the most, if not *the* most, amazing trumpet solos I have ever heard." I don't know what piece it was, and don't recall Ellington announcing it, but I think it must have been *Frantic Fantasy*. Anderson began "very smoothly and simply," then "worked his way with an incredible crescendo" to "a most exciting climax of power and height. At the beginning of the last chorus he reached high Fs and Gs, and got quite ornamental—in a wild sort of way. Via some deft scale work and glissandos, he reached altissimo B flat and ended, in one last desperate effort, on an F above high F" ♪ . I added that it "was not mere screaming or screeching, but played with a perfectly legitimate tone, so high that I could barely whistle it." My diary recorded that we were all emotionally exhausted, "glad to see the men leave the stage for an intermission. I couldn't have taken any more."

That was not only the first time I heard "Cat" Anderson but also the first time I ever heard anyone play an octave *above* the then-attained upper range of the trumpet, which at the time was around concert F, G, and A flat ♪ . That range was considered the Mount Everest of high notes, and players such as Snooky Young, Paul Webster, Eddie Tompkins, and Al Killian had shown for some years that you didn't need oxygen tanks to play in those upper high-altitude regions. As for classical trumpet parts, I knew that Strauss had written a (mere) C# ♪ at the end of *Rosenkavalier* (which Wohlgemuth had played so beautifully in our Cincinnati recording of the *Rosenkavalier* Suite), and that Stravinsky had written high Ds and E flats in his *Rite of Spring*, but these were meant to be played on a small piccolo trumpet, on which altissimo high notes were considerably easier to get than on regular B-flat or C trumpets. Thus Anderson's stratospheric tour de force on a normal (although small-bore) B-flat trumpet was for me, as a brass player, an impossible accomplishment.

At one point Lawrence Brown, whom I had met briefly the year before, spotted me near the end of the set and winked to me to come backstage. He wanted to introduce me to Ellington and led the three of us to the maestro's dressing room. He told Duke that I was first horn with the local symphony, but also very interested in jazz, especially "our music," as Larry put it. I told Duke that I had transcribed about a dozen of his compositions from the recordings, at which point he suddenly perked up. "Really? How do you *do* that?" I said: "Well, laboriously—just note for note." He looked genuinely surprised, not so much at the fact that such a thing could be done as wondering why anyone would want to do it and have the ear and patience to do it. I didn't realize at the time but found out some years later that Ellington, for reasons of his own, never planned to publish his music or disseminate it in any way. Indeed, for a long time he initially kept his music, his scores and parts, hidden from the rest of the world.[4]

All the while I noticed that Ellington was eyeing my two escorts, especially Margie. I was to learn that when it came to beautiful young ladies, Ellington was one of the world's greatest and linguistically most versatile and eloquent flatterers. The stories about this side of the Ellington persona are legion.[5] He also seemed to be rather intrigued with me. Twice he asked me whether I was really only eighteen, as Larry had told him. What happened next really surprised me. After we had been with him for about ten minutes, I thought surely he would now usher us out, needing to get ready for the next set. Instead, he sat down at the upright in his dressing room and started playing what turned out to be the beginning of a new composition he said he was working on for Paul Whiteman. (That piece turned out to be *Blutopia*.) He also asked me some questions about the horn, and said that next time I should play something for him. I was amazed at how cordial he was. Was it me or the two young ladies that kept him extending what was initially surely intended to be a very brief encounter? I didn't take his invitation too seriously; it was the kind of thing one might say to be polite. And when would the next time be that I would see Ellington?

In any case, I asked *him* if in the next (last) set he could play a couple of my favorite Ellington pieces, *Dusk* and *Cotton Tail*, which to my delight he did play; he did not forget.

Even more surprising—I could hardly believe my ears—he asked Gussie to sit in with the band to play *C Jam Blues*, which she had told him was one her favorite tunes. (That invitation was not fulfilled.)

After the dance, as we said our goodbyes, he told us that he would be back in Cincinnati next Wednesday—that was in a mere four days—and that he hoped to see us all again. It was like a dream, so unbelievable; and I must admit that, years later, when I sometimes thought back to that evening, I wondered whether it had all really occurred. I might doubt it even now, except for the fact that those diary pages confirm that it is true.

I was so lucky to hear Ellington again so soon. This time he was playing at the new Ezzard Charles Coliseum in the West End (on November 1).[6] Here the band was playing not for a white audience but for a black audience; and that was the first time I realized what a noticeable difference there was in how black bands played for their own audiences, and how those audiences reacted to the music. There was only one other white couple in the ballroom besides Margie and me. (White folks did not go to the West End much in those days when Cincinnati was one of the most segregated big cities in the country.) We had a table very close to the stage where we could hear the whole band, even Freddy Guy's unamplified guitar. Here people were not hesitant to show their appreciation, whether in screams of ecstasy or in their wild, contortive dancing. In this supercharged atmosphere, the orchestra and the audience inspired each other, fed off of each other, symbiotically producing a constantly spiraling intensity, like 7.5 on the musical Richter scale. Here both the decibel and emotional levels, whether in slow steamy ballads or up-tempo "flag wavers," were maintained at such a fever pitch that it transported you to another realm.

"Junior" Raglin, stationed out in front of the band this time, was in top form. I could hear every beautiful, rich, joyful note he played, almost as if I was inside his instrument. He told me that "it makes such a difference to have somebody in the audience who is a musician, who listens intently," and fully appreciates "what we are doing." I loved it especially when, in his wonderful walking bass lines, he would climb all the way up to high Ds and E flats, always in perfect intonation. This was playing that went beyond technique; it was transcendent *feeling*, where the fingers and mind, technique and content, were one and the same.

Hodges and Brown were only a few feet away from our table. It was that proximity perhaps that made me realize that those two musicians, who played the most exquisitely elegant and sensuous solos, were also the ones who (as my diary noted) "never moved a muscle, their faces completely expressionless, motionless, as if made of stone. And yet the warmth and expressiveness of their playing was unsurpassable."

Lawrence Brown had me mesmerized once again, especially when I noticed—watching and hearing him at such close range—that Ellington constantly "gave Larry the most important trombone parts, whether a high lead part," or some "blistering hot solo, full of trills and turns, crackling like flashes of lightening," or in the "bass range below Joe Nanton and Claude Jones." Ellington had lost his former third trombone, Juan Tizol, a few months before, and although Brown was the section's titular leader and high-register player, Ellington had him at times also play the low third part—very unusual. I also noticed that Brown's vibrato, so pure and expressive, was produced "in the throat, not with the slide—a precious rarity among trombonists" in those days.

As Lawrence Brown sat with us during one of the breaks, I learned how unassuming and modest he was. When I asked him how he managed to play so easily in the entire range, particularly in the technically more awkward low register, he simply said, "it's just a matter of getting used to it." He spent quite some time extolling the virtues of Tommy Dorsey, and the Dorsey and Harry James brass sections. He also told me—and what a shock that was—that he was thinking of leaving the Ellington orchestra soon. He had been with the band twelve years.[7]

I had decided to take Ellington up on his suggestion to bring my horn along the next time and play something for him. Ellington had told me how much he loved the horn, how he always wanted to have one in his orchestra, and that his son Mercer played the horn for a while as a second instrument. When we went to see Ellington backstage during a break and he saw my horn, he told me to play something—jazz or classical, "it doesn't matter." I should have been nervous as hell, but I just said "sure," got my horn out of the case, and played most of Hodges's alto part in Ellington's beautiful 1940 ballad tone poem, *Warm Valley*. He nodded gently, smiling approvingly. I was too excited (or afraid?) to give him a chance to say anything, and quickly told him that I had arranged *Warm Valley* for symphony orchestra, and that we had just played it a few weeks before in one of our pop concerts. Then I mentioned that I had been working on Hodges's brand-new solo vehicle, *Mood to be Wooed*, but had given up playing it since it was virtually impossible to play Hodges's glissandos and expressive pitch scoops on the horn's rotary valve system, so totally different from the piston valves on a trumpet.

As the break came to an end, he said to me—I swear—"Why don't you join my orchestra? I told you, I've always wanted the color of a horn." As he put on his jacket, aided by his valet, checking if everything was in full sartorial splendor, he winked at me and said: "Think about it." I didn't say anything. Frankly I didn't know *what* to say, I was so stunned. Was he just kidding, teasing me? Or did he mean what he said?

I've thought about that scene many times over the years, and usually concluded that he must have been kidding. First of all, the very idea of a white kid playing in an all-black orchestra, especially on the road and in those days of segregation, was preposterous and unrealizable. It is true that blacks had begun to occasionally play in white orchestras since about 1940 (Cootie Williams, for example, with Benny Goodman), but the reverse seemed to be unthinkable. Equally preposterous was the notion that the nearly one hundred pieces or so that Ellington constantly kept in his repertory, many of them dating back to the 1920s and 1930s, would now have to be rearranged to accommodate a horn part.

After the dance I invited Duke and Larry to join me and Margie at the nearby Cotton Club for some food and drinks. They agreed, but when we got there the place was closed, and because the Ellington orchestra was moving on to the next one-nighter at eight thirty in the morning, we all decided to call it a night. But Margie and I stayed up the rest of the night, both of us not wanting that evening to end.

I had no idea at this point that I would see Ellington so soon again, this time in Cleveland, where his orchestra (I learned accidentally) was going to play for a whole week, November third through ninth, at the Palace Theatre on Euclid Avenue.[8] That visit turned out to be not just a matter of catching a few of the band's shows at the Palace but also—believe it or not—staying, living with Ellington and the orchestra for a couple of days.

As chance would have it, I had previously planned to travel at week's end to Rochester for a pop concert Sunday evening, in which my new conductor friend, Paul White, had programmed two of my symphonic arrangements. When it dawned on me that, by sheer luck, I was also going to have Monday and Tuesday free, my next Cincinnati Symphony rehearsal having been, exceptionally, postponed from Tuesday to Wednesday afternoon, I realized that I would be able to squeeze in a quick visit to Cleveland.[9]

The next five days were pretty hectic. After playing Saturday evening's two symphony concerts (Mozart's "Jupiter" Symphony and Rachmaninov's Second Piano Concerto, with Alec Templeton as soloist, and Stravinsky's *Firebird* Suite), I took a night train to Rochester so that I could attend the (one and only) Sunday morning rehearsal of my *Mood Indigo* and *Night and Day* arrangements for symphony orchestra, which I had been asked to make for the pop concerts of the Cincinnati Symphony. The program also included Paul White's newest composition, *Lake Placid Suite*, not surprisingly quite beautiful but also a bit too placid.

The performances of my pieces under Paul's direction were first-rate, well prepared. I was also pleasantly surprised to hear the horn solos that I had written for myself played so well and swingingly by the Rochester Philharmonic's first horn, Morris Secon. (We were to work quite often in the upcoming years in New York.)

Cleveland was only a stone's throw from Rochester. I headed there the next morning by train and arrived in early afternoon, just in time to catch one of the early afternoon shows at the Palace Theatre. But oh, what a terrible disappointment! I hardly recognized anything I heard. The orchestra sounded tinny and blarey, their ensemble ragged and disjointed. I just couldn't relate this to the orchestra's musical and technical perfection that I had by now come to take for granted. But two shows later I had figured out what was wrong: it was the acoustics in the Palace Theatre. They were horrendous, and in bad acoustics musicians need some time to adjust, to let the ear adapt to the stage's sonic characteristics. It is quite amazing how quickly and effectively the human ear can figure out the acoustics, adapting to where it feels relatively comfortable. However, the sound on the stage and in the auditorium may vary considerably, leading to the possibility that, while the musicians may adjust to the stage acoustics success-fully, what actually comes off the stage may still not sound very good in the audience. It was interesting to me, having already experienced dozens of different acoustics (from very bad to very good) and having learned to aurally adjust to these diverse conditions, to see how over the course of the afternoon the Ellington orchestra began to sound better and better, increasingly at ease with the acoustics.

The program, the usual blend of early Ellington hits and newer works, also featured one of the greatest of the black comedians, Dusty Fletcher. His hilarious "Open the Door, Richard!" routine was about a thoroughly inebriated character coming home hours late, in the middle of the night, unable to find the keys to his place. He staggers around blindly—he's so drunk he can't even find the front door—as his cries for his roommate, Richard, to let him in become ever more desperate, rising a couple of octaves and many decibel levels by the end of the rou-tine. I saw the Dusty Fletcher show many times over the next few years, and it never failed to reduce me to stomach-aching, eyes-tearing surrender.

I wanted to see Ellington and the musicians, of course, and headed for the stage door after the third show. The stage door guard wouldn't let me in, so I decided to wait until someone in the orchestra came along. That turned out to be Raglin, who was surprised to see me, and immediately took me inside, past the puzzled doorman. I asked Junior if he thought I could see Ellington, because I wanted to tell him about the success of the *Mood Indigo* performance in Rochester. On the way up to Ellington's room I began to see many of the players, and then I realized that they all were staying and, in fact, living in the theatre. It dawned on me that blacks could not stay in the white downtown hotels like the nearby Statler on Euclid Avenue. (Even many years later—I think it was in 1953—I witnessed an altercation and shouting match in the lobby of that same hotel between Nat King Cole and the hotel staff that was clearly racially motivated.) They could have stayed in hotels or with friends in the black section of town, but that was way out at the eastern end of Euclid Avenue, about five miles away, too far to allow the musicians to commute back and forth between their stage shows during the time that the movies, usually just ninety minutes long, were on. So they all stayed in the dressing rooms of the theatre, the management providing cots and other amenities (quite a few of the musicians had their own portable Bunsen burners for cooking), living and sleeping there for the entire weeklong engagement.

This time it was Ellington who was surprised to see me, so soon after his Cincinnati date just five days earlier. He had two fairly large connecting dressing rooms, one of which had an upright piano, at which he was seated when I arrived, composing. When he found out that I had not yet gotten a place to stay and that I was hoping to hang out for a few days, he suggested that I stay in the theatre, like the orchestra, in one of the dressing rooms. He sent Tom Whaley[10]—Ellington's librarian and copyist, whom I had met briefly in Cincinnati—to arrange for a room and a cot for me. I was thrilled. I, a white kid, a nobody, staying with the world's greatest jazz composer, and one of my absolute musical idols!

And I did stay in my little cubicle room that night, right next to Ellington's, a fact that in retrospect seems more like a dream than reality. There I learned first hand one of the basic facts about Ellington and his prodigious creative productivity, namely, that he almost never— never—stopped composing. He sat at that upright every possible minute, between shows as well as at night—all the time. I was told that he rarely went out. Food was brought in either by his valet or by Tom, or sometimes Carney would cook up something on his little stove and share it with Ellington.

I am proud to relate what few can claim, namely, that I actually heard, from my next-door cubicle, Ellington compose. Between sets and after the shows at night, he would put on his beautiful maroon silk bathrobe, his nylon stocking cap, sit down at the keyboard, and start working. He would just play, improvising, more or less fooling around, ruminating, as it were, sometimes for long periods of time, working on some melody or motive, trying out some harmonic progression or a chain of chords, always so beautifully voiced. Then, every once in a while there would be silence, and I would hear the scratching sound of a pencil. Duke had heard something he thought worthy of committing to paper. Then the keyboard ruminating would commence again.

I learned that night that the stories I had heard about Ellington *always* composing—on trains and in train stations, in cars, buses, restaurants, hotel lobbies, anywhere—were true. Ellington was larger than life, and his appetite for playing, but also for creating music, was enormous, unquenchable. And if we want to understand why Ellington had bags under the bags under the bags of his eyes, one explanation would be that he hardly ever slept. In those two days with him in Cleveland I witnessed with my own eyes and ears that after the last show, which ended at midnight, he stayed up for hours at the piano—composing, writing, improvising, exploring. He was ruthless with himself. Around four or five in the morning he'd finally lie down to catch a few hours of sleep, then get up around ten thirty to hand out some music to Tom—maybe only twenty or thirty bars. And then, at the usual eleven o'clock warm-up rehearsal, the music that he had composed earlier that night (and which Tom had in the meantime copied out) would be read through by the musicians. Ellington, sitting at the piano, still in his bathrobe, would listen intently, while one or two of the musicians would quietly make some interpretive suggestions.

And if one wants to understand why Ellington kept his orchestra going for fifty years—even when there was no work for the band, at his own personal expense—then one must appreciate what a unique luxury it was for him to compose something and only a few hours later have it come to life in the hands of his musicians. (I doubt that even Papa Haydn at Count Esterhazy's cstate could hear the next morning something he had composed the day before.)

By the second day, Election Day, the band began to sound like its old self. My diary recounts that I was particularly impressed by an extended Jimmy Hamilton solo in *Blue Skies*, rating him "not as outstanding as Hodges, but always uniformly good, absolutely reliable." And one of the most beautiful tunes Ellington played in Cleveland was the then quite new ballad *Don't You Know I Care*. I called it a "masterpiece of saxophone writing," and daydreamed about how fantastic it would sound played by five horns. There was also an extended version of *Frankie and Johnny*, which contained a long solo by Al Sears. I had heard him previously "only in the wildest, roughest solos, full of groans and shrieks." But in *Frankie* he played very softly and delicately, which, of course, he certainly could do, coming out of the lineage of perhaps the greatest saxophone balladeer of all time, Ben Webster. "Tricky Sam" Nanton astonished me with one of his patented plunger "talking" solos, in a poignant blues-ish mood, "full of star-tling wah-wahs and onomatopoetic word imitations." He finished on a "very slow, elongated upward *glissando* from A flat to D flat, and as he hit the tonic, he dropped his plunger, which left only the pixie in the bell. He faded to a barely audible quadruple *piano (pppp)*, with Junior Raglin finishing up with a beautiful ringing double-stop fifth."

Between shows I once or twice went up to Whaley's library, where he was constantly copy-ing parts. At one point Rex Stewart came up with Duke, and the two of them worked out some details on a new tune for Rex. What a treat for me to hear these two great musicians—Duke at the piano, Rex with his cornet—finalizing something they would play in public a few days later. In the meantime, wherever I went in the building I would hear Jimmy Hamilton playing, practicing—continually, incessantly, obsessively. As Duke never stopped composing, so Jimmy never stopped practicing.

Later that day, after the last theatre show, the whole orchestra went for a while to a club next door, the Stage Door Canteen, a USO club, for an impromptu performance for the armed service men and women gathered there, all in uniform. The sound in that place was much superior to the theatre, which really helped. The high point of the set was an extended version of *On the Sunny Side of the Street*, with two extra-long solos by Hodges and Brown. The audi-ence, out to have a good time, certainly helped; they really ate it up, which in turn inspired the musicians to even greater heights.

To this day I thank my lucky stars that on that three-day trip I was able to squeeze so many memorable experiences into what amounted to only sixty hours. I realize in retrospect that those three days were an early example of what happened hundreds of times in my life: I moved precipitously within a short time—or even on a given day—between and among mul-tiple musical professional areas.

I took advantage of the Symphony's scheduling anomaly by staying in Cleveland long enough to hear the Ellington orchestra into the late hours of Tuesday evening, then, with hardly any sleep, returned by train at the crack of dawn to Cincinnati in time for my Wednesday afternoon rehearsal. In those days, young, eager, and undauntable, spending a night without sleep didn't bother me in the slightest. Being with Ellington as much as pos-sible was what mattered!

Ellington's offhand suggestion to join his band—teasing, kidding, or genuine, I'll never know—was I guess the first time I caught a glimpse of what many people regarded as an enigmatic, elliptical, elusive aspect of his personality. As I came to know Ellington better in succeeding years and heard him in countless concerts and ballroom engagements, including Carnegie Hall, the Zanzibar Club on Broadway, the 400 Restaurant on Fifth Avenue, or the Aquarium on Broadway, I began to learn that Duke, with his supreme verbal and linguistic skills, could spin words so elegantly, so dexterously—and elusively—that you sometimes didn't know what he had said, or even whether he had said anything specific at all.

Legions of Ellington admirers and observers, especially interviewers, have tried over the years to fathom this side of Ellington's persona and public image. Psychologizing theories abound by the dozens. On the one hand, the notion has been advanced that Ellington was a profoundly private person whose interior self was almost entirely engaged with creating music and that, as a bandleader having to constantly lead a public life, he wanted to keep his private self—his real self—completely screened from his public. On the other hand, there are those who say that Ellington loved to put audiences on, as for example in his thousands of introductory explications of his compositions; or—even more whimsical—that on many occasions he really did not know what to say or just did not care to say anything, and simply allowed his extraordinary verbal adroitness to cover the void. Still others have theorized—more seriously—that Ellington's aston-ishingly prolific creativity, both in quality and quantity, caused him to live in a kind of fantasyland that constantly fed his creative imagination while at the same time protected him from others being able to penetrate his inner persona, and that provided him with an impossibly charming, elegant, ducal show business facade. Perhaps all these suppositions are valid to some extent or another. I'm not sure myself, for, as well as I knew Ellington, I felt that I really never *truly knew* him, except perhaps on one occasion that I will relate further on.

Ellington drove interviewers crazy with his evasive answers—although, God knows, many of them, when they plied him with stupid or embarrassingly simplistic questions, deserved nothing better. Many was the time when, say, after a concert, a fan or critic or reporter would ask Ellington some inane question—which he would have heard hundreds if not thousands of times before—he would launch into a most exquisitely worded, elliptical verbal barrage. With an enigmatic Mona Lisa smile on his lips, never looking at his interrogator, addressing instead everyone else in the room, Ellington would, in a much practiced faux-professorial tone, throw up a gigantic verbal smokescreen, spiked with beautiful-sounding quadrisyllabic words, that would leave the interviewer totally awed while frantically scrambling to note down every precious word. It didn't take much to have the interviewer leave minutes later, scratching his head, wondering: but what did he say? Many are the reporters or critics who foundered on one of Ellington's slippery verbal slopes.

On some occasions he would duck questions entirely, humbly disavowing any knowledge of the questioner's subject, and with the same benign smile point to me, suggesting: "Oh, I'm sure my friend, Professor Schuller here, can answer *that* question." Since the questioner would never have heard of Professor Schuller and wanted only to hear the word of God himself, that usually ended the matter abruptly. Then he'd wink at me, kind of asking for forgiveness. He just loved playing these ducal games. With female fans, pretty or not, it was quite another matter. There he was usually all charm and poetry, often to the point of deliberate unctuousness. It was so perfectly carried off that it was most of the time impossible for a young lady to tell whether Ellington's flattering attention was real or just another one of his flights of verbal hyperbole. It was masterful and magnificent—and in its own unique way, perfectly genuine.

There are film and video interviews of Ellington in which, with an inscrutable, enigmatic, faraway look and constantly roving eyes, he manages to completely avoid any serious answer to the interviewer's earnest questions. This was never done in a spirit of meanness or condescension; there was no malicious intent. And I don't think it ever was or could be taken as such, because it was always carried off so suavely; it was so elegantly and smoothly executed that the interviewer usually felt more flattered than affronted—as well as bewildered. It was as impossible to feel offended by Ellington as it was for him to offend somebody. Despite some grouching at times from some of his players, of which he must have been aware, he seemed to have found a way of entirely ignoring any unpleasant matters with a beatific unconcern. Most tellingly, in his career as bandleader spanning some fifty years, he was never known to have fired anyone (with the grand exception of Charles Mingus). He seemed to be congenitally incapable of doing such a thing.

I am proud to have known this most remarkable, unfathomably genial human being. I bask in the knowledge that I was privileged to work with him, to have had those precious days with him in Cincinnati and Cleveland, to occasionally appear on the same stage with him, to have at least one all-night serious musical discussion with him, and to cherish in my memory the various times when I was in attendance at his concerts. Whether in Paris or Berlin or Washington or Santiago de Chile or Rockefeller Center's Rainbow Room, or anywhere else, he always had the kindness to introduce me to the audience, always in the most generous way.

Needless to say, Ellington's orchestra wasn't the only big band I heard in my years in Cincinnati. The various ballrooms and clubs, such as the Lookout House, Castle Farms, and the

Beverly Hills Supper Club, played host to most of the reigning jazz orchestras of the day; most important for me, those of Count Basie, Lionel Hampton, Jimmie Lunceford, and Earl Hines. I already owned recordings by all these orchestras, but because I had concentrated primarily on Ellington, Basie, and Armstrong, I was less familiar with the work of some of the others. But just to hear big band jazz in acoustic reality, with its rhythmic, sonoric spontaneity, not to mention the visual, kinetic aspects of watching great musicians produce music of the highest order, was for me a great thrill as well as a wonderful education.

The words "of the highest order" may raise some eyebrows. Can jazz really ever be on the high order of Bach or Beethoven or Stravinsky? Well, yes. It definitely can be and is on the order of high art in the hands of its greatest players, composers, arrangers, singers. That "mere" dance music could be and often was high art was something I began to realize with full force when I heard the music of the great Swing Era bands live in those Cincinnati dance palaces and ballrooms. Ninety percent of the people in attendance were dancing, only dimly aware of the importance and the beauty of the music; but the other ten percent stood close to the bandstand, listening intensely, soaking in the remarkably serious sounds coming from the stage.[11] What younger readers may not realize is that, especially during the stressful years of World War II, jazz and all entertainment was appreciated with a particular depth and fervor. That was serious business—both the war and the music.

The frenetic pace of those war years, generated by an entire nation involved in the most ambitious war effort in human history, was reflected in the popular and jazz music of that era, particularly so, for example, in the frantic driving music of, say, Lionel Hampton and his orchestra. I heard Hampton's orchestra several times in those years. From the conventional sixteen-piece band of the early forties, Hampton's orchestra had grown to twenty-one by 1944: five trumpets (at one point even six), five trombones, five saxophones, and a six-man rhythm section (including Hamp, of course). The decibel level of their playing had also tripled or quadrupled in the intervening years. Trumpet players had lately extended their upper range by at least an octave, in some cases an octave and a half. Early high-note players such as Paul Webster, Tommy Stevenson (known as "the Screamer"), Snooky Young, the young "Cat" Anderson, the amazing Al Killian, a bit later Ernie Royal and Maynard Ferguson—they all were completely at ease in the stratospheric upper range, a region in which previously only piccoloists, flutists, and violinists had been able to venture.

All this made the jazz of those peak war years incredibly exciting in a visceral, physically palpable way that didn't necessarily always add up to great art, but surely made lots of folks very happy, offering as it did some temporary escape from their stressful daily lives.

I'm not a person to be easily impressed by sheer power, even less by fast and loud music, which is what usually thrills most audiences. But according to my diary I was quite overwhelmed by the playing of Hampton's powerhouse band one December evening in 1944, exemplified by pieces such as *Flying Home*, *Screaming Boogie*, *Loose Wig*, and the deep, richly textured *Million Dollar Smile*. I was also intrigued by the number of duet improvisations I heard that night, a relative rarity in jazz, then and now. I'm not referring to what are called "fours" or "eights" (in which players chase each other, exchanging four- or eight-bar phrases), but to real duets. I was particularly impressed with a lengthy, mostly improvised trumpet duet during what was, in all but name, an extended jam session. The two trumpeters were Joe Norris—so young that I called him "a mere boy"—and Snooky Young. In the manner of Dorsey's and Sy Oliver's popular 1942 hit, *Well, Git It*, Norris and Young, after an unbroken round of back and forth exchanges, ended up on high Gs and E flats in thirds. Eventually Norris's lip gave out and Snooky continued alone to a climactic conclusion. As a brass player, listening to these two players tease and battle each other, especially in the final high-note climax, my own lips were beginning to hurt in empathy. But in my diary I wrote that those high "shrieks" were "beautiful, clean shrieks."

Other duet improvisations I heard that night were by two saxophonists (George Dorsey and Arnett Cobb), as well as several drum duels between Fred Ratcliff, Hampton's regular drummer, and Lionel himself. (Hampton played hardly any vibraphone or piano that evening.) The Hampton band was not generally known for subtlety, to put it mildly. But to hear two drummers compete with each other in the power-plus-acrobatics department—Radcliff alone could be heard *in the next county*—was something I had never before considered a particularly *musical* option. But impressed I was nevertheless, noting Radcliffe's "powerful beat," especially his two-and-four afterbeats, which I described as having enough power "to keep all the bands in the country supplied with rhythm for several years." When Hamp joined Radcliff in this drum duel to the death, we were more in the realm of show business and musical calisthenics. Hampton was fond of jumping high off the ground while playing, then landing with his full weight (and the benefits of the law of gravity) while simultaneously throwing his drum sticks high into the air, always catching them in flight; an alternative to such high jinks was entertaining the audience with a three-drumstick juggling act: two sticks seemingly always in the air, the third one disappearing into his coat pocket, and still somehow keeping some kind of time on his cymbals.

Hamp's two bass players, Charles Harris and Ted Sinclair, were another duet combination; it was the first time I had actually seen two bassists in a jazz orchestra (although I knew that Ellington had used two players simultaneously off and on since 1934). In the case of Hampton, I really think he had two players not for musical reasons, but to provide twice as much support for the enormous sound of his twenty-one piece band, this, of course, in the days before bass amplification. And Harris and Sinclair certainly worked hard to be heard, mostly playing in unison. Both happened to be tall and gangly, they hovered over their instruments in a seemingly mortal embrace—as I wrote in my diary, not unlike "two gigantic tyrannosaurus rexes."

I also noted in my diary that a woman played the piano that evening, mostly *standing* at the keyboard, who was also a fine singer. Could that have been Dinah Washington? Or was it Dardanelle Breckenridge (later known only as Dardanelle, who for a while led a fine trio with Tal Farlow as guitarist, competing effectively with Nat King Cole's trio)? Whoever it was, I heard her in some superb improvising in a duet with the remarkable Fred Beckett, a quite advanced trombonist for that time, whose beautiful tone I especially singled out.

All in all, that evening stands out as possibly one of the most frenzied, frantic evenings of music making I ever experienced. I remember looking forward to a somewhat calmer night of music the very next day, when the King Cole Trio and the Benny Carter Orchestra were both in town. As I wrote in my diary at 6:36 p.m. that evening, "The day is just starting for me: tonight some great music!"

While my diary is, for whatever reason, silent on Cole and Carter, it offers some salient commentary on another band, which has become legendary only in retrospect, but that, ironically, hardly anyone actually heard or paid any attention to at the time. A partial explanation might be that that orchestra, along with hundreds of others, was not permitted to make any recordings during a fourteen-month recording ban between July 1942 and September 1943, during the strike by the American Federation of Musicians. I am speaking of the 1943–44 Earl Hines Orchestra. Its importance lies in the fact that at various times in those years the Hines orchestra harbored an amazing array of young talent that represented the breakthrough leadership in the upcoming bebop revolution. The names are now legendary: Charlie Parker, Dizzy Gillespie, Sarah Vaughan (as second pianist and singer), Benny Harris, Wardell Gray, Dexter Gordon, trombonist Benny Green, Freddie Webster (briefly), Al Killian, Shadow Wilson, trombonist-arranger Gerry Valentine, and Hines's star attraction, singer Billy Eckstine. In fact, in March and April 1943 the first six musicians mentioned were *all* in the Hines band simultaneously, constituting a remarkable breeding ground for the new music that was about to take over from swing.

Hearing the Hines band live on the road was a real rarity; it had been in residence for eleven years, from 1928 to 1939, at the Grand Terrace Ballroom in Chicago, never touring, which, of course, most Swing Era bands did, and constantly. Hines, himself the most dazzlingly talented and innovative pianist of the time—only Art Tatum can be equated with him—always had an eye and an ear for fresh young talent. But, paradoxically, once he had them in the fold, he generally failed as a leader to forge his ensemble into something distinctive and original, to personally guide its musical growth. He always left such matters to his arrangers, most recently, from 1939 on, to Budd Johnson. But Johnson, a major talent himself, had left the band in late 1942. And because no comparably gifted arranger was found to take his place, the orchestra, though burgeoning with all this fresh young talent, failed to develop and coalesce into a single new stylistic voice. By mid-1944 all the young turks had left Hines and had become the core of Billy Eckstine's new orchestra, with Dizzy Gillespie as its musical director and Gerry Valentine its chief arranger—in effect the first orchestra, along with Woody Herman's "First Herd" band, to fully embrace the new bop language.

All this is not to say that by the time I heard the Hines band in the fall of 1944 in Cincinnati's Coliseum it didn't offer evenings filled with excellent challenging music. What differentiated the Hines band from most other major orchestras of the time was its emphasis on ensemble, on arrangement and composition, rather than improvisatory solo work (like Basie's, for example). Indeed, the main reason for the protoboppers leaving Hines's band one by one between late 1943 and mid-1944 was that they were not given the solo space that most of them wished for. As the pianist-leader, Hines was the prime featured soloist, along with Eckstine. Thus the other players found themselves mostly locked into arranged ensemble playing, unable to sufficiently expand their improvisational skills, their soloistic visions.

Yet, when I heard the orchestra, Wardell Gray and Bennie Green were still in the band, and in their playing as well as that of the slightly older "Scoops" Carey and Bob Crowder, I could hear that something new and innovative had definitely left its mark on the orchestra's style and sound. Well, that "something new" I realized a few years later had been Parker, Gillespie, and Valentine.

Mind you, at the time I had no idea who these fine players were, nor did I know that the Hines band had recently lost, as mentioned, a whole contingent of young, innovative talent. I did bring with me a clear memory of how the orchestra's harmonic language was chromatically spicier, more advanced, than that of most other jazz orchestras of the time, and that there was a different, sleeker rhythmic drive and energy, with lots of little double-time interjections quickening the pace of the music. I heard some new sounding, rich, soulful saxophone playing on alto and tenor, finding out years later that those players were Wardell Gray, Scoops Carey, and Robert Crowder, who along with trumpeter Shorty McConnell had played next to Parker and Gillespie for many months.

At the end of that evening Crowder played himself almost to total exhaustion—that was very much a part of the scene in those war years—starting at f and $f\!f$, and building from there with a "Bolero-like crescendo." For the finish, Crowder held a single note (B flat) for four solid choruses, piercing through what would appear to have been an "impenetrable wall of sound" produced by the other seventeen players. Crowder's solo was, by the way, the first time I ever witnessed or even heard of circular breathing—breathing simultaneously while playing—on a wind instrument, a commonplace nowadays. In my diary I called it "breathing through the corners of the mouth while playing."

I was really impressed by the orchestra's excellent ensemble in the arrangements and compositions, mostly by Gerry Valentine, and its "beautifully balanced canvas of sound." I was particularly fascinated with the clean playing and elegant blending of the five trombones Hines had in his band at the time.

In view of the fact that Hines was not particularly interested in leading an orchestra and shaping its style and artistic vision—as compared to simply fronting it—it is interesting that I noted that Hines sat "perched very high on his piano stool, seemingly uninvolved (or bored?) with his work." In quite a few numbers Hines didn't play at all. Was that a momentary lapse that night or a constant condition?

As I say, I had no idea who these players were. Places like the Coliseum, Castle Farms, or the Cotton Club had no programs that listed the numbers played or the names of the musicians in the band, something classical concert hall programs did automatically. But I remember thinking that I was hearing a new kind of music, especially harmonically. And that was very exciting for me as a composer writing already highly chromatic or atonal music. Harmony is the lifeblood of music, and rhythm and pulse are its beating heart, just as melody, theme, motive are to music what the skin, our integument, is to our bodies. I had been impatiently waiting for years for some advance in the harmonic language of jazz. The young protoboppers I heard in Hines's band—or just missed hearing, in the case of Parker and Gillespie—turned out to be the new leaders only one year later who moved jazz forward in exciting new directions. By late 1945, by which time I was back in New York, Parker's and Gillespie's recordings had become the creative centerpiece of my expanding record collection. They and the other beboppers were becoming household names.

The fourteen-month strike by the American Federation of Musicians permitted no recording for over a year, except for the so-called V-discs, made by a few of the most popular bands for the armed services during the war. This left a huge gap in recording history, precisely at one of the most crucial historic junctures in the development of jazz. What great recordings would have been made in that year just as the bands of Billy Eckstine, Charlie Barnet, Woody Herman, Stan Kenton, Boyd Raeburn, Alvino Rey, and several others were all developing a new jazz language!

In all these encounters with jazz orchestras in Cincinnati I inevitably met many of the great young players of the day such as Joe Newman, Gerald Wilson, Lucky Thompson, and my favorite, Eugene "Snooky" Young. I saw Snooky a lot in those days because he seemed to be constantly shuttling back and forth every few months between Basie and Lunceford. One time I'd see him with Basie, and then three months later with Lunceford, holding down the lead trumpet chair, only to reappear in the Basie trumpet section half a year later.[12]

I had started to spend a lot of time in Cincinnati's black section, known as the West End. Apart from the fine jazz that I often heard in the dance halls and jazz clubs, mostly by excellent local musicians, there were many other manifestations of the cultural and social life of the West End that I found very exciting and rewarding. It was there that I learned so much about blacks as people, not just as musicians, and about the reality of their lives. I had read and learned a lot about America's history of slavery, the ongoing oppression of blacks even after emancipation, and the dismal social and economic conditions under which the vast majority of blacks still lived in the 1940s. What I didn't know but learned virtually overnight was that almost every black man or woman I met was unreservedly warm and friendly, genuine and earthy, in ways that I had not encountered to such an extent and so uniformly as I did there in Cincinnati. It puzzled me that these people, who had suffered indignities, verbal and physical, and years of economic and social deprivation, seemed so inwardly happy, secure, and proud, evincing no outward bitterness, no raging hatred of their white oppressors. Nor had I ever heard such rich, deeply seated, uninhibited, infectious laughter as I witnessed there. I kept asking myself: Why don't they hate me? How, after all that we Whites have done to them over three centuries, can they be so friendly and tolerant of us, of me?

I pondered such questions for weeks and months—and, to tell the truth, still have not found an appropriate answer. I have had to conclude that perhaps it is not for me or for Whites to know. Perhaps it is the African American's secret: you can only know how to contain your anger and feelings of recrimination and vindication if you *have* experienced such sufferings, collectively or individually.

I have been in lots of jazz clubs and dance halls all over the country, and I can say that the mood and atmosphere, the general feeling of well being in the black clubs, was something amazing to me. I'm not talking about merely having a good time; everybody does that (or presumes to). It is rather the prevailing spirit of a general euphoria, of true communal camaraderie, as well as a deep appreciation and enjoyment of the music. It was immediately clear to me—*audibly* clear—that the black bands played with a special enthusiasm, commitment, and depth of expression when playing in their own community environment, for their own people.

I should add that in places like the Cotton Club or the many after-hours "breakfast clubs" I would sometimes see the most stunning looking women, often flamboyantly dressed to the nines, yet always with taste, obviously loving to be admired. I found in those clubs a relaxed, maturely uninhibited freedom of behavior that was at once subtly sensual and erotic, yet never lewd or vulgar. Even the pimps that sometimes frequented these places—with their dazzling white suits, jauntily cocked fedoras, Al Capone spats, a gold watch dangling ostentatiously from their vest—strutted and sashayed around with a certain undeniable elegance and irresistible allure.

The Cotton Club was the center of Cincinnati's black West End universe. It was one of the few clubs, along with the downtown Barn and Hangar, where the races could mix freely, where colored and white could both come to hear great music and enjoy the good times that awaited there. You also knew that the place was clean and safe, unlike the many mobster-run clubs and joints across the river in Newport, Kentucky. I learned soon after arriving in Cincinnati that you did not go over to the Kentucky side for your fun and entertainment, because you might be caught up in some blackmail affair and actually never come back. Most of the Newport and Covington taxi drivers were in cahoots with the Kentucky mobs, and were paid extra for steering customers to certain places where, as Will Wilkins once put it to me, "you could be turned upside down like a salt shaker." He told me that Cincinnati was a pretty clean city as far as prostitution and gambling were concerned. There was evidently a neat arrangement whereby Cincinnati could send folks out for a good time across the river to Covington, where a plethora of casinos and brothels would take good care of them while Cincinnati remained a clean and proper town.

The integrated Cotton Club, named after its famous forerunner in Harlem, was everybody's favorite place for music, for dancing, for spectacular shows. Besides the club's musical offerings of local groups I heard many players there from the Basie, Hampton, and Lunceford bands. They came there after their main gigs at Castle Farms or Lookout House to do a little jamming and play in the club's famous dawn dances. These shows were very exciting and at a high professional level, featuring tap dancers, exotic dancers, comedians, and—new to me—the terrific dancing of the club's customers.

There was a certain earthiness and frankness in the Cotton Club's shows, especially in the work of the featured star performers and exotic "shake" dancers. I particularly remember one named "Torchie," who danced with snakes—pretty sensuous stuff. Another dancer—her billing was "Lady Ecstasy"—could rotate her hips and twist her body into the most unbelievable shapes and contortions, even as her act was making love to an imitation pulp tree. Another exotic dancer actually appeared naked, except that she was painted bronze all over, and danced and gyrated sensually in a transparent celluloid garment. It was heady stuff for an innocent like me; I was strangely moved by what I saw, not just momentarily aroused but deeply stirred by the entertainment's earthiness, its—shall I say—seriousness, and the utter absence of show business routine and artificiality. I was to learn many times in later years that there were exotic dancers who really felt and meant what they were doing and, on the other hand, those who were just putting it on, as fake as the papier-mâché props they would use. There was something real happening when blacks danced those exotic routines for their own audiences.

Those Cotton Club shows also featured great black comedians such as Redd Foxx or Moms Mabley, or venerable comedy teams such as Butterbeans and Suzie. Until I saw and heard Sid Caesar, Jonathan Winters, Red Skelton, Buddy Hackett, Lucille Ball, and Tim Conway years later, comedic geniuses all, those early black comedians were without equal. How a woman as ungodly ugly as Moms Mabley could pack so much outrageous streetwise humor into her fifteen-minute routines of drunkards or wisecracking mammas, one devastating punch line after another, until your stomach hurt from laughing, well, that was something to behold. And what struck me again was that those comedy routines of Moms Mabley, George Kirby, or Redd Foxx were earthy, honest, and above all profoundly connected to the everyday life of blacks in their segregated ghettos; they found the happy, funny side to their lives, laughing so as to keep from crying, as it were. It was all so much like the blues, which sang so radiantly, so positively, and yet so unsentimentally of the hardships of life in a segregated society.

In retrospect there were two people, two blacks, whom I regret never having met in my years in Cincinnati. One was Artie Matthews, the great ragtime composer-pianist, and the composer-publisher of some of the earliest blues (including the all-time enduring standard, *Weary Blues*).[13] The other was George Russell, famous for his work with the early Dizzy Gillespie band and his pathfinding theoretical work, the *Lydian Chromatic Concept of Tonal Organization for Improvisation*, recently republished in its updated third edition.

I became very involved in the early 1970s with ragtime music. Indeed, along with the American musicologist Vera Lawrence and the pianist Joshua Rifkin—not Marvin Hamlisch, by the way!—I was largely responsible for the revival of ragtime in those years. As a teenager I knew very little about ragtime, the forerunner of jazz that by the 1930s was a completely forgotten music. Artie Matthews, one of ragtime's most inspired creators—Scott Joplin, James Scott, and Joseph Lamb were the other major ragtimers—was not only living in Cincinnati but had also founded a music school in the West End, the Cosmopolitan School of Music. It provided training in theory and voice and offered instrumental lessons for black kids—who were at the time unwelcome at the white Conservatory on Highland Avenue or at the College of Music. When ragtime was replaced by jazz as America's popular music in the years right after World War I, Matthews turned his musical talents toward classical and sacred music, becoming one of Cincinnati's leading church organists. His school was dedicated "to the glory of God and Beethoven."

Years later, in the twenty-five-year existence of the New England Ragtime Ensemble, which I founded and which performed several of Artie Matthews's ingenious, remarkably advanced *Pastime* rags hundreds of times, I often thought with a sad twinge how I wish I had known about Matthews in the 1940s. Matthews kept his school going until his death in 1958 at age seventy.

That I never met George Russell in those years in Cincinnati is rather strange. Two years older than me and already a working jazz drummer in local clubs and a budding composer, it seems odd that I wouldn't have met him, even casually, in those two years; or conversely, that he wouldn't have been aware of my symphonic jazz arrangements being performed regularly by the Cincinnati Symphony and receiving wide, ultimately national, attention. It is strange that we never met at the Cotton Club or other jazz hangouts, of which Russell must have been a regular. I heard Russell's early pathbreaking compositions with Dizzy Gillespie's band (*Cubana Be/Cubana Bop*) many times in the midforties, and finally met him through my friend John Lewis in 1948. In 1969 I brought George Russell to Boston on the faculty of the New England Conservatory, where he taught theory and composition until 2004.

There were two future celebrities that I did meet in Cincinnati; one was Doris Day. She was working at Cincinnati's great radio station, WSAI, singing on a regular sustaining show. What a stunning beauty she was! One couldn't take one's eyes off of her. Even then she had that beautiful, lilting, natural voice, and I can understand how she was irresistible to Hollywood. I also heard and met Rosemary Clooney, the same way, but at WLW, where I went several times because, as with hundreds of radio stations around the country, it had a fine ten-piece jazz group permanently on staff—as public service!

Once I discovered Cincinnati's little Harlem and its musical treasures, it was inevitable that word got around in the orchestra that Gunther Schuller was spending all his evenings and nights in the West End, the implication being that he was quickly going to the dogs. Even my parents were called and alerted to my impending moral degeneration. This not only alarmed them unjustifiably, but also caused me to spend many hours on the phone, convincing them that I was not morally corrupted, had not entered some Bosch-like hell or Dantesque inferno (not even *Tannhäuser's* Venusberg), that I was playing my horn better than ever—and that I was still a virgin. A few in the orchestra looked at me darkly, disapprovingly, unable to forgive my scandalous behavior. Most others, like Walter Heermann and Reuben Segal and some of the old-timers, viewed me approvingly, secretly happy that I was finally sowing some wild oats—as they had done in their youth.

At first I hesitated to take Margie to the Cotton Club or the Hangar. We decided that on the few evenings that she could afford to be away from her heavy load of studies and practice, we wanted to be alone—dinner or a movie, or by ourselves somewhere. Besides, we had our weekend afternoons listening to records, which almost always included healthy doses of Ellington and Nat King Cole.

Along with hearing many of the great jazz orchestras and my constant visits at the Hangar and the Cotton Club, I was reading every book about jazz and its history that I could get my hands on. Most important were the Belgian jazz aficionado Robert Goffin's *Jazz: From the Congo to the Metropolitan* (1943), Hughes Panassié's *Hot Jazz* (1934) and *The Real Jazz* (1942), both rather too opinionated and retrogressive but nonetheless largely informative and fascinating, Wilder Hobson's *American Jazz Music* (1939), and from the same year *Jazz Men* by Frederic Ramsey Jr. I was also getting *DownBeat* and *Metronome*, the two major jazz magazines, regularly, and in that way kept myself pretty well informed as to what was currently going on in jazz.

Soon my increasing involvement with jazz took me in two different directions. One became a lifelong preoccupation: the transcribing of jazz recordings into full-score form, the other was writing symphonic arrangements of jazz works for the orchestra's pop concerts. The desire to transcribe jazz recordings was motivated by my interest, as a composer who had been writing and studying hundreds of classical works in full score for some six or seven years, to see the great jazz creations in a similar format.[14] My ears are very good, so that I could certainly hear what was going on in an Ellington composition or recording. But hearing music and seeing it in a notated visual form offers quite different although complementary perceptions and responses. One should not forget that music exists in a time continuum; one cannot stop a piece of music in performance to say: wait a minute, I want to hear that bit again. Even when you can play a given passage in a recording or, for that matter, the whole recording over and over again—which is, incidentally, what makes transcribing music possible—such repeated listening is not the same as being able to study a score in all its myriad internal relationships, not to mention at some leisure. It happens all the time that one *sees* something in a score that one has not been able to hear by just listening, sometimes because what one is seeing is not well represented in the recording (through faulty balances, an inadequate interpretation of the work, a technically poor recording), or because in listening holistically to a recording or performance one is not always bound to pick out some structural or orchestrational detail as the piece flashes by in real time, which one *would* see in the more leisurely visual perusal of a score.

I began transcribing some of Ellington's recordings as early as 1943, very soon after my arrival in Cincinnati. I think I was the first person to notate a recording in full score, in *all* its details—not just a trumpet or saxophone solo. Jazz musicians had been doing that for some time, as a means of learning what their favorite soloist had done. But my transcribing consisted of the accurate notating of every note, every sound on that recording: pitches, rhythms, dynamics, instrumentation (of course), including the drum and other rhythm parts, and, as far as I was concerned, also all improvised solos. That's a pretty tall order, especially if one is transcribing from earlier recordings—from the twenties into the forties—when microphone and recording techniques in general (and the actual disc production) had not yet attained the high quality that recordings achieved, say, in the LP era. Furthermore, to try and hear and then notate correctly all eleven notes in an eleven-note chord or ensemble passage, not to mention a very fast moving running passage, is not easy. Transcribing music from recordings takes a good ear and a certain musical intelligence, as well as extraordinary patience. The faster the tempo of the music, the harder the transcribing. It takes a strong desire and willpower—and *lots* of time (hours, days, weeks)—to arrive at an accurate, reliable transcription.

The first transcription I undertook was of Ellington's 1930 masterpiece, *Mood Indigo*. I chose it not only because I was haunted by its poignant, melancholy beauty—it must surely be the first "tone poem" in jazz history—but also because I felt it would be relatively easy to transcribe, being in a moderately slow tempo, its textures very clear and transparent, and comprising only an eleven-piece ensemble, not yet the later standard sixteen-piece big band. From there I graduated to much more complex compositions from the early 1940s such as *Ko-Ko*, *Cotton Tail*, *Dusk*, *In a Mellotone*, *Warm Valley*, and many, many more.

Dusk gave me the hardest time because its rich ten-part harmonies in the full-ensemble passages were so perfectly balanced and blended among the ten players (not counting the rhythm section) that I could not be sure I was allocating a given note or inner line to the right instrument or player. (It is always easy to hear the highest and lowest notes in a mixed ensemble, but the inner voices—well, that's something else.)[15]

Transcribing these wonderful works was an incredibly inspiring experience, even though it was quite time consuming and emotionally exhausting. It certainly was a remarkably educative experience to see deeply inside the music (as opposed to merely hearing the exterior surface of the music), to fully comprehend Ellington's inspired and sometimes highly original, unconventional voice leading, to observe at really close hand how ingeniously Ellington would mix the instrumental tone colors and timbres of the different choirs in his orchestra.

During the transcribing of *Dusk* that first time in 1943 I had a most extraordinary experience. I had been working for four or five hours on my second day of transcribing, making good progress, when around two a.m., remembering that I had a rehearsal of a difficult Haydn symphony with the orchestra at nine thirty later that morning, I decided I had better turn in for the night. I stopped my transcribing just as I was approaching the forty-third measure of *Dusk* (the third bar of the bridge in the third chorus), and went to bed. I was awakened from a dream with a start a few hours later with a remarkably precise, almost photographically accurate image of the next four bars, precisely the point where I had left off. I saw these four bars in perfectly detailed full-score format—as if in an engraved, printed score by Beethoven or Stravinsky. And it was so vivid in my mind—and remained so for some minutes—that I was able to quickly write down what I had dreamt in all significant details, partly in musical notation, partly in verbal description. Amazingly, my dream had transcribed the next four bars for me. That afternoon, after my symphony rehearsal, I wrote out what I had dreamt in full score, and when I checked the result with the recording I saw that it was 100 percent correct, at least pitchwise. It included—and this is *really* amazing—even a minor performance error that Juan Tizol, one of Ellington's three trombonists, had committed on the recording. Tizol played a valve trombone and was usually given the third and lowest of the three trombone parts, and so also on this recording. As it happened, Tizol did not take a phrasing breath on his low C flat in bar forty-four, as everyone else in the band had. My subconscious mind in its dream state had recognized and registered even that tiny accidental flaw.

It is an interesting by-product of my jazz transcribing, and my deepening interest as a brass player in the great variety of mutes that jazz trumpeters and trombonists used, that I began to wonder how I might acquire or develop similar mutes for the horn. I deplored the fact that there were no cup or harmon mutes for the horn. So I decided to do something about it. When we were scheduled to play Gershwin's Piano Concerto (with José Iturbi as soloist), I asked Goossens if he wouldn't mind if I played the opening three-bar horn solo of the second movement with a cup mute, rather than with the normal horn mute. He was rather fascinated with the idea, and asked me where on earth I had gotten a horn cup mute, knowing that there really wasn't any such thing. I told him that I was going to make one. I borrowed a trombone cup mute from my friend Ernie Glover, second trombone of the orchestra, whittled away at the corks on the outside of the mute and shortened the length of the tube until it fit neatly into the bell of my horn. The resulting sound was warm and velvety, and I like to think Gershwin would have loved it. Goossens certainly did.

With all this transcribing, mostly of Ellington and the Nat King Cole Trio, and shuttling back and forth, almost daily, between the two musical worlds, classical and jazz, and constantly encountering the deep-rooted prejudice against jazz among many of the Symphony musicians, I began to formulate the notion that the best of jazz was not only as great as the best of classical music—I had already reached that conclusion years earlier—but that it too was an art music. I realized that while classical music considered itself an art music, intrinsically non-functional, intended to be enjoyed and valued on its own terms *as art*, jazz in its first thirty, forty years was an inherently functional dance and entertainment music. But over the decades jazz developed—year-by-year, step-by-step, creative effort by creative effort—into an art form. This became really clear in the 1940s with the emergence of bebop and the trend away from big bands toward small chamber groups, as well as the loss of jazz's prime function as dance music and the dramatic move toward an essentially instrumental music and the performance of *compositions*. At the same time jazz abandoned another important earlier function as the main purveyor of vocal literature, that is, in the hundreds of thousands of Broadway show tunes and songs that constituted the basic repertory of the big band Swing Era. That side of jazz moved away to become its own separate genre.

The other fact, arguably the most crucial, is that a whole roster of tremendously gifted, innovative players—Charlie Parker, Dizzy Gillespie, John Lewis, Ben Webster, Max Roach, Lester Young, to name just a handful (out of thousands)—came along in the 1940s and transformed jazz into a wholly creative, serious, essentially noncommercial form of music that could only be defined as an art form. Armstrong may have been too humble to consider himself an artist, but I know the young, breakthrough, come-hell-or-high-water beboppers began to think of themselves as artists.

Be it noted that nowadays every famous rock and roller, rapper, hip-hopper considers himself or herself an artist and is so considered by the industry.

As for the second direction in which my broadening interest in jazz took me, I don't remember precisely what or who initiated it. I have a sneaky feeling that it was Reuben Segal who, knowing of my interest in jazz and my fascination in particular with Ellington's music, suggested to Reuben Lawson, leader of the second violins and also the conductor of our pop concerts, that

Gunther should be asked to make some symphonic arrangements of real jazz, not just Broadway show tunes. However it happened, the next thing I knew I was asked to do just that. And I chose Ellington's *Mood Indigo* as my first effort—that was in late January 1944—to be followed by seven or eight more during the course of my two years in Cincinnati.

The Cincinnati Pops played typical pop concert fare consisting of light classics, tuneful pieces by Leroy Anderson, Victor Herbert, Oscar Straus, and Ernesto Lecuona, a fair amount of George Gershwin, and pieces such as David Rose's *Holiday for Strings*, Louis Alter's beautiful *Manhattan Serenade*, and Peter DeRose's extremely popular *Deep Purple*. It also played some arrangements by Robert Russell Bennett and Morton Gould (*Star Dust* and *Body and Soul*), and Gould's catchy hit *Pavane* (from his Second Symphonette). But they had never played any real jazz material. The Cincinnati Orchestra in the early 1940s was not what the Cincinnati Pops is today, or what lots of American orchestras can now offer in the way of a swing, jazz-related repertory. The orchestra was certainly one of the best in America when it came to standard classical fare, but with its high percentage of elderly German immigrants, the vast majority of whom (especially the string players) had no interest whatsoever in jazz, who, in fact, were deeply biased against it, considering it a low-class, irrelevant nonmusic, the orchestra was certainly not destined to come to grips with a sophisticated, advanced, swing-style jazz. What's more, Lawson was a rather unimaginative, pedestrian conductor, at best a sort of time beater. Sammy Green called his conducting "slow and slower."

There were no jazz or jazz-interested players in the orchestra at that time except for myself. But in my second year, two new players came into the orchestra who were really interested in jazz. They were Hilbert Moses, the new third horn, and Tommy Thompson, a percussionist. I could now write some jazz licks for Hilbert and rely on Tommy to lay down a good swinging beat, more or less à la Joe Jones or Buddy Rich. What was still sorely missing was a bass player who could swing, who could play what we call "walking bass lines." (There was one young bass player in the orchestra, on the last stand, who could have done it, and was very eager to do so, but there was no way the two elderly gentleman on the first stand, quite good players in classical terms, were going to let the youngster play any solo jazz parts.)

In writing those first arrangements, obviously I faced some formidable challenges in attaining some semblance of jazz or swing. I had no choice but to leave the real jazz parts to myself. Not that I was such a great jazz player, but at least I knew what jazz was, what it sounded like. I loved its rhythmic energy and spontaneity of expression, and was close enough to it stylistically that I could give a good representation of it. I was hopeful that by my playing, and with the help of a handful of other younger players scattered throughout the orchestra, I could shake the orchestra out of its rhythmic lethargy, and that we could give these performances some kind of authentic jazz sheen.

The model for my arrangements was the high-class, sophisticated symphonic treatments of popular music that Andre Kostelanetz, Morton Gould, and David Rose had pioneered some years earlier. (Gould's and Kostelanetz's arrangements were not available and remained unpublished for many years.) I did my best to write my arrangements in such a way as to prevent the deadly string sogginess and leaden brass ponderousness that one usually heard in symphony pop concerts in those days. I did this by using lots of single solo instruments, as in chamber music, rather than using whole massive sections, so as to guarantee a certain textural transparency and lightness. I thought of my orchestrations as preventative and preemptive, and (I hoped) a fail-safe way to counteract the orchestra's rhythmic stiffness and inflexibility in regard to jazz.

My other worry was that pop concerts traditionally got only one rehearsal, so my arrangements would probably get no more than fifteen or twenty minutes rehearsal time, at best two quick run-throughs. Had I been able to conduct them myself I might have been able to coach and influence the orchestra to play in a lighter, looser style. But that was out of the question, because Mr. Lawson was not about to relinquish his conducting post to me, even for one number, and I was desperately needed in the orchestra to provide whatever swing and flexibility I could bring to the performance. But I must say that, in the end, the orchestra and Lawson rallied rather well to the challenge inherent in playing this new genre of symphonic music.

Besides *Mood Indigo* I also arranged Ellington's *Warm Valley* and *Don't You Know I Care*—Hodges's original alto solos made beautiful horn solos—as well as *Sophisticated Lady*, two very fine hit songs of the time, *My Ideal* and *Besame mucho*, also Liszt's *Liebestraum* (yes, in a jazz treatment), and as my crowning achievement in this genre, in early February 1945, a medley of hard swinging, up-tempo Count Basie tunes. I was quite proud of this arrangement, because it was a minisurvey of Basie hits from that band's great late-thirties period,[16] *and* because it was the first time that any symphony orchestra had ever ventured to play the music of the Basie band.

To make the Basie symphonic arrangement I first had to transcribe the music from the recordings. In those days the Basie band played mostly "head arrangements," that is, pieces created not by an arranger in notated form, but assembled collectively by the musicians in the band, usually consisting of a few ensemble passages and lots of freshly improvised solos.[17] Once I had transcribed the recordings, I could then set about rearranging the music for a symphony orchestra, with the original saxophone parts assigned to the horn section.[18]

I wound up the arrangement with a climactic ending featuring a screaming horn duet for me and Hilbert, with me ending on a high F#. I'll admit that was modeled after the spectacular two-trumpet ending of Sy Oliver's *Well, Git It*. I was so busy with all the stuff I had given myself to play—at the same time worrying about Lawson getting the right tempos for the five different Basie band tunes—that I don't have much of an idea of how well the arrangement went, how jazzy it actually was—or wasn't. All I remember is that there were no real catastrophes, that Hilbert and I didn't clam a single note, and that Tommy Thompson provided the appropriate rhythmic drive and energy in the Joe Jones manner. In jazz parlance, he played his ass off.

The performance received a tremendous ovation, perhaps because Hilbert and I played our duet *standing up* as in a jazz band, rather than sitting down as in a symphony orchestra. As the saying goes, audiences hear what they see.

News of a symphony orchestra playing music of the Count Basie band[19] was considered so novel at the time—so outrageous—that it made the two major wire services, United Press and Associated Press, with the result that practically every newspaper in the country carried a notice of this event, not on the front page, of course, but somewhere back on page seventeen or thereabouts. (I still occasionally meet people who had read the two little paragraphs about me and my Basie arrangement in 1945.)

I should add that I wrote these more than half a dozen arrangements for the Cincinnati pop concerts absolutely gratis. I was not offered any fee; nor did I ask for any. I simply did it for the love of doing it, and as a learning experience. I not only wrote the arrangements but also copied out a nice clean conductor's score and all the fifty or so orchestral parts myself. I doubt that there are many people who would have done what I did so freely and—as some more business-oriented people might argue—rather foolishly. But I was very young, and unknown, and obviously had no known track record as an arranger. It was one of the earliest of countless instances in my long life where I have done things for nothing, including sometimes rather huge undertakings that, if I were to calculate their total fiscal worth in paid fees or honoraria over a lifetime, would amount to several millions of dollars (without any inflationary recalculations).

It was obviously my choice to live and work that way much of the time, and as long as I was able to afford such altruistic magnanimity, I was happy—even proud—to do it. In that way

I have been able to do many, many worthy things that, had they been required to be financially compensated, would in most cases never have happened. And I would not have had the opportunity, the pleasure, the rewarding experience, of making these varied contributions to a greater cause, while in turn learning from the experiences.

Money isn't everything, and it certainly isn't the main thing—which is evidently a hard thing for many people in our basically commercial, consumeristic, materialistic society to understand and appreciate.

Chapter Five

FIRST YEARS AT THE
METROPOLITAN OPERA

As HAPPENED SO OFTEN in my young life, some event or chance meeting came to rescue me from some bad or worrying situation, in this case picking me up out of my conflicted doldrums. Suddenly in mid-September I received a call from the personnel manager of the Philadelphia La Scala Opera Company to join them on first horn for a two-week tour in the Midwest. My Italian connections were evidently at work again here, as my colleague Mimi Caputo had recommended me for the job. It was a perfect prelude and preparation for my joining the Met orchestra. The La Scala Opera Company had a fine reputation, particularly in the popular Italian and French repertory: Verdi, Puccini, Bizet, Gounod, and the two ever-present perennials, "Ham and Eggs" (*Cavalleria* and *Pagliacci*). Like so many east coast regional opera companies of the time, it had access to the best singers, including singers from the Met.

It was wonderful to reacquaint myself with many of the operas I would soon be playing regularly at the Met. But also, once again, I indulged myself in my favorite habit of collecting friends. There were some really outstanding musicians in that orchestra, mostly quite a bit older than me, who became cherished colleagues. I remember particularly Luigi Penza, an amazingly dexterous cellist (whom I later frequently ran into in New York playing Broadway shows), and Arno Mariotti, not only a fabulous oboist (first chair with the Detroit and Pittsburgh Symphonies, successively) but also a man of high intelligence, with a deep philosophical turn of mind and wide-ranging artistic and intellectual interests. Arno and I really bonded deeply; we became inseparable and spent endless hours together exchanging our life stories and experiences, philosophizing, analyzing, arguing, and engaging in the proverbial desire to solve all the world's problems. I also met a wonderful, innately gifted trumpet player, Dominic Kampowski, one of those warm, easygoing, funloving personalities whom one found simply irresistible, and who in addition was a great connoisseur of Italian gastronomy. In every city he knew the best Italian restaurant, was friends with the owner or chef. They were rarely the fanciest or most expensive places, but, oh my, such authentic Northern Italian cuisine of the highest quality. It was from Dominic that I first learned what great Italian cooking could be, a domain with which I had had very little contact, given my family's exclusively German culinary background, and the fact that the best restaurants in Cincinnati, in the two years I spent there, were all in the German tradition.

Considering my great love for the string bass, readers will perhaps understand how thrilled and moved I was the first time I heard the remarkable duet "Quel vecchio maledivami!" in the first act of *Rigoletto*, a duet not only between Rigoletto and Sparafucile, the professional assassin, but also, more remarkably, a duet in the orchestra for a solo cello and a solo bass. It was a most daring thing to do in 1851—the first extended string bass solo in all of opera. But then all of *Rigoletto* represents a strikingly new phase in Verdi's development, a whole new level of music and dramatic characterization, expressed so remarkably in that act 1 duet: two bass-register singers and two bass-register instruments—unprecedented in the history of music.

The tour was a momentous event for me, and that is an understatement. When you are facing many weeks of unemployment—my job at the Met wasn't going to start until late November—things that come your way can be very momentous. A few weeks later I got another important phone call, this time from one of the all-powerful musician contractors on Broadway, Morris Stonzek. He wanted me to immediately take over the horn part in *The Song of Norway*, which, as one of the most successful musicals of that era, was now in its second year at the Imperial Theatre. (It eventually ran for 860 performances, from August 1944 to September 1946). That job was going to tide me over until late November, when the Metropolitan Opera's preseason rehearsals would begin.

The show was loosely based on the life of Norway's great composer, Edvard Grieg, and featured much of his beautiful music, only slightly adapted and reorchestrated for a thirty-five-piece pit orchestra (by a very fine arranger named Robert Wright), including Grieg's then tremendously popular Piano Concerto. To be hired by Morris Stonzek was almost like gaining an audience with the Pope. Hundreds of New York freelancers sat by the phone for days and weeks on end, hoping to get a call from the almighty Stonzek. A Broadway show in those days was quite a lucrative proposition, especially if the show became a real hit and ran for several years.

Stonzek had heard from some of his musicians and also from Mr. Schulze that I had just been hired by the Met. I was thrilled not only to make the money entailed in eight weeks of work on Broadway, but also enthralled at the prospect of getting to play every night the many beautiful horn solos scattered throughout Grieg's Piano Concerto, especially in the slow movement. They are perfect in the sense that they are at once technically easy—virtually impossible to misplay—and exquisitely melodic and poignantly expressive. They are also emblematic of the kind of "romantic" horn writing in which, if you are an intelligent, tasteful, musically sensitive player, with a beautiful tone, you can communicate the deepest feelings and probably melt the hearts of the most stone hearted audience—that is, of course, if you have an equally sentient and cooperative conductor. And that I had in *The Song of Norway*, a fine conductor named Franz Allers.[1]

I was determined to give those solos all that I had, not with the intent of showing off how good I was, but to see whether I could, eight times a week, make my playing equivalent—expressively synonymous—with the perfection of Grieg's haunting music. It was more than a professional obligation, it was a matter of honor, and of giving back to music what music had already in my short life given me. Those were moments in which I really learned what I already vaguely knew: that playing music, playing an instrument (or singing), must involve—a healthy confidence and personal individualism notwithstanding—a high degree of humility vis-à-vis the music and the art of music. Now I truly understood the role of humility in making music, whether creating or re-creating it, and being privileged to do so. And I can say in all modesty that in those wonderful Grieg-enriched weeks I achieved my goal—eight times a week for nearly seven weeks. I simply had to!

Beyond that I was much gratified to be gainfully employed, playing a very successful, high-quality Broadway show. I enjoyed myself immensely, not only feasting on Grieg's beautiful music but also enjoying very much Irina Petina's excellent singing (as Grieg's wife, Nina) and the generally high professionalism of the entire cast. It was all a new and wonderful experience for me. I played *The Song of Norway* right up to the time that my rehearsals at the Met began, with only a three-day respite. The first rehearsal at the Met took place on November 20, and opening night was six days later, with *Lohengrin*, conducted by Fritz Busch.

Margie arrived in late September and, also around the same time, to my surprise, so did Gussie, Nell Foster, Paula Lenchner,[2] and Jean Geis—what many thought of, erroneously, as my little Cincinnati harem. Gussie's arrival in New York was a complete surprise, as I had had absolutely no contact with her for several months. Was she too following me to New York to continue a possible competition with Margie? As it turned out Gussie had come to the Big Apple looking for greener musical pastures, having pretty thoroughly exhausted most professional opportunities in Cincinnati. She quickly found good work as a rehearsal pianist and coach in a number of Broadway shows, an arena in which she spent the rest of her working life, eventually becoming the first woman conductor on Broadway. Somehow she had found out that Margie and I had gotten together again and that, whatever her original intentions vis-à-vis myself had been, she had lost out. Margie and Gussie remained good friends, at least until Margie and I moved to Boston in the late 1960s, at which point we pretty much lost touch with her.

As another kind of link back to Cincinnati, my much admired colleague and friend, Walter Heermann, provided a wonderful surprise in a big package I received from him. It was an enlarged 18 x 22 photograph of Brahms, with a note that this was a very rare picture that only he and a few other people in Germany had or even knew about. Walter had brought it with him from Germany in 1905, and had it hanging in his living room all those years in a prominent place. (I had seen it there, and knew how much he treasured the picture.) His note said that he now wanted me to have it as a gift of friendship and admiration. I was so touched that I almost cried, I was so choked up. What a dear man and wonderful musician!

When Margie arrived in New York in mid-October she still had no idea where to live in the big city. She certainly couldn't stay with me at my parents' home, an idea that had briefly been contemplated—and accepted by my parents as a possibility—but quickly rejected by Margie's parents. Nor could they give her any advice about where to stay, since they knew very little about New York except for the garment district in midtown Manhattan where Mr. Black conducted business on buying trips to New York (while staying at the Paramount Hotel near Times Square). But at the last minute the Lenchners took Margie in—which was very kind of them—until she could find a permanent place to call home. That took longer than hoped for because it was clear to us that her parents would never allow their daughter, although now twenty-one years old, to stay in an apartment by herself, and probably not even with some of her Cincinnati girlfriends. The latter wasn't an option because as it turned out all those friends had already found places to live before Margie ever got to New York. And in any case, apartment hunting would have been a nightmare, what with New York overrun in the fall of 1945, just a few months after the end of World War II, with thousands of people, especially GIs, returning to New York. After a couple of weeks the Lenchners could no longer have Margie stay with them; they had a small apartment and two daughters, and Paula had moved into her sister's room in order to make a place for Margie. Margie's parents, in desperation, reluctantly told her to stay at the Paramount. This was obviously not a happy solution for them, but a welcome one for me—for us.

I was more or less an innocent bystander throughout this initial period of Margie's move to New York, but I knew that her staying at the Paramount could not, for all kinds of reasons, continue much longer. I eventually found the ideal place for her, with *everyone's* approval, namely, the Studio Club, located on the East Side in the seventies—long gone now, but in those years a kind of combination dormitory and hotel, strictly for young ladies, especially those already in the theatre or the performing arts. Most of its so-called studio rooms were quite large and equipped with pianos and little kitchenettes. One slight drawback was that the Studio Club allowed no male visitors, except in the ground floor lobby, and even then only to pick up or drop off someone.

I was living at home in Jamaica, Queens, with my parents and brother Edgar. Now that I had a good, well-paying, steady job, I paid my parents a modest rent for my room and board, even though my heavy schedule at the Met—on average four or five morning rehearsals per week plus five or six evening performances—meant that my parents' home was essentially a place for me to sleep. The trip from our house to the Met took well over an hour by bus and subway. That trip four times a day—in and out for the rehearsals in the morning and again back and forth for the performances in the evenings—added up to about five hours on New York's transportation system, rather much on a weekly basis over an eighteen-week season. Instead of going home every afternoon, I often stayed in Manhattan, going to the main branch of the New York public library at Forty-Second Street and Fifth Avenue, very near the Met, to research more music, especially works that could not be taken out but could be studied there on reference. Alternatively, I spent many of my afternoons at the Museum of Modern Art, always with Margie, especially at its daily afternoon film showings, then under the remarkable curatorship of Iris Barry. As for my board at home, that was thus pretty much limited to breakfast and an occasional dinner, with otherwise free access, of course, to the kitchen refrigerator.

It is fascinating for me in retrospect, and altogether impressive, how proactively Margie plunged into the musical and cultural life of New York from almost the minute she arrived. And in those aesthetic adventures I was her constant guide. It was within only a few days of her arrival that we went—she for the first time—to the New York Philharmonic to hear Artur Rodzinski conduct a great program of Mahler's First Symphony and Prokofiev's marvelous Third Piano Concerto. I also recall that a week or so later, by which time she was staying at the Paramount Hotel, we heard Duke Ellington broadcast from the Zanzibar Club one evening, playing, among other things, *Ko-Ko*, *Ultra Blue* (a new piece), *Riff Staccato* (with the wonderful nineteen-year-old Joya Sherill), and, of course, *Take the A Train*, all in terrific performances. Another evening, when I was with Margie at the hotel, Stokowski's recording of Scriabin's *Poem of Ecstasy* came on the radio—the perfect musical ambience.

Once Margie moved to the Studio Club she was pretty much confined to her room, what with all her practicing and studying for her voice and piano lessons, the latter with Edward Steuermann, and voice with Lotte Leonard, who had also moved to New York. Despite both of our busy schedules we did manage to see a lot of each other, meeting for dinner on most of my free evenings at the Met, or going to a movie or a Philharmonic concert, sitting way up in the fifth balcony of Carnegie Hall. Margie also started going to many Met performances— standing room only—as often as time and her father's allowance permitted. She came not only to hear me play but also to become acquainted with operas she didn't yet know, especially Wagner—we did a lot of Wagner that 1945–46 season—and Verdi, of which she knew only the most famous soprano arias, such as "Ah! fors' é lui" and "Pace, pace!" She was very often accompanied on such evenings by our mutual friend from Cincinnati, Paul Bransky. Paul had also moved to New York to find a more stimulating artistic environment than the Queen City of the West could offer in those days.

As the Met season progressed Margie and I found our way more and more frequently around Manhattan's amazingly rich cultural scene, often with Paul in tow; we discovered the countless jazz clubs up and down Broadway and Seventh Avenue and on the famous Fifty-Second Street. After the opera the three of us, sometimes as a foursome with Gussie, would go as often as we could afford to hear the astonishing wealth of jazz fare that New York offered at the time. Given the sad deterioration of interest in jazz in the United States over the last thirty years, only older readers will remember what a rich profusion of jazz clubs flourished in almost all major American cities in the 1940s and 1950s, but above all in New York. My only problem was that the last Union Turnpike bus left the Kew Gardens, Queens subway station at 2:25 a.m. If I missed that, I had to walk about three or four miles to my house or take a taxi, which I could ill afford. Once I moved out of my parents' house a year later, that particular problem disappeared, permitting us to stay up even longer, exploring New York's rich scene.

My first Met season began officially on November 26, 1945, with a week or so of preparatory rehearsals. I had been given a contract basically as third horn, the only opening in the horn section, created by the departure of my friend Mimi Caputo. But early within that first year my contract was amended by the term "etc.," and was soon thereafter, to my surprise, reamended and specified "and general horn," implying the potential inclusion of principal horn, but only in two-horn operas (such as Mozart and Rossini).

The Met orchestra had a six-man horn section for many years, including, unlike most symphony orchestras of the time, two principal horns and two third horns. The Met generally presented seven different operas a week (six evening performances and one Saturday matinee); if virtually daily rehearsals are counted, this workload is almost twice as heavy as that of any symphony orchestra.[3] Four other horn players were hired on an on-call basis to perform in the stage bands that many operas call for and to play the so-called Wagner tuben in Wagner's *Ring* operas (which call for eight players), or to play in six-horn operas such as Strauss's *Salomé*.

The two principal horns at the time I joined the Met were Richard Moore and David Rattner, who divided their weekly performances between them more or less evenly. I was quite content playing third horn, happy enough to be playing in such a fine orchestra at all at age nineteen. But the augmentation of my contract came about as the result of an impression among the Met's conducting staff that Richard Moore, a very secure player with what might be called a "heroic," powerful, somewhat brash style of playing, was considered unsuitable for the Mozart and Rossini operas that the Met performed regularly. Dave Rattner, a wonderfully intelligent musician, with a very refined, musically sensitive style, somewhat on the light side compared to Moore's powerhouse playing, had therefore been given as much of the "lighter" Mozart-Rossini repertory as possible. However, that division of labor by style of playing sometimes created serious scheduling problems for the management and conducting staff. The operas were assigned at the beginning of the season by the conductors and the management, but that schedule of preassigned operas, if strictly maintained throughout the season, could sometimes result in a given week in an overbalance of either Moore's or Rattner's weekly performance duties. Since optional switching between Moore and Rattner in order to maintain a balanced weekly schedule was allowed only in the most familiar, most often-played operas (Puccini, early Verdi, Mozart, Rossini), they often found themselves quite suddenly in each other's stylistic territory. When, for example, Moore ended up with a couple of Mozart operas, and Rattner with some heavy Wagner and Strauss, the results were not always the happiest—Moore too heavy in the Mozart, Rattner too light in the Wagner.

The solution that the management came up with, unbeknownst to me, was to ask that I play the first horn in all the Mozart operas and Rossini's *Barber of Seville*. And that explains how and why near the middle of my first season I was approached by John Mundy, the orchestra's personnel manager, with the offer to amend my contract accordingly. I happily agreed to the new terms, which also included a small raise. I certainly did not want to antagonize my two colleagues, especially my friend, Dave Rattner, by creating the impression that I wanted to encroach upon their territory. Mundy assured me that my "promotion" would be effectuated only with the approval of my two colleagues and "with the utmost in diplomacy."

Mundy, an English cellist, had come to America in the 1930s with the Doyle Carte Gilbert and Sullivan Opera Company and then settled here; in 1944 he became the Met's contractor and personnel manager. He turned out to be one of my staunchest supporters and defenders (when on occasion I got into trouble), and privately, I gathered, was eager to see me become full principal horn. He had been present at my audition for George Szell earlier in the year, and apparently had been impressed by my playing. I found out over time that Mundy's friend John Barbirolli had told him about young Gunther and his musical talent as early as my days as a choir boy at St. Thomas. Mundy had also heard about me in laudatory terms from his friend Eugene Goossens—all examples of how connections, professional relationships, and a bit of luck can play a crucial role in one's career. A further push toward playing first horn came from Fritz Busch, who, I learned from Mundy, had become very fond of my playing in Wagner's *Lohengrin*.

When I was formally promoted, after rather delicate negotiations with Richard and David, the latter welcomed me with open arms as an equal colleague. Dick, alas, became quite upset with me, and our friendly collegial relationship was severely damaged for years. I tried to convince him many times that the idea of having me play some first horn did not originate with me, but came from the staff and management (which he either disbelieved or discounted as a lie on my part), that I wasn't after his job, that I was very happy playing the great third horn parts in *Walküre* and *Rosenkavalier* or whatever (which he also disbelieved), and that I hoped he would at least understand that the management's offer to me was one that I really couldn't refuse (a notion Dick rejected out of hand).

In any event, that is how I came at times to play first horn in my first four years at the Met, before becoming full-fledged principal horn in 1950, when Rattner retired from the co-principal position and moved down to third horn.[4]

As third horn in the section my closest colleague was our fourth horn player, Silvio Coscia, a most remarkable musician who became one of my best friends in the orchestra.[5] He had emigrated to America in 1928, along with his brother Carlo, who sang in the Met's chorus. I say "a most remarkable musician" because, although his style of playing was a bit old fashioned and not particularly refined technically, in the fifteen years I heard him play almost every night— some two thousand performances all told—I heard him miss a note only twice, and then only slightly, what we horn players call a "scratch." Silvio was also a composer, although very much stuck in a conventional mid-nineteenth-century pre-Verdi (not even post-Verdi) style, but certainly competent as a graduate of the Milan Conservatory. What impressed me most over the years was Silvio's vast knowledge of the entire history of Italian singing, especially the *bel canto* era, and a concomitant, alas, somewhat overly biased dislike—even hatred—of German singing and vocal technique. He was even aurally blind to the many German singers at the Met—mostly the women—who sang with taste and beauty of voice, with a *bel canto* line, and who *didn't* bellow and hoot. Many was the night that, sitting next to Silvio, I would hear him explode—*sotta voce*, of course—into a string of Italian expletives at some German or Austrian singer's barbarian desecration of proper (meaning Italian) singing.

Silvio amassed over the years a voluminous manuscript on *bel canto* and Italian vocal style(s), including extensive original interviews with every great singer from Amato and DeLuca to Bori, Raisa, and Ponselle, and dozens of others singing at the Met or living in New York. It was the first time I heard, for example, of such long-ago first-rate tenors as Luigi Colazzo and Carlo Albani, plus a dozen or so others, whose names and artistry are now all but forgotten (except by specialist collectors of ancient turn-of-the-century recordings). Coscia's book was a comprehensive history of nineteenth-century Italian singing in the era of Garcia, Marchesi, and Melba—all in all an incredibly valuable compendium on the art of singing, vocal technique, and style. It was never published, alas, primarily because—so some publisher and editors told me—Silvio could never organize the material into a manageably sized, coherent, practical guide to the subject. He was never willing to eliminate the considerable redundancies in the sprawling text, particularly in the interview sections.

Because of Silvio's great knowledge of Italian operatic history and his own excellent singing (strictly avocational), I asked him to join the voice faculty of the New England Conservatory when I became that school's president in 1967, and then also tried to get his book published. But even then Silvio could not bring himself to make the necessary changes and revisions to make it publishable. I believe it still exists somewhere, probably in his son's care—unpublished.

Apart from the very good horn section, the rest of the Met orchestra was, as I soon discovered, an altogether outstanding aggregation of fine musicians, notwithstanding a few weaknesses here and there—as every orchestra almost always has. There is no question that

James Levine has made the present-day Met orchestra into one of the best orchestras in the land—opera or symphony—by a variety of approaches. But it is therefore unfair to assume that the Met orchestra, including during my time (often called "the great Bing years"), was a mediocre or average pit band. As general manager from 1950 to 1972, Rudolf Bing led the Met in the opinion of many to one of its highest artistic and popular heydays. The orchestra was well populated with a host of first-rate musicians who were passionately devoted to the operatic repertory and, unlike many symphony musicians, did not look down upon opera as a sort of aberration of the true mainstream of classical music. Of course, the Met orchestra was on any given night, as with any orchestra, as good as the conductors caused or permitted it to be, which, considering that some of those conductors were the likes of Reiner, Busch, Böhm, Stiedry, Kempe, Perlea, Walter, Mitropoulos, and Rudolf, guaranteed—all in their different ways—a pretty high standard indeed. Recordings that the Met has issued in recent years of performances from the 1940s and 1950s provide ample evidence of the high standards of performance.

This is not to take anything away from the many fine symphony orchestras in the world. It is simply to say that opera orchestras are not, by definition, a lesser breed, as is commonly assumed. There is one characteristic of opera orchestras that is unique to them: they play essentially the same basic repertory year in, year out, and that repertory is more or less limited to the seventy or so standard operas that constitute the basic operatic repertory. What that means is that opera musicians *really* do know that music intimately,[6] and are in addition remarkably flexible, instantly able to contend with any variant interpretation by any singer or conductor, no matter how strange or aberrant. By contrast, symphony orchestras—less so now than in former days—play new, lesser known or unknown repertory almost every week, not always with sufficient rehearsal time, which, of course, requires of them astonishing sight-reading and quick assimilation abilities. It is therefore not that one type of orchestra is inherently better than the other; rather, they are, despite certain obvious similarities, different animals serving divergent functions and therefore not really easily comparable.

At one time, earlier in the twentieth century, the Met orchestra had been almost 100 percent Italian and German, with a few Frenchmen sprinkled in among them and virtually no Americans.[7] In the late 1930s, however, a fair number of American-born, American-trained musicians joined the orchestra (such as my two colleagues Moore and Rattner), all of them dramatically improving the overall quality of the orchestra, bringing into it a stylistically more flexible, technically more technically advanced way of playing. Among the more outstanding of these recent American inductees I must mention our superb first trumpet, Isidor Blank, and our first violist, John DiJanni. Later, in the Bing years, the orchestra received another beneficial facelift with the arrival of Ray Gniewek (concertmaster), Godfrey Layefsky (violist, later for many years principal viola of the Pittsburgh Symphony), Henry Aaron (violist, a very intelligent musician and for many years conductor of several regional orchestras—Bridgeport, Wheeling), Janos Starker (principal cellist, although only for a few years), James Politis (flute), William Arrowsmith (oboe), Stephen Maxym (bassoon), Richard Horowitz (timpani), Harry Peers and Joseph Alessi (trumpets), and Roger Smith (trombone)—to name a few of the most important ones—all Americans.

There was one non-American player whom I must single out most especially: our Italian-born co-principal clarinetist, Luigi Cancellieri. Brought to the Met in 1930, Luigi—Gigi as his friends called him—was in certain ways perhaps the most remarkable player in the entire orchestra during my fifteen years at the Met. Relegated by the management and in part by his own consent to mostly the Italian repertory, the beauty of Gigi's playing was such that it always brought tears to my eyes. His tone was rich and perfectly centered, with a gently expressive edge, every note a pearl; his legato was like melted butter, smooth and elegant, absolutely crucial in Italian *bel canto* playing. His timing and phrasing, with the subtlest of rubatos, the line and flow in his playing were miraculous. As often happens in early or middle Verdi (leaving aside for the moment Puccini's glorious clarinet solos), the clarinet will have brief *a cappella* interjections, sometimes just four simple notes, that, when Gigi played them, would leave you—not just me, but many of us—all choked up. How I always awaited those precious, miraculous moments!

While, like anyone else, I was interested in making a decent living and thus a commensurately appropriate salary, making money was far from my main concern or ambition. I was thrilled to be in the Met orchestra, one of the world's dozen or so best, playing the great opera literature, which comprises some of the world's most remarkable, most profoundly moving music. My initial annual salary of around $5,000, a good one for that time, was more than enough for me to indulge in certain luxuries, such as the purchase of music and recordings, books, art and literary magazines, even some original paintings and the occasional splurge on dinner in a fine restaurant—with Margie, of course. By the time I left the Met in November 1959, I was making almost three times that amount, at the time a typical principal chair salary in a major symphonic ensemble. The Met's season had also been extended by then, mostly by Rudolf Bing, to thirty-two weeks, including an eight-week countrywide tour.

My first season at the Met was rich in superior musical experiences, perfect for me as a young, developing composer, with so many great operas scheduled: not only *Lohengrin, Rosenkavalier, Fidelio, Tannhäuser, Don Giovanni, Magic Flute, Meistersinger, Walküre, Tristan, Götterdämmerung,* and *Parsifal,* but also the heart of the non-German repertory: *Tosca, La Bohème, Madama Butterfly, Carmen, La Traviata, Barber of Seville, Ballo in maschera,* and *Rigoletto.* These were conducted in my early years at the Met by many fine conductors such as Fritz Busch (justly famous for his legendary Mozart opera recordings at Glyndebourne in the mid-1930s), Bruno Walter, and George Szell, as well as solid routiniers such as Cesare Sodero, Pietro Cimara, and Wilfred Pelletier; and they were sung by the likes of Helen Traubel, Lauritz Melchior, Herbert Janssen, Kerstin Thorborg, Jarmila Novotna, John Brownlee, Rose Bampton, Jussi Björling, Leonard Warren, John Garris, Jan Peerce, Ezio Pinza, Eleanor Steber, Martial Singher, Salvatore Baccaloni, Bidu Sayao, Raoul Jobin, Licia Albanese, Richard Tucker, Robert Merrill, Astrid Varnay, Joel Berglund, and Gerhard Pechner—to mention only some of the most outstanding artists, regulars at the Metropolitan Opera around the time I arrived there.

I was in heaven, not only playing the great operas and learning all that immense body of music, but also because I was absorbing it from inside the orchestra, soaking up those glorious sounds, literally feeling the vibrations of the music in my body. These are experiences one can gain only in an orchestra pit or on a stage—not in the tenth row or first balcony of an auditorium. More than that, I was constantly studying the scores of all the operas we played.

Learning to play such a vast repertory was not difficult for me. First of all, I had played almost all the Italian and French repertory before, in some cases several times. Second, I had studied almost all the Wagner and Strauss operas as a composer, both in their orchestral and piano-vocal scores, and owned much of that music on recordings. Third, I was a very good, quick, sight-reader, and quite at ease with horn transpositions, an annoying bugaboo for many horn players. I seem to have constantly amazed Silvio, who couldn't believe that I played all those new operas as if I had been playing them for many years. On the other hand my ease with the music annoyed Dick Moore, especially when he saw that I never seemed to count the empty measures (with which many horn parts tend to be filled), and that I never seemed to miss any entrances. It was just that Dick Moore, alas, had a habit of counting empty bars on his fingers, even though he had played all these operas already for about four or five years.

Dick and I had a very checkered relationship during the fifteen years we worked together, particularly volatile on his part the first five years. Once I became a full-fledged first horn, coequal with him (equal except in terms of his higher salary, based on his seniority of service), he seemed to relax with me, and we eventually became rather good friends, even socially. But prior to that he always seemed to feel threatened by me, constantly prey to strong outbursts of jealousy. He knew or sensed that I was (and I don't deny it) eager to move up to first horn—who wouldn't be?—but he took that to mean that I was specifically out to take *his* job, which in fact never entered my mind. For one whole year he wouldn't talk to me, and behind my back called me "the fucking genius." That didn't exactly endear him to me, but I kept trying to maintain at least a civil, respectful relationship with him. But he couldn't accept that, cynically believing that my attempts to remain his friend and respectful colleague *must* be insincere, intended only to butter him up. In later years, especially after I left the Met, and even when I had moved to Boston in 1967, we made it a point to meet fairly often for dinner, with our wives. When he too was retired from the orchestra in 1979, we met at least three or four times a year at La Scala Restaurant on New York's Fifty-Fifth Street whenever I happened to get to New York.

I respected Dick very much as a player and an excellent teacher, so much so that in the 1980s I published two of his fine study and horn excerpt books with my publishing company, even though we were so different in our musical outlook and style of playing. He was violently opposed to almost all modern music, ranting and raving, for example, against Britten's *Peter Grimes* and Stravinsky's *Rake's Progress*, operas that he was assigned to play. He hated liberals with a vengeance (which included me, of course), while he drove himself crazy following the stock market at every turn, constantly running out at every rehearsal intermission to the nearest phone to call his broker to see how his stocks were doing. He also was a serious drinker and smoker, and ultimately developed so many stomach ulcers and other ailments that in the end he had to leave the Met orchestra—after a solid career of over thirty-five years.

Although my first season at the Met was certainly a most exciting and professionally fulfilling one, it wasn't all a bed of roses. Within three weeks of the beginning of the rehearsals, Szell, who had hired me just months before with great enthusiasm and fervent expressions of approval, suddenly in the final stage rehearsals of *Rosenkavalier* began to ride me mercilessly and at inordinate length—of all places in a beautiful repeated three-note solo in the third horn

part near the end of the opera . Szell was clearly not happy with the way I was

playing that passage and showed his irritation impatiently, I must say to the utter consternation of my colleagues, even Dick Moore. Neither they nor I could figure out what was bothering Szell, what he wanted, or how he wanted me to play it. I certainly didn't miss or crack those notes—how could one miss such simple notes, located in the safest, easiest middle register—and I certainly didn't play out of tune. It was my phrasing that somehow bothered him; and even though he sang the three notes for me at least a half dozen times, when I imitated what he sang, he still was never satisfied. He tortured me like this for two rehearsals. It was utterly ridiculous and embarrassing. I didn't know what was happening, and began to think that I was going to get fired after only three weeks. (Szell was the unofficial but de facto music director that year at the Met.) In the second stage rehearsal, when Szell tackled me again, the mood in the pit became audibly tense. Eventually after what seemed like hours of torture by Szell—obviously only some minutes, but enough to rattle me completely—John Mundy interceded, suggesting that Szell go on with the rehearsal, since only seven minutes were left in the alloted time.

To my surprise, I was not asked to go to Szell's room, something I had fully expected. In fact, nothing more happened. I played the premiere performance of *Rosenkavalier*, and although Szell glared at me off and on, I played the offending passage with nary a look from him. Nothing further was ever said about the matter. I suspect that Mundy and Rudolf told him to "bug off."

Like so many conductors, Szell was an odd mixture of good and bad. I got to know him fairly well through the years, observing him at rehearsals (at the Met and with the New York Philharmonic), playing regularly under his leadership and, eventually, even directly *for* him, when he asked me several times to conduct his Cleveland Orchestra in the 1960s. Indeed in those years, when I also conducted a lot in London, I used to see him quite often at the Carlton Towers Hotel, where I regularly stayed, and where we had lunch or dinner together several times. Szell reminded me, glaring at me through his thick brown horn-rimmed glasses, and with his stern, humorless demeanor, of a typical stiff-backed, bemonocled Prussian general, epitomized by Erich von Stroheim in the early silent movies and in *Sunset Boulevard*. Szell was the closest thing to an intellect among the Met conductors, an excellent pianist (who incidentally could sight-read astonishingly well from a full score, transpositions and all) who claimed to have studied and to have actually played *every* orchestral instrument at the Vienna Academy—whatever "studied and played" might really mean. His solid knowledge of the orchestral literature and the basic chamber music repertory did not, however, extend as thoroughly to opera, a not insignificant gap in his artistic arsenal that, combined with his penchant for obsessively repetitive rehearsing, often caused his work at the Met to turn rather sour. I remember particularly his *Rosenkavalier* and *Götterdämmerung* of that 1945–46 season, when he would rehearse the orchestra again and again and again—and yet again (often, incidentally, in certain passages in which he himself was somewhat insecure)—eventually to the point where the music would become stale and mechanical and lose all its bloom and vitality.

With his superior intellect and technical knowledge Szell liked to take a piece of music completely apart—horizontally, vertically, clinically, scientifically—painstakingly excavating every little note, dissecting every little phrase or phraselet, and then tried to pull it all back into some preordained shape. The trouble was that many times Szell couldn't put Humpty-Dumpty back together again, especially when his obsessive overrehearsing was in the first place unnecessary. To make matters worse Szell would sometimes, in sheer panic, misconduct in a performance, glowering at us, while we, the unrattled orchestra, covered up for him. (Such mishaps never happened with Reiner or Leinsdorf or Monteux.)

I don't know who or what persuaded Edward Johnson, the Met's manager, to give Szell so many excessive rehearsals, which the Met orchestra certainly did not need. And why Szell picked on me in that innocuous three-note *Rosenkavalier* solo, particularly after I had negotiated so many much more difficult and precarious exposed passages in the first and second acts of *Rosenkavalier* without a hitch. No one in the orchestra could fathom it either.

The episode was over as quickly as it had arisen. It was like a bad nightmare that, thank God, quickly vanished. But I was deeply shaken by the experience. Here I thought that Szell was satisfied with, perhaps even pleased with, my playing, judging by the audition with him. After all I had wowed him in my audition in all kinds of dangerous third horn solos, including several of the trickiest third horn parts in *Rozenkavalier*. Instead, he turned on me and tried to publicly humiliate me in front of the whole orchestra and cast. Within days I lost my confidence in playing, for the first time ever in my four-year horn-playing career. I began to lose my nerve; my tone started to shake a little, and I really thought I was going to lose it all. Many of the players tried to bolster my spirits, praising my playing, helping me to survive those two torturous encounters. "Don't let that son of a bitch get you down." "Don't pay any attention to him, just ignore him," and so forth. But real help and support came from, of all people, Dick Moore. He seemed to have detected some vulnerability in my playing, although to this day I don't know precisely what that was, or what he thought it was. But he took me under his wing, gave me some lessons for about two weeks and some long-tone exercises, presumably to strengthen and stabilize my embouchure. Fortunately, Dick's treatment, whatever it was, worked, for within a few weeks I was healed, and returned to my earlier secure and confident self. Suffice it to say that I have been eternally grateful to Dick, for he may very well have saved my career as a horn player, at least at the Met. In view of his generous help to me in that episode, it was all the more disappointing that some four months later our relationship became so frayed.

I estimate that in my first season at the Met I encountered a whopping 75 percent of the great, most popular, and most enduring opera repertory. It was an artistic feast and an incredible learning experience. I cannot describe what an emotional and intellectual high I was on. Margie was inevitably drawn into this learning, artistic maelstrom. On free days she would come out to Jamaica for the day, and we'd listen to recordings of the operas for hours, just as we used to in Cincinnati. Or I would accompany her at the piano, in arias and recitatives that she was working on. In the evening we'd head back to Manhattan for dinner or a movie or a jazz club. A few times we even went to the opera together, obviously operas that I was not assigned to play.

In that first season there were a number of towering operatic highlights for me that rose above the already high level of the total twenty-eight-week experience. Among these I would have to count my first living, breathing encounter with three of Wagner's *Ring* operas, plus *Parsifal* and, above even these, *Tristan und Isolde*. I came to understand why that last opera is considered by so many as Wagner's most astonishing breakthrough work, completed as early as 1857—utterly remarkable when you think of it—around the time that Brahms, Wagner's twenty-year younger contemporary, was then just beginning to unfurl his more traditional personal language; and equally remarkable, when you consider that Claude Debussy, the other great late nineteenth-century innovator, was born a full five years *after* the creation of *Tristan*. That opera is in many ways Wagner's ultimate artistic testament, clearly pointing the way forward to a new world of music, a legacy that to a large extent determined the future of music for the next half century or more.

On another level, but closely related to the Wagner phenomenon, was my introduction to Puccini's *Il Tabarro* in the Met's revival of this remarkable opera. It is to my mind unjustifiably neglected by opera houses, and is a better work than the overperformed *Turandot*. In any case, I had never heard a note of *Il Tabarro* before then—I don't think it existed on recordings in 1945—and was thus simply bowled over by the daring of its harmonic language and Puccini's stunningly modern orchestration. I had not realized how thoroughly Puccini had by 1915 absorbed and digested the recent developments in extended chromaticism and bi- or polytonality, all used brilliantly by him to great dramatic effect in this passionate, moody, triangular tale of love, seduction, and murder, with a kind of sinister film noir quality. I was so excited to discover this truly twentieth-century music that during the rehearsals I borrowed one of Sodero's scores and copied dozens of its most daring passages into one of my notebooks. The opera was sung to perfection by Licia Albanese (as always), Frederick Jagel (in the twilight of his fine career, but with his age-weakened voice perfectly cast as the powerless, cuckolded husband), and Lawrence Tibbett as the irresistibly high-testosterone macho lover.

Another unexpected revelatory experience occurred for me in Offenbach's *Tales of Hoffmann*, not exactly considered one of the top operatic masterpieces. Nonetheless, besides a lot of tuneful, instantly accessible music, it contains moments of real genius, and, in one instance, arguably one of the dramaturgically and musically most original and inspired flights of imagination in all opera. It is the famous "Barcarolle," of all pieces. In the second act of Offenbach's opera this extremely popular piece, overperformed in the first half of the twentieth century to the point of total tedium—mostly in tawdry, cheapened arrangements—functions in the work as the most dramatic turning point in the whole opera. Its elegant melody, inspired by traditional Venetian gondoliers' songs, so harmless in its lovely lilting innocence, is in fact the setting for a saber-rattling duel between the two male protagonists fighting it out in two gondolas on a Venetian canal. The vivid contrast between the gentle, clinging music and the brutal swordfight to the death, amid shouts and screams, was for me, as I watched and heard it in the dress rehearsal, a powerful experience. That episode is unique in the history of nineteenth-century opera, and is inimitable, nonreplicable.

Of the many, many vocal thrills the Met's generally excellent roster of singers provided that first season, I will single out (in the interests of brevity) only the gorgeous silver-toned singing of Jussi Björling (in *Rigoletto*) and the great Brazilian artist Bidu Sayao (in *The Barber of Seville*). They were the best of the best.

As often as possible, Margie and I also went to Philharmonic concerts. The 1945–46 season was once again under the musical directorship of Artur Rodzinski. It was his third season with the orchestra and, as in the two previous ones, he not only brought some much-needed discipline to the orchestra, he also—of special interest to me—programmed a fair amount of twentieth-century music. Highlights for me were a week with Stravinsky as guest conductor, premiering his *Symphony In Three Movements*, *Scénes de ballet*, and his rarely heard early Op. 4 *Fireworks*, also (under Rodzinski's direction) Bloch's *Schelomo*, magnificently played by Leonard Rose. But the most overwhelming musical experience for me was the performance of Szymanowski's Violin Concerto with the Philharmonic's new concertmaster John Corigliano as soloist. All these performances ended up in my record collection, thanks to the rather curious circumstance that a record collector friend of mine, Zeke Frank, whom I had first met at the Elaine Record Shop on Forty-Fourth Street, had, somehow, in 1944 managed to open up a tiny cubicle-sized recording studio right in Carnegie Hall, on the second-floor balcony, near the hall's own broadcast booth. The primary purpose of that studio was to record, privately and noncommercially, the New York Philharmonic live, direct from the Carnegie Hall stage. How this was possible—and why it was allowed—I have no idea, although I assume that such a thing was not considered particularly contentious in those days. Now, and for many past decades, any recording made of *any* group playing in Carnegie Hall must pay that ensemble at full union recording rates in addition to paying thousands of dollars to various other unions that work there (stagehands, electricians, etc.). Nowadays such ad hoc recordings are prohibitively costly and, beyond that, considered ethically, morally wrong—exploitative of the talents of the people working in Carnegie Hall. Rightly so.

But it simply wasn't an issue in those days, either financially or morally, to make and acquire such recordings. They were made on what were called transcription discs, twelve- or sixteen-inch acetates; and Zeke sold these at reasonable rates to his customers, developing it gradually into a rather lively business. His customers ranged from Carnegie Hall recitalists to composers who wanted a recorded memento of their performance, as well as, ironically, hundreds of orchestra musicians, including those in the New York Philharmonic—especially the wind and brass players—who sought a record of their playing of a concerto or some piece in which they had a prominent solo. Knowing that many Philharmonic musicians lined up at Zeke's studio after almost every concert to pick up their acetates, I certainly had no compunctions about buying recordings from him. Indeed, in time I became one of his best customers. Of course, what interested me was adding to my growing library of recordings, important contemporary works, performed or premiered at Carnegie Hall, mostly by the Philharmonic, works that because of their newness had not yet been commercially recorded. And there were plenty of them. Thus it was that I accumulated a sizable record archive of contemporary music for my own study purposes, music that in many cases did not become available on recordings until perhaps one or two decades later. I should add that, when a commercial recording of a certain contemporary work was finally issued, I discovered that my private recordings were often much superior. In this way I was able to study all kinds of modern music that was commercially unavailable. Two of the three works I mentioned above (by Stravinsky and Szymanowski) were among my first acquisitions.

Among the dozens of performances and recordings of the Szymanowski Violin Concerto that I have heard in my lifetime, that February 1946 rendition stands out most vividly and unrivalled in my memory. Both Rodzinski and Corigliano loved this music with an almost delirious passion, and produced a performance of electrifying, intoxicating power and beauty, carrying the whole orchestra along with them, as if all the musicians on that Carnegie Hall stage had been fused into one single entity. I can still hear Rodzinski at climactic moments singing almost at the top of his voice, wildly humming and moaning, lost in the ecstasy of the moment.

Unfortunately, I discovered years later that the six sides of that acetate recording were severely damaged; I foolishly had failed to store the discs properly, and they had baked together in one of New York's famously humid summer heat waves. The records can still be played, but you have to listen through a constant blizzard of static noises caused by the damaged grooves. I did listen to the recordings again recently, and even through the static one can hear the almost physically palpable passion, drama, and fervor of the performance.

My father was not a record collector, but he did every once in a while visit a record store in Yorkville specializing in imported German-label 78s. Some of these recordings constituted important learning experiences for me and for Margie. One of my father's most prized possessions was a recording of the ravishingly beautiful Arabella-Zdenka duet, "Aber der Richtige—wenn's einen gibt (But the right one—if there is such a one)" from Strauss's *Arabella*, an opera that was only a few years old and had not yet been performed in America when I first heard that recording. This duet aria is one of Strauss's most resplendent creations, comparable to the great three-soprano trio near the end of *Rosenkavalier*. On that Telefunken recording Marta Fuchs and Else Wieber sing with the most beautiful exquisite blend and line and ease of production. It is heartbreakingly beautiful. (And these were singers no one in America had ever heard of.)

Arabella is no longer a new work, and has been performed hundreds of times since the 1930s, including at the Met in my days there. I particularly cherish the memory of that *Arabella* duet with Eleanor Steber and Hilde Güden (in 1954), and Lisa Della Casa and Güden (in 1958); in the latter instance Erich Leinsdorf drew exceptionally fabulous performances out of the orchestra and the cast.

Another revelatory recorded performance in my father's small record collection, which I played for Margie on one of her overnight stays in Jamaica, was the great "Einst träumte meiner sel'gen Base (My late cousin once dreamt)" aria from Weber's *Freischütz*, sung by Erna Sack. Although Sack was primarily famous for her spectacular upper range—high altissimo Gs and As, even the double high C—and her rather showoffy virtuoso coloratura singing, this *Freischütz* recording showed that she could also sing beautifully with taste and style. But what really bowled me over was the extraordinarily sumptuous playing by Rudolf Nel (evidently principal violist of the Deutsche Oper in Berlin) of the aria's extensive viola obbligato. I had heard such secure viola playing and such a rich, full, appropriately dark tone only once before (Joe Sherman in Cincinnati), halfway between violin and cello—as it should be, but nowadays rarely is, since so many violists want to sound brilliant and bright like a violin.

It was once again a chance encounter that provided me with an introduction to a most remarkable piece of music, of which I had previously been totally unaware, but which became almost immediately one of my most revered musical traditions and abiding interests. Through a Japanese graduate student at Columbia University—I have no memory anymore of his name, nor any idea of exactly when and through what circumstances we met—I discovered Gagaku (or as it is called in its danced form, Bugaku), the ancient court and ceremonial music of Japan, as well as the related Noh dance-drama. What was really extraordinary about this encounter was that it happened sometime in the winter of 1945–46, a few months before the surrender of Japan, and thus a period when anything Japanese was generally rejected and reviled in the United States. But I didn't think I was being unpatriotic in refusing to regard this Japanese student as my mortal enemy; I was merely indulging my habit of instantly making almost anybody I met my friend.

This young man had a stack of recordings of Gagaku music and even of complete Noh plays. (Gagaku in Japanese means "noble music.") As I soon found out, this ancient music, dating from the Heian period (794–1185), was subsequently banned and suppressed for seven centuries by a long succession of Japanese emperors. Then suddenly—inexplicably—it was revived in the nineteenth century, although permitted to be performed only at the Imperial Court and on very special state occasions.

I don't know how my new friend acquired acetate recordings of this music, since—as I also learned—by edict of the Imperial Court Gagaku was originally not allowed to be commercially recorded. Either that restriction was withdrawn in the late 1930s or my Japanese friend had somehow obtained some illegal pressings. All I know is that he lent me his entire collection of records so that I could in turn copy them for myself for further study. I still have those acetates on big sixteen-inch transcription discs.[8] The collection includes a piece called *Etenraku*, reputed to be the oldest extant example of Gagaku, dating from the ninth century. After I heard *Etenraku* that first time at my new friend's university dormitory, I told Margie that I had just heard the most sublime, heavenly music I had ever come upon. I haven't had any reason to change my mind. Many years later, in 1973, I conducted Konoye's *Etenraku* transcription as the opening work in a special monster concert at the New England Conservatory presenting music covering over a thousand years, from about 850 to 1962.

I was completely mesmerized by this music's indescribable beauty, its stately elegance and unusual timbral chromaticity. I knew that sooner or later, somehow, I would have to incorporate elements of Gagaku in my own music. This eventually occurred in 1958, when in the third movement (a set of variations) of my *Contours* for chamber orchestra one of the variations pays loving homage to ninth-century Gagaku.

Speaking of Japanese culture I am very proud of the fact that Margie and I were among the very first New Yorkers, certainly of our generation, to explore Japanese cuisine. The first Japanese restaurant to open in New York after the war was Miyako, on Fifty-Fifth Street between Fifth and Sixth Avenue, and Margie and I went there two weeks after it opened in January 1946. We fell head over heels in love with Japanese food, especially sukiyaki, a beef and vegetable dish prepared at your own table. During the years we lived in New York we had dinner at Miyako's at least once a month. For some time it was the only Japanese restaurant in New York; now there are over three hundred.[9]

As if all these exciting experiences and discoveries were not enough, there was an abundance of great jazz to hear in the clubs up the street from the Met: on Broadway, on Seventh Avenue, and on Fifty-Second Street between Fifth and Sixth Avenue, as well as in hotels such as the Pennsylvania (later the Statler) and the Edison. They all had a real jazz policy in the 1940s. With its dozens of jazz clubs, New York was a musical paradise in 1945—and within a few years there was the addition of Bop City, Kelly's Stable, the Royal Roost, the Aquarium, and, in 1949, Birdland. Even restaurants such as the 400, Jack Dempsey's, and the famous Child's restaurant chain offered good jazz featuring the big bands or the best smaller combos. Margie and I spent countless evenings in the Pennsylvania Hotel's Café Rouge, listening for hours to Woody Herman's "First Herd" or Stan Kenton's dynamic midforties band, the two reigning white orchestras in those postwar years. Or we'd go to the Hurricane Club on Broadway and Forty-Ninth Street to hear Duke Ellington or Louis Jordan's hot little jump band, with their big hit *Caldonia*. On Fifty-Second Street (which was simply called "the street") we heard Charlie Parker, Miles Davis, and Dexter Gordon (at the Spotlite), Errol Garner and Slam Stewart (at the Three Deuces), and Ben Webster and Sarah Vaughan at another of the half-dozen jazz clubs there.

Imagine my good fortune to be able to enjoy the following musical scenario time and time again: play some great opera with a fine conductor and a stellar cast, then at eleven or eleven thirty meet Margie at the Met's Fortieth Street stage door and walk northward on Broadway to choose between Basie, Sarah Vaughan, and Snooky Young, or Andy Kirk (with Joe Williams) or John Kirby's remarkable little band (with Charlie Shavers), or Cootie Williams's new band (with Ella Fitzgerald)—to name just a few. It was a special thrill for me now and then to encounter a horn (or two) in a jazz orchestra: my friend Billy Brown in Howard McGhee's band, or John Barrows with George Paxton. I had not yet met Barrows, but had heard a lot about him as not only a terrific player but also a virtually self-taught "American original," well outside the predominantly German-based horn tradition. And on the radio I'd often hear Elliot Lawrence's outstanding young, streamlined bop band from Philadelphia—with *two* excellent horns. I also recall one evening hearing in a small club an amazingly versatile girl pianist who also sang well and played the vibraphone. I never got her name, but I think she was Margie Hyams, who contributed so notably to Woody Herman's "First Herd" band.

That first year in New York, we heard Tommy Dorsey's (at that time) very great orchestra on a dozen different occasions at the 400, a restaurant-supper club that had recently opened on Fifth Avenue, near Forty-Second Street. (It was the only venue on Fifth Avenue that ever offered jazz. It lasted only two or three years.) Margie was especially impressed by Charlie Shavers's trumpet playing, his consummate technique and elegant stylings. (He had moved over from Kirby's sextet to Dorsey's band.) In one diary she noted how she had "finally felt" and begun to "appreciate the element of spontaneity and freedom in jazz," so significantly different from performances of classical music. She added that the playing of Charlie Shavers was inspiring her "to take risks" in her singing, particularly in regard to high notes. Most singers always worry about their high notes—which in the business are called the "money notes"—and she, too, was having trouble fairly often with her high Cs and Ds. The day after one of those evenings spent with the Dorsey band Margie asked in her diary: "Why can't a classical singer profit from the jazz musicians' gift of terrific, forceful drive and yet at the same time spontaneous looseness? If singers could be released from their 'literal' bond, they would be freed to do so many unbelievable things." She went on to say: "Like Charlie Shavers, I'm just going to pick those high notes out of the sky, no matter what, with no care. It's *got* to work. Mixture of love and will!"

During all this time my involvement with jazz grew exponentially, largely through the issuance of a number of breakthrough recordings by Dizzy Gillespie's Sextets (several featuring Charlie Parker); Woody Herman's revolutionary big band releases (especially *Apple Honey*, *Caldonia*, and *Happiness is a Thing Called Joe*, the latter arranged by Ralph Burns and beautifully, poignantly sung by Herman's young twenty-year-old vocalist, Francis Wayne); and Billy Eckstine's band, featuring Dizzy Gillespie and Sarah Vaughan. These were not just another batch of run-of-the-mill good jazz recordings, they were the first inklings of a musical revolution that, so I learned, had been fermenting since 1942, particularly in Ellington's, Eckstine's, and Charlie Barnet's bands, but which in late 1944 and in 1945 burst onto the scene seemingly overnight, a music soon to be called "bebop" or "modern jazz." What I heard on those new recordings, and what excited me enormously, was a more advanced version of what I had heard a year earlier in Cincinnati in the Earl Hines band—a dramatic revamping of the harmonic, melodic, rhythmic language of jazz.

Incidentally, even in the fall of 1945 I still didn't know who Gillespie and Parker really were, or how important their contribution to this musical revolution was, and that *both* had been at one point in that Hines band, which was later often called the "incubator of bebop." Just a few months later the whole world began to hear about Dizzy Gillespie and Charlie "Bird" Parker, and their pathbreaking roles in the evolution of this new music with the funny name "bebop."

Obbligato

In my desire to give not only a truthful account of my life and career but to also comment on the broader cultural context in which that life has occurred, I feel an obligation to reminisce about some of the fine jazz I heard in my younger years, in this instance played by orchestras of the time that were, for whatever reasons, consistently underappreciated, underrated, and have been regularly ignored in jazz histories, jazz criticism, and jazz discographies. We all remember and are constantly reminded of the great music of Goodman, Basie, Shaw, Gillespie, Herman, Kenton, etc., while we never hear about certain orchestras that were almost as good—or as good—but which happened somehow to be not as popular. They shouldn't be forgotten because for their time—and for a while—they produced some wonderful music, definitely in the vanguard of important jazz developments.

That midforties period, incidentally, was especially fertile and productive in reflecting the exciting developments that seized jazz at the end of the war, as it converted from swing to bebop. It was a difficult and controversial time for jazz, as the entire formerly unitary field began to splinter into a number of discrete arenas. First, big orchestras were replaced by much smaller groups—six major bands suddenly disbanded in late 1946, mostly for economic reasons—and small combo jazz took over the field, much to the dismay of the majority of erstwhile swing band fans. Second, former band singers (from Frank Sinatra and Sarah Vaughan to Perry Como and Ella Fitzgerald) evolved into singles and took half of the prevailing jazz audience with them. Third, concomitant to those developments, ballrooms and social dancing, so intimately associated with swing bands, faded out, superseded by small clubs and concert halls in which dancing was no longer a part of the scene.

There are four orchestras I heard fairly often between 1945 and 1947 that I would like to bring back to memory in no special order of preference: Sam Donahue, Gerald Wilson, Bob Chester, and Alvino Rey. What I particularly admired in these orchestras, and what they all had in common, was their big, full-bodied sound and richly chromatic harmonic language, in compositions or arrangements, that significantly expanded the scope of jazz artistically.

The Sam Donahue Orchestra was for a few years (in the midforties) one of the very best jazz orchestras around. This is not just my opinion; it was one of the groups most respected by musicians and critics. The problem was that in those postwar years, when even some of the most famous and successful jazz bands were forced to disband, Donahue's orchestra, a newcomer to the scene, managed to survive only a few years. Eventually it was also forced to disband.

I heard the band four or five times in 1946, when it played regularly at the Aquarium, one of the best jazz venues in New York. Donahue's orchestra, primarily an ensemble group, featured excellent arrangements and a host of terrific players such as Eddie Bert, Conrad Gozzo, and Manny Albam (later a very much sought-after arranger), all inspired by the stylistic revolution that had begun to overtake jazz since the early 1940s. The band swung like mad, almost like Basie's, and was truly a "big" band, with a big, rich sound. Its instrumentation included five trumpets, four trombones, and six saxophones, with a strong rhythm section. Donahue himself was a terrific arranger, an inspiring leader, and an exciting improviser (tenor saxophone), playing a hard-swinging jump style with a virile, warm tone. In my diary I called one of the evenings with the Donahue orchestra "a thrilling experience," and on a later occasion, "I have not yet heard a single bad arrangement"—laudatory language that I did not use very often. On one of those visits to the Aquarium I sat with three of the major jazz critics of the time: Leonard Feather, Barry Ulanov, and George Simon. All three were raving about the Donahue orchestra.[10]

Another fine band, led by Bob Chester (1908–77), is unfortunately never mentioned in jazz histories or encyclopedias. I already owned a few of its recordings, and had copied Bill Harris's (of later fame with Woody Herman's "First Herd") great solo on *From Maine to California* into my notebooks. Chester's band always featured topnotch arranger-composers such as Dave Rose, Frank deVol, and Paul Jordan, fine soloists such as Stan Getz, Herbie Steward, John LaPorta, Johnny Bothwell, and hard driving lead trumpeters such as Alec Fila (later with Benny Goodman) and Louis Mucci (subsequently of Claude Thornhill fame).

In some ways the Alvino Rey (1911–2004) orchestra was perhaps the most exciting and innovative of the four groups under consideration. For a few years Rey seems to have employed practically every outstanding young, upcoming, hotshot player and arranger that he could get his hands on. And collectively that orchestra produced some of that era's most remarkably creative big band jazz. Many readers, even those knowledgeable about jazz,[11] will think such a statement a gross exaggeration, but it is true, as any retrospective listening to the Rey band's recordings will confirm.

It remains incomprehensible to me why and how a band this good, comparable to anything that the Woody Herman, Stan Kenton, Boyd Raeburn, and Dizzy Gillespie orchestras did in the way of breakaway jazz, can be so roundly ignored in the jazz literature. Alvino Rey is not even mentioned in Grove's *Dictionary of Jazz*. I did what I could in my 1989 *Swing Era* history to rectify that situation, but was much hampered by the fact that there were so few recordings of the Rey band still extant, and some of those I couldn't even find.

I heard the Rey orchestra very often on the radio when I was still in high school, and became even more enamored of the orchestra's work later, when his band acquired some of the most important modern arrangers: Frank DeVol, Nelson Riddle, Billy May, Neal Hefti, Ray Conniff, and George Handy. What a fabulous list! Rey encouraged his arrangers to "go way out" if they wanted to, and not to worry about the audience. The evidence is in the recordings that have been reissued since the 1980s, in which one can hear the band exploring all kinds of new, fascinating instrumental groupings and timbral combinations, constantly reaching out stylistically into bitonality and even atonality, always in very original, creative ways. Despite the fact that the orchestra experienced frequent personnel changes, it always maintained excellent ensemble and always had players with a good, strong beat, producing clean, hard-driving swing. The 1946 orchestra's personnel included such outstanding new-style players as Chuck Peterson (trumpet), Johnny Mandel (trombone), Hal McKusick (alto sax), Al Cohn, Zoot Sims (tenor sax), Don Lamond (drums), and the band's two most outstanding players, Roger Ellick (lead trumpet) and Rocco Coluccio (piano), Ellick with an amazingly agile and secure high-register technique, Coluccio dazzlingly virtuosic and stylistically very advanced. And Alvino Rey was a most remarkable guitarist, one of the early experimenters with the electronification of the instrument, who should at least be given credit for converting the "steel" or the "Hawaiian" guitar (previously never heard in jazz) to a legitimate jazz instrument. I heard him play many excellent modern, protoboppish solos, only with a "Hawaiian steel" sound, a fascinating new color in jazz.

I heard the Gerald Wilson Orchestra twice in Los Angeles on tour with the Met (in 1946 and 1947), and was thunderstruck not only by how good it was but that it was also stylistically a true bop orchestra, like Dizzy Gillespie's. (There weren't many yet in those years.) In fact, I thought that Wilson's band was in some respects better than Gillespie's orchestra of the time. It was more disciplined, played more in tune and with better section ensemble. Wilson's arrangements and compositions were first-rate, hard-swinging, and harmonically advanced. I was very happy—and surprised—to see Snooky Young, my friend from my Cincinnati days, in the trumpet section, and even more surprised to see a young lady trombonist in the band—she was nineteen years old—who turned out to be Melba Liston. (The only female trombonist I knew of before was Dorothy Ziegler, principal trombone of the St. Louis Symphony.) Snooky introduced me to Melba, whom I later encountered frequently in New York, when I got to know her work as an excellent arranger, sometimes working in that capacity for Charles Mingus and playing in his workshop bands.[12]

*   *   *   *   *

These were wonderful times for Margie and me; we were so deeply in love—in a kind of emotional delirium stimulated by New York's artistic bounties and challenges. Our insatiable appetites for the fullest possible life were constantly being whetted. But in this aesthetic whirlpool there was, frustratingly, no access to what we sometimes most wanted: absolute privacy and the expression of our love in its most intimate physical manifestation. Margie was confined to the Studio Club and I was restricted to my parents' home in Jamaica, Queens. But in the shrewd and wily ways of young people in love, we did find various ways of satiating our libidinal urges, but of course only rarely in the ultimate physical act. Dark places—movie houses, taxicabs—had to serve as surrogate venues, allowing us to find some release for our pent-up needs. Eventually we were occasionally able to stay overnight at Paul Bransky's bachelor apartment, sometimes well into the next day, while Paul went off to work at Sloane's on Fifth Avenue, where he was in charge of the great window displays. On other occasions we stayed overnight at the Edison Hotel, one block north of Times Square, or at a couple of other hotels on the Upper West Side. One night at the Edison we listened for two sets to the quite good Henry Jerome Band, which I learned many years later had in its sax section Alan Greenspan and Leonard Garment, both later world famous in economics and politics, the former as longtime head of the Federal Reserve, the latter as Richard Nixon's lawyer during the Watergate hearings.

I know that I came up with some clever white lies trying to persuade my parents that I needed to stay in Manhattan overnight. The rationale went something like this: there is some important jazz I have to hear after the opera. But I have a Met rehearsal early the next morning and there's no chance to catch the last bus out of Kew Gardens. I don't know whether they believed me or knew what I was up to. I think they realized that, having reached the age of twenty, they had better let me occasionally roam free.

For Margie those first few months in New York were an incredibly stimulating, exciting, inspiring time. It was thrilling for me to see how she began to open up intellectually and emotionally as a result of the constant stimulation of New York's incredible artistic and cultural abundance. Her life in Fargo had been so sheltered, even restrictive, and limited to the relatively meager offerings of her hometown. Now, in New York, she gave herself over to the limitless inspirations that the city presented. On all sides, she found herself immersed in totally new experiences, discoveries, and revelations. I was amazed how she took it all in her stride, and thrived on it.

Her diary recounted in considerable detail the relentless onslaught of those new experiences, and her feelings and reactions to them. Occasionally she wrote—and also expressed to me—that it was just too much, too overwhelming; she couldn't absorb and digest it all. In truth we were on the go practically every day. We went to the New York Philharmonic concerts each week, often on Friday afternoons, when I was normally free of any obligations at the Met. They were mostly wonderful concerts, conducted by Rodzinski and Szell, in which Margie heard many great orchestral works for the first time in her life, at least in acoustic reality, not merely on recordings—*and* in the glorious acoustics of Carnegie Hall. Imagine hearing for the first time in the span of, say, sixteen weeks, Mahler's First and Ninth Symphonies, Prokofiev's Third Piano Concerto, Ravel's *La Valse*, Strauss's *Sinfonia domestica* and *Don Quixote* (with the preeminent Leonard Rose as soloist), act 3 of Wagner's *Walküre* (with Helen Traubel and Herbert Janssen), and, of course, fine performances of the more familiar repertory of Brahms, Beethoven, and Mozart symphonies. We also listened together to Schönberg's *Pierrot lunaire* during one of our many visits to John Clark's home. We appreciated and understood the work so much more than two years before in Cincinnati. In her diary she wrote, "I'm learning so much about music here in New York—in my lessons with Steuermann, and from Gunther, and all the music I'm hearing almost every day."

In addition we went to many performances of the Ballet Theatre's fall season, seeing our beloved *Romeo and Juliet* (Tudor's great choreographic creation), also his *Lilac Garden* (with Nora Kaye), Stravinsky's *Apollon Musagète*, William Schuman's powerful *Undertow*, Morton Gould's *Interplay*, and, of course, the inevitable *Firebird*. In fact, we went to see *Firebird* three times, primarily because of Chagall's sumptuous, magical stage décor. Margie was surprisingly knowledgeable about ballet and modern dance. I wasn't aware of this in our Cincinnati years, because there weren't many dance offerings presented there. In those many ballet evenings in New York Margie taught me a lot about what to look for, what to appreciate in great dancing. She was especially keen on studying and appraising what she called a dancer's "line," something that in my three months with Ballet Theatre in 1943 I hadn't learned to appreciate at all. Now, with Margie's insights, it all made so much more sense to me, now that I was able to analyze the solo dancers' different styles and techniques. And I began to see the relationship between line in ballet and in music. Our only disappointment on many of those ballet evenings was the playing of the orchestra, which didn't deal too well with the great variety of very difficult and demanding scores.

In another field—art, painting, sculpture—she was much more the novice. Fargo had no art museums, and if it had had one it would not have been able to offer any significant selection of important works of art. And in our two years in Cincinnati neither of us had concerned ourselves much with the visual arts, being so deeply involved with music. (I had visited a few museums in other cities when on tour with the Cincinnati Symphony, but that was all.) In New York Paul Bransky became our guide to the best art galleries, and, of course, there was the Metropolitan Museum and our favorite, the Museum of Modern Art (MOMA). I was very touched when I saw how Margie took to MOMA's art treasures. She kept saying, "I get such a tremendous thrill out of seeing great paintings and learning so much about them." She especially loved and admired the expressionist and surrealist works that I loved: the Tchelichevs, the Mattas, Dalis, Tanguys, Calders, and the remarkable "strength," as she put it, in the works of Stuart Davis and the Mexican social realist painters Diego Rivera and David Siqueiros.

One problem surfaced during this period. I have mentioned that Paul Bransky often joined us for dinner or at one of our favorite hang-outs, an ice cream parlor and restaurant called Cerutti's on Fifty-Eighth Street near Fifth Avenue. Margie called it our "New York Hangar," because we spent so many evenings there, and because two very talented black duo-pianists were in residence there for almost a year, playing light classics and very hip, sophisticated jazz arrangements of Broadway show tunes. As I mentioned, Paul occasionally took Margie to the movies and the ballet when I was busy at the Met. Paul was gay and lived with a painter friend. It was therefore a considerable surprise to both Margie and me that Paul at one point started making all kinds of subtle overtures toward her. At first I thought it was unwitting on Paul's part, but after a while these expressions became more and more overt, less and less platonic. He was clearly falling head over heels in love with her.

It was very awkward. At the time I didn't understand how this could be happening. Paul was a homosexual and had known for more than two years that Margie and I were in an intimate relationship. Moreover, he was such a kind, gentle, generous, honest person that I couldn't fathom how he would express his feelings for Margie so openly in my presence. It would have been more comprehensible if his attraction to Margie had been declared in some secrecy, in private, instead of right under my nose.

This strange triangle situation lasted only a few weeks. Eventually it resolved itself, almost imperceptibly. I can say without bragging that we—all three of us—acted rather maturely. There were no hysterical blowups, no shouting matches, not even any heated exchanges. I must admit that I occasionally felt some small pangs of jealousy, a fear that Paul might somehow be able to draw Margie away from me. But then I saw that she in no way reciprocated his feelings, and that she, with extraordinary composure, received Paul's increasingly ardent sentiments with a beautiful smile, but without responding or even acknowledging them. She was magnificent, the way she handled this rather tricky situation, assuring me that she could only love me and had no feelings of love for Paul. She just liked him very much, as I did, as a person. She felt sorry for Paul and, above all, did not want to hurt his feelings.[13] That was the Margie I knew during all our life together: always helpful and kind to others, always concerned for others, always deeply sympathetic for other peoples' problems, whether physical, medical, emotional, or whatever.

For reasons not clear to me—it is a very rare experience to know, to *really* know, what induces a particular dream—I began to have some horrible dreams involving Margie around this time. I have had these dreams off and on throughout my entire life, even sometimes in the fifteen years since Margie's death in 1992. It baffles me that, although we had such a wonderful, deeply loving relationship, I would have these terrible dreams in which she would become suddenly very cold and mean to me, rejecting me with a diabolical grin, verbally abusing me—none of which she ever did in real life. What could cause such totally refutative dreams?

It did occur to me that maybe, in some perverse way, the episode with Paul might have provoked those dreams. Who knows? Some of these dreams were amazingly realistic and specific in the sense that they involved real people, real situations. One such dream, which, surprisingly, I remembered in considerable detail and recounted in a letter to her because it was so nightmarishly real. It took place in Cincinnati in a real place, near the back entrance to the College of Music at the corner of Elm Street and Central Parkway. Margie's parents, my nemeses, had just arrived in Cincinnati, whereupon Margie instantly changed into another person: nasty and cold, fuming with hatred, which not only shocked me but also shocked my friends Paul Bransky and Sammy Green—as it surely would have in real life. In an incriminating outburst, in a voice full of bitterness, Margie said that she was going to have a baby by me, and she knew "what to do about that," implying she was going to rush out to some abortionist downtown. I offered to take her there, but Paul and Sammy tried to prevent me from doing so, at which point I awoke in a fit of heavy breathing, my whole body shaking.

I was so frightened by that dream, it was so vivid and lingering in my mind, that the same day I wrote her a special delivery letter from Philadelphia (during a performance of *Tosca*)—we wouldn't be able to see each other the next day—to assure her of my undying love, "running the complete gauntlet from the physical to the mental, from longing for your lips and your body to the heights of spiritual happiness."

Of the several torturous dreams that I remember quite vividly (usually dreams evaporate within seconds or minutes, making retention of their content practically impossible), one of the strangest and most convoluted involved, once again, Margie and others close to both of us. Amazingly, it was a dream conceived in four scenes, like an opera or some four-movement symphony. I was swimming in a lake with Margie, Gussie, and Nell, suddenly holding in my hands a little puppy that was a cross between a dog and a cat. But then the pup escapes me, runs up the sloping shore and scurries up a tremendous tree, leaving tiny bloody footprints in the snow. The puppy sits down on one of the highest branches, when an enormous python comes crawling up the tree trunk and swallows him. In scene two I am again swimming with my three friends, although Gussie is mostly sitting on the beach. A curious interlude (scene three) takes place in an old nineteenth-century trading store, such as I had often seen in the Adirondacks. I was negotiating with the old wizened store clerk about acquiring some very ancient coins made of California redwood timber. In another scene change, all four of us are trying to escape some unseen enemy who is chasing us. It is pitch dark and we are all naked. All of a sudden a blindingly bright light is thrown on a group of people ahead of us, which suddenly includes my parents. This audience of enemies is watching me kiss Nell, whose face is nevertheless Margie's. My father asks me whether I like this woman, whereupon I proudly point to her full voluptuous bosom. With a vigorous nod of approval from my father I awake.

The last part of that dream—which I had in Rochester, New York, on a one-night stand with the Met—must have been inspired by a remark that Josie White's father, Bohumir Kryl, had made at dinner that evening, to the effect that Margie's face was one of the most beautiful faces he had ever seen, with the kind of body he loved to sculpt. (The old lecher!)

It was clear to me that Margie was gradually becoming more liberated sexually, freeing herself progressively from the restrictive mores of her family. It was so exciting to behold how, by degrees, she learned that enjoying sex, especially when it was entwined with a deeply felt love, was not something sinful, not something about which one was in retrospect supposed to feel guilty. She was beginning to lose her erstwhile shyness and timidity about mentioning the subject of sex and related matters. In Cincinnati we had never talked about such things. I sometimes wanted to approach the subject, very gingerly, but always thought better of it, thinking it was inappropriate or too early, or that I might offend or upset her. Although I was an ardent reader and student of the subject, sex was not a subject I dwelt upon very much. I was too preoccupied with my various musical pursuits. Now, in New York with all its stimulations, not only artistic and intellectual but also sensual and erotic, Margie was gradually opening herself up to such other attractions. I first became aware of this, for example, one day right after we had gone to see *Ecstasy* (1933), starring Hedy Lamarr, a film that had achieved considerable notoriety because of its brief nude scenes, and had been banned in America for almost a year. At dinner after the movie she told me she liked it immensely, especially for its imaginativeness, its symbolisms, and its fascinating focus on pictorial, visual detail. Pretty astute analysis, I'd say. She thought that the nude scenes were beautiful and she couldn't understand why anyone would want to ban the film because of that. (She committed more or less the same words to her diary because she also wanted to make it into something to be documented and remembered.)

On another occasion we went to see Garbo's *Camille* (1936). She was very interested to see it not only for Garbo, but also because the story by Dumas about a Parisian courtesan was the basis for Verdi's opera *La Traviata*, whose arias she had studied and sung. We had heard many of the legends about Garbo and the controversy that always swirled around her. In *Camille*, Garbo and the director, George Cukor, had been criticized for turning Camille into a scandalously indecent, unbecoming, even vulgar character. That upset Margie terribly, and she fumed that Garbo wasn't repulsive or vulgarly sexual at all. "Besides, what did these critics expect?" Margie wrote in her diary. Marguerite, Dumas's heroine, was after all a courtesan, a high-class call girl. The Hays Office with its production code—a form of film censorship—exerted tremendous power over the movie industry in those years, including indirectly over the critics and even audiences. For Margie, Garbo was "very refreshing, sincere, reserved. Garbo was beautiful as a soft white gardenia. Her portrayal made me cry—on Gunther's arm."

I remember especially one occasion when she had come out to Jamaica for an evening of listening to records. My parents had gone to Carnegie Hall for a Philharmonic concert. We listened to lots of jazz (Ellington and Herman), but also Debussy (*Images*), Ravel (*Gaspard de la nuit*) and Ibert's *Escales*. I remember her telling me how overwhelmed she was by so much great music. It was a magical evening, sitting there in the special intimacy of semidarkness, in silence, the music the only communication between us. She didn't leave until about eleven o'clock, taking the bus and subway back to Manhattan. As we said goodnight, I rather untypically didn't approach her in an intimate way, whether because of my brother Edgar's presence in the house or because I was still lost in the haze of all that sublime music, I don't know. In any event, thinking nothing of it, I was rather surprised when the next day at dinner in town she calmly mentioned that she had expected more from me as a late-night goodbye. I was quite impressed by the forthrightness with which she expressed herself. But there were more changes of attitude to come. Two days later, as chance would have it, Margie came out to Jamaica again, this time intending to spend the whole evening and night there. I must confess that I was somewhat hesitant to go to her guest room, fearful that my parents, who *were* home that evening, would catch us in *flagrante delicto*. But wonder of wonders, she "could not resist the irrepressible desire," as she put it in her diary, to come to my room, "despite the dangers, and we spent the whole night together in an incredible state of happiness." This was indeed a new Margie.

Many months later when Margie showed me her diary—we occasionally exchanged diaries—chronicling her first year in New York, I was surprised to read, in reference to that evening, how, privately, she could sometimes still be conflicted about sex. "Last night Gunther didn't come near me; I was expecting more. But that makes me angry. Am I so vulgar and low as to be so influenced by physical attractions, which get so strong in me at times? That truly worries me. Must my thoughts be governed by this animal instinct? Maybe other women have this too—but they just won't admit it."

During the next twelve months, until Margie finally moved out of the Studio Club, we spent many a night at my parents' home. They were often away in Webatuck, and Edgar was now in the army, having been drafted. Thus we often had the house to ourselves. I know that my parents understood and accepted what was going on between us. Whatever they knew or thought, they never said one word to me and never interfered. It was amazing, especially for that time, the 1940s, when premarital sex was severely frowned upon, an absolutely forbidden sin. In truth, my parents welcomed Margie into their home almost as one of the family, and had simply rationalized that these two young people really loved each other, and now in their early twenties ought to be allowed to live and relate to each other as they wished. Perhaps they also remembered that *they* had sown some wild oats in their youth, and had almost fallen into the trap of producing an illegitimate child—namely, me.

We were living extraordinarily full days in those early months in New York. Besides working very hard on our primary commitments, there was all the concert going, the visiting of museums and art galleries, and staying up so often into the wee hours listening to jazz. To this already huge thesaurus of activities we now, mostly under my instigation, began to add the world of film. In Fargo Margie had been allowed to see a movie maybe once a month and then only certain movies that met with her parents' approval. In Cincinnati we hadn't gone to the movies very much because it took me a whole year to feel that I knew Margie well enough to ask her to go to one. Also, there was only one art house theatre in Cincinnati, and I was not particularly interested in spending my time watching the generally lightweight film fare that came out of Hollywood. But now in New York, where there were already dozens of art house theatres, offering the best films that had been made in Europe in the 1930s and early forties, we practically lived in those theatres.

We also went to see some of the best earlier Hollywood productions, classics such as *Camille* and films such as John Ford's *The Informer* (with John McLaughlin) and *Mutiny on the Bounty* (with Clark Gable and the incomparable Charles Laughton)—which Margie hated because of all the realistically depicted cruelty and torture—or films such as *Wuthering Heights*, with Laurence Olivier, on whom Margie had a huge crush.

The cinema became for a while our most passionate pursuit, I suppose because film was an exciting new artistic realm for us to explore. I had already developed a keen interest in film for some years, seeing it as a close corollary to music, especially in the sense that both music and cinema are forms of expression that occur and function uniquely in time, and are fully understood and experienced only in the passage of time. So when I discovered that there was an ongoing series of film showings at MOMA that changed programs daily and presented in a systematic way the great film masterpieces of the previous fifty years of cinematic history, I knew that this was a field I *had* to add to my growing collection of artistic interests.

I was aware that, while most Americans went every week to see a Hollywood movie, they were generally quite unaware of the great cinematic masterpieces created over many years in almost all the European countries, starting in the 1910s.[14] Most Americans thought that because Edison had "invented the film camera" (they never heard of William Dickson, who really invented the kinetoscope), therefore America and Hollywood had created the movies, and that was all there was to it. I had read enough to know that that wasn't so, and had seen several outstanding foreign films in my young teenage years at St. Thomas (Harry Baur's 1937 *Rasputin: La Tragédie imperiale*, for example). Thus, when I discovered that the MOMA film showings regularly presented a broad cross-section of historic French, German, Russian, Danish, and Swedish films, as well as the best of American films, I knew that I would have to spend a lot of time in the inviting darkness of the MOMA's five-hundred-seat theatre. And what hundreds and hundreds of inspired hours of education and brilliant entertainment Margie and I spent there!

Aside from attending the film showings at MOMA, we also became regular visitors at the museum's many different galleries and frequently changing special exhibitions. It was at MOMA that Margie and I really became aware of the most recent twentieth-century developments in the visual arts. In 1945 the twenty-one-year-old MOMA was already a fantastic treasure house of the best in modern art, even just in terms of its own holdings. But these were then regularly complemented by stylistically wide-ranging special exhibitions. It was at one of these that I fell in love with the work of Loren McIver, especially his *Votive Lights* series. But it was also in that show that I saw my first Dali—live, so to speak—his stunning *Illumined Pleasures*, as well as several Yves Tanguys and my first Motherwells.

One may wonder how, after spending so many afternoons in MOMA's theatre (or alternately at the Forty-Second Street public library), I kept my horn playing at the requisite high level demanded by my position at the Met, and by my own professional standards and pride; or—even more astounding perhaps—how Margie made any progress in her studies with Steuermann and Mme Leonard. As I look back on those years from this great distance, I really do not understand how we did all that we did—except by youth, love, and a limitlessly motivated joie de vivre.

As good fortune would have it, we became aware of MOMA's film showings at precisely the point at which Iris Barry, the brilliant director of the museum's film division, had decided to present a more or less chronological history of cinema from its very beginnings in 1894–95: from one of the first kinetoscopes, only twenty seconds long, *The Beheading of Mary, Queen of Scots* (1895), to Georges Méliès' legendary semisurrealist *Trip to the Moon* (1902) and Edwin Porter's *The Great Train Robbery* (1903), to the German *Possibilities of a War in the Air* (1910) and *Queen Elizabeth* (1912), with Sarah Bernhardt.[15] These are not films you would ever see in an ordinary cineplex movie house; although you might see them—if you pursued the matter—once every five years in the dozen or so art film theatres in the United States, or in some special film festival.

Seeing these very early, sometimes rather crude and primitive beginnings of what before long (for example, in the hands of D. W. Griffith) became a new twentieth-century art form was very important to me, especially since I have always been interested in and fascinated by how things get started—any thing: ideas, projects, concepts, technical and medical-scientific advances, the early lives of all kinds of creatures (how and why they became what they are), not to mention the beginnings of life and our universe. I have many friends who are not particularly interested in the birth of things; they are interested only in the ultimate outcome, the zenith, of a given development. I am interested in that too, of course; but that is usually already well established and profusely analyzed, whereas the initial impulses that propelled some human activity or evolution forward is almost always, at least at first, beclouded with mystery and unanswered questions. Thus I have been almost more interested in, for example, a composer's earliest works, or the earliest innocent, fumbling efforts in a given quest. What captivates me to this day is not so much *what* has been achieved—that is usually pretty clear—but *how* it was achieved and *how* it started, where it came from.

In succeeding days and weeks we saw almost all of Griffith's great films, from the early *Corner in the Wheat* (1919) and *The New York Hat* (1912) to the later *Intolerance, Birth of A Nation*, and, above all, *Broken Blossoms*. And thence on to Von Stroheim's films, such as *Foolish Wives* and his incomparable *Greed* (1925), a magnificent breakthrough film masterpiece, even in the truncated, mutilated version in which it was originally shown.[16]

Before our three- to four-year religious attendance at Iris Barry's film programs had ended, we had seen almost every film of value and historic importance, from Buster Keaton, Charlie Chaplin, mid-1930s Busby Berkeley, and Gene Kelly's innovations as a dancer and director, to many of the great films of Sternberg (*The Blue Angel*), Lubitsch (*Trouble in Paradise*), and Raoul Walsh (*High Sierra*)—the silent ones accompanied by Alex Klein, one of the last great silent film piano accompanists. We saw post–World War I German cinema from Robert Wiene's *The Cabinet of Dr. Caligari*, Murnau's *Nosferatu, The Last Laugh*, and *Sunrise*, Fritz Lang's *Metropolis* and *M*, to G. W. Pabst's *The Joyless Street, Pandora's Box*, and *Threepenny Opera*. We saw as well the films of Max Stiller and Victor Sjöstrom in Sweden, Eisenstein and Pudovkin in Russia, and Carl Dreyer's *The Passion of Jeanne d'Arc* (1928); not to mention Dali's, Bunuel's, and Cocteau's midtwenties surrealist films, René Clair's *Entr'acte, À nous la liberté, Sous les toits de Paris, The Last Millionaire*; and last but certainly not least, Jean Vigo's incomparable masterpieces *L'Atalante* and *Zéro de conduit*. The list could go on for another page or two. Seeing, studying, and appreciating all these cinematic masterworks provided a crucial element in my creative and artistic development. I learned very important lessons in regard to managing narrative continuity (pacing and timing) and matters of form and structure.

Thus I became an avid student of the cinema as an art form, rather than a mere entertainment. I subscribed to all the film magazines and journals (such as *Sight and Sound, Film Art, The Penguin Film Review*, and the French *Cahiers du Cinema*); and by 1950 I probably could have named not only every director worth talking about in the history of the movies but also every assistant director, scriptwriter, cameraman, lighting director—and maybe even the costume designer.

To live so many times in that incredible celluloid fantasy world, sitting undisturbed in the wonderful isolation of the darkened museum auditorium, was the purest possible encounter with the magic of human creativity. We were undisturbed and temporarily liberated from ordinary real life, except when sometimes, annoyingly, the audience would insensitively spoil our total absorption in what was on the screen by giggling and laughing, when by contrast Margie and I were about to cry or were seized by goose bumps. That happened in, for example, Theda Bara's and Frank Powell's films (such as *A Fool There Was*), which much of the audience saw as high camp or just bad overacting, or when it viewed Lillian Gish's or Mary Pickford's innocent fragility and Victorian sentimentalities as hopelessly naïve. They couldn't appreciate the essential magnified theatricality in early silent films, so remote from our modern, slick, hard-core realism. In their stark black-and-whiteness and their strong dramatic force, the best of these early silent films pack an emotional wallop that can be—and certainly was for us—truly overwhelming. But I guess for some people it was too hard to take. So they giggled and squirmed in embarrassment, while we sat there thunderstruck by the power of the images and the intensity of the acting—even *if* by our modern standards somewhat overdone.

Thinking further about *A Fool There Was*, I certainly didn't think it came up to the towering standards of Griffith's greatest films (*Intolerance, Broken Blossoms,* and *Way Down East*). But neither was it some inane curio from Hollywood's earliest years, deserving only ridicule. I felt—and still feel—that *A Fool* was a basically serious film, much more serious than thousands of 1930s Hollywood musicals full of superficial, fast-talking banter and smart-alecky boy-meets-girl, boy-loses-girl, boy-gets-girl-back plots. Moreover, although most of the audiences at MOMA didn't seem to realize it, a film such as *A Fool There Was* advanced the same morality as Griffith's, and a lot more honestly than the hypocritical exploitation of pseudo-sex and fake morality that the typical Hollywood movie has excelled in ever since films began to talk. Looking at *A Fool* from a technical, cinematographic point of view, appreciating its great skill in editing, lighting, even in its symbolism—these are achievements that are anything but a cause for giddy laughter. The horrors depicted in that film were gripping and really disturbing to Margie and me. And Theda Bara's real sexual presence—she was the first femme fatale, the first sex object in movie history—was refreshingly honest as well as potent.

One of the most impressive and unendingly haunting films we saw during that summer at MOMA's series of French cinematic masterpieces was the 1924 silent film *Menilmontant*, most highly regarded by film scholars and critics but, alas, little regarded by the general public, and rarely shown nowadays. Less than an hour in length, written, directed, photographed, and edited by a Russian émigré, the cellist Dimitri Kirsanov, it is remarkable for its use of early 1920s montage techniques and early zoom and close-up devices. It represents with almost brutal honesty murder, seduction, jealousy, prostitution, set in Menilmontant, a working-class suburb of Paris. Kirsanov directed and photographed the film as a complex narrative that verges on the abstract, the dreamlike. It is poetry—and yes, even music—all achieved, incidentally, without any intertitles, normally *de rigueur* in those days of silent films.

It fascinates me that among the many hundreds of film masterpieces that I saw in those years, a dozen or so films—not necessarily always the most creative or most important—continue to stand out vividly in my memory. One such film is *Carmen*, a French film from the midforties with the sensual, fiery Viviane Romance in the lead role, and one of the better film versions of Prosper Merrimé's novel, on which Bizet's famous opera is based. What attracted me particularly to the film was how excellently and tellingly the director integrated Bizet's *Carmen* music in the soundtrack; it was done so impressively that I went to see the film three more times. Especially in the final scene, when in desperation Don José kills Carmen, Bizet's powerful fourth-act music underscores the film's action as rivetingly as any film music I know of, perhaps even Prokofiev's famous score for *Alexander Nevsky*.

By the time I saw that *Carmen* film I had played Bizet's opera dozens of times. In the fourth act, after the orchestral prelude, the trumpets and trombones leave the orchestra pit to play backstage. The noisy crowd-scene music in the bullring arena, coming from a distance (on stage), leaves only the four horns as brass instruments in the orchestra pit. The contrast between the lively, brassy, high-register backstage music celebrating the toreador Escamillo and the heavy, often darkly ominous, mostly low-register music in the orchestra is one of the greatest dramaturgic inspirations in all of opera, comparable and similar (in its use of musical, dramatic synergism) to that duel scene in Offenbach's *Tales of Hoffmann* mentioned earlier. The *Carmen* film affected me profoundly, making me realize what the full potential for a true synthesis of the visual and aural arts might be. And that cinematic experience caused me to play that fourth act *Carmen* music with an even deeper understanding and emotional involvement.

When Margie was busy in the afternoons with voice and piano lessons, I would spend the time at the Forty-Second Street library, only two blocks from the Met. There I spent many a happy hour discovering music that I had never seen or heard of before, and which in many instances was only accessible there. It was during that time that I became very interested in medieval and Renaissance music, especially in the fourteenth-century *Ars nova* and the madrigals of some of the late sixteenth-century composers such as Willaert, de Rore, and the chromatic madrigals of Marenzio, Gesualdo, and Gastoldi. I spent untold hours consuming those precious treasures, copying much of the music directly into my music notebooks. I also discovered there the numerous voluminous encyclopedic collections devoted to certain national musical heritages or particular periods in musical history, such as the fabulous *Denkmäler der Tonkunst in Österreich* (*Monuments of Austrian Music*), or Torchi's similar *La Musica istromentale in Italia nei secoli XVII e VVIII* (*Italian Instrumental Music in the Sixteenth Through Eighteenth Centuries*), copying the works I considered most important into my notebooks, or if the works were too long I had the music photostatted.[17]

It was also at the New York public library that I discovered the remarkable music of Oswald von Wolkenstein in *Denkmäler der Tonkunst in Österreich*. Wolkenstein (ca. 1377–1445), born in Tyrol, was one of the last of the German minnesingers. (In France they were called *trouvères*, i.e., troubadours.) There are at least five reasons for Wolkenstein's importance as a composer: (1) We have more of his works, both text *and* music, than of any other mastersinger or of any pre-Renaissance musical figure. Of most other minnesingers, such as Wolfram von Eschenbach (made famous in Wagner's *Tannhäuser*) and Walther von der Vogelweide, we have either only the poetry or the scantiest examples of the actual music. Wolkenstein composed nearly three hundred songs, which he notated fully and issued in various manuscript editions (called codexes). (2) In these editions he specified the instrumental accompaniments for instruments such as the lute, lira, shawm, harp, and even the sackbut. (3) He composed not only monophonic songs, including many passionate love songs, but also polyphonic pieces in two, three, and four parts, and thus became one of the earliest innovators in this new technique, in effect one of the most creative forerunners of the golden age of polyphony. (4) His songs encompass an enormous range of genres and types, that is, drinking, dancing, spoofing, farcical, fighting, and battle songs, and, most amazingly, numerous autobiographical songs. (5) As a result of which, we know more about his life than any other pre sixteenth century musician. And what a life that was! As a knightly poet he served numerous kings and dukes, including King Sigismund (crowned emperor of Germany in 1433), and as such was obliged to travel with his ruler-employer. It was thus that he often found himself in faraway places such as Portugal, Morocco, eastern Europe, the bordering area of Asia, and even on a pilgrimage to the Holy Land.

Beyond that, and the reason I got so excited about Wolkenstein's music way back then in the late 1940s, is that it is incredibly inventive, adventurous, and individualistic. There is very little (if any) music like it in the entire Middle Ages. I had never seen anything like the up-tempo two-part onomatopoetic song, *Der Mai mit lieber zal* (in old medieval German), or the *Number of Birds in May*, with its wildly virtuosic imitations of birds (nightingales, cuckoos, doves, and such). The four-part song *Frölich geschrai* (*Merry Shouting*) is just that, an ingenious, frantic babble of yelling and shouting for two voices and two instruments, including a flautino and a piccololike recorder. And the song *Du auserweltes* (*Thou Otherworldy*) for one voice and three instruments is one of the two Wolkenstein pieces I copied into my notebooks and some years later not only transcribed for English horn (substituting for the voice), harp, flute, and tenor trombone but also performed in a series of concerts that Edgard Varèse asked me to produce at the Greenwich House Music School in lower Manhattan. (More of that later.)

My dozen or so notebooks from that period are tangible evidence of the catholicity of my musical tastes. To instance just one of those notebooks, it contained (mostly in excerpts), all written in beautiful ink manuscript: (1) the slow-movement cello solo from Brahms's B-flat Piano Concerto; (2) the first violins, flute, and horn solos from Shostakovich's Fifth Symphony first movement; (3) the final forty-five bars of Strauss's *Ein Heldenleben*; (4) an excerpt from the final tableau of Stravinsky's *Petroushka* and some very challenging horn passages from Strauss's (at the time brand-new) opera *Daphne*; (5) a series of chords from Stravinsky's *Capriccio*; (6) a beautiful passage from Jacques Ibert's *Divertissement*; (7) part of Marcel Grandjany's *Rhapsody* for harp; (8) excerpts from the horn parts (transcribed by me from the recordings) of David Rose's fetching little masterpieces *Our Waltz* and *Poinciana*; (9) excerpts from Holst's *The Planets*; (10) excerpts from one of Hindemith's Organ Sonatas; (11) the entire horn part of Alexander Mossolov's *Iron Foundry* (which the Philharmonic played quite often at the Lewisohn Stadium summer concerts); (12) Samuel Barber's *Essay No. 1*; (13) Tommy Dorsey's trombone solo from *Marie*; (14) excerpts from Prokofiev's Third Piano Concerto; (15) Dizzy Gillespie's trumpet part from *Groovin' High* (I used to play and practice that a lot on the horn); (16) various selections from Stravinsky's *Firebird*; (17) Bill Harris's great trombone solo from the Woody Herman Band's recording of *Apple Honey*, as well as Chubby Jackson's entire bass part (for his five-string bass with the high C string); (18) excerpts from that band's recordings of *Northwest Passage* and *Goosey Gander*; (19) excerpts from Delius's *Paris*; (20) huge chunks from the first movement of Mahler's Ninth Symphony; (21) Duke Ellington's *Dusk* and *Jack the Bear*, and the King Cole Trio's *I'm Lost* and *This Side Up*; and (22) five pages (in piano reduction) of excerpts from Stravinsky's *Sacre du printemps*. Quite a collection!

I filled many notebooks in a similar manner and with similarly varied content, the later ones with a great deal of medieval and Renaissance music. In the meantime I was reading Charles Burney's histories, Romain Rolland on Beethoven, both Chrysander and Rolland on Handel, and Burney's wonderful writings on Johann Friedrich Fasch and Reinhard Keiser, several books by André Pirro (the great French writer) on Heinrich Schütz, Adam Carse on the eighteenth-century orchestra, and—most fascinating of all—Curt Sachs's *History of Musical Instruments* and Gustave Reese's *Music in the Middle Ages*.

To give an idea of what a workhorse I was as a twenty-year-old, I found in my diary the following entry for August 2, 1946: "Got an incredible amount of work done today. Finished *Till's Boogie* and *Lady Be Good*" (one a composition, the other an arrangement of Gershwin's famous tune for brass sextet and rhythm section). "Then copied Kenton's terrific recording of *Just a-Sittin' and a-Rockin'* off the Capitol record, and arranged that, too, for a twelve-piece ensemble (five horns, three trombones, and rhythm section). In evening, copied all the parts for *Just a-Sittin.*"

That seems like an amazing series of accomplishments for one single day. But truth be told, that wasn't particularly unusual, for I have filled many a day in my long life in similar ways. It is clear that I did such things easily and with considerable speed. But the real explanation is that I enjoyed such work immensely—anything to do with music—and thus was tremendously motivated. On such occasions the rewards and gratifications of real accomplishment were instantaneous.

It was around this time that I was given the opportunity to play the Brahms Horn Trio for the first time in New York. It was to be in Town Hall, the city's second concert hall, and, more important, I was to perform with Rudolf Kolisch and Edward Steuermann. Our rehearsals were a remarkable eye and ear opener, a fascinating deep probing into the piece, and a rewarding follow-up to our Kenyon performance. Alas, Kolisch suddenly became ill, and more or less at the last minute Bronislaw Gimpel, another fine, intelligent musician, took his place. I was a bit nervous; it was going to be my first fully professional major outing in New York as a soloist, and the program was scheduled to be broadcast over WQXR. Fortunately I acquitted myself well, garnering a favorable review in the *New York Times*:[18] "Mr. Schuller's horn playing was remarkably free of tonal blemishes, squarely on pitch and well integrated with the other instruments."[19]

Among my most wonderful learning experiences was an invitation by Steuermann to attend all of Marjorie's piano lessons. I did that as often as I could for a period of four or five years, sitting in a corner of his large studio—like a fly on the wall—listening to this great man's teaching, both technical and musical, interpretational. Just sitting there and listening to Steuermann's specific advice, suggestions, analyses and insights into the music, his detailing and dissecting of all kinds of notational and textual matters, brought my own awareness of such things to a significantly higher level—as it did, of course, for Marjorie.

If there was time at the end of the lessons before the next student arrived, Steuermann would escort us to the elevator, and he and I would have a brief chat about various musical subjects, which often ended in his questioning me about matters in that big wide world of music that he felt I was part of. I think he was rather intrigued by me as a sort of American curiosity, different from other young Americans he had met, and someone who seemed intellectually literate, musically knowledgeable, and who already at age twenty occupied an important major position in the music world. On top of that, this American spoke fluent German, and—wonder of wonders—admired Schönberg's music.

I realized after a while that Steuermann, although a legend to me, was unheralded and unappreciated in New York. With no possibility of a concertizing career, as he had enjoyed in Germany before emigrating to the United States, Edward eked out a living giving piano lessons some sixty hours a week. Steuermann's highly successful career in Germany and Austria in the 1920s and early 1930s had been abruptly aborted with the coming to power of the Nazis. He had been a much sought after singers' coach in opera and Lieder. Steuermann, a Polish Jew, fled to the United States; but here no one knew who he was nor what an important career he had had in Germany. His long association and friendship with Schönberg and others of the "twelve-tone crowd"—as it was often facetiously referred to—didn't help matters. As newcomers they were considered intruders and not particularly appreciated.

In his isolation Steuermann saw me as a link to that vital, exciting professional world in Europe that he had once been a part of. Many times he asked me about famous artists—singers, pianists, violinists, composers—and how they were doing, especially about other European refugees from Hitler's Germany, whom he knew and had worked with in Europe but had lost virtually all contact with in America. Steuermann was particularly curious about conductors at the Met, especially Busch, Walter, and Szell, and singers in the Met's German wing. I was not surprised to learn that his knowledge of the opera literature was vast. But I *was* surprised by his almost sheepish curiosity about Puccini. He seemed much relieved—and amazed—to learn that I was a great admirer of Puccini, particularly his unique orchestrational talent. And when I asked why he would be so surprised about that, he revealed that among his German colleagues, especially composers and most especially those of the Schönberg school, Puccini was more or less frowned upon as a talented but ultimately second-rank composer. In our little exchanges I discovered that we shared a mutual fascination for the music of Franz Schreker, particularly his operas. Steuermann called him the German Puccini, especially in respect to Schreker's colorful, scintillating orchestration and his highly chromatic language—and also Max Reger. When Steuermann found out that I was also a jazz fan—which puzzled him, as it did most German refugees—he asked me what I thought of Gershwin, and was happy to hear that I considered Gershwin a major figure of genius rank.

I soon learned that Steuermann was also a composer, indeed a very good one.[20] Unfortunately, due to his abrupt departure from Europe and his precarious financial circumstances in America, he had been more or less forced to give up composing, consigned instead to a daily diet of eight to ten hours of teaching piano. But he was able to return to his first love—composing—in the early fifties. It was during Marjorie's lessons that I began to hear about one of his highly gifted young students, a fifteen-year-old lad named Russell Sherman, already known then as Buddy.

Unlike many European refugees who had to leave all their belongings and possessions behind, often getting out with only the clothes on their backs, Steuermann had contrived to bring almost his entire tremendous library of music and books with him to America. What was especially significant to me was that his library had almost all relevant works, in full score or in piano reductions, of the entire repertory of Schönberg, Berg, and Webern. This repertory was virtually unobtainable in the United States at that time. Steuermann was kind enough to lend me many of his most precious scores, to duplicate or to copy them out note for note, as, for example, I did with Alban Berg's *Altenberg Lieder*. It is thus that I obtained much of the great, important works of these composers for my personal library, works such as Schönberg's *Orchestra Variations Op. 31* and his masterful opera *Erwartung* (of which Steuermann had made the published piano reduction), excerpts from *Wozzeck*, and a dozen pieces by Webern. It gave me instant access to very important compositions in the development of twentieth-century music that almost no other young composers of my generation in America could obtain—again, the result of a fortuitous encounter with a great musician who played an influential role in my life.

In the midst of all this hectic professional and personal activity, I managed to accomplish a fair amount of composing, and a lot of self-study. I wrote an orchestral work that united music with my longstanding interest in the visual arts—painting, sculpture, drawing, design—and my constant attendance at the Museum of Modern Art. In the midforties there were two paintings that for me dominated the museum. They were *Hide and Seek* by the Russian-American Pavel Tchelitchew, and *Le Vertige d'Eros* (*The Madness of Eros*) by the Chilean Echaurren Matta. I was finally so drawn to the latter that I knew I had to somehow synesthetically translate my impressions and feelings for that picture, with its surrealist fantasy world, into musical terms. I was so fired up that I composed the work in a fever pitch in what amounted to about fourteen days, betwixt and between all my other commitments and activities, rehearsals, and performances. Although the piece clearly reveals various musical influences, above all, of my twin heroes Stravinsky and Schönberg—even a few vestigial reminiscences of my earlier obsession with Scriabin—I feel that these influences were already well subsumed into my evolving personal style and language. *Vertige d'Eros* is a work of which I am very proud, even though it shows those early influences. But for a self-taught twenty year old it also shows real talent, especially in its handling of the orchestra. In retrospect, I realize that it was by far the best work I had done up to that time, a quantum leap forward for me.

In those midforties years my insatiable appetite for the acquisition of ever-greater knowledge manifested itself in one curious by-product: the filling of dozens of little pocket diaries and notebooks with lists of works with statistical information and reminders for further explorations. I was particularly fond of making lists of composers or works in less regarded musical fields, for example in Renaissance and medieval music. Such music was rarely represented on records in those days, and totally ignored in ordinary concert life. This little mania of mine developed out of a three-pronged set of related experiences: primarily the thirst for knowledge and a deep curiosity about the world around me, but also an irresistible need to somehow *own* that acquired information (not only in memory but also in a more concrete, instantly accessible form), and my concern that in cramming so much knowledge into my brain day after day my memory cells would not be able to retain it all. Thus the need to write everything down, to commit it to paper so that it could be easily referenced. This technique of getting information onto paper worked well for me. In some of my fields of interest I became a virtual walking encyclopedia. Whatever I had acquired in my extensive reading, especially in encyclopedias, dictionaries, and monographs, I never wanted to lose; and that required having immediate access to this accumulated information.

For example, I made a list of books in 1946 that I felt I must read (and own), consisting mostly of French literature: Balzac's *La Comédie humaine*, Racine's *Phèdre*, Flaubert's *L'Éducation sentimentale* and *Madame Bovary*, Baudelaire's *Les Fleurs du mal* (*The Flowers of Evil*), de Sévigné's *Letters*, the Goncourt Brother's *Diaries*, the great seventeenth-century satirist and historian Charles Sorel's *Le Berger extravagant*, and several works by Stendhal. That particular list even included Choderlos de Laclos's *Les Liaisons dangereuses*, later (in 1960) made into a remarkable film with Jeanne Moreau and Gerard Philippe. Be assured that I did eventually read all those books. Other listings encompassed fields ranging from musical performance (how often a given composer was performed on WNYC and WQXR) to automobiles (how many of a given car make I had seen when traveling with my parents), and in jazz, listings of bandleaders and sidemen (how many performances each had on the radio). I was almost always more interested in the most obscure or less performed composers (such as Inghelbrecht or Loeffler or Turina), or in custom-built cars (such as the Cord, or a Ferrari). I would tabulate the listings or sightings with bullets or hatch marks.

What I learned from these compilations was that when you write something down, commit it to paper, it is much more likely to stay with you. I know that I have carried a large amount of such factual data and knowledge with me all of my life, sometimes very profitably indeed. Because you never know when some bit of knowledge, stored away somewhere, will come in very handy!

A new phase in my family's life developed late in 1945 when my parents heard about some land for sale an hour and a half north of New York City near the small hamlet of Webatuck, a kind of suburb of Wingdale, New York, about three miles from the New York-Connecticut border. Twenty-five acres of prime undeveloped land was available—unbelievably—for twenty-five dollars an acre. Before the year was out, my parents had sold their Rocky Point bungalow— a sad moment for Edgar and me, and my friend Willy Manthey, remembering all the happy times we had there—and bought the twenty-five acres in Dutchess County.

By the spring of 1946 my mother, who had a natural talent for architectural design, was drawing up detailed blueprint plans for a one-room cabin, which was to become the family's new summer home. The property my parents had bought was pristine, hilly, wooded land— mostly cedars—on the highest point of which, after some clearing, the summer cottage was to be built. My parents, typical frugal Germans, decided to build the cabin mostly themselves, cleverly pulling in everybody from our extended family of cousins, uncles, friends, and colleagues—including even many of my new Cincinnati "family," such as Sammy, Paul, Gussie, Paula, and her sisters. All were conscripted, variously enticed to help in these labors by my mother's famous German cooking. She fed everybody royally, for which the guests would be expected to put in a certain number of hours of work.

To house not only my family but also this veritable army of helpers that summer of 1946, while the cottage was gradually rising, Julian Hunt (the proprietor of the Hunt Country

Furniture Company, famous throughout the Northeast), from whom we had bought the property, offered us rooms in his beautiful, old, fifteen-room house—built in the early eighteen hundreds—right on the banks of the Ten Mile River.

My father and I were very busy with our various professional obligations, and were thus somewhat limited in the amount of time we could devote to building the cabin. Nevertheless, by the end of the summer the basic structure was up, and it soon had a roof as well as a big double fireplace, indoor and outdoor. But since there were as yet no washroom and toilet in the cabin (we built an outhouse about fifty feet away on the slope of the hill), or electricity, and only a few pieces of Hunt furniture, we still had to stay at Julian's big house throughout most of 1946.

I went to Webatuck as often as possible between jobs in New York, always with Margie, to help with the building of the cottage. By the fall we started to add an L-shaped extension to the cabin, which eventually housed a small kitchen, bathroom, laundry room, and a tool-storage and carpentry workshop. I remember being asked to dig a hole, with the help of Edgar and Sammy Green, about eight feet deep and wide, to house an electric pump that would bring the water up from a well nearly a hundred feet below. The well had been drilled through solid rock. On most of our hilltop—so we were told by the well drillers—the layer of earth was only three or four feet deep. Underneath that it was all solid granite. We were situated, in effect, on a gigantic rounded boulder, probably left there at the end of the last Ice Age. The place where I was asked to dig the hole was one of the very few places where there was a slightly deeper crevasse in the rock formation, thus allowing us to go deeper than a few feet.

That job was relatively easy compared to a bigger and more dangerous one, namely, building a twenty-foot-long, ten-foot-high stone wall for the L-shaped cottage extension. Margie and I worked on that wall over a period of several weeks in October, virtually without interruption from eight in the morning until nine at night, well after dark. We had to turn on my father's car lights in order to see what we were doing. The next day my hands were painfully sore from the rough, pebbly cement, and from lifting those boulder-size stones into place. I could hardly practice the horn, for my fingertips (with which one manipulates the valves) were sore with cuts and blisters. I look at that wall and a couple of its biggest rocks nowadays, and wonder how Margie and I lifted some of those heaviest sixty-pounders into place four or five feet up, midlevel in the wall. Although it is not the most elegant looking stone wall ever built, I'm still mighty proud of our work as stonemasons.

Building the cabin mostly by ourselves had its hazards. One fine summer morning, working on the half-finished peaked roof, I fell about twenty-five feet to the ground, landing with my right foot smack on a big penny nail, which penetrated halfway through my heel. A quick trip to the hospital in nearby Pawling and a two-hour drive later that afternoon to Manhattan, and my father and I were busily working our way through a ballet program at Lewisohn Stadium, Efrem Kurtz conducting. It never occurred to me to call in sick!

We finally had a housewarming in our new cabin, all six of us—my family of four plus Margie and Janet Putnam (my harpist friend from the Met orchestra who was visiting us for the weekend). All of us slept in the one room, like so many sardines in a can, on an assortment of bedrolls, mattresses, and cots.

We saw Gussie a few times that summer. On one occasion—it was Easter Sunday—the three of us had dinner with Paul and our mutual Cincinnati friend, Gene Selhorst, whom I hadn't seen for almost a year. In order to dine with us, Gussie had broken a date with her newest boyfriend, Neil Hidalgo, a Bolivian who had recently immigrated to the United States. We had a great time, Gussie and I showing off with our little battles of sarcastic teasing banter, probably to veneer over any remembrance of our brief fling the year before, and generally reminiscing about the good old days. After dinner, when the four of us saw Gene off at the bus depot—incredibly, in a city of eight million—we ran into Neil, of all people, who had just bought Gussie some Easter flowers, still expecting to spend the evening with her. One can imagine how Neil felt when he saw Gussie in the company of two other men, Paul and me.

It got worse. We all gathered in the bus depot's restaurant for some coffee and dessert. At first Neil seemed pleasant enough, but when Gussie—unfathomably—more or less ignoring Neil, began reminiscing excitedly about our Cincinnati days, also casually mentioning some jazz news she had just read about in a new magazine called *Jazzway*, he suddenly turned on her and in a nasty, bossy tone of voice told her to stop reading and talking about music—of which he evidently didn't understand anything. Gussie, in a reckless mood, shouted at him to shut up. Whereupon Neil got up, and with a menacing, steely look, turned on me, shouting several times, insinuatingly, "I've heard *so* much about you," and then stormed out of the bus station. I got a clear sense that this man could be dangerous. Angered, his face took on a frightening hardness, like some mean-faced gangster in a Hollywood crime film or in the television drama *Miami Vice*. (The only thing missing was a big sallow scar on his cheek.)

Now suddenly Gussie felt really bad, realizing that she had been foolish to rebuff and ignore Neil so incautiously. She cried on Margie's shoulder, asking her what she should do. We took her to the 400 Restaurant, where Gene Krupa's orchestra (with the young Red Rodney) was playing, and we had a long talk in which I tried to comfort her and gently suggest that Neil was not the right guy for her. But she claimed that she loved him, which I couldn't understand at all. This was not the very talented, carefree, fun loving young lady that I had come to know in Cincinnati.[21]

The big excitement for me in mid-April of 1946 was the start of the Met's annual spring tour; we were scheduled to perform in some dozen cities. As an inveterate traveler, I was looking forward to seeing much of the country again, deploring only that we weren't going to get to the West Coast; Dallas was the farthest west we were to venture on that particular tour. The whole company lived in two roomette-equipped trains that the Met acquired for the entire tour—one for the singers, chorus, and dancers, the other for the orchestra musicians. We stayed in hotels only during longer stopovers in the bigger cities such as Chicago, Cleveland, Minneapolis, and Dallas; in shorter layovers such as Chattanooga or Milwaukee we slept in our roomettes.

Aside from the sheer pleasures of traveling, seeing new places, new sights, meeting new people, and encountering some wonderful culinary experiences along the way, I looked forward most of all to the prospect of hearing a lot of good jazz on the road. For in those days not only were the big bands still traveling, playing in theatres, clubs, and hotel ballrooms, but the better hotels all had lounges, sometimes even two, where the many smaller groups—trios, quartets, and quintets—could be heard regularly. Over the fourteen years I toured with the orchestra I got to hear a lot of great jazz that way, courtesy of the Metropolitan Opera. The minute we arrived in a city I'd check the newspapers to find out who was playing. If time and my performing schedule permitted, I'd head straight for the theatres, then still featuring, along with movies, the big bands in their stage shows. Most of these theatres, built in the 1920s (but now mostly gone or converted into other venues), had uniformly great acoustics. Some of them were in the black sections of town, such as the Paradise in Detroit, the Regal in Chicago, and the Howard in Philadelphia. In addition, there were the Fox and Loews chains, spread all across America.

How rich this culture of theatres, clubs, ballrooms, and lounges was in those days! Now, nearly seventy years later, very little of that remains. Old-timers like me can attest to the fact that some of the very greatest, some of the most sublime, perfectly played music heard—often even greater than what was produced on recordings—occurred in those theatre shows or hotel ballrooms. It could be the third stage show, just before dinnertime, when the whole band—or maybe one particular soloist—was afire with inspiration, or it could be the last dance set, when the musicians were feeling really good, in anticipation of some great *jamming* in an after-hours place, or some great home cooking at a friend's house, or some fantastic sexual encounter in the offing. You would then hear some incredible jazz that would never be heard again, though it remained in your memory for the rest of your life. I can certainly attest to that. I have quietly thanked the Met for those thirteen spring tours. Life on the road could have its great excitements and enticements!

The only real hardship for me in the six weeks of touring was caused by the painful prospect of not seeing Marjorie for a seeming eternity. But then we figured out that she might be able to come to nearby Boston (where we played a whole week every year) for a brief visit, and that, if she went home to visit her folks in Fargo, she could come to nearby Minneapolis for two or three days about midway through the tour, and thus break up our long separation.

After three or four weeks on the road the level of my own libidinal frustrations, not only unassuaged for all that time but also subjected to all manner of temptations, easily encountered on the road—I might as well be absolutely candid about it—would easily reach uncontrollable heights of intensity.[22] What to do about that? There certainly was no easy answer. It took a few years before I could develop some reasonable, realistic, accommodative modus vivendi.

As much as I had been looking forward to the Met's spring tour in 1946, I was terribly disappointed, even shocked, at what I found in Baltimore, our first stop. With all the traveling I had done since the Ballet Theatre tour in 1943, I had seen a lot of inner cities but nothing as depressing and disturbing as downtown Baltimore. In fact, in all of my six decades plus of peripatetic traveling, I have never seen anything as depressing again (except in New Orleans in the black ghetto and the legendary Storyville section of town, and another time in the shantytown outskirts of Rio de Janeiro). I knew, of course, about port cities, and that their waterfront districts were usually the sleaziest sections of town, but I was not prepared for what I encountered in Baltimore. Not that I was specifically looking for anything like slums. It was rather that the opera house, the Lyric Theatre, a huge wooden rambling barn of a place (with, however, wonderful acoustics—I loved playing there), was located quite close to both the waterfront and the nightclub area, the latter known as "sin city." (Fortunately, in the 1980s, Baltimore's waterfront, following Boston's example, was completely sanitized, modernized, and beautified.)

On my first day there, heading from my hotel for the Peabody Conservatory of Music, I got lost and found myself suddenly in one of Baltimore's several slum areas, what I gathered to be the "white trash" part of town. It was gruesome: nothing but run-down, often windowless houses, garbage strewn everywhere, alleys littered with abandoned stoves, broken-down sofas, beds, piles of age-old moldy lumber, and yards filled with automobile parts, broken bottles, and more garbage. It was for me, shielded by my sheltered middle-class background, a terrible example of American twentieth-century civilization. Even in the black section of Cincinnati I never saw anything as horrific. I was told in our subsequent annual visits to Baltimore that during World War II the city had experienced a tremendous influx, in the thousands, of what were called "hillbillies" from the mountains of West Virginia, who found well-paying work in the wartime plants. But now that the war was over, most of them were out of work and living in utter poverty. I should point out that what I witnessed in those days in Baltimore was not what occurred two decades later in hundreds of American inner cities, what came to be called the "white flight." The Baltimore slums I saw in 1946 had nothing to do with white flight or inner city abandonment; the area was fully populated, in fact, probably over-populated—meaning that many thousands of people actually lived in that squalor and social chaos. The next day, I did find the Peabody Conservatory without any trouble, and heard a very nice rehearsal of the school's orchestra. After seeing more of Baltimore I felt better about the city. Margie and I were fortunate to have three wonderful days together in the first few weeks of the tour when, between her voice and piano lessons in New York, she was able to come to Boston. It was for both of us our first time in that fair city, the legendary "Athens of America," the country's first great citadel of culture, and the place Margie and I would some two decades later make our permanent home.

In the midforties Boston was still very old-English, so different from the frantic hustle and bustle of New York. We couldn't get enough of Boston's vast array of cultural offerings, from its renowned Museum of Fine Arts, its old-world downtown, so rich with the historic beginnings of our country, and its splendid harbor, to its extraordinarily lively jazz scene. We visited most of the jazz clubs near Copley Square. Vividly embedded in my memory is the soulful, stylistically pure artistry of Frankie Newton and Vic Dickenson. I can see and hear them as if it were yesterday: profoundly moving, expressive music making—not just displays of technical virtuosity—and at the same time wonderfully entertaining.

We also spent a great evening at the famous Totem Pole in Noremberg Park, billed as the "smartest and largest dance hall in the country." The Les Brown Band was in residence, featuring the beautiful Doris Day and the band's outstanding comedian-vocalist-saxophonist, Butch Stone, enthusiastically offering the orchestra's signature hits, *Bizet Has His Day* (a swinging take-off on one of *Carmen*'s most fetching themes), *A Good Man Is Hard To Find*, and *Sentimental Journey*, Doris Day's big hit. Although we spent a fortune in cab fares getting to the Totem Pole—some fifteen miles west of Boston—and back again to our downtown Statler Hotel, it was well worth the effort and expense just to see the place. As I revisit it in my memory's eye, it was in the shape of an amphitheatre and encompassed a huge dance floor, with a long, massive, slightly tilted pole holding up a gigantic sloping tent ceiling. The entire circle of rising tiers was furnished with hundreds of little couches (just for two) with a table and lamp, very dimly and seductively lit. When we arrived at the Totem Pole, the place was mobbed with several thousand dancing couples pressed together like herrings. We had to slash our way through this mass of humanity to the bandstand in order to hear the music, the throng of milling bodies acting like a soundproof wall. I think it was a wise policy at the Totem Pole, unusual back then, to sell only soft drinks, absolutely no liquor. There would otherwise have been murder and mayhem most nights.[23]

Our Museum of Fine Arts visit was an especially revelatory experience, as it introduced me for the first time to the paintings of Constable and Turner in a special exhibition gathered from many American and European collections. I was fascinated by Turner's prophetic, visionary abstractions of sky and cloud pictures, such as *Rain, Steam and Speed*, or *Rockets and Blue Lights*. Even the titles sound rather twentieth century. They reminded me immediately of Debussy's *Images*. It seemed to me, so my diary suggests, that Turner must have been "the first major artist to be primarily concerned with the painting of light, while relegating the main subject matter to a secondary status." I had seen similar paintings only by late nineteenth-century impressionists, especially Monet and Pissaro. Here Turner was doing a similar thing almost a whole century earlier. And, of course, as someone addicted to a love of color, Turner's pastel-like use of yellows, whites, pinks, light blues, and grays fascinated me no end. As for Constable, at first I didn't get the connection usually made between his work and Turner's. But in that exhibition I saw that Constable also concentrated on the skies and weather and light, which in turn influenced his depiction of nature, of trees and broad English landscapes. In contrast to Turner, Constable did not veil and camouflage his intended subject matter, but suffused it with an infinite variety of shadings and gradations. My diary notes that "I had never seen such lyrically and limitlessly nuanced inflections of greens."

As if exploring that exhibit wasn't overwhelming and exhausting enough, we plunged ahead to examine the museum's famous collections of Oriental and Asian art, Persian fourteenth- to sixteenth-century paintings and manuscripts, and Egyptian tombs and statues. Our senses were reeling from all this magnificence; and I can't explain how we had the energy and persistence to take it all in—all in one day. To confirm how truly crazy I was—and perhaps still am—my diary recounts that after that museum visit, I copied quite a bit of Stravinsky's *Symphony of Psalms* into one of my notebooks—that is, before dining at O Sole Mio, one of our favorite Italian restaurants in Boston, then catching a show at the Casino Burlesque, and *then* heading out to the Totem Pole—all in one day!

The next morning, still exhausted from our extensive museum visit, we nonetheless went sightseeing in the old historic section of town. We visited most of the important points of interest along the so-called Freedom Trail: Benjamin Franklin's birthplace, King's Chapel and the Old Grannery burying ground, the Old Market section, Faneuil Hall, Old North Church (of Paul Revere fame), and so forth. We climbed up the North Church tower and had a wonderful view of Boston harbor—at a time, mind you, when Boston was still a *very* busy seaport, with many major transatlantic passenger ships docked at its piers. It is in the Grannery burying ground that I first saw the great American sculptor Augustus Saint-Gaudens's famous bas-relief sculpture, *Col. Shaw and His Colored Regiment*, celebrated in the first movement of Charles Ives's orchestral set *Three Places in New England*—a work that I had not heard of then, but which I programmed many times later in my conducting career.

On a second visit to the museum, after Margie had returned to New York, I discovered several superb, virtually photographic still lifes of one of the greatest seventeenth-century Flemish painters, Pieter Claesz. And then by chance I stumbled into a whole room full of Millets, the painter whose work I had fallen in love with and written several papers on in my one year at Jamaica High School.

A very important discovery for me was Boston's Central Public Library (on Copley Square), where I found a stupendous, all-embracing music collection. I had no choice but to spend much of the remaining days of my Boston stay at the library, frantically copying into my excerpt books everything from pieces by Guillaume Dufay, Philippe de Vitry, and Gilles Binchois to Henry Eichheim and Arnold Bax, and parts of a beautiful, little-known Villa-Lobos song cycle (*Serestas*), as well as Schönberg's astonishingly visionary *Herzgewächse* (for high soprano, celesta, harp, and harmonium).[24] Additionally, in connection with the special prerelease showings of Laurence Olivier's *Henry the Fifth*—which we saw quite by chance on our first day in Boston—the library had thoughtfully pulled together an exhibition of music from that era, including certain songs associated with the battle of Agincourt in 1400. The Boston Central Public Library was more like a great museum, and through the years continued to be one of my favorite haunts in Boston.

Apart from picking up and studying lots of music previously unknown to me at the library, I discovered a fabulous music store in Boston, Homeyer's. For me it was like a five-year-old's toy store; everywhere I turned my eyes fell upon wonderful and extraordinary things, especially many foreign-published scores. I bought a rather sizable miscellany of scores as diverse as the Palestrina Preludes of Pfitzner, several works by Paul Gräner and Albert Roussel, Milhaud's wonderful jazzy *Piano Concertino*, Stravinsky's brand-new *Scènes de ballet*, Miaskovsky's *Sinfonietta for Strings*, and, most gratifyingly, because I had been trying to buy it for years and could never find it, one of my absolute favorite Scriabin works, his Op. 65 Etudes—all this music, as I recall, cost a mere twenty dollars.

On a second visit to Homeyer's, I more or less cleaned out their stock of four-hand piano arrangements, things such as Respighi's *Pines* and *Fountains of Rome*, Rachmaninov's Third Symphony, Ravel's *Rhapsodie espagnole*, Strauss's *Sinfonia domestica*, Ibert's *Escales*, Eichheim's *Oriental Impressions*, and more—all for twenty-three dollars.[25] Those were the days!

In cities such as Boston or Cleveland or Chicago, where we stayed typically for a week, the Met's offerings would include some of the "big" operas, such as *Rosenkavalier*, *Walküre*, and

Tristan, with some of the most outstanding and challenging virtuoso horn parts. On such evenings in those major cities, the local symphony horn players would usually be in attendance. In Boston that spring of 1946, the entire horn section of the Boston Symphony showed up for *Rosenkavalier* and sat very near the pit, where they could see and hear us best. (I don't know how they were able to afford those expensive orchestra seats, usually reserved for the wealthiest dressed-to-the-nines opera patrons; perhaps they had some pull with the Boston Opera House management.) That's where I first met Jimmy Stagliano, Harry Shapiro, Harold Meek, and Hugh Cowden, the outstanding BSO horn section of that time. And like many horn sections that I've known, this "gang of four" was quite a notorious drinking bunch, led by Stagliano, their irrepressible leader, whose playing I admired very much.

After the performance they all came to the stage door and invited me to go out with them. They were my seniors by several years and already famous players, so, as a relative unknown, I was flattered to be asked to join them. Little did I know what I was in for. I was never a member of the typical hard-drinking horn fraternity. These Bostoners quickly sensed this and tried to do something about it. I was clearly too innocent for them. They began to ply me with straight scotch, a drink I generally avoided—preferring gin or wine—primarily because I easily got sick on scotch. I wanted to keep up with my famous quaffing colleagues and not show them what a timid drinker I really was; but there is something special about hard-drinking horn players (and other brass players), namely, when they sense that one of them is averse to tilting a few (with what they consider an unmanly reticence), they zero in on their victim, doing their best to shame him into a fine state of inebriety. It was quite a struggle, but I survived fairly well by invoking a technique I had learned on the Ballet Theatre tour. There, when some of the musicians and dancers had attempted to get me drunk, or at least a bit high, the more and the faster they drank—and began showing it—the more I slowed down the pace of *my* imbibing. That night in Boston was not the last time I had to pass this particular horn fraternity ritual and macho test!

By unanimous consensus the Boston Opera House, located on Huntington Avenue a few blocks from Symphony Hall, was considered one of the top three opera houses in the United States, especially renowned for its extraordinary acoustics. I recall vividly how much we in the Met looked forward to playing there, especially as compared to some of the "barns" or gargantuan municipal auditoria we had to perform in on tour. Admittedly, the Boston Opera House, built in 1908, was not the most inspired edifice architecturally; and its musicians' quarters, a dark, labyrinthian, dungeonlike cavern directly below the stage, was a horror. Six feet tall, I had to lean forward and down in order to negotiate among the steamer trunks, bass and cello cases, etc., so as not to hit my head on the vast accumulation of steam pipes, electric conduits, and ducts protruding from the low ceiling. It also seemed that the place had not been dusted or cleaned in half a century, and there was no musicians' lounge or locker room to escape to. But the acoustics were glorious, we could hear everything clearly—singers and the whole orchestra—no matter where we sat in the pit, which more than compensated for all the other inconveniences.

What most of us musicians and Boston opera lovers have bemoaned for many years is the fact that, through a shady political deal with the city and local real estate people, the Boston Opera House was suddenly razed in the early 1950s and the land ceded to Northeastern University. The only slight homage paid the departed opera house is that the name of the street on which it was located, Opera Place, was retained. I have driven past that street hundreds of times since I moved to Boston, and rare is the occasion when I don't shed a silent inner tear.

The most memorable experience during Margie's three-day Boston visit was a trek out to Walden Pond, the famous, almost hallowed place about fifteen miles west of Boston where Henry David Thoreau built a cabin, living there in solitude for two years, applying his doctrine of self-sufficiency, of living with, learning from, and respecting nature.[26] We happened to pick a perfect time to visit Walden Pond, early April on a mildly overcast day, a late spring frost still hanging in the air. There wasn't a soul out there besides us: no sign of modern civilization, only nature in its most pristine perfection. As we stood there on the banks of the pond, in awed contemplation of the utter faultlessness of the sight before us, we could feel and hear nature breathing. It was so beautiful—and so spectacular in its quiet grandeur. I remember one particular experience. Standing there in this virginal sanctuary, the slow movement of the "Heiliger Dankgesang" section of Beethoven's Op. 132 Quartet suddenly floated into my mind, one of the master's most perfect contemplative and introspective statements—and the most profound expression of individualism.

What a relief it was to see Margie again several weeks later, in early May on the Met's three-day weekend in Minneapolis. I can't express how thrilled I was to see her step off that train from Fargo, how absolutely beautiful she looked. I could hardly contain or restrain myself. Only common decency and propriety kept me from crushing her in my arms as the taxi drove us to the Curtis Hotel.

After more than forty years of the so-called sexual revolution and the general loosening of sexual mores, only older readers will remember that unmarried couples were not permitted to stay in the same hotel room, could barely even visit in daytime, and that a host of house detectives—sardonically called and aptly named "house dicks"—and front-desk personnel saw to it that such assignations did not take place. (Hollywood films could not at that time even show a *married* couple sleeping in the same bed!) Margie and I dutifully checked into two separate rooms, on two separate floors, and then did what we felt compelled to do to pacify our immediate needs—house detectives notwithstanding.

We had three glorious days together with luxuries like breakfast in bed and room service more or less around the clock. But we also visited the Walker Art Center, a wonderful museum with (originally) a famous collection of paintings of the so-called Hudson River School by George Innes, Thomas Cole, and Frederic Church, all favorites of mine.[27] We also climbed the twelve-story Foshay Tower, at that time the tallest building in Minneapolis, and indeed in the entire Midwest. The Foshay Tower is now virtually invisible, surrounded as it is by a dense throng of gigantic skyscrapers.

At one point, most surprisingly, I had three days off from the Met tour. So I decided to fly to Cincinnati. I was mightily drawn to the city where I had spent two wonderful years, and now could visit once again with my many friends there. I was received like a combination prodigal son and returning hero. I also made one new friend who was to play a significant role in my life, since within not too many years she married one of Margie's cousins, William Bunce, thus becoming "family" and part of the large Black clan. I met Nancy Freeto the first time on that Cincinnati visit, a beautiful girl and, like Margie, musically doubly talented: concert-mistress of the college orchestra and additionally blessed with a lovely rich mezzo-soprano voice. I was quite taken with her, and during the three days I was in Cincy, I took her out several times, including a wonderful return visit at the Hangar and an evening of great jazz. In his youth, Margie's cousin Bill Bunce loved Dixieland jazz, and for a while took a swing at playing the trombone, just for fun. (Both Bill and Nancy, now senior citizens and still happily married, are enjoying a life of retirement and leisure in sunny Arizona.)

On that Cincinnati visit I also met for the first time Roland Johnson, a very talented conductor, who was for many years music director of the Madison (Wisconsin) Civic Orchestra and of the local opera company. Within hours of getting to know Roland I knew that he was a musical soul mate, and particularly one whose interests in music and the other arts were almost as wide-ranging as mine. We knew instantly that we were destined to be close, long-time friends.

I heard one bit of disappointing news, namely, that Emil Heermann had been fired both at the Symphony and at the College of Music. It was sad because his playing at age sixty-one was still at a very high level (as can easily be heard on the Cincinnati Symphony's wonderful recording of Stravinsky's *Le Rossignol* Suite, with its many tricky little violin solos). Of course, he had been playing in Cincinnati for over thirty years, but still. Even sadder was the news that Walter, Emil's brother, decided, probably in sympathy, to resign from the orchestra—two of my best Cincinnati friends gone.

The Met tour continued on to Milwaukee, Chicago (giving seven performances in the famous Insull Opera House), St. Louis, Dallas, Memphis, and ended in Chattanooga on May 22. In St. Louis, while wandering around downtown near the Mississippi River levee, I suddenly realized that I was walking on hallowed ground. Only someone interested in jazz and its predecessor, ragtime, would have been aware that some of the bars and clubs on the old waterfront, including the legendary Rosebud Café, were the old haunts where ragtime first flourished at the start of the twentieth century, and where Scott Joplin reigned supreme. Of course, no ragtime was being played there in 1946, and the Rosebud and other former hang-outs where all the great turn-of-the-century ragtimers had played—showing off their pianis-tic bag of tricks, competing in "cutting contests"—were now reduced to pretty seedy looking bars. But the rundown condition and bleak atmosphere of these places, some of them now offering sound movies and mildly sexy peepshows, did not keep me from conjuring up Tom Turpin (bartender-owner of the Rosebud and early ragtime composer), Scott Joplin, James Scott, Joseph Lamb, and Artie Matthews—even the great "Jelly Roll" Morton—beating on the ivories all night long, playing in smoke-filled rooms for a conglomeration of card sharks, gamblers, pool hustlers, pimps and prostitutes, Mississippi levee workers and longshoremen. Little did I realize then that many years later I would help bring about the revival of ragtime.

Another retrospective jazz vision came to me in Dallas when I stayed at the Adolphus Hotel, where famous to me Alphonso Trent, one of the three greatest jazz orchestras of the 1920s—perhaps *the* best of them all—held forth for almost two years. What was unusual, indeed unheard of, was that Trent and his orchestra were black. It was unprecedented back then for black musicians in the Deep South to be engaged to play in a white hotel—and cer-tainly not for two years. Though barely remembered nowadays, Trent's orchestra was legend-ary among black musicians in the Midwest and Southwest, who considered it even better than the two big east coast orchestras of Fletcher Henderson and Duke Ellington. But by staying almost entirely in the Southwest, not playing in the East until the midthirties, the Trent band was overlooked by the eastern record companies; they ultimately recorded only nine titles on a poorly distributed label. (Ellington and Henderson made *hundreds* of recordings.)

I had read about the Trent orchestra, and that Jimmie Lunceford and Fletcher Henderson felt that the Trent band was the greatest, the one they tried to emulate, the most advanced, the most perfected in its ensemble work. Moreover, the Trent orchestra sported an amazing roster of soloists, this at a time, by the way, when the extemporized jazz solo as such had just barely been "invented" by Louis Armstrong. I realized I was on hallowed ground when one morning I stumbled almost by chance onto the Adolphus Hotel ballroom, looking for a piano so that I could do some composing. As I sat there in that huge empty space I could envision the Trent band, dressed impeccably in silk shirts and immaculate uniforms, which they changed several times in the course of an evening. I could see them pulling up to the Adolphus in a fleet of Cadillac touring cars, proud and erect, enjoying their tremendous popularity and basking in the knowledge that they were making $150 a week, when other bands, white or black, were earning between $25 and $45 weekly![28]

When the Met got to Chicago, I began my exploration of the city's famous South Side, where, as in mid-Manhattan, there were dozens of jazz clubs, many legendary ones dating back to the twenties, when great jazz pioneers such as King Oliver, Louis Armstrong, Sidney Bechet, Earl Hines, Jimmy Noone, Bessie Smith, and Jelly Roll Morton were shaping the Golden Age of jazz. I had already read about Chicago's remarkable history during the early days of jazz: the legendary clubs and dance halls where the greats of that era plied their craft. Many of these venues were still around in 1946—so that I could really appreciate where so much great music had been created.

Sentimentalist and nostalgist that I am, it was something special to walk into the basement Apex Club, where Jimmy Noone had held forth for years with legendary companions such as Kid Ory, Johnny St. Cyr, Teddy Weatherford; or the old Sunset Café, later renamed The Grand Terrace, where Armstrong and Earl Hines once had revolutionized jazz. But there were also dozens of newer smaller clubs that had sprung up during the recent war years, when jazz and dancing and floorshows were among the absolute necessities of life to escape the hardships of war-related work and double factory shifts. There were also a few big, fancy, ostentatious nightclubs, such as the Rhumboogie and the Club de Lisa, all located in a relatively small area bounded by Thirty-Fifth Street and Calumet Avenue.

I didn't sleep much during that week in Chicago, preferring to spend as much time as possible on the South Side, not just to hear whatever jazz I could stumble upon but also to observe the whole exciting nightlife, to soak in the heady wide-open atmosphere for which Chicago was renowned. This part of Chicago never seemed to sleep; the entertainment went on around the clock. I had experienced the same kind of scene in Cincinnati, but not on Chicago's heightened scale. There was no way that you could exhaust Chicago's nightlife in one week. Unlike in New York or Cincinnati where I would have almost daily rehearsals in the mornings, with the Met on tour we never had any. So I took my fill of that frantic Chicago scene, either not sleeping at all or finally plopping into bed sometime around nine in the morning. In those days nightclubs, jazz clubs, restaurants—what have you—stayed open until four a.m. But that was the hour when the South Side came truly alive, when the after-hours jam sessions started and the dozens of breakfast clubs began their operations. My memories of that week are now a grand blur, but there is among all that fast-paced dizzying excitement one event that stands out even after all these many years, because it meant so much to me. That was meeting, quite by chance, the great Joe Williams, long before he became known as "the great Joe Williams."

I had heard that the Andy Kirk band was playing at the Club de Lisa, a cavernous, lavish entertainment palace with floorshows, ballroom dancing, and name jazz acts. I had been quite taken with Kirk's band, owning many of its recordings from the early Mary Lou Williams days and one of my favorite tenor players, Dick Wilson, to more recent 1942 discs, two of which were so popular that they were on jukeboxes all over the country for two years. (That's the equivalent to now being high up on the charts for weeks and months). These two new compositions had become a big hit; *Boogie Woogie Cocktail* was by Kirk's pianist, Kenny Kersey, the other, *McGhee Special*, was composed by the modern proto-bebop trumpeter Howard McGhee. As a brass-playing colleague I had hoped to hear and meet McGhee at the de Lisa, but he had, unbeknownst to me, just left the Kirk band to form his own group.

When the last regular show finished at four a.m., the club's house band of local musicians took over for the breakfast club part of the entertainment. I wasn't ready to go home to my hotel, and am I glad I stayed. For suddenly I heard a beautiful rich baritone voice among the general din of clinking glasses and animated conversations, delivering some typical ballads (not blues) of the day. During a break I went up to the singer and invited him to a drink, telling him how much I admired his singing, and that I was here in Chicago with the Metropolitan Opera, and that I dug jazz. Acting a bit diffident at first, he perked up at the mention of the Met, I suppose assuming that I was also a singer. He said his name was Joe Williams. (I found out later that his real name was Joseph Goreed.) When I told him that I played the horn and had hoped to hear McGhee, that I was practicing some of the Dizzy Gillespie trumpet licks I had heard on the new Billy Eckstine band recordings (especially *Opus X* and *Blowing the Blues Away*), and *how much* I loved Eckstine's singing, he seemed amazed that this white kid with a horn was digging his music.

As we continued to talk, it turned out that Joe had already sung and toured with the Kirk band some years earlier, but now preferred to stay in Chicago, his hometown, and sit in with the de Lisa's house band, singing for tips. All his life he had dreamt of becoming a classical singer, performing at the Met. He knew full well that that was impossible. And yet, rather timidly, he asked me whether I could introduce him to somebody, perhaps one of the coaches at the Met. On second thought he admitted what a wild pipe dream that was.

Hearing him sing several times that morning—and again the next night—I realized that here was a black man in his late twenties, with a beautiful, natural, perfectly placed voice, who could easily have sung at the Met or some other major American opera house—if the world were right.

That Joe was good enough and more or less ready to enter the world of classical music was clear to me when the next night I went again to the Club de Lisa, mainly to hang out with him some more. He suddenly asked me if I'd like to hear him sing some classical music, since he knew several arias from Verdi's *Trovatore* and *Traviata*. Sure, I said, I'd love to. He took me backstage into the kitchen, where everyone knew him—"Hey, big Joe. How'ya doin'?"—probably wondering, who's this white kid with Joe? Whereupon, far off in a corner where food cartons and supplies were stacked, he sang—not quite in full voice—bits of the opera arias he had mentioned. Yeah, he could have been at the Met; it was a fully matured voice, not unlike that of Leonard Warren's, but with a more vibrant resonance.

We eventually parted company, feeling that we had known each other all our lives.[29] We promised—and hoped—to see each other again soon, perhaps on my next trip to Chicago. As it turned out, we became lifelong friends, often went out together with our wives whenever Joe, in later years, got to New York, especially during his Basie years when he appeared at Birdland many, many times.

The last time I saw Joe, his voice at age eighty-four (!) still perfectly intact (no strain, no wobble, pure and open, beautifully projecting, and with his always impeccable diction) was when I invited him to sing at my Sandpoint Summer Festival in Idaho in 1988.

Around the middle of that Met tour I felt the urge to write again for the cello. In retrospect I find this rather surprising, since I had already written a big, difficult two-movement Cello Concerto, and one would think that I might now have preferred to choose some other instrument. But once again it was a convergence of influences that prompted me to return to the cello. It was just about my favorite instrument, with its rich, mellow, middle-register warmth, so close in many respects to the horn. (My transcription of Bloch's *Schelomo* might be considered reasonable evidence of that.) Furthermore, pieces such as Kodaly's remarkably innovative Sonata for Solo Cello, Bach's six suites, Beethoven's cello sonatas, of course the Dvořák and Boccherini concertos, as well as the beautiful cello ensembles by Verdi (*Otello*) and Puccini (*Tosca*)—were all somehow constantly in my mind, in my ear. And I seemed to be continually surrounded by outstanding cellists:[30] Ernst Silberstein and Marcel Hubert at the Met; Leonard Rose, later Laszlo Varga, at the Philharmonic; Frank Miller, principal cellist of the NBC Symphony, later the Chicago Symphony; Walter Heermann in Cincinnati; not to mention the many superb Emanuel Feuermann recordings in my record collection. So when Silberstein, the Met's principal cellist at the time, approached me on the tour about writing something for him, I could not resist.

Beyond that, I was lured toward writing a sonata-form piece by my haunting memory of Krenek's Third Violin Sonata, the premiere of which I had heard the previous summer at Kenyon. I had really fallen in love with that piece while attending all of the preparatory rehearsals, turning pages for Steuermann at the premiere, and listening to Krenek coaching the performers, that is, *really* getting to know it intimately. What fascinated me especially about Krenek's piece was that he had connected the very new, modern composing technique of twelve-tone with fifteenth-century isorhythmic concepts. It was a totally novel idea to me. What was also unusual in Krenek's piece—which I was now tempted to emulate—was his use of long meters, that is, notating his music in breves rather than quarter notes, in meters such as 4/2, 3/2, 5/2, as opposed to 4/4, 3/4, 5/4. I hadn't seen such meters since my choir-boy days at St. Thomas, where we sang a lot of older music notated in that breve manner. I knew that most modern and, for that matter, most nineteenth-century symphonic music had abandoned the old ecclesiastic modes of notation, and that writing in breves had lingered on only in church music. I decided to try that in the cello piece. Krenek had also experimented with vertically uncoordinated meters and bar lines to make visually clear in some of the more polyphonic sections of the work the relative independence and metric diversity of the individual contrapuntal lines.

Much of my new piece—I called it *Duo Concertante*—was composed during our four-day stay in St. Louis, and a little bit more in Memphis. I discovered on tour that most hotels would let me use their ballroom piano, especially in the mornings or early afternoons. The fact that waiters and other hotel personnel would be rather noisily busy, cleaning up from the previous evening's dinner dance, didn't bother me at all; I always had the ability to mentally isolate myself from outside noises and concentrate totally on my work. On the other hand, I did often wonder what the waiters thought about some guy sitting at the piano, occasionally eliciting totally unintelligible, weird sounds from the keyboard. (After all, I wasn't playing Irving Berlin songs or something they might know or like.)

The work that evolved in those weeks on tour, composed in the Schönberg-Krenek twelve-tone technique (my very first attempt at this), was stylistically and formally much more severe than I had at first anticipated: the first movement full of rigorous contrapuntal and canonic designs, the second a set of half a dozen rather strictly organized variations, and the last movement a Passacaglia. But as I worked on the piece, while I felt that much of what I had written was quite good, I also felt that maybe it wasn't really me, and instinctively, gradually, in the middle of the last movement Passacaglia I lost faith in the piece and abandoned it.[31] There it lay, undisturbed on the proverbial shelf for fifty-five years, until sometime in 2001 when a dear friend of mine, Ken Radnofsky, who had a talented cello-playing daughter, heard about the work and asked me whether it was something his daughter could play in her graduation recital. I told Ken the sad saga of the work, whereupon, undaunted, he begged me to have another look at it, suggesting that "maybe you'll find it to be better than you think." Well, lo and behold, when I looked at it I discovered that I had been too severe in my judgment fifty-five years earlier; in fact, the work really looked quite good. I decided to make some revisions, as necessary. It turned out that the first movement required largely cosmetic, minor editing, while the second movement needed more critical repairs (corrections, reconstructions, prunings), and serious and extensive revisions were made in the third movement. The upshot was that my long-suffering *Duo Concertante* was finally premiered and played in late 2002 and early 2003 by about sixty cellists all over the United States and Europe, in multiple, virtually simultaneous world premieres.[32]

Our 1946 Met tour ended in Chattanooga—not much jazz there! All I could think about was getting back to New York to see Margie after nearly three weeks of separation. I was so frantic to see her that instead of taking the train with the rest of the company, I flew directly to LaGuardia Airport at my own expense. Our joyful reunion made our lives whole again, the tensions and frustrations of loneliness on the road evaporating in no time.

It was exciting to look forward to a summer of composing, studying, and plunging back into New York's exuberant cultural life. But there was one concern: would I find any work in the summer? The 1946–47 Met season wouldn't start until late October. Would anybody call me for jobs? As luck would have it, those concerns were almost immediately laid to rest.

Chapter Six

PLUMBING THE DEPTHS OF NEW YORK'S CULTURAL SCENE

EVEN ON MY VERY FIRST DAY back in New York, after six weeks of touring and a passionate afternoon reunion with Margie—I wrote in one of my rare diary entries, "what a relief to get even with Mother Nature"—that same evening we went to the Three Deuces on Fifty-Second Street to hear Bill de Arango's[1] Quintet (with the fine supportive pianist, Tony Aless) and a Charlie Ventura group featuring the young Danish-American trombonist Kai Winding and the wonderfully gifted, constantly inventive (only twenty-year-old) Shelly Manne.

All kinds of momentous things were happening in jazz at the time. The transition from the Swing Era to bebop was in full force. Recording companies that had sprung up after the war, several of them only months old, were discovering the new music and saw enough economic potential in it to invest in these young turks and their novel music. For me, having waited for years for advances in jazz (harmonic, melodic, rhythmic, formal-structural) that would, I hoped, supersede the increasing stultification and commercialization of swing music, the mid-forties were incredibly exciting. In addition to the Gillespie Sextet and Quintet recordings, some with Charlie Parker, that came out at midyear on Guild and one year later on Ross Russell's Dial label, there were the first Tristano discs, many breakthrough recordings by the Herman, Kenton, and Boyd Raeburn bands, and, of course, in late 1946 Dizzy's exciting new big band. (An earlier attempt in 1945 to maintain a big band was short lived.)

One of my new friends at the Met was Bob Boyd, the new first trombone in the orchestra, and he was also very interested in jazz. He and I used to play famous bebop licks together during rehearsal intermissions, passages from Dizzy Gillespie or Billy Eckstine recordings. Our playing annoyed some of the elderly European born musicians who hated jazz, thought it was a cheap, noisy, primitive music that should certainly not be allowed in the hallowed precincts of an opera house. It was through Bob Boyd that I met Barry Ulanov as well as George Simon, the two major jazz writers and critics of the time (along with Leonard Feather), writing in *Metronome* magazine, the more progressive competitor of *DownBeat*. One day in late 1946 Barry called me, saying that he had an advance acetate pressing of an incredible new recording that Dizzy and his band had recently made. It was called *Things to Come*. When I heard that music that evening at Barry's house, I couldn't believe my ears. I had never heard six trumpets (in unison) play running eighth notes so fast. (I had, in fact, never heard *any* music written at such a fast tempo, about ♩ = 366, ♩ = 72). The sheer virtuosity and energy of the performance was matched by the daring of the composition's zigzagging musical gestures. Coming away from Barry's house, shaking my head in disbelief at what I had heard, I thought to myself that these guys were breaking the sound barrier in music, and that no classical musicians I knew could play music that fast—and that well.

Barry also told me that he had been at a rehearsal of Lennie Tristano's Trio for a recording that was going to come out in early 1947 on the Keynote label, and that it included atonal versions of *I Can't Get Started* and *Out on a Limb*. This was exactly the kind of news I had been waiting and hoping for. Somebody might say, well, what's so good about atonal jazz? What does atonal music have to do with jazz? The answer, like it or not, is that ever since jazz arose as a new musical idiom in the 1910s and 1920s, it gradually and systematically replicated the whole harmonic-melodic development in classical music, from the simplest diatonic-triadic language to tonal atonality, as in today's "free jazz" improvisations and other works no longer based on traditional chord changes. These harmonic developments were initiated most prominently by Duke Ellington already in the 1930s, and soon thereafter by various other forward-looking jazz musicians. In 1933 Red Norvo composed and recorded the first (partly) atonal piece in jazz that I know of, a quartet for marimba, guitar, bass, and Benny Goodman on bass clarinet, called *Dance of the Octopus*. And Jimmie Lunceford in 1934 composed and recorded *Stratosphere* with his band, daringly reaching out several times toward bitonality and atonality.

In any case, it was in those 1946 to 1947 years that experiments in stretching the harmonic language of jazz (as well as its rhythmic and structural syntax) really evolved on a wide concerted front. Not *all* of this music was necessarily great; how could it be? But some of it surely was. For many of us young folks it was an exciting time in that jazz exploded in all kinds of different stylistic directions, including at last harmonically.

My record collection was growing by leaps and bounds, and, of course, Margie and I took in as much live jazz as we could, feasting on all the remarkable music that was available in the world capital of jazz, New York. One evening in 1946 at the very popular Café Society Uptown stands out in my memory because it combined a great disappointment with an otherwise wonderfully exhilarating evening of fine music, made even more memorable by enjoying it in the company of Joe Williams and his wife. The disappointment was that Sarah Vaughan, whom we had expressly gone to hear, had had a fight with the club's owner and had canceled the rest of her engagement. But we were compensated for Sarah's absence by an alternatively great show. It featured the black comedian Timmie Rogers, whose hilarious routine "Good Whiskey and a Bad Woman," with its half-dozen hilarious sense-twisting title inversions and variations, I had already seen and heard twice before on the road. I enjoyed it all over again. (I had never heard Margie laugh so loud, and, as a singer, her bell-like laugh was resounding, to say the least). We also heard the great pianist Hank Jones—live the first time for me—accompanied by George Treadwell, Café Society's house drummer. As if that weren't enough, Joe introduced me to Billy Strayhorn (oddly enough, the only time I ever met him) and Pete Johnson, two other outstanding pianists who had also come to hear Sarah and Hank. This was just one of many similar evenings that Margie and I could enjoy almost any time, any evening; it was exemplary of the kind of high-level entertainment one could regularly experience in New York in those years.

In the meantime, I hadn't been home more than a few days from the Met tour when I was called for two substantial horn-playing jobs. First, I heard through Mr. Schulze that I had been invited back to play first horn with the New York Philharmonic at Lewisohn Stadium. I guess somebody there liked my playing, but this time I was invited not for the whole summer season, just from early July to early August. Two days later—I shall never forget it—as I was wondering whether there might be some other work for me in June, in advance of the Philharmonic gig, I was rehired by Morris Stonzek to return to *The Song of Norway*. What a godsend! Stonzek told me that he and the orchestra had missed me during the seven months I had been playing, as he put it with a smile, "in that other pit, down there on Broadway and Fortieth." I must admit I was filled with pride. It was not the kind of talk one ever heard in the tough, sometimes rather cynical music business.

I played *The Song of Norway* show until my contract with the Philharmonic required me to move literally overnight from Broadway and Forty-Fourth Street northward to the amphitheater at 138th Street and Convent Avenue. In retrospect, I wonder whether I fully appreciated how fortunate I was to be so continuously employed during the summer, which in those days was generally a fallow period of employment for musicians, and to be able to perform first-rate music and at the highest professional levels.

I shifted quickly from Grieg's music to the full range of the Philharmonic's repertory. The first two conductors I encountered were Laszlo Halasz, with whom I had worked so satisfyingly two years earlier at the New York City Opera, and Pierre Monteux, in my first chance to work with him. Halasz was a good conductor, but somehow he had changed in the intervening years. Although he was quite pleasant with me, he seemed to be much more short-tempered and cynical working with the Philharmonic. I was disappointed.

Monteux was very special. Already a legendary hero to me for having brought Stravinsky's *Rite of Spring* to life in its world premiere in Paris, I realized in my first rehearsal with him that he was really stunningly gifted—what we call a born conductor. His wonderfully clear, simple yet expressive beat, his incredibly sharp ears (which to me meant sharp mind and deep knowledge), his gentlemanly, unostentatious podium behavior, the friendly twinkle in his eyes, the feeling he exuded that all of us on the stage were equals and that he was not superior to us just because he had a long stick in his hands—all these qualities were not only impressive but totally endearing.

Monteux's four programs with the Philharmonic were filled with superb music: Stravinsky's *Petroushka*, Debussy's *Afternoon of a Faun*, Ibert's 1922 *Escales* (one of my big favorites), and various Beethoven, Brahms, and Tchaikovsky symphonies, all done with impeccable taste and Gallic lucidity.

A somewhat lesser but nonetheless very welcome high point occurred when Leonard Bernstein conducted his new *Jeremiah* Symphony—with some wild, challenging horn parts, which I and my colleague Morris Secon (playing third horn) really relished and nailed with cocky exuberance, much to Lennie's delight. He also did Strauss's *Don Juan* and the inevitable *Firebird Suite*. Lennie winked at me when it came to the B-major horn solo near the end of the suite, remembering our meeting in Parkersburg, West Virginia.

The rest of the season comprised a lot of fairly mediocre evenings with Alexander Smallens, some popular light classics nights, several ballet evenings with Efrem Kurtz, whom some of us called "l'homme qui danse" because he danced on the podium almost as much as the dancers on stage. One early August concert brought all my Cincinnati friends who had moved to New York to the Lewisohn Stadium because Paula Lenchner had been engaged as guest artist in the "Letter Scene" from Tchaikovsky's *Eugene Onegin*. She sang very beautifully that night.

Meanwhile, many late evenings (after the Stadium concerts) were filled with great jazz, not only at the Pennsylvania and Statler hotels (Woody Herman and Stan Kenton) but also at the Aquarium (on Broadway and Forty-Seventh Street), where the Count Basie band was ensconced for weeks on end. In various other venues, we heard such bands as Buddy Rich's big band, John Kirby's Sextet, Andy Kirk's band (with Joe Williams), and the Sam Donahue and George Paxton orchestras.

The very day that the Stadium season ended, August 11, I was called to fill in on first horn in WOR's resident symphony orchestra, an engagement that developed into a lucrative and very interesting series of weekly evening broadcasts that lasted, conveniently, right up to the last week of October, when the Met preseason rehearsals were to start. An indication of how seriously the managements of these New York radio stations took their staff symphony orchestras is evident from the programs and the caliber of the music that was presented. No light classics here, or ephemeral dumbed-down arrangements of pop concert fare, but music of the highest quality, ranging, for example, from an all-Wagner program (with excerpts from *Tristan* and the *Ring* operas) to Beethoven's "O Du Abscheulischer!" aria from *Fidelio*, one of the most challenging horn excerpts in the entire nineteenth-century symphonic-operatic repertory. The soloists in the series were the likes of Eleanor Steber, Lawrence Tibbett, Gertrude Ribla, and the young African-American soprano Camilla Williams, who did a remarkable job with the formidable and at the time rarely performed "Casta Diva" aria from Bellini's *Norma*—an aria made world-famous years later by Maria Callas in her Met debut in 1956.

I was also fortunate to be asked to play on quite a number of recordings later that summer. I remember particularly a fine session of all-Mozart arias with Ezio Pinza and Bruno Walter, and, above all, a double session with Erich Leinsdorf and a top-notch freelance pick-up orchestra, recording Haydn's "Farewell" Symphony. I had been hired as second horn for the Haydn dates, with Joe Singer, the new co-principal horn of the New York Philharmonic, as first horn, but only for the morning session because he had a conflict with the afternoon date. Dick Moore had been engaged for that second session. The recording went well all day until, in the afternoon, we got to the very difficult last movement of Haydn's famous symphony, where the musicians leave one by one until only two violinists are left playing. What most people don't realize is that in that movement there is a series of the most precariously slippery horn passages in the entire late eighteenth-century orchestral literature. The first horn part lies very high in the altissimo A transposition, which for nonhornists may mean nothing—and which will hardly give present-day hornists, with their descant horns, a second thought—but for us, sixty years ago, playing our big double horns, it was quite a challenge to negotiate those high-lying Haydn horn parts with ease and absolute security.

Dick did not, as already mentioned, have a very easy high register, especially if the part required playing softly and delicately. When after three or four tries it became clear that he could not manage those final treacherous A horn passages, a ten-minute intermission was called, during which Leinsdorf suddenly asked me to take over the first chair. I was really torn, knowing that Dick would be deeply offended and would probably never forgive me, even though he had just been officially asked to move to second horn by the orchestra's contractor. On the other hand, I realized, and Leinsdorf reminded me, that the recording of the symphony could not be finished unless I or someone else stepped in and rescued the session—Haydn's symphony was composed for two horns, and thus it was either Dick or me, the only two horn players in the studio—which in the end is what I did. The solos went very well for me, and we were able to finish the session in time, just minutes before its scheduled termination. I was a hero to Leinsdorf and the recording supervisor, for I saved the company thousands of dollars by not having to reengage the entire orchestra to finish the recording some other day. To show that you can't always win, while most of the musicians congratulated me on my playing, happy that we were able to complete the recording, some others grumbled at me because they figured that had I not come to the rescue they would have had to be rehired for another session, and in that way would have made some extra money. Dick, of course, never forgave me—or at least not for a very long, long time.

Another recording came my way when I was called to play and appear—visible only in the distance, far back in the orchestra—in several sessions for the movie *Carnegie Hall*, with Leopold Stokowski conducting various orchestral excerpts including the slow movement of Tchaikovsky's Fifth Symphony. In the first date, a rather short session, they recorded us not in some famous piece of music but only in the tuning of an orchestra, as if just before a concert. They made four takes of us tuning and wasted a lot of time. We all fooled around a bit, showing off with various excerpts, and I recall playing a certain brief horn passage from the Beethoven

Fifth: an octave higher than written, and a loud lip-trill on a high

C. Many, many years later, watching that movie by chance on late-night television, I suddenly heard myself amongst all that orchestral din, playing that Beethoven lick, having never thought that what I played would actually project through.

The second session turned out to be one of the strangest and perversely ludicrous musical experiences I can recall in my long and varied career. I have already mentioned that Stokowski was one of the more eccentric and egotistic conductors of the twentieth century, an era when there was no shortage of ego-driven maestros. Having worked often with Stokowski, in a variety of circumstances, I will go further and state that he was 50 percent a remarkable sui generis genius,[2] and fifty percent a bona fide charlatan.

In the Tchaikovsky Fifth's slow movement there are any number of *ritardandos* and *ritenutos* in which many conductors—including Stokowski—were apt to indulge themselves in great distortive stretchings of tempo. One such passage occurs about three-quarters of the way through the

movement, where the soulful 12/8 melody in the strings

is accompanied by four horns, oboes, and clarinets in 4/4 (!) in sixteenth notes (four per beat), thus creating a fine four-against-three composite rhythm. Tchaikovsky writes *animando* in the third measure of the phrase, followed in the fourth measure by a counterbalancing *ritenuto*, thereby returning the phrase to its original tempo. We had all played "Tchaik Five" (as it is called by seasoned professionals) many times, and had long ago learned to follow conductors' tempo modifications, no matter how extreme or irrational they might be. Indeed, with John Barrows (one of our stellar horn players in New York) as leader of the horn section in that recording session, it was with great pride that in the first run-through of this passage the other three of us in the section—I was playing third—stuck resolutely with Johnny (all the while watching Stokowski), intent on keeping the four sixteenths per beat absolutely together, while accelerating and ritarding perfectly with Stokowski. Rather proud of ourselves, we couldn't believe our ears when Stokowski, having suddenly stopped conducting, *berated* us for playing with him, and—incredibly—asked us instead to maintain absolutely the initial speed of the sixteenth notes, no matter how his tempo and beat might vary. In other words, he was asking us to ignore not only what Tchaikovsky had written but also his beat and to play *against* it.

That is not only totally crazy and arrogantly contemptuous of Tchaikovsky's score; it is extremely difficult, indeed almost impossible, to execute. When you are trained as an orchestra musician from your earliest days to follow a conductor through thick and thin—indeed your job and your career depend on it—to then suddenly be asked to *ignore* a conductor's tempo and, additionally, to ignore what a composer had written is really very, very difficult—and perverse. It would be difficult for one player to manage such a rhythmic distortion, but to ask eight players (four horns, two oboes, two clarinets) to stay perfectly together as a group in such a situation is simply ridiculous. Instead of playing sixteen sixteenths in that *ritenuto* measure, we were being asked to play some unknown indeterminate number of notes, depending on how much *ritenuto* the maestro might take. It might be nineteen notes instead of sixteen, or twenty-one and a half, or some other strange, unanticipatable number. What made the situation really bizarre was that in the three takes we recorded of that passage, the amount of Stokowski's *ritenuto* was never the same. I don't know how many sixteenths we played to fill out Stokowski's stretched-to-the-breaking-point *ritard*, but it might have been twenty-one or twenty-three and a half—who knows. The trickiest part was that there are three different changing harmonies in each of those measures, which means that, however aberrant the relationship of our sixteenths was to the tempo, we still had to fit them into the music's harmonic changes per beat.

I should make it clear that had we refused Stokowski's crazy demand, or had we been unable to accomplish what he asked for, we would have been fired on the spot and instantly replaced. (Talk about an unfair playing field.)

It was one of the most nightmarish recording sessions any of us had ever been through. You can believe that all four of us headed straight for the Carnegie Hall Tavern after the session; I don't recall any of us leaving sober.

In any other profession such aberrant behavior as Stokowski's would be regarded as inconceivable and intolerable—the ravings of a madman. Imagine an analogous situation in a surgeon's operating room, or a chef's preparation of a meal. The tragedy is that Stokowski, who had no sense of humor whatsoever, wasn't joking in these perverse episodes. He was deadly serious, and if you didn't take his outlandish wishes seriously, no matter how weird they were, or if you appeared to be resisting him—not that anyone ever dared to think along those lines— you were peremptorily fired. I invite the reader to stay tuned, for he will encounter several more Stokowski anecdotes in the course of this narrative that, though absolutely true and factual, are so outrageous as to defy belief.

I was also asked to play on occasion with one of New York's best chamber orchestras of that era, the New York Little Symphony, led by its founder Daniel Saidenberg, who in the 1930s had been solo cellist of the Chicago Symphony. Saidenberg's programs were always adventurous, exploring the lesser-known, often neglected literature ranging from the baroque to the contemporary. It was with Saidenberg's orchestra that I had my first opportunity to play Bach's *Brandenburg Concerto No. 1*, in those days one of the half-dozen supreme pinnacles of achievement for horn players because of horn parts' high tessitura. In the intervening years, the work has lost some of its terrors, partly because it is nowadays played on smaller horns, so-called descant horns, which makes the altissimo register much easier to control and more secure. In my day we played the *Brandenburg Concerto* and other Bach, Mozart, and Haydn high horn parts on our big double horns simply because there was no alternative.

The reunion with Margie in New York after the Met tour made my life whole again, although we were not living together. Margie was still staying at the Studio Club, while I slept twenty miles away in Jamaica, Queens. The constant struggle to find time together was very frustrating, so quite naturally we began to think about finding some place where we could live together as husband and wife. While such a situation has now been commonplace for nearly fifty years, it was unheard of back then in the forties. Even just the *thought* of an unwed couple living together was an extremely daring concept—it was called living in sin—and if attempted would certainly have to be done in secret. In our case, what with Margie's inordinately conservative Fargo family, we would simply have to share a place in absolute secrecy. But where?

By this time I knew that my parents would not be upset by such a quasi-marital arrangement. They had become very fond of Margie, and had begun to treat her like a daughter, inviting her often to our house in Jamaica—frequently even to stay overnight. Indeed, my parents were remarkably generous in inviting quite a few of my Cincinnati friends to their home—including Gussie, Nell, Paula, and Paul Bransky. My mother, a terrific cook and fond of offering the hospitality of her home, would spend most of the day in the kitchen preparing fabulous German dishes, such as sauerbraten or Rhenish potato pancakes with sour cream and apple sauce, and always some wonderful homemade plum or rhubarb pie. My émigré friends from Cincinnati became, in effect, my extended family.

It was in New York that our relationship took on a clearly different character from that of our years in Cincinnati. There, except for that final month and a half during which we drew apart from each other, our love, our relationship, was characterized by a wonderful pureness and innocence. In Cincinnati it was astonishingly free of the tensions and problems that so often interpose themselves upon teenage relationships. There was a certain natural independence and separateness that our busy work-a-day lives—I at the symphony, she as a double major at the Conservatory—imposed on us. In Cincinnati, we often didn't see each other for days or weeks. When we could be together it was as if we had known each other all our lives; the emotional rapport was instant and direct, unblemished by outside concerns. And our love was chaste—literally—and inherently void of the emotional and psychological strains so often associated with adolescent explorative sex. In retrospect, even considering what a close, deep, and happy relationship we had for nearly fifty years, I believe that our years in Cincinnati were ultimately the very happiest and purest of all. I also think that this unencumbered relational pureness was possible because in Cincinnati we were both free of any parental supervision or interference. Very private and discreet persons in our behavior, we kept very much to ourselves; it was no one else's business *how* we related to each other. Though Margie wrote two or three letters a week to her parents, she only rarely mentioned my name and not at all our growing relationship.

By the time we had both moved to New York in 1945 the character of our personal relationship had changed noticeably. It had become much more complex, partly because of the whole new level of intensity and dedication she had to bring to her musical studies, and partly as a result of the myriad cultural and intellectual interactions New York interposed on her—and me. The tempo of our lives virtually doubled, which in itself introduced certain stresses in just trying to keep up that New York pace and making our two respective schedules mesh. Beyond that, our slightly different capacities for absorbing and digesting so much new information and so many new experiences, even our differing levels of physical and intellectual energy, became occasionally an issue to be resolved. And, of course, we were now sexually intimate and as sexually explorative as our busy daily lives would permit.

What is described here is a not-so-unusual example of how even the purest, pristine love relationship can be put under pressure from varied outside forces, forces that can be so subtly invasive as to be initially indiscernible. For example, in our life in New York the parental situation eventually became a source of constant worry and concern, not on my family's side—they had quickly accepted certain inevitable realities—but on Margie's. The very idea of moving to New York was enough to sound alarm bells with her parents, especially Mr. Black, who considered New York a disreputable, morally corrupt, dangerous place that might be okay to visit for three-times-a-year buying trips, but certainly not a place to live. He thought of New York as a Communist outpost, ruled by the *New York Times*. As much as Margie tried in her letters and occasional visits home to give the impression that ours was only a casual, platonic, musical relationship, we could not help but worry that they suspected more than that, and probably imagined the worst. This put considerable pressure on Margie because she was very devoted to her parents and truly loved them. She hated to lie to them and in any way upset them or hurt their feelings. Worse yet, her Fargo visits, which were intended to be happy family reunions, turned out to be more often than not stressful, strife-torn situations, as her parents put enormous pressures on her to allay their own worst fears: My God, their daughter living in sin in New York—*with a musician!* I gleaned a lot of this from letters and her occasional desperate midnight phone calls.[3]

It was a collision of two quite contrary, irreconcilable worlds, and that alone put a heavy burden on our relationship, a constant needling irritant impinging on our love. The constant pressures from her parents often caused her to experience periods of self-doubt or self-recrimination. With these constraints and emotional wranglings, Margie would sometimes lose all self-confidence and become very irritable—with me, with herself, with everyone. At times like that her contrariness and capriciousness could be very difficult to live with. Nothing like that had ever happened to her—or to us—in Cincinnati. Additionally, Margie would experience bouts of depression whenever her voice or piano lessons went badly. She would chastise herself for not working hard enough on her music; this was a serious issue for her since the whole rationale presented to her parents for coming to live in New York was the opportunity to work with the best teachers in the undisputed musical and cultural capital of the country. She would even feel guilty for living in New York, for *enjoying* being away from Fargo and actually relishing life in New York and the feelings of freedom it offered. But then she would get upset with herself, feeling guilty for her emotional and financial dependency on her parents.

Disapprobation from her parents clearly affected Margie's moods and confidence. On one occasion Margie had inadvertently and in all innocence written her mother that she had just bought several pairs of nylon stockings tinted in various colors (black, brown, rose), which just then were all the rage in women's fashions. Her mother shot back a much-displeased letter, chastising Margie for indulging in such questionable taste. That really hurt her. Reprimands like that from her mother came far too often, especially on her visits to Fargo, where she was easy prey to constant parental haranguing.

But Margie gradually did learn to deal more rationally with these various pressures, learned even to ignore and fend off her parents' reprimands. And in turn her parents began to realize little by little that their daughter was not going to the dogs in New York, that my relationship with her was not causing her personal ruination, and that, lo and behold, she was still the loving, equable, proper young lady who had left Fargo two years before.

While Margie couldn't help dreading her visits home, I regarded my trips to Fargo more as a slight inconvenience, a sacrifice that I had to make. I primed myself to be the kind of nice young man, the sort of suitor that Margie's parents would approve of, avoiding as much as father Black would allow all discussion of his favorite subjects: politics (Communism), race and religion (Jews, blacks, Catholics), Franklin Roosevelt, modernisms of various kinds. It was not easy to hold my tongue, but I eventually learned to do just that for the sake of peace and harmony. Not that this presented an insuperable hardship for me. I knew how to be patient and tolerant, for I had long ago learned that one didn't have to hate someone in eternal unforgivingness if one didn't agree with their politics or religion or social views. Besides, I could not help but show a certain respect for Margie's parents; they were after all Fargo's first family, and George Black's remarkable business achievements had been attained through a long life of dedication, selflessness, and hard work.

Margie's mother seemed to me a much gentler, kindlier, less assertive personality—and *very* handsome. I could see where Margie inherited some of her own radiant beauty. As I got to know her better, I came to like Mrs. Black a great deal, especially when I saw that she often tried to act as a mediating, balancing force between her husband and her daughter. Mrs. Black would have been much happier—and relieved—if Margie and I had gotten married right away, as Margie's sister Anna Jane had done within months of meeting her husband-to-be, William Schlossman.[4]

Bill gradually took over Mr. Black's business, expanded it substantially, and, as a man of the highest, uncorruptible principles, became one of Fargo's leading business and civic leaders, as well as a major, most generous yet unostentatious supporter of the arts in North Dakota.

On a one-day visit to Fargo during the Met's 1946 spring tour (when I had an evening off), I was taken to all of Mr. Black's business properties—stores, hotels, office buildings, parking lots—including the ten-story skyscraper, the Black Building, which George Black had built in 1930, inspired, so he told me, both by the building of the Empire State Building in New York and the Foshay Tower in Minneapolis. I must say it was all very impressive—and good. On that day we also surveyed the many places in town where that year the seriously flooded Red River, winding its serpentine way through Fargo, was just then making many sections of Fargo and Moorhead totally inaccessible. West of town, the Cheyenne River had also crested and created an immense lake, three feet deep, inundating vast areas of previously absolutely flat North Dakota farmland. (Some years later Bill Schlossman built an immense, extremely successful shopping mall nearby called West Acres—the first in Fargo.)

One sign that Mrs. Black's attitude toward me was mellowing somewhat was that on one of these Fargo visits she gave me a collection of Ned's letters home, letters in large part dating from his two years in Brazil as an exchange student and also, of course, from his service in World War II. I took this to be a wonderful, warm compliment, and a gentle gesture of reaching out to me.

There was one incident that really puzzled and irritated me again and again during my visits with the Black family. Being strict Presbyterians and principal patrons of their church, regular attendance on Sunday mornings of the entire Black clan was expected, including non-churchgoing visitors like me. I certainly didn't mind; indeed I looked forward to hearing the minister's sermon, which over the years I always found to be intelligent, thought provoking, and well delivered. What puzzled me was that at the subsequent, also mandatory, Sunday brunch gathering, *no one* ever referred to the minister's talk—as if it had never occurred. It was left to me, the alleged heathen, to mention the minister's sermon, to often praise him for his wisdom, and it was left to me to initiate a discussion on the sermon's topic. Most of the time I felt that no one had really listened or understood, let alone been inspired by, what had been said. I found that very strange.

As much as I tried to enter the Black family's world, I never fully succeeded. I could not imagine how I could ever share their type of life, where money and more or less platitudinous social activities were central, epitomized mainly by a "pleasant noncommitment," as I put it once in my diary.

Margie and I kept our own council, so to speak, sensing that her family's world, though not necessarily bad or wrong, was inherently too remote from ours and from the one to which we aspired. In New York we could be free to search for our true inner selves, more or less unfettered by customs, traditions, and life patterns. And, of course, beyond that, the saying "true love triumphs over all" is not without validity. Margie and I managed, through all the vicissitudes, fluctuations, and mutations of daily life in the wearing, hectic atmosphere of New York to maintain an enduring, loving relationship—a few miscalculations now and then not-withstanding. Our love grew steadily, all the while maturing, expanding, exploring, and testing whether our relationship would be lasting, and whether it would withstand the inevitable pit-falls and unexpected twists and turns that life somehow seems always to interpose.

Several times during this period I ran into my old high school buddy, Tony Acquaviva. We hadn't seen each other ever since I dropped out of high school in 1942; nor had I heard anything about him, except one time via some vague rumor circulating among musicians at Nola studios that Tony was now big time, had a touring swing band based in Los Angeles, and that he and the band were transporting drugs (probably marijuana) back and forth across the country. When Margie and I met Tony quite by chance at Luigino's, one of our favorite Italian restaurants in midtown Manhattan, we naturally exchanged news about our careers, mostly the usual musicians' shoptalk. But when I asked him about the rumors I had heard about him and his band, he pleaded absolute innocence. He was clean, he said, but then expanded elaborately on what he called "the narcotics racket in the band business." He rather grandly admitted that he too for a time had had some dealings with a few big racketeers, even with "Lucky" Luciano, and could have had more. He told us some harrowing tales of the murders, bribes, and payoffs in the popular music business, really big money dealings. I had occasionally read about Murder Inc. in New York's *Daily News* and the *Police Gazette*, and I had seen *Scarface*, the famous Hughes-Hawks film about Al Capone. But to hear about these things first hand from Tony in rather graphic, Italian-opera dramatic detail was another matter. He told us that for these people human life means nothing and that they play around with fifty grand as we would with nickels and dimes. Margie nodded knowingly. She always had a weakness for conspiracy theories and a strong inclination to find a gangster or the Cosa Nostra behind every otherwise inexplicable mysterious act or event. She often chided me for my naïve and idealistic gullibility. (She wasn't entirely wrong about that.)

In some scraps of diary that survived from that time, I had written rather cryptically—as if trying not to give away some dark secret—that "this" (meaning Tony's stories) "all makes that story of Bix Beiderbecke's death quite probable, and explains much about the 400 Restaurant and the Aquarium," "and those hook-nosed, cigar-chomping Woody Herman bosses I had met there." Whom exactly I met there I don't now remember, but it surely was some Mafia types, who clearly were active in the big band business.

I saw Tony only twice more, very briefly, when he and his touring band did some rehearsing at Nola studios and I sat in with the band, making up (i.e., harmonizing) my own horn parts. I remember being quite impressed with the quality of the band's arrangements, which turned out to be mostly by Ted McCrea. It was quite a coup for Tony to snare a very talented saxophonist and arranger like McCrea, who had been a stalwart of the great 1930s Chick Webb band, and had worked for Ella Fitzgerald when she took over Webb's band after his death. After that encounter at Nola's Tony dropped out of my life; I never saw him again, never heard any further news about him, except that he had married the fairly successful pop singer Joni James, who had a couple of big hits in the fifties (such as *Your Cheatin' Heart*).

In early summer Nancy Freeto, who had just graduated with flying colors from the College of Music, wrote us that she was also coming to New York to pursue her musical studies. This news acted as a signal for Margie to move out of the Studio Club, with its restrictive women's dormitory atmosphere, and to look for an apartment for Nancy and herself. They soon found a furnished one on West Ninety-Fifth Street with four rooms, providing privacy for both girls; amazingly, it had an upright piano. But the best news for me was that I would now have easier access to Margie, and Bill Bunce, Margie's cousin, who had also moved to New York, could more effectively pursue his courtship of Nancy. They were—in gossip column parlance—getting to be quite an item. (By the end of the year they announced their engagement and were married in April 1948).

With Margie leaving the Studio Club, I decided that I would also move out of my parents' home in Jamaica. It was about time; the main benefit of a move to Manhattan being that I would no longer have to suffer the daily one-way hour-and-a-quarter bus and subway trip to my job at the Met.

My search for an apartment unfortunately coincided temporarily with the lowest ebb in my financial condition. I cannot remember why that should have been so, especially since I recall that the previous year I had amassed over $2,000 in savings. Perhaps it was my continual splurging on recordings, constantly haunting the big midtown record stores as well as the several second-hand record shops on Sixth Avenue. I certainly found lots of bargains in the latter, but I doubt that I was able to resist the various more costly temptations; I threw fiscal caution to the wind, feeling that I just *had to have* that special Louis Armstrong English Parlophone import, or that twenty-year-old vintage recording of Feuermann playing the Dvořák *Cello Concerto*. I had this obsessive desire to *own* everything (books, records, journals, etc.). I felt I needed these things for my musical, aesthetic development. (In retrospect, I was right.)

In any case, after weeks of fruitless apartment hunting for something I could afford, I found a large one-room furnished apartment on Ninth Street, just off Fifth Avenue—and, how nice—only three blocks from the Fifth Avenue Cinema and ten minutes by BMT subway from the Met. The room, with a tiny kitchenette and adjoining bathroom, was part of a much larger apartment belonging to the super of the building, a friendly, jovial chap with a strong Swedish accent, who reminded me immediately of George Marion, Greta Garbo's barge-owner father in the 1930 Marie Dressler-Greta Garbo *Anna Christie* film. The rent was only fifteen dollars a month, a godsend considering my pitiful financial situation. As spacious and as comfortable as the room was, it also came free of charge with a sizable family of cockroaches, who would make maximal use of their room when it was dark, and scatter *allegrissimo* when the lights went on, cleverly heading for and hiding in an instant behind the refrigerator. They were typical, well-experienced New York survivors. The granddaddy of the clan was a three-and-a-half-inch

Figure 1. The author at seventeen months.

Figure 2. With mother and father and friend Elizabeth Kühling (at right) on a farm in Long Island, 1929.

Figure 3. Gebesee 1936, with my best friend, Jürgen Pascheu (middle), and one of my many teachers (left). Schloss (castle) in the background.

Figure 4. Gebesee, view from the Schloss (castle) towards the main gate tower, classroom and dormitory buildings, left and right.

Figure 5. Chalk drawing of kiwi by the author.

Figure 6. Rotogravure section of the *New York Times*, December 19, 1937. The thirty-six voice boy choir of St. Thomas Church, NY. Gunther fourth from left, in lower transverse row.

Figure 7. With mother, Elsie, wearing Eton collar, part of the dress code at St. Thomas Church Choir School.

Figure 8. Gunther at age seventeen as the new principal horn of the Cincinnati Symphony. Gustav Albrecht, assistant horn (left) and Reuben Lawson, violinist and Cincinnati Pops conductor. In background, close friend and admired colleague, Reuben Segal.

Figure 9. Marjorie, 1948; photo by violinist friend and amateur photographer Alexander Levenson.

Figure 10. Playing horn duets with my co-principal horn Richard Moore outside the Loew's Grand Theater in Atlanta where the Metropolitan Opera played every year in its eight-week national tours, and where *Gone with the Wind* premiered in 1939.

Figure 11. Best Met Opera friends, James Politis (left), trumpeter Harry Peers (right).

Figure 12. Marjorie with one of our first bookshelves in the background, which my very handy brother Edgar made for us (1948).

Figure 13. The first bite of the three-foot tall wedding cake.

Figure 14. With violinist friend Gabriel (Gaby) Banat, rehearsing *Recitative and Rondo*, 1953. Paul Cordes, photographer.

Figure 15. The young family in Webatuck in 1955, Edwin not so happy.

Figure 16. Father and son in a duet (horn and toy trumpet) in Webatuck.

Figure 17. Webatuck cabin and main house, with stone boulder wall that Marjorie and I helped build.

Figure 18. Marjorie with sons Edwin (left) and George (right), 1960.

Figure 19. Edwin and George, in Webatuck, early 1960s.

Figure 20. Gunther Schuller, early 1950s. Photograph by Metropolitan Opera oboist and friend William Arrowsmith.

Figure 21. Composing.

monster, a veritable speed king, and tough as nails. One evening, after dinner, when I had had enough of this little minotaur, I pursued him with a rolled-up newspaper, hitting him hard nine times—yes, *nine times*—before I was finally able to stop him from reaching the safety of the refrigerator.

The best thing about my new apartment was that Margie could visit me freely, at will. She came over often in the afternoons after her voice and piano lessons, and then stayed over many times, especially when I had a free evening at the Met. And, no question, the traveling time for her from Ninety-Fifth Street or midtown Manhattan to Ninth Street was one third that of the trek all the way out to Jamaica, Queens.

I will always associate that apartment with the one poverty-stricken period in our early years together in New York. Margie was surely better off financially than I was. But quite apart from the fact that she was living on a strict, limited allowance from her parents, we had decided long ago, in Cincinnati, that we would always go dutch and split all joint expenditures down the middle. Of course I wasn't going to let that idea extend to meals in my apartment. I remember clearly that for weeks she and I survived on small cans of Campbell soup, bits of cheese, and Ritz crackers. Our one dining out splurge for the week was to go to Longchamps, a fine, relatively pricey chain of restaurants—there was one kitty-corner from the Met—where all we could afford was their delicious $1.25 vegetable dinner, with a fried egg, sunny-side up, as its centerpiece. I also recall with considerable embarrassment that I was so poor at the time that I could afford to give Margie only a single orchid for her birthday on September 29.

Despite my penurious situation, we still somehow pursued our obsession with film art, which in turn became entwined with our love life. If an important film was showing at the Thalia at Ninety-fifth and Broadway, I would stay overnight at Margie's apartment, half a block away. Conversely, if there was a film playing at the Fifth Avenue Cinema, Margie would stay with me at my Ninth Street lair—despite the cockroaches (which, by the way, with the help of the super, we eventually managed to send to cockroach heaven).

Just when we thought we had solved our respective apartment problems, the Ninety-Fifth Street landlord, a Mrs. Guise, a rather hysterical, crazy harridan, tried to impose on the girls an unwarranted, indeed, as it turned out, illegal rent hike. Rather than fight with this insane woman and legally contest her groundless demand, both girls moved out, glad to be rid of Mrs. Guise's harassments. Margie moved fully into my Ninth Street place while I, ostensibly anyway, moved back out to Jamaica, and Nancy moved in with Bill Bunce. All of this moving about was eventually resolved when, about a year later, I found a new home for us, quite by chance, in an abandoned Greek Orthodox Church on Houston Street and Second Avenue, where finally Margie and I were able to live together unobstructedly, no longer obliged to plot and scheme as to where and when we could meet.

I had been talking with Joe Marx for some time about forming a woodwind quintet with him and three other Met orchestra players, which we eventually did in late 1946. Over the next half dozen years we called ourselves the Metropolitan Woodwind Quintet, with James Hosmer, flute, Luigi Cancellieri, clarinet, and initially Arthur Weisberg, later Steve Maxym, bassoon. We played all the obvious quintet literature of Danzi, Reicha, Taffanel, Hindemith, Milhaud, and Ibert, as well as works such as Mozart's K. 452 Quintet for Piano and Winds, performing in various concert halls and schools in New York, and then, more actively, on our Met tours on the university and college circuit. Our proudest achievement as a group was making the first recording of Schönberg's Woodwind Quintet Op. 26 in 1951.

In December we had our very first rehearsals, specifically of various well-known woodwind pieces by Milhaud, Ibert, Danzi, Reicha, and Hindemith. We continued working on the basic repertory off and on throughout the opera season in preparation for a series of concerts that Joe had managed to book for us at various universities during our 1947 spring Met tour.

As we worked, Joe and I realized that the available quintet literature was rather limited, both in quantity and quality, a realization substantiated by an extensive search in dozens of publisher's catalogues. How many times could you play Mozart's Quintet for Piano and Winds, as wonderful as it is, when on the one hand it required engaging a pianist, at the same time disengaging the group's flutist—there is no flute part in Mozart's K. 452 Quintet—and when, on the other hand, by its very greatness it makes any other works on a given quintet program sound inferior. Even the rather pleasant early nineteenth-century woodwind quintets of Danzi and Reicha are no match for Mozart. And as for contemporary or twentieth-century works, after you played a few adequate lightweight pieces by, say, Milhaud, Hindemith, Ibert, or Ropartz, you had pretty much exhausted the field. It always brought Joe and me back to the Schönberg Quintet, perhaps not one of his very greatest works—and certainly not one to bring audiences running to a concert—but nevertheless a work of high quality and of distinction and historic importance.

The crux of the problem is that there are no woodwind quintets by Mozart and Haydn (the medium did not yet exist in their time), nor by Beethoven or Brahms or Schumann or Tchaikovsky or Wagner or Stravinsky—the list goes on. Moreover, an ensemble (a group of musicians), needs over the long haul to play music that will challenge it artistically, that will constantly test its standards and further its growth and evolution—something ordinary competent works can in the long run not do. I felt that we should test our mettle on music by the greatest masters.

And that is how, as de facto leader of our quintet, I came to two decisions: one, with Joe's enthusiastic support to start working on the Schönberg Quintet in the hope of giving within a year or two the first performance of the work in the Western hemisphere; and two, to embark on an extensive program of transcribing all kinds of great and outstanding music, both older and modern, in the hopes of significantly expanding the woodwind quintet repertory. Schönberg's Quintet had a fearsome reputation as virtually unplayable and far too difficult, composed as it was in that "incomprehensible" twelve-tone technique. At the time, the Quintet, composed in 1923, had had only two performances, one in Vienna in 1924 and another at the Zurich ISCM Festival in 1926.

Had I been a pianist, I would have tried to play Schönberg's many outstanding piano compositions. I didn't see any chance of playing Schönberg's orchestral music, certainly not at the Met. But wishing urgently to perform some of his music, *any* of his music—to learn it from the inside, as it were—the Woodwind Quintet seemed the most logical and immediately accessible work. Furthermore, since it had never been performed in the United States, there was the additionally enticing prospect that we might end up playing the American premiere of the work. We had heard rumors that five Los Angeles-based players, under the leadership of the wonderful horn player and local musical inspirator Wendell Hoss, had begun to study and rehearse the work in the hopes of performing it at the prestigious Monday Evening Concerts. But we also heard that they had struggled for months and months to conquer just the second (Scherzo) movement, and that Schönberg, who had been invited to hear them play through the movement, had discouraged them from continuing to work on the piece. I must admit that made me all the more determined to perform the work. I was also intrigued to conquer the Quintet's very challenging horn part, considered to be unplayable by most horn players at the time. But I didn't think so.

I can't remember whether the parts for the Quintet were temporarily unavailable in 1946 or whether there was another reason that I undertook to hand copy them from the score. I think it was probably my realization that copying out the parts by hand would be the best way for me to study and learn the work. I started copying in mid-October and worked on it intermittently as often as I could. It took me the better part of three months to finish all five parts. We had our first reading rehearsal in early January, after the holidays.

In two hours we got through only about eighty bars of the first movement, although rather thoroughly. Much encouraged, we now began studying and rehearsing Schönberg's Quintet in earnest, both separately (our individual parts) and eventually collectively, as a group. I spent a lot of time with my horn part. It was very difficult and long (some twenty pages, about thirty-five minutes in playing time), with many tricky passages that required lots of woodshedding. One curiosity about the horn part is that it had been printed and published by Universal Edition in Vienna in concert pitch, not in the usual F horn transposition. That was one big reason why, even among those few horn players who were interested in Schönberg's music, and perhaps in playing his Woodwind Quintet, almost all of them shied away from tackling the music because the part was in C, what they thought of as a C transposition. They considered this too much of an obstacle in learning to play the work. But since I always read horn parts in concert pitch, no matter what transposition they were written in—as a composer I was interested in the actual pitches—I copied out the part in C, in actual pitch. (It took another five years and several hundred hours of rehearsing—with, of course, constant interruptions and postponements—until we finally had the honor of producing the first recording of the work, for Ross Russell's Dial Records.)

In the summer of 1947, right after returning home from the Met tour, I decided to relieve the dearth of quintet literature by making arrangements or transcriptions of all kinds of great and outstanding music.[5] In that summer alone I took almost a dozen outstanding compositions of considerable stylistic variety and transcribed them for quintet. In retrospect I can't fathom how I managed that much work over a period of just six months, not only making the transcriptions but also copying out the individual parts. It wasn't as if I did nothing else; I was busy with all my other professional activities and pursuits.

One of the first of the transcriptions I made was Ravel's *Le Tombeau de Couperin*. Mason Jones, principal horn of the Philadelphia Orchestra, had also made an arrangement, but of only four of the six movements, probably taking his lead from Ravel himself, who had orchestrated *Tombeau*, a work originally for solo piano, with two movements unarranged, the Fugue and the Toccata—I suspect because the latter is a brilliant but technically very challenging tour de force, a perpetual motion of four minutes of continuously running sixteenth notes. (I was always surprised—and disappointed—that Ravel, surely one of the greatest orchestrators of all time, had shied away from tackling the Toccata.) In any case, I decided to accept the challenge of transcribing all six *Tombeau* movements, including the Toccata, an awesome task for a variety of reasons, the most obvious being that any number of passages are located in the low register, an octave or more below middle C. The inescapable problem is that in such a passage two of the five quintet instruments, flute and oboe, are automatically eliminated from consideration, for the simple reason that both instruments cannot reach below middle C. That leaves

the clarinet (although its lowest note is only a C sharp [musical notation] , and Ravel's music ventures

well below that), the horn (with the problem that fast moving low-register passages are far from its best feature), and of course the bassoon (no problems there).

A similar but converse transcriptural problem was that all his life Ravel loved writing high-register, scintillating tinkly passages. We are told that this stems from Ravel's special love for birds, both live and mechanical. (His villa, particularly his study, in Montfort-l'Amaury was filled with music boxes, small mechanical toys and contraptions, many of them with chirping birds.) The problem in such high-register passages was that the bassoon's highest note is an

E or F (in the staff), and definitely has to be approached prudently, not really of much use in, say, a fast moving or rhythmically boisterous passage. Similarly, much of *Tombeau*'s music is set above the uppermost range of the horn. Even the three remaining instruments—flute, oboe, and clarinet—were not entirely free of certain problems, especially in regard to dynamic control. When Ravel wrote a very high-lying but soft (*pianissimo*) passage, say, in the third octave above middle C (which he did quite often), the flute and clarinet would be hard pressed to play it softly, and, depending on which notes, they might even be beyond the oboe's usual range.

But the trickiest, most difficult-to-solve problem in transcribing Ravel's *Tombeau de Couperin* lay in its rich chromatic, often bitonal, harmonic language. How would one take one of Ravel's nine- or eight-part chords, so easily played by two hands on the piano, and reduce it to only five notes, an uncircumventable limitation, since the five instruments of a woodwind quintet can—unlike, say, a violin or a piano—sound only one note at a time, offering not even any double-stop possibilities.[6]

To make my task even harder, I had set myself two important, indeed for me mandatory goals. One was to respect and adhere as much as possible to Ravel's orchestration, particularly in regard to his choice of solo or leading instruments. (His orchestrated version of the four *Tombeau* movements features the oboe most generously, making the work virtually an oboe concerto.) I definitely wanted to preserve the particular instrumental colorations, the timbral choices that Ravel had made in his orchestration. Here, of course, the Fugue and Toccata could not be of any guidance. I was also determined not to ever change Ravel's registral placing, as Mason Jones had done rather freely by moving certain passages an octave lower or higher. I felt that such octave displacements, though convenient, would to some degree do damage to the always most meticulously specified sound and texture of Ravel's music. This decision affected particularly the horn part, which had to climb at times to well above the accepted upper range of the instrument. If, for example, Ravel had written the following high-register

four-part chord , there was no choice but to give the lowest note (G) to the horn,[7]

a risky but unavoidable choice since, particularly in those earlier days, very few horn players could (or cared to) venture beyond the normal confines of the upper range. But since I was going to be playing the horn part, and since I had an easy, reliable high register, I simply wrote those altissimo notes, thereby avoiding the whole question and temptation of octave transposition.

An even more challenging task confronting me was the problem of what to do with the hundreds of chords in the entire *Tombeau* that contained more than five notes, even when there weren't any registral or range complications. There I must pat myself on the back, and say that I unraveled (*Nice pun!*) that problem about as well as it can be resolved. Without divulging the fullness of my secret, I will say only that the ultimate pitch choices were primarily made on the basis of which five notes would best and most fully portray the chord in question, and secondarily determined by certain voice-leading considerations. Intertwined with such decisions, I took into account and relied heavily on a musical-acoustic phenomenon in which the sounded notes in certain aggregate forms produce harmonics or overtones that, though not in fact played, nevertheless resonate in varying degrees of projection, in the best instances creating the illusion that somehow those implied sounds were actually played, and thus actually heard.[8]

Despite these formidable transcriptural problems, I was determined to solve them all, undaunted in my belief that I could muster sufficient instrumentational ingenuity to meet these multiple challenges.

I set to work early in the summer of 1947, completing the score and parts of the entire *Tombeau* by late September. Our Metropolitan Quintet began playing my transcription in concerts in 1948, after some strenuous protracted rehearsing. Nothing had ever been written for wood-wind quintet that offered that many diverse and new performance and interpretive challenges. When after some time other quintet groups asked permission to play my transcription, I had to deny them the opportunity, the reason being that Ravel's *Tombeau de Couperin* was at the time still under copyright with Durand in France. Mason Jones, I assumed, had gotten permission to make his arrangement, which pretty much precluded my also obtaining the rights to make an alternate arrangement. I also assumed that my colleagues in the Philadelphia Wood-wind Quintet would not be too keen on having another arrangement competing with theirs. And so I kept my transcription very much to myself and to our small group, quietly perform-ing it only in fairly obscure places around the country on our sporadic quintet tours.

By the rules of international copyright law, it would have been illegal either to publish or record my transcription without permission from Durand. However, as the underground interest in my *Tombeau* transcription grew, I decided that as soon as the copyright ran out and the work entered the public domain, I would publish my transcription with Margun Music, thereby making the music widely and legitimately available—all of which did happen in 1995.

In any event, by the time the summer was over and the new Met season was in the offing, I had completed, besides Ravel's *Tombeau*, transcriptions of Schönberg's Op. 19 *Sechs kleine Klavierstücke* (Six Little Piano Pieces), Scriabin's Op. 63 (*Étrangeté*) and all the Op. 69 and Op. 74 Preludes, the Scherzo movement of Schumann's First String Quartet, the famous Scherzo from Mendelssohn's *Midsummer Night's Dream*, Bartók's *Romanian Dances*, and Rachmaninov's Prelude in E Flat, Op. 23, no. 6.

Subsequently I transcribed the *Pavane and Chaconne* by Henry Purcell, the Menuet from Mozart's K. 421 String Quartet, Gabriel Fauré's beautiful "Pavane" from *Pelléas et Mélisande*, Erik Satie's first *Gymnopedie*, Dvořák's *Notturno* (for strings) Op. 40, and the second and third movements of Bartók's Second String Quartet, a work I had come to love passionately through the recording of the Budapest Quartet. My transcribing binge ended with Ravel's *Valses nobles et sentimentales* (which, however, for reasons I can no longer remember, I never finished—probably no time), and, most important, Beethoven's Op. 71 Sextet for Winds.

There was a nineteenth-century published arrangement of the Beethoven work (by Robert Stark) that had become very popular with woodwinders. It was an okay arrangement, but after we had played it a number of times—it was a sure-fire attraction to have a Beethoven work on a program—I decided to make a new transcription for our group. My problem with the Stark arrangement was that it veered sonically and orchestrationally too far from Beethoven's original. The original Op. 71 is a sextet for pairs of clarinets, bassoons, and horns, and is in effect a major vehicle, almost a kind of concerto, for the first clarinet. But the Stark arrange-ment had turned the piece into a veritable flute concerto. Also not quite to my liking was the fact that in Beethoven's original sextet the slow movement's rather substantial bassoon solo had been converted into a horn solo. Most horn players, I'm sure, would welcome the oppor-tunity of playing an almost one-minute-long solo in a woodwind quintet, and of all things in a Beethoven work. To some extent I did, too. Yet I felt that it deviated too much into serious stylistic and instrumental inauthenticity. This sextet was a very early, youthful Beethoven work, dating from the 1790s, still the time of so-called natural, valveless, and not yet fully chromatic horns. The point is that the sextet's second movement is in the key of B flat, and therefore there is no way that Beethoven's E-flat horn could have played idiomatically well the notes the composer had written for the bassoon.

There were also other anomalies in Stark's arrangement that I found stylistically too adverse. But even more important, my overall aim was to restore the work as much as pos-sible to its original sonoric patina and texture, dominated by the timbre of the clarinet. I was even more keen on this idea than I might normally have been because our quintet boasted that most remarkable clarinetist, Luigi Cancellieri, one of my great musical heroes in the Met orchestra.

I believe I attained this lofty goal in my transcription, although at a bothersome and yet, to me, unavoidable price: namely, by holding the flute to a minor role. There was for me no alternative. In order to reclaim the piece for the clarinet and at the same time fully represent Beethoven's basically six-part harmonies—reducing continually from six to five notes was in itself a hard enough task—and preserve at the same time as much of the original horn and bassoon colorations as possible, I simply had to reduce the two other instruments in the quintet—flute and oboe—to a much lower status than in the Stark arrangement—lower both in range and ranking. But at the same time, I was determined to preserve Beethoven's pitches as faithfully as possible, two thirds of which were originally located in the two horns and two bassoons. This meant—I called it earlier the price to pay—that I had to constantly keep the flute in its lowest range, rarely letting it out of its low-register captivity into the higher, more brilliant atmosphere, where the flute is accustomed to reign. It was quite unfair to the flute and to flutists, especially those who were used to leading a woodwind quintet or performing leading roles in an orchestra. Flutists were understandably unenthusiastic about my Beethoven transcription. (Please forgive me, flutists, but for me the choice I made was the lesser of two evils.)

Fortunately, the one flutist who not only didn't mind being constantly stuck in the low register but actually enjoyed it was the great Jimmy Politis, who, when he became co-principal flute of the Met orchestra in 1950, replaced the quintet's original flutist, James Hosmer. Politis had a naturally big, healthy, virile tone, and an especially overtone-rich low register, which, in addition, he could vary timbrally—chameleonlike—from gentle and warm to hard, almost metallically nasal sounds. It was amazing!

I am astounded to find that in the midst of this transcribing and arranging orgy, I still managed to do a fair amount of composing. I wrote an *Adagio for orchestra*, inspired by the slow-movement of Schumann's Second Symphony. I remember sending the work to Rodzinski through the intercession of my father. Rodzinski seemed to really like the Adagio and mentioned something about possibly programming it with the New York Philharmonic. But this tantalizing hope evaporated quite suddenly when, in the middle of the 1946–47 Philharmonic season, Rodzinski resigned, accepting the position as music director of the Chicago Symphony.

It was during this period that Margie and I virtually lived at the Fifth Avenue Cinema, at Twelfth Street and Fifth Avenue, almost around the corner from my Ninth Street apartment. The Fifth Avenue Cinema was in those days one of the two or three premier art film houses in New York. It was widely known for presenting surrealist films, which the other art theatres rarely or never presented: films such as Jean Cocteau's 1930 *Le Sang d'un poète* (*Blood of a Poet*), and Watson and Webber's *Lot of Sodom*, the latter featuring a terrific chamber ensemble score by a little-known composer named Louis Siegel. We must have seen those two films at least five or six times. They were incredibly fascinating to us young cinema fans—at times teasingly incomprehensible and irrational, while exploring strikingly new cinematic frontiers. As someone just beginning to come to grips with modern poetry—at the time for me still a rather remote and obscure art form—*Blood of a Poet* showed me how the magical can exist in the real, how poetic and dreamlike imagery can find its logical expression in film art, and, even more significant, how film related so intimately to music and composition. I saw that the absence of explicit, literal definability in such films and in much modern poetry—not to mention James Joyce's stream of consciousness—had its parallel in music, an artistic expression that, like abstract art and poetry, can imply so much *precisely* because it cannot say anything explicit, anything concretely definitive.

Other important surrealist and nonobjective films Margie and I saw at the Fifth Avenue Cinema were several of Maya Deren's works (*Meshes of the Afternoon* and *At Land*), Joseph Schillinger and Lewis Jacobs' *Synchronization*, and two films by Oscar Fischinger, *Allegretto* (an abstract film set to jazz music) and *Optical Poem* (to Liszt's *Second Hungarian Rhapsody*), as well as a most ambitious feature-length color film, Hans Richter's *Dreams That Money Can Buy*, which featured visions and scenarios by Max Ernst, Fernand Leger, Marcel Duchamp, Man Ray, and Alexander Calder, with music by John Cage, Paul Bowles, Darius Milhaud, and Edgard Varèse. What a visual and sonic feast that film was! This is where we first saw Duchamps's *Nude Descending a Staircase* in motion, since Richter included a life animation of the famous painting in his film. It was also in the Fifth Avenue Cinema, long gone now, that I learned that Fischinger, the great German (pre-Hitler) experimenter and film avant-gardist, had created the original sequence of Bach's *Toccata and Fugue* for Disney's *Fantasia*, but that it was eliminated from the final film for being too abstract.

Somehow over most of this very active period—betwixt and between all these diverse activities—I composed two pieces that have received little attention, but that I consider among my loveliest, handsomest, and most unusual creations. They are both entitled *Fantasia Concertante* and both are for a trio of instruments accompanied by piano: one for three oboes (in which two of the oboes double on English horns), the other for three trombones and piano. The inspiration for the oboe *Fantasia* was threefold: first, through my early extensive study of sixteenth- and seventeenth-century music, where I discovered and read about hundreds of consort pieces (for ensembles of viols, shawms, recorders, etc.), in other words families of like instruments; second, more specifically Beethoven's two trios for two oboes and English horn (Trio Op. 87 and Variations on Mozart's "Là ci darem la mano" aria from *Don Giovanni*); and third, my friend and colleague Josef Marx's deep involvement with contemporary music and his enthusiasm for meeting the musical and technical challenges that such music presented, challenges that most professional oboists of the time tended to avoid.

Both *Fantasias* date from a time in my stylistic and linguistic development as a composer when I had become completely familiar with and enamored of Alban Berg's music, not only his Violin Concerto but also his Chamber Concerto, his remarkably pathbreaking *Altenberg Lieder*, the Lyric Suite string quartet, his Op. 6 Three Pieces for Orchestra, and, of course, his opera *Wozzeck*. Both of my *Fantasias* reflect the strong influence Berg had on me at the time.

I believe the *Fantasia* for a trio of oboists has, sadly, never been performed in public, and has certainly never been recorded. The trombone *Fantasia* has fared a little better, especially because of a fine trombonist named Dennis Lambert. Over a period of years, first as a graduate student, later as a freelance professional, he brought together two other trombone colleagues and a pianist several times, giving the work at least a half dozen very good performances. But there has been no recording—yet.

Margie and I had now been together in New York for almost a year, and it was clear to me that the move to the big city and the whirlwind diversity of its attractions were having a profound effect on her and on our relationship. I was a born New Yorker and probably had in my bones a real sense of what this incredible experiment in democracy, high-level commerce, and social acculturation had to offer any curious, diligent, explorative individual. But for Margie, coming from Fargo, North Dakota, the combination of the constant bombardment of artistic stimuli and my own fervid appetite for expanding my creative and intellectual horizons gradually wrought a considerable, even dramatic change in her. It was so exciting to see her grappling to absorb the vast array of aesthetic enticements that New York proffered. Her lessons with Steuermann, enlightening and inspiring beyond anything she had previously experienced, were one thing. My involvement with the opera, so close to her own singing aspirations, added another dimension. There was no opera company in Fargo, but here she was going several times a week to one of the best opera houses in the world, hearing for the first time some of the most sublime music ever composed.

As I became in the first few years after my return from Cincinnati more and more professionally involved in the New York music scene, and began in an ever widening circle to explore and feast greedily on New York's cultural riches, Margie was drawn inevitably into this maelstrom, becoming ever more deeply involved in my interests and my life. She frequently gave me gifts that she felt would be useful in my two careers. I remember being deeply touched and very excited when, around the time that I was trying to catalogue my growing jazz record collection, she bought me a jazz discography, actually the only one in existence at that time.[9] It was Charles Delaunay's 1938 *Hot Discography*, published in America by the famed Commodore Record Shop in mid-Manhattan. I pored over that book for hours, days, weeks, eager to identify all those jazz players I admired so much.

Soon Margie also began to read many of the art magazines and books (even Joyce and Tolstoy) that I was reading. At one point she actually began to play the horn, for which she showed considerable talent, although in the end, not surprisingly, she couldn't keep up with it—just one thing too much. I dare say this immersion in a much wider cultural scene, as was possible at that time in America perhaps only in New York City, immensely broadened and deepened her intellectually. It was so exciting to know that my life's companion, in addition to being an extraordinarily beautiful woman, was also growing into my closest musical, intellectual, and spiritual soul mate. Constantly stimulated by all that the New York scene offered—and that it virtually compelled us to experience—we became gluttonous in our cultural appetites. The constant thrills of discovery, the joys of creativity and of making music, the almost relentless onslaught on our senses, enriched both of us, bonded us in ways we had never previously experienced.

Our mutual transformations, individually and conjointly, were fascinating to observe. We had so much to learn from each other. She was more passive in her behavior and reactions, more mysterious, more complicated (or was it a trifle uncertain?), while I tended to be more active, more direct, more assertive, more determined. I knew instinctually that if we were to come closer together in our emotional and sexual understanding of each other, we would have to be very sensitive and patient with each other. We both understood that living together, whether officially married or not, was going to be serious, hard work, and essentially a work in progress.

We didn't talk much about such matters. I think we didn't have to. We seemed to quietly digest and absorb what we learned from and perceived in each other. Over time we adjusted to each other, meeting each other half way—and then, plunging on ahead from there.

It was not hard for me to be gentle and patient with her. I was (and am) a basically gentle type to begin with; but more than that, I had seen enough scarring rancor, disaffection, and estrangement on far too many occasions between my own parents. So I vowed I would never let such clashes destroy our relationship. I knew with a high degree of certainty, deep down inside me, that my love for her was indestructible, that it could not be tampered with, no matter what might emerge or intervene, either from her or anyone or anything else. My love for her had one main agenda: *to make her happy*, in all the ways that that could be done. I knew that I would devote my life to that objective.

I know that I awakened Margie—I say this as humbly as I can—to the full joy and pleasures of sex, mainly by thinking primarily of *her* happiness. Even in my teens, long before I became sexually active, I knew deep down that I would never be able to regard sex with a woman as a one-way ticket to my own personal gratification. If my instinctual and intellectual belief in absolute, nonnegotiable equality between people wasn't enough, the callous, arrogant, self-satisfying talk I heard as a teenager from most of my peers would have in itself convinced me that such a self-indulgent one-sided approach to sex was anathema to me. I heard lots of crude bragging that last year in high school and from some of the guys in Tony Acquaviva's band. I suspected that it was just bragging or wishful thinking, the blabber of puffed-up adolescent egos. To me such talk sounded subhuman. That a girl, a woman, was in their minds a slave, an object to be used, that a woman wasn't much more than a vagina, and that the sex act was solely a matter of conquest, was beyond my comprehension, and something I found totally repulsive and rejected innately. I knew with absolute certainty that that wasn't love. There was no tenderness involved, no beauty, no warmth. And if tenderness, sensitiveness, and gentleness were not involved, then it couldn't be love.

In the early days of our life together, even before we were living together in the Houston Street church, when we were still exploring and savoring each other physically, emotionally, psychically, I knew that in regard to a sexual relationship, I would have to be the initiator: cautious, gentle, persuasive rather than coercive. Though this sometimes didn't satisfy my own needs, I learned to accept that. Somehow I knew that the road to a rich, imaginative, truly reciprocal sex relationship lay not in impetuous or precipitous behavior, probably producing in the aftermath silent, unspoken recriminations, but rather in a patient, graduated, mutually respectful approach. For me that meant one thing, whatever it might require of me: to make *her* happy! I quickly discovered that this gave me indescribable pleasures, and brought me satisfactions I had never experienced before. I hasten to add that it had nothing to do with any sort of masochistic subjugation to her, for that was not what I could ever construe as equivalence between partners.

Love is one of those things that we human beings, even with our (presumably) superior brains and unique capacities for high intelligence, can't rationally understand or analyze objectively. At least I know I couldn't. But I knew our love was right, it felt right, and that the feeling of supreme mutual satisfaction was genuine. It didn't need to be understood or analyzed. It just was.

As I say, Margie and I didn't talk much about such matters. I think we were both too inhibited to bring such issues up for verbal dissection and intellectual psychologizing. We were too naïve; we were novices, two young experimenting kids. What did we really know when even the world's greatest experts knew very little! Theories, opinions, guesses: yes; but some all-embracing, irrefutable knowledge: no. For my part, I sensed somehow that talking about sex was futile. One could only learn what there was to learn by doing, or at least one could learn infinitely more by doing than by talking. I knew—I'm not sure how or why—that one best learned about one's partner from subtle, silent reactions, from tiny moves and sounds of pleasure, sounds of satisfaction or their opposites: irritation, discomfort, annoyance. This took great sensitivity and attention to minutiae and detail, a recurrent theme in my life.

In a larger sense, what we were doing, without even consciously realizing it, was testing our potential for a life together. Without ever mentioning the subject, we both knew that it would be best to try out our marriage, to test whether our love for each other was strong and deep enough to withstand the pressures, the inevitable trials and tribulations of life that would certainly intrude somewhere along the line. It is in the nature of such interventions that they do not announce themselves, they don't come with any warnings. Yet that is where I learned to respond calmly, unconfrontationally, treading as delicately as my emotions—and my vocabulary—would allow. (It is amazing how one ill-chosen or slightly too-harsh word—or even a not-so-harsh word harshly spoken—can totally thwart any further rational discourse.) I went out of my way in general to avoid arguments, especially ones that I was sure would be a senseless waste of time, solving nothing and just creating tension. Our demands of each other had to be thoughtfully expressed and thoughtfully received, while we tried always to maintain a mutually responsive, equipoised relationship.

Though Margie was docile and generally composed by nature, this should not be construed as her being spineless, without temperament or without strong convictions. She could stand her ground with unwavering firmness. At the same time she was unpresumptuous enough to be open-minded and most eager to learn, to explore, to venture further—even if sometimes cautiously—into new untested realms, be they intellectual, emotional, or sexual.

By the time we found a way to live together—as if married—we had begun to learn to adjust and to give in to each other for the sake of a deeper and more beautiful union. When we did finally marry in 1948, by which time we had known each other for nearly five years and had lived more or less intimately together for two-and-a-half years, we knew, we could feel, that we had worked out most of the problems we had faced. We learned in later years that we hadn't gotten all the wrinkles out of our relationship, and realized that even under the best of circumstances there might be areas of incompatibility that might never be completely reconciled. We knew that achieving and maintaining a successful marriage—whether officially sanctioned by church and state or not—was a work in constant progress. Exercise tolerance and patience, and you will arrive at (one hopes) such a deep ensouled bonding that nothing can break the relationship asunder.

We both had problems and flaws that we could never fully surmount. Mine haunt me to this day, and some of them will in due course become part of this narrative. If I mention one of Margie's problems now, it is only because it led to our first really serious fight, our first terribly wounding altercation.

Margie had one unfortunate and intractable habit: she was constantly late. She seemed to have no sense of time, and she could easily confuse five minutes with half an hour and not know it. It was not a matter of meanness, orneriness, personal defiance, or sense of superiority that would allow her to ignore the concept of being somewhere on time. And it certainly wasn't disrespect for me. I truly believe such negative impulses were simply not part of her nature. As often as she was disastrously late and as often as it irritated and hurt me deeply, she was never able to break this insidious habit. I realized in the end that it was like an addiction. I suppose if she had achieved her dream of a career as a singer or pianist, she would have learned to get to a rehearsal or appointment on time; she would have had to, or else she could not have survived professionally.

Not being on time was something incomprehensible and intolerable to me. On that one subject the gulf between us was very wide. For my life was completely dominated and controlled by the discipline of time. One of the earliest primal lessons one learns as a professional musician is that one has to be absolutely on time to jobs—no exceptions—whether to a rehearsal, a concert, a recording session, or an audition. One learns very quickly to live by the clock, it becomes as natural as brushing one's teeth every day. The memory of the two times I was inadvertently late to a Met performance makes me wince to this day and sticks in my mind as among the most dreadful experiences I've ever had. Nightmares about being late to a job are the two or three of the most recurrent and most common to musicians. I *still* have such nightmares; my most recent one occurred just a few months ago. In those dreams I am not only late; when I finally get to the rehearsal I don't have my horn with me and can't find it.

It was in those first months in New York when almost every day involved meeting somewhere that I became painfully aware that Margie—like Marilyn Monroe—was virtually incapable of getting anywhere on time. I can't count the number of times that I waited for her on some street corner or at some restaurant for an hour, sometimes two hours; or, in later years, returning from, say, an extended trip to Europe and being almost beside myself with longing for her, having daydreamed over and over again of feasting my eyes on her extraordinary beauty, she would arrive to pick me up at Logan Airport more than an hour late, not once but many, many times.

That is enough to try any man's patience. There I stand, patiently, still filled with the exciting anticipation of our imminent reunion. But little by little as the minutes turn into a half hour, then into an hour, my patience dwindles to nothing. I am so frustrated (emotionally, psychologically, sexually) that I can't think straight. I can't even manage a smile when Margie finally arrives. My heart is dark, and I can't even bring myself to hug her, because this is now something like the 112th time that she is late.

It was inevitable that my sense of discipline regarding time and Margie's real difficulty in keeping appointments would lead to a major collision between us. As mentioned, it was the subject of our first big fight and, alas, the cause for the majority of our quarrels, a recurring theme with endless variations over the ensuing years. I write about this matter out of a mixture of pain, confusion—and apology. Considering my deep love for Margie, I wish, nineteen years after her death, that we wouldn't have had those terrible fights that tore at our psychic innards, the wounds of which would sometimes take days to heal. That night, at the climax of a horrific screaming match, Margie said that she could no longer stay with me, that she would have to leave me. That flash of sheer hatred and fury was devastating; it burned deep into me. I had in the heat of the battle never anticipated that my criticism of her lateness habit would wound her so deeply, and that the depth of her anger could lead to a threat of leaving me. At last, in a sudden precious moment of silence, momentarily exhausted from our shouting match, I told her that I would always love her, that even if she left me, I would never—could never—stop loving her. I think she was too angry, too heated to hear me. But somehow, deep down, in her innermost recesses, she must have heard my call of anguish. Whatever hurts I may have caused her from time to time in our fifty years together, she knew that my love for her was inviolably enduring—as the touching phrase goes: Till death do us part.

Months later, at dinner, one of us—I can't recall who—thought that our little spat (as we then thought of it) was right out of the third act of *La Bohème*—without, fortunately, the same aftermath.[11] That searing fight was the first serious testing of our love for each other, of our hopes of spending a lifetime together. There were to be more tests through the years, some similar, some frighteningly different, some unexpected, others embarrassingly redundant, and always at first seemingly irresolvable. And yet, as stubborn and as convinced as we both were of our individual righteousness, we did gradually learn to resolve these matters, not by divorce but by quietly adjusting and forgiving each other. In the long perspective these occasional altercations were tiny blips on a very large screen. Both of us learned that such shouting matches were devastating experiences in which no one emerged victorious, and that, if prolonged, could destroy our love. It was a matter of giving in, of swallowing our pride—not always easy—of pulling back from the brink of combat, and thus avoiding the impact of a direct head-on emotional collision.

I have often thought that we were protected from having too many fights by our incredibly involved and busy exploration of New York's rich cultural scene. That may sound disingenuous, but I really think there is some truth in it. It was as if we had *no time for fights*, for negative distractions. It was like a gigantic joyride into a whole new universe, the impact of which matured us, gave us a solid intellectual and emotional foundation, and a whole arsenal of implements with which to navigate through life's obstacle course.

Everything we experienced, separately or together, we discussed, analyzed, argued, reexamined, and usually also shared with close friends such as Joe Marx or the Clarks. John and Jeannie Clark had moved out to River Edge, New Jersey, and we seem to have visited them at least twice a month, which meant that each of our visits involved three or more hours of travel. But the effort was worth it, for our evenings with the Clarks were filled with many happy hours of listening to great recordings, often exchanged from our respective record collections, followed by wonderful conversations and discussions, all the while watching their first child, Dickie, grow from a tiny baby into a constantly clambering toddler. We could never seem to tear ourselves away; nor can I recall that the Clarks ever kicked us out. We always seemed to stay until at least two a.m. and thus never got home till four or so, sometimes not until the crack of dawn.

I remember especially my first hearing of Ravel's *L'Enfant et les sortilèges* and many Berlioz recordings from that time, including some marvelous ones by Munch and Beecham, Berlioz being one of John Clark's favorite composers. John had a sizable collection of Albert Coates recordings, arguably—for me certainly—the greatest conductor of the early twentieth century. (Yes, greater even than Toscanini.) The Coates recordings John had were mostly Wagner opera excerpts (almost always with the greatest Heldentenor ever, Lauritz Melchior, and other great Wagnerians such as Frida Leider and Friedrich Schorr). But he also had fantastic performances of Ravel's *La Valse*, Respighi's *Fountains of Rome*, and all of Tchaikovsky's symphonies. I could write many pages of encomiums about Coates (born in St. Petersburg, died in Cape Town, South Africa, 1882–1953), but will for now simply affirm that, as a larger than life figure with voracious appetites and an insatiable zest for life—one British writer once called him "a vast whirlwind of a man"[10]—his recordings are always enormously exciting, ranging from the explosive and powerfully dramatic to the most tender, lyrical, and warm. He also had the largest, most broad-ranging repertory of any conductor I know of. Perhaps—to make just one musical-technical point—the most outstanding quality of his more than a hundred recordings is the near perfect acoustic-dynamic balance that he constantly achieved with his London Symphony Orchestra.

Reading Tolstoy might not ordinarily be considered one of those obstacle courses. And perhaps that is not quite the right way to describe my prolonged encounter with the writings of the great Russian novelist and humanist philosopher. But it was certainly prolonged, for I read over a period of about a year virtually every word that Tolstoy ever wrote.

Most people associate Tolstoy with his masterful novels *War and Peace* and *Anna Karenina*, and are not aware that he wrote several hundred books, essays, articles, pamphlets, tracts, and short stories—ultimately the preponderance of his literary output—which, collectively, dealt in a more focused and didactic way with a whole series of human, ethical, moral, and social issues, ranging from marriage, love, and sex, to politics and religion, and human relationships. I had earlier read his two famous novels, but through Söndlin on a brief visit in Cincinnati I had been alerted to that other side of Tolstoy's work. I started with *The Kreutzer Sonata*, *Family Happiness*, *The Death of Ivan Ilyich*, *Confession*, *Master and Man*, and worked my way through *Resurrection*, *What Is Art?*, *On the Relations Between the Sexes*, and many other essays, as well as his powerful play *The Power of Darkness*.

I became totally entranced by the force of his language (even in English and German translation), the laserlike brilliance of his mind, his uncannily observant eye and ear for human dealings and for realistic dialogue and persuasive dialectic argumentation, and above all by the passion of his convictions. I was caught up in an irresistible compulsion to pursue his thinking to whatever ends it might lead. I fell completely under Tolstoy's spell.

That turned into an extraordinary psychic journey, during which I underwent a strange and eventually very conflicted personal transformation. I became totally enmeshed in his philosophical, moral, ethical, and social concepts and judgments, some of them intrinsically—it is quite ironic—foreign to me. On the one hand I reveled in Tolstoy's libertarian social ethics, in his indictments of czarism and his bitter railings against the Russian aristocracy, against the rich and powerful, and autocratic rule in general; in short, his exposition of the whole range of social and political evils festering in Russian society, and his corollary ennoblement of the peasantry and serfs. On the other hand, I am surprised in retrospect that

I gradually succumbed so completely to his moralistic preachings on sex and marriage, given my own intense, innate yearnings for a rich, liberated sex life. I am astounded that I could become so ensnared in Tolstoy's extreme moralistic, judgmental views, such as demanding absolute chastity of men and his belief that marriage was the only justification, the only permissible outlet for man's sexual urges, or his claims that sex relations are only justified in order to produce children. Tolstoy proclaimed all this even as he admitted that in his own life he could never meet his own dictates, and that what he preached was an unrealizable ideal that should nevertheless be striven for.

In *My Religion* Tolstoy acknowledged, after castigating the wealthy aristocratic class for its vices, avarice, and materialism, that he had also lived a complete life of sin in his youth, but that he was now inspired by his reading of the Bible and particularly Christ's Sermon on the Mount to preach and live a life of self-denial and self-renunciation. He wrote that he had been strongly influenced by reading about a particular ultrachastity movement that flourished in America in the last decades of the nineteenth century.

It was crazy. Here I was trying to reconcile Tolstoy's demand that I become some sort of Christlike creature in my life as a normal, well-rounded male, enjoying a regular healthy sex life. Part of me was trying to figure out how I could practice sexual continence when deep down I knew that that was not only impossible to achieve but also pretty idiotic—completely against human nature. Furthermore, how could I reconcile total continence with my love for Margie and the sexual attractions she represented to me?

Eventually my faith in Tolstoy's reasonings began to waver when in some of his late stories, such as "Evil Allures, But Good Endures" and "The Devil," he condemned even his own previous fiction (even *War and Peace*), flagellating himself for the realism of his earlier novels, and suggesting that man's sole salvation lay not only in sexual denial but also in the rejection of all forms of pleasurable gratification—even the intellectual and emotional satisfactions and delights of the arts. And when I read *What Is Art?* and *The Prostitution of Art*, in which he roundly condemned *all* modern art, I began to consider that perhaps his teachings and credo, besides being untenable, were the fanatic ravings of an octogenarian in his second childhood.

The final turning point came for me through a most adventitious intervention when, during my reading of Tolstoy's deprecating view of modern art, I was at the same time playing Moussorgsky's *Boris Godunov*, an undeniably great and unique masterpiece, a work that always stirred unknown depths in me. I wrote in my diary that "I didn't believe Tolstoy would have so mercilessly condemned modern art had he heard that opera, which above all celebrates Russia's peasantry and serfs as the land's true nobility." The tremendous contradictions in Tolstoy's judgments suddenly became crystal clear to me. I began to understand that Tolstoy's strict moral interpretations had to be ascribed to a form of artless fanaticism, a strain of zealotry, which—I also realized—actually runs like a thread through Russian nineteenth-century literature.

The only way I can rationalize what happened to me during this Tolstoy addiction is that—apparently, in my youth—I tended at times to become swayable in often contrary directions by the sheer diversity of my readings and interests. But it also must have been a kind of relapse into that strange religious illumination I experienced at St. Thomas, when, like Tolstoy, I thought that I must live a life of absolute moral purity and resist all sexual temptation.

In the end, I didn't totally regret my yearlong encounter with Tolstoy and his judgmental writings. It was a useful exercise, as one often learns more from one's problems and mistakes in being misled temporarily into some strange alien attitude and behavior. Above all, I realized in retrospect that what struck me most deeply was the beauty and power of Tolstoy's language, and the incredible clarity and persuasiveness of his detailed argumentations. I was simply hypnotized, and any resisting rational thinking was temporarily suspended. I was hypnotized just as several years earlier I had been by the music of Scriabin. I recall, with some bemusement, that as an antidote to my immersion in Tolstoy's writings, I began to read books such as D. H. Lawrence's *Lady Chatterly's Lover* and Shaw's *Man and Superman*, dialectically 180 degrees in the opposite philosophical, moral direction.

When I came out of this bizarre episode—a weird mental detour—I returned to my original concept that sex was all about beauty: the irresistible attraction of beauty, whether physical or sensual, of the mind or of the spirit, outward or inward. I realized that I was in love with beauty itself, whatever form it might take: human, artistic, intellectual, and—naturally—physical love.

Of course, I wasn't recovering with only Drs. Lawrence and Shaw. In retrospect, I marvel at the range of literature that captured my attention, from Oscar Levant's riotous, wittily cynical *A Smattering of Ignorance*, George Bernard Shaw's *The Perfect Wagnerite*, two books on Rasputin (I couldn't shake my fascination with the Russian mystic and sybarite), to Aldous Huxley's brilliantly satirical *Antic Hay*, Oscar Wilde's *Dorian Grey*, Daniel DeFoe's *Moll Flanders*, and François Rabelais' *Gargantua and Pantagruel*.

As a wonderful literary bonus, I discovered a remarkable program aired every Sunday morning for almost twenty-five years called *Invitation to Learning*. (Can you imagine such a program—or a program with such a title—on *today's* network television?! I don't think so.) It was hosted by an astonishingly knowledgeable literatus, Lyman Bryson, who led highly informative discussions on great world literature with other bibliophiles such as John Mason Brown, Muriel Rukeyser, Sidney Hook, Clifton Fadiman, Alfred Kazin, and Quincy Howe. It was an incredible learning experience presented by CBS as a public affairs broadcast. It dealt with a wide, comprehensive spectrum of literature and drama: Aeschylus's *Prometheus*, T. S. Elliot's poetry, Spengler's *Decline of the West*, Joyce's *Ulysses*, and many a great classic in between. Moreover, these highly intelligent and informative discussions were transcribed and made available in print for the grand cost of ten cents. (Several dozen of these pamphlets still grace my rather substantial library). *Invitation to Learning* was followed every Sunday morning by *Invitation to Music*, programmed by Oliver Daniel, conducted by Bernard Herrmann, and played by the station's excellent CBS Symphony Orchestra. These public service programs— no sponsors, no commericals—were a real inspiration to me, what church might be for others.

Near the end of August, when it seemed there would not be any further work for the rest of the summer, Margie and I decided to spend some time in Lake Placid visiting with the White family and Walter Heermann. I had told Margie about my two previous visits to Lake Placid, about Paul White and his wonderful family, also about Walter Heermann, and, of course, about the grandeur and sublime beauty of the Adirondacks. This time I argued that piano and voice lessons or not, she had to come with me for a brief vacation away from the city.

Because of prior commitments to her teachers—which she felt she really couldn't break—I ended up going to Lake Placid *twice* within a two-week span; Margie joined me only on the second trip. That splitting of what we had hoped would be a full two-week vacation together also became necessary because I was called at the last minute to play on the *Carnegie Hall* movie recording session, which paid top dollar. At the time I could ill afford to turn the job down. But I had also promised Paul White to play horn in two of *his* concerts in Lake Placid, for which he had programmed, especially for me, Mozart's *Musical Joke* and Haydn's "Farewell" Symphony, with Pouny White playing second horn. I just couldn't let Paul down.

I raced to Lake Placid and played the two rehearsals and two concerts, finding out that the "Farewell" Symphony had been programmed in honor of and as a fond farewell to William Shirer, the famous World War II CBS correspondent and great writer. Why honor someone musically just because he was going off to New York City for a few days? First of all, Bill

Shirer was in his day as beloved, admired, and respected nationwide as Walter Cronkite, his younger colleague at CBS, was to become a few decades later. Bill, a passionately devoted music lover, attended every concert and almost every rehearsal at the Lake Placid Club. Performing Haydn's "Farewell" Symphony, one of Bill's favorites, was a sly, witty way of bidding him a fond farewell—even though he was going to be gone less than a week—and was a token of their appreciation for his devoted presence and support of the club's musical activities.

On that brief stay in Lake Placid I also managed to squeeze in a visit with Artur Rodzinski, who had his summer home there. Rodzinski and I had a long talk about conductors and orchestra musicians, from which I came away with the impression that he hated musicians, and seemed to hate even music. I had never heard him talk like that before. This was not the person I associated with his hair-raisingly beautiful Berg Violin Concerto recording, or the passionate New York Philharmonic performance of the Szymanowski Violin Concerto. After a while he talked to me only about money. I wondered, *what is wrong with this man?* Then rather suddenly, he broke off the conversation and asked me to help him do some underbrush clearing in the woods behind his house. I felt that I must oblige him. While we were working in the woods I suddenly heard some goats bleating nearby. Rodzinski told me that they were his goats, that he milked them himself every day, and that he was allowed to drink only goat milk because of his stomach ulcers and his nervous disposition.

After about an hour—when he was much calmer—he released me from duty, so to speak. It was one of the more bizarre afternoons I ever spent in my life. The only nice moment occurred when I saw Rodzinski's young son, Richard, a chubby, red-cheeked boy who was playing with some toys in the front of the house. (Richard Rodzinski has been for many years the managing director of the world famous Van Cliburn piano competition.)

I rushed back to New York to play that crazy film date, and two days later I headed back to Lake Placid, this time with Margie in tow. Instead of staying with the Whites in their huge compound, we elected to stay in Lake Placid Village in a cute little rooming house located near the town's public golf course and parklike woods with hiking trails. We rented two adjacent attic rooms, in effect a bedroom and a living room. There was a tiny kitchenette that we rarely used, since we preferred to buy a picnic lunch of bread, cheese, salami—and wine—and enjoy that in the nearby park or at the edge of the golf course.

It is impossible for me to describe how happy we were in that small, modest place and in our semi-isolation. We could do as we pleased and we were inseparable, deeply in love in all the ways that could be expressed, brimming with youthful energy, eager to conquer the world.

After all the relatively busy work of the earlier summer, I had really looked forward to some totally uninterrupted time to compose and study. But what I ended up doing instead was some jazz transcribing. Sometime earlier that summer I had acquired a few Harry James recordings, which impressed me so much that I felt I had to transcribe them off the record—just as another learning experience. They included *The Mole* (1941), *Friar Rock* (1945), and *Easy* (1946), three compositions by Leroy Holmes, one of the James Orchestra's best arrangers. I had my small Columbia portable record player with me and over a period of several days (especially on rainy ones) transcribed those three records—cooled by the breezes coming in from the woods, several times working long into the night, while keeping my record player at the lowest audible volume so as not to disturb the other tenants.

If some of my more jazz-interested readers wonder, in sardonic astonishment, why I would bother transcribing some Harry James recordings, I happily respond that James was not only one of that era's very finest jazz musicians, he was also its most stunningly gifted trumpet player, a most inventive and fiery improviser, and a technically (trumpetistically) supervirtuosic instrumentalist. These qualities were, alas, never recognized or appreciated by jazz critics or historians and the public. Most of the former never forgave James for his early 1940s superstar popularity and his overindulgence (admittedly) in far too much inane Tin Pan Alley pop tune repertory, worse yet, often played in a whiny, saccharine hotel dance band manner. A sad part of the Harry James story is that no one noticed that he dramatically changed course in 1945 and 1946, adopting a strong jazz policy that, unbeknownst to most of the world, he maintained through hard and easy times, until the end of his life in 1983. James remained a remarkably explorative and imaginative jazz player, as much or more so than many more famous jazz celebrities. He should even be appreciated and admired for keeping successive big bands going and recording with them in the sixties and seventies when big bands (jazz orchestras) were virtually extinct.

As early as 1941 James had added a small string section and a horn to his orchestra, another thing certain intolerant jazz critics never forgave him. The strings were used by James not as some sentimental overlay (as was so often the case in some jazz and most pop music), but ingeniously as another instrumental color; and it expanded the upper register of the band with high notes simply not available in the standard jazz orchestra. James even used string harmonics, and had the string players play the backgrounds with little or no vibrato. This sound brought a novel organlike or harmoniumlike quality to the orchestra's sonoric palette. The bad reputation that clung to strings, especially violins, as inherently sweet and sugary, was quite definitely a result of the constant *misuse* of strings in popular music that relentlessly catered to the basest public tastes and lowest forms of sentimentality. Had those critics who constantly criticized the use of strings in jazz ever listened to a Beethoven, Brahms, or Bartók violin concerto, or for that matter to Stuff Smith's or Ray Nance's violin playing, they would never have come up with the idea that strings—violins—are inherently sweet and sugary. Come to think of it, those writers probably never forgave James for marrying Betty Grable, either.[12]

Naturally Margie and I went regularly to the Lake Placid Sinfonietta's concerts, and visited a lot with Walter Heermann and Paul's family. Josie, the matriarch of the family, to whom I, of course, had to introduce Margie, heartily approved of her, albeit in her somewhat haughty, superior manner. She even urged me in a motherly way to "marry her soon; you don't want to lose her." I cockily assured her that I didn't think there was any chance of that.

In the evenings there were almost always chamber music concerts at various friends' summer homes or cottages. Several of these musicales were held at Bill Shirer's place, even when he was away for a few days. I particularly remember a wonderful evening of relaxed music making, featuring Brahms's glorious Clarinet Quintet (with Stanley Hasty, the newly appointed principal clarinet of the Rochester Philharmonic). As I had my horn along I was invited one evening to play the Brahms Horn Trio at Carl Lamson's cottage, with Carl and Millard Taylor, concertmaster of the Rochester Philharmonic. But more exciting were the two dinner evenings Margie and I spent with Bill Shirer. He not only reminisced about his experiences in Germany before and during the war, but we also got into long discussions about Proust and Tolstoy, both of whose works I was reading at the time.

Bill throve not just on the popular three Bs repertory (Bach, Beethoven, and Brahms) but also loved modern twentieth-century music, and had an interest in the German-Austrian tradition. On one of the evenings we spent together he started—to my surprise—to talk about *Wozzeck*, Alban Berg's great opera, based on a drama by Georg Büchner. Perhaps I shouldn't have been surprised, because Shirer, as I well knew, had spent many, many years in Germany, and was in fact very knowledgeable about Germany's cultural history. We both got so excited talking for hours, exchanging views about our favorite subject, German culture (music, literature, art, history), and, inevitably, by dramatic contrast, the agonies and horrors—and incomprehensibility of—Germany's more recent history, in which he had been so personally and critically involved.

I told him that I had never heard or seen *Wozzeck* because it had been performed only once in America, in 1931 by Stokowski and the Philadelphia Orchestra. (The great breakthrough performance in America was a few years later, in 1951, by Dimitri Mitropoulos and the New York Philharmonic.) Paradoxically, some weeks later I had occasion to write Bill a long letter about *Wozzeck*; by an amazing coincidence, I heard a beautiful performance of three excerpts from *Wozzeck* broadcast on CBS's *Invitation to Music*, performed by the CBS Symphony and conducted by Bernard Herrmann. I was overwhelmed by this beautiful, heartbreaking, gripping music. In my letter to Shirer I called it "the deepest music of our age." I had that CBS performance recorded off the air by my friend Zeke in Carnegie Hall, and that recording is still one of my most prized possessions. Herrmann and the orchestra's rendering of those *Wozzeck* excerpts, officially called "*Drei Bruchstücke* (Three Fragments)," was superb, still one of the best performances I have ever heard, especially considering that Berg's music was still totally unheard and unknown in this country. But then, Bernard Herrmann was a very gifted musician and conductor, knowledgeable in this kind of modern repertory. He was very much underappreciated in his time, probably because his career as a Hollywood film composer overshadowed his work as a conductor and a serious composer. That *Wozzeck* performance also featured some extraordinarily beautiful playing in important extended solo passages by a great trumpet player of the time, Harry Freistadt, and by Fred Klein, first horn of the orchestra, both admired friends and colleagues of mine.

Ever since I had first gone to Lake Placid in 1944, I had dreamed of climbing Whiteface and Mount Marcy, the Adirondack's two highest mountains, located about ten miles northeast of the town. Although looming majestically in the distance, Whiteface was actually a lot closer to Lake Placid than Mount Marcy. On certain days the air was so clear that Marcy appeared to be only a twenty-minute hike away; but that was a visual atmospheric illusion.

In 1945 I had tried several times to organize a climb of Whiteface with some of the Sinfonetta musicians—it is a full day's venture—but had no such luck. They worked a fairly heavy schedule and were busy with rehearsals and lots of little concerts scattered through the week, which left very few free days. When I finally did get a few folks set to make the ascent with me, we were rained out and beset with heavy fog and thick low-lying clouds—not for just one day but for *three in a row*. That's the way it often is in the mountains. Finally, in the last few days of my stay, we did get both a clear weather day *and* a free day, and climbed Whiteface with five companions: Jack Holmes, the Sinfonietta's oboist (who was about to join the Boston Symphony as co-principal oboe and the youngest player in the history of that orchestra), George Humphrey, violist in the Boston Symphony,[13] his son, Lee, and for female companionship, two orchestra wives.

It was a glorious day in every way, one to make your heart leap with joy, only a few wispy clouds in the sky—a rarity in the mountains. Everything shone and glistened in the clear, pure Adirondack air; we were blessed with cool, dry weather and a south breeze. I had been told that some of the Whiteface trails were not in the best condition; they had been neglected during the last three years because many park rangers had gone into the armed services. There were, in fact, some bad patches now and then, mostly muddy, slippery, washed-out trails or paths blocked by fallen trees and such. But that just energized us even more; it upgraded the challenge.

The view from the top of Whiteface, westward across the Finger Lakes and eastward over the long stretch of Lake Champlain well into Vermont and northwestern Massachusetts, was fantastic, and its 360-degree grandeur was awe inspiring. The simple lunch we had at the summit—Walter and his daughter Polly had fixed mine—was almost an equally inspiring experience, since a meal on a mountain top is a unique event. But what I remember most lovingly was the wonderful all-day conversations—even arguments—with Jack, all about our love for music, our favorite pieces, favorite recordings, and conductors. We were both young and music was our passion; a way of life, not just a profession or a business. Up there, in those pristine forests, we bonded almost as in a love affair. It was so exhilarating. I was indulging in two of my great loves: nature and music. That was in 1945.

Now, on this 1946 Lake Placid visit, I hoped once again to get some mountain climbing in—this time with Margie—and to tackle Mount Marcy, the Adirondack's highest peak. But again, that adventure had to be abandoned several times because of poor weather and low-hanging clouds. (Climbing around on a mountain in dense clouds isn't much fun.) Instead we drove with Walter Heermann to Montreal, only a few hours away, and ate at two of my favorite restaurants: Chez Pierre and Aux Delices. On our return to Lake Placid—a wonderful drive home, lit by a clear, bright full moon—we saw the most spectacular northern lights (aurora borealis), near the Canadian border. It was my first time. What a spectacular sight to behold!

Despite the almost daily foggy, drizzly weather, Margie and I did manage to squeeze in occasional hikes and short walks to some of the special sights around Lake Placid, such as Mirror Lake, Heart Lake, and Cobble Hill. This certainly whetted our appetite for the opportunity to do some real climbing, which we finally did the following year.

The other work I did that summer of 1946 that comes under the heading of musical creativity was the completion of a series of jazz compositions and arrangements I had started earlier in the summer in New York. I was so eager to play some jazz—somewhere, somehow—but as the horn was still not considered a bona fide jazz instrument, I obviously wasn't getting any calls to play or sit in with anybody. I didn't try the jam session route because I was a little afraid at my embryonic stage of playing to face such a challenge (fear of rejection?), and because at that time I hardly knew where jam sessions took place in New York, except late at night at Minton's and Small's Paradise in Harlem. And I certainly didn't think I could make it in that scene. Then I remembered what Josef Marx had told me several times on the ballet tour in 1943 (paraphrased): If there's something wrong or something missing, or something you'd like to do or see done, don't just sit around complaining and bitching about it; *do something about it*, make it happen yourself!

I decided to form a group with some of my close brass player friends and colleagues. I settled on an instrumentation of four horns—I love the sound of four horns in close harmony—two trombones and three rhythm (piano, bass, and drums). I anticipated that the pieces I was going to write would be mostly fully written, with only here and there some room for improvisation, for the obvious reason that I was not yet personally acquainted with any real (improvising) jazz musicians (as I had been in Cincinnati). The colleagues I was hoping to involve were essentially all classically trained; like me they had a keen interest in and love for jazz, and had at least a feeling for it, but were not yet ready to do any serious improvising.

These brass sextet plus rhythm section compositions-arrangements were my first attempt to write real jazz. The symphonic arrangements for the Cincinnati Symphony pop concerts, the one-and-a-half arrangements I made for harp (and bass) in the spring of 1945 for Linda Iacobucci, and the jazz Harp Concerto for Gloria Agostini were by their nature basically for a symphonic instrumentation, a kind of quasi-jazz at best. The new brass arrangements were of Gershwin's *Lady Be Good* and *Summertime*, and Ellington's *Just a-Sittin' and a-Rockin.'* I also made an exact transcription of Ellington's *Dusk*, in which I played Rex Stewart's solo and Gordon Pulis played Lawrence Brown's solo. My originals were called *Till's Boogie* (obviously based

on Strauss's famous *Till Eulenspiegel* horn theme)

and a slow blues called—what else?—*Brass Blues*. I felt I had to do something on *Till* because

Thelonious Monk's *Straight, No Chaser* was so simi-

lar to *Till's* horn theme, which relationship I brought out a few times in my piece.

I was inspired to write for four horns because by now I had met a few other young horn players who also aspired to play jazz, or at least to play with a modicum of jazz or swing feeling. One of them was my longtime friend and colleague Art Holmes, who, since I had last seen him, had played for a while with the Charlie Barnet band. The other was Bobby Brown, fourth horn in Toscanini's NBC Symphony. If I could find one more horn player, I could assemble what would undoubtedly be the first four-man jazz horn section ever. For the two trombones I chose Gordon Pulis, first trombone of the New York Philharmonic, without a doubt one of the finest classical trombonists ever,[14] and my great friend from my Ballet Theatre days, John Clark. For my rhythm section I initially chose Walter Hendl, at the time pianist and assistant conductor of the New York Philharmonic, who alleged an interest in jazz. But after a couple of rehearsals both Walter and I realized that jazz piano was not really his cup of tea. I replaced him with, guess who—Gussie! As bassist I hoped to get Doc Goldberg, a fine all-around musician and veteran of the jazz scene, having played for years with two fine Swing Era bands: Will Bradley–Ray McKinley and Will Hudson–De Lange. I had first heard him on a 1941 Metronome All Star recording. The drummer I had in mind was Brad Spinney, who was on the staff of WOR, while Doc played with both the CBS Symphony and that station's full-time small-group jazz unit.

I planned to record my brass-plus-rhythm pieces at the famous Nola Studios on Broadway between Fiftieth and Fifty-First Streets,[15] and also to rehearse there over a period of weeks starting in late September. But by mid-September I still had only three horn players ready to work on the music, and unfortunately one of them never showed up for a crucial rehearsal. But eventually we managed to have one terrific rehearsal with everyone present, including, luckily, Vinny Jacob, whom I was able to snare at the last minute for second horn. I loved Vinny's playing, as he had a beautiful warm tone, and had played with the Claude Thornhill, Harry James, and George Paxton bands. For the final rehearsal date, however, Doc Goldberg and Brad Spinney couldn't free themselves from their staff jobs. So I quickly drafted Clarence Totten, a fine bass player at the Met who was interested in jazz, and the young Walter Rosenberg, in his first year as percussionist with the New York Philharmonic. It was nightmarish at times to get—and to keep—this group together. All eight players were willing to do this work gratis, out of friendship and respect for me; but of course they first had to take care of their primary jobs. In the end, I was successful, but now, instead of recording at Nola's, I went to a studio at New York University, which I could lease for practically nothing because my brother Edgar worked there as a recording engineer. This in turn meant that he, with his fine musical ear, could supervise the session, and that was a lucky break.

In retrospect, I consider it a minor miracle that these brass ensemble sessions occurred at all. I still have those acetate discs, now sixty-five years old and worn, but still playable. As I recently listened to them for the first time in decades, I found them remarkably ambitious and mostly successful. The horns are nicely swinging, while the rhythm section at times sounds a bit stiff and labored. Again, learning by imitation, I borrowed a lot of licks from Dizzy Gillespie and Tadd Dameron, Gerry Valentine, Pete Rugolo, and Ralph Burns, transferring them in some cases more or less literally to the horns, often in my own lead parts.

I had an easy, secure high register, a great asset in horn playing, and therefore, in an attempt to come as close as possible to emulating Dizzy or Howard McGhee or Conte Condoli, my lead horn parts in these pieces were full of high F sharps, Gs, A flats, As. These notes were all considered to be above the operative upper range of the horn. I remember (in *Till's Boogie*) fooling around just for fun in a rehearsal with Strauss's famous horn call, in a truly stratospheric range: *a ninth higher* than where Strauss had originally set it. But what I was really proud of was the sheer sonic opulence of those pieces; all that rich four- and six-part close harmony writing, clad in the new emerging bop language, produced a truly exciting brass sound.

It was a great learning experience for me, and we all enjoyed making these acetate recordings. Like so many of my early endeavors, this one was a modest undertaking, without a commercial objective. My only aim was to explore new musical territory and learn from the experience. I value them for their nostalgic interest and the happy memories of the interesting experiment they represent.

One seemingly innocuous occurrence during those Nola rehearsals led to an incalculably important relationship. It was there that I met a man who became my very closest and now oldest still-living friend: the composer, flutist (earlier in his youth, jazz alto saxophonist), and superb teacher, Robert Di Domenica. Bob had been urged by his navy buddy, Roland Johnson, when both were stationed in 1945–46 at the U.S. Navy Sonar School in Key West, to "look up Gunther Schuller when you're back home in New York." Bob did just that, showing up at Nola's one of those September rehearsal days, thinking that it was the most likely place to find me. Thus commenced a deep, long friendship.

Josef Marx had joined the Met orchestra as English horn and third oboe in 1944. He had always been, along with his oboe work, a music historian and musicologist, a great admirer and friend of Alfred Einstein, the German-American musicologist. He was an ardent devotee of baroque and early classical music; among his multiple intellectual interests and talents this was probably his real forte. So it was that in the midforties Josef started a publishing company, McGinnis & Marx (McGinnis being his first wife's maiden name), specializing in woodwind music and literature, and what is now broadly called early music, European classical music from the Middle Ages and the Renaissance, including the baroque.

Josef had studied the oboe in London and in Amsterdam in the late 1930s. During that time he had become acquainted and friendly with some of the British baroque specialists, especially Arnold Dolmetsch, Adam Carse, and the young Robert Donington. He had also examined the superb early instrument collections in the British Museum in London and the Stedelijk Museum in Amsterdam—many decades before the emergence of the early-music, period-instrument movement. At the time he was the only oboist in America who specialized in baroque literature, and he was an avid student and proponent of the different embellishment and improvisational practices of the baroque era. His very personal and sometimes eccentric way of playing the oboe, technically and interpretationally, was well suited to the more individualistic, extemporaneous interpretation of baroque music, more than to the tradition-bound, codified opera repertory. At the Met Josef was a bit of a square peg in a round hole, and, in fact, didn't last long there. He was let go in 1948. But he was a wonderful player in baroque and contemporary music. That's why I wrote two pieces for him, my Oboe Sonata, which he premiered, and the *Fantasia Concertante* for three oboes and piano.

I worked with Joe in his McGinnis & Marx Company on his publication of Mozart's *Twelve Duets for Two Horns*, K. 487. We collaborated on this edition, I as a horn player and student of the late eighteenth-century horn, and Joe as the musicologist and historian. It was a fascinating undertaking because most Mozart scholars of the time, including Alfred Einstein, assumed these pieces to be for two basset horns. But Joe and I thought the work was in fact for two (French) horns. The duets are certainly playable on horns, including the natural horns of Mozart's time. They certainly would have ranked very high among the virtuosically challenging works for horn of that entire era. What finally gave me great confidence that these duets were indeed for two horns was the knowledge acquired in many months of independent research in the New York Public Library, where we found any number of works (well known in their time) by many other composers that presented similar technical and virtuosic demands: to wit, a number of Haydn symphonies, as well as his spectacular (though little known) "Concert Aria" for two sopranos, tenor, horn, English horn, bassoon, and orchestra in E major;

various works by Johann Dismas Zelenka; Friedrich Zachau's concert aria cantatas; Leopold Mozart's spectacular *Concerto for Two Horns*; Antonio Rosetti's horn (and two-horn) concertos; not to mention Mozart's highly virtuosic horn writing in *Così fan tutte* in the "Per pietà" aria. We also took into account Mozart's daring and rangy vocal demands in his soprano concert arias, and the amazing technical challenges in "Per questa bella mano," a work for double bass and vocal bass. All these compositions feature daunting demands, equal to any in Mozart's K. 487 Duets. Moreover, we established from other research that Mozart's close friend and leading horn virtuoso of that era, Ignaz Leutgeb, would have easily met any of the challenges offered in those twelve duet pieces.

My contribution to the publication was to show that certain nondiatonic notes and very high notes, always considered unplayable or too difficult on the natural horn of Mozart's time by nonhorn playing musicologists, were in fact not only playable but existed in a fairly wide range of literature by major composers, as suggested above, and even by Mozart himself. The high-lying notes contained in the duets—written Es, Fs, and Gs—were relatively common in the virtuoso horn writing of the period. All our research was elaborately documented by Josef in a brilliant foreword to the publication.

Our publication probably had little impact on musicologists and Mozart scholars at the time, since Josef was not taken seriously by professional musicologists in academia. Joe was considered more of an amateur dabbler. (A 1953 edition of the K. 487 Duets by the German musicologist Kurt Janetsky, published seven years after our edition, made no mention of our publication.) Joe and I decided not to worry about any of that, but I must admit that I was rather disappointed that my American hornist colleagues ignored our Duet publication, and rarely programmed those wonderful pieces composed by the mature Mozart.[16]

Other assignments for Joe as editor were a quintet for winds by Henri Brod (an early nineteenth-century French oboist and composer), as well as some Johann Ernst Galliard bassoon sonatas, the Karl Stamitz Quartet Op. 8, no. 2, and various other editorial tasks. All of my work for Joe was done unpaid; I worked for him because I wanted to and because I saw it as another valuable study and learning experience.

I recall from this time a rather special musical experience, namely, the first time I heard Josef Szigeti live. It occurred at a New York Philharmonic Stadium concert, one in which, paradoxically, the omens for any kind of a special performance were not particularly propitious. First of all, the microphones were distorting Szigeti's sound, a problem that was only rectified in the last movement of his Brahms Concerto performance. Second, Alexander Smallens was conducting that evening, and had just delivered himself of a particularly deadly, wooden Brahms Fourth Symphony performance. Szigeti saved the day by taking over completely in the finale of the Concerto, when the microphone problems had finally been resolved. It was absolutely thrilling to hear how he made every note of the piece a personal experience. As Margie said afterward, it was as if he was drawing his bow across your body. His double stops, so expressive and meaningful, were a special thrill because of his fine harmonic tuning. He didn't just play in tune, he *felt* the harmonies, the intervals' special unique nature. That was a rare experience.

As encores Szigeti first played two Bach solo violin pieces, music he always did superbly. But I was surprised when he launched into a couple of Paganini *Caprices*, undoubtedly wanting to show the audience that he could not only play all that serious stuff, such as Bartók, Bach, and Beethoven, but also some of the flashier virtuoso repertory. His performance did not have quite the mechanical perfection and natural ease of, say, a Milstein, but it had a timing and pacing that brought out both the music's inner expressive content and its extraordinary harmonic invention, an important aspect of Paganini's *Caprices* that is ignored in most performances of these technically *and* harmonically daring pieces.

The other fascinating artistic event that Margie and I were privileged to witness was a three-day visit by the Joos Ballet at the City Center. I had heard for some years about the famous German Joos Ballet and its renowned position in the world of dance, as a result especially of its groundbreaking 1932 dance drama, *The Green Table*. I had met Fritz Cohen, the company's music director and composer of virtually all its ballets, the year before at Kenyon. And now this legendary company was right on our doorstep. They presented most of their repertory, from *The Green Table* and *Prodigal Son* to *The Big City*, the latter with a fine ragtimey score by Alexandre Tansman. The Joos Ballet had no orchestra; all the music was for two pianos. The company's work—its dance style, choreography, and subject matter—were radically different from that of the Ballet Theatre or the other Russian companies that were current in America at the time. Joos's balletic language was very simple and direct, even stark, technically intricate and highly disciplined. It featured plain, unadorned costuming and the scantiest scenery, "expressing in dance the dramatic events of human life" (as the program book put it)—themes both contemporary and actual, yet also timeless.

Some time in the midst of all these myriad activities, I began reading H. L. Mencken, the all-time great debunker of pretentiousness. I immensely enjoyed his no-holds-barred satiric polemics, especially in *A Book of Burlesques* and *Prejudices*. I also kept pace as time allowed with my many film and art journals, in the process becoming more acquainted with Eric Bentley's brilliant writings. Meanwhile, the two books on musical subjects that I especially cherished (both in German) were a marvelous study of Stravinsky's compositions (up to the *Symphony of Psalms*) by Herbert Fleischer, a major and most perceptive German music critic of the time, and a fascinating, incredibly detailed and well-researched history of the early development of the horn up to Bach's time by Fritz Piersig. That was a subject about which most of us twentieth-century hornists knew next to nothing. Nowadays, half of all professional hornists own and play a variety of authentic replicas of baroque and early classical horns.

I also remember with what excitement I discovered the cantatas and oratorios of Friedrich Zachau (1663–1712) in the New York Public Library, in *Denkmäler der deutschen Kunst* (*Monuments of German Art*). Zachau was not only an important predecessor of Johann Sebastian Bach, but also the teacher of the young George Frederic Handel. Zachau's numerous church cantatas presented an interesting crossover format between vocal cantatas and instrumental concertos. Indeed, he called them concerto aria cantatas. And as a bonus, I found that many of his cantatas had very interesting, highly virtuosic solo or concertante horn parts. (More expensive photostatting followed!)

All this left little time for composing. The only productions from this 1946 period were an initially unnamed atonal composition for a twelve-piece jazz ensemble, and the two *Fantasias Concertantes*. These may seem to be odd choices until one realizes that young unknown composers often have to write for players of their acquaintance, on the assumption (and hope) that one can always prevail on one's friends to at least read through a new work, and thus gain some aural idea of its quality. In my case, I had many oboe and trombone playing friends, notably Josef Marx, Wally Bhosys, Gordon Pulis, and John Clark.

The jazz ensemble piece was a follow-up to the brass-plus-rhythm nonets I composed in 1946. I believe it was the first full-fledged through-composed atonal jazz piece in history—unless Bob Graettinger, the outstanding composer-arranger associated with Stan Kenton, beat me to it with some piece that I don't know of, and that was never performed or recorded.[17] My piece, eventually called *Jumpin' in the Future*, was scored for flute, oboe, three saxophones, trumpet, trombone, two horns, and piano, drums, and bass, and was, as others of my early efforts, never performed around the time it was written. Composed for an atypical ensemble, certainly not the standard fifteen-piece jazz orchestra, there wasn't even an existing group to whom I could have sent it, to give it a read-through. (Jazz groups in those days didn't have an oboe and a flute.) So, like many of my early works, *Jumpin'* remained unperformed for years. That didn't bother me, what was important was to have had the chance and privilege of creating something new.[18]

Near the end of September I received a call from the manager of the Montreal Symphony (Orchestre Symphonique de Montréal) to play a concert in early October, replacing the first horn, who had suddenly moved on to another orchestra. I was thrilled when I heard that the program included Ravel's *Mother Goose Suite* and the Glazounov Violin Concerto, which is to this day one of my most favorite violin concertos. Besides its inherent beauty and originality, it has some of the most delicious horn solos in the whole late nineteenth-century repertory. I recall the rehearsals and the concert as one of my happiest performing experiences of that time. Wilfred Pelletier was the conductor, a fine musician with whom I also worked many times at the Met. He was a very sensitive, gentle person, and a bit shy on the podium, lacking the kind of commanding authority that conductors are generally expected to have. I not only admired and respected him for his cultivated unaffected musicianship, but I was also touched by his modesty and self-effacing approach to conducting, which, alas, certain musicians saw as a vulnerability and on occasion abused woefully.

I was in heaven those two days in Montreal. My playing was secure and confident, and I recall with some pleasure how in the rehearsals heads would turn toward me in surprise, as some prominent horn passages would sail through the hall, with that look of: Wow! Who is this kid?

My second Met season began in the late fall of 1946 with a whole series of revelatory experiences. Within the first month I had the great privilege of rehearsing and playing for the first time not only Verdi's *Otello*, Moussorgsky's *Boris Godunov*, Wagner's *Siegfried* and *Walküre*, but also—on first horn—Mozart's *Marriage of Figaro* and *The Abduction from the Seraglio*.

My most overwhelming experience occurred in the second week of rehearsals, during the first few minutes of the initial orchestra reading rehearsal. It was Verdi's *Otello*. Although I was only twenty, I knew a substantial amount of music pretty thoroughly, not only as a professional and already experienced orchestral player, but also as a composer and an indefatigable student of all kinds of music. I was, moreover, a dedicated but still dilettante music historian, and as such quite knowledgeable in an immense amount of music ranging from Perotin in the twelfth century to the early twentieth-century moderns (Stravinsky, Schönberg, Berg, etc.), and most everything in between, whether operatic, symphonic, or chamber music. But thus far Verdi's *Otello* had somehow eluded me, mainly, I suppose, because most American opera companies at the time shied away from late Verdi and concentrated on the more popular middle operas such as *La Traviata*, *Il Trovatore*, and *Rigoletto*. Even on recordings, operas such as *Don Carlos*, *Otello*, and *Falstaff* were sparsely represented. I had only heard Iago's "Credo" aria on recordings played on the radio.

What exploded onto my ears in those first fifteen minutes of that *Otello* rehearsal was—despite Stravinsky's *Rite of Spring*, Wagner's *Tristan*, Debussy's *Jeux*, Ravel's *Daphnis*, Shostakovich's *Fifth Symphony*—like nothing I had ever heard before. Sitting in the midst of *Otello*'s twelve-piece brass section, at full *ff* throttle, and hearing for the first time Verdi's powerful, roaring, rhythmically driving storm music—as Otello arrives in Venice from his decisive victory in Cyprus to the ecstatic acclamation of the Venetian populace—the whole tumultuous scene hit me with such an overpowering aural, palpable force as I had never experienced before. I was stunned. I realized that part of what made the experience so overwhelming was the fact that I was not hearing this incredible music on a recording or sitting in a concert hall, but right *in the midst* of the music, in the brass section, surrounded and enveloped in it. I could feel in my feet the vibrations of the music coming through the floor of the orchestra pit.

But there was some deep, unearthly, sustained sound that I couldn't immediately identify. After a few minutes of mystified consternation I figured out that it was a very low register sound cluster, probably played on an organ. None of the musicians in my immediate neighborhood (most of them Met veterans who had played *Otello* dozens of times)—not even Coscia—knew what it was. That surprised me. Wouldn't anyone want to know what that extraordinary sound was?

As soon as the first intermission broke I rushed up to Fritz Busch's podium; looking at his score I saw that Verdi had indeed included an almost four-minute-long pedal point, a three-note semitone cluster ![musical notation], played on a sixteen-foot organ stop. Verdi called it a "contrabassi and timpani" stop. It was a powerful, terrifying, earthshaking sound, which I suddenly realized no composer before Verdi had ever used.

I was really surprised because, as a student of twentieth-century compositional developments and experiments, I had learned years ago that Henry Cowell had invented the cluster in 1912, first using it when he was only fifteen years old in one of his early piano pieces, *The Tides of Nanaunaun*. Needless to say, Verdi never heard of Cowell, and Cowell was four years old when Verdi died in 1901.[19] Cowell, who never studied music until he was twenty (in 1913), and who certainly never heard *Otello*, came upon the cluster by sheer accidental experimentation, trying to imitate on his upright piano the angry sounds of the Irish sea, dominated by the ancient sea god, Nanaunaun.

I hope the reader can understand how thrilled I was as a composer to experience the sonic roar of that raging storm music, with Verdi's brilliant, high-energy instrumental virtuosity in that opening scene. I can still recall my hair bristling when that first *ff* G-minor seventh chord over a low C pedal hit me. Of course, there was another three hours of incredibly great Verdi music to come in that rehearsal. When it ended, I was in a virtual daze. I couldn't understand how, with all the music I already knew, loved, and had studied, I had completely overlooked *Otello*, and for that matter *Falstaff* and *Don Carlos*. The next few days I spent copying about a dozen of the most startlingly original *Otello* passages into one of my notebooks, borrowing a score from our Met librarian, Harry Shumer.

Fritz Busch was the conductor for *Otello*, a fine choice for a number of reasons. He led the work with his very special, animated, nervy energy, keeping the music moving in the big choral scenes and, most interesting, achieving a certain leanness of sound, so appropriate in Verdi and so different from the thicker Wagnerian sonorities with which a lot of Verdi is often played. He approached the opera not from the usual Italian tradition-bound interpretations that most conductors imposed on Verdi's operas, but as if he had never heard or conducted the work before—with a clear, incisive sound and texture. For this Busch encountered a lot of resistance from the singers in the initial cast rehearsals, especially from Stella Roman, that season's Desdemona. But by the time the *Sitzproben* (German opera lingo for semifinal rehearsals) rolled around, Busch had all the singers with him. He even rehearsed the chorus separately, something that hardly ever happened in my fifteen years at the Met. Busch was dead right; the chorus needed lots of rehearsing—intelligent, critical rehearsing—because in those years it was in terrible shape. Kurt Adler (not the Kurt Herbert Adler of San Francisco Opera fame) was a terrible chorus master. The chorus sang without any real rhythmic precision or balance; many of the tenors and sopranos bellowed, trying to outshout each other, and the whole chorus was a wild jumble of big vibratos, the very thing choruses should not be. They all probably thought they should be soloists, singing leading roles. Busch did get them into pretty good shape over a period of a week. He told us in the orchestra that "it was a bit like cleaning out the Augean stables."

I also found out from some of the older Germans and Austrians in the orchestra (such as Hugo Burghauser and Ernst Silberstein), some of whom had played with Busch in Dresden in the 1930s, that it was Busch and Fritz Stiedry who had brought about the revival of middle and late Verdi in Germany in the late twenties and early thirties.

Busch must also receive credit for one even more remarkable achievement. Coming from Germany, he was unaccustomed to and indeed offended by American opera audiences' disgusting habit of breaking into loud boisterous applause right after a famous singer's high notes, near the end of arias. By doing so they made it impossible to hear the beautiful music that great composers such as Verdi and Puccini appended to many of their arias' brief instrumental postludes.[20] Busch told me during the *Otello* rehearsals that he was determined to keep the audience from breaking into applause right after the final *pp* high A flat of the fourth act's "Ave Maria." I wished him lots of luck. I knew, as we all did, that it was the claques, paid by the singers to start applauding immediately at the end of arias, regardless of how well or how badly the aria had been sung, who would initiate the applause and start the "bravo, brava" yelling in the house. I even knew who the various claqueurs were; I used to see them pick up their miserable little ill-gained payoffs at the stage door. Busch and all of us musicians knew that the applause directly after the "Ave Maria" high A flat was particularly disruptive and callously insulting to Verdi, because he had composed at that point some of his most poignantly expressive and most original music, cast in soft upper strings, as Desdemona sadly foresees her imminent death at Otello's hands. The high strings are followed by string basses playing (all alone) their lowest note, as Otello furtively enters the room. This sequence is one of Verdi's greatest strokes of genius; it moves abruptly from the key of A flat to the dramatically distant key of E, all via a four-octave downward leap from the high strings to the sepulchral low-register basses. But Met audiences never heard any of this musical-dramatic miracle.

Ultimately, Busch was successful in stopping the unwanted applause and yelling. He had persuaded the Met's management to keep the claqueurs out of the house during all scheduled *Otello* performances, no mean trick. In the first performance, some idiot opera fans who had just gotten their jollies during the soprano's high A flat—or were probably in love with Stella Roman—started to applaud despite the claque's absence. But Busch instantly swerved around to the house, loudly shushing the audience—which was, of course, itself disturbing to the music. But it did get the applauders to stop. For the first time in decades Verdi's sublimely inspired music was actually heard by a Met audience.

More remarkably, for the second performance, a Saturday broadcast matinee, word had gotten around in the audience that there was to be no applause while the music was still playing. It was a stunning victory for Busch—and for Verdi.[21] Alas, this cease-fire between audience and Busch didn't last long. By the seventh performance of *Otello*, the "Ave Maria" applause had filtered back in. At this point Busch gave up in disgust and actually stopped conducting. He waited for the audience to quiet down and then continued with the basses' low E, having to make an unwanted minute-long break in the music, thereby destroying Verdi's fantastic dramatic inspiration. As a result Ramon Vinay, our Otello, who wasn't supposed to enter the stage until the basses' entrance, came on much earlier, since neither he nor anyone backstage realized that Busch had stopped conducting, waiting for the applause to die down.

My second season at the Met actually began for me with a *Boris Godunov* rehearsal on October 28, an opera I knew pretty well from recordings, including Chaliapin's several hair-raising dramatic renditions of the "Death of Boris" scene and Stokowski's *Symphonic Synthesis* with the Philadelphia Orchestra. I was bowled over by the direct power of this music, even in the Rimsky-Korsakov version.[22] As miscast as Emil Cooper was in conducting Mozart, I must say that he did *Boris* very well. His massive way of conducting somehow suited the work. In fact, it gave some Moussorgskyan weight to Rimsky's sometimes over-brilliant, over-slick rewritings.

Boris Godunov was another stunning revelation for me. To sit in the pit and to feel the power of this music all around me, at once so simple, steeped in the Russian folk vernacular, and yet harmonically so daring, so explorative, almost crude at times (although Rimsky-Korsakov had removed much of the earthy coarseness of Mussorgosky's original conception), produced another overwhelming experience. And with Pinza (as Boris) leading the cast, Baccaloni (as Varlaam), Lazzari (as Pimen), and De Paolis as the oily, unctuous Prince Shuisky, electric sparks could almost be palpably felt on the stage. The only weak link in the cast was Risé Stevens, who, with her ostentatiously sexy scooping and exaggerated vibrato, sang the role of Marina more as if it were the seduction scene in the first act of Bizet's *Carmen*.

Rehearsing and playing multiple performances of *Boris Godunov*, as well as (in due course) *Siegfried* and *Walküre*, were totally inspiring experiences. I knew those two Wagner *Ring* operas well from recordings and from having thoroughly studied the scores. The two conductors, Emil Cooper for *Boris* and Fritz Stiedry for *Siegfried* and *Walküre* (the latter's debut at the Met), were well chosen. Cooper, a Russian, certainly knew *Boris* in and out. I admired his approach to *Boris*, despite the fact that for no discernible reason he often picked on me and three other musicians (Bob Boyd, Cecil Collins, Josef Marx), all of us by coincidence young newcomers to the orchestra. Most of my orchestra colleagues theorized that Cooper picked on me so relentlessly because in rehearsals I was wearing, quite by chance, a red flannel shirt that Margie had recently given me, and that therefore—so they reasoned—Cooper, who had left Russia soon after the 1917 Soviet Revolution, hated anything red and resented my obviously intentional attempts to irritate him. Nothing, of course, was further from my mind. But for several weeks the tale of Gunther's red shirt kept circulating in the pit and our locker room with a kind of malicious glee. As silly as it may all seem now, I thereby became a hero, for nobody liked Cooper. What *really* may have irritated Cooper was that I seemed not to be paying much attention to him; many conductors' egos demand that you constantly watch and admire them.

All in all the *Boris* performances went well, largely due to the immense talents of Pinza, Baccaloni, and my idols, Virgilio Lazzari and Alessio de Paolis.

From *Boris* that season's repertory progressed to *Walküre* and *Siegfried*, *Rosenkavalier*, *Tristan*, *Otello* (the former two with Stiedry, the latter three with Busch), and most important for me, Mozart's *Marriage of Figaro*, again with Busch and a superb cast of Pinza, Baccaloni, Steber, Risé Stevens, and Herta Glaz. Both Stiedry and Busch gave new life to their respective operas, most of which had been more or less strangled the year before by Szell's over-rehearsed, overintellectualized "scientific" approach.

I think Stiedry's spirit and deep understanding of Wagner's *Ring* music gave the Met's orchestra a considerable lift in its performances of late Wagner—probably the highest level since the two great earlier Wagner eras at the Met: the first under Anton Seidl (in the 1890s) and the second with Artur Bodansky (in the 1930s), in the latter era with Kirsten Flagstad and Lauritz Melchior in the main roles. But Stiedry's conducting could at times also be uneven, his beat unclear and erratic, his pacing occasionally lacking in drive and certitude. As I got to know Stiedry better I realized that part of the problem was that his eyesight had deteriorated and had started to give him problems—a fact little known, since Stiedry obviously tried to keep this matter secret, lest it affect his career as a conductor. He had trouble seeing not only the score, which in any case he knew very well—none of his scores had a single marking in them and he was proud of that—but also the stage and most of the orchestra clearly enough. It didn't help matters that Stiedry was too vain to wear glasses. Despite all that, over the long haul, Stiedry steered us through very exciting performances of *Walküre* and *Siegfried* that season.

Indeed, for me Stiedry's arrival at the Met was like a breath of fresh air. However, many in the orchestra were less than impressed.[23] In his first year he took over the late-Wagner repertory from Szell, who had in the interim become music director of the Cleveland Orchestra. I

was impressed not only by Stiedry's thorough knowledge of the score but—even more important—his obvious deep love for the music, even though he couldn't always express what he
felt technically, gesturally. For example, Stiedry sometimes had considerable trouble setting
new tempos, a basic and very common requirement in all opera conducting. This blemish in
Stiedry's conducting caused many of our Met musicians over time to make fun of him relentlessly and generally to play rather indifferently for him. Indeed, most of the orchestra thought
Stiedry to be a bit of a *meshuggener*—Yiddish for a fool or a crazy person.

I often felt sorry for him when this happened. As first horn (after 1950) I was in a fairly
prominent leadership position (as the horn almost automatically is in any orchestra), and took
it upon myself to help him whenever possible set the changes of tempo, which Stiedry then
would follow—with a big childish grin of relief on his face, as if *he* had accomplished the
tempo change all by himself. I tell this anecdote not to brag; I simply cared more about getting the music right than complaining about or making fun of Stiedry. Over the twelve years I
worked with him, I know that he appreciated my playing and my support of him. That his beat
was at times erratic, overly fussy and nervous, didn't bother me much, because I played more
with his facial expressions, his body language, than with his baton.

My initial impression of Stiedry was that he felt music more warmly, more deeply, but also a
touch more freely than Busch, and certainly more humanly than the overly rigid, rather "Prussian" George Szell.[24] However, I was to change my mind about Stiedry many times over the
next dozen years, even as we remained friends beyond our Met years.

What helped Stiedry a lot was the fact that the Met had a strong German wing at the
time, with well-established Wagner singers such as Melchior, Traubel, and Herbert Janssen.
But there were also others, younger newcomers such as John Garris, a most musical, elegant,
technically secure and consistent artist. He was especially good in his portrayals of Mime in
the *Ring*, David in *Meistersinger*, and Cassio in *Otello* (with perfect Italian diction).[25]

Stiedry also conducted Wagner's *Parsifal* for many years—with great love and care and a
veritable religious fervor. In the fourteen years I played *Parsifal*, three or four times a year
around Easter time—Dick Moore wasn't too keen on playing that opera, which automatically caused it to fall into my hands—the best cast I can remember was the one of 1947: the
fabulous Rose Bampton as Kundry, Mack Harrell as Amfortas, Joel Berglund as Gurnemanz,
Gerhard Pechner as the mean-spirited, revengeful Klingsor, and Torsten Ralf as a pretty good
(but a bit wimpy) Parsifal. While Stiedry always had trouble keeping the flower maidens (in
act 2) together, the almost sensual love he evinced for the *Parsifal* music made these performances very special experiences for me. But my feelings were not shared by many in the Met
orchestra, although that may have been as much a dissentient reaction to Wagner rather than
to Stiedry. Wagner's music, especially his late operas, the *Ring* and *Parsifal*, have always been
controversial and polarizing. You either love them or hate them.

New and different thrills came my way when I was given first horn in the two Mozart
operas scheduled that season: *Figaro*, with Busch, and *Seraglio*, with Cooper (unfortunately),
who kept trying to make Mozart sound thick and heavy, more like *Boris Godunov* or Wagner.
It was pretty bad, and I can't imagine why the Met management gave Cooper, of all people,
a Mozart opera, when there were conductors at the Met like Max Rudolf, one of our best, or
Paul Breisach, not to mention Busch and Stiedry. Cooper kept asking for bigger, fatter sounds,
urging the strings to play with "more bone"—his broken, Russianized English for "more bow."
I was so annoyed and bored with him and his ponderous ways that I took to reading during the
rehearsals. In one of his ghastliest five-hour rehearsals, I managed to get through a huge chunk
of Rousseau's *Confessions*.[26]

Rehearsing and playing Mozart's *Marriage of Figaro*, with Busch conducting, was a highlight
of the season for me. It was my first *Figaro*, having previously played only excerpts from it. The

assembled cast was topnotch, all legendary veterans of the Met's Mozart productions: Pinza, Baccaloni, Sayao, Steber, and John Brownlee. It was a wonderful experience to be finally playing this miraculously perfect music and to be playing first horn. Busch played all the recitatives himself at the piano (not a harpsichord), often in very ingenious and creative ways, yet very much in style and with a lively *parlando* approach. (While this is much more common nowadays, conductors accompanying the recitatives themselves were a relative rarity back then.)

A special thrill for me was to play from a horn part that had been annotated, surprisingly, by none other than Bruno Walter, in respect to slurs, articulations, *staccato* and *tenuto* designations, all very neatly amended in blue pencil. Since it was in Mozart's and Haydn's time a convention not to include such notational nuances in brass parts—that was left to the musical intelligence and good taste of the players—I feel so fortunate to have had in this way the perfect introduction to how one has to play Mozart horn parts. By simultaneously studying the score of *Figaro*, I quickly learned that Walter's annotations were based on correlating the horn parts to the woodwind parts, which usually *were* notationally complete in all respects. It was an important lesson for me.

There was an episode during the *Figaro* performances where I almost got in trouble, not for my playing, but because of what was considered a misdemeanor in professional orchestral behavior. Because most of the musicians in the orchestra pit could be seen from above by the audience, the management had forbidden reading in the pit during performances. This applied especially to the woodwind, brass, and percussion players, who tended to have many more rests and empty measures than the strings, even entire numbers tacit. (Reading was allowed in rehearsals; everything from *Time* and *Life* to girlie magazines and stock market reports could be seen on the musicians' stands.) During the *Figaro* performances I brought my full score into the pit in order to follow both the score and Busch's conducting. It was a rash, perhaps foolish thing to do. Even though I was as discreet as possible about this, suddenly in the fifth performance I saw Busch staring angrily at me. In the ensuing intermission I was ordered by John Mundy to see Busch in the conductor's room. I don't know how Busch could have seen through my music stand and the thick book of the horn part that I was reading something other than the music. Maybe somebody snitched on me. In any case, I received a terrific bawling out, in German. After a minute or so of this tirade, I got up enough nerve, knowing that Busch basically liked me and my playing, to tell him (in German) that what I was reading was the score of *Figaro*. At which point, to my amazement and relief, he quickly softened and said, in effect: "Oh well, that's something else, that's alright." And with a smile and wink, he added: "But don't do it anymore," and, almost apologetically, "I can't allow it, even if it's a score." I came away unscathed. But I often wondered what would have happened had the conductor been George Szell, an inflexible martinet type, or Karl Böhm.

One other event during that period stands out in my memory as very special and exciting. That was the premiere and, alas, the only set of performances of Bernard Rogers's opera *The Warrior*, inspired by the Samson and Delilah story from the Bible. I had already met Rogers in Cincinnati in 1944 on the occasion of our May Festival premiere of his oratorio *The Passion*, a work that I admired very much. And I had also visited Rogers in Rochester, where he was Professor of Composition at the Eastman School of Music.

Mack Harrell, a wonderful, beautifully voiced, intelligent musician, was the superb Samson in our *Warrior* performances. John Garris sang the part of the Captain, and Regina Resnik was a good Delilah. And it was excellently conducted by Max Rudolf. But I have a feeling that I was almost the only one in the orchestra who liked *The Warrior*. Certainly Dick Moore ranted and raved against the work, with every expletive he could think of. And the press roasted the whole affair, unfairly. Of course, it wasn't another *Tristan* or *La Bohème*; but it wasn't so bad that it had to be crucified and blasted so mercilessly, especially by Olin Downes, chief music critic of the *New York Times*. The work was never played again, and the experience broke dear Bernard's heart. He never got over this failure.[27]

This was also the time that I really became aware of the phenomenal talents of Alessio de Paolis, the greatest character actor singer the Met may have ever had, who had a tenure there of twenty-five years. In the decade and a half I played at the Met, I never once heard De Paolis—and his sidekick, George Chehanovsky—sing with less than impeccable taste and style—and perfect diction, regardless of what opera tradition or language. Even in his early sixties, when De Paolis's voice began to decline, it didn't matter, because he somehow managed to unfailingly project his part stylistically correctly and yet imaginatively, individualistically. He was a true complete artist. In *Otello* he was a superb Cassio; in *Boris* a sly, insinuating, scheming Prince Shuisky. And De Paolis and Chehanovsky were an incomparable pair of bandit smugglers, Dancaïro and Remendado, in Bizet's *Carmen*. They were in top form in every one of the almost thousand *Carmen* performances I played, whether on tour or at home at the Met. Both were very great artists, and although underappreciated (or taken for granted), they were way at the top among my all-time heroes at the Met.

Two singers that I heard for the first time in that 1946–47 season who impressed me mightily were Jarmila Novotna and Herta Glaz. Both sopranos, now alas forgotten, were highly intelligent musicians with radiant, thrilling voices. Novotna had a huge range, enabling her to sing both soprano and mezzo parts. She sang many major roles at the Met, such as Octavian in *Rosenkavalier* and Violetta in *La Traviata*, the latter a part that, with its difficult brilliant coloratura passages, she delivered with more musicality and ease than anybody else, except possibly Maria Callas and Licia Albanese. Glaz, a spirited, fetching personality—I think I had a crush on her, from a distance—was a superb Amneris in *Aida*, and she absolutely owned the part of Annina in *Rosenkavalier*. The whole orchestra used to wait for her spectacular two-octave sixteenth-note high-speed run, halfway through the third act of *Rosenkavalier*. Eventually, over the years, most of the orchestra began to *sing* the run along with Herta. To my surprise, no conductor seems to have ever objected to this orchestral participation, and it is now a solid Met tradition, even tolerated by the great Carlos Kleiber in his guest appearances at the Met in the midnineties.

I immensely enjoyed playing *Rosenkavalier* with Busch that year, especially after the grim experience with Szell the year before. Busch restored the score to its full luster and Viennese charm. Somehow even Hofmannsthal's sparkling libretto came into its own, not, as so often otherwise happened, buried beneath Strauss's sometimes very busy orchestra. Busch's conception seemed so natural and right that he managed to make *Rosenkavalier* seem actually easy to perform. Could that have been because he had conducted *Rosenkavalier* (and many other Strauss operas) for thirteen years at the Dresden State Opera, renowned for its special long-time association with Strauss as a conductor *and* as a composer? I think so.

Busch had a characteristically brisk and energetic, slightly fretful yet disciplined baton technique; it had a way of invigorating the orchestra. The musicians generally liked him, especially when he let us out of rehearsals early several times. He knew that we did not need endless rehearsing à la Szell.[28]

Busch's *Tristan* was still another illustration of how a very demanding, emotionally draining opera could somehow feel almost relaxed and compliant, even the wild, feverish, almost atonal music of the third act, with which Wagner underscored Tristan's delirious near-death ravings. *Tristan und Isolde*, which I had studied already in my midteen years, was always a special musical aural banquet for me. Except for Harry Peers, I may have been the only musician in the orchestra who, as a composer, realized what a crucial role this trailblazing work had played in the development of music. To this day it is still difficult for me to understand how Wagner was able to create something so prophetic, so radical, so original that it dramatically changed the course of music— yet so perfected—*and* as early as the 1850s. Of its many, many wonders I particularly looked forward every time to Brangäne's warning ("Einsam wachend") in the second scene of act two, with its sublimely diaphanous, transcendent accompaniment in muted tutti strings and eight melodically entwined *un*muted solo violins and one viola. But then also the profoundly moving and totally different "King Marke Monologue"; or, for that matter, Brangäne's last utterance in the opera: a lofty, vaulting phrase ("Sie wacht, sie lebt!") that always gave me the goosebumps, and that Blanche Thebom used to sing so beautifully night after night.

It was also during this time that I twice met up with Ellington, whom I hadn't seen since late 1944. The first time was at the Aquarium, where I got to see him very briefly during a break between sets. When he spotted me, he smiled and said, "ah, here's my horn-playing *professor*," the last word enunciated with an effusively vaulting inflection, as only he could devise.

The second occasion was on one of his annual Carnegie Hall concerts, November 23, 1946. I did not actually see him that time, not wishing to battle the Carnegie Hall stage doorman and a huge postconcert crowd of autograph seekers. Of the concert I remember above all being quite disappointed in Django Reinhardt's guest appearance with the orchestra. Having previously marveled at Django's spectacularly inventive, sensitive, and harmonically rich playing, particularly on the 1939 Rex Stewart Quartet sides (elaborately praised in my *Swing Era* history), and his innovative work with the Quintette du Hot Club de France, I was looking forward to hearing him for the first time in the flesh. He seemed ill at ease and nervous in the Carnegie Hall atmosphere. On the other hand, I remember liking Ellington's *Flippant Flurry* very much, a little compositional gem featuring Jimmy Hamilton's fluent clarinet; and, even more, Ellington's outstanding *Golden Cress*, featuring my idol Lawrence Brown in a gorgeous lengthy solo that brought down the house.

I was—to my surprise—not particularly impressed by several of Strayhorn's collaborations, especially some movements from the *Deep South Suite*. With his considerable background in classical music (especially the French moderns, from Debussy to Ibert and Milhaud), Strayhorn was synthesizing elements of those styles with Ellington's harmonic language. It is too long ago for me to remember with any precision what I found lacking in some of his pieces, but it probably was that some of the fusing of classical and jazz elements seemed a bit forced, and that the jazz side of the stylistic equation had lost something in the process. As the apostle (later) of Third Stream—broadly speaking, the fusion and cross-fertilization of two musical mainstreams, classical and jazz—I always felt that, as in any true and successful synthesis, the two (or more) fused elements should survive in the new product in some degree of equivalence. I guess I must have thought, right or wrong, that that was not the case in those particular Strayhorn pieces.

What did impress me very much all evening was Harold Baker's beautiful trumpet tone, in his lead playing as well as his solos, but also Oscar Pettiford's remarkably original bass playing. It really intrigued me because his tone was lean and clean; virile, but somehow lighter than that of most Blanton-influenced bassists of the time. And I was amazed by Pettiford's incredible left-hand dexterity. It was like Charlie Parker's speed had suddenly been transferred to the bass. (I didn't hear anything like that again until Scott LaFaro came along.)

For all of my longtime admiration of Ellington's music, that night I felt for the first time that there was really something to the rumors beginning to circulate—the word on the street, so to speak—that a certain unevenness had crept into both Ellington's creativity and the performance level of his orchestra. It was puzzling, and I felt somewhat conflicted.

On the classical side, New York's rich concert life yielded its usual cornucopia of wondrous gifts. I'm sure I've forgotten more than half of what Margie and I were able to attend and experience, the range of offerings was so expansive. But what stands out particularly in my memory (and in my diary) were a whole series of superb concerts and recitals by Jennie Tourel ("thrilling," "a wonderful blending of intelligence and emotion") in her favorite repertory: early twentieth-century French vocal literature; a gala concert of the Philadelphia Orchestra, featuring its great flutist William Kincaid ("a tone like pure silver"),[29] a concert, I swear, attended by all the flutists on the East Coast; a superb recital by Lili Kraus and Symon Goldberg (former concertmaster of the Berlin Philharmonic under Furtwängler); Maggie Teyte and Raoul Jobin with the New York Philharmonic in excerpts from Debussy's *Pelléas et Mélisande*; also the first of several now legendary concerts of John Cage's music, in this instance featuring his new compositions for prepared piano ("very interesting," "reminds me of a Javanese gamelan orchestra"); and finally, above all, the New York City Symphony concert series led by Leonard Bernstein. His programs were masterful and ingenious in their sweeping stylistic range, including a broad sampling of contemporary works by predominantly European composers. One typical program—all English—which I remember particularly well, started with several of Purcell's *Fantasias*, including the remarkable *Fantasia on One Note*, continued with William Walton's racy, sprightly (slightly jazzy) *Portsmouth Point* Overture and Benjamin Britten's rarely played Violin Concerto, and ended with Elgar's *Enigma Variations*. Lennie's concerts were for the three years he presided over them the consistently most exciting, stimulating concerts in New York. I have often over the years come back to the thought that, just maybe, what Bernstein achieved in those three years, now mostly unremembered and unappreciated, may be the best thing he ever did, even including his highly successful Omnibus and Young People's Concerts telecasts. And if not the best thing, at least one of his very best.

Around this time I was also hired to play an all-Wagner concert with Toscanini and the NBC Symphony, the first of many to follow in the ensuing years. Among Italian conductors the maestro was the best Wagner interpreter (with the possible exception of Victor de Sabata), and the "Rhine Journey" from *Götterdämmerung* was one of the maestro's favorite warhorses. I greatly admired the remarkable line and flow Toscanini was able to get from the orchestra. It was magnificent; I sat there in awe. But what was not so magnificent was when he blew up in one of the rehearsals and cursed the entire orchestra in one of his famous tirades in outrageously foul-mouthed Italian—I should add, undeservedly so. On that occasion I didn't hear anything that ought to have prompted his tirade, nor did anyone else in the orchestra that I spoke to. But that was life with Toscanini. The irony is that his intemperate outbursts rarely included any actual instructions or explanations of what he found wrong or wanting. A flow of scatological Italian is not necessarily very informative as to what needs to be corrected or improved—particularly when most of the orchestra doesn't speak Italian. The saving grace was that we all knew that Toscanini's tantrums were mostly the expression of a typically uncontrollable Italianate temper, that it was more habit than purposeful exhortation. It was simply a part of almost every rehearsal.

Exciting compositional discoveries for me in that period were Prokofiev's 1924 Quintet for Violin, Viola, Oboe, Clarinet, and Bass, with its (for the time) startlingly challenging high-register bass part; four of Bartók's string quartets, still very rarely heard in New York at that time; a number of flashy Ravelian works (*Fête du vin, Musique de table*) by Manuel Rosenthal, guest conducting the New York Philharmonic.

My life was far from limited to my work at the Met. In retrospect I have to be amazed at how much and on how many fronts I pursued my quest for greater knowledge and growth, not only in music but also (almost as much) in the other arts. And there wasn't a better place than New York (at least in America) to engage in such pursuits, particularly the New York of the forties and fifties. The main problem was to *find the time* to savor all that New York had to offer. My schedule at the Met filled most evenings, of course, and a good part of each day was taken up with rehearsals, mornings or afternoons. That left little free time except night hours; but those hours had to be reserved, at least to some extent, for other essential nighttime activities.

Margie and I went to New York Philharmonic concerts practically every week, where we heard wonderful works mostly still new to me, such as Debussy's *Pelléas et Mélisande*, Prokofiev's stunning *Scythian Suite*, or Messiaen's *Hymn for Orchestra* (the latter two conducted by Stokowski and ravishingly played by the Philharmonic), as well as fabulous performances of Berlioz and Debussy brilliantly conducted by Charles Munch. We were also regulars at many Madison or Fifth Avenue art galleries (Knoedler, Wildenstein, Janis, Valentin, Matisse, etc.), and, of course, New York's great museums (the Metropolitan, Frick, Whitney). We also joined Lincoln Kirstein's new Ballet Society, and saw there for the first time Ravel's *L'Enfant et les sortilèges* and Stravinsky's *Renard*, beautifully choreographed by George Balanchine. How then, on top of all that, we managed to go to hundreds of Museum of Modern Art film showings and lots of other movies is beyond my understanding.

I was so obsessed with the other arts that I actually embarked and for several months worked sporadically on the compilation of an encyclopedia of the arts. What possessed me to think that I had not only the knowledge but also the time to squeeze such an immense undertaking into my already impossibly crowded life, I can't imagine. I guess it was to some degree overconfidence, but also the overt expression of an intense love of the subject. This is one project that eventually fell by the wayside—not surprisingly.

Our sex life had to compete a lot with the great jazz that could be heard almost everywhere in New York. One can imagine that we never got much sleep, and I remember being constantly energized by my awareness of New York's myriad cultural attractions; at the same time I was always kind of sleepy or tired—and yet I attempted relentlessly to quench my thirst for new intellectual and artistic adventures.

The one thing I fiercely protected from any outward intrusions was my horn playing, which I managed to keep at top level—an occasional tired lip notwithstanding. In the midst of all these other interests and preoccupations I took up practicing the piano again, and rather diligently, which meant hours of practicing Cramer and Clementi studies, easy Mozart sonatas, Bach inventions, Scriabin preludes and études.

Around this time Margie left her voice teacher, Lotte Leonard. We both finally realized that Leonard was more a vocal coach than a voice teacher, in the sense of someone who could work on voice production and vocal techniques. In that department Margie was not really making any noticeable progress. She seemed unable to break the pattern of taking two steps forward and then falling three steps back. We had learned that good musical singers and musicians don't necessarily make good teachers—a lesson one can usually learn only from experience.[30] I had found her a new teacher, Carlo Monetti, and lo and behold within weeks her voice began to recover, to such an extent that I was encouraged to record her with my new recording equipment, my brother Edgar doing the engineering. My piano practicing now stood me in good stead, as I decided to accompany her and coach her for the sessions. When over sixty years later I hear Margie's singing at that time, in Puccini's "Vissi d'arte," and "Un bel di," and in Mozart's "Deh vieni" and "Ah, lo so," I can hear her natural musicality: her sensitivity and musical intelligence, everything in proportion, no exaggerations or bad musical habits. But I also can hear the occasional slight strain and tightness in the voice, especially around the break—vestiges of not fully resolved technical problems. On that day Margie also recorded a beautiful rendition of Scriabin's Op. 63 "Etrangeté" Etude.[31]

I had one rather big disappointment around this time, when a score of my *Vertige d'Eros* that I had sent to Mitropoulos in Minneapolis (where he was music director of that city's orchestra) was returned without comment and, worse, seemed not even to have been looked at. I knew from Mitropoulos's programming, especially as guest conductor with the New York Philharmonic, but also from Ernst Krenek in St. Paul and Rudi Kolisch in Madison, that Mitropoulos was very sympathetic to modern music, especially that of the Second Viennese School. And thus I had held out some hope that he might be interested in my music. Obviously, as an unknown composer with only one obscure public performance to my credit (my Horn Concerto in Cincinnati), my hopes were somewhat premature. But it is in retrospect interesting that my faith in Mitropoulos was not entirely misguided, for, as is now well known, a decade later he conducted *two* of my works in the 1956–57 New York Philharmonic season, in effect putting me on the map as a composer of some note and promise virtually overnight.

On the other hand, a very nice thing happened when I got a message from Lawrence Brown that I should go to see Mack Stark at Mills Music in the Brill Building at Forty-Ninth and Broadway, a publishing company founded by Irving Mills, which in the 1930s became the publisher of Duke Ellington's compositions. Larry thought that Stark, Mills's second-in-command, in charge of acquisitions and publications, might be interested in publishing some of my music. When I got there I was surprised to see Larry himself, and learned that he had already strongly recommending me to Stark. This meeting led in due course to my very first beautifully engraved publication: my *Nocturne* for horn and piano. I found out later that Morton Gould, already a big success with Mills, had also recommended me, having heard favorably about my pop concert arrangements in Cincinnati. (Two of them had been on the same program with several of Gould's own arrangements and compositions.)

One day while I was cleaning up my room[32] and listening to the radio, I suddenly heard something strangely familiar. It was a concert on WJZ by a string orchestra with harp, celesta, and piano, and at certain points featuring in some solo spots two of my favorite musicians, the marvelous trombonist Charlie Small and the famous cornetist Bobby Hackett. On this broadcast Paul Whiteman was conducting a group of symphonic arrangements of popular songs such as "Body and Soul" and "Sweet Sue, Just You." Suddenly, in the middle of "Embraceable You," in a fast double-time section, my ears perked up at some very familiar sounds. I quickly realized that the harpist was Gloria Agostini, in WJZ's staff orchestra at the time, and that some staff arranger had cribbed some of my best jazzy licks from the Harp Concerto I had written for Gloria and Paul Whiteman two years earlier, but which was never performed by them.

That's some nerve, I thought: Gloria not even telling me that my composition served as an inspiration for a WJZ staff arranger, probably Glenn Osser. On the other hand, it was a strange thrill to unexpectedly hear my own music *on the air*. Gloria was supposed to have returned the orchestral parts to me, which she never did. I suppose they are still in the ABC library or some warehouse. But more likely, they were thrown out one fine day with the trash. I wrote Gloria a rather irritated letter, which, of course, soured our relationship for a few years. But eventually I let bygones be bygones, and we have been good friends and colleagues ever since, for more than half a century.[33]

My unquenchable appetite for the visual arts was partially satisfied during this period, not only at the Museum of Modern Art and our second visit to the Frick Museum, but also, most spectacularly, at the Knoedler Gallery, one of our favorite haunts. In one thrilling exhibition of "Twenty-four Masterpieces" we finally got to see two El Grecos: *The Saviour* and *The Despoiled (El Espolio)*, the former a painting that the artist is reputed to have worked on for nearly a decade. I had never seen anything like the expression on Christ's face in *The Saviour*: at once beautiful, exalted, solemn, and virile—and those intense (Greek?) eyes. Two particular aspects of *The Despoiled* riveted my attention, in part because they translated almost one-to-one into some of my then current explorations of orchestral timbres and polyphonic (or vertical) complexity within a consistent metric patterning. I marveled at El Greco's colors that I felt had never been seen before in a painting: the ruby-red of Christ's robe juxtaposed directly next to the grey-violet of a soldier's armor, the subtly differentiated shades of ochres, browns, and blues (i.e., timbral). And then the picture's dramatic, almost chaotic, intricacy of composition, as soldiers and the crowd surge forward toward Christ to better witness his despoliation.[34]

I don't remember all the great pictures we saw in the Knoedler show, but my diary mentions particularly Rembrandt's extraordinary *Visitation*; Vermeer's *Lady Waiting* (which, unlike most Vermeers, with their smooth, lean texture and cool detachment, seemed to project a certain misty, almost impressionistic feeling); some portraits by Frans Hals and Hans Holbein the Elder; several fifteenth-century Dutch painters, including Petrus Christus and Gerard David of the Flemish school; and a stunningly detailed *Birth of the Virgin* by Fra Carnevale, a painter I had previously never even heard of.

The reader can now well imagine what a permanent high Margie and I were on (without benefit or need of drugs, need I add), the continual exhilaration of floating in a swirling aesthetic, artistic maelstrom. Inevitably all these glorious experiences drew us ever closer together. I felt that we seemed to have fully recovered the pristine, uncomplicated first love of our Cincinnati days. I was incomprehensibly fascinated with her inner and outer beauty, her affecting gentleness, her large-hearted devotion to me, but all of it now fortified by the sexual dimension. In Cincinnati Margie was for me still partially veiled in mystery. Now I was in awe of her.

I worshiped her body; I always had, since I first laid eyes on her. I loved a fulsome figure, what my Jewish friends called *saftig* (Yiddish-German meaning, literally, "juicy," and figuratively, "sumptuous," "luxuriant"). I didn't like—still don't like—skinny girls, the fashion model type, which most of my young friends and colleagues lusted after. Oh well, *chacun à son goût!* When I was young, fashion models had to be narrow-bodied, totally vertical, angular, breastless creatures. At least nowadays they are permitted to show some curves.

From time to time Margie would feel that she was too chubby—which she wasn't—and would diet briefly, especially when for a few years she did modeling for a fashion house in New York's garment district, only to return in due course to her former shapeliness.

Margie had exquisite taste in clothes. She undoubtedly acquired that in her father's Store Without a Name, which featured only the finest, elegant, classic, yet moderately priced women's garments. She knew that I had provocative, couture tastes in clothing; nothing extravagant or extreme, let alone weird. (I saw too much of that at contemporary music concerts, art galleries, and the MOMA film showings.) But Margie sensed that my interest in how a woman dressed had to do first and foremost with my craving for beauty—beauty in all its myriad manifestations. If a dress, a hat, a pair of high-heeled shoes, if some special lingerie would beautify a woman and bring out her sensuality, well, all the better. Given Margie's love for me, her docile, accommodating nature (which she lavished on everyone she came into contact with, not just me), she had no problems in obliging me without abandoning her own firmly held criteria of tastefulness and aesthetics. One thing was sure: both of us were definitely not going to be constrained by society's platitudinal, generally prudish attitudes.

Our idyllic happiness was only briefly disrupted when Margie had to go home to Fargo, where her parents would recurrently work on her to break off with me. They had one or two suitors in mind for her. The name of some Dan—he had been at high school with Margie—came up a lot. Her visits home always generated several very unhappy letters telling me of the nagging pressures her parents put on her to abandon her relationship with me, and at times even to reconsider the whole idea of staying and studying in New York. They wanted her to come back home—like her (now married) sister, Anna Jane. It became clear also that her parents were worried that I would surely get Margie pregnant. In fact, her mother had dreams and nightmares to that effect.

I know Margie looked upon these visits home with great trepidation, knowing that once again she would be caught up in the tensions between their opposition to me and her innate love, loyalty, and gratitude to her parents. I agonized with her, especially in my letters. I never dared telephone her, although she, in sheer desperation, would sometimes call me at one a.m. or some such hour, when her parents had long ago gone to bed.

In the meantime, there were some rather weird things going on at the Met that couldn't help but generate some feelings of insecurity in me. Suddenly neither Moore nor Mundy would talk to me; all I got were sullen stares from both. What the hell had I done now? I had been led to believe that Mundy was quietly, behind the scenes, pushing for me to move up to full principal horn. I had even heard backstage scuttlebutt that he and both Busch and Rudolf had been quite impressed with my playing in *Figaro* and other operas. Now Mundy seemed to be freezing me out! As for Moore, tensions were always high between us. He could never seem to rid himself of the thought that I was constantly agitating to take over his job as principal horn. In fact, Izzy Blank confided to me that Moore, in some whispered locker room tirade about me addressed to one of his trombonist drinking buddies, especially resented my playing *Figaro* so well, because that could only mean that I must be after his job. I guess Dick couldn't comprehend, couldn't accept the notion, that I might want to play well out of sheer personal pride and for the sake of representing Mozart's glorious music as beautifully as I could.

Besides, the perversity of Dick's ravings becomes even clearer when one realizes that it was David Rattner's increasingly insecure, shaky, nervous playing that the conducting staff was concerned about. To the extent that I was being considered to move to first horn, it was to replace Rattner, not the solid, technically reliable Moore. And, as I've already mentioned, I was most hesitant in any way to go after Rattner's job, because I had such a high regard for him as one of the most intelligent musicians and most tasteful horn players that I had ever heard.

But suddenly, a month or so later, there was an announcement that there would now be an audition for first horn. I was really quite conflicted about auditioning for the first horn position and thereby possibly precipitating Rattner's retirement from the orchestra. But as in the case of auditioning for Mimi Caputo's third horn job two years earlier, I finally persuaded myself to take the audition. Several players, especially Izzy Blank, had urged me to do so and not to be quite so reticent. The fact that Rattner was having problems playing, as a result of a rather extreme case of nervousness or stage fright, evoked only sympathy in me. I knew how he was suffering and how courageous he was in facing his playing problems every night, trying through his musical intelligence to play well enough to somehow survive.

Just when I thought that Mundy had also turned on me, along with Moore, he suddenly appeared, smiling and cheerful, inviting me to an audition for Busch, Rudolf, and himself. I played very well, and it would have been a perfect audition if I had also nailed the final high F of the Siegfried Call, always the ultimate test in a horn audition. Although I got the note, it was a bit strained and wimpy, not the heroic, confidant hurrah it should be. I was disappointed with myself, remembering that four years earlier at Reiner's house I had played the call so easily and securely at nine in the morning—even without a warm-up—and also later with Szell in my initial audition for the Met.

After the audition Mundy asked me to wait in an anteroom. Fifteen minutes later he emerged, looking rather pleased with himself, wearing his best (but noncommittal) manager's smile. He quietly explained that they were very happy with my audition, as well as my general work as third horn and occasional first horn, but that they had now decided to keep David Rattner on for another season or two, because of his many years of honorable service. They asked me to be patient, that my time would come, and—a nice surprise—that I would immediately receive a raise of twenty dollars per week (something like eighty dollars in today's terms), a very welcome gesture.

I was delighted with the outcome of this whole episode, really happy for Rattner and very pleased to have a little extra money to spend on recordings, books, literary and film magazines, and the like. But in a somewhat unusual aftermath, which only fate could have provided, both Moore and Rattner became ill at different times in the next few weeks, which resulted automatically in my temporarily taking their places as first horn. I remember that two of the operas in which I substituted were *Otello* and *Lohengrin*, both with wonderful and very prominent horn parts.

By way of painful contrast, I heard that my dear friend from Ballet Theatre days, Cecil Collins, a first-rate trumpet player holding the second trumpet chair at the Met since 1944, was suddenly fired. I could not find any possible reason for this action, for Cecil, still quite young, was playing beautifully.[35]

As Max Rudolf became increasingly active as conductor at the Met, moving from the back of the house as Eddie Johnson's musical advisor and administrative assistant to the orchestra pit, not only substituting as needed for Busch or Stiedry but also taking on operas such as Bernard Rogers's *The Warrior* or Humperdinck's *Hänsel und Gretel*, I became increasingly impressed with his conducting work. As I found out over the many years that I got to know Rudolf rather well, he was a modest, unpretentious, unassuming man. His work as a conductor would never be called exciting, flamboyant, or charismatic. Those who would want to see more extrovert, gymnastic podium behavior probably considered Rudolf too sedate or rather dull. I, on the other hand—and most of us in the orchestra—admired his work, appreciating his high musical intelligence, his calm, secure leadership, his impeccable taste in matters of style (whether Wagner or Strauss or Verdi or Mozart). His knowledge of the scores that he conducted was consummate, down to the minutest notational details. And in his quiet, unostentatious way, he made *us* respect those details and adhere to them—in case we didn't.

Since Rudolf was rarely assigned (and therefore rarely got to rehearse) any of the big or standard operas—those were automatically given to Stiedry, Reiner, Cooper, Antonicelli, and the rest of the core conducting staff—it was amazing to me how, when he took over a performance on a day's or a few hours' notice, *always without rehearsal*, he would calmly correct the misinterpretations or exaggerations perpetrated (or allowed) by the other conductors, just through his manual gestures and podium demeanor, and suddenly everything seemed right and secure. He reminded me a lot in his basic conducting approach of Pierre Monteux and Fritz Reiner (without, to be sure, the latter's sadistic touch). Efficient routiniers such as Sodero, Cimara, and Cellini also knew their scores very well, but they lacked either the musical imagination or the appropriate baton-technical skills to get the right and best results. Rudolf exuded a reassuring imperturbability, and in a no-hassle way would just let us—invited us—to play our best. It was such a pleasurable experience playing for him.

Such distinctions in conductorial quality became very clear that season when we made a recording of *Hänsel und Gretel* that turned out to be that opera's very first complete recording. It was initially assigned to Stiedry, but sad to say, old Fritz had no feel for this work at all. His direction was unnecessarily fussy and insecure, lacking all the easy charm that this beautiful, happy music embodies. When it came time for the recording in June, after our spring tour, we learned that it would not be Stiedry conducting, but Rudolf. What a relief! I was obviously not in on the decision to relieve Stiedry of this assignment, but I would like to imagine that Johnson and Rudolf realized that, with Stiedry at the helm, the recording's quality would be in serious jeopardy.

Although I have some minor quibbles with Risé Stevens's and Nadine Conner's rendition of the lead roles—no quibbles with John Brownlee (in the role of the father) and Thelma Votipka[36] (our witch)—the recording came off very well indeed, and the orchestra acquitted itself admirably under Rudolf's benign direction.[37]

The occasional encouraging tokens of support from Busch, Rudolf, and Mundy did not entirely outweigh my continuing feelings of frustration with the general state of affairs at the Met and my own place in that situation. I felt that, except with our best conductors that year, the orchestra was allowed—or encouraged—to play at ever-louder dynamics. There was this feeling in the orchestra that it really didn't matter whether Mozart or Wagner wrote *p*, while we played *mf* instead. It was often a kind of rough, careless playing, which annoyed me no end. This generally rather crude way of performing was aggravated by my section leader, Dick Moore, whose unsubtle heroic style flourished under these conditions. I was also annoyed with myself for allowing him to constantly intimidate me, personally and musically. It was thus some relief when I was able to play first horn in the three Mozart operas I was assigned that year, *Magic Flute*, *Figaro*, and *Abduction from the Seraglio*, where I was able to at least control the dynamic levels in the horn section and the rest of the brass section (three trombones in *Magic Flute* and trumpets in all three operas), and even, to some extent, of the whole woodwind section.

My partner on second horn that year was Alan Fuchs,[38] new at the Met that season, and a very talented, clever, and intelligent player. Fuchsie, as we called him, clearly enjoyed matching his first horn partners—it is one of the essential requirements of a good second horn—and I must say, the two of us delivered some beautifully blended horn duettings throughout the season. Dick Moore took an immediate dislike to Fuchsie, immediately considering him—without reason—arrogant and a brownnoser, and another threat to his position.

I also began to resent the fact that I had to miss so many other concerts in New York, simply because I was busy at least five or six nights a week at the Met. Margie was, of course, free to go to these concerts and recitals, but hearing from her about some great performance or some important composition I had never heard before became increasingly frustrating. I had to miss, for example, hearing not only Schönberg's Third Quartet and Webern's *Five Pieces* Op. 5, but also Bartók's Fifth Quartet, all in their first performances in New York, and played superbly by Rudolf Kolisch's Pro Arte Quartet, which was without question at the time the finest interpreter of such music. When at the same time I had to suffer through some particularly mediocre performance at the Met, I felt that I was perhaps wasting my time staying there. But what were the alternatives? Maybe getting into the New York Philharmonic, or playing some Broadway show. (The freelance recording scene was not yet as fully developed in the midforties as it was half a dozen years later.) On the other hand, the Met job offered a certain financial security.

I was aware that there was increasing criticism in the press, lamenting the fact that Met performances had become quite uneven, in large part due to the constantly changing casts and the resultant inability to develop any real vocal or acting ensembles. Only very rarely would we have a perfect cast that would also be maintained more or less throughout the season.[39]

I remember a particularly scathing attack in *Time* magazine on the Met and Edward Johnson's administration. Even the *New Yorker Staats-Zeitung und Herold*, New York's German newspaper, delivered itself of a lengthy analysis—written by Wolfgang Stresemann (who later became manager of the Berlin Philharmonic during Karajan's regime, and was the son of Gustav Stresemann, the president of the Weimar Republic in the pre-Hitler days)—of what ailed the Met, and how its former high artistic standards might be regained.

Also, like any young capable horn player, I naturally wanted to advance to a principal horn position, not only for the better salary, but also—here the composer in me was speaking—to lead a horn section; not so much to put *my* stamp on it, but rather to achieve some closer respect for the individual composer's notation, style, and ethos. Dick Moore played everything the same way, *his* way (not necessarily the composer's way), with the same sound, the same heroic, somewhat rough and unsubtle manner, whoever the composer: Wagner or Puccini or Mozart or Gounod. This, of course, obliged me as third horn and as his section partner to match him, and thus to play, against my will, in the same brash manner. Our relationship had reached an absolute nadir; and to work in the same section with him night after night, rehearsal after rehearsal, became quite unbearable, especially since I never seemed able to satisfy him.

I was much bewildered and bothered by the managerial policies and artistic decisions of the Met's general manager, Edward Johnson, especially his arbitrary policy of mix-matching casts in the bread and butter standard operas, which were rarely accorded any follow-up rehearsals when casts changed, so that a particular opera almost never developed any well-built, truly musical ensemble sense. While I rather loved the musical challenge of matching, following, and blending with a constantly changing parade of tenors, say, in the Puccini operas (the horn being so often partnered with the leading tenor), from the perspective of achieving the best ensemble standards it was too casual a directorial approach. It seemed to me—and many others—that this was not a way to run one of the world's leading opera houses.

Cumulatively, all those mediocre and confusing musical experiences also constituted the first hesitant glimmerings in my mind that some day, off in the future, I would want to write a series of articles—or even a book—on the allowable limits and intrinsic meaning of interpretation, and, even more important, the issue of maintaining an absolute irrecusable respect for the composer and the specific notation of his work. Those glimmering thoughts eventually evolved into what I believe is one of the more important—and seemingly most controversial—achievements of my life, the publication half a century later of my book *The Compleat Conductor*.

Worse yet, I became aware that to some extent my playing had lost some of its high consistency; it had become a little uneven. Precisely how and which of these various circumstances affected my playing and my professional standards in the orchestra I cannot now fully reconstruct. Undoubtedly, my pursuit of other cultural and artistic interests (cinema, literature, jazz—and, of course, composing and studying) must have to some extent affected my playing. But the uninspired, pedestrian conducting of Fourestier and Cimara and Sodero must also have been a factor. I think I lost my artistic and professional bearings for a while, not practicing regularly; I lost some of my consistency in endurance (important in operatic work because of the length of most operas), and my intonation was occasionally erratic. I became worried that I could get myself out of what in baseball is called a slump.

Eventually I realized that somehow or other I had to pull myself together, regardless of surrounding circumstances or influences. I had to figure out how and why I had lost my sense of confidence and security, how it was that in Cincinnati I had played virtually flawlessly for two entire seasons, playing most of that repertory for the first time. And why did I play so well and with such confidence in jobs outside the Met—Broadway shows, radio concerts, pop concerts, chamber music, but not at the Met. It made no sense.

Ultimately I understood that in everyone's existence situations arise that may have a conflictingly critical effect on one's career, one's life, one's relationships. I understood in particular that one must find a way to immunize oneself from one's surroundings and to irksome external circumstances. I came to an understanding that I must never let my own playing be influenced by other circumstances or conditions, that I must uphold my own highest standards of performance, no matter what else might be going on in the pit or on the stage with a given conductor. I had found out that it was too easy to let my own work slip to the lesser levels that sometimes surrounded me. I can honestly say that once I formed this protective idea, I never again let my playing suffer. Indeed the worse the conductor was, the better I played; the more ridiculous the singing was on stage, the more I resisted participating in it, and the more I fought to maintain my own highest standards. I was not going to allow some mediocre outside situation make me descend to its lower level.

In all this confusion it didn't help matters that by mid-December I had to face once again Margie's imminent departure for Fargo for the holidays. I could not fend off my loneliness and frustration without her. Worse yet, the disgusting year-end Christmas commercialism destroyed in me any sense of the true festive Christmas spirit. I was nothing without Margie, and spent the last few weeks of the year listless and more or less brain dead, barely functioning at the Met, and waiting impatiently for the year to end.

My downcast spirits must have become noticeable to some of my colleagues. One day, Izzy Blank, who had befriended me ever since my arrival at the Met, took me aside in a fatherly way—he *was* twice my age—and admonished me "not to get too despondent; it's dangerous." He buoyed my spirits considerably when he told me: "Don't you realize that you're the best horn player we've had in this orchestra for years and years." (We all can use a compliment now and then, especially when young and trying to make one's way in the world, and especially when the compliment comes from a peer whom one greatly respects and admires.) Izzy told me that "no one, in all the years I've been here at the Met, has played that difficult third horn solo in the first act of *Meistersinger* as beautifully and as easily as you have—not even close."

I must confess that I was particularly proud of my rendering of that rather difficult horn passage (in unison with the first clarinet and the tenor, on stage). It was always followed by a shuffling of the feet, our musicians' way of complimenting a player on a well-played solo or a very difficult passage.[40]

The mention of this *Meistersinger* passage reminds me of a very trying occasion in the early days of my first season at the Met, another not-so-pleasant encounter with George Szell. On several occasions Szell had bragged to the orchestra that as a student in Vienna he had not only studied but had also played every instrument in the orchestra, and that he still knew all the fingerings for the modern double horn. That was particularly odd information, since in Vienna they have never played and do not to this day play the modern double horn. (They play a single F horn.) I had played this first-act passage already many times without a blemish. Thus Szell had no reason to complain about my playing of it, nor to admonish or address me in any respect—except perhaps to compliment me. Nonetheless he looked sternly straight at me, and told me that the "easy way to get that high E" (in m. 4) was to "use the thumb valve." He looked at me, evidently waiting for me to acknowledge his advice, or perhaps even thank him for it. I could do no such thing, since his fingering suggestion was in fact quite wrong. And I surely did not need his stupid advice as to what fingerings to use on my instrument, since I had been playing the horn professionally for about four years, and had played several thousand high Es without benefit of his advice. Szell began to lose the respect of many in the orchestra that day.

Fortunately, life apart from the Met continued at its usual challenging New York pace. Outstanding in my memory are several special exhibitions at MOMA, particularly one consisting entirely of Titians and El Grecos, and some great evenings at Lincoln Kirstein's Ballet Society, where I noticed for the first time what a terrific conductor Leon Barzin was. I was also utterly fascinated by two quite different books on jazz: Mezz Mezzrow's (and Bernard Wolfe's) brilliantly written, anecdotal, quasi-autobiographical *Really the Blues* (1946),[41] and Winthrop Sargeant's 1938 *Hot and Hybrid* (what a great, accurate title!), unquestionably the first serious study of the history of jazz from a musical, analytical point of view, rather than the usual social, anecdotal, biographical approach.

I knew of Sargeant (1903–86) only as a very conservative, antimodern music critic at the *New Yorker*. So I was rather surprised—and impressed—by his clear-minded, unbiased analysis of the musical elements of jazz, what he referred to frequently as the "anatomy of jazz." It was exactly the way I was looking at jazz, noting the similarities between it and classical music, at the same time fully aware of the differences between the two art forms. The only thing I could seriously quibble with was Sargeant's rather cavalier dismissal of the possibilities of some sort of rapprochement or crosspollination between the two disciplines. Having already introduced some concepts from contemporary classical developments into a few of my own jazz works (such as *Jumpin' in the Future*), and being aware that others (such as George Handy, Ralph Burns, Will Bradley, Pete Rugolo, Bob Graettinger) were also experimenting with bringing the two musics into a closer, mutually fructifying relationship, I was pretty certain that on that particular point Sargeant was somewhat shortsighted. In his defense I rationalized that he was writing *Hot and Hybrid* in 1938, a time when hardly anyone was dreaming of bringing jazz and classical music together, while I was reading Sargeant's book nine years later in 1947, during which intervening years a whole lot had happened both in jazz and in modern classical music.

I'm sure that reading *Hot and Hybrid* helped to generate in me my first thoughts and dreams of some sort of musical style or concept that would bridge the gap between classical music and jazz, a concept that some ten years later I baptized with the term "Third Stream."[42]

In the meantime I continued my voluminous reading of great literature. I had started Marcel Proust's *Remembrance of Things Past*, which I finished about a year later while playing the Broadway show *Annie Get Your Gun*. I even tackled Joyce's *Ulysses* for the first time, being inspired to do so by reading Harry Levin's marvelous Joyce biography as my introduction to the works of Joyce. But I confess I had to give up on *Ulysses* after a few weeks; it was just too much for me. It wasn't until many years later that I managed to get through the book, realizing even then that as beautiful and fascinating as Joyce's language was, there was much that I couldn't unravel and understand. Instead, I turned to Joyce's early works, *Dubliners* and *Portrait of the Artist as a Young Man*, a thrilling experience because so much in those works resonated with my own interests and my own search for enlightenment and eternal truths. The other revelatory reading for me was Ernest Jones's two-volume biography of Sigmund Freud, which came out in 1947.

It was during this period that, on one of my weekly midtown art gallery explorations, I couldn't resist buying a painting by one of my favorite surrealist artists, Yves Tanguy, at the Pierre Matisse Gallery on Fifty-Seventh Street, near Fifth Avenue. It was a beautiful gouache titled *La Jupe* (*The Petticoat*). I paid $200 for it. It is now worth around $50,000. After over fifty years of owning it and looking at it almost every day, I still love it, and can't even think of selling or parting with it.

My midwinter and holiday feelings of frustration and depression were somewhat alleviated in the new year by increasing signs that the Met could still rise to very high performance standards, if it so chose. Perhaps much of this had to do with the addition of Giuseppe Antonicelli to the Met's conducting staff—undoubtedly the all-around best conductor of Italian repertory we had at the Met in my entire fifteen-year tenure, even a cut or two above Fausto Cleva (who succeeded Antonicelli in 1950). I say this even though Antonicelli was at the Met only three years. The proof of my assertion can be heard on the splendid recordings we made of *La Bohème* (with Bidu Sayao and Richard Tucker) and Verdi's *Un Ballo in maschera*. Those recording sessions were exciting, inspiring learning experiences, in drastic contrast to the dismal recordings we made of *Tristan* excerpts under the totally amateurish direction of Charles O'Connell. We all knew that O'Connell had been asked (or allowed) to conduct not because he showed any talent for conducting, but because he was at the time music director of Columbia Masterworks—in other words he essentially appointed himself to direct the recordings—

and had been prior to that for nearly twenty years head of the Artist and Repertory (A&R) division of RCA Victor, in charge of their Red Seal records. In my diary I called those *Tristan* sessions "probably the most horrible records ever made."

After many years of allowing the Italian repertory to languish in the hands of unmemorable routiniers such as Cesare Sodero and Pietro Cimara, Antonicelli's arrival in the late fall of 1947 brought a breath of fresh interpretive air to the Met's stale, rusty, haphazard treatment of the Puccini and Verdi operas. I remember very well how Antonicelli in his very first rehearsal—of *Tosca*—instantly affected and inspired the orchestra. It was quite amazing. After a few bars of bewilderment, we all realized that we were face to face with a great conductor, perhaps a genius. He reminded me immediately of Mitropoulos, with his priestlike demeanor, his engaged, illuminated expression, his ascetic-looking, tight-necked rehearsal frock. He proffered a bright, kindly personality, which somehow one was immediately compelled to respect. Several times in that first rehearsal he apologized for correcting us. We could hardly believe our ears. Even Dick Moore, inherently suspicious of newcomers, seemed to admire Antonicelli, declaring that *Tosca* was being "completely de-Soderized." He was right; *Tosca* in Antonicelli's hands suddenly became again the living, surging masterpiece we knew it to be. Without saying much, he showed us with the simplest of manual gestures all the score's wonderful nuances, and unified the orchestra into a single pliable, receptive instrument. And when Tibbett took over the role of Scarpia, the Met suddenly seemed to rise to its full grand potential. Though Tibbett's voice was by this time almost completely shot[43]—he sometimes coughed the notes out—he brought to the Scarpia role a realistic, truly demonic, sadistic realization, the like of which I never saw again in any of our other Met Scarpias (even with Tito Gobbi, for example).

Another Metropolitan Opera veteran whose voice was starting to go was Lauritz Melchior. His had been for decades one of the greatest voices of that era; indeed, it was a voice that can only be described as unique. I feel so privileged to have experienced Melchior, in *Lohengrin* and in *Tannhäuser*, and, of course, in Wagner's *Ring*. Even though Melchior would sometimes, late in his career, sing a bit flat or rush tempos (especially in less heroic high-tessitura parts, such as the "Rom Erzählung" (Rome Narrative) in *Tannhäuser*), I could tell that he was simply saving his voice. It was a continual thrill for me to hear that rich, fully centered, baritonal tenor voice. He was the ultimate Wagnerian *Heldentenor* (heroic tenor), and I doubt that there will ever be anyone like him again.[44]

Another musical thrill for me was the chance to hear the debut and subsequent four years of outstanding singing of the now completely forgotten Florence Quartararo (in *Traviata* and Mozart's *Figaro*), one of the most beautiful young soprano voices I heard in my years at the Met. But, unfortunately, she also was a prime example of how a singer can be professionally, managerially exploited and seduced into oversinging until the voice (the larynx) gives out and the career is prematurely aborted.

I was also very happy to reencounter two longtime favorites of mine: Charlie Kullman, whose radiant voice and elegant artistry had captivated me ever since I acquired Bruno Walter's seminal recording of Mahler's *Lied von der Erde* eight years earlier, and Virgilio Lazzari (in *Boris Godunov*), whose virile voice and impeccable musical taste I had admired since my days with the Cincinnati Zoo Opera in 1944.

Speaking of great singing artists, Rose Bampton, who had returned to the Met in 1946 after an absence of several seasons, provided incomparable musical thrills not only at the opera house but also in her other New York appearances. At one of Leonard Bernstein's New York City Symphony concerts, she sang in a performance of Alban Berg's three *Wozzeck* "Bruchstücke." I was deeply moved and impressed by her touching portrayal of the betrayed Maria. Bampton's German diction was superb, as was her heartbreaking interpretation of the "Sprechstimme" passages, so different from Erika Wagner's approach on the 1940 Schönberg *Pierrot lunaire* recording—and, in my view, so much more faithful to Berg's implied pitch indications and gestural contours.

Obbligato

Rose Bampton had joined the Met way back in 1932, where she enjoyed great successes for a number of years in a remarkable variety of roles. In the late thirties she decided to sit out several seasons, but eventually returned to the Met in the 1946–47 season, succeeding Kerstin Thorborg, particularly in roles such as Kundry in Wagner's *Parsifal*. For me she was one of the relatively few complete artists—interpretationally, technically, dramatically—during my fifteen-years at the Met; there are more adulatory Rose Bampton entries in my diaries by far than on any other singer. I had already filled my (lost) Cincinnati diaries with numerous encomiums to her.

What I found so especially wondrous about Bampton was that, in addition to her superb musicianship and stately, rare beauty—much like my Margie—her acting was, no matter in what role, an inborn part of her singing, second nature, not something studied or separate or tacked on. She seemed to feel the music organically, holistically. One was never conscious of her thinking about or planning, calculating her singing. And yet, as with any truly great artist who bares his or her soul to the audience, her work was the result of painstakingly meticulous preparation and study. She completely lived the part and lost herself in it.

There was one other aspect of Bampton's persona that I particularly appreciated. Whereas the vast majority of singers kept themselves segregated and aloof from the orchestra, took little notice of us—except occasionally to complain—and were essentially unapproachable, Rose Bampton was one of the few who recognized our orchestra's important contribution to the overall artistic and dramatic result. For her it wasn't us and them; she went out of her way to show and tell us orchestra musicians how much she appreciated our work, individually and collectively. She seemed really to care about the orchestra and, miracle of miracles, actually listened to the orchestra. She made music with us, instead of just singing over the top of the pit to the audience.

I am proud to have had the privilege of working with her and learning so much from her about the art of music.

*   *   *   *   *

Once again, in mid-December, Margie and I had to go through the agony of another parting: her annual two-week Christmas visit home to Fargo. We managed to spend the three evenings and nights before her departure together out in Jamaica, and what wonderful, really close, happy times they were. But that also made the final hours and the farewell at Pennsylvania Station all the more unbearable—so cruel, so impossibly final. Suddenly she was gone. How many more times would we have to endure this gut-wrenching torture!

In a way the next two weeks somehow never happened; they didn't exist for me, they were an empty blank. Oh, yes, I played the operas, and I tried to do some reading, and some cataloguing of my accumulated jazz records. But my heart wasn't in it. It was as if I were absent, somewhere else, in some faraway empty space. But then, the long wait, the big emptiness, was suddenly over. Margie got back on a Sunday morning after a long overnight train trip with two stopovers in Minneapolis and Chicago. But as fatigued as she was, she wanted to go to the New York Philharmonic afternoon concert, *right away* after arriving at Penn Station. Rodzinski was conducting, and that particular program of Beethoven and Gershwin was well worth the effort, mainly because of a stunning performance of Beethoven's Seventh Symphony, a piece for which Rodzinski had a special affinity. That same evening I gave Margie her Christmas presents, which included a very high-quality Tanguy reproduction. To my delight—I was not quite sure how she would react; surrealist art was not something one could experience in Fargo, North Dakota—she loved it. In her diary she wrote that "the abstract desert-like, horizon-less expanse, with a few molten objects scattered through its lunar landscape, gave me such a beautiful calming feeling— like some gentle, serene *adagio* music."

In my occasional moments of self-doubt, being at heart a bit of a worrier, I also wondered how much my extensive reading of Tolstoy accounted for my confused state. Was my seeming inability to puzzle out the contradictory impulses that constantly gnawed away at me an offshoot of my struggles at some kind of reconciliation with Tolstoy's writings? Moreover, I realized that in character and personality I was not like any of my acquaintances. I seemed to take everything more seriously, at times morbidly so, and found that in a host of ideological and philosophical matters many of my friends couldn't understand me, and probably thought I was kind of weird.

I thought of myself as an undaunted individualist, clinging sternly to my attitudes and opinions gathered over years of studying, reading, learning, and questioning. I felt strongly that in this world of ours, which I saw to be so full of fake feelings, superficial presumptions, intellectual dishonesty—not to mention a pervasive, wide-ranging anti-intellectualism—I had to represent something deeper, something unmaterialistic and purer. And I was very impetuous (the impetuosity of youth?) and impatient in regard to these matters. Was this a premonition of my later famous outspokenness? I saw myself quite alone, and rationalized that the life and death of Christ had taught us that in order to gain perfection—apparently unattainable, but something to be at least always striven for—one first had to suffer through all manner of trials and tribulations, probably as a result finding oneself a "lonely voice in the wilderness."

The one bright beacon of hope, whenever I fell prey to such periods of self-doubt, of soul-searching inner struggle, was offered by Marjorie, who seemed to understand me, and who was, in her quiet, trusting way, committed to support me in my multiple endeavors and interests.

Chapter Seven

COLLECTING FRIENDS AND MENTORS

THE MET'S NATIONAL TOUR in the spring of 1947 was divided into two segments, the first two weeks in Baltimore and Boston in March, the second part from early April to late May through the South and Midwest. For the week between those two segments we returned to New York, primarily to give our annual Good Friday performances of *Parsifal*, a work I loved so much that I would have been happy to play it ten or twenty times a season, as opposed to the two or three performances we gave every year.[1] I realized that many of my Met colleagues regarded *Parsifal* a big bore (too slow, too long, nothing happens), a fact that bothered me terribly. But they were not experiencing *Parsifal* as I, a composer who had been weaned harmonically on late-Wagner's super chromaticism, experienced it. With the exception of a handful of close friends in the orchestra who were really interested in the music—Harry Peers (trumpet), Ernst Drucker (violin), Henry Aaron (viola), David Rattner (horn), Dick Horowitz (timpani)—most everybody else thought *Parsifal* was an afternoon- or evening-wasting exercise in tedium. I remember with a special nostalgia the feelings of religious fervor that pervaded the atmosphere at the Met during those pre-Easter days, generated by Wagner's music. Even the most bored musicians couldn't quite escape that feeling; one could palpably feel the mystical, sacral atmosphere in the air.

A great part of the magic of those performances was provided by the generally excellent casts the Met gathered for its *Parsifal* performances in my early days there, especially Melchior and the beautiful Rose Bampton, the most musical of all the Kundrys I ever heard (except possibly Thorborg). Bampton's understanding of that demanding role—one of Wagner's most mysterious and complex heroines—was so deep that I sometimes felt that she was singing that glorious music as if she herself had composed it. I used to marvel at how she made her voice fit into the instrumentation, particularly in the second act, which is for long stretches exclusively for strings and solo clarinet. It is an example of Bampton's musical sensitivity and intelligence that she blended in and sang as if she were a partner with the clarinet.

I always had what you might call an emotional orgasm every time we played the heavenly third act Good Friday Spell music. And when Melchior sang "Es lacht die Au" (All nature smiles), it all connected with the passion and resurrection of Christ and the long-awaited return of spring, the balmy fragrances of nature reborn.

The Met's visit to Boston that spring encompassed a full ten days, with a dozen opera performances. During that period Margie managed to get to Boston twice, each time for three days. Those days with her were among the happiest and most exciting times we had in those early years. We did a lot of sightseeing, enjoying particularly the quaint, old English atmosphere of Boston. We revisited the city's marvelous Museum of Fine Arts and the central public library, the two cultural sanctuaries in which we had spent so many happy hours on our visit the year before. We also took our first trip to Cambridge, mainly to have a look at Harvard University, the legendary citadel of learning that was like hallowed ground to us.[2] We spent many hours at Harvard's Museum of Natural History, especially the glass flowers exhibition.[3] We couldn't tear ourselves away, marveling at the hundreds of dazzling glass masterpieces by the famous Czech-born Blaschka brothers, Leopold and Rudolf.

We stuffed ourselves at Boston's legendary Durgin Park Restaurant with roast beef and the world's biggest strawberry shortcakes, whilst enduring the insults and surly service of its notorious waitresses—all part of the entertainment.

Following up on our pilgrimage to Walden Pond the year before, this time I talked Margie into making an all-day bicycle trip to Salem, about thirty miles northeast of Boston. The full round-trip excursion from downtown Boston to the Massachusetts north shore and back, solely by bicycle, was too ambitious to accomplish in one day. So we took a bus to Melrose, a town about seven miles north of Boston, and then headed for Marblehead and Salem on our rented bikes for another fifteen to twenty miles, mostly taking the many charming back roads. I recall, when we reached the ocean near Swampscott and Marblehead, how refreshing and bracing it was to breathe in the brininess of the sea. Marblehead with its seventeenth-century charm and curious crooked streets seemed an idyllic refuge, safely tucked away from the advances of modern civilization. After Marblehead the going got rather tough with lots of long hills that would be nothing in a car but on our bicycles was painfully knee straining. Huffing and puffing, we finally made it to Salem. There we visited the town's most famous sites, the House of the Seven Gables and Hathaway House, wonderful bits of early American history that we had learned about in school. Unfortunately the visit at Seven Gables was somewhat spoiled by the droning, lifeless voice of our guide, making it hard to savor the old-world atmosphere of the place.

I thought of bicycling over to nearby Rockport, where Dr. Noble, my beloved choirmaster at St. Thomas, was living in retirement. But since Rockport was another twenty miles further north, I realized that we would be pushing ourselves beyond our limits—and would never get back to Boston before dark.

The trip back to Melrose, although on a more direct route, was more difficult because of a strong afternoon headwind, and it was beginning to get dark as we went through Lynn. I was worried about Margie getting tired, but good trooper that she was, she remained strong and controlled, except for a short stretch on a dark, swampy road with no other human beings anywhere in sight, where for an instant she became a little hysterical.

Our joy encompassed not only the liberating feeling of getting away from the city into the countryside but also seeing many Massachusetts historic sites on the way, and tasting the region's old-world charm and architecture—all packed into one day; it was an almost dreamlike experience. Call me crazy, but even though we were half dead when we got back to Boston around dinnertime, it was one of the most exhilarating days we ever spent together.

By contrast to these "healthy, normal" pursuits, we indulged in a quite different type of recreation: we went to the two famous Boston burlesque houses, the Old Howard and the Casino, both on or near the equally legendary (and now longingly remembered) Scollay Square.[4] Though the Casino was the bawdier of the two ecdysiast palaces, they both had a certain Bostonian class, even elegance—unlike the raunchier, cheaper burlesque houses and nightclubs in Baltimore (another but much rougher navy town in those days). The featured stripteasers at the Howard, the special chorus line, the unusually brainy comedians—after all they had to cater to Harvard undergraduates—all were the classiest and best paid on the whole vaudeville and burlesque circuit. Even the pit band wasn't some pitiful out-of-tune duo of piano and drums, but a seven-piece orchestra, led by a stand-up violinist (sporting a bow tie) and featuring a pretty good trumpet, trombone, and saxophone.[5]

Down the street from the Howard, at the Casino, Peaches reigned supreme (real name, Georgia Southern—so one was told). She was undoubtedly the most daring of all the stripteasers, at a time when the Hays Office in Hollywood was still rigidly controlling what parts of a woman's anatomy could be revealed. Peaches was fearless, brazen, and earthy. She wanted to be real. She was a heroine to the Casino's clientele—I suppose a kind of Madonna of her time, although a bit less crazy—even a martyr for all those who couldn't resist her devilishly teasing charms. Peaches was always being arrested by the police; she spent many a night in jail, but was always quickly bailed out and returned in triumph to her adoring Casino fans the next day. Most Bostonians knew that their city government and its officials were among the most corrupt in the country,[6] and felt it was a game the police played with the Casino: they eagerly collected payoffs, but then put Peaches in jail—thus appearing to be upholding the laws of the land—and as quickly as possible released her so that the cycle could start all over again.

Peaches was a wonder, in her way an artist, uniquely endowed for the art she practiced. Her stunning body was usually covered only in a black wide-net costume (which might as well not have existed, it was so transparent), with seven or eight red roses strategically placed to hide the "hot spots." She moved with an exuberant energy, slow enough that her movements could be fully appreciated and savored. She had a rhythm in her maneuverings around the stage, at times slinky, at times brazenly striding, that prompted Margie to suggest that Peaches must have been part Negro. It seemed that every part of her body could move independently at will, in its own orbits. Indeed, her body seemed to ride and undulate on a series of ball bearings.

We went to see Peaches many times over the years, and were, I'm sure, among her most ardent admirers. Some readers might be shocked that my Margie, from rural North Dakota and a strict Presbyterian background, would go to something as low as a burlesque show. Only depraved men go to those horrible places. Well, that doesn't quite jibe with the facts.[7] Burlesque shows have been around at least since the early twentieth century, along with the first attempts at erotic films. It has been the common man's entertainment forever, the plebeian nether end of the theater, although also enthusiastically attended by the rich, by intellectuals and artists—even if a bit more covertly. More important: burlesque is, in its guileless, unpretentious, and honest viewpoint about sex, a theatrical entertainment and amusement equivalent to light reading.

I always preferred the honesty of burlesque to the hypocrisy of most Broadway musicals and Hollywood movies. The one was exactly what it was, no pretension; the other pretended to be some form of higher entertainment, but used enormous injections of sex—or faux sex—to prop up some inane boy-meets-girl plot. It is ironic that the disrobing of dancers in burlesque was called striptease, when in fact what they did was quite forthright, quite plain to see—they *undressed* (as far as the law allowed)—while in musicals it was all suggestive teasing, without ever delivering. The one was real, the other was sham.

In one of my sporadic diary entries from 1947[8] I ranted and raved against a Gertrude Niesen show on Broadway and its total emphasis on sex and sexual innuendo: all tease, no consummation (analogous to the wonderful crack about Hollywood cowboys: "all hat, no cow"). I delivered myself of a fairly heated diatribe, deploring that the already "questionable morals of audiences keep sinking lower and lower. Sex humor has reached the final stages of obviousness." I couldn't understand why "all evening long" I was forced "to see nothing but sex, paraded either glamorously artificially or bluntly (in vulgar bumps and grinds). Niesen might just as well have lifted her skirt and shown all she owned. Joke after joke, song after song, girl after girl—it all leads to one focal point: sex!! As skirts get shorter and jokes dirtier, women march on, breasts (mostly false) pointed outward, in this endless vicious circle of degradation of women and a kind of moral prostitution to men and their perverted humor." (I was, if anything, outspoken.) In another entry I suggested that perhaps the recent war had brought on "all this delusory sexual hypertension, the frayed finality of postwar emotions," and wondered where it all would lead next.

It was also on this Boston visit that we discovered not only a few excellent Chinese restaurants in Chinatown, but also a couple of good Italian ones in the north end of town. But our absolute favorite was the Athens Olympia, offering wonderfully authentic Greek cuisine. The Athens Olympia was run by two elderly Greek-born brothers, who served up not only a fine authentic Greek cuisine but also wonderful bouzouki mandolin and zither music, and the typically sensuous, quietly intense Greek dancing and singing. That's where I discovered

Greek egg and lemon soup, moussaka, lamb kebab (on a skewer), real kalamata olives, bak-lava, and one of my all-time favorite appetizers, taromasalata, a pinkish caviarlike paste made from mullet roe. In those earlier days I had the impression that proper Bostonians regarded eating well as rather sinful, something irresponsible, even immoral. Except for the Athens Olympia, Durgin Park (good, but a limited, unimaginative basic menu), and Lockober's (a virtual English private men's club—women were only allowed in a small barless room on the second floor), where the typical favored dish was English-style roast beef, or the Ritz (very good but also *very* snobbish, and so expensive that no mere mortal could afford to dine there), the best, most popular eating place in Boston was Howard Johnson's. Ethnic cuisines and menu diversity were totally unknown, and (probably) also considered improper or some sort of moral transgression.

How Boston's culinary ambiance has changed since then! A dramatic revolution took place in the 1970s, led by two women, Julia Child (on WGBH, public television's flagship station), and Lydia Shire, who not only opened a superb restaurant in the Bostonian Hotel, but also founded a cooking school that in a short span of time spawned several successive generations of chefs who now provide greater Boston with a vast array of superb, sophisticated cuisines.

After Boston, the tour headed westward, through Cleveland, Minneapolis, and Chicago, and thence to the South (Atlanta, Memphis, New Orleans, Texas), ending up eventually in Rochester in mid-May. Because of days off in my own performing schedule, I was able to again take a few side trips, two to Cincinnati and one to Fargo, most of them by air.

I started flying fairly regularly as early as 1943. I loved it; the feeling of freedom, of not being earthbound, the sense of quiet isolation, a feeling of specialness. Flying was still something few people undertook in those days. The planes were small by comparison to our jet-age giants; the largest plane I flew in seated only forty-four passengers. And, of course, planes flew at much lower altitudes and therefore at slower speeds than nowadays. But the service was exceptional; one received a lot of personal attention and the food was excellent, first-class quality, competing with the superb dining one could enjoy in those days on America's super-trains. In flight, the crew, the stewardesses (as they were then called), and passengers became for a few hours like family, sensing that all of us were engaged in something unique. Since planes weren't very wide and had only two rows of seats lengthwise, with a comfortable aisle in between, *everybody* had a window seat; and, since viewing the world from several thousand feet up was still a novel experience, one spent almost all the time looking down at the wondrous sights below.

By today's standards of long-distance flying, flights like the one I took that spring from LaGuardia Airport to Cleveland (on United Airlines) will seem quaint and a bit circuitous. (I flew to Cleveland to meet the orchestra, preferring to fly rather than spending so many hours on the Met's tour train.) It took four hours, flying at a speed of about 170 miles per hour, generally between five and ten thousand feet above ground. Soon after lift-off I was thrilled to see Lewisohn Stadium directly below me, filled with tiny little figures playing football. We flew southwest over the swamps of New Jersey to Princeton and Philadelphia, where we picked up additional passengers, thence over the mountains in eastern Pennsylvania to Harrisburg, then on to the southwestern corner of New York State, and over Akron into Cleveland. I was astounded to see how compact and toylike everything looked from on high: railroads looked like scale-model electric trains at home, fields with their beautiful quiltlike patterns looked like fine abstract paintings, even the foul-smelling swamps and oil dumps of New Jersey looked attractive, somehow clean and inviting. Then there were the many ribbons of rivers cutting through the Pennsylvanian mountains, especially the Susquehanna, reflecting and glistening brightly in the sunlight. I was astonished to find that one could clearly see the Ohio-Pennsylvania border, an absolutely straight north-south line, marked variously by roads, fences, stone walls, or edges of forest, a line visible as far as the horizon.

Flying high over Wisconsin on another flight, I saw what extraordinarily beautiful patterns and varied colorations were created by the hundreds of individual fields below. Shouldn't these splendid designs—no two alike, fairly complex and yet so simple—be considered a form of art, the work of artist farmers? On another flight a few weeks later, from Fargo to Chicago (via Minneapolis), we flew mostly over a huge plateau of brilliant, blindingly white clouds; and I think it must have been the first time that I had the impression of flying over the North Pole.

On this Met tour my two side trips to Cincinnati were made possible by postwar advances in air travel speed and accessibility, and by the chance circumstance of having several free evenings in my schedule while we were still in the Midwest. Once again, I was very drawn to the Queen City to visit my many friends there, both on the classical and jazz side: Eugene Selhorst, August Söndlin, Walter Heermann, Reuben and Bobbie Segal, Sammy Green, Hilbert Moses, Roland Johnson, and, of course, my three jazz buddies at the Hangar. As soon as I arrived in Cincinnati's brand new airport (in northern Kentucky), I headed directly for Music Hall, luckily just catching the end of the concert: Eleanor Steber in some encores, and in absolutely glorious voice. Everybody in the orchestra seemed thrilled to see me: the return of the hometown hero, as it were. I caught up with doings at the college and was very impressed with Roland Johnson's work as conductor of the college orchestra, now populated with quite a few more male instrumentalists than in previous years, most of whom had returned to school under the GI Bill after service in the war.

I was pleased to see Roland do quite a bit of contemporary music. In the two days I heard him rehearse his orchestra, he worked on pieces by William Schuman, Paul Hindemith, and Goossens (*Rhythmic Dances*). I was particularly struck by the exceptional talent of two of the younger students, Dennis Larsen and Conrad Crocker, both of whom became principals in the Cincinnati Symphony within a few years (oboe and flute, respectively) and longtime close friends of mine.

My visit with Söndlin turned out to be a rather melancholy affair. He was now retired from the symphony and very much at loose ends, although taking some solace in his superb library, reading mostly poetry and the German philosophers. Many times during that long evening at his house he had tears in his eyes; he said that I brought out things in him that he hadn't thought about in years, even since his youth in Berlin. He felt very lonely, had no real friends in Cincinnati. And he complained that he almost never saw his wife, Karin Dayas,[9] since due to their poor financial situation she was forced to teach some sixty hours a week, which I knew had to be a pretty horrible life. (It reminded me of Steuermann's situation in New York.) Long after midnight, it was still hard for me to tear myself away from these dear friends, for they represented the musical world that I lived and breathed.

It was clear to me that in the relatively few waking hours during my two Cincinnati visits it would be impossible to visit all my friends and respond to the slew of dinner invitations I got after my arrival. I had no idea that I was that popular and well remembered. So I began to organize a schedule of lunches and dinners, at the YMCA and the Alms Hotel—both old haunts of mine—eating two meals at one sitting, each with a different set of friends. (In those days I was as thin as a rail, and there was little danger of my gaining excessive weight. Indeed, many people remembered my frequently eating two full meals in a row at restaurants like Pohlar's or Mecklenburg's, or finishing a big meal with two or three deserts.) My scheduling scheme worked out well, because I managed to see practically everybody, in many cases reestablishing contacts with colleagues I hadn't seen for three or four years.

During the first of my two Cincinnati visits I went several times to the Hangar, hoping especially to see Will Wilkins. To my surprise he wasn't there, having been fired, as I quickly found out—although it was never revealed why. Lee Anderson, who had been the pianist in the trio during my earlier two years in Cincinnati, was now playing bass, and very well indeed. The piano chair had been taken over by Jack Surrell, a good player, but not quite the possessor of Lee's fine touch and tone and brightly swinging rhythmic feel. The Hangar had also changed dramatically in one particular respect. Whereas earlier it was frequented by jazz fans and the most attractive, sharp, foxy ladies, it had in the interim turned into a very noisy gay bar with— sad to report—hardly anybody listening to the fine music coming from the bandstand.

Will, whom Lee had called to say that I was in town for a few days, promised to come down to the Hangar a bit later to visit with me, but he never showed up. I finally saw him on my second trip to Cincinnati, two weeks later—as it turned out under the most terrifying circumstances.

For my second visit to Cincinnati Margie had flown in from the Midwest, having visited her aunt Harriet in Omaha. She was very excited about spending a few days with me and about returning to Cincinnati for the first time since her graduation from the College of Music. Everybody was so eager to see and visit with her that, at first, we had a heck of a time finding even a few minutes to ourselves. Walter Heermann helped several times by sneaking us off to his apartment, where we eventually ended up bedding down for the three nights we had together in Cincinnati.

After several failed attempts to hook up with Will Wilkins, it finally happened on our last night in Cincinnati, indeed during our final hours there. We met at two in the morning at the Cotton Club, my old stomping ground. And what a joyous reunion, to bask once again in the warmth of Will's friendship, and to reminisce about my "thousand and one" nights at the Hangar, and about our mutual love for the Nat King Cole Trio. Will told us that he was fired when he happened to express his mild upset to the club's new owner for turning it into a gay hangout. Life had been very hard for Will since then, although he was managing to eke out a marginal existence, gigging as a freelancer.

When the Cotton Club closed at four a.m. the three of us walked over to Fountain Square, where we expected to find cabs to take us to our respective abodes. Just as we were entering the square—eerily silent and empty at that time of night—chatting about the show at the Cotton Club, Will suddenly froze in mid-sentence, and in a sudden panic he grabbed the two of us and told us to run for our lives. Margie and I had no idea what had happened to put Will in such a state of fright; this was not the gentle, relaxed Will we knew. As he began to run at breakneck speed, heading for an all-night cafe some three hundred feet away on the other side of the square, the only place in sight that was open, Margie and I—she in hysterics, I suddenly also panic-stricken—ran after Will. I remember seeing Will's legs directly ahead of me moving so fast that they became just one whirling visual blur.

A few seconds later something came flying past me, hitting Will in the small of the back and shattering into pieces. He stumbled, almost falling, but somehow managed to right himself and keep running. Looking back, I saw in one frightening instant of recognition an open convertible with three young men, careening around Fountain Square[10] in drunken zigzags, yelling obscenities at us, and other endearing epithets such as "nigger lovers" and "mother-fuckers." Instantly, two more objects came flying our way, which I could now see were big gallon jugs, with jagged edges where the neck had been broken off. Christ, these guys were out to kill us, maybe Margie and me more than Will, because *we* were the "nigger lovers." I'm convinced that if they had decided to drive diagonally *across* the square, rather than staying on the streets trying to catch up with us, I might not be here writing these words. Margie threw off her high heels, running like mad, almost faster than me. It is amazing what fear and danger can do to galvanize and adrenalize the human mind and body.

All three of us reached the cafe across the square just in time as the convertible, tires screeching wildly, lurched past us at breakneck speed. Our hearts pounding like jackhammers, and totally out of breath, we staggered into the cafe, only to see, wonder of wonders, two cops sitting at the counter. As soon as I could catch my breath I explained to them what had happened. They immediately dashed out onto the street, just as the three rednecks—we now could tell they were quite drunk and completely out of control—came screaming around the corner again, barely missing a couple of lampposts. Now the cops took up the chase in their police car, their siren frantically yowling, and within minutes pulled the trio over, right outside the cafe. The three hoodlums were not only drunk and virtually incoherent but also—unbelievably, to me in my innocence—cockily unapologetic, still fuming and cursing at us, obviously frustrated that we had been able to escape them. They kept shouting that they had come from Kentucky, across the river, to "have us some fun." Some fun, indeed! "Let's kill us a nigger and a couple of nigger lovers." It was clear that they were especially exercised that a white girl would be at ease in the company of a "nigger."

The policemen finally got the three rednecks calmed down, but instead of arresting them, they told them to "get the hell" out of here. Worse, to our disgust, all of this was said in the calming casual tone of voice that a father might use to chide his four-year-old son for some minor infraction. We couldn't believe our ears, having assumed that the cops would quickly cart these three creeps off to the nearest stationhouse. But nothing of the kind. The scene turned truly bizarre. When Will and I started to yell at the two cops to arrest these bastards, they—unbelievably—turned on us and told *us* to shut up. Now, suddenly, *we* were the perpetrators, the culprits. *Sotto voce*, Will reminded me that Cincinnati was still very much "in the South."

As the cops went about persuading our three bigots to leave the scene, Margie and I, now totally cowed and fearing that *we* might actually be arrested—it was like something out of a Kafka novel—began to think only of getting out of the cafe and home as quickly as possible. When I suggested getting a cab and dropping Will off at his house, he, keenly sensitive as a Negro to the danger of his situation, quickly put a stop to that idea. He knew that our three frustrated pursuers would in fact be not on their way to Kentucky, but rather lying in wait for us in some dark alley, out to wreak their final revenge on us. I realized then that Will's psychological antennae, ever alert to the constant perils of life for a black man in America, had in a matter of seconds picked up the scent of danger, even when still at a considerable distance. Many years later, when I wrote my opera *The Visitation*, a conversion of Kafka's *The Trial* to an American setting of racial hatred and bigotry, I felt compelled to incorporate my Cincinnati nightmare, with its close parallel to one of Kafka's episodes, as one of its most relevant scenes.

Will called a black cab driver friend of his, who had a reputation for being the fastest cabbie in town, and who generally worked Cincinnati's West End. Will was sure that Charlie would be able to elude our three drunken pursuers, if it came to that. And so it was. The three drunks *were* waiting for us, only two blocks away from Fountain Square. But Charles, speeding at sixty or seventy miles an hour through Cincinnati's empty streets, quickly lost the Packard convertible. Finally home, unable to hold back our tears, we desperately hugged and kissed Charles, knowing that he had probably saved our lives.

On my many visits to Cincinnati since then, often staying at the Westin Hotel, located exactly where that all-night cafe once stood, I am still haunted by the memory of that nightmare in April 1947. When I look out over Fountain Square I remember that that night was the closest I ever came to being killed or at least severely beaten. The square's placid appearance at night, with its lovely nineteenth-century German fountain gurgling away unconcernedly, belies the continuing reality that Cincinnati (I hate to say it) is still a place where racial tensions can erupt any time in grizzly scenes, as they have in fact several times in recent years.

We got home around five thirty in the morning, needless to say quite unable to sleep. All we could do was to cuddle up to each other, hold each other very tight, realizing how precious and transient life can be. As it was, I had to get up in a few hours anyway to catch a plane to Atlanta to play a *Figaro* that night. With Margie heading back to New York by train, we had an especially painful farewell, tinged with feelings of profound gratitude that we were still alive and, thank God, unharmed.

My two-hour flight to Atlanta was a very wild and bumpy one, precluding a brief shut-eye. I probably couldn't have slept anyway, for burning into my consciousness was a new awareness of the kind of fear and deep-down anxiety African Americans lived with—constantly, relentlessly—knowing full well that their very lives were continually in jeopardy. In the coming years our country was to see abundant proof that such fears and anxieties were not unfounded.

The rest of the Met tour certainly had nothing to offer in the way of high drama that would match that incident in Cincinnati. But it provided many other memorable experiences, especially in the benign realm of the arts. I was, for example, fortunate to have enough free time in Chicago to roam for two entire days through virtually all of the fabulous Art Institute, as well as, several weeks later, the superb Art Museum in St. Louis. The visit to Chicago's Art Institute was particularly rewarding because its enormous, wide-ranging collection allowed me to see not only several hundred of the world's greatest works of art, but also to significantly expand my knowledge of some of my favorite works by artists such as El Greco, Chagall, Caravaggio, Tintoretto, and Titian. As I worked my way through gallery after gallery, it was like visiting old friends one hasn't seen for a while, and, in almost all cases, a confirmation of my previous high impressions.

As an ardent El Greco fan, I was fascinated by his mysterious, disturbing, turbulent art. But seeing his *Assumption of the Virgin* showed me another softer, gentler, more open side. I also was mesmerized by the almost photographic detail and precision of Pieter Claesz's still lifes, such a contrast to other Dutch masters like Rubens or Rembrandt. But the latter's powerful *Christ in the Storm* affected me particularly as memories flooded back of my spellbound Bible readings of this New Testament episode while at St. Thomas's, and of hearing the Dresdener Kreuzchor's performance of Günter Raphael's *Christ, Son of God* way back in 1938.

I remember wondering whether the voluptuous hedonism of Caravaggio's *L'Amour sacre et l'amour profane* wasn't, for once, too much of a muchness. It was also the first time I saw Chagall's startlingly ascetic yet refined *The Rabbi*, as well as one of Dali's greatest technical and creative achievements: *Invention of the Monsters*, with its weirdly burning giraffes.

Another happy encounter on those two days at the Art Institute was a reacquaintance with the work of George Innes, a whole roomful of landscapes. It led to a lifelong fascination with his serene Hudson Valley landscapes and his exceptionally meticulous capturing on canvas of the most miniscule details: leaves on a tree viewed from a distance of a mile or two, blades of grass, the ears of wheat stalks. Some thirty years later I fulfilled a long-held dream of translating an Innes painting into musical terms: *Peace and Plenty*, the third movement of my *Four Soundscapes (Hudson Valley Reminiscences)*.

And then there were the inevitable Cézannes and Monets. It was the first time that I saw a significant number of their paintings. I recall the overwhelming effect upon me of seeing not one but *several* of Cézanne's *L'Estaque* and *Le Mont Sainte-Victoire* pictures, and, similarly, a whole series of Monet's *Haystack* paintings. I had never before seen a whole sequence of pictures on the same subject; it of course reminded me right away of the concept of variation in music. With my intrinsic love of "colors" in music—timbre, sonorities—seeing several of Monet's *Haystack* pictures in a row, hanging on the same wall, each in different colors and shadings (mauve, blue-gray, brownish, etc.), was in its way a wonderful confirmation of my own musical-visual predilections. But beyond their thrilling surface attractions, those Cézannes and Monets reflect the perfection of nature, and called up hidden emotions in me that brought me to the point of tears.

My pursuit of the visual arts on this Met tour reached another apogee when I visited the St. Louis Art Museum and, upon entering the great vaulted main hall, I practically ran into one of Ivan Meìtrović's monumental sculptures, occupying not only pride of place in the center of the hall but also pride of place in my heart. For Meìtrović was at the time my absolute favorite sculptor. I couldn't seem to see enough of his larger-than-life, sensuously rich figures. I also was able to revisit, quite by chance, two remarkable works that had previously been on view for many years at the Museum of Modern Art: a glorious Lyonel Feininger, called *Die Marktkirche in Halle* (*The Market Church in Halle*), and a beautiful 63 x 90 inch rug by Stuart Davis, entitled *Flying Carpet*.

My pursuit of the art of jazz was just as vigorous and determined as that of the visual arts. I took full advantage of the numerous opportunities that presented themselves by traveling to many midwestern cities, where great jazz flourished in that postwar era. I can't remember it all, but I can definitely dredge up memories of hearing Sy Oliver's new band (in Chicago) and its great brass section that included Dickie Wells, Paul Webster, and Lamar Wright; also the great Joe Mooney Quartet (in St. Louis), with its most delicious chamber jazz sounds—possibly the most original and stylistically sophisticated group in jazz after the King Cole Trio—at least before the advent of the Modern Jazz Quartet in the early 1950s, and Johnny Moore's Three Blazers, a fine blues group and one of the most talented progeny of the Cole Trio.[11]

Perhaps the most unforgettable musical evening for me on that spring tour occurred at Chicago's Chez Paree. I went there to hear Lena Horne. I had heard about her for many years, owned a few of her recordings (with the Charlie Barnet band), and had seen her in two films, *Cabin in the Sky* and *Stormy Weather*. But nothing prepared me for seeing and hearing her in person. Ravishingly beautiful, she was dressed in a spectacular full-length white gown with one shoulder bare, and a long, narrow, Chinese-style skirt slit to the hip, teasingly exposing just enough of her flawless light-brown skin to create the most beautiful total design. She was a perfectly sculpted, statuesque work of art. Vocally, Lena was in superb voice, a wonderful blend of timbral clarity and warm, caramelized mellowness, all delivered with the most impeccable diction.

I am convinced that Lena must have had one of her very best nights musically that evening. Although I knew that everything she sang had been well rehearsed—very little was left to improvisation—she made it all sound totally spontaneous and fresh. I had never heard her sing with such a catchy beat and irresistible infectious swing, as during those two sets at the Chez Paree, whether it was in medium-tempo ballads like *Lonesome Gal* or *Old-Fashioned Love*, or her signature number, Fats Waller's *Honeysuckle Rose*. She was everything: sophisticated, hip, elegant, distinctive, natural. There was in her singing a subtle undercurrent of restraint that made the climactic moments in her songs all the more potent and overwhelming.

I feel that she owed much of her success that evening to her husband-to-be, Lennie Hayton, the excellent pianist-arranger who first came to my attention as one of Paul Whiteman's stable of outstanding arrangers in the late 1920s and in his work for Artie Shaw. All the songs that Lena sang that night were arranged by Hayton, and were played superbly by the Chez Paree orchestra—something I wouldn't necessarily have expected from a typical house band, even in a fairly ritzy nightclub like the Chez Paree. But most impressive was how Hayton supported Lena with the most tasteful, modern, swinging, full-chordal accompaniments.

It is odd that the jazz and popular music press could never make up its mind how to label Lena Horne. Most jazz writers were reluctant to call her a jazz singer, I guess because she didn't normally improvise (as Sarah Vaughan or Ella Fitzgerald did). But in the end everyone settled on the more neutral term, "singing star." Being no great fan of any kind of labeling (pigeonholing, typecasting), I prefer to think of her simply as a consummate artist. To me it didn't matter that she wasn't a natural improviser. All I knew was that she was—and is—a perfectionist, a superb performer whose artistic integrity was, as far I know, never compromised.

I happened to have heard Lena in 1999 at age eighty-two on television, and I wasn't surprised that everything was intact: her voice, her beauty, her artistic taste.[12]

I was to hear Lena Horne many more times, mostly in New York, headlining shows at various Broadway theatres such as the Capital, the Roxy, Paramount, and at Cafe Society. And although she was never less than flawless—what in the business is called a "class act"—I think that night in Chicago represented a kind of artistic zenith. There was some special electric atmosphere and energy palpable in the club. Lena seemed invincible, and incredibly happy. Romantic that I am, I think she was deeply in love with Lennie Hayton. That evening they were making love to each other in public—through their music.

In the late spring of 1947, with the Met tour over, I was facing a long summer of unemployment. This time the Philharmonic's two principal horns were available to play the Lewisohn Stadium summer season, so no opportunity there for me. But luckily several contractors and conductors remembered me favorably, and hired me for some recording sessions, as well as a variety of light summer-fare dates: Naumburg concerts at the Central Park Mall, outdoor pop concerts at Jones Beach, New London, Bridgeport, and Staten Island.

Of the conductors I worked with that summer I remember particularly Dean Dixon and David Broekman. The Naumburg concerts were mostly done with one rehearsal; with seasoned freelancers and a good sprinkling of Philharmonic and Met players, given the usually very familiar repertory, that was never a problem. What was a problem at that first mall concert was the temperature. I remember that clearly, because Dixon had programmed Ravel's beautiful *Pavane*, a short piece filled with extensive prominent horn solos. It was so cold that night—my mouthpiece felt like a clump of ice—that I wondered how I'd get through the piece. But good fortune was with me and it went smoothly, without a single glitch. Although Dixon got mixed up a few times during the evening, I got the impression that he was quite talented and, above all, sincere. He also seemed to have a slight persecution complex, but whether that was really so, or whether I was influenced by the generally received opinion about him, I'm not sure.

The worst conductor I encountered that summer at a pop concert was Jack Shaindlin. We musicians all knew that he was terrible; but we also knew that he was one of New York's major employers of musicians. Shaindlin was music director and conductor of the so-called March of Time newsreels, shown regularly in all movie houses in those days. They were produced three or four times a week, thus representing an immense amount of consistent work for those musicians who belonged to Shaindlin's inner circle. With such a powerful position in New York's music scene, he had no problems having a few pop concert bones thrown his way.

In an all-Gershwin concert in Bridgeport, Schaindlin not only got continually lost but also stayed lost, and couldn't even seem to follow us, the orchestra, as we continued without him. I sat in the bus with our concertmaster on the trip back to New York. His first comment was: "Man, we saved his ass once again!" Luckily the concert was saved from total disaster by the beautiful singing of Muriel Rahm in a group of *Porgy and Bess* excerpts.

D'Artega, another pops conductor that summer, wasn't much better, his participation made more ridiculous by his strutting around in a Cab Calloway costume, white tails and all.[13] That concert sticks in my memory especially because my father had also been hired, not only as violinist but also doubling as pianist, accompanying a couple of singers in some operetta numbers. During a brief sound check rehearsal before the concert, my father discovered that half a dozen piano keys—in the middle register, of all places—would not come back up after being depressed.[14] During that segment of the concert it became my job to pull up the misbehaving keys the split second my father's fingers left them. I did pretty well, except when, as often happens in piano music, certain keys had to be reactivated several times in very quick succession.

The best conductor of the lot was David Broekman, unfortunately now long forgotten. A violinist and composer, Dutch-born Broekman had found employment in the 1930s
as conductor and arranger in the burgeoning orchestral music scene on radio. It is hardly
remembered nowadays that the 1930s saw the emergence of a whole new genre of conductors,
working exclusively on radio, names like Andre Kostelanetz, Morton Gould, Howard Barlow,
Paul Lavalle, Don Vorhees, Erno Rapee, David Broekman. While Broekman and many of the
radio conductors became over time popular household names, they were not considered to be
really important or serious by the profession. There was a certain stigma attached to musicians working primarily in radio, as compared to those who conducted the proper symphony
orchestras such as the Philharmonic, the NBC Symphony, the Metropolitan. What was not
appreciated, except by us musicians who worked for these radio conductors, is that most them
were really *quite* good: they were equipped with a clean, clear, unfussy baton technique, excellent knowledge of the scores, a quick mind, and a no-nonsense efficient rehearsal method.

More than that, they all had one important skill in common: a superior sense of timing.
They had to, because the music had to be perfectly fitted into a radio program's exact half-
hour or sixty-minute duration. If you had twenty-six-and-a-half minutes to do *x* number of
selected pieces, allowing for a two-minute introduction and a one-and-a-half minute closing
by the announcer, well then, you had to come out *exactly* on time, whether you were doing a
movement of a Schubert symphony, or Tchaikovsky's *Romeo and Juliet*, or some operatic aria.
There was no room for some sudden willful interpretational whim. Those conductors delivered the program exactly as it was timed and rehearsed. They may not have been the world's
greatest, most profound, deep-thinking interpreters, but by God they knew their business. It
was a pleasure to work with most of them because, unlike certain much more famous maestri,
you could absolutely rely on them. They rarely screwed up and they exuded a reassuring feeling of confidence.

David Broekman reached his professional zenith in the 1950s on television, when he
was appointed conductor of CBS's *Wide World*. Around the same time Broekman also created and directed a contemporary music series at New York's venerable Cooper Union in
downtown Manhattan, a series that ran the entire then-known stylistic gamut from classical avant-garde music to modern jazz, presenting many important New York and world
premieres. Broekman took me on as his assistant and subsequently turned many of his
concerts over to me.

It is thus curious that our relationship started on a most peculiar and, for me, potentially
precarious footing. During the rehearsals for an all-Gershwin pops concert at Jones Beach,
Broekman within minutes, spying a new face in the horn section and, of all things, in the first
chair, began immediately watching and listening to me, intent, as I quickly realized, on catching me in some mistake or other. As I've mentioned before, in those days when conductors
reigned supreme in the music world many of them played these kinds of games with their
musicians, teasing, toying with them like a cat with a mouse. In their varying ways they were
all imitating Toscanini and Reiner, then the most famous tyrants in the music business.

I had learned about these conductors' ploys as early as my days with Dorati at age seventeen
on the Ballet Theatre tour. I knew those *Porgy and Bess* excerpts very well, having played them
many times over the previous four years. I could practically play my horn part by heart, enabling
me—my old trick—to look straight at Broekman, eyeball to eyeball, instead of looking at the
music. It was a game of "chicken," I was daring him to catch me. He really did try to catch me off
guard, at the same time showing off a bit for some of his friends in the string section. One of his
tactics was to purposely vary the tempo every now and then, stretching or compressing certain
phrases, playing around with *ritards* and *rubatos*, to see if I would follow him. I was ready for all of
Broekman's little tricks and games, I found it exhilarating to spar with him.

I won that initial skirmish hands down. You had to. As silly and childish and antimusical as it sounds, it is how you survived in the music business. By intermission time I had Broekman smiling and silently congratulating me. I later learned that he asked his contractor, who had hired me, who this "young horn player kid" was, and then told him that I was someone "we should keep around."

Halfway through that first rehearsal, seeing that he couldn't trap me and also getting a little bored with his game playing, he let up on me. By the time of the concert the tables had turned, in that Broekman was now clearly looking at me with considerable admiration. Through mutual eye contact we made music together, not as adversaries but as comrades, mutually enjoying Gershwin's rich, sensuous harmonies and marvelous melodies. I know that Broekman henceforth constantly asked for me for his concerts; eventually we became not just good colleagues but also dear friends.

Muriel Rahm was again the superb vocal soloist, outstanding in *My Man's Gone*, singing with a wonderful mixture of warmth and intensity, also extraordinarily tasteful in the quarter tone wailings and long upward glissando at the end of *Summertime*—effects in which so many singers often sound vulgar and awkward.

It was also in that summer of 1947 that I made my first visit to Tanglewood, the Boston Symphony's summer home, a wonderful place where I was years later to become deeply involved as artistic director and head of the composition department of the Berkshire Music Center. While most of my young musician friends had gone to Tanglewood and from there on to positions in major orchestras, I had bypassed it, primarily because as an already fully active professional at an early age I never had the time or leisure to consider studying there. But that summer, before heading for Lake Placid, I said to Margie that we must go to Tanglewood. What primarily prompted this urge was that Koussevitzky had programmed Honegger's Second Symphony for strings, a work I absolutely revered, having first heard it on a recording by Charles Munch.[15]

We went to Tanglewood twice that summer, traveling by train, since we didn't have a car and never thought of renting one. (Car rentals were not as common at that time as now.) The rather slow chug-along ride was very pleasant and picturesque. The train wound its way leisurely through the splendid countryside of western Connecticut and southwestern Massachusetts. For long stretches we traveled along the beautiful Housatonic River, and stopped at dozens of quaint villages, their graceful white New England church spires peaking out above the treetops, arriving eventually, after four-and-a half hours, in Lenox.

Poor as church mice at the time, Margie and I felt that we just couldn't afford the four-dollar admission charge to the Tanglewood grounds. I am embarrassed to reveal that we decided to sneak in, and discovered a loophole to clamber through in the hedge enclosing the Tanglewood estate, in back of what years later I came to know as the rehearsal stage. Miraculously, we were not caught, but the search for an unguarded opening in the hedge almost caused us to be late to the concert, which started with Honegger's Symphony. It was an absolutely magical moment as we approached the shed just in time to hear the sweetly melancholy opening of the Sym-

phony, with its gently undulating viola theme 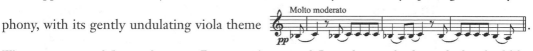.

The gorgeous and famously warm Boston string sound floated serenely through the shed like some ancient incantation. It is a sound that has tangibly stayed in my memory to this day.

In view of the work's formidable technical difficulties, including its rhythmic complexities, the whole performance of the Honegger Symphony went remarkably well, taking into account also that this was the first performance of the work in America. Truth be told, the performance was considerably better than Munch's recording with the Paris Conservatory Orchestra. The rest of the concert, alas, did not fare that well. The Brahms Second Symphony, played with eight horns (!), was a rather raucous affair, and the concert-ending *La Mer*, the BSO's millionth performance, was, that time at least, rather lackluster.

Among the highlights of that first Tanglewood visit, besides reuniting with Roland Johnson, Jo-Jo Leeds, and several other Cincinnati friends studying there, I count especially my first meeting with Aaron Copland, who gave a very informative lecture on American opera (mostly Thomson, Menotti, and Blitzstein). There were also several superb lectures by Hugh Ross,[16] who spoke about pre-Bach choral works (from Perotin and Gabrieli to Orazio Vecchi) and Allessandro Scarlatti's cantatas. There was also a rehearsal and concert of Copland's brand-new and very strong Third Symphony.

As the first American music festival to also incorporate a school for young advanced instrumentalists and singers, Tanglewood attracted from its very beginnings in 1940 the finest musical talents from all over the country. We happened to hear several students who stood out dramatically, even among this elite, and were soon to become world famous artists; for example, the young Adolph Herseth[17] played superbly in Poulenc's treacherously difficult Trio for Trumpet, Horn, and Trombone (a piece that I had already struggled with several times). We also discovered the beautiful tenor voice and tasteful singing of David Lloyd, who was many years later to sing the lead in one of my operas; as well as the exquisite singing, in a Goldowsky Opera Department concert, of two young ladies, Adele Addison and Mildred Miller, both also soon to achieve international stardom. Tanglewood was loaded with superior talent.

On our second visit to Tanglewood a week later, we again saved the four-dollar entrance charge by sneaking into the grounds. But this time we got caught, which, embarrassed and stung with guilt, put us in a horrible mood, to the point of barely being able to enjoy that evening's Bernstein concert. But still, I recall being very impressed by Hindemith's rarely played, astonishingly "romantic" Violin Concerto, and by Haydn's Symphony No. 102. Hindemith's 1940 Violin Concerto, from his American period, really surprised me, as it is so different—a stylistic anomaly—from most of his later quartal-modal works. And I was also overjoyed to again hear Ruth Posselt as soloist, whose playing I had greatly admired in Cincinnati. The Haydn Symphony, which I had already heard many times, amazed me all over again. Perhaps it was Lennie's excellent direction that brought out the work's startling modernity, its sudden harmonic changes and zigzagging modulations, not only in the development section but also, unusually, already in the exposition.

On this second Tanglewood visit I heard Bud Herseth again in a stunning performance of Copland's *Quiet City*, one of my all-time favorite Copland works, in a solo trumpet part that usually gives trumpet players two weeks of worrisome sleepless nights. We also enjoyed, in another opera department evening, the glorious baritone voice of Frank Guarrera, soon to be one of the most reliable, consistently artistic stalwarts of the Metropolitan Opera.

We had more occasions on this Tanglewood visit to hear the student orchestra, and we were amazed to find that the student orchestra at times and in some respects sounded better than the Boston Symphony. And I began to gain some appreciation of what Koussevitzky had really created at Tanglewood: a wonderful sanctuary—a Walden Pond of music—where young talented instrumentalists, singers, and composers could work and study with master teachers, unencumbered by the obtrusions of either the outside professional and commercial world or the sometimes overwhelming requirements of academia. I had no idea that I would some day become artistic director of the Tanglewood school, that I would devote more than twenty years of my life to preserving the sanctity of Koussevitzky's prophetic vision.

Our last day at Tanglewood was a very long one, beginning with a Sunday morning student chamber music concert, then an afternoon BSO concert (with Stravinsky's *Symphony of Psalms* and Ravel's *Bolero*, the latter not a particularly good performance—quite a few accidents along the way), followed by a four-and-a-half-hour train ride back to New York.[18] And yet, after eating at Lum Fong's, our favorite midtown Chinese restaurant, Marjorie and I went to the Hickory House next door and spent the next three hours—till two a.m.—listening to Dardanelle and her Trio. Tanglewood had really energized us.

It was directly upon the heels of that first visit to Tanglewood in late July that I had decided to write, of all things, a quartet for four double basses. I am astonished in retrospect to read in my diary that I began work on the quartet that last day of our Tanglewood visit, around ten thirty at night, at the end of a very long, exhausting day that began with attending a rehearsal of the Boston Symphony in the morning, a student orchestra rehearsal in the early afternoon, followed by a nearly five-hour train ride to New York, and then, at home, listening to that afternoon's Boston Symphony Tanglewood concert in a delayed broadcast on WQXR. Absolutely crazy!

I was truly inspired, and work on the quartet went exceptionally well. By the end of one week I had finished both the first movement and the second movement Scherzo. Then, after an eight-day hiatus, prompted by an extremely busy week in New York, I wrote three quarters of the final (Adagio) movement in one day, August 14, and finished it the next evening. The music literally poured out of me. It was an astonishing experience.

The reader may well wonder what possessed a young composer to write a quartet for double basses. For almost two centuries it was considered *de rigeur* for a young composer to prove himself first with the writing of a string quartet—meaning, of course, a standard quartet of two violins, viola, and cello. I bypassed this implied mandate without a second thought, and did not at all consider it a strange or unusual thing to do. I also knew that it had never been done before, and that, of course, intrigued me quite a bit. But beyond that, what brought me to the point of wanting—actually needing—to write for a group of basses were several factors, at first glance seemingly unrelated.

Factor one: I have already mentioned my fascination with low-register instruments. There is something in my physical makeup and particular aural capacities that inclined my ears to unhesitatingly focus in on the lower octaves of the human audible range, especially the particular sonoric quality of cello and bass, with their comparatively darker color and full-blooded sound. I remember well that even in my childhood I was always attracted to those two instruments. I remember vividly how excited I was when in 1945 I discovered at the Forty-Second Street public library, for example, a piece by Mozart—mind you, not by some obscure minor composer, but by Mozart!—featuring the bass as a solo instrument. It is an aria for bass baritone, double bass, and orchestra called "Per questa bella mano," K. 612.[19]

I also had seen several motets for four basses at the library by two great sixteenth-century composers, Cipriano de Rore and Orlando di Lasso, but, of course, for bass voices. I copied three of these four-part works—one was called "Latin Ode"—into my notebooks, simply because they were written in that low register I loved so much. (I later transcribed them for four trombones.)

From very early on I learned that the low-register and bass-range instruments provided the acoustic foundation, the basic fundamental, on which all musical sounds are built. This is a physical reality, determined by the laws of acoustics. A fundamental pitch generates and contains within it a whole superstructure of overtones, known as partials. Another manifestation of this concept is that the lowest note of a chord is called the root, analogous to the roots of a tree; the higher-lying notes of a chord are like the branches or the crown of a tree. For me, as a performer and interpreter, and especially as a conductor, one of my quintessential performance touchstones is to make sure that harmonies, chords, are built from the bottom up, and, as in a house or a building, the foundation is strong enough to hold up the upper structure. (That, by the way, was one of the secrets and absolute fundamentals of Stokowski's concept of conducting, of interpretation, as it was also Albert Coates's: establish a good bass foundation and the rest of the musical structure will more or less take care of itself.)

Factor two: I had been noticing for some years that bass players' technique had undergone an astonishing evolution. A whole new generation of young players, inspired by a handful of major teachers in New York, Los Angeles, and Rochester, had arrived on the scene, playing with a cleaner, more refined tone, greater technical facility, much better intonation, and a freer expressivity. I knew quite a number of such players in New York, many of them my friends; and I could hear in their playing an ease and fluency so different from the past and more akin in concept to that of a cello. But I also knew that these talented young players had very little to play, on which they could exercise their newly won technical prowess and challenge their expanded musical horizons.[20] So I wondered, why not write something for these players to cut their teeth on, not some light little entertaining bagatelle, but a serious, substantial multimovement composition. That turned out to be an eighteen-minute three-movement work, and I approached it exactly as if I was going to write a proper string quartet, only casting it exceptionally for four string basses.

Factor three: There was a particular orchestral bass passage that had haunted me ever since I first came across it in a score I saw in Steuermann's apartment during one of Margie's piano lessons. I had subsequently bought that music at Patelson's so that I could study it in complete detail. That was Schönberg's remarkable breakthrough work, *Five Pieces for Orchestra* (1909), and the bass passage occurs at the very end of the fourth movement. It is arguably one of the most startling and original endings in all of music; the last sounds one hears are eight basses

divisi à four, alone, in the very highest bass register, playing tremolo and *fortissimo* .[21]

On the spur of the moment I decided to *start* my *Bass Quartet* with the very sounds with which Schönberg had *ended* his piece—my tiny private tribute to his creative imagination.

Factor four: The most immediate impulse that prompted me to begin the *Bass Quartet* that late evening after a day at Tanglewood came from hearing Honegger's Second Symphony earlier that week. Why? Well, again it has to do with the bass. In that work bass players get a major technical and musical workout. Honegger wrote many precipitously leaping, uncompromisingly difficult bass passages, often identical—although in octave unison—with the cello parts. (But what may be reasonably manageable on a cello is significantly more problematic on a bass).[22] The Boston Symphony bass section, one of the strongest in the orchestra, played most of the Honegger Symphony bass part so well, so cleanly, that I could scarcely believe my ears. But what I really carried around with me in my inner ear those four days at Tanglewood was one of my most favorite passages in that Symphony, a high-lying, intensely expressive, four-bar exposed passage for the basses near the middle of the second movement. Incidentally, the Bostoners did *not* play that so well in tune on that occasion, an excusable blemish, since it was brand-new for the players, and since that passage lies in the stratospheric upper range of the bass, above middle C, a range that had never been tested up to that time in orchestral bass music. It is beastly hard, and a real challenge for a section of eight or nine basses to play with absolute, perfect uniform intonation.

Those were the variety of inspirations and influences that led me, with nary an equivocating thought, to compose my *Bass Quartet*. Thinking back to those heady days almost sixty-five years ago, I am proud of my *Bass Quartet* and the breakthroughs it achieved. It was the first of its kind. There are no known previous compositions for four basses. And that such a piece was written by a twenty-one-year-old—and in a matter of days—is rather unusual, and signifies that there was a remarkable fusion of varied inspirations that drove the creation of this work.[23] Stylistically, linguistically, the work explores no new ground, although it is an interesting amalgam of Bartók, Stravinsky, and Schönberg/Berg, and is surprisingly well put together, in terms of form and continuity and the flow of ideas. On the other hand, it proposes several fairly startling technical breakthroughs. The most impressive is that the second and third movements require each bass to change to a special tuning of its four strings, in what we call scordatura. There is nothing radical per se about that, since scordatura has been a device employed on string instruments since the seventeenth century,[24] but it is the specific retuning of the strings in my case that is unusual and that had never been attempted before.

The reason for my resorting to scordatura arose from the desire, as I planned out the Scherzo movement, to make use of lots of double-stop harmonics, especially in the Trio section. Since the bass is tuned in fourths (G, D, A, E), double-stop harmonics, particularly so-called natural harmonics, would naturally come out in fourths. I have nothing against fourths per se, but an overabundance of that interval in my basically tritone-laden language was something I knew I had to rule out. So I devised a scordatura retuning for each of the basses, in which the first and second bass would have two of their strings tuned in tritones, the third bass in a major third, and the fourth in a minor third, thereby permitting not only a greater variety of readily available double-stops, but also, more important, a greater variety of double-stop harmonics, which would otherwise be totally impossible or, at best, extremely awkward to produce.

The scordatura opened up a whole new vista of harmonic and chordal possibilities. My favorite accomplishment in this respect is an eight-part chord near the end of the piece, in which six of its constituent notes are played in double-stop harmonics 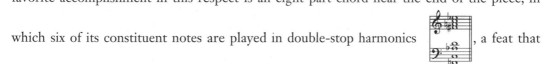, a feat that would be totally impossible in a nonscordatura situation. The other breakthrough impelled by my *Bass Quartet*—so lots of bass players tell me—is that it was *the* piece that in the 1960s really made it imperative to switch from gut to steel strings.

My *Bass Quartet* did not have its premiere—its baptism—until April 26, 1960, almost thirteen years after its genesis. Assessing what happens to a work of art when its early history seems to be fraught with impediments is not a precise science. It could be that my *Bass Quartet* was too far ahead of its time, technically, or perhaps even conceptually. It may be related to my reluctance to push my own music, but it also could be the decidedly lukewarm reception my piece received during a quick visit to Rochester in October 1947, when Oscar Zimmerman (formerly principal bass of the NBC Symphony and subsequently a renowned member of the string faculty at the Eastman School of Music) organized, at my request, a read-through of my *Bass Quartet* with four of his best students. Although I had privately worried about the work's technical demands, I was impressed by the relative ease with which the four students played through the first two movements, the inevitable mistakes and misreadings notwithstanding. (They rebelled at tackling the third movement, claiming that they couldn't deal with its far-out difficulties.)

But what was discouraging to me was that they not only didn't like the music, they didn't even appreciate the fact that someone had written a substantial, serious, uncompromising work for their instrument, something I considered to be my token of affection for the instrument and a compliment to the new young generation of players. The Eastman kids and their teacher's lack of enthusiasm for the work—or even for the effort involved—was indeed discouraging. It seemed that they almost resented my writing such a challenging work. And I surely had not expected that bass players, of all people, would more or less ridicule the very idea of writing a quartet for basses.

With my tail between my legs, I returned to New York later that day and put the piece aside, adding it to the growing pile of unperformed, presumably unperformable, compositions.

There it lay for about ten years. In retrospect, I realize it was stupid of me not to mention my *Bass Quartet* to any of my many excellent New York bassist friends. I cannot fathom why I kept the piece such a secret. Was I ashamed of it? Not likely. Was I too shy to promote the piece? Probably. Was I discouraged or intimidated by the reaction of the Rochester players—and even Oscar, my supposed friend? Possibly. Or was I so busy with a thousand other things and constantly writing new pieces? Very likely.

Ultimately, I owe the rebirth and eventual highly successful debut of my *Bass Quartet* to one man—a great man—who had, among his many accomplishments as the major bass teacher in New York for many years, a tremendous influence on the development and evolution of bass playing: Fred Zimmerman (no relation to the Rochester Zimmerman). Fred was one of the teachers who in the 1940s and 1950s spawned a whole new generation of superior bass players.[25]

Fred was the inspired and inspiring leader of what I have characterized for years as a bass revolution, the word "evolution" being insufficient to describe how dramatic and radical those technical, conceptual advances in bass playing were at the time. Fred brought a whole new aural and intellectual sensibility to his teaching and playing—in sound, intonation, style, and musical vision. He was in these respects the heart and soul of the New York Philharmonic's bass section, and to the extent that many of his most talented Juilliard students began to join the Philharmonic, he wrought a very noticeable melioration in the sound and artistry of the entire section.[26]

It was in the early 1950s, when I was playing often with the Philharmonic, that Fred and I became very close friends, musical soul mates, as it were. I visited him and his wife Dorothy often, enjoying festive dinners with them and marveling at his amazing collection of paintings. Fred had a huge five- or six-room apartment on Fifty-Fifth Street near Carnegie Hall with very large, spacious rooms. It was, in effect, a small museum; all the walls were literally covered with paintings. One large room was entirely devoted to Klees and Kandinskys, another to very large floor-to-ceiling Beckmanns. Fred was in his quiet, modest way proud that he had bought most of his collection as a young man, in the twenties and early thirties, when these painters were still little known; when, I suppose, a small Klee might have cost only a few hundred dollars.

On one of my visits to his apartment—this must have been in late 1957—while he was showing me his newest about-to-be-published collection of interval studies, something I saw reminded me suddenly of a certain passage in my *Bass Quartet*, which I mentioned to him. He nearly jumped off the sofa: "What?! You've written a Bass Quartet? You mean a quartet for four basses?" His voice rose even higher. "Why didn't you ever tell me about that?," he almost shouted in excited exasperation.

Within weeks after I had given him a set of score and parts, he had talked his three best Julliard students—Bob Gladstone, Orin O'Brien, and Alvin Brehm—into starting rehearsals of my quartet, with the full intention of preparing for a premiere performance—somewhere, he didn't know where, but he hoped soon.

It fell to me to find an occasion and a venue for the performance. By that time, the late fifties, I had made good connections with a number of organizations that regularly performed new music, for example, the New York chapter of the International Society of Contemporary Music (ISCM), or Charles Schwartz's new music series presented in the Nonagon Gallery on lower Second Avenue, another at the McMillan Theatre in Columbia University. But when I approached them about premiering my *Bass Quartet*, I learned that their programs for the coming season were all set and already announced.

Happenstance—fate, chance—once again came to the rescue. Walking down Fifty-Seventh Street one day, I bumped into Norman Seaman just as he was coming out of the Little Carnegie entrance (now Weill Hall), where he presented concerts from time to time. "Hey," he said, "I've been wanting to call you about an idea I had for a series of concerts in Little Carnegie.

You know how painters have one-man shows at galleries? Well, I want to put on a series of four one-man shows with four composers, and I want you to be one of them. What do you think?"

"What do I think? Of course, I'd love to be involved." It was like manna from heaven. I immediately thought that I might be able to premiere the *Bass Quartet* in a concert devoted entirely to my work. "I want you to suggest the other three composers," he said.

A few days later I called Norman with what I thought was a novel idea. "Let me pick three composers who are also performers, instrumentalists, like me. And each of us will compose a short piece for one of the concerts that the four of us will perform. I propose Ezra Laderman, who plays the flute, Meyer Kupferman plays the clarinet, Robert Starer the piano and harp, and I'll play the horn. That way we'll have four new pieces for that quartet combination, and all four of us will be presented in a one-man show not only as composers but also as performers." Seaman loved the idea.

After something like two months of tenacious practicing and rehearsing, with me coaching and conducting, the four players—Bob Gladstone tackling the difficult high-lying first part, Fred Zimmerman[27] playing second bass, Orin O'Brien and Alvin Brehm playing the third and fourth, respectively—had the work ready for performance. It was thus that my *Bass Quartet* finally received its world premiere on April 26, 1960, in a concert that also included my first String Quartet and *Fantasy Quartet* for four cellos (1950), in effect four quartets, for three different string combinations—as well as a three-minute newly composed Quartet for flute, clarinet, horn, and piano called *Curtain Raiser*. The whole Seaman series, by the way, was a huge success.

The performance proved that my *Bass Quartet*, considered by Oscar Zimmerman and his students to be too difficult, and in part unplayable and impractical, was in fact eminently playable[28]—although by four of the country's finest professionals and after seven or eight weeks of intermittent but intense rehearsing. And the *Bass Quartet*'s progress from alleged unperformability to its first acoustic realization continued in leaps and bounds when four Juilliard graduate students, including Gary Karr, performed my Quartet two years later, this time without benefit of a conductor, coached by Stuart Sankey, *and* a half-dozen years after that when four high school students played two of the movements at Interlaken's summer academy.

So much for the work's unplayability. Many hundred performances later—all over the world—the piece is still very difficult, very challenging, testing even the best players' mettle. In that respect my *Bass Quartet* is in very good company, one of a long list of works that were initially declared to be unplayable, or too difficult, which sooner or later became standard repertory pieces.

As my summer jobs began to dwindle, Margie and I decided to head once again for Lake Placid. This time it turned out to be a real vacation. We spent most days swimming in nearby Mirror and Saranac Lakes, playing tennis—Margie was quite good, I was terrible—and taking long walks on the numerous hiking trails that encircled the town of Lake Placid and its famous namesake lake—for me a whole week virtually without music. Oh, we managed to attend a few of the Lake Placid Sinfonietta concerts, and—crazy me—I decided on the spur of the moment to learn to play the cello.

Not that I thought I had any real aptitude for the instrument, but I loved its innate lyric, expressive nature and its sound so much, especially when I heard Walter Heermann play. Also, the cello is close in range and character to the horn. I took a few short lessons with Walter, and practiced about an hour, early every morning. By the third or fourth day I was beginning to develop a rather attractive warm sound and vibrato. But, so typical of my restless, constantly explorative nature, that's how far I got with the cello: a lovely but brief flirtation, abruptly terminated by a four-day hiking and mountain climbing tour that Margie and I had been looking forward to since the year before.

The Adirondacks are, of course, one of the most beautiful mountainous regions in the entire northeast, incorporating large tracts of primeval forest (at least back then in the 1940s) and, as its centerpiece, Adirondack Park, a pristine six-million-acre wooded area. I had mapped out a hiking and climbing tour that would cover most of the highlights of the region just south of Lake Placid, comprising not only most of the MacIntyre Range but also Mount Marcy, the highest mountain in New York State. It was a glorious four days in this pure nature paradise, just the two of us, all alone (except for a passing hiker now and then). There is nothing like being alone on a trail in the deep quiet of a forest, lost in one's thoughts, in mute communion with oneself, yet intimately in touch with nature's transcendent wonders.

Our first day's goal was to climb to the top of Mount Marcy. David van Heusen, the new principal bassoonist of the Rochester Philharmonic, drove us to Heart Lake, whence the Hoevenberg Trail took us through dense forest, past Marcy Dam to Indian Falls. From there the trail became significantly steeper, twisting and turning, requiring us to clamber over all kinds of rocks and boulders, and patches of muddy, slippery, washed-out trail. Unused to mountain climbing, we were really huffing and puffing,[29] and mighty glad to reach a high ridge, from which we had our first clear view of Mount Marcy's peak straight ahead of us. But, with no rest for the weary, the most grueling climb came next, until we finally reached the bare slopes of Marcy's cone-shaped peak. So much of climbing is psychological; motivation is crucial, and once we came out of the forest and saw our goal directly ahead, though still several hundred feet above us, we almost *ran* up the boulder-strewn slope.

I don't think there can be anything as delicious as a simple lunch on top of a mountain, especially after a strenuous hike or climb. The milk in our thermoses, which Walter had given us, tasted like the nectar of the gods. After basking in the sunshine and enjoying the clear mountaintop breeze, we descended on Marcy's south side to the beautiful emerald-hued lake, Tear of the Clouds, and from there, via an excruciatingly precipitous descent, to our destination for the evening, the Feldspar lean-to, situated perfectly near the junction of two sparkling, rushing brooks. The lean-to was furnished with a coffeepot, a frying pan, and plenty of firewood, allowing us to treat ourselves to a delicious dinner of vegetable soup, cheese sandwiches, a good Chianti wine, and apples and bacon roasted on a skewer. For refrigeration, we kept some of our food in one of the brooks. This simple, rugged camp was so enchantingly located that my mind kept recycling a wish to stay there, to live there forever, and—in memory of Thoreau at Walden Pond—to compose my music in this heavenly spot.

The following morning it was impossible to tear ourselves away, but we finally broke camp just before noon. I had sketched out a more leisurely paced itinerary for the next two days, during which we explored several long, narrow, and reputedly very deep connected lakes, nestled between two parallel mountain ranges. It was a fascinatingly wild area, consisting mostly of steep thousand-foot rock cliffs that dropped straight down into the lakes on both sides, leaving room for neither woodland vegetation nor any trails. Most of the time we were climbing up and down on ladders, walking on boardwalks, planks, or little log bridges. Only occasionally was there enough space for a small narrow sand beach and a few trees struggling to survive along the rock cliffs. It was relatively dark at the lake level because the sun was blocked by the mountains on either side, except for a few hours around high noon.

We encountered all kinds of fascinating natural wonders. On a short midafternoon detour, heading away from the lake toward a towering waterfall that I had located on my U.S. Geological Survey maps, we suddenly found ourselves looking down at a rushing stream, which for several hundred feet ran along far below us in a deep flume, underneath a huge overhanging rock ledge. Every once in a while the stream would broaden out into tiny, beautiful green or aquamarine pools.

We soon came to the second of the string of lakes, Lake Colden, and continued on its east shore to Avalanche Lake, both at the foot of Mount Colden. In the late afternoon, not finding any lean-to in which to overnight, we decided to make camp at the foot of a bare rock slope, near the spot where a famous campsite (Caribou) was destroyed in a 1942 avalanche. When we realized that we would have two or three more hours of daylight, we decided to explore the other side of Lake Avalanche, another paradisiac site, again with steep vertical rock walls, but this time cleft with huge "chimneys" that, we were told by a park ranger, were the most favored routes for climbing to the top of Mount Colden. The natural serenity we felt on all sides, with the deep black waters of Lake Avalanche as our constant companion, was haunting in an almost eerie way: the mystery of nature. It was so beautiful it hurt.

When we headed back to our campsite, we made a little bed of pine branches, and fixed another simple, delectable dinner, topped by apples and bacon. In the twilight I tried to climb the rock slope directly above us, but got only a little way up; it became too steep for me. We lay awake in the dark for several hours, gazing at the star-studded heavens. It made me think back to my reading, years earlier in high school, Robert Louis Stevenson's *A Night in the Pines*.

On our third day, we couldn't resist the temptation to try an ascent of Mount Colden via one of those chimneys. Fortunately, we found one that was not at quite so steep an angle. Still, it was a climb straight up, almost six hundred feet. The view from atop Colden was spectacular, the huge expanse of Lake Champlain to the east, Mount Marcy directly to our south, and to the north, way off in the distance, Mount Whiteface and Lake Placid, southward down to Fort Ticonderoga and westward to Tupper Lake. I was quite excited to have even a bird's-eye view of that final stretch of train ride from Big Tupper Lake to Lake Placid, where three years earlier, I had that wonderful experience of inhaling the sweet scent of the Adirondacks' ancient primordial pine forests. In the afternoon we descended to Lake Avalanche to overnight in our pine-bed campsite and to be near our next trail, which would lead us northward toward Lake Placid.

On our final day we awoke to a foggy, thickly overcast sky, a surprise after another clear starlit night. It was time to head home. Our trail took us along the top ridges of Boundary and Algonquin Peaks, where we found ourselves unexpectedly enveloped in near-gale-force winds. Up there, near the timberline, the small wind-stunted spruces could offer us no protection from the elements. It was quite scary, alone up there in thick fog and clouds, and howling winds. We both got terrific chills, but luckily were able to find shelter under a rock ledge, where we not only warmed up but also had a quick lunch, which included delicious blueberries that we had picked the day before on the north slope of Mount Colden.

Finally the winds stopped, the fog and clouds lifted, and the sun broke through. Further down, as we reached beech and birch woodlands mixed with hemlocks, we were presented with an incredible fall color spectacle.

In the early evening we ended up in the tiny village of North Elba. Having consumed all the food we had brought along, we were lucky to find a log cabin inn, and splurged on some terrific steaks. The place was jammed with people, a very excited crowd, mostly fishermen and hunters. We soon realized they were talking about one of them having shot a large bear earlier that day. I don't know whether I heard correctly in the jumble of agitated chatter, but I thought they were talking about making steaks from the dead animal for everybody. We had heard that there were brown bears in the Mount Marcy and Colden region, but because we hadn't encountered any we thought that maybe those stories were mere huntsmen yarns. But now we knew better. (We did not have any of the bear meat.)

From North Elba we took a taxi back to Lake Placid, packed our things, and took an overnight train to New York. As tired as we were, we started planning to tackle the Adirondacks again the following year. That following year, however, didn't occur until 1950, when we did indeed spend a whole week of quite ambitious mountain climbing.

The only thing that could interrupt our fervent preoccupation with the cinema would have to be a week of mountain climbing or some other physical activities in the great outdoors—there aren't many movie houses on mountain ranges. On the very day that we got back to New York from Lake Placid, dead tired—at 7:40 a.m. after a mostly sleepless night on the train—we still went to see two films: Orson Welles's *The Stranger* and *The Man Who Could Work Miracles*, a terrific British movie based on H. G. Wells's classic story, with Ralph Richardson and Roland Young; it had, for that time (1937), some amazing special effects. What drove me to both films, one brand new, the other almost ten years old, was not merely my obsession with the art of film, but, in this instance, an urgent, virtually irrepressible desire to see two of my absolute film heroes, Orson Welles and George Sanders (the latter in only his third screen appearance). I would go to almost any lengths to see those two remarkable, unique actors. Welles, the boy genius creator of one of the dozen most important, most original films ever made in Hollywood, *Citizen Kane*, has been widely celebrated and lionized; and his genial yet at times flawed body of work has been scrutinized and analyzed in such exhaustive detail that there is very little left to say about the subject. As a composer and creative musician, my fascination with his work stems from the capacity of his best films to coalesce materiality with the imagination, that is to say, to take what is concrete and factual and transmute it into the sacrosanct mystery of feeling and emotion.[30]

What George Sanders and Orson Welles had in common was their uniqueness: nature made no duplicates of either of them. And that is what always compelled me to run after every film they made. In the case of Sanders that was quite a chore, considering how dreadful most of the films were. (The exceptions are *All About Eve*, *Moon and Sixpence*, *The Picture of Dorian Gray*, and *Hangover Square*.) But Sanders always shone through all the surrounding theatrical flatus; and it is hard to figure out how he could keep his composure through such a long film career, which encompassed three-and-a-half decades and some sixty-five pretty bad movies.

As the quintessential unflappable Britisher, Sanders' roles rarely changed: always the ultimate, superelegant scoundrel, at all times sporting perfect manners in impeccable sartorial splendor, his drawled speech and expression set in perpetual condescension and skeptical disdain. He floated loftily above any and every fray. The point about Sanders—and the point of my abject bewitchment with him—is that he was not really an actor: *he didn't have to act*. He *was* exactly what he portrayed on the screen—uniquely so.

Our fanatic devotion to creative cinema sometimes compelled us to go to not one, not two, not three, but to four films that were showing at MOMA on a single afternoon, four gems of the French avant-garde: René Clair's legendary *Entr'acte* (1924), as well as his satiric masterpiece, *À nous la liberté*, and Luis Buñuel's *L'Âge d'or* (*The Golden Age*, 1931). What a cinematic feast! Two days later we were watching five more surrealist masterpieces: Alberto Calvacanti's *Rien que les heures* (*Nothing But Hours*, 1926), Marcel Duchamp's *Anaemic cinema* (1926), Man Ray's *The Mysteries of the Chateau of Dice* (1929), as well as *Emak Bakia* (1926) and *Étoile de mer* (*Starfish*, 1928). (Now you know how really crazy I was.)

My preoccupation with the art of the film extended to spending many hours in MOMA's film library, poring over issues of *Sight and Sound*, *Cahiers du Cinéma*, and *Hollywood Quarterly*, reading up on subjects such as Czech, Hungarian, and Yugoslav films, even on one occasion on the state of the film industry in Guayaguil, Ecuador!

It was on the evening of one of these heavy movie days that I heard the Claude Thornhill orchestra in person for the first time, at one of our favorite haunts, the Café Rouge in the Pennsylvania Hotel. I had been listening to this remarkable orchestra ever since my high school days, at that time chiefly because Thornhill had carried two horns in his band since 1941 (a tuba was added in 1947), and also because he recorded a fair number of jazzily arranged classical pieces for his seventeen-piece band in 1942, including excerpts from the Grieg Piano Concerto.[31] That really intrigued me. Were these the first primal stirrings of Third Stream? Perhaps. Also, one of my first jazz recordings—I bought it in 1941, when I was fifteen—was of Claude Thornhill's lovely three-minute tone poem for solo piano and jazz orchestra, *Snowfall*. I have heard it since then hundreds of times—it also was the Thornhill band's theme song— and I know that I would never tire of hearing it again and again. It's one of those simple but perfect miniature compositional gems.

By the time Bill Borden and Gil Evans joined the Thornhill orchestra as arrangers, I was really hooked. Borden was responsible for the arrangement and stylistic conception of *Sunday Kinda Love*, Fran Warren's remarkable breakthrough vocal of 1946. Gil Evans, of course, goes down in jazz history as one of its all-time greatest, most innovative composer-arrangers, as well as the cocreator, with Miles Davis, of the legendary *Birth of the Cool* nonet, that amazing small-band offspring of Thornhill's 1940s orchestra. When I was sitting there in the Café Rouge with Margie, listening to the band, I didn't know that a few years later I would have the privilege of participating in some of those famous classic nonet recordings.

Hearing the Thornhill orchestra live in acoustic reality was an astounding experience for me. Those eight brass and five saxophones provided such a perfectly blended sound that you almost couldn't pick out any single instrument—something I had previously experienced only with the Ellington orchestra. That rich symbiotic blend was possible primarily because of the presence of one of the finest lead trumpet players ever, Louis Mucci. Unlike most lead trumpeters, whose job it is to scale the stratospheric heights of the audible range, and who therefore resort to smaller bore trumpets and mouthpieces, Louis Mucci didn't do that. His playing gave the brass section a rich, warm, velvety sound—in the sonic direction of the horn or the flugelhorn—and a tone that never stood out, but still gave the orchestra its unique, sumptuous sound.

That night at the Café Rouge was the first time I heard not only Louis Mucci in person, but also Red Rodney (trumpet), Bill Barber (tuba), Barry Galbraith (guitar), Joe Shulman (bass), and, above all, the amazing alto saxophonist Lee Konitz—all of whom I later worked with quite often and most felicitously.

I remember being approached around this time by various classical instrumentalists and singers to make small group arrangements of solo pieces intended very often for debut recitals. One of the first of these was a cellist named Bergen—I can't recall her first name—who asked me to arrange two pieces for cello and a small string group: one, a violin sonata by the eighteenth-century French composer Francois Francoeur (1698–1787), and the other, Two Pieces for Cello and Piano by Dimitri Kabalevsky. They were performed at Bergen's recital in Little Carnegie Hall.

I did a lot of such arranging gigs over the next half decade—including for Met singers such as Mildred Miller, Rosalind Eilas, and Inge Manski—and always did the work gratis, including copying of all the parts. I never thought about the money; I did it for the love of it and as a useful learning experience.

The singer Ruth Kisch-Arndt asked me in 1951 to arrange some psalms by Salomone Rossi (1570–1630), an early seventeenth-century Italian composer and contemporary of Monteverdi. Rossi composed a considerable amount of instrumental music and madrigals. He is important in the history of Renaissance music for composing a major Jewish liturgical work entitled *Hashirim Asher Lish'lomo* (*The Songs of Solomon*). It was Rossi's only sacred music, an extensive polyphonic setting of some thirty Hebrew psalms. Kisch-Arndt was a very interesting figure on the New York musical scene because of her semiannual recitals in Town Hall (and later Times Hall) devoted entirely to medieval and early Renaissance music, this at a time when there was little or no knowledge and hardly any performance of such early literature. She created the Early Music Foundation in the mid-1940s, and must be considered an important forerunner of Noah Greenberg and his trailblazing work with Pro Musica Antiqua.

I don't remember exactly which psalms from Rossi's *Songs of Solomon* Mme Kisch-Arndt gave me to arrange, except that they were for four voices and I was to arrange the music for mezzo-soprano and three accompanying instruments. At first glance it was a very intriguing assignment, the main challenge being that I didn't have access in those days to any players who were versed in Renaissance music. In any case, I decided to transcribe the music for viola, bassoon (both to be played without vibrato), and bass trombone. I really looked forward to working on this material, partly because it was the first early music I encountered written by a composer of the Jewish faith, and partly in the hope of discovering something truly astounding with specifically Hebraic stylistic elements. I was very impressed when Mme Kisch-Arndt told me that Rossi was one of the very earliest composers to write basso continuo parts and figured basses. But then I recall being a bit disappointed when I found the music to be rather conservative for its time, compared, for example, to the music of Monteverdi. Rossi's music reminded me of some of the simpler madrigals of Luca Marenzio and Jakob de Wert.

Mme Kisch-Arndt asked me to hire the instrumentalists needed for the concert beyond her core group, Bernard Krainis's Recorder Ensemble. To enrich the program I added two of Andrea Gabrieli's *Ricicares* for brass quartet. All in all, her concert was a quite amazing musical event. It was the first concert I ever heard or was involved with that consisted entirely of music from the fourteenth to the early seventeenth century, featuring works by composers quite obscure at the time, such as Francesco Landini, Jacopo da Bologna, Orazio Vecchi, and Constanzo Festa, although the program also had pieces by Monteverdi and Palestrina.

One of these arranging jobs led to one of my first conducting jobs. The occasion was when Rosalind Elias had me do a whole multimovement suite of the most popular excerpts from *Carmen*, reducing Bizet's original orchestration to a core string group and a few winds. What with all the tempo changes and instrumental and vocal *rubatos*, the players thought it necessary to have a conductor. I was happy to oblige. (Roz actually paid me—very generously—for this one.)

In October I was happy to be called once again, the third time, to play a short tour in Toronto and Detroit with the Philadelphia La Scala Opera Company. I was glad to see many of my good friends in the orchestra—Mariotti, Kampowski—and also newcomers such as Henry Bove, a terrific solo cellist working in several orchestras in the Philadelphia area, and Luigi Antonelli, another fine horn player from Philadelphia.

Playing first horn gave me back a lot of confidence, psychologically and technically, some of which I had lost at the Met under the intimidating pressures of Dick Moore's section leading, and maybe also under the sinking standards at the Met. After only a few days of rehearsals and performances with La Scala (*La Traviata, Tosca, Lucia, Il Trovatore*), my tone and my embouchure felt as good as they had ever been in Cincinnati. I don't think I was just imagining this, for several players, especially Mariotti, whom I respected so much, offered me some very gratifying compliments. And after our initial performance in Toronto of *Lucia*, an opera that features many exposed horn passages, including several prominent extended horn quartets, the critic on the local newspaper singled out my playing most positively—rather unusual since critics are normally busy writing about the star singers and the conductor, rarely bothering to mention anything good that might occur in an orchestra.

It was on this tour that I first heard Herva Nelli (a fine singer and musician who a few years later was to become quite famous working with Toscanini), as well as the seemingly ageless

Frederick Jagel, then already in his fifties and a twenty-year veteran of the Met. His singing, including all high notes, was remarkably secure and free—a great artist.

Preseason rehearsals at the Met began at the end of October, and on the face of it the schedule of operas to be presented looked very promising. The big news was that we were going to perform *Tannhäuser* plus the entire *Ring Cycle*. That certainly excited me, especially as a composer. I had not yet played *Das Rheingold* (with its incredible three-minute opening tone picture of the Rhine River, played by eight horns in undulating arpeggiated figures) and *Götterdämmerung*. Then there was Puccini's *Tosca*, to be conducted by Giuseppe Antonicelli, about whom we had heard excellent reports. Two other fine operas I looked forward to playing were Mozart's *The Magic Flute* and Humperdinck's *Hänsel und Gretel*. And in February the Met was going to stage Benjamin Britten's *Peter Grimes*, which had received its American premiere six years earlier at Tanglewood.

Exciting new voices—new to America—were also on tap: the remarkable velvet-voiced tenor Giuseppe di Stefano, the wonderful baritone Giuseppe Valdengo (whose superior musicianship I had already experienced with La Scala), and the dynamic, powerfully voiced dramatic mezzo-soprano Chloe Elmo, whose splendid work I knew from a few imported Italian recordings.

Fritz Stiedry's conducting in several of Wagner's operas gave me much opportunity to revive my ambivalent feelings about him. He stunned me in the first rehearsal of *Tannhäuser*—an opera that Busch had led, I thought, rather perfunctorily the year before—by approaching it not as one of Wagner's early harmonically tame operas, but from a post-*Tristan* point of view, especially in the Venusberg scene and the Bacchanale, which Wagner had, in fact, drastically rewritten and expanded (*after* his completion of *Tristan*) for the Paris premiere of *Tannhäuser* in 1860. The string writing in the Bacchanale is some of the most consistently challenging and virtuosic—almost orgiastic—that Wagner ever wrote. It is enormously difficult technically, and relentless in its demands of concentration and endurance. I was thrilled when Stiedry rehearsed the strings alone, repeatedly practicing some of the more hair-raisingly exciting passages, allowing us all to hear that amazing music exposed and fully audible in a way that one can never hear in a performance, where the winds and brass tend to cover much of that string writing. Now I knew where Schönberg's fantastic string writing in *Verklärte Nacht* (*Transfigured Night*) came from. I also wrote in my diary that "such revelations justify my staying at the Met—a priceless experience, to be had nowhere else in the country."

The next day Stiedry rehearsed *Tannhäuser*'s second and third acts, and even there, in that more conventional style, he managed to instill a modern post-*Tristan* approach, rehearsing again with unusually meticulous care all kinds of details that Busch had more or less glossed over. All that excellent rehearsing, instilling new life into an old warhorse, more or less came to naught a few weeks later when a miserable cast headed by Torsten Ralf (who crooned his way through the whole opera like a bad Irish tenor), and the even more miserable Met chorus—*Tannhäuser* being a big chorus opera—dragged the entire performance down to a most mediocre level.

The work on *Tannhäuser* showed the good side of Stiedry. Alas, a few months later when we started work on the *Ring Cycle*, I was beside myself with frustration in Stiedry's rehearsals. It was hard for me to understand how this man, whose work I had admired on so many occasions, could suddenly hold a rehearsal that I called in my diary "a ridiculous farce," could make the most "shameful mistakes," could seem not "to know the music at all." It was *Rheingold*.

I didn't know how to reconcile the conscientious, almost inspired work Stiedry lavished on *Tannhäuser* and his inept, disorganized approach to the *Ring* operas. Was he ill? Was he overworked? Was it encroaching senility? I have sometimes thought that perhaps it is my memory playing tricks on me. But no, that can't be, because my diary recounts in considerable detail how upset not just I but the whole orchestra was. It came to the point where *we* had to enlighten him as to the nature of his mistakes: a wrong tempo, an ineptly managed tempo change, a wrong cue. It remains a mystery to me, especially since Stiedry did some really fine work again in the early 1950s, most notably with excellent and loving interpretations of Verdi's *Don Carlos* and Mozart's *Così fan tutte*.

A great revelation for me was my discovery of Jules Massenet's *Manon*. Except for Bizet's *Carmen* and Gounod's *Faust* (and an occasional *Roméo et Juliette)* there wasn't much French opera done by American opera companies. When I was young the received opinion about Massenet's music was—and probably still is—that it wasn't particularly important, consisting as it did primarily of some thirty mostly obscure, rarely performed operas, and sixteen orchestral suites. I was therefore all the more surprised to become instantly enamored of this composer's music in our first *Manon* rehearsal. What really got to me was a certain voluptuousness, a subtly sensuous undertone, expressed not only in Massenet's rapturous melodies but also in his rich orchestration.[32] I was quite overwhelmed by the profusion of totally unexpected revelations that this remarkable music offered. I did not realize, for example, that Massenet had been strongly influenced by Wagner's late post-*Tristan* chromaticism and by his use of the leitmotif as a thematic character identifier. I was surprised by Massenet's copious use (in 1884) of augmented and major seventh harmonies, even more surprised by dissonant

chords such as , quite often unresolved. Massenet also

invaded the then not-yet established territory of bitonality. Right away, in the opera's Prelude (and all through the fifth act), we hear chains of harmonically unrelated "horn fifths":

. Even Wagner and Liszt did not dare anything quite as

modern as that.

On the other hand, Massenet's creative mind and manifest knowledge of musical history enabled him to include several delicious recreations of eighteenth-century Menuets and Gavottes. He even managed to incorporate a loving tribute to that most sacred of French operatic traditions, the mandatory ballet sequences (a tradition that goes all the way back to Rameau and Lully in the seventeenth century), by introducing in the third act a tiny miniopera with its own ballet sequences.

I was impressed by the way Massenet adapted Wagner's melodic-harmonic ethos to the particular inflections of the French language, especially as couched in the eloquent, often languidly sensuous libretto of Henri Meilhac—one of the most linguistically elegant librettos in all of opera. In that regard, I loved Massenet's extensive use of spoken dialogue over quiet orchestral accompaniments, a practice I first learned to admire in Offenbach's *Tales of Hoffmann*. And what can one say about the poignant pathos of Massenet's three great *Manon* arias: the searing, tormented "Ah! fuyez," and the two intimate ariettas "Adieu, notre petite table" and "En fermant les yeux," so deeply touching in their utter simplicity.

Another surprise for me was when I realized that Massenet's *Manon* brought to the world of opera, famous for its fascination with gods and ancient mythologies and its impossibly convoluted plots, a welcome touch of realism, to a large extent already contained in Abbé Prévost's 1731 novel from which the *Manon* libretto was drawn. This was something Margie and I, as young lovers, could fervently relate to, and associate in mood and feeling with the French films we saw at MOMA, especially those of Marcel Carné. What also helped to make the whole *Manon* experience so wonderful was the perfect casting—for once—of Licia Alba-nesi, Giuseppe di Stefano (in his absolute prime), and my two favorites, Alessio de Paolis and George Chehanovsky. The only drawback was that Louis Fourestier, at best a pedantic routi-nier, was the conductor. But even he could not seriously undermine the power and expressive glow of the music.[33]

After many months of frustrated efforts to find an apartment that Margie and I could share, I suddenly heard in November about the availability of two apartments on the fifth floor of a building on the corner of Houston Street and Second Avenue that had been a Greek Orthodox church. As it turned out, the fifth floor consisted of two clusters of rooms on opposite sides of the building, separated by a very large, empty, gymnasiumlike area. Both sets of rooms had been the bishop's quarters. The entire area comprised nearly five thousand square feet, and the rent, we were told, would be an amazingly modest $275 per month.

I asked Joe Marx, who had just gotten divorced from Maggie McGinnis and was now going to be living alone, if he'd be interested in moving into one of the two apartments and splitting the rent with me. He jumped at the opportunity, thus helping me to realize my goal of living with Margie, of ending the constant frustrations of having separate places. In late November we moved into our new quarters, which in itself was no easy undertaking. There was no eleva-tor in the building, which meant that everything had to be carried, pulled, and dragged up 162 steps to the fifth floor. The biggest problem, apart from moving my furniture in, some from Jamaica, Queens, some newly acquired, and getting my huge record collection[34] and even huger music library up those infernal stairs, was *how to get my piano* up to the fifth floor. The piano movers inspected the four flights of stairs and quickly declared them unsafe, incapable of supporting the weight of my very heavy Sohmer upright piano. Eventually, having noticed the very tall six-foot-high windows in the gymnasium facing Houston Street, the movers decided to lift the piano with pulleys and fly it in through one of the windows. An excellent idea, except that evidently none of the four windows had been opened for several decades. It took over two hours to get one of them open, but then—three hours later—we did see the piano, in its heavy blanket covering, float into the room, like some huge elephantine carcass.

The entire floor, including the gymnasium, had been unoccupied for many years. But the two unfinished apartments were in fair shape, just very dusty from years of neglect. The church, built in the late 1800s, was well constructed, and—no doubt about it—had a certain elegance; some turn-of-the-century carpenter's decorative artistry had been lavished on the bishop's extensive quarters: rich wood wall paneling, huge closets with shelves, even ornamented ceilings and a few small gargoyles on the walls of the living room. Still, we had to do extreme cleaning. We pitched in with the enthusiasm and energy of newlyweds, and in a few days we had our apartment in wonderful shape. Since almost all the walls were paneled with beautiful rich-brown wood, we hardly had to do any painting, a considerable work, time, and money saver.

The state of the gymnasium was another matter. The huge floor—fifty by eighty square feet—was caked with half an inch of what must have been ten or fifteen years of New York soot, dust, crud, all kinds of mysterious vegetable matter, even fungi and other growing things. We really didn't have any idea initially of how to utilize the gymnasium's four thousand square feet in some useful way. But I knew we would have to clean it up, no matter what. It took the three of us—Joe, Margie, and me—three or four days spread over several weeks, with all kinds of scrapers, brushes, and brooms, plus tons of water, to remove all the accumulated grime. We then saw that the wood of the floor was in great shape; and I immediately thought of turning the room into a dance studio and renting it out to ballet companies as a rehearsal space. But when I realized that I would have to get another piano, install dancers' bars along the walls, and add washroom facilities and other accoutrements, I abandoned that idea.

I did, however, turn part of the space into a recording studio. I bought a lot of professional recording equipment, such as several 7B RCA microphones—then state of the art—and a Rekokut disc cutter (this was still before the widespread commercial use of magnetic tape), and over the next year or two produced quite a few recordings for friends and colleagues, not for commercial purposes but for personal or archival use. One of the first recordings I made was of rehearsals of the then newly formed New Music Quartet with Broadus Earle, Matthew Raimondi, Walter Trampler, and Claus Adam, rehearsing Anton Webern's Op. 28 String Quartet and the fourth Bartók quartet. I also often recorded rehearsals of our Metropolitan Woodwind Quintet, including our early rehearsals of the Schönberg Quintet.

Having thus far lived almost always at home, I owned relatively little furniture—no bed, no tables and chairs, no kitchenware or utensils, nothing. So, in addition to buying some of the most basic items, a double bed mattress (still no bed), a small table, a couple of chairs, we were given a few pots and pans and kitchen utensils by my parents. Thus we got off to a reasonably comfortable start.

Margie and I lived in that apartment for nearly six months—as far as I can tell undetected by Margie's parents—until we got married in June 1948. This does puzzle me a bit in retrospect because Margie's father must have come to New York at least once in that period on one of his buying trips. For that visit Margie moved in with Paula Lenchner's family for a few days. I still have occasional guilty feelings when I recall how we were compelled to invent such devious stratagems. I'm amazed that we got away with these deceptions.

We were very happy in our bishop's quarters because we could work together and interrelate musically without having to rent studios on Forty-Eighth Street or at Nola's. But more important, we were—without thinking about it much—trying out our marriage, exploring how we would relate to each other in such constant intimacy, which you cannot experience when you are living separately.

Although our sacerdotal apartment could only be described as elementary, even primitive in some ways, we were more than happy to finally be living together, not just physically as husband and wife but also in a close spiritual relationship, which we probably could not have maintained dwelling apart. As a result, we could share all our varied experiences, which brought us closer and closer, strengthening and animating our love. We were pioneers in premarital sex—and, in retrospect, mighty proud of it.

My hope that the overall performance level at the Met might improve was a silly one. Why should the mere arrival of the new year bring about an artistic amelioration? I was not alone; seemingly everyone interested in opera felt increasingly that Eddie Johnson had lost his touch, and that his managerial policies and decisions, especially in regard to casting and conducting assignments, had become stale, capricious, and ineffectual. One lackluster performance after another—not terrible, but not worthy of one of the supposedly great opera houses of the world—seemed to be the norm, not the exception. God knows, most of us in the orchestra did our best to compensate for some of our conductors' shortcomings. But an orchestra cannot sustain such efforts for very long and not become eventually demoralized, despite doing its best to maintain professional pride and standards.

Even Busch and Stiedry, in charge of some of the most important repertory of the season, seemed to be floundering; this after both of them had brought a breath of fresh air to the Met just a year earlier. Were they now perhaps already past their prime, or were they, too, defeated by the generally phlegmatic atmosphere in the house? And why was Emil Cooper given operas such as *Peter Grimes* and *Abduction from the Seraglio*? He couldn't even handle *Aida* or *Louise*. The only saving grace was Antonicelli. I excitedly looked forward to working with him, but unfortunately I was assigned to only two of the four operas he was conducting that season.

Johnson's casting was consistently uneven. You'd have a good Traubel and Melchior a few times, but then Set Svanholm or Torsten Ralf would take over the Heldentenor roles. Svanholm, a handsome Swede, certainly looked the part of the youthful Siegfried, although mostly when he was standing still, singing straight at the audience—seldom when he was moving about on stage. His whiteish voice and scooping singing left anything but a heroic impression.[35] As for Ralf, he was no Heldentenor at all, what with his smallish voice and wimpy style. He was well past his prime, which had been in Germany of the mid-1930s.[36] That season Risé Stevens, Ferruccio Tagliavini, Eugene Conley, James Melton, Stella Roman, Mimi Benzell, Pierette Alarie—to name just a few—dominated the Met's repertory too much.

Undoubtedly some readers will be shocked (and annoyed) that I include Risé Stevens in my list of Met mediocrities. She was certainly considered the most glamorous and popular mezzosoprano of the time, but glamour and popularity do not necessarily equate with great singing. For all I know Stevens might have sung with taste and style in her early years at the Prague Opera House, or at the Met after Eddie Johnson brought her on board in 1938. I can only judge her work in opera from the perspective of my years at the Met, the mid-1940s and 1950s, and by that time Risé had accumulated an alarming array of tasteless, even vulgar and histrionic vocal habits. Along with scooping notes, exaggerated vibratos and portamenti, excessively melodramatic stage displays, it bothered me that what some of my colleagues heard as bad habits were not that at all, and certainly not the result of a lack of talent. She was, in fact, very talented and intelligent, with a quick, alert mind. No, her vocal vulgarisms and pushy, exaggerated stage deportment were shrewdly calculated for maximum effect with the audience. And those intentions became increasingly suggestive, which, unfortunately, appealed to audiences.

Perhaps Risé reached her behavioral nadir one night in *Carmen*, always the role in which she most blatantly indulged her bent for exhibitionism. In this particular performance, during the final scene of the last act, she had (obviously) decided to dispense with a more or less transparent top that she had worn in all the previous performances, and which was designed to help hold up her well-wired costume, leaving her shoulders and most of her bosom well exposed. In the final scene a desperate Don José, now a weak, starving, hunted, derelict army deserter, pleads unsuccessfully with Carmen to come back to him. It is a very intense, active scene in which Don José is finally impelled to kill Carmen, after a chase all over the stage. In all that running around and stooping down Stevens very cleverly managed to almost bare her breasts by constantly pushing them up to the bulging point above her wired bodice. It was quite a show and took a lot of nerve; no burlesque stripper could have teased more effectively. The audience went wild. It was hard to concentrate on the music with such a riveting scene on stage. I sat there wondering what such tawdry exhibitionism had to do with one of the most inspired and powerful scenes in all of opera.

To be fair to Johnson and the Met's administration, those postwar years were not the best of times in which to manage a major opera house. There were financial problems and a shortage of European artists. Many were not yet as available to the Met as they would be a few years later for Rudolf Bing. Of course, sprinkled in among the mediocrity were some great performances—far too few for my taste—which only proved that, at its best, the Met could still produce at the very highest levels. *Rheingold* (with Gerhard Pechner's great Alberich portrayal), and several wonderful *Walküres* (with a superb cast of Lauritz Melchior, Helen Traubel, Herbert Janssen, Kerstin Thorborg, Rose Bampton, and Mihály Szekely as Hunding), were highlights among so much surrounding dross.

Hearing a spate of superb concerts at the New York Philharmonic under Charles Munch's brilliant direction made me wonder again whether I should stay at the Met. Munch inspired the Philharmonic players, always a tough bunch to stimulate, whether it was in Berlioz's *Symphonie fantastique* (one of Munch's favorite warhorses) or Mozart's *Adagio and Fugue* (for string orchestra), Beethoven's Eighth Symphony or Ravel's *Daphnis et Chloé*. I wondered why we couldn't have an inspiring conductor like that at the Met.[37]

Eventually I stopped worrying about the Met's problems, realizing that there was little—in fact, nothing—I could do about them. I busied myself with various other activities: composing, studying, more research into medieval and Renaissance music. I also began work on several new pieces more or less simultaneously, none of which, however, came to fruition. They turned out to be momentary infatuations rather than well-thought-through projects. For example, reading George Bernard Shaw's *The Perfect Wagnerite*, a wonderfully succinct and clearheaded treatise on Wagner's *Ring Cycle*, brought on an irresistible urge to write an opera, something I hadn't thought about very much. That urge led to the idea of basing an opera on Shelley's *Prometheus Unbound*. The Prometheus legend had always fascinated me, ever since encountering it in my readings at St. Thomas School. I started on a libretto and sketched out a few thematic ideas, but again I became distracted, this time by reading James Joyce's *Chamber Music*. Now I found myself embarking on a series of choral settings of Joyce's poems, some with rather exotic instrumental backings, such as six flutes, strings, and celesta. But I never finished that work either. I was diverted from the Joyce project by a request from Roland Johnson to write a work for his College of Music orchestra.

The six-flute idea from the Joyce music survived in Roland's piece, the idea of using six flutes having been stimulated by several other motivations and influences. I had recently restudied not only Schönberg's *Five Pieces for Orchestra* in its original 1909 version with its lavish consortlike instrumentation, but also his remarkable Op. 22 *Seraphita* song settings, in which some of the instrumental accompaniments include sections of five flutes, six clarinets, twelve solo cellos, and six-part divisi violin sections. But a more pragmatic reason for using such an unorthodox instrumentation came directly from Roland, who let me know that even two years after the end of the war his 1947–48 student orchestra still had a rather unbalanced woodwind section. There was still a serious shortage of male students, many having acquired other skills in the army during the war that took them away from music; in some cases they were still finishing their tours of duty. As a result he had in his woodwind section six female flutists, five oboists (including only two boys), a mere two clarinets and one bass clarinet, and only two bassoons (no contrabassoon). On the other hand, he had six horns in the brass section. Roland wasn't even sure that he could field a better-balanced wind section the following fall (in 1948), when he wanted to premiere my piece.

That's why my *Adagio for Orchestra* (soon renamed *Meditation*, but eventually ending up with the more prosaic title *Symphonic Study*),[38] sports such an oddly balanced wind section. In effect, I simply accepted the odd instrumentation of Roland's orchestra. I could have settled for a typical Mozartean orchestra of winds and horns in two, but I became fascinated with the idea of having the luxury of six flutes, five oboes, and five horns, never mind that this produced a strangely unbalanced wind and brass section. This has been, of course, a serious impediment to further performances, since orchestra managers, always mindful of the financial bottom line, are rather reluctant to hire three extra flutists, two extra oboists, and two extra horns while one of the orchestra's clarinetist and one bassoonist sit idle and receive their usual salary.

A few months later another one of these enthusiastically undertaken composing projects that soon fell by the wayside was another attempt at an opera. This time I decided to start one based on the great Marcel Carné film, *Les Visiteurs du soir* (*The Devil's Envoy*). After Margie and I had seen the film three times, I was so moved by its enchanting fairy-tale mood (the story takes place in medieval times), its visual beauty, and its deeply spiritual esthetic that I felt I must translate this work of art into an opera.[39] Alas, it too was a creative effort that was predestined to remain unfulfilled. While I immediately set about finding the original film script by Jacques Prévert—where else but at my favorite midtown foreign language bookstore,

Adler's—and feverishly started working up a libretto, I gave no thought whatsoever—how naïve I was!—to the fact that there were author's and film rights to secure. And who knew whether they were obtainable?

One day it occurred to Joe Marx that we ought to start a series of evening musicales every couple of weeks—chamber music, of course—inviting small audiences of friends and colleagues. On our first such evening we played two Karl Stamitz pieces, the Oboe Quartet and the Quartet for oboe, horn, viola, and cello (a work that Joe had dug out of some library in Holland years ago and published in his McGinnis & Marx woodwind catalogue), as well as one of Schubert's string trios. On our second musicale, we programmed an all-baroque evening, prompted by Joe's considerable knowledge of little-known baroque literature, including two delightful quintets by Johann Christian Bach for flute, oboe, and string trio. We continued these concerts for several months, until Margie and I got married and we abandoned the old Greek Orthodox church.

I've mentioned before that Joe had a sardonic bent, and he constantly teased and mocked people, especially those people he actually admired. One Sunday evening, a few weeks later, we were sitting around after dinner, talking about the state of American music and the place of American composers. The only two composers Joe had anything good to say about were Stefan Wolpe and Elliott Carter, although I knew he actually admired many more composers (including me). In any case, he suddenly teased me with taunting mock-derision, suggesting that I thought I "was pretty hot stuff" as a composer, but "I betcha you can't do what Bach and Vivaldi and Mozart could do, write a new piece in three or four days."

Once again I fell for Joe's tease and rose to the bait. "Of course I can. Whadaya mean, I can't?"

"Alright then; write us a new piece for next Thursday's musicale."

I swallowed hard a few times, but took him up on his dare. Four days later—on Thursday—we read through and rehearsed my new three-movement twelve-minute Trio for Oboe, Horn, and Viola, with Joe, myself, and the Met's first violist, John DiJanni. Even Joe was impressed. For not only did he concede defeat, but he also even allowed that it was "a damn good piece." I thought so too, by the way. I was amazed that I could actually write something quite good on such a tight deadline and have it turn out so well. Even more astounding in retrospect is that those four days were not free for me. I was extremely busy with many other commitments. On Monday I had committed myself to working on one of those songs based on Joyce's *Chamber Music* poems, in this case poem XXXV. That took most of the day. In the evening, Margie and I went to an ISCM concert, in which the Juilliard Quartet was going to play the New York premiere of Bartók's Sixth Quartet, an event I was determined not to miss. The program also offered Harold Shapero's String Quartet (1941), Roger Sessions's Piano Sonata (1946), and a setting of Anacreon lyrics by Luigi Dallapiccola. I was so inspired by the Bartók Quartet—I called it a masterpiece in my diary, and likened it in its depth and originality to Beethoven's late quartets—that I rushed home and started immediately on my new Trio, and finished half of the first movement by around two a.m. The next day, Tuesday, I had a long rehearsal with our woodwind quintet, preparing for two concerts the following day at the Bennington School in Mount Vernon. That same evening I played *Götterdämmerung* at the Met, and finished the Trio's first movement and most of the second movement later that night. Wednesday evening I played in a concert in Brooklyn at the Schwabenhalle, a German beer hall and club, with a conductor, so my diary notes, who acted like "a small-time Hitler," constantly barking at us musicians and asking for the most ridiculous things.

Thursday I had a long *Parsifal* rehearsal at the Met, spent some time at the public library looking for some Guillaume Dufay pieces, then not only finished the second and third movements of the Trio but also copied two movements of the viola part and one movement of the oboe part by opera time. DiJanni studied most of his part during the opera (*La Bohème*), while I finished copying his and Joe's parts during the opera's three intermissions (and even a little during the performance in bars rest).

Our Thursday musicale began around midnight, first with a read-through of the Hanns Eisler String Quartet, and then, around two a.m., we embarked on the first rendering of my Trio, with me playing the horn part from the score.[40] I think it is of some interest that the viola part is in a way the most difficult of the three parts, because the viola is, by the nature of this somewhat unusual instrumentation (with no real bass instrument), forced to play a triple role: one part lyric melodist, another part keeper of the music's bass lines, and a third part the supplier of harmony, being the only one of these three instruments capable of producing two or more notes simultaneously.

That was the last time Joe Marx baited me, having lost every bet with me including the famous ice cream sundae incident in Toronto five years earlier. Not that I was ever offended by his mock testing of my character; our friendship and mutual admiration was never breached. Indeed, ten years older than I, and a remarkably intelligent, original, thinking person, Joe (and his first wife, Beulah) became in those years a kind of moral and intellectual mentor to me and to some extent for Margie.

Joe and his wife, like many artists in that postwar period, were ardent Freudians and devotees of psychiatry. They had recommended various doctors to us, including a leading New York psychiatrist and medical practitioner, Henry Richardson. I was never sick and never had any medical problems. I didn't know any doctors, let alone a psychiatrist, and Margie, coming from Fargo, of course knew no doctors in New York. Thus we were grateful for any advice and recommendations the Marxes offered us in matters medical. And so it came to pass that Margie, trying to cope with the changes in her life, especially in regard to our new relationship and her unease in balancing a demanding schedule of musical studies with the constant tension with her parents, was persuaded to seek the psychiatric care of Dr. Richardson.

Although not actually opposed, I wasn't really enthusiastic about the idea. I was skeptical about the actual effectiveness of psychiatric treatment. My feelings were not helped by the fact that I had seen and met so many strange and disturbed people in New York, especially in artistic circles—many much more troubled than Margie—who were constantly seeing their shrinks (as the phrase went), but didn't seem to receive much help. Oddly enough, George Black approved of his daughter's seeking psychiatric help. I assumed that he, the archconservative, would think dimly of psychiatry initiated by that "sex fanatic" Freud. He really surprised me—as he would do a few more times over the years in other matters.

My misgivings to the contrary, Margie was helped by her sessions with Dr. Richardson. Over a period of several months she regained a sense of confidence, of self-esteem, which she had lost at times since coming to New York. I couldn't tell whether this was related to her disappointing development as a singer (under Mme Leonard), or even in her work with Mr. Steuermann, where her lack of self-assurance and mounting dissatisfaction with her progress sporadically undermined her will to work hard, or whether it was a mixture of her own innate modesty and some innate sense of insecurity.

In any case, under Dr. Richardson's benign care Margie seemed to sort out her various anxieties, and she began to blossom mentally and emotionally. Soon her occasional bouts with depression virtually vanished.

I cannot fail to mention my first meeting with one of the most important musicians and dear friends in my life, Dimitri Mitropoulos, whom I had wanted to meet ever since his (and the New York Philharmonic's) electrifying performance of Strauss's *Sinfonia domestica* way back in 1941. In 1944 and 1945 I had briefly worked with him in special summer concerts sponsored by the United States Rubber Company, but I had never gotten up enough nerve to approach him. Eventually I met him in 1947, at one of his Philharmonic concerts in which he delivered a most stirring performance of Strauss's *Alpine Symphony*. I was so moved that I told my father that this time I just had to meet the great man.[41]

I congratulated Mitropoulos on the performance, enthusiastically comparing it to his *Domestica* performance six years earlier. But there must have been something in my tone of voice, or something I said, that made him realize that I didn't regard the *Alpine Symphony* as one of Strauss's greatest works—which was indeed my opinion. He asked me what, as a young composer, I thought of the work. A quick wink from my father, standing by Mitropoulos's side, signaled to me: Be nice, don't criticize. Tell him it's marvelous. I was really in a quandary, knowing that this man had just drained every fiber of his being in generating this extraordinary performance of a work that—I could tell—he loved deeply. And yet I also knew, not being very good at lying or dissembling, that I was going to have to tell him something of my own true feelings—as diplomatically as possible. Doing my best to somehow sound positive, I told him that compared to so many Strauss masterpieces—*Salomé, Don Juan, Till Eulenspiegel, Rosenkavalier, Ein Heldenleben*—the *Alpine Symphony* had, along with its many brilliant ideas and inspirations (I remember using the German word *Einfälle*), some stretches of bombast, overextended development, even of relatively weak thematic material. I even dared to mention some plagiarizing—stealing, borrowing, whatever—because Strauss had borrowed the main theme from the slow movement of Max Bruch's Violin Concerto. Why did a great man like Strauss stoop to that?

Mitropoulos looked pained. But my biggest problem with the work, I told him, was that it looks backward aesthetically, linguistically; that after *Salomé* and *Elektra*, both fearlessly, daringly forward-looking works, heading toward an almost atonal chromaticism, the *Alpine Symphony* seemed regressive, afraid to look forward. I added, as if to soften my criticism, that I thought the opening of the work was pure genius: a sustained twenty-two note, four-octave sound cluster, played *pp*, depicting the awesome stillness of night and the heavy mists clinging to the mountain slopes and the valleys. In that opening, Strauss was heading for atonality, as he did in *Elektra*. Why then did he back away already in the eighth measure?

I was feeling *very* uncomfortable, certain that I had hurt Mitropoulos's feelings. He seemed lost in thought. Finally, all he said, with a sigh and a sad tone of voice, was, "Ah, you young people," as if to say, you're never satisfied, always criticizing.

Several times in later years, when we were together so often, including dozens of dinners at La Scala in mid-Manhattan or on the road on Met tours, Mitropoulos reminisced about our first encounter. He told me he remembered it well, and that he was disappointed in my critique of the *Alpine Symphony*, an opinion that he realized was shared by many, but that at the time he thought was unjustified. He said that despite the hurt my comments caused, he respected me for honestly stating what I thought, and not prevaricating, not inventing what he called some evasive, polite "green room platitude."[42] Little did I know at the time what a crucial role Mitropoulos would play in my life and career in future years.

Addendum: By coincidence, the score of my *Vertige d'eros*, which I had sent to Mitropoulos almost a year earlier, in the hope that he might take an interest in my music, had just been returned, without having been opened or looked at. I did not mention that to Mitropoulos.

As I got to know Mitropoulos better, musically as well as personally, I learned that Greek-born, as a young adult he had lived and worked in Berlin for four years, studying with Busoni and working as a repetiteur under Erich Kleiber at the Berlin Staatsoper. It was there that he was exposed to many of the major creative figures (Strauss, Schönberg, Furtwängler), who so brilliantly represented the central European cultural and intellectual tradition—of which in turn Mitropoulos became such a faithful representative.

But there was an additional element in Mitropoulos's artistic and cultural makeup and in his music making—something galvanic and elemental, even uncontrollable. Mind you, it was never self-indulgent or ego-driven, as it was so often with Leonard Bernstein. On the contrary, it came out of some sacrificial, self-denigrating impulse. Many people called it—too simplistically—undisciplined. It was much more complicated than that. His sometimes volatile podium behavior came out of the strange confluence of an unusual background and upbringing and a high-strung, nervous, extremely sensitive temperament. I choose my words very carefully, to avoid any negative profiling, when I say that at times I thought there was something temperamentally East European or Slavic—certainly not central European—in Mitropoulos's character and bearing, and thus in his music making. I often thought this was all some complicated reaction to his monastic, reclusive upbringing in the famous monasteries of Mount Athos, or perhaps part of some genetic Byzantine or Asia Minor heritage of four centuries of Turkic cultural domination. In any case, whatever Mitropoulos did in music, he always did it with an incredible intensity and energy that I, having worked very often in Greece and knowing many Greek musicians, associate with a particular Greek temperament.

Perhaps I need to justify the use of the word "extreme." I cite one instance (out of many) in which this aspect of his personality and work ethos was expressed in a most forceful and intense way. In 1944 Mitropoulos had programmed, on one of those summer Carnegie Hall concerts, one of his specialties, Rachmaninov's Second Symphony. It was clear from the first moments of the rehearsal that Mitropoulos loved this work passionately; he subjected his entire self fully to the music in all its wide range of expressions. At one of the more climactic moments in the Symphony's first movement, a series of heroic, fanfarelike *fortissimo* calls are initiated by the horns, followed by canonic responses in other brass and woodwind instruments. It is always a hair-raising moment, especially if you are sitting *in* the orchestra, enveloped by the full acoustic onslaught of the music. But Mitropoulos raised the experience to a maximum, almost terrifying level, and with an unimaginable intensity that I had never witnessed before. As he turned to the horn section, his deep-set blue eyes shone with an extraordinary clarity; they seemed to be on fire. Moreover, suddenly the skin on his bald head, shiny with the reflected glow of Carnegie Hall's ceiling lights, began to move, crawl back and forth across his pate. I could hardly keep playing; it was such an astonishing sight. But, believe it or not, when the horn fanfare is repeated a few bars later, but now a minor third higher, with even greater intensity, Mitropoulos's *eyes crossed*!

I am convinced that he was having an emotional orgasm. The man was caught up in ecstasy, a paroxysm of emotion so powerful that it must have been almost like an out-of-body experience.

To be continually enveloped in New York's boundlessly protean cultural life was a constant inspiration. Just keeping up with the plethora of offerings, not to mention trying to successfully digest and absorb it all, was an immense challenge. Needless to say, we did our best, much aided by the sheer narcoticlike irresistibility of these enticements. Our passion for film art alone kept us fully enraptured. By 1948 and 1949, more and more important Italian and French, even English and German (including East German), films were being imported to satiate New York's growing art house market. This substantial influx of European—and soon Japanese—films was added to our already full diet of historic cinema at the daily film showings at the Museum of Modern Art. It was expanded even further when I discovered new postwar Czech and Mexican films. My rather elementary Spanish, mostly siphoned off from the elementary Italian I had acquired over the years playing opera, sufficed to appreciate the content and quality of the Mexican films. While I soon discovered that they were often rather melodramatic and soap opera-ish, Margie and I were fascinated by their forthright, no-nonsense, sensuously realistic approach to sexual mores and male-female relationships, free of the prudish hypocrisy of Hollywood films.

In the process I also made an interesting discovery of a most talented composer, for it seemed that half of the Mexican films we saw had excellent supporting scores by one Gustavo Pittaluga. When I tried to find some music by him or even any information about this composer, I ran into a stone wall of ignorance and indifference, even with Mexican musician friends.[43] There were no recordings of Pittaluga's music in those days, neither on 78s nor LPs. It was only in the recent CD era that one—and only one—of his works was recorded: a 1933 ballet called *La Romeria de los cornudos* (*The Pilgrimage of the Cuckolds*). It was very good music.

As for the Czech films, mostly shown at the New Europe Theatre on First Avenue and Seventy-Ninth Street, many of them were very impressive, often more in the manner of French and German expressionist films. The language being incomprehensible to me, I got myself a couple of good Czech to English and Czech to German dictionaries; and soon, with the aid of publicity blurbs, synopses, handouts, and reviews in film magazines, I felt quite at ease in adding a goodly dose of Czech films to our regular cinematic diet. It also was good training in intuiting a film's message or subject matter primarily from its visual content, a skill I have developed into a fine art in the last thirty years. I have watched hundreds of movies on airplanes, always without the sound. (I'm a very good lip reader by now.) Watching a movie in silence is also a good way to assess a cast's acting abilities.

Of the dozens of films we saw, mostly foreign, just in the late winter of 1947 and spring of 1948, the ones that stand out in my memory are Carné's *Les Portes de la nuit*, *Hotel du Nord*, and *Visiteurs du soir*; also *Panic*, written and directed by the Duvivier brothers (Julien and Pierre), with a stellar cast of Michel Simon, Viviane Romance, and Paul Bernard, and a haunting, appropriately eerie score by Jean Wiener.[44] The next day we saw *Volpone*, with Harry Baur and Louis Jouvet, featuring a brilliant scenario by none other than Stefan Zweig and Jules Romaine, and brimming with typically daring French satire (although some parts, alas, had been cut for American more prudish tastes).[45] Henri-Georges Clouzot's *Le Corbeau* (*The Raven*), a stunning, subtly antifascist documentary chronicled man's bestial behavior under the stresses and terrors of wartime. (The film was actually—and heroically—shot during the Nazi occupation of France). From Italy, we saw *Furia*, a powerfully acted, sex-charged film on adultery in an Italian farm village, and the De Sica masterpiece, *Scuscia* (*Shoeshine*), one of the many grim but gripping postwar Italian films that began to reach our shores, starting with *Open City* (1945) and leading to *Paisan* (1946) and *Germany, Year Zero* (1947).

As for Hollywood movies, I mention only Garbo's and Gielgud's rather glib, depthless *Crime and Punishment*, which, however, featured one of my favorite Hollywood character actors, Russian-born Vladimir Sokoloff, as Porfiry;[46] and Ernst Lubitsch's hilarious *Ninotchka* (1939), with Garbo and a wonderful trio of Hollywood character actors—Sig Ruman, Felix Bressart, and Alexander Granach (all German refugees from Hitler's Germany)—whose silly antics as totally incompetent Prussian bourgeois functionaries were so marvelously exaggerated as to achieve a whole new level of comedic artistry.

Arguably, the most controversial American film that came out in 1947 was Chaplin's *Monsieur Verdoux*. It was banned and vilified in many quarters, but hailed by others as Chaplin's ultimate and most personal *chef d'oeuvre*. The controversy over the film and Chaplin's probably rather muddled sympathies for Communism prompted the House Un-American Activities Committee to subpoena him to testify about his alleged political affiliations. This contributed to a very limited distribution of the film. Margie and I saw *Monsieur Verdoux* finally in 1948, in of all places Catholic French Canada, in a little town, Gatineau, outside of Ottawa, when I happened to be in Canada with the Goldman Band. I must say, I thought it was a somewhat flawed film, too complex and convoluted in its satirical takeoff on the Bluebeard story, with various preachings of pacifism thrown in, apparently as a countercharge to his conservative critics.

But perhaps the most outstanding film we saw all summer, surpassing even the many French and Czech offerings, was the Danish director Carl Dreyer's *Day of Wrath*, in which he showed again, as he had in his previous masterpiece *Joan of Arc*, that he was one of the two or three top directors of the time—let's say, the Ingmar Bergman of that earlier period. He consistently moved his films into the pure realm of art, way beyond mere entertainment and technical expertise. I sometimes felt that viewing a Dreyer film was like seeing a superb time-extended Rembrandt painting unfold before one's eyes. His camera shots were grouped and designed with an austere simplicity, yet with the intensity of the great Dutch master's art, producing a unique filmic pictorial beauty. In *Day of Wrath* Dreyer worked with unusually long close-ups to tell his story of moral conflict and witchcraft in seventeenth-century Denmark. With his daringly deliberate cutting and editing, he created an incredible tension that, unfortunately, many American viewers saw only as slow, dull, and heavy. But one critic had it right when he wrote that Karl Anderson's photography "was lit by that flame which reveals layers of inner meanings, and which gives [the film] its wondrous mixture of mysticism and realism." A special masterful touch for me, as a musician, was the haunting effect of hearing pure boys' voices chanting *Dies irae* (from which the film takes its title) at the funeral, while an ancient manuscript scroll of *Dies irae* slowly unfolds on the screen.

One might think that under the circumstances of my obsession with films, other things would have to play a secondary role. Not so. I spent as much time and money at several midtown bookstores, the Gotham Book Mart, Adler's Foreign Books, and various libraries. I was always finishing some major literary work, and immediately plunging into whatever was next on my "masterpiece" list. I must have read with considerable ease and speed in those days. In that same spring of 1948 I remember reading Baudelaire's *Les Fleurs du mal*—also learning, incidentally, that he was among the first in France to recognize Richard Wagner's genius and the importance of his innovations. I read Frank Wedekind, especially his *Music* and *Dance of Death*; some beautiful Rilke poems in the *Duino Elegies*; Sartre's great essay "Portrait of the Anti-Semite"; also books on Berlioz and Johann Mattheson, books on and by Furtwängler, and Adam Carse's *Orchestra of the Eighteenth Century*.

I also discovered *Partisan Review* around this time, adding it to my subscriptions for *Commentary*, *Horizon*, and the *Atlantic Monthly*, all quite important in my intellectual and political development.[47] It was in *Partisan Review* that I began to reconnect with Europe during the time of the Marshall Plan and the Berlin Blockade, and began to learn about something called "Stalinism" as differentiated from Communism or Marxism—hot topics in the late 1940s, about to become a lot hotter with the McCarthy and the House Un-American activities Committee hearings. Reading *Partisan Review* with its thorough coverage of European political and cultural issues made me uncomfortably aware how ignorant I was in that field. It was in *Partisan Review* that I first read about the massive purges of writers, composers, and artists by Stalin and his cultural henchman, Andrei Zhdanov, starting in 1946. As a counterbalance, subsequent issues had extensive articles by the editor in chief, Philip Rahv, on European and American literature, and on many American writers in the 1930s who fervently espoused Marxist-Communist ideologies. That movement reached its apogee during World War II, when the United States became an ally of the Soviet Union, but then in the late forties, in a counterconversion, it broke away from Stalinism and Communism. *Partisan Review* also offered many writings by and about Jean-Paul Sartre, who was a regular contributor and almost the house editor. I especially remember a revealing article on the history and early functions of literature ("For Whom Does One Write"), which discussed the eighteenth-century emancipation of literature from the aristocracy and the church, and the creation of a new reading public within the bourgeoisie.

Apart from *Partisan Review*'s extensive cultural and political reportage from Europe, its pages also regularly included works of America's major poets and writers (much as Mencken's *Smart Set* and *Mercury Review* in the 1920s and 1930s, and the *New Yorker*, in later decades, had done), as well as brilliant articles, most often by Clement Greenberg and Eric Bentley, on the newest developments in the visual arts and drama/theater, respectively.

I knew how important all this reading was for me and how I had, ever since my Cincinnati days, lost touch with the European political and cultural situation, concentrating so determinedly on the New York and American scene. Once the United States entered the war after Pearl Harbor, my parents and I lost whatever contact we had maintained in the late thirties with our German relatives. When I was at St. Thomas, happily isolated there and busy with my various studies, I was—as I realized only later—hardly aware that we were hearing less and less from abroad, whether from our relatives in Krefeld and Burgstädt, or my parent's close friends, or, for that matter, even a few of my Gebesee schoolmates. In the late thirties our relatives in Germany became more entangled in Hitler's war preparations, willingly or not. Once the war started, we heard very little or nothing from them. We Americans, on the other side of the Atlantic, in our relative isolationism (political and otherwise), became less and less curious about the deteriorating situation in Europe, regarding much of what was happening over there either with disbelief or outright dismissal: Hitler can't be *that* bad, *that* crazy. It's got to be exaggerated. Or: Well, Hitler won't last!

Amongst the little news we did get, we heard that my Aunt Ilse in Burgstädt had gotten married, that she and her husband had two children, and that my Aunt Gretel had also found a husband, a shipbuilder working in a boatyard on the Rhine River, and that they had moved into a house in a new housing project on the outskirts of town. Still later we heard that there were lots of children on the way. My correspondence with my favorite Gebesee teacher, Bobby Schneider, broke off suddenly in 1939, and for almost a decade I didn't know whether he was dead or alive.

I also did not know for a long time—nor did my parents—that Ilse's husband, Günter Friedemann, had disappeared on the Russian front in 1942, and that both my grandmothers had died. We heard nothing of our relatives' state or whereabouts until late 1945 and early 1946, when news did begin to trickle in that all hands were safe (except Ilse's husband), but were living under the direst conditions and deprivations. That initiated a long period, extending well into the late 1980s, of my parents and I sending so-called care packages to Germany three or four times a year (coffee, tea, butter, sugar, soap, and so forth), to our Burgstädt relatives who, alas, ended up in Stalin's Communist East Germany.

As I look back on that half a decade, encompassing the World War II years, I experience pangs of guilt over the fact that I hardly concerned myself with the circumstances under which my relatives in Germany were living. Not hearing from any of them certainly should have made me worry; but I became so preoccupied with my own burgeoning career that I just did not think about such seemingly remote matters.

Obbligato

The one person from my childhood in Germany that I cared most about and admired the most was my Gebesee teacher, Bobby Schneider. I really began to worry about him when, in the immediate postwar years, as other names began to resurface, I heard nothing from him, and feared that he had been killed in the war or had ended up in a concentration camp.

I loved my relatives, of course, but Bobby had been my idol, and my mentor. He was a highly intelligent, superbly educated person—an intellectual in fact, but not a rigid professional academic. As young as I was that last year in Germany—ten going on eleven—I sensed two things about him: that he had no truck with Nazi ideologies and, as far as I could tell, had not joined the Nazi Party. (Whether he was forced to do so during the war I don't know.) I also sensed that he admired me. He seemed to think that I had talent, and always encouraged me and tried to stimulate my inquiring mind.

Then, one day in early 1948 I did receive a letter from Bobby, as a result of which we embarked on what evolved into a two-decade-long correspondence. Unfortunately, after surviving the war years he too had ended up in Soviet-controlled Communist East Germany, in a small city called Salzwedel. After facing Nazi political coercion for years, he now found himself harassed to join the Communist Party, an honor that he vigorously declined. The problem was that, under Chairman Walter Ulbricht's repressive Stalinist regime, you were not permitted to work, especially to teach, unless you joined the Communist Party. But Bobby would not capitulate. Oh, I was so proud of him, even though I knew that he and his family would live a miserable physical existence, continually near starvation. For years he eked out a subsistence living, writing articles for friends and colleagues more or less in the same political predicament, and doing translations from French to German, primarily of certain great classics that the authorities somehow felt had sufficient Marxist-proletarian interpretational appeal.

I sent Bobby care packages regularly, mostly the things that were unavailable even for money: coffee, tea, butter, sugar, etc. Magazines, newspapers, books—intellectual property—were all disallowed, and were confiscated by the border guards and the post office, the intended recipient probably hauled off to jail or worse. I knew that 85 percent of the people Bobby had known were fanatic Nazis, especially the numerous party functionaries and government officials one constantly had to deal with. Overnight, they had all become Communist Party functionaries. A worse political brew, combining Nazi and Communist ideologies, cannot really be imagined.

Starting in the fifties, I eventually was able to visit Bobby a few times in East Berlin. (He was never allowed to go to West Berlin.) We kept up our unusual correspondence and friendship until his death in 1972. He was a heroic figure, with a brilliant mind that was completely wasted by the two totalitarian regimes under which he lived and suffered. I so deeply cherish his memory; and his letters occupy a sacred place in my library.

*   *   *   *   *

In our continuing pursuits to savor all the rich treasures accessible in New York, we certainly did not neglect the city's great art museums and art galleries. Many a day we spent the whole afternoon gazing at great Renaissance or impressionist masterpieces, until our feet couldn't stand it any more, literally. We typically caught several new exhibitions and one-man shows at the many Madison Avenue galleries. We now hankered to not just view great art but also to actually own it, a financially preposterous notion. Not that I had any idea of becoming a serious art collector, as Fred Zimmerman, my bass player friend, and, to a lesser extent, Joe Marx had become. It was more a compulsion I had to own things, which I had recognized in myself even in my early teen years; not, to be sure, as an investment or a financially valuable acquisition, but simply to have great art and books near at hand, to which I could have instant access. I think it was also my feeling that to own a book or a work of art signified a certain cultural awareness and discriminating taste, perhaps even sophistication; I wanted these things to be an integral, permanent part of my life—like family.[48]

Two gallery visits stand out in retrospect, both linked in my memory, although in different ways, to Josef Marx. He had recommended a Dutch-born dentist living in New York to me, Frederick Franck by name. Fred turned out to be not only an excellent dentist but also a first-rate painter. I had seen some of his work in his office, but then found out one day that he was about to have a show at the Van Diemen Gallery, one of Madison Avenue's most prestigious galleries. By the time the summer rolled around, I had bought a couple of his paintings, one from the Van Diemen show, a very successful affair (considering that Fred was a totally unknown artist) that sold six of the twenty pictures shown on the very first day. That painting, called *Brooklyn Nocturne*, is a semiabstract view, through a window, of the Brooklyn Bridge at twilight, with a bright yellow daffodil on the window sill in the foreground. The other painting was a still life with a rocking chair and a big flower bouquet, which I got from his private collection. Though not great art, both paintings were skillful, expressive, and professional in the highest sense, and have given me much pleasure for all these many years.

In my many visits to the Marx's village apartment (before the move to the Greek Orthodox church), I had very much admired a painting that Joe owned, by a very fine Israeli painter named Mordecai Ardon Bronstein, representing a view of *Mount of Olives by Day Near Jerusalem*. Joe and Bronstein had become friends when Joe lived in Palestine in the late 1930s.[49] Now, in 1948, Bronstein was visiting New York for his show at the Jewish Museum. Of course I went to see that exhibition, and found two rather somber El Greco–like paintings especially irresistible to me: *Bethlehem*, and what turned out to be the twin to Joe's picture, *The Mount of Olives at Night*. When I told Joe I wanted to buy the *Mount of Olives* at the museum, he called Bronstein, who, to my astonishment, wanted to *give* me the picture as a present. But I talked him out of that, and eventually paid him $1,500 in three installments. I am proud to say that it still hangs in my living room gallery, opposite the Tanguy and a Chagall lithograph.

The annual Met Opera tours provided welcome opportunities to visit many of the great art museums throughout the country. Another important encounter with artistic creations occurred on the 1948 spring tour in Boston. There Margie and I made our first of what subsequently became annual visits to the famed Gardner Museum, with its grandly diverse collection of paintings, tapestries, furniture, sculptures, and, of course, its resplendent inner courtyard garden.

One of the musically happiest, most exciting nights we spent during that 1948 visit in Boston was with the Nat Pierce Band at the Raymor Ballroom, long gone now, but at the time one of the best places to hear great jazz. Ironically, it was located right next to Symphony Hall and more or less kitty-corner from the New England Conservatory, where, nineteen years later, I was inaugurated as its president. I always had a pretty good nose for ferreting out interesting jazz scenes. One day, walking along Huntington Avenue past the Raymor, on the way from the Museum of Fine Arts back to the subway stop at Symphony Hall, I saw that a certain Nat Pierce Band—then totally unknown to me—was playing a dance there that night. (Yes, believe it or not, in those days lots of people still danced to jazz.) Something told me that this was a band worth hearing; I could smell it. And was I right! We stayed all night, heard three complete sets, stood there transfixed by the amazing sounds coming from that bandstand. Pierce was the orchestra's pianist and its chief arranger—and what a talent! That night I wrote in my diary: "this band is as good as Woody Herman's—and that's saying something."[50]

That 1948 spring tour, my third with the Met, offered another remarkable succession of new experiences and encounters. What was special on this particular tour was that Joe Marx and Steve Maxym had managed to arrange quite a few Woodwind Quintet concerts for us, in places such as St. Louis (Washington University), Bloomington (Indiana University), Sandusky, and Toledo, among others. And so I suggested that, having worked on the Schönberg Quintet off and on for almost two years, particularly the first two movements, in one of those concerts—it turned out to be at Indiana University—we would play, in fact premiere in America, the Quintet's Scherzo movement. I had hoped to play some of it before that for Schönberg himself in Los Angeles, when the Met was scheduled to be out there for more than a week. I called Schönberg, Steuermann having by then introduced me to him in several letters, telling him among other things to be nice to me. But I could not arrange a meeting or coaching with Schönberg, as he was at the time very busy and preoccupied with rehearsals in connection with the annual Ojai Festival near Los Angeles.

Our dress rehearsal for the Bloomington concert was bad, indeed disastrous. Joe Marx's playing had deteriorated during that season, both at the Met and in our Quintet rehearsals, a situation that led to much frustration and rancorous arguments among us. Steve Maxym threatened to quit several times, and the mood in some of our on-tour rehearsals was prickly, to say the least. But somehow, miraculously, after that calamitous final rehearsal, Joe pulled himself together, leaving the hysterics of the morning behind, and cooled off enough to get through the concert surprisingly well. To put it quite objectively, the whole concert, including the Schönberg Scherzo, went remarkably well. Many of our Met colleagues who were free from the opera that evening came to the concert and were full of compliments. Our rather good and challenging program included, beside the Schönberg, one of the twenty-four virtuosic Anton Reicha quintets, my own Suite for Woodwind Quintet (with the Blues movement), and Mozart's sublime Quintet for Piano and Winds, with an Indiana University faculty member, Walter Roberts, playing the piano part. During the intermission, right after the Schönberg, we found Hendrik de Vries, the Met orchestra's second flute, in tears. He was deeply moved by the performance and his nostalgic recollection of his participating in the Schönberg Quintet's world premiere performance in 1924, twenty-four years earlier.[51] Unfortunately, almost nobody else liked the Schönberg, although some of the Met guys and a few of the university faculty praised us for our courage and the seeming assuredness of our performance. Somewhat to my chagrin, my Suite was the big success of the evening, and many people wanted to get a copy of the score. To Joe's evident discomfort he told me that I had stolen the show—which he somehow felt a burning need to tell to me, as if that was my fault. What a character!

Later, during the summer, when Jim Hosmer decided to retire from the Quintet, I suggested Charlie Ehrenberg, whose playing I had admired so at the Manhattan School of Music, to replace Jim—even though Charlie wasn't in the Met orchestra. But in several try-out rehearsals, we discovered that he did not fit in with our already established ideals of woodwind quintet playing. We were aghast when he let us know that "all this stuff you're trying to play"—my transcriptions of Bartók, Scriabin, Schönberg, Messiaen, etc.—"is crap." It was clear that he was not a viable candidate to replace Hosmer. Our Quintet lay fallow for about a year, until Jimmy Politis came to the Met in 1950 and joined our group.

I should mention one interesting (and funny?) incident that occurred in Bloomington. When we got there just before our *Rosenkavalier* performance, I was surprised to find half of my Cincinnati College friends there: Roland, Ruth Duning, and the other three "Terrible Four" (Linda Iacobucci, Jessamine Campbell, Helen Miller), also Paula Lenchner, Conrad Crocker, Dennis Larsen, and Mary Jo Leeds (for a couple of years concert mistress of the College of Music orchestra). I was so touched that they had come to see me and hear me play, and, of course, to hear *Rosenkavalier*. After the performance we all piled into two cars, and by chance Paula ended up on my lap. I became strangely excited by her buxom voluptuousness, and promptly had two delicious spells of tumescence.

It was on this trip that I first became aware of Southern cooking, at places like the Old South Restaurant in Atlanta and several other southern fried chicken joints, there and in Chattanooga. In fact, one time I was utterly surprised to discover that I could actually eat and enjoy hominy grits! It was also the first time that I really became conscious of the extraordinary, lusciously healthy beauty of Southern women. I made a connection, probably illusory, between Southern cooking and Southern female beauty. Indeed, I conjectured that the former must be conducive to the growth of mammary glands and various other curvaceous *accoutrements* of the female anatomy. I wrote in my diary: "they must give the law of gravity quite a struggle."

It was on tour in the South that I got to do some interesting sightseeing, to Stone Mountain (near Atlanta) and Lookout Mountain in Chatanooga, marveling at the Stone Mountain's form, essentially a huge, round, single-granite boulder, seven hundred feet high—but also sadly recalling that both places were favorite sites for the Ku Klux Klan to carry out their lynchings.

After my considerable discontent with the Met's performance levels during the winter season, I was astonished at how many fine performances actually took place on our tour. This was, I concluded, the consequence of some fortuitous cast scheduling, resulting in several superb ensembles, most notably in an inspired Antonicelli-led *La Bohème* (with Albanese, Jussi Björling, Nicola Moscona, and Frances Greer—I was in tears most of the time), also a very fine *Meistersinger* (in Cleveland, with Charlie Kullman and a very sensitive, expressive Irene Jessner), as well as several *Rosenkavaliers*, mostly because of Max Rudolf's beautifully paced, virtually flawless leadership. (Rudolf had taken the opera over from Fritz Busch.)

Another great performance took place in Los Angeles: Massenet's *Manon*, with Bidu Sayao and the twenty-seven-year-old Giuseppe di Stefano. It was one of the first times I heard him sing. What a gorgeous voice it was, with its lovely, warm, velvety patina. (It reminded me of Mel Torme's voice in jazz, only richer and bigger.) That night I heard him do what is called *messa voce*, where one starts a high note with full voice and very gradually, without any break, turns it into a falsetto or head tone. (It's analogous to seeing a chicken slowly rotating on a roasting spit.) I would hear di Stefano do that *messa voce* so smoothly and elegantly, hundreds of times, and I don't think I ever heard anyone do it better. (Most tenors don't even try it.)

Two other Los Angeles experiences stay in my memory. One was seeing Rita Hayworth at one of our performances in the downtown Municipal Auditorium—but what an unexpected disappointment; I almost didn't recognize her. I had seen her in practically every movie she ever made, including the sensational *Gilda*. On the screen she always was the most glamorous vision one could imagine. But here she was with her hair quite disheveled, her face apparently without makeup, rather grayish looking, in a very ordinary, slatternly dress. Even so I couldn't take my eyes off of her. Neither could others in the orchestra; many of them gawked at her and said, "is that really Rita Hayworth?" The other was a remarkable culinary experience, noted in my diary, at a Jewish delicatessen, where I had a shrimp cocktail, a delicious cold borsht, authentic German sauerbraten with potato pancakes, salad, and a strawberry shortcake—all for $1.25—and a beautiful, intelligent waitress to boot.

After our week together in Boston, Margie and I were not to meet again for a seemingly interminable six weeks, and this time not in Minneapolis, as in previous years, but in Chicago. We met there in early May at six a.m. in the vast Union Station. I was coming overnight from Cincinnati, Marjorie from New York on the Empire State. Together we then took the Burlington Zephyr to Minneapolis, with its brand-new glass-dome car, where from the upper floor one had a 360-degree view, while traveling in luxurious comfort at maximum speed in an unprecedentedly smooth ride. It was sheer heaven. Although Margie was really on her way to Fargo, we had dreamed up a way to spend at least some thirty hours together in Minneapolis. There we stayed at the Raddison Hotel and spent the afternoon reacquainting our minds and bodies with each other. It was unbelievably exciting. For all the myriad happy times we had already experienced, we had never belonged together as perfectly as we did that time. Those were very special magical moments.

That evening Margie came to our *Rosenkavalier* performance in a new ice-green satin dress and a pair of smartly elegant high heels, sitting in the front row right near the horn section. All the orchestra musicians were so glad to see her—and I was quite proud of her. After the opera we went to hear Dardanelle and her Trio on her last night in town. We were lucky to catch her, for it was wonderful to hear, on the one hand, how marvelously and with what subtlety and sophistication she played that night in her Ravel-like impressionistic, coloristic, lyrical style, and on the other hand, equally impressively, the more dynamic proto-boppish jump tunes, in beautiful, elegant harmonizations. I was also impressed—and flattered—that she remembered me from when we met briefly the year before, in Detroit, while I was there with the Philadelphia La Scala Opera Company. I really think that, like several other female trios of the time, Dardanelle was never sufficiently appreciated.

The next day, after some shopping for our mothers—Mothers' Day was just around the corner—we ate at Charlie's, reputedly the best restaurant in Minneapolis. It was curious that about twenty minutes into our dinner, in some deliriously happy mood, we virtually simultaneously said to each other: "Let's get married. It's time. Let's do it in June."

The euphoria of the evening was broken when Margie had to leave for Fargo—another painful parting. To console myself I worked until two a.m. on my orchestral *Adagio*. The next morning I wrote a long letter to my parents, announcing our plans to marry. By midafternoon I heard from Margie that her folks were delighted—and relieved—and that they immediately offered to have the wedding in Fargo in their spacious home. (I hoped *my* parents wouldn't mind.) I certainly thought it was a fine idea, and took it as the Black's ultimate sanction of our proposed union and of their full acceptance of me as their son-in-law.

Meanwhile, there were two more weeks of Met tour to fulfill. I kept getting lots of compliments from my orchestra colleagues on my Woodwind Suite—and lots of complaints about Joe Marx's playing. During the few remaining rehearsals (for the two Ohio concerts) he was impossible: argumentative, sarcastic, embittered; and finally in a hysterical outburst he blamed the recent breakup of his marriage on the Quintet and us four ingrates. At one point, in a terrible huff, he threatened to resign. We did not accept his resignation—actually, we had little choice, with two more concerts in the immediate offing—but decided to have him retire from the Quintet in the summer, and to replace him with Bill Arrowsmith, a wonderful, sensitive, quiet-tempered player, who was scheduled to become one of the Met orchestra's two principal oboists in the fall.

I recall becoming increasingly friendly on this tour with another newcomer, Harry Peers, a protégé of Saul Caston, the famous principal trumpet of the Philadelphia Orchestra. Harry assumed the orchestra's third trumpet chair. An intelligent and superbly knowledgeable musician, passionately enthusiastic about all great music, in those waning days of that 1948 tour Harry began to stand out among my colleagues as a kind of intellectual: extremely well-read, ardently engaged in all the other arts, and, like me, an avid record collector. He also displayed at times charmingly weird tastes in all sorts of exotica (including very strange foods), and harbored a fascination for high-quality dirty limericks that had to rhyme in the traditional AABBA pattern. Harry exhibited a definitely eccentric sense of humor. How could I resist him!

I kept myself generally busy on the rest of the tour with copying parts for various works for which there had been only scores, my own atonal jazz piece (still at the time untitled, eventually to be called *Jumpin' in the Future*), the Dauprat horn Quartets and Sextets, as well as making a four-hand piano arrangement of that prophetically visionary third movement of Schönberg's *Five Orchestra Pieces*. I also did a lot of nightclubbing with some of my colleagues (Bob Boyd, Harold Bennett, Joe Alessi), particularly in wide-open cities such as Chicago and Cleveland. Between the copying and the after-hours diversions, I seemed to be living entirely by night and sleeping during the day.

The opera the last night of the Met tour was *Rosenkavalier* and, as happens often on last concerts of a season, the performance was terrific, a euphoric experience—"virtually flawless," I wrote in my diary. That's saying something, when it comes to a very difficult, complex opera like *Rosenkavalier*, where a thousand things could go wrong at any time. I felt that it must have been the best performance of the entire season. Apart from the almost giddy mood in the orchestra—the prospect of finally heading home after a long, exhausting, eight-week tour—there was also the realization that half the Rochester Philharmonic Orchestra and many Eastman School students were in attendance that night (including a very young Dale Clevinger, the renowned first horn of the Chicago Symphony for the last forty plus years). One can well imagine that when the Met (or for that matter any major musical organization) comes to a city for a few nights and presents a rarely heard major work like *Rosenkavalier*, the entire musical and cultural elite of the city turns out. This always spurs an orchestra on to its greatest performance heights. To know that out there in the hall or auditorium there is an audience of aficionados, who really appreciate what you're offering, is always a tremendous turn on. When Dick and I spied the entire Rochester Philharmonic horn section and the Eastman School's horn faculty in the audience, seated close by the orchestra pit, there was an unspoken sense between us: okay, we'll show them; all the more since *Rosenkavalier* is one of the greatest performance challenges—technically, musically, interpretationally—of the entire operatic repertory. As for its horn parts, let's say they constitute practically a concerto for four horns.

I should add that another significant reason the performance was so top-notch was that it was conducted by Max Rudolf. Of the more than one hundred *Rosenkavalier*s I played in my years at the Met, with a great variety of conductors, Rudolf's was the best (with the possible exception of Reiner). High praise indeed!

After the opera, Buff (Jim Buffington) took me and a few of my Met friends to hear the Jack End jazz orchestra at some downtown club. It was another marvelous musical experience, not quite on the level of *Rosenkavalier* perhaps, but nonetheless wonderfully compelling, especially considering that it was a totally unknown local band, made up entirely of students. Jack End's arrangements were first-rate and impeccably played. I had the feeling that the players—who had also been at our *Rosenkavalier*—were inspired by Strauss's music and our performance, and were on their best musical behavior, eager to show me that, in their own way, their music could match what took place earlier that evening.

Back in New York in late May, it was all about various levels of preparation for our wedding: lots of shopping, buying clothes, Joe and I working out how to break our lease at our Houston Street quarters, helping to move Margie's music, books, most of her wardrobe, some dishes and kitchenware, to a tiny two-room apartment we had rented so that she would appear to be living in her own place when her parents came to town. Margie had spent most of her time with me at the Greek church, although not while I was on tour.

Only five days after my return to New York, I had to leave again, this time for Madison, to perform Schubert's great Octet with Kolisch at the University of Wisconsin. Kolisch remembered my horn playing from Kenyon, and hired me to join him and his Pro Arte Quartet, which included a local bassoonist named Fred Church, and Bill Willet, a wonderfully musical, warm-toned clarinetist from Fredonia College in New York. Margie and I took the Pacemaker from New York, a terrific train with comfortable roomettes, arriving in Chicago at seven in the morning. Although we were dead tired and sleepy, since we hadn't slept much during our brief five-day stay in New York, I persuaded Margie to do some sightseeing with me in downtown Chicago for a few hours. Ever since my first visit to Chicago, years before, I had been impressed by the city's uniformly outstanding architecture. This time, with my brand-new Olympia camera in hand, I took quite a lot of pictures of some of the major buildings, especially in and immediately north of the Loop.[52]

Sadly, by late morning we had to part again, Margie off to Fargo, I on to Madison. There I was met by Kolisch, and during a quick lunch we discussed Fritz Stiedry's work as a conductor. I was interested to hear that Kolisch was the only one of the inner Schönberg circle willing to admit that Stiedry, despite his many admirable attributes, suffered from "some serious limitations"—as he put it—and "occasional senile behavior."

By two o'clock that afternoon we were plunging into a four-hour Octet rehearsal, the first of three extensive, thoroughly explorative probings of that magnificent masterpiece. Working with Kolisch during that entire four-day period was a truly inspirational experience, very much like our work on the Brahms Horn Trio at Kenyon. I know that all week long I did my best playing. Rudi did that to you. His own richly expressive, meticulously informed playing compelled everyone around him to rise to his level. I found it such a deep pleasure to finally be able to play real *pianissimos*, as well as the whole wonderful range of dynamics. Although I had played the Octet several times already, exploring the work under Rudi's benign guidance and insightful direction was another matter. It made me realize that I had not fully understood what a pure and perfect work Schubert's Octet really is.

After our last rehearsal we all traipsed over to the local radio station for an acoustic sound check in preparation for a broadcast performance the next day. That turned out to be a very frustrating and annoying experience. The very small studio was rather dry acoustically, poorly equipped, and a bit ramshackle. When we started rehearsing the microphone pick-up made my most delicate *pianissimos*—and believe me I could play *pp*—boom out almost *f*. It was awful. I finally had to move about twenty feet away from the mike and the other players, which fixed the transmitted balance for the radio, but made it much harder for me to play ensemble. Thank God, by the next day the engineer had tinkered around with some other mikes and the broadcast balances were much better. The horn part of the one-hour Schubert Octet is hard enough, but especially if the horn is to really blend with the inherently softer clarinet and bassoon, and to keep a certain unity of sound in the three winds. I knew now that I had to play the soft dynamics even softer—like *ppppp*!

Eventually the broadcast went very well. I was really happy, quite proud of myself. Rudi, who was not given to lots of complimenting, nor to appreciative smiling—he always wore an earnest, philosophical, contemplative expression—almost couldn't stop smiling at me. To my utter surprise Margie heard the broadcast way off in Fargo, and she said it sounded most beautiful. The actual concert in the university's concert hall went even better, helped by the favorable acoustics in the hall.

It was also great to work with Rudi's quartet partners: the quietly elegant Albert Rahier (second violin), the highly intelligent Bernard Milofsky (viola)—I had first met him at that Haydn "Farewell" Symphony recording date with Erich Leinsdorf—and the brand-new quartet cellist, Ernst Friedlander. By the time I left Madison, Ernst and I had gotten together socially several times, and he insisted on my sending him my cello-piano *Duo Concertante*. Ernst assured me that it would be no problem for him to arrange performances of the work. Famous last words!

My visit to Madison also offered a number of unexpected bonuses. One was discovering Rudi's extensive music library. I was like a little kid in a toy shop. First I made a list of all the twentieth-century music Kolisch had that I didn't already own, actually in some cases music that I had never even heard of. I didn't know, for instance, that Honegger, one of my favorite composers, had written three string quartets. Rudi also had a lot of Webern music, still unknown to me in 1948, as well as Ingolf Dahl's Woodwind Quintet and René Leibowitz's String Quartet. Rudi let me borrow some of these scores, and that same evening I started hand copying Honegger's Third Quartet and finished the first movement the next morning, the day of our Octet performance. I also copied Webern's Op. 9 *Bagatelles* into my notebooks. It is a most remarkable work, whose extreme lyricism and subtle sensitivity I found absolutely fascinating. I had never seen anything like it. For the first time I really began to fathom Webern's music. I photostated some of the other scores in the ensuing days. Relentless crammer that I was, exploiting every minute of every day, I also started composing a *Perpetuum Mobile*, a quintet for four muted horns and muted tuba (or alternatively bassoon), on one of those Madison days. It is a short piece with one long, unbroken chain of babbling sixteenth notes, inspired by one movement in Jean Françaix's delicious and perfectly made String Trio. I finished the short work in the next two days.

I need to mention two rather interesting evenings spent with some of Kolisch's university colleagues. In the one instance, at Rudi's request, Bernard Gilson, head of the music department, had gathered all the local academic intelligentsia together to meet with me. Perhaps I misjudged most of them, but I had the distinct impression that in their relative cultural isolation in Madison they felt compelled to impress me with their most avant-garde notions. There was a kind of cultish atmosphere in the room, something I found very off-putting. But what saved the evening for me was hearing a great deal about one of their former colleagues, Harry Partch. It was the first time I had heard his name—we later became good friends—and of his invention of a microtonal scale of forty-three equal tones. This was a decade before Partch became nationally known during his long residency at the University of Illinois in Champaign, and still some years before he invented all his forty-three tone instruments. When Harry was in Wisconsin he was just beginning his experiments in microtonal and Asian-influenced music. He had set his music mainly to Oriental poetry, using chanting and wailing, mostly accompanied by a "prepared" viola. Gilson, whose favorite hobby was making recordings, had the finest disc cutting and playback equipment I had ever seen up to that point, on which he played some of Partch's very early incantational pieces for me, all very impressive and eerily beautiful.

The other remarkable musician I met through Rudi Kolisch was Gunnar Johansen, a Norwegian-born pianist on the faculty in Madison. He lived about ten miles outside of town, in what is undoubtedly the most idyllic secluded spot I had almost ever been in. It was located in a landscape of rolling hills and babbling brooks; there were no neighbors within a mile or so. The back of the house was built right into a fifty-foot rock ledge; in fact, the rock ledge *was* the back wall of the house, and their bathtub was built right into it.

The huge combined living and music room was a very spacious, circular, three-tiered affair; the outer perimeter held three grand pianos: two Steinways and one Hans Barth quarter-tone piano. Gunnar specialized in quarter-tone music, especially that of Alois Haba, the Czech composer who began to experiment with microtonal music in the early 1920s. But Gunnar was best known for his Liszt playing; he was, I believe, the first to record over a period of many years Liszt's entire piano oeuvre. Gunnar and his wife were Norwegian, and the entire house was decorated with Scandinavian furniture, rugs, vases, colorful plates on the walls, and, of course, paintings. Although quite modern in style, it reminded me of the grass- or thatched-roof houses I had seen depicted in my fairy-tale books as a child.

Gunnar and Rudi both wanted me to leave New York and join the faculty of the University of Wisconsin School of Music. "How thrilling it would be to work with Kolisch all the time," I wrote in my diary. We also talked about collaborating the following year on a Schönberg festival in Madison. Both ideas were never fulfilled, but it is an interesting twist of fate that some twenty-odd years later, when Rudi had to retire at age seventy from the university, I immediately invited him to join the faculty of the New England Conservatory.

But perhaps the most memorable bonus of my Madison sojourn was the visit to Frank Lloyd Wright's Taliesin in Spring Green, a visit that was a life-changing experience. Rudi had arranged for a private tour of the entire house and its gardens, including areas to which visitors usually had no entry. It was the first time I saw and really understood how architecture can be holistically integrated in a single building and in its natural surroundings—in Taliesin's case the moundlike hilly terrain—and how everything in a building ought to be derived from one or two basic thematic ideas, just as in a classical symphony movement.[53] I was surprised to find such a strong oriental influence in Taliesin's design and color schemes, also in the subdued glow of the templelike lighting in the theatre and music room, and, of course, in the seemingly boundless, open spaciousness of the rooms.

When I left Madison it was exactly five days before our wedding. I flew to Fargo via Minneapolis. What hit me forcibly when I got there was the dramatic change from the warmth and openness of the Kolisch household to the inhibited, deadening, repressed atmosphere of my in-laws-to-be. It made me feel quite out of place. Even Margie seemed to change into someone else when back home in Fargo, feeling restrained and constantly aware of having to behave in a certain predetermined, predefined way. I got very depressed. The only relief to this stifling atmosphere came from Bill Schlossman's nimble-witted, relaxing sense of humor. There didn't seem to be much for the groom to do. I was shown off around town to my in-laws' friends and business associates as the celebrated *artiste* from the East Coast, and, of course, to many of Margie's high school friends. As someone not given to small talk, I had never been obliged to carry on so much bland, small-town prattle, nor to meet so many people outside of my own world. I had a lot more fun one day when I was drafted to make the individual place cards for the bridal dinner. In one eight-hour stretch I produced nineteen of them, each with a different floral design—four short of the total required. Mother Black loved them. In the meantime Marjorie was, of course, feted all over town in a whirlwind of showers, sometimes three a day.

On the Sunday of that week, the entire Black clan was herded off to church. And once again I noticed that hardly anyone in our group listened particularly intently to Presbyter Hohn's excellent sermon on tolerance; nor did the sermon or the subject come up during a sumptuous lunch at George Black's Graver Hotel private dining room. I was impressed that Hohn would tackle such a complex and controversial topic, and do it so intelligently and broadmindedly. I was once again greatly impressed by the simplicity and general absence of ritualistic pomp and rigamarole in the Presbyterian service.

In the meantime gifts were streaming in by the carload, eventually filling both the entire library and sitting room. I began to feel a bit guilty at not participating in all these feverish prenuptial preparations. I really wanted to do some composing, but I didn't quite dare; I felt it would shock everybody and break all conventions if I were to be so uninvolved and calmly collected as to do something like that. So I wasted time all day, although I did listen to a couple of baseball games. Oddly enough, at one point I found myself leafing through Hitler's *Mein Kampf*, which I found, much to my surprise, on one of the bookshelves in my bedroom. Eventually, I did sneak in some composing on a string quartet. I had found two late Webern works, the Op. 20 String Trio and Op. 28 String Quartet, the week before in Rudi Kolisch's score collection. It was the first time that I had laid eyes on any late (1930s) Webern. I was fascinated by what I saw there, in the way of Webern's particular kind of modern polyphonic writing and almost pointilistic textural fragmentation. I simply had to try writing something like that, even if only as an exercise. And an exercise it remained, because the actual wedding and our honeymoon came along two days later and I never got back to the quartet. However, what I took from that brief encounter resonated within me very deeply, and showed up in subsequent works, especially in my *Brass Symphony* and *Dramatic Overture*.

My parents arrived the day before the wedding. Elsie immediately got involved with all the elaborate nuptial preparations: flowers, all kinds of decorations. Arthur and I sat in the garden and watched the hectic to and fro from a distance, me telling him of some of the good musical experiences on the recent opera tour. On the eve of the wedding day, June eighth, the magnificent bridal dinner was followed by a rehearsal of the wedding, with lots of crying, which, after all the smiling everybody had expected me to do for four days, I found rather a great relief. I kept thinking that this ceremony should mean something deep and special, not just an occasion for a lot of vapid smiling and cute platitudes. After the rehearsal, father Black took the bride and groom aside, and sermonized us with a heartfelt presbyterial catechism—going regularly to church, no drinking, and the like—and then surprised us by telling Margie that she was going to receive a number of monetary gifts, partly inheritance, partly to support her music studies, and $500 for us to buy furniture. I had never experienced such overwhelming generosity.

Finally the big day arrived. After hours of waiting around all morning while the bride, segregated, was engaged in all manner of sartorial and beautifying rituals, the wedding took place at two in the afternoon in the Black's spacious living room, surrounded by a veritable garden of bouquets and ceiling-high floral decorations. The procession, led by the flower girl, four-and-a-half-year-old Marjorie (Anna Jane's daughter), was truly beautiful. And my Margie looked radiant in a gorgeous, richly embroidered white dress with a long train. Minister Ratz's ceremonial admonishments and blessings were so sincere; it was very touching. Of course, there was the virtually mandatory crying. Papa Black could hardly talk, he was so choked with emotion, his eyes moist with tears. As for myself, I don't remember much at all. The whole ceremony sort of floated by me, as if I was in some vague, far-off dreamscape.

Eventually the ceremony ended in interminable picture taking, lots of congratulations, and more endless how-do-you-do-ing with all the guests, some thirty Fargoans whom I hardly knew. I did a lot of smiling. And then, suddenly, it was all over. Somebody tossed a bouquet into the crowd. It was caught by a teenage girl. With hardly any time to say our good-byes, we rushed through a phalanx of guests bombarding us with showers of rice, toward a waiting car, and were whisked off to the train station and our long-awaited honeymoon.

Margie's parents had really exerted themselves to make our wedding a most beautiful and memorable occasion. And it certainly was that. I also saw and took away with me, as a kind of bonus of that Fargo visit, the realization that my new in-laws were not really such simple-minded philistines as I had sometimes thought. Yes, they were saddled with certain deep-rooted prejudices and dogmatisms, but so were millions of their fellow Americans in those years of political and social isolationism. My God, my own father, a gentle, kindly man, delivered himself often enough of unthinkingly foolish anti-Semitic remarks, all the more ridiculous since his three absolutely very best friends and boon companions in the New York Philharmonic were Jews. And how many times had I already heard German Jews pontificate deprecatingly about East European Jewry. Racial, ethnic, and class discrimination were rampant in the United States—and are certainly not yet eradicated. As I got to know the Blacks better in their own family and social environment, I was chastened to realize that they were basically good, decent folks, with some familiar human foibles—was I so cheerily free of them?—basically intent on living honest, virtuous lives.

Black senior took on a much more human side when, for instance, he told me about his visits to the Metropolitan Opera in the 1920s, when he first started to travel to New York on buying trips, and how he loved Giuseppe de Luca's and Marcella Sembrich's singing, and Verdi operas such as *Trovatore* and *Rigoletto*; or similarly—the rumored family secret—how George had never missed a chance to visit Radio City Music Hall to gaze at the leggy precision dancing of the Rockettes.

And there were major virtues to be seen in his own life's struggles; he rose from the poorest of farm boys by dint of unflinchingly hard, honest work to become a highly successful businessman, indeed Fargo's leading citizen and most generous philanthropist. I also witnessed how Alice, his wife, tended to nag him on all kinds of behavioral minutia, and easily fell into hysterical fits directed at him. Religion was not so much a matter of pious faith to George Black as it was one of personal modesty and discipline. I could certainly understand and respect that. It became clear to me that in his simple, sincere way he fought for his way of life, a way that would favor his financial circumstances and the welfare of his children. Thus I came away from our wedding visit in Fargo with the happy realization that I need not feel so defensive with my in-laws, and the further perception that I would henceforth proactively reach out to them and meet them more than half way in any potentially disputatious situation.

Our honeymoon was not a typical one of heading for some southern or Caribbean resort and lolling around on a beach for days on end, while engaging in as much marathon sex as nature and physical energies might permit. Our honeymoon was pretty short, only five days. Why? Because I had rehearsals starting with the Goldman Band on June fourteenth, just six days after our wedding. We had decided that we would spend one day in Chicago, to engage in our favorite twin pursuits: spending most of the day at the Art Institute and in the evening going nightclubbing on notorious West Madison Street, and also having a great dinner at Jacque's, at that time one of the reigning multistar restaurants in Chicago. We would spend the remaining three days in Rochester with my surrogate family, the Whites, and at the same time hook up with Jim Buffington, Morris Secon, and my other Rochester friends.

Chicago's Art Institute yielded to our gaze its usual amazing fill of great masterpieces. From room to room, there were the finest Picassos (the famous *Guitarist*) and many Klees, including one of my all-time favorites, *Garten auf Trümmern* (*A Garden of Rubble*); Monet's brooding *Old St. Lazare Station*; an extraordinary, very early (1884) Gauguin, made up unexpectedly of only parallel lines; El Greco's famous *Assumption of the Virgin*; another gruesomely detailed Tiepolo *Saint Jerome*; the marvelous and astonishing satirical *A Grave Situation* by Roberto Echaurren Matta; as a complete surprise, a remarkable painting by E. E. Cummings, *Tree and Moon*; and of course, many other beauties whose names have now escaped my memory.

When we told the typically snooty maître d' at Jacque's that we were newlyweds—and after slipping him two dollars (a lot of money then)—he seated us out in the garden near the fountain. What could have been more idyllic?

West Madison Street was one of three Chicago areas where, as far as late-night entertainment was concerned, almost anything went. It was, in the near-final heydays of burlesque, the home of some of the finest ecdysiasts in the world, and the natural habitat of some of the greatest, funniest, and most outspoken comics: legendary names like Red Forrest, Benny Moore, and Billy Hagan. (This was, of course, decades before Lenny Bruce, George Carlin, and the HBO roster of "anything goes" comedians.) Prudish readers should know that Margie loved every minute of that evening, generally reviewing the ladies and their terpsichorean talents approvingly. (There was not much to criticize.) We had our fill of female beauty that night—and a deep feeling for the awesome power of feminine lure. As for the comics and MCs, we—especially Margie—laughed so much that our stomachs hurt and we felt we couldn't take anymore. They were top of the line, as befits Chicago: brilliantly vulgar, crude, provocative, fast-talking, creative. When Margie laughed—singers learn how to project—she could be heard in downtown Chicago. A sort of Chicagoan bonus was the music that accompanied these floorshows, a subject I wouldn't normally mention. But Chicago's nightclubs, which had after New York and New Orleans the longest history of great jazz, dance, and entertainment music, could field the best and most well-paid musicians of this genre. For all I know some pretty good, older, former jazz musicians, tired of the road and wishing to settle down in their hometown, were sitting in those bands we heard that night.

We finally got to bed at the Stevens Hotel around four thirty a.m. and slept, well satiated, till noon. In the afternoon we left for Rochester, where we were met at the train station by the four White girls: Teenie, Pouny, Louly, and Pooky. After a fabulous dinner with Paul and Josie, it turned into another long night of wonderful familial comradery, the entire White family—

all six of them—congratulating us on our marriage. Josie White kept telling me: "See, I *told* you!" It was getting light at four a.m. when we finally got to bed, but somehow not at all tired.

The next three days were filled with all kinds of music making, mostly organized by Buffington, which included reading through my new hot-off-the-press *Perpetuum Mobile* and rehearsing my Brass Scxtet jazz arrangements. Also, somewhere in those hectic three days we met with the Leventons. Mr. Leventon was concertmaster of the Rochester Philharmonic and, later, when retired, became a professional photographer. We had him take a whole slew of nuptial pictures, which are among the very best we got of our marriage. The photo session was made all the more interesting for me by Mr. Leventon telling me all about Alexander Scriabin, whom, as a young musician in Russia, he had gotten to know quite well through family and violin teacher connections. I, of course, told him of the enormous impact Scriabin's music had made on me.

Through Buff I met some more of his fellow students at Eastman. Fine musicians all, many ending up in New York, and with whom I often had occasion to work later on. In fact, once the Buffingtons moved to New York in 1949, their Greenwich Village apartment became the local hangout for all the Eastman graduates. From what I could gather, many of Buff's Eastman pals were the nucleus of a small group of insurgents, constantly rebelling against Howard Hanson's rather conservative musical tastes and educational policies. The fact that these students were interested in jazz was an automatic black mark against them in Hanson's book.

That is also when I first met Ruthie Kramer, a terrific violinist, Buff's girlfriend and wife-to-be; Ed Gordon, a fine bass player with a big rich tone, especially in his pizzicato jazz playing; Larry Rosenthal, an immensely gifted composer and pianist who became a successful film composer in New York and in Hollywood; and Tommy Goodman, a jazz pianist, who for many years worked the upstate New York territory. (By an amazing coincidence, very recently—some sixty-five years after I first met Tommy in Rochester—he hooked up with my bass player son Edwin, and hired him for a series of gigs in the Hudson Valley region.) All of these multi-talented musicians were members at one time or another of the aforementioned band, led by Jack End, who later became head of the jazz department at Eastman.

On that three-day Rochester visit I was particularly impressed with Larry Rosenthal's piano playing. I quickly realized that this was a superbly trained pianist who was not just a good composer-improviser, but was also an outstanding virtuoso pianist with a classically honed technique to burn. This was further confirmed the following day when, at a reading session of my brass sextet arrangements, Larry sight-read the piano parts flawlessly, and then, after a quick lunch, played Ravel's *Tombeau de Couperin*, *Valses nobles*, and a piano reduction of Ravel's *Introduction and Allegro*—beautifully, sensitively, intelligently. Obviously, Larry also relished Ravel's sumptuous harmonic language as I did, and he played all this music totally from memory. This was a major, major talent!

When I got back to New York, after what amounted to a long absence of twelve weeks, I had a lot of catching up to do in my reading of accumulated mail and the magazines, especially *Partisan Review* and *Commentary*, *Cue* (film and theatre listings), *DownBeat*, and *Metronome*. In the latter periodical I was quite surprised to read that Will Bradley,[54] one of my most favorite jazz trombonists, had turned completely away from jazz and made an extensive study of Alban Berg's music, and had begun to compose with the twelve-tone method. A trombone sonata, called *Arithmetical*, was performed at one of the League of Composers concerts in 1948. He had also written pieces for eight clarinets (including contrabass clarinet) and for thirty-seven trombones. I heard the latter pieces performed a few years later, but was, alas, disappointed; the work, although well constructed in an orthodox twelve-tone technique, seemed rather abstract and cold, inexpressive, too calculated.[55]

The Metropolitan Opera House was closed annually from late May and early June to late October, a very long stretch to be unemployed. (Nowadays the Met offers a fifty-two-week contract to its musicians.) So it was incumbent upon each of us to find some interim work. In 1947 I had managed to scrape by with a variety of pop concerts and a series of radio broadcasts, the latter very well paid. Now, in the summer of 1948, I was offered what amounted to two months of work as principal horn with the famous Goldman Band, playing outdoor concerts in Central Park (at the Mall) and in Prospect Park in Brooklyn. I was very lucky to be offered that job, for my finances were, as usual, in a sorry state from overspending on books, records, music, paintings, and marathon movie going. In 1947 I had not been financially responsible for Margie, but now I certainly was.

Fortunately, my reputation as a "damn good horn player" continued to spread among musicians and, most important, among contractors.[56] Bill Miller, the Goldman Band's contractor and fourth horn, had heard about me, and reached me by telephone while I was still on tour. He hired me as first horn over the phone, just like that, no audition, no haggling about salary, no back and forth negotiations. Bill Miller saved my life that summer, and perhaps even my marriage. He was a first-rate, experienced fourth-horn player—a special niche in a horn section—and a wonderful person, honest as the day is long, with an uncanny nose for picking out fakes and brummagems in the music business. While a few contractors were well known for wheeling and dealing, and all kinds of underhanded shenanigans, Bill Miller was as straight as an arrow.

One would not think of the Goldman Band, founded by Edwin Franko Goldman in 1911 and supported to a large extent by the Naumburg Foundation (the concerts in the parks were free to the public) as one of New York's stellar musical organizations. It was a motley crew, ranging from some very fine musicians to a few too many run-of-the-mill players and well-beyond-their-prime old-timers. But it was a job, and it paid the bills. A big part of the problem with the job was Goldman himself. One could not call him a conductor; he was a time beater, and directed in the stiff-armed manner, akin to a railroad semaphore, of most military bandmasters. His head was constantly in the score, occasionally darting abruptly upward to give a cue to some player—often too late—who usually didn't need such a cue. It was downright comical. I never could figure out what he heard or *how* he heard music. When, quite rarely, someone made a wrong entrance, he seemed never to know who or what instrument it was. On one occasion a substitute percussionist came in with a loud cymbal crash one whole bar too early in a rather quiet moment in the music. For the next five minutes Goldman, beating away furiously, glanced angrily left and right at all the different sections of the band—including me, by the way—hissing loudly under his breath: "Who did that? Who was that?" He was absolutely frantic. (How can you mistake a loud cymbal crash?)

My first rehearsal with the band was quite an interesting experience. It so happened that the first piece to be rehearsed was a new composition by Eric Leidzen, Goldman's main arranger and transcriber at the time. My horn part began with seventeen bars rest, but the eighteenth bar was encased in a heavy lined rectangle with the word SOLO above the notes in big block letters. It was meant to alert a player that he or she had an important solo coming up. Here was my golden opportunity to show Goldman and my new colleagues what a fine player I was. In the last bar of rests I took a deep breath, my mind thinking, now listen to this, when suddenly at least another dozen players burst in *fortissimo, with the same solo notes that I had*. I couldn't even hear myself. If I hadn't needed to keep on playing, I would have burst out laughing. Why my part was marked SOLO, I have no idea. During the rehearsal intermission I looked at the other dozen parts and saw that they too were all marked SOLO. Ridiculous!

What was worse—and what I had to learn to live with during the seven years I played with the Goldman Band—was that right behind me sat our lead baritone-euphonium player, blowing directly into my back and ears. The problem was that Colucci—that was his name—played not only with a vociferous, very pronounced and undeviating vibrato, but also almost a quarter-tone sharp, *and* constantly a split second ahead of the beat, ahead of everybody else. He was in his early sixties, and had been in the band for almost thirty years; and I knew there was no way his playing was ever going to change. We became good friends and I was *very* fond of him, because like so many Italian musicians that I worked with in America (or later in Italy), whatever their flaws, they loved music—deeply—with total commitment and devotion. Calucci was like that. That intense vibrato of his was all ardor and fervor, and love of music. And in his thick accent he would always say, with a paternal gesture: "I lika your playing; you play bravo."

That first rehearsal, which included the Berlioz *Symphonie funèbre et triomphale* and a wind symphony by Miaskovsky, was conducted by Goldman's son, Richard (who later became president of the Peabody Conservatory in Baltimore). Richard reminded the band several times that there are such things as *ps* and *pps*—alas, to little avail. The average dynamic level of the band went from *mf* to *fff*. You can believe that I developed a strong lip in my weeks with the Goldman Band!

The band played mostly transcriptions (what are called bandstrations) of famous and popular classical works: Wagner overtures, Liszt tone poems, symphony excerpts (especially from Tchaikovsky's Fourth and Fifth Symphonies), and the like. (I had to play the famous Fifth Tchaikovsky "Andante cantabile" horn solo several times a season, although half a tone higher, in E flat.) But we also played a fair amount of original band and wind ensemble music: several works by Gustav Holst and Vaughan Williams, a symphony by Francois Joseph Gossec, the Gounod and Hindemith symphonies, the *Symphony for Band* by Miaskovsky, works by Morton Gould, and, of course, lots of Sousa marches, as well as some very good marches by Goldman himself. One particularly snappy one that I loved playing and never tired of was called *On the Mall*.

One time Goldman invited Percy Grainger to conduct the band, which was a mighty interesting experience. Grainger made a striking figure with his flaming red hair, long flailing arms, and his unusually witty, rather eccentric comments and admonishments—altogether an astonishing presence! Unfortunately we didn't get to play any of his masterful, innovative, modernistic works such as *Lincolnshire Posy*, *Marching Song of Democracy*, and *Hill Song*. (They were almost never played in those days, but were eventually revived in the 1960s by the younger generation of wind ensemble directors such as Bob Reynolds at the University of Michigan and Frank Battisti at the New England Conservatory.)

Perhaps the most legendary musician in the Goldman Band was Gus Helmicke, well into his late seventies during my tenure there. Gus, as a young man, had played bass drum for many years in Sousa's world-famous concert band (with a violinist and soprano soloist), touring all over America and Europe. Gus was reputed to be the ultimate keeper of the true Sousa performance tradition, especially in the percussion parts of Sousa's marches, which in that tradition were embellished with little extra and often showy fillips.

Jimmy Burke, the Goldman Band's cornet soloist, played all the turn-of-the-century virtuoso cornet pieces by Herbert L. Clarke, Arthur Pryor, Walter Smith, and Bohumir Kryl. Jimmy was an excellent player, very secure and reliable, with a fine, elegant style; I can't recall him ever missing a note in all the years I played with the band. One day I asked Jimmy and Goldman if they would consider playing a piece of mine. I mentioned that it was not terribly modern or dissonant, that it was rather short, about five minutes in duration, more or less in the style of Ravel. In fact, it was an homage to Ravel; I was thinking of the *Pavane* that I had written for horn and piano back in 1942. I thought it would go well for cornet. So they said, "make the arrangement; we'll read through it, and then we'll see." I spent a whole day copying out all the parts for the band and brought the piece to the next rehearsal, during which we played it through. It went very well and everybody liked it. I thought, what's not to like? It's in the style of Ravel: nice plush ninth and eleventh chords. Well, the upshot was that Gold-man never got around to programming my *Pavane* that summer. He did schedule it a couple of times the next year, in 1949—although I had the impression the old man did so without much enthusiasm. I guess it was a little too subtle for him. But Jimmy really liked it, especially its jazzy Ravelian flatted fifth harmonies, and played it beautifully.

When it rained our park concerts were, of course, canceled. This resulted over the course of eight weeks in quite a few free evenings, which Margie and I put to good use by going to see a movie or to hear some jazz. But the tricky part was that we musicians were obliged to show up at the bandstand on time, in case the rain stopped and the concert was delayed but not canceled. Sometimes we would start a concert and halfway through it would start to rain; then we'd all run at full speed to the nearest subway stop, a quarter mile away.

Our most immediate concern now became finding a proper house or apartment. After hunting a whole month for something in Manhattan, and learning that everything was either too small, too large, or too expensive, we thought we had found our dream place for a mere $110 a month rent, plus $3,000 for the apartment's exquisite modern furniture; as a bonus, the band leader Boyd Raeburn (whom I already knew) and his wife Ginnie Powell lived in the apartment next door. But it slipped out of our grasp at the last minute when a couple outbid us by $1,500 for the furniture. After a number of other near misses we decided to give up on Manhattan and started searching in Queens. Two months later, in mid-September, we found a darling apart-ment, unfurnished but with a thirty-by-twenty-foot sunken living room and two bedrooms, for only $95 rent, in a spanking new eight-story building, half a block from the subway line that would take me to mid-Manhattan and the Met (or Carnegie Hall) in thirty-five minutes.

We now moved out of our Ninth Street room, almost reluctantly—the Lindstroms were so good to us—and with the help of my brother, my parents, and our Solari movers, we man-aged to get everything over to our new apartment at Pershing Crescent, although not without some difficulties. Solari had been our movers for a year or so. They were three brothers, Ital-ians, with a cheerful, happy-go-lucky attitude, never complaining or showing any annoyance with their varied schlepping tasks, even the difficult move the year before up five flights on that ancient rickety staircase in the Greek church. This time their antediluvian truck broke down on Queens Boulevard, one of the main arteries in Queens. It took about three hours for them to get the old beast going again, and eventually, at five in the afternoon, they arrived at Pershing Crescent. For moving half of our belongings, including my piano and the 150-pound record collection, they charged us, as I recall, only forty dollars.

Now began the furniture hunting for our nearly empty apartment. We started at Sloane's, where our Cincinnati friend, Paul Bransky, helped us find some of the necessary furniture, including a fine double bed at a great discount, since he was a Sloane employee. (To give the reader an idea how the world—and our culture—has changed, while we were looking at fur-niture with Paul, we heard Mahler's *Lied von der Erde* played over the store's public-address system, piped in from station WNYC. Now where in the world would you hear Mahler's *Lied* in a public place today!)

At Bloomingdale's we found two modern, curvaceous twin sofas, covered in a deep-red looped pile. To complete the living room's centerpiece, we bought an extraordinarily hand-some coffee table at the Museum of Modern Art, designed by the great Japanese-American sculptor, Isamu Noguchi. It was made out of a triangular two-inch-thick glass plate, set upon two beautifully sculpted, black ebony supports—truly a work of art. I also wanted to buy a Jean Arp rug; several of his famous paintinglike rugs were on display at MOMA in those years, occasionally for sale. But the price of one of Arp's rugs, several thousand dollars, was a bit too much for us at the time. We had already stretched our finances beyond the breaking point by acquiring six cubistically wood-sculpted Charles Eames chairs,[57] also on display at MOMA, but mass produced by the Herman Miller furniture company. I think of these furnishings as works of art, which still grace my living room to this day.

My favorite color has always been turquoise or some blue-green blend. Happily, at Bloomingdale's we found woven cloth draperies in an exquisite abstract geometric design of several shades of turquoise and beige, with tiny contrasting, oddly triangular brownish patches. I myself contributed a very simple but smart looking bookshelf for our living room, about four-and-a-half-feet tall, assembled out of eight-foot-long shelf boards, painted black, each shelf supported by three twelve-inch glass bricks. It all sat on a pedestal of brownish-red clay bricks—no nails, no screws, no carpentry of any kind. It probably didn't cost more than two or three dollars in materials.

My brother Edgar also contributed significantly to the enhancement of our apartment. He was always extraordinarily handy, able to build, fix, or repair almost anything, even in his teen years. I can't think of anything mechanical, electrical, or technical that is beyond his ability to deal with efficiently. As the Norm Abram of our family, Edgar built quite a few pieces of furniture for me once I moved away from our home in Jamaica, Queens: cabinets, bookcases and shelves, various encasements for my growing record collection and recording equipment. And everything he built in those years was so well and beautifully made that I still have and use it all, sixty-plus years later. For Christmas in 1948, he surprised us with a shapely, modernistically curved, multipurpose cabinet in a rich tomato red, adorned with an attractive ribbed veneer and red trimmed edgings. We used it initially as a breakfast bar, for which my aunt Lydia, obviously in collaboration with Edgar, gave us four red bar stools.

As for the mountains of wedding gifts we had left in Fargo, they were gradually brought to New York bit by bit, trunk by trunk, over the course of the next six months, every time George Black came to Gotham City on his buying trips.

I must admit we were pretty proud of our living room; in its harmonious color scheme and stylistic congruence it looked, from its entrance, if you squinted a bit, like a big painting or sculpture, or perhaps a large Max Ernst collage. But it also killed our finances, meager enough to begin with, even with my in-laws' wedding gift of $500.

To make matters even more precarious fiscally, I suddenly heard at the very end of July that our musicians' union—rather weak, and most musicians said corrupt—having bungled the contract negotiations with the Met management, announced that the orchestra would immediately go on strike. Miraculously, some kind of divine intercession came to the rescue. In early September my friend and horn colleague Mike Glass[58] called to say that he had recommended me to the contractor of the big Broadway hit show *Annie Get Your Gun* (with Ethel Merman), to take over his chair at $120 a week. (Mike was moving on to another musical.) Little did I realize at the time how Providence in its mysterious ways had just interceded to dramatically expand and enrich the course of my life in the form of a prophetic meeting with one of the most remarkable jazz musicians of the mid- and late twentieth century.

Mike had just saved my life, so to speak. But then, well after its season had finished in mid-August, the Goldman Band also came across with two more jobs; one providing the music for the inauguration ceremony of Dwight Eisenhower as president of Columbia University, the other a weeklong engagement in Ottawa and Toronto at two late summer outdoor fairs. What I remember most about that latter job was the continuous muggy, hundred-degree temperature and baking sun in Canada, which made my horn (made of brass) so hot that I could hardly hold it in my hands.

In the meantime there was one hitch in taking over for Mike at *Annie Get Your Gun*. I suddenly had a problem with the inside of my lower lip; I had accidentally bit into its soft inner flesh and the resulting abrasion was not healing properly. The blood vessels on the inside of my lip had grown into a gnarly, swollen lump. It is not much fun to play with a swollen lip. I struggled along as best I could in the heavy blowing of the Goldman Band, but when the swelling and discomfort in my lip intensified, I knew I would have to have my lip operated on. But what if the surgery was a failure? It might ruin my embouchure permanently. Thanks to the skillful hands of Dr. Sutton at New York Hospital, after four shots of Novocain and a few quick incisions, three stitches to hold the blood vessels in their intended place—followed by one somewhat doped up overnight stay in the hospital—it was all over. Well, almost. In the operation's aftermath my lower lip felt completely numb for about nine days. I now realized I couldn't start playing *Annie* as soon as Mike and the show's contractor wanted me to, namely, in two days. In desperation I promised them I could start six days later, on the next Saturday matinee, and that Lennie Klein, also in the Met horn section, would be able to cover for me in those five intervening shows. I'm sure that the contractor, Philip Nano, not a very nice guy (I had heard), told Mike to forget about me and get someone else. But Mike fought for me and persuaded Nano to let Klein substitute for those five nights, and the job was saved for me.

That summer of 1948 Margie and I spent many, many evenings and nights at the numerous jazz clubs on Broadway and Seventh Avenue. One of our most frequented was the Royal Roost (also called the Metropolitan Bopera House). Indeed, one could say that we practically lived there, because that summer Dizzy Gillespie's and Tadd Dameron's orchestras were in residence there for long periods. The Roost also offered a double bill by bringing in as relief groups to the main acts such outstanding small ensembles as the Lennie Tristano and Bud Powell Trios, and the Thelonious Monk Quartet.

Dizzy's orchestra, alas, didn't sound as good as his 1946 band. The playing of the new group, while exciting and featuring many new arrangements and compositions, was sometimes wildly out of tune (especially in the brass) and poorly balanced in the three main choirs. But Dizzy himself was in top form. Those late forties years were his heyday. His playing was fresh and lively, borne by a tremendous physical and creative energy, constantly explorative, and at times wonderfully rambunctious. He certainly reestablished for me that, with his spectacular improvisations and his phenomenal technique, tone, and range, he was the most vital voice in the new postwar jazz (along with Charlie Parker, of course).[59] Unfortunately, Dizzy's high standards and boundless creativity were not matched by the rest of the orchestra. Maybe it was unrealistic to expect as much. Though spirited, the orchestra was severely limited by ragged ensemble playing and poor tone, especially in the brass. Teddy Stewart, the orchestra's drummer, had interesting ideas but played much too loudly. This all made a somewhat messy impression, especially in the orchestra's playing of some of the extremely difficult new repertory, such as Tadd Dameron's *Soulphony* and *Symphonette*.

A week later, when we returned to the Royal Roost and found in the first set the same performance sloppiness, especially quite bad intonation in the lead alto, I got so disgusted that I pulled out a notepad and started to write an article, intended for Barry Ulanov at *Metronome*, about how such poor playing doesn't help the cause of modern jazz and bebop. But then, miraculously, in the middle of the second set things suddenly improved when a bunch of jazz celebrities (Noro Morales, Woody Herman, Charlie Ventura, among others) suddenly showed up. With such an audience, Dizzy's band seemed quite transformed and really came to life. Ensemble and tone improved dramatically, and the true quality of the music appeared suddenly in all its power. Cecil Payne played several excellent well-formed baritone solos, and Dizzy was spurred on to the most tremendously imaginative, daring solos I had ever heard him do. I was to witness many more times in my career the inspiring effect that knowledgeable and truly appreciative listeners can have on performers.

That same evening at the Roost, Monk's Quartet was virtually flawless throughout two sets, what with Shadow Wilson's tastefully discreet, yet deeply engaged drumming, John Simmons's quietly impeccable bass artistry, and Monk's wondrously unorthodox harmonizations and piano technique.[60] Oh, how I loved those right-hand "empty" ninths and tenths, and widespread bitonal chords. I remember thinking that Monk was the Hector Berlioz of modern jazz, with a similar quirkiness of ideas and unpredictability and adventurousness.

On our next visit to the Roost, I was amazed to find some chairs in the back of the room, where you could just listen to the music without having to drink—just like going to a concert. That was the first time I heard Tadd Dameron's Sextet, which soon came to be the house band of the Royal Roost. I thought it was just about the best jazz one could hear in those days. Milt Jackson was playing vibraphone, Allen Eager was the very young tenor player (with a fine, centered tone and good, clear ideas), and above all was the inspired Fats Navarro with his beautiful golden tone and rich ideas. Sometimes I thought he equaled Dizzy. Navarro's fast runs were so beautiful, every note a little gem: wonderfully clean, smooth, and effortless. The word "effervescent" was constantly in my mind. His high register—always a matter of great pride with trumpet players—was in his hands not just virtuosic display, but also a truly inventive, personal statement of real substance. That night I also heard Fats play an impossibly difficult, long, whole-tone trill (not a shake) on a high F, something I had never heard anyone do, including Dizzy, let alone any classical trumpeter.

Dameron's Sextet was backed by the ever-creative Kenny Clarke (drums) and Curly Russell (bass). The latter did some incredible high-speed bassing—still a relative rarity in those days—in some twenty-five to thirty choruses on Gillespie's *Dizzy Atmosphere*. In the midst of it all, there was Tadd Dameron's relaxed, light, and rhythmically intricate piano playing. The unity of the group's rhythm section (Dameron, Clarke, Russell) was sometimes breathtaking, it was so cohesive. But what was perhaps most impressive to me was that, although Dameron's Sextet featured such outstanding players, they were not presented as stars or featured soloists, but rather as parts of a tightly knit ensemble, an integrated whole in the finest traditions of chamber music.[61] A surprise bonus came our way when Dinah Washington sauntered onto the bandstand and sang some terrific blues, as only she could do, with her young, bright, well-projecting soprano voice.

When Dizzy's orchestra returned to the Roost months later, in October, they were a much-improved outfit. The sax section was much more in tune, although John Brown, the lead alto, still stuck out too much. The trumpets were surprisingly clean, in tune and clinkerless. The trombones were still the weakest section in the band and, if I recall correctly, remained so as a section in different incarnations of Dizzy's bands for many years. The arrangements were mostly new or updated earlier ones, very modern and innovative; and they played everything with their usual exhilarating spontancity. That was also the night that I heard Dizzy's new singing find, Johnny Hartman, a marvelous baritone with deep, full, low notes and great ease in the high register.

We went several more times to hear Dizzy during that three-week October engagement, and the orchestra continued to improve, virtually from day to day. I especially loved it when Jesse Terrant, the lead trombone, many times switched to bass trumpet to play the bottom part in what then became a five-man trumpet section, with Dizzy's big tone on top—a most glorious sound.

Dizzy played his favorite ballad, Vernon Duke's *I Can't Get Started*, almost every night, one night even twice. He seemed to be especially intent to work on a rhythmically free, highly chromatic, almost atonal introductory solo break. He kept exploring it again and again. (Unfortunately, on his two recordings of *Started*, Dizzy never managed to produce the wonderfully inventive, sinuously twisting lines that he did so often at the Roost.)

As the alternate group on Dizzy's last night we heard a Miles Davis-led nonet, which turned out to be the first public performance of what a decade later came to be known in its LP recording as *The Birth of the Cool*. What I heard quite by chance that evening were the initial attempts to present some of that now legendary repertory in public. (I had no idea that some three years later I would be playing and recording with that ensemble.) That first evening, sorry to report, I was less than impressed with what I heard. It all sounded underrehearsed, ragged, and out of tune. Balances were also off; for example, I couldn't hear Bill Barber's tuba at all, nor Junior Collins's horn, except in one little written-out solo. I felt that the group had not come to grips with the rather unfamiliar modern harmonic language of the compositions and arrangements, or with the unusual voicings for the uncommon ensemble of alto, baritone, trumpet, horn, trombone, and tuba, plus a three-piece rhythm section. Players in those days were very good at blending and balancing in the customary section work, but much less adept at playing ensemble as six different soloists. The music I heard that evening consisted entirely of brand-new compositions by Gil Evans, Gerry Mulligan, John Lewis, and John Carisi, all so radically different from the then-prevailing jazz. It took a few more years of on and off rehearsing, two recording sessions, and a few more gigs at the Royal Roost for the group to successfully assimilate this remarkable new music.

On September 29, Margie's birthday, we went again to the Roost to hear Dameron's group, and, as second billing, a sextet led by Wardell Gray and Dexter Gordon, with Milt Jackson—Milt was in demand by everyone—J. J. Johnson (my first time to hear him live), Max Roach, Al Lucas (playing bass), and the outstanding pianist Lou Stein. As a fellow brass player and a longtime student of jazz trombone playing, I was astounded to hear a real bop trombone close up. With his amazing facility, J. J. had by then assimilated most of Dizzy's ideas and technical advances, including those previously considered impossible on the trombone: lighting-fast sixteenth and thirty-second note runs. The young Max Roach's solos were more than the usual impulsive percussion bombardments; they were intelligently constructed statements—little compositions, in effect—exploring the varied colors and sonorities of the modern drum set. I was also quite impressed by Lou Stein's playing; he contributed beautiful harmonic support when needed, combined at times with daring melodic lines, all couched in a rich saturated tone. I recalled in my diary that the group played a "seemingly inexhaustible fifteen-minute" *How High the Moon*, in a truly inspired performance. As a bonus we heard three numbers by the inimitable Anita O'Day, certainly the hippest, most natural, uninhibited and relaxed singer of the day. She made it all sound so easy, while with her contemporary, June Christy, there was still always that slight sense of struggle, of vocal difficulties and intonation problems.

In Dameron's group I was again most impressed by Fats Navarro's playing. I feel so privileged to have heard Navarro in his prime. As I heard him many times in those years, sometimes on the same night as Dizzy, I began to see and hear the distinction between the two. Although influenced and inspired by Dizzy, Navarro's playing was in a noticeably more relaxed mode, given more to beautiful lyrical lines—as Dizzy could also do on ballads like *I Can't Get Started*, but didn't do all that often. Fats lacked some of Dizzy's flash and charismatic personality, but he projected a particular kind of poignant beauty and tenderness, even expansiveness, that Dizzy by nature tended to eschew. And when Fats would spin out his irresistible melodic lines—not just the top notes of chord progressions—it was absolutely breathtaking.

Dizzy's long, intermittent residence at the Royal Roost was coming to an end. He and his orchestra were about to embark on an extensive tour. We couldn't miss Dizzy's last night at the Roost, nor could a lot of famous jazz folks: Stan Kenton and June Christy, disc jockey Fred Robbins, trumpeter Kenny Dorham and Billy Eckstine, most of whom began to show up around midnight to see Dizzy off. It was a great evening, the orchestra playing all its big numbers really well—*Manteca*, *Things to Come*, *Salt Peanuts*, *Emanon* (in John Lewis's fine arrangement)—with plenty of Dizzy's antics and clowning thrown in for good measure.

On one of the Roost's Sunday afternoon matinees (from four to eight) we heard, besides Dameron's Sextet,[62] Lennie Tristano's Quintet. The latter group played new versions of my favorites from their recordings on the Keynote label, numbers such as *I Can't Get Started* and *Out on a Limb*, as well as wonderful performances of standards such as *Sweet Lorraine*, *Tea for Two*, *What Is This Thing Called Love*, pieces that the group never recorded, as far as I know.

Tristano was a remarkable pianist and musician, far ahead of his time, equipped with a solid, advanced technique, a vivid musical imagination, and, so valuable in trio or small group ensemble settings, an uncanny ability to pick up at any moment on what his partners were doing and integrate that into his own improvisations. Billy Bauer, the guitarist, had developed significantly in the interim since the Trio's first recordings into an equivalent partner to Tristano, especially in the ensemble's often beautifully intertwining contrapuntal work.

That was also the very first time I heard Lee Konitz in person, whose already highly distinctive alto seemed to fit remarkably well with the Trio, to a large extent because Konitz, unlike most alto saxophonists of the time, played each note, no matter how fast, with a subtly punchy, thrusting articulation, which fit perfectly with the quasi-percussive piano and guitar. Konitz's improvised florid lines, often with a subtle internal double-time feeling, had shapes and contours that I had not heard before. On the other hand, the bass and drums (Arnold Fishkind and Shelly Manne) did not yet integrate in terms of ensemble as well as they did later. (Manne had just joined the quartet a few days earlier.) Nonetheless, Fishkind contributed many nicely inventive bass lines, which made for some ear-catching polyphony with the two melody instruments. And Manne, one of the most amazing drummer talents of that whole era, occasionally added (as my diary put it) "many little wizardous, subtle percussion touches, like a great colorist painter."

One day, in the midst of all this hanging out at the Royal Roost, I suddenly found myself sitting in with Boyd Raeburn's orchestra. I was ambling down Broadway with my horn in my hand toward the Imperial Theatre, where *Annie Get Your Gun* was playing, when, passing by the Strand building, I heard some wild jazz floating down from the top floor. I couldn't resist investigating those interesting sounds, and was told that it was the Raeburn orchestra in a week of rehearsals, trying out some of their new charts, (jazz lingo for arrangements or compositions). I had to check it out further. When I snuck into the studio, Boyd spotted me and stopped the orchestra: "Man, am I glad to see you." Those charts turned out to be by his main arrangers, George Handy, Eddie Finckel, and Johnny Richards, and had been written to include two horns. But one horn player had not shown up for the rehearsal. So Boyd asked me to sit in, which, of course, I did eagerly. He told me that the orchestra had a week of one-nighters booked for the following week, and asked me if I could join him for that tour. I had to tell him that I couldn't, because I was contracted to play *Annie Get Your Gun*, but that in the meantime I would be happy to rehearse with him until he found another horn player.

It was a thrill to be playing real jazz again, although (in what I was told was the first rehearsal of a newly formed orchestra) the playing was still pretty shaky. The charts were, like the ones the orchestra had recorded in 1947 (*Boyd Meets Stravinsky*, *Tonsilectomy*, *Yerxa*, *Dalvatore Sally*), very modern and difficult, in a strongly chromatic, at times atonal style. While things improved over the next few days, I saw that Boyd did not know how to really rehearse these complicated compositions. It puzzled me that the respective composers were not rehearsing their pieces themselves. I found it a bit frustrating, as I was used to always working with musicians who could sight-read far-out music with ease. I was, however, impressed by Johnny Bothwell's playing, and by some incredible stratospheric high-note trumpeting. That, I quickly learned, was the twenty-year-old Maynard Ferguson.

Some weeks later Margie and I went several times to hear Woody Herman's new Second Herd. What I heard there was simply stunning, overwhelming. In contrast to the Raeburn orchestra and Dizzy's orchestra, Woody's virtuoso musicians played so well and were so well rehearsed that it reminded me of the heyday of Ellington's orchestra in the early forties or Woody's First Herd at the Pennsylvania Hotel in 1945. At the time I didn't know who the sax players were in Woody's new band,[63] but they were superb in their ensemble playing as well as their solo work. Everyone in the band seemed to be a major, original soloist. In the brass there was one of my great heroes, Bill Harris, plus Shorty Rogers, Red Rodney, and the great lead trumpet, Ernie Royal. That was the first time we all heard Jimmy Giuffre's *Four Brothers*, Ralph Burns's *Keen and Peachy*, Bill Harris's *Everywhere*. I recall being especially intrigued by Rodney's playing, as it retained many swing or pre-bop elements—bends, scoops, and a certain rough, swaggering tone—that sounded quite original in the general bop context.

A few weeks later we heard Stan Kenton's orchestra in Carnegie Hall. The Kenton orchestra sounded great in Carnegie's superb acoustics, but Margie and I found the program a bit uneven, not as satisfying as their previous concert in February. The program ranged from hard swinging numbers like Rugolo's *Unison Riff* and a hilarious knockout band improvisation on *Tea for Two*, to overly "progressive" and rather pretentious pieces like *Chorale for Brass*, *Bongo*, and *Piano*, and the excruciatingly grinding and perhaps too well-named *Monotony*. As always, there was a lot of excellent, technically secure, virtuosic playing, both in ensemble and solo work. Especially notable were several of Laurindo Almeidas's guitar solos, including a lovely *a capella* introduction to David Raksin's *Laura*; also Ray Wetzel's many witty vocals and trumpet solos, Harry Betts's trombone, some spectacular Conte Candoli trumpeting, and—as expected—Bart Varselona's incomparable solid-as-a-rock, full-toned bass trombone anchoring the brass section.

But the great surprise of the evening, as noted in my diary, was an outstanding creative effort by a trombonist named Parker Groat. I had never heard of him at the time; and frankly, he was someone that I never heard about again in all the intervening years. Did I dream up this name?[64] His extended improvisation on *September Song* was a marvel of beautifully sustained continuity—I could hardly believe it was extemporized—including the most intelligent use of the entire trombone range (i.e., no avoidance of the low register), all delivered with great swing and drive. I was very taken by this performance.

But that evening was also the first time I began to worry about the direction Kenton was taking his orchestra, not so much in regard to its repertory—there were the remarkable works of Bob Graettinger and many fine pieces by Bill Russo and Johnny Richards yet to come—but rather its performance style: the virtual elimination of vibrato, and the development of a steely hard, often cold sound and timbre. It left me puzzled and not a little frustrated.

To round out the year of jazz encounters at the Royal Roost, we went to hear Charlie Parker's Quintet and Charlie Ventura's Trio, a fine evening to be sure, but I recall that I preferred the latter's group. This surprised me, since I regarded Bird, ever since his 1945/1946 recordings and the amazing Red Norvo sessions of 1944 (*Congo Blues*, *Hallelujah*, *Slam Slam Blues*, etc.), as the supreme artist of the new bebop idiom, equal or even superior to Gillespie. (We now know that in those late forties years Parker's playing was often uneven, due mainly to his substance abuse problems.) We happened to catch him on an off night. There were occasional flashes of brilliant musical ideas—shapes and gestures that only he seemed to be able to invent—delivered at a blazing double double-time speed with his patented snaggy, sharp-edged articulation. But I complained in my diary that too often there were intonation problems and that he played with a lackluster tone, quite untypical for Parker. Some one at the table next to me—he must have been a saxophone player—whispered to me that Parker's alto was probably in a hockshop, and that he was playing on some out-of-shape instrument. I mention my puzzlement and disappointment because I had decided some years before, after acquiring most of Bird's early recordings, that he had one of the two most beautiful alto saxophone sounds ever produced on that instrument, the other by Johnny Hodges. And I have had no reason too change my mind about that, with the possible exception of adding Eric Dolphy to that distinguished group. What these three players had, albeit in quite different and highly personal ways, was a pure, perfectly centered tone, that is, no gratuitous or extraneous sounds, a luminous shine or bloom, rich and warm in expression, neither too thin nor too fat, neither too edgy nor too diffused. That description certainly represents the innate beauty of Charlie Parker's sound, of his personal tone. But that night it shone only rarely; I was surprised.

I was also disappointed that evening because I missed Miles Davis, who had evidently just left the Parker Quintet; and Kenny Dorham, his successor—soon to become an admired colleague and dear friend—on his first outing with the group, hardly seemed to know the book. Also, I was annoyed that I could barely hear Al Haig (bad miking?), who was one of my favorite pianists of the time. By contrast, Ventura's group was well rehearsed, and played everything with great fluency. Ventura was in fine fettle, a new sort of Coleman Hawkins, to my ears. Jackie Cain and Roy Kral sang a few numbers in their hip new stylings, wonderfully clean and smooth. But I did wonder whether they weren't sometimes a little too hip, too clever, perhaps lacking in depth and substance.

At the same time that Margie and I were engaged in this summer-long jazz marathon, we partook of quite another musical world by pilgrimaging almost every Sunday morning to the Cloisters, a museum way up in the northernmost part of Manhattan overlooking the Hudson River, to hear the noon concerts of medieval music in recordings. In that wondrously peaceful, restful atmosphere of the Cloisters' inner garden courtyards, we heard music ranging from early Gregorian chant and pieces by Pérotin le Grand (twelfth century) to a Guillaume de Machaut Mass and his beautifully austere *Hoquetus David*, on through works by John Taverner and some German minnesingers (such as Walter von der Vogelweide), to Machaut's *Chasse*, *Se je chant* (with its ingenious musical emulation of barking dogs), and works by Pierre de la Rue, Jacob Obrecht, and Clément de Janequin. These concerts were aural feasts of fascinating instrumental sounds new to our ears, such as fourteenth-century musettes, oboe-ish sounding viols, narrow-bore wooden trumpets (Zinken) and sackbuts (trombones) and medieval harps.

Speaking of Perotin, my conductor friend Roland Johnson breezed into town one day (on his way to Tanglewood), and asked me to help him in his research on Perotin and Giovanni Gabrieli, whose works he wanted to feature in the fall at the Cincinnati College of Music. This research led us variously to a big music publishers' gathering at the Juilliard School, to the Metropolitan Museum's ancient instrument collection, hoping to meet its famous historian-curator, Edward Winternitz (no luck on that front), to an East Fifty-Sixth Street music shop, where Roland found some beautiful fifteenth-century vellum manuscripts, and finally to the Forty-Second Street library for its extensive collection of Gabrieli publications. A bit later we ended up at a "World's Fair of Music" held at Grand Central Palace, unfortunately a disappointing commercial affair, which reached its nadir when Passantino, a manufacturer of music manuscript paper, presented Winnie Garrett, a famous stripper, in two shows that were replete with suggestive slogans of "perfection in form, feel, and texture," while another music publisher offered Joan Brandon, one of Billy Rose's star showgirls, to help sell its sheet music.

Quite a different musical discovery, the memory of which, for all its relative obscurity, I dearly cherish, occurred at two places, the Gramophone Record Shop and the Broude Brothers publishing offices. In the first instance I found a recording of a remarkably beautiful quarter-tone piece, *Ainsi Parlait Zarathustra* (*Thus Spake Zarathustra*) for four pianos (eight hands), by Ivan Wyschnegradsky (1893–1980), a Russian émigré composer living and working in Paris,[65] and five days later, by sheer coincidence, the score of this same music in Broude's store, in a beautiful edition published by Oiseau Lyre Press in France. If one wants to hear how beautiful and emotionally expressive quarter-tone music can sound, this music will provide a superb introduction. It sounds like late Scriabin in microtones, or as if Wagner had written *Tristan und Isolde* in quarter tones.

Another unusual but very meaningful musical encounter took place at that rarity of rarities (at least in those days): a double bass recital, in this case given in New York by Ludwig Juht, an Estonian-born bass player in the Boston Symphony. I've already mentioned my love for the bass, and so it was inevitable that, once I saw the ad for Juht's Town Hall concert, I was definitely going to be in attendance. The audience consisted mostly of bass players, as might be expected. I know I was the only horn player there and also the only composer. I don't remember everything that Juht played that afternoon—I'm sure he must have included the Dragonetti Concerto or one of the two Bottesini concertos—but, as my diary put it, "it was definitely a most interesting concert." That's saying a lot, considering that at the time the solo bass repertory was not only extremely limited (compared to the immense literature for the three other string instruments), but also of fairly average quality. What I do remember finding so interesting were three pieces that Juht presented, all of them new to me; one by Reinhold Gliére, *Two Pieces for Double Bass and Piano*, another by Alexander Glazounov, *The Minstrel's Song* for cello and piano (which Juht had transcribed for bass), and a third by the Estonian composer Eduard Tubin, an outstanding concerto. That one really impressed me, and I remember telling everyone about this remarkable composer from Estonia, of whom none of us had ever heard before.[66]

Around the same time I heard another most memorable concert, this one given by Nell Tangeman (whose husband had favorably reviewed my Horn Concerto premiere), the fine mezzo-soprano I had met three years earlier in Cincinnati, singing in Mahler's *Lied von der Erde*.[67] I thought Nell was just about the most intelligent and most musical of the young American singers. Her program was wonderfully unconventional and explorative, consisting of an aria from Berlioz's *Damnation of Faust*, Jocasta's aria from Stravinsky's *Oedipus Rex*, Milhaud's *Chants populaires hebraiques*, and a closing American group of songs by Ned Rorem, Leonard Bernstein, and (the obligatory) Theodore Chanler, as well as a beautiful group of Mahler songs, including "Liebst Du um Schönheit (Lovest Thou For Beauty)" and "Ich Atmet einen Lindenduft (I Breathed the Fragrance of Linden Blossoms)."[68] The latter song was our personal love song, ever since Margie had learned and performed it on one of her recitals at Kenyon in 1945. What a joy it was to hear such a challenging program sung so well.

Another most exciting and musically inspiring event of the new fall season was the visit by Charles Munch and his Orchestre Nationale de France (as it was then called). I admired the orchestra especially for its near-perfect ensemble, which rather surprised me, having grown up on dozens of recordings made in Paris in the thirties and midforties that, though spirited and lithe in style, were often blemished by balance problems and questionable intonation. Munch's program was a brilliant blending of the familiar with the unfamiliar, beginning with an electrifying rendition of Berlioz's *Corsair Overture*. I'll never forget how that stunning opening *fortissimo* run in the strings burst onto our ears, clean as a whistle, contrasting so beautifully with the ensuing warm and radiant Adagio. In the rest of the Overture, the orchestra's French-style brass section showed what brilliancy and virtuosity could achieve. Honegger's *Symphonie liturgique* followed in an inspired, luminous performance, fully expressing the meaning of the work's finale, "Dona Nobis Pacem." After that came Walter Piston's ruggedly rhythmic *Toccata*, and an elegant shimmering performance of Ravel's *Tombeau de Couperin*. As if that wasn't enough, Munch finished the concert with one of his favorites, Roussel's lusty *Bacchus et Ariane*.

I was happy to note that my father and quite a few other members of the Philharmonic were also deeply impressed. I don't know if the Orchestre Nationale always played that well and always that disciplined. Probably not. All orchestras can be uneven in their day-to-day performance; that is simply a human condition. But most times orchestras play their best when on tour in a foreign country, and especially when visiting New York. But even if we subtract a healthy quotient of adrenaline induced by the specialness of the occasion, we would still be left with superb ensemble playing, which the New York Philharmonic, for example, had lost to a noticeable extent in those late-forties years.[69]

One could describe the entire history of the New York Philharmonic from 1930 to the Masur years of the 1990s as an extended series of seesawlike oscillations from one extreme of conductorial deportment (tyrannical) to another (benign). That history begins with the six-year reign under the uncontrollable temperamental dominance of Arturo Toscanini (as remarkable a musician as he was), swinging suddenly, in 1936, to the benign regime of John Barbirolli, a courteous English gentleman. There was another dramatic shift to a very volatile and destabilizing period under the dictatorial Rodzinski. (It didn't help matters that Rodzinski began his tenure by attempting to fire thirty-seven of the orchestra's musicians). There followed a few uncertain years of generally equivocal leadership under various musical directors (including Bruno Walter and Leopold Stokowski), in another dramatic cyclic swing. Then came eight years under the saintly Mitropoulos; and on to Bernstein, whose buddy-buddy relationship with the orchestra and an inordinate personal need to be loved by everybody led to an even greater deterioration of discipline. Thence to one more 180-degree turnaround with the rather stern, aloof, unsmiling (and also somewhat limited) Pierre Boulez. Next came Zubin Mehta, whom everybody called "Zubie-baby," and who developed many personal friendships and favorites with individual orchestra members (not necessarily a healthy thing); and finally, in yet another leadership turnover, to Kurt Masur, part of whose mandate was to restore personal and musical discipline in the orchestra, a job he fulfilled rather well.

Of course, the New York Philharmonic has fundamentally been a great orchestra since the mid-1920s, blessed with many immensely talented musicians. (Listen to Mengelberg and the orchestra's superb recording of Strauss's *Ein Heldenleben* made in 1928.) But orchestras are like human beings; they are all different and sometimes they feel good and sometimes they don't, sometimes they work well and sometimes they don't. But the verdict on the Philharmonic unfortunately has been too often: Yeah, they sure can play! But only when they want to—and too often they don't want to.

When Mitropoulos arrived for his spate of concerts in 1948, the orchestra was in a rather dispirited and fractionalized state, which manifested itself in part in a gradually spreading, cancerous cynicism and apathy about making music, expressed partly in certain players' antagonistic behavior toward the conductor (whoever he might be), and partly in some players' desire, those with rather excessive egos, to in effect take over the directorial leadership of the orchestra. (I could easily name the main culprits, but they are gone from the scene, and I would rather let them rest in peace.)

Mitropoulos exacerbated matters inadvertently by programming a great amount of new or "contemporary" music,[70] to which many in the orchestra offered a strong, flagrant resistance.[71] While some were captivated by Mitropoulos's phenomenal capacity for memorization and knowledge of all scores, and by his total, passionate, self-denying commitment and devotion to the music, others complained about his unclear beat and his erratic podium behavior. Yes, his baton technique was somewhat unconventional, but not bad or inept. (I prefer to call it free, unorthodox, and personal.) And I must say that in the six years I played with Mitropoulos, both at the Philharmonic *and* at the Met (where he was a regular guest conductor for about four years, 1956–60), I never had any problems following his beat. I should add that Bruno Walter's beat was sometimes unclear and unconventional, to put it euphemistically, but I never heard anyone complain about his beat.

Real trouble began with Mitropoulos's third set of concerts, when in that week's Friday afternoon performance he (unfortunately) allowed the orchestra to blast its way through

Schumann's *Rhenish Symphony*—the Philharmonic being known at the time as the ultimate powerhouse band.[72] It was therefore an almost miraculous turnaround to hear what a great performance of Schönberg's *Five Pieces for Orchestra* Mitropoulos elicited from the mostly recalcitrant orchestra in the same concert. Of the five movements, the least successfully realized was the third, the prophetic "Der Wechselnde Akkord (The Changing Chord)," which consists of five sustained chords that are gradually and slowly transformed through a long succession of overlapping, dovetailing tone color exchanges. This radical idea, first conceived by Schönberg in 1909 (at least in such an expanded form), was beyond the comprehension of most Philharmonic players of that time.[73] Thus, given the usual limited rehearsal time, it was inevitable that the several hundred dovetailing connections during this three-and-a-half-minute movement—which have to be subtly and sensitively handled—were beyond the orchestra's ability to realize.[74] On the other hand, it was an astonishing victory for Mitropoulos to get the orchestra to play the other four movements as well and as convincingly as they did.

In Mitropoulos's fourth series of concerts, he programmed Webern's Op. 1 *Pasacaglia*, a poignant and sometimes intense expressionistic work, which must be the most remarkable opus one ever created. It's filled with rich, romantic, yearning melodies (already using the major seventh as the most important melodic interval) and surging climaxes—and a special joy to my ears—a number of high-lying lyrical horn solos, exquisitely played by Joe Singer. Once again, the performance Mitropoulos drew from the orchestra was magnificent. But again, some of the players' behavior during rehearsals was disgraceful and totally unprofessional. Certain leading loud-mouth musicians had the audacity to openly boycott Mitropoulos by purposely not playing when they were supposed to, or by playing intentionally out of tune, as if in this atonal music, which "doesn't make any sense anyway," you don't have to bother to play in tune, or by openly chatting with their stand partners when they had a few bars rest. The harpist, Cella, added more mistakes by his sheer incompetence.

I felt so sorry for Mitropoulos. My father and many others in the orchestra were furious—and embarrassed—at some of their colleague's behavior. After one of the rehearsals we went to see Mitropoulos so that we could commiserate with him. With tears in his eyes he asked: "Why, oh why, do they treat me like this?" It was incredible to hear Mitropoulos in one of the rehearsals excuse his conducting and ask one of the players to correct him. It was so humiliating! Why couldn't they see how he was suffering, and why couldn't they work positively with him, who, even with his faults, was not only one of our truly great conductors but, above all, was a man whose generosity and sincerity was already legendary.

During the rehearsal intermissions I often went to the musicians' locker room to seek solace with some of my friends and colleagues who admired or even revered Mitropoulos. But I couldn't help overhearing here and there little cliques of malcontents who stood there griping about everything: their job, Mitropoulos, rehearsals, the music they had to play, including Brahms and Tchaikovsky ("always the same stuff")—the reader can add the explicatives—and, of course, "this modern crap." What *did* they want to play? Maybe nothing; just collect the check at the end of the week? I was so depressed; it reminded me of when, a few years earlier, I had been hired to play seventh horn in the Mahler First Symphony and had heard the same kind of cynical, hateful talk amongst some of the musicians who hated Mahler's music, the conductor, the length of the rehearsal. Now, still the same stupid litany.

In his three final concerts Mitropoulos programmed Mahler's Seventh Symphony, most of which was beyond both the orchestra and the audience—I loved the mysterious Scherzo and the beautiful melancholy fourth movement—as well as Poulenc's witty *Concert champêtre*, two of Erik Satie's hauntingly beautiful *Gymnopedie*s, and in his final concert Arthur Schnabel's really thorny twelve-tone *Rhapsody for Orchestra*. I found it at first hearing somewhat uneven, but also at times, especially in its calmer moments, quite beautiful. Yet I also got the feeling that too often Schnabel let the twelve-tone systematization determine the music, rather than being guided by the ear. It seemed that as long as it fitted into the twelve-tone rules Schnabel let it stand, regardless of how it sounded to the ear—eye and mind music rather than of and by the inner ear. Mitropoulos did not endear himself to either the orchestra or the audience with this work, so lethargic and apathetic to begin with. It was clear that Mitropoulos's future with the Philharmonic was not to be an easy one.

One other concert from around that time that I remember with great pleasure was given in late December by Ernest Ansermet and the NBC Symphony. While Munch was featuring Honegger's symphonies in his concerts, Ansermet (French-Swiss like Honegger, and an old friend of the composer) performed his early 1920s work, *Horace victorieux*, a strong, rhythmically muscular work that is, along with lots of other early Honegger compositions, very much neglected.

Of a lesser order of musical encounters, but still of significant import in my formative years, was my meeting and getting to know musicians like Frederick Prausnitz[75] and René Leibowitz,[76] a French conductor-composer and author of an excellent book, *Schönberg et son école* (*Schönberg and His School*), which had a startling success, especially in France, where it single-handedly almost overnight penetrated the iron curtain of resistance to the twelve-tone school. Another encounter of considerable significance was my discovery of the Elaine Record Shop, a specialty store whose unique catalogue contained even the most obscure and least favored items, including a sizeable amount of imported recordings otherwise not generally purchasable in New York.[77]

That summer in New York, after our wedding, was another protracted period of wonderfully rich and varied cultural and artistic experiences. On the cinematic front we saw at least forty films, often on evenings when the Goldman Band concerts were rained out. We saw many new French films, new films from East Germany, several outstanding Czech and Mexican films, and also some American or British classics, such as Hitchcock's trailblazing *Blackmail* (1929) and Chaplin's *Monsieur Verdoux*—oh, and also the very first Hanna and Barbera *Tom and Jerry* cartoon, called *Solid Serenade*, featuring a delightful and superbly played jazz score. This spate of moviegoing also included my first Billy Wilder film, the mildly satiric *A Foreign Affair*. Wilder was soon to become one of my most revered Hollywood directors.

Of the many great French films—Duvivier's *Golem* (1937), with Harry Baur; *Blind Desire* with Louis Barrault and the very exciting, fascinating Edwige Feuillère; Marcel Pagnol's classic, *Baker's Wife* (1940), as well as his *César*, the third of his great trilogy, starring the incomparable *Raimu*—the most outstanding were the masterful *Non Coupable* (*Not Guilty*) with the great Michel Simon, and Jean Delannoy's intense, disturbing *Symphonie pastorale*, based on André Gide's novella of the same name and starring the extraordinary Michele Morgan as the pathetic blind girl. Bosley Crowther (a very good *New York Times* film critic of that era) wrote: "Morgan's performance is an exquisite piece of art—tender, proud, and piteous in the comprehensions of the feelings of the blind."[78]

Passionelle, with Odette Joyeux, although not quite in the same class, possibly because it was based too literally on a somewhat hard-breathing, overwrought novella by Émile Zola (*For a Night of Love*), captivated me more for its very fine musical score by Jean Wiener, so much so that Margie and I watched it a second time, just to hear the music again. While most of Wiener's film scores had previously been light and witty, this was sensuous, powerful music, reminiscent of Honegger's Second Symphony (for strings). It was the first time, I believe, that I heard a feature film score in which the *musical* continuity and form, rather than the film's scenario, was predominant; it featured very clear thematic material, constantly varied and developed into a full rich continuum.

Among the German films, there was the rather good *Kreutzer Sonata* (1933), based on Tolstoy's masterpiece, and a very corny Erna Sack costume drama called *Nanon*, which, however, featured one of my favorite German villainous characters, Oskar Sima, and some truly spectacular virtuoso singing by Sack. At one point she sang an amazingly smooth *glissando* from a high altissimo G to an A below middle C with absolutely no audible break! We also saw the brand-new East German *Mörder Unter Uns* (*Murderers Among Us*), with the young Hildegarde Knef, and *Ehe im Schatten* (*Marriage in the Shadows*). Both films were, in my opinion, Germany's strongest cinematic contributions since the war.

Ehe im Schatten was a remarkably moving and terrifying documentation of life under the Nazis; it told the story of a famous Berlin stage star and his Jewish wife, and of their ultimate suicide. Aside from its importance as a relentlessly realistic, uncompromising portrayal of how Hitler and his dehumanized henchmen drove their victims to their "final solution"—extinction either by murder or by suicide—it was a jolting reminder of how we Americans, in our prewar isolationism and complacency (myself included), couldn't see or wouldn't believe what the fearsome realities in Hitler's Third Reich actually were. *Ehe* also teaches us that it is unwise for the artist to ignore or consider himself outside of or immune to politics.

We also saw several Fritz Lang films, such as his thriller *Woman in the Window* (1944) and *The Last Will of Dr. Mabuse* (1933); and at MOMA, for the third time, von Sternberg's *Blue Angel* with Marlene Dietrich. Amazing how two fabulous legs garbed in black garters and stockings pulled in the crowds to the often half-empty MOMA film showings—or is it so amazing? On another occasion, when we saw Murnau's *Nosferatu* (1923) at the Museum of Modern Art (like *The Cabinet of Dr. Caligari*, one of the great German avant-garde expressionist films of the 1920s), most of the jaded, supercilious audience laughed and giggled throughout, quite ruining the experience for me and Margie.

As for American cinema, the most memorable films we saw were a whole series of masterpieces by D. W. Griffith—in a three-day Griffith festival at MOMA, ironically occurring two days after Griffith's death. But there was also Robert Flaherty's extraordinary documentary *Nanook of the North* (1922), on the life of the Eskimos in Labrador; Orson Welles's directorial tour de force, *Lady from Shanghai*, with a stunningly beautiful Rita Hayworth in possibly her best ever performance; and Paul Szinner's *Dreaming Lips*, with Elizabeth Bergner and the excellent, but now sadly forgotten Romney Brent. William Walton's revamping of Beethoven's Violin Concerto in *Dreaming Lips*, heard as a thematic thread throughout the film, added greatly to the congruousness of the film. But even more compelling, as one of the great marriages of music and filmic drama, was Lauritz Melchior's singing in a *Tristan und Isolde* excerpt, the climatic theme just before Tristan's death, in which he raves, delirious with pain from the heavy wounds he has sustained, of his longing for Isolde. The powerful double experience of the interaction between the visual and the musical affected me most deeply; for me as a budding composer, that third-act *Tristan* music was, among all the trailblazing wonders of that opera, the most boundary shattering sequence in the entire work, what with its constant 5/4 meter changes and breakthroughs in extreme chromaticism and virtual atonality. I still get goose pimples even in the mere recalling of the experience.

As for the Griffith film festival, it was so overwhelming that I had the feeling that cinema fascinated me almost more than music. The festival began with Griffith's earliest film (as an actor, with Edwin Porter directing), *Rescued from an Eagle's Nest* (1907), an incredibly naïve but somehow fascinating example of Griffith's and Porter's fledgling efforts at creating narrative in the film medium. It was followed by four early pictures (with Griffith directing, and alternatively starring Mary Pickford and Lillian Gish) that showed an immediate improvement in continuity, freer movement (of both camera and acting), terser editing, and thus a more realistic approach. The series continued with a badly cut and censored version of *Birth of a Nation*

(1915), a flawed masterpiece (if there can be such a thing), the Ku Klux Klan scenes and other racist embarrassments gone in this cut. What we saw mostly were the brilliant panoramic battle scenes and such amazing episodes as Sherman's march on Atlanta; an iris in the top corner of the screen detailed a mother and her three children sitting in the charred remains of their burned-out home. From there the series progressed to the great 1920s masterpieces *Broken Blossoms*, *Way Down East*, and *Intolerance*.

Even this relatively brief set of showings was a startlingly revelatory exposition of Griffith's creative development, and thus, by extension, of the early evolution of cinematic art. It demonstrated that all the most important and artistic technical innovations were his: the first full shot (in *For Love of Gold*), the first attempt to show what goes on in actors' minds not just by their facial expressions, the emancipation of film acting from stage acting, the first use of shadows (in *Drunkard's Reformation*), the daring idea that a scene does not have to be the same length as in real life, the first use of vast panorama shots (in *Ramona*), the first moving camera shots (*Lonedale Operator*), the expansion to two and three or four reelers—all this in five short years! But then, what a tragic disintegration after *Intolerance*. He was the first great artist in movies, just as Louis Armstrong was the first great artist in cinema's sister art, jazz.

The three Mexican films we saw were all comedies with the beautiful Maria Felix and the ingeniously hilarious Cantinflas, Mexico's Charlie Chaplin. But several Czech films were among the very best we saw that summer, especially *Merry Wives*, with its outstanding photography and original camera work, and its uninhibited, down-to-earth portrayal of Czech-Bohemian life centuries ago. *Pana Kulinaholych* was another historically factual film about a miner's struggle in the sixteenth century against a group of corrupt mine owners and town officials. As is well known, Czech artists (writers, playwrights, filmmakers, musicians) were always very politically courageous and singularly adept at subtly hidden or satirically expressed protests against their many oppressive political regimes, but especially in the post–World War II decade when Czechoslovakia was under the domination of the Soviets. From the evidence of what Czech filmmakers seemed to get away with, one has to assume that the Communist censors didn't regard themselves as part of an oppressive political regime, in that they pretty much left most Czech films intact. But even more astounding was the fact that in *Pana Kulinaholych*, the story of protesting miners who are led in their fight by a defiant, dashing poet and libertine Don Juan motivated the film's writer and director to insert all sorts of subtle symbolic and metaphoric sexual innuendos and sensual insinuations, cleverly overlaid with a diverting comedic veneer—all well-established cinematic stratagems and feints that the censors in Moscow would probably not have tolerated.

I also remember another Czech film of particular interest to me, *Bohemian Rapture*, because it was an elaborate cinematic rhapsody about an actual Czech musician, the violinist and composer Josef Slavik (1806–33).[79] The film not only recounted rather realistically and authentically Slavik's brief career—he died of typhoid fever at age twenty-seven—and his encounters with Schubert, Mendelssohn, Chopin, and Paganini, but also his many love affairs and his struggles as a musician to preserve his artistic integrity against life's realities and temptations.

It is the superb cinematography, its earthy mood of realism and the sometimes daringly uninhibited acting (especially by its female stars) that gives almost all Czech films of the period its distinctive flavor. (I had sensed some of that when I saw the controversial *Ecstasy*, with the young Hedy Lamarr, even in its censor-mutilated and much delayed American release.) The photography usually was slightly rough-textured (reminding me stylistically of certain Stieglitz photographs); the use of shadows and darkish hues created a lyrical mood and depth, the complete antithesis of Hollywood's generally slick, shallow, bright camera work. Closely related to the cinematography were the expressionist (but unmannered) sets. There was the unrestrained directing and acting style that perfectly mirrored (in the case of *Pana Kulinaholych*) the exuberant and uninhibited pace of life in the sixteenth century. We found the major actresses, such as Jirina Stepnickova or Hana Vitova, absolutely fascinating, in that they displayed their natural assets in a manner that would have wreaked havoc with the moral code of the Hays Office in Los Angeles. I remember Margie saying, "what empty shells most Hollywood dolls are by comparison." My enjoyment of those films was further enhanced by the beautiful lyrical sound of the Czech language, even though it looks so spiky and thorny to us Americans. I immediately thought of composing some songs in Czech.

Although we were at times a bit less active on the museum and gallery front, our visits there were often richly rewarding. I am thinking particularly of a remarkably wide-ranging MOMA photography exhibit that included the first photographs ever made (dated 1845), some of Matthew Brady's superb Civil War work, many early Stieglitz photographs, Steichen's great *Rodin*, Paul Strand's *Driftwood* (1929), two of Ansel Adams's incomparable Yosemite scenes, to my special delight a fine portrait by Adams of Furtwängler, a Bernice Abbot picture of New York City at night, and much more: altogether fifty outstanding photographs. We also saw that amazing 1887 precursor of movies by Edward Muybridge, *Analysis of Motion*, depicting in movement through the use of three cameras an extremely daring (for the time) striptease.

On one day, November 9 it was, we visited three eastside galleries, one after another: Van Diemen had fifty Paul Klee drawings, starting with the early *Sailboats* (1911), through the touching *Tear*s (1920) and *City of Cathedrals* (1931), to the late *Little Blue Devil* (1933) and the frightening *Revolution of the Viaducts* (1937). In the hallway entrance there was a wonderful Lyonel Feininger painting, *Gothic Spires*—on sale for only twenty dollars. Oh, how I wanted to buy it and add it to our growing collection, but we were so broke at the time that we couldn't even think of it. Then on we traipsed to the Janis Gallery to see its retrospective Kandinsky show. The paintings ranged from an early (1908) expressionist fauve landscape to his nonfigurative work and later abstractions of the 1940s that were often based on musical forms and concepts. It was startling to be reminded that both Klee and Kandinsky were at the Bauhaus in Dessau in the 1920s.

In view of this multiplicity of activities I read relatively little of what one might call grand literature. Once I discovered *Partisan Review*, I tended more toward reading it and some of the other literary and cultural magazines, and I perused the daily columns of political and social commentary (what we now call op eds) by such brilliant columnists as Max Lerner in the *Post* (a totally different paper then) and Murray Kempton in *PM*, a new daily that lasted only a few years; it was considered too brainy, too intellectual. But there were two new works that did catch my attention and made quite an impact on me: Sartre's essay "Portrait of the Anti-Semite," and—by dramatic contrast—a collection of love letters written in the seventeenth century by the Portuguese nun Marianna Alcoforado to a French soldier, translated from the Portuguese into German by Rainer Maria Rilke. It reminded me of the erotic poetry of Juan de la Cruz, which I had read some years before, except that the Spanish mystic's love was directed with overwhelming religious fervor at a Christlike human vision, whereas the Portuguese nun's letters suggest a fanatic and virtually masochistic subservience to her lover—very disturbing to read, but strangely beautiful and poetic in its odd perverseness.

Sartre's philosophical and historical analysis of anti-Semitism was much closer to my own experienced reality. I was fascinated, but also made somewhat uncomfortable by Sartre's extraordinarily cold-blooded rationality, which had already given me much trouble when, earlier on, I had encountered his writings on existentialism in *Partisan Review*. The wide acceptance of existentialism in the postwar period was disconcerting to me, since it seemed, among other rationalizations, to disavow any certainty of what is right or wrong. The phenomenon of anti-Semitism certainly refuted that uncertainty—even eventually for Sartre.

One major musical preoccupation that summer and fall involved a young lady who in due course became a dear friend, and who played one of my favorite instruments, the harp. That was Janet Putnam, a student of Salzedo at the Curtis Institute (for many years now Mrs. David Soyer, of Guarneri Quartet fame). Janet had joined the Met orchestra in 1943, the only female in the orchestra and a very attractive one at that. But since she sat at the other end of the pit, some forty or fifty feet away, I didn't get to know her particularly well until late 1947. That was the year she left the Met, a decision she made when the management put us all on strike, at a time when she was getting enticing offers to join the staffs of several radio stations and also from freelance contractors. In those days it was not unusual for New York's radio stations to present short fifteen-minute noonday recitals, more often than not by harpists. Janet loved jazz, but knew relatively little about it; yet she had the idea to play some jazz rather than the usual gloppy arrangements of Debussy's *Girl with the Flaxen Hair* or *Clair de Lune*. She had heard of my involvement with jazz, and when she was offered a job as staff harpist at WNEW, she asked me to make a few jazz arrangements of popular tunes for her. In the course of the summer I not only updated the two arrangements I had made for Linda Iacobucci in Cincinnati years before, but also fashioned a dozen more for Janet, initially just for harp alone. But I quickly realized that if my arrangements were to be harmonically and stylistically (i.e., chromatically) up to date, and if at the same time I didn't want to overwhelm Janet with too many pedal changes, it would be very helpful to have the support of a string bass to play all the bass lines.[80] Once again, all this work—arranging and copying of parts—was done for nothing; no money was exchanged. In those days I was happy to do things for the love of music. I didn't think commercially.[81]

Janet, a quick study, developed rapidly into a good jazz student. She worked hard on these very demanding arrangements. I recall that one day she practiced without a break for seven hours. When it came to coaching and rehearsing with her, I had to travel all the way up to 189th Street in Manhattan—180 blocks from our Ninth Street apartment. Her favorite arrangements were *Night and Day*, *Body and Soul*, *Star Dust*, *Sunday Kinda Love*, and *How High the Moon*, especially the latter two. I fashioned the arrangement of *Sunday* after the Thornhill orchestra's recording, which was quite a challenge. Because of the song's rich chromaticism and, on the other hand, the harp's rather limited capacity to deal with chromatically shifting harmonies (chords), I resorted to retuning one or two individual harp strings a half step lower or higher.[82] The other arrangement I was very proud of was *How High the Moon*, in which I based a Tristano-ish contrapuntal, bitonal or mildly atonal introduction on the song's rather innocuous verse, enlivening it with some really beautiful, ahead-of-their-time harmonizations.

Near the end of the summer we recorded two of my arrangements, *Body and Soul* and *Sunday Kinda Love*, at Zeke's studio, with Ed Gordon playing bass. Janet was thrilled with Ed's big rich tone, and so was I. It took two sessions to get both pieces recorded. Some friends of Zeke's happened to drop in at his control booth. After listening a while they asked, "Who is this genius arranger?" That genius arranger was sweating it out in the studio—it was a nerve-racking day for me—watching helplessly as take after take passed while time and money were fast slipping by. I recently heard those recordings for the first time in sixty-three years. I was thrilled and amazed at what I heard.

As a small compensation for Janet's hard work and indefatigable energy, we took her over the summer to a number of French and German films—she had never before seen a foreign movie—and to a couple of Fritz Lang's American masterpieces, including *You Only Live Once*.[83]

That summer wasn't all an endless involvement with the cultural and artistic life of New York. We had our pure fun days when we went swimming at Jones Beach on Long Island's South Shore—it was so exciting to battle the endless onslaught of huge incoming waves, nature supplying its own uncanny entertainment. Once in a while we forgot all about movies, muse-ums, and music, and took day trips (by subway or bus) to the Palisades on the other side of the Hudson River in New Jersey, or went by train to Huntington in mid–Long Island to visit Walt Whitman's birthplace.[84] I also remember going to the opening and dedication of Idlewild Air-port (now Kennedy) and the International Air Exposition held there. We saw hundreds of planes of all types and sizes, including jet planes, many years before commercial jet travel, and the new six-engine B36. We went boating on Long Island's South Shore several times, at the invitation of my friend and great Met colleague, Luigi Cancellieri;[85] and of course there were the many trips to Webatuck, to just relax, lie in the sun, or hike along the Ten Mile River. We loved to watch the cows that my father had borrowed from a neighboring farmer; they munched away on our several acres of meadows (incidentally saving us the job of mowing and cutting the grass), and we watched *them* stare at *us*. Cows are so nosy! We also enjoyed work-ing in my mother's beautiful garden, or helping with the roofing on the extension of our cabin, which was soon to house a small lavatory, a laundry room, and a combination workshop and tool shed, and which would in turn lead eventually to the big two-story winterized house that my parents started to build in 1949.

For sheer fun and another kind of excitement, we would occasionally go on nightclubbing binges to see famous showgirls of the time—that is, whenever we could afford such indul-gences—showgirls such as Winnie Garrett, Baby Lake, and Jessica Rogers, at places such as Lou Walters's high-class Latin Quarter (Lou was Barbara Walters's dad), or at Billy Rose's, or at other clubs with silly names like the Ha-Ha Club, Club Samoa, and The Frolics. I don't know whether Margie was inspired by some of those visits to New York's nightclubs or by the generally liberalizing ambience of New York, but she began experimenting with more venturous, more provocative attire in shoes, in the cut and length of dresses and skirts, in more attractive and suggestive lingerie. She also bought some half-bras, a new fashion trend that arrived along with the so-called new look in those post–World War II years; and at one point she got some fascinating results by dispensing altogether with bras and playing around with a diaphanous black scarf. I took all of this—I know she meant it that way—as an extra expression of her love for me.

That summer we saw quite a bit of Gussie, who had for some time disappeared into the orchestra pits of Broadway shows, and who was taking occasional work in Los Angeles. When alone with us she was very friendly and affable. But we found out that she was allegedly mar-ried to Neil Hidalgo, the Bolivian madman we had met earlier, and that he, like a pimp, took all the money that she made in her theatre work. We also heard that the irascible hothead would often beat her, and that she was deathly afraid to leave him. Mutual friends told us that he was intensely jealous of me and had several times spoken of wanting to kill me. Neil contin-ued to make threats to kill me for many years.[86]

By this time the correspondence between Bobby Schneider and myself had multiplied enor-mously. To keep me au courant with musical and cultural matters in East Germany, he would constantly send me reviews of concerts and theatre productions in East Berlin and other cit-ies in the DDR. For example, I had earlier written him of my love for Scriabin's late music, whereupon he sent me several reviews of a Dostoyevsky play, during and after which a pianist played Scriabin's *Vers La Flamme* and the Tenth Sonata, as well as Prokofiev's *Five Sarcasms*. In the continuous flow of letters over the years Schneider wrote me of his thoughts on Ger-man films and literature, and of the new cultural endeavors in his country as it was trying to recover from the total destruction of the final years of the war. At one point he sent me *fifteen* clippings of film and concert reviews. Another time he sent me several issues of a new West German music magazine, *Melos* (how did he get hold of that?), for many years the best such journal in Germany; it dealt especially seriously with contemporary music. Bobby sent me a copy of his lecture on Shakespeare's *Hamlet*. He was also very taken with Sartre's philosophy of existentialism, mostly likely, as with Sartre, because of his experiences in the Hitler era and the war years.

Eventually I could not keep up with the relentless flow of mail from him, and I remember finally writing him a seven-page thank-you and apology letter, which in itself took me—with many interruptions—over a month to write.

It was also around this time that I became very involved with baseball and the various team standings. My hero Stan Musial's batting average in mid-June 1948 was around 405. The age-old rivalries between the Dodgers and the Giants, between the Red Sox and the Yankees, were both really heating up, with the Red Sox for once on a long winning streak—but of course to no avail. In my enthusiasm I designed two graphs, one for each league, horizontally plotting the rise and fall of every team, each with its individual color (blue, green, red, etc.). Over a period of three months the eight often-crisscrossing lines stretching out horizontally made a rather pretty picture, much nicer, I thought, than the daily stock market graphs in the *New York Times*. Rex Barney and Bob Lemon both pitched no-hitters that season; and to top things off Satchel Paige, the great black pitcher—arguably the greatest of all time—at age forty-two was strutting his stuff every few days.

With my daily tracking of the games in both leagues, I soon had almost everybody's batting averages, earned runs, and home run statistics memorized. If any of my friends had a question about team and player standings, they knew they could come to Gunther and immediately get the answer.

By the time the World Series arrived between Cleveland and the Boston Braves, I was glued to the radio every possible moment. We even had a radio on—surreptitiously—in the orchestra pit at *Annie Get Your Gun*. With Lou Boudreau, Gene Bearden, and Bob Feller in top form, I predicted that the Indians would win the series. And for once I was right. However, I began to have my doubts when the Indians lost the first game of the World Series 1–0, and lost the penultimate game, in which Satchel failed to put out a six-run Boston attack in the fateful seventh inning, 11–5. But what ultimately won the series for Cleveland was an absolutely amazing number of double plays.

Suddenly, it was all over, and I was both sad and glad—glad because now life could return to some degree of normalcy, and sad because life suddenly seemed rather boring and meaningless.

Speaking of *Annie Get Your Gun*, I found in that orchestra pit at the Imperial Theatre an amazing array of superb musicians, and very few of the cynical constant gripers I knew from the Philharmonic. My brass partners included Alvin Glantz (nephew of the legendary Harry Glantz); Ralph Kessler (our lead trumpet), a fantastic musician, versatile in both jazz and straight playing (which the show, of course, required); Larry Todd, a very fine trombonist; our resident veteran banjoist-guitarist Tony Gianelli, who told me many fascinating stories about working with Joe Venuti, Jack Teagarden, and Bix Beiderbecke in earlier days; and several other musicians, whose names and instruments I can no longer recall.

We all played really well. After my lip healed from the lip operation, I felt really good, and remember playing faultlessly for twenty-six shows in a row. (On the twenty-seventh evening I allowed a teensy-weensy fluff that was barely audible.) We also had a lot of fun, especially the brass players. Al Glantz had an unbelievable repertory of jokes, and kept our corner of the pit in stitches. Al and Ralph constantly brought in new jokes and limericks, and passed them around. One has to understand that some of these guys had played *Annie* from its inception, which amounted to nearly a thousand shows—indeed the thousandth performance occurred on October 7, 1948, which was only my twenty-third show—and they were bored with the show and the music. They had long ago stopped reading the music, and played the entire book by heart. Thus one can understand that they had to occupy their minds with *something*. Most of us, myself included, read a lot—during those many sequences in *Annie* where there was no music, no singing, just acting on stage.

Both Al and Ralph had a real talent for drawing cartoons—and did so relentlessly. Ralph produced a whole series of me, real goofy ones, but intelligently ludicrous. He also made a series of cartoons of Margie—she came frequently to the show and sat in the front row—having her looking dopily, dreamily lovesick at her hubby; Ralph dressed her up with crazily spiked hair. (I still have most of those cartoons.)

All of this fun and reading came to a crashing halt when, during an intermission of a Wednesday matinee, Ethel Merman called the entire orchestra on the carpet, screaming as only she could, furious at our reading in the pit. If she caught anyone reading again, she yelled at us, the person would be instantly fired. We quickly figured out what had happened. The night before, as was her wont, she had come to the front of the stage, almost standing *on* the footlights, belting out one of her monologues, and had suddenly spied a few of us reading. Her demand that we stop reading was really silly. It wasn't that she felt it looked bad to the audience—no one in the audience when seated could see into the pit, which was set quite low. No, it was that, with her mighty ego, she wanted all of us to be watching her, admiringly.

Things got even more tense and weird as Merman continued on her warpath with the entire cast: the orchestra, the actors, even her stage manager and the orchestra contractor, Philip Nano. For no discernible reason Merman fired one of the best and most talented chorus girls, and raised hell with several others. Even my Margie was at one point bodily thrown out of the stage door by Charlie, the doorman. I was furious but impotent to protest. I desperately needed the job, and in no way could I afford to be fired. I began to feel like we were in some kind of a prison.

Ethel Merman's strident voice and slightly out of tune singing dominated the show. What saved it for me was Irving Berlin's wonderful music, arranged and orchestrated by Robert Russell Bennett, especially top songs such as *I Got the Sun in the Morning* and *They Say It's Wonderful*. Merman was known on Broadway among musicians, dancers, and actors as a real bitch, with a voice like a fire engine siren. I cannot disagree with that assessment, but I have to say that she could, and did, deliver what the audience wanted, as vulgar and musically crude as it was. In her way she was really amazing. Indeed, one time she had a severe case of laryngitis and could not talk at all. And yet this tough broad marched to the front footlights, and in the old tradition of "the show must go on" (there were no understudies for her), belted out her songs as if there were no tomorrow. Sheer willpower and ego!

As the reader can undoubtedly imagine, most of the female singers and dancers in *Annie* were tantalizingly beautiful, incredibly well shaped. It wasn't long before a few of those foxy ladies started making eyes at me—whether out of sheer well-practiced flirty habits, or because that's how you got ahead on Broadway, or that as a fairly handsome, slender youth they found me attractive. Who knows? But I suddenly found myself ogled at from the stage and during intermissions, particularly by a girl we knew only as Rosalynd. The area below the stage where we all had to congregate between acts was rather small, making it difficult to avoid someone you didn't want to see. But Rosalynd's behavior—I remember her name well because of its odd show-biz spelling—was very strange and made me distinctly uncomfortable. I was puzzled by her attentions and, in any case, not interested in her at all. I had my hands full enough with Margie, and happily so.

Rosalynd eventually approached me directly during an intermission, all smiles and charmingly flirtatious. But to my astonishment, two days later she haughtily snubbed me when I greeted her. I didn't mind her snub, but I just found it a very odd behavior, especially since on stage in the very next act she returned to smiling invitingly at me. Was she just another one of those famous showgirl teases, what in the pit was called a cock teaser, or was she just a nut case? I was too inexperienced in such show business shenanigans to know *what* was going on. It was disturbing—and perplexing.

Eventually—thank God—she lost interest in me and in her weird teasing games. But as soon as the episode with Rosalynd ended, a girl named Janice, with beautiful legs and breasts, started on me. I thought, what is going on here? A kind of nightly staring-at-each-other cold war ensued, which, however, came to a grateful end a few days later when I suddenly had to leave *Annie* in order to start my rehearsals at the Met.

One evening at *Annie*, in mid-November, during the period of those Rosalynd and Janice episodes, when I happened to be downstairs in the common room, sitting on one of the uncomfortably narrow wooden benches in our scrimpily appointed lounge area, a young man sat down next to me, and introduced himself as Leon Bibb. I had noticed him many times from my vantage point in the pit, from which I could see everything on stage.[87] We couldn't talk long because the intermission was almost over, but two days later as we continued our exploration of each other's histories, Leon was surprised to discover that I was very interested and knowledgeable in jazz, and that I was an avid record collector and idolized Dizzy Gillespie, Fats Navarro, Milt Jackson, and John Lewis, among others. But then, *I* was astonished when he revealed that he was John Lewis's brother-in-law! Was this destiny speaking or what?

I told Leon how much I idolized John's playing, not only his musical ideas, his modern bop style blended with a certain classical refinement, but also his beautiful tone and touch, so rare among jazz pianists. I told Leon that I *must* meet John. Could he arrange that for me? "Of course, I can," he replied. "But right now John is on the road with Lester Young. However, I know he'll be back home just before Christmas." That was quite a few weeks in the future, but Leon said he'd let me know very soon when exactly the visit with John could take place.

Leon and I went a few times to the Royal Roost, one time with his wife, Marilyn, John Lewis's sister. Through Leon I found out that John was very interested and knowledgeable in classical music, which I sort of knew, though not to what extent. I was pleasantly surprised to hear that John had wanted to study with Arthur Honegger, and that when he was in the army during the war, serving in France, he heard a lot of classical music performed by various orchestras in Paris, including—amazingly—Alban Berg's opera *Wozzeck*. That *really* surprised me. *I* hadn't even heard *Wozzeck* live or complete.

The new Met season (1948–49) opened after more than a months' delay on November 29—preseason rehearsals had begun two weeks earlier—with Stiedry and Busch again presiding over the big operas: *Otello*, *Walküre*, *Götterdämmerung*, and *Louise*, *La Bohème*, and *Mignon* (with Cooper, Antonicelli, and Pelletier, respectively). This time I was not particularly impressed with Busch's *Otello*, and wished that Eddie Johnson had given it to Antonicelli. I got the impression that Busch had lost interest in working at the Met, or perhaps in America altogether. (As it happened, Busch left the United States in 1950 for Denmark, where he spent the last years of his life.)

Stiedry seemed to have become even more senile since the previous season. Our mercurial, curiously hot-and-cold relationship stumbled along fitfully. On the one hand, I appreciated that he thought I was a better player than Dick Moore, not necessarily technically, but musically, and that he wished for me to become principal horn. At his first rehearsal (*Götterdämmerung*) Stiedry took me aside and asked me "to behave" myself this year—though I must say in a kindly, inviting manner. A few days later he called me the "gentleman of the opposition." But he also told me that ever since he heard me play and rehearse the Schönberg Woodwind Quintet on tour in Los Angeles, he had revised his opinion of me—more favorably.

On the other hand, as much as I wanted to cooperate with him—and in performances I always did—I knew that he had no idea how difficult it was to fully cooperate with him in the face of his often silly, senile remarks to us, or his at times unbearably condescending attitude to the orchestra ("these poor American fools; what do they know about Wagner!"). And what could you do in the way of cooperation when he intended to make an *accelerando*, as indicated by Wagner, but made a *ritardando* instead?

I often felt sorry for him, particularly on one occasion in a *Götterdämmerung* rehearsal. In the rhythmically precarious Siegfried's "Funeral March," Stiedry had great trouble because of his own uncertainty with the famous nine-note upbeat runs in the strings in a rehearsal, so much so that even his wife, Erika, and her friend Alma Mahler—yes, *the* Alma Mahler—were laughing in embarrassment. When Stiedry, in a *Walküre* rehearsal, began to criticize and yell at Marcel Hubert, our superb new first cellist, as if he were some mediocre conservatory student, I really lost it. As I say, we stumbled on in this peculiarly lopsided relationship. I really did do my best to help him and to behave myself, but it wasn't always easy.

Opening night with *Otello* was televised, a historic first at the Met, especially when one realizes that in 1948 television was in its absolute infancy. And, as always, on opening night New York's upper four hundred came to display their (probably ill-gained) wealth and gaudy finery. By the way, they weren't all septuagenarians; there were some real beauties, decked out in thousand dollar Balenciaga and Dior designs. It always amazed me how sexy and downright wanton some of these wealthy debutante girls tried to look. They seemed to get a sort of sadistic pleasure out of making men gape at their allurements.

Licia Albanese triumphed in that *Otello* performance. All along in the rehearsals, Albanese had been superb, both in her singing and acting, apparently completely recovered from her recent illness. Her "Salce" and "Ave Maria" (in the last act of *Otello*) were simply magnificent. Albanese was also glorious in *La Traviata*. One of the very finest performances of that great opera in my fifteen years at the Met took place on that New Year's Eve (1948). After having played *Traviata* with many competent but rather uninspired conductors (Sodero, Cimera, Cellini), it was a joy to see Antonicelli give the opera a great lift with his marvelous pacing and lightness of touch. Albanese was always a little uneasy about the difficult first-act aria, "Ah! fors' è lui," one of Verdi's most brilliant and vocally virtuosic creations. But that night she was fearless; the music flowed out of her with such ease and naturalness. As we say in our business, she really nailed it that night. She was partnered with Jan Peerce, always a most intelligent, tasteful singer, and Leonard Warren. Although Warren always sounded the same, no matter what role he played, he was still one of the best Germonts we ever had in those years. And when those three glorious voices, Peerce, Warren, and Albanese, launched into one of Verdi's great ensemble pieces, it was truly thrilling—and unsurpassable.

Of special interest to me was the one more or less contemporary opera presented that season, Italo Montemezzi's *L'Amore dei tre re* (with Virgilio Lazzari in the lead role), which I was fortunately scheduled to play.[88] Montemezzi was present at all rehearsals and several performances. Although not original in the grand Beethovenian or Brahmsian sense, Montemezzi assembled an ingenious concoction of Wagner, Puccini, Strauss, and Moussorgsky with great skill and effectiveness. It was a thrill for me to be literally enveloped in this wonderfully sensuous and highly dramatic music. And the cast was exceptionally good: Lazzari, Robert Weede, Kullman, and at a slightly lesser level, Dorothy Kirsten. The latter's portrayal of Fiora, though vocally resplendent, was just too calculated, too studied and postured—as was often the case with her performances. Even worse, when she took her bows she slinked on and off rather sexily, provocatively, like some stripper. It certainly was not the way she normally walked, and clearly was an act to attract attention. She was too attractive a woman to have to emulate Mae West's sexy slinkiness.[89]

Whenever Mr. Black came to town on one of his buying trips, he took us to dinners in the fine hotels he frequented, such as the old Vanderbilt Hotel—he had many high-level hotel connections since he owned the two biggest hotels in Fargo—and was otherwise very generous, sensing without us having to tell him that we were not exactly swimming in money, especially in the lean summer months. On these visits I got to know George Black much better, particularly on one occasion when he and I had dinner alone. (Margie happened to be occupied with one of her piano lessons with Steuermann). Although he was not one to wear his troubles on his sleeve—he was a private person and a noncomplainer—on this occasion he did let on that he was worried about Alice, his wife, concerned that as she got older she seemed to be getting increasingly nervous and irritable, usually over nothing (according to him), and that she nagged him an awful lot. Not wishing to make matters worse and possibly create more tension and friction, he implied that he had just learned to live with the situation. This rang true to me, for never once in the four years I had known him did I ever hear him lose his temper, or even get particularly excited. I think I had probably attributed that to a certain dullness of character. I saw in those visits a different side of George Black than the more stereotypical view I had held up to then; he was a kindly, generous, unpretentious gentleman, his racial and religious prejudices notwithstanding. When he found out that Margie and I were occasionally in financial straits that first summer, he did not lecture or berate me, but without hesitation offered to help us out—mind you, in frugal moderation. (He certainly believed in fiscal discipline and restraint, and would never have been overly ostentatious in his generosity.) In recompense for his help to us I tried very hard to be the kind of son-in-law he imagined his daughter deserved and the fine person he remembered in his own son, Ned.

I would never have wanted to disappoint or upset him by, for example, neglecting to go to church with him on Sundays—which I did several times that summer. As it turned out, far from being a merely dutiful experience, the minister (an Englishman named John Short) at George's favorite New York church, the Fifth Avenue Presbyterian Church at Fifty-Fifth Street, just two blocks north of St. Thomas Church, gave such marvelous sermons that I was enthralled and mentally fully engaged.[90] He spoke about God and pure religion, rather than selling the church or a particular religious faith or dogma, and also about a sound, unhypocritical relation to God. He laid bare man's selfish idea of God as a sort of "cosmic Santa Clause," as he put it. His sermon, beautiful in its form, its exquisite language, and its obvious sincerity, was completely free of pompous pronouncements and hollow rhetoric.

Meanwhile, as newlyweds that summer of 1948, certain tensions began to surface from time to time. As two people grow and mature together, not always in an exact parallel match, previously invisible differences—of habits, of perspectives, of tastes—can suddenly obtrude. Our occasional financial problems began to create tensions, and Margie's inability to be on time was another constant irritant. Twice we missed the train to Webatuck because she was late, which put us both in such a sour mood that for the entire two-hour trip we could not find anything to say to each other. Despite her generally equable and docile nature, Margie sometimes became quite irritable and easily offended, especially before her monthly period, a condition to which I was sympathetic, but which nevertheless brought on some dark moments between us. Margie would get quite irritated with me over what she perceived to be my compulsion to always want to be right. It is hard for me at this great distance to objectively assess the accuracy of her complaint. If I did feel such a compulsion, I could maybe trace it, in part anyway, to a kind of rebound from my mother's continuous nagging and belittling of me when I was a boy. But I rather think it was also a feeling of being very well and broadly educated, in the two superb schools I was privileged to attend as a child, and by my own industriousness and unquenchable appetite for the acquisition of knowledge. I'm sure I was right a lot, but obviously not always. I do know that I never said or pronounced the words "I am right." It was rather that I said things with such seeming authority and conviction that it sounded unarguable—and probably arrogant to others.

Margie also thought I was often too critical, that I reasoned too much, that I didn't—in her words—let myself go. Maybe she was right; I had many, many times thought about such questions myself, and often had my own doubts about my behavior. But one thing I knew with certainty: I believed unalterably in the need to balance subjectivity with objectivity, even as I knew how hard it is to be truly objective—about how objective one actually is. Another conundrum!

That summer and fall was for Margie an arduous and frustrating period. There was the absence for several weeks of her two teachers, which left her somewhat unrooted for awhile. The months of apartment hunting, followed by the time-consuming search for new furnishings, took their toll. As a new wife and as an idealistic, perfectionist housekeeper, she worried, more than I felt she needed to, about making that new home the most beautiful, tasteful, elegant domicile she could imagine for us.[91]

Added to her concerns was the unexpected realization that she had married a husband of relatively modest financial means with, however, rather rich tastes. And in truth, with all that moviegoing, dining out, reckless purchasing of books, journals, recordings, and music scores, I was in fact guilty of spending quite a bit beyond my means. On top of that, for some reason, that summer everyone I knew seemed to be running out of money, including my parents and my brother. Somewhere in my diary there is a note that I had to lend my father $150, money that I desperately needed myself. It was odd, since he was more steadily employed than I was. I am embarrassed to relate that for Margie's birthday I had wanted to buy her a terrific dress she had seen in a shop on Fiftieth Street, but was unable to do so because I had also lent my brother thirty dollars the week before, which put an unexpected hole in my funds for the week, until the next *Annie Get Your Gun* paycheck came around. Consequently, our beloved dinners at Longchamps, at our Fifty-Fifth Street French restaurants, and at Miyako's were more or less replaced by the humbler Horn & Hardart around town, where you could have a really good meal for fifty or seventy-five cents.

All these financial problems worried Margie—me too, of course—and as a result, she decided she had better look for work. It had often been suggested to her, when accompanying her father on his buying trips to New York's garment district, that she should do some modeling, beautiful as she was. In due course she did get a job modeling in one of the couturier houses on Thirty-Seventh Street, only three blocks from the Met. Unfortunately—or fortunately—that job, which she loved and which paid well, ended abruptly after five weeks when one of the two elderly brothers who owned the establishment made improper advances to her while she was momentarily in dishabille while changing into a new dress.

But three days later she got herself another job, this time at G. Schirmer, the big music publishing house (which, coincidentally, became my main publisher some years later). But that job lasted exactly twenty-four days, after which Mr. Schirmer himself fired her, for reasons best known to himself. However, by that time the Met was in full operation again, the strike having been finally settled, and we could once again breathe the air of relative financial stability.

On December 6 Margie discovered that she was pregnant. All good and well. But when she went to see her psychiatrist, Dr. Richardson, and one of New York's leading gynecologists, Dr. Abraham Stone, she was advised to have an abortion. I was told that going to full term there was a strong possibility of serious physical complications, for both her and the baby.[92]

In early December I had heard from Leon Bibb that John Lewis wanted us to visit him on December 19 at his home in St. Albans, the next town over from Hollis, Queens, where we were now living. Marilyn, a great cook (so Leon told me), would have a late dinner ready around eight thirty. But it is here that fate almost intervened to prevent the impending meeting of Lewis and

Schuller. For on that day New York decided to have the greatest blizzard in twenty years. It was a truly epic storm. By late afternoon some fourteen inches of snow had fallen, and more was pouring down without any end in sight. Bus and taxi service in Queens was for all intents and purposes suspended. For a while, watching the heavy snow from our apartment, we were doubtful that we would be able to keep our appointment. But then we decided to brave the storm. Margie was all for going; she knew how much the meeting with John Lewis meant to me. Fortunately, from our house to his place in St. Albans was only about fourteen blocks.

So off we went. Margie wore her knee-high boots, while I didn't even have any overshoes. The first three or four blocks downhill to Queens Boulevard weren't too bad, mostly free of drifts. But on the other side of Queens Boulevard things got much, much worse. There hadn't been any attempt to snowplow the streets on that side, typical of the nonservice accorded black sections of town like St. Albans. (Louis Armstrong was a near neighbor of John's, so were many other black musicians; and the pianist Cyril Haynes owned the house in which John lived in a spacious basement apartment.)

We now began to struggle through streets covered with three or four feet of soft snow. With every step we would pull ourselves out of almost hip-high mounds of snow, only to sink back into the next one. Luckily, every once in a while Mother Nature had managed to shape the drifts into little valleys, only two feet high, which made walking almost normal and easy. Now and then the winds had piled the snow into huge wall-like drifts. Thank God the blocks were short, but it still was a gigantic struggle to keep moving forward. Fortunately the fierce winds of the earlier afternoon had subsided somewhat.

I was worried about Margie. How could she—how did she—keep going? At one point, about half a dozen blocks from John's house, with my shoes completely filled with wet snow, my corduroy pants sopping wet, its ribs clogged with ice, I turned to her: "This is ridiculous. Shouldn't we turn back? It's almost eleven o'clock. I'm sure they've given up on us." "No, let's keep going. We've gotten this far; it would be pointless to give up now."

I was so proud of Margie; she was heroic. Mind you, this was two days before she was to go into the hospital to have her abortion! More than that, I saw how strong and tough she was. She hadn't wintered seventeen years in Fargo's famous minus-forty temperatures for nothing. So we struggled on, arriving—finally—around a quarter of twelve, exhausted, sopping wet, ice and snow everywhere in our clothes, our hair. Wonderfully, our hosts had *not* given up on us. In fact, Marilyn had kept the food hot without parching it. It was one of the most rewarding and revivifying meals of our lives.

Had this ordeal been God's or nature's way of preventing a great and important friendship from taking place? Well, it couldn't. John and I immediately reached a deep brotherly bonding that held for some fifty years until the end of his life—a relationship that ultimately had a profound effect on the course of certain aspects of American music. It was as if we had known each other for years, instantly anticipating each other's thoughts and feelings, reading each other's mind. There was a dignity in John's manner, a seriousness and directness that I found so entrancing. And there was no mincing words. When I happened to mention that so far I was not very impressed with Miles Davis's playing on records, he shot back at me: "Well, then I'll have to get you to hear some of his newest recordings on Savoy. You'll like *them*." And I did, a fortnight later at my house. John was right. I just had never heard Miles play that well on records or in person.[93] My problem with Miles's playing was partly on the technical side. His tone was rather thin in those early days, poorly centered and with fuzzy attacks; as a result he fluffed a lot of notes. Be it said that Miles's playing in those respects improved considerably over the next decade, through a series of gradual transformations. However, truth be told, even in his heyday, say the fifties when I played with him on the *Birth of the Cool* and *Porgy and Bess* recordings, Miles still had occasional embouchure (chops) problems.

For a man of already such singular accomplishments I found John to be self-effacing and shy. But I also quickly found out that in certain discussions, he could be quite firm and unyielding. I also mentioned that I thought Dizzy's band sounded at times rather ragged or under-rehearsed. He agreed, and then countered with: "But you should have heard that band in Sweden. You can't imagine how relaxed, in the right way, the band became in Sweden's different social climate, and how that showed in their playing."

Around two a.m. we went to John's basement music room and listened to records, first of Fritz Reiner and the Pittsburgh Symphony's recording of Bartók's *Concerto for Orchestra*, and then a recording of Respighi's *Pines of Rome*. A little later he played some air checks of the Claude Thornhill Orchestra of recent arrangements of Gil Evans—really recompositions—of Parker's *Anthropology* and *Donna Lee*, as well as Gil's reworking of *The Old Castle* from Moussorgsky's *Pictures at An Exhibition*. Although these air checks were staticy, crackly, hissy things, I could hear some absolutely amazing music through the noise, and relished Gil's wonderfully rich harmonic palette and fantastic orchestrations.

I told John about my own burgeoning jazz and classical record collection, and invited him to our house two days hence. That time we listened to records all evening long: Bartók's *Music for Percussion, Strings and Celesta*, Messiaen's *Hymn for Orchestra*, three of Honegger's symphonies, my *Wozzeck* excerpts (from Bernard Herrmann's CBS broadcast), and Webern's Op. 28 String Quartet.

What a wonderful evening that first encounter was, despite the grueling effort to get to John's home. We left about four thirty in the morning. I don't remember how we got home, but somehow we did. I know, because I had a *Madama Butterfly* rehearsal at the Met that same morning, at eleven.

Obbligato

It is amazing how certain seemingly unrelated events or encounters can link together into a series of connections that lead to some event of enormous importance, which in turn decisively affects the future of one's life and career. It was such a chain of unforeseeable coincidences that led to the meeting with John Lewis that crucially influenced both our lives and careers. And beyond that, John was my closest ally in the battles over a whole new genre of music located halfway between classical music and jazz, the so-called Third Stream concept.

In tracing the genealogy of such a process of unexpected linkages one may pick several points of inception. In one scenario, I would choose the dozens of times that I and my hornist colleague Mike Glass spent at the Carnegie Deli developing a very close friendship of mutual admiration. That led to his recommending me, out of possible fifty other horn players, to replace him at his show, *Annie Get Your Gun*, loyally engineering the postponement of my actual starting date (because of the injury to my lip), and thereby preserving the job for me. Then, quite by chance and after playing the show for almost a month, I met someone named Leon Bibb, who turned out to be the brother-in-law of John Lewis, the soon-to-become famous pianist and composer and the founder of the Modern Jazz Quartet.

Or, I could go still further back, to another point of incipience for this mysterious process I am describing: my hearing Duke Ellington at age eleven or so, and becoming converted at that moment to a conviction that jazz was a most important creative art form. I unhesitatingly determined that I would have to incorporate in my life and career some kind of deep involvement with jazz. That pivotal moment in my life initiated an expansion of my musical horizons, which prepared me for the encounter with John.[94]

*   *   *   *   *

Margie went to Roosevelt Hospital four days before Christmas—she was in her third month—and had the operation. The next day, when I visited her, she looked quite weak and pale, but said that she felt fine. Two days later, Christmas Eve, Margie left the hospital, in time for us to buy a Christmas tree together in Kew Gardens, and for me to still get to the Friday afternoon Philharmonic concert, where Munch conducted superb performances of Ravel's *Valses nobles et sentimentales* and Roussel's Fourth Symphony.

My parents picked Margie up in the evening to go to their home in Jamaica, where we would have, according to our long-standing German Christmas custom, the so-called *Bescherung*, the sharing of gifts, late at night on Christmas Eve. I had to play *Aida* at the opera that evening—musicians (and other performers) usually end up working on holidays because that is, of course, when all other folks wish to be entertained—and got to Jamaica around midnight. (*Aida* is a longish opera that usually lasted until eleven fifteen.) My mother had decorated her home most exquisitely; the living room's centerpiece was a large, perfectly shaped spruce tree, direct from Webatuck, trimmed with candles and a wealth of glistening German ornaments (mostly from Lauscha). She had also prepared one of her marvelous goose dinners, replete with German knödel (dumplings) and—my favorite—red cabbage. Our reciprocal gift giving was very modest and centered on practical things, actual necessities—which is actually the way it should be.[95]

After the exchange of gifts and singing of carols, Edgar drove Margie and me home, where around two thirty a.m. we had our own private little *Bescherung*. It was our first Christmas as husband and wife—which my diary recorded as "a very, very happy one!!"

Chapter Eight

GREAT YEARS AT THE MET

"FIFTEEN-MINUTE DEMONSTRATION follows last night's performance at the Metropolitan." Thus spake the *New York Times* in a headline. And indeed, it was one of the greatest triumphs in the sixty-five-year history of the Metropolitan Opera, maybe even the ultimate pinnacle of artistic achievement and audience approbation up to that time—a sustained wild ovation, the likes of which I had never previously witnessed, nor had any of my veteran orchestra colleagues. To put this in proper perspective, one has to realize that audience acclamations in the 1940s were not yet the overly ostentatious, instant standing ovations of today.[1] The event produced an outpouring. And for once, it was well deserved. I feel very privileged to have been a small part of that absolutely remarkable performance. On the goose-pimple meter, it outranked even the *Otello* experience I have described earlier. The two artists primarily responsible for the electrifying excitement, integrity, and sovereignty of that performance were Fritz Reiner and the Bulgarian dramatic soprano, Ljuba Welitsch. Some of my older readers will realize that I am talking about that legendary evening of February 4, 1949, at the old Met, when the season's opening performance of Strauss's *Salomé* took place.

For me, as a young composer and an ardent admirer of Strauss's music, getting to actually play *Salomé* was an extraordinary experience, heightened by my deep love and intimate knowledge of the music for almost a decade. I knew practically every note of that score, not just the horn parts but the whole score from top to bottom, from the first C-sharp minor clarinet run to the final spastic C-minor outbursts[2] signifying the deathblows with which Herod has Salomé executed.

My life with Strauss's *Salomé* began around age twelve, when I came upon my father's piano score of the opera and started, stumblingly, to work my way though the whole score over a period of weeks, savoring every delicious, dramatic, exciting moment in that work. It was an incredible experience, way beyond the kind that you might have in a music history or analysis class, where the time spent on *Salomé*, if at all, might be two hours and one listening assignment. On my own schedule I could linger on any passage for minutes, for hours, again and again. There is a bitonal chord combining F# major and an A-major dominant seventh near the very end of the opera that I fell in love with at age twelve, and that I must have played on the piano hundreds of times.

The next revelatory experience with *Salomé* occurred a few months later, when I found a recording in my father's library of the final scene of *Salomé*, sung magnificently by the great Australian soprano Marjorie Lawrence, and valiantly accompanied by the Pasdeloup Orchestra of Paris, with Piero Coppola conducting. Lawrence's realization of that staggeringly demanding music—arguably the most perfect twenty minutes of music Strauss ever wrote—is also to my mind the most moving, dramatic, and beautiful rendition on records, sung in the most exquisite French. When Lawrence sings "J'ai baisé ta bouche; elle avait un âcre saveur (I have kissed thy mouth; it had a bitter taste)," it is a moment in the history of singing one can never forget. I must have played those four RCA Red Seal 78 shellac sides hundreds of times through the years. (Fortunately they were of a very high technical quality and withstood repeated playings astonishingly well.)

When my father saw how many hours I was spending on the *Salomé* music (which was also just about his favorite opera), he began to make time to play through the score with me, he playing the right-hand part, I the left hand. I could not find a full score of the opera; none was purchasable at that time. (Scores were available only on a rental basis to opera houses, along with the orchestral materials.) But a few years later I did find a secondhand copy of a full score of the final scene of *Salomé* at Patelson's.[3] I was ecstatic.

The next stage in my total absorption with Strauss's *Salomé* occurred when, at age fifteen, I had progressed enough on the horn to be able to play and practice the most important, most exposed horn passages in the opera—in all six horn parts. They were in one of my many symphony and opera excerpt books, from which one learned and studied the repertory. So that by the time of my first *Salomé* rehearsal with Reiner in January 1949, I not only knew every note of those horn parts, but also *almost* all the other parts as well, having been able to buy in 1947 the entire opera in full score when Boosey and Hawkes finally made it available for purchase.

Obbligato

It is unlikely that many of my readers, even older readers, will know that Fritz Reiner had a fearsome reputation among musicians as one of the most tyrannical conductors of that entire era, when almost all conductors' podium behavior was in varying degrees authoritarian, autocratic, despotic. The two reigning tyrants were Reiner and Toscanini, whose behavior, especially Toscanini's, was shamelessly imitated by most of the other famous conductors of the time, such as Stokowski, Szell, Leinsdorf, Dorati, Rodzinski, Cleva, and even (although in a more subtle, milder form, but just as dangerous) Walter and Böhm. Dangerous, because in those days it was not just that a conductor could be nasty or irascible, have countless temper tantrums, humiliate you in front of the whole orchestra; a conductor also had the power to hire and fire you. In those days musicians' unions were notoriously weak, corrupt, or self-serving, that is, before the creation of orchestra committees. Conductors had your life, your career, in their hands. For all the respect one had for Toscanini and Reiner, one lived every day—rehearsal after rehearsal, concert after concert—in fear that today or tomorrow or some day they would single you out for some perceived (or real) musical misdemeanor, and would berate and humiliate you publicly. That was bad enough; if they really disliked you or were clearly unhappy with your work, they had it in their power to have you dismissed—instantly.

The respect for Toscanini and Reiner was real, because in no way could you ignore or refute the fact that they were *remarkable* musicians, uniquely gifted, near-genius in their knowledge of music and their command of their craft. The fear and, in many instances, the hatred of them as human beings was just as real, since you heard about their tyrannical behavior and terrorization of orchestra musicians already in your student days. On the one hand, your respect for them and their relentless pursuit of what seemed to many musicians to be a virtually unrealizable demand for perfection made you play your very best. On the other hand, your fear of them often made you so nervous that you could hardly play; your bow would shake, your breathing was uncontrollable, your lips quivered, and your confidence was shaken.

In the case of Toscanini and Reiner, there was a significant difference in the character and nature of their podium behavior. I worked with both of them a great deal over the years, and realized that Toscanini, the quintessential Italian with the commensurate explosive temperament, was not a mean, nasty man, not even particularly arrogant. Off the podium Toscanini was, so one heard continually, a typically kind, proud family man, quite normal in his behavior and relations with those around him. But on the podium, driven by his obsession with perfection, he simply could not control himself. How often I witnessed his impulsive explosions in rehearsals—screaming in withering scatological Italian—when the playing he was berating had, in fact, been perfectly fine, or when the object of his wrath had only committed some obviously inadvertent and minor error. We all learned that Toscanini's temper tantrums would pass quickly, like a brief summer storm, and that he had meant nothing personal with his outbursts.

Reiner's terrorization of musicians, on the other hand, was of a quite different nature, and in its way much more dangerous. He clearly had a sadistic streak in him, and truly enjoyed making musicians uncomfortable, making them squirm, humiliating them. He was the type, so brilliantly analyzed and described by Krafft-Ebing[4] in his books on various forms of psychopathy, that inflicted his particular sadistic gratifications in a coolly clinical, perfectly controlled manner, a type we have all seen many times in films caricaturing Prussian or Nazi officers and the like. Reiner never exploded, like Toscanini; his criticisms were couched in cutting sarcasm, in a devilish desire to make you feel inferior. When Toscanini exploded, he was *very* unhappy, but with Reiner I clearly sensed that he was deriving a certain emotional and intellectual pleasure from torturing his victims. Another difference, as far as I could tell, was that Toscanini never held grudges, and he never relentlessly hounded a particular player. Indeed, usually he almost immediately forgot whom he had just cursed out in Italian. Reiner, on the other hand, would not only deliver his stinging sarcasms in utter calculated calm, but would also pursue his victim until the person broke, it being symptomatic of this type of verbal sadist that he can easily sense a weakling who is unable to stand up to the abuse; this type of sadist hunts down his prey until the kill has been accomplished.

Yes, it could be rough working for Reiner, unless you found some way to stand up to him—successfully. It is in the nature of these types of intellectual sadists, usually highly intelligent and exceptionally talented—attributes that certainly apply to Reiner—that they back off when they see that they have been effectively challenged, and that their intended victim has not been cowed into submission. The game consists of meeting the tormentor's attacks with an equivalently strong and intelligently confident response. But you had better be unerring in your counterattack, and know what you're doing. I found that out when Reiner started to work on me a few years later. I managed to survive Reiner's assaults successfully by standing up to him each time, face to face—to the point where I eventually became one of his favorite players and he never bothered me again.

You could ignore Toscanini's raging and ranting because, as I say, it was never meant as a personal attack. Because his tirades went on for minutes at a time, there was no way you could interrupt him to respond. You could maybe dismiss his ravings as those of a madman, but you couldn't do that with Reiner. He was too calculating and controlled; it was almost as if he waited for your response, baiting you, daring you to respond. It was his clinical way of testing your mettle, your temperament—and your intelligence.

*   *   *   *   *

Getting back to the Met's 1949 *Salomé*, already in the very first orchestra-only "reading" rehearsal, you could feel the bristling, electric excitement engendered by Reiner's mere presence, as he sat there Buddha-like—he was quite portly in those years—sour-pussed and glowering and immobile. It was as if the entire orchestra had been suddenly charged with an electric current that produced instant alertness and solicitude—as well as a large dose of self-preservation. I don't think there was anyone in the orchestra who hadn't diligently woodshedded his part. I must say that, to the orchestra's collective surprise, during those particular *Salomé* rehearsals we saw rather little of Reiner's anticipated nastiness. He was remarkably patient and generally helpful, instructive rather than destructive. As Reiner sat there, almost motionless with his miniscule beat (but oh, so precise, so clear), impassively peering through his trifocals, calmly surveying the orchestra like some omnipotent potentate, the sounds that came out of the orchestra were clean and balanced, as if purified. It was an amazing transformation.[5] I could tell right away that Reiner would be able to chase away the Eddie Johnson doldrums.[6] What impressed, in fact amazed me the most, is how Reiner with his tiny beat (we called it the "postage-stamp" beat), got the orchestra to play with a very wide dynamic range. He did not really conduct the dynamics. And yet we supplied them, we played them. I don't know any other conductor-orchestra relationship in which that occurred so automatically (except again with Stokowski). Something in Reiner's demeanor made us do it, out of that combination of fear and respect. We played our hearts out for him, secure in the knowledge that with his impeccable beat and prodigious knowledge of the score—not just the obvious leading voices or main thematic ideas, but all the rich details and inner workings of the score—we were in totally reliable hands, and, in a way, could do no wrong.

Things got even more exciting in the rehearsals with the full cast of singers. I'll never forget my first glance of Ljuba Welitsch, her flaming red hair framing a beautiful face and topping a lush, sensuous, curvaceous body balanced on remarkably slim, tapered legs. She was youthful and seductive, and amazingly lithe on her feet, surprisingly so in the famous *Dance of the Seven Veils*. Although history tells us that the real Salomé was seventeen years young and slim, I knew of no Strauss Salomé that was young and slim (except perhaps, later, the great Felicia Weathers in Germany). It takes a hefty dramatic soprano to sing Strauss's incredibly demanding part, but Welitsch, then thirty-seven, certainly created the illusion of a young, flirty, temperamental spoiled brat. More important, Welitsch owned that part vocally. She had the range, the subtly erotic timbre and feeling, as well as the clarity of voice, and—so crucial—the completely natural vocal projection that carried the voice easily over Strauss's huge orchestra. And she had the innate talent to sing even Strauss's difficult music with a well-sustained bel canto line.

Welitsch seemed perfectly cast in another very specific way, related to Hofmannsthal's highly fanciful, chimerical libretto, which I knew pretty much by heart, having read through it many times. In the opera's first scene, Narraboth, a young captain of the guards in Herod's palace, in love with Salomé, rhapsodizes about her; she is "a rose, reflected in a silver mirror," or "like a silver flower in the moonlight." Amazingly, Welitsch, floating onto the stage in her gauzelike, gossamer, silver-white peignoir, had this amazing alabaster, almost translucent skin, as her fairly well-exposed body clearly showed. From my vantage point near the outer edge of the orchestra pit, I could easily see the entire stage, and I'll never forget how Welitsch delivered certain moments in Hoffmansthal's text. When Salomé tries to seduce Jochanaan (John the Baptist) with alluring beseechings such as, "your body is as white as the snow of Judaea's mountains" (she glorifies his hair and mouth next), seducements which he vehemently rejects, she excoriates him with a volley of scathing denunciations such as, "your body is gruesome (Dein Leib ist grauenvoll)," and, "it is like a tinctured wall, through which snakes have crawled, and where scorpions have their nests (Es ist wie eine getünchte Wand, wo Nattern gekrochen sind, wo Skorpione ihr Nest gebaut)." The way Welitsch spat out those nasty words in her slight Bulgarian-tinctured German has influenced every *Salomé* since then.

Equally unforgettable was that remarkable passage in the final scene, when Salomé, sensing her imminent doom, laments that "the mystery of love is greater than the mystery of death (Das Geheimnis der Liebe ist grösser als das Geheimnis des Todes)." The phrase ends with a low B flat and G flat, low notes that 95 percent of all sopranos don't possess—and dread, usually muttering them pitchlessly, voicelessly. But Welitsch sang those notes in pitch, with a ghostly, hollow, wan sound that caused your skin to crawl. Although there have been a few Salomés from time to time who learned how to soar seemingly effortlessly over Strauss's mighty orchestra and complex orchestration, none, I believe, has been able to surpass Ljuba Welitsch in that regard—with the possible exception of Felicia Weathers and Marjorie Lawrence.

I have mentioned that Reiner hardly ever moved when he conducted. This was not just some meretricious matter of style or podium manner; it was, for Reiner, a matter of conductorial discipline and control. His ironclad conducting maxim and the absolute credo by which he taught conducting at the Curtis Institute in Philadelphia (where one of his students was Leonard Bernstein),[7] was based on the following postulate: the best conducting technique is that which achieves the maximum result with the minimum physical effort. And Reiner certainly practiced what he preached. When he conducted standing in front of an orchestra, he was virtually immobile.[8] But he was even more stationary when he conducted operas, where he sat down—an old tradition in opera houses.[9] But what really fascinated (and confounded) me over the four years that I worked with Reiner at the Met was that, intrinsic to his economical baton technique (of minimal manual movement, albeit with a rather large baton), the *size* of his beat, even its character, hardly ever changed. And yet we played with the entire dynamic range, from mysterious whisper-soft *pianissimos* to the most heroic *fortissimos*. How and why we did that with Reiner I can't really figure out, when with almost every other good conductor the size and character of the beat visually showed the given dynamic indications. My own baton technique, which I gleaned from some of the finest conductors of that era, is based on the principle that a conductor's beat should gesturally reflect and represent the constantly variable expression and character of the music. Reiner felt that such baton-technical, physical expression was superfluous, and that it was up to *us musicians* to supply the appropriate sound, dynamic, and character. He also gave very few cues. That was the extent of his contribution; the rest was up to us. Although he seemed to divide his attention between the score and the stage and the singers, you somehow felt that his eyes were on you all the time—and not just you but on everybody in the orchestra.

In the end, whatever that mesmerizing power Reiner exercised over an orchestra worked, I know that I—and most of my colleagues felt the same way—never played better than when I played for Reiner.

As glorious and emotionally charged as that hour and a half of near-perfect music making was, there was one moment in that 1949 *Salomé* performance where the orchestra almost fell in love with the world's most hated conductor. True to form, Reiner sat through the hour-long main part of the opera, virtually immobile, calmly in sovereign control of things on stage as well as in the pit. His discreet beat was barely visible; only his head moved sometimes slowly from left to right, in the direction of one orchestra section or another, his eyes coolly observing the entire scene. But then, suddenly, in the seconds just before the final scene, as Jochanaan's severed head rises out of the cistern prison on a silver platter, to the accompaniment of an ominous tension-building tremolo in the high violins and violas, Reiner—all five-foot-six of him—rose from the podium like some giant, while his short arms unleashed a tremendous orchestral outcry, in that amazing all-embracing, sweeping upbeat gesture that precipitates the final scene. I do not exaggerate when I say that I felt I was swept along in some incredible emotional paroxysm. When moments later Welitsch came soaring in on her high G-sharp, "ah, your mouth, now I will kiss it," my hair stood on end, and my skin started crawling. For a few seconds I seemed to be caught in some emotional swirling vortex, and I wondered how I could keep on playing.

Perhaps some medical genius or behavioral scientist can explain categorically what happened there, in that moment. Obviously, there were some incredible chemical reactions or adrenaline charges at work. Reiner, the generally impassive, outwardly unexcitable "Mr. Imperturbable" had been deeply inspired and smitten—as he admitted to us some days later—by Welitsch's singing and the dramatic ferocity with which she conveyed Salomé's perverse desires. But she too had been inspired by the extraordinary passion of that performance, and, probably, by the whole hullabaloo and excitement with which she had been greeted by the New York press and musical circles. Reiner and Welitsch had turned each other on in some magical way.

There were many exciting evenings to come in my years at the Met, especially in the Bing era, but none quite as overwhelming as that first *Salomé* performance. Ironically, it came in Eddie Johnson's last two lame-duck seasons.

With *Salomé* thus restored to its pride of place in the great standard opera repertory,[10] my hopes were raised that maybe this artistic success could engender a turnaround in the Met's overall artistic direction and standards. The *Salomé* performance was roundly praised for fine ensemble work and for its well-balanced cast. Perhaps Eddie Johnson would now try harder to assemble casts of higher and more uniform quality. But that hardly ever happened, except by some fortuitous coincidence, as in the case of Montemezzi's *L'Amore dei tre re*. The relatively rare performances of this very demanding work more or less relegated the choice of cast to the few Montemezzi specialists in the world, in our case Virgilio Lazzari and a cast otherwise of Americans (Dorothy Kirsten, Charlie Kullman, Robert Weede), who happened to have performed this opera already several times, in Cincinnati and Chicago. The five performances we gave of *L'Amore dei tre re* that season were (along with *Salomé* and *Peter Grimes*) among the very best of the entire year, largely due to Lazzari's dominating presence and the great conducting of Giuseppe Antonicelli.

Alas, my hopes and those of many of my colleagues were not fulfilled, except now and then in a few isolated performances and in the work of some excellent newcomers such as Frank Guarrera, Jacques Jansen (a wonderful Pelléas), and, of course, Welitsch, who among her other roles that season brought true Verdian distinction and grandeur to our *Aida* performances. And although there were still stalwarts like Melchior and Traubel, di Stefano, Thorborg, Albanese, Bampton, Baccaloni, Sayao, and a few others, there were too many poor, indiscriminate casting choices, as well as conductor assignments. For management to assign Emil Cooper to premiere *Peter Grimes*, or to give someone like Osie Hawkins, with his big, oafish, uncultivated voice and stiff amateurish acting, the role of Gunther in *Götterdämmerung*, was the height of incompetence. Many a time I wrote in my diary: "Poor performance tonight. It's no fun to have to play this way."

Something rather unusual happened to me around this time. At this stage in my life I was not at all interested in orchestra and union politics; I was much too busy with my music and my various other artistic pursuits to think that I should waste my time on such mundane matters. I was pretty cynical about the very thought of it, although the orchestra strike the year before had awakened in me some vague questions as to why there should be such a basically adversarial relationship between management and orchestra.[11] In any case, I was doing so many things gratis—arranging, playing, editing, copying music, thousands of hours of work—that money or financial compensation rarely entered my mind. It certainly wasn't a major issue with me.

But suddenly, during the elections for two newly formed (poststrike) committees, one the overall orchestra committee, the other the five-person review committee, whose function was to review the management's contract terminations, that is, firings, I found myself nominated to both committees without ever having submitted my name. Quite a surprise! In due course I was elected to both committees, placing fifth highest with sixty-three votes in the orchestra committee. On the review committee, largely because of my opposition to some of the management's decisions, I was able to save Coscia's and Rattner's jobs. I was incensed that Silvio was on the pink slip list; he was too good as a totally reliable player to justify termination. I was also saddened to find Adolf Schulze (my teacher's brother) on the list. But I didn't oppose his termination, since he had previously told me that at sixty-eight he really wanted to retire. He had been playing in orchestras for fifty-two years, four in his native Germany, forty-eight in America. He was not only a thirty-eight-year veteran of the New York Philharmonic (having also once played in the Metropolitan Opera orchestra for six years in the 1910s), but also one of the best second horns I ever worked with. I also didn't oppose Joe Marx's termination. For all my admiration of his many virtues and talents, I didn't see how I could defend his playing at the Met—stylistically he was a square peg in a round hole.

In the ensuing years, especially after I became a full-fledged principal horn, I served often on the Orchestra Committee and did some royal battling with Rudolf Bing and Erich Leinsdorf, both of whom in later years confided to me that, though they often didn't agree with my positions, they respected my balanced, no-nonsense argumentations.

As for the 1949 spring tour, it was for me, the inveterate traveler, a wonderful change of scenery, but also a welcome break in the daily routine: no rehearsals for two months, leaving me lots of free time to go sightseeing, or to work on my compositions and arrangements, which I was increasingly being asked to make, including for various singers at the Met. The tour also offered me time to do lots of reading, particularly in my swelling collection of literary, political, and music journals. Of the books I read I remember most vividly Thomas Mann's *Doctor Faustus*, which I read in the original German. I found some of Mann's writing on musical matters a bit labored—not how a real musician would write about such things. But nonetheless it was engrossing reading for me, especially in the context of the controversy that erupted around the book when, early in January 1949, Schönberg attacked Mann in the *Saturday Review of Literature* for inappropriately appropriating his twelve-tone system, without mentioning or crediting him, ascribing it instead to a fictional composer named Adrian Leverkühn. It was silly and childish of Schönberg to try to start a feud with Mann, one of Germany's great twentieth-century literary figures. But one can perhaps understand how, out of his by then well-developed persecution complex, nurtured by decades of rejection, neglect, and miscomprehension, Schönberg felt slighted and insulted. Happily, it never developed into a long-standing feud (except perhaps among some of the sycophants surrounding both men), primarily because Mann wrote Schönberg a gracious and implicitly apologetic letter, even though Mann had really no reason to apologize. Also, Mann, out of respect for Schönberg and eager to assuage the composer's hypersensitive feelings, immediately had a statement inserted in his book that gave due credit to Schönberg for the creation of his "method of composing with twelve tones." That statement did not, however, respond explicitly to the question that Schönberg had petulantly and, I think, childishly raised in his public attack on Mann, as to who was whose contemporary.

Speaking of Schönberg reminds me that around this same time (1948) I read Dika Newlin's superb *Bruckner, Mahler, Schönberg*, an important and timely book about the modern central European (read German-Austrian) musical tradition, especially timely in the 1940s, when both Bruckner's and Mahler's symphonies were roundly ignored or rejected. For most readers this may be hard to believe now, half a century later, when you can hardly go to a symphony concert or turn on a classical radio station *without* encountering works by both rejectees, especially Mahler.

Schönberg's music (except for the early *Verklärte Nacht*) was, of course, even less performed, and therefore totally unknown in America. Newlin's book was bound to have little impact, except with a small cadre of music lovers who were aware of the historical importance of the so-called Second Viennese School (Schönberg, Berg, and Webern). But it was, along with René Leibowitz's *Schönberg et son école* (1946), another early pioneering effort to try to rectify this severely imbalanced situation, and it was certainly encouraging, invigorating reading for me. Not that this in any way affected my profound admiration for Stravinsky's music. I had long ago decided that both Schönberg and Stravinsky were equally great masters; they were the Brahms and Wagner of their time, twin giants of early twentieth-century music. I had much to learn from both.

There was one bit of information in Newlin's book that really floored me, namely, that in his younger years, even before his First Symphony, Mahler had composed a work called *Das klagende Lied*. One may well ask how could I not have known that? Primarily because *Das klagende Lied* did not exist on records,[12] and had never been performed in America. Add to that, there were at the time that I acquired Newlin's book (1948) no biographies of Mahler in English, not until 1953, when a biography by the Dutch writer H. Rutters, published in 1919 in Holland, was translated into English.

My discovery of *Das klagende Lied's* existence released a flood of memories of how I had been haunted for months in my childhood in Germany by that melancholy tale. Of all the stories and fairy tales I read in those years *Das klagende Lied* affected me more profoundly than anything else; somehow that woeful tale of murder and retribution touched me very deeply. I was much affected by learning that my much-admired Mahler had also been fascinated by this melancholy tale, to the extent of composing a work based on it. I was tempted to do the same thing, and, in fact, started work on a text outline, a kind of libretto. But once again my initial enthusiasm for the project waned, in part because I knew I had to finish work on my newest composition, *Meditation* (*Symphonic Study*), which I finally completed around Christmastime; Roland Johnson had scheduled the premiere in Cincinnati in the spring of 1949.

Another aborted composition project that I regret not having completed was my dream of setting some of the poetry of San Juan de la Cruz to music. I had come across his poems and a series of articles about him in *Horizon*, one of my favorite literary magazines. In conjunction with the de la Cruz project I also reread the Old Testament's *Song of Songs*, marveling at its rich, imaginatively sensuous language, so direct and so strong. I did some sketching in my composing notebook, including an expansive melody and theme for horn, courageously starting softly on a high F (written C), then descending and ultimately covering a range of over three octaves, down to a low E ♭. But once again I was

diverted by other equally interesting creative distractions.

One work that I did finish was an arrangement for four basses of Gershwin's *The Man I Love*. I intended it mainly for Ray Brown, whom I had already admired for many years as the rightful heir to Jimmy Blanton's legacy, and whom I had recently met through John Lewis. I just loved Ray's big, beautiful tone, and his remarkable ability to produce long resonant pizzicato notes, sometimes four slow beats long ♩, almost unheard of in those early days

before the extensive use of amplifiers. With classical bassists, by contrast, you got a short, dry-sounding, thumpy, eighth-note pluck. I also had Percy Heath and George Duvivier in mind for my quartet, both of whom I had also met through John Lewis. I knew Duvivier's playing for some time, having heard him as early as 1946 when he was the bassist in Sy Oliver's short-lived band. I also thought of Nelson Boyd, one of Gillespie's and Tadd Dameron's favorite bassists, whose work I heard a lot at the Royal Roost, and appreciated, particularly his ability to negotiate interesting, imaginative walking bass lines in the new updated harmonic bop language.

Although I finished *The Man I Love* arrangement—all in pizzicato, sounding like a gigantic, oversized guitar—and sketched out a few other pieces (*How High The Moon* and *I Can't Get Started*), it was never performed, and I think it is now lost. I could never get my four idolized bass players together in the same place at the same time—it turned out to be just another one of the many things I undertook that ended up being a valuable explorative experience.

It was also around this time that I met Ross Russell (of Dial Records fame),[13] again through John Lewis. Both Ross and John had come to one of the Met's *Tristan* performances, and after the opera Ross invited us all up to the legendary Minton's in Harlem. I hadn't ever been there, but I knew, of course, that this was bound to be a wonderful musical treat, no matter who would be playing. I insisted that we pick up Margie at Beulah's apartment, and then we headed for Harlem. As we approached the stage, I could hardly believe my ears; I thought I heard a horn. Well, it *was* a horn, and it turned out to be—of all people—Julius Watkins playing. Could Ross Russell have picked a better night for me to be taken to Minton's, and to hear the finest jazz hornist of that time? I don't think so.

In 1949 I had not heard of Julius Watkins. He had not yet recorded and was out on the road in the Midwest, not in New York. Moreover, he was playing mostly trumpet, not horn. None of my New York horn colleagues had heard of him either. Here was an African-American horn player improvising fluently in the new bop style. As I listened to him that night at Minton's I was amazed at the agility and absolute note security with which this young man played; his technique seemed impeccable and effortless.[14] I kept thinking, gee, this guy doesn't seem to know that the horn is a difficult instrument. As I got to know Julius, when we worked together in ensuing years (most notably on the Miles Davis and Gil Evans *Porgy and Bess* recording) and when he studied with me at the Manhattan School of Music in the early 1950s,[15] I began to understand why he could play with such ease and fearlessness. He simply played the instrument as if it were a trumpet;[16] it wasn't a big deal for him. He didn't know—or care—what the range and limitations of the horn were supposed to be. Julius had a tremendous high register, and whatever he heard in his inner ear he could instantly produce on the instrument.

Julius was one of the nicest, friendliest, most unpretentious persons I ever met. He always wore a beautiful, gentle smile, and seemed to be perennially happy, content with life. This was all the more remarkable since he lived with a lifelong drug addiction, as a result of which he always had money troubles. His health began to deteriorate seriously, especially affecting his teeth and gums, which is disastrous for a brass player. Julius was constantly broke; half the time he came for lessons with me he didn't have his horn because it was in the hockshop. Sometimes he'd come in with some dirty, beat-up instrument; who knows where he got it. Often I just had him play on my horn.

I felt so bad for him. But given his lifestyle, I really didn't know how to help him. I felt even worse when I heard that he had died—at age fifty-six. We had, sadly, lost touch when I moved to Boston in the late sixties.[17]

Ross Russell had come to New York from California on that 1949 visit not only to hear *Tristan* at the Met but also to attend two concerts by the Kolisch Quartet, which played Schönberg, Berg, and Webern. Ross was one of those very rare individuals who, although primarily involved with jazz and having no actual background or training in twentieth-century contemporary music, nonetheless loved and admired it, instinctively. It was as if he had some sixth sense that let his mind and ear automatically appreciate even the most complex, challenging, atonal music.

After the two Kolisch concerts, Ross decided to branch out with his Dial label to record some of the most advanced new music, rejected by almost all other record companies at the time. I became Ross's private adviser in that literature, steering him to some of the best performers of that repertory. Eventually I also had the great privilege of making the first recording (in 1951) of Schönberg's Op. 26 Woodwind Quintet for Ross's Dial Records with my group from the Met.

Above all, 1949 was the year in which a deep abiding friendship and long-standing collaborative working relationship developed between John Lewis and me, which had a profound impact on both of our lives and careers. Together we made very important musical history. I knew at our first meeting, that snow-bound December night in 1948, that ours would be a very special reciprocal affinity. We seemed to be on exactly the same intellectual and musical wavelengths. We were constantly learning from each other, he about various aspects of classical music, I about aspects of jazz that were still remote to me. I felt that I had known John all my life, that we were true soul mates. Of the many black musicians I had gotten to know in the previous five or six years, in Cincinnati, New York, or on the road, I had not yet met anyone who was so knowledgeable in classical music as John was. I was surprised to find out that he had enrolled at the Manhattan School of Music, and was now taking courses in fugue and counterpoint, studying the music of Bach and the early classical styles and forms of Mozart and Haydn. He said he was, in turn, amazed to discover how involved I was with jazz, especially with the music of Ellington and Basie, and the new bop styles of Parker, Gillespie, Monk, and Gil Evans. He was intrigued that I was already writing music in the advanced languages of Schönberg and Stravinsky.

In the ensuing months, in what must have been literally dozens of phone calls, usually about two hours long—often to the dismay of my dear wife—we embarked on a great voyage of mutual exchanges and discoveries. Once we got on the phone, it seemed impossible to tear ourselves away. It was so exciting to learn from each other, to constantly have new revelations. We found that we had many things in common, including a virtually identical work ethic based on discipline and an unflinching commitment to hard work, and an unquenchable thirst for greater knowledge.

We also shared a certain unyielding stubbornness. Half jokingly I often called it my German stubbornness—probably true. John didn't consider it stubbornness in his case, as much as a kind of rock-solid, disciplined, reasoned way of thinking. And indeed, while John was very shy, very quiet and gentle—and impeccably respectful—it was often impossible to argue with him, to convince him of something other than what he already believed—even by a fairly persuasive persuader like me. There would come a moment in our discussions where his resistance to persuasion would translate into a sudden deprecating wave of the hand and an impatient frown, which signaled that no further discussion was necessary or possible. With all his shyness and gentleness, John could also be quite implacable.

One important way in which we exchanged information and musical experiences was by checking out each other's record collections, and also by playing through my rather extensive collection of four hand piano arrangements. That was tremendous fun and a great learning experience. John was not the most fluent reader, but he was obviously a better pianist than me. I could read very fluently, even if digitally constricted and stumbling. We sometimes staggered along at a slower tempo than suggested by the composer, one that we could manage, even lingering many times on some gorgeous eleventh-chord harmony or some incredible modulation, as in Stravinsky's *Rite of Spring* or Respighi's *Pines of Rome*.

It was very exciting for both of us to introduce our respective colleagues and friends to each other. That's how I first met many of the most important jazz musicians of the time, who knew John and respected him highly. These included his seniors, Coleman Hawkins, Earl Hines, Lester Young; his contemporaries, Miles Davis, Milt Jackson, Lee Konitz, Oscar Peterson, and so many others. I must say that, if you were introduced to someone by John Lewis, along with a complimentary comment or two, you were "in"; you automatically became a member of the jazz inner circle. John's word was trusted implicitly, his opinion unquestioningly respected. (The same was, of course, true of Dizzy or Bird, or many other major figures of the jazz fraternity.)

For my part, I introduced John to many of my instrumentalist colleagues at the Met and the New York Philharmonic, many of whom in the coming years were to participate importantly in recordings and performances of John Lewis's music. I also introduced him to some of my conductor friends—Dimitri Mitropoulos, Léon Barzin, Walter Hendl, Paul Wolfe, David Broekman, and to close friends like Steuermann and Kolisch.

John took me several times to rehearsals that he participated in, to which I would other-wise have had no entree, or wouldn't even have known about. One such occasion involved a long rehearsal with Dizzy Gillespie's orchestra in which they were trying out some new compositions and arrangements, including one by John. That's not only where I met Dizzy but also J. J. Johnson, John Coltrane (for a short time in Dizzy's band), and Al McKibbon. The rehearsal took place in Harlem, in a studio at 131st Street and Lenox Avenue, a part of town I rarely visited. I remember the band rehearsing Lester Young's *Jumpin' With Symphony Sid* (in Gil Fuller's arrangement), but I never heard John's piece, because unfortunately the parts had not yet been copied, as John had been promised. He was quite annoyed, although he tried not to show it, permitting himself only a slight frown. I don't remember what else was being rehearsed, but I do recall how slow and ineffective the rehearsing was. As I had witnessed that time with the Boyd Raeburn band (and on many other occasions at Nola studios), most arrangers—Gil Fuller too—did not really know how to rehearse, not with the kind of efficiency and clarity with which classical conductors generally rehearsed. Of course, jazz arrangers weren't trained conductors; they were time beaters at best, and pretty elemen-tary ones at that. But what surprised me most was that arrangers (and composers) in jazz rarely made any precise, specific, really instructive comments or corrections. Jazz musicians in those days didn't read so fluently, and the main method of rehearsing consisted of con-stant, often rather boring and time-consuming repetition, interspersed with interminable discussions, trying to figure out how to get some particular phrase rhythmically together or get some ensemble passage in tune.

John and I left the rehearsal after a few hours, rather frustrated. We escaped to my house, where we treated ourselves to a marvelous—*and beautifully rehearsed*—Busch Quartet record-ing of Beethoven's Op. 135 and the "Moonlight" Sonata, played by Wilhelm Backhaus—accompanied by a few snifters of Courvoisier.

I was disappointed that I couldn't attend the premiere of my *Meditation* with Roland John-son's orchestra at the Cincinnati College of Music. Although in all three previous Met spring tours I had been able to sneak off to Cincinnati for a couple of days, this time I couldn't get away because the *Meditation* date conflicted directly with opera performances to which I was committed, and from which I could not free myself. But Roland had the performance recorded on a 78 disc, which I was able to hear when I got back to New York in late May. The perfor-mance was very good, considering that Roland was working with a student orchestra with some weaknesses in certain sections. I knew that he would be very exacting in his rehearsing and respectful of my very detailed notation, and that the performance would accurately reflect what I had composed.

I have always been objective and self-critical of my work—I still am—and I recall that I wasn't entirely happy with the overall continuity of the piece. I had conceived it in the form of a palindrome, where the ending of the piece is a literal retrograde of the opening, an idea I had borrowed from several of Alban Berg's compositions. I thought this aspect of the piece worked beautifully. So did the slightly unusual orchestration (with its six horns, six flutes, five oboes, four trombones, etc.). The harmonic language is very Bergian—he had such a strong influence on me—especially in the several stretches of rich polytonal six- or five-part chords. But the Allegro middle section was too short, too undeveloped, and therefore it seemed like a gratuitous interruption of the overall Adagio, rather than a full-fledged B episode, as in a basic ABA form. I realized later that the lopsided form was due to the fact that the Allegro section had been interpolated a year *after* the original single-section Adagio had been composed. The piece then lay around for months, half forgotten, until Roland asked me how it was coming along. When I went back to work on it, I must have thought that it needed a lift in the middle, in contrast to the undeviating Adagio. In my haste I shortchanged the Allegro section; it is only eighteen measures long, lasting some forty seconds, compared to the surrounding Adagio, *one hundred* measures long, with a duration of about eight and a half minutes.

In the end it was a good learning experience. It made me realize that with all of my various talents in orchestration, in using the orchestra imaginatively, idiomatically, and in the use of a quite attractive and compelling harmonic language, I was still weak in managing larger forms. I realized that this was an aspect of composing that, with virtually no formal education or training, I had never seriously explored. It was one of those learning experiences that sent me back to Beethoven and Brahms, among others, to see how they handled form so perfectly, with such superb inner logic and infallible pacing.

For a while I toyed with the idea of revising *Meditation*, of expanding that middle section. But in the end I made a decision in principle not to engage in revising, a rule that I have respected to this day. Rather than correcting mistakes by revising, especially mistakes of form and continuity, it is better to learn from these mistakes and avoid making them again. Under a revisionist philosophy one might always—I mean *always*—find errors of judgment, something to correct even in some earlier work.[18] I think constant revising can be a slippery slope, since, as you develop and mature, you will always discover lapses in your earlier works or even in more recent ones. That is inherent in what we call progress. Where and when would you stop revising and correcting? It could turn into an endless process, which in its extreme form might lead to interminable revising, every few years updating the same piece, striving for some probably never attainable perfection, and probably never getting around to writing a new work.

Sticking to my rule, when I recorded *Meditation* some fifty years later, in the 1990s, I left it as conceived in 1948/1949, even though I had thought of any number of ways of improving the piece, including removing the B section altogether, restoring the work to its original single-form Adagio. But I preferred to present the piece as an early work, and as a work in the context of a longer process.

The 1948–49 Met season, my fourth year with the orchestra, had introduced Fritz Reiner and Ljuba Welitsch to American opera audiences, and had produced *the* outstanding highlight of the season. Almost as important to me, albeit in a completely different and saddening way, was the realization that one of my great operatic heroes was in his farewell years, not only at the Met, his primary home for well over twenty years, but also in the opera world in general. I am speaking of Lauritz Melchior,[19] who had become one of my most admired vocalists in my teen years when I acquired many of his superb Wagner recordings, especially those from the 1920s and 1930s conducted by Albert Coates and Felix Weingartner. The 1949–50 season turned out to be Melchior's last; he sang only four *Tristans*, two *Walküres*, and two *Lohengrins*. It also meant that his last *Götterdämmerung* had already taken place in late 1948. I mention this because *Götterdämmerung* was to my mind always the musically most challenging of the four *Ring* operas for the tenor.

Obbligato

Melchior's voice was a kind of miracle, a great rarity in the whole history of singing. He was originally a baritone and had begun his career in Copenhagen in 1913. In the early 1920s Melchior started to switch gradually to tenor parts, scoring his first great success in that capacity in 1924 at London's Covent Garden in *Walküre*. (The only possible parallel would be Jean de Rezke, who also began his career, though not particularly successfully, as a baritone; after switching to tenor he became the outstanding interpreter of Wagner's Heldentenor roles.) What is special, perhaps unique, about Melchior's transformation was that it took almost six years to accomplish, a period during which, judiciously pacing his performing schedule, he studied successively with four of the world's major voice teachers of the time (in London, Berlin, and Bayreuth), including Anna von Mildenburg, the preeminent Wagnerian soprano. (Compare that with the often too hasty career advances in more recent times, which have so often led to abbreviated careers.)

Melchior was a large man with a robust, corpulent physique, who had a *huge* lung capacity, enabling him to sing with such clarion power and yet with relative ease. You rarely felt that he was out of breath at the end of a lengthy phrase. But the most miraculous quality of Melchior's voice, besides its sheer quantity and size, was its special sheen, which critics called its golden quality, and which one can hear in all the early recordings, even those of rather primitive technical quality.

Admittedly by the time I came to the Met, Melchior's voice had darkened a little, a natural process, yet it did not lose its inherent brilliance. Remarkably, that golden sheen was blended with a certain weightiness of voice, a kind of vocal gravity, that I would assume was the residual baritone element in his voice. It was this rare vocal mixture that enabled Melchior to color his voice from the most thrilling, shining brilliance to the darkest covered quality, and virtually every shade of timbre in between. Part of that remarkable vocal blend was its focus and projection. I am quite sure I have almost never heard any male voice so concentrated, so perfectly centered, as Melchior's,[20] which gave it its wonderful projection.

Of the many thrills and chills Melchior gave me in those final years of his Met career I single out only one occasion, which is well etched in my memory, and which even got the entire orchestra excited. The occasion was Melchior's very last *Götterdämmerung*, on December 20, 1948. Of the many wonders of that performance—and of that opera—one stands out in particular. It was a tenor high note, a high C. Now, I am not a high-note chaser, as are almost all die-hard opera fans, who come far too often to see whether their favorite soprano or tenor makes that final high note. But the high C in *Götterdämmerung* (in the second scene of act 3) is something special, indeed unique, in Wagner's operas. It is one of those *Hoi-ho* greet-

ings that Wagner sprinkled throughout the *Ring* . There

are thousands of high Cs in Italian and French operas, but relatively few in the German repertory. And there are no other tenor high Cs in Wagner's operas, at least not in his mature post-Rienzi operas. I cannot calculate how many times during the years I heard Melchior nail that high C, head-on—no scooping,[21] no hesitation. That is not only hard, but also very risky. (Melchior did crack it wide open one time years earlier). That particular high C is much more difficult to hit because it is a short eighth-note, rather than a longer note value. We all knew that it was Melchior's last *Götterdämmerung* that night; and at age fifty-eight—late in an opera singer's career—things can happen, especially in one of the most brutally tiring Wagner roles. But once again Melchior rose to the occasion, and produced a glorious, ringing high C that could have stopped traffic out on Broadway. If we could have, we in the orchestra would have shouted our own congratulatory *Hoi-ho* greeting; we were so happy for him. Truth is, we also liked him. He was a regular, unpretentious guy who also had the most wonderful dry Danish sense of humor.

I sorely miss Melchior and his remarkable voice. No tenor since Melchior has ever come close to filling his shoes, and I have often thought, listening to Wagner performances at the Met or Bayreuth, you know, one really shouldn't do mid-to-late Wagner until another Melchior shows up. But then one would miss all that glorious music.

*   *   *   *   *

One of that season's happiest encounters for me—and I think for most of the orchestra—was the arrival of Jonel Perlea, one of the best conductors to grace the Met's podium during my years there. Romanian-born, but trained in Munich and Leipzig, where he studied with Max Reger at the Hochschule (he must have been in the same classes with my father, both being the same age), Perlea had already enjoyed a distinguished conducting career in Europe, including leading the first performances in Romania of *Rosenkavalier*, *Meistersinger*, and *Falstaff*.

At the Met Perlea was given four operas to conduct: *Rigoletto*, *Carmen*, *Traviata*, and for his American debut, *Tristan und Isolde*. In his very first rehearsal we could tell that we were in the hands of a superior musician. (I found out later that he was also a fine composer, more than just a conductor-composer.) He managed to bring to that ecstasy- and hysteria-laden score a wonderful calming restraint. With Fritz Stiedry the more frantic episodes in *Tristan*, especially in the third act, could easily spin out of control. It is incredibly intense music, sometimes more intense than it can readily tolerate. Perlea treated the music with an almost chamber music transparency—lyric, eloquent, even elegant—without diluting the drama and emotional excitement of *Tristan*, or for that matter of *Carmen* or any of the operas Perlea was given.

All this was all the more amazing since Perlea had had a heart attack and a stroke, and as a result was paralyzed on most of his right side; he conducted only with his left hand. This is highly unusual and takes some getting used to—which we did very quickly. We really loved this man. Alas, Perlea was at the Met for only one year. All year long we kept hearing backstage rumors that certain conductors, especially Alberto Erede, also new at the Met in 1949, were agitating with the management to have Perlea retired. If true, it was but another typical example of what is known far and wide in the music world as "opera intrigue." I saw Perlea several times in the 1950s in the hallways at the Manhattan School of Music, where both of us were on the faculty, and I could never resist telling him how much we missed him after he was let go.

Near the end of the 1949 Met tour we began to hear rumors that our orchestra might be hired to play a two-week season—at the Metropolitan Opera House—of the visiting Sadler's Wells Ballet. The rumor turned out to be true, and the two weeks with Sadler's Wells were a wonderful musical and educational experience. It brought back many happy memories of my days with the Ballet Theatre, six years earlier; and now I was fortunate enough to witness with my own eyes the brilliant work of England's premier ballet company, with its outstanding, oh so graceful prima ballerina, Margot Fonteyn. (This was a special bonus for Margie, who was so keenly interested in great ballet. She came to almost every performance, accompanied by Jeannie Clark, my dancer friend from Ballet Theatre.) But for me the two major highlights of the Sadler's Wells visit were the discovery of Prokofiev's extraordinary *Cinderella* music (in its first performance in the United States), and the amazing experience of working with Constant Lambert.

I really looked forward to playing with Lambert, for I admired him greatly as a composer, and for years had heard that he was a marvelous conductor. In England he was generally considered a lightweight composer, I assume owing to his very jazzy 1929 *Rio Grande* Suite and his catchy, devilishly clever ballet *Horoscope*. I thought of him more as a kind of British George Gershwin, a high compliment. And I didn't like it when some of our musicians, realizing that he was a homosexual, kept calling Lambert "Constance"—under their breath, giggling like little children. It was embarrassing.

I was thrilled with his conducting; it was so intelligent and sensitive, although I noticed that sometimes in certain performances his beat, his direction, would be kind of wavering, wobbly. I began to realize that the man was at times not entirely sober. It got worse when, in the middle of the second week, disaster struck. Halfway through Tchaikovsky's *Hamlet* music (which Lambert had turned into a ballet), completely befuddled, he simply broke down in tears and slumped over the podium. We tried to keep playing; Felix Eyle, our concertmaster, beat time with his bow. But it was no use; we barely knew the music (none of us had ever played *Hamlet* before), and we certainly didn't know the dancers' tempos. We never finished the performance. It was a truly tragic occasion; I felt so bad for Lambert. We now all knew that he was a raging alcoholic, and wondered how he had held up so long.

Discovering Prokofiev's *Cinderella* music was a much happier experience. It was completely new to me—the first recording (of only excerpts of that ballet) didn't come out in England until a year after the New York performances. I was so taken with the sheer melodic, harmonic beauty of the music, with Prokofiev's seemingly boundless creative imagination, that I knew I had to somehow get a look at the score. When I found that none was available for purchase, I did the next best thing: over a period of fours days, in every intermission during the six rehearsals we had of *Cinderella*, I copied out, either fully or in a shorthand of mine, a dozen of my favorite excerpts from Lambert's conducting score—which, bless him, he always left on his podium in the pit.

Dick Moore, hating the music, thought I was crazy. (He was playing first horn, while I was on third.) I couldn't understand how one could hate such stunningly attractive, instantly accessible music. But Dick had no use for any new or modern music. Since I was sitting only five feet away from him, it was an incredible annoyance to constantly hear his under-the-breath bitching obscenities.

I was now approaching my fifth year at the Met. Two major events loomed ahead, which made my life there much more agreeable, much more rewarding musically, professionally, and artistically. One such event was my full promotion to co-principal horn. David Rattner was relieved of his position near the end of the 1949–50 season, and I was told sometime on the spring tour that Max Rudolf, Fritz Reiner, and Fritz Stiedry had all recommended that, without need for an audition, I be moved up to first horn—with an appropriate and, I thought, rather generous raise in salary. "Would I please accept the offer?" Would I? Well, of course I would. I was thrilled and gratified that my work as third horn (and first horn in Mozart and Rossini operas) had truly been appreciated. It was nice to know that the conducting staff and the management valued my particular way of playing, which contrasted considerably with Richard Moore's generally more boisterous, extroverted style. I think they recognized that I brought a composer's insights to my playing, an intimate awareness of the music's inner workings, structurally, orchestrationally, conceptually, particularly in regard to ensemble considerations. For me it wasn't just a horn part, which one could use to display one's soloistic and technical prowess. My horn part was just one of some thirty other voices that in toto yielded the complex and constantly variable ensemble relationships in an orchestra. I can truly say that there was no ego involved in my playing—pride yes (when justified), but ego, no. I knew that I and my horn part were just one small cog in a great wheel that required constant flexibility and pliancy in adjusting to the myriad and diverse collective demands of the composition. Fitting in—rather than standing out—gave me the greatest pleasure—and still does to this day, a commitment I ardently pursue as a conductor as well.

The other event that not only affected my life as a musician but also significantly enlivened New York's musical scene, and probably, by extension, the entire opera field in the United States, was the ascendancy of Rudolf Bing to the general manager throne of the Metropolitan Opera Company. I use such language because, in my view and that of most others in the opera world, Bing was an authoritarian aristocrat, virtually a dictator, certainly not a pleasant man to work for and with. He had a rather severe don't-mess-with-me look about him all the time. Indeed, with his balding head, piercing eyes, and hawklike nose, he always reminded me of Max Schreck in *Nosferatu*, Murnau's famous vampire film of 1922. His twenty-two years at the helm of the Met were marked by continual strife, altercations, feuds, and controversy—although they weren't always his fault or his creation. He was roundly disliked by many of his employee subjects, and several rather scandalous affairs occurred on his watch, which were, however, hushed up and very cleverly suppressed, never reaching the outside world or the press. (I could write about them, but out of respect for him as a remarkable impresario I will desist.)

All that said, one has to acknowledge that he was in the end an extraordinarily talented, genial impresario–general manager. He really knew his stuff. Bing was what we call in German a real *Opernhase* (opera hare), richly experienced as managing director (*Intendant* in German) of the Stadttheater in Darmstadt, Germany, the Charlottenburg Opera in Berlin (that city's second opera house), and as artistic director of Glyndebourne in England, literally bringing that institution to international prominence in the 1950s. In 1957 he helped organize and then managed the Edinburgh Festival.

Bing was remarkably knowledgeable in musical matters, especially in his primary function and responsibility of bringing to the house the best and most appropriate singers. He set the highest standards in selecting and hiring the casts himself, a skill that had eluded Edward Johnson in his later years. It is not enough to know that a certain role is for a soprano or baritone, and then hire the most famous soprano or baritone in the business. Every part, every role, has its own characteristic requisites: questions of range, timbre, size, and quality of voice. In the category of soprano alone there are officially three kinds: dramatic, lyric, and coloratura. But the Italians make further distinctions, such as soprano *acuto* (high soprano) and soprano *leggiero* (light soprano), and—I like this one—soprano *sfogato*.[22] Furthermore, the Italian vocal tradition is significantly different from the German, and even from the French and English. In addition, not all composers always conformed in their vocal works to these basic categorizations. The same distinct differentiations exist in the other four vocal types: alto, tenor, baritone, and bass.

So the opera manager must know particular singers' voices really well in order to choose someone with the right quality, timbre, and expressive character—not to mention acting ability and stage presence, another aspect of casting decisions that Bing addressed very seriously and successfully. In these matters he engaged a whole roster of singers in his first year as manager who, by their presence and artistry, raised the overall artistic level of the Met. To name a few: the galvanic mezzo-soprano, Fedora Barbieri; the outstanding (but woefully underappreciated) Lucine Amara, who sang important roles at the Met for another incredible twenty-seven years, still in beautiful voice to the very end; Hans Hotter, in the twilight of his career, but one of the greatest Inquisitors ever in Verdi's *Don Carlos*; Roberta Peters; Mario del Monaco; Victoria de los Angeles; and, above all, Cesare Siepi, one of the *very* greatest vocal artists I had the privilege to work with in my fifteen years at the Met.[23]

Another major reform Bing brought to the old Met was to reach out beyond the well-known cadre of established stage directors to outstanding figures from the worlds of theatre and film, most notably Margaret Webster, Garson Kanin, Tyrone Guthrie, Alfred Lunt, and Cyril Ritchard.

Bing also made me very happy when I read in a *Times* interview that one of his main goals was to revamp the Met's casting system, and turn the Met, like the opera houses he had presided over in Germany and England, into an ensemble house, where the initial cast would be kept together for the entire sequence of performances in a given season.

It didn't take Bing long to also enliven the repertory, which had grown rather stale in the preceding decade. Within a few years he brought back Verdi's great opera, *Don Carlos* (after a nearly thirty-year absence); Mozart's *Così fan tutte* (with a stellar cast of Eleanor Steber, Blanche Thebom, Richard Tucker, Frank Guarrera, and one of my all-time favorites, John Brownlee); also Strauss's *Arabella* (in its U.S. premiere). Add to that the American first performance of Stravinsky's *Rake's Progress* (with Stravinsky in attendance). But perhaps Bing's greatest triumph was scheduling Johaan Strauss's *Die Fledermaus*, which became a *huge* hit, both artistically and financially, spawning in turn a highly successful road company that crisscrossed the country for several years.

The reader will gather from the foregoing that the remaining nine years of my tenure at the Met were very happy ones, musically, artistically, and professionally. That fact, in conjunction with my ever-increasing involvement in the jazz world, where I started to work with such giants in the field as Dizzy Gillespie, J. J. Johnson, Miles Davis, John Lewis, Lee Konitz, etc., and my increasingly expanding and successful career as a promising young composer, made that decade truly metamorphic for me.

Bing's first season was transformative, not only for the Met but also for opera in America in general. It was particularly exciting for me as a keen observer and eager participant in all the great things that were happening at the venerable old company. The first thing I realized as I received my personal principal horn schedule of opera assignments was that I had been given just about every one of the big operas in the repertory; I mean the entire Wagner *Ring Cycle*,[24] Verdi's *Don Carlos* (the great new hit of the season), Wagner's *Flying Dutchman* and *Rosenkavalier*, both with Reiner, and *Fidelio* and *Magic Flute* with Bruno Walter and Fritz Stiedry, respectively. I have often wondered why I was given such an array of great operas, all with some of the most inspired and demanding horn parts in the entire opera literature. Was the conducting staff testing me to see how I would do? Or were they complimenting me? Whichever it was, I was once again in musical heaven.

Don Carlos, neglected for so many years at the Met (and in lots of opera houses around the world), did indeed turn out to be Bing's first great success, largely because of a superb cast of Cesare Siepi, Jussi Björling, Fedora Barbieri, Robert Merrill, and Hans Hotter, as well as the very effective staging by Margaret Webster, and—not to be underestimated—Verdi's inspired music. (Incidentally, *Don Carlos* was a real discovery for the critics, too.) The conductor was Stiedry, whose major prior claim to fame had been that he and Otto Klemperer were the two conductors who, in the early 1930s, initiated a major revival of the late Verdi operas in Germany, including *Don Carlos*. Stiedry told me that he had personally lobbied Bing, an old friend, to schedule *Don Carlos* and to open the season with it. Stiedry did this opera very well, with a deep understanding and love of Verdi's astonishing music, which in my humble opinion, in balance, ranks with the other two late Verdi operas, *Otello* and *Falstaff*, even though in its form and continuity it isn't quite as perfectly put together as those two masterpieces. But to compensate, it has some of the most inspired and heartbreakingly beautiful music Verdi ever wrote.

Of all the wonders of that music and of our performances of it, I will single out only the first two scenes of act 3, incorporating King Philip's great aria "Ella giammai m'amò (She has never loved me)," referring to Elisabeth, his wife and Queen, as well as the scene between Philip and the Grand Inquisitor. "Ella giammai" is possibly Verdi's grandest, most inspired aria conception. It is remarkably expansive in its form and outline, from its plaintive cello and oboe introduction and Philip's gloomy recitative to the aria proper, in two full stanzas, separated by a brief instrumental interlude. It is not just a great aria; it is an acute psychological study, a profound philosophical contemplation of a kind that is relatively rare in opera. King Philip sits alone in his vast study, forlorn in his emotional isolation, meditating on his own mortality and his frustration that even as the most powerful ruler in the world he cannot control all the conflicting forces unleashed by wars, religious persecutions, and political power struggles that fester under his dominion. Worse yet, his own son, Carlos, is his wife's lover, and the Grand Inquisitor is trying to threaten his regnancy.

As moving, as inspiring as the music was for me, it was Cesare Siepi's rendering of it that was so overwhelming. I was almost in a state of shock in our first stage rehearsal, when Siepi uttered Schiller's simple words: "Gia spunta il di (Already day dawns)." That moment and the hundred recurrences of it in ensuing years, when *Don Carlos* stayed uninteruptedly in the Met's repertory, is one of the three or four most indelible impressions on my mind and ears and psyche during my twenty years playing opera. I'll never forget Siepi's magnificent, rich, saturated voice in those four simple words, racked with pain and despair and foreboding.

That Verdi was one of the most genially gifted opera composers is common knowledge. But in *Don Carlos* he even trumped himself by creating in the third act an astonishing twenty-five minute sequence of music and high drama that not only may be in one respect unique in opera history, but which also in its daring exemplifies the highest levels of inspiration and imagination—in short, of musico-dramaturgic creativity. Verdi follows the already high-powered bass aria "Ella giammai," which opens act 3, with an even more powerful dramatic scene, cast—amazingly—as a bass duet. How many opera bass duets can you name? Philip is visited by the Grand Inquisitor, who demands in a stormy altercation that Rodrigo, who with Carlos has been fighting for the freedom of the Flemish people oppressed under the yoke of Spain, be turned over to the Inquisitor and burned at the stake. The music is set in a dark and menacing F minor, its ominous main theme presented not by the violins or cellos but by the basses and the contrabassoon. It is in effect a bass trio, three low-register voices—a first in opera.

Hans Hotter, our Grand Inquisitor, had had a long and distinguished career in Germany, including at Bayreuth,[25] but by 1950 his voice was in some initial decline. Never mind! The resultant slightly raspy coarseness and signs of struggle in his voice were transformed by Hotter into an artistic triumph, expressing as I never encountered again the aging, blind Inquisitor's wrath and wily determination to bend the King to his will. In the climax of the scene, as the irate Inquisitor warns Philip that "even kings can be brought before the Inquisitor's tribunal," the exchange between the two dark but slightly different-timbered bass voices was a revelatory experience.[26] Marveling at what I was witnessing, I almost felt myself transported to sixteenth-century Spain and King Philip's Escurial.

I was so privileged to work again and again with Siepi, accompanying him from my humble place in the pit, enjoying his ravishingly beautiful voice, not only in *Don Carlos*, but also in *Don Giovanni, Marriage of Figaro*, and *Barber of Seville* (in which he was a hilarious music teacher, Don Basilio). Siepi was a great, great artist, blessed with an uncommonly resplendent voice and musical intelligence. The Met was most fortunate in having Siepi grace its stage for a full twenty-two years, during which his work was undiminished in its perfection and artistic integrity.

I have often thought in retrospect that Siepi's "Ella giammai m'amò" aria that opening night and the Grand Inquisitor scene, in fact the whole *Don Carlos* experience in Margaret Webster's large-canvas human-realistic staging, symbolized a new era in the Met's history. It also showed the extraordinary power of opera; a great work of art based on history—in this case Schiller's drama on the plight of the Flemish people under Spain's rule and the horrendous excesses of the Inquisition—was brought to life in a virtually perfect realization.

Except for the two early productions of *Don Carlos* (a truly demanding, long, four-act opera) and *The Flying Dutchman* (probably the most strenuous first horn part of them all),[27] the really heavy part of that 1950–51 season for me started with six operas all put on the boards within a span of five weeks. I must say I loved it; I couldn't get enough of all this astonishingly great music. What was particularly challenging but also nerve-racking was that two of those operas, *Dutchman* and *Rosenkavalier*, were with Reiner. I knew that he had a particular thing about first horns; he loved to tease and test them. I was almost continually on trial with him. And, of course, a first horn part is *always* one of the consistently most audible, most exposed parts in an orchestral ensemble. You have no place to hide, compared to a second clarinet, a third flute, or a fourth horn, although given Reiner's sharp ears and intimate knowledge of the score, no one was really ever safe from his sharp scrutiny.

I mentioned earlier that Reiner tended not to move his head much, something most conductors do as they direct the traffic, so to speak. He rarely looked at any particular player. (For a man who knew his scores so well, he did an awful lot of looking at the score, and not much at the stage.) But horn players were an exception. I don't know why, maybe because of some bad experiences with horn players early in his career. Anyway, he would glower at me with his patented dour look, puffing his cheeks, whenever an important passage came along. Reiner had enormous jowls, like a big bullfrog; it was a really disgusting look. And you had better not ignore him; he expected you to look at him, so that he could lead you, inspire you. He wanted to know that you were paying attention. If you didn't look at him at least every few bars, and looked instead at your part, he would assume that you didn't know it very well, and that could mean trouble.

I wasn't going to get trapped by such a silly peccadillo and decided, already in the previous year, in *Salomé*, to look at him whenever and as long as he would look at me, in a sense staring him down. I remember that at first—I could read it in his eyes—this puzzled him. But in due course he seemed to accept my throwing the gauntlet back at him. His look seemed to say that I knew my part. I played this silly game with him for the next four years (when he left to become music director of the Chicago Symphony). In effect I was beating him at his own game. It led to an interesting relationship between us,[28] one of mutual admiration and respect. But in the 1950–51 season, in *The Flying Dutchman*, there occurred one strangely interesting episode. In that opera there is one of the only two rather awkward and unidiomatic horn solos Wagner ever wrote. Like the one in *Meistersinger*, it is high lying and more suitable for a clarinet than for a horn. It is what we horn players call "slippery" or "nasty." Needless to say, I was prepared—you were *always* prepared for Reiner!—and in the first rehearsal I negotiated that tricky passage not only without a mishap but actually with a certain ease, surprising even to me, considering that I was somewhat nervous. Reiner gave me a quizzical look, evidently not yet ready to give me a sign of approval. In all subsequent rehearsals, the premiere, and the next six performances, the solo went beautifully, without a hitch. Starting around the third performance Reiner began to salute me—his way of complimenting a player. By the sixth performance he was smiling and saluting, although his smiles—rare occurrences to begin with— were always a bit reluctant and uncomfortable looking.

Well, in the eighth performance it happened. I got the first three or four notes, but after that what came out of my horn was completely unrecognizable. As Joe Alessi, one of my trumpet player friends, said to me in the intermission: "Man, you sure shat all over that solo!" He said there was an audible intake of air in the pit as the disaster unfolded. My mind and ears had gone more or less blank, but as I tried to regain control I realized that Reiner was still saluting me. Then, after the debacle, he looked at me with a terribly pained expression on his face, as if to say, how can you do that to me?

After the show I went to his room and apologized, telling him that I didn't really know what happened to me. He patted me on the shoulder, and in his Hungarian German mumbled something about the "cross you horn players have to bear."

I don't really know what happened to me that night. Some, like Reiner, will say, well, that's the way the horn is; you can never completely conquer it. True enough. But I have a hunch it was a combination of a bit of overconfidence on my part, and a little too much red wine. I remember feeling very good at dinner at one of my favorite restaurants right across from the Met's Fortieth Street stage door, run by a German chef who had the best steaks, a great wine cellar, and the best apple crumb cake (which he pronounced "ebbel kroomkake"). I had just polished off a perfect four-hour matinee performance of *Magic Flute*, and was sitting there with Margie, enjoying a great steak dinner and a fabulous burgundy. The upcoming *Flying Dutchman* performance crossed my mind, but—heck—I had easily dealt with that little problem passage a number of times. Not to worry!

That was the last time I drank too much before a performance. But the moral of the story is that you *could* win over a type like Reiner by beating him in those little skirmishes and standing your ground while playing his game, looking him straight in the eye. Occasionally you could carry it so far that he thought you were the best, that you were invincible.

The Reiner story continues in the sense that, of course, you were never really completely out of the woods with him. He had a pesky way of intermittently testing your character and mettle. One particular episode occurred in early 1952, a year after the *Flying Dutchman* incident, when quite suddenly I had to undergo one of Reiner's occasional cross-examinations. But my story really begins two seasons before that, in my first *Salomé* rehearsal; and it must begin by reiterating that Reiner knew his scores and every notational detail in them as well as any conductor I can think of. One should not overrate this accomplishment, because when Reiner came to the Met in 1949 he had been conducting *Salomé* for at least thirty years, hundreds of times, starting in Dresden in the 1910s. Considering that, shouldn't one expect a conductor to have gained complete intimate knowledge of a score? Of course he should, even though we know that many conductors don't come even close to reaching that goal. If you don't know the score to *Salomé* after conducting it for thirty years, then you shouldn't be on the podium. Conductors, I may add, expect us musicians to know our parts *perfectly*.

On a related matter, Reiner had learned over the years, since he first came to Dresden in 1914, what mistakes the original publisher, the engraver, had made in the printed orchestral parts.[29] Reiner knew the printed errors in the parts for all the Strauss operas, and probably in the rest of his conducted repertory as well. He also had very good ears; he heard very clearly. But he had the weakness of wanting to show off how *really* good his ear was, and how well he knew the score and each musician's part. It was an unnecessary bit of braggadocio; he didn't have to *prove* that he had sharp ears. And yet Reiner could not resist the temptation (every once in a while) to show off *how* well he knew the music. The first such instance occurred in the preseason rehearsals for *Rosenkavalier*, the 1949–50 season's opener. At one point in the second act, in a Presto section for the full *fortissimo* orchestra, with the clarinets scurrying around full speed in sixteenth-note runs (as was often Strauss's wont), Reiner suddenly stopped the orchestra and berated our first clarinet player, Gino Cioffi, for playing a wrong note in that run. Now, dear reader, believe me: no one—*absolutely no one*—could possibly hear one wrong sixteenth-note on a clarinet, flying by—one instrument out of about eighty-five—especially in all the surrounding orchestral din of that particular passage.

Reiner was caught in a trap, but didn't yet know it. Cioffi, very agitated, in his broken English protested: "Ma maestro, senti—listen—I maka no mistaka. Wasa errore in part, ma we correcta longatime ago." And Cioffi was right. Reiner didn't realize that most, if not all, of the printed errors in the *Rosenkavalier* parts had long ago been caught by astutely knowledgeable conductors such as Leinsdorf and Bodansky. Reiner became very silent. "Four bars after twelve," he grumbled.

He tried the same wile on me during a *Salomé* rehearsal, one of the many that preceded the great musical triumph in February 1949. At one point Reiner stopped the orchestra, peered at me with his beady eyes, and said in his broad Hungarian accent in a rather annoyed tone: "Schullair, vy you play B flet?" With my heart in my shoes, I somehow rose to my feet and with a shaky voice managed to respond: "Herr Doktor, that's what is in my part." Reiner: "Vell, eets wrong. Play E natural." With that he pointed upward with his finger, meaning an augmented fourth higher. "Oh, okay." I took my pencil and made the correction in my part. Reiner knew that the third horn part at that point had a misprint, although not a *completely* wrong note. The B flat fitted very nicely into Strauss's B-flat diminished seventh chord. (So, of course, does the E.) Here again Reiner felt the need to show us how well he heard things and how well he knew the music. As in the *Rosenkavalier* case, he knew that the part had been originally printed wrong; I had indeed played a B flat.

That rehearsal was what we called an "orchestra reading rehearsal," usually scheduled in opera houses early on—in this case in December 1948—for very difficult or brand-new or less familiar operas. For some reason the next spate of Salomé rehearsals did not take place until late January 1949. Fast forward to five weeks later, when in that same spot—I couldn't believe my ears—I hear a voice saying: "Schullair, vy you play B flet?" This time I was really scared. But still, I wasn't going to take this sitting down; I would have to embarrass him—a risky business. "But Herr Doktor, I played an E, just like you told me in the first rehearsal." He had been caught again, this time not remembering across the five intervening weeks that he had already corrected me and the part. He looked darkly at me, but said nothing. "Fifteen minute intermission!"

I had stood up to him; and I can only assume that in doing so and by playing my part well, with every nuance of Strauss's notation in place, he probably thought twice about bothering me again. He did look at me a few times with a slightly puzzled look, wondering, who *is* this kid?

The two *Salomé* skirmishes and, two years later, the *Flying Dutchman* disaster, were encounters in which I managed to assert myself vis-à-vis Reiner; and as I look back at those incidents, I have to believe that I *won* those rounds because he never tackled me again, and went instead after other prey. Indeed, I seemed to become the apple of his eye.

In Reiner's fourth and final season at the Met he was given *Meistersinger*, and as luck would have it, I was assigned first horn. I was thrilled to play it again, this time on first horn. It is an opera I love dearly—it is as close to comedy as Wagner ever got—although Wagner's pontificating about the German Reich at the end of the last act is something I could have done without, both the text and the music. (Happily, that section was often cut at the Met.)

In the beginning of the second act there is some of Wagner's most rapturously, mystically beautiful music, the so-called *Fliedermusik* (lilac music), in effect an ode to spring and the magic of nature. It is scored primarily for four horns in lovely euphonious parallel thirds. I always looked forward to that music, and here was my chance to interpret it through my lead part, playing it with the most beautiful legato and with a gentle tonal (lilac?) coloration that would evoke the mysterious beauty of spring. I must give full credit to my three section mates, Allan Fuchs, Arthur Sussman, and Silvio Coscia, who blended so perfectly with my lead voice. Reiner was actually smiling—and this time with a real smile. To my amazement he stopped the orchestra at the end of the passage, looked straight at me and my section, and then said to the orchestra: "Gentlemen, I want you to know that in all my years of conducting this music, I have never heard it played so beautifully." He gave his signature salute and then—even more amazing—said to the orchestra: "Gentlemen, I want you to hear that again." I was aglow with pride and a sense of victory, so were my three partners. Reiner was such a formidable opponent; he rarely said such things.

I tell this anecdote in part because another Reiner-Schuller story that has circulated among orchestra musicians, especially in the Chicago Symphony, is a total fabrication. When some years ago I was in Chicago to attend Jimmy Levine's and the orchestra's recording of my *Spectra*, a group of my Chicago orchestra friends, led by Gordon Peters (timpanist of the orchestra), asked me during a lunch break if a story they had heard was true. I was supposed to have had some accident in one of Reiner's *Meistersinger* performances, for which I am alleged to have apologized to him, supposedly saying that I had never played *Meistersinger* before. To which the maestro is said to have responded: "What? How could you *not* have played *Meistersinger* before?" The story did not include my response to Reiner's peculiar comment. All three claims are completely false, and more than that, literally *can't* be true, since by the time I played *Meistersinger* with Reiner in 1952, I had played that opera at least thirty times, and had also recorded various excerpts from it. Beyond all that, I had learned that music in my father's lap, so to speak, studying it as a teenager and playing it many times on the piano (four hands) with my father. Reiner had a strange sardonic Hungarian sense of humor, but I think even he could not have invented such a weird fallacy.

In his last year with the Met, Reiner also conducted Strauss's *Elektra*, which I would loved to have played. But I realized that I already had a heavy load, and Dick Moore, with his senior status, was justifiably given *Elektra*. I did play one performance, though on short notice and at sight (without rehearsal), when Mario Ricci, fifth horn, became indisposed. It was pretty exciting and challenging, playing that very complex music without a rehearsal, but it was the kind of challenge I thrived on.

Another welcome challenge in those years was the opportunity to play Beethoven's *Fidelio*, with its famous virtuoso soprano aria, "Abscheulicher (Abominable One)," accompanied very soloistically by three horns and a bassoon. Kirsten Flagstad was Leonore, and Bruno Walter was the conductor. I eagerly looked forward to working with Walter, whom I had admired for so many years because of his seminal Mahler recordings and some fine Mozart performances with the New York Philharmonic. It was a thrill to play Beethoven's prophetic music six times within a period of two weeks, especially since in the "Abscheulischer" aria everything went very well every time. In that piece you are a hero if you play it without a hitch; but you're a schmuck or a schlemiel if you flip a note or two. There's no in between.

Speaking earlier of Dick Moore reminded me that one of the surprising, unexpected turn of events that occurred soon after I became full-fledged principal horn was that Dick changed his whole attitude toward me. We never talked about his conversion to look upon me musically and personally much more favorably, but I suspect it had something to do with his recognition—finally—that I was not, indeed could not be, in view of the changed circumstances, after his job. Instead of seeing me as a rival, he now saw me as a respected colleague and a friend in a cordial relationship that, as mentioned, we maintained even after I had moved to Boston until his death in 1988.

One way in which his cordiality toward me manifested itself, although in a rather curious way, was that I began to be invited on our spring tours to the daily late-night drinking bouts that Dick and two of his closest buddies, Lester Solomon (hornist) and Earl Leavitt (trombonist), staged every night, either in their hotel rooms or in the roomettes on our all-night train rides. I think Dick thought he was bestowing some special honor on me by inviting me into this closed circle of heavy boozers. Most of the time I begged off, pleading that I needed to do some composing or copying of parts. I was not much of a drinker, and knew that I never could keep up with those guys. Nor would I want to. They were truly serious drinkers, especially of scotch and bourbon, and more or less drank themselves into a stupor most nights.

Lester was another matter; he was legendary as a drinker who could ingest a half-gallon of whiskey in one sitting, and though a bit glassy-eyed and a tad wobbly on his feet, still function reasonably well. Many a time on the road, when Lester had been hitting the bottle most of the afternoon and there was an evening performance of, say, *Marriage of Figaro*, I would have to walk him into the pit, steadying him along the way, then prop him down on his chair and hand him his horn. And you know what? He would somehow sit straight, and play that second horn part in *Figaro*—not at all an easy one; there are always tricky horn passages in Mozart operas—and play it without a serious hitch. Unbelievable! I don't know how Lester could do that. If I had ever gotten that stewed, I wouldn't even have been able to remember my fingerings, let alone any of the right notes.

My friend Jimmy Politis speculated that the only explanation for Lester's extraordinary capacity for absorbing such awesome quantities of booze lay in his body, in his build. Lester was short, with a stocky, stout, fleshy figure. Jimmy would say: "You see all that fat on that guy? That's full of thousands of pores and capillaries that soak up all that liquor. It never gets to his brain."

It was absolutely amazing to me how fanatic and devilishly clever Dick and his drinking buddies actually were on the road about having their daily ration of booze. They brought their supply of liquor for the tour with them in our traveling trunks, big steamer trunks especially built for shipping our horns from city to city. Lester and Dick would *carry* their horns with them, and then fill their huge, well-padded five-by-four by three-and-a-half foot trunks with enormous two- or five-gallon jugs of scotch or bourbon, further protecting their treasure from breakage by wrapping each jug in thick bath towels. Halfway through the eight-week tour, when the trunks were nearly empty, they would replenish the supply with a second round.

On the relatively few occasions when I joined the boozing trio, I was, of course, a most cautious imbiber. Although I liked a good scotch, it didn't like *me*. I had learned on my Ballet Theatre tour in 1943 that my stomach couldn't take much scotch; I would quickly get sick and I didn't find that much fun. There was a brief period—a couple of weeks—on one of the tours in the early 1950s, when I was being particularly strenuously wooed by Dick and Lester to join their nightly drinking bouts in their roomettes. Typically, the Met's two private trains, on which we more or less lived for the entire tour, wouldn't leave until around three or four in the morning—it usually took that long to get all the scenery and wardrobe from that evening's performance stowed away on the train—and usually did not arrive at the next destination until the following afternoon. That left lots of time to drink oneself into a stupor and still sleep it off before arriving at the next city, ready for another evening performance.[30]

Of the various drinking bouts to which I was witness, there is one that is particularly memorable. It took place in St. Louis, where Margie had joined me for a few days. On our last night there, after a performance of *Traviata* that I had to play, Dick, who was kind of sweet on Margie, invited both of us to his hotel room for what he called a "quick nightcap." (As it turned out, there was nothing quick about it.) When we got to Dick's hotel after the performance, we discovered that he and several of his boon companions—Lester and Earl, of course—had already been going at it all evening, drinking not scotch, their usual fare, but beer and some of the vilest manhattans that I've ever had to deal with. They were not only sickeningly sweet; worse yet, they were lukewarm. Dick evidently had long ago run out of ice, and was already well beyond the point of remembering where to get some. Along with the manhattans, Margie and I were served some warm, sweaty camembert cheese and some limp Ritz crackers. Both had seen better days.

This didn't bode well, but not to be discourteous to our host, drunkenly egging us on, we agreed to stay for one or two quick ones. That was a big mistake; I should have known better. It dragged on and on, and I couldn't find a way to extricate us. But finally, two hours and three or four manhattans later I could tell that the party wasn't going to wind down soon. Everybody was getting glassy-eyed and verbally incoherent. It was a hot, sultry, sticky summer night, and several folks were now in varying degrees of undress. The room was thick with the stale smell of beer and manhattans—and sweat. Although Margie and I had been drinking very cautiously, even we were beginning to get a bit woozy. When my stomach started to turn and the room began to reel, I knew it was time to make our exit.

We all had to catch a train to Toronto at nine a.m. for a long, all-day trip. I had promised Dick to pick him up in a cab on our way to the train station. I told Lester to remind Dick, who had by now dozed off in a corner of the room, that we would pick him up in the hotel lobby at eight fifteen a.m.

Margie and I were more sick than drunk from those saccharine manhattans. What little sleep we got was fitful and sporadic. At seven we staggered out of bed, still not feeling too well, packed (as best we could), checked out, and taxied to Dick's hotel. Not seeing him in the lobby, we headed for his room, but got no response when we knocked on the door. As luck would have it, the door was not locked. I rushed in, but there was no Dick Moore. The room was a total mess, with clothes, bed sheets, towels, food (leftover cheese), and empty bottles strewn all around. It looked like a garbage dump. Desperate, thinking that we might now miss our train, we decided to leave. To hell with Dick! But as I rushed past the half-open bathroom door, I saw him there, asleep, all six-foot-three-inches of him, lying naked in the bathtub, with the rubber bathmat pulled over him. Frantic now, we somehow got him up and dressed, packed his bag and helped him check out. The three of us just made it to the train seconds before it pulled out.

I could have killed Lester when I saw him later, looking quite sober, and he asked me if I "had slept well." Grrr!

I lost sleep around this time over a much more serious event. In May 1950 my parents were nearly killed in a horrible auto accident. Driving up to Webatuck late one night on the Saw Mill River Parkway, a car coming from the opposite direction suddenly swerved into my parent's lane, smashing head-on into their car at high speed. The front of my parents' auto was totally crushed; much of the motor was pushed into the front seats. My father had been driving, and it was his side of the car that received the brunt of the collision's impact. When he was extricated his left leg was lying, just short of being fully severed, on top of his right leg. That my father's upper body, including his hands, was unharmed is a miracle. Obviously, had his hands—even one—been crushed or even slightly injured, his violinist career would have been history. My mother, sitting in the right front seat, sustained multiple injuries to her head (a partially crushed skull over her left eye) and her chest (many broken ribs), and all kinds of internal injuries. It was clear that she had been thrown forward into the windshield and dashboard (their 1947 Plymouth had no seatbelts.)

Fortunately, there was the very good Grasslands Hospital in Valhalla only a few miles from the accident, where both were kept for almost two months.[31] As horribly injured as my parents were, the numerous operations they underwent were so amazingly successful that by the end of the summer it was almost impossible to tell that they had ever been in a serious accident. Indeed, my father was able to play most of the Philharmonic's Lewisohn Stadium season that summer and continue his career as an orchestral player. (He worked professionally with many different orchestras until he was eighty-seven.) My mother never fully recovered from her many injuries—her head and face remained a little disfigured, she had fairly serious chest pains off and on for the rest of her life—but as valiant and determined as she was, she did not let that hinder her from pursuing her various artistic interests and housewifely duties as vigorously as before.

It was very clear that the accident was the other driver's fault—he, ironically, sustained only minor injuries—and an insurance settlement was easily reached.

In the 1952–53 Met season the big event, particularly for me as a composer, was the American premiere of Stravinsky's *The Rake's Progress*. We heard that the seventy-year-old composer was going to be in attendance at all rehearsals and at the first few performances. Reiner was the conductor, although when we recorded *Rake's Progress* for Columbia Records only four weeks after the February premiere, it was Stravinsky himself on the podium.[32] As my senior, Moore had first call on playing the *Rake* (as most of us began to call it), and since the score called for only two horns, Fuchsie was set to play second horn. I anticipated that I wouldn't participate in the *Rake* performances, except in the case of Dick's possible indisposition. But Max Rudolf and John Mundy, realizing that I was dying to be involved, especially in the rehearsals, had the wonderful idea of assigning me to assistant first horn for the entire run of rehearsals and at least the premiere performance. I was very grateful for this bit of largesse, because, frankly, the *Rake's* first horn part is very light endurance-wise, and really does not require an assistant. Mundy later told me they wanted to involve me as a sort of insurance. Since Moore's antipathy for modern music was well known, and if Reiner was not happy with Dick's rather heavy style of playing, which the rather transparent chamber music-like Mozartean idiom of the *Rake* might not tolerate, I would be prepared to step in. (Although Dick constantly grumbled about Stravinsky's music, he played his part very well throughout.)

Our initial rehearsals were held in the Met's so-called rehearsal room, just large enough to accommodate a normal-size orchestra. But now, word had gotten around town that Stravinsky was going to be at the rehearsals, with the result that all kinds of visitors, including famous musical celebrities, came—Aaron Copland, Samuel Barber, William Schuman, Alexander Tansman (a close, longtime friend of Stravinsky)—as well as Chester Kallman and W. H. Auden (the *Rake's* librettists), George Balanchine (hired by Bing to provide the stage direction), Lilian Libman (Stravinsky's secretary), and all their various entourages. The entire assemblage of visitors was seated along the four walls of the room, completely surrounding the orchestra. It was a lucky thing Rudolf and Mundy had engaged me to play in the *Rake's* rehearsals, otherwise I would never have been able to attend; there wouldn't have been room for me.

The rehearsals went very well. Every musician in the orchestra was well prepared, not only because of Reiner but also because of Stravinsky's presence. And while the initial orchestra rehearsals were exciting enough, the full beauty and perfection of the *Rake* music was revealed to me only in the final stage rehearsals and actual performances. Between the singing of the excellent cast, in particular Hilde Güden as Anne and Mack Harrel as Nick Shadow, and George Balanchine's superb staging, the *Rake* was a great artistic triumph and a deeply moving experience.

I was able to play *The Rake's Progress* the following season (1953–54), although, alas, not under Reiner but under Alberto Erede, a conductor for whom I could never muster much admiration. Still, the music was so wonderful—Stravinsky's last hurrah and farewell to neoclassicism, and what a refulgent adieu!—that even Erede's dry, pedestrian approach could not really mar the music. By then we had made the recording with Stravinsky, and we knew how he wanted the music to feel. And that's what we played, regardless of what Erede did on the podium.

Of the many fond memories I have of the whole *Rake's Progress* experience, the most indelible is of Hilde Güden's beautiful rendition of the role of Anne, especially in the last three of the eight scheduled performances. She really grew into the role. For me the artistic and interpretive zenith of Güden's performances was the Lullaby, a loving farewell to Tom Rakewell near the end of the opera, which is arguably the most moving, touching, heartbreaking music Stravinsky ever conceived. (Was it, like Anne's poignant farewell to Tom, also Stravinsky's farewell to tonality?) The memory of that gentle music and Güden's singing of it brings tears to my eyes; an uncontrollable heaving simply wells up in me, even now over half a century later—an instance of memory touching a person's soul through music.[33]

Hilde Güden was also one of the most beautiful women that ever graced an opera stage. I say that in full knowledge that there has never been a shortage of beautiful sopranos and mezzos, since the very beginnings of opera in the late sixteenth century. But I think I could argue that it couldn't have been too often that an opera house had on its roster contemporaneously four such beauties as Hilde Güden, Lisa Della Casa, Irmgard Seefried, and Elizabeth Schwarzkopf (that was just in the Met's German wing!)—all of them as gorgeous as any highly touted Hollywood star. Because I more than a few times happened to express my great admiration for both Güden's artistry and her extraordinary beauty, before I knew it the talk in the orchestra was that "Güden is Gunther's girlfriend." Hah! What strange (surrogate?) wishful thinking! More likely they were thinking of themselves, for whenever one of these guys teased me about my alleged affair with Güden, there was an unmistakable glow in *their* eyes. I sort of played along with this silly game. Truth was, of course, that I never even met the lady, never said a word to her. I wish I could have. The moral of this little story is that orchestra musicians, to while away the time, can on occasion be as silly and simpleminded—harmlessly so—as any other species of humans, even when they are fine or great artists.

The recording of *Rake's Progress*, with Stravinsky conducting and with the original cast Bing had put together for the premiere (Hilde Güden, Eugene Conley, Mack Harrell, and Blanche Thebom), took place in March 1953, only a few weeks after our premiere performance on February 14. It was a fascinating experience, working with the "old man" (as we affectionately thought of Stravinsky), noting how different the composer's approach in conducting was from Reiner's. Fascinating because, as is well known, Stravinsky was not a great conductor. And yet the way he expressed himself verbally and even with his sometimes clumsy gesturing, he conveyed the feeling and expressive essence of the music, as *he* heard and felt it. His gestures looked cold and dry—especially in rhythmic matters—and yet the music came out warm and expressive. This is remarkable because Stravinsky didn't like warm, resonant sounds; I think he thought it was too romantic, too sentimental. He loved a dry, clear, sharply etched sound, an unadorned, uninterpreted representation of what he had written. It was very difficult in the warm, resonant acoustics of Liederkranz Hall, with its well-aged wood paneling, to give Stravinsky the tart, taut sounds he wanted. (We all loved playing in those generous, musician-friendly acoustics.)

Stravinsky was really obsessive about articulation. For him it couldn't be dry and graphic enough. He kept after us with an amazing persistence to play, for instance, staccato eighth notes *extremely* short. We didn't seem to be able to satisfy him. I'll never forget the vision of him bent over his huge music stand, staring at the score, exhorting us winds and brass in his high, tight, pinched voice, gesticulating pointedly with his right hand, to show *how* short he wanted things: "Gentlemens—*secchissimo, secchissimo*—more *secchissimo*." Each reiteration rose in a crescendo. The problem was that we were already sucking the notes back in; that's how clipped short we were playing. It felt very unnatural. Thank God, the reverberant acoustics of Liederkranz Hall fleshed out the sound rather nicely on the recording.

We loved and respected the great composer so much that whatever conductorial foibles Stravinsky might commit we compensated for them: we played the dynamics he had written that he couldn't quite conduct; we played the expressive lines that he, in his vertical time-beating, could not quite show. In the end I think there was a kind of subtle compromise: he conducted and heard what he wanted to hear, and we played more or less what we felt was natural, although in the direction of the textural clarity that he was after. From my point of view the *Rake's Progress* recording sessions were a great success, and a fabulous experience for me, one that I am very grateful to have been involved with.[34]

One of the many privileges and musical pleasures in my Met years was playing Mozart's *Così fan tutte*. *Così* had not been done at the Met since 1922 (!) and was for a time completely neglected worldwide. But Bing knew and loved the work from his days at Glyndebourne. And it turned out to be one of Bing's great early success stories. It had a stellar cast that stayed together for that opera's entire five-year run at the Met. And I had the pleasure of playing *Così* for four of those five years, totaling some thirty performances. The conductor for *Così* was my pal Stiedry. For all that I've said both good and bad about him, I must say that in *Così* (and *Don Carlos*) he really came into his own. He did both operas amazingly well; we were all quite surprised. With Stiedry, the more deeply he loved a work the more effectual and efficient he became. It was as if in those two pieces the music cleansed him of his usual foibles. Sometimes in *Così*, especially in the incredibly beautiful act 1 E-major Quintet—in its serene mood one of Mozart's most inspired creations (and that's saying something)—Stiedry seemed to be transported by the music to another realm. Almost in a trance, his hands would weave the most beautiful musical gestures. It was moving and inspiring. Many years later, when I brought Eleanor Steber to the New England Conservatory and worked with her many times in various ways, we often reminisced about the special mood and aura Stiedry created in those performances of *Così*. That spirit was something akin to a love affair. That's the best way I can describe it.

Così fan tutte was special for me in another way. In that opera Mozart composed an aria for Fiordiligi, "Per pietà, ben mio," which prominently features the winds, but especially two horns (often with a third voice in the bassoon), in true concertante fashion. It is what in our horn world is considered a difficult piece; not horrendously difficult or impossible, just quite challenging, requiring a high level of technical skill and dependability, the kind of writing composers save for solo concertos. The horn part is quite exposed, several times completely *a capella*. I loved the challenge of it; it is incredibly rewarding, psychically and professionally, to play a certain difficult piece or passage, or for that matter a whole opera, some thirty times in a row without a blemish.[35]

There is one aspect of my life at the Met in those first few years as principal horn that intrigues me in retrospect. It is that my playing, which was already quite good—obviously, or else I wouldn't have lasted there very long—was even more consistent, more secure, more confident, when I stepped up to first horn and, in effect, became leader of the section. Being very self-critical, I had often chastised myself during my first five years in the orchestra for certain slight inconsistencies in my playing. It wasn't anything that anybody had reason to complain about; it was more that some aspects of my playing didn't meet *my* very highest standards.

Sometimes I couldn't control my intonation as perfectly as I wanted to. By intonation I mean what I call "harmonic" intonation, that is, tuning every note to the precise tuning that the harmony, the chord in which the note is located, requires. The lay reader may not realize that musicians (on any instrument, except keyboards) play with what is called "equal temperament tuning."[36] But beyond that predefined tuning, musicians playing wind instruments must fix the intonation of notes, of pitches, in minute adjustments, so as to correspond to the absolutely precise pitch positioning that a given note in a given harmony, a particular harmonic-melodic context, requires. Playing would be quite simple if it were merely a matter of pushing down some key or valve, and playing that pitch always with the same single identical intonation. Instead, it is that every note we play—*every note*—needs some degree of infinitesimal pitch adjustment in order to be true to the harmonic function and structure at hand. To put it another way—and this is the most fascinating and challenging aspect of fine playing—every note on our instrument, say, an F just above middle C, has to be adjusted in pitch depending on whether it is the third in a chord, or a fifth, a minor seventh, or whatever, or whether it is a leading tone, whether that F is in an ascending or descending posture, and so on. This sounds incredibly complex—and it is.

It was that high degree of fine tuning that I sometimes could not control as precisely as I wanted to. But it was just such refined precision adjustments—of intonation, of tone, of timbre—that I learned to bring into complete control as I took on the principal horn position. And when one reaches that level of playing and consistency, it is an incredible high that beats anything a drug might induce. Musician readers will know exactly what I mean.

The other playing and performing challenge I conquered in those early years as first horn regards a problem particularly endemic to opera. Operas are, with few exceptions, considerably longer in duration than any symphony and even any normal symphony concert. Many of the greatest operas are four hours long, some (by Wagner, for example) even longer. Thus opera playing, particularly on an instrument such as the horn, requires unusual physical, labial stamina and endurance. With experience and intelligent pacing in the use of one's energy one can learn to cope with such extraordinary physical—and, by the way, mental—demands. Playing the first horn part of even one heavy opera such as *Meistersinger* or *Götterdämmerung*—even with an assistant—is quite a "blow" (brass players' talk). In fact, if you're not careful you can kill your lip in the first act. But to play *two* such heavy operas on the same day is another matter—a not entirely uncommon occurrence in a major opera house such as the Met, which every Saturday presented a matinee in the afternoon (also broadcast on radio in my day) and a second performance in the evening. Many was the time that, because of the chance vagaries of performing schedules, I had to play *Götterdämmerung* in the afternoon and *Rosenkavalier* in the evening; or a doubleheader of *Siegfried* and *Così fan tutte*.

In regard to *Götterdämmerung* and physical endurance, I remember loving that music so much that, being young and strong, I wanted to play *every* note, despite the fact that I had an assistant, Mario Ricci, at my side, whose job it was to spell me in long, heavy, full-orchestra passages; the idea was that the principal horn should be able to save his lips for the more exposed parts and prominent solos. In my unbounded enthusiasm I would have none of that, especially in a remarkable section in the second act of *Götterdämmerung*—a particular favorite of mine—where the music is for about five minutes unrelievedly loud, in full orchestral cry, with virtually no rests, no empty bars.[37] In opera orchestras that have an assistant horn available, that whole third scene is played almost entirely by the assistant, giving the main player a nice long rest;[38] there are another three hours to the end of the opera. But I was so entranced by that music that, crazy as I was, I would not deny myself the experience, the pleasure, of playing every note of that scene. Mario Ricci was confounded. He could not understand how I did that, and *why* I would *want* to do that.

In 1947/1948, after a Communist government had been installed in Hungary with the help of Russian troops and tanks, and its borders sealed off to emigration, many Hungarians nonetheless managed to escape to the West, and eventually to the United States, among them many musicians. Most of them were members of the Budapest Philharmonic and National Opera, graduates of the famous Franz Liszt Academy, and readily found work in American orchestras. This was especially true of orchestras led by Hungarian-born conductors, such as the Dallas Symphony with Antal Dorati at the helm and the Met orchestra during Fritz Reiner's tenure. That is how we acquired Victor Aitay as assistant concertmaster, and in 1949 János Starker, the world-famous cellist. Another great cellist, Laszlo Varga, became solo cellist of the New York Philharmonic around the same time. Still another Hungarian escapee, Georg Lang, landed in the Dallas Symphony as a violinist, and played there for several years—he also built some rather fine violins—and then moved to New York and changed professions to become one of the world's most sought after restaurateurs.[39]

It must have been destiny that, in its uncanny way, brought me together with these four Hungarians. Aitay and his wife Eva (who happens to be George Lang's cousin) lived quite by chance in an apartment on the same floor as ours in Rego Park, Queens, where Margie and I moved in 1950; Margie and Eva became very close friends. George and his first wife, Dorothy, lived on the floor below us when we moved a few years later to a huge ten-room apartment on Manhattan's Upper West Side. And Laszlo Varga was someone I saw almost every week at the New York Philharmonic. I became close friends with this Hungarian "gang of four," as we quickly bonded in a sort of musical mutual admiration society. I think they related rather readily to me with my European background—we often spoke German, they after a fashion, with a pungent paprika-spiced accent—and they sensed that I respected and admired their cultural background. It impressed them no end that one of my all-time favorite pieces was Zoltán Kodály's Solo Cello Sonata, or that I knew and had thoroughly studied Béla Bartók's six string quartets, or, even more amazing, that I knew what a great teacher and composer Leo Weiner was, with whom all of them (except Eva) had studied in Budapest.

We soon became virtually inseparable, going out to dinner together, all seven of us, or spending free evenings at Czardas, an eastside restaurant and nightclub, where for many years a phenomenally gifted gypsy violinist named Béla Babai held forth.[40] One evening at Czardas, in a state of euphoric camaraderie, after a pirkilt (paprika goulash) and spätzle dinner and several bottles of tokay, my six Hungarian friends—Margie, visiting her parents in Fargo, was not with us—declared me an honorary Hungarian in a relatively elaborate handholding and embracing ceremony that stopped just short of declaring blood brotherhood.

János Starker is, of course, one of the world's most celebrated cellists and teachers, blessed with an astonishing technical facility, a terrific precision ear, and high musical intelligence. When he came to the Met in 1949 as principal cellist, we became friends almost instantly, bound by a hearty mutual respect. We always had good solo cellists in the orchestra in my time, but I must say that when he played the lead part in the cello quartets—in Verdi's *Otello* (first act) and Puccini's *Tosca* (last act)—the music took on a wonderfully clear sheen and a sense of absolute security that was wonderful to behold.

While at the Met, Starker made his first moves toward establishing a solo career, primarily by making his first recordings and, secondly, by planning his New York debut recital. He asked me to be involved with both ventures, in the first instance helping him in his two recordings of Kodály's 1915 Cello Sonata, Op. 8.[41] He wanted me to be musical supervisor in the control room, and to help with the editing—this was in the early days of magnetic tape recording—a flattering indication of how much Jançi trusted my judgment, my ears, and my knowledge of the piece. I was thrilled to do this for him—of course gratis. Both recordings came out in 1950 and were inevitably, given Starker's extraordinary technique, the best recordings of the Sonata at the time—even though he was not completely satisfied. (An artist of that caliber is rarely—if ever—completely satisfied.)

I think it was in the fall of 1951 that Starker came to me during a rehearsal and asked me if I'd be willing to write a solo piece for him, to be the new work on his debut recital in Carnegie Hall in early 1952. Terrific! I eagerly accepted the invitation. "But now listen," he said—and I'll never forget his words, astonishing as they were—"I want you to make this very difficult, really virtuosic. You know my technique. You like the Kodály Sonata. Well, I want you to make your piece even harder than that."

I was stunned by his words. Until now, when players asked me to write something for them they always said, half cajoling, half seriously: "Now, don't make it too hard!" Here was Starker asking me to make it *really hard*. I was skeptical. Did he really mean that? On the other hand, it was sort of nice for once to hear from someone who was encouraging me to make a piece really challenging. But then came the capper. "You know the Kodály. Well, write your piece a twelfth higher, like a violin part." I knew that I had heard correctly, but still it was hard for me to believe what he said. "OK," I said, with feigned conviction. I decided to take his last remark with a grain of salt, certainly not too literally.

By now the reader knows how much I love the cello. I had already written two big challenging pieces for the instrument, and was eager to write another. Moreover, by chance, a few weeks earlier I had been inspired in a superb recital by the prodigiously talented (and ravishingly beautiful) Raya Garbousova, and was quite ready for another cellistic challenge. Despite being very busy at the Met—all those heavy operas I've mentioned—and teaching every week some twenty-five students and two wind ensemble classes at the Manhattan School of Music, I wrote the piece for János in a couple of weeks, and handed it to him one morning at a rehearsal at the Met. I had called it *Fantasy for Unaccompanied Cello*.

János said he would look at it in the next few days; he seemed quite excited. But here's where the story takes a weird 180-degree turn. Two days later, again at a rehearsal, rather stony-faced, he blurted at me something like: "I can't play this thing," with a tone of voice that seemed to say, this piece of crap. I was stunned, speechless. I stammered something to the effect: "Jançi, what's the matter? What's happening?" His quick, unequivocal response: "I don't play this kind of stuff; I don't play any twelve-tone music. I'll never play this. Thank you very much." And with that he threw the manuscript onto the table.

I stood there dazed, numb. How could my friend treat me this way? And didn't he know that I was composing in the twelve-tone concept? And besides, what was so horrible about that? And how could someone so intelligent, so brilliant, such a remarkable musician, be so deeply prejudiced? Why couldn't he in some more friendly or temperate way explain that he really didn't like or understand twelve-tone music, didn't know that the piece was going to be in that style, and please forgive me, I just don't think I can play this piece. It still would have hurt, but the rejection would have been handled in a less cold-hearted manner.

I could hardly look at Starker the next few days; he was now my enemy. A few days later he rubbed more salt into my wound by cornering me in the locker room with a final insult, his *coup de grâce*: "Besides, you know, I looked at the whole piece, and it's *much too hard*. It would take me four months to learn this thing; and my recital is in six weeks." This after he had enthusiastically encouraged me to write a technically difficult piece, more difficult than the Kodály Sonata. It was a crazy, surreal situation, impossible to salvage.

There is further irony in his recriminations in that the *Fantasy*, although certainly created in the twelve-tone concept, is also clearly located in C major. There are any number of junctures or cadence points scattered throughout the piece where the music comes to rest on C major, a point of tonal resolution. The middle section starts on a high G and is basically located in G major (the dominant of C), and I used the cello's low C string in many ways, despite the composition's basic atonality (or high chromaticism) to subtly anchor the music in C. (All this was done deliberately, and without diffusing or undercutting the basic twelve-tone principles.) That Starker did not see the centrality of C major in the piece is surprising to me. All he evidently saw was that the *Fantasy* started with a full statement, craggy and jagged as it is, of the twelve-note set.

I more or less got over my hurt in due course, though a bit humbled, I have to say, wondering what would happen with my cello *Fantasy*. But once again, fate intervened. One day in late February I got a call from Herman Newman at WNYC, who asked me if I had anything recent that he could put on in his annual "Contemporary American Music Week." A few days after telling him that I didn't think so, I remembered my new cello piece—I think I had sort of pushed it out of my mind as a lost cause—and told him that I would immediately try to get someone to learn it. On the phone at the other end I heard the following words: "Well, he's got to learn it pretty quickly, because the only spot I have left on my programs is a week from now." "Oh my God" was my only possible response. The technically redoubtable Starker had declared that it would take him four months to learn the piece, and now someone was going to have to learn and play it in *one week*!

I knew only one cellist of my acquaintance who could possibly accomplish this awesome task, the new principal cellist of the New York Philharmonic, Laszlo Varga, who had just succeeded the great Leonard Rose, and was already one of my much-admired colleagues and Hungarian brotherhood friends. I immediately called up Laçi and told him what was up. Could he in his busy Philharmonic schedule take on my *Fantasy*? "You remember, the piece I wrote for Starker, which he has now rejected?"[42] "Well . . . sure," a bit hesitant. "When do you need it? How much time have I got?" I gulped, and hemmed and hawed a bit, and gingerly suggested: "Uh, about one week." My voice rose to turn it into a question.

"One week!," Laçi cried. "Are you crazy? Besides, this is the worst time for me. I'm playing a new concerto by Ghedini[43] in three weeks with Mitropoulos, and then in April I've got the *Arpeggione Sonata*.[44] Gunther, I just can't do it!"

I was sunk. But somehow I ratcheted up enough nerve and courage to say: "Wow, that's some schedule. But couldn't you do this? Just look at the piece, read through it, and then decide whether you really can't do it. It would mean so much to me. Newman has been after me for several years to get me on his WNYC festival, and I've never been able to offer him anything, because I've mostly written orchestral music and pieces for largish ensembles. He can't handle these in his small WNYC studio." Pleadingly, I said: "Please, just look at the piece for an hour or so." With a sigh of reluctance, he told me to bring the part over right away. "It's Monday, and I have a free day; I'll look at it this afternoon."

I don't know exactly to what extent the silent rivalry with Starker indirectly figured subconsciously in Laçi's decision to undertake the premiere of my *Cello Fantasy*. Perhaps it was that he might be able to show the world that he could play a piece that a more famous colleague, with several acclaimed recordings to his credit (Varga had none at the time), had declared too difficult. But I know that Laçi also did it out of friendship for me and in admiration for some of my recent compositions that he had heard. He must have worked extremely hard during that week, along with four Philharmonic rehearsals and three concerts (more than twenty hours right there), because on Sunday he called me and said, "Gunther, you're in luck. I think I can play it next Tuesday. Come over as soon as you can, and give a listen. Coach me on it. By the way, it's a terrific piece—difficult, but rewarding. Really cellistic."

I don't think I can describe how happy I was, how grateful to Laçi. But even more important, the performance Laçi gave that evening live in a studio at WNYC, which was taped (I still possess that tape), was so good that I am tempted to say that, of all the performances the *Fantasy* has had over the last fifty-eight years, his is still one of the very best, certainly musically, interpretively.[45]

News of Bing's and the Metropolitan Opera's great successes in the early 1950s spread throughout the country, and by the midfifties had resulted in an expansion of the Met's season at home to almost thirty weeks, and the annual spring tour from six to seven weeks. This came along with an increase in salary, of course. What was nice about the expanded tour was that some cities, such as Oklahoma City, Montreal, and Des Moines, were added to the schedule, and our sojourns in some of the bigger cities (Chicago, Houston, St. Louis) were extended. This was very welcome; the longer our stays, the more free evenings I would have, allowing me in turn to explore more thoroughly the cultural and architectural offerings of the cities— museums, parks, theatres, book shops, music stores—and, of course, friends.

Many of these cities also offered a quite exciting night life, if that was your bent. And one can well imagine that by letting some eighty wifeless males loose on the road for six or seven weeks, the attractions and temptations of the night became incrementally more than a bent. They fulfilled an often desperate need, provided an outlet for pent-up emotions and feelings. I know whereof I speak, being neither immune to such seductions nor opposed to some form of transient release. Places such as Dallas and Houston, Chicago, Atlanta, and St. Louis, provided a plethora of options, which many of us availed ourselves of.

In a certain sense I perhaps strayed a little farther than most of my colleagues—I became very interested in the social and political environment of some of these famous American cities. I wanted to know how all these basically illegal and, many would say, immoral activities were able to exist and to function unperturbedly, to defy the law and authority. As if I didn't know the answer: corruption, payoffs, political and fiscal. It's not that I hadn't read the many *Inside* exposé books by John Gunther, or the novels of Nelson Ahlgren and James T. Farrell dealing with the seedier side of American urban life. But I wanted to see with my own eyes and learn through direct knowledge about the raw realities of big-city underworld life.

In several cities—Atlanta, St. Louis, Houston, especially Chicago and its wide open sub-urbs, Cicero and Calumet City—I had quite by chance gotten to know and become friendly with certain night-shift cab drivers, and, in St. Louis, a newspaper reporter whose beat was the red-light nightclub district on the eight p.m. to four a.m. shift. His title was city reporter. My main cab driver contact in St. Louis was a young fellow whom I knew as Morty, who must have known every cop, every prostitute, every club owner, every doorman, every pimp in town. He was liked—and trusted—by everyone, a congenial charmer: convivial, easygoing, with a healthy Yiddish sense of humor, remarkably philosophical and unjudgmental about what he witnessed every night. Morty had some kind of inherent native wisdom, what we might call street smarts. He had neither contempt nor pity for the lowlifes he beheld every night, and in whose world he made his living. He saw them dispassionately as human beings who somehow were destined to live at the lower end of the human existence spectrum, who in various ways had been dealt a bad hand by fate—consigned to a world that "proper" society looked upon with hypocritical, snobbish contempt. Morty's reporter friend (his elegant name was Garnett) was of the same unjudgmental, philosophical turn of mind.

So was I. Through my voluminous reading of great literature and history—even the Bible—it was clear to me that man was capable of expressing the entire range of human behavior, from the noblest good to the grossest evil. While I personally didn't want to necessarily experience the low end of that behavioral scale, I felt it was part of a full, richly observant life to be realis-tic about the limitless range and potential of human existence. I invented a metaphor for this viewpoint, which likened life to a big tree that reached all the way from its beautiful crown to its invisible roots, in endless unpredictable and unduplicatable variety. No two trees, no two flowers, and no two human beings are or have ever been identical. Since the roots are as important as the crown and the tree's branches, I wanted to see and to some extent experience life in the same holistic way—to see the whole tree, as it were. (I realized later that my simile didn't quite stand up to unconditional scrutiny, since it seemed—by implication—to be unfair to the tree's roots, as if there was something dirty about them.)

Making the nighttime rounds in St. Louis was an amazing experience. Some of my friends in the orchestra thought I was crazy, that what I was doing was downright dangerous. Per-haps. But I felt really safe in Morty's and Garnett's hands. We'd drive around all night, Morty, of course, picking up fares along the way, but also checking in on various hot spots—strip clubs, bordello districts, police stations, the all-night bus depot—chatting with various types of inmates. Around two thirty a.m. we'd usually stop at an all-night restaurant, which served the best eggs, tomatoes, and bacon—almost an English breakfast. (By the way, after my first year with Morty, he never again charged me cab fare.) It was all a little like being on a kind of strange high, enveloped in a surrealistic experience, driving around in this endless neon-lit jungle.[46]

In Montreal, another interestingly open city[47] (with a French touch, of course), my guide was Alfie (Alfred Wade), a young black jazz musician who seemed to have a dazzling array of other interests and contacts. I had hooked up with him at some jazz club that Harry Peers and I had come upon. The jazz wasn't very good, but we both took a terrific liking to Alfie, who was hanging out at the bar. A happy-go-lucky, always smiling, adventurous, enticingly enig-matic character, Alfie was an extraordinarily handsome fellow, clean looking, always dapperly dressed. For all we knew, he might have been some small-time pimp. If so, what an elegant, well-mannered one. We were pretty sure that Alfie was involved with drugs, but I suspect only marijuana, which wasn't a big deal in those days, since virtually all jazz musicians were on drugs, usually marijuana. Why, even in the Met orchestra we had, as far as I could determine, at least a dozen or so who regularly lit up on the weed. Like Morty, Alfie knew everybody, spoke a fluent Montreal French patois, and kept Harry and me royally entertained. I can't recall how many night haunts of all kinds the three of us visited, but everywhere we went Alfie was greeted like the prodigal son. He proudly introduced us around, mentioning our association with the Metropolitan Opera as if we were some legendary visiting potentates. But I often wondered whose hands I was shaking, what stories lurked behind those easy smiles and small-talk amenities. I also often wonder what became of Alfie—such a charmer!

One opera that I always enjoyed playing and, as a composer, was particularly fascinated with, was Mussorgsky's *Boris Godunov*. I even enjoyed it when Emil Cooper conducted it in 1947. He had a way with that music, which he knew intimately (in the Rimsky-Korsakov version), having had one of his biggest early successes as a conductor premiering *Boris Godunov* in England at Covent Garden in 1909. In 1953 Fritz Stiedry took over *Boris*, having persuaded Bing to commission Karel Rathaus, a Polish-born composer teaching at Queens College in New York, to edit and restore Mussorgsky's original orchestration of 1872. *Boris* is an astonishingly personal and original work, and I thought that Rathaus managed to preserve Mussorgsky's bold, unorthodox, idiosyncratic writing and orchestration very respectfully. There was none of Rimsky-Korsakov's technically brilliant but often rather glitzy reorchestration, not to mention his constant recasting of Mussorgsky's allegedly simplistic, crude harmonizations. Most of Russia's musical intelligentsia, including Rimsky-Korsakov, called them inept and illiterate.[48] Whereas Rimsky-Korsakov skillfully fleshed out and updated every chord and orchestration that he considered incompetent and lacking in sophistication, Rathaus left Mussorgsky's original conceptions intact in all their folk sparseness and boldness. I especially appreciated Rathaus's restorations when Mitropoulos conducted *Boris* in two different seasons. As a Greek and a kind of spiritual monastic with a healthy appreciation of artlessness and primitivism, Dimitri had a very close, natural consanguinity with Mussorgsky's music. In that opera the peasants, the people of Russia, represented by the numerous choruses, are the real stars of the opera, the real heroes and protagonists. I also like to think that the plasticity, even the occasional lack of discipline and control, in Mitropoulos's conducting style fit remarkably well with Mussorgsky's vagarious, often unorthodox, yet inspired musical language. I found it thrilling to play *Boris* under Mitropoulos's hand, savoring as a composer the strange little oddities and clumsinesses, but also the music's overwhelming power and original inspirations—especially when Cesare Siepi sang the Tsar Boris part.

It was in those midfifties years (1956–57, to be precise) that Erich Leinsdorf returned to the Met,[49] a most welcome event for me because his conducting provided some of the most revelatory and inspiring experiences of my years at the opera house. I had worked with Leinsdorf only one time before (on that Haydn "Farewell" Symphony recording in 1947), when he arrived at the Met in 1956. I had heard lots of talk among musicians that he was a "pretty good" musician—that's already high praise coming from orchestra musicians—and that he was very exacting; also that he was often caustic and mordant in his podium behavior, that he had been undergoing psychiatric care for about twenty years, and that he had a history of never being able to hold on to a job. This latter point seemed really to be true; most of Leinsdorf's career was characterized by an initial euphoric honeymoon with an orchestra, followed by a gradual souring of relationships, ending sooner or later in mutual detestation.

Thus, Leinsdorf's coming to the Met was not the kind of news conducive to putting us at ease. But instead, to our surprise—certainly mine—he seemed to have undergone a major transformation. I saw right away that he had a flawless baton technique, clean and clear, and a stunning knowledge of the score, indeed of all aspects of the music. Best of all, he exuded the kind of confidence that we had experienced with Reiner, but in a more benign manner.

No wonder people had marveled at his previous work at the Met in the late thirties. Gosh, I thought, this might turn out to be fun!

And indeed, so it was. The two operas that were a particular thrill and privilege for me to play with Leinsdorf were *Arabella* and *Madama Butterfly*. *Arabella*, compared with *Salomé* and *Elektra*, is a stylistically much more conservative work, Strauss, having by 1933 (the date of *Arabella*), and even some twenty years before, recoiled from his near-encounters in 1905 and 1909 with atonality, retreating to his earlier tonal language. But Strauss, the great virtuoso orchestrator, had certainly not moderated his technical instrumental demands, especially in the horn parts. *Arabella* is filled with rangy virtuosic passages that push beyond almost anything he had attempted before, the kind of writing one would expect in a solo concerto. I had never played *Arabella* and was eagerly looking forward to the challenge of playing that music; and it turned out to be a marvelous experience, primarily because of Leinsdorf's supreme handling of that complex, extraordinarily busy score—and also because two of my favorite singing beauties, Hilde Güden and Lisa Della Casa, headed the cast, along with George London.

I can say that I played *Arabella's* daunting first horn part with great relish and ease, making it sound effortless. I knew it virtually by heart, and played the same game I had played so often with Reiner: looking straight at Leinsdorf any time he chose to look at me. After one or two rehearsals those visual contacts lost their feeling of mutual challenge, of testing, and devolved to the joy of making music together, of communicating our reciprocal respect and admiration through the music. A major factor in Leinsdorf's consummate management of the multiple musical and conducting challenges in *Arabella* was his flawless, elegant, uncluttered baton technique. It was a joy to see and to hear the confident, relaxed results it allowed and in fact produced. You felt that you were at all times cradled in the security of his musical talents. It was an amazing experience, free of any anxieties whatsoever, one that I never felt to quite the same extent with any other conductor. (The closest runner-ups that I can think of are Monteux, Rudolf, and Perlea.) And it was such genuine fun!

Another special treat that Leinsdorf provided was his conducting of Puccini's *Madama Butterfly*, and the complete interpretational transformation he brought to his performances of that opera. I don't think I know exactly how he achieved that conversion but, put in the simplest terms, that music sounded symphonic, not operatic with him, far from the long-standing, ossified traditional interpretations that *Butterfly* generally received. (*Butterfly* was what we called a "warhorse" of the repertory; in my relatively brief career in opera I must have played the opera about two hundred times.) I know that one thing Leinsdorf did was to remove all the extraneous tempo and dynamics liberties that had been superimposed on Puccini's remarkable score over the fifty-four years since its creation. There was something uncanny about how Leinsdorf, without saying a word, got the orchestra to play this thrice-familiar music in quite a different way than we were used to. It sounded cleaner, and its usually rather thick, gluey texture was suddenly lighter and transparent, although not bodiless, empty. The multiple colors of Puccini's orchestration, usually alloyed together in some undistinguished amalgam, now shone vividly in their beautiful diversity. It is possible that Leinsdorf's treatment caused *Butterfly* to lose some of its drama and pathos—but I don't think so; and in any case, much of that aspect was mostly in the hands of the singers. But the orchestra's role gained in clarity and distinctiveness. It sounded like a new piece.

All this was accomplished without a word uttered; it all came out of Leinsdorf's hands, his gestural molding of the sound, and his alert eyes as they roamed around the orchestra. It was rather amazing, too, that the singers, especially the various Cio-Cio-Sans who sang the lead role (during that season Victoria de los Angeles, Kunie Imai, Renata Tebaldi, Licia Albanese), had to a large extent also relearned their roles, whether reluctantly or cooperatively I know not.

I'm fairly sure that I was the only one in the orchestra to appreciate and to some extent understand what Leinsdorf had wrought, and how different *Butterfly* now sounded and felt, mainly because I was listening and observing as a composer, knowing the score very well, and being intimate with the tools of the creative craft. Leinsdorf had his troubles with almost all the orchestras and musical organizations he was involved with, especially in the case of the bitter adversarial relationship with which his tenure ended with the Boston Symphony, after the original two-to-three-year honeymoon. But I have to think that the six years he spent at the Met must have been the happiest and most uncontentiously productive engagement he ever had.

Among other outstanding musical experiences of those midfifties years, I must not neglect to mention working with Pierre Monteux, a longtime hero of mine.[50] By the time Monteux came to the Met in 1953, I had kept up with his career through his fine recordings with the San Francisco Symphony.[51] And now, here he was conducting one of my most favorite operas, Debussy's *Pelléas et Mélisande*. It was a special thrill for me to play this profound masterpiece with him, particularly since I still had a very bad memory of doing *Pelléas* with Emil Cooper. Monteux's cast was a good one, headed by Victoria de los Angeles, the excellent musician Theodore (Teddy) Uppman, and featuring Martial Singher as Golaud.

Of the many things I admired about Monteux, I would put at the top of the list that he was certainly the most equable and even tempered of all the conductors I've known and worked with. He was so economical in his baton technique, so simple and clear—the exact opposite, for example, of Bernstein. Monteux's composure on the podium, his calm control, were beautiful to behold. Of course, some audiences thought Monteux lacking in charisma; there was nothing to see, he looked boring. There is no question that because he eschewed any type of exhibitionism he was never fully appreciated by audiences.[52] What we musicians also saw looking at Monteux was that wonderful, almost constant twinkle in his eyes. It was so inviting.

What I thought was particularly winning was that Monteux knew every repertory work he conducted by heart, yet he never conducted without a score on his stand, occasionally looking at it, even though he never really needed to. It seemed to me that he wanted to have that beautiful score near him, like a dear friend.[53] A score is in itself, especially when handwritten by the composer, but even when engraved and printed, a work of art. It was so touching the way Monteux turned the score pages. He did it in a way that I never saw with any other conductor, but that I had often seen in my years in Germany with some of my elderly relatives, even with my own father—a way of turning a page that I believe is unknown in America. Monteux (French, of course) would lick, that is, moist the forefinger and thumb of his left hand, and then v-e-r-y leisurely turn the page. It was the unhurried, simple, modest way that he turned the pages that I found so affecting. The *Pelléas et Mélisande* score has 409 pages. Since he knew the score intimately, including its entire pagination, he didn't have to look at it to see when the last bar on a page arrived in order to turn it in time. I saw a certain humility in those gestures and a deep love for the music.

Monteux had many remarkable talents. Perhaps most exceptional was his uncanny ear. I mean his ability to unerringly hear details and minutiae in music, an ability that was way beyond any other musician that I can think of. I offer one extraordinary example. In Monteux's first year at the Met he conducted Gounod's *Faust* and Bizet's *Carmen*. In a rehearsal of *Faust*, at one point I suddenly heard a slightly out of tune note—a relative rarity in our orchestra. The note was an F above middle C, which in Gounod's particular orchestration of that moment of music was played, as I saw by looking at my score, in unison by seven different woodwind and brass instruments. Monteux stopped the orchestra and—in a kindly way—said to our second bassoonist that he was a little sharp. I was amazed; Monteux was dead right. The bassoonist sat right in front of me, and I had heard that he was slightly out of tune. But how had Monteux, at a distance of some thirty feet, with a full orchestra playing directly at him, heard exactly what *particular* instrument, out of some seventy, had produced the offending note? And how could he have aurally isolated it from the six other players playing that same F? That was really astonishing to me. If the seven players involved had been sitting far apart from each other, or if the bassoonist had played his note louder than the other six, Monteux's picking out that one player would not have been quite such a remarkable feat. But the fact that those seven players, including the third and fourth horn (intrinsically louder than a bassoon), were all sitting within a few feet of each other, proves that Monteux had an uncannily discerning and sensitive ear. Nothing got by him.

What was also appealing about Monteux was that when such little errors occurred, he never got irritated, never lost his temper, never took it out on the musician, as so many conductors were prone to do. I learned so much from working with him and from his many recordings, not only about conducting but also about what constitutes a really great, superb, score-respecting performance. He often said: "I have no interpretation; I play the music." I loved and respected so much that he never conducted for the audience, and never revised or touched up a score.

Beyond all these particulars—or perhaps because of them—Monteux had an uncanny ability, undoubtedly innate, to infallibly find the absolutely appropriate tempo(s), and to elicit from an orchestra the right ensemble balance(s), which I regard as the ultimately most important and critical areas in the full realization of musical works. His tempos always seemed so right, never too slow, never too fast; and even though they were steady—he saw no need to vary the tempo except very subtly, according to character and mood—they never seemed inflexible, rigid. In regard to ensemble balance, he effortlessly fulfilled the ideal of hearing everything the composer had written in its proper proportions. It is almost impossible to find a Monteux recording where these two aspects of re-creation are less than flawless. And above all, Monteux saw each piece of music as a whole, as a single entity, rather than as a collection of movements, segments, or episodes. All quite amazing!

I never heard a single musician say a critical or negative word about Pierre Monteux. That is phenomenal, musicians having generally no hesitancy in criticizing or bitching about conductors.

There was one encounter at the Met with a much-admired musical figure, Bruno Walter, which surprisingly turned rather sour. The reader will recall that Walter had long ago earned my admiration for his late-1930s seminal recordings of Mahler's works with the Vienna Philharmonic. In the interim I had heard many fine performances with Walter conducting the New York Philharmonic, especially the Mahler Second Symphony, the Brahms *Requiem*, and several rhapsodically lyrical performances of his favorite Mozart symphonies. But vaguely lingering in the back of my mind was a remark my father had made a few years back at dinner one night, after a day of rehearsing with Walter at the Philharmonic, to the effect that "sometimes I can't stand that guy, he's so"—he reverted to German—"*scheinheilig*."[54] I remember being surprised when he said that, but I had not at that time worked with Walter and could neither contest nor confirm my father's remark.

I had played *Fidelio* with Walter in 1950 and had some hazy memories of him making some slightly condescending remarks to the orchestra in one or two rehearsals, which seemed to imply—it was the first time he had conducted the Met orchestra—that we didn't really understand Beethoven's style and didn't appreciate Beethoven's greatness. But I hadn't taken his remarks particularly seriously, concentrating mainly on playing my first *Fidelio* really well and to his satisfaction. Walter did give us horns a perfunctory nod of approbation after the famously challenging "Abscheulischer" aria, and that was good enough for me. But Hugo Burghauser, former chairman of the Vienna Philharmonic, who had played under Walter in those 1938 Mahler recordings, and obviously knew him well from working many years with him, was quite upset with Walter's condescending attitude toward the Met orchestra.

In the 1956–57 season I was assigned to play Mozart's *The Magic Flute* with Walter. I was really looking forward to it, thinking that Walter ought to be an ideal interpreter of that wonderful work. But there was trouble right away at the beginning of the first rehearsal. There were only three rehearsals scheduled—orchestra and stage—since the orchestra had played *The Magic Flute* many, many times, and Walter himself had done it in the previous season. There was no need to have any extended rehearsal period. But it so happens that the Overture of the opera presents a famously challenging conducting problem, well known for a long, long time to musicians and conductors. The very beginning starts with a thrice iter-

ated introductory call  , stated in the entire orches-

tra, recapitulated at midpoint in the Overture in a slightly varied rhythmic configuration

 , this time only by the wood-

winds and brass. The trick is to get those sixteenth notes, after the *fermatas*, together in all the instruments. It is not exactly easy, but in the right conductor's hands it has certainly been done well many, many times. A conductor has to give a very clear, rhythmically precise, well-controlled beat, which was something, for all of Bruno Walter's many good qualities, he did not have. When rhythmic precision was required, his beat was often unclear, wiggly, erratic, in the manner of many German and Austrian conductors. When the music was more flowing and melodic, its flux and pulse well established, in other words when beat precision was not absolutely required, Walter's manual gestures were quite expressive.

It was that second set of calls that gave Walter the most trouble at this particular morning rehearsal; he seemed quite anxious about it, and his beat was even more wandering than usual. We all tried hard to be together on those first two notes, but it just didn't happen.[55] With each new attempt to get it right, but with little success, Walter got more and more annoyed—not with himself, but with us. After four or five more tries, he got even more irritated and launched into a lengthy exasperated diatribe. I quickly whispered and hand-gestured to my brass and woodwind colleagues, in effect telling them: listen, I'll give you two eighth notes with my head, breathe with me, and I'm sure we can be together. After one more failed try, we did get it together. Walter, surprised, gave us an unctuous smile, pointing with his finger to himself, as if to say: you see, if you watch me and follow me, it all works out fine. Yeah, sure! It was pathetic. (We played that little trick all through the season, successfully.)

Later in the same rehearsal, Walter, obviously annoyed with something he thought the orchestra was doing wrong, stopped rehearsing and began a rather moralizing sermon, solemnly delivered in his thick Viennese accent with pontificating emphases, to wit: "You know, my frrrriends"—the Viennese really roll their *r*s very vigorously—"Mozart vas a verrry grrreat composa." As if we didn't know that! "And you moost play his music with grrreat rrrespect. Iss verry serrious." He went on for quite a while in the same vein, interspersed with several more "my frrrriends," at high points shaking his finger at us ominously. What came across to us in both his condescending tone of voice and the substance of his lecture was that he was treating us like a bunch of little children, as many Central European refugees often did, considering all Americans more or less cultural illiterates who couldn't possibly know anything about the "grrrreat Kultur" of Germany and Vienna. It was an embarrassing display, and Walter lost a lot of respect that day among the orchestra. I must say that he didn't do this sort of thing often, but every once in a while he felt the need to preach at us uncultured musicians.

Sometimes Walter had a look on him as if he were wearing a halo. And somewhat hidden under his generally pleasant demeanor was a certain aloofness. You had the feeling, despite the Viennese politesse, that he thought orchestra musicians were something beneath him in worthiness, that they had to be kept in line, like children. He hardly ever knew any musician's name—you were an oboe or a horn—in contrast to Reiner who knew *everybody's* name and addressed us personally.

So I guess my father was right, there was something *scheinheilig* about Walter. I don't mean to imply that he was a fool or a bad conductor. These preaching incidents occurred sporadically, and in the end they were meaningless and harmless. He was often quite inspiring, and, like Stiedry, deeply in love with the music. We learned to play with him not by following his beat so much as his eyes, his facial expressions, his body language.

It was especially interesting for me that Burghauser, my senior by some forty years, who had early on befriended me—we always spoke German, and I loved the typical Viennese lilt of his Austrian dialect—told me many anecdotes about Walter in his four-year tenure as chief conductor of the Vienna Philharmonic, confirming many of the impressions we at the Met were beginning to gain of him. (We began to hear similar stories from our colleagues at the New York Philharmonic, where Walter was co–music director for a few years.) Burghauser, who was vehemently anti-Nazi (who had to leave his home country precipitously right after Hitler's *Anschluss* of Austria), did point out that Walter, from the very beginnings of his career (going back to the 1890s), had constantly encountered anti-Semitism, and as a result had lost many an important conductor post over the years. Likewise, the Vienna Philharmonic in the thirties was a hotbed of Nazi and Hitler sympathizers—after all, Hitler was an Austrian by birth—and often made life miserable for Walter. On the other hand, Burghauser confirmed that there was often about Walter this sense of holy superiority, and a kind of unctuous false modesty and artificial courteousness, which hid the fact that he was often just as short-tempered as any of the other famous conductor despots.[56]

I played with Walter often over the remaining years of my horn playing career, even recording with him several times. These anecdotes about Walter exemplify the lessons that I had to learn so often with the many great and celebrated conductors of that time; that he, too, was flawed and fallibly human—not quite the saint so many people thought he was.

Another conductor with whom I worked quite frequently, who also wasn't much of a saint, was Leopold Stokowski. I would define Stoky (as we called him—not to his face, of course) 50 percent genius, 50 percent charlatan. Several experiences that I will relate in the course of this narrative will substantiate that statement, which (I understand perfectly well) must appear quite outrageous and completely unbelievable to the lay reader, the average uninitiate music lover and Stokowski admirer. Indeed, the one story that I have already related and the ones I will occasionally share with the reader are on their face truly unbelievable. But they are true, proving once again that truth is very often stranger than fiction. Besides, although I have a fairly creative imagination I am certainly not capable of inventing tales so strange, so close to evil. Some of these incidents are so unbelievable, so bizarre, that they have over the passing years from time to time prompted my own disbelief in them. Did these things really happen? In consequence, I have on occasion, when beginning to doubt my own memory and intelligence, even my sanity, felt compelled to check the actual facts, the hard evidence, which in every case confirmed and reconfirmed the reliability of my recollection.

One day in early November 1954 I got a call from Joe Fabbroni, at the time the most powerful, most influential contractor in New York, for a record date with Stokowski, substituting for one of the horn players who had suddenly become ill. Fabbroni told me that RCA Victor was in the process of recording the complete second and third acts of Tchaikovsky's *Swan Lake* ballet. Luckily I happened to be free at the Met that morning, and of course accepted the engagement. The orchestra I found assembled at the studio, the famed Manhattan Center on Thirty-Fourth Street and Eighth Avenue, consisted partially of the officially announced and advertized members of the NBC Symphony, together with some of New York's finest freelance elite.[57] I was quite flattered to be in such august company.

Having already worked with Stokowski several times over the years (including in that 1947 crazy film date, *Carnegie Hall*), I wondered what strange things he might make us do this time. If there was one thing one could always rely on with Stoky, it was that he would preside over a rehearsal or a recording date with an icy autocratic assertiveness—some called it arrogance or an unfettered, puerile willfulness—which would inevitably entail some pretty weird interpretive demands. On this occasion, however, I noticed that Stokowski seemed to be not quite as magisterial in his demeanor as usual. Even his beat, which normally was very clear and economical—if rather inexpressive—seemed indecisive, capricious. It led from time to time to some noticeably ragged playing in the orchestra, mostly in the strings, which Stokowski either didn't hear or didn't care to do anything about, but which is clearly audible on the issued recording.

I also got the impression that Stokowski and Richard Mohr, the session producer, were trying to cram a lot of music into the three-hour session, because many numbers were considered acceptable after only one take, even when there were discernible performance blemishes that one usually wouldn't allow. For example, in the four-bar introduction to the so-called *Danse napolitaine* in act 3, some musicians in the woodwind section had completely neglected to play, while a few others (two oboes and one clarinet) did play something—except that it was from the wrong piece, the number *after* the Neapolitan Dance, the Mazurka—which was in a different key and a different tempo. This blunder is clearly audible on the recording; you'd have to be deaf not to hear it. But there was no call for a retake. Stokowski clearly had not heard the screw up.

In another number, "Espiègle (Waggish),"[58] Stokowski took so many tempo liberties, with constant *accelerandos* and *ritardandos* (not indicated by Tchaikovsky)—never quite the same in repeated takes—that even these very experienced orchestra musicians, well aware of Stoky's penchant for changing and distorting composers' music at will, had trouble following him. It took three takes to get that short movement reasonably together.

The worst incident of all occurred near the end of the recording session, where, in a transition from one of *Swan Lake*'s many waltzes to the final scene of act 3, Stokowski suddenly conducted the last six bars of the waltz in a totally different and, at first glance, quite incomprehensible beat pattern. Within a few seconds the orchestra fell apart, coming to a whimpering standstill. The waltz in question was one of Tchaikovsky's most popular and familiar ones, and this orchestra could have played this thrice-familiar music in their sleep. So what could have brought us to a complete stop? We all had played the *Swan Lake* music many times, myself included, particularly on my 1943 Ballet Theatre tour, when excerpts from either *Swan Lake* or *Sleeping Beauty* were on the schedule almost every night. Looking quite annoyed, Stokowski gruffly announced: "Back to the beginning!" Off we went again; but to our consternation, exactly the same thing happened at the tempo and meter transition. We tried to keep going, some of us trying to ignore Stoky's strange, confusing beats. Again the music broke down. Really annoyed now, Stokowski called an intermission, and stormed off toward the control room, where Mohr and Fabbroni were supervising the session. Through the control room window we could see what seemed like some agitated repartee, Stokowski probably screaming, what the hell is the matter with these musicians?

We were all completely confounded as to what was going on. What was the matter with the old man? In all the many times I had worked with him, I had never seen him perpetrate anything as inept, as confusing, as we were witnessing that morning. Was he on some kind of a sedative or some mind-twisting drug? Half the time he seemed to be in a trance.

That second time around I had figured out what Stokowski was doing. The waltz (in 3/4) shifts abruptly to a faster tempo 6/8, *allegro vivo* (conducted in two) with additionally a brusque key change. Instead of staying in one in the waltz and simply changing to a faster two, Sto- kowski had conducted the half notes in the last six hemiola bars in some undecipherable beat pattern. Perhaps it was intended to be a group of 2/2 bars, conducting the hemiolas rather than the basic 3/4. He had also made an *accelerando* into the *allegro vivo*, and then beat the 6/8 in 4/4, that is, one bar of 4/4 equaling two bars of 6/8 *allegro*.

I remember getting into a little huddle during the break with Julie Baker, Bob Bloom, Eli Carmen, and a few others, trying to figure out what to do. We knew we couldn't talk to Sto- kowski about the situation, since you could never criticize Stokowski, even indirectly by impli- cation. It was even dangerous to congregate like this; Stoky had eyes like a hawk. And what if one of the nearby mikes was open? We tried to look as casual as we could, under the circum- stances. I happened to spy Hugo Kohberg, the session's concertmaster that day, on the other side of the studio. He too was in a huddle with some of his violinist colleagues—the whole orchestra seemed to be in little huddles—gesticulating wildly as if to say, Lord, what's hap- pening with Stoky? Hugo, a friend of mine, was a former concertmaster of the Berlin Philhar- monic under Furtwängler, and one of Stokowski's favorite concertmasters, whom he regularly asked for in his recording sessions. I thought that Hugo and Stokowski must be close enough that maybe he could talk to him, quietly, privately, before we continued recording. It was worth a chance. I ran over to Hugo—the intermission was almost over—and suggested as much to him. I should have known; he looked at me aghast, throwing up his hands: "Are you kidding? I'll be fired! He'll never hire me again. Oh no!!" This great man, this wonderful, kind, intel- ligent, superb musician was frightened to death at the very thought of my suggestion.

I ran back to my huddle, and told Julie and the others around him what I thought Stokowski had been beating. Julie said: "Ok, if he does that again, ignore his beat and just keep on play- ing. I think we all know how this music is supposed to go. Come on, let's quickly spread the word." There was no time to discuss or argue the point. In a succession of hurried whispered communications the word was spread from section to section. When Stokowski came back into the studio, I thought he looked strangely calm and pensive, not uttering a word except "twelve bars before 73." Had Mohr talked to him? But that seemed inconceivable, because even Mohr would have been fired. But why was Stoky so relaxed, so impassive?

It was now six or seven minutes before one o'clock, when the session was scheduled to end. We started again, many of us hoping that Stokowski would beat what Tchaikovsky had actually written. But no, he conducted exactly what he had done before, and we—now prepared for this eventuality—kept playing, doing our best to ignore his beat. And here's where the story gets really bizarre and ugly. I swear, about ten or twelve bars into the *allegro* 6/8—I was watching Stokowski—I suddenly saw a glint in his eyes, a tiny glimmer of recognition. I'm convinced that at that moment he had just realized that he had been compounding two bars into one 4/4 pattern at the 6/8 *allegro*.

At this point, most of the several dozen conductors I knew or worked with—in fact, any conductor I have ever heard of or read about—would have stopped, maybe hit his head with his fist, as if to say, oh, what a dummy I've been, and would probably have apologized to the orchestra. (Although that might be going a little too far, given most conductors' egos and their inborn tendency to never relinquish their sense of superiority.) Not Stokowski. With incredible sangfroid, a steely determination to never admit a mistake, he unflinchingly continued to conduct in four; and, as hoped for, we all played through the 6/8 section and on to the end of act 3 without a breakdown. It's a good thing, too, because it was the last take of the recording session; no time for any retakes. What one hears on Victor Red Seal LM-1894, issued some time in early 1956 (and later reissued on the Quintessence label),[59] is, believe it or not, what we produced on that day under these very strange circumstances.

I need to make it clear that Stokowski never—that I know of—made what one would normally call errors or mistakes accidentally, out of some momentary uncertainty, as all conductors, even the best of them, are apt to make from time to time. Whatever interpretational transgressions and aberrations Stokowski perpetrated—and in the several thousand recordings and performances he conducted over a career that lasted a phenomenal eighty-three years, he committed an uncountable number of such transgressions—they were never accidental, inadvertent, or the result of some actual incompetence or plain misconducting. No, they were willful misinterpretations, driven by an unparalleled ego and arrogance, decisions that Stokowski in his supreme sense of himself felt he had the absolute right to make; and he believed that his interpretations always made the music better, more successful, greater, more important.

One could write volumes about Stokowski's seemingly irrepressible propensity to regularly change, revise, and distort composers' notations, most notably in the realm of dynamics and tempo. He was unique in his ability to unwaveringly ignore what composers had actually composed, had laboriously written in their scores. Mind you, this applied to any and all composers, greater or lesser, whether Beethoven and Bach or Geminiani and Lekeu. Any interpretational whim he might have would immediately be put into practice, without questioning.

One other aspect of the *Swan Lake* recording that needs comment here is that it was announced and marketed as offering the complete act 2 and act 3 of Tchaikovsky's four-act ballet. That was simply not true. Not only were many numbers or movements in both acts left out completely, but some from act 1 were added. Stokowski also made dozens of cuts, sometimes huge ones, in almost all the movements. In the process he eliminated many structurally critical repetitions, as well as some of Tchaikovsky's finest music, including a few of his most beautiful waltzes. Beyond that, many times he arbitrarily, willfully, for no discernible musical or structural reasons, changed the sequence and ordering of set numbers as originally conceived by Tchaikovsky and obviously based on the ballet's scenario and story line. (I have no quarrel with a decision to make some cuts in order, for example, to get the music onto two sides of an LP, but then don't promote the recording as containing the complete second and third acts of the ballet.) This is just another symptomatic example of the extraordinary, absolutely uncontestable power that Stokowski wielded.

I have said that Stokowski was equal parts charlatan and incomparable genius. His genial side will also be well represented in this narrative. For I owe so much to that side of him. I learned much from him and his many great, virtually unique, accomplishments, starting with the fact that in my formative years as a teenager and young man, at least one quarter of my sizable record collection, covering a vast spectrum of the orchestral literature, consisted of recordings by Stokowski and the Philadelphia Orchestra.

Returning to my final years at the Met—and turning from the ridiculous to the sublime—I must recount one of the most thrilling artistic revelations I was privileged to experience there. It concerns one of the supernovas of the musical history of the last century: Maria Callas. I had, of course, heard of her spectacular triumphs in the European opera world, especially at La Scala and Covent Garden. So when Bing engaged Callas to open the 1956–57 season with Bellini's *Norma*, one of her signature roles, I was pretty excited. Callas was world famous and controversial, always in the news, a favorite target of Italian and American tabloids and paparazzi. But by the midfifties reports had begun to circulate that her voice was going or gone, that she was past her prime, finished. Well, did she ever prove her naysayers wrong that opening night!

Obbligato

Maria Callas (originally Maria Anna Sofia Cecilia Kalogeropoulos), born in New York of Greek parentage, had one of the most extraordinary but also controversial careers in operatic history. An incomparable artist and a feisty, fiery diva, she was married to Giovanni Meneghini (her patron and manager) and had a relationship with Aristotle Onassis (the millionaire shipping tycoon). She was a legend in her own time. Her relatively short life—she died at age fifty-three—encompassed an even briefer career of hardly more than a dozen years. Originally quite overweight at 220 pounds, Callas slimmed down to 170 in the early 1950s. In some circles arguments still rage over whether the premature loss of her voice and the rapid demise of her singing career were precipitated by this dramatic loss of weight, or by her affair with Onassis, or her (presumed) profligate life as a jet-set celebrity. The truth is that it was, as most knowledgeable commentators have affirmed, a combination of precipitously losing that much weight (in less than half a year), and as her fame escalated to unprecedented heights, the attendant emotional pressures gnawing away at her inner life, driving a wedge between her career and her personal life—between the singer and the woman. On the first point, the fact is that the metabolic changes that resulted from her weight loss gradually caused the size and range of her voice to shrink, in turn responding less readily to the intensifying vocal and artistic demands she persisted in placing on it. The well over one hundred recordings (commercial, live, and pirated), ranging from her early performances of Wagner (Brünnhilde, Kundry, Isolde) and her engagements in Mexico to the final recordings and concerts in the 1960s, unambiguously trace the trajectory of her meteoric rise, her relatively brief heyday, and the harrowing decline of her career.

Most informed people know that Callas not only had a remarkable voice (replete with a stunning coloratura technique),[60] but that she was also arguably the greatest dramatic actor on the operatic stage. What is less appreciated, but to which I can personally attest, was the way those two aspects of her art arose out of her instinctual feeling for music, in whatever style she was singing. In other words, her much admired acting was developed from or through the music, and out of her deep understanding of it. Callas also was notable for her no-nonsense professionalism and disciplined work ethos. She loved hard work. In her contracts she demanded and was almost always given copious rehearsals. I was amazed to see her always sing with full voice in rehearsals, much to the dismay of many of her colleagues, who always wanted to save their voice by what is called "marking."

I saw those qualities and talents at work in the rehearsals and performances of *Norma*, *Tosca*, *Lucia di Lammermoor*, and *La Traviata*, the four operas she sang in her two seasons at the Met. My friend and much admired colleague, Jimmy Politis, co-principal flute of our orchestra, happened to be the one designated to play the flute part in *Lucia's* Mad Scene cadenzas, and as a consequence was with her on stage during all the rehearsals, saw her work at close range, confirming my own experience.[61] On stage, in rehearsals, she was as tough on herself as she was on others. Like anyone who is direct and outspoken, Callas evidently incurred the animosity (or the jealousy?) and resentment of many who were not quite so committed and professional.

By the time Bing was able to engage Callas at the Met, anyone with discerning ears and a real appreciation of her supreme artistry would have been able to detect the first slight, sporadic indications that her voice had lost something. (Ironically, New York really never got to hear Callas in her absolute prime.) If the invidious claims of Callas's detractors that she was now already over the hill were grossly exaggerated, it was nonetheless a fact that, though she was only in her early thirties, minute hints of strain had begun to creep into her singing. Her vibrato at full voice, especially on high notes, had begun to widen, to slightly wobble, and what had sounded easy and effortless just a few years earlier, was now, especially in certain more difficult passages, showing signs of strain and undue exertion. At times the radiant beauty of her naturally rich voice would take on a slightly unpleasant hard edge.

But leaving those fairly rare circumstances aside for a moment, what I loved and admired so much about her remarkable vocal endowments was the rich texture of that voice, what I can only describe as the weight, the richness, of her voice. It was a thrilling, vibrant sound. It also explains how at age twenty she could sing Leonore in Beethoven's *Fidelio* and Wagnerian roles such as Isolde and Brünnhilde. Now, some of that weight, that gravity, was no longer there; the voice had become a little thinner, a little paler. Knowing her singing from some of her best recordings and now listening to her rehearsals, I had the impression that her voice wasn't quite as responsive as before, not quite as ready to do anything she wanted to do with it. It now seemed to require extra effort and concentration. And at times I thought she seemed a bit anxious, even annoyed with herself, worried about her high notes.

Of course, even with these caveats, Callas's singing at the rehearsals, especially in terms of the sonic splendor of her voice, the astonishing expressive diversity and subtlety of her musicianship and interpretations, was still at an artistic level simply unreachable by most of her contemporaries. I marveled at the way she shaped and colored her voice in relation to the text or the dramaturgic context and the orchestral accompaniment, not to mention her clear, expressive diction.

What impressed me was her incredible breath control, enabling her to spin very long phrases with complete ease, with never a sense of running out of breath. There was also the subtlety and beauty of her *portamenti*,[62] and again, her willingness, indeed her eagerness, to rehearse. Callas obviously saw rehearsals as supplying the necessary time and practice opportunities to arrive at the levels of perfection that she aspired to. What affected me the most, indeed filled me with awe and wonder, was Callas's willpower, the sheer indomitable determination to succeed at the highest artistic levels, to overcome any difficulties and adversities. I don't think I ever saw or knew of anyone who had that quality in such abundance (except perhaps Judy Garland). This became clear to me during the many rehearsals Callas had insisted on with Rudolf Bing for her Met debut, a wonderful exemplar of the never-one-to-shirk-hard-work professional.

Being almost brutally self-critical and honest with herself, the encroachment of slight vocal difficulties was, of course, of considerable concern to Callas. Watching her in rehearsals (and performances) from my perch in the pit, I could almost palpably feel the energy expended to overcome any problem. Unlike the majority of singers who, say, at mid-to-late career develop vocal-technical uncertainties or bad habits, especially in regard to vibrato, but who then simply go into complete denial of their problems, Callas fought back with every fiber of her body and mind, determined through mental concentration and sheer willpower to not let her problems intrude upon her singing and her lofty artistic standards. When some of the difficulties showed up during the rehearsals, I could see her annoyance and frustration with herself. I gathered from others on stage with her that, once in a while, it would turn into a little temper tantrum, which some people erroneously took to be directed at them, and which on one famous occasion was quite disruptive to the rehearsal.

Whatever vocal annoyances Callas had encountered during the *Norma* rehearsals, she overcame them completely in the opening night performance through sheer willpower and an iron determination that I had never witnessed to such an extent. She was resolved not to let the public, the critics, the singers, hear any of her problems. She actually *made* any problems go away. I could literally feel the energy, the adrenalin, the extra concentration that Callas brought forth, from what inner psychic resources I know not. It was as if in such moments she just shifted into another gear as she made her voice do what *she* wanted it to do, not what *it* wanted to do. I was spellbound. The gritty fierceness with which she applied herself to the task at hand reminded me of a mother bear fiercely protecting her cubs. That night she was a not-to-be-denied bundle of egoism-driven energy (not egotistic) and determination. It was a phenomenon I was to observe many times during Callas's two years at the Met.

I happened to be assigned to all four operas she starred in during those two seasons, some thirty performances, and was thus able to witness her superhuman efforts to successfully hide the gradual fraying of her voice. Equally impressive was what I learned from her about the true Italian *bel canto*, as expressed particularly in *Norma* and *Lucia de Lammermoor*. There I also learned something about real accuracy, the kind of technical accuracy where every run, every *fioritura*, is as perfect as a string of pearls, where every pitch is produced with the right intonation and color. And what can I say about her *Tosca*. For me, no one ever delivered that final line of act 2, just after Tosca has killed Scarpia—"*Avanti lui tremava tutta Roma* (Before him trembled all Rome)"—more grippingly, or with the warmth and passion she exuded so ideally in the first act love aria, "Non la sospiri," both dramatically and vocally.

I deeply cherish the many fine memories of her singing that I carry with me to this day. I sometimes get chills up and down my spine just thinking about her work. For my sixtieth birthday Marjorie gave me four high-quality cassette recordings from Callas's prime years. On the way back from the birthday dinner at our favorite Boston restaurant, I decided to give myself a little taste of Margie's present on the car stereo. The first piece was "Vissi d'arte." I lasted about twenty seconds, then got all choked up, sobbing, unable to stop the tears from welling up in my eyes. I couldn't take any more, it was just too beautiful!

Callas's fame has unfortunately been shamelessly exploited by many record companies that issue pirated tapes of her singing, acquired by hook or crook (mostly crook) from late in her life, when she was struggling to keep some kind of a presentable career going. On many of these recordings (especially the many duet appearances with di Stefano) her singing is terrible, excruciating compared with her earlier glorious work. These CD companies take some tape made on nonprofessional equipment, maybe by someone in the audience or back stage in some opera house, and sell it to unsuspecting customers, who buy the thing just on Callas's name and fame.

This is a good place to discuss Renata Tebaldi (1922–2004), since both she and Callas were at the Met the same time, and were considered by many to be fierce sparring rivals. Actually, deep down they respected each other very much, although their zealous fans, split into two polarized camps and spurred on by the sensation-loving press, made sure that the rivalry was kept continually at a boiling point. In my view both were great artists, almost equal; and I like how one writer—I forget who it was—put it so well: Tebaldi was the second *numero uno*.

Tebaldi had an unquestionably beautiful and naturally calibrated soprano voice, in a way more innately beautiful than Callas's. One might say they both had extraordinary voices and were equivalently endowed vocally, but with different capacities and a different sonic quality. The differences between them arose from their respective training and early musical inculcation. Callas's teacher, Elvira de Hidalgo, taught her gifted pupil the art and technique of *bel canto*, with its pure lines but also its technical agility, the ornamental roulades, trills, virtuoso scales that enabled Callas to reintroduce the previously neglected early nineteenth-century *bel canto* repertory, what used to be called in opera houses "nightingale music," sung by lightweight *soprani leggieri*. Callas also reinvented the *soprano d'agilità*, and took on the dramatic roles of the more rebellious opera heroines—Medea, Norma, Lady Macbeth, Tosca, even Wagner's Sieg-linde and Brünnhilde. Tebaldi's teacher, Carmen Melis, on the other hand, taught Tebaldi the ins and outs of the true *verismo* style and repertory, with its more fragile, innocent heroines, as in Verdi's Leonora, Aida, and Desdemona, in *Adriana Lecouvreur*, and *Wally*, and, of course, Puccini's Mimi.

The rivalry engendered by these two divergent styles and concepts of singing—projected by the public and the press back onto the two ladies' personae—took on, especially in New York when they were both at the Met, a very nasty tone. It was a silly feud; they were in their different ways both great artists. Ironically, they both began to develop vocal problems: Cal-las, in the mid-to-late 1950s, and Tebaldi, in the 1960s, when she tried to make her already remarkably lush voice even larger, which in the end impaired her high register control. She left the Met for about a year to repair her voice, and was able to make a comeback, but never at her previous high artistic levels. She retired from the Met in 1972.

Another singer whose work I loved and admired very much was Antonietta Stella. Although I would not claim that she was, ultimately, at the level of a Callas—I don't think anybody in the Italian or *bel canto* repertory would be able to claim that—she came very close. I had fallen in love with her singing in Puerto Rico, a few years before she came to the Met, when I played several two-week opera seasons during the summer in San Juan.[63] Stella sang in *Trovatore* and *Don Carlos*, two roles perfectly suited to her lush, rich voice and artistic temperament. In her years at the Met in the middle and late 1950s she sang those two roles plus *Aida* and *Tosca*. I was irresistibly drawn to her singing in two ways: intellectually, in admiration of her secure, totally reliable vocal technique, a completely balanced two-octave range; and emotionally, in love with the sheer beauty of her voice and her exquisite musical intelligence and taste. Her pure clear voice and her musical intelligence reminded me of Rose Bampton's beautiful sing-ing, only located half an octave higher. There was in Stella's no-fuss, no-nonsense approach something so simple, so at ease, so apparently effortless and natural—and certainly free of any prima donna antics or tantrums—that many people, more impressed by artists' extravagant reputations and behavior, didn't appreciate what a superb artist she was.

I was fortunate to have been assigned to all four of her operas in the last three years of my tenure at the Met. I don't recall her singing ever being anything but beautiful and flawless.

Writing one's autobiography, as personally fascinating as it may be, is also in many respects very difficult and challenging. Perhaps the knottiest, most complicated of these challenges is how to write about one's achievements in an objective, duly modest way, to find just the right tone that avoids self-aggrandizement on the one hand and an exaggeratedly apologetic tone on the other. I have done so many different things in my life, pursued so many different interests in the arts and education, in effect maintaining six or seven different careers simultaneously for most of my adult life. Many people who know my work know this to be true, but wonder how such a thing was possible. When asked that question, I often quip, "well, I just didn't sleep very much," which is actually true. I sometimes add, "I've also worked very, very hard; more than most people." But among my many admirers I would guess that at least half of them know me only in regard to one of the six or seven arenas in which I have been active. Some people know me only as Mr. Ragtime, the one who "brought back" that wonderfully happy music by Scott Joplin that had languished in complete oblivion for about fifty years.[64] But most of those who appreciate my work in ragtime know nothing about me as a classical composer, or as a jazz historian, or about my work as an educator and an activist on behalf of many diverse musical causes. Even the fact that I am writing this memoir, to which I am devoting as many of my waking hours as is physically possible, surprises and disappoints many people who know me only as a jazz historian, and who desperately want me to write the third volume of my history of jazz. Those readers are quite unaware of and uninterested in my work as a composer and conductor, which happens to be the primary means by which I make my living. (Writing books, in my case, is the opposite of making a living.)

I am not complaining. Not at all! I am the last to suggest that people should appreciate *all* aspects of my multifarious career. That said, and to return to my work at the Metropolitan Opera as a horn player, I want to note, with all the modesty and objectivity I can muster, that I was considered pretty good—which is musicians' lingo in public for very good. (In private they may upgrade that to, oh, he's terrific.) Anyway, I *was* pretty good or very good, certainly good enough to maintain my position as one of the Met's two principal horns for many years, good enough to achieve a growing reputation in New York as a reliable, versatile player, with the result that I must have played on at least several hundred recordings (both classical and jazz) during the 1950s and the early 1960s.

I was not the world's greatest technical or virtuoso player; there were a few hornists in New York who could play rings around me in that respect. (Mind you, there was very little in the standard operatic and symphonic repertory that required such supertechnical virtuosity.) What I contributed as a player was, first, a composer's insights and understanding of the music, in regard to how it was put together and its personal stylistic characteristics; second, a meticulous, rigorous attention to all details of a composer's notation; and third, a way of playing that audibly expressed my love and comprehension of the music, of whatever kind or style or language.

Another interesting aspect of my playing that developed during my fifteen years at the Met, which both pleased and surprised me, was that I found that I could play for months, even a whole season, without cracking or clamming a note. But not to make too much of it, I would add that, apart from my constantly striving for something close to perfection, when you play the same, rarely changing repertory over a period of years, you get so familiar with it at every level, particularly technically and learning how to pace yourself in three- or four-hour operas, that you can avoid every pitfall and anticipate every difficulty—something you can't acquire as easily playing in a symphony orchestra. There the programs, over a thirty- or fifty-two-week season, change every seven days. In that sense playing in an opera orchestra is easier than playing in a symphony orchestra, simply because of the element of familiarity and repertory constancy inherent in an opera setting.

In view of the high level of assuredness I was able to achieve, the very few times that I did allow an accidental blemish to creep in haunt me to this day. One particularly embarrassing accident occurred of all times on one of our weekly Saturday matinee broadcasts, sponsored nationwide by Texaco and heard all over the country. I bobbled a couple of notes in a very exposed spot in the famous "Micaela" aria in Bizet's *Carmen*, a piece I had by then played probably three or four hundred times without any accident. I don't know why I clammed those notes. Was I for a split second not concentrating? Was I somehow overconfident? It was an especially embarrassing moment for me, since one of my most favorite conductors and dear friend, Dimitri Mitropoulos, was on the podium. He was not used to me missing notes, and to this day I see before me his puzzled, rueful expression, right after the accident.

In both the orchestra and the Met's management, including the conducting staff, I was increasingly regarded as not only an outstanding player and thus a kind of musical leader, but also as someone whose judgment on musical issues (such as artistic standards in performance) and professional and political questions (particularly in connection with the annual contract negotiations) was very much respected, and thus I was considered an especially valued member of the orchestra. As a result I found myself continually on several orchestra committees, dealing with issues related to our daily work as orchestra musicians and the conditions under which we labored, and during contract negotiations with problems arising out of the normally adversarial relationship between the management and the orchestra. Apparently, both sides trusted me as someone who was levelheaded in his judgments on disputatious matters. I often enough ended up in an arbitrative role, which was not always easy, since everybody was always tugging away at me, hoping to persuade me to join one side or the other. I'm sure there were now and then people on both sides who suspected me of harboring ulterior or expediently self-serving motives. But in the end I am proud that I was, for the most part, regarded as someone whose judgments were considered equitable, objective, and constructive.

It was inevitable that over those final years of my tenure at the Met, I got to know some of the conductors rather well, in some cases even developed a collegial social relationship. Leaving aside for the moment my close friendship with Dimitri Mitropoulos, and my gradually expanding relationship with Erich Leinsdorf, there were two other conductors with whom I developed a personal affinity and genuine feelings of mutual respect. One was Fausto Cleva, with whom I first worked in Cincinnati at the Zoo Opera in 1944, where he immediately won my respect for his astounding knowledge of the opera scores he conducted.[65] At the Met, in the roughly five hundred performances and rehearsals I played with Cleva over a period of ten years, I never saw him come even close to making a mistake. He also had, like (or perhaps even more than) Toscanini, a basic unconditional respect for the printed score.[66] This, of course, put him at odds with many singers, who were intent on taking all kinds of liberties with the music, rhythmically holding high notes longer than written, or holding any *fermata* three times longer than taste and common sense would dictate, dragging or rushing tempos, and the like. It put him in constant strife with haughty prima donnas and arrogant divos. Sadly enough, most of those singers ignored him, knowing full well that audiences came to see and hear *them*, not some little five-foot-four conductor in the pit, who was paid a lot less than they were. Many times I felt truly sorry for Cleva, as he struggled, mostly in vain, to protect Verdi's or Puccini's music from the usual interpretational aberrations, so many of them sanctified by something called tradition.

But there were two problems with Cleva: one was that he had an ingrained mistrust of musicians' ability to achieve the kind of interpretive perfection that he aspired to. This innate distrustfulness led to a flaw in his conducting; an excessive habit of what is called subdividing, which we musicians, feeling expressively strangled and overcontrolled, tried our best to ignore. But that was hard to do, since it was an immutable constant of Cleva's baton technique. Most 4/4s were conducted in eight; moderate tempo 12/8s were conducted in twelve. He simply didn't trust us to do the subdivisions ourselves, and when we did—which we almost always did—he just didn't appreciate it.

His favorite outcry was "Non scappate" (Don't rush). We heard that endlessly. His insistent subdividing led to a degree of rigidity, a certain lack of flow in the music. Subdividing generally does that. However it did produce rhythmic accuracy, if a tad on the mechanical side. Fausto didn't realize that he would have gotten the same rhythmic accuracy from us if he could only have trusted us to deliver it. That was a lesson he could have learned from his revered idol, Toscanini, who did not subdivide that much, and who, especially in moderate and slow tempos, generally created a fine lyrical line and flow.

Cleva's knowledge of the scores was awesome. He knew every note intimately, every notational flyspeck, every minute detail, as only very few conductors ever have. And, bless his soul, he possessed and always maintained an innate respect for the great composers' scores and the textual minutiae contained therein, constantly fighting against the multitude of bad traditions that infest the opera repertory, most of them never sanctioned by the composers. In my mind's eye, so many years later, I still see poor Fausto trying for the umpteenth time to get some singer off of a high note—unsuccessfully—the singer callously ignoring him. Eventually Cleva would give up in disgust, muttering a stream of Italian curse words under his breath. At such times I really felt for him.

Orchestra musicians can never indulge in the kind of interpretational excesses that many singers routinely get away with. Indeed, it would never occur to an orchestra musician to do that. We are trained from the outset to follow a conductor religiously, with no allowance for any personal deviations. The Cincinnati and Met opera orchestras, the two orchestras in which I was able to work with Cleva, were no different in that respect. And thus, when Cleva conducted, with his clean technique and commanding control, we always played well for him. In that sense, over the many decades, including his twenty years at the Met, Cleva usually got consistently good, clean performances. I for one respected that enormously, but I think he was in the end underappreciated, probably taken for granted, both by audiences, the press, and even many musicians.

On the podium, in rehearsals or performances, Cleva always looked like a very, very unhappy man. He always had a pained expression on his face. And indeed, in all the years I worked with him I hardly ever saw him smile or relax, and that was when one of our least beloved singers, the tenor Kurt Baum, a pompous, unbelievably arrogant ass, screwed up royally in a *Carmen* matinee, at which point Cleva broke into a big, gleeful, sardonic grin, as if to say: you see what a dumb, pathetic, hopeless jerk you are![67]

My fourth horn colleague, Silvio Coscia, who was an old friend of Cleva's, told me one day: "You know, just like Toscanini, off the podium Fausto is a really nice, relaxed guy." That was hard to believe, but I eventually learned it to be true. I knew, ever since my days of working with Cleva in Cincinnati, that he liked and respected my playing. I think he realized that I was as meticulous in adhering to a composer's score as he was. I don't recall him ever—*ever*—in all the years that I played for him, correcting me or asking me to play something louder or softer or differently. Still, we never talked or met in any way. I was therefore rather surprised when one day John Mundy came to me during a performance and told me that Cleva wanted to see me in his dressing room during the next intermission. For a moment I wondered if I had done something wrong. What it turned out to be, to my amazement, was an invitation—still with no smile—to come to dinner with his family at the Ansonia, a great big ornate residential building, with huge apartments, on Broadway in the Seventies, where half the Met's singers and conductors lived.

I don't think readers will realize how absolutely unusual such an invitation was (and still is). Conductors and orchestra musicians live in two different social worlds; they generally don't fraternize. Certainly in the past, musicians would never think of asking to meet or socialize with a conductor; it just wasn't done. If word got out, you would forever be suspected of playing up to a conductor in the hopes of protecting your job. Conversely, conductors wouldn't invite a (mere) musician to dinner or some social event because, with a few rare exceptions, they thought themselves so superior and so importantly busy that they could not deign to stoop that low. A segregative class system, keeping artist singers and conductors well separated from musicians, especially on tour, was a sternly maintained policy in Rudolf Bing's opera house.

Cleva's invitation led to two dinner evenings at his home a year apart; the first time just me, the second time Fausto and his signora invited Margie as well. He said, with almost a smile, "that way we won't only talk about music." Margie and I tried valiantly to reciprocate with invitations to our home, but unfortunately our mostly conflicting schedules never allowed that to happen. When I say dinner evenings—the emphasis on the latter word—I mean to say that these were enormous three- to four-hour feasts, which I learned in later years on my many visits to Italy was an Italian tradition, a national pastime of elysian culinary experiences and extraordinary hospitality.

Silvio was right. Cleva was such a different person when surrounded by his family; he was downright charming. He obviously doted on his four children, including two beautiful teen-age daughters. His wife must have slaved for two days over the preparations for that immense seven-course dinner, climaxing in a most delicious homemade tiramisu. It turned into a lovely relaxed evening of exchanging stories and anecdotes about our backgrounds, his student years at the Milan Conservatory and early days at the Met in the 1920s (as assistant chorus master). I learned that Cleva had been brought to America by no less than Gatti-Casazza himself, the famous artistic director of the Met at that time. When Cleva heard that I had made my professional debut at age sixteen with Toscanini, he was quite impressed—and smiled!

Getting to know Fausto and his family was a revelation; it afforded me one of my earliest opportunities to learn that many of the conductors I worked with, mostly all famous celebrities in the world of music, were often off the podium regular folks—there weren't many female conductors in those days—with all the virtues, contradictions, and fallibilities of any human being. It was a good thing to learn.

Another conductor whom I admired and with whom I was able to develop a relatively close relationship—more professional and musical than personal—was Jean Morel. He was brought to the Met by the two Rudolfs (Bing and Max) in 1956 to conduct two Offenbach operas, *The Tales of Hoffmann* and *La Périchole*, both considered by Bing a kind of French counterpart to Johann Strauss's *Die Fledermaus*, with which he had had such a huge success. (It didn't quite work out that way, although, both works being operettalike operas, they did enjoy a continuously successful three- to four-year run at the Met.)

I had already learned that as a very young man Morel had played in the Paris premiere of Darius Milhaud's marvelous *L'Homme et son désir* (*Man and His Desire*), a ballet created, like his jazz-influenced masterpiece *Creation of the World*, for Les Ballets Suédois (The Swedish Ballet) in Paris. That placed Morel automatically in very high esteem with me, which was quickly confirmed in the first rehearsal I had with him, in *La Périchole*. He not only knew the score intimately and respected it, he also brought to his re-creation the endemic (and mandatory) French charm, sparkling wit and elegance, sustained by a typically Rhenish-German sophistication.[68] I loved the alacrity of his mind, his sparkling wit. Unlike Cleva, Morel constantly wore a slightly smirky, bright, intelligent smile. It was fun working for him and intellectually stimulating to spar with him, not through argument or discussion, but through eye contact and testing our reciprocal reactions.

Although I never had dinners or lunches with Morel, we corresponded off and on after I left the Met, when he was head of the conducting department at the Juilliard School. In those days I heard often enough that Morel was a real martinet, a cruel taskmaster with the students, wearing a perpetual scowl. That is hard for me to believe. Persistently demanding and severe, yes; cruel, no. With his very high standards and sharpness of mind, I'm sure that what he wanted to inculcate in some of those often cocky students was that they had a bit more to learn, and that playing music was a very serious, challenging business. If Morel felt that you weren't serious, that you were too casual in your behavior and not really paying attention, not concentrating, he would cut you down to size. And he could do that with a typically Gallic caustic wit; you'd feel about two inches small. Some may have thought that was being cruel. It wasn't cruel, because in Morel's case it wasn't about him, about his ego; it was about the music. He couldn't stand it if someone didn't take the music seriously, didn't concentrate, appeared not to be completely committed, fully engaged in the task at hand. I admired that about him.

We kept in touch from time to time after I left the Met. When I conducted Milhaud's *L'Homme et son désir* in 1962 in my Carnegie Hall series "Twentieth-Century Innovations," I wrote him about it, reminding him that he had played in the world premiere of that work.

Three days later I had a postcard from him, thanking me for telling him about the performance, wishing that he had known about it—"I would have come to hear you"—and appending (I assume from memory) one of the main themes of the piece. That postcard is one of my little treasures among the sizeable collection of memorabilia I have of famous people I have admired, and with whom I was fortunate to develop fine collegial relationships.

I did eventually get to play Offenbach's *Tales of Hoffmann* with Morel, but I wish I could have played Gounod's *Faust* and Debussy's *Pelléas* with him. Alas, he was not given those operas until after I had left the Met.

In the midfifties the Met commissioned Samuel Barber to write an opera, which turned out to be *Vanessa*, with a libretto by his close friend Gian Carlo Menotti. Mitropoulos was assigned to conduct the work, which premiered on January 15, 1958.[69] In early 1957 I got a phone call from Barber from his home in Mount Kisco, New York, asking me if I could help him with a little problem he had, writing a particular thing for the horn. He needed, according to Menotti's libretto, to imitate the howling of a dog near the beginning of the third act, and wondered whether that could be done somehow on a horn. He said he was stuck, and would I be so kind as to help him with that problem. "Of course," I said. "I'd be glad to." He added something about how impressed he had been with my brass writing, especially for the horns, in my *Symphony for Brass and Percussion*, which he had heard on the radio a year earlier, when Mitropoulos conducted the piece with the New York Philharmonic.

I was quite surprised and flattered by Barber's call. I had never met him, although he had written me a very complimentary letter after that performance of my *Brass Symphony*. To me he was one of those remote, very famous, and very successful composers who, along with Copland and Schuman, seemed to live in a different, exalted world. Barber evidently did not know that I was, in fact, a hornist in the Met orchestra, and that I might end up playing the first horn part in *Vanessa*. (As it turned out, Dick Moore was assigned to play that opera in its premiere performances. I played *Vanessa* the next season, having hoped to play the dog howling part, but by that time Barber had put it into a separate horn part, played backstage.) A few weeks after his phone call, Barber invited me to his brownstone house on East Sixty-First Street. I brought my horn along, ready to try out whatever he had so far envisioned. What he showed me were a few notes in the high register, just about in the range where dog howling would occur—generally in the octave above middle C. I had guessed that this is what Barber had in mind, and so I showed him how, with lip and embouchure adjustments and what we call "half-valve" positions, you could imitate the howling of a dog (or a wolf). I also talked him out of using three horns—initially he had in mind to have several dogs howling—telling him that what we were working out would be unusual and difficult enough for one horn, but too risky to coordinate between three players. I played several versions of this howling for him, using his pitches as a point of departure, and suggested to him that the rhythms he had written for this effect at his designated tempo were perhaps a bit too fast, that at a slower tempo the bending of the notes to sound like a howl would be more effective and realistic. I also told him that what I had shown him was not exactly easy to produce on a horn, that it was the kind of thing that classical horn players were never asked to do, that I knew of no such passage in the entire horn literature, and that what he had in mind would be much easier to play on a trumpet, which has piston valves. With horns, which have rotary valves, pure *glissando* effects were hard to produce. But the trumpet's timbre was intrinsically too bright, too narrow, to reproduce the sound of a howling dog. I felt that with some diligent experimentation and a bit of practice it could be done on a horn.

Barber seemed delighted with my suggestions and demonstrations of the effect, and thanked me profusely. But as it turned out, in the rehearsals and performances the effect didn't work all that well. Barber had designated both dog howling passages to be played offstage, which meant that one of the horn players from the Met's second horn section (which was responsible for all the many incidental backstage horn parts that are scattered throughout the entire opera repertory) was assigned to play the calls. Although I tried several times to show Mario Ricci how to produce that effect, he never could really do it well. It just sounded strange and clumsy, and not very much like a dog.

When a few weeks later, after the premiere, I ran into Barber by chance at a Philharmonic concert, in which Mitropoulos was conducting Barber's *Medea's Meditation and Dance of Vengeance*, we both commiserated over the fact that what I had suggested wasn't being realized effectively. I suggested that perhaps the best solution would be to record a dog howling on tape, and have the tape played offstage, exactly like the recording of a nightingale that is played in every performance of Ottorino Respighi's *Pines of Rome*.

Barber wrote me a lovely letter, thanking me for my help, and especially for advising him to have the effect played by only one horn. He said: "I dislike sound effects in general, and the less rumpus they entail the better." He had wanted to send me some money, but I told him that that was quite unnecessary, that it had been enough of an honor and pleasure to meet him and work with him. His response was: "I'm going to take you at your word, but you must promise me that if you are so kind as ever to help me again, it must be on a strictly professional basis, for I cannot intrude on your time. But please accept my most sincere thanks and the esteem of a colleague."

As far as I know, Barber left the dog howling effects in the stage horn part. I wonder how often it has been rendered effectively, realistically.

Another conductor with whom I worked at the Met is Karl Böhm, whose major musical talents were intertwined with rather dubious and expedience-driven professional behavior—once again an interesting case of high artistry marred by human fallibility.

Böhm arrived at the Met in 1957, having been handed a huge welcoming gift by Bing:[70] the season's opening night opera, *Don Giovanni*. I was assigned that opera, and I have to say that although I could never muster much affection for Böhm, and although I had played *Don Giovanni* at least a hundred times with most of the famous Mozart specialists of the day (Busch, Walter, Leinsdorf), Böhm's *Don Giovanni* was ultimately the best.

How and why was it the best? Good question, especially when one considers that the conductors just mentioned were easily three of the finest and most celebrated Mozart conductors in the world at the time. Furthermore, Mozart's operas were so popular—really never out of the repertory since their creation in the late eighteenth century—and their language and style were so fixed and so intimately familiar to conductors, singers, and orchestras, that performances of Mozart operas (and Mozart's works in general) were consistently the most authentically rendered performances in perhaps the entire classical repertory. In Mozart's music hardly anybody takes the wide liberties that conductors generally visit upon, for example, Beethoven, Brahms, and Schumann's masterpieces. So, if all renditions of Mozart's operas are at such a high level, what made Böhm's performances so superior? I don't think I know the complete answer to that question, but I think major credit must go to Böhm's extraordinary, uncanny sense of pacing, of working with the time continuum. With him one experienced the entire three-and-a-half-hour opera as one magnificent, unified entity, rather than a string of twenty-four separate set pieces. I also think that Böhm's slightly brighter, yet unhurried steady tempo helped the flow and pacing of the whole piece.

But it is not simply a matter of brighter tempos. In listening some years later to Böhm's recordings of Mozart's last seven symphonies, made between 1959 and 1966, and played superbly by the Berlin Philharmonic, I realized that what he did so perfectly and so consistently—and did it also in our Met *Don Giovanni*—was to move or relax the tempo ever so slightly (we are talking about two or four metronome points either way), usually some twenty or thirty times per movement, without ever losing the inner pulse of the music, the most important expressive element of all. The result was that every change of mood and character got its own perfect tempo, not some "perfect" metronomic sameness, but a most subtle shifting of tempo inflections that never undermine the basic underlying pulse.

I'm convinced that this is how Böhm created such a wonderful grand line. I could feel it, sense it, in each performance as it unfolded.[71] I also admired Böhm for avoiding the sometimes sentimentalized, over-romanticized interpretive approach to Mozart's music that we sometimes experienced with Bruno Walter. Böhm was right when he said somewhere that "you will find every emotion in Mozart's music, but he is never sentimental."

That represented the good side of Böhm. The darker side manifested itself in two ways, one relatively harmless, the other much more serious and, in my opinion, difficult to ignore or forgive. Regarding the former, in rehearsals and performances, Böhm was, frankly, unpleasant to work with. He spoke with a particularly vulgar Austrian dialect, in curt, impersonal *Kommandant* instructions. He wore an incessantly sour expression on his face, a permanent deadpan expression of dissatisfaction, no matter how well we played for him. In his mind we were definitely inferior. But we could live with that, being rather used to superior-minded conductors' attitudes, which one just learns to ignore over time. But Böhm was not liked for other more serious reasons. We knew from several musicians in our orchestra who had played with Böhm in the Vienna Philharmonic in the 1930s—Wittels, Geringer, and Burghauser— that Böhm, as an early Nazi Party member, had been appointed to a number of the most prestigious conducting positions directly, personally, by the "Big Three": Hitler, Göbbels, and Göring. The most notorious instance of this transpired when Fritz Busch in 1935 resigned from the position of chief conductor of the Dresden Staatskapelle because he felt he could no longer work in the oppressive political and cultural environment bred by the Nazis. Busch abruptly left Germany. Böhm asked Göring for the Dresden job and was immediately installed as Busch's successor. Burghauser also told me that Böhm, who often conducted in Vienna, was regarded by most of the Vienna Philharmonic musicians the same way he was viewed by the Met orchestra: haughty, aloof, and unfriendly. Hugo added, "my friends in the Vienna Phil tell me now that he hasn't changed a bit: still the same old grouch."

Böhm's sourpuss attitude on the podium and his Nazi past concerned many of my colleagues, especially the Jewish refugees, who knew that he was the type of conductor who enjoyed firing musicians. Actually that could never have happened, at least not easily, because Bing never gave any conductor, even his old Darmstadt friends, that kind of official authority, and also because our orchestra committee gained in influence and strength during the first half-dozen years of Bing's tenure as general manager. Nonetheless, some wag in the orchestra, inspired by the Hollywood cliché that had every German U-boat captain commanding his crew to "fire one!," started a rumor about Böhm as "the U-boat captain."

For me, having as a young boy been suddenly forced to join the Hitlerjugend without any choice in the matter, the question of Böhm's close association with the Nazi Party was, now as an adult, a matter of considerable concern.[72]

When I began to hear rumors that Bing was going to schedule Alban Berg's *Wozzeck* in the near future, I naturally assumed that Dimitri Mitropoulos would be engaged to conduct the work. Instead I soon found out that Bing had chosen Böhm, of all people. This really infuriated me. Here Mitropoulos had had the greatest triumph during his years at the helm of the New York Philharmonic with four glorious concert performances of *Wozzeck*, which were turned by Columbia records into the very first recording of the work. And I know that Dimitri, who had hoped—and rightly expected—to conduct *Wozzeck* at the Met, was deeply hurt by Bing's decision. But what made me, and Harry Peers and Hugo Burghauser and our concertmaster, Felix Eyle, and quite a few others who knew about Böhm's political past in the 1930s and 1940s, really mad, was that Böhm, the Nazi sympathizer, would now have the privilege of conducting this great masterpiece by a composer whose music was banned by the Nazis as degenerate art, and who was officially declared a noncitizen by the Austrian Nazi authorities.

I was not surprised that Böhm would accept the assignment. But many of us in the orchestra could not understand how Bing could be so callous and hypocritical as to ignore Mitropoulos and give *that* opera, of all operas, to Böhm. I was also shocked to realize that none of the critics or anyone in the press made even the slightest reference to this gross injustice—another example of how career expediency prevailed over professional integrity.

The conductor with whom I enjoyed the closest personal and professional friendship was Dimitri Mitropoulos. Even before I actually met and got to know him well, I had often thought that a close relationship with him was somehow inevitable, given my great admiration for him as a musician and as a human being. If I have called Max Rudolf a wise man, I would have to call Dimitri a saint (one of the only two or three persons I have known to whom I could apply that laudation). Naturally I also greatly admired Dimitri for his unwavering commitment to the best, most important contemporary music of the time, both in Minneapolis and in New York. He programmed many works never previously performed in America, and most especially the thoroughly rejected and officially despised music of the Second Viennese School.

For me as a young composer, Mitropoulos's commitment to new music was crucial, since it enabled me to finally hear with my own ears, and absorb and digest in my own mind, so many works that I had read about, but never had a chance to actually hear: Berg's *Wozzeck*, Schönberg's *Variations for Orchestra* and his opera *Erwartung*, Webern's Symphony Op. 21, and many more. Here they were—now finally—not only available to be heard in glorious acoustic reality but also played by an outstanding, virtuosically endowed (although sometimes still rather recalcitrant) orchestra, and led by a passionately committed and genially knowledgeable conductor. These were revelatory experiences. But even more important, they provided me a more balanced, comprehensive view of the "new music" terrain. It enabled me to fill in the huge void left by the realities of America's concert life at the time, where someone like me could hear regularly and know practically every work by Stravinsky and Copland, by Barber, William Schuman, and Roy Harris, but nothing by Berg, Webern, and Schönberg (except the latter's very early *Transfigured Night*).

Thus I had early on hoped—even naïvely assumed—that Mitropoulos might also be interested in my work as a composer. I was thus rather disappointed when, despite various overtures made to him on my behalf by my father, by Morton Gould, and by Artur Rodzinski—not to mention my sending him in Minneapolis on two separate occasions some of my early orchestra works—he seemed to show no interest in my music. The scores were returned unopened, unexamined. I have to assume that they were never passed on to Mitropoulos. As I later got to know him personally, it is inconceivable to me that he would not have looked at the scores, had he been shown them.[73] I was also surprised, and a bit hurt, by his seeming disregard of me in the early 1950s, when in fact I should not have been unknown to him. We had first met in 1947, when Mitropoulos conducted Strauss's *Alpine Symphony* and my father introduced me to him after the concert; and several times I actually worked with him in the horn section of the Philharmonic. Subsequently I had seen him often at rehearsals and concerts as he began performing so much music that was completely new to New York, not only Schönberg and company, but also composers such as Ernst Krenek, Roger Sessions, Max Reger, Milhaud, even Monteverdi. So he must have known (and could hardly have forgotten) that I was a composer, and that I was particularly interested in all the music he was so courageously presenting.

Mitropoulos finally did become interested in me as a composer. It may have been through David Diamond, a close friend of his, or Max Rudolf, when Mitropoulos joined the conducting staff at the Met in 1954. All I remember was that sometime in December 1954 I was suddenly asked by one of the librarians of the New York Philharmonic to send one or two of my scores to Franco Autori, the Philharmonic's associate conductor. But what may also have caused Mitropoulos to put two and two together was when he saw me sitting in the first horn chair at the Met, in the rehearsals for Verdi's *Un Ballo in maschera*, which he had been assigned to conduct.[74] I remember that he looked at me in surprise, with a somewhat hesitant smile of recognition and greetings. Had he also forgotten that I was a horn player?

Things now began to move very quickly. I sent Autori my 1949 *Symphony for Brass and Percussion* and my *Dramatic Overture*, the work I had composed in one week in the summer of 1951 and of which I had been able to make a recording. A few short weeks later, Mitropoulos called me to his room at the Met, and told me he had programmed *both* pieces with the New York Philharmonic in the 1956–57 season. I was stunned, especially when he, the dear man, apologized for not being able to program my compositions earlier, in the immediately upcoming season. I told him I understood that with an orchestra like the Philharmonic one has to program works at least two years ahead of time, and that I was thrilled he would even consider doing my music, and so soon. Thrilled? My God, I could hardly believe what I was hearing, especially since he was planning to conduct both works in the same season. It turned out that that was the first time ever in the Philharmonic's 114-year history that an unknown composer was introduced to the music world with *two* different compositions in the same season. What a break! What an honor!

It was only some time later that I realized what a major watershed moment in my life Mitropoulous's presentation of my music actually was. The performances of those two works with the New York Philharmonic were heard not only in Carnegie Hall, but also nationwide on the weekly Sunday afternoon CBS network broadcast. That literally put me on the map as a new talent and someone to really watch. Suddenly I was getting highly complimentary letters from some of the leading names in American music: Aaron Copland, William Schuman, Roy Harris, Samuel Barber, and Randall Thompson; I was being acknowledged as an important up-and-coming talent by these composers who probably had never heard of me or my music. Besides, the American compositional scene was sharply divided between two camps: the tonal neoclassicists, following in the footsteps of Stravinsky and Copland, and on the other hand, a young burgeoning group of composers writing in a strongly chromatic or atonal language. The neoclassic camp more or less dominated the musical scene for some fifteen years, and constituted America's official music establishment. In effect, it determined what got performed, what got recorded, and what got published. In one fell swoop, Mitropoulos made it possible for my music to be heard—twice, within a few months—on widely heard national broadcasts as performed by one of the premier orchestras of the land. I was suddenly welcomed into the greater community of established composers.

It was a nice feeling, although a mite strange, since I felt that I had been up-and-coming for at least a decade or so, except that nobody seemed to know about it. It was what in show business is called an overnight success. For someone like me, writing in a widely repudiated style and language, suddenly being recognized as even existing, to say nothing of receiving considerable praise for my work—that was an enormous career breakthrough.

Mitropoulos's advancement of my work as a composer, and the chance to work consistently with him at the Met and the New York Philharmonic, led quickly to a very close collegial friendship that lasted until his death in 1960. I also soon became the beneficiary of his legendary generosity. Probably the most widely held perception about Mitropoulos, exceeding even any appreciation of his musical achievements, was his lifelong passion of charitably expending almost all he earned on other people. He was famous for helping musicians buy new or better instruments when they couldn't afford to do so themselves, or to pay their doctor or dentist bills, and to underwrite interesting musical projects that came to his attention. In this he was often too generous and sometimes—one could argue—a bit too indiscriminate. As a result he often found himself in financial straits, suddenly unable to pay his taxes or his rent. It was well known that he lived a rather ascetic lifestyle, imbued with the spirit of sacrifice and self-denial, which also manifested itself in his total unostentatious devotion to music. In this he was inspired in his young years by the life and teachings of St. Francis of Assisi, particularly his belief in the essential insignificance of materialism and the acquisition of worldly goods and wealth.

Mitropoulos's generosity to me manifested itself in many ways, but most significantly in his determinate devotion to my music, including the commissioning in 1958 of what was to be one of my best and most important early compositions, *Spectra*. The commission was given to me at his request and on his behalf by the New York Philharmonic, and premiered in Carnegie Hall in January 1960. The three performances given were remarkably good, considering the difficulty and complexity of the work, which was in a style that most of the Philharmonic musicians had neither experienced nor liked nor understood. But I know the performance was as beautifully played as it was because of Mitropoulos's obvious devotion and commitment to my music, not to mention his intimate knowledge of the work. I also like to think—I could feel it at the rehearsals—that the musicians liked and respected me; having played with them so often over the last fifteen years, they thought of me as one of them. They also all liked and respected my father. So, it was almost like a family affair. But in the end it was Mitropoulos who once again extracted from those musicians not only a technically secure but also a highly expressive performance—a kind of miracle.

Mitropoulos also sponsored and lavishly subsidized several of my trips to Europe when he was championing my music in places like Cologne and Salzburg. Starting in the midfifties, he began inviting me to join him in what turned out to be literally hundreds of dinners over the remaining years of his life. I lost track of how many times I was privileged to enjoy his company and the always inspiring conversations we would have at La Scala, his favorite restaurant in New York, famous for its superb North Italian cuisine. La Scala was in effect Mitropoulos's second home. He also invited me, on the road during Met tours, to many fabulous upscale restaurants like Justin's in Atlanta or the Golden Pheasant in Memphis.[75]

In my last five years at the Met I had the opportunity to play some hundred performances with Mitropoulos, in operas ranging from *Tosca* and *Carmen* to *Boris Godunov* and *Masked Ball*. It was an interesting experience for me because of the different interpretive approaches he took toward these stylistically and dramatically quite dissimilar operas. Mitropoulos had not done much opera in the United States (except occasionally in nonstaged concert performances), concentrating primarily on the symphonic literature. No one, including myself, could anticipate how he would fare in opera, working with haughty prima donnas and brainless tenor divos. But I quickly discovered that he knew his way around the opera world, and that he had a forceful personal take on all the operas he conducted. This was especially the case in the Italian repertory, where he brought out fresh aspects of these works, through timing and pacing, by highlighting all kinds of important orchestrational aspects, and in general eliciting a richer, darker, more intense sound from the orchestra, all in all accentuating things that one had not heard or noticed before in the more routine, codified renderings typically accorded most of the Italian opera repertory.

Sometime in the late 1950s Mitropoulos wrote a short biographical sketch in which he commented on his distinctive approach and relationship to opera. Contrasting himself with self-appointed specialist opera conductors, who only deal with one limited area of the repertory, he thought of himself as a Greek, who was "good for everything." One finds those routinier types in almost all opera houses: Italian specialist conductors for Italian repertory,

German specialist conductors in German repertory, and so on. Mitropoulos eliminated many long-standing but not particularly valid interpretive traditions—which, of course, upset some of the older Italians in the orchestra and other Italian staff conductors. But many others found it exciting to finally encounter a different slant on these thrice-familiar works.

Most interesting for me was the emotional power and stark realism Mitropoulos brought to Mussorgsky's *Boris Godunov* (in the Rathaus edition), where it seemed to me that his Greek and monastic heritage and background[76] gave him a special affinity for that opera's basic subject matter: the eternal suffering of the Russian people under the feudal Czarist regimes, so realistically captured in Mussorgsky's astonishing music.

Finally, of the many fine conductors I worked with in my twenty-one years as a horn player, the one that may be the least remembered nowadays and least appreciated during his lifetime is Max Rudolf.[77] I came to greatly admire Rudolf over the years for both his musical skills and his personal qualities. As a musician and conductor, the two words with which I would primarily characterize him are wisdom and knowledge. He possessed many of the attributes that I most admire in musicians: a comprehensive intelligence, great sensitivity, an innate comfortable modesty coupled with a wonderfully poised self-confidence, and, above all, an intrinsic respect for and fidelity to the composer's text, regardless of what style or language or repertory. As our chief artistic administrator at the Met he was an absolute straight shooter, no hidden personal agendas—as evenhanded and equitable as can be.

I have already praised Rudolf's work. I would like to recap his philosophy of conducting, particularly in regard to the "question of musical allegiance to composers," as he once put it in an address given at the Curtis Institute.[78] In that talk Rudolf stated his artistic beliefs and concepts and expressed his values in regard to the profession *and* art of conducting about as comprehensively and succinctly as is possible. His list of values, judgments, criticisms, suggestions, and counsels began head on with his pronouncement that too many "conductors excel in ego trips." (How very simple—and so true!) He reminded musicians and conductors that they should unequivocally respect the "great musical minds" and the "works of the great composers," living or dead, and develop a deep sense of obligation to them, for without them we "performers could not make a living." He especially reminded younger musicians and conductors that the art of interpretation and re-creation is a lifelong pursuit, humbly adding that even as an octogenarian he still had not finished his studies. "I am still a student."

For me one of Rudolf's most important tenets (by which I have also tried to live my life and career)—indeed the centerpiece of Rudolf's philosophy—was that we performers must determine "not only what the great masters of music wrote, but why they wrote it in that specific way and no other." He deplored the notion harbored by far too many conductors that they could "serve the composers best by creating something new each time they perform one of their works," and he would add—so crucial—that he did not believe that "as interpreting musicians we have the right to 'create' music." He suggested instead that we should unequivocally "love" and "respect" the composer and his works. Rudolf was also fond of quoting Stravinsky's admonishment "to treat the composer with loving care," and, paraphrasing from the Bible, "thou shalt love the composer as thyself."

Rudolf also deplored the notion of "the definitive reading" claimed by so many conductors and critics, saying, rightly, that "there is no such thing." I remember that when I was with him years later in Cincinnati, when he premiered my first Piano Concerto, we happened to talk one day about the notion of a definitive recording. Rudolf, who was a very calm and gentle person, exploded in reaction: "I despise that idea." (Despise was a word that rarely passed his lips.) He also thought that the term "style" is bandied about too carelessly and unjustifiably, since most of the time the word "fashion" would be more accurate. His intent here was that a composer's style—Mozart's or Beethoven's, for example—does not and cannot change. What changes are the various fashions with which that style is interpreted. A lot of wisdom and professional integrity in his words and thoughts!

In conversations with Max he several times told me how long it took him to unburden himself of the influence of the "legends that I grew up with, the sacred cows in musical interpretation—like Furtwängler." Max and I were both Furtwängler admirers; in my younger years I worshiped his recordings and learned a great deal from them. But in later years, as people who have read my book *The Compleat Conductor* know, for all my basic admiration and respect for Furtwängler, I had to single out the numerous untenable liberties he took in his interpretations, as convincingly as he may have done them. Max did not hesitate to state that Furtwängler, though one of his idols too, "nonetheless strayed too often from his favorite composers' intentions." Max was also against the idea that composers of the past would, if "they were living now, welcome the changes in interpretation" that conductors visit upon their works. He thought that such often-proffered arguments were speculative at best, arrogant at worst, and in any case could never be empirically demonstrated to be true or valid.

I cherish the many memories of my working with Max Rudolf all those years and of our growing collegial friendship, which blossomed particularly generously on our spring tours, when there was more leisure time for relaxed and private associations than during the hectic winter season. He and I often happened to end up in the same hotels. (Unlike most of my orchestra colleagues, who tried to save money from their per diems by staying in the cheaper hotels, I tended to frequent the better hotels, where the upper echelons of the Met's staff also stayed.) Max and I would occasionally run into each other, or he would ask me to join him for dinner. On such occasions we realized that we did indeed have a lot of ideas and feelings in common about making music. I appreciated that he became quite interested in my compositions and in my growth as a composer. Several times he even dropped by at rehearsals of my woodwind quintet or at run-throughs on tour of some of my newest orchestra compositions, impromptu rehearsals in hotel ballrooms that I sometimes was able to organize with my Met colleagues.

One time I found myself playing the celesta part on tour in three *Rosenkavalier* performances, with Max conducting. The regular celesta player, Julius Burger, had became indisposed and had to leave the tour for a week and a half. (By a strange coincidence none of the other assistant conductors were available to fill in for the missing colleague.) I knew the entire celesta part—not particularly extensive, with long periods of rests—almost by heart, because I had been playing excerpts from *Rosenkavalier* on the piano ever since my midteen years, just for fun or showing off a little. I especially loved those magical superchromatic, quasi-atonal celesta passages near the very end of the opera, embedded in the sublime G-major duet of Sophie and Octavian

Twenty-three years my senior, Max Rudolf was someone I looked up to, and in many ways—perhaps unknowingly—tried to emulate.

On my last tour with the Met, in the spring of 1959, I undertook a brief adventure that almost ended in a minor disaster for me. I had wanted for some years, in addition to my excursions on free days to Galveston, El Paso, Ciudad Juarez, and Tijuana, to also visit Havana, both for its Spanish colonial cultural and architectural splendors and also to taste a bit of its famously lively nightlife. When I found a three-day loophole in my performance schedule, I flew from Atlanta to Havana. One of my first destinations was the beautifully ornate Teatro Principal, where the first Western hemisphere performance of Mozart's *Don Giovanni* took place (in 1818), and where the Orquesta Filarmonica, founded in 1924, regularly held forth, renowned for attracting many of the world's most distinguished maestri as guest conductors, artists such as Erich Kleiber, Igor Markevich, Arthur Rodzinski, Thomas Beecham, Fritz Busch, Sergiu Celibidache, Jascha Horenstein, Antal Dorati, and many others. The Teatro was also where, in 1860, the legendary New Orleans-born pianist-composer Louis Moreau Gottschalk conducted and premiered his *Night in the Tropics* symphony, with a monster orchestra of some four hundred musicians, augmented by several brass bands totaling another hundred players, plus a solo percussion quartet especially imported from Santiago de Cuba, who improvised in the indigenous Tumba Francesa style.[79] What an occasion that must have been! Four thousand people are said to have attended the concert; another large throng was out on the central Plaza, unable to get into the packed-to-the-gills hall.

Among the many impressive sights I saw in my wanderings around Havana, most astounding was Morro Castle, the fort that has guarded Havana's harbor for centuries, and is one of the very oldest edifices built by Europeans in the whole Western hemisphere, dating from the mid-1490s, soon after Columbus landed in Cuba and claimed the island for Spain. I was surprised to see that Havana's old capitol building, built in the 1700s, looked very much like our capitol in Washington. I also loved walking along the Malecon, a beautiful palm tree-lined boulevard running along the coastline, reminding me very much of Nice's Quai du Midi, facing the Mediterranean.

I tried to avoid the more touristy Las Vegas type of show entertainment, but was not too successful there. I really didn't need to see another Sally Rand fan-waving, totally factitious, sexless show. I was looking for some authentic ethnic Cuban music, and some of the sensuous, exotic, uninhibited dancing so inherent in the Spanish-tinged Caribbean Latino culture, which I knew well from Mexican films. But I found none. Not that it wasn't available in Havana. I just didn't have enough time or information for locating, in the forty-eight hours I was able to spend in Havana, the kind of places where I could hear good indigenous popular music making, along with some classy, sophisticated stage shows. Still, I felt good about having made the jaunt to Cuba, and getting a fairly good impression of Havana's special cultural ambience. Little did I know that eight months later all that would change when Fidel Castro's revolutionary forces took over the country and turned it into a Soviet-style socialist state.

It was on my way back from Havana to the Met tour in Birmingham that I almost got into really serious trouble. But I was saved, in a manner of speaking, by Old Father Time. I left Havana around one p.m. on a sixty-minute flight to Miami, expecting to continue on to Atlanta after a forty-five-minute layover. But the Miami-Atlanta flight left over an hour late. I now knew I was in trouble, because with that late departure I was definitely going to miss my connection in Atlanta for the flight to Birmingham, and thus never make the eight o'clock curtain of *Tosca*. I was desperate; my stomach was in knots during the whole two-and-a-half-hour flight to Atlanta. In the airport there I was about to call Dick Moore or Dave Rattner to cover for me, when I saw a sign for an air taxi service. I suddenly realized that if I could rent a plane, I could still make it in time because Birmingham was on central time, that is, one hour earlier than Atlanta. I ran as fast as I could to the air taxi office, and immediately found a pilot there ready to fly me to Birmingham—the rental was about $350, which I paid by credit card—and within a half hour of having landed in Atlanta, I was heading westward in a one-engine Piper Cub. We landed in Birmingham about five after seven, and a fifteen-minute cab ride later I was changing into my tuxedo and warming up for the evening's performance. (I hadn't touched my horn for three days.)

I told no one of my escapade, and no one, above all John Mundy, ever knew that except for that time zone advantage, I would never have made that *Tosca* that evening!

By late 1957 I was beginning to have renewed thoughts of leaving the Met. Not that I was unhappy there. Quite the contrary; I loved my job. I loved playing the horn and playing all that wonderful music, working with a lot of excellent singers and interesting, sometimes even great, conductors. I was also playing off and on with the New York Philharmonic, and on many recording dates, incidentally doing quite well financially. Nonetheless, my recent successes as a composer reminded me of what I had known from my early teen years, that my first love was composing, that I was captivated with the fascination and challenge of creating, with the miracle of filling those blank sheets of music paper with lots of little black dots that would someday produce beautiful musical sounds. Now I was no longer composing in total obscurity; my compositions were beginning to be played with some regularity, both in America and in Europe. My music was also being heard on the radio and produced on recordings; and several New York music publishers began publishing my compositions in beautifully engraved editions. Still more crucial, I was beginning to receive commissions with some regularity from instrumental colleagues and soloists, from orchestras and chamber music groups and university ensembles. This provided not only encouragement but also professional recognition, and—wonder of wonders—extra income. People were actually *paying* me to create, and usually with a guarantee that what I created would be immediately performed. Too often in the past the pieces I composed ended up, unheard, in the proverbial drawer.

All this greatly increased interest in Gunther Schuller, the composer, prompted me to wonder how Gunther Schuller, the busy horn player, was supposed to deal with all these tempting opportunities and commitments. Although I had occasionally dreamed of being able to make a living as a composer, I knew deep down that it probably would be a long time, if ever, before I could survive professionally as a composer. Anyway, that was in the future; that time had certainly not yet come. For now I would have to continue my life as a gainfully employed professional musician. But the question that didn't seem to want to go away was how could I answer the greatly increased demands upon me as a composer, and still maintain the heavy, time-consuming schedule at the Met, clearly my main secure source of income.

There was no easy answer, considering that each day was only twenty-four hours long, and that my job at the Met, plus some thirty hours of teaching the horn, consumed nearly sixty hours each week. Apart from practicalities, I was really torn between my two great loves: composing (creating) and performing (re-creating). I also knew deep down that I truly wanted to do both. To add to this interesting dilemma, I was becoming more and more involved and in demand as a player and writer and lecturer in the field of jazz, and experiencing the first inklings that there might be a part-time career in conducting in the offing. I sensed that soon something would have to give, and my innermost feelings told me that that would undoubtedly have to be the horn, as much as that idea was anathema to me. The fleeting thought that perhaps I could be a part-time horn player was quite unrealistic, for you cannot physically and mentally uphold the rigorous standards required at the highest professional levels if you don't keep at it daily.

Eventually I arrived at a reasonable—and I hoped temporary—compromise. Even with my recent successes as a composer, there was still no guarantee in the precarious world of contemporary music that I could maintain my arrived-at standard of living and also support a wife and a growing family. Our first child was born in 1955; another was on the way in 1958. I knew that there were only two or three American composers who did not also have a teaching job at a college or a university. Two of the three, Samuel Barber and Elliott Carter, were independently wealthy; and Aaron Copland, the lone composer whose success and fame guaranteed him a steady income, did not have a family to support. I also knew that as a high school dropout, without diplomas or certificates of any kind, there probably was no chance of getting a teaching job as a composer.

The compromise I decided upon was to leave the Met, but to continue the horn career as a freelancer in the New York studio and recording scene—a solution that worked out very well for the ensuing four years. I discovered that I loved playing the horn so much that I simply could not give it up—at least not yet. I decided to give the Met at least a one-year notice. When I met with John Mundy, Max Rudolf, and Erich Leinsdorf, and told them that as much as I loved my work at the Met, I felt that I must now give priority to my composing career, they were practically in a state of shock. "Oh you can't do that; you're one of our most valuable players. You *can't* leave us." I must say I was flattered, realizing now how much the conducting staff appreciated my playing and my meditative role on the Orchestra Committee. When Stiedry found out about my intention to leave, he too pleaded with me to seriously reconsider my decision. But I was adamant.

There now ensued endless weeks of negotiation, which produced several offers of generous raises, even talk of somehow reducing my weekly or hourly schedule. I didn't see how that could work, since it would surely place an extra burden on several of my colleagues in the section, or else require hiring an extra horn player. Moreover—*really* unthinkable—it would set a dangerous precedent, which other first-chair players would certainly try to exploit. But it was clearly an indication of how desperate the management was to keep me in the orchestra. The discussions continued off and on for more than a year. Rudolf and Leinsdorf tried every kind of flattery, cajolery, and bribery to get me to stay on. Eventually, since all these negotiations were completely amicable, and I was really deeply touched by their genuine desire to keep me on board, I agreed to Leinsdorf's offer that the Met would let me go at the end of the 1958–59 season if I would seriously help to find a replacement who could maintain the high standard they felt I had set, if I would promise to coach that player in the opera repertory, especially if he were someone who had little or only sporadic experience in opera, and if I would be prepared to finish the 1959–60 season if my successor somehow did not work out to their satisfaction.

I checked with a number of my close horn colleagues, including Jim Buffington, John Barrows, and Tony Miranda, to see if any of them might be interested in coming to the Met, but all three—very successful freelancers with lots of lucrative work in the New York studios—were uninterested. One of them considered it being "buried in an opera pit." Eventually I chose my best student at the time, Paul Ingraham, to take my place; though still young and relatively inexperienced, he was a first-rate musician, a quick learner, a player with a secure technique and a beautiful tone. Paul was hired. He did take over and did very well, much to the relief and satisfaction of Rudolf and the conducting staff. But ultimately Paul was not happy at the Met—it was never clear to me exactly why—and at the end of that one season he left the orchestra, eventually becoming one of the finest and most successful freelancers in the New York scene, where he is still active to this day.

There is a postlude to this story. In my attempts to convince Rudolf and Leinsdorf that they ought to let me go, I asked them repeatedly what they would do if *they* were offered an opportunity to advance, to expand their career options. Wouldn't you want to go forward? They always dodged the question, mumbling some evasive platitudes. The irony is that both of them also left the Met very soon after my departure, for what they surely thought of as greener pastures. Indeed, Rudolf left the Met in 1958, actually the same year that I left, becoming the Cincinnati Symphony's music director. Leinsdorf stayed a little longer at the Met, but took over the music directorship of the Boston Symphony in 1962. In later years I kiddingly chided both of them for trying to prevent me from moving forward, when at the very same time *they* were already plotting their own next career moves.[80]

The last time I saw Rudolf Bing was in the mideighties, sitting alone at Fontana di Trevi, a first-rate Italian restaurant on Fifty-Seventh Street. It was one of Bing's favorite restaurants in midtown Manhattan (as it was for me since 1957), located practically next door to Ronald Wilford's Columbia Artists offices, where, incidentally, Bing was employed for some years after his contract with the Met expired in 1972. I was shocked to see how frail, how haggard, Bing looked, so different from the authoritative, quick-witted, spry-looking figure I had come to know in my years at the Met. I couldn't believe my eyes. Although I was sitting only two tables away from him—about fifteen feet—he did not recognize me or even notice me. No surprise there perhaps, since we hadn't seen each other for nearly thirty years, and even then only sporadically, during the annual contract negotiations.

As I watched him I realized that he seemed to be barely conscious; he wasn't eating, just sipping some wine from time to time. I had a strange feeling that he didn't know where he was, that his mind was lost in some vague distant place.[81] As much as I had had sufficient occasions to dislike the man in the past (for all that I also admired his managerial accomplishments at the Met), I was saddened to see him in such a pitiful condition. I sat there in amazement, the phrase "Oh, how the mighty have fallen" coming to mind over and over again.

There is no question that my fifteen years at the Met constituted one of the most fulfilling periods in my life, in part because they cover my still youthful, formative years. It was there, in that decade and a half, that I assembled and began to fuse together most of the constituent components of my later career as a multifaceted musician. It was there that I developed and consolidated my artistic and aesthetic philosophy of life. It was the professional and financial stability and unbroken continuity that my employment at the Met provided that enabled me over time to pull the various strands of my diverse interests together. And it was the period during which I became fully established as a composer and a performer at the highest levels. It was also the time when I was in effect instinctively, almost unknowingly, exploring and preparing for most of my future pursuits as a conductor, educator, writer, jazz historian, lecturer, music publisher, and record producer.

And then there was, of course, all that glorious music at the Met, night after night: Mozart, Verdi, Puccini, Strauss, Wagner, Bizet, the occasional Beethoven and Debussy. And in the performances of those magisterial works there were often inspired, revelatory realizations by this or that artist that I shall carry with me to my grave.

There are five most special, precious, and unforgettable moments that still give me goose bumps just thinking about them, reliving them in my memory—even decades later. Hilde Güden's heartbreakingly poignant rendering of Anne's farewell to Tom Rakewell; the sublime Lullaby in Stravinsky's *Rake's Progress*; Cesare Siepi's agonized ruminations in the great "Ella giammai m'amò" aria in Verdi's *Don Carlos*, alone at night in his palace chambers, about to face the cruel, heartless Grand Inquisitor; Luigi Cancellieri's touching, brief clarinet asides in *La Traviata*—which not once but *every* time brought a lump to my throat; Maria Callas's deeply affecting, heroic rendering of Bellini's "Casta Diva" aria in her Met debut; and the electrifying opening night performance of Strauss's *Salomé* with Ljuba Welitch and Fritz Reiner.

I knew that I had to move on in my life, and say good-bye to the Met, but it was also a sad and reluctant farewell.

Chapter Nine

THE THIRD STREAM

DURING THE EARLY FIFTIES so much of my involvement with jazz came about because of my close friendship and professional relationship with John Lewis. We talked just about every day on the telephone, sometimes for hours on end. We discussed all sorts of musical matters and issues and problems, in a sense educating each other about our different professional areas, but also beginning to plan all kinds of collaborative ventures—new musical organizations, concerts, recordings, workshops—all with the intent of bringing classical music and jazz (also classical and jazz musicians) together, in a variety of mutually creative ways.

It all began very simply with exchanging and borrowing from our respective large and diverse record collections, also going to jazz and classical concerts together, comparing our sometimes divergent impressions, and hanging out a lot at the Carnegie Hall Tavern, where, incidentally, Charles Mingus soon joined us on a regular basis. Our mutual interests and activities led eventually over the next dozen years to our organizing a whole range of innovative joint enterprises, such as the creation in 1956 of the Jazz and Classical Music Society (the first such organization ever). The list of these collaborative endeavors is substantial. It included—most important—the founding in the late 1950s of the Lenox School of Jazz (a first in the history of that music), and the creation of a workshop-rehearsal band with a mixed group of jazz and classical musicians, an ensemble we maintained for about three years, but which we never presented in public. Also, in a broader sense, there was the emergence and development of a new musical genre called "Third Stream" (a term I coined in a lecture at Brandeis University in 1957), representing the growing rapprochement between the two musical mainstreams, jazz and classical, which when married and merged produced a third stream—that is, a creative fusion of classical and contemporary jazz techniques and practices.[1]

John began asking me to make arrangements or orchestrations of some of his new extended compositions (again for jazz and classically mixed ensembles), as well as to organize recording dates for him, on which I soon became involved as a conductor, as the music he was composing increasingly demanded such directional supervision. John also offered me through his contract with Atlantic Records and Finnadar (an Atlantic subsidiary) multiple opportunities to record some of my jazz-infused Third Stream compositions, and to make seminal recordings of works such as Schönberg's Chamber Symphony Op. 9 and the Op. 29 Suite.

In late 1952 John founded the Modern Jazz Quartet with his colleagues Milt Jackson (vibraphone), Percy Heath (bass), and Kenny Clarke (drums). (Clarke was replaced in 1955 by Connie Kay.) That was at the time a rather novel instrumentation, which John had experimented with a year earlier, with Ray Brown as bassist. And in 1958 John formed MJQ Music, with me as editor in chief, a publishing company dedicated to bringing out in elegantly printed editions jazz and Third Stream works in complete sets of score and parts—still a great rarity in those days. I was in charge of editing and engraving, and in general preparing the works for publication. I held that position—unpaid—until the mid-1960s.

As a horn player, my first professional jazz recordings took place in 1950, and included the last of the three recording sessions of the Miles Davis Nonet, the whole series eventually becoming known as the *Birth of the Cool*.[2] I was invited to play on the March 13, 1950, recording date by Miles, a session that, as luck would have it, included one of the all-time masterworks of jazz: Gil Evans's remarkable recomposition of Chummy MacGregor's ballad *Moon*

Dreams. Junior Collins and Sandy Siegelstein had preceded me in the horn chair on the two previous recording sessions, Junior in January 1949, and Sandy in April 1949. I was particularly enamored of Sandy's playing—I knew it well from his many recordings with the Thornhill Orchestra—particularly with his particularly beautiful rich, warm tone and elegant phrasing. When neither Junior nor Sandy was available for the third Nonet session, I was asked to take over at the recommendation of John Lewis.

By that time I had acquired the previously issued six sides, and knew the music very well. I did not, of course, know the four new pieces we were about to record. But Miles arranged for us to have several rehearsals, starting in February. A good thing, too, because Gerry Mulligan's *Rocker*, with its tricky syncopated rhythms, at a very bright tempo, and Gil's complex *Moon Dreams* score certainly could not be recorded properly without some serious prior rehearsing. Also, memories were now in 1950 a bit rusty, to say the least, since the group had not played together for over a year. There hadn't been any gigs for the group; this new kind of jazz had thus far been a decided nonsuccess. With its cooled-off sounds and sleek modern lines, as well as the "strange" instrumentation, it certainly wasn't straight ahead bebop; nor was it the more familiar swing of bygone days. There had been no demand for the group to tour or even to play in New York, except for a couple of dates at the Royal Roost, and those had been a whole year earlier.

In any case, I was thrilled to be able to participate in the recording. I was particularly excited to be working with Lee Konitz, whose playing with Tristano and the Thornhill Orchestra I admired greatly; and also, of course, with J. J. Johnson. He and I—it was John Lewis, once again, who had brought us together—had already become close as composers via our mutual enthusiasm for the music of Hindemith, Bartók, and Stravinsky. J. J. was a real composer in the classical sense, that is, not just a writer of thirty-two-bar tunes or twelve-bar blues, but also of extended multimovement works, with varying tempos and meter changes, and instrumentations that prominently featured brass instruments. I also looked forward to playing with him because his full, rich trombone tone, expressed with little or no vibrato, was very close to a horn sound. I knew we would blend together beautifully. And then there was Bill Barber, an amazing tuba player, who had such a beautifully clear, lithe tone and remarkable agility on the instrument, this at a time when most tubaists were more or less content to pump out the *oom* of the stereotypical *oom-pah* accompaniments that most tuba parts consisted of.

I recall that a few weeks prior to the scheduled sessions Miles actually came to the Met to meet with me, to personally check me out, since he had never heard me play, and to go over the horn parts with me. (I have to think that Miles may have been the first jazz or black musician to ever set foot in the musicians' locker room in the then lily-white, sixty-seven-year-old Metropolitan Opera House.)

The Nonet's presession rehearsals went quite well, especially on *Rocker*, *Deception*, and *Darn That Dream*, although much less so for *Moon Dreams*. The problem there was that Gil Evans's recomposition of MacGregor's ballad included a Coda, where two things happen: (1) the weight of the heavy atonal chords in the six "horns" completely overpower the simple quarter-note time on the cymbal (in the drum part), thus in effect quashing any sense of a jazz or swing beat, so central to jazz playing; and (2) to complicate matters further, the "horns" split into six separate polyphonic lines, with some of the most intricate, vertically uncoordinated rhythmic anticipations and suspensions ever heard in jazz up to that time. We kept falling apart in that section, except one time, when I asked Max Roach—for rehearsal purposes only—to play his quarter-note beats really loudly, with sticks rather than brushes. That, however, was not what Gil had intended. I'm sure Gil did not realize how difficult those last twenty or so bars of *Moon Dreams* are. By the way, strangely, Gil was never at any of our rehearsals.[3]

I got to the record date a half hour early. I was really anxious, not only because it was my most important involvement with jazz to date—a virtual nobody, suddenly working with some of the finest jazz talents in the world—but also because, as a very experienced musician in classical preparation procedures (rarely exercised in jazz in those days), I was worried about how we would be able to record so much new and difficult music in a three-hour record session. And so were J. J. and Bill Barber. We were especially worried about how we were going to get through that Coda in *Moon Dreams*.

A few minutes after I got to the studio I went to Miles and said, "Please, Miles, you know how difficult that *Moon Dreams* is, and you also know how tiring that piece is for our chops, especially for me and J. J., and probably for you too." He nodded a yes. "So, please, don't do *Moon Dreams* last, that'll be dangerous. You don't have to do it first, but maybe second—just to get the most difficult piece out of the way early in the session, when our minds and chops are still fresh. *Please*, please, don't leave it for last!" A bit later I saw Miles go into the control room to talk to Lee Gillette, who was A&Ring the recording.[4] Of course, I couldn't hear what he was saying, but I assumed it was something like: the guys in the band would like to do *Moon Dreams* fairly early on, not at the end of the session; it's the most difficult piece for us. Ok?

Well, for whatever reason, my request, my suggestion, was ignored.

We recorded Gerry Mulligan's *Rocker* first, and it went very well. When Gillette announced from the control room that we should do *Deception* next, I looked at Miles, questioningly. He merely shrugged his shoulders, as if to say: I'm sorry, it's not my call. Lee wants us to do *Deception* now. There was no time to argue, and I didn't feel I could intervene. I was only a sideman, not the leader. I was lucky to be on the date.

Gerry's *Deception* also went well, although for some reason we did three takes, even when some of us thought the second one was really quite good. (Maybe something went wrong in the control room.) My heart sank when I heard that *Darn That Dream*, with Kenny Hagood as vocalist, was scheduled next. It took a while to get the microphone levels and balances set between Kenny and the band, and again we were asked to do more takes than we thought necessary. *Darn That Dream* is a good song, in fact one of Jimmy Van Heusen's best, and it was the easiest piece to record. But in the context of an essentially instrumental ensemble session, it seemed to me that this one vocal piece was odd man out, so to speak, maybe even expendable, and certainly didn't warrant making more than two takes. We had only three hours for the entire session, but one has to subtract at least twenty minutes for intermission breaks. And here we were spending precious extra time on that song, rather than saving our energies and chops for the most tiring piece on the docket. (Slow tempo pieces with lots of long notes are always more tiring for brass instruments). And now we had only thirty-five minutes left in the session, and the most difficult piece by far yet to do.

During a five-minute break, J. J. turned to me and said, "I hope I can get through this thing. My chops are beat." "Yeah, mine too." Things were also made more difficult by the fact that the studio where we were recording was quite small, almost claustrophobically so—and everything sounded very dry. There was little reverberation in the room, no acoustic aura to the sound. I felt that the notes I played dropped immediately to the floor, with hardly any projection.

The reader can probably anticipate what happened next. The first take of *Moon Dreams* started out very well, barring a few ragged moments and some questionable balances—except that we broke down, as I had feared, in the Coda. We got through the piece a little better on the next two takes, but with note fluffs, some bad intonation, and again various rhythmic inaccuracies in the Coda. Even on the issued recording[5] you can hear the strain in our playing, especially at the beginning of the Coda, where Miles's high F sharp is out of tune, and Lee's takeover of the same note is even more out of tune, very sharp. You can hear how Lee—a great player, whose intonation was usually impeccable—is hanging on to that F sharp for dear life. J. J. sounds tight and strained, very unusual for him. And I sound a tiny, tiny bit flat at one point. To this day I can feel how tired my lip was; I just barely got through that last take.

The atmosphere in the studio was now getting really tense. (Miles mentions this also in his autobiography.) What I had worried about if *Moon Dreams* was left to the end of the session was coming true. I really felt we weren't going to make it, especially when Gillette announced over the studio intercom: "Gentlemen, there's no overtime; don't even think about it! Capitol Records is not going to give us any!"

It was now ten minutes before the end of the session. During the final five-minute break I decided, in desperation, that in order for us to get through the Coda somebody would have to conduct, to keep us together rhythmically. And that someone was going to have to be me. I told Miles that's what we should do, to which, thank God, he readily agreed. I moved my chair and stand forward a foot or two, and told everyone to also move a little so that they could see me. (So far the six "horns" had all sat in a straight row, with virtually no eye contact between us.)

Very few readers will know that playing the horn and conducting at the same time is a rather awkward and precarious business, for the simple reason that we hornists play with our right hand in the bell of the horn. If you take your hand out of the bell, your playing will automatically go a little sharp in intonation. To partially avoid that I pulled out the main slide on my horn, and hoped that with some additional lipping down I would be able to conduct with my right hand and still play in tune.

That's exactly what happened, and that is how we got through the piece in the last five minutes of the session without breaking down, and with at least an acceptable rendering of Gil's complex rhythms, although the intonation could still have been better.[6]

I remember that none of us left the studio right away, something musicians normally do. We all stood around, sort of half dazed by what we had experienced, but relieved that somehow we had made it through.[7] The last time the Miles Davis Nonet played together was on October 30, 1950, in Birdland, seven months after that final record date. That was a Monday, the "off night" when new or lesser-known groups would be engaged for a one-night stand. I remember it well, because we played two of the three sets to a virtually empty house. A few people straggled in from Broadway every once in a while, and mostly left soon again. The only musician that I can remember coming to hear us was Charlie Mingus, and he left after one set, without saying much. It was a dismal evening; it is very depressing to play to an empty house. We joked among ourselves: "Since there's nobody listening, let's turn this into a rehearsal." The response, of course—unstated but deeply felt—was: "Rehearsal for what?" We all knew that this was the end of the Nonet. The music was just too far ahead of its time, too radically different, with its cool sounds, soft darker textures, and its advanced harmonic language. I remember that one of the renditions of *Moon Dreams* that night was the best we ever played it, nearly perfect. I also recall that that night we played some of the pieces written for the group that were never recorded. My memory fails me as to their titles.

I mention this date because to my knowledge it has never been referred to in any writing on jazz or in historical accounts, and its very existence has been disputed. Unlike the Royal Roost date in 1948 (with Symphony Sid officiating as MC and announcer), the 1950 Birdland evening was not broadcast, therefore not air checked, and probably not advertised. Whenever I have mentioned this Birdland date, people who claim to know about such things—jazz writers, researchers, discographers—have stated flatly that I have dreamed it up. After some years of this, even I began to wonder whether my memory was playing tricks on me. But in 1956 I received a letter from a Roger Dunn, a member of the Institute of Jazz Studies (now located at Rutgers University), who, referring to that evening—giving the date, listing the musicians who played—asked me for the name of "one long composition played that evening," that "gassed" him, as he put it. (I'm sure it was *Moon Dreams*.) Dunn remembered that evening "as one of the greatest" he ever had "at a jazz club!" He went on to suggest that if I could record the unrecorded pieces, I should get "Barber, Lewis, Konitz (or Gigi Gryce if Lee were not available), Gil Evans (on piano), Art Farmer, Urbie Green." He urged me to do this "for posterity." Dunn's letter would appear to be proof that I didn't dream up that concert.

The experience of playing the great *Birth of the Cool* music stayed in my memory and my consciousness for a long time. The desire to encounter that music again, somehow, somewhere, never left me, and eventually expressed itself in two ways: not too many years later I started to perform and re-create the music in jazz repertory concerts, and I made arrangements for different instrumentations, especially for woodwind quintet, sometimes with, sometimes without rhythm section. I did this primarily for my own Metropolitan Quintet, with the idea of also making the arrangements available to other groups.

Some of the *Birth* pieces were clearly not reducible to five voices. But I first tackled Carisi's *Israel* and Denzil Best's wonderfully sprightly composition *Move*. I particularly loved John Lewis's arrangement of *Move*, a masterpiece of its kind, with its clean, sleek, classic lines and Mozartean clarity. Arranging it for woodwind quintet was not an easy task, reducing its six harmonic lines to five or four—don't forget that I had to somehow take care of the bass lines as well—while also transcribing the originally improvised solos. We played *Move* fairly often in our concerts, mostly as an encore. It was always a huge success.

I also wanted to arrange *Boplicity* for quintet, but I soon gave that up, because I realized that in Gil Evans's superchromatic harmonizations leaving out even one of the six notes would do severe damage to the music.

No less a personage than Mitch Miller hired me for a Sinatra date in October 1950.[8] I was thrilled to participate in one of Sinatra's recording sessions, for by that time I had been an unconditional admirer of Sinatra's remarkable jazz-oriented singing for many years. And I was thrilled to find myself in the company of many of the best New York freelancers and studio musicians. Mitch and Axel Stordahl (Sinatra's main arranger for many years) had decided on a twenty-six-piece orchestra, including five woodwind doublers, one horn, a harp, and a five-piece string section. Here I was suddenly sitting right next to so many great heroes of mine: Billy Butterfield, Chris Griffin (trumpet), Hymie Schertzer (clarinet), Larry Altpeter (trombone), Julie Held (violin), George Ricci (cello), and Trigger Alpert (bass). Except for Butterfield, they may not be household names, but they were definitely among the cream of the New York freelancers who could read down an arrangement flawlessly the first time around: no studying or rehearsing needed, playing perfectly in tune, religiously observing the dynamics, instantly achieving section balance, and most important—getting the feel and swing of the music right away. If by some remote chance one of them would make a mistake, it would be instantly corrected without a word spoken, never to occur again. I mention this because I know that the lay reader, music lover, record collector has no idea how extraordinary the musicians in the studio recording world of New York (and in the Hollywood film studios) were, and still are—to the extent that there still is a studio recording scene in New York. (It is, in any case, very diminished.) In that highly competitive world you *had* to be the best, or you just wouldn't survive. One or two bad moments, and the contractor wouldn't hire you back. He couldn't take that risk, because mistakes, besides being upsetting, waste time. And time is money. Perfection (or in any case near-perfection) was the only way to go. I was proud and felt very privileged to have been active in that world at the very highest levels.[9]

It was a good thing the orchestra was that versatile and quick because on that day, about two-thirds of the way through the session, Sinatra developed serious vocal problems. I had noticed that he sounded a bit tired, strained, although nothing that would jeopardize the recording date. But a half hour later, in the next song, Sinatra began cracking on the high notes. (As best as I can recall, they were high Fs.) He became very upset with himself, and called a halt to the session. At that point most of us assumed it would have to be aborted, and we'd be sent home. We were waiting around for final word as to our fate, when suddenly we were told that Sinatra wanted to give it another try, *but a tone lower*. We were, in effect, told—not asked whether we could—to transpose more or less at sight the whole arrangement down a whole tone.

We were given a few minutes to prepare, to scribble a few things into our parts. For most of the group the transposing of what was not a particularly complicated or demanding arrangement wasn't much of a problem. For me it wasn't any problem at all, because horn players learn from the very beginning to transpose *all the time*, all the standard horn literature being written in any one of the twelve different transpositions. For us to go from an F horn part to one a whole tone lower (E flat) is what we do every day.[10] But for Elaine Vito, our harpist, it was another matter. Transposing a harp part at sight is a virtual impossibility (unless it is ridiculously simple), because harpists have to prepare and mark almost every bar with pedal-change indications. But Elaine, though young—and by the way, extraordinarily beautiful (she was a famous beauty in the New York orchestral world)—was already an old pro, and in a matter of minutes had her part figured out.

In this way we were able to finish the date—and in time. Frank got through the song well enough, having also simplified his part here and there, successfully negotiating (although just barely) the few climactic E flats. He thanked us profusely. Well that he did, because it was really an impressive performance by the orchestra, which—no question about it—saved Columbia Records a lot of money that day.

A year later (August 13, 1951) another Columbia date, again organized by Mitch Miller, featured Alec Wilder's *Jazz Suite* for four horns, accompanied by harpsichord (!), guitar, bass, and drums; the horn quartet consisted of John Barrows, Jim Buffington, Ray Alonge, and myself, on fourth horn. I *loved* playing low horn parts, providing the all-important bass foundation on which harmonies are built.[11] The four movements of the Suite ("Horn O'Plenty," "Conversation Piece," "Serenade," and "Horn Belt Boogie") are quintessential Wilder, some of the best, most cohesive and compelling music—and, for all I know, the jazziest—Alec ever wrote. I published the *Jazz Suite* in the 1980s with Margun Music. The third movement "Serenade" has one of the most gorgeous and irresistible theme melodies ever composed. (Yes, I include even Schubert, Schumann, and Gershwin in the comparison.) I can't remember how many times I have said that I would give anything to have composed that melody! And John Barrows played it so beautifully. The date went extremely well, and showed, if proof were needed, that horns could function in jazz not only in their traditional songful, lyric, romantic role, but could also swing as hard and as driving as any of the best swing band brass sections.

Unfortunately, the four 78 sides remained virtually unknown and unappreciated, and were reissued only briefly and limitedly on 45s.

I consider it one of the great fortunes and honors of my life that I, coming from the world of classical music, was so warmly received and welcomed into the inner circle of jazz. This would not have happened without the introductory imprimatur of a John Lewis—or a Miles Davis or a J. J. Johnson, for that matter—but particularly John. He was held in such high regard in that community of musicians that his word on any musical matter was automatically and completely trusted. This was also true of all those now legendary figures—Dizzy, Bird, Miles, Lester, Ben, Roy, Hawk, Duke, the Count—just to name a few of that great jazz pantheon. John was especially respected, for he had already proven himself not only as a pianist (with Dizzy's orchestra, with Lester Young, Charlie Parker, Illinois Jacquet, Ella Fitzgerald—in the 1940s), but also as a composer and arranger, and soon thereafter as a leader, an innovator, an intellect, a thinker—as someone whose serious, cultivated demeanor commanded unquestionable respect.[12] Already well educated at the University of New Mexico in Albuquerque, where he majored in music and anthropology, after service in the army during World War II, John pursued his studies at the Manhattan School of Music in classical music, graduating with a master's degree in 1953. Such an accumulation of rich, hands-on, practical experience, coupled with a high-level academic education, was still extremely rare in the jazz field in those days, and was thus very much admired and respected—and probably not a little envied.

For my part, I held all those great jazz masters of that period in such high esteem, in such awe, that it would never have occurred to me to introduce myself to any of them. I was quite shy in that regard, and considered the idea of simply going up to one of my music idols (whether in jazz or in classical music) at a club or a concert, or in passing on the street, as an unwarranted intrusion into their lives. Introducing myself to Joe Williams at the Club de Lisa in Chicago, as I did in 1946, was a behavioral anomaly for me. Likewise, I would never have approached Duke Ellington on my own in Cincinnati. In that instance, it was Lawrence Brown, who had spotted me avidly listening to the music, who took me to meet the great man. In later years, as I gained more self-confidence, I overcame my shyness and became a quite willing initiator of new collegial friendships.

John was my entrée to the jazz world, and from him the word about Gunther spread to all the many, many others I was privileged to work with and get to know, not just in passing but in close, long-lasting friendships. I don't think many classically oriented musicians can say that, certainly not from that era. I owe so much to John, not only in that sense but also in how much I learned from him and, through him, from his many remarkable colleagues and collaborators.

It was fascinating to be so instantly accepted into the jazz fraternity as one of them; you don't get into that inner jazz community without prior endorsement by at least one of its major figures. That may sound a little snobbish or paternalistic, but it really isn't. It is just unequivocally honest. In earlier days the jam sessions and cutting contests in jazz—now long gone—were the traditional process for sorting things out as to who would belong and who wouldn't, separating, as it were, the wheat from the chaff. The jam session helped to preserve the integrity of the art in a way that doesn't exist (and never did in any serious way) in classical music. At its highest levels, jazz, an essentially improvisatory—that is, creative—art[13] has been constantly refining and purifying itself by a self-regulatory, self-cleansing process. That kind of pride and artistic integrity is much less prevalent in classical music, partly, and I suppose somewhat understandably, because it deals with much larger organizations and personnel, that is, symphony orchestras, opera companies. They can be more easily infiltrated by less than top-level talent, especially in the typically large string sections that need to be filled with sufficient bodies, and where the individual creativity native to jazz is simply not a prerequisite. The kind of high standards generally maintained in jazz are to be found more readily in the classical world in chamber music. In jazz the individual player's involvement is more personally and creatively contributive—at the highest levels, even innovative—and thus also more exposed. There is really no place to hide. Playing in a symphony orchestra, an essentially *re*-creative enterprise, makes no such creative or inventive demands. To survive relatively easily it is sufficient to have acquired a certain high-level technical proficiency and to participate in a more or less functional manner—to be a tiny cog in a big wheel. I'm not suggesting that symphony orchestras consist largely of average, medial talents. I *am* suggesting that it is possible—and is often enough the case—that many secondary, less exposed positions in an orchestra are held by modestly gifted, less inspired musicians, who are never required to be creative or innovative.

While I was tooting my horn—literally—at the Metropolitan Opera in the early 1950s and in innumerable recording dates (of jazz, opera, and symphonic repertory) and concerts on radio, John Lewis was spending most of his time and energies on his studies at the Manhattan School of Music, avidly studying classical theory and compositional techniques and styles. For a well-established major jazz figure in the forefront of the whole bebop and modern jazz movement, John was surprisingly well informed in the classical repertory. More than half of his record collection and his library were devoted to classical music, from Bach through the romantic era and well into the twentieth century. But even so, he felt his knowledge in that field to be still too limited and scattered. And as someone who always knew what he wanted and needed to do, he took full advantage of the recently enacted GI Bill to fund his four years of studies at the Manhattan School of Music. The only alternative would have been to go back on the road as a sideman for someone like Lester or Ella, or to plunge into the rat race of gigging in New York.

John especially loved the music of Haydn and Mozart, and, of course, Bach and Scarlatti. He concentrated most of his studies on Bach's prodigious achievements in counterpoint and fugal composition, which John then utilized to such wonderful effect in his work with the Modern Jazz Quartet, not only in his own pieces (such as *Little David's Fugue* and *Concord*), but even more compellingly in the hundreds upon hundreds of contrapuntal duet improvisations that John and Milt Jackson executed over a period of forty years—perhaps the Modern Jazz Quartet's most memorable hallmark. I'm referring to those many, many passages where what normally would have been set aside as a vibraphone solo chorus was turned into a duet improvisation by John partnering himself with Milt. I mention this in particular because what resulted in these duet choruses was virtually unique. Other than a few obscure exceptions, I don't know of any such duets in jazz,[14] certainly not in the particular manner and style that John and Milt did them. First of all, they invariably occurred within a limited range (rarely more than a fifth or an octave), and in the upper middle range, what we call the top of the staff. Second, within that limited range the two players' lines, usually single-line melodies or riffs, would twist around each other in freely crisscrossing tendrils, rhythmically and motivically independent, yet blending into a dynamically balanced sound. Third, that blended sound sang forth with an almost magical, luminous quality, given that Milt and John drew from their respective instruments two of the most beautiful sounds ever heard in jazz.

John was famous for his warm, refined, full-sounding tone and touch—he never recorded on anything less than the finest Steinway sound, and Milt produced that pure, rich, centered sound of his with those huge homemade mallets, each weighing about half a pound. He must have had incredibly strong wrists to manipulate those "boomers" as easily as he did. Put two such shining sounds together, and you'll get a uniquely beautiful sonority that could never happen but for the union of the two. It was one of John's creative strokes of genius, one of several that contributed so vitally to making the Modern Jazz Quartet over the long haul one of the most admired jazz groups of all time. I think this sort of collaborative chamber music playing was intrinsic to John Lewis's conception of the Modern Jazz Quartet; namely, oriented more toward the notion of composition, with its essentially integrative sharing concept, rather than, as more common in jazz, the considerable (and sometimes only) emphasis on the solo and the individual. What played into these ideas was the fact that John was a superb accompanist, one of the best ever in jazz. Great soloists such as Lester Young and Ella Fitzgerald loved John's playing because as an accompanist—not a competing soloist—he seemed almost always to know *exactly* how much or how little to play, how best to support a soloist, when to fill in with little perfectly placed connecting phraselets. Although a fine soloist, given to reasoned understatement rather than overwhelming digital displays, he preferred sharing the musical experience as in a true dialogue, modestly contributing to it. In that sense he was the perfect foil for Milt Jackson's brilliant virtuosic inventions.

I have dwelt on this Lewis-Jackson duet specialty at some length because it was so unique to the Modern Jazz Quartet's style, and because it has rarely been discussed or written about in any appreciation of the quartet. I have found nothing else in jazz, nor for that matter in classical music, like this particularly imaginative idea, except in the several concertos for two violins by J. S. Bach, where the crisscrossing of melodic lines by the two soloists produces a similarly joyous sonic effect. I wonder whether John got the idea from his extensive studies of Bach's music. It could very well be.

By the time John founded the Modern Jazz Quartet as a cooperative group in late 1952, I had already met the other three members several times while on the road with the Met. I also knew them musically through recordings, in my own record collection and through daily jazz programs on the radio. Younger readers of today cannot imagine how much jazz was available on radio, not just in New York but also in other major midwestern cities such as Chicago, Cincinnati, and St. Louis, where stations with enormously tall and powerful transmitters could send broadcasts practically across the entire country. Most of the jazz programs were hosted by very knowledgeable disc jockeys who had access to huge record collections. So that when I was traveling around the country on those Met tours I could hear great jazz, both locally produced and on nationwide network broadcasts, literally everywhere. I could be in Des Moines, Iowa, or Chattanooga, Tennessee—or Fargo, North Dakota—and I could hear good jazz of all kinds without any trouble, especially in the evenings and even all night.

Both the big bands and the smaller combos were all still touring a great deal in those days; and unlike the present, all cities and towns of any reasonable size had at least half a dozen jazz clubs or ballrooms where the big bands—Ellington, Kenton, Herman, Gillespie, etc.—would play. If I wasn't assigned to play an opera that night I was in those jazz clubs and ballrooms, including those in the black section of towns, where usually white classical musicians were hardly ever seen.

That's how I ran into Miles Davis several times on the road, also Percy Heath and Ray Brown (who was accompanying his then wife, Ella Fitzgerald) and Dizzy Gillespie. There was one encounter with a whole bunch of top-notch musicians when by chance two different jazz groups were in St. Louis, playing in two different clubs. I remember that they included Jimmy Heath and J. J. Johnson, Sonny Rollins, Nelson Boyd, and Roy Haynes. I happened to have two successive nights off from the opera that week, and spent both evenings at the two clubs, conveniently located a few blocks apart on the same street. It must have been in 1952 or 1953 because I had with me recordings of both my *Brass Symphony* and *Dramatic Overture*. Somehow on one of those evenings the conversation turned to some of my music: "What'cha been writing lately?" When I mentioned those two pieces, J. J., himself very interested in modern classical music, asked, "Gee, how can we hear those things?"

I had in previous St. Louis visits hooked up with a jazz disc jockey at one of the big radio stations, with whom I then arranged to use one of the station's unoccupied studios to play my recordings for everybody. Although jazz musicians love to sleep late, almost everybody showed up at the station at eleven in the morning. After the usual greeting banter, during which I heard for the first time the deathless words, "man, he sure wails with them pots and pans!"—a laudatory reference to the culinary prowess of one of the Heath brothers exhibited the night before—we listened to my two tunes. I wondered what they would think of my stuff, knowing that, with the exception of J. J., they rarely, if ever, got a chance to listen to such modern, atonal, free-form music, which was quite removed from their usual musical fare.

When the *Brass Symphony* ended, there was almost a minute of stunned silence. I saw Percy break into a big broad smile—he had one of those radiant smiles that could light up a room[15]— and heard him blurt out, "man, this cat don't need no shit; he's high all the time—*very* high!" It was one of the nicest compliments I ever got.[16]

It was clear right away, from the very first recordings of the Modern Jazz Quartet (released in 1952 on Prestige), that here was something new and totally different in jazz—in its sound, style, and expression, in its clean classic beauty. I don't mean classical eighteenth-century music (Haydn, Mozart)—although that enters into it as well—but rather a highly refined artistic expression, espousing lucidity, balance, harmonious proportions, and a certain tempered moderation.[17] There had been interesting chamber groups before in jazz; one thinks of Benny Goodman's Quartets and Sextets, John Kirby's Sextet, the Nat "King" Cole and Tristano Trios, the Joe Mooney Quartet, and those superb recordings made in Paris in 1939 with Rex Stewart (cornet), Barney Bigard (clarinet), Django Reinhardt (guitar), and Billy Taylor (bass). But the Modern Jazz Quartet's unique sound, in particular its gently percussive bell-like clarity, its emphasis on the merging of composition and improvisation, its classy demeanor on stage (in full dress), and its insistence on performing not in night clubs but in concert halls—all this was new and different, and appealed to a new audience that hadn't yet taken jazz, with its somewhat casual and relaxed atmosphere, all that seriously. For many of these new converts, bringing some discipline and professional dignity to jazz was a good thing. So was getting away from the idea of jazz as a generally loud, rather raucous music, devoid of dynamic nuance and shading. But for others, the Modern Jazz Quartet's music was at best puzzling, at worst annoying, especially when by the midfifties it became associated with the new Third Stream movement, a concept that was in itself quite controversial and contentious in those days. Now, decades later, Third Stream is generally accepted as an important development in postswing-era jazz, as an optional alternative and a new direction.[18]

As for the varying reactions to the Modern Jazz Quartet, it was simply that in any given population there are always going to be those who resist change and deplore anything new and different. Beyond that, it was inevitable that much of the denunciations of the work of the quartet (and of Third Stream in general) came from two sides: many folks in jazz felt that even the slightest influence from classical music would contaminate jazz, undermine its spirit of freedom and individualism, dilute its special energies; while on the other side, classical critics and musicians feared that their precious, noble classical tradition would be corrupted and polluted by any association with this low-life, crude, inferior upstart called jazz. It was sheer prejudice and ignorance on both sides. In between these extremes many jazz fans found the Modern Jazz Quartet's music making, including John Lewis's compositions, completely ingratiating and surprisingly accessible.

Some people—even fellow musicians and some critics—took the quartet to task for its stage presence, making fun of the musicians in their tuxedos or tails, their supposed proper, stiff, serious demeanor that suggested (to the critics) a bunch of funeral directors at a wake. Even within the group, Milt sometimes complained about John's deportment mandates. But John ignored such complaints and criticisms, from within the group or without. Although a shy and gentle person, John could be incredibly firm in his beliefs and convictions; he always defended himself (if driven to it) by saying that he was not indulging in silly formalities, that it was a matter of showing respect for one's art, for the music, and for one's profession, the same level of respect and dignity that was accorded classical music but that jazz generally did not receive. Since for John jazz was not some inferior form of music, it deserved full respect and seriousness, in whatever ways that could be expressed. I think that John was quite right for not equivocating about such matters, for he also realized that in a still largely racist society and culture, where not only black and white musicians but also their respective music were still kept segregated, black musicians and their music were rarely accorded the homage and respect that their white counterparts received automatically.

More serious was the groundless criticism, put forth as an accusation by some, that the Modern Jazz Quartet didn't swing, and probably couldn't. Anybody who thought that Milt, and for that matter Percy and Kenny, couldn't swing must have been clinically deaf, as countless recordings by the quartet clearly showed over and over again. It wasn't perhaps the solid, weighty, overt swing of, say, the Basie band, but rather a more subtle, inner-directed kind—

there are many types and degrees of swing—with a lighter touch. John dismissed all such mongerings with his famous deprecating wave of the hand. But if he thought it worth responding, he would calmly suggest—as Duke Ellington also had to counsel on many occasions when his band was unfairly accused of not swinging—that not all jazz needs to swing, that in fact lots of very fine jazz in the past did not and was not meant to swing, and that he, John, sometimes wrote music that would swing and sometimes not. End of discussion!

Regardless of all these quibblings, the Modern Jazz Quartet was a remarkably successful group, whichever way you might want to measure their success: popularity (i.e., success at the box office), musical creativity, quality of performance, or longevity of existence (more than forty years).

John invited me to the quartet's early recording sessions and the preparatory rehearsals, starting in 1953, saying that he wanted another pair of good ears in the control room. There usually wasn't much advice for me to offer because John really knew how to rehearse—including not rehearsing too much—down to the minutest details of balance and timbral nuance. This study of a new piece of music was a novel approach in jazz, and was sometimes a bit annoying to his three colleagues, who were used to a more casual, relaxed, unpremeditated approach. But John persevered, so that after a year or so of working together the quartet became such a finely tuned instrument that comparisons to some of the finest string quartets, such as the Juilliard, the Budapest, and Busch quartets, with their long traditions of superb ensemble playing, were being invoked with some regularity. John wisely concentrated most of his rehearsals on his own compositions (such as the *La Ronde* Suite, *Vendome*, *Queen's Fancy*), leaving tunes such as *Autumn in New York*, *But Not For Me*, and *I'll Remember April* to his quartet companions' individual spontaneous inspirations, with superb results.

One problem did arise during the quartet's first three years; it concerned drummer Kenny Clarke—"Klook," as he was known—much revered as one of the pioneer innovators in the bebop movement, and one of John's oldest, closest friends from their days together in the army during World War II. Kenny, a strong, richly inventive drummer, ideal in big band settings, began to feel uncomfortable and too hemmed in by the small group setting and by John's more controlling, superrefined chamber music approach. By mutual agreement and under the most amicable circumstances, Kenny ceded his chair to Connie Kay, and returned to Paris, where he spent the rest of his life, much of it as coleader of the very successful Kenny Clarke–Francy Boland Big Band. I missed Kenny a lot; his was such a kindly, likeable, simpatico nature. I saw him only once more, in Paris a few months before his death, playing at the Club Saint Germain. He had never lost his beautiful beaming smile.

John clearly saw the Modern Jazz Quartet as a vehicle for the presentation of his own compositions, modestly surrounding them in well-constructed programs with generous doses of beautifully fashioned arrangements of the great American song literature—Gershwin, Porter, Kern, Vernon Duke, Rodgers, Berlin, Arlen. But it wasn't long before John began to envision hearing his music in expanded orchestral versions, not necessarily in the standard jazz orchestra (i.e., big band) format, but in variously configured ensemble settings, incorporating classical instruments, such as oboe, bassoon, harp, and horn, along with the standard jazz triumvirate of trumpet, trombone, and saxophone. Such instrumentations may be commonplace nowadays, but half a century ago this kind of timbral-sonoric intermixing was virtually unheard of in jazz—in "real" jazz.[19]

As John's main link to the classical world, I soon found myself in the role of contractor for his recording dates, bringing him the top-level classical woodwind and brass players in New York who were actively interested in jazz. The next step was his asking me to arrange some of his latest pieces for these larger mixed ensembles. The first of such collaboration occurred in March 1955, when John and I set up a recording date for Verve, Norman Granz's label, in which five of John's recent compositions and, it was hoped, one of J. J. Johnson's new works would be recorded. John asked me to arrange two of these new compositions, *Midsömmer* and *Queen's Fancy*, for a twelve-piece ensemble consisting of clarinet (alternately Tony Scott and Aaron Sachs), tenor saxophone (Stan Getz and Lucky Thompson), three rhythm (John, Percy, Connie), trombone (J. J.) on the jazz side; on the classical side, flute (Jimmy Politis, from the Met orchestra), Loren Glickman (bassoon), harp (Janet Putnam), and horn (me). It was a lot of new, not entirely easy music to produce in two sessions, in an unfamiliar type of instrumentation, more complex than the typical four- or five-piece combo or standard big band. Balance and ensemble problems would be especially serious, given the basic fact that instruments such as the saxophone and trombone, even the clarinet (as used in jazz), were inherently louder, more overtly projecting than, say, a flute, bassoon, or harp. This prompted the idea of having several presession rehearsals, obviously a good idea except that, with this particular grouping of musicians, there were bound to be serious scheduling conflicts. It had been hard enough to find a date for the recording with everyone available. To now, in addition, find compatible rehearsal times, given so many conflicting schedules, turned out to be very difficult. We already knew that Stan Getz would not be able to make any rehearsals, no matter when they might be, because he was two thousand miles away in Oklahoma on a weeklong club engagement near Tulsa that ended on the twelfth of March; our recording date had been set for the fourteenth. I privately worried whether Stan would be able to get to the date in time, coming from such a great distance. (This was in the days before jet travel.) We could have hired someone else, but both John and I were so taken with Stan's playing that we really didn't want to consider anyone else. In my arrangement of *Midsömmer* I wrote some prominent lines specifically with Stan's special sound and lyric style in mind.

We rehearsed the music as best we could, mostly in sectionals, unable to ever get everybody together at the same time. I took the woodwinds and Janet; John worked with the jazz players—without Stan, of course. J. J. briefly rehearsed his *Turnpike* a couple of times, but soon realized that it wasn't going to be ready to be recorded. Norman Granz also thought that to put one J. J. piece on the record against five by John was a bit odd and imbalanced.

In the end, the two recording sessions went very well, and were issued by the Modern Jazz Society label. The real hero for all of us was Stan Getz, who did make the afternoon date, although more than an hour late. His trip east from Oklahoma was almost scuttled by the death of Charlie Parker on March 12. Stan was so distraught by the news that, as he told me later, he immediately thought of calling us to say that he couldn't possibly think of playing his horn when the greatest horn of all time had just been silenced. We didn't know that those weren't the worst of Stan's worries. His wife and two children had just been in a terrible car accident; his son David's skull was crushed and his entire left side paralyzed—he lay in a coma for a whole week—while his wife, Beverly, thrown into the car's windshield, sustained two fractured vertebrae and had to undergo many weeks of rehabilitation. It was thus truly amazing that with all these concerns and distractions, and getting to the session late and dead-tired, therefore having to sight-read the music without the benefit of a quick run-through, he played magnificently in the two pieces we had assigned to him, *Midsömmer* and *Queen's Fancy*.

A few months later I got a call from Gigi Gryce, a marvelous alto saxophonist and composer-arranger, to play on a recording date in Rudy Van Gelder's famous studio in Hackensack, New Jersey. I was particularly interested to work with Gigi because John Lewis had played me some big band recordings Gigi had made in Paris in 1953 for the French Vogue label. I was quite impressed with Gigi's compositions and by the playing of the band, which featured trumpet players Art Farmer, Clifford Brown, Quincy Jones (Quincy also played piano on some pieces), as well as the cream of the crop of French jazz musicians (such as Pierre Michelot and

Henri Renaud). Then I found out that Gigi had originally studied classical music with Daniel Pinkham and Alan Hovhaness at the Boston Conservatory, and later in Paris with no less than the legendary Nadia Boulanger and—my great favorite—Arthur Honegger. As one of the very best Charlie Parker disciples, and with his dual interest and training in both jazz and advanced classical styles, I saw Gigi as a kindred spirit and as an important, original, new voice in jazz.

The date, issued as *Nica's Tempo* (on LP), certainly lived up to my high expectations. We did two of Gigi's compositions and an interesting recomposition of the famous traditional Irish Jig, *Kerry Dance*. The instrumentation was modeled basically after the Miles Davis Nonet: two saxophones (alto and baritone: Gigi Gryce and Danny Bank), four brass (trumpet, horn, trombone, tuba: Art Farmer, me, Jimmy Cleveland, Bill Barber), and a rhythm section of Horace Silver, Oscar Pettiford, and Kenny Clarke. It can't get much better than that.[20] And Gigi wrote me some very fine, challenging horn parts.

I find it difficult to comprehend, in retrospect, how it is that I had so relatively little contact, professional or social, with Charlie Parker, compared with the many other major jazz figures of the time that I was constantly involved with. A partial explanation can be that I did not actually meet Parker until rather late—in May 1950—when John Lewis took me to hear Parker and his Quintet (with Fats Navarro and Bud Powell) at Café Society in midtown Manhattan, by which time I had already acquired a sizeable collection of Bird's greatest recordings and thus knew his work very well. I remember how the three principals turned each other on that evening, inspired each other. It was one of those relatively few occasions at which I heard Parker at his very best, comparable to the incredibly high standards he had set on innumerable recordings (such as *Anthropology*, *Relaxin' at Camarillo*, *Yardbird Suite*, *Confirmation*, *Ko-Ko*).

But there is also the fact that Parker's several bouts with illness during the last five years of his life led to his working very irregularly. Worse yet, opportunities for him to work in New York were seriously curtailed during one two-year period, 1951–53, when his New York cabaret license (in effect a work permit) was revoked by the narcotics division of the NYPD, preventing him from playing in nightclubs. By 1954, Parker, having less and less work, his health deteriorating (physically and mentally), and in serious financial straits, attempted suicide several times, and at one point even committed himself to Bellevue Hospital.

It is ironic that it was only during those last years—he died in March 1955 at age thirty-four—that I began to see him more frequently, not playing the saxophone but as a result of being invited by some of my friends (Tony Scott, Kenny Dorham) to attend the regular evening gatherings that took place at the huge loftlike apartment of the Baroness Pannonica (Nica) de Koenigswarter, where Parker had recently been living off and on.

The last time I saw Parker—it must have been in January 1955—was at one of the Baroness's parties. I must say that the times I went there I never felt particularly at ease; the atmosphere was very strange for me. Musicians didn't seem to come there with any particular purpose; it was just a place to hang out, to get high, to maybe see somebody—or maybe not. The rooms were dimly lit; the sweet scent of marijuana was everywhere. You could cut the air with a knife. I was always afraid of getting a contact high. One of the rooms had almost no furniture, no chairs, no tables; instead it had lots of mattresses or futons.

Finding no one to talk to on one of those evenings—I think I had come too early in the evening—I lay down on one of the mattresses, when, a bit later, who came along and sat down on the mattress next to mine, but Charlie Parker. I was so in awe of him that I found myself quite tongue-tied. What I dearly wanted to talk about, using this rare opportunity alone with him, in a moment of unexpected closeness and intimacy, was what I considered the most important of his several technical and expressive breakthrough achievements, namely, his fundamental transformation of the role of rhythm and tempo in jazz, what musicians simply call "time."[21]

But I couldn't think of a simple way of asking him about this remarkable innovation, having found out over the previous half dozen years of getting to know dozens of the leading jazz musicians of the time that whenever I asked one of them about some outstanding thing they had done on a recording or in a concert, none of them ever knew what I was talking about. What they had done—whatever it was—they did by pure instinct, unconsciously; it was never a planned or predetermined intellectual decision. This is so true of the great innovative jazz musicians; they do things intuitively, out of their natural talent and intuitive inspirations.

While I was hesitating as to how to ask him my question, Parker, as if suddenly remembering something, mentioned that John Lewis and Miles Davis had for some time been telling him about me, a major classical composer and a fine horn player who was very deeply involved with jazz. He had vaguely heard about my experiments in Third Stream, and about the recent initiatives in fusing jazz and classical concepts and techniques.

What developed next really startled me. Bird began expressing his extreme frustration with where jazz was going; he felt that it was stuck in a rut, in routine and stultifying formulae. More personally, he expressed his frustration with what he felt he was forced or expected to play by the business, the commerce of jazz, the demands of the market place, audiences, and record companies. It was not dissatisfaction with his own playing per se, certainly not from a technical and expressive point of view, but rather from what he saw as the severe stylistic, linguistic limitations of jazz. He expressed this in two distinctive ways. At one point, with a lot of anguish and pain in his voice, he asked if I realized how many thousands of times—and ways—he'd played the blues. He'd had enough of that. He felt that there had to be something else out there. It wasn't just the blues; it was, he said, the exhaustion of the thirty-two-bar song form, the increasing codification and delimiting conformism of harmonic changes, the boring, fettering, stereotypical standardization of jazz performance and form, i.e., the head, followed by a series of improvised choruses, and repeat of the head.

The other way he expressed his frustration and concern was even more unexpected. He told me that lately he had been listening increasingly to modern classical music, mostly on recordings, music of Bartók and Stravinsky, and how exciting and refreshing that was, how he wanted to explore more of that kind of music. He said something like: I know there's a whole lot of great music out there, I want to know more about that. Can you help me? I'd like to study with you. He said this in such a pleading tone, as if this would be his musical salvation. I of course said yes, I'd be more than happy to get together with him whenever he wanted. He should just let me know when.[22]

Alas, that was never to happen. I never saw Bird again. He died a few months later, on March 12, 1955.[23]

I cherish the memory of this encounter with Charlie Parker. It touched me very deeply, because he spoke with such passion and devotion in his concern for the future of jazz.

Parker is one of the three greatest and most important giants of jazz; the other two are Armstrong and Ellington. Parker dramatically advanced the art and language of jazz, being arguably even more widely influential than Armstrong. He became a legend in his own time, this in a career that lasted less than twenty years. Yet, sad to say, he and his astonishing innovations are all but forgotten nowadays, and his work is considered of little or no relevance. Jazz is a much-diminished art form by virtue of the recent nearly total disregard of the profound lessons that Parker's colossal artistic contributions tried to pass on.

The year 1955 was, in relation to my activities in jazz, big for me. It was the first time I attended the Newport Jazz Festival, founded only the year before by George Wein, where I heard not only a tremendous amount of great music, including what turned out to be a most important Miles Davis comeback appearance,[24] but also met all the leading critics and writers on jazz, such as John Wilson (of the *New York Times*), Whitney Balliett (of the *New Yorker*), Nat Hentoff, Martin Williams, George Simon, Marshall Stearns, Dan Morgenstern, and, most important, Sheldon Meyer, who in due course became my editor at Oxford University Press for all of my books since 1967. (Sheldon passed away in 2006.)

This was also the year John Lewis and I founded the Modern Jazz Society (later to be renamed, more accurately, the Jazz and Classical Music Society), under whose aegis we began to present over the next half-dozen years a series of concerts offering an intermixture of jazz (primarily John Lewis's compositions, mostly in arrangements for variously expanded instrumentations) and classical works (by early composers such as Mozart and Bach and contemporaries such as Charles Ives and the modern Italian composer Luigi Nono). Our performance on November 19, 1955, of Nono's *Polifonica-Monodia-Ritmica* was the first time any music by Nono (or for that matter by any of his European avant-garde contemporaries, such as Boulez, Stockhausen, Berio, Henze) was ever heard in America. No such concert featuring three distinctly diverse periods and kinds of music had ever been presented anywhere, as far as I know. The concert was a real breakthrough that attracted considerable attention, including a very favorable account and review of the event in the *New York Times* (by John Wilson). But it also generated considerable consternation and puzzlement—even outright hostility—in other quarters, where the very idea of intermingling jazz with "that modern stuff from Europe" was totally incomprehensible, unacceptable, and offensive.

The first Modern Jazz Society program was constructed in five segments, beginning with the Modern Jazz Quartet minus Milt Jackson, but aided and abetted by Tony Scott, Lucky Thompson, and J. J. Johnson, in Lewis's *Sketch*, and their improvised versions of ballads by Richard Rodgers, Harold Arlen, Matt Dennis, and Charlie Parker. Second, there was a short set by the Quartet in three Lewis compositions (*Concorde*, *Fontessa*, and *Versailles*). Third, in the classical centerpiece of the program, we performed the Nono piece, played by a mixed group of Jimmy Politis (flute), Jack Kreiselman (bass clarinet), Charlie Hartman (alto sax), myself (horn)—I also conducted the piece—Tony Scott (clarinet), John Lewis, and Connie Kay, the latter skillfully manipulating the tricky percussion part for four different-pitched suspended cymbals. (Nono always used four or more cymbals, playing with soft felt mallets, creating in effect shapely melodic lines). The fourth segment presented my own *Twelve By Eleven* for a mixed ensemble of three woodwinds, horn, harp, tenor sax, trombone, plus the Quartet. (I had premiered the work earlier that year in one of David Broekman's Music in the Making concerts at Cooper Union, with the young Jimmy Knepper playing trombone—my first encounter with him.) *Twelve by Eleven* was followed by my arrangement for a similarly mixed ensemble of John Lewis's masterpiece, *Django*. The fifth and final segment of the concert featured four of the Lewis compositions we had recorded six months earlier for the Verve label.

In his review of the concert John Wilson called the program "brilliant and adventurous," praising especially the "superb performance of John's *Fontessa*," with its "many classical illusions, yet definitely and strongly jazz in its rhythmic concept."[25] Wilson called Connie Kay "a paragon of jazz drummers" who displayed "delicacy, taste and extremely effective reserve, even while supplying an undeniably insistent beat." He called my *Twelve By Eleven* "the most completely realized" of all the performances by the augmented mixed group, adding that my making the "mixture of jazz and classical musicians swing with ease and naturalness" was "a minor marvel." The review ended by declaring that the "concert marked a definite step forward in jazz concert presentations. Thoroughness and imagination were evident in every aspect of it." (Wilson did not mention the Nono work. I believe he felt that this kind of advanced free-form atonal music was beyond his expertise—a wonderful honesty.)

In due course, we gave many more equally adventurous concerts, all along the same lines. I recall one at Hunter College, where I programmed in the midst of a healthy dose of jazz repertory the Mozart Divertimento in F Major, K. 247, for two horns and strings, a long six-movement work with two slow movements and two menuets. All our Jazz and Classical Music Society concerts offered a hearty mixture of jazz and classical works, performed by an aggregate of classical and jazz musicians. We wanted to show our jazz listeners that the music of a Mozart (or a Bach or a Vivaldi) could, if performed correctly, have a kind of swing and rhythmic drive that was inherent in jazz; we also wanted to offer great tunes and at the same time show our classical audiences something about the freedom and ad hoc spontaneity intrinsic to jazz. What was exciting about this process was that all of our musicians on either side of the musical fence learned so much from each other—technically, stylistically, conceptually—at a time when ignorance and prejudice between the two fields was still very high.

I first heard of Bill Evans around 1955 from Tony Scott and George Russell, who both told me about this amazing young player who had come to town. I didn't quite know what they meant until I heard Bill the first time, at a Randall's Island (New York) Jazz Festival in 1956, where I was playing in an afternoon concert with Dizzy Gillespie's short-lived midfifties big band. Someone told me that Bill Evans was scheduled to play a set later that afternoon in another venue. I hied myself over to that tentlike place, and heard a remarkable combination of highly articulated rhythmic playing (à la Bud Powell, but somehow cleaner, clearer, firmer) and a wonderfully warm, lyric, "singing" style. I also heard some unconventional, more chromatic harmonizations. I remember thinking, this is someone I'd love to work with and write for.

My next encounter with Bill's playing was on an LP recording that came out in late 1956 and prominently featured Bill as a major soloist. It was one of the most important jazz recordings to be issued in those years, a sextet led by George Russell, featuring a number of pieces written by George expressly for Bill (e.g., *Concerto for Billy the Kid* and *The Ballad of Hix Blewitt*).[26]

I soon learned that Bill was not only a prodigiously gifted improviser, obviously with such a formidable technique that he could immediately translate any musical idea that might come to his mind into acoustic reality, but that he could also read any written part with consummate ease. In fact, he was an amazingly good sight reader. He had that ability common to all good sight readers of anticipating what will appear in the next few bars, a remarkable trick of the mind by which you can be in two places at once: both in the bar you're actually playing and in what lies directly ahead. It was a kind of prescience that I knew from my own sight-reading of horn parts, but I had never encountered this particular talent in any jazz musician. I also heard in Bill's playing a reaching out into more advanced chromatic harmonizations, especially in his left hand chordal comping.[27] This was very exciting for me. Here was someone in jazz whose personal style was close enough to my own chromatic language so that his improvisations in one of my compositions would not engender a stylistic break in the continuity of the piece, but would in fact partake more or less of the same basic harmonic language as mine. Also, here was someone who would not be daunted by the (possibly atonal) written piano parts that would be regularly found in my compositions.

The harmonically limited style of jazz musicians (not just pianists) of the 1940s and 1950s, which was then essentially still located in tonality (though somewhat chromaticized), presented a performance problem in the early years of the Third Stream movement. When the language of the composer and of the improviser were at variance with each other—as was almost always the case when it came to my atonal and twelve-tone pieces—there was apt to be a stylistic discrepancy between the composed and improvised parts.[28] As much as I admired John Lewis's playing, there was always the problem that his improvisations (and for that matter those of his Quartet partners, Milt and Percy) were in a frankly tonal conservative style that could never really match my atonal compositional approach. That presented me with some interesting challenges because I was determined to not allow any stylistic inconsistency to show in the performance of the work. It made no sense to me to end up with a piece, a performance, in which the improvised elements would be in the harmonic language of a Haydn or Mendelssohn or a Ravel, while the composed framework surrounding the improvisations would be in an advanced atonal or highly chromatic style. I faced that challenge in all of my Third Stream works in a variety of ways, which I generally dealt with by accompanying—or, so to speak, clothing—the improvisations with orchestral or ensemble backgrounds that would disguise and cloak the inherent stylistic incompatibility—paper it over, as it were. With Bill Evans, and other younger players such as Eric Dolphy, Ornette Coleman, Scott LaFaro, and Eddie Costa, with whom I worked in those years, that kind of camouflaging was no longer necessary. They could improvise in a manner and style that would fit in with the embracing composition and would meaningfully relate to it.[29]

The problems inherent in merging musical styles and categories took some time to be resolved. One cannot expect a brand-new form of musical or artistic expression to be perfectly conceived and developed from the very outset. In any new union or marriage there are kinks to be ironed out, so also in the marriage of jazz and classical. The stylistic and linguistic divergencies between and among musicians from the two different fields were real, and had to be blended and integrated. There is no question that the occasional stiffness and discomfort in performance was a problem in the early days of Third Stream, but over time these problems were resolved. That certain critics and antagonists of Third Stream pointed to these works as failures was unjustified. They were unable, in those early days of Third Stream, to separate the *performance* difficulties from the work itself. They pounced on these issues negatively, with no understanding of the problems involved, and were certainly not constructive in their criticism.

My musical affinity to Bill Evans blossomed over time into a deep friendship and, as with John Lewis, into something akin to a mutually reciprocal teacher-pupil relationship, both of us learning from each other about the two different musical worlds we occupied. I recall with great pleasure and nostalgia one rather special manifestation of our musical collaboration. For almost an entire year, in 1959, Bill came to my apartment at Ninetieth Street and West End Avenue every couple of weeks—it must have been altogether some twenty times—for the two of us to join in a rather extraordinary undertaking, namely, to play through all of Wagner's four *Ring* operas as well as *Parsifal*, four hands on the piano. This all came about when Bill mentioned one day how much he loved Wagner's late superchromatic music. I must say that this really surprised me. Not that I thought Bill incapable of appreciating classical music, for I could tell from his awesome piano technique that he must have studied a lot of the classical repertory.[30] But that his interest in classical music extended to Wagner operas was pretty unusual. I had never known any jazz musician to express an interest in Wagner's music, even John Lewis (although I found out years later that Paul Desmond owned a lot of Wagner recordings).

When I told Bill that I had piano scores of all the Wagner operas, Bill asked whether he could borrow some of them. He wanted to play through them and study them. I said that I couldn't lend them to him because the scores were very old and in some cases beginning to fall apart, although still usable, and that they really belonged to my father, who had bought them in Germany when he was a young man. I suggested instead that he come over to my house, and that we could read through the operas, playing four hands, Bill the top staff, I the bottom staff—I would also handle the pedaling—similar to what I had done in my teens with my father, and later, in Cincinnati, with Margie and Gussie.

So that's what happened. Bill came over every few weeks in the afternoons, whenever he had free time, and we would play Wagner for about two or three hours. Sometimes, in the easier parts, he would play alone, and I would sing the Wotan or Siegfried vocal parts. It was such fun making music together—*great* music—that we both loved so deeply. In many of the more fantastic advanced chromatic passages that we particularly dug—there were so many—we'd play them several times or in slow motion, lingering on them, in order to savor the incredible beauty and potency of those harmonies. When we got through all the Wagner operas, we continued with some of the many four-hand piano reductions I owned. I remember particularly playing through Rachmaninov's *Isle of the Dead* and Scriabin's *Poem of Ecstasy*.

I mention this episode in our friendship because I know that this almost year-long immersion in late-Wagner chromaticism and the styles of post-Wagnerian composers such as Rachmaninov, Respighi, Szymanowski, and Rimsky-Korsakov was a fascinating learning experience for Bill. I am not claiming that this encounter with late Romantic and early twentieth-century classics was a completely novel discovery for Bill. That would be silly, for Bill had been using richly spiced-up changes ever since I first heard him—and probably even before—and, of course, quite copiously in his late-1950s Trio recordings. This is one of the things that intrigued me so in Bill's playing. I also am not claiming that our "harmony lessons" (as Bill started to call our get-togethers) were the only influential development in Bill's artistic evolution. He was always an avid learner and listener. I knew he was also listening hard to Tristano and Bud Powell, and probably Cecil Taylor. I am merely suggesting that what we did together those many, many afternoons acted in effect as both a confirmation and an enrichment of already well-developed stylistic tendencies.

I also remember us talking about atonality as an evolutionary extension of bitonality and polytonality. In the course of these discussions I showed him my piano reduction of Schönberg's opera *Erwartung*, and in particular the many instances in the work of what some of us younger composers were beginning to call the "*Erwartung* chord," because it appeared so consistently and in so many different musical and dramatic contexts in that opera. I told Bill that I thought of it as the new triad, the modern successor to the major triad (e.g.,). In Schönberg's case the three-note chord was made up of a perfect fourth and an augmented fourth, spanning a major seventh (i.e., or) and its four-part cousins . I photocopied some of the more salient pages of the *Erwartung* piano score for Bill, passages in which this chord appeared most prominently and in many different guises. He seemed very intrigued by these note groupings and thought that he had, in fact, often used something like them in his playing, in his left-hand comping.

The new *Erwartung* triad has now been for many decades a staple of modern atonal-chromatic dominant-oriented music. (It does not—almost cannot—appear in modal music, whether jazz or classical, because of that style's concentration on perfect fourths and fifths, and pentatonic formations.) I have used the *Erwartung* triad thousands of times in my own music. What is fascinating to me is that with this trichord and its various relatives (as shown above) modern classical harmonization and jazz finally met on common ground, stylistically speaking. When did this happen? In the 1940s and 1950s, when bebop chordings (with the famous flatted fifth) caught up with the chromatic, bitonal-to-atonal harmonies that Ravel, Debussy, Schönberg, Stravinsky, and many other composers had been using ever since the earliest 1900s. (Be it noted that Ellington had been using bitonal and polytonal harmonies ever since 1932, and sporadically even before then as early as 1928—although with little appreciation and notice by the rest of the jazz community.)

The specific way in which this type of jazz chording relates to the *Erwartung* triad is that the following five-part chord used by a host of classical composers in the early twentieth century came into common usage in jazz in the bebop and modern jazz era. That chord and

its six- and seven-part expansions is, for example, the constantly recurring

harmonic centerpiece of Debussy's extraordinary piano composition *La Puerta del vino*, written

around 1911. In proper classical notation that chord would be spelled , where it would

be called a D-flat dominant seventh with an added minor third. In jazz it is called a raised
ninth chord, whether spelled as Debussy notated it or not. If you look at the top three notes

of the chord in question , you recognize it as the *Erwartung* triad, whichever way you

spell it. The fascinating history of its three-hundred-year development toward total independence as a freestanding primal chord begins with its use in the early eighteenth century, especially in Bach's music, and later very conspicuously in Mozart's works. There, however, this

"dissonance" had to be resolved melodically through three passing notes

(minor ninth, octave, minor seventh) to a tonic chord. This harmonic usage progressed in the
late nineteenth century toward full emancipation by first dropping the chord's root note, that
is, the bass D flat, using the chord in its first inversion; and then, still later, by also dropping
the A flat, which left the top three notes in free-floating unrestricted autonomy.

The way this history and harmonic analysis connects up with jazz is that the harmonies
under discussion came into full use in the 1940s and 1950s as five- or six-part chords in
arrangements and compositions, or as emancipated trichords in accompaniments and substitute changes, especially in the left-hand comping of pianists. And Bill Evans was one of the
first to use them prolifically.

His encounter at my house, with this specific harmonic material and its history and its
usage in works such as Debussy's *La Puerta del vino*, Schönberg's *Erwartung*, as well as much
of Ellington's music (most prominently in *Dusk* and *Azure*), encouraged him and confirmed
for him the need to explore it further, and to make it a prominent component of his harmonic language.

The *Erwartung* trichord works beautifully in jazz not only because its top note happens to
be one of the "blue notes" of jazz and the blues but also because for a pianist in a trio, quartet,
or other small-group setting it provides the three absolutely essential most important pitches
to produce a beautiful rich "dominant" chord: namely, the third, the minor seventh, and the
blue note minor third (or raised ninth), while the bass supplies the root notes.

By way of example, in the key of E flat with the bass playing the root E flat , the

midrange trichord would be F sharp, D flat, G . In the tritone substitute for

that chord in the F sharp, C sharp, and G functions as the sixth, the third, and the

minor seventh, respectively. If we add one more pitch to the trichord, namely, B flat, we then
add the enriching fifth in the E-flat chord, and the even more enhancing minor ninth in the
A-major chord. We have thereby clearly landed in the land of bitonality. The right hand in

is in F-sharp major, the left hand in E-flat major. A different version of such a bitonal

chord is   , where we still have F-sharp major in the right hand, but now C major in

the left hand. That chord even has its own personal name: it is called the "*Petroushka* chord" because Stravinsky used it very prominently in his ballet *Petroushka*.

Eventually, Bill Evans and I both felt that we had exhausted the subject of high chromaticism, bitonality, and its potential harmonic implications. He disappeared out of my life; I didn't see or hear from him for a couple of years. It was strange. But one day, perhaps in 1963—I recall that it was springtime—Bill suddenly showed up at my front door asking me to lend him some money. I didn't have to ask what for. The person standing in front of me was not the clean-cut, wholesome, well-groomed young man that had sat next to me at the piano for all those many months. Instead of the quiet half-smile I was used to see playing on Bill's lips, he had a haunted, haggard, hungry look, and definitely seemed to be in a hurry. I gave him fifteen dollars, knowing nothing about drugs, what exactly they were, what they cost. I just felt so sorry for him. Bill took the money and left quickly, with barely a smile, only a muttered thank-you.

To my surprise Bill showed up again two days later and asked me to help him out again. I really didn't know what I was doing when I gave him some more money. I didn't seem to have the strength to turn my admired friend down. I was very conflicted, part of me unable to refuse him, part of me realizing that what I was doing was wrong and was not helping him, that it was probably making matters worse. Nevertheless the softy in me won out. Bill kept coming back almost every day, always, with amazing punctuality, around four o'clock. For many days I didn't tell Margie; she was almost always out in the afternoon shopping, or with the children, or at her voice and piano lessons. I knew she would disapprove and think that I was nuts. Eventually, she found out what was happening. We had a couple of fights, but somehow I just couldn't stop giving Bill money for his daily fix. He looked so helpless, so desperate.

After a few months, I did come to my senses and told him that I had to stop the handouts, that I was gonna go broke. To my amazement—and relief—he calmly said, "I understand," completely impassively, without any feeling. A few days later it finally occurred to me—I was that naïve—that I could not have been Bill's only financial source for supporting his habit.[31]

Bill Evans had a brilliant career as one of the most original and innovative pianists and composers in jazz, providing dozens of superb recordings right up to his passing in 1980. Working with him at the Brandeis Creative Arts Festival in 1957 was an absolute joy. Of all the outstanding musicians involved with that project, Bill was the best prepared to cope with the wide range of musical, interpretational, and technical challenges that this concert of six world premieres presented. It was clear to me that he was the ideal pianist for any jazz-related work I might produce in the future, whether in concerts or on recordings, whether for my own music or that of similarly advanced composers. It was my great fortune that Bill was available to work with me on several important occasions, including the Circle in the Square concert, the *Jazz Abstractions* album (with Ornette Coleman, Eric Dolphy, Scott La Faro), and John Lewis's film score for *Odds against Tomorrow*.[32]

A most important series of recording dates for me as a composer and as a conductor occurred in 1956. It combined on one LP my modern classical nonjazz atonal *Symphony for Brass and Percussion* on one side, and on the flip side three jazz pieces: John Lewis's *Three Little Feelings*, J. J. Johnson's *Poem for Brass*, and a work by Jimmy Giuffre entitled *Pharaoh*. That album, eventually called *Music for Brass*, came about in a somewhat circuitous way. The four compositions were originally scheduled to be performed at Town Hall in our Jazz and Classical Music Society's second concert in the fall of 1956. I had also programmed two of Giovanni Gabrieli's *Sacrae Symphoniae* to showcase some of the remarkable large-ensemble music created during the High Renaissance at St. Mark's Cathedral in Venice nearly 350 years earlier. But that concert was canceled (and postponed to the fall of 1957) at the request of the New York Philharmonic when Mitropoulos scheduled my *Symphony for Brass and Percussion* for performance in November 1956. The Philharmonic didn't want to be scooped in that premiere by a freelance group. But I had already begun rehearsing my Symphony in June, soon after my return from the Met's spring tour. June was the one month in the year when, the regular performance season being over, one could most likely get musicians from New York's various top musical organizations (the Met, the Philharmonic, the NBC Symphony) together for a spate of rehearsals.

As a result of the Philharmonic's intervention John and I now faced the dilemma of being stuck with a schedule of further rehearsals, but for what? A concert a year and a half away? The possibility of a recording had been vaguely considered but nothing definite had been set. Now, suddenly, my friend and Columbia Records producer George Avakian came to the rescue by organizing a recording session for my Symphony in mid-June, at the same time committing to recording dates for the three other works (by Lewis, Johnson, Giuffre) in October that year.

It was an important breakthrough recording in that it was one of the very first—if not *the* first—to present on the same disc not only classical *and* jazz pieces but also classical and jazz musicians working together, side by side. For it was still uncommon (in the 1950s) to put classical players in jazz concerts and recordings, and, vice versa, to hire players labeled as jazz musicians for classical gigs. It was a time when the long-standing artificial barriers between jazz and classical music still kept the two musical worlds segregated, but were just beginning to break down. And I like to think that John and I had a lot to do with bringing about the rapprochement that eventually brought the two musics together.

What was also particularly gratifying to me as a young, little-known composer was the fact that the world-famous Dimitri Mitropoulos, then music director of the New York Philharmonic, agreed at my request to conduct the *Brass Symphony* on the recording. It took place on June 14, 1956.

I handpicked the musicians for the three recording sessions not only with an eye toward getting the very best players New York could offer but also—to me almost more important— to bring together as broad a mixture of jazz and classical players as possible. Thus I chose some colleagues from the Met (including Joe Alessi Sr., Izzy Blank, and timpanist Dick Horowitz), from the New York Philharmonic (principal horn Joe Singer, trumpeter Johnny Ware, trombonist Gordon Pulis, as well as trumpeter Mel Broiles, just out of Julliard), and from the NBC Symphony (my old friend John Clark, bass trombone). On the jazz side I selected great trumpet players such as Bernie Glow (one of the finest lead trumpets in New York at the time) and Joe Wilder, trombonists J. J. Johnson and Urbie Green, and, specifically for the three jazz pieces, Milt Hinton (bass) and Osie Johnson (drums). I played fourth horn in my *Brass Symphony*, and conducted the three jazz works. Miles Davis was a special guest soloist, playing flugelhorn in John Lewis's *Three Little Feelings* and J. J.'s *Poem for Brass*.

I prerehearsed all the music, leaving the final rehearsal of my Symphony to Dimitri, who knew the piece extraordinarily well. He had as usual memorized the work down to the minutest details, and drew a stunningly exciting, dynamic performance from this stellar ensemble of players. The recording has been hailed for decades as the finest brass ensemble recording of its time.

Given the great roster of players I had assembled for the two recording sessions in October, they were destined to be pioneering breakthrough performances, especially in consideration of the fact that there had never before been any jazz compositions for a large brass-only ensemble. The interpretational and technical challenges presented by these four compositions were largely unprecedented, yet they were met brilliantly. If you listen to those recordings of fifty-five years ago with any degree of objectivity and historical perspective, you have to be amazed at what you hear. Those musicians walked into brand-new territory, faced the challenges they encountered head-on, and emerged victorious.

It was so exciting for all of us to explore these new musical soundscapes. As certain as I was that my chosen musicians would pass the various tests they were facing, I was still amazed at how quickly and easily the musical and technical problems were solved. Clean intonation, blending and balancing the rich, full-bodied euphonies, especially in J. J.'s *Poem for Brass*, was automatic with these players. One didn't have to rehearse such things. I could feel how they relished being allowed for once to seize the limelight and not be merely secondary to strings and woodwinds. They were particularly intrigued by J. J.'s sumptuous Hindemith-influenced jazz sonorities. (J. J.'s favorite classical pieces were Paul Hindemith's *Mathis der Maler* and his 1930 *Concert Music for Strings and Brass*.) I loved the way he exploited the luxury of a large sixteen-piece ensemble, using the opportunity to spike his already richly harmonic language with lots of polytonal seasonings: G major over A flat, D major over E-flat minor, D major over C major, and the like—adventurous harmonies that J. J. could hardly muster in his small groups, for example in the J. J. & Kai Winding Quintet. His ultimate polytonal triumph can be heard in the final climactic fifteen-part chord, compiled out of three tonalities: A major (in

the trumpets), D major (in the horns), and G major (in the lower brass) 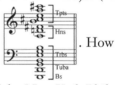 . How

Johnny Ware—later for several decades the stalwart principal trumpet of the New York Philharmonic—hit that final high C sharp again and again in several takes at around half past three in the morning, at the end of a lip-withering session, is still incomprehensible to me as a fellow brass player. I know something about tired lips.

In contrast to J. J.'s homophonic work, John Lewis's *Three Little Feelings*—the three movements are entitled "Of Hope," "From the Heart," and "Majesty"—is more intrinsically melodic and theme oriented. It also swings more, and represents—undoubtedly inspired by the availability of so many powerful brass instruments—a more forceful side of John's musical personality than the chamber music setting of the Modern Jazz Quartet would allow. John also left more room for improvisation (by Miles and J. J.), and made room in the third movement for a majestic declamatory solo (written) for horn, played beautifully and authoritatively by Jim Buffington. Though Miles here occasionally played slightly out of tune, especially on the flugelhorn in the first movement—the instrument was new to him at the time—John's nostalgic, poignant music in the "From the Heart" section elicited from Miles the most touching, heartfelt playing any of us had ever heard from him. He sounded like a new Miles. Thereby hangs a tale.

Obbligato

I have mentioned that I had sometimes found Miles's trumpet playing somewhat wanting, primarily from a sonic-technical point of view. His best, most distinctive musical ideas were so often undercut by a thin, fuzzy sound, untidy slurs, and a subtle but fairly consistent sense of insecurity. One could never be quite sure that he would get that high note he was striving for.[33] One day in late 1955 or early 1956, John Lewis and I got onto the subject of Miles's playing, and how he was still so entrapped in the tempting desire to be another Dizzy Gillespie. We felt that Miles had certain technical limitations that Dizzy, a more natural player, never had to contend with, which would prevent Miles from ever following in Dizzy's footsteps. Yet Miles had it within himself to be a totally different, distinctively original, quintessentially lyric player. John decided that perhaps we, as two of Miles's closest friends and work colleagues, should share our thoughts with him. And so, over an extended period of time, we very subtly worked on him, using every possible approach, from cajolery and teasing flattery to deadly serious argumentations and technical analyses—my department, as a fellow brass player—to try to persuade him of the wisdom of our words. I remember spending one whole night with him in a Chinese restaurant in Boston talking about these matters: embouchures, mouth pieces, breathing, and so on. To his credit Miles admitted that he was often frustrated by the pesky little problems he sensed in his playing, that they really annoyed him, but that he didn't know what to do about them.

We had turned a corner with Miles.[34] I told him that I thought I could help, an offer he readily accepted. He trusted me, having heard from Julius Watkins and Bob Northern, two black horn players and students of mine at the Manhattan School of Music, that I had quite a reputation for fixing (correcting) players' embouchures, helping with better-fitting mouthpieces, and working on problems of breath support. One of the first suggestions I made to Miles was to get a cornet (which has an inherently warmer, rounder tone than a trumpet) and a flugelhorn, an even larger and bigger-bored instrument. (That is why Miles ended up playing his solos on *Three Little Feelings* on the flugelhorn.) I was sure that playing on these two relatives of the trumpet would over a period of time give him an aural sense for the fuller, deeper sound, which he could then replicate on the trumpet.

But beyond that elementary suggestion I made three attempts over a period of several years in the late 1950s to change Miles's embouchure, basically to move his mouthpiece higher on his upper lip so that he could play in the high register with greater ease and security, perhaps even extend his upper range. He would come over to my house, and I'd sit him down opposite me in the dining room (where I did all my teaching) and size up his lips and mouth. Then I'd take his mouthpiece and place it on his pursed lips, so that its upper rim would sit just above the red of the lip, in the little indentation that we all have there. This better placement of the mouthpiece gives you a kind of leverage on the pressure of your lip that enables you to play high notes with greater ease and accuracy. If the mouthpiece sits too low—in the red of the lip—you can still get high notes but only with greater effort and heavier pressure on the lips, with the result that the tone sounds strained and forced. Eventually the lip muscles rebel, and become stiff and inflexible.

It was such a joy to see Miles's smile of relief when, with the new mouthpiece position, a high B flat or high C floated out of his horn with the greatest ease, with a nice open sound and without any strain.

But now came the hard part; nothing good really comes that easily. I had to tell Miles that what he now needed to do was spend at least three or four days a week taking no gigs and just playing lots of soft long tones and easy exercises until the lip muscles could adjust to the new position and different feeling of the mouthpiece. That's where Dr. Schuller's prescription and practice regimen ran up against Mr. Davis's impatience—or call it a want of discipline—with the full process, staying with it to its conclusion. The first two times, I'm sure, Miles did not practice the long tones to stabilize the new embouchure, and probably played some gigs or jam sessions. When I saw him the next time, his mouthpiece had slipped right back to its former position. But whatever Miles did the third time, it worked much better. His playing became more relaxed and technically secure, his tone a little fuller. But those slight changes coincided with a much more important shift in Miles's performing. That was when he came up with the idea of playing, almost permanently, with a harmon mute, close into a microphone.[35]

*   *   *   *   *

Jimmy Giuffre's *Pharoah* is in many ways the most unusual, the most original, of the three *Music for Brass* compositions. It is a prime example of what in the 1950s was beginning to be called "cool" or "West Coast" jazz, polyphonic in conception, primarily linear-melodic, and thus more or less devoid of any harmonic undergirding. What little harmony occurs in *Pharoah* results vertically from the multiple layers of melodic-thematic lines. *Pharoah* is also completely written out, fully notated, precluding any improvisation. It is also unusual in that the entire piece is in a single tonality, the key of F, alternately minor and major—except for a brief middle section built on the dominant C.

   Pharoah is a kind of tone poem; certainly in Giuffre's mind the title and the imposing heraldic opening timpani passage were intended to conjure an imaginary "procession in ancient Egypt of a great pharoah and his court," as Giuffre put it.[36] In contrast to J. J.'s homophonic work, with its massive vertical harmonies and density of textures, everything in Giuffre's piece is horizontal, linear; and despite his use of the full sixteen-instrument ensemble, there is a lightness, a transparency of texture, a clarity, which enables the ear to hear and follow all the various contrapuntal lines. Every instrumental section functions melodically and independently, that is, polyphonically. There is a relaxed, cooled-off feeling—a kind of casualness—that is unique to Giuffre's understated style, whether as a player or a composer. Arthur Statter, principal trumpet of the New York City Ballet orchestra, and one of the six trumpet players I had hired for this recording date, at one point quipped: "Man, I didn't know these old Egyptians spoke with a Texas drawl," alluding to Giuffre's Texan background and low-keyed, leisurely manner—even in his music.

   Tucked away here and there in *Pharoah* one can find strangely original little passages that are unique to Giuffre. One that I love particularly is for the six trumpets *a cappella*, featuring

six widely spread, contrapuntally independent lines, which then suddenly pull together into a deliciously spicy resolution:  . And I can still thrill to the central climax of the piece, where two trumpets climb in unison to a very high F (sustained in Bernie Glow's golden-toned

lead trumpet)   , over a monumental six-

part chordal pillar.

It may be that of all my various involvements with jazz and Third Stream in the 1950s the most important was in connection with the Brandeis Creative Arts Festival in June of 1957.[37] It is certainly the artistic and creative achievement of that period of which I am most proud. The concert and the seminal recording that resulted from it were unprecedented events, firsts in the history of music; and they more clearly and firmly clarified what the Third Stream concept meant, what it could be at its best, what it could produce, what its aesthetic potential as a new genre of music really was.

I'm not sure how the idea of including jazz in the 1957 festival came about. Since its founding in 1952, the festival had celebrated classical music, dance, poetry, and painting. I think it must have originated in President Abram Sachar's office, with support and input from Arthur Berger and Irving Fine, both on the music faculty at Brandeis. Fine was also head of the arts council that provided funding to the School of Creative Arts. Aaron Copland was very likely also involved as an advisor;[38] and so was Nat Hentoff, the major jazz critic and writer on jazz at the time. All I know is that one day late in 1956 I was approached by a Mrs. Milton Steinberg, director of public relations at Brandeis, and Max Kleinbaum, administrative assistant to President Sachar, asking me if I would be interested in creating and organizing a "really special jazz concert" for the upcoming festival. In our first meeting I got the impression that they wanted me to think big, to have "some large dreams," as they put it.

Wow! What an opportunity! I came up with the idea of putting on a concert of six newly commissioned compositions: three by jazz composers and three by classical composers. I chose Charles Mingus, George Russell, and Jimmy Giuffre, at the time, in my mind, the most progressive, innovative composers on the jazz side, and Milton Babbitt (of Princeton University) and Harold Shapero (on the Brandeis composition faculty) on the classical side. By common consent I was also asked to compose a piece for the occasion. In addition, I programmed two other works: Duke Ellington's *Reminiscing in Tempo*, as the all-important historic forerunner in jazz of multisectional, completely through-composed, extended-form composition, with a duration of fourteen minutes; and Thelonious Monk's *Eronel*, as arranged by André Hodeir, who by 1957 had already written (and recorded) a whole series of extended-form pieces that incorporated many ideas and techniques propounded by the European twelve-tone avant-garde.

I also chose a basic mixed instrumentation for which all the works would be composed: two woodwinds (flute and bassoon—Robert DiDomenica, Manuel Zegler), three saxes (Hal

McKusick, John LaPorta, Teo Macero), two trumpets (Louis Mucci, Art Farmer), trombone (Jimmy Knepper), horn (Jimmy Buffington), harp (Margaret Ross), guitar (Barry Galbraith), piano (Bill Evans), vibraphone (Teddy Charles), bass (Joe Benjamin, most recently bassist in Duke Ellington's orchestra), and drums (Teddy Sommer)—fifteen musicians in all. For the Ellington and Hodeir pieces additional saxes, trumpets, and trombones were brought in, but I do not recall who they were.

As diverse as the six compositions were in form, harmonic language, and style (within the larger concept of Third Stream), they had one thing more or less in common: all six pieces were to some extent based on or developed out of *thematic* ideas, a long-standing concept intrinsic in classical music, but not really endemic to jazz.[39] It came about quite naturally, I think, because of the association with classical composers in the project, and because the theme happened not to be entirely foreign to the three chosen jazz composers.

While in standard jazz improvisation normally overrides composition, in this instance it was outbalanced by composition, a dramatic shift of emphasis. Three composers (Giuffre, Shapero, and Babbitt) eschewed improvisation, two others (Mingus, Schuller) called for relatively little, and only in one (Russell) were there any substantial improvisations. Another important distinction is that in Mingus's and my pieces, to the extent that improvisation was required, very little of it was in an outright solo format; most of it was instead in an ensemble context, that is, only as part of a larger ensemble complex. In Mingus's *Revelations* the thematic-motivic idea manifested itself in the building of the piece, in what Mingus called "voice lines," polyphonically layered lines. In my piece, *Transformation*, the theme idea took the form of a Passacaglia, first stated linearly in twelve-tone as a *Klangfarbenmelodie*, and then gradually turned on its end to produce a vertical twelve-note chord. Similarly, the brief improvisatory sections were all intimately related to the basic twelve-tone row-*cum*-theme. In Shapero's *On Green Mountain* the main theme was a melodic line borrowed note for note from a Chaconne by Claudio Monteverdi.[40] In Russell's *All About Rosie* the music is based on a motif taken from a catchy black children's song from Alabama, a theme that functions prominently, though in various guises, in all three movements. Giuffre's *Suspensions* is clearly based on and developed out of two themes. Composed in the classical Sonata-Allegro form, it has a "principal theme" and a "second subject." In much of Giuffre's writing, whether in *Four Brothers* or his *Suspensions*, the thematic-motivic lines are always inherently melodic.

In Babbitt's *All Set*, although there is no theme or motive as such, the "theme" idea is represented and deeply embodied in the music *in the set* (i.e., the twelve-tone row), which functions persistently in *all* aspects of the work—vertically, horizontally, diagonally, interrelationally. In essence, a set—a row—is an especially fertile kind of thematic material; it is with its row of twelve pitches a linear quasi-melodic structure that determines every musical detail (harmonic, melodic, rhythmic, etc.) in the resultant composition.

The stylistic diversity and varied complexities of the six pieces presented enormous technical and performance challenges. Foremost in this respect was Babbitt's *All Set*, a most remarkable jazz-related work by the world's leading twelve-tone (or serial) composer. The only musician who took this music completely in stride was Bill Evans. At the first rehearsal of the piece he already played his part perfectly, including the constantly changing dynamics. (In Babbitt's music virtually every note—not just every four- or eight-bar phrase—has its own independent dynamic, an integral part of the serialized procedures with which Babbitt works.

There was no such awareness in the case of, say, Art Farmer or Joe Benjamin. When they encountered Babbitt's *All Set*, they nearly freaked out. They had never seen such music before: one horrendously difficult, unfriendly looking page of music after another. But to their unbounded credit, they worked endless hours deciphering and practicing those parts. It was truly heroic. I cannot praise them enough for their dedication and devotion to that awesome task, unprecedented in their lives. That Art and Joe ultimately turned in such very creditable performances of the Babbitt piece is almost in the realm of miracles.

For that matter, the whole Brandeis concert was a kind of miracle, given the enormous difficulties presented by the eight works performed that evening, all of them brand new to every one of the musicians. Under the circumstances, the performances were surely not perfect, especially in the case of *All Set*. We played all the notes correctly, but not with the ease and relaxed feeling that greater familiarity with the music would have made possible. In those early days of the Third Stream movement there was one fundamental problem that could not be quickly overcome. Even the best jazz musicians tended to tighten up, to freeze, when confronted with having to read lengthy, rhythmically complex parts. To make Babbitt's *All Set* swing, which was certainly my hope and intention, took years to achieve.[41] *All Set* can be played, assuming for the moment note perfection and very experienced musicians, in two ways. If played by straight classical musicians unfamiliar with jazz, it will sound like any very advanced modern classical music, but in no way like jazz. If played (especially nowadays!) by jazz musicians, it will become a jazz piece. It is not the notes per se; it is *how* the notes are played that will determine in which direction the performance will go stylistically. And this is true of many compositions that attempt to amalgamate classical and jazz stylings.

That said, if we take into consideration what the six composers intended and hoped for, then three of them (Babbitt, Russell, Giuffre) absolutely require jazz players. The other three (Mingus, Schuller, Shapero) need players who are versed in *both* idioms.

The reviews of the Brandeis concert ranged from mildly, cautiously favorable and bewildered puzzlement to outright rejection, along with the inevitable split-decision reactions, that is, liking one or two of the pieces and condemning the others. Hardly anybody knew what to make of Babbitt's piece and more or less passed it over, offering a few noncommittal platitudes. the *New York Times* sent Ross Parmenter instead of John Wilson. His review was at best ambivalent, since on the one hand he characterized the whole concert as "producing neither outstanding jazz"—he must not have heard Russell's *All About Rosie*—"nor particularly impressive concert music," while on the other hand he praised my *Transformation* as "the tautest and most authoritative," "the one piece that blended the idioms most convincingly." Parmenter referred to myself, Babbitt, and Shapero as "longhair" composers, and this in the august *New York Times*! He passed off Russell's *All About Rosie* with one sentence, as "exhilarating in its soft sections," and considered Mingus's *Revelations* "the least successful in finding convincing middle ground."[42]

Although annoying, such reactions didn't surprise me, given that most of the works explored radically new musical territories, an acceptance of which the average critic and listener was simply not prepared for. I can readily understand how the degree of stylistic diversity in the program, ranging from Babbitt at one end of the spectrum to Mingus and Russell on the other, would be for most critics bewildering and hard to assimilate on a first hearing. What was baffling—and disappointing—to me was that almost all the critiquing and evaluating was based on the wrong criteria: namely, to what extent the works were or were not jazz, rather than whether there was a balanced fusion of classical and jazz elements. For that is in one way or another exactly what each of these six composers achieved. Such criticisms completely missed the point that the six pieces were not intended to be either purely jazz or purely classical, but rather an amalgam of the two, in whatever special way each composer saw and imagined such a fusion.

Part of the issue in assessing the worthiness, the artistic viability of any new musical creation is that of performance problems, which inevitably present themselves in any new genre or idiom or style, and which may not be immediately solvable. Performers have to become familiar with the music's untried technical and conceptual demands, which will in some cases take time and cannot be expected to be instantly unraveled. There is no question that our performances that first night were to one degree or another rather tight and tense. The next morning, when we played the whole program again, in connection with a symposium and discussion period, our renditions of the six pieces were already much less constrained, more at ease and inwardly relaxed—performances that were, of course, not reviewed. It is an essential part of the history of music performance that it often takes years, perhaps decades, for the new to be assimilated, to be finally rendered in a fully comprehending and feeling way. It took about a hundred years for Beethoven's Ninth Symphony to be performed correctly and with full intellectual and affective understanding.

Whatever the quality of the performances in the Brandeis concert may have been, the recordings we made of all six commissioned pieces were quite naturally better, more representative, partly because by then we knew the music better, and partly because in recording we could improve the performance by making repeated takes and then, of course, by postsession editing. The editing process was particularly useful in the Babbitt work, which, by the way, George Avakian, the producer, let me edit myself—with Columbia engineers, of course. There was also a personnel change on the recording date for one of the pieces. Whereas Joe Benjamin had played the bass part on Mingus's *Revelations* in the concert at Brandeis, Mingus wanted to play the part himself on the recording. There was, needless to say, no objection to that, fabulous bass player that Mingus was. There is, however, a very prominent extended bowed passage in *Revelations*, which Mingus backed out of playing, saying that "my arco chops are not up to it right now." By common agreement Fred Zimmerman, from the New York Philharmonic, Mingus's sometime teacher and my close friend, played the bowed parts—and beautifully. It was good to have Mingus aboard, for no one could deliver the shouted exclamation—"Oh yes, my Lord!"—in the gospel music section of the piece with the ecstatic exultation that he brought to it.

For all that is good and worthy on the Brandeis Festival recording, the absolute high point for me is Bill Evans's solo on Russell's *All About Rosie*. It is not only one of his finest moments in an altogether sterling career, but is also one of the greatest piano solos ever in the whole history of jazz. It has to be heard to be believed.[43]

Wherever I may go in this world of ours—and I have had the good fortune to set foot on every one of the six continents that adorn this globe—I am bound to meet many people, including complete strangers who, if they have heard of me, will know one thing, and usually *only* that one thing. This is typically expressed in a heartfelt exclamation: "Oh, you're the one who played with Miles Davis," their face aglow with the delight of recognition and appreciation. It often seems to me that the only thing considered important in my life and worth knowing about me is that I worked with Miles. Well, yes I did. And I count knowing Miles and working often with him among my most significant artistic experiences and relationships. But perhaps even more important in the long view is the fact that it was through Miles that I got to meet two other great men: Gil Evans and George Avakian.

I could write a whole book about Gil Evans, and if I live long enough, I will very likely do just that. Meanwhile, suffice it to say that Gil clearly belongs near the top of the list of genius-level jazz composers (with emphasis on the word "composers")—a hall of fame graced by a trinity of Duke Ellington, Charles Mingus, and Jelly Roll Morton. I fell in love with Gil's work when, as a twenty-two year old, I first heard his early arrangements—we now call them, more accurately, recompositions—for the Claude Thornhill orchestra of pieces such as Charlie Parker's *Yardbird Suite*, *Anthropology*, and Mussorgsky's *Arab Dance*. It is a sad commentary on the jazz community, including its critics and writers, that Gil's early work was mostly unappreciated and ignored for so many years, with the result that he worked in relative obscurity much of that time. It is thus rather ironic that his great talents were finally accorded serious recognition only when he became associated with Miles Davis in 1957 through three remarkable recording projects: *Miles Ahead*, *Porgy and Bess*, and *Sketches of Spain*.

That's where George Avakian comes into the picture, because the three Gil Evans-Miles Davis collaborations were initiated and conceived by Avakian (although he was able to produce only the first one, *Miles Ahead*). He should be as celebrated for those achievements as Miles and Gil, because without George's visionary role as producer (at Columbia Records), those recordings would in all likelihood not have been realized.

George Avakian has, in fact, initiated more firsts in the jazz recording field than anyone else I can think of. To list just a few, in 1939 he was the first to produce jazz reissues (for Columbia), a concept that a few years later he expanded into extensive overview reissue programs of Louis Armstrong and Bessie Smith (eight LPs in toto). He brought major artists such as Johnny Mathis and Dave Brubeck to Columbia, whose successes, financial as well as artistic, enabled him to undertake ambitious and costly projects such as the Miles Davis-Gil Evans collaborations. George was also the first to record jazz festival performances (starting with the Newport Festival of 1956). He pioneered ingenious new splicing techniques for working with magnetic tape, among other things creating performances collated from two or more takes. (Editing was unknown—indeed impossible—in the pre-LP 78-rpm era.) George was also crucially influential in establishing the early recording careers of Dave Brubeck, Sonny Rollins, and Keith Jarrett. (I first met Jarrett at George's home on Central Park West, where John Cage, a close friend of the Avakians, was often on hand, and where Cage and I began our friendship.)

Equally important is the work George did in the field of jazz criticism (as an early contributor to *DownBeat*, *Metronome*, *Esquire*, and many other magazines), and in jazz history and research, as chief editor in revising, updating, and significantly expanding Charles Delaunay's pathbreaking *Hot Discography* for its first American edition in 1948. I cannot emphasize enough how indebted I am—as are so many of us in the fields of jazz history, research, criticism, and record collecting—to George Avakian's selfless, lifelong devotion to jazz.

Sometime in March 1957 I got a call from Miles, asking me to participate in a recording in late May or early June, "some new things I'm doing with Gil," as he put it. It turned out that Avakian, an ardent admirer of the "new" Miles Davis—new after a dramatic comeback success at the 1955 Newport Jazz Festival—had signed Miles up at Columbia, and was planning three major recording projects with him, to be spread over three years. To George the word "major" meant, among other things, using a large orchestra rather than the usual small-group quintets or sextets.

At the time, the only thing settled in George's mind for the first of the three albums was its title, *Miles Ahead*, along with a vague notion to create a sequel to the Miles Davis nonet recordings, which had deeply impressed him. Still annoyed and baffled by their critical and public rejection, he wondered how he might now, in his leading position at Columbia, pursue the idea of an enlarged variant of Miles's nonet.

George himself has recounted that in 1956, when he was supervising the recording of my *Music for Brass* album, which featured Miles's balladic, lyrical soloing on John Lewis's and J. J. Johnsons's compositions, mostly on flugelhorn ("a wonderful surprise" for George), several ideas began to jell for him into a plan for recording a nineteen-piece orchestra (including four woodwind doublers rather than only brass), mixing jazz and classical elements. When he mentioned this idea to Miles, he also proposed that Miles should choose as composer-arranger for the project "between Gil and Gunther, the only two," in George's words, "who could do this most effectively."[44] Miles chose Gil—and a better choice could not have been made.

As for being one of the three horns on the proposed *Miles Ahead* date, I found myself—alas—having to turn George and Miles down, since in May I would have to be on tour with the

Metropolitan Opera. I was sick about not being available, but I recommended that my buddy, Jim Buffington, take my place.

When many months later I got an advance acetate copy from George of the *Miles Ahead* LP, I was amazed at what I heard. I was especially taken with Johnny Carisi's *Springsville*, with its amazing full-throttle block-chord ensembles, and—by complete contrast—Kurt Weill's *My Ship*, with those haunting languorous dense "sound clouds," drifting by ever so slowly (one of Gil's patented specialties). I was also surprised to find on the program Léo Delibes' *Maids of Cadiz*, which I knew well in its original incarnation as a chanson that Margie used to sing occasionally. But beyond all that—apart from Miles's beautiful playing—what impressed me the most as a composer were the little bridges that Gil had composed, linking the ten pieces together into a kind of Suite. That was a breakthrough idea that no one had ever used before, at least in a jazz context, and that, to my knowledge, has never been emulated.[45]

Miles and George had intimated that there were more collaborations with Gil in the offing. I kept hoping they were right. For in the treacherous profit-driven record business, nothing as venturous as what Gil and Miles were planning could ever be considered a sure thing. But as it turned out, a year later I was called for a spate of recording sessions to be held in late July and August 1958, a call this time not from Gil or Miles, but from Calvin Lampley, who had succeeded George as producer-editor at Columbia Records. The plan was to record a dozen or so numbers from Gershwin's opera, *Porgy and Bess*, as recomposed and re-created by Gil Evans, with an instrumentation very much like that of *Miles Ahead*, and with Miles again as soloist. Lampley told me that he expected Julius Watkins and Willie Ruff to complete the three-piece horn section.

I was elated at the good news. What evolved eventually has long been acclaimed as one of the most astounding artistic and creative achievements in the history of jazz. Gil's recasting of that already remarkably beautiful and virtually perfect Gershwin music is for me—and I know for many others—an almost inexplicable triumph of inspiration, invention, and creative originality.[46] And I can say for myself that, had I been offered the assignment to reimagine Gershwin's music, I would have turned the offer down. I would not have wanted to tamper with something that was already perfect. Gil Evans's unique genius lay precisely in that he could reenvision Gershwin's music at an equally high level of inspiration and invention, though in a quite different context and idiom. Gil produced many passages, scattered throughout the thirteen movements of the Suite, that created in their originality a new magical sound world that had never been heard before—even in *Miles Ahead*. I can't think of another similarly creative transference from one great master, George Gershwin, to another, Gil Evans.

As acclaimed and as artistically and commercially successful the *Porgy and Bess* recording was, it should not lead one to think that it was a perfect realization of what Gil had actually written, what he had really envisioned. Fifty-three years ago Gil's score presented a considerable challenge (technically, conceptually, interpretationally), even for some of the best musicians in New York—challenges that in some instances were never fully met. That said, one still has to regard what *was* achieved on that recording as a minor miracle.

Since I am now one of the few living survivors of those recording sessions, I feel it incumbent upon me to give as accurate an account of what transpired as possible, not with the intention of denigrating the recording and its achievements, but, on the contrary, to signal what a heroic achievement it was, despite certain shortcomings in the realization of Gil Evans's score.

Attentive listeners with keen ears will hear in the recording at various times moments of rhythmic raggedness (most notably in the "Gone" section), of poor ensemble balances, of serious intonation problems, and a certain uneasiness with Gil's music—all of which could have been remedied if, for one thing, we could have been given more recording time, which Columbia was, however, unwilling to provide. The *Porgy* recording was given much less recording time than the relatively easier *Miles Ahead* album. The disparity of approach and scheduling between the two is, in retrospect, rather startling. I remember overhearing trombonist Jimmy Cleveland and bass clarinetist Danny Bank, both of whom played on all three Davis-Evans collaborations, during a break in one of the *Porgy* sessions complaining about having much less time on this date than on the *Miles Ahead* date. What they were talking about is confirmed in detail by Phil Schaap's exhaustive discographical research presented in the 1996 box-set reissue of the original recording. Specifically, on the *Miles Ahead* date only two or at most three titles were recorded per session, as compared to three, four, and five on the 1958 *Porgy* date. These circumstances were determined—I must assume—by the fact that on *Miles Ahead* there were only ten numbers to be recorded (with a total duration of about thirty-nine minutes), as compared to thirteen *Porgy* numbers (with a total duration of over fifty minutes).

In the end, we had only ten hours (when you subtract intermissions and breaks and other interruptions) to record thirteen separate pieces of music. Morever, the *Porgy* music was inherently more difficult, more challenging, more unfamiliar stylistically. That in itself should have resulted in allowing more time for retakes, for overdubbings by Miles, which in turn would have offered a greater choice of takes and additional editing options. *Miles Ahead* was heavily edited because there were many more takes and retakes available, not to mention rehearsal takes (which on the *Porgy* date we never had), thus ultimately achieving a cleaner, better performed result. Similarly, on the *Porgy* sessions we never did more than five takes, and many of them were short and incomplete because of serious breakdowns, making them of course unusable. Compare this to the ten to twelve takes—in one case, *I Don't Wanna Be Kissed (By Anyone But You)*, even nineteen!—that almost every piece on the *Miles Ahead* sessions was accorded.

The musicians on the *Porgy* date were virtually the same as on the *Miles Ahead* album. But we were not given enough time to learn and assimilate the much more demanding *Porgy* music. Considering its difficulty and the sheer amount of it, we should have had one more session, optionally with at least an hour overtime. That would have sufficed to clean up the ragged spots with what we call "insert" or "patch" takes; or at minimum it would have provided more editing and splicing opportunities. I thought so back in 1958 and I still think so today.

I am embarrassed when I hear us horn players fumbling with the syncopated background rhythms on *It Ain't Necessarily So*. We were never given another chance to rectify things. There were only three takes for that piece: on take one the beginning was never recorded (a faux pas by the booth), take two was a false start, and the third one was the one used on the original release (CL1274), unedited—because there was nothing to edit with. Did Cal Lampley really think that take three was good enough to be used? The irony is that on the first take we sight-read our background compings perfectly for long stretches, in any case much better than on take three. I figure that the later take was used because on take one several full-ensemble passages came off rather poorly, and it had no ending, having broken down completely near the end in the last chorus. There again, one more take would have saved the situation.

I believe there is a second reason, a crucial one, why the *Porgy* sessions did not turn out as well as they should have. We had to cope with a very problematic stage and microphone setup.[47] I consider the orchestra's seating plan that had been decided upon to have contributed seriously to our problems in achieving good ensemble playing, which is always dependant on easy visual and aural contact between players.

Columbia's Thirtieth Street recording studio, located in a former church, was a spacious pentagonal room with good acoustics. (I recorded there dozens of times, especially with the Met orchestra.) When I arrived for the first *Porgy* session I saw to my dismay that the orchestra had been set up in a gigantic 360-degree circle, divided into four widely separated groupings (woodwinds, trumpets, horns, trombones, and tuba), with Miles, Paul Chambers, and Philly Joe Jones (or Jimmy Cobb) way off in one corner of the room. Gil's conductor podium was in the center of this circle. It was all designed to provide as much acoustic and spatial separation between the various instrumental choirs as possible, to thus allow for greater microphonic and balance control in both the recording and editing process.[48] While this setup was ideal for the recording engineers, since separation between the various choirs would minimize leakage from one microphone position to another, for us musicians, accustomed to sitting close together so as to hear one another better, it was a considerable disadvantage. Imagine trying to hear someone with whom you are supposed to blend and balance in dynamics and sonority to produce beautiful, sensitive ensemble sound, when that someone is sitting forty feet away on the other side of the room—the acoustics of which are already a trifle too reverberant, too blurry. Moreover, at such a distance there is also a tiny yet significant time delay.

Cannonball Adderley and the three woodwinds, the nearest group to us three horns, were about twenty feet away to our left. The four trombones were facing us, allowing at least some visual contact, but they were nearly forty feet away. The trumpet section was seated about ten feet to the right of the trombones, but even further back across the room, maybe fifty feet away from the reeds and horns. Paul Chambers and Jimmy Cobb were partly hidden in baffles and virtually inaudible to me. Miles, as I recall, played sometimes in a booth, at other times outside of it, which, I think, had to do with whether he was playing open-horn trumpet, or harmon muted, or on flugelhorn. When Miles was in the booth, I could just see the top of his head, nothing else.

Implied of course in this set up was the idea that to help us hear better we were expected to play through earphones—what musicians call "cans." But earphones are a pretty limited substitute for hearing the real unmiked and unamplified sound. I always hated playing with cans. Not only did they give you a crude replication of the original pure sound, but when you had earphones over your ears you could not hear your own playing very well, *and* there was the risk that what you were fed on the earphones, namely, the sounds of the total orchestra, wasn't mixed or balanced correctly in the control room. Most of the musicians didn't use the earphones.

Musicians, as a lot, are pretty good in adjusting to bad or problematic acoustic conditions, and we all did our best to deal with this less than ideal situation. But in the end, we couldn't always solve the various problems that arose, especially given the limited recorded time.

The reader must know by now in what high regard I hold Gil Evans. So it is with all due respect—and with much reluctance—that I point out that Gil was not a particularly good conductor. He was basically a time beater—that is, lacking any real baton or gestural technique—and not always with particularly good time.[49] His head was often buried in the score, so that we had little eye contact with him. (Of course, the way many of us were positioned we could see mostly only his back.) But we all loved and admired Gil, and worked extra hard for him, doing our best to compensate for his conducting shortcomings. That the playing on *Porgy* was rhythmically as together as it was must be credited to all of us hanging on for dear life to our rhythm section's beat, especially to Paul Chambers's impeccable playing, knowing very well that in jazz the drummer and the walking bass are the real conductors. But there again, Paul was at least fifty feet away from where I was sitting. When there were no drums, especially in slow or free-tempo passages, it was a real struggle to stay together.

Many of us wished—and pleaded with Cal Lampley—to have one more recording session added. We knew that with Gil's extraordinary but rather difficult music we were making history, and felt that with one more session we could make what was already pretty good even better, perhaps near-perfect. Miles also wanted another session because he wasn't entirely happy with everything *he* had played. (The considerable amount of overdubbing he did is a clear sign of that.) But Lampley told us that an extra session or overtime was not in the financial cards that Columbia had dealt the project. He must have felt that with judicious editing and tape splicing he could produce a result that would do full justice to the music and to us players.

In truth, Lampley did remarkably well in the postsession editing, considering the limited number of takes he had to work with. In many instances, he had no way to edit out minor note and rhythm mistakes, or clean up ragged ensemble attacks. In some cases all he could do was to suppress an errant note or a wrong entrance as much as possible, so as to make it inaudible to all but the most attentive ears. Several such "ghost" sounds, pushed way into the background, are still discernable if you listen real carefully.

As for Miles, the only soloist in Gil's recasting of Gershwin's music, much of his part was written, which left relatively little wiggling room for improvisation. It may sound easy on the recording, but a lot of blood and sweat went into his achieving that generally quite beautiful performance. And here again, the relatively new overdubbing and tape editing techniques were a tremendous boon. I mention blood intentionally, because at one point Miles developed a split lip, which started to bleed. Thank God, it was near the end of that particular three-hour session. Miles immediately called a break and came running to me—his personal lip fixer—crying for help: "What can we do? It hurts. How can we stop the bleeding?"

His upper lip looked pretty bad, as if Mohammed Ali had hit him right smack on the mouth. I told him there wasn't much we could do, except to abandon what we had started to record, which happened to be *There's a Boat Dat's Leavin' Soon for New York*, a section that had a string of high notes in his part, which I knew Miles wouldn't be able to handle, and which, if attempted, could perhaps further damage his upper lip. I suggested that we could finish *There's a Boat* in the next session (scheduled two weeks later), and for the rest of this session rehearse and record something else, preferably something without Miles, or at least something with an easy low or middle register solo part. I also told him that I would try to find some balming salve to cover the cut on his lip, and thus enable him to continue playing—not comfortably, but manageably. Luckily, I got some salve from Dick Hixson, our marvelous bass trombone player on the date. The session ended without further incident, and two weeks later Miles delivered *There's a Boat Dat's Leaving* in splendid form—without a split lip.

The solo trumpet part was exceptionally tiring, even when broken up into four separate sessions. I didn't realize until many years later, in the nineties, when I started to program the *Porgy* Suite in some of my jazz repertory concerts, that the trumpet part when played in one unbroken continuity is a real lip killer—or, as musicians say, "a chop buster." None of the trumpet soloists with whom I performed the work could get through it all without taking some parts down an octave, not holding notes as long as written, and often leaving certain brief passages out altogether—thereby providing a few moments of relief and allowing the blood to return to the lips.[50] It was in my performances of the *Porgy and Bess* Suite (in Europe) that it became really clear to me what a severe endurance test the solo trumpet part presents when played in its full thirty-five minute continuity, with its perpetual emphasis on long sustained lines, very few rests, and very little use of the trumpet's low register—which would bring welcome and much needed relief to the lips.

As physically tiring as the solo trumpet part is, there are also several lip-killing movements for the tutti brass that are even more tiring. In the case of "Prayer" and "I Loves You, Porgy," Gil, who always loved to give his brass and woodwinds slow moving, sustained music to play,[51] wrote two long passages at a very slow tempo, which will test the endurance limits of even the strongest player. "I Loves You, Porgy," for example, opens with a kind of recitative or aria for the solo trumpet, accompanied by soft undulating trills and warblings in the woodwinds and muted brass, which continue unbroken, with nary a place to even breathe—one can only sneak in a catch breath—for slightly over a minute.[52] After a brief respite of only thirty seconds for the trumpets and horns (although not the trombones), there follows a three-minute stretch (!) of heavy, sustained quarter notes in rising and falling patterns, again with hardly a place to breathe. Three minutes may sound like nothing to the lay reader, but three minutes on a brass instrument without being able to take the mouth-piece off the lips, that's quite another matter. I remember thinking as I got to the end of that passage, happy that we had all made it through without a clam, whether Gil really knew how hard that was and fully appreciated what we had just accomplished. On a piano or a synthe-sizer—Gil's instruments—you push a key and the note comes out, guaranteed. That's not the way it works on a horn or a trumpet or a trombone.

But what about Miles in that section? He did well enough. *But he was improvising his part,* which means that he could take little rests, choose to play in an easier, less tiring register, or even lay out altogether for a few seconds. That's something we in the brass section could not do, bound as we were to Gil's specific demands. We did get through the "I Loves You" move-ment well enough—mind you, after several stumbling rehearsal takes—but only by dividing it into three separate takes (all listed as take one in Phil Schaap's discographical notes). When we attempted a second take, it broke down after a while from sheer collective lip fatigue. On brass instruments you can't do this type of relentlessly lip-punishing three-minute endurance test more than once or twice.

Speaking of endurance, among the many heroes on the *Porgy* date I must particularly single out our three lead trumpets: Ernie Royal, Louis Mucci, and Bernie Glow. Ernie handled the really stratospheric parts with amazing aplomb and control, in ten hours of high-register hero-ics he hardly ever missed a note; while Louis and Bernie dealt so sentiently with those lead parts requiring a more lyrical, expressive-sounding approach.[53] And what can one say about Paul Chambers? Rock-solid, always gently swinging, and that beautiful sonorous sound of his.

Earlier in the summer of 1958 I attended the Newport Jazz Festival, where I met for the first time many of the European musicians that were playing in Marshall Brown's International Youth Band, which was one of the big hits that year in Newport. Some of these players, such as Albert Mangelsdorff, Ronnie Ross, and Dusko Goykovich became lifelong friends, and I also worked often with them over the years in Europe. In particular, Ronnie and Albert played in the jazz septet called for in my opera, *The Visitation,* Albert in the premier per-formances at the Hamburg State Opera in 1966 and Ronnie in the BBC's 1970 television production of the opera.

I began organizing jazz repertory concerts with some regularity as early as the 1960s, hav-ing occasionally pioneered this idea even a decade before by performing certain Ellington compositions (such as his prophetic 1930 masterpiece, *Mood Indigo,* and the even more innova-tive extended-form work from 1935, *Reminiscing in Tempo*) in authentic re-creations. It wasn't long after the 1958 *Porgy* recording date that I developed a strong desire to include Gil's *Porgy and Bess* masterpiece in some of the concerts I was increasingly being asked to organize and conduct (with, for example, Orchestra USA, or my Carnegie Hall "Twentieth Century Innova-tions" series, or in certain pop concerts). I called Gil one day and asked him whether he had kept the set of parts for *Porgy,* and if so, could I borrow or duplicate them. And if he didn't have the parts, did Miles have them—or perhaps Columbia Records? To my astonishment Gil told me that as far as he knew the parts and score were lost, and that technically they belonged to Miles, and that he evidently had lost them. Several searches of Miles's apartment had turned up nothing.[54] For those relatively few people who were interested in performing or studying Gil's *Porgy and Bess* music, every inquiry as to how and where to obtain a score or a set of parts was met for years with the same answer: no luck, pal, the parts are lost. This eventually prompted the thought among a number of Gil's admirers—including myself—of transcribing *Porgy* from the recording. Starting in the late 1980s several attempts at transcrib-ing the music were made, although, as far as I have been able to piece together, for only five or six of the thirteen movements.[55] I had for many years—actually decades—contended that, as valuable and salient as recordings are, if great music is not performed live or published in some readily accessible form, it will eventually vanish, cease to exist. Consider this: were it not for some fourteenth-century monk, laboriously writing out on parchment a motet by, say, Philippe de Vitry or a chanson by Machaut, which was then preserved in some monastery, that music might have been lost forever, and we, seven centuries later, would not even know of its existence. It is in that sense that hundreds (if not thousands) of jazz masterpieces—Gil Evans's *Porgy and Bess* certainly high among them—need to be preserved for posterity in some tangible form and in live acoustic reality.

By the mid-1990s I had become rather impatient with the fact that after nearly forty years this musical masterpiece was still not available for purposes of study and possible re-creative performance. So I decided to contact some of these transcribers with the idea of collaborating to produce in transcription a beautiful engraved set of score and parts, just as in classical music. I offered to assume all the financial burdens involved (or most of them, in case one or two of the collaborators were willing to share some of the costs) if the transcribing, engraving, printing, and publishing were done through my company, Margun Music (if no other party was interested). I tried to make clear that I didn't want to hog the whole enterprise for myself, that I wanted rather to share the effort with other Gil Evans and *Porgy and Bess* admirers. I did this out of respect and profound esteem for Gil's work, and in deference to our long friendship. I just wanted to be of service and to help break the deadlock that prevented this wonderful music from being available for people to study, to learn from, and to hear in live performance, in true acoustic reality. I was willing also to participate, in whatever way might be necessary, in the predictably complicated (and therefore costly) negotiations with the rightful owners of the musical materials, whether Anita Evans (Gil's widow), or Columbia Records, or the Davis and Gershwin Estates.[56]

Sadly, the response to my offer was at best tepid, at worst completely rejective—very disappointing. So I decided to go it alone, although not quite so ambitiously as originally intended. I transcribed the entire work—all thirteen movements. It took me most of one week, working long hours every day, capturing in explicit detail every audible sound on those LP grooves: not just the notes, but all nuances of dynamics, phrasings, and specific instrumentation. (For example, with his love for timbral variety and unusual tone color combinations, Gil used at various times three alto flutes or three bass clarinets, amazing sounds quite missing in some of the other transcriptions that I had seen or heard.)

P.S. It was a stunning surprise to hear in 2005 that the original *Porgy and Bess* parts *were* in fact found, in a basement room of one of Miles's apartments, and that Anita Evans is now making the music available on a rental basis.

In late 1958 John Lewis was approached by Harry Belafonte to compose the music for the Robert Wise film, *Odds against Tomorrow*. A few months later John called to tell me that he had finished the score for the film, that copyists were producing the parts, and that he wanted me to gather together the orchestra for recording the music in early summer.

Belafonte and Wise had given John not only lots of space for background underscoring, but also a generous-sized twenty-two-piece orchestra to work with: four trumpets, four horns, a trio of low brass, two percussion, two cellos, a harp, a flute, Bill Evans, Jim Hall, and John's three Modern Jazz Quartet colleagues, Milt, Percy, and Connie. In contracting the musicians I did my usual mixing and matching of classical and jazz players: in the trumpets, for example, Mel Broiles/John Ware and Joe Wilder/Bernie Glow. I also brought into the horn section the young Paul Ingraham (my most talented student at the time), and on tuba, because Bill Barber wasn't available, the great (now virtually legendary) Harvey Phillips. We recorded the music on three days in mid-July 1959.

I remember being especially impressed by John's music: nineteen "cues" (as we call them in the film business), totaling almost forty-five minutes of original music, tailor-made to the specific narrative demands of the film's story line. I thought it was some of the strongest and most powerfully expressive music John had yet composed. Listening to it again recently, both on the United Artists sound track recording and watching the film, after not hearing it for many, many years, I found no reason to rescind my original feelings. In fact, knowing a lot more now than I did then about what makes good or great film music, I am astonished to hear how perfectly John had trod the fine line between artfully supporting and mirroring the film's narrative on the one hand, and yet, on the other hand, not distracting from the visual filmic experience. The best appropriate, compatible film music has to be in some sense original, to some extent compelling and interesting enough to be a worthy parallel to the film and its underlying scenario—it can't be bland, clichéd, inept—but it also can't be so strong, so powerful, so original that it will overwhelm the film, push it into the background.

John fulfilled all these contradictory demands perfectly. What impressed me was that John, clearly inspired by the film noir scenario and the filmed sequences Robert Wise had given him to see, had written the most dynamic, harmonically and chromatically advanced music I had ever heard him compose. For the many ominous, qualmy episodes in the film,[57] John used the eleven-piece brass section to great dramatic effect: massive sustained chords loaded with dissonances of harsh, bristling minor seconds and major sevenths. Equally effective is the way John used Milt Jackson's vibraphone and Jim Hall's guitar in the more lyrical, melodic sections of the score, and, above all, Bill Evans's piano. One of his extensive improvised solos, in the so-called "Social Call" sequence, seems to parallel in its two-fisted, richly chordal style the massive brass structures just mentioned, exemplifying Bill's firm authoritative touch and assured command of highly chromatic yet euphonious harmonizations.

John also wrote some beautiful waltz music in the sequence called "Skating in Central Park," led by the two cellos and two horns. All in all, he covered a wide range of human expression, whether (as I was quoted by Nat Hentoff in the LP's liner notes) "sad or powerful or noble, haunting, bitter, or playful."[58] This was quite an achievement, at a time when it was still rather unusual to engage jazz composers to write music for films,[59] especially since John (unlike Ellington in his film scores, which remained well settled in his personal, long-established musical language) stretched out in *Odds against Tomorrow* beyond jazz into stylistic regions he had rarely touched upon before, certainly not in his works for the Modern Jazz Quartet.

When the film and the sound track recording came out, there was considerable controversy as to whether John's music was really jazz—as if that mattered. Such questions still arose in those days because many people on both sides of the fence did not want the two genres to fuse and cross-fertilize. People were reluctant to accept the fact that some composers were no longer content to be boxed in and limited to one idiom or the other. John broke through these archaic prejudices and barriers in *Odds* by writing in a variety of musical conceptions for a variety of dramatic situations. There is nothing logical to the notion that the music accompanying a bank robbery must be jazz or jazz-related. Instead of dwelling on such primitive partisan considerations, the discussions should have recognized that the time had come for film companies to optionally use jazz or classical modes of expression or both, regardless of what the script or story line described. The answer to the question of whether a film score had to be in a jazz or a classical idiom was now going to be: neither or both.

That divisive question, is it really jazz, was now even sillier, and in many ways unanswerable, since the lines between the two idioms had become blurred, beyond any clear, unequivocal demarcation. Which composer and which performers with which stylistic backgrounds will determine whether something is jazz or classically oriented? Some of the brass passages that John wrote sounded jazz inflected simply because they were led by Bernie Glow and Joe

Wilder. No one, least of all John, ever said to us: play it like jazz, or play it more classically. Had John Ware and Mel Broiles led the brass section in that passage, it would have sounded subtly different, more classical. I think the written horn solo I played in the "Main Theme" sequence is neither jazz nor classical, but arguably both, located somewhere between the two idioms. On the other hand, whatever John wrote for guitar or vibraphone was bound to sound more like jazz by virtue of the particular inflections with which Jim Hall and Milt Jackson played John's music. On the other hand, the cello theme of the waltz music (in "Skating in Central Park") inevitably emerged with a classical feeling because it was played by Harvey Shapiro and Joe Tekula, who could not have turned it into jazz even if they had wanted to. If the same phrase would have been played by Eric Friedman and Fred Katz, two well-known jazz cellists, the result would have been markedly different.

What was quite unusual in recording the *Odds against Tomorrow* music was that, whereas a film score is typically recorded with the conductor synchronizing the music to the images projected on a screen, we performed the music ad hoc in a recording studio (not a sound stage), and absent any screen images. We never saw the film. The independently recorded sequences, captured initially on magnetic tape, were then later transferred to film.[60]

Among the many fortuitous circumstances that were beginning to influence the direction of my life and career around this time, none were more auspicious than the opportunities John Lewis gave me to record my own music. He did this by inviting me over a period of five years to record half a dozen of my works that I'm quite certain would otherwise not have been recorded (or at least not that early on). What was truly special and unusual was that in all these instances John was allowing me to piggyback, so to speak, on his personal exclusive contract with Atlantic Records. To fully grasp how remarkable this act of generosity was, even given our close friendship, one has to understand that this arrangement had serious financial implications for John, in that the substantial costs ascribable to recording my music were debited to John's account with Atlantic. These expenditures constituted monies that were no longer available to him for recording his own works, and were, in fact, charged against him, that is, subtracted from his royalty income. It also needs to be mentioned that none of this would have happened without Nesuhi Ertegun's blessings. I can well imagine that there were others high up at Atlantic Records who considered taking my music on a pretty foolish enterprise, a risky business at best. For my part I readily understood that I was not going to share in any royalties or income that might accrue from my pieces. That was a small—and really insufficient—acknowledgment of my gratitude to John.

The first work of mine to be recorded by Atlantic under this arrangement was my *Conversations* for string quartet and jazz quartet—in this case of course the Modern Jazz Quartet, for which it was written. That was in September 1959. *Conversations* is all about how two separate worlds of music, initially opposed to each other, gradually find various ways of coming together, of conversing with each other and learning from each other—like Third Stream itself. Over the course of the piece, these conversations take on a variety of forms and expressions, the most interesting of which (and at the time the most novel) is when the eight players break out in a series of collective extemporizations, brief minicadenzas in effect, each one showing off his distinctive stylistic wares. The strings engage in their own brand of improvising a classical counterpart to jazz improvisation, which was first developed in Europe in the midfifties under the name "aleatoric," that is, chance procedures. *Conversations* was the first of my so-called Third Stream pieces to be recorded and was released in 1960, along with John Lewis's *Sketch*, for the same double-quartet instrumentation.[61]

In short order there followed two LPs released in 1961. The first of these included three of the pieces I had premiered at the Circle in the Square concert: *Abstraction* (with Ornette

Coleman as soloist), and the two *Variants* (the one on Monk's *Criss Cross*, the other on John Lewis's *Django*), all with a stellar cast of Ornette, Eric Dolphy, Eddie Costa, Bill Evans, Jim Hall, Scott LaFaro, George Duvivier, Sticks Evans, and the Beaux Arts String Quartet (led by Gerald Tarack). The album, which also featured Jim Hall's *Piece for Guitar and Strings*, carried John's imprimatur and the proud title "John Lewis Presents Contemporary Music: Jazz Abstractions."

For the other recording—in June of 1961—the Modern Jazz Quartet and I traveled to Germany, where Wolfgang Röhrig, head of jazz programming at the Stuttgart Radio, had invited us to record (for Atlantic) my three-movement eighteen-minute *Concertino for Jazz Quartet and Orchestra* (issued as SD 1359). We also recorded André Hodeir's *Around the Blues* and the young German composer Werner Heider's, *Divertimento*, both pieces featuring the Modern Jazz Quartet as soloists.

I also had an influential hand in several of Johnny Mathis's early dates for Columbia Records, when George Avakian had just signed him up and had asked John Lewis to make some of the arrangements. On the roster of fifteen musicians I hired nine of my classical colleagues: two flutes, an oboe and a bassoon, a bass clarinet, two horns (myself and one of my horn students, George Nadaf), a tuba, and a harp. The jazz side was represented by Tony Scott and Hal McKusick (clarinets), Herb Ellis (guitar), John Lewis (piano), Ray Brown (bass), and Connie Kay (drums).

John's interest in all kinds of contemporary classical music, as well as in my burgeoning side career as a conductor, prompted him to invite me to record Schönberg's Op. 9 *Chamber Symphony*—another courageous and idealistic undertaking. Although recorded under Atlantic's aegis, the record was issued on Finnadar, Atlantic's classical affiliate (Finnadar was headed by the Turkish-born composer Arif Mardin.) There was even a plan to have me record Schönberg's Suite Op. 29 for piano, three clarinets, and string trio, but for some reason (which I can no longer recall) that recording ended up with Period Records, a company headed by Bela Bartók's son, Peter. A decision to record anything by Schönberg was something close to financial suicide, given that his music was considered strictly *persona non grata*. But John, in his quiet self-confident way, never paid much mind to critical reactions, favorable or unfavorable. One always sensed with John that the firmness of his decisions was grounded in an uncanny blend of intelligence, sensitivity, and independence—*his* three little feelings.

One can see that 1960 was a pretty busy year for me. But there was much more. Having left the Met and its strenuous performance commitments behind in November 1959, I was now more available to engage in New York's voluminous recording scene. It was also in late 1959 and early 1960 that I had the very important premieres of two new orchestral works: *Spectra*, commissioned by the New York Philharmonic and Dimitri Mitropoulos, and my *Seven Studies on Themes of Paul Klee*, commissioned by Antal Dorati and the Minneapolis Symphony. *Spectra* premiered in January 1960 in Carnegie Hall. *Seven Studies* premiered in November 1959 in Minneapolis, and was subsequently taken on a Middle East tour, and finally recorded in Minneapolis in May 1960.[62] In 1960 I was also in my third year of hosting not one but two separate weekly one-hour shows on WBAI in New York: one on modern classical music, called "Contemporary Music in Evolution," the other on jazz, called "The Scope of Jazz," cohosted with Nat Hentoff, with guest hosts Martin Williams and John Hammond.

There were also lots of recording sessions that I participated in as a horn player or a conductor that were not associated with Atlantic Records or John Lewis.[63] The most important and satisfying of these were Lalo Schifrin's *Gillespiana*, a five-movement Suite featuring Dizzy Gillespie as soloist; Dizzy's *Carnegie Hall Concert* (1961), not really a recording date per se, but an LP release on Verve of the actual Carnegie Hall concert of March 4, 1961; J. J. Johnson's *Perceptions* (1961), a kind of trumpet concerto, again for Dizzy; four great dates with Judy Holliday and Gerry Mulligan, also in 1961, for which Gerry pulled together an array of superb arrangements by some of his most talented arranger colleagues: Bob Brookmeyer, Ralph Burns, Al Cohn, Bill Finnegan, and, of course, a few of his own; also three dates with Julius Watkins (for Philips), with arrangements by Billy Byers, where the terrific five-man horn section of Barrows, Buffington, Bob Northern (one of my students), myself, and Julius outnumbered the rest of the orchestra.

One late afternoon in January 1958 when I happened to have some business with Nesuhi Ertegun at Atlantic Records, I noticed a young man sweeping floors in the offices, someone I had not seen before in my many previous visits. As I walked by him he looked at me, almost as if he recognized me. When I asked Nesuhi, who's the kid out there sweeping the floor, he said: "Oh, he's a student at Bard College; he plays the piano. A few weeks ago he asked if we had any work for him. He said he loved jazz, and would just like to be around musicians and hang around at our offices." When I asked Nesuhi whether he had heard him play, he said: "Yeah; but, boy, it's a *very* strange kind of jazz—if it even *is* jazz."

That was my first encounter with Ran Blake, one of the most remarkable and original pianist improvisers in the last half century; his playing was located stylistically halfway between modern jazz and modern classical music—in other words, what I was calling Third Stream. There was something—a purely instinctual reaction—that intrigued me about Ran that first time, heightened by what Nesuhi had said about his playing. There had to be something special about someone who was willing to spend his entire school vacation cleaning and sweeping floors just so he could be around jazz musicians and soak up the atmosphere of a major record company.

It didn't take me long to ask him to play something for me. I was dying to know what Nesuhi had meant by some kind of strange jazz. What I heard in that first get-together with Ran was the most interesting free-form extemporizing that I had ever heard, especially since it was stylistically, harmonically, rhythmically expressed in a fusion of two distinct musical languages, jazz and classical. What fascinated me particularly was that Ran's playing was loosely based on a composition of his own. Even more interesting, his compositions were never written down, written out, as composers had traditionally done for centuries. I learned that Ran, although he had briefly tried writing his music in full notation, preferred creating his compositions out of his inner ear and putting them together at the piano, in constantly reinvented improvisations. Once the piece was more or less set in his mind, with certain moments or ideas fixed but others less precisely specified, he would then extemporize on that material. It would be recognizable as a particular composition, and yet always evolving each time, reshaped, reinvented, and reimagined.

I had never heard anything quite like it. Ran's harmonic language fascinated me, as it ranged from free atonality through varying degrees of polytonality to standard jazz changes of the postwar bop period. I was amazed at how easily and naturally Ran traveled back and forth between these divergent musical worlds. An eight-part widespread atonal chord, such as Schönberg or Stravinsky had originated fifty years earlier[64]—or as Thelonious Monk was now occasionally experimenting with—might be right next to a rich, more familiar flat-five thirteenth chord, miraculously causing no stylistic discrepancy. Indeed, these divergent harmonies seemed to enjoy each other's company. I couldn't figure out how Ran managed these harmonic juxtapositions with such artlessness and logic. I still find it kind of miraculous. (If Elliott Carter or Schönberg had ever committed such contrarian juxtapositions, it would have been considered a serious stylistic breach, a lapse in judgment.)[65]

What I found so astonishing about Ran's playing—and still do to this day—is the deep stylistic interpenetration of the several musical worlds that Ran's improvisations occupy. I had never heard such a close, seamless fusion, while also allowing both vocabularies to speak from time to time in their own tongues, side by side. It reminded me of a bilingual person effortlessly shuttling back and forth between two languages.

There was one serious weakness at the time in Ran's improvisations, a certain formlessness, a lack of control of overall form. But I was so taken with his basic talent and the originality of what he was striving for that I decided to help him with this problem by coaching him, in effect taking him on as a student. Ran worked with me over a period of two or three years, although somewhat sporadically, due to his commitments at Bard College. In general, I made him listen to a lot of well-constructed music, from Beethoven to Stravinsky and Schönberg and Bartók, with an emphasis on how these great masters dealt with form, with logic and proportionality, with continuity and the development of ideas. I wanted him to hear and realize how with the greatest composers nothing in a piece is ever too long or too short, or, to put it another way, under or overdeveloped. Everything is always perfectly balanced in its proportions.

At Bard Ran had gotten to know a young woman named Jeanne Lee, a psychology majoring who was also a fine singer, with a rich, warm mezzo voice. The two soon became friends and formed a duo while still at school, and when I heard them a few years later I was greatly impressed. They functioned incredibly well together, like two sides of a coin. The overall outline of a piece would be more or less set, but much of the inner details and how to get from one passage to another was left to impromptu extemporization, they fed off of each other's ideas and gestures in constant close communication. I mentioned their work to George Avakian, who by that time had moved over to RCA Victor as an A&R producer. Before I knew it, George had arranged for a recording of the fledgling duo, and then asked me to supervise the sessions, which took place in November and December 1961. Originally intended to be simply a Blake-Lee duo album, I suggested that one or two of their pieces would benefit from adding an extra voice, namely, a walking bass, to give those songs a little more of a jazz feeling. I hired George Duvivier, with whom I had already worked quite happily on several of John Lewis's Atlantic albums. They recorded eleven titles ranging all the way from *Blue Monk* through *Lover Man* and *Laura* to Jeanne Lee's most moving, deeply felt *a cappella* version of *Sometimes I Feel Like a Motherless Child*.[66]

That was the beginning of a long, professional relationship and friendship with Ran Blake. The rest is history, which included my bringing Ran to the New England Conservatory when I moved to Boston and became the conservatory's president in 1967, eventually creating a Third Stream department there for him to head, as well as inviting him many times to Tanglewood, in my capacity as artistic director of the summer school. At age seventy-six his legacy resides in over forty remarkable (primarily) solo piano recordings, which occupy a world all their own. Ran remains a unique figure in the recent history of American music—under whatever label one might place him.

It was on January 11, 1955, that the great event had occurred: the birth of our firstborn, Edwin. It was not an easy birth, and this after three earlier miscarriages, in 1950, 1953, and 1954. I don't remember what the specific causes of these miscarriages were. Perhaps I was never told the circumstances in full; one didn't talk a great deal about such matters in those days—at least we didn't. And Margie was never one to complain much about any personal or physical problems she might have, even, in later years, during her twenty-one-year battle with three different cancers. I learned that a big part of her attitude about such matters was a strong desire to avoid worrying me or distracting me from my work because of *her* problems.

I can only surmise that the miscarriages were not of the most serious or life threatening kind, since her doctor encouraged her—us—to continue trying for a successful pregnancy. At our fourth attempt things seemed to be going very well, until at the very end, when in the last few hours of labor it developed that the fetus was about to be strangled around the neck by its own umbilical cord. The baby was turning blue. Edwin was delivered prematurely by cesarean section at 5:01 a.m., after it was discovered that he was in danger of being asphyxiated. At birth his condition, according to the hospital's medical records, was poor and required resuscitation with oxygen. He weighed five pounds and was nineteen inches long, and was immediately transferred to the hospital's premature unit.

Amazingly, I didn't know anything about the situation until almost twenty-four hours later. Because I knew I was going to have a very full day on the eleventh (including a trip to Philadelphia with the Met to play an opera there), not wanting Margie to go to the hospital alone in a cab, I had checked her in a little early on the evening of January 10, slept a few hours, got up around eight in the morning for a three-hour rehearsal, squeezed in two horn lessons in a studio on Forty-Eighth Street, and from there headed directly for Penn Station and the train to Philadelphia for a performance of Verdi's *Ballo in maschera*.

I found out what had happened when I called the hospital around one a.m. upon my return to New York (i.e., in the early hours of January 12) to see how Margie was doing, neither of us having had any expectation that there might be a problem in Edwin's birth. I was a bit stunned by the news that greeted me, although I was also told that mother and child were fine. Margie, the nurse said, was asleep, and it would be best not to wake her. So I didn't see or talk to her until later that morning, and finally saw Edwin Gunther[67] in the afternoon, although only through a huge glass window, half hidden in his crib on the other side of the ward for premature babies.

Margie and Edwin were kept in the hospital for another eleven days, by the last three of which Edwin had gained enough weight to be transferred back to the main nursery to be with his mother. It was then that I was finally able to actually hold that precious little bundle in my arms—an indescribable feeling.

An unexpected collateral offshoot of Margie's pregnancy and her hospitalization was her decision to stop smoking. It had nothing to do with her pregnancy, but rather a casual, almost accidental remark I made on one of my visits with her in the hospital. She had asked me to pass her a cigarette from the drawer in her bedside table. As I fished for the cigarette pack amongst the various personal paraphernalia, I must have expressed—very subtly—a certain reluctance or hesitancy. I handed her the cigarette and match folder, but instead of lighting up she looked at me kind of questioningly.

Margie was a casual smoker at best. It was something she had picked up inadvertently at Shimer College, as something young girls were supposed to do to be hip, to be with it, as the saying went. And though I, an inveterate nonsmoker, wasn't particularly fond of her smoking, as casual and intermittent as it was, I had never said anything to her about the matter. The subject had simply never come up.

Now she was looking at me quizzically, her fine intuition reading my mind: "Why—you don't want me to smoke?"

I said somewhat hesitatingly, not wanting to hurt her feelings, "Well—no." Pause. "You really need to?"

"Not really," she said after a while. "Would you like me to stop smoking?" She looked at me lovingly.

"Well—yes," I said gently. I didn't want to actually demand it. "I would love it."

"Ok. I'll stop it," she said firmly.

And that was the end of her smoking. Just like that. It was another one of her many expressions of unselfishness, of generosity, of her spirit of humility.

A little later she asked me why exactly I didn't like her smoking. I said, "Well, for one thing, when I kiss you after you've had a smoke, I don't like the smell of your breath. It's awful. I just hate the smell of smoke." (This was long, long, long before anyone ever brought up the fact that smoking was actually harmful and dangerous.)

Nearly four years later, our second son, George Alexander, was born. Although we definitely wanted another child, hoping this time for a girl, the complications with Edwin's birth had been very intimidating. Dr. Greeley also was hesitant, advising us to at least wait a while. But Margie was getting older, heading toward her midthirties. The quandary was eventually resolved by deciding *a priori*—if and when—on delivery by cesarean section. But then fate intervened anyway. A C-section became absolutely necessary when, after a few hours of labor, Margie's contractions began to slow down until they stopped altogether. After fourteen hours of no progress in her labor, a cesarean section was done. Baby George was born at 7:36 a.m. on December 29, 1958, delayed just enough to allow Margie to celebrate Christmas at home and not in a hospital. She *did* miss New Year's that year.

By the midfifties, having by then met most of the leading jazz writers, critics, editors, and publishers, I was increasingly invited to contribute articles on jazz and that new thing called Third Stream, and to participate in symposia and panel discussions, such as those held at the Music Inn in Lenox, Massachusetts, and at various universities around the country. If memory serves me rightly, I believe that my first important, published article was for the *Saturday Review of Literature* in 1957, "The Future of Form in Jazz."[68] It was commissioned by Irving Kolodin, a contributing editor to *Saturday Review*, and one of New York's ablest music critics. The article dealt with some of the newest advances in jazz in respect to form and language, recent trends in the growing rapprochement between contemporary classical music and modern jazz, and the expanding role of composition in jazz and its relationship to improvisation. In that context, I extolled certain composer-performers (and their works), who seemed to me to be at the leading edge of these developments: Charles Mingus (citing especially his *Pithecanthropus Erectus* and *Love Chant*), Jimmy Giuffre (*Side Pipers* and *Down Home*), John Lewis, George Russell—and in Europe, André Hodeir, for his remarkable cross-fertilizations of jazz and swing with certain advanced formal-technical concepts spawned by the European avant-garde. The article attracted much favorable attention as well as its share of controversy and antipathy.

A year later a major breakthrough in jazz scholarship and criticism occurred with the founding of *The Jazz Review*, which many regarded as the best and most important jazz magazine of its time. Its creators were Hsio Wen-Shih (publisher), Nat Hentoff, and Martin Williams (coeditors). The journal maintained the highest standards of reportage and critical writing for some three years, when, alas, it was forced to abandon publication for lack of financial and circulation support. One can only conclude that, like so many good and valuable things in life, *The Jazz Review* was far ahead of its time. While it lasted, it not only raised the level of intellectual discourse in matters relating to jazz, but it also brought forth a whole cadre of younger writers with fresh perspectives and a keen appreciation of some of the more important new developments in jazz. These included Larry Gushee, Max Harrison, Don Heckman, Harvey Pekar, and musicians such as Bill Russo, Lou Levy, Dick Katz, Bob Brookmeyer, Cecil Taylor, and Benny Golson. Asking musicians to write critical essays, often about their colleagues and friends, represented a new trend that was initiated primarily by *The Jazz Review*.

I was very honored to be invited to serve as associate editor, and am proud of some of the articles I was able to contribute over the years, such as "Sonny Rollins and the Challenge of Thematic Improvisation" (1958), or a review of the early work of Cecil Taylor (1959), or a piece about Thelonious Monk, not to mention three extensive discussions of Duke Ellington's early work, which some years later became the impetus for the first installment of my history of jazz, *Early Jazz: Its Roots and Musical Development*.

In early 1957 I began to think about shifting some of my writing and teaching activities in the direction of radio. Margie and I were avid radio listeners, and regularly tuned in to the many good jazz programs one could hear in New York, notably the 1280 Club, nicknamed Robbin's Nest (hosted by a very hip disc jockey named Fred Robbins), and Symphony Sid's All Night Jazz. I heard a lot of good music that way over the years, more than in clubs. I was getting so busy with varied activities and professional commitments that going out to jazz clubs became more difficult, especially after the birth of our son Edwin.

I kept up with what was new in jazz by listening to the many jazz programs on the radio. One day it occurred to me that while it was interesting and useful to be given the titles and personnel of the recordings, it would be even better to have explanatory and critical commentary along with the playing of the music. This was fairly common on classical radio. Classical disc jockeys such as Edward Tatnall Canby and David Randolph had been producing music programs with background commentary on WNYC for many years. They were remarkably knowledgeable, in effect great teachers. I know that so much of what I learned in my teen years about music, about the classical repertory, I owe to their weekly programs. In the midfifties two more music programs came along, one in jazz, the other in classical music, which inspired me to do something similar. Leonard Altman hosted the program that dealt exclusively with medieval, Renaissance, and early baroque music. The jazz program, produced at San Francisco's Pacifica station, KPFA, presented mostly very early jazz in extremely rare recordings, along with superb informative commentary by Phil Elwood.[69]

These were my models for what I wanted to do. So I decided—as if I wasn't already busy enough—to create two weekly shows, one on twentieth-century classical music, called "Contemporary Music in Evolution," the other on jazz, called "The Scope of Jazz." I approached Nat Hentoff to cohost the show with me, and he was the one who suggested WBAI as the logical home for the program, after I had been turned down by Herman Newman at WNYC, whose schedule was already completely filled. We invited Martin Williams and John Hammond as a regular guest hosts, and over the three and a half years that the show ran we invited many other writers and musician colleagues. The programming was entirely thematic, each show devoted to a particular theme or subject. I am very proud that over time we covered the entire history of jazz, from its very beginnings—even its prehistory—to the latest developments as they occurred. It was an immense territory to cover, quite ambitious not only in concept but also in its realization—and, I believe, unprecedented at the time. The programs generally consisted of forty minutes of music, twenty minutes of commentary. All this was, of course, limited to some extent by the current availability—or nonavailability—of recordings. In that respect we were fairly lucky, for it was in those peak years of the LP era that the major record companies—especially the older ones such as Columbia, Victor, Decca, with their enormous jazz holdings—embarked on the most ambitious and comprehensive reissue programs in the history of the record industry, in the process filling in countless gaps of historically important recordings.

WBAI was always on the brink of insolvency, surviving primarily through subsidies from the Pacifica Foundation in California and a few private sources.[70] Since WBAI's jazz record library was rather small, Nat and I had for the most part to supply our own recordings, which we were, of course, happy to do. In that respect, having Nat as my host partner was a tremendous boon, since he, as one of the major jazz critics and record reviewers, was sent all new releases every month—free.[71]

But we were so determinedly committed to presenting the most complete picture of whatever subject or period we were covering in a given program that when we could not find an obscure but nonetheless important recording in our own collections, we would borrow records from John Hammond, who had a huge collection, having begun buying records way back in

1928, and also from Marshall Stearns's extensive library.[72] And if those resources failed us, we went so far as to buy rare 78s from Jacob Schneider, who at the time was reputed to have the largest collection of 78 records in the United States, perhaps in the world. It filled an entire four-story brownstone house—wall to wall, floor to ceiling—in the upper seventies on New York's West Side. Many of the recordings I purchased from Schneider came in handy in the mid-1960s when I started to work on my *Early Jazz* history, where one of my fundamental principles was to systematically listen to every—and I mean *every*—recording ever made by any musician or orchestra under consideration. Even if a particular record was eliminated from the discussion, at the very least it had been heard, and not ignored and rejected out of hand.

When Nat and I started "The Scope of Jazz" program, WBAI was in its infancy, so small and poor that it was housed in two tiny, windowless, claustrophobic rooms on the forty-first floor at the top, the very crown, of the Hotel Pierre. Fortunately, after several months in those cramped quarters—with only two turntables—WBAI was able to move to a brownstone on East Thirty-Seventh Street. The station remained so poor for many years that quite often the ten-inch tape reels on which we produced our programs were reused by the engineering staff or by other program producers. Once I realized this, I began to hold on to the tapes of our programs, particularly the reels that Nat or I had bought at our own expense. Occasionally we assembled our programs at our homes, for convenience sake—I on my big professional Tape-sonic tape recorder and state-of-the-art RCA Victor 74BX ribbon microphone, considered the best in the business, and normally used only by the big record companies and high-fidelity radio stations.

In this connection, it is worth mentioning that Nat and I did all this work gratis. We never received a penny for three and a half years of producing some of the best-recorded programs on jazz—there were no pennies to give. We didn't mind not being paid for our efforts—we never even thought about the possibility of remuneration, we just wanted to do something important and very much needed. I confess that I wondered whether we shouldn't at least be reimbursed for the personal expenditures we incurred, such as the tape reels. For my part I probably spent around $1,500, a lot of money half a century ago, in taxi fares alone, back and forth from my home on Ninetieth Street down to Thirty-Seventh Street. To go by subway was unfortunately so circuitous—three changes of trains, plus walking some blocks at both ends—as to be quite impractical and too time consuming.

I started the classical music show "Contemporary Music in Evolution" sometime in 1959. The basic concept and format of the series was to take the listener chronologically through the entire history and development of twentieth-century music up to the present (which turned out to be late 1962), in weekly one-hour programs. The show ran for 151 programs over a period of three years. Inspired by Leonard Altman's series on medieval and early Renaissance music, the idea was to play recordings of the most important, pathbreaking works and offer commentary on each piece, which might include the history of its creation or an analysis of its form or style. Generally I offered the listener information as to the importance of the work in the development of twentieth-century music, the most significant breakthrough elements of a given piece, and the logic and inevitability of the step-by-step progression by which modern music developed—to show that it was not some random, capricious, wrong turn in the evolutionary road. In effect I was offering live program notes linked directly to hearing the music.

The point of presenting the music in a strict chronological order was to demonstrate that what was often considered to be a revolutionary or radical step forward was really only the result of an *evolutionary* process. In this respect, it was particularly important to me to show how the transition from late nineteenth-century chromatic tonality, evolving over the next twenty to thirty years into atonality, was in fact transitional, logical, and as inevitable as the sun rising every morning.

Besides wanting to cover in my discussions and recordings as much of the great and important twentieth-century literature as possible (as the availability of recordings permitted), inclusion in the series was determined not so much by stylistic considerations or the degree of modernity—let alone its popularity—but by the quality and the individual distinctiveness, originality, and technical mastery of the work.[73] In addition, I was most keen on playing only recordings that were interpretationally truly representative. I had long ago learned that even note-perfect recorded performances could result in unrepresentative and misleading performances, given the interpretive whims and liberties assumed by so many conductors. An even more serious problem for me was that in the late 1950s and early 1960s, many works that I would love to have included had not yet been recorded, or had been recorded only once, and then perhaps in an inferior performance.[74] In some cases I was able to substitute a recording from my private collection of performances, as recorded by Zeke Frank in Carnegie Hall of the New York Philharmonic and other visiting orchestras. Many was the time when I bought at my own expense a recording that neither I nor WBAI owned, so that I could present a really important work to my audience. As in the parallel running jazz series, this often meant that I had to purchase recordings from a collector of rare or no-longer-in-print recordings, often at considerable expense.

But it was all worthwhile, if only as a tremendous learning experience—for me as well as the audience. The program was immensely successful, downright popular, judging by the favorable audience response to it, not only at the time but also through the years. I have been enthusiastically thanked for presenting that program series hundreds of times, either in letters or in meeting someone for the first time: "I am so grateful to you, because you opened my mind and ears to the beauty and validity of contemporary music," or "you really helped me to understand this modern music, and that it isn't just a bunch of meaningless noises." What could be more gratifying!

Early in 1950 a bassoonist friend of mine, Ralph Lorr, who had recently founded *Woodwind Magazine*, asked me to become his main contributing editor. Over the next half-dozen years I wrote many articles for him, everything from reviews of woodwind quintet concerts to research on woodwind publications and literature to specialty articles on the individual instruments of the woodwind family.[75] Lorr's magazine was the first of its kind, a heroic undertaking that I believe he privately subsidized. It had—no surprise—a small circulation, so that all of us who contributed to the magazine did so pro bono. Like many of the noncommercial endeavors that I have been involved with over the past sixty years, it eventually folded from lack of financial support.

Probably the biggest brouhaha the magazine experienced in its six-year history was a review that I wrote in 1953 of a performance in New York of Schönberg's Op. 26 Quintet by the Philadelphia Orchestra Woodwind Quintet. I really roasted their performance. While it was technically neat and clean, as was to be expected from five such outstanding players, it had practically no understanding of Schönberg's harmonic language, its twelve-tone workings, and its Brahms/Wagner-derived expressive style. In their recording that Columbia put out a year or so later, the innocuousness of their performance is plainly audible. It also includes a few serious editing gaffs, where, for example, one two-bar phrase is heard twice, while the two measures that were recorded are missing.

In retrospect, I can't imagine what possessed me to ever write a review of the Philadelphians' Schönberg performance. They were after all my universally esteemed colleagues, especially Mason Jones, one of my most admired fellow horn players. Besides, it was clearly a conflict of interest, and I'm surprised that Ralph either asked me or allowed me—I can't remember which—to do such a stupid thing. At the very least, I should have used a more moderate tone, or, having already performed and recorded the work two years earlier, recused myself. I clearly must have been on some momentary, ambition-driven ego trip; on the other hand, given my intense love for Schönberg's music, I must have felt that I was obliged to point out that their performance was a serious misinterpretation of this remarkable work. I'm sure I was more intent on defending and protecting Schönberg's music than I was on criticizing my colleagues.

The aftermath of the situation is rather interesting. In the ensuing months there was an endless, back-and-forth editorial skirmishing in Ralph's magazine. Then, many years later, I learned that Sol Schoenbach, the bassoonist in the quintet (and legendary principal bassoon of the Philadelphia Orchestra for some thirty years), had been carrying my review of the concert with him in his inner jacket pocket *for decades*, showing it to his bassoon and woodwind colleagues all over the United States and Europe. It seems that Sol could never forgive my review, and wanted everyone to know how hurt he was and how dastardly my critique had been. It is therefore doubly ironic that Sol and I, late in our lives, not only became the closest of friends, but also partners and coworkers in a whole series of associations and musical enterprises (Tanglewood, the Pro Musicis Foundation, my Summer Festival in Sandpoint, Idaho), bonding in a kind of two-man mutual admiration society. Neither of us, in all the years we worked together, ever brought up the subject of my negative review, an amazing thing, considering the original intensity of his reaction and his feelings—a great credit to Sol, a man I came to love as my own father.

One of the more unusual projects that I undertook in the late 1950s was to produce a recording of a remarkable jazz musician whose playing I admired a lot, but who was at the time a pretty much forgotten figure living in relative obscurity in Dallas, Texas. I'm speaking of Buster Smith, known only to die-hard jazz aficionados, serious record collectors, and a few enlightened jazz writers who knew that Buster had been a major influence on the young Charlie Parker.

I had become aware of Buster sometime in the late forties on one of my regular haunts of a cluster of second-hand record shops on Sixth Avenue in midtown Manhattan, where I had picked up quite by chance two recordings, one (*I Want a Little Girl*) from 1940 by Eddie Durham (the great Kansas City arranger, trombonist, and guitarist), the other a 1939 Pete Johnson recording of *Cherry Red*. I knew Johnson and Durham as important figures in the history of Kansas City and Southwestern jazz, and was quite pleased with what I heard on my new purchases. But what really made my ears perk up was the sound and phrasing of the alto saxophone player. I looked up who that might be in my discography, and saw the name Henry Smith, nickname Buster. What fascinated me about Buster's playing was that his tone reminded me a lot of Charlie Parker's sound and his expressive warmth, and I also heard a similarity with certain turns of phrase that I clearly associated with Bird's early work when he was playing with the Jay McShann band and on the mid-1940s Guild and Dial recordings.

With further reading and research on Buster, and after acquiring more of his recordings (for example, with the legendary Blue Devils of 1929), I learned that he had also been very busy as an arranger for many Kansas City bands, including Basie's. Buster had become Parker's mentor in the mid-1930s, at a time when Parker's playing with various bands in Kansas City clubs was roundly rejected and ridiculed. The information I gathered on Buster also indicated that he had not recorded since 1942, and that he was more or less retired from the music business. That, fortunately, turned out not to be true.

The second phase of my involvement with Buster began quite accidentally when, in 1957 near the end of the Met's annual spring tour, on the train leaving Dallas I heard several of my colleagues rave about a "terrific colored band" they had heard a couple of nights before. The occasion had been a lavish Texas-style ball the Dallas Grand Opera Association had given the Met at the Baker Hotel. They thought the band leader's name was something like Buster

Smith. It was in that incidental way that I learned that Buster was not retired, in fact still active in the Dallas area. I decided that somehow—I didn't know how or when—I would like to produce a recording of Buster or, at the very least, talk someone else into recording him—perhaps Nesuhi Ertegun and Atlantic Records.

I resolved to find and meet Buster on my next trip to Dallas, in May 1958. When I got there I learned rather quickly that finding him was easier said than done. The search for Buster turned into an incredible three-day saga, occupying almost every waking minute of my entire Dallas stay. Luckily I was free for two of the four opera performance we gave that year, which afforded me quite a bit of time to devote to this search. As soon as I arrived in town, on a Friday afternoon, I looked in the phone book, assuming that, as an active bandleader in Dallas, Buster would be listed there. The first surprise was that there were *three* Buster Smiths listed, but none of them were musicians. I decided to call the local musicians' union, and was surprised to find out that there was a separate colored local. But when I tried to call there I learned that although it had a phone, it was not listed in the phone book and that it could be reached only through its white counterpart. But even via that route, despite repeated calls, there was never any response at the Negro local. (In this whole process I learned that very few blacks in the South had telephones.)

That evening I called a couple of well-known Dallas nightclubs that I knew from previous visits occasionally employed black musicians. But neither place could offer me any help. I was getting quite discouraged.

The annual Dallas Grand Opera Association ball was scheduled that night, after the opera performance. I went there hoping that Buster's band would be one of the two orchestras normally hired for the occasion. (It was customary to hire one white orchestra, a very polite society-type orchestra, and one colored dance band, playing something much closer to real jazz, so that some of the rich opera longhairs could let their hair down a bit.) It turned out that Buster had not been engaged, but one musician in the black orchestra that was there thought he knew where Buster was working that night: at a place called Pappy's Showland, a popular Dallas dance hall.

By this time it was nearly one a.m. Undaunted, I decided to head for Pappy's. However, when I told the cab driver where I was going, he said that I was too late. "Pappy's is already closed." Closed at twelve forty-five on a Friday night? That didn't sound right. Then I found out that according to Texas law you had to bring your own liquor to a club, where you would then be served your set-up. But set-ups could not be served after midnight, which meant that people generally started leaving around that time, and consequently all dancing and musical activity also stopped. So there was no point in going to Pappy's. Frustrated again! It was a strange sort of consolation to find out the next day that Buster hadn't even been at Pappy's. He had been on a gig in Fort Worth.

On my way back to my room at the Hilton, an interesting coincidence occurred. I bought a paper, and for some reason—I seldom did this—I read the gossip column, where I came across a little item that "one of the best-informed jazz enthusiasts hereabouts is Stumpy Jones, at the shoeshine parlor Columbia Hatters on Evary Street." I figured that this fellow would know where Buster might be reached.

The next morning—Saturday—I headed for Columbia Hatters, but, of course, Stumpy Jones was not in and wasn't expected. Nobody knew where he lived, and, naturally, he didn't have a phone. Another complete impasse. Repeated visits to the shoeshine parlor eventually turned up Stumpy Jones, but he said he hadn't seen Buster in months, and couldn't really say where he might be working. Stumpy gave me one of the greatest shoe shines of my life, accompanied by a lengthy lecture on how Buster had really written *One O'Clock Jump*, not Basie, and that Basie had simply appropriated the copyright.[76]

After my matinee performance of *Rosenkavalier*, I went to a restaurant near the Fair Park Auditorium where there was a whole crew of black waiters. Since they looked pretty hip to me, I thought of enlisting their help. A few of them promised to ask around for Buster, as did some white jazz musicians who had come in for a bite to eat. But none of those people ever came up with any ideas of how to find Buster.

By Saturday evening, I was becoming desparate. A day and a half was already gone, and we were scheduled to leave Dallas the next day. I happened to be free that evening, and decided to go to some nightclubs where I knew local musicians might be working. Finally—at about the third or fourth joint—I met a bass player named Jim Bell, who knew Buster was working that night at a dance hall over in one of the black sections of town. Bell assured me it was okay for me to go there. But the cabdriver refused to take me. It was only after a lot of grumbling and rather dubious glances at me—plus a promise to grease his palm a bit—that he finally decided to drive me to the place.

At the front door I asked if I could come in and listen to the music. I was told that ordinarily it would be all right, but this happened to be a private dance given by the Shriners, and it would not be possible to come inside. I could hardly believe my ears. Standing there in the tiny entrance vestibule, I argued with the man, telling him that I was from New York, visiting here with the Metropolitan Opera, and that I had come all this way to hear Buster Smith. He was not impressed in the slightest.

It was now beginning to rain. Couldn't he make an exception? "No," was the answer. "Nothin' doin'!" He was very officious, determined to do the right thing.

Luckily, Jim Bell had given me a message for one of Buster's baritone players, Grady Jones, who was also secretary of the local. I told the doorman that I had a message to give to Jones; couldn't I at least hang around until the band had a break? I could actually hear the music through the inner door, and was determined not to give up. He agreed that I could wait there, rather than out in the rain. But then, after about ten minutes, he softened and said that he would speak to someone about this situation.

Lo and behold, at the next break, Buster himself came to the door and promptly fixed things with the officious doorman, who turned out to be the owner and manager of the place—and probably also the bouncer. Buster took me in, and said I should sit right by the bandstand. What I heard that night confirmed for me that this man definitely had to be recorded; Buster's alto fascinated me as it soared effortlessly above the rather raucous, rocking, Southwestern-style band. One could hear that pure distinctive sound that Charlie Parker's ears must have absorbed in Kansas City over twenty years ago.

Buster was overjoyed, although not without a touch of disbelief, to hear that I—that *any-one*—wanted to record him. I told him I would try to arrange something for next spring.

The third and final phase of what I was calling "Operation Buster" occurred in June 1959. I had talked to Nesuhi about my idea of recording Buster, and he readily agreed to let me record him in Dallas at the first opportunity if we could find a good recording studio there. I told Nesuhi I didn't think I could squeeze in a recording session during my stay in Dallas with the Met, given my own performing commitments that weekend—three opera performances in two days—but that I was going to be in Phoenix, Arizona, in June for a lecture at the annual convention of the American Symphony Orchestra League. I could record Buster then, stopping off in Dallas for a few days on the way back to New York.

In due course, Nesuhi located a good studio in Dallas, highly recommended by Tom Dowd, Atlantic's chief engineer. But Nesuhi's repeated efforts to reach Buster to tell him about our plans to record him in early June were unsuccessful. So were mine when I got to Dallas in May. The best that I could find out was that Buster was out of town—nobody knew exactly where—and that right now he was unreachable. Great news!

That should have worried us. But we assumed, being used to organizing record dates in New York on fairly short notice, that I would be able to set things up with Buster when I got back to Phoenix in June, only a few weeks away.

On my first day in Phoenix, I immediately contacted the studio in Dallas and, of course, also endeavored to reach Buster. This is where trouble began anew. The studio sounded fine; the engineer turned out to be a horn player who loved jazz—a real comrade in arms—but, incredibly, the studio was not available. That week, of all times, the organ in the studio had to be repaired. The repair crew was hired and set to go. Somewhat reluctantly, my horn player friend was kind enough to recommend his biggest rival, but in Fort Worth, the only other place that had the requisite recording equipment to meet Atlantic's very high technical standards. Another phone call, and I had arranged for the recording session in a studio in Fort Worth.

On the other hand, my attempts to reach Buster to tell him that a recording date was now set were foiled by one mishap after another. To contact someone who has no phone is not an easy matter to begin with. Thank God Buster had given me his brother Josea's phone number, but when I called there and talked with several relatives, none of them had any idea where Buster or Josea were, or when Josea might be back. I left word with them that I wanted to record Buster next Monday, five days hence, and that Buster needed to round up his band, to think about repertory, and that, above all, he should call me collect any time of day or night. That was Wednesday evening.

By Saturday morning I had not heard a word from Buster. I called the Josea number again. This time I was told that Buster had gotten my message, but was away on a Saturday night gig in the northeasternmost corner of Texas, in a town I had never heard of. In desperation I decided to call him directly at the dance. I waited until about eleven o'clock, hoping to catch Buster during a break. When the receiver was lifted at the other end of the line, my ears were assailed by an unbelievable din. It seemed as if everybody in the place was also on the line, but through the noise I could hear fragmented snatches of music, including an unmistakable alto sound, telling me that I was within earshot of Buster. Yelling into the phone at pitch voice, I tried to make the man at the other end understand that I needed urgently to talk to Buster Smith. But he had never heard of anyone by that name. I told him he was the guy blowing the alto saxophone not more than fifty feet away, and that he was the leader of the band.

"Well," he said, "I'll look for him." After what seemed an eternity, the voice returned: "There's no Robert Smith here!" I shouted so loud that you could have heard me in northeastern Texas: "BUSTER Smith." "Oh, ok. I'll look for *him* then." I tried to tell him to go to the bandstand, but his voice trailed off into the ear-deafening cacophony. When he returned after another seeming eternity, he told me—believe it or not—that there was "no Robert Smith here." Before he could hang up, I shouted at him to talk to the leader of the band, "tell him his brother is on the phone," I lied. He seemed to finally understand. But after more waiting I was told—now by a female voice—that I should leave my number and Buster would call me back at midnight, at the close of the dance.

Needless to say, I received no call that night. It wasn't until two the next afternoon that Buster finally telephoned. After apologies as well as a litany of unkind words about "last night's place" and the people that ran it, we talked about personnel and repertory.

The repertory question worried me. I was pretty sure that Buster at that point in his career was no longer playing jazz in the sense of an art music, a music to be listened to, in the sense that his protégé Charlie Parker had played jazz. Not that Buster couldn't play that way anymore; it was rather that the relatively limited number of players he could hire in the Dallas area for his band would in all likelihood be playing something more akin to rock and roll or rhythm and blues, rather than jazz in the more creative, improvisational sense. What was required in the dance halls and clubs of Dallas was a strictly functional, solidly rocking rhythmic music to which people could dance, not sophisticated, improvised, melodic, harmonic flights of fancy. Buster told me, somewhat ruefully, that he was losing lots of work lately to smaller three- and four-piece rock and roll groups.[77] With all of that, I had good reason to worry that Buster's musicians wouldn't really be familiar with what he and I would consider real or true jazz repertory. Furthermore, I found out that two of Buster's pieces that I had hoped to record were committed to another record company. (But that was only a pipe dream, for, as far as I know, Buster never recorded again after our Atlantic date.)

Another potential problem with personnel might well be that the sidemen I had heard with Buster a year ago, while adequate for an ordinary dance, were hardly the kind of imaginative soloists one would look for on a record date. But Buster assured me he would get the absolute best players in the whole Dallas–Fort Worth area, and he promised me a real surprise in the baritone player. I told Buster I wanted to make the date Monday night, the next day. Could he round up his men that quickly? He thought he could, and would call me at the Hilton in Fort Worth.

My hopes were rising. Early Monday morning I visited the Fort Worth studio, discussed microphone set-ups, questions of stereo separation, and told them, as a hedge against more unforeseen problems and surprises, that the date would be either tonight or tomorrow. I'd let them know during the day. By midafternoon it was clear that tonight was not going to happen. Buster called me to say he couldn't get his band together on such short notice. "Almost none of the men have phones, and it takes a lot of time driving around to each of them."

We reset the date for eight o'clock Tuesday night. That evening I was at the studio early, eager and excited. All the chairs, music stands, and microphones were neatly set up. I looked forward confidently to a fine session, which would show the world that a man like Buster Smith should not have been allowed to go unrecorded for seventeen years.

I really didn't expect anybody to be on time, having for years heard horror stories of jazz recording dates starting late, musicians showing up hours after the appointed time. But by eight thirty I was getting restless. I went outside in the vain hope that by waiting near the main road their arrival would be accelerated. My engineer read several Dallas and Fort Worth newspapers from cover to cover, while I stood outside watching two motorcycle cops use a dark side street as a hiding place to catch speeding motorists. They made a rich haul that night, about one every ten minutes. And I was there to see it all!

I called Josea's home at nine thirty, and was told that he and Buster were on their way, but would be a little late. "Couldn't locate some of the boys." But by ten o'clock I was really beginning to wonder. I kept thinking back to the story John Hammond had told me of how one of his greatest recording sessions, with the Fletcher Henderson band in 1933, was scheduled to begin at nine a.m., but didn't get started until eleven thirty. But somehow or other I retained what in retrospect was an extraordinary degree of patience and optimism.

At ten thirty still no sign of the band. At eleven the motorcycle cops left off chasing speeding Texans, and checked in at the nearby station house. By eleven forty-five I was measuring time not in minutes but in quarter-hour segments. The engineer and the studio's owner said they had never heard of anything like this. We waited until twelve thirty, but then I gave up, thoroughly beaten. I decided if I didn't hear from Buster in the morning, I would forget the whole thing and fly home to New York that afternoon.

Buster did call—at eight forty-five in the morning, no less. He explained that he "couldn't get the boys together." They lived in entirely different parts of greater Dallas, and since they had no phones, he had to drive to each man's house to get them all. Working music gigs generally only on weekends, and therefore never expecting to hear from Buster *during* the week, two of his best men had gone off fishing! Poor Buster had traveled up and down Dallas and its far-flung suburbs all afternoon and evening, finally pinning down his last man around eleven. I felt my wrath melting into sympathy. He said his boys were all alerted now, and would definitely be on hand at nine tonight.

The miracle finally happened; that night his men *were* on hand, although they came trickling in a few at a time, the rhythm section at nine thirty, the two brass fifteen minutes later. Leroy Cooper, the baritone, didn't arrive until after ten because he had a day job in Dallas until nine and couldn't get to Fort Worth any earlier.

So as not to waste all that precious time, I decided to record Buster in several ballads with just rhythm. But to my surprise—and disappointment—he was very reluctant to do that, and eventually I could only coax the lovely *September Song* out of him. He said he preferred to play on blues tunes.

The whole band was finally assembled around ten thirty, with the arrival of Cooper. His fine playing immediately lifted my spirits, and probably those of the other musicians. The more I heard him play, the more eager I was to get as much of him on tape as I possibly could. I loved his solid musicianship, gutsy sound, great energy, and good-humored attitude. As for Buster, he really came alive on the up-tempo riff tunes. And I was happy to hear that warm, glowing tone of his, and especially those twisting, serpentine lines that I had first heard years ago with Charlie Parker. All in all things went reasonably well, with most tunes requiring only one or two takes. It was after one when we started our last tune, which accounts for the *Late Late* title. The session finished around two a.m. Once underway, it had taken four hours.

For a recording date whose outcome hung in the balance so many, many times and in so many odd ways, it was miraculous that it came off as well as it did. Through it I came to know personally a fine gentleman and a remarkable musician, and I am proud of my tenacity and patience, but above all grateful that I was given a chance by Nesuhi Ertegun to produce a recording that paid tribute not only to a most admirable musician but also to an older style and an earlier period of our unique American musical heritage.

It was in the midfifties that one began to hear about all kinds of interesting activities relating to jazz stirring in a little town in western Massachusetts named Lenox. This was quite surprising to many people, since Lenox had been known for many years as the premier citadel of classical culture, the summer home of the Boston Symphony and its famous summer school at Tanglewood. Jazz had never been allowed to enter or even come near those sacred precincts; but then suddenly, not more than a mile from the Tanglewood grounds at a place called the Music Inn, there were jazz concerts, and symposia, and panel discussions on jazz. This interest in jazz, and the idea of creating a summer home for jazz on a smaller scale than Tanglewood, was being fostered by Stephanie and Phillip Barber, owners of the Music Inn.

It all began very humbly in 1950 with the Folk and Jazz Roundtables, headed and moderated by Marshall Stearns and Willis James,[78] and involving both traditionalist musicians such as Wilbur de Paris, Willie "the Lion" Smith, and Sammy Price, and representatives of the newer postwar modern jazz developments. I was invited in 1955 to a couple of the roundtables and, as I recall, the panels were *very* lively, at times even contentious discussions as to where jazz was going and why, and should it take that direction.

In 1955 the Barbers had met John Lewis at a Modern Jazz Quartet concert in New York, and had been charmed by both John and the Quartet's sophisticated, engaging music. They soon invited him and the Quartet to give annual concerts in their Berkshire Music Barn, located on the Music Inn grounds. (They also brought the Brubeck Quartet and the Giuffre Three to Lenox.) These concerts and a host of other jazz-related activities gradually led to making recordings at the Music Inn[79] and, in 1957, to the creation of the Lenox School of Jazz.

Soon after my roundtable participation John Lewis mentioned the possibility of creating a jazz school in Lenox, indicating that the Barbers were interested in offering their Music Inn as the home for such an enterprise, maybe for a few weeks in late summer or early fall. John and I were constantly working together in concerts and recording projects, and the subject of a school for training in jazz—a still radical idea in those days—came up more and more frequently. If I had the idea of creating a summer school, asked John, what form might it take? I told him the answer lay just around the corner from the Music Inn, namely, at Tanglewood. The basic idea was to bring a faculty of master musician-teachers together with a group of talented young people selected by audition—which was simply the venerable, century-old master-apprentice concept. It was in essence Koussevitzky's vision in creating Tanglewood, as well as Serkins's and Casals's for Marlboro. But I suggested as an additional refinement of that basic concept the idea of master and apprentice actually performing together, in rehearsals and concerts, as differentiated from the more standard approach of teachers merely coaching students in preparation for a concert.

I had seen this method work so well at Kenyon in 1945, and more recently at Darmstadt, Germany, in the summer courses there. It inevitably brings student and teachers much closer; they work side by side on the same problems, and effectively the same level. Teachers would not just talk and offer advice, they would teach by example, in continuous face-to-face contact. In practice a group of students would be assigned to one or two teacher-leaders for the three weeks of the session, and then perform in public. I also felt that it was most important to have required courses for all the students in composition and arranging and the history of jazz.

Late in 1956 John and I started on the actual plans for the Lenox School of Jazz in collaboration with Stephanie and Phillip Barber. Given John's close friendships and long-standing connections with virtually the entire jazz elite, he had no problem in assembling a stellar faculty. There had never been anything like it, certainly not in jazz. Imagine that you are a young player in 1957, and you hear that there is going to be a jazz school with a faculty of a dozen of the world's most famous jazz musicians who will not just be teaching a one- or two-hour class once a week, but would be living at the school—you could be hanging out with your idol—and you'd be seeing and hearing them work the whole three weeks. Best of all, you'd be working and playing directly with at least one of them, rehearsing and preparing a concert. It was like a dream come true.

In 1957 the faculty included Dizzy Gillespie, Oscar Peterson, Ray Brown, Herb Ellis, Jim Hall, Jimmy Giuffre, Bill Russo (composition), Marshall Stearns (jazz history),[80] and, of course, John Lewis and his three colleagues from the Modern Jazz Quartet. In 1958 Max Roach, Booker Little, George Coleman, Kenny Dorham, and George Russell (composition) were added. In 1959 Bill Evans joined the faculty, and in 1960 composer Ed Summerlin and violist John Garvey came aboard, while J. J. Johnson and Freddie Hubbard visited the school for about a week.

If that wasn't enticing enough, every evening was filled with special events: concerts by guest artists such as Mahalia Jackson, Lennie Tristano, the Oscar Peterson Trio, Bobby Hackett, and Ray Charles, and guest lectures by Fela Sowande ("Music of Africa"), Nesuhi Ertegun ("Problems in Jazz Recording"), Wen Shih ("The Problems of Acoustics"), Eric Larrabee ("Jazz and Its Place in American Culture"), Willis James ("Primitive Beginnings of Jazz"), John Wilson and Nat Hentoff ("Functions of the Critic in Jazz").

John Lewis wanted me to be involved in the school right from the start, but I wasn't able to join the faculty until the 1957 and 1958 sessions because I was on European trips in connection with performances of my classical works. In 1959 John asked me to present a jazz history course based more on the music's stylistic development than on purely historical events, which Stearns continued to teach in parallel with my course. I also did some teaching in composition and analysis, and led, coached, and performed in one of the ensembles. That year the group I was in charge of included Perry Robinson (clarinet), John Eckert (trumpet), and David Baker (bass trombone), all of whom later developed substantial careers in jazz. (Some of the other outstanding students in 1959 who also became well-known in the jazz field included Steve Kuhn and Larry Ridley.) I programmed David Baker's *Lone Ranger and the Great Horace Silver*, a piece titled *Aristocracy* by Sandy Schmidt (one of the student pianists), and Monk's *Straight, No Chaser*. (As a horn player, I especially loved that piece because of its close thematic relationship to the famous opening horn motive in Strauss's *Till Eulenspiegel*—almost exactly the same pitches. Also, on the spur of the moment David wrote a piece for me called *Song for Gunther*, and we added that to the program at the last minute.

In 1960 John invited my friend John Garvey from the Walden String Quartet to the school to head up a string program to teach jazz playing to young string players. Garvey played on my ensemble concert, along with violinist Alan Grishman (then a student, but later the first-rate concertmaster of the Pittsburgh Ballet Orchestra for many years), a concert that also featured J. J. Johnson, Jim Hall, and John Lewis as guest soloists. In that program we premiered my *Variants* on Lewis's *Django* and Hall's *Piece for Guitar and Strings*, as well as John's brand-new *Milano*. In addition, my protégé and great friend, Ran Blake, a student for two summers at the Lenox School, performed—that is, improvised—one of his early compositions, *Vanguard*.

The students were, as in any school, of varying levels of talent and technical accomplishment, and varying degrees of experience. Quite a few were already very advanced and subsequently developed important and successful careers. Among these I would list Al Kiger, a wonderfully gifted lyric trumpet player, David Young (tenor sax), Joe Hunt (drums), both of them most impressive talents, and David Lahm, a pianist-composer. The following year they all, along with David Baker, formed George Russell's highly successful Sextet of the early 1960s. Other later famous students were Don Ellis (trumpet), J. R. Monterose and Ted Casher (tenor sax), Jamie Aebersold (alto sax), Vera Auer (a forty-year-old vibraphonist from Austria who had attained a successful career in Europe before coming to Lenox), Gary McFarland (a most talented vibraphonist and composer-arranger), Margo Guryan (a gifted pianist and songwriter), and Attilla Zoller (guitar), who went on to a most distinguished career, working with Oscar Pettiford, Herbie Mann, and the 1968 great duo of Lee Konitz and Albert Mangelsdorff.

But unquestionably the most famous of all the students in the four-year existence of the Lenox School of Jazz was Ornette Coleman. Ornette could hardly be called a student by 1959, but John and Nesuhi were most eager to bring him east from California, and one way to do that was to enroll him in the school on a scholarship. John had been alerted to Ornette's outstanding talents by bassists Red Mitchell and Percy Heath, both of whom had participated in a recording with Ornette and Don Cherry in Los Angeles in early 1959 for Contemporary Records. Percy came back to New York raving about Ornette, not necessarily fully understanding everything he was doing, but definitely sensing that this was a very special talent, very likely a successor to Charlie Parker. I remember him saying many times, with a blend of awe and puzzlement in his voice: "You gotta' hear this guy!"

Nesuhi had committed to signing up Ornette and his Quartet (with Don Cherry, Charlie Haden, and Billy Higgins) for Atlantic Records,[81] and it was easy enough for him to arrange a scholarship for Ornette. It was no surprise to John and me that Ornette was not particularly welcomed at the school. As a twenty-eight-year-old professional, he was considered a bit of an intruder. Initially there were feelings of envy among the students generated by all the attention and praise he was receiving in the jazz press; and, of course, very few of them could relate at all to what they regarded as Ornette's out-of-tune, erratic, fragmented, makes-no-sense kind of playing. In the microcosm of the school one heard the same complaints and denunciations as in the macrocosm of the outside world. There was much snickering behind his back, which Ornette ignored with remarkable philosophical aplomb.

Ornette gave an astonishing performance in the session-ending final concert, playing three of his own compositions and a happy little song by Margo Guryan called *Inn Tune* (of all titles!). The group was led and coached by John Lewis and Max Roach. By that time some of the other students began to realize that maybe—just maybe—there was something about this guy that commanded respect.

I began to sense the tide turning after one very long late-afternoon jam session that took place on the Music Barn stage. It is one of three episodes relating to Ornette that have stayed vividly in my memory. It was a Saturday, a mostly free day with no rehearsals and classes. Inevitably some of the kids with nothing better to do started a jam session. It was a typically lackadaisical affair, with a few special moments scattered through what was otherwise a collection of cliché-ridden licks in the standardized bop vocabulary or the show-off type of grandstanding.

I was sitting with Martin Williams, listening, chatting about this or that, when we saw Ornette come into the Barn and quietly sit down a few rows in front of us, off to the side. He seemed to be listening rather diffidently, maybe wondering what these kids might be able to produce. I was sure that Ornette wasn't going to sit in, and said so to Martin. But I was wrong. For, after about twenty minutes of this casual listening, he grabbed his plastic white alto and headed for the stage, waiting patiently for the two players already lined up to play to finish.

What suddenly burst out of Ornette's horn was one of those moments in music that you never forget. It was one of his patented blazing, swirling runs, the notes flying by so fast that you didn't hear them as individual pitches, more like some gigantic cluster or a dense cloud of sounds. It was Ornette signaling—not arrogantly or angrily,[82] just dramatically—hey kids, listen up. It nearly shook up the rhythm section, which came almost to a standstill—as in: Whoa! What was that?! After a few more blistering, attention-getting salvos, and after the rhythm section had recovered, Ornette settled down in a calmer mood, spinning many lovely lighthearted arabesques, as only he could contrive. Most of the kids who had already played, and who were probably thinking about leaving the scene, now decided to stay and see how the afternoon would end with Ornette up there.

Ornette kept on playing, as if in a world by himself. What now transpired was an amazing demonstration of seemingly inexhaustible improvisational inventiveness, but beyond that, to our astonishment, also something totally unexpected. As Ornette kept building one blues chorus after another, he was also—I swear it—giving a lesson on the history of the saxophone. Was he doing this for Martin and me, the two history buffs at the school, and clearly two of his (rather few) fans who would surely understand and appreciate what he was doing? Maybe so. We both remembered seeing Ornette's eyes and face light up in my history classes—where he was, incidentally, the most attentive, the most fascinated of all students, listening very hard—when I would talk about and present recordings of the early days of jazz, the 1920s and 1930s, great recordings of Armstrong and Jelly Roll Morton's Red Hot Peppers, and, of course, of many of Ornette's saxophone predecessors: Coleman Hawkins, Ben Webster, Chu Berry, Dick Wilson, Lester Young, Frankie Trumbauer. Here, unbelievably, in this jam session, Ornette was now tracing that long beautiful history, subtly modifying his sound as needed, darkening, brightening, choosing lines and figures that harkened back to those earlier times without losing his own identity. It was an amazing tour de force.

Ornette was obviously having a ball. He played on and on, and in the process wore out three rhythm sections. I lost track, but he must have played at least forty or fifty medium-tempo blues choruses. It all came to a kind of whimpering stop when the last of the three drummers threw up his hands and quit. That was the very young John Bergamo, a very talented percussionist, although more experienced in contemporary classical techniques than in jazz. (I brought John to Tanglewood a few years later when I took over the contemporary music program there.) John told me later, at dinner: "Man, I just suddenly couldn't keep going. I couldn't keep up with Ornette. I didn't want to drag him down, and further embarrass myself." (John played beautifully for Ornette a week later as the drummer in Kenny Dorham's group.)

Did Ornette's live history of saxophone really happen, or was it wishful thinking on our part? I don't think so. I'm so glad that Martin was sitting with me, hearing the same thing I was hearing, or I might think that I dreamed the whole thing. Were Martin alive, I'm sure he would confirm my account.

The two other episodes that relate to Ornette involve, respectively, Jimmy Giuffre and my then three-and-a-half-year-old son, Edwin, better known now, fifty years later, as Eddie, and as a pretty damn good bass player—speaking obviously as a proud father.

At Wheatleigh, the palatial mansion to which the school had moved in 1958, there was at one end of the building a glass-enclosed greenhouse conservatory called the potting shed where some of the larger indoor plants and flowers were grown and cultivated, and which the students often used for small group jam sessions. Ornette and Don Cherry had for some time been very gently needling Jimmy Giuffre about always playing music that was—so they felt—too formalistic, too disciplined, too circumscribed. Ornette is the kindest, gentlest soul and would never openly criticize or denigrate someone else's playing, certainly not face to face. It was mostly Don who kept nagging the quiet, imperturbable Jimmy whenever he got a chance: "Loosen up, man. Don't you want to be free?," and similar teasing entreatments. Ornette would chime in every once in a while.

Eventually this constant baiting got to Jimmy. Whether he was fed up with their harassments, or whether he wanted to face their challenge and find out what they were talking about, or whether he undertook it as a lark, I don't really know. All I know is that one late afternoon in the last week of the 1959 session, Giuffre grabbed his tenor and headed for the potting shed, where Ornette and several students who were interested in exploring a harmonically and melodically freer type of jazz were holding forth in an impromptu jam session, in the process getting—as I was told later—into some pretty wild, completely unintelligible stuff.

I happened by pure chance to pass by some time after the session had started, when suddenly Jimmy Giuffre showed up with his tenor and joined in. After a few minutes it became clear that Jimmy had decided to rise to Don Cherry's bait and, instead of playing in his usual cool, folksy, modal style, was now trying to emulate Ornette's atonal, fragmented, wailing, gliding, swooping style. As Jimmy's playing became more frantic—and, frankly, incoherent—he gradually slid to the floor from his initially standing position, rolling around on the stone floor in a kind of hysterical paroxysm, as if he'd been bitten by a tarantula. His feet were up in the air, gyrating in frenzied, twitching movements, while he was blowing like mad into his tenor, holding it high up in the air above his head, producing the most God-awful cacophony of cracked notes and screaming, screeching, honking sounds. For a while Jimmy kept blasting away at his lowest A flat, much to the delight of the gathering crowd of onlookers. (All saxophone players know what a gross honking sound that A flat, the lowest note on the tenor, can make.) In between Jimmy would intersperse crazed, zig-zag runs at a ridiculous dizzying speed, trying to replicate Ornette's lightning-stroke takeoffs. Jimmy's face was now as red as a beet; he was beginning to froth at the mouth, and I was getting worried that he might somehow crack up mentally. I couldn't tell whether he was still enjoying himself, or whether he was under the spell of some satanic ritual, becoming completely unhinged.

Suddenly Jimmy stopped, I think from sheer exhaustion, not just physical but emotional. He didn't seem to be able or want to talk. All he kept saying, out of breath, was, "Whew! Whew! Whew! . . . Whew! . . . What was that?"

At dinner later, the whole dining room talked about nothing else but that incredible jam session. (Would that it had been taped or recorded!)

Much later that evening, sitting by the fireplace in Wheatleigh's main lounge, I asked Jimmy the least intrusive question I could come up with: "Hey, how'r'ya doing? How'd'ya feel?" He said: "Oh, fine"; then, with a little more emphasis: "OK." When I probed a little further—about the jam session this afternoon—he said, almost matter-of-factly: "Oh, it was a kind of cathartic experience." And after a pause: "Yeah, it was liberating, a kind of release of something." But he said it with the tone of voice that made you feel, that's all I'm gonna say, end of subject.

One day, when I got to dinner right after a late-afternoon rehearsal, Margie, sitting at our table with a big grin on her face, greeted me with: "You'll *never* guess what happened with Edwin this afternoon." As the tale unfolded, Margie, who generally spent most of her time at Lenox taking care of our two young kids, Edwin and eight-month-old George, had left Edwin asleep in our room to run a quick errand in Stockbridge (ten minutes away), telling a few folks also staying in the dorm, including Ornette, to keep an eye on Ed. Wouldn't you know, while she was gone, Edwin woke up, calling for his mom because he had to go to the bathroom. Guess who came to the rescue? Ornette. The story of how the great and famous Ornette Coleman had patiently cleaned little Edwin up was told again and again in our family once the kids were older, with considerable pride—and lots of laughter. But what we didn't expect—nor do I know how the story was leaked out—that when Ed, in his midteens, started to become known as a fine bass player, the whole jazz world seemed to know that he had had his ass wiped by none other than the great and famous Ornette Coleman!

It was shocking news to suddenly hear and read in the jazz press in early 1961 that the school's plans for the coming summer had to be canceled for lack of funds to finance another three-week session, particularly at the high level and quality that had been attained. The broader support that the Barbers and the school's trustees had hoped for never materialized. The small inner circle of patrons, mostly jazz enthusiasts and musicians, and very little corporate support—except for Atlantic Records, Broadcast Music Inc., and a small grant from the Schaefer Brewing Co.—was simply not large enough to maintain the operation. Although I had very little to do with the school's fiscal affairs, I am sure that the brunt of its financial support was borne by the Barbers, and that they probably took some losses that they could no longer bear.

Those were the hard economic realities. But I feel that, as with so many good things and excellent ideas, especially in the realm of the arts and humanities, the Lenox School of Jazz—its concept, its mission—were too far ahead of its time. The world wasn't ready yet for the idea of teaching and training in jazz.

Perhaps the most influential—and controversial—concert John Lewis and I presented (in collaboration with Charles Schwartz's "Jazz Profiles" series) was the one given on May 16, 1960, in downtown Manhattan at a venue called Circle in the Square, offering an all-Schuller program of seven of my new Third Stream pieces. The reason it was both influential and controversial was that John Wilson, in his *New York Times* review of the concert, used the term "Third Stream" in the headline.[83]

I had coined that term a few years earlier in a lecture at Brandeis University to identify a growing rapprochement between jazz and classical music. When Wilson used it in the headline of the review, it became a slogan, a sellable label, a postulate—and a battle cry. The same headline in *DownBeat* magazine or any other newspaper in the United States would not have had the tremendous effect it had in the *New York Times*. Why? Because the *Times* is by far the most widely read and influential newspaper in the world; and if anyone anywhere read a second newspaper other than their home town or regional paper, it was the *Times*. It can instantly generate a nationwide buzz on almost any topic. Soon lots of folks were talking about Third Stream, pro or con, as "the new thing," even when they knew little about it or didn't even know what it was.

Wilson was just being a good journalist, reporting accurately what had occurred at the concert, but his use of the term "Third Stream" became a catchword. We live, after all, in a society that thrives on labeling, on promotion and advertisement.[84] What may also have made the event and the announcement of this new thing called Third Stream an issue, and a controversial one, was that all the music performed that night was by a reputedly classical composer (with major performances by the New York Philharmonic under his belt) and horn player at that temple of classical grandeur, the Metropolitan Opera. To many people in jazz, the concert, with its seven pieces that were clearly trying to break down the musical and aesthetic barriers keeping the two mainstream genres apart, represented an invasion from an alien world. It had to be stopped, and one way to stop this musical miscegenation was to pronounce it a miscarriage, to claim that jazz and classical, like oil and water, could never be mixed. It was an alchemical impossibility. Within less than a quarter century both assumptions were proven quite wrong.

Considering that those seven pieces of mine[85] represented brand-new musical challenges even for the best musicians on either side of the musical divide, the performances were remarkably well played. I was so privileged—and lucky—to have sixteen such outstanding musicians playing my music. I say privileged because they all were not only very great players but also close friends and among my most admired colleagues; and I say lucky because, by circumstance of my birth in New York and living and working there, I was active in the very highest echelons of the music field.

On the jazz side, imagine working with the likes of Eric Dolphy, Ornette Coleman, Bill Evans, Eddie Costa (a phenomenally talented vibist and pianist, who unfortunately died far too young at age thirty-two), Scott LaFaro (the same fate as Costa's), Buell Neidlinger, Sticks Evans (drums); and on the classical side, a string quartet consisting of violinists Charlie Treger and Joseph Schor, both major freelancers—you'd rarely see a recording date string section without them sitting in the front chairs—John Garvey, viola (member and founder of the great Walden String Quartet, in residence at the University of Illinois), himself so passionately involved with jazz that he promptly created a special department at his school specializing in the training of string players in jazz, Joe Tekula, cello (another omnipresent freelancer), Bob DiDomenica, great flutist, and finally, my harpist friend, Janet Putnam.

Quite a few of this stellar cast, mostly then in their twenties and early thirties, became legends in their own time. But one name in that list is now virtually unremembered, and, strangely, was not even well known and widely appreciated back then: Sticks Evans. I must pay homage to him here because he was an amazingly versatile set drummer and percussionist. No one at the time could read my very demanding, stylistically hybrid drum parts as easily as he could. I was astounded. I was even more astounded when I learned that Sticks was one of the busiest rhythm and blues drummers in the country, and among other things the house drummer for Atlantic Records for many years, when Atlantic was recording Ray Charles, Aretha Franklin, Ruth Brown, Stevie Wonder. Given that background, one can understand how gratified I was that Sticks could read my drum parts perfectly at sight, including dynamics and other stylistic nuances that I always incorporate in my compositions.

But then I discovered that Sticks was also a part-time professional photographer, both film and still. He showed me some of his work, which was of a very high artistic quality. I also found out that Sticks wrote poetry and occasionally, when time permitted, short stories. He was an intellect, extremely well read, and socially and politically very engaged. With all of that there was not—as there well might have been—an arrogant bone in his body. He was much too intelligent and wise to be conceited. (Sticks is also not even mentioned in *The New Grove Dictionary of Jazz*.)

Audience reaction to the concert, judging by the applause, was very favorable, and was particularly enthusiastic for Ornette Coleman. But reviews of the concert were mixed, some of them severely negative. Typical of the naysayers was their inability to accept even the basic premise of Third Stream, which of course relieved them of having to deal in any specific way with the actual music. Moreover, their rejection of the Third Stream concept was in turn based on their verdict that none of the pieces were jazz. Well, yes—they *weren't* jazz. And they weren't intended to be jazz. Nor were they classical. They were conceived to be an amalgam of both. The arguments in the jazz press were almost always the same, rooted in various negative attitudes about classical music and a sense that jazz must be protected from any infection from the classical virus. And then there was the main offense committed by anything classical: that it didn't swing—it *couldn't* swing. Ellington had been crucified with the same accusations many times, so I realized I was in good company.

By effectually disallowing any appreciation or assessment of the classical side of the Third Stream equation, this rigid ideological stance predestined such reviews to concentrate only on the jazz elements. Jazz players were praised; improvisation was the only thing valued. On the other hand, composition—the composed elements—were disparaged or simply ignored, considered not even worthy of discussion. And the absolute worst thing that Third Stream could do was to use strings. The anticlassical, anti–Third Stream camp found everything they perceived to be jazz exciting, brilliant, fiery, invigorating, convincing, while anything that smelled of classical was considered irrelevant, academic, artificial, inert, and a host of other epithets. Oddly enough, I was also upbraided for writing and presenting pieces that were far from complicated, where there was nothing that would startle or confound the listener.

The vehemence of the attacks and the depth of the prejudices often led to the weirdest sophisms. One critique, which sticks in my memory and can stand for other similar instances, pounced upon the Coda of my *Transformation* in order to ram home the point for the umpteenth time that classical music doesn't swing. Well, whoever said that it could or should? No one! But even more embarrassing was that this writer, hell-bent on trashing the piece, had missed the raison d'être for the special ending of *Transformation*, which, I believe, had never occurred before in music. Beginning as a classical piece with a long-lined twelve-tone *Klangfarbenmelodie*, the music is gradually, almost imperceptibly, transformed into jazz and several improvised choruses over a walking bass and highly chromatic changes. (George Russell always raved about Bill Evans's solo and the atonal changes I gave him to play on.) As the improvisers continue to hold forth, the classical players—wanting to get in on the fun—quietly sneak in with a riff, in typical swing band fashion, which leads to the climactic Coda, where the two genres, classical and jazz, are juxtaposed in close encounters and do battle with each other, each trying to assert its sole leadership. The idea was for the two distinct worlds of music to firmly stand their respective ground, with the one (jazz) swinging vigorously, the other (classical) holding to its own long rhythmic tradition—in other words swung and unswung rhythms duking it out in ever closer, alternating juxtapositions, neither side winning, and finally ending up together, in the sense of a musical handshake, on the same twelve-tone chord that started the piece. All that this critic heard was that classical rhythms didn't swing, missing the whole point of the piece. His conclusion was that third streaming could only lead to a dead end. Well, history and the next half century of developments in music have proven him not quite right.

Of the goodly number of favorable reviews of my Circle in the Square concert, the most perceptive and potentially influential were John Wilson's in the *New York Times* and Whitney Balliett's in the *New Yorker*.[86] In contradistinction to the many music critics who spend most of their time promoting their knowledge of the subject, or engage in bouts of ideological warfare, Wilson reported what actually occurred at the concert, including the fact that "an enthusiastic audience filled" the hall; he called the concert "a rousing success" and offered an accurate, succinct definition of Third Stream. Whereas those who opposed the very idea of Third Stream deplored what they perceived as the total lack of swing in the concert, Wilson had no problem describing several works as "successfully swinging." In my *Variants* on John Lewis's *Django*—which others found to be a "disaster," with its "schmaltzy saccharinity"— Wilson liked that I had retained the original's "jazz feeling" and had given it "extremely provocative expression." He held that "Mr. Schuller's compositions reveal a highly provocative mind at work, for he composes not only with a sense of adventure but also with a fine sensitive feeling for proportion and balance," and followed this observation with a touching bit of wisdom that also contained a subtle hint of warning, to wit: "At this stage in the use of techniques from both jazz and classical music both of these qualities are all-important."

In parallel to Wilson's article, Balliett began his review of the concert with a brief prehistory of Third Stream—although without mentioning the name—going back to the 1920s, pointing out that the earlier one-way traffic (classical composers reaching out toward jazz) had more recently broadened into a two-way street, as jazz had recently "begun to adopt the forms, the harmonies, the instrumentation, and even the discipline of classical music." But since "set designs" of classical music "cannot swallow the fluidity of jazz whole, and vice versa, or each will simply turn into the other, a compromise," something new was now in the offing: "a new music consisting of the most durable elements of both."

The reporter in Balliett pointed out that my concert presented "the first program ever devoted entirely to this new music" and provided "a bold and exciting evening." The poet and imagist in Balliett offered several of his patented verbal personifications, recalling Ornette Coleman's first solo on my Monk *Variants* as "two fluttering, whimpering downward runs that totally disarmed one, and that devolved into a typical tangle of squeaks, freshly coined notes and rhythmic displacements," or Eric Dolphy's entry on bass clarinet as having "a tone that alternated frighteningly between black moos and an out-size hubble-bubble," Dolphy and Coleman "jostling each other noisily, dissonantly, and marvelously, providing a singular example of dual improvisation." (I always loved duet improvisations and incorporated lots of them in my composition.) Balliett admired Coleman's "bucking solo" in *Abstraction*, and the work's "coherence and light resiliency" resulting from its "written and improvised interplay," clearly showing that "composition and improvisation had been organically and inextricably linked."[87]

One week after the Circle in the Square concert I had the great distinction of rehearsing and conducting Charles Mingus's *Half-Mast Inhibition*, one of his earliest, prophetic compositions (1960) in a highly chromatic, advanced harmonic language that unmitigatedly mingled jazz and classical elements. The eight-minute piece was definitely the kind that needed a real conductor to negotiate all the many tempo and meter changes, to direct the dynamics and balances between and among the twenty-six instruments for which Mingus had written the piece: two woodwinds (flute and oboe), five saxes, five trumpets, four trombones, tuba, three rhythm (including Mingus's bass), plus three extra percussion (including Sticks Evans and Max Roach), and, most important, a cello soloist.[88] Among the musicians Mingus hired for the date the most prominent were Eric Dolphy, John LaPorta, Danny Bank, Jusef Lateef, Marcus Belgrave, Ted Curson, Clark Terry, Eddie Bert, Slide Hampton, Jimmy Knepper, Roland Hanna, and Dannie Richmond. Since Jackson Wiley wasn't available for the recording session, I suggested Charles McCracken for the solo cello part, at the time principal cellist of the Metropolitan Opera.

I'm quite proud of the recording (issued on EmArcy in 1960), a near-perfect rendition of Mingus's highly complex, individualistic work.

To select one single event from all the great and wonderful experiences I had in jazz and with jazz in the 1950s is really impossible. But among those that I would rank near the zenith would be a certain television show that many of us feel is without doubt the finest hour that jazz ever had on television. That telecast was *The Sound of Jazz*.[89] This program was the brainchild of Whitney Balliett, who was able to persuade Robert Herridge, the producer of an excellent television series called *The Seven Lively Arts* (seen on CBS every Sunday afternoon), to include jazz—with Balliett's firm promise that such a program would show jazz to be the liveliest of all the arts. As conceived by Balliett and Nat Hentoff, the program was built around the Basie band as its nucleus, and was augmented by various instrumental groupings and such established jazz giants as Coleman Hawkins, Ben Webster, Lester Young, Billie Holiday, Gerry Mulligan, Rex Stewart, Milt Hinton, Pee Wee Russell, and a dozen other greats; to represent one of the newer, more modern developments in jazz, it had the Jimmy Giuffre Trio and the Thelonious Monk Trio.

Usually, when describing or commenting on a jazz program (or concert), one ends up pointing out its highlights. Critics do it all the time. But you can't do that with *The Sound of Jazz*. There were too many highlights; in fact the whole program was one sustained, near-perfect highlight.[90] The Basie band quickly set the tone for the whole program, bursting onto the scene with a riveting, driving, up-tempo blues, promptly launching Ben Webster on a fiercely charging, brimming solo, while his friend Coleman Hawkins—the camera caught him—listened, his eyes aglow with happy admiration. How often did one get those two masters on the same stage? I cannot describe what a joy it was to hear and see in this program the amazing Basie rhythm section of Joe Jones, Freddie Green, and Eddie Jones at work, with Joe Jones tossing off one hard-swinging catchy figure after another with the most impeccable timing and such consummate ease, and Freddie Green's beautiful rock-solid chordings, to which, I swear, I could listen all day. In its utter simplicity, is there anything more perfect in music?

Among the many things that made *The Sound of Jazz* unique was hearing Basie suddenly playing not his famous plinky, aphoristic asides (as fetching as they always were), but reverting instead to the old virtuoso stride-piano style of his youth. It was something to behold. Basie had been one of stride's renowned masters back in the late twenties and early thirties, but he had abandoned the style around 1935 when he took over the leadership of the Bennie Moten Band. To see Basie's left hand flying back and forth at full speed in two-octave leaps at a clip of metronome ♩ = ca. 260, and to hear him never miss a note, while the right hand was sprinting along even faster, at double-speed eighth notes—well, that was something that none of us had ever seen or heard Basie do in the last twenty years.

The second group,[91] led by Red Allen, featured Hawkins, the grand master (with his full-throated, bursting-at-the-seams sound), Rex Stewart (in one of his most ebullient, look-what-fun-I'm-having-solos, replete with wild shakes and half-valve moans), and the inimitable, incomparable Pee Wee Russell, delivering one of his wonderfully quirky solos in which nothing was ever predictable. His debonair, patrician demeanor on-screen—looking like Hollywood's Charles Bickford in one of his roles as a reticent suitor—cannot be easily reconciled with what came out of his amazing clarinet. Pee Wee was always exceptional!

Allen's rhythm section retained Joe Jones, but changed over to Danny Barker (guitar) and Milt Hinton (bass), offering another stunning lesson in what it is to swing. Come to think of it, all you had to see on the screen was Milt Hinton, bent deep over his bass, as if in love with it, with his ever-present blissful, radiant smile, working so hard to draw that last drop of sound from his instrument, and you knew what swing was. It defies comprehension how three musicians, who had rarely, if ever, played together, could produce such a perfect dynamic, timbral, sonic fusion of their three distinctive sounds as to become instantaneously a wholly new instrument—one might call it a "guidruba"—at the same time producing a totally irresistible, lilting swing. If you could sit still during Allen's *Wild Man Blues* and not tap your feet, there probably was something seriously wrong with you.

The Monk Trio, with Ahmed Abdul Malik and Osie Johnson on bass and drums, played a version of *Blue Monk*. What made that set very special was seeing Basie on camera, standing right next to the piano, listening admiringly to Monk's playing, amazed at what he heard, given Monk's unorthodox piano technique. I'm sure that Basie had heard Monk on recordings, but I doubt that he had ever witnessed Monk playing in person and at such close range.

Much of *The Sound of Jazz* as planned by Hentoff and Balliett was about reunions, reuniting musicians and old friends who hadn't worked together in years. Jimmy Rushing, for example, had left the Basie band seven years earlier, Joe Jones three years earlier. Billie Holiday hadn't worked with Lester Young in nearly twenty years. But beyond such specifics, the whole program was a kind of reunion, a coming together of some of the greatest musicians of that era, all of whom had made music together at some time or other, but in many cases not recently.

In the studio the love and respect for one another was palpable, but especially in the Billie Holiday *Fine and Mellow* segment of the show. What transpired there in those eight minutes has to go down in jazz history as one of the most—perhaps *the* most—inspired, touching, and moving blues performance of all time. I have rarely been able to listen to those twelve choruses without choking up, overwhelmed by the sheer beauty—the humanity, the artistic integrity—of those simple, soulful, heartfelt sounds. The eleven players chosen to accompany Billie were given one chorus each, to be interspersed between Billie's five stanzas. They were (in order of appearance) Ben Webster, Lester "Prez" Young, Vic Dickenson, Gerry Mulligen, Coleman Hawkins, Roy Eldridge (with two choruses).

But those eleven almost ended up being only ten. During the two rehearsals earlier in the day,[92] it became clear that Prez was in bad physical shape,[93] his playing weak, out of tune, fumbling, and meandering; he was unable to rally enough strength to sustain even a short two-bar phrase. The decision was made that Prez would not be able to participate in the telecast.

But sometime between the rehearsals and the show the tide turned. Everybody began to realize that it was really unthinkable for Lester Young to be cut out of the show. Prez was one of the giants of jazz, of the blues, and more than that, he was, as everyone knew, Billie Holliday's longtime closest friend. How could he be left out? It was just too cruel. Both Billie and Prez were not well, no longer functioning at full capacity, their careers fading; and it was clear that this could well be the last time they might ever be able to work together. The feeling now was that if there was one piece on the program that Prez could manage to play—he would have only one twelve-bar chorus, and hadn't he played thousands of them in his life?—it would be *Fine and Mellow*, and it would be with Billie Holiday.

And so it came to pass that he did play. And what a magical, spiritual, noble triumph it was. Everybody played their hearts out, for Billie—and for Prez. They all knew that this was a most special occasion, brought on by a remarkable confluence of circumstances. Even Eldridge behaved pretty well, allowing himself only two high-note squeals. Gerry Mulligan, the youngest in the group, subtly set his chorus in a more modern, bouncy double-time, and came up with what must be one of the most perfect twelve bars he ever played, not only in the way he built his solo, starting quietly in the low register, gradually climbing upward, but also at its climax in the impeccable choice of notes and beautifully contoured shapes and lines.

But the ultimate artistic triumph in those dozen sublime blues choruses belonged to Billie and to Prez. Even with her weakened voice, ravaged by years of drug abuse, now further shrunk in what even in her prime had been a very limited range, her intonation no longer controllable, Billie somehow—on this day—sang out with a pure and clear voice, the edgy hardness of late gone, a voice aglow with warmth and love. She suddenly seemed years younger.

Lester Young's transformation was even more miraculous. For days he had been so sick that he could hardly stand; he sat slouched much of the time on a chair in a corner of the room, almost totally incommunicative. But there he was, suddenly, the second to appear in the round of solos (right after Ben Webster's chorus), playing his twelve-bar aria with a heartrending expressivity, but stated so simple and economically—and quiet, all in *p* or *mp*. He was too weak to play any louder.

In my book *The Swing Era* I pointed out that in four short, halting phrases Lester played "a mere forty-five notes (not counting another eighteen embellishmental or passing tones), about half of Webster's majestic, ornate solo." It seemed to me that he was "expressing his innermost feelings about Billie, looking straight at her with half-closed eyes, and keeping his solo, like her singing, intimate and pared down to essentials."[94]

Margie and I watched *The Sound of Jazz* that afternoon of December 8, 1957. We both cried, we were so moved. And in many viewings of the video since then and listening to the sound track recording, I have never been able to get past Lester's seventh bar without tears welling up in my eyes. Nor can the image of Billie looking at Lester with such profound affection ever be erased from my memory.

Oh, go ahead, call me a sentimentalist. But then tell me, what kind of transformative power was it that enabled those two racked bodies and souls to heal long enough to produce such a perfect musical communication. Was it their love, made almost palpable on that soundstage? The camera suggests just that. Was it the love and admiration and respect that was radiating out from all the musicians in the room? Was it the transcendent power of the music itself, those beautiful vibrations that those musicians produced on that day? Who can say? But it was *something*—probably beyond categorization and analysis.

Chapter Ten

REENCOUNTERING EUROPE

IT WAS IN 1949 that I composed a work that several years later would bring me my first major recognition as a most promising new talent, as a composer of considerable significance. Thus spake some of New York's most respected and powerful music critics about my *Symphony for Brass and Percussion* in 1956. Prior to that, all the music I had written in Cincinnati and then in New York had either never been performed at all or only in private, among a small circle of friends and colleagues (as was the case, for example, with my *Trio for Oboe, Horn, and Viola* and *Duo Sonata* for clarinet and bass clarinet.)

Two thirds of the *Duo Sonata*, the second and third movements, were written under a three-fold inspiration: (1) the artistry of clarinetist Jack Kreiselman, a freelancer in New York and, by coincidence, the son of my father's best friend in the New York Philharmonic, and of bass clarinetist Sidney Keil, a splendid young musician in the Met orchestra; (2) the little known *Sonata for Two Clarinets* by Francis Poulenc, and some brilliant early works by Jean Françaix; and (3) Stravinsky's wonderful Symphony for Strings in D Major. The first movement of the *Duo Sonata*, a very serious affair, is the real developing Gunther Schuller, probing increasingly into a highly chromatic, partly atonal language. At the time I couldn't quite carry that style into the other two movements, which clearly ended up in a more lighthearted tonal idiom. In that sense the piece is dichotomous, the experiment of a twenty-three-year-old composer who may have been a bit impatient, unwilling, or unable to give the effort enough time. It is ironic and amusing to me that, to the extent that the piece is played at all, especially on university and conservatory student recitals, it is precisely because everyone really enjoys playing the last two movements, which are quite tonal and, respectively, Poulencish and Stravinskyish.

I have already confessed that, as a high school dropout without any formal musical training, self-taught and learning mainly by imitation, the occasional paraphrasing of some music that I particularly adored was my way of learning—without engaging in any direct plagiarism or outright duplication. I have always had a soft spot for many pieces by those two devilishly clever, artful, instantly accessible French composers: Poulenc and Françaix. I also recall finding Stravinsky's neoclassic language and playful creative fluency totally irresistible. I knew that if you're going to crib a few ideas from earlier models, at least let them be very good ones, a qualification that certainly applies to Stravinsky, Poulenc, and Françaix. Kreiselman and Keil premiered the *Duo* in 1951 at an ISCM concert. Peggy Glanville-Hicks, a composer and one of New York's major music critics at the time, wrote in the *Herald Tribune* that "Schuller's Sonata for Clarinet and Bass Clarinet is a cheerful little opus, brilliantly written for the instruments."[1]

News of whatever compositional successes I had enjoyed in Cincinnati (with my Horn Concerto and my symphonic arrangements), although garnering good local reviews, had certainly not reached New York or any other major musical center. More than that, I was much too shy and modest to push my work, even though I had already composed a few rather good orchestral pieces such as *Vertige d'Eros* and my Cello Concerto. I felt that I had no connections with well-established conductors and performers who might be inclined to take an interest in my music, and could not even consider approaching anyone. I also felt that in the aesthetic and stylistic climate for modern music in America, so completely dominated by Copland's and Stravinsky's neoclassicism, my atonal language fused, with highly chromatic ingredients derived from Scriabin and Ravel, would find little resonance or acceptance. I was quite realistic about that and content to be patient, thinking deep down that someday my time would come. The two works that generated my eventual career breakthrough were *Symphony for Brass and Percussion* (1949–50) and *Dramatic Overture* (1951). The *Brass Symphony* (as it came to be informally called) owes its existence to my two-year sojourn in Cincinnati, especially to a dear friend and colleague, Ernie Glover, second trombone in the orchestra and director of wind ensembles and bands at the Cincinnati Conservatory of Music. In the summer of 1949 he wrote to me, wondering whether I could write a big piece for him and his Conservatory brass players. (He called it a commission, but, of course, there was no fee involved.) I eagerly accepted the invitation; writing for brass would be right up my alley. Ernie was hoping to have my piece ready for a pre-Christmas concert to end the semester featuring his various brass and wind ensembles.

As busy as I was with my numerous horn playing obligations, I plunged right in, having quickly decided to write for a largish ensemble of six trumpets (divided into two trios), four horns, three trombones, and a trio of bass instruments (optionally either one baritone [euphonium] and two tubas, or two baritones and one tuba). And within a few weeks I had finished three (of four) movements, completing the fourth movement about six weeks later. The piece just flowed out of me; I was surprised—and delighted, although I don't know exactly why it came to me so easily. Indeed, I'm not sure that we composers can fully comprehend how and why a piece sometimes has such an easy birth, while other works exact a considerable struggle. There are too many variable circumstances in one's life during the days, weeks, or months that it takes to create a new composition for anyone to know definitively why one work is realized more easily than another.[2] But I do have a sense that the opening chord of the symphony, a fulsome ten-note chord—that is, a chord that vertically contains ten of the twelve notes of the chromatic scale, and is played at full force (*fortissimo*) by the entire sixteen-piece ensemble—is the syntactic, stylistic, I almost want to say, the symbolic generator of the whole piece. It's

a dramatic hit-you-in-the-face opening, if there ever was one, and it somehow unleashed for me all that was to follow. In some mysterious way it inspired the whole first movement. The Symphony is a full-fledged twelve-tone work, although slightly loosened up in method and application from the initial strict orthodoxy of Schönberg's earliest twelve-tone compositions. I used the row (or set) in varying ways in each of the four movements. In the second movement Scherzo, for example, the twelve-tone row is for the greater part of the movement triplicated into parallel trichords made up of a pair of fourths, that is:

At the time I wasn't particularly interested in the strictest twelve-tone orthodoxy, being determined to find my own more personal, slightly less fettered approach, without—I hasten to add—undercutting the organizational premise of that system. Even then, at that early stage of my development, I thought of twelve-tonality more as a method, a process that would inherently produce a high degree of chromaticism that was linguistically freed from functional tonality yet subliminally still related to it. I was not interested in the mere note counting that unfortunately a lot of orthodox twelve-tone composing fell prey to in those early days. By tripling each pitch into a trichord—getting three notes for the price of one, as it were—I was in fact augmenting the chromaticism to a heightened intensity. Because of my use of parallelism in the melodic-thematic lines (as shown in the second example above) the music retained a greater textural clarity, avoiding a more-difficult-to-follow density of multilayered polyphony.

I was also very pleased with the outcome of the slow (third) movement, marked "Lento desolato." I composed it in a single day, which is perhaps not *so* remarkable, since it is only two-and-a-half minutes long; but still it is an indication how fluently the movement composed itself. In retrospect, I am impressed by how logically the leisurely paced eighth-note phraselets flow into each other, making one grand line, and how the two climaxes in the movement (symmetrically placed: one fairly early on, the other just before the end) produce a fine formal balance. Among the movement's more original ideas is that it is played in its entirety very quietly by only six soft, muted trumpets—with two tiny exceptions, one a *fortissimo* single-chord blast in the four horns and three trombones, the other an A-major triad in the three bass instruments.

Oddly enough, although the slow movement makes absolutely no technical, virtuosic demands—it is entirely in slow motion rhythmically and in conjunct stepwise motion melodically—it is *the* movement in which, consistently over the years, the most miscounting accidents have occurred, especially near the end, where I overlay a four-eighth note melodic pattern on the underlying 6/8 meter. It seems to always confuse musicians. I have often thought to myself, an awful lot of musicians can't even seem to count to six.

I was particularly proud of the last (the fourth) movement, in which, after a *cadenza*-like introductory section, prominently featuring the first trumpet, the rest of the finale is one continuous *perpetuum mobile*, featuring at all times, somewhere in the ensemble, for 114 measures, the relentless chatter of running sixteenth notes.

I was intent on writing a substantial work that would avoid the typical brass instrument clichés and conventions of the day, creating instead a composition that would challenge even the best virtuoso players in New York.[3] The *Brass Symphony* was premiered by Ernie Glover's Conservatory Brass Ensemble in Cincinnati in early 1950, a few months later than originally planned, although without the finale. (It is by far the most difficult of the four movements, and in the end there wasn't enough rehearsal time to prepare it properly.)

The next performance—this time of the entire work—took place in New York in April 1951 at an International Society of Contemporary Music concert, with a personally handpicked group of New York's finest brass players[4] plus Dick Horowitz (from the Met) playing timpani and percussion, all conducted by Leon Barzin.

David Broekman conducted the next performance (in 1954) at one of his Cooper Union concerts, once again an excellent outing for the work. David and I assembled another stellar group of New York brass players, including quite a few who had played the piece in the ISCM concert and were thus somewhat familiar with it.

The *Brass Symphony* performance that pleased and touched me the most (after Dimitri Mitropoulos's with the New York Philharmonic) was Pierre Monteux's, in a marvelous realization in 1959 with Thomas Sherman's Little Orchestra Society of New York, in part because it was the only time in this great conductor's career that he conducted a twelve-tone work. In conversations with me he certainly never made an issue of it, or even mentioned it; he just took my work at face value, based entirely on his study of the score. Monteux was eighty-two at the time, and could easily have rested on his many laurels acquired over a long, brilliant career, and not bothered with exploring new musical territory (as most conductors in the twilight of their career often choose to do). I was particularly grateful to Sherman for assenting to Monteux's request to program my *Brass Symphony* because his Little Orchestra, as its name implies, normally used only two horns in its concerts, sometimes two trumpets, and very rarely a trombone. Here suddenly there was a call for a total of *sixteen* brass. It must have cost the Little Orchestra Society a pretty penny to hire some dozen extra musicians. Such a thing was unheard of in orchestral circles.

Monteux was really committed to my work and had extensive plans to program it in his future concerts, including right away with the Boston Symphony, both in Boston and Tanglewood. But that plan never came to pass. Some weeks after his New York performance I received a very sweet letter from Monteux, telling me that his intention of doing the piece in Boston and at Tanglewood had to be abandoned because of Charles Munch's plan for a series of concerts devoted exclusively to the music of Tchaikovsky and Stravinsky, one of which was to be conducted by Monteux. And, quite logically, he was asked to do *Sacre du printemps*. In order to play my work in Tanglewood, he felt that it would first have to be done in Boston because, as he put it, "only in Boston can I have the necessary rehearsals. You know, in Tanglewood there is only one rehearsal!! And as I have only one concert this time in Boston, I cannot do both the *Sacre* and your wonderful symphony." Then he added: "But nothing will prevent me from playing it in other places in the next few seasons. With my regrets for now, very cordially—Pierre Monteux."

I can honestly say that I was not disappointed; I knew and understood that the exigencies of symphony orchestra scheduling could often cause cancellations of one kind or another. Besides, there was no way I could be upset, given such a gracious, beautiful letter. Indeed, I felt honored that my work would be replaced, as it were, by as great a masterpiece as *The Rite of Spring*.

Despite the *Brass Symphony's* technical and musical-interpretive challenges, considered especially thorny in those years, it has been performed quite successfully many times, all over the world. I am proud that it is, more than half a century since its creation, still considered a preeminent performance challenge, genuinely admired and loved by brass players.

Reviews of the work (and of its recordings and performances) have not always been able to assess its artistic quality correctly or its overall importance in the brass and wind literature. They range from the astutely appreciative to the inanely uncomprehending. Two critics take the cake for missing the whole point of the piece. Jay Harrison, for example, made the ridiculous suggestion that my *Brass Symphony* was "obviously influenced by numerous similar brass works of Paul Hindemith," a composer that Harrison much admired.[5] To begin with, this is patently untrue, certainly stylistically.[6] But besides that, a few sentences later he contradicted himself, when he felt that my piece "was limited by its instrumentation"—so Hindemith's wasn't?—and that an "undue emphasis on sonority for its own sake fatigues the ear." What sonorities did he expect from an all-brass group? And yet he evidently missed the fact that the "Lento desolato" movement, with its velvety muted sonorities, sounds more like six clarinets than a sextet of trumpets.

John Rockwell, never a fan of my music, lamented that my *Brass Symphony* had little or nothing to do with jazz—which it definitely (and intentionally) did not.[7] Veering into amateur psychology, Rockwell found its only "happy moments" to be the "self-assertions of a beleaguered orchestral brass player." Me, beleaguered?

On the other hand, Robert Sabin, writing in *Musical America*, found the *Brass Symphony* to be "a splendid work, firmly organized, fascinatingly scored and emotionally inspired. Schuller knows how to make the brasses speak a new language, and the harmonic texture and design of his work reveal a major creative talent. To put it briefly, it is a masterpiece. The score (with its virtuosic handling of brass instruments) is uncannily right for dancing."[8] Similarly, Carter Harman, another *Times* critic—and composer (a student of Roger Sessions)—offered a very sympathetic view of the *Brass Symphony* by calling it "a stunning finale" to a "very exciting concert," describing it as a work "of delicate nuance as well as brilliant shattering climaxes."[9]

Years later, Carl Apone of the *Pittsburgh Press* found that my "splendid symphony . . . brings out the best in the brass, and the sorrowful 'Lento desolato' may well be among the loveliest modern music ever for brass."[10] An English writer, in an article on "the Symphony as a Genre" for the BBC's *Radio Magazine*, found "much finesse of aural detail and a strength of total conception" in the *Brass Symphony*; while in a 1974 review of the Philip Jones Brass Ensemble's recording of the work, the critic Alvin Lowery called it "this venerable classic of our time."[11]

The *Brass Symphony* also enjoyed for some years a separate existence as a modern dance and theatre piece. In 1954 José Limon created a work titled *The Traitor*, based on the biblical account of Judas's betrayal of Christ, danced brilliantly by Limon's company in his dramatic, highly realistic choreography, especially by Lucas Hoving in the lead role. Limon's company took *The Traitor* on a five-week tour of South America, for which Limon asked me to arrange the work for four-hand piano.

I did so rather hesitatingly. How could a piece for sixteen brass, with all its vibrant sonic colorations, work for the singular sonority of a piano? Also, I never really thought of my music, my style, as being adaptable to modern dance or ballet—as Stravinsky's so notably was. But in the end the piano transcription worked very well, which I like to think meant that the piece had real musical substance beyond its special brass sonorities and effects. (I was very happy to hear that my close friend and admired colleague Russell Sherman was going to be one of the pianists.)

On a second tour (in 1955) Limon commissioned me to arrange the work for a string orchestra, which, surprisingly, also worked quite well.

My harpist friend Janet Putnam invited Margie and me one day in the summer of 1951 to spend, as a sort of vacation, a whole week at the home of her close friends the Stedmans, who lived on Captree Island in the Great South Bay on Long Island's south shore. For Margie it was a real vacation, no worries about housewifely chores; she was able to relax, lie in the sun on a beach chair, read a book or catch up on recent *New Yorker* issues, go boating or water ski-ing with the Stedmans. She was so happy; it reminded her of long ago summer vacations at Detroit Lakes, southeast of Fargo, in Minnesota, where her parents had a summer cottage and where she had spent many carefree, playful days.

I was supposed to join in all this fun and relaxation, away from music for once. But it didn't happen that way. I was obsessed with composing—composing *something*—even while tempo-rarily escaping the hectic life of the city and enjoying the relative tranquility and easy pace of life on Captree Island. What possessed and inspired me with a depth and force that I had never experienced before were two recent musical experiences. One was my getting to hear Schön-berg's *Variations for Orchestra*, Op. 31, which Mitropoulos, in a powerfully expressive perfor-mance, had conducted just half a year earlier with the New York Philharmonic, and which Zeke Frank had recorded for me on acetate discs directly from the stage of Carnegie Hall. I had in the meantime listened to the work umpteen times, and became completely fascinated with the music and also with how Mitropoulos had inspired the Philharmonic musicians to play this totally unfamiliar and most difficult music as well as they did. It was a music that, I'm sure, the vast majority of them didn't understand and didn't like. I couldn't get those beautiful rich harmonies out of my mind, and *had* to do something to have that music become a part of me, to course through me, and to experience it vicariously through the act of creation.

After one day of indulging in the lavish hospitality of the Stedmans, and enduring Janet's constant teasing admonishments to relax and take it easy, "you can't work all the time"—little did she know—I couldn't resist the emotional pressure building up in me (like some geyser about to burst forth) to put pencil to paper, to assuage this uncontainable hunger for compos-ing. And what a surge of creativity it was. The work, subsequently titled *Dramatic Overture*, poured out of me in a mere five days. By the end of that vacation week, the short score—con-taining all significant details of notation (dynamics, orchestration, articulations and phrasings), that is, not merely a sketch—was finished. I was truly amazed by the fluency with which the work was achieved.

The other experience of major impact on me at the time was a performance of Berlioz's *Corsair* Overture in a brand new, wonderfully expressive and virtuosically brilliant recording by Beecham and his London Royal Philharmonic.[12] The *Corsair* and several other Berlioz concert overtures (such as the *Roman Carnival*) have a distinctive form, which, I believe, is special to Berlioz. It consists of three parts, fast-slow-fast, but in this case not in the format of established classical symmetry, where the different sections of a piece would be balanced in relatively equivalent proportions. Here the form consists of a very brief Presto section, with a tremendous burst of rhythmic and sonic energy, quickly followed by a much larger and quieter lyric Adagio episode. The rest of the Overture returns to the original Presto tempo, and is by far the largest section of the work. This ten-and-a-half-minute Overture equates to a time sequence of roughly 0:30–2:00–8:00, or in proportions of 1–4–16. Some would consider that a decidedly lopsided and idiosyncratic form, and not very classical. But how well it works, in Berlioz's hands.

In any case, I modeled my *Dramatic Overture* after Berlioz's *Corsair*, in effect drafting my music onto that particular form. Linguistically the piece is indebted, as just mentioned, to Schönberg's dodecaphonic harmonic language, essentially a more flexible, somewhat loosened-up approach compared to his earliest syntactically more delimited twelve-tone works such as the Op. 26 Woodwind Quintet.

In composing *Dramatic Overture* there was an additional specific kind of inspiration, prompted by the talents of two extraordinary musicians whose playing on their particular instruments I admired inordinately. Those two instruments were the clarinet and the tuba, and the two players were Luigi Cancellieri, about whom I have already written glowingly, and Bill Barber, my new tuba player friend from the Miles Davis Nonet.[13] My love for their work inspired me to include not one but two major extensive solos for both instruments. And when in 1952 I undertook to privately record the *Dramatic Overture* with a handpicked orchestra, both Luigi and Bill were able to participate in the recording, playing the solos I had written with them in mind.

The reader may wonder why a recording, and why a private recording? And what is a private recording? Simply put, it is a noncommercial recording not produced, financed, or issued by a corporate record company. As to why I wanted to make such a recording, it is simply that a composer, especially a young one, needs to hear the music he or she has written in acoustic reality—one hopes sooner rather than later—to assess the work's quality and to adjudge its strengths and weaknesses. By 1951 I was already twenty-five and had not yet heard any of my orchestra music in live performance; I had heard only one piece, my *Symphonic Study (Meditation)*, on a recording in a performance by a not fully professional student orchestra.[14] Furthermore, while it is obviously a great help to hear one's work in a live performance, it is still ultimately a fleeting, unrepeatable experience. A recording can be listened to repeatedly, can even be stopped at a certain critical point and checked out in detail and as often as might be necessary. That is a much more valuable experience than what can be gained from a single live hearing, when, let's face it, a young inexperienced composer is likely to be rather tense or nervous and not particularly objective.

I was desperate to hear some of my orchestral compositions, but fairly certain that, given the then prevailing musical and stylistic environment, there was little chance any of my orchestral works might see the light of day. I decided to take a drastic step—I believe an unprecedented one and, even years later, still, as far as I know, unreplicated—namely, to assemble a handpicked, top echelon orchestra of about seventy-five of my best New York musician friends and colleagues, and record the brand new *Dramatic Overture*, with Leon Barzin conducting. Given Barzin's great talent, his considerable experience and ease with contemporary music, and given the unstinting respect musicians had for him, I felt that Barzin would be the ideal person to conduct the recording session.

Obbligato

Leon Barzin (1900–1999) was in the early 1950s a recent addition to my growing collection of friends and admired colleagues. I had heard about Barzin even in my childhood; my father would occasionally mention his name and praise him as the outstanding principal violist of the New York Philharmonic in the 1920s and early 1930s. I became personally aware of Barzin as a remarkable conductor in 1947 when Margie and I started attending the performances of the newly founded Ballet Society, of which he was the music director and conductor. A year later, upon the founding of the New York City Ballet, Barzin assumed its musical directorship. In 1930 he had also become chief conductor of New York's National Orchestral Association, a training orchestra for young advanced (primarily postgraduate) musicians.

Barzin had a remarkably clear and elegant baton technique, and was highly respected by his musicians; he became also a much sought after teacher of conducting. Around 1948 I began to attend Barzin's thrice weekly rehearsals of the National Orchestral Association fairly regularly, which over a period of three or four years became an enormous learning experience for me. It was very exciting to watch Barzin's rehearsal technique, to see how he worked with the excellent young talents, molding their playing little by little over three or four weeks of rehearsals into concert performances that were quite often every bit as good as those of the New York Philharmonic.

In this molding and training process Barzin had the outstanding help of a whole cadre of New York's best orchestra musicians—generally principals of the Philharmonic, NBC Symphony, and Metropolitan Opera—one for each section of the orchestra. They came to all rehearsals and coached the young musicians in stylistic and technical matters, performance, and traditions relevant to the works Barzin had programmed.

I must have gone to several hundred of those Barzin rehearsals, score always in hand, always listening carefully, watching and learning. Although Barzin was rather haughty and aloof in his relationship to other musicians, he somehow took a real liking to me, undoubtedly noting that I was an unusually loyal attendee at his rehearsals, and that I was really very serious about observing his work with the orchestra. Indeed, he seemed flattered by my attention to him and his work. (We all knew that he had quite a vain streak.) After a while he began to exaggeratedly show off his baton technique and excessively berate his young musicians, I thought often quite unfairly, all seemingly for my benefit. He would turn around—I always sat behind him, facing the orchestra—to see whether I had caught his latest exhibitionistic peccadillo.

I certainly didn't like that side of Barzin; it was embarrassing. But I soon realized that this was part and parcel of his podium behavior, at least with young, not yet professional musicians.[15] In the end I stopped watching him, doing my best to ignore his podium antics, and kept my head intently buried in my scores.

*   *   *   *   *

When I told Barzin that I was going to put an incredible orchestra together, and that the session would not go longer than two hours, he readily consented to participate. We agreed on a date, a Thursday afternoon, a time when most symphony musicians were likely to be free.

There is an adage among New York musicians that if one stood for a couple of days on the corner of Fifty-Sixth Street and Seventh Avenue, at the stage door of Carnegie Hall, one would in a few days meet every musician in the city. I trusted that adage, and parked myself on that corner for about ten hours a day, and, believe it or not, between that and several dozen phone calls, I managed to assemble in two and half days a truly fabulous orchestra of the best players in New York—all friends and colleagues, mostly young, who I knew were good sight readers and not averse to modern music. My father and Leon helped me with selecting the best violinists and violists. Hardly anybody turned me down, even when I told them that I wouldn't be able to pay them anything. Would they do this for me as a favor? I promised everyone that they would be out in two hours, guaranteed.

It was amazing. There wasn't a weak musician in that whole group of seventy-two players. I provided everybody with the parts about a week ahead of time, and hired Stanley Tonkel, an engineer at Columbia Records, who had excellent portable state-of-the-art recording equipment, to do the taping. And Barzin arranged for us to use his NOA rehearsal hall in the City Center building (the old Mecca Temple) free of charge.

The recording came off perfectly. Barzin rehearsed the piece for about an hour and ten minutes in considerable detail; he knew it *very* well. We took a fifteen-minute break, and then made two complete takes of the nine-minute *Dramatic Overture*, the second of which was the better of the two. We finished four minutes before the hour—as promised.

The whole occasion was an extraordinary experience for me. Luigi Cancellieri and Bill Barber excelled in their solos, and the orchestra's and Barzin's work was virtually perfect; the result was that I now had a superb recording of the Overture. But beyond that I was deeply touched and flattered by the willingness with which all those fine and very busy musicians offered me their talent and time. Many also did it for Barzin; he was so respected and admired. Had I chosen some other conductor, I think there would not have been as much enthusiasm for the project.[16] I could not help but feel that everybody had paid me a huge compliment as a composer and as a musician colleague. I was able to use the recording quite effectively in acquainting various conductors and composers with a good example of my music; listening for nine minutes to a recording had a tremendous advantage over having to find the time to study a score in detail.

There is no question in my mind that the performances of *Dramatic Overture* with the New York Philharmonic in 1956 and at the famous Darmstadt Summer Courses Festival in 1954 (my composer debut in Europe) came about as a result of that recording.

Nineteen fifty was also the year of my *Fantasy for Unaccompanied Cello* (the saga of its creation and rejection by its commissioner has been told earlier), as well as the completion of my Oboe Sonata, written for Josef Marx. I had started the piece in 1948 and had nibbled away at it from time to time. Joe had even premiered parts of it—without telling me (believe it or not)—at a small private musicale somewhere on Cape Cod. (I found this out through our mutual friend and Margie's doctor, Henry Richardson). I finally worked on the Sonata seriously starting in July in 1951 and finished it in late August.

Joe really took the Sonata to heart. He had the technique and right mindset for this at times rather difficult piece, with its atonal style and twelve-tone conceptions. Keen ears will also detect an underlying inspiration of Beethoven's Violin Concerto, a work I knew well, not only from my father's almost daily practice of it during my teen years, but also from many live performances and recordings. A wonderful new recording with Yehudi Menuhin, Wilhelm Furtwängler, and the Lucerne Festival Orchestra had jolted me into a renewed examination of the Violin Concerto, especially in respect to its formal design. Some of what I learned in that process found its way—subtly—into my Oboe Sonata. But it was also inspired by Schönberg's recently composed Phantasy for Violin and Piano. The Oboe Sonata's public premiere took place a year later at an ISCM concert, with Joe and with Russell Sherman as the pianist.

It was around this time, 1950 to 1952, that I became more widely involved with New York's contemporary music scene. This took a variety of forms, most prominently, of course, as hornist, performing (as much as my schedule at the Metropolitan Opera permitted) in concerts of new music, especially those offered by ISCM, the Composers Forum, and Charles Schwartz's Composers Showcase, and sometimes even those of the more conservative League of Composers. Because of my good connections with hundreds of New York's finest instrumentalists, including those particularly interested and skilled in playing challenging new music, it wasn't long before I was asked to choose and hire the musicians for such concerts. In this way, too, I came to know personally almost all the most famous and active composers living and working in New York at the time—everyone from Varèse, Carter, Babbitt, Perle, Wolpe, on one side of the stylistic spectrum, to William Schuman, David Diamond, Robert Ward, Jack Beeson, Carlos Surinach, on the other, and many more, both young and old, well established or still little known.

I am pretty sure that I met Milton Babbitt in 1950 at the premiere of his *Composition for Viola and Piano* (played by Abe Loft and Alvin Bauman), and then again a year later, when Milton invited me to help with the rehearsals of his 1948 *Composition for Four Instruments*, for which I had engaged the players. We also met often at Philharmonic rehearsals, when Mitropoulos was doing such Schönberg pieces as *Erwartung* and the Opus 31 *Orchestra Variations*. When Milton became president of the New York Chapter of ISCM, I was appointed secretary-treasurer, a position that occasionally got me in trouble with some of the musician friends I had hired; ISCM was almost always broke and I was unable to pay them on time or, on one occasion, in full.

It was also around this time that I first met Bethany Beardslee, fresh out of Juilliard, and her pianist friend and husband to be, Jacques-Louis Monod. We all worked together many, many times in subsequent years, and I'll never forget so often listening in awe to Bethany's silvery-toned soprano voice, sauntering through all those supposedly impossible-to-negotiate twisting melodic lines in Webern's *Lieder* or, some years later, in Babbitt's *Philomel* with such apparent ease and absolute accuracy.

In the next two years I composed what I consider to be two of my best early works: *Five Pieces for Five Horns* (1952) and *Recitative and Rondo for Violin and Piano* (1953). I feel that the five-horn quintet is perhaps the piece in which one can begin to hear my personal language in its first flowering. It was also, I like to think, my first attempt in a long, long, long time to write some really serious, innovative, challenging horn ensemble music, far beyond the traditional cliché-ridden horn quartets with their hunting calls, fanfares, and simplistic fake chorales, almost always in a solid (or stolid) F and B-flat major.[17] The *Five Pieces* are in a truly contemporary style and language, incorporating all manner of recently developed techniques, such as *glissandos*, quarter tones, alternate fingering tremolos, and a variety of different mutings. I love particularly the second movement, which, with its muted horns in delicate sonorities and canonic patterning, sounds more like a section of clarinets than horns. The last movement, a Toccata, all written in five-part unison (except for a few bars at the end), is a particularly intriguing challenge for all five players to produce absolutely cleanly.

Five Pieces was premiered in New York at an ISCM concert in 1953 with myself and John Barrows alternating on first and third horn, Jim Buffington on second, Ray Alonge on fourth, and Weldon Wilber on fifth horn, with Leon Barzin conducting. The piece was finally recorded forty-one years later in 1993 by the NFB Horn Quartet with my much-admired friend Barry Tuckwell in the lead part (issued on my own GM Recordings). I am quite proud that the piece has been played fairly often in England, most notably by Dennis Brain's fine horn ensemble.

As for the *Recitative and Rondo for Violin and Piano* (or *Orchestra*), it came about, oddly enough, by way of the Janos Starker *Fantasy for Unaccompanied Cello* incident recounted in chapter eight. Starker had requested a solo piece that would be the new contemporary work on his debut recital at Carnegie Hall in early 1952, and had then rejected it. But Gabriel Banat, a very talented young violinist, heard about me as a very talented up-and-coming composer from his close friend and colleague Laszlo Varga. Gabi, who was planning to make his Carnegie Recital Hall debut around that time, then asked me to write a piece for him. Gabi not only premiered *Recitative and Rondo* in New York, but he also performed it often in Europe in its orchestral version,[18] most notably with the Residentie Orchestra in The Hague (Holland).

Interestingly, the work was in part stimulated by twin musical experiences, this time in two different musical worlds: jazz and classical. One was hearing Dave Brubeck (for the first time in person) at George Wein's Storyville Club in Boston's Kenmore Square. During the course of that evening Dave, fresh from his studies with Darius Milhaud at Mills College in California, offered one of his amazingly inventive, patented extemporizations, building it slowly from a tiny simple musical cell to an immense, rousing climax. It was better than Ravel's *Bolero*—and shorter. My piece employs a similar idea for its climatic ending. The other influential experience, whose aftereffect is discernable in the *Recitative and Rondo*, was turning pages for Edward Steuermann in the New York premiere (and all the attendant rehearsals) of Schönberg's beautiful *Phantasy for Violin and Piano*, in the process really getting to know and study that work thoroughly. Any perceptive pair of ears will be able to hear the linguistic relationship.

The music-interested reader may have noticed that I was, even in my teen years, fascinated with the three big preclassical Western musics, in reverse chronological order: baroque, Renaissance, medieval. I don't quite know what caused my fascination with these early musical forms almost from the very beginning of my musical development. This was rather unusual—and still is—although somewhat less so today; people in general tend to be more broadly oriented in their musical tastes than in the past. But back then none of my friends and colleagues evinced any interest in the history of European music or in any other musical tradition than the one they were professionally involved with. (This included my father.) Their view of music was thus limited to about two hundred years of musical history, from 1750 (Mozart, Haydn, Beethoven) through the Romantic era to the middle of the twentieth century.

I do not fully understand why I was so deeply interested in the *whole* world of music flowing side by side in two gigantic streams: one from the earliest beginnings in European music through all the successive eight centuries to the newest and most modern of twentieth century manifestations, the second, running in parallel, a host of other ethnic, vernacular traditions, sometimes thousands of years old, and (of more recent vintage) American jazz. My record collection and music library did in fact grow open-endedly and chronologically, and expanded stylistically and idiomatically, more or less embracing the whole known musical universe. On the ethnic and vernacular front, I spent a lot of time and money acquiring recordings of Near Eastern and North African Arab music in record stores on Flatbush Avenue in Brooklyn, or Turkish Zeybek or Greek Bouzouki music in downtown Manhattan, or indigenous South American (Peruvian, Brazilian) music in Upper Manhattan and the Bronx, not to mention Alan Lomax's *Folk Song* collections and Moses Asch's huge Folkways library. Lomax and Asch covered just about all the vernacular and folk music recordings on the face of this globe.

The only explanation I can offer for my interest in preclassical European music and so many ethnic musics is that I have always been intrigued and fascinated by the *origins* of things. It seems to be something inscribed in my DNA. Once I became really interested in music at age eleven, the musical language of Mozart and Haydn and Beethoven was a known quantity to me, a received knowledge already embedded in my consciousness. I didn't have to wonder what it was; it just was. But knowing that Bach and Mozart and Haydn were not the beginnings of European or Western music, my mind was soon asking where did their music come from? Who did they learn from? How did it all get started? Well, that search brought me via my encyclopedias and histories back through the centuries to Perotin and Adam de la Halle of the twelfth century, and even before that to the very earliest treatises on music by Boethius and Guido d'Arrezzo. It was rather unusual that I didn't view all that earliest music as mere dry-as-bones history, and that my ears connected so readily with it. In the process I discovered the Ars Nova and the music of De Vitry, Machaut, Jacopo da Bologna, Solage, and several dozen other composers, and I was hooked. Having found my way back to the beginnings, I now traced the evolutionary trail forward, step by step, to Bach and Mozart and Haydn. It was a fantastic journey.

As so often happened in my life, a seemingly incidental confluence of circumstances and connections led to an episode in my career, an undertaking of which I am very proud, but which is among the least remembered, the least acknowledged of my many professional enterprises. In my work with various contemporary music organizations (such as ISCM and the Composers Forum) and in my general concertgoing, I had met Edgard Varèse a few times. I was very much aware of his important contribution, beginning in the early 1900s, to the contemporary music scene (first in Paris and Berlin, and after 1915 in America) as a leading composer and as a conductor, lecturer, and concert organizer. Yet, I had heard hardly any of his music. As of the late 1940s, only two of his works had been recorded (*Ionisation* and one movement only of his *Octandre)*, and his music, which was generally regarded as being much too radical and incomprehensible, was now just beginning to be performed in concerts. I was thrilled when in 1950 four of his 1920s compositions were issued on Columbia Records.

Varèse had been present at the first performance of my *Brass Symphony* in New York, and had been, as he himself told me, very impressed. He closed his hand into a tight fist, as if to signal a really strong piece. Subsequently, he and his wife Louise invited me a few times to their home on Sullivan Street in the Village. That's where I first glimpsed, hanging on several coat racks and on the walls of his studio, hundreds of strips of magnetic tape of sounds produced on his beloved Ampex tape recorder, which were destined to play a significant role in the electronic music Varèse was composing at the time, in particular his famous *Déserts* for wind, percussion, and electronic tape (premiered in 1954 in Paris). On one of those visits, at afternoon tea (which Louise always insisted on serving), I mentioned by pure chance that I was working on some arrangements of Ars Nova and early Renaissance music and how excited I was about this amazing music, some of it sounding so modern to me, sometimes almost like Stravinsky. At that point his ears really perked up. I didn't then know that in the 1940s Varèse had founded and directed the Greater New York Chorus for the performance of Renaissance and baroque music. But I *had* heard casual comments now and then that Varèse didn't like string instruments, except for the bass, that he loved brass and woodwinds, also that he loathed Romantic music and thus most of the music of the nineteenth century.

The next thing I knew, I received a call from Maxwell Powers, head of the Greenwich House Music School on Barrow Street in the Village, asking me if I'd be interested in creating and directing a series of concerts at the school, and that he was calling me at the recommendation of Varèse. Varèse was associated with the Greenwich School as a teacher and was on the school's board. At the ensuing meeting it was Varèse who did all of the talking. He asked me if I'd be willing to produce three concerts a year, for which I would choose the programs and the musicians; and only contemporary music and music from the Renaissance and the Middle Ages, up to about 1600—none from the nineteenth century! I agreed without hesitation, although I was inwardly surprised at the slightly odd request.

A week later I telephoned Varèse to ask him if it would be okay to do these concerts mostly without singers, that is, almost entirely with instruments. I knew lots of singers, but they were almost all in opera. I heard Varèse groan on the other end of the line—at the prospect of having to deal with singers. I said: "I know hardly any singers who do this old music." "Bien sûr. Ça va; c'est bien." And that was it. (Varèse was always amazingly direct in his responses.)

I ran that series of concerts under the heading of "Early Masters and Contemporary Composers" for two seasons, from the fall of 1952 through the spring of 1954, dividing each concert into two more or less equal halves, the first half devoted to the early music, the second to the new music—by which I meant mostly music composed since 1945. The twentieth-century works—about twenty-five over the two years—ranged from Ernst Krenek's 1922 *Symphonic*

Music For Nine Instruments, the oldest new music performed in the whole series, although even then it was still an American premiere, to more recent works by New York composers Marc Wilkinson and Arthur Berger, European composers André Casanova (French), Riccardo Malipiero (Italy), and Hans Erich Apostel (Austria), along with occasional sprinklings of Stravinsky (his brand new 1953 *Septet*, for example), and Schönberg (*String Trio* and *Phantasy* for violin and piano), to name just a small sampling.

The early music segments of the programs were the most interesting and certainly the more unusual; most of those pieces had never been heard or performed in New York—or, I dare say, anywhere in the Western hemisphere. One needs to remember that there was as yet no ongoing early music movement in this country, such as there has been for the last twenty years or so, nor any early music ensembles, as there were already in Europe (in England and Belgium). However 1952, the year I started my early music concerts, was also the year that Noah Greenberg founded the vocal and instrumental ensemble Pro Musica Antiqua, unbeknownst to me at the time. Within only a very few years, under its new name, New York Pro Musica became the leading early music ensemble in the United States and arguably the world.

In any case, the interesting challenge for me was to take this centuries-old music and bring it to acoustic life, sonically and stylistically, in as authentically representative a re-creation as I could envision. Nobody knows exactly how that music, in all its remarkable variety, was performed and how it *really* sounded in its own time. We know a lot, to be sure, but in the end we are all guessing and hypothesizing to a greater or lesser extent.

At the time that I embarked on this venture, I had studied just about anything and everything I could lay my hands on that dealt with music in the five centuries between 1100 and 1600. Those materials included Gustave Reese's magnificent *Music in the Middle Ages* (1940), Curt Sachs's *The History of Musical Instruments* (1940), and the pathbreaking, multivolume German encyclopedia *Die Musik in Geschichte und Gegenwart* (*Music in History and the Present*), to which I had subscribed in 1949. Although by 1952 only two volumes (of the fourteen) had appeared, even that comprised 1,930 pages containing several dozen articles on medieval and Renaissance music and composers, including an all-important, extensive entry on Ars Nova. That remarkably informative article was written by Heinrich Besseler, one of two preeminent German musicologists and early music scholars, the other being Friedrich Blume, the chief editor and major contributor to the series. One couldn't be in better hands.

For the actual music my two prime sources were: (1) Willi Apel's *French Secular Music of the Late Fourteenth Century* (1950), which contained the most precise, detailed notation of eighty-one compositions (mostly Ballades, Virelais, Rondeaux) by five of the most important Ars Nova composers and, as always in such publications, about thirty pieces by that ubiquitous composer named Anonymous; and (2) Johannes Wolf's *Music of Earlier Times* (an American edition of Wolf's original publication of 1926), containing sixty-six compositions by virtually every composer of note from the thirteenth century to Bach. I also owned almost all the recordings of music of the Renaissance and the Middle Ages available at the time, especially those of Safford Cape's various Pro Musica Antiqua groups in Brussels (on Curt Sachs's L'Anthologie Sonore label), and some of Marcel Couraud's recordings of prebaroque music. From these and a few other scattered recordings I learned about the sounds the instruments of that earlier time produced—presumably the recordings were authentic to the original.

My main contribution, apart from selecting the individual works to be performed, and rehearsing and conducting them in the concerts—there were anywhere from ten to twenty pieces per program, depending on their durations (rarely more than two minutes)—was to assign them specific instrumentations, then orchestrate them accordingly, and copy out the scores and parts. This was necessary because before the 1600s specific instrumentations were almost never designated by the composers, the assumption being that *any* instruments that happened to be available in a particular situation could be used, and because of the very close correspondence between the technical, expressive characteristics of the music and, reciprocally, the instruments of the time.

The most interesting and difficult challenge I faced was how to approximate authentically the sounds made by the ancient rebecs, recorders, shawms, sackbuts, and medieval harps. The problem was that in the 1950s there were no period instruments to be had, either original or replicated, whereas now there are thousands of such instruments available, just as there are uncountable numbers of players who play professionally on nothing but period instruments. As far as I knew the only such existing instruments in my day were in museums, and were simply not available to be played on. Therefore the challenge for me—and in turn for my musicians—was to variously prepare or modify their modern instruments, and adjust the sound through their aural imagination, through their ears, as well as their embouchure, fingering, and bowing techniques, so as to produce the desired sound. It also meant virtually eliminating—or at least greatly minimizing—the use of modern vibrato.

It was very exciting to see how eagerly the musicians responded to these novel demands. To emulate the sound of the sackbut and cornet or zinken, for example, my brass players resorted to whatever smallest-bore instruments and mouthpieces they owned (or could get their hands on), further modifying their sounds aurally through minute embouchure adjustments and in their breathing techniques. The appropriate sounds of the shawms and krummhorns were pretty easily achieved by playing on oboe d'amores, English horns, and bass oboes (one of my players, Wally Bhosys, owned two different bass oboes and a heckelphone), as well as playing with lighter reeds and creating a more nasal tone, and through embouchure and breathing adjustments.

The string players—this was long before the time that players owned baroque or gamba bows—played with much less bow pressure and bow speed, nearer the fingerboard, and with no vibrato, thereby producing a less weighty, less brilliant, slightly darker, but quite beautiful sound.

Since the pieces in which I used a harp were quite limited in range, and confined pretty much to the two middle octaves, my harpists dampened their instruments' sound by applying wads of cotton to the few strings they had to use, and then played quite softly, low on the strings, near the soundboard, thus producing a thinnish, clear, drier sound.

Occasionally I did use singers, in particular the versatile Paul Mathen (in a group of Machaut *Ballades* and some songs from the German *Glogauer Liederbuch*) and Bethany Beardslee (in *both* the early and new music segments).

All in all, it was one of the most stimulating, rewarding—and educative—musical adventures I ever undertook, exciting even in the fact that the early music that we brought to life was some five or six centuries removed from my own music. That we premiered about fifty pieces from that long bygone era, music probably heard for the very first time in centuries, was, I think, quite a singular achievement.

It was in 1951 that I became increasingly aware of a burgeoning contemporary music scene in Europe, particularly in Germany, but also in England and France. During the war and for several years afterward we in America had lost almost all contact with Europe in regard to cultural activities, especially on the Continent. Now, as Europe was digging out of the detritus of war's destruction, it was also beginning to revive its cultural pursuits, rebuilding and repairing concert halls, opera houses, and theatres, especially in bombed-out Germany. A number of major figures in music, theatre, film, and literature were now returning to Europe, or at least visiting and touring there. Music festivals were springing up all over, answering a huge hunger for too-long denied musical and cultural nourishment.

But what particularly attracted my attention was the emergence of contemporary music festivals or of newly reactivated concert series exclusively devoted to new music, now lavishly presented by state-supported radio stations. In music journals such as the German *Neue Zeitschrift für Musik* and *Melos* or England's *Score*, I began to hear about new works composed during and directly after the war by Olivier Messiaen and his students Pierre Boulez and Karlheinz Stockhausen, or about new works by Luigi Dallapiccola and the young Luigi Nono, and about a growing musical avant-garde in countries such as Poland and Sweden. This all sounded pretty exciting to me, especially since it appeared to be inspired mainly by the three prime creative lineages of Bartók, Stravinsky, and Schönberg.

I felt that I had to experience and engage in these developments, to see and hear things with my own eyes and ears. Words and descriptions are one thing, but becoming personally, intellectually and emotionally involved is something else; it is inherently more reliable, more affecting. It was clear to me that the most proactive, exciting programs in the furtherance of new music were the International Summer Courses for New Music in Darmstadt and the Donaueschingen Music Days for Contemporary Music, both in Germany.

I hadn't been in Germany since my early school days in the 1930s, and naturally hadn't seen any of my relatives or Bobby Schneider. By around 1951 I had decided that I *must* get to Europe as soon as feasible—with Margie, of course—and I set my sights primarily on Darmstadt and Donaueschingen. One festival was usually in July, the other in October; they both fell before and after my eight-weeks work with the Goldman Band and before the customary opening of the Met season in late October. Besides the prospect of visiting my relatives there was the further enticement—a special request of Margie's—of spending a week or so in the Black Forest, one of Germany's most beautiful regions, and as luck and geography would have it, within easy driving distance of both Darmstadt (two hours to the north) and Donaueschingen (only a half hour to the east).

The first opportunity for the European venture came only in the late summer and fall of 1953, allowing us to visit the Donaueschingen Festival, but eliminating any chance of getting to the Darmstadt Festival. Beyond that, we had a wonderful two-month sightseeing tour of six countries: Holland, Switzerland, Austria, France, Spain, and, of course, Germany; and we enjoyed many concerts and opera performances in Berlin, Munich, and Vienna. It was filled with fascinating, at times overwhelming experiences, ranging from some very great theatre and opera in West Berlin and my first live encounters with the Berlin Philharmonic and Wilhelm Furtwängler, to Granada's Alhambra, Antoni Gaudi's Sagrada Familia church in Barcelona, our first visits to the Swiss and Austrian Alps, as well as a few amazing evenings in the nightclubs of Paris.

At the midpoint of our tour, on our way to the Black Forest, I visited the offices of the Darmstadt Musikinstitut and its director, Wolfgang Steinecke, to inquire as to how one might apply for the festival it sponsored. I found out that it wasn't just a festival of contemporary music; as its full name implied, it was also a school for both performers and composers. Since I was both, I was torn between applying as a horn player or as a composer. I rather assumed that as an already seasoned player in major New York orchestras I would be easily accepted in the former category. But that issue was quickly resolved by the disappointing news that the horn was not one of the instruments included in Darmstadt's curriculum. So I applied as a composer. Anticipating a swift rejection, since I was completely unknown in Europe, I was stunned to hear back from Steinecke that I was not only accepted and promptly enrolled as a student (for a fee, of course), but was even invited to submit a few suggestions of recent compositions that could be scheduled for performance in 1954. Wow! I had really not expected such a quick and favorable response. I wondered whether it was because my letter had been in fluent German, or because I had also mentioned being very interested in and influenced by the Second

Viennese School, or because I was a major instrumentalist in New York City, heavily involved in the contemporary music scene. I found out later that it was all of those things, including Steinecke's astonishment that a young, unknown American composer would be writing in such a fluent and correct German, and writing music *outside* the neoclassic idioms prevailing in America. But he also revealed that he had consulted with Kolisch and Steuermann—neither of whom, by the way, I had mentioned in my letter—who, unbeknownst to me, had already been teaching and performing in Darmstadt for the past several years.

The 1954 Darmstadt Festival more than lived up to my highest expectations. I had never heard so much new and very good, often exciting music (mostly world or European premieres), and so well played as in those two weeks. The schedule of lectures, workshop sessions, analysis classes, open rehearsals, and concerts (usually four or five a week) was very tight and concentrated. I loved it. It reminded Margie and me of the structure and organization of the Kenyon Institute in 1945. Within a few days I had met Stockhausen and Boulez, the Italian triumvirate of Nono, Berio, and Maderna, and many of the so-called students: from England Alexander Goehr and Harrison Birtwhistle, from Sweden Bengt Hambreus and Bo Nilsson, from Holland Peter Schat, from France the two Michels, Fano and Philippot, and from Switzerland Jacques Wildberger. Krenek, Leibowitz, Kolisch, and Steuermann were also there that year as faculty, and it was a real pleasure to encounter Steuermann as both a performer and composer. Normally, in New York, Steuermann rarely talked about his composing; he was either too modest to mention it, or too depressed about his killing teaching schedule that left no time for composing. So it was an extraordinary experience to hear a lot of his remarkable music, including a beautiful song cycle for soprano and the world premiere of a recent Piano Trio.

The visit to Darmstadt in 1954 became very important in my life as a composer. It was there, in a concert on August 22, that a work of mine was performed for the first time in Europe. My *Dramatic Overture* was played by the Hessian Radio Orchestra of Frankfurt, under the direction of Ernest Bour. My *Overture* ended the program, which also included a stunning array of world premieres and German first performances by Ernst Krenek, Bruno Maderna, Hans Werner Henze, and Giselher Klebe. I was in pretty distinguished company, to say the least. The *Overture* performance went quite well, considering that the piece, set almost entirely in a fast-moving *alla breve* tempo, is technically quite demanding. But I found Bour's interpretation of my piece, while meticulously rehearsed, rather rigid, dry, and expressionless—producing only what one might call a mechanically correct rendition.

The half dozen German radio orchestras were famous in the postwar years for being the best in the land, generally because they were the highest paid (except for one or two private orchestras like the Berlin Philharmonic) and attracted the best players. They were renowned for their expertise in advanced contemporary music, the propagation of which their employers, the government-supported radio network, were particularly committed to. Thus I ascribe the clinically cold quality of the performance not so much to the orchestra as to Bour. He was one of those specialists in contemporary music who could intellectually assimilate the most complex scores with great ease, but from whom one could never expect a warm, glowing, emotionally expressive performance. (This was especially noticeable in the nineteenth-century romantic repertory, although he did—exceptionally—make one superior recording of a later-period opera, namely, Ravel's *L'Enfant et les sortilèges*, in 1948.)[19]

Bour was famous for editing and correcting any score that came into his hands. It seems to have been a habit of his to never return a score unemended. When my *Overture* was returned to me, I discovered that he had made about a hundred little corrections, meticulously inserted in minuscule, very light pencil markings. It must have taken him many, many hours to do this. I had heard from several other composers whose works Bour had conducted that his correcting of manuscript scores was a kind of hobby, very near to an obsession. As far as I know he never mentioned the matter to any composer—certainly not to me—and apparently never wanted any thanks for this unexpected gift. The irony in my case was that 98 percent of the corrections he made were insignificant: minor omissions (that any orchestra musician would consider self-correctable), or the insertion of a staccato dot (that had been omitted for lack of space) over a notehead, where all other instruments but that one *had* the dot. If there was no vertical space to insert the dot, Bour would put it next to the note head, with a tiny little arrow—which *really* looked wrong and confusing because putting a dot to the right of a note-head changes that note's duration and produces a more serious error.

Although I had already heard my *Overture* music on the private recording I had made of it, I was thrilled to now have it played in a public performance, a very important one to boot, in Europe.[20] It was a real breakthrough for me, even though the immediate reaction to the piece turned out to be rather lukewarm. Some critics considered the work old-fashioned, or worse, not even worth mentioning. The most interesting review appeared in the English contemporary music journal *Score*, written by David Drew.[21] After suggesting that the entire concert might be entitled "Aspects of Contemporary Romanticism," he referred to my *Overture* as "neo-Straussian"—which I decided to take as a compliment (whether or not he meant it that way). He also pointed out that my *Overture* "aroused a storm of well-deserved applause." He singled it out as "brilliant and unsubtle" and "worlds apart" from the other three young composers (Klebe, Maderna, Henze). Whether "worlds apart" was meant to indicate that he preferred my music, I couldn't tell. Nor could I be certain as to what Drew meant by "unsubtle," since the word "subtle" already has several somewhat conflicting connotations, ranging from "ingenious" and "refined" to "obscure," the negative of subtle was thus doubly conflicting. (In one of Sandy Goehr's letters to me he offered the thought that "Brilliant is the mind that can appear unsubtle to critics of modern music"—which I took to be another compliment.)[22]

Years later, when David and I had become good friends, I finally asked him if he could recall what he meant by "unsubtle." Unrefined? Crude? Too clever? Too obvious? "Oh," with a dramatic wave of the hand, "I was being a smart-ass; just beginning to write criticism. I was only twenty-three. No, I liked your piece the best." I told him that I was surprised that he considered the *Overture* "neo-Straussian," gently chiding him for not realizing that it was much more Schönbergian.

As for Steinecke, he had by 1954 become a fanatic devotee of anything extremely complex and flamboyantly avant-garde. Noting that some of the reviews of my work were rather dismissive, he suggested: "Next time you better put some more pepper in your music."

The early history of the Darmstadt Summer Courses for New Music is an interesting and positive one, but not without its problems. The festival was an offspring of the Kranichsteiner Musikinstitut, the institutional base for the summer courses. Both entities were founded in 1946 by Wolfgang Steinecke. Since two-thirds of the city of Darmstadt had been destroyed in 1944 by Allied air forces in a single night of bombing, including all of the city's concert halls and its opera house, its schools and government buildings, the first three years of the institute's existence were spent mostly with organizational matters and rebuilding infrastructures for the eventual housing and presentation of its future performing and educational activities. Although in those early years there were a few concerts presented in makeshift halls as early as 1946, the institute's main goal was, perforce, to catch up with the rest of the world in developments in modern music going back to about 1935, to try to overcome the decade-long moratorium on new music imposed by Hitler and Göbbels. All composers of Jewish faith as well as those Aryans whose music was decried as "degenerate art" had left Germany and Austria by 1939 for other parts of the world, particularly America and England. Performances of their works had been strictly prohibited for many years; it is hard to imagine now that no music of Milhaud, Hindemith, Mahler, of course Schönberg and Berg, of Weill, Bloch, Schulhoff, Gruenberg, Copland, Gershwin—even Mendelssohn, Meyerbeer, Offenbach, and Saint-Saens—was permitted to be performed.

Those musicians—conductors, composers, teachers, musicologists, critics—who remained in Germany during the decade-long reign of Hitler's Third Reich had absolutely no idea what had transpired elsewhere in new music since the early 1930s. Under the prevailing political exigencies many German and Austrian composers, such as Karl Amadeus Hartmann, Werner Egk, Boris Blacher, Gottfried von Einem, Carl Orff, Günther Raphael, Hugo Distler, and Wolfgang Fortner, withdrew from public activities by going underground and staying out of the Nazi's way.[23] Most of them composed very little or nothing during that entire period. Thus, after the war, they and Germany in general had to rediscover the music not only of its own composers but also those of the rest of the world. Darmstadt and Donaueschingen played the most significant role in that recovery and revitalization process.

The disconnect from musical and cultural developments on the Continent was not quite so dramatic in America and England; still, we didn't know what fascinating compositions Messiaen had been composing during that time—for example, the *Quartet for the End of Time*, his *Trois petites liturgies*, or even the *Turangalila-Symphonie*. Only now, in the early 1950s, were we beginning to hear Boulez's early compositions—his wonderfully precocious Sonata for Flute and Piano (1946), his first two piano sonatas, or the beautiful *Le Soleil des eaux* (1948). Nor had we been able to keep *au courant* with the new works of, say, Dallapiccola or Petrassi in Italy, or what was going on in the Scandinavian countries. We did, however, know lots and lots of recent Russian music, huge quantities of Shostakovich, Prokofiev, Kabalevsky, and Khachaturian. Our continuous acquaintance with Russian music—at least the music that was sanctioned by Stalin and his cultural czar, Aleksey Zhdanov—was in large part because the Russians were for those brief four years our allies.

A very important aspect of my Darmstadt attendance was my meeting two young British composers, Alexander (Sandy) Goehr and Harrison (Harry) Birtwhistle. They and I bonded quickly into an inseparable trio, keen observers of all that went on in Darmstadt, not only in 1954 but also in subsequent years. Sandy, a marvelous composer, became and has been one of my closest, most admired longtime friends.

After more or less digesting and absorbing the music of the older, previously well-established composers such as Milhaud, Hindemith, and Bartók, who were still writing in a basically tonal language, Darmstadt began to tackle atonal and twelve-tone music, principally by Schönberg, Berg, and Krenek. Then in the very early 1950s there was the emergence of young talents such as Stockhausen, Boulez, and Nono, who were writing in a much more advanced style. The discovery of Webern had to wait another year or two. The big Webern years in Darmstadt were 1953 through 1955, the year in which quite suddenly fifteen of his most challenging chamber and orchestral works were programmed. (The year 1955 was also when Webern's music finally broke through in America.) Those first Webern concerts were accompanied by extensive introductory exegeses, mainly by Herbert Eimert (from the West German Radio in Cologne), and by Nono and Stockhausen. It was in 1953 that not one, not two, but three all-Schönberg concerts took place in Darmstadt, offering all four of the composer's string quartets and a number of his major late chamber works. In addition, that was the year in which a whole new genre of music, musique concrète and electronic music, then still in its infancy, was first presented.

In its early years Darmstadt had been abuzz—in rehearsals, concerts, and classrooms—with the genuine excitement of encountering new, never-before-heard music on an almost daily basis. One could savor a cornucopia of new aural, emotional, and intellectual experiences that had been bottled up far too long and were now finally released from their long censorship in Germany. So far, so good.

But it was in the ensuing three years that Darmstadt became increasingly doctrinaire and dogmatic in its programming, and politicized as a major battleground over who or what particular style or system or technique would emerge as the new leadership. I suppose it was inevitable that the temporary creative vacuum left in Europe by the war and postwar conditions would motivate some composers and their publisher publicists to try to fill that void. For a while it appeared that Krenek was ascending to a leading central position, given the great number of Krenek works and lectures that were scheduled not only in Darmstadt but also all over Germany and Austria. But in 1953 and 1954 it was Stockhausen and Boulez who were beginning to move into commanding positions; and by 1957 they had definitely emerged as that new leadership—one might even say dictatorship—now strongly invested in and promoted by a triumvirate of the powerful German radio station network, a small but influential circle of critics, and certain major music publishers, especially Universal Edition (in Vienna and London).

Beginning in 1956 and 1957—I went back to Darmstadt those two years—and for another decade or so thereafter, Darmstadt was dominated not so much by a sense of artistic discovery (and rediscovery) as by constant, often vicious skirmishes between the various stylistic, ideological factions. By the mid and late fifties the content and substance of the lectures, classes, and performances seemed to be primarily determined by a continual jockeying for positions of power and influence in the narrow world of contemporary music—with Steinecke (not a composer or practicing musician) obediently following every twist and turn of the changing stylistic winds. Worldwide, Darmstadt came to be known as the citadel of extreme avant-gardism. A footnote: this power struggle took place in the most remote periphery of conventional musical life. It was completely ignored not only by the average music lover and concertgoer but also by the vast majority of musicians, conductors, and performers, for whom it was totally irrelevant who would dominate the contemporary music scene, not being the slightest bit interested in new music in the first place.

Karlheinz Stockhausen's enormous prominence and influence in the German and international contemporary music scene at the time (much less so in recent decades) is hard to imagine now. There is nothing quite like it in the more fragmented music world of today. Karlheinz and I were close friends in those early years, and it might be well to recount his precipitous rise to worldwide fame, as well as my vacillating relationship with him. To begin with, his half dozen earliest compositions, especially *Zeitmasse* (*Time Measures*) and *Gruppen* (for three orchestras), are unquestionably masterful works, astonishingly innovative breakthroughs. Karlheinz sought me out, and we often sat together at lectures or at dinners. I think he was rather intrigued by my considerable knowledge of the total musical repertory, also by my fluent German. (Remember that most Germans, even relatively intelligent ones, thought that most Americans were cultural and intellectual illiterates.) And he was impressed enough with my *Dramatic Overture* to consider befriending me. I was very impressed by his music, by his brilliant mind and his absolute sense of self-assurance. But that was to change dramatically within a few years.

Nineteen fifty-six was my second time in Darmstadt, a banner year of fascinating concert programming. There was the usual profusion of world premieres, including Stockhausen's trailblazing *Zeitmasse*, performed brilliantly by a quintet of players from the Cologne Radio Orchestra;[24] Boulez's *Le Marteau sans maître*, in its second version (not played all that well by a group of students enrolled at the festival); Gigi Nono's *Canti per tredici*; a fine string quartet by Bruno Maderna; my friend Alexander Goehr's *Fantasia for Orchestra*, Op. 4; a valiant performance of Schönberg's Woodwind Quintet (again Cologne Radio Orchestra musicians), and his

Violin Concerto, magnificently played by Rudolf Kolisch; and, finally, one of Luciano Berio's best early orchestra works, his 1954 *Nones*, unfortunately not played very much nowadays.

All in all it was an exciting, stimulating festival. But Sandy and I began to sense that Boulez and Stockhausen, particularly the latter, were becoming more authoritarian, more domineering in their ad hoc *pronunciamentos* to the assembled students, artists, and publishers. This was not Stockhausen's aforementioned self-assurance; rather, his preachings seemed increasingly removed from any kind of reality. In one particular series of classes he introduced and elaborated endlessly upon what he called his *Formantentheorie* (formant theory), something he had, I think, derived from his work with electronically produced sounds, as in his *Gesang der Jünglinge* (*Song of the Youths*). As he went on about his sonic formants, he kept filling several blackboards with incredibly elaborate mathematical formulas and equations, every day new ones. Sandy and I spoke fluent German, but we really didn't understand a word of what Stockhausen was talking about. And we got the distinct impression that no one else in the room understood anything either. But I noticed that all the younger German composition students were eagerly writing down every precious word uttered by Stockhausen and every mysterious formula. Sandy and I looked at each other, mighty perplexed, and finally decided after three days of this barrage of verbal and mathematical complexities that most of it sounded like poppycock.[25]

I found it all rather discouraging. It seemed that Darmstadt was heading into a kind of authoritarian doctrinairism, with Steinecke clearly in ideological tow or, for all I know, simply oblivious of what was happening. And it got worse that year because it got very political, meaning music-political and nasty.

In my youthful innocence and naïveté, viewing music, composing, and performing as an art and as a basically idealistic pursuit, I was shocked by what I saw and heard. What happened in that year of 1956 was that Stockhausen and Boulez began to disassociate themselves from Nono, those three having been for the previous four or five years considered *the* triumvirate of leaders in regard to the future direction of modern music. Now, suddenly, one began to hear veiled (and sometimes not so veiled) attacks on Nono in classes, lectures, and in the nightly freewheeling discussions that took place in the Marienhöhe, a restaurant and bar located in a woods on a hill above the city, where we all hung out after concerts, usually for half the night. It was clear to me that a power struggle was in the works. Gigi's great successes at Darmstadt every year—he had several commissions from Steinecke—and the admiration in which he was held by just about everybody,[26] apparently presented a problem to Stocki and Pierre. They were longtime friends and comrades-in-arms in the postwar cultural wars, ever since their days as fellow students in Paris under Messiaen. Gigi, a student and protégé of Hermann Scherchen, came from a different intellectual and musical aesthetic. So Pierre and Stocki ganged up on him in their lectures and classes, using not so subtle innuendos, accusing him of a creative naïveté amounting to ineptness, an obsession with simplistic, formulaic, or mechanical patterning—all of this somehow also related to Gigi's membership in Unitá, the Italian Communist Party.

Many of my friends from the United States and England, not only Sandy and Harry, but also Kolisch, Steuermann, and Krenek, were very dismayed at these politicizing shenanigans, and eventually, like me, stopped going to Darmstadt. For his part, Gigi more or less ignored these attacks on him. He simply shrugged them off as silly games, which he would not dignify with a response. He had more important things to do, such as finishing his wonderful, powerful masterwork *Il Canto sospeso* (*The Interrupted Song*) for chorus, three soloists, and orchestra, using as texts excerpts from heartbreaking last letters of European resistance fighters condemned to death during World War II. Every day Gigi lent me some more pages of the score. It looked just marvelous, and fascinating. As I was unable to hear the *Canto sospeso* world premiere by the West German (Cologne) Radio Orchestra with Scherchen conducting, Gigi sent me a tape of the performance. Many years later, I was privileged to give the work its American premiere at Tanglewood—unfortunately still its only performance in this hemisphere (as far as I know).

Sandy, Harry, and I could hardly believe our ears. We had heard about jealousies and rivalries among composers, but we had never experienced anything this aggressive in any academic setting or artistic colony. We were disgusted, not only with these fratricidal goings-on, but also with the doctrinairism that had begun to creep into Darmstadt's concert presentations, programs, and classes. The three of us looked at all this with an increasingly jaundiced eye, finding it either quite sickening or really laughable. We became the "rebellious three," tending not to take Mr. Stockhausen's preachments and pontifications all that seriously. The occasional bluntness of these attacks and political maneuverings, cleverly disguised as serious aesthetic and philosophical symposium discussions, was amazing. I count Boulez and Stockhausen as among the shrewdest, cleverest, most brilliant polemicists I have ever encountered.

Even more disturbing and perplexing was Stockhausen's at times absurdly irrational behavior. One of the most startling of such incidents occurred one afternoon during a dress rehearsal for a concert that same evening featuring works by Schönberg, Milhaud, Ives (his *Unanswered Question*), Hindemith, and, most prominently, Webern's Op. 14 *Six Songs*, after Georg Trakl poems. I happened to be sitting with Stockhausen at that rehearsal, in about the tenth row of the auditorium, when suddenly, during the third Webern song, he stood up, turned to the audience attending the rehearsal, and started ranting and raving against Webern's music—yes, even Webern's. This was ironic and incomprehensible, since Webern's serialism had been sanctified by him just a few years earlier as "the way to the future," and the only way. As far as we all knew, he had considered Webern's music the be-all and end-all of new music—the "only true beauty," he once called it. But here he started shouting hysterically, like Hitler in one of his Nürnberg Party harangues. It was ridiculous and outrageous; he had completely flipped out.

The rehearsal, of course, broke up—in consternation. Screaming, not always intelligibly, Stockhausen was saying something to the effect that this music was hopelessly obsolete, that this music is nothing to build upon, that we must create a radically new art, a new order that must divorce itself totally from the past, even the most recent past.

I grabbed Stockhausen and tried to pull him down. "What's the matter with you? You're breaking up the whole rehearsal." It took a minute or two to calm him down. He then stormed out of the hall and did not attend that evening's concert. I realized that what had triggered his sudden outburst was that Webern's Opus 14, a relatively early work, was worlds away from the later 1930s serial works (such as the Op. 28 String Quartet and Op. 20 String Trio). The Trakl songs, though stylistically and linguistically very adventurous and extreme for their time, still cling basically to traditional concepts of form and continuity, of structure and internal relationships. This was something Stockhausen could no longer tolerate.

That concert happened to be the final one of that year's festival. I was going to leave two days later, but something made me decide to see or meet with Stockhausen once more, partly to say good-bye, and partly to find out if he had perhaps recovered from his hysterical implosion. (Or was it some strange out-of-body experience?) We had lunch on that final day—his wife Doris had come along—but no mention was ever made of the rehearsal two days earlier, not by Stockhausen or Doris and therefore certainly not by me. We talked about other matters. Stockhausen had often picked my brains about music in America, about our orchestras, but especially about any new and important American music. He seemed to be genuinely interested and hoping to hear about some recent, more radical, compositional developments. Like most Germans (and Europeans in general), he had long ago written off the works of what he called "the Copland crowd," that is, Schuman, Diamond, Barber, Harris, Hanson, etc.—of which, by the way, he could not have actually heard very much by 1956.[27] In any case, during this long and very friendly lunch meeting, I happened to tell Stockhausen about John Cage and his explorations with chance methods, with tape and electronic media. I was quite surprised that he seemed to know nothing about Cage, particularly since some of Cage's music had already been presented two years before in Donaueschingen. I told him that although I personally thought of Cage as more of a philosopher, a visionary, and an aesthetic gadfly, rather than a particularly talented "true" composer in the traditional sense, I greatly admired some of his early completely original experimental works with nontraditional instruments and concepts, such as his several *Constructions* for percussion and *Imaginary Landscapes*. I also told him that Cage had by now developed a considerable following and prominence in the American musical scene.

Stockhausen seemed fascinated, entranced particularly with Cage's experiments with chance elements and extemporization, with which Stockhausen had also already experimented in *Zeitmasse*, his solo percussion piece *Zyklus*, and several of his *Klavierstücke*. I am certain I wasn't the only one to inform Stockhausen about Cage. But I may have been the first one; and, if so, I am at least to some extent responsible for Cage and Earle Brown being invited to Darmstadt from 1957 to 1959.

Earlier I mentioned Stockhausen's self-assurance, his sense of absolute certitude. Unfortunately these attitudes developed over the course of a few years into an enormously inflated ego, an arrogance of truly Wagnerian[28] or perhaps even Hitlerian proportions. He became in a sense the new Führer—thank God only in music.

I can't help but think that Stockhausen's attempts to control the modern music scene have their direct parallel in his obsession to achieve total control of all musical materials and component elements in his music. By 1957 he had conceived the radical notion—he loved that word "radical"—of composing music without form, as he put it, "against form." Form per se, not just the old classical forms, had become a hopelessly old-fashioned concept for him, one that belonged on the garbage heap of history. In his radical view of a new contemporary music world—which seemed to me and others not far removed from Hitler's concept of "New German Reich"—music should no longer proceed from the idea that one musical event follows another; musical continuousness (in his mind already once removed from the conventional idea of continuity in music) should not be—*must* not be—the consequence of what had preceded it. It seems to me that this is not only a bad, even a stupid idea, but also that it is in fact and in reality impossible, unachievable, an unrealizable figment of his imagination. For, at the very least, there is the reality *that music exists in time*; and there is no way anybody (except maybe Albert Einstein) can stop the second of two successive events from following its predecessor, thus producing a continuity, which, wanted or not, will produce a form of some kind, good or bad.

It is this arrogance of radicality that I can't stomach, not only because it is such a totally irrational concept, but also because it is, I am sorry to say—and perhaps I can say this better and more believably because of my German background and my close knowledge of German mentalities—that this kind of arrogance is very German, and is found in no other country in such abundance.

Is this perhaps related to the fact that of the four major European countries Germany is the only one that never achieved its social revolution toward democracy until—possibly—the post–World War II era, and even then through evolution rather than any actual revolution. (The one brief attempt at a revolution occurred on June 17, 1953, and only in Communist East Germany.) It is no accident that Hitler and Nazism occurred in Germany, not in France or England or Scandinavia. There is an innate arrogance, an inherent sense of superiority, in Germans—thank God, for the most part either under the surface or in manageable, small, unthreatening dosages. In my several dozen visits to Germany since World War II, I have never failed to witness this typically German conceit and insatiable craving for superiority. One sees it at all levels of German society, but most noticeably and often exaggeratedly among males in everyday life, with ordinary folks such as cab drivers, waiters, store clerks, the whole range of civil servants, and, of course, politicians—happily less so among musicians.

I went back to Darmstadt one more time in 1957. Although the festival's whole atmosphere had become quite stifling and uninviting, with very few interesting performances or premieres that year, it still turned out to be another important visit for me. I had the European premiere of my First String Quartet that year, which led almost instantly to the engraving, printing, and publication of the work by Vienna's Universal Edition, right in the company of the most celebrated works of Stockhausen and Boulez. The Quartet was performed wonderfully by the Ortleb Quartet, four members of the Berlin Philharmonic, terrific dedicated players all of them: Heinz Ortleb, second violin in the orchestra, Karl Plenge, violin, Siegfried Ricklinkat, viola, and Wolfgang Böttcher, cello, later one of the members of the celebrated Berlin Philharmonic Cello Octet.[29] On the same program there was the world premiere of Luciano Berio's String Quartet, a most excellent work, unfortunately overshadowed by some of his more sensational and more publicized compositions. (I have never heard it again, and it seems never to have been recorded.) Significantly, no music of Luigi Nono's was performed that year at Darmstadt. He was there, however, as composer-in-residence and lecturer.

My dormitory roommate that year was the young but already precociously and strangely gifted June Paik, later to make a big career as a world famous video artist. It was also the year I first met György Ligeti, just recently escaped from Hungary, as well as a group of talented young Italians, Luc Ferrari and the two Francos, Evanglisti and Donatoni. That same year there was a veritable invasion of Polish composers, including Henryk Gorecki, Wlodzimierz Kotonski, and Wojciech Kilar; the Communist regime had recently loosened its policies and regulations relating to artistic freedoms and permissions to travel outside the country.

I also met the twenty-six-year-old Toru Takemitsu that summer. When I told him about my great enthusiasm for Japanese gagaku, the ancient court and ceremonial music of Japan dating back to the ninth and tenth centuries, I was much surprised to discover that he knew nothing about that most beautiful of musics, even of its very existence. (He did, of course, soon acquaint himself with his homeland's great historic musical tradition.)

There is one other aspect of the Darmstadt Festival's history that needs to be mentioned. It deals again with something very Teutonic. One of the most common (and most accurate) sayings about Germans is the one that credits them with what is called *Deutsche Gründlichkeit* (German thoroughness). It is a very apt adage. The question is, which ends, which aims, is this thoroughness directed toward: good or evil? Hitler's Third Reich was a staggering example of thoroughness gone totally awry, especially the Nazi's so-called Final Solution, which attempted the total elimination of Jews from the face of the earth. In the works of Goethe and Beethoven one sees the other, the wonderful side of German thoroughness. A corollary to this characteristic of thoroughness is the strong German tendency of going to extremes. Ironically, sometimes these related characteristics manifest themselves in contradictory ways. I saw this happening over the years in Darmstadt. In the beginning, right after World War II, Darmstadt (and Germany in general) started out at an absolute nadir in the presentation of contemporary music. But only a decade later Darmstadt had outperformed every other organization (and country) in that regard, having zoomed through several decades of compositional creativity, crowned with the additional feat of taking over full leadership in the "new music" arena. In its haste, the festival swallowed whole most of what it gobbled up, without ever digesting it thoroughly. That was a typically German example of extremism, paradoxically vitiating the very thoroughness with which Darmstadt had caught up with the rest of the world.

These attitudes expressed themselves in Darmstadt not only in a much too hasty digestion of all that was presented in all of those hundreds of concerts, lectures, and classes, but also very often in a rather shameful rejection of some of the finest works presented in those years. One of the earliest and worst instances of such mindless rejection by the Darmstadt attendees (mostly German rabid Stockhausen admirers), accompanied by extremely rude behavior, was in 1954, after a fine performance of Alban Berg's Violin Concerto. German audiences love to boo at concerts, but this particular audience carried the practice to an extreme. The concert was held up for about ten minutes, as the clamor led almost to a riot. What were these kids thinking? Were they thinking at all? Margie and I were so upset by this stupid and malicious behavior that we almost couldn't sleep that night. At the Marienhöhe afterward a lot of people thought the near riot had just been great fun, not to be taken too seriously. But most of the older folks—Sessions, Krenek, Kolisch, and Steuermann—were outraged. Steinecke thought it was a good, "exciting" evening.

The same thing happened a week later to Dallapiccola's touchingly lyric *Quaderno musicale di Annalibera* (only a bit less raucously), and to Hindemith's Op. 36 *Kammermusik*, as well as to several other works deemed too conservative, too unradical by these young punks. For them anything that sounded even faintly familiar, that wasn't radical, or weird, or crazy, was of no interest. By their rabid behavior they made it impossible for the rest of the audience to enjoy these works. It was very disturbing. Even Steinecke finally got upset!

It was on our second European trip, in 1954, that Margie and I attended the Donaueschingen Festival in its entirety. In 1953 we had been able to get to only one of its three concerts, which featured Luigi Nono's beautiful *Due Espressioni*, Blacher's artful *Orchester Ornament*, and a first-rate performance of Schönberg's *Orchestra Variations*. Unlike Darmstadt, the Donaueschingen Festival[30] encompassed only two days of one weekend, during which, typically, three orchestra concerts were presented. There were no classes or students, only a Sunday morning lecture or roundtable.

The orchestra in Donaueschingen in residence was (and still is) the Southwest German Radio Orchestra in Baden-Baden, a city famous for being the most popular spa resort in all of Germany. Hans Rosbaud, one of the finest conductors of that era, was the conductor. The uniformly excellent programs were put together by Rosbaud, and by Heinrich Strobel, the head of the Southwest German Radio's music division. Strobel's 1953 lecture was entitled "New Music and Humanitas," a brilliant and most enlightening oration, placing new rules and trends in the broader contemporary cultural and aesthetic context.[31] The discussion in 1954 was called "An Open Disputation: How Will it Continue?"; it asked in effect where the future was going to take music. There was no agreement on that, but it was a very lively, at times even heated, discussion.

For me, attending the Donaueschingen Festival over many years, well into the 1960s, was in its own way a tremendous musical education, given Strobel's wide-ranging catholic tastes—and without the contentiousness and creeping doctrinarism of Darmstadt. It was at Donaueschingen that I heard, just in the 1950s (my first four years there), many excellent works, mostly in their world premieres, by Jacques Wildberger, Giselher Klebe, Karel Husa, Karl Amadeus Hartmann, Gilbert Amy, Boris Blacher's *Orchester Ornament*, Nono's *Due Espressione*,[32] Messiaen's *Réveil des oiseaux* and *Oiseaux exotiques*, works by Nikos Skalkottas, Matyas Seiber, Iannis Xenakis (the fabulous *Metastasis* for orchestra), Berg's *Three Orchestra Pieces*, Stravinsky's *Agon*, Elliott Carter's *Orchestra Variations*, a whole evening of Honegger's music, and much, much more.

Beyond all that, in 1954 and again in 1957 jazz and jazz-related works were presented for the first time in Donaueschingen's programs.[33] In 1954 I heard Stravinsky's *Ebony Concerto*, in a flawless, stylistically perfect performance by Kurt Edelhagen's Baden-Baden Jazz Orchestra, as well as the world premiere of Rolf Liebermann's *Concerto for Jazz Band and Symphony Orchestra*, an interesting, ambitious—and instantly controversial—but not unflawed work, which quickly became a worldwide hit.[34] When jazz returned to Donaueschingen in 1957, it did so in full force (although leaning more toward the Third Stream genus) with four works by Eddie Sauter (who was by now arranging for Edelhagen's orchestra), Friedrich Gulda's *Dodo* (dedicated to the amazing pianist, Dodo Marmarosa), Duke Jordan's *Jordu*, André Hodeir's *Parodoxe* (in its world premiere), and as the concert's pièce de résistance, three compositions by John Lewis from his *Fontessa* Suite, played by the Modern Jazz Quartet.

Beyond these pioneering jazz presentations, the 1954 Donaueschingen Festival offered another breakthrough event, added ad hoc to that weekend's concerts. Because it was not listed in the official program, it did not receive much public or media attention, and as far as I know was never mentioned or officially reviewed in American jazz publications. I learned about the concert only by chance, in talking with some of the younger brass players in the Southwest German Radio Orchestra who were avid jazz fans. It was a concert presented as a combination open rehearsal and lecture demonstration, featuring Edelhagen's Jazz Orchestra. It turned out to be a most exciting event, especially in that it featured not only superbly performed advanced jazz compositions and arrangements, leaning very much toward Third Stream—mind you, several years *before* that concept acquired any currency—but also, most amazingly, in one instance, what surely must have been the first twelve-tone improvisation ever. The high point of that concert for me was an atonal composition based on a twelve-tone row, which sounded quite a bit like the early contrapuntal Tristano Trio recordings (such as *I Can't Get Started*), and featuring—astonishingly—an improvised solo on the underlying row by the orchestra's alto soloist, Franz von Klenck. At least it was so announced.

I say "astonishingly" because, as the only twelve-tone composer involved with jazz at that time, I had often enough thought about the possibility of improvising on a row, on a set. But in the end I had always come to the conclusion that such a thing was really a practical impossibility, at least in any strict application of the twelve-tone principle as articulated by Schönberg, one of its main tenets being that none of the pitches in a given set may be reiterated until all twelve have been sounded. (That particular concept was later loosened by Schönberg himself in a variety of ways.) But in either case, I thought there was no way a player would be able to keep track of whether he had repeated a certain pitch before he was supposed to, or had included all the other eleven pitches—especially in a rapid-tempo multinote running passage.

There is obviously no way that I or anyone else would be able to tell in a florid, fast-moving improvised solo whether absolutely strict twelve-tonality was adhered to or not. All I could tell in von Klenck's solo, especially in the more leisurely passages, was that certain recognizable, recurring set groupings were used as motivic connecting material, and that tonal, key-related references were avoided. This was already a major achievement and is, in fact, very much what one of the twelve-tone system's ultimate goals is: the consistent preservation of full chromaticism. But even this presents quite a challenge, especially if in your daily work you are improvising tonally with traditional harmonic changes.

What was so impressive to me was that von Klenck was able—however he did it—to maintain on the one hand this feeling of a total chromaticism, and on the other hand show that his playing didn't forfeit anything in the way of swing—not perhaps the kind of deep, overt swing of the Basie band, but the more subtle, cooler swing of, say, the young Lee Konitz or Gerry Mulligan. It was quite a tour de force.

I made it my business to meet von Klenk after the concert, telling him how impressed I was with this remarkable, unprecedented accomplishment. He confirmed what I had more or less assumed, namely, that he had taken the row and had then improvised on segments of the row in his spare time, every day for weeks on end—trichords, tetrachords, hexachords, whatever.

At first, he admitted, he stumbled a lot; there was the seemingly unavoidable intrusion of tonal elements. But as he became more familiar with the row's component subsets and with its variant forms and transpositions, he could play with them, either separately and repeated in various groupings or pulled together into longer segments, virtually at will. The material had over time become as familiar to him as blues changes or songs such as *Body and Soul*. In fact, he said, after a while he was so at ease with the set and its intervallic content that he began to dream about it and practice it in his dreams. He slept it, ate it, drank it, breathed it. He said he was very excited about the prospects for tonally freer improvisations, and that in the next stage of development he would be working with not only transpositions of the row but also its inversions and retrogrades.

It was also at that concert that I met two persons who were quickly to become very close friends, and who played very important jazz-related roles in my life. One was Joachim Behrendt, in the 1950s and 1960s the most influential jazz critic in Germany, whose *Das Jazzbuch* (1953), an excellent succinct history of jazz, was to Germany and Europe in general what Marshall Stearns's *The Story of Jazz* (1956) was to America. The other was Horst Lippmann, a concert impresario who first brought the Modern Jazz Quartet to Europe in the early 1950s, as well as many other jazz groups, and later became, with Philip Rau, through their joint concert agency, the major presenters and promoters of blues artists and rhythm-and-blues groups on the European continent.

Behrendt had provided the introductory commentary at that Donaueschingen jazz concert, and so informatively that I felt I must get to know this man. I sought him out the next day and, as happened so often in my life, embarked on what developed into a lifelong professional friendship.

It was John Lewis who first told me about Horst Lippmann, whom he had met in 1948 in Frankfurt, when John was on tour in Europe with Dizzy Gillespie's big band. I heard so much about Horst's heroic behavior during the war as part of a small resistance group in Frankfurt, and what a wonderful, generous person he was, that by the time I met him in 1954, it was as if I had known him all my life. Horst did become one of my closest and most admired friends. As a young man he had, in 1942, joined a small group of mostly amateur musicians who were fascinated with American jazz, and who held forth under the name "Harlem Club" in one of Frankfurt's better bars—this at a time when jazz "in the black mode" (called "Nigger-Jew" music by Nazi authorities) had for already many years been condemned as degenerate music. Anyone having any association with it as a performer or listener risked harassment by brown shirt functionaries or, much worse, arrest and incarceration, and disappearance in Nazi death camps.

Horst, whose parents owned one of the best hotels in the center of Frankfurt, played the drums, but occasionally also doubled on bass. His fellow players in the Harlem Club, mostly upper-middle-class teenagers, were Emil Mangelsdorff, saxophonist and accordionist, Hans Otto Jung (an economics student), pianist, and Carlo Bohländer, trumpet. These young musicians, including Emil's younger brother, Albert, were ardent believers in social democracy and hated the Nazi dictators. The group members expressed their protest not only by courageously continuing to perform at the club, in defiance of Göbbels's oppressive policies regarding jazz and the Gestapo's constant surveillance, but also in various acts of civil disobedience and sabotage. Horst and Emil told me that they would disable city street cars during rush hours, pile large rocks on train tracks to obstruct troop trains, puncture tires on police and Gestapo cars—dangerous activities at the height of the war. Just listening to the news or to jazz on the BBC could earn you instant incarceration. In the end the Gestapo did manage to suppress the Harlem Club. Horst was subjected to endless personal harassment; Emil was jailed for a couple of years and released only to be drafted and sent off to the Russian front.

After the war Horst inherited the Hotel Continental from his father, which was quite profitably located smack in the middle of Frankfurt (always Germany's major banking and commercial center), and only a few hundred feet from the city's immense central railroad station. Horst was provided with sufficient fiscal security, permitting him to indulge in his pioneering efforts of bringing jazz groups from America after the war and touring them throughout Germany and Austria. Indefatigable in his efforts on behalf of jazz, Horst created the German Jazz Federation, and founded two jazz clubs in Frankfurt: Storyville (in 1956, with Carl Bohländer) and, in 1949, the Jazz Keller (Cellar) in a basement club near his hotel, which quickly became *the* hangout in Frankfurt for jazz musicians and jazz lovers. That's where I first heard the late Albert Mangelsdorff, the phenomenal jazz trombonist, and David Amram, pioneer jazz hornist and composer. The reader may imagine my consternation—and delight—on one warm summer evening in 1954, walking toward Horst's hotel, hearing jazz sounds—of all things on a horn—floating toward me from some basement cavern. It was Amram playing in the Jazz Keller. In the German context of that time it was an almost surrealistic experience to find an American jazz hornist in a German jazz club.

As John Lewis had told me, Horst was indeed a most generous person, paying musicians very generous fees and putting them up at his hotel almost always gratis. On all the numerous occasions that Margie and I—later with our two children—stayed at his hotel, Horst never let me pay one cent, except for the meals we might take there. One of the truly great human beings I was privileged to meet in my life, he died nineteen years ago, after decades of enduring serious liver and kidney problems, which even the best doctors in Germany and the most expensive medical treatments could not cure. I miss Horst terribly.

I also owe him 225 German marks, which he lent me once in 1960, and never allowed me to pay back.

I relish the memory of those first trips to Europe; like any first experiences they are indelibly impregnated in my mind. I will not attempt to recount all that Margie and I saw, encountered, and heard in the way of music. These trips were filled with very enjoyable experiences and they were also, for us youngsters, profoundly enlightening and informative. As I think back, I realize that we approached them the same way we had assailed New York's cultural life in our first years together there. But Europe was another matter, a much larger territory. Driven by that insatiable curiosity that we both were blessed with, we never spared ourselves in applying our full energies to exciting new experiences—no casual, relaxed sightseeing for us. Each twenty-four-hour day was already by definition too short.

On our first visit to Europe, in 1953, we crossed the Atlantic on the Statendam, one of the Holland America Line's smaller ocean liners. Those seven days alone were a wondrous, most relaxing experience—wondrous because what the Dutch line provided, even in third class, was staggering to us. The Statendam's five-course meals, with multiple choices in each course, were something we had only heard and dreamed of, but never thought we would ever actually be able to savor. After our hectic around-the-clock life in New York, lolling around on deck chairs in the sunshine, swimming in the pool, playing shuffle board, leisurely reading in the lounge or the well-stocked ship's library was in itself a whole new experience.

We spent five days in Holland, split between Rotterdam, The Hague, and Amsterdam, overwhelmed by the natural beauty and amazing neatness and cleanliness all around us. We were finally seeing the legendary windmills, the myriad canals, the endless tulip fields, and, everywhere, the millions of bicyclists. To see at every major street crossing in the morning rush hour some three or four hundred bicyclists lined up, waiting for the light to change, filling the entire width of the road and backed up twenty deep, ready to sprint forward, is an amazing sight to behold—very much like the amassment of humanity at the start of a Boston or New

York marathon. The fact is that in Holland and many other European countries (Belgium, Germany), for many years after the war the vast majority of people did not own cars and rode to work on bicycles. Although nowadays one may still see lots of bicycles in those countries, almost everyone, starting in the 1960s, began to acquire automobiles, thus relegating bicycle riding to a secondary status.

Our first two days in Holland were spent in Scheveningen, a kind of suburb of The Hague, and Holland's most popular seaside resort. We stayed at the four-star Kurhaus, the largest and most venerable of the thirty or so hotels that line the mile-long beachfront. Looking down from our fifth-floor balcony, as far as the eye could see, the beach was jam-packed with people. (The scene was reminiscent of those famous pictures of mass crowds at Coney Island in the 1920s.) Not surprising, of course; it was the end of August, and everyone was trying to take advantage of the waning summer days. We quickly abandoned our original intention of heading immediately for the beach, and went later on a long, magical, late-night stroll, in moonlit semidarkness, a calmed North Sea constantly at our side. The only sounds, except for some Dixieland music wafting over from a nearby hotel jazz club, came from the ripplings of little wavelets washing onto the beach—there was just the two of us, lost in our own thoughts, marveling at how beautiful life can be.

A really big surprise was to learn, right after our arrival, that The Hague's Residentie Orchestra was giving a concert that night in the Kurhaus's concert hall, conducted by none other than my new friend Antal Dorati. I managed to reach Tony, who was also staying at the Kurhaus, to get us tickets in the balcony directly overlooking the stage and the orchestra. Whether it was our general state of euphoria—the excitement of our first night in Europe, luxuriating in one of Europe's grandest old-world hotels—or whether it was really as outstanding a concert as we thought it was, I can no longer parse out. But it sure sounded good. It was a typical Dorati program, the kind he always excelled in: Rimsky-Korsakoff's *Russian Easter* Overture, Tchaikovsky's Fourth Symphony, and ending with Kodaly's *Hary Janos* Suite—three of his best warhorses.

Of the many highlights of our five-day stay in Holland, the one that stands out most vividly in my memory was a visit to Madurodam, in The Hague. This parklike wonderland contained in perfect miniature replication virtually all of Holland: its many great cities (in composite), harbors, canals (replete with bridges, barges, and sightseeing boats), immense tulip fields, windmills, magnificent churches and museums, even its famous airport, Schiphol, with cars, ships, planes, and trains all moving at exactly the relative speeds that one would observe in a bird's-eye view of the country. The park is crisscrossed with a network of walking paths, most of them sunken and thus invisible to the sightseer, and ingeniously set at varying levels, so that, for example, in the exhibit's section devoted to agriculture and rural canals one sees everything at eye level as if one were driving by in a car, gazing at huge stretches of tulip fields, each tulip actually only a millimeter high. One didn't even have to squint one's eyes to get the feeling one was viewing the real thing. Talk about virtual reality!

We visited Madurodam many times again, later with our children. On every visit we were fascinated to see that the park had been once again updated and expanded, replicating some of the newer high-rises and skyscrapers in Rotterdam and Amsterdam, and huge new business complexes (like Philips). Even the constant expansion of Schiphol airport has been kept pace with.

The strangest episode in our entire Holland stay occurred on our last day there. We were advised by our New York travel agent, Hendrien de Leeuw (born and raised in Amsterdam), to be sure to have dinner at the Five Flies, "the best restaurant" in Amsterdam. We made a reservation on our last night there, and when we were ushered to our table in a corner booth, I saw that it was adorned with, of all things, a large plaque reading "George Szell's Personal Table." Aghast, I told the maitre d' that I couldn't sit there. "Please give us another table."

Puzzled and rather offended, he said: "But this is one of our most prized tables!"

"I don't care. Please give us another table; otherwise we'll have to go somewhere else." Amazed at my adamancy, he offered: "Well, you'll have to wait about a half hour, but we could have another booth then."

"We'll wait."

When we came back a half hour later, he took us to a booth, named for—of all people—Pierre Monteux. We couldn't stop laughing.

"Is this one okay?," the maitre d' said, with a touch of sarcasm in his voice.

"You bet. This one is *fine*."

The maitre d' walked away, shaking his head, probably thinking: these Americans are mighty strange people.

Half a century later, my behavior seems rather churlish and silly. But it was a clear indication that I hadn't forgiven Szell for his malicious torturing of me my first year at the Met, and, conversely, my great love and admiration for Monteux.

From Amsterdam we went by train via Nijmegen to Krefeld to visit, for the first time in almost twenty years, my mother's three sisters, Lulu, Hedwig, and Gretel. We brought them all kinds of gifts from America, mostly very practical things—all three families lived very humbly at near-poverty level—and they in turn lavished their choicest culinary skills on us, each trying to outdo the others in the baking department. It was a remarkable example of how much human creativity could be achieved with the most modest of means.

I was really astonished one evening when Hedwig and I engaged in an extensive discussion about modern music, actually initiated by her. She wanted to know more about my music, and about contemporary music in general in America. I was surprised at her interest in this subject. At least once a year I had sent her care packages around Christmastime, as Margie and I and my parents did with all of our German relatives. But in her letters Hedwig had never mentioned anything about music. She was not in any sense a musician, not even as an amateur; and yet, she was, as I now learned, a seriously knowledgeable music lover. It wasn't long into our discussion when I heard her expound enthusiastically about the music of Schönberg and Berg. When I expressed my amazed surprise, she said it was because of the German radio network, especially the nearby WDR (*Westdeutcher Rundfunk* [West German Radio]), which programmed a lot of new music all the time, and which she had come to find very interesting. I had a remarkable conversation with her about Schönberg and many of his orchestral works. She confessed that she loved Schubert and Brahms more, but that she found much of *diese neue Musik* (this new music) quite intriguing, even though she didn't fully understand it. "You know," she said, "repeated listening brings a certain familiarity." Over the years I was to discover that Hedwig's interest in contemporary music wasn't really all that exceptional, that lots of people listened regularly to the modern music programs the German radio stations presented as a matter of course. I tried to imagine such a two-hour discussion in New York with my music-loving friends, even with most of my musician colleagues, and couldn't envision it at all—except with someone like Milton Babbitt or Elliott Carter or Harry Peers.

Some time before our trip to Europe I had received a letter from a horn player in the WDR orchestra, Fritz Straub, who said that he had heard great things about my *Symphony for Brass and Percussion* and wanted desperately to perform the work, sight unseen, in Germany—this at a time when the piece had had only two performances, three thousand miles away: the premiere in Cincinnati and one in New York. The enthusiastic, enterprising tone of Straub's letter intrigued me, and so I decided to contact him. I had a sense, reading between the lines, that this man was somebody unusual, and an interesting character.

In Cologne, being only a forty-five minute trolley ride from Krefeld, we headed for the radio station, I to a rehearsal of the orchestra, Margie to the *4711* store (the famous German perfume), located right next to the radio station. I arrived just when the orchestra was having its half-hour break. The stage was empty—all the musicians were in the canteen (the radio station's cafeteria)—except for a strikingly handsome young man with tousled curly black hair who was sitting at the edge of the stage, legs crossed nonchalantly, eating an apple. Could that be Straub? I was really struck by the appearance of this young fellow, apparently in his early twenties. He didn't look German; wasn't dressed like a German.[35] He looked Italian, a bit dandyish. Even sitting there unmoving, munching calmly on an apple, there was something instantly attracting about him.

Well, it wasn't Straub. It turned out to be the first oboe of the orchestra, Lothar Faber, and as I was quickly to find out, a terrific oboist with a flashy virtuosic technique and a wonderfully expressive, rich, warm tone—the kind of exciting playing it was impossible to ignore. I was astonished to learn that he was a very close friend of Dimitri Mitropoulos. (I had heard that Mitropoulos had been conducting the Cologne Radio Orchestra for quite a few years, that it was his favorite orchestra in all the world, and that the love affair was reciprocal).[36]

Lothar introduced me to Straub, fourth horn in the orchestra. As anticipated, he was a real live wire, a fast talker bristling with energy, overconfidence, and career ambitions. Margie, with her sensitive intuitions, less gullible and more cautious than I, warned me after she had met Straub a few times to be careful, "that man is out to exploit you and your name—you know, first horn at the Met, famous American composer—obviously out to garner the European premiere of your *Brass Symphony*." That judgment may have sounded too harsh, but it was essentially correct. I soon learned that some of Straub's musician colleagues were also leery of him and his braggadocio ways. To this day, I don't quite know what to make of him. He could bedazzle you with his charm, his sassy, witty repartees; and he could overwhelm you with what often turned out to be merely big talk. And you could never tell whether he was just exaggerating and fantasizing.

For all his crazy bragging, Straub was a very good horn player, a good, solid musician, and an avid advocate of contemporary music. I don't know what kind of a conductor he was, but since he had studied with Hermann Scherchen for a couple of years, I assumed that he must have some talent and proficiency. He also seemed very well informed about goings-on in Donaueschingen and Darmstadt, both pro and con, and was most enthusiastic about Luigi Nono and his music, and also about Giselher Klebe—enthusiasms that I shared. When I wrote him that I was somewhat disappointed in the Darmstadt rendition of my *Dramatic Overture*, he suggested that there were only two or three German orchestras and conductors that could interpret a contemporary work authentically and convincingly, and that the Frankfurt orchestra under the direction of Ernest Bour was not one of them.

Straub was a great admirer of my *Brass Symphony*, or at least constantly said so, and also showered me regularly with lavish compliments in his letters. (Margie again wondered how much one should trust and believe him.)[37] I also liked Straub's passionate antiauthoritarian views, a distinct rarity in Germany in earlier times, although attitudes have dramatically changed since then. In all of his many varied enterprises Straub never sought support, financial or otherwise, from any governmental agency or bureaucracy, which was usually done automatically in Socialist countries such as Germany. There, almost any activity or enterprise in the arts is subsidized by the government. Fritz Straub was proud of his artistic independence.

He was a master at organizing a variety of unusual musical groups and educational projects. He loved managing things and people. I thought of him as an entrepreneur, at a time when entrepreneurship was practically unknown in Germany. One of Straub's early, rather unusual undertakings was to acquire a bargelike boat on which to train and conduct various-sized brass or wind ensembles while cruising up and down the Rhine River.[38] And that is what Straub had in mind for my *Brass Symphony*: a performance on his barge. I wondered how he, three thousand miles away, could have heard about the piece, which was only three years old. The answer offers a striking example of how personal connections and coincidence can cause something important to happen that otherwise could never have occurred. It was my friend Roland Johnson, to whom I had previously sent an acetate recording of one of the *Brass Symphony*'s earliest performances, who told Straub about the piece, extolling it highly. Roland and Straub, I found out, had both studied conducting with Scherchen in Switzerland and knew each other. At some point Roland heard that a performance of the *Brass Symphony* had taken place somewhere in the Rhineland, but didn't know by whom, until I told him half a century later when the subject came up—again by pure chance—in a phone conversation.

Straub's groups were always made up of talented young players, mostly students but also accomplished amateurs, nonprofessionals. He was both the conductor and coach-teacher. I never knew him to use professionals or any of his orchestra colleagues; I think he didn't hold many of them in particularly high regard, right or wrong, probably out of a sense of his own superiority. He financed most of his projects with his own money, although in some of his more ambitious enterprises he charged the students a modest fee. In one of his first cruise-touring ventures the concerts took place outdoors on the deck of his flatboat barge. The players slept and ate in youth hostels in towns along the Rhine.

He eventually played my *Brass Symphony* at several of those concerts. I don't know how well things went, since I didn't hear any of the performances or anything about them—even from him. Very strange! He never mentioned the performances in his letters. I only knew from a few Cologne colleagues, such as Lothar Faber, that some performances had taken place, and that the group Straub had put together was rumored to be very good.

A year or so later, Straub exchanged the barge for a larger boat, which he called a yacht. Actually, in a little photo he sent me it looked more like a tugboat, maybe fifty feet long, with two tiny, cabinlike housings (one was the bridge), and a few bunks below deck, with two masts for sails. With this he planned to sail the Rhine and the Maas (in Holland) with a thirteen-piece group, so he could do Mozart's *Gran Partita* and Dvořák's *Serenade for Winds*. This time the concerts were going to take place in concert halls, theatres, movie houses, and hotel lounges along the Rhine and the Maas. He wrote to me that he had booked some twenty-five concerts for a four-week tour. But in his subsequent letters he never mentioned whether that tour actually happened.

Straub's dreams and visions grew ever more grandiose and ambitious. For the next stage, he and Ingrid bought a real yacht, an eighty-foot motorized sailboat for $16,000, with seventeen beds and, if absolutely necessary, accommodations for a dozen more. The boat's cruising range, he bragged, could take him nonstop from Cologne to New York. He named his yacht *Pro Musica*, hired a sixty-two-year-old retired captain (who wanted no salary, just bed and board), and one young crewman. Ingrid would be the *chef de cuisine*. Also on board, he had a blind dog. In order to purchase the yacht, Straub and Ingrid sold their house and all its furniture, and most of their clothes and all kinds of other belongings, essentially pulling up their roots in Cologne; Straub also left the orchestra, with its reliable, steady employment. The pair intended to spend the rest of their lives on their yacht, sailing the high seas, and even dreamed of a cruise around the world.

Straub wrote me that he had already booked twenty concerts in South America with an agency in Buenos Aires, which was promising at least twenty more bookings along the entire east coast, mainly in Brazil and Uruguay. In a newspaper interview he spoke of planning a months-long cruise tour to Holland, Belgium, France, and Spain; from there a side trip circling the Mediterranean, and thence via the Canary Islands to Africa, eventually sailing to

Lambaréné in Gabon to visit Albert Schweitzer and play Bach brass transcriptions for him. Straub even knew that the last leg of that trip would have to be done in a boat smaller than his yacht, since the Ogowe River, with its many hidden sandbars, would be impassable for the *Pro Musica*. He had already written Schweitzer, who wrote back that he was looking forward to his visit. Straub told everybody he was "in final negotiations" with a film company about making a documentary of the event, to be called *Serenade in the Jungle*.

To me, however, he wrote of even grander plans. He wanted me to help him organize a six-month course of study and performance on a cruise "for American students," visiting "many countries and continents" and meeting with composers everywhere. He was very particular about *my* selecting the young American woodwind and brass players, all to be unmarried and therefore able to sign up for extensive tours. He asked me to find especially good players who would, on the side, be willing to learn German and immerse themselves in German literature, culture, and history. Since his "floating academy" or "miniature swimming hotel," as he called the *Pro Musica*, would not be bound to any particular city or country, he envisioned traveling to "the most remote regions of Europe, encountering different cultures, always at the same time honing our musical skills." He expected the many Amerika Houses, located in all of Europe's major cities, to help in organizing the itinerary and in booking concerts. I was to help him with publicizing and promoting his plans in American music schools—just my cup of tea, as if I had nothing better to do. He also hinted that he hoped to be invited to come to the States to help with the planning and, as he put it obliquely, "to kind'a look around." (Margie said, "You see, he wants you to help him get a job here.")

At this point my memory fails me and I can't recall the rest of the saga. I don't know whether I ever responded to his letter about the American expedition. I'm pretty sure I wouldn't have wanted to respond, and I probably didn't. I never heard from him again, except that he once sent me a quite favorable review—with no letter—about a concert he conducted in Nippes, a suburb of Cologne, given by his Cologne Orchestra Society, evidently another amateur group he had formed—a "music lovers' association," the reviewer called it. But this time it was Straub leading a full symphony orchestra, in a program of the *Meistersinger* Overture, Grieg's Piano Concerto, and Schumann's "Rhenish" Symphony.

I never found out what happened to Straub and his yacht. As quickly as he waltzed into my life, he vanished just as suddenly: the strange case of Mr. Fritz Straub.

From Krefeld Margie and I traveled to Berlin. On the way we were held up a long time in Helmstedt at the West-East border by the Soviet and East German border guards—sheer lawless chicanery—causing us to arrive two hours late in Berlin. I was so excited to be in Berlin, among other things hoping somehow to meet my idol, Wilhelm Furtwängler. Hendrien de Leeuw had gotten us a room in a very nice pension in Charlottenburg, one of the finest districts of the city, with easy access to West Berlin's many theatres and opera houses. To our surprise the opera on our first evening in Berlin was Gottfried von Einem's *Der Prozess* (*The Trial*), based on Franz Kafka's masterpiece of the same name. We both loved it, and were especially overwhelmed by the glorious singing of Elfriede Trötschel, with her rich, warm, expressive soprano voice, and Erich Witte as *K*, and the superb staging by Günther Rennert, at the time Germany's reigning opera director.[39] I was particularly impressed by the orchestra, conducted by Arthur Rother (a seasoned old hand at opera), and by the outstanding horn section. My heart lept with joy, hearing the wonderful ensemble balance of the four horns—rather than the usually overly prominent first horn accompanied by three barely audible satellite horns. Although I didn't know von Einem's opera, hearing it for the first time that night, I thought I detected some most remarkable fourth horn playing. This turned out to be the case, as I heard the orchestra in further rehearsals and performances over the next six nights, including

Beethoven's *Fidelio*, as well as three of Wagner's *Ring* operas. In *Rheingold* the opera starts on a low E-flat pedal point, the fourth horn initiating a series of successive rising, canonically staggered E-flat arpeggios in all eight horns, musically depicting the waves of the Rhine River. I had never heard that *Rheingold* opening played so well in all eight horns—even with my horn section in the Met.

It never was a problem in Germany or Austria for me, a German speaker and principal horn of the Met, to gain free access to any opera performance or rehearsal through my horn colleagues. I arranged to meet the opera's horn section on our second night in Berlin, in the canteen, the house cafeteria, after a terrific performance of *Fidelio*, in which the three horns had played superbly in the "Abscheulicher" aria. We had such a good time together that we closed up the place at two a.m. The fourth horn player, with the impeccable control in the low register and a beautiful rich tone—as big as a house yet not obese or heavy—was Paul König. He played with a cultivated tone that even my teacher, Bob Schulze, and Silvio Coscia, my partner at the Met—as good as both were—could not have matched. König had been in the famed Dresden State Opera for many years before coming to Berlin. The first horn was Hans Streuber, whose playing was completely secure and relaxed, as well as beautifully expressive. He never used an assistant in the heavy, long Wagner operas—meaning he had tremendous endurance—and I never heard him miss a note. It was enough to make one envious. The second and third horn were Oskar Tuchs and Günter Köpp, both excellent, who helped to make that quartet one of the most homogenous horn sections I have ever heard. What I particularly admired was that Tuchs and König were true "low" horn players, as in the classic horn playing tradition that goes way back to the early nineteenth century, but which began to vanish in the 1950s and 1960s when the trend among horn players was to want to play only first horn—for more fame and more money. As a result, with some very rare exceptions, horn sections in general have for a long time not been sonically well balanced.

My fondest hope was, of course, to hear the Berlin Philharmonic, either in rehearsal or concert, and, above all, to perhaps get to meet Furtwängler. Since you can't just walk into a rehearsal of an orchestra, uninvited, unknown—the usual job of the forbidding-looking stage door guards is to keep strangers out—I asked Streuber to call his colleague, Martin Ziller, his counterpart at the Berlin Philharmonic, to see if he could sneak me into the Philharmonic's first rehearsal of the next week, offering to meet him at the stage door a half hour before the rehearsal. And so it was arranged. Ziller assured me that there would be no problem in meeting Furtwängler after the rehearsal.

The rehearsal turned out to be the one and only rehearsal for a concert that same evening of an all-Schubert program, the *Rosamunde* Overture and the "Great" C Major Symphony. The orchestra had played these two pieces, I would guess, at least a dozen times in the years since Furtwängler took over the orchestra's reins in 1922. It was an epiphanous experience for me, hearing that remarkable orchestra and watching Furtwängler rehearse. How many people can claim to have witnessed a Furtwängler rehearsal? And then meeting him and chatting with him for almost half an hour after the rehearsal.

The rehearsal began with *Rosamunde*. I could hardly believe my ears when the strings sang on

that most beautiful opening theme,  ,

near the beginning of the Overture. It sounded so beautiful to me, that rich, pure, saturated string sound for which the Berlin Philharmonic was so famous, further enhanced by the warm acoustics in the empty auditorium. But to my astonishment Furtwängler stopped conducting a little more than half way through that melodic statement, with a slightly irritated, wiggly gesture of the hands. He turned to the first violins with an expression that managed to combine a somewhat injured look with a benevolent paternal smile, and said: "Aber, meine Herren, das muss doch schön sein (But, gentlemen, this has to be truly beautiful)." Another impatient gesture. "Noch einmal! (Come on, once again!)" If the first time had been inordinately beautiful, the second was magical, luminous, transcendent. Furtwängler smiled, gratified; his men had not let him down. I don't know what he considered unsatisfactory the first time, it sounded more than satisfactory to me. I queried Ziller about the matter. He said: "You know, he often teases us, chides us, especially at first rehearsals after a couple of days off. You know, the typical Monday morning rehearsal—where sometimes we aren't quite with it yet; cobwebs in the brain."

I was thrilled beyond words to have this chance to hear Furtwängler rehearse, of all pieces, Schubert's great C Major Symphony. I knew that Schubert was his favorite composer, even above Beethoven and Brahms, and that he had a special affinity for this particular work. I have already related what a revelatory experience it was for me when, in 1942, at age sixteen, I heard the Berlin Philharmonic and Furtwängler in this piece on my father's shortwave radio. Now I was going to hear it live, in full acoustic reality.

Many of the wondrous sounds of that Monday morning rehearsal are still in my mind, my inner ear—even after more than half a century. Most of what I heard in that rehearsal surpassed anything in previous performances or recordings of that work, including even Toscanini's and Beecham's renditions, which, though very good, don't quite catch the magical mood and feeling experienced in that rehearsal. I saw and heard with my own eyes and ears what people often called the "quasi-hypnotic power" that Furtwängler could exercise over his musicians and audiences. The rehearsal was a perfect example of what we musicians sometimes experience when a rehearsal rises to an unforeseeable, inexplicable level of transcendence that can never be replicated.[40] What stands out most in my memory is that rich, pure sound of the strings—yet not thick or heavy. There was something luminous, a kind of inner radiance in the sound; and they all seemed to really *feel* the music, making it sing, especially in cantilena passages. I also saw and heard Furtwängler's legendary way with slow or moderate tempos, endowing them with a deliberate, expansive grandeur, without the feeling of dragging the tempo. Similarly, it was the first time that I saw his famous hard-to-understand wiggly downbeat gestures, not only in certain agitated, urgent passages, but also in single-stroke downbeats; that's why the orchestra was sometimes not quite together. Indeed, I wondered how the musicians played as well together as they did, but I soon realized that they watched the concertmaster a lot and often just ignored Furtwängler's jittery, erratic gesturing. Ziller told me: "I somehow don't watch his beat; I watch his eyes and his face. Anyway, we know him so well. He could probably stand on his head and we could still follow him."

Although I was well aware of Furtwängler's renowned penchant for taking considerable liberties with tempo indications and pacing, I was rather surprised that he took so few, but that, on the other hand, the two liberties that he *did* take were rather extreme. (For the record, there are no tempo variations, such as *accelerandos* or *ritards*, indicated in the entire score, except for the one major tempo change in the first movement.) But as so often happened with Furtwängler, as one sat there thinking, "gee, that's not right, that's not in the score," one realized that it was accomplished so beautifully, so convincingly, that one felt compelled to accept the deviation. That's what happened with a huge, long *ritardando*—not in Schubert's score—that Furtwängler made in the second movement. I remember thinking of Schumann's famous encomium regarding Schubert's Ninth: "diese himmliche Länge (this heavenly length)." The *ritard* took forever, but it was so beautiful.

Furtwängler stopped only three or four times in that entire rehearsal of the fifty-two-min-
ute Symphony. One of these pauses concerned a particular interpretational cliché—which
some famous conductor must have adopted somewhere in the distant past; maybe it was Furtwängler himself—that is definitely not indicated in Schubert's score. It is that place in the very
beginning of the third movement (Scherzo), well-known to all orchestra musicians—I already
knew about it in my early teen years—where conductors have made a tiny caesura, like a hic-
cup, before the fourth bar. That theme statement is repeated five more times in that movement. When Furtwängler came to the second iteration of that phrase, he suddenly stopped,
smiled at the orchestra, and said: "You know, it's not good to repeat a joke twice; it is never
funny the second time." Then, shaking his head, baffled: "But why do I like it so much," referring to the inserted caesura, "that I want to do it again and again (*immer wieder*)?" "I can't help
myself," he said with a sigh.

In that same (Scherzo) movement there was another very special moment, a downward cas-
cading five-bar passage, starting in the first violins and ending in the low basses. It looks easy,

, but it is very difficult to bring off

perfectly with each section playing its six notes at exactly the same dynamic level and exactly
the same feeling and identical tiptoe-light articulation. As the Berlin strings played it that
morning, flawlessly every time—it is repeated four more times—I could only think of a beautiful necklace, with thirty identical pearls strung in an impeccably spaced sequence. I have never
heard that passage played that well again, not even on the Berliner's commercial recording of
the Schubert Ninth—and, yes, including in my own performances of the Symphony, although
I have tried so hard every time to achieve the same pearly effect.

One of the Symphony's many magical and ingenious passages occurs in the finale movement,
where its second subject (played by the woodwinds) is accompanied by a vivacious, bouncy,
sparkling triplet figure in the first violins and violas, and by cellos and basses in a vaulting piz-

zicato line [music notation] .[41] In all

the performances and recordings I have ever heard, this dancing triplet figure is barely audible,
either underplayed or underrecorded, or played with such a flabby articulation that it might
as well be left out. Furtwängler realized that this sprightly repetitive figure, along with the
underlying rising and falling pizzicato line in the basses and cellos, is the rhythmic motor that
drives this music forward in such a catchy way, energizing the winds' melodic line. This second
subject runs on for seventy-nine bars each time it is recapitulated, and one is overjoyed as a
listener when it keeps coming back. The Berlin strings delivered that triplet figuration with an
amazingly crisp, crystal-clear articulation and almost jazzlike swing that has to be heard to be
believed.

After the rehearsal Ziller took me to see Furtwängler, where instead of the hasty five minutes I expected to have with him, he kept me for nearly half an hour. I don't know whether he
was taken by my fluent German or whether he was pleased to meet a young American musician admirer—Ziller had told him that I was not only an ardent fan, but also first horn at the
Met—or whether it was my reminding him that my father had been his principal violist in
Mannheim in 1919, and had played *The Rite of Spring* with him in New York in 1927. Maybe it
was all three. In any case we had a marvelous chat. He wanted to know all about his conductor

colleagues, most of whom he had not seen or heard from for decades—Reiner, Walter, Stiedry, Mitropoulos, Szell—as well as other émigré musicians, some of whom were Jews he had helped to escape to America. This included former players in his orchestra such as Szymon Goldberg, Hugo Kolberg, and Joseph Schuster. He also asked about his old friend Hindemith, and eventually about the state of new music in America. I filled him in about some of our leading lights (Copland, Schuman, Piston, Perle, Carter, Babbitt, the young Kirchner, etc.), and our two warring stylistic camps, the neoclassicists and the twelve-toners. At one point he interrupted me with: "Verstehen Sie diese neue Musik (Do you understand this new music)?," mentioning Boulez and Stockhausen. When I told him that I not only understood and admired much of it, but that I also wrote in this particular style, he looked a little dismayed. I told him, "but I also admire very much Blacher,[42] von Einem, Egk, Raphael." In all this time he never mentioned his own composing and that he had recently recorded two of his symphonies. I knew it was a painful subject for him, his own music having never been considered very favorably. I was glad that he didn't bring up the matter.

Although he seemed rather animated in our little session, I could sense that this was a very lonely man who felt rather rejected and isolated from much of the music world, a hero to some but a villain to many more who never forgave him for staying in Germany and, allegedly, collaborating with the Nazi regime.

As I said my good-byes and wished him "toi, toi, toi" for tonight's concert, he invited me and my wife to sit in his box. I had to excuse us since we had tickets, very expensive ones, to *Waiting for Godot* at the Schlosspark Theatre. I walked all the way back to our Charlottenburg pension, floating on a cloud. Had this been just a dream?[43]

Beckett's *Waiting for Godot* that evening was *the* artistic event of our entire 1953 trip, the supreme highlight, even surpassing Furtwängler's Schubert rehearsal. I consider it the most remarkable theatre experience of my life (along with Brecht and the Berliner Ensemble's *Galileo* a few years later). *Waiting for Godot* is one of the very greatest and most original works in the entire history of theatre. I have seen *Godot* several times since that evening in Berlin, including in Paris (where the work was premiered earlier that year), in Zurich, and at its American premiere in New York. But never have I beheld such perfection of acting and staging as in that Berlin performance. The four actors were flawless in their pacing and timing; their masterfully understated acting made every line—every quip, every enigmatic aside—all the more powerful. In too many American presentations Beckett's mock humor and oblique commentaries on the world are turned into slapstick.

The only way that I can begin to explain why that production of *Godot* was so very good is that it belonged to a time-honored, virtually unbroken history of superior theatre in Germany, equal to that of England, but entirely different, which is little appreciated in the rest of the world. It is a tradition that goes back to Goethe and Schiller, and Schikaneder (the great theatre and opera impressario of Mozart's time), and was expressed at a particularly innovative and high artistic level in the Weimar Republic era of the 1920s, and then again in the post–World War II theatre of West and East Germany.

We had known for some time that we would be meeting Bobby Schneider in Berlin, but the question was when and in which Berlin, West or East? The city was divided after the war into four sectors: French, English, American, comprising West Berlin, and the Soviet sector in East Berlin. Schneider had settled in Salzwedel after the war, a small town in the East Zone about an hour by train from Berlin. He had not been out of the Soviet Zone in all these years, and was dying to see what the much-recovered West Germany looked like. He feared that because he was deemed insufficiently cooperative—mainly for having refused to join the Communist Party—by the Communist authorities, who controlled all travel in East Germany, he would not be able to get a travel permit, and certainly not for travel to West Berlin. We were thus surprised when (as he told us later) after many weeks of bureaucratic wrangling, filling out one "stupid form" after another, he was finally given permission to spend part of one day in West Berlin. He had wanted to bring his wife along, but that permission was denied—the government's tactic for trying to stem the tide of emigrations from East to West.[44]

It was wonderful to see Bobby, even though it was only for a short time; his visa limited his stay in West Berlin to eight hours. We took him on extensive walks through central Berlin, showing him the completely rebuilt inner city; our walks were interspersed with rounds of window shopping and lavish meals in two of the best restaurants and cafés on the Kurfürstendamm, Berlin's Champs-Élysées or upper Michigan Avenue. Bobby was bedazzled by the elegance and opulence of the West Berlin stores, and the seemingly unlimited abundance in the window displays of foods and fashions and material goods. There was nothing even remotely like it in all of East Germany.

It was not so wonderful to hear about Bobby's terribly restrictive life in drab little Salzwedel, more or less unemployed—his wife was the family breadwinner—and prevented from pursuing his earlier career as a multilingual educator and pedagogue. He told me that one of the few remaining joys in his life was playing his violin once a week in Mozart, Haydn, and Beethoven string quartets with three other amateur musician colleagues. In the entire time we were able to be with him we spoke only English, since he wanted an opportunity to practice his English, which he hadn't been able to use during the last fifteen years.

The eight hours passed in a flash. It was a sad farewell, not knowing whether we would ever see each other again, given the awesome realities of the expanding Cold War. Oddly enough, we did see Bobby several more times in the 1960s, but in East Berlin and at *our* peril.

On our last day in Berlin Margie and I went to a rehearsal at the Berlin Opera, where Heinz Tietjen was conducting *Tannhäuser*, and to my surprise I was quite impressed by his work. I knew of him only as the *Intendant* of the Deutsche Oper, and was thus surprised that, although here and there a bit pedantic and lethargic, he was otherwise fully in command of things, and had a solid, clear baton technique. And he certainly knew the music inside and out. (Other opera director-managers I have known, who doubled as conductors, were mostly embarrassingly bad in the pit.)

The *Tannhäuser* rehearsal was followed by a farewell lunch with my four horn buddies from the orchestra. By the time we had had many beers and killed several bottles of wine—it was a mostly liquid lunch—half the orchestra's brass section had joined us. They all wanted to meet the kid from New York. Then Margie and I went over to Ziller's apartment on the elegant Fasanenstrasse in midtown Berlin for afternoon Kaffeeklatsch, where I was introduced to Hans Peter Schmitz, Ziller's close friend and onetime first flute of the Berlin Philharmonic, also Germany's foremost authority on baroque ornamentation practices.[45] We became good friends over the years, corresponding frequently, and I learned much from his writings and research; occasionally I even used his findings in some of my own works, most notably in the "Italian" movement ("Lamento") of my 1958 *Contours* for chamber orchestra. Many years later, in the 1990s, I asked Schmitz to write the program notes for the three CDs of flute sonatas—by Bach, Bach's sons, and the young Mozart—for my GM Recordings.

On an entirely different level, probably our most exciting, dramatic experience during our stay in Berlin was in relation to an event that occurred there on June 17, 1953: the uprising of hundreds of thousands of East German workers against the Communist DDR regime.[46] It counts as the most critical political conflict in Germany in the entire Cold War period. For many years after the end of World War II I had closely followed political developments in postwar Europe, especially in the divided Germany. I did this primarily through my reading of two important literary and political magazines, *Partisan Review* and *Der Monat* (*The Month*), the latter created under the Marshall Plan and supported by the Ford Foundation and various German-American exchange initiatives. *Partisan Review* and *Der Monat* were among the first in the late 1940s to call Soviet-style Communism by its true name: Stalinism. Both magazines were in the forefront of alerting its readers to the fact that the Soviet Union was now, under Stalin's tyrannical rule, a totally oppressive regime, as evil as Hitler's Nazi empire, and that the Soviet Union kept a dozen Eastern-block countries (Poland, Czechoslovakia, East Germany, etc.) under total subjection.

Margie and I happened to arrive in Berlin only a few weeks after the June 17 uprising. We had read about it in American newspapers, but it wasn't until we got to Berlin that we realized how momentous an event this had been. It was, in fact, tantamount to a people's revolution of major proportions, erupting not only in East Berlin but also in almost the entire DDR, in some six hundred cities, towns, and villages. And if Soviet tanks had not quelled the revolt, the Ulbricht regime and all its Stasi functionaries (secret police) and Vopos (*Volkspolizei*, peoples' police) would have been toppled in two or three days.

This rebellion was essentially peaceful; several hundred thousand unarmed workers demonstrated and marched on government buildings, offices, police stations, etc. By the end of the first day, most government officials had joined the marchers; the rest ran for their lives, hiding out in the woods and countryside around Berlin. Ulbricht cowered for days in a Soviet army barrack.

In 1952 Stalin had imposed on East German workers, who were already slaving under intolerable conditions, even harsher increased production quotas, combined with equally severe wage reductions. Simultaneously Stalin also initiated a countrywide wave of persecutions that almost always ended in executions. Under such conditions it would take only the tiniest spark to set off a conflagration of some kind. In this instance that spark was as harmless an event as a weekend excursion in which five hundred building workers and their families were invited by a local workers' union to spend two days at one of the many lakes near Berlin for sailing, picnics, and other weekend relaxations. During the first day discussions (accompanied by lots of beer and schnaps) gradually centered, ever more aggressively and irritatedly, on the recently effected 25 percent wage *losses*, linked to demands for a voluntary 15 percent *rise* in production requisitions. The general mood darkened throughout the afternoon, so that by dinnertime one laborer suddenly jumped up on a table and shouted: "We're not going to work on Monday!" It was a call to strike, which *did* go into effect on Monday. By Tuesday morning about forty workers had marched down the Stalinallee toward the West Berlin border, but by evening the demonstrations had grown to *forty thousand* workers. On Wednesday, June 17, all of East Germany had declared a general strike.

At midday hundreds of Russian tanks advanced on the workers, dispersing the marchers with machine gun fire flying overhead. Most protesters fled into the side streets, while many young men and boys stood their ground, heroically hurling rocks at the oncoming squadrons of tanks—to no avail, of course. It's clear that if the Russians had not interceded, the DDR government would have fallen in those few days, as it finally did forty-six years later with the breach and destruction of the Berlin Wall.[47] The June 17 uprising was a triumphant moment for Germany and German democracy, even though Ulbricht's despotic regime survived and prevailed for almost another half century.

Ultimately, it wasn't only Soviet military might that won the day by crushing the rebellion, it was also the fact that the East German demonstrators had no organized guiding leadership, no charismatic Lech Walesa (as in Poland) or Zoltan Nagy (as in Hungary), and no thought-out unified plan for how to proceed after the initial marches. The protest movement had been improvised on the spur of the moment, was too fragmented throughout the whole country, and had no commanding voice in charge. The Soviet tanks scattered the rebellion to the four winds, and the only thought—the only hope—the marchers had was the misguided assumption that the West would somehow come to their rescue. But the West (Great Britain, France, the United States) was not going to risk a third world war with the Soviet Union as a result of a local uprising three thousand miles away.

Many times in human history certain events occurred too early, only to be fulfilled some years later. Such was the case of the June 17 minirevolution. It was one of Germany's very rare, unified mass assertions of democracy and freedom, the last previous such expression—also thwarted—had occurred 105 years earlier, in 1848.

During that whole week that we were in Berlin, we were intoxicated with a spirit of triumph, of emancipation that came from finally standing up and fighting back against an intolerant, oppressive regime. Even though it was some weeks later, both Berlins were still abuzz with the excitations and emotional fervor everyone felt in those few days. It was still palpable in the air. Yes, the German workers had lost, but they had finally *done it*, had finally fought back and not sat meekly by as with Hitler twenty years earlier. I can only say that I was deeply moved, and very proud of my German compatriots.

I was also proud of my Bobby. He and his wife and two teenage children had marched in protest in Salzwedel.

From Berlin Margie and I flew to Hamburg, and in two days there covered a wide range of experiences, from Hindemith's opera *Mathis der Maler* to the exciting erotic entertainments of the legendary Reeperbahn, Hamburg's famous St. Pauli red-light and nightclub district, in between not neglecting to savor Hamburg's famous culinary delicacy, smoked eel, at the city's finest hotel, the Vier Jahreszeiten (Four Seasons). We also visited Hamburg's world-renowned zoo, heard a wonderful all-Bach organ recital in the famous Nicolai Cathedral, did some rowboating in the Alster (Hamburg's huge, mostly manmade lake, dating from the sixteenth century), and ended both days on the outdoor patio of the Alster Pavillon, the most splendid of the dozen or so cafés that line the Alster. There we sat, gazing at the starlit heavens, and all around us the city's panoramic late-night light show. It was enough to fall in love all over again.

The next day was spent in nearby Bremen, visiting the thousand-year-old marketplace, with its famous Roland statue[48] and magnificent fifteenth-century late-Gothic city hall, followed by a quick dash to Bremerhafen, the port city I became so familiar with as a child on my three round-trips to Europe, where the Hapag-Lloyd ocean liners disembarked their passengers.

We were indefatigable in our desire to press as many new experiences and adventures as possible into each day. Perhaps we achieved the ultimate in cramming a maximum of travel activity on that first 1953 trip when on one day we visited four different places in Germany. Margie thought I was crazy to try for such a sightseeing homerun, but I was motivated by an irrepressible desire to revisit four particular places of which I had especially happy memories from my childhood years in Germany. Because of previously made travel commitments all four towns would have to be visited on the same day. Always the optimist, I hoped that since the four towns were located relatively near one another—in the densely populated Germany there is no such thing as enormous distances between towns and cities—and if train schedules cooperated, we would actually be able to achieve that goal. I must give myself a bit of credit for rather ingeniously figuring out the day's itinerary from various train schedules, which involved not three (as I had hoped for) but five different successive train trips. Since German trains are famous for running on time, I was quite certain we would be able to get to all four cities.

And so it was. We started out from Bremen by train around seven in the morning. Two hours and one change of train later,[49] we arrived in Hameln (Hamlin in English), a picturesque city on the banks of the Weser River famous for the legend of the Pied Piper of Hamlin. I showed my wife all the sights I had visited almost twenty years earlier, including the several Pied Piper statues and fountains scattered throughout the town. I looked for and ultimately found a Gasthaus, a café, on a hill overlooking the town, where Bobby Schneider had taken us kids for a memorable picnic years ago, and where now Margie and I enjoyed a most terrific breakfast.

A few hours later we were on a train to Höxter, wending our way mostly along the Weser, with its many sloping vineyards on both sides, much as in the Rhine and Mosel Valley. I had also been in Höxter as a kid on that same hiking tour; it was a medieval town with the magnificent Gothic cathedral of St. Killian and the famous Benedictine abbey of Dreizehn Linden (founded in 822), named after the thirteen linden trees that surround the monastery. We had enough time to sit for a while in one of its cloistered courtyards in absolute seclusion and silence, only the quiet steady gurgling of a nearby fountain reminding us that we weren't really transported back in time eleven hundred years.

It was almost impossible to leave this magical place, but leave we did. In fact, we ran most of the way to the train station for fear of missing our connection. Our next stop, only about forty-five miles away, Bad Gandersheim, was reached by a little chug-along milk train that must have been built in the late nineteenth century. (I had seen trains like that only in my father's model train collection, which he had inherited from *his* father.) In Gandersheim (population 2,700) I had two objectives. One was to revisit the Romanesque abbey-church dating from the end of the eleventh century, where my mother had taken me when I was nine. The nun Roswitha (a colleague and contemporary of Hildegard von Bingen) wrote her poetry and music there, and some of her illuminated manuscripts were on view in the church's little museum. I had been so deeply moved by the visit to that church so many years earlier.

The other goal in Gandersheim was to find the little villa called Waldschlösschen (Little Castle in the Woods), only a ten-minute walk from the village, where I had stayed in 1936 and played with my little brother in the surrounding woods and gardens. I was looking forward to recapitulating the experience of having some delicious cherry pie and coffee out on the villa's terraces. But to my dismay the terraces were gone, along with all the flowers and gardens, and the place had been turned into a completely cheerless, drab-looking home for the elderly.

It was late afternoon when we embarked on the last segment of our marathon journey, which took us to Kassel, a city I had never been to, but was fascinated to visit because it was the site of the famous Wilhelmshöhe—again one of those sights every German child and adult dreams of seeing sometime in their life. I heard about it often from both of my grandmothers, one of whom had spent part of her honeymoon there in the late 1890s. We had to change trains again on this last jaunt, running from one platform to another, and finally arrived in Kassel around eight thirty in the evening, in enough time to celebrate our surviving that hectic day with a terrific dinner of Wiener schnitzel at the best hotel restaurant in town. The Wilhelmshöhe would have to wait until the morning.

We rose very early in order to spend at least three or four hours at the Wilhelmshöhe. It is essentially a huge park (about three times larger than Central Park in New York), covering an entire thirteen-hundred-foot hill. At the top there are not only two castles and an obelisklike statue of Hercules, but also four different waterfalls (one of them 130 feet high) and, descending from one of the castles (named the Octagon), a 200-foot-long series of water cascades, lined on both sides by 842 steps. (I assure the reader we arranged our sightseeing so that we *descended* those stairs).

But ultimately, what fascinated us most was the utter sublimity of the wooded park itself. One gets from Kassel to the top of the Höhe in large, roomy trolley cars, provided with special gear and brake systems to negotiate the Höhe's relatively steep slopes. Thus in a round-trip ride we were immersed for a half hour, each way, in a huge forest of beech trees, splendid in their yellow and orange fall colors, all the more beautiful since forests, woods, and parks in Germany (and most European countries) are cleared of all underbrush. This lends them a kind of classic grandeur and clean elegance. (It also prevents wildfires.)

In retrospect, for me that Bremen to Kassel trip was both an exhilarating and exhausting experience: exhilaration at achieving the intended goal, but physically and mentally exhausted by the day's frantic pace. What was it for Margie? I'm not sure. All I know is that she showed no resistance and amazingly little fatigue. She was never a complainer, and I know that she understood how much this particular nostalgia trip into my childhood past meant to me. I should add that this sightseeing tour de force was an anomaly in our European travels. Most of the 1953 trip was planned at a much more leisurely pace; we stayed in many of the targeted cities at least a few days, sometimes even longer.

From Kassel we headed for Mainz, to visit the home of the Alexander horn factory—Alexander being the make of horn I played.[50] Margie rested at the hotel, while I headed for the factory. On that first trip I had come to Mainz to pick out horns for nine of my students at the Manhattan School of Music and one for Margie.[51] But the following year, 1954, I bought and brought back to New York a total of thirteen horns, all hand-picked by me at the factory, for students and a few colleagues, but also one for myself. It was on that occasion that I found hanging on the rack the horn that I was to use for the rest of my playing career (another nine years), and then kept for another thirty-two years because I couldn't part with it—it was my best friend, and part of the family. I finally sold that horn in 1995 to one of my favorite Tanglewood students, Rick Todd. It was a truly fantastic instrument; it had no bad notes—highly unusual. Everyone who ever played on it called it a magic horn (*Ein Wunderhorn*).

Herr Philip Anton Alexander proudly showed me around the various shops of the factory where the horns were constructed and sequentially assembled. Herr Alexander was also a very knowledgeable wine connoisseur, specializing in German and Alsation wines. Mainz is only a half hour's drive from one of the finest wine regions in Germany going back to Roman times, the renowned Rheingau, famous for its dry white wines. But Mainz is also not far from the Mosel River, whence the other most popular German wines come. After lunch Mr. Alexander drove us to Erbach, Eberbach, and Eltville, where we visited several of the oldest vineyards in the region; we met some of their owners—all of them his friends—and spent the whole afternoon in leisurely wine tastings. We fell in love with the Erbach Reinhartshausen Riesling. It is a truly noble and elegant wine, with a delicious touch of tartness, amazingly consistent from year to year, and I've been drinking it ever since that first visit to the Rheingau.

Off and running again, we headed for Heidelberg, visiting the university and the city's famous castle, and thence via Karlsruhe by bus to Triberg in the Black Forest. In the evening we took the short train ride to Donaueschingen, and spent one and a half days there, just enough time to hear one of the two concerts given that year during the Donaueschinger Musiktage. Of the five pieces on the program, played remarkably well, as far as I could tell, by the South West German Radio Orchestra—works by Malipiero, Blacher, Messiaen, Schönberg, and Nono—I was most impressed by the latter's work, *Due espressione* (as recounted earlier).

Heading further south toward Switzerland, we stopped over for one day in Freiburg at the southwestern foothills of the Black Forest. Freiburg is world famous for its great university, actually one of the very oldest and most prestigious in Germany, where even the legendary Erasmus of Rotterdam once taught. Freiburg is also proud of its magnificent Münster (the old German term for cathedral), right in the town's main square and marketplace. We had been told by Strobel to be sure to check out the wonderful organ in the Münster and, above all, to stay and eat at the Oberkirch, the most wonderful picturesque inn and restaurant in all of Freiburg. Strobel knew what he was talking about. Oberkirch (old German for "above the church"), a historic inn in *Fachwerk* (half-timber) style,[52] probably dating back to the late fifteen hundreds and perfectly preserved (so we were told), was all that had been promised. It wasn't just the fabulous food, a true epicurean delight, it was the whole atmosphere of the place: the dimly lit low-ceilinged dining room with its crown-shaped chandeliers, rich wood carvings everywhere, candlelit tables and booths, many-colored *Butzenscheiben* windows, flowers everywhere, the waitresses all in local period costumes. It was like stepping back several centuries in time.

We were equally lucky regarding the organ situation. While we were exploring the cathedral, marveling at its enormously high vaulted ceiling, we suddenly heard music at the other end of the church. It sounded like Mozart or Haydn. What we were fortunate to hear was a dress rehearsal for a concert the following day of one of Mozart's early sacred works, *Vesperae solennes* (*Solemn Vespers*), written when he was twenty-three for Hieronymus von Colleredo, the archbishop of Salzburg. I had at that time never heard any of Mozart's youthful masses and church sonatas, as they are only rarely performed, even in churches. *Vespers* is a work for four soloists, chorus, and orchestra (featuring, somewhat unusually, two trumpets and three trombones). I remember being rather astounded by the inordinate beauty of the music and being particularly impressed by Mozart's trombone writing,[53] an instrument we don't find that often in his music. (It does not appear in any of his forty-one symphonies.) And I was very impressed with the sound of the organ, its clear silvery timbre, especially with the particular stops the organist was using. There is also something special about hearing great sacred music in the spacious ambience and reverberant acoustics of a great cathedral, especially one with high ceilings, as the sounds travel slowly around the vast space.

Margie was disappointed, as was I, to have spent so little time in the Black Forest. We had driven through it (by bus and train), stopping off in only three places, although including a majestic but rarely visited waterfall, hidden deep in one of its extensive forests, which I had read about in my father's Baedeker travel guides. We couldn't help but marvel at the endless pine forests and the beautifully shaped, gently sloping mountain ranges and valleys, as if some gifted sculptor had tried to create the most eye-pleasing contours and designs. (I understand that in the last twenty years much of the Black Forest's pine trees have been destroyed by environmental degradation.) We promised ourselves that either next year or sometime soon we would spend some serious time in the Black Forest—a promise that was kept in 1954.

Our next destination was Switzerland, specifically Interlaken, Lucerne, Zurich, and in the mountains, fabled places such as Lauterbrunnen, Grindelwald, and the region around the Jungfrau, one of the Alps' most famous mountains. That was all at Margie's request, since the Swiss part of her 1936 trip to Europe as a twelve year old with her parents still generated the happiest memories of the entire two-month tour. No resistance from me, needless to say.

For us, living and working in the crowded canyons of New York, Switzerland appeared like an enchanted fairyland, the perfect toyland, everything in miniature—beautiful, pristine, and perfect. Our rather ambitious sightseeing plans for our four days in Switzerland were, alas, partially foiled by two days of very uncooperative weather: dense fog, heavy rains, and low-lying clouds that filled the valleys to the brim, making even walking and hiking tours more or less pointless. But we did manage to salvage visits to some of our most cherished goals. Among the highlights was taking the funicular to the top of five-thousand-foot Rigi, that unusual perpendicular, cone-shaped mountain near Lucerne, strangely left standing there, isolated, by a meltdown at the end of the Ice Age. From the top we had a spectacular view of what seemed like half of central Switzerland. In fact, being so isolated, many miles away from the high Alps, the view from Rigi on a good day is some three hundred miles in all four directions, an absolutely amazing sight.

The next day we headed for the Jungfrau and Eiger region, which has some of the most spectacular and most visited mountains of the Alps, staying one night in Interlaken, another night in Lauterbrunnen. It was Margie's turn to make a nostalgic voyage into her childhood past. We devoted one day to the Jungfrau and Grindelwald mountains, taking the cog railway to Klein Scheidegg, a ridge halfway up the Jungfrau, from which one has an unforgettable view of the Grindelwald Valley, over three thousand feet below. More than that, all around us, in a huge circle, we could view one dramatic range after another, especially to the south, where the awesome twin towers of the Jungfrau and the even more fearsome Eiger, with its *Eigerwand* (Eigerwall), so legendary in mountain climbing history, were visible. Between the dozens of peaks, wherever we looked, there were huge snowfields and broad glaciers. At first sight that gigantic panorama is so overwhelming that you can't really take it all in.

We wanted to stay there all day, but still needed to reach our next goal, the beautiful village of Grindelwald, a three-hour descent over well-kept winding bridle paths, permitting grand, ever-changing views of this magnificent alpine terrain. In Grindelwald we stayed in a beautiful chalet-inn with one of those perfect postcard views of the entire river valley, the alps high up on either side, from whence, amazingly, in the quiet of the evening we could hear miles away the fascinating composite rhythms and delicate ringing of cowbells.[54]

On one of the heavy rain days we headed off intrepidly for the Lütschine Gorge, a very narrow, awe-inspiring steep-walled canyon, at the end of which there is a majestic waterfall. We reached the gorge completely drenched after a ten-kilometer walk in the rain, mostly wading through puddles on the dirt roads and paths. But it was well worth the struggle. The gorge was a sinister place with its jagged, craggy walls and huge boulders strewn helter-skelter everywhere. The turbulent scene made one mindful of the powerful force that must have plowed its way through what originally was only a tiny fissure in the rock formation, but that ultimately left a deep gash and twisted chaos in its wake. It was not easy to negotiate one's way through the jumbled terrain in the semidarkness, even with the aid of a network of boardwalks and planks; I had to help Margie quite a bit to get us through the half-mile gorge. Finally, at its northern end there was a series of bridges and galleries affording a dizzying view back down into the deep rocky chasm four hundred feet below.

From there it was only a relatively short distance to a place called Unter Gletcher (Swiss-German for under glacier), which is literally what it was: a natural cave or grotto inside and under a long glacier tongue. On this rainy day there was no one else there, just the two of us. Even with no sun the sky's light shown through the grotto's ceiling in whitish blue—probably deeper-hued on that day for all the heavy, dark clouds. It was at once beautiful and eerie, there all alone in the creepy silence, except for the occasional drip-drip of melting ice. It was a bit scary, and I remember trying hard to stave off the fear that the glacier might collapse and bury us alive. It also made me think of *Avalanche* and *White Frenzy*, two late-1920s German films (one with the young Leni Riefenstahl) that we had seen at the Museum of Modern Art about life among the snowbound mountains and alpine glaciers.

Despite the incessant rain we soldiered on, and as the valley widened we came to a large lake. Tired of walking—more psychologically than physically—we decided to rent a paddleboat, a crazy idea in a storm (thank God, there was no lightning). We ate our lunch of cheese and wine circumnavigating most of the lake. By the time we returned to the boathouse, the thought of walking all the way back to Grindelwald was more than discouraging. It occurred to us to try to rent a couple of bikes, but in the middle of nowhere we weren't going to find a bicycle rental place; there was no alternative but to start walking, drenching rain or not.

But now, suddenly, luck was with us. After a half hour of trudging along rather listlessly, we saw a farmer on a large hay wagon, heading toward us on a side road. He noticed our tired, bedraggled look and asked: "Gähn's nach Grindelwald?" "Ja," we both shouted enthusiastically. "Kommen's mit." It turned out that he was bringing some bales of (wonderful smelling) hay to his brother-in-law, who had a small farm right at the outskirts of Grindelwald, with cows and horses but no meadows to produce hay. Perfect! We scrambled aboard and covered ourselves with the tarpaulin with which he kept the hay dry. As the wagon lumbered along shakily through the puddles and potholes, we snuggled together, unable to believe our good fortune.

That night the forecast in all of central Switzerland was for more rain and fog. So we reluctantly decided to cut our stay in Switzerland short, heading instead via Interlaken and Zurich to Innsbruck and finally on to Grainau (in Germany), a village near Garmisch-Partenkirchen and the German-Austrian border. Neatly nestled at the foothills of the Zugspitze, Germany's highest mountain, Grainau was the place where my mother had spent all of her many summer vacations in Germany. I had telephoned Herr and Frau Maurus from Grindelwald, hoping that we could come and stay with them two days earlier than originally planned. The Mauruses owned a small chalet-inn in Grainau, where my mother had always stayed. They treated her like a daughter, and consequently also accepted us with open arms. We stayed with them off and on for many years, always enjoying their superb hospitality.

We also met my mom's close friends, Peter and Karina Strauss, in Garnmisch-Partenkischen. Three years later, these fine people were to open their hearts to us and our baby son, seventeen-month-old Edwin, not only giving up their bedroom for Margie and me, but also taking care of our sick child while we were, of necessity, in Darmstadt attending the Contemporary Music Festival.

After that lovely touch of southern Bavaria, our next target was Vienna, the fabled city of Mozart and Beethoven and Brahms—and of Schönberg—as well as the latest battleground for the burgeoning rivalry between Karajan and Furtwängler. (Margie and I were to find ourselves suddenly, although only peripherally, in the midst of that famous controversy.)

From Grainau we bussed to Mittenwald, just a few miles north of the German-Austrian border, a town where for two centuries the famous Klotz violins were made, of which my father owned two fine specimens. Announced as principal horn at the Metropolitan Opera and the son of a New York Philharmonic owner of several Klotz violins, I was greeted like foreign royalty and taken around several of the shops, where we were shown how the violins were assembled at various stages of development. We sent my father an oversized postcard, with greetings from the Klotz family.

In the afternoon a bus took us to Innsbruck, where we were going to catch the train to Vienna. Can you imagine my astonishment when, as we were about to board the train, I spotted Furtwängler on the platform, three or four cars ahead. I ran over to him to say hello. He recognized me immediately, and invited me to come visit with him in his first-class compartment. I couldn't believe my ears. "It's a long eight-hour trip to Vienna," he said; "we can pass some of the time together—that is, if your lovely wife doesn't mind. Or bring her along, too."

Margie thought it better not to join me, and so I spent six hours with the great man, covering a whole range of subjects: as I recall, modern music and his concerns as to where it's all going, his great admiration for Arthur Nikisch (whom he succeeded in the Berlin Philharmonic)—more than for von Bülow and Weingartner—and his inability to always understand Toscanini. "He's an incredible technician, but it's such a different temperament than mine." After a long, thoughtful silence, he added: "We admire each other, but can't agree on so many things." Lost in thought, after a long pause he concluded: "Very strange."

I remember also that somewhere in that extended conversation he went on about how long it took him—"in my youth"—to appreciate and fully understand the Brahms symphonies.

"Now I think he's as great as Beethoven." And then with a little chuckle, raising his finger in caution: "Almost!"

I told him that I had almost all his Berlin and Vienna Philharmonic recordings, and how much I learned from them, how I loved especially the Tchaikovsky Sixth and the extraordinary Beethoven Violin Concerto with Menuhin, and how much I appreciated Menuhin's recent defense of him against some of the more scurrilous attacks on him in certain American musical circles. "Aber das is 'ne lange Geschichte (but that's a long story)," he sighed, somewhat evasively.

As we were approaching Vienna I said that I had better get back to my wife, and how much I appreciated the opportunity to spend this much time with him. As I left his compartment, he suddenly said: "By the way, on Sunday there's a Karajan concert with the Vienna Symphony, an eleven o'clock matinee. I'm going to that concert. Would you and your wife like to join me?" Stunned, I managed to mumble my acceptance of his invitation. "Meet me next to the box office. I'll come at the last minute." I must have looked puzzled. "You understand?," with a wink. Then I understood.

We were so excited. Could it really be true that we would be taken to a concert by one of the most famous musicians in the world? Sunday morning we got to the Konzertverein a half hour early. I assumed from what Furtwängler had said on the train that we wouldn't see him until about five of eleven. But five of eleven came and passed; no Furtwängler. What if he didn't show up? We had no tickets, and there wouldn't be any to buy, because any Karajan or Furtwängler concert in Vienna would be sold out weeks ahead of time. Word had been leaked out that Furtwängler was going to attend Karajan's concert. The two maestros' much publicized rivalry was kept roiling more by the press and the tabloids than by the two principals. And the famously gossip-loving Viennese could never resist the temptation of witnessing some scandal-prone situation, such as these two conductor titans in the same concert hall.

We were now almost the only two people left in the foyer; everyone else had gone into the auditorium, and ushers were beginning to close the concert hall doors. But one minute *after* eleven a car suddenly pulled up, and out stepped our Furtwängler. He spotted us: "Kommen Sie schnell." He grabbed us, one on each side; an usher opened the door, and there we were: Furtwängler accompanied by two young strangers, heading calmly—he was setting a leisurely, appropriately dignified pace—toward three empty seats right in the center of the auditorium. I could hear a huge rustling noise of several thousand heads and bodies turning toward us, and a wave of whisperings: Look, there's Furtwängler. But who are those two kids with him?

I learned later from a few of my acquaintances in the Vienna Philharmonic, including Freiberg, that the whole episode—Furtwängler arriving late and entering the auditorium in full sight of the entire audience, making his grand entrance—was all prearranged, allegedly by Furtwängler himself; and that the Vienna Symphony management had been specifically asked to start the concert five to ten minutes late. This was based on the assumption that there would certainly be some latecomers, whom it would be best to seat late and have the concert start five minutes late. But that explanation sounded a bit hollow to me. Concert halls everywhere in the world, virtually without exception, rigorously insist that latecomers wait in the foyer until *after* the first number has been played. Whatever the truth of the matter, all the talk and rumors—even after the event—clearly indicated how heated the rivalry between the Karajan and Furtwängler factions was, how much the Viennese public was engaged—and how much the Viennese tabloids loved it all.

Karajan's concert, by the way, was really quite good! I had only heard the Vienna Symphony (the "second orchestra" in Vienna) on recordings, and had not been particularly impressed. It was nowhere near the quality of the Philharmonic. But I must say I thought that Karajan whipped that orchestra into pretty good shape, and—amazingly—did so in an all-French program of Debussy, Ravel, and Dukas—not exactly that orchestra's usual repertory. Karajan got this rather rough-and-ready, raw-sounding orchestra to play with a French-refined sensitivity that was really remarkable. I like to think that Furtwängler must have been impressed, and perhaps surprised. Sitting right next to him, I don't remember noticing any particular reaction from him, pro or con. It may just be that as a sensitive, philosophical person, not particularly given to peevishness, getting on in years and having enjoyed a really spectacular career as one of the world's most revered and respected conductors, he was now beyond expressing childish, caviling recriminations.

We parted company after the concert. I thanked him for inviting us to experience it in his company, and, above all, for letting me spend those six hours with him on the train. At which point he turned to Margie, and with a gallant flourish and an admiring smile, apologized to her—in good English—for having "borrowed your husband for such a long time." (It was well known that Furtwängler always had a keen eye for an attractive female.) I told him that we planned another trip to Europe next year, and hoped that we could then meet again. That was not to happen. Furtwängler died on November 30, 1954.

We stayed in Vienna about a week, seeking out all the famous places, among them the Hofburg Palace (residence of the Habsburg rulers of Austria for seven centuries), the Burg Theater, St. Stephen's Cathedral, some of the places where Mozart, Beethoven, and Schubert had lived and worked, and the city's beautiful parks. We spent a few evenings at Vienna's legendary Prater, listening to the nostalgic zyther music and imagining that we might be sitting at the very same table that Brahms and later the young Schönberg might have occupied as their *Stammtisch* (private table), listening to the same zyther music, drinking some fine Styrian wine.

Of course we went often to the opera, eager to know how its performances would stack up against Berlin or New York. We wondered whether we could get free passes for the performances through the good offices of the opera's horn players. I contacted Freiberg—Herr Professor Gottfried von Freiberg—the veteran principal horn of the Vienna Philharmonic and State Opera (since 1932), who instead of providing us with tickets or passes invited us to sit right at the entrance to the orchestra pit, just a few feet behind the horn section. From that vantage point we were able to see both the stage and the conductor—with just a slight craning of our necks.

Freiberg was known as "the king of the horn players" in Vienna, and, as such, was a living legend to Viennese music lovers. (They really prize their world-famous leading musicians as much as Americans love their baseball or basketball players.) I admired Freiberg's playing greatly, having heard him hold forth on many Vienna Philharmonic recordings, especially on the two superb 1930s Mahler recordings of the Ninth Symphony and *Das Lied von der Erde*.

In general, the Viennese horn players were known in America and England—perhaps a bit maliciously—mostly for their plenteous *kicksing*, Viennese lingo for fluffing, cracking, or missing a note. Horn players, as a lot, more than any other instrumentalists, have always been the butt of much kidding for their cracking notes, to which horn players respond, half-jokingly: "Folks, it's not us; it's the horn." And there is some truth in this response, whether given jocularly or seriously. The fact is that the horn is the most potently projecting instrument in the orchestra, not only dynamically but also in the unusually rich intensity of its sound. As a result, if a horn player cracks a note, everyone, even the most tone-deaf person in the audience, will hear it. (Horn players joke that you can hear it two blocks away.) Whereas if, say, a flutist fluffs a note, or a violinist in a section plays a wrong note, only the most *incredibly* attentive and knowledgeable ears will hear that mistake. There is also the fact that the horn, especially the so-called double horn, is more accident-prone than any other instrument in the orchestra, even the other brass. The reason has to do with certain structural features of the instrument, which cause some technical and mechanical compromises, making the horn in effect, unlike a violin or a flute or even a trumpet, an imperfect instrument.

The Vienna Philharmonic horn players are exceptional in the orchestral world—indeed unique—since they play, and have played forever, the single F horn, as opposed to the double horn (in F *and* B flat) that is generally played everywhere else in the world. The single horn is by definition, by its nature, a simpler, purer, more structurally perfected instrument, and is therefore in theory less prone to kicksing accidents—although, as I've indicated, this is not always borne out in actual performance. In any case, it is amazing to most of us double horn players how remarkably accurate and consistent the Viennese hornists actually are—or can be when on their best behavior. And, of course, they never kicks on recordings.

In the early 1950s Furtwängler had decided to try to introduce the double horn to Vienna. Since he was also the Vienna Philharmonic's (and the Salzburg Festival's) music director, it wasn't much of a problem to have his favorite hornist, Hans Berger (longtime principal horn of the Berlin Philharmonic, later also of the Berlin Staatsoper, as well as principal horn in Bayreuth), to join—to infiltrate—the Vienna Philharmonic's horn section. His hope was that in this way he might be able to persuade the Viennese to switch to the double horn, or at least to begin to play alternately on both types of instruments, the single and the double, as the orchestra's diverse repertory might dictate or require. But nothing doing. As the tale was told to me by several reliable sources, not only was Berger quite unable to incline his colleagues toward the double horn, but he was treated so inhospitably by his Viennese colleagues that he found himself increasingly isolated, musically and personally, and after a year or so left the orchestra and returned to Berlin.

This version of the situation is vigorously denied by various partisan members of the horn fraternity, including the Viennese. But it is true. When I saw Berger briefly on one of my Vienna visits, he was terribly depressed, bemoaning the fact that his colleagues were so intractable, so stubbornly tied to their long-standing conservative traditions, and that the only attempt to introduce the double horn into the Vienna Philharmonic was abandoned. The matter was forgotten, and the group has, as far as I know, lived happily ever since then. The Viennese hornists still play everything on the single F horn, and do so astonishingly well. They unequivocally believe that the tone of a single horn is indisputably the best, the only true horn sound—and there is some truth to that claim.[55]

Irony of ironies, Hans Berger's son, Roland Berger, a marvelous horn player, joined the Vienna Philharmonic's horn section in 1955 as an extra or substitute player, and half a dozen years later succeeded Freiberg as principal horn. Roland had one of the most beautiful tones on the horn that I have ever heard, equivalent in its purity and sonoric elegance to Bruno Jänicke's, my idol.

When I told Hugo Burghauser, my Met orchestra colleague (and former chairman and manager of the Vienna Philharmonic), about the Hans Berger case, he said without much hesitation that that was "but another symbol and example of a typically Austrian archconservatism and monarchical authoritarianism." Meanwhile, it's unlikely that the arguments, as to which of the two types of horns is more reliable—more versatile, easier to play, better sounding—will ever be settled.

The first opera we saw at the Staatsoper was *Otello*, which I found at best to be a middling performance, both on stage and in the pit. Though disappointed, I was not entirely surprised, since my Viennese opera colleagues at the Met had all told me that performance levels at the Vienna Opera could be extremely variable, more than at the Met. You could within a given week hear two absolutely terrific, virtually perfect performances, followed by two awful, sloppy ones, in which nobody even seems to have tried, and then, in between, three average good ones, merely OK. That was certainly borne out by our own experience over a stretch of a week and a half. What was more surprising to me was that the myth about the Viennese horn players and their proclivity for kicksing wasn't a myth at all; it was in fact a persistent reality. They could produce more kicksers per performance than anything I had ever heard before, or even thought possible, in a professional context. I should add that it wasn't the principal horn—Freiberg, in the case of *Otello*—but the other three in the section, who kicksed a lot that first night. What was truly staggering to me was that most of the time those players laughed or giggled (not audibly, of course) when they clammed. It was all fun to them. Had that happened at the Met in such abundance as in that *Otello*—inconceivable to begin with—we would have tried to hide our heads in shame, hoping to shrink into oblivion. Not so in Vienna. Furthermore, had any one of us at the Met, or any other American orchestra, delivered such an embarrassing flurry of fluffs more than two or three times, we would for sure have been fired, and in total disgrace. Even more astonishing to me was the fact that no one, including the conductor, showed any upset or particular concern at the amount of performance calamities, not only in the horns but also in other instruments, and in a general sloppiness and raggedness of ensemble.[56] Had we sat in regular seats in the main part of the house, say, in the twentieth row or in one of the balconies, we would never have heard and seen what we couldn't help but notice sitting so close to the pit. (The pit in Vienna in those performances was generally set rather low, well out of sight of the audience.) As a musician, I certainly would have heard the horn clams, but I might not have caught the giggling and generally casual attitude of everyone involved.

After the *Otello* performance, Freiberg and two of his section colleagues invited us, along with a few other musicians, including an elderly violinist who had been a close friend of Burghauser back in the 1930s, out to a nearby wine bar for an evening of Heurigen.[57] It was a lively time—*Otello* was completely forgotten, unmentioned—there were several hours of trading anecdotes, jokes, and weird experiences, unique to life in an orchestra. The three horn players, especially Freiberg—who always had a sly twinkle in his eyes—kept plying me with wine, generously refilling my glass, even when it was still half full, never asking me if I wanted more. Not wishing to offend his hospitality or appear to be a reluctant imbiber, I kept drinking away, mainly because the Heurigen, which I had never drunk before, tasted so fresh and sparkly, wonderfully effervescent. After a while it began to dawn on me that Freiberg and his two drinking buddies were testing me to see what kind of a boozing horn player I was. It was too late. I felt my stomach turning, my head starting to swim. It was awful—and embarrassing. I ran for the bathroom in the basement, down the narrow fifty-step staircase, the whitewashed walls moving up and down, surrealistically leaning in on me—like something out of Robert Wiene's *The Cabinet of Dr. Caligari*. I just made it in time and threw up for about five minutes. The thing about Heurigen is that it's pretty harmless at first; you feel nothing. But then, an hour or so later, it catches up with you—and how!

While I was drinking the stuff like water, Freiberg, an old hand at drinking bouts, was pacing himself, watching me go down the primrose path. He finally had pity on me, and took me and Margie, who was also feeling a bit woozy but who had been more cautious than I, home to our hotel.

I don't remember all the operas we saw on that visit to Vienna, but what stands out in my memory is a fine *Magic Flute* (no horn kicksing), a pretty bad *Trovatore* (like the *Otello*), and a wonderful *Der Prozess* (*The Trial*), Gottfried von Einem's wonderful opera, very well sung and played, with a different cast and staging than the one in Berlin. I preferred Berlin's Elfriede Trötschel over Vienna's Irmgard Seefried.

As a break from a week of operas, we undertook two excursions outside Vienna. First a one-day roundtrip to Salzburg, mainly to see the famous Schloss high above the town and the river Salzach, and also the grounds of the Salzburger Festspiele, including its most unusual concert venue, the famous Felsenreitschule (the old academy riding school), where Karajan and Furtwängler staged all their opera productions. (I hadn't the slightest inkling that four years later my music would be played at the Salzburg Festival.) The other one-day excursion took us south to Semmering, Austria's popular summer and winter resort in the mountainous southeastern corner of the country, right near the Hungarian border. Semmering is not only a mountain village, comparable, say, to Lake Placid or Vail, Colorado, but there is also a Semmering Pass, sitting right on the border of Lower Austria and Styria, at a height of almost three thousand feet. It is spectacular country, different than the Alps in Switzerland and western Austria, where there is a certain neatness and organic naturalness; the southeastern region of Austria is wild and rugged, a lot more jumbled and cluttered. Almost every sight was a dizzying, puzzling experience.

Semmering is famous in Europe—I even read about it as a kid in Germany—for being the site of the first mountain climbing railroad in the world, built in the 1840s. It features twenty-three tunnels—one of them a third of a mile long—and almost as many viaducts. The road across the pass was first built in 1728; and that's before Washington and Jefferson—or Mozart—were born!

But much of our visit in Semmering was spoiled by the ubiquitous presence of Austrian and Soviet border guards and military police, the Russians with their Kalishnikovs and machine guns, always looking threateningly at everyone, as if we were all some kind·of public enemy or terrorist. It was quite unnerving.

One strange little episode, just as we were about to board the train back to Vienna, reflects so typically the small-mindedness of Austrian-German burgher mentalities—inconceivable in modern America. We both had been on the go all day, and had had no chance to go to a bathroom. We were desperate. About thirty yards from the tiny railroad station, itself nothing more than a dilapidated shack, I spotted what looked like a row of four wooden outhouses, guarded by an elderly, wizened, mustachioed fellow, who was in full uniform. As we headed for the toilet doors, the man stopped us, and in his barely intelligible Styrian mountain dialect asked me what we were doing. What an idiotic question! "What do you think we're doing?," spurted out of me. A brief, stupid, heated verbal exchange ensued, but eventually he let us proceed. Now it turned out, to our utter amazement, that there was no toilet paper in the outhouses. You had to acquire that from the guard—for a tip. The situation got more surreal when, instead of getting a roll of tissue, the man handed each of us two—yes, *two*—very rough patches of paper, about six by eight inches square. Believe it or not, that's all that each person was allowed to get. What another world!

After Austria, we spent two days in Munich, again with evenings at the opera, where we saw splendid performances of Strauss's *Arabella* and *Capriccio*. I was particularly moved by the latter, which along with his *Four Last Songs* is Strauss's most touching, nostalgic look back at his own past; a musical memoir of his youth, as it were.

I also met there the opera orchestra's principal bass, Franz Ortner, a remarkable virtuoso, and in his day one of the first to perform and record bass concertos (by the likes of Dittersdorf and Wanhal). We became close friends over the years, and on many later visits I stayed at his house; I also corresponded frequently with him until his death in the late seventies. There is in my library in manuscript an unfinished concertante piece for four solo strings (violin, viola, cello, and bass), which was primarily inspired by Ortner and his elegant playing.

After Munich we traveled via Saarbrücken to St. Avold in France to pay our respects to Margie's brother, Ned, killed in the Battle of the Bulge and buried in the gigantic military cemetery there, a most beautifully kept place. Margie's parents had arranged with the cemetery keepers to constantly have flowers at the foot of Ned's white cross. It was the first time anyone in the family had been able to visit Ned's grave.

From nearby Frankfurt we flew to Barcelona for our five days in Spain. In the interest of experiencing as many of Europe's historical, cultural, and artistic treasures as physically feasible in a six-week tour, we had early on decided to include a brief visit to Spain, with four prime targets in mind: Madrid's Prado, one of Europe's great art museums; Toledo, where one of my most admired painters, El Greco, had lived and worked; the Alhambra in Granada; and above all, in Barcelona, the many architectural masterpieces of one of the most original, uniquely gifted architects in history, Antoni Gaudí. I had already read several books about Gaudí, and was so fascinated with his extraordinary work that I made Spain, not usually the first country one thinks of visiting in Europe, one of our absolutely primary goals.

Talk about cramming. We did a lot of walking in Barcelona, seeking out and then inspecting every—and I mean *every*—edifice Gaudí created, whether it was his many apartment houses (especially the famous Casa Mila) or the great unfinished Sagrada Familia cathedral, or the totally astonishing, almost surrealistic Park Güell. The Sagrada Familia, begun in 1883, was left unfinished at Gaudí's death in 1926. Since then, over the last ninety years, work has continued intermittently as an ongoing work in progress—a frustratingly slow progress, the ultimate goal of which is to complete Gaudí's dream cathedral in strict adherence to the plans and designs he left behind.

To encounter the Sagrada Familia even in its unfinished state—at most only one third of what was originally conceived—is an awesome spiritual experience, for which it is impossible to find any analogy. Since the entire project is open to the public, even as work continues on a daily basis, we were able to explore it all in its beautifully extravagant free-form heterogeneity; we climbed around in its two-hundred-foot towers, sat on their huge projecting gargoyles overlooking the entire fifty-thousand-square-foot project—and saw most of Barcelona in the bargain, all the way to the Mediterranean. Gaudí's Park Güell, sometimes called a "genius's charming folly," is indeed a phantasmagoric fairyland retreat, with its voluptuous leaning tunnels, weirdly shaped arbors and grottos, bizarre towers, balconied patios—mostly fashioned out of glass and ceramic mosaics, where the placement, size, shape, and color of every stone had been selected or supervised by the master himself.

The whole Barcelona visit was like living on some incredible extended high; it's a feeling I've had the good fortune to experience several more times with repeated visits to that great Catalan city.

On the way to Granada we stayed for two days in what has to be the most enchanting lodgings I ever encountered in my life. Located high above the tiny fishing village of Castelldefels on the Costa Brava, only about fifteen miles south of Barcelona, this small hotel offered all conceivable modern comforts and service, and was situated directly adjacent to the ruins of a medieval tower fortification. The little fortress looked rather like a windmill, which made us feel that we were transported back to Cervantes' age of chivalry. I count our stay at Catelldefels among the happiest, idyllic, carefree times on that entire trip, a brief interval of serendipity and quietude; we were serenely isolated from the turmoil and noise of the world somewhere out there, just taking things easy and enjoying the superb food and wines the inn served. The only slightly strenuous venture we undertook was clambering down—and up—the fairly steep two-hundred-foot cliffs to the beach below, where to our amazement we discovered that the hordes of bathers, enjoying the famous Costa Brava, were all German tourists; not a Spaniard in sight.[58]

The Alhambra in Granada is the largest and best preserved of all the alcazars (Moorish-built palaces and fortresses) in Spain. Its commanding presence, looming high above the city, with its magnificently sculptured red brick walls and thirteen imposing towers, is impossible to imagine until you've actually viewed it, especially on approach from the valley below. And what can one say of the majestic architectural splendors of its palace chambers and the famous inner courtyards: Moorish art at its highest development—another overwhelming experience.

From Granada we headed by train for Toledo, a city I insisted on visiting for a number of reasons: El Greco lived and worked there for nearly forty years; the Alcázar of Toledo and its much celebrated majestic cathedral, which contains paintings by El Greco and Goya; and Toledo's spectacular geographic location. The first sightings of Toledo are truly awe inspiring. For the city is perched high on a huge, round, granite hill (a humongous single boulder) less than a mile across, rising nearly a thousand feet above the river Tagus, which, uniquely, surrounds Toledo on three sides in an expansive 270-degree arc. The city is densely crowded and cannot grow or expand. Its streets are very narrow, and around its circumference the houses sit straight up and cling to the precipitous rocky slopes rising up from the river below. One nineteenth-century travel writer recorded that the sight of Toledo from a distance is wild and striking. This impression is brilliantly seconded in El Greco's greatest painting, *Toledo*, a dramatic protoimpressionistic long-distance view of the city. I don't think any landscape like that had ever been painted before. It has haunted me ever since my years at St. Thomas, when I was taken to the Metropolitan Museum of Art the first time, where *Toledo* was then on exhibit. It is one of El Greco's darkest, most active, wildest paintings, all somber blues, blue-greens, turquoise,[59] and black-green. The town's topography is strangely rearranged—the Alcantara Bridge is on the wrong side of town—while the alcázar and cathedral are lit with a ghostly, whitish, grey-blue. The sky above the city is rent with angry, bulging, lightning-surrounded clouds. And that is exactly what we saw, as our train approached Toledo in late evening.

We could only spend one day there, but managed to visit all four of our intended sites. The Cathedral of Toledo, the city's chief glory, one of the largest in Europe, was most impressive, comparable to the Cologne Cathedral. We had been advised to visit the cathedral in the late afternoon, when the morning masses and some of the midday services were over, and to await the time just before sunset when most of the altars, the nave, and aisles would be almost dark, and the beautiful stained glass windows would glow with a sunny, fiery brilliance—advice we certainly followed. We were also lucky to see Greco's amazing *Espolio de Jésus* in the sacristy, as well as great paintings by Goya (*The Betrayal of Christ*) and by Titian and Rubens. Imagine such a collection of treasures in a local church! The only disappointment was that the cathedral is so hemmed in on all sides by tall buildings and narrow streets that it is impossible to get a good long view of it, let alone a good photo.

We saw still more Grecos in the Casa del Greco, where the great master lived and worked during the last decade of his life (he produced *Toledo* there). But it was quite a disappointment to see with our own eyes that Toledo's great alcázar, which had for many centuries towered over the city—it was also the castle where most of Spain's kings presided—was nothing but a ruin, having been destroyed during the Spanish Civil War in the 1930s.

Our final two days in Spain were spent in Madrid, and can be described at once as rather peculiar as well as quite disappointing. The peculiarity occurred when I failed to make a hotel reservation, thinking that we could do so in the Madrid train station. (That is a long-standing tradition in Europe, where every major train station and airport offers extensive hotel reservation services.) It happened that for those particular September days Madrid was overrun with tourists, mainly Germans and Italians. After many phone calls the reservation bureau did finally find a room for us, which they told us candidly was rather simple, even primitive—far from first class. We had no choice but to accept. What the heck, just two nights; and we would hardly ever be in the room anyway, mostly out sightseeing. What they didn't tell us was that the hotel was right in Madrid's red-light district.

The disappointment was also due to a lack of proper planning on my part, for I had misjudged the vastness of the Prado, allowing us only one day there. We seriously ran out of time, not to mention that our feet gave out completely. We did manage to see about a dozen El Grecos and a room full of paintings by Velasquez, a painter I knew virtually nothing about. It's a special thrill to discover a great master's art for the first time; like first love, but particularly so when it is work of such classic eloquence and elegance. We never did get to the Prado's huge Goya collection of over a hundred paintings.

From Madrid we flew to Paris and spent five hectic days and nights there, assaying the full range of cultural and entertaining diversions that the legendary City of Lights had to offer. During the day we covered most of Paris's famous sights: the Eiffel Tower, the Notre Dame Cathedral and the Sacré-Coeur Basilica, Napoleon's Tomb, the Louvre and Museum of Modern Art, also—*de rigeur*—a Bateaux Mouches trip up and down the Seine, and, of course, the mandatory shopping at Galeries Lafayette and Printemps. The evenings were for concerts or the opera or the theatre, and after that, well into the night, the city's notorious nightlife. We didn't sleep very much.

The musical offerings in Paris were mostly disappointing, sometimes bafflingly so, given the city's reputation as one of the great cultural centers of the world. A concert at the Théâtre des Champs-Élysées, with Hans Knappertsbusch and the famous Orchestre du Conservatoire (its members largely the conservatory's faculty), was so wretched that it was for the most part downright laughable. Knappertsbusch's intolerably slow, lugubrious, inert tempos were bad enough. But the sounds that came out of that orchestra—thin, edgy, raggedy, often out of tune—were something to behold. But the funniest, weirdest sound emanated from the orchestra's contrabassoon in the Brahms First Symphony; it was 90 percent buzz and about ten percent tone. Margie thought it sounded like the rattling, scraping noise that old-fashioned window shades made.

On the other hand, a concert by Karajan and his Vienna Symphony, this time with an all-German program, fared much, much, better.

We got pretty excited when we saw that Debussy's *Pelléas et Mélisande* was being given at the Opéra-Comique. Hoping to hear a really beautiful, authoritative representation of that remarkable opera, we were offered instead an only fair performance (except for a very good Golaud—the French have always had very good baritones and basses)—rendered by a listless, bored orchestra in the pit. Given our great love for this music, it was a rather painful experience. But the most notable memory we took away from that *Pelléas* performance was not the opera itself, but an inadvertently comical aspect of our attendance at the venerable old Opéra-Comique. Built in 1840 and, as far as I know, updated or renovated only once (in 1879), it is in many ways an oddly constructed building, stingily furnished, not given to creature or body comforts. It was as if, along with one's entertainment and amusement, one should also have to suffer a little. The third balcony, very high above the stage, was precariously steeply banked and equipped with ancient wooden unupholstered folding seats. That may not sound very funny—and it wasn't—but the hilarious part was that the seat aisles were so narrow that only people with abnormally short legs could sit with their legs straight ahead. All others had to slant their legs at least thirty or forty degrees to the left or to the right, which meant that if any one person in that row wanted to shift from left to right or right to left, *the entire row* had to shift, whether it wanted to or not. There was one elderly, very tall man in our row, obviously a seasoned visitor to the Opéra-Comique, who, sitting near the end of the row, would every once in a while signal that it was again time to shift. You didn't have much choice about it. By the fourth and fifth acts of *Pelléas*, Margie and I were more concerned with when the next leg-shifting signal would come than what was happening on the stage and in the orchestra pit.

Only in France!

As for our nightclubbing, that was spectacular. Paris has been world famous for its risqué nightlife ever since the late eighteen hundreds, when its theatres began presenting cancan dancing in public, at a time when merely revealing a well-turned female ankle was considered an outrageous act of exhibitionism and, for the viewer of such lewdness, a mortal sin. The invention of the striptease in the 1930s raised an evening's pleasurable amusement to a whole other level, and by the 1950s Paris had become the world's capital of erotic entertainment, not only in its public nightclubs and private bordellos—its *maisons de plaisir*, as they were euphemistically called—but also, in a more subtle and yet perhaps insinuating way, in its cinema.

The center of such activities was located in and around the infamous Place Pigalle (dubbed "Pig Alley" by the hordes of American GIs and sailors who began to flock there), offering just about every form of female entertainment that human ingenuity was capable of devising, ranging from the mildest floor shows and cabaret acts to which even the primmest of proper American tourists might be taken (incidentally by the busload), and to which you could even take your maiden aunt without fear of offending her, all the way to the wilder, more explicit, erotically enticing entertainments.

There is something special, indeed unique, about the way the French, as a people, as a nation, deal with eroticism and sex. They see these human impulses and activities as completely natural, that is, as something basic to nature, inevitable and essential, not sin-ridden, morally conflicted, or sordid, and certainly not a human aberration. They treat the subject and bestow on its varied manifestations a certain elegance and style, an ease of manner. You also see that in the way French women dress—always stylishly, in impeccable taste. I was always struck on my many visits to France over the years—not just in Paris, but even in the most remote country village—how women were always well dressed. They carried themselves with a natural grace, a high sense of style and distinctive but unostentatious fashion—a certain artful sophistication virtually unknown in, say, Germany or England. French women do not need to dress provocatively. Even the ordinary middle-class housewife emits a subtly alluring, subtly sensuous attractiveness.

The same can be said about the Parisian brand of erotic entertainment. There was always a certain sophistication, a stylishness, an inherent sense of naturalness, of normalcy. Because sex is not considered something dirty, there never was anything course or vulgar in the shows. Whether in some small strip club or the larger variety shows, the productions were almost always ingeniously creative in costume, dance routines, décor, in skits and tableaux—mandatory attributes in Paris in a highly competitive field. They were created, produced, and executed as a seriously entertaining performance art.

Even though Paris's nightclubs offer variations on the one same theme—sex—the variety of approaches among them is simply amazing. We enjoyed them all—the Eve, the Mayol, Midi Minuet, the Casino de Paris. But one stood out among all the others: the Crazy Horse Saloon. Talk about ingenious and original. The Crazy Horse was new in 1953, but soon became the most popular club in Paris, a gold mine for the owners. We returned to it often in ensuing years, always finding block-long lines outside hoping to get into one of its three nightly shows. Once inside, with the relatively few seats and tables all taken, you usually found yourself standing in a tightly packed throng of three or four hundred people, like sardines in a can. (I am sure the club broke every fire law every night.) The Crazy Horse was always jam-packed with visitors from all over the world. You never knew who you'd be brushing up against. For example, it turned out one time that Margie found herself next to a Saudi prince, and another time I discovered that my standing room partner was the minister of culture from Norway.

I shan't divulge all that Margie and I attended and experienced in Paris. Suffice it to say that it was all wonderfully exciting, challenging, unprecedented, and liberating.

Which reminds me that we had another unprecedented experience on our last day in Paris. We discovered that the great, reasonably priced steaks that we had many times for lunch at a restaurant near our hotel on the rue de la Boétie turned out to be *horse meat*. It certainly fooled us, as it tasted quite fabulous. We noticed that the restaurant always seemed to be filled with cab drivers, and subsequently learned that it was one of four restaurants in Paris that openly served horsemeat instead of beef, and that it was indeed a favorite hangout for Parisian cabbies taking advantage of the amazingly cheap prices.

Then it was time to go home. In less than a week rehearsals would start at the Met and I had not touched my horn in over two months. But I wasn't too worried about getting back into playing shape; I had only five rehearsals of relatively easy operas such as *La Bohéme* and *Rigoletto* that first week.

A two-hour train trip took us from Paris to Luxembourg, where we boarded an Icelandic Airlines plane. Two stopovers later—one in Reykjavik, Iceland, the other in Goose Bay, Labrador (in predawn darkness)—we landed in Idlewild Airport; it was a fairly grueling flight in those prejet-age days. Neither of us was looking forward to facing an empty apartment with no food in the refrigerator. So we were much relieved when my parents invited us to stay with them in Jamaica, Queens for the first few days, allowing us to unbend a bit from the rigors of our European jaunt. We were welcomed like conquering heroes by all our friends, and invited out to dinner and long visits every day for a whole week: Joe Marx, Janet Putnam, John and Jeannie Clark, the Buffingtons, my brother and his wife Doris, even Margie's new voice teacher, Whitfield Schanzer—one after another. They were all dying to hear about our trip. Those were very long evenings, what with trying to tell it all and show our hundreds of photos and slides. Many evenings we simply stayed over at our guests' houses, slept on couches or on the floor rather than struggling to get back to Jamaica at two or three in the morning.

I got my horn out of the closet, took it down to the Met and practiced for a few hours every day, getting my lips back into reasonable shape. By Monday afternoon I was ready to tackle *La Bohéme* without any embarrassments. Margie was thrilled not to have to do any cooking or housecleaning. But, of course, this respite was brief, and soon we were once again fully entangled in the hectic pace of life in New York.

One awesome, indeed frightening, reality we became immediately aware of upon our return was the extent to which the McCarthy hearings had widened into a full-blown witch hunt that used every foul demagogic tactic—false accusations, presentation of unsubstantiable "evidence," playing on deeply held popular prejudices (such as anti-Semitism; most alleged Communists were assumed to be Jewish), ignoring or suppressing contesting testimony—to intimidate witnesses, critics of the hearings, and the press. I don't think there had been anything in American history to match McCarthy's capacity to invent lies, to obfuscate facts and bend the truth, and by these means to acquire more and more dictatorial power.

By late 1953 the daily televised hearings began to totally dominate life in America, much like the O. J. Simpson trial forty years later. People were strangely mesmerized, even in partial disbelief, by what they witnessed. It seemed impossible that a trial by innuendo, by threats and harassment, with contrived accusations against a sizable segment of our population could be taking place in this country—of all countries—in front of our very eyes. McCarthy and his henchmen (Roy Cohn and Richard Nixon) were completely out of control. And yet in the climate of fear generated by McCarthy's uncanny ability to twist truths into outrageous but somehow persuasive lies, any opposition to this blatant attempt to destroy our democracy remained intimidated and fettered for months. Even the Congress and President Eisenhower were cowed, too afraid to openly oppose and expose McCarthy.

I was horrified by what was happening to our country. It was particularly unnerving, having just months before, in Berlin, seen how demagoguery, aided by brute military force, could squelch a peoples' uprising and its pursuit of freedom from oppression. Worse yet, thinking back to my years in Germany, it was frightening to realize how much McCarthy reminded me of Hitler, in his arrogance, his lies, and his insidious tactics. The only thing that was different was McCarthy's voice: baneful, twisted, wickedly insinuating, squealy like a bad tenor in pain, compared to Hitler's raucous, raspy, screaming baritone tirades. It also seemed to me that too many Americans were caught in a vise of unawareness, of disbelief and intimidation, just as Germans had been in the 1930s—until it was too late.

It is a matter of history how many careers and lives were ruined by McCarthy, how many friendships were shattered. (Witness the case of Arthur Miller and Elia Kazan.) And who knows how much further McCarthy might have progressed in demolishing liberty and democracy in America, had not—finally—some courageous voices spoken up, most prominently Edward R. Murrow, warning on his nightly CBS broadcasts of what was befalling us. From there other voices soon rose in protest, until a groundswell of resistance poured forth.

I will never forget Joseph Welch's tormented cry—on television—flush with the deep pain of what had been allowed to fester for so long, directed straight at McCarthy and thrice reiterated: "Have you no shame!? Have you no sense of decency!?" Even McCarthy was stunned speechless—for once.

That was even in its anguish a moment of triumph, a moment in which every decent American breathed a sigh of relief, a moment that spawned an amazing turnaround. Within a few months the McCarthy hearings were terminated, McCarthy was censured by the senate, after which he fell quickly into obscurity and died three years later. The lesson that I learned from that whole experience was that there is in our democracy, in our DNA, an inherent element of self-cleansing, of protection of that most precious basic right: free speech. The problem, however, is that in that same democracy, a deteriorating, liberty-threatening situation has to get really, really, really *very bad* before enough people come to their senses and realize that everything they truly cherish might, at the next step, be lost.

Our second trip to Europe (in 1954) was even more extensive than the year before, a full nine-and-a-half weeks, covering primarily four countries: England (including Scotland), Germany, Italy, and France. The highlights were Scotland, including the Edinburgh Festival, and my attendance at both the Donaueschingen and Darmstadt Festivals, the latter featuring my debut performance as a composer in Europe. I also managed to build into that trip, as I had promised Margie the year before, many days of driving around and hiking in the Black Forest, and climbing its two highest peaks. One was the Feldberg (nearly five thousand feet high), with an incredible 360-degree view of the entire Black Forest range and all the way to Strasbourg thirty miles to the northwest, and almost to the Swiss Alps fifty miles south. The other mountain was Schauinsland (Look Down into the Land), only a few hundred feet smaller than the Feldberg. To see the forest in the fall was a special treat, the yellow and orange-brown colors playing off the deep dark-green of the Black Forest's famous pines. It is not only their beauty, their natural perfection—each one a work of art—but also the unique scent. (I have always theorized that Black Forest's pine scent should be made into a perfume.) Margie was so happy. I think she would have divorced or killed me if I hadn't fitted those precious days into our itinerary. Even at that, I can't claim to be much of a hero, since Donaueschingen, our next stop, was on the eastern edge of the Black Forest, only twenty-five miles east of the Feldberg.

If Scotland and the Scottish Highlands impressed and excited us even more, it was partly because we were somewhat familiar with Germany and its geographic, physical splendors; I certainly was. Whereas our knowledge of Scotland was virtually nil (except for reading Sir Walter Scott or Robert Louis Stevenson and learning about all those thousand-year feuds between different Scottish clans). We spent four days in Edinburgh, mainly at the Edinburgh Festival attending various chamber and orchestral concerts.[60] The one that captivated me the most featured Dennis Brain as the horn soloist with Paul Sacher's famous Basel Chamber Orchestra, in the Otmar Schoeck Horn Concerto. That was also the evening that I first met my revered colleague. We did some very pleasurable reminiscing about working often (although literally worlds apart) with Eugene Goossens, and of our great admiration for him. Dennis had made his first important recording of Britten's *Serenade for Tenor, Horn, and String Orchestra* with Goossens as conductor in 1943, the same year that I started working with Goossens.

Margie and I also took an extensive tour of the Edinburgh Castle, perched high on a gigantic perpendicular 430-foot rock, almost within the city, physically and visually towering over it. While we were being shepherded around the castle, we were lucky enough to witness the daily military tattoo presentation of the famous Black Watch, Edinburgh's legendary bagpipers band, in kilts and full clan regalia. I say lucky because if we had returned to America confessing that we had failed to see the Black Watch in Edinburgh, we could never have escaped the outraged reproaches of our relatives and friends. It is the one—and only—thing that most people associated with the Edinburgh Festival wanted to hear about.

Our travel agent, Hendrien de Leeuw, who had served us so well on our first visit to Europe, had told us weeks before our departure, with the most infectious enthusiasm, that we "*must* spend at least a couple of days in the most heavenly little village in *all of Scotland*, Ballachulish." Who could resist such a recommendation! Apart from the fact that there are surely several hundred equally heavenly villages scattered throughout Scotland, Hendrien was dead right. Ballachulish was indeed one of *the* most picturesque places on the face of this globe that I in my extensive travels had ever seen or could possibly have imagined. With a population of less than a thousand, it was nothing more than two parallel quarter-mile rows of low-slung whitewashed thatched-roof houses, and one cobblestone street between them. I don't know how many times the word "darling" crossed Margie's lips, but she was right. Everything was in miniature, our room modestly yet perfectly appointed—and the food, in its homegrown simplicity, was absolutely superb.

The four-hour train ride to Ballachulish from Edinburgh via Glasgow and through the western Central Highlands to Fort Williams, and thence by bus (twenty minutes) to Ballachulish, had been a spectacular experience in itself; the route wound through endless vales and glens and straths, past half a dozen lochs and lochans constantly surrounded by rugged, barren, treeless mountains (mostly three thousand footers). It had given us a very good idea of what to expect on our upcoming hiking and sightseeing ventures. That train trip had taken place on a bright, almost cloudless sunny day—a great rarity in Scotland—and when we settled in our little second-floor room that first evening, we could see Ben Nevis, Scotland's highest mountain (4,406 feet) from our windows, in all its bare, somber glory. But that was the last time we saw Ben Nevis. As we wandered and bicycled around the Highlands the next three days, we did so in unbroken mists, in drizzling rains and low-hanging clouds that covered the tops of the hills. At first I thought, just our damn luck! But you know what? By the second day, I knew that *this* was the way to see Scotland. To walk in these ancient eternal mists, which have shrouded and colored the whole history of Scotland, to look down at these endless secluded glens, no living thing in sight, enveloped in moraine-smoothened sloping hillsides—that is to capture in a pristine way the whole flavor and spirit of this land. There was something beautifully eerie and mysterious about the experience that is hard to put into words.

It unleashed the imagination. We often just stood there in awe, peering through the rolling fog, and seeing in our mind's eye the ghostly figures of storied legends, of feuding, battling clans—as if in some Olivier or Hitchcock film—especially in Glencoe, the scene of the fabled massacre of the MacDonald clan in 1692. The rain was never heavy or drenching, as in the Swiss Alps the year before. More mist than rain, it actually felt balmy, soothing on the skin, inviting. It was uncanny: at every turn of a winding hilly road another spectacular sight broke into view down some long valley with a tiny babbling brook trickling down the middle.

It is a strange thing about the Scottish Highlands; when you're out there in some remote, unpopulated valley, all alone, you see all these beautifully paved winding roads, as far as the eye can see. But nobody's on them. Once in a great while you see one lone bicyclist, off in the distance, almost hidden under his tentlike cape to ward off the rain, pedaling—it seems—to nowhere. Another time, we saw a farmer on a horse-drawn wagon, heading for the only house in the valley, a house that was actually, untypically, bordered by a short line of trees; a flock of sheep milled around nearby. For us there was something magical in experiencing such splendid isolation, contemplating in this awesome silence these vast antique spaces, just the two of us. I think we were never closer.

Those day trips, eastward to Glencoe and to the hamlet of Lochlinleven (as picturesque and darling as Ballachulish), another along the western shore of the beautiful Loch Linnhe[61] (near which Ballachulish is located), and each evening's return to home and hearth in Ballachulish were the highlight of that entire 1954 European trip. Whenever in the last fifty years a conversation turned to those early trips, what inevitably popped into our minds was that visit to Scotland's Highlands, and our sojourn in little Ballachulish.

Next, a short bus ride took us to Oban on the Scottish west coast, where we boarded a large car ferry to Glasgow—a circuitous ten-hour cruise past hundreds of islets and estuaries, and some of the most rugged, wild, rocky scenery we had ever seen—followed by a four-hour connecting train ride to our next major destination, Manchester. The trip to Manchester was mainly to visit with Kenneth Hopper, one of Margie's Irish cousins. When we found out that the next evening there was going to be a performance by the Hallé Orchestra of the Verdi *Requiem*, conducted by John Barbirolli, we knew we had to go. I got in touch with the first horn of the Hallé, a man named Maurice Handford, who told me that the concert was completely sold out. But he said he would try his darndest to find some way of getting us into the concert, especially after I told him that Barbirolli and I had known each other for many years. He asked Barbirolli if the Schullers could sit hidden in the back of the orchestra, to one side, near the brass. Barbirolli acceded happily, adding something like: gosh, I haven't seen that little tyke for years![62]

What we didn't know was that the only space that could be found for us was indeed near the brass, but also right next to the bass drum, with us jammed in between it and the side wall of the auditorium. But you see: it wasn't an ordinary bass drum. It was, in fact, the *biggest* bass drum I've ever seen in my entire life. It was at least twelve feet tall, and the percussionist who had to play this monster—ironically, a smallish fellow—had to stand on a high stool so that he could reach the center of the drumhead, which is where you have to play the drum. We were almost completely hidden; we could just barely see Barbirolli around the front of the drum. But we were happy to be there at all. And thank God, Verdi used the bass drum in only one movement, in the terrifying music of the "Dies irae." When the big drum let loose, it was a truly shattering, apocalyptic sound, promising doom and perdition. We could feel the stage tremble under our feet. When we thanked Barbirolli after the performance, particularly for that *very* special sonic experience, Barbirolli offered: "Yes, it does make a jolly good noise, doesn't it." Cool British understatement!

Maurice Handford, a wonderful friendly chap, drove us around Manchester and environs to see some of its interesting sights, including the Royal College of Music (where Sandy Goehr had studied for several years) and the Free Trade Hall (where many years later I was to conduct the Hallé Orchestra for several seasons).

On to London, mainly to visit Sandy Goehr and his new bride, Audrey. However, we also made it to London's three great museums: the Tate, the British, and the National, one each day—another feet-killing venture, but so worth the pain. But perhaps in an unexpected way our most memorable London experience occurred on our first morning there. It had to do with two of our three greatest loves: music and food. When we awoke in our splendid High Street hotel, I ordered breakfast from room service, while Margie turned on the little room radio. On came the most heavenly music from the BBC: Elgar's *Dream of Gerontius* oratorio, which I had never heard before. It put us in a mesmerized trance, especially when in parts it reminded me of my beloved *Parsifal* and Delius's *Sea Drift*. As for the food, if you've never had an "English breakfast," you haven't lived. It's the thick English ham and the wonderful grilled tomatoes that make the difference. We were in double heaven.

From London we headed for Berlin via the English Channel by ferry, and Calais, Brussels, and Cologne—more great theatre and opera, but no Furtwängler this time. And thence on to Munich (with still more opera), and a brief stopover in Mainz to buy another thirteen Alexander horns that I had promised to get for various students and colleagues.[63]

Although Margie and I disliked going on organized tours, wanting rather to be on our own, Hendrien (who never misled us in any way) had managed to talk us into joining a ten-day tour of Italy. And was it ever worth it. For a tour that was limited financially to a mere ten days, it was near perfect, encompassing four of Italy's most famed cities: Verona, Rome, Florence, and Venice. As promised by Hendrien, a good many of the renowned sights—churches, museums, monuments, statues, fountains—were all on the tour's itinerary. Indeed it was such an overwhelming sightseeing marathon that in the end—even though we absented ourselves occasionally from the group to get some sleep or to pick our own (often more musically related) sights—we couldn't take in any more. And to chronicle all that we did see and experience could take another chapter, all by itself. Suffice it to mention a very few of the most memorable of our Italian experiences.

Maybe it was for both of us nothing more than our first visit to Italy, or perhaps it was a special twilight light show Mother Nature had arranged for our arrival in Verona. I guess it was both. Having checked into the Albergo Due Torri, in a beautiful room in one of the hotel's two towers, before we could even unpack our bags we were startled by the amazing sight from our tower windows. Before us lay the entire city of Verona, directly below us the river Adige, the whole scene bathed in an incredible, luminous, orange-rose. The show was going to last only a few more minutes; the sun was sinking fast. We stood there transfixed, never having seen anything like it. I can still see it now very clearly in my mind's eye. What was especially fascinating for me, with my painter's eye for color, was to see the multiple shadings of orange-rose. Verona is a city located south enough and in very warm climes to have been constructed in lighter materials and colors: mostly sienna and yellowish brown, ochre, beige, and amber. When this range of colors and textures is aglow in the orange-rose of a setting sun, it is in its myriad tints and hues a sight that even the most subtle and fantastic colorist painter could not have envisioned. (Mother Nature is ultimately the greatest painter.)

We could not resist going to an opera at Verona's famous open-air amphitheater, and saw their typical cast-of-thousands *Aida*, elephants and all, spectacular in its way, but musically, vocally quite average. Of the numerous beautiful sights we beheld in our three days in Verona, I will single out only the extraordinary ten-foot-high sculptured bronze door to the church of San Zeno Maggiore, which Luigi Nono had urged us not to miss.

Rome was another matter. For all there is to see in the Eternal City, in all its bewildering profusion, we found the constant juxtaposition of ancient Rome with the insanity of modern Rome annoying, frustrating. With its millions of tourists crowding every square inch and every sight one might want to see, not to mention its crazy Italian drivers racing down the far-too-narrow, convoluted, ancient streets, not to mention the sheer noise of the city—it was all a bit too much. It was downright ludicrous to see how our tour bus had to fight its way through all these congestions and obtrusions.

Margie and I skipped St. Peter's and the Vatican, visiting instead the four fountains of Rome, which Respighi celebrated in his same-named orchestral masterpiece, and—also musically related—the famous Castel Sant' Angelo, towering above the Tiber River, a sight I had seen a hundred times as a backdrop in the third act of Puccini's *Tosca*, from which Scarpia, Tosca's tormentor, ruled Rome.

And what can one say about Florence in a paragraph or two? We saw most of the official sights to see, including the five-hundred-year-old Ponte Vecchio, the famous bridge crossing the Arno. In modern times the bridge became a kind of huge shopping mall; there were some thirty or forty little shops, designed to entice the tourist trade, on a bridge only 275 feet long. Margie was proud that she didn't buy anything more than a few postcards. Of all the magnificent sights we saw in Florence the one that fascinated me the most was the great square of Piazza della Signoria, in the center of Florence, where Savanarola, the fifteenth-century religious reformer, was burned at the stake as a heretic in 1498. I was very interested in Savanarola (as I had been years earlier in Rasputin), and was contemplating writing an opera on his life, an idea also instigated by the remarkable auto de fé Inquisition scene in Verdi's *Don Carlos*.[64]

On to Venice and its incredible wonders. I had wanted to visit Luigi Nono in his home in Giudecca, the big island across the Canale Grande known as the workers' district. But Gigi, I found out, was in Gravesano, Switzerland, with his teacher and friend, Scherchen. (We caught up with Gigi a few weeks later in Paris, attending a performance of his *Due espressioni*.) Hendrien de Leeuw had booked us in a second-floor room in the cutest little hotel, the three-star Marconi, replete with balcony and flowering hibiscus trees, only a few yards from the famous Rialto Bridge, overlooking a long stretch of the Grand Canal and its endless gondola and vaporetti traffic. The best way to see Venice in a limited amount of time is to travel in its many canals, and not in expensive gondolas but in the modestly priced vaporetti, Venice's famous water taxis. It is the only way to really get around, other than with lots of walking. We mostly absented ourselves from the tour group, and saw St. Mark's Square and Cathedral and the famous Campanile Tower on our own. And yes, we also fed the pigeons! But, almost like Rome, Venice was so overrun with tourists, most prominently fat-bellied Germans and (much slimmer) Japanese, both with at least three cameras hanging around their necks, that it was almost impossible to really enjoy Venice's incredible splendors. Even worse, Venice was having one of its famous stiflingly humid September heat waves.

It was actually a relief to head northward for Vienna, to see some of the sights we had missed last time, especially the spectacular palace of Schönbrunn and its dozens of magnificent fountains, but also to visit with my horn player friends Hans Berger and Freiberg. (This time we were careful about the Heurigen!)

Then to Paris via Donaueschingen and the Black Forest, to climax our trip with another taste of Paris's legendary nightlife, but mainly to visit with Nono and attend a few rehearsals and the performance of his *Due espressioni*, which I had heard and admired so much in Donaueschingen the year before. But what a disappointment that was. The Orchestre Nationale behaved miserably toward Nono; they obviously hated his music, but worse, they callously and arrogantly expressed their venom in all kinds of ways in order to sabotage the performance, as only French orchestras can get away with. (They are all civil servants, and can't be fired.)[65] As disgraceful as it was, neither the conductor nor anyone else in the directorship of the French Radio could do anything about the situation. To be fair, in the concert the orchestra rallied to some extent, I guess out of Gallic self-pride. But still, the performance was far from what it could have been.[66]

We did have one mildly scary experience in Paris. It had to do with the black market, which even nine years after the end of the war was still very big all over Europe. Sandy Goehr had told us to be sure to see his friend Alain, who made his living in the black market, and who would give us a terrific deal in changing our dollars into French francs. We had never dealt in the black market, and in our innocence felt a certain unease about getting caught by the police. Meeting secretly in an alley in Paris's Jewish ghetto, arranged through hand signals and recognition of what Alain was going to wear, was not exactly our cup of tea, and ending up in a French jail was not a prospect we looked forward to. But Alain turned out to be one of the handsomest men either of us had ever seen—he could easily have been a superstar in films—who spoke the most elegant, perfect English, American English to boot. *He was a charmer!* The transaction was over in a few minutes with no incident of any kind. "See you again, I hope," he said cheerily. "You have my phone."

With the money we saved, we had ourselves a couple of wonderful meals in a cafeteria we discovered near our hotel—it was the first American-style cafeteria in Paris—and Margie bought herself some beautiful embroidered stockings and a very sexy pair of shoes on the rue de la Paix, Paris's answer to Los Angeles's Rodeo Drive.

We had to separate now because I had to get back to New York in a hurry, by air, since my first rehearsal (*Meistersinger*, of all pieces—a very heavy blow) was in less than a week. Margie had decided to take a more luxurious, leisurely mode of travel back to the States, on the fabulous *Nieuw Amsterdam*. As I headed for Le Bourget Airport, she took the train to Rotterdam and a weeklong relaxed crossing of the Atlantic.

More European trips followed in subsequent years, indeed more or less regularly throughout my life, most often, of course, in connection with my composing and conducting commitments. What was special and unusual about our 1956 trip to Europe was that we took our eighteen-month-old son, Edwin, along. It is the kind of thing that nowadays would be frowned upon, maybe even legally forbidden, but hardly questioned in the 1950s. It was a courageous, daring thing to do, in fact a heroic decision for Margie to make, since the burdens of taking a baby along on a three-month roving tour of Europe clearly would fall mostly upon her shoulders. For months she was quite torn between two awful prospects: being without her dear baby or being without her husband for a whole three months. The thought of staying in New York while I would be gallivanting around Europe alone was simply intolerable. On the other hand, taking care of a baby still in diapers and in constant need of proper infant care for all that time, in five different countries, was a truly daunting prospect. We allayed her basic concern of traveling without any help by hiring a German-speaking nanny—German was by now Margie's best second language—to accompany us on the entire trip, except for a two-week period during which the two of us would go off on a little vacation of our own while Karina and Peter Strauss in Garmisch-Partenkirchen took care of baby Edwin.

This solution worked out very well. Upon our arrival in Holland we rented as big an Opel station wagon as we could find, with plenty of room for a good-sized crib, a collapsible baby carriage, and several suitcases filled with various baby necessaries that Margie didn't want to have to buy in Europe.

The main targets of the 1956 trip were Darmstadt (for eleven days)—no Donaueschingen this time—a few weeks in southern France, including Avignon, Nice, Cannes, the music festival at Aix-en-Provence (not to mention the great Rhône Valley wines); a vacation outing (at Margie's request) to visit Rothenburg Ob Der Tauber in Franconia (arguably the best preserved, most romantic medieval town in all of Germany); the Italian Tyrol, especially Merano and Bolzano, and a quick three-day visit to nearby Venice, primarily to attend certain events of the Venice Biennale and to see our friends the Nonos; a visit in late August to the Salzburg Festival, mainly to see Mitropoulos and hear a few Mozart operas (it was the two hundredth anniversary of Wolfgang Amadeus's birthday); and, of course, the mandatory visit with my relatives in Krefeld and Burgstädt.

Of all those encounters and experiences, I will single out only three: one, undoubtedly the highlight of the whole trip, another, an important musical event, the third—well, that was quite another matter.

It was our little private vacation that ultimately topped the list of happiest times among so many on this trip. To visit and explore Rothenburg Ob Der Tauber was a dream come true, maybe even more for me than for Margie, because as a young boy in Germany my Burgstädt grandmother had often talked about her visit there with her father, back in the 1890s, and what a special place Rothenburg was in Germany's history. It was founded in the late 1100s by the Holy Roman Emperor Frederick Barbarossa. She would always finish with the admonition "some day you *must* go there."[67] One of the things that makes Rothenburg unique is that the entire town (of some eleven thousand inhabitants) is completely encompassed by a six-foot-thick wall towering above the Tauber River, in some places three hundred feet high. The wall is topped by covered walkways from which one can look down into the enclosed town and the surrounding terrain in all directions. Entry from the outside to the inner Rothenburg is possible only through eleven gate towers that, as part of the wall system, encircle the town. These towers are so iconic and so unique to the town's medieval architecture that I'm sure there isn't a single German household that doesn't have a picture, drawing, or etching of these imposing edifices hanging in the living room.

I think we inspected every prominent sight in the town and covered every inch of accessible ground, including a one-hour picture-taking stroll around the whole perimeter of the town. There, on its west side, where the wall is at its highest, we saw some odd looking, slightly protruding openings high up in the wall. Looking in our guide book, we were amazed (and amused) to learn that these were what passed for medieval privies, installations which, so the guide book said, only the wealthiest burghers in the town could afford to have (like the burgomaster and town councilors). Evidently, the accumulated waste would eventually be dropped down the three hundred feet into the river valley.

But perhaps our greatest surprise was to find—right in the town square, the marketplace next to the town hall—a stunningly good nouvelle cuisine gourmet restaurant named Lucculus, after the legendary Roman epicure. It was, as far as I know, the first such restaurant in Germany, for it took French haute cuisine a long time after World War II to infiltrate its neighbor country—for various political and economic reasons.

I took advantage of Margie's request for a vacation within our vacation by piggybacking onto it two ideas of my own. One arose out of my keen interest in medieval music, greatly spurred on by concerts of Ars Nova and early Renaissance music that I had organized and conducted for several years in New York. I had become very interested in acquiring a particularly important fourteenth-century manuscript facsimile known as the Bamberg Codex, a collection recently published by the Schloss Library in Weikersheim, a town only seven miles from Rothenburg. To my delight, the library allowed me to make a photocopy of the entire Codex, some sixty pages, for a minimal cost. It was for many years one of my rarest manuscript treasures, and in later years I performed works from the Codex several times.

The other idea was on a much grander scale: it was to visit—and in some cases to stay in—a series of nine castles and palaces, all built early in the second millennium by the Habsburg, the renowned royal family that held thrones in central Europe from the thirteenth century until 1918, when the last Hapsburg relinquished his title at the end of World War I. None of the castles we saw in Franconia were ruins, as you found, for example, so often in the Rhineland. In the 1950s most of the twentieth-century Hapsburg descendants still owned their castles, but had them converted into hotels or hostels. And what very comfortable and charming hostelries they were.

We were fortunate to meet one of these Hapsburg descendants early on in our nine-castle tour, a handsome, distinguished looking elderly lady with the proud title Therese Freifrau von Gebsattel.[68] The average American never gets to see, let alone stay in, a fifteenth-century castle. I had lived in one, albeit of somewhat later vintage, for four years, as a boy in

Gebesee. But for Margie, visiting these Hapsburg castles (all in the region of Bamberg and Würzburg) was an incredible experience. Walking across a drawbridge over a centuries-old moat into a cobblestone castle courtyard, and suddenly finding yourself surrounded on all four sides by imposing four-story edifices and towers, can be a very impressive, awe inspiring experience. As in our stay in Scotland, it fires the imagination to sit and dine in some ancient vaulted Weinkeller, hewn right out of the rock, where perhaps a few hundred years ago some emperor or duke held forth at an enormous banquet with all his courtiers and ladies-in-waiting in attendance.

One night, in one of these castles, we were fortunate enough to be given a beautifully furnished room with an amazingly ornate canopied bed, on one of the upper floors of the castle's main tower. I often had dreamt of such things but never thought they would ever come true.[69]

Shortly before our trip I had heard that Stravinsky's most recent work, his *Canticum Sacrum* (*Sacred Canticle*) was going to be premiered sometime in September, during the Venice Bienniale. It was one of his new twelve-tone pieces, only the second in the new style to which Stravinsky had converted in 1953. I had hoped to sandwich in a stopover in Venice to hear the work, and also to visit with Gigi and Nuria Nono, who were constantly entreating us to stay with them in Giudecca whenever we might be in the neighborhood. When we got to Bolzano in Tyrol, I suddenly realized that we were only about eighty miles from Venice. So we decided to cut our Tyrolean visit short by three days, not at all an easy decision, since the region around Bolzano offers some of the most spectacularly beautiful scenery imaginable. But I felt that duty called, as it were, especially for me as a composer for whom Stravinsky's music had already meant so much, and from whom I had learned so much. And now there was the additional sense of curiosity about how Stravinsky was using the newly adopted twelve-tone technique. (At the time I had not yet heard *Agon* or *In Memoriam Dylan Thomas*, his two previous works in that style.)

We called Gigi to let him know that we were coming to Venice after all, and would he be so kind as to get us two tickets for the world premiere concert at St. Mark's Cathedral. It turned out that that concert was completely sold out—as Gigi put it, "even the Pope wouldn't be able to get in at this point"—but Gigi did get us a free pass to the second-to-last rehearsal, as a famous composer from America. (Even if not true, it worked). In that prepenultimate rehearsal, it seemed that half of the European contemporary music world was present. I found out later that the Stravinsky concert was in fact only one of a series of seven concerts given in Teatro La Fenice and other concert venues as a week-long international festival of contemporary music presented under the auspices of the Bienniale—in other words, a minifestival within the larger Venice Festival. This naturally brought all the usual suspects of the modern music hegemony to the legendary city.

One slight disappointment for us was that this *Canticum* rehearsal was not conducted by Stravinsky but by Robert Craft, when we, of course, had expected to see the old man himself on the podium. I was also surprised to see no violins or cellos on the stage; the orchestra consisted primarily of woodwinds and brass, with only small sections of violas and double basses.[70] I always loved that clear, lean, uncluttered, rather ascetic sound that Stravinsky got in his string-reduced pieces. It was certainly one of his signature sounds.

I was eager to hear how the great man would deal with the twelve-tone technique; I didn't really know what to expect. Thus I was surprised, as the rehearsal progressed, Craft occasionally repeating certain sections, cleaning up ragged attacks and poor ensemble balances, that not all of the music was atonal, and I assumed, therefore, not twelve-tone; that in fact some of it, near the beginning of the work—what I later saw, once I was able to acquire a score, was the "Euntes in mundum" section ("Go ye into all the world")—was entirely tonal (it sounded like pure B-flat major to me), while the actual opening of the piece sounded like Gregorian chant. Yet all of it—all of it—sounded unmistakably Stravinskian. What especially impressed me was that the parts that were clearly and distinctively atonal and twelve-tone, such as the "Surgo, aquilo" ("Awake, northwind") and the third movement "Caritas" ("Charity"), sounded unequivocally like Stravinsky, not like Schönberg or Webern, let alone Berg—which is exactly what many critics and other observers had expected and predicted.

So much of *Canticum Sacrum* kept reminding me of the *Symphony of Psalms* and *Oedipus Rex*, written twenty-five and twenty-eight years earlier, respectively, in part because Stravinsky had once again used his favorite language, Latin. He loved the abstractness, the remoteness (to twentieth-century ears) of Latin. For Stravinsky Latin's archaism was ossified, but not dead. Indeed he saw it as a pure, live, phonetic material, especially rich in vowels, which he could, if necessary, dissect, reassemble, and reconstruct polyphonically. In his oratorio *Oedipus Rex*, the ultimate oracular Greek legend, Stravinsky set it not in Greek (or French or Russian), but in Latin.[71]

For me one of the most brilliant touches in *Canticum Sacrum* was (and is) the work's brief eight-bar introduction, which I considered to be an allusion to Gregorian chant, and which was subtly echoed later in the work. As I realized upon perusal of the score months later, those eight bars are in fact the dedication of the composition to Saint Mark, in Latin: "Dedicated to the City of Venice, in Praise of its Patron Saint, the Blessed Mark, Apostle." The dedication was composed right *into the work*, brilliantly set in a style and language removed enough from Stravinsky's own to function as something separate from the rest of the composition and yet somehow still a part of it,[72] set distinctively and very simply, humbly, for two male voices and three trombones. What a stroke of genius!

The one aspect of that rehearsal that I thought was a bit absurd—and insulting—was that Robert Craft conducted the entire rehearsal not with a baton, but with a no. 2 yellow pencil. Unbelievable!

Obbligato

Stravinsky's sudden conversion to twelve-tonality around 1953 sent enormous shock waves through the music world, especially, of course, for the thousands of adherents to the longtime prevailing neoclassic style, which Stravinsky had almost single-handedly forged in the early 1920s. Across the entire range of the neoclassic field in its many stylistic manifestations—from Aaron Copland to Nadia Boulanger—everyone was in a state of shock, unable to comprehend how their revered Igor could abandon them all. A traitor to the cause, and, worse yet, as if to rub salt into their wounds, he deserted over to the detested enemy camp of Schönberg and his followers. Many people were especially surprised when word got out that it was an unknown named Robert Craft, a recent Juilliard student, who had been singularly influential in persuading Stravinsky to reassess the whole concept of twelve-tone and serialism as an important, valid form of musical expression.

It was all too much, impossible to believe and to accept. Many musicians and composers—even some critics—went so far as to question Stravinsky's sincerity in making such a dramatic stylistic switch. But Stravinsky's conversion was certainly genuine, proven by the fact that in the last fifteen years of his life he wrote at least another dozen masterful works in the twelve-tone idiom. But it is also confirmed in his writings and comments in interviews and other evidentiary information, which includes, most convincingly, an account of a meeting in Paris in the early fifties between Stravinsky and one of his oldest, closest friends from boyhood—the name Pyotr Souvchinsky lingers in my memory—a gathering to which, by chance, Stockhausen and Boulez (who happened to be in Paris visiting with their former teacher, Olivier Messiaen) were also invited, although only for after-dinner drinks.

As it was told to me by Stockhausen, it was a long evening of reminiscences about the old days in Russia and the 1920s in Paris. (Souvchinsky, like Stravinsky, had also fled to Switzerland and then to France after the Russian revolution.) By the time Karlheinz and Pierre and a few other friends and colleagues (such as Madeleine Milhaud and Ivan Wyschnegradsky) arrived, the two septuagenarian friends were, as the saying goes, well into their cups, having imbibed enough wine and cognac to put them on the mellow side. At some point the subject of composition, musical styles, the latest developments in music and the like came up, and eventually—probably inevitably—the words "twelve-tone" and "serialism" entered the discussion. Stockhausen said that Stravinsky just sat there for a long time, saying not a word, quietly listening to the banter crisscrossing the room. Then suddenly, as if coming out of a long reverie, Stravinsky, now in a very melancholy mood—I remember Stockhaussen's exact words: "in einem ganz melancholichem Ton (in a thoroughly melancholic tone)"—slowly raised his hand, quieting the discussion. Seemingly lost in thought, he soliloquized, and in a somewhat apologetic tone (here I am obviously resorting to reconstructive paraphrase, since I wasn't present at that occasion, and Stravinsky was speaking in French, but Stockhausen was telling me the story in German): You see, I now realize that in all these years I have been going in the wrong direction, and that of all of us composers the one who had the right idea from the beginning was Webern, even more than Schönberg. I made a gigantic detour—I think a very beautiful one—but it led eventually to a dead end.

Stunned silence in the room. If that doesn't confirm that Stravinsky's conversion was genuine, I don't know what would or could. It is, of course, also proven by the fact that for the rest of his life, nearly another twenty years—he died in 1971—he never wavered in his conviction that the twelve-tone concept would henceforth govern and inspire his musical creativity.[73] What is most interesting and important to understand is that Stravinsky immediately developed a very personal, individualistic approach to the twelve-tone way of composing: no mere imitation or adherence to the methods used by the Second Viennese School triumvirate. The astonishing result is that all of Stravinsky's late twelve-tone works sound not in the slightest like Schönberg, Berg, or Webern (three composers who, by the way, also sound *completely* different from one another—a truism very often forgotten or purposely ignored), and that, in fact, all those compositions are instantly recognizable as Stravinsky's, and only his. There's no way they can be confused with the music of the three Viennese. Which shows both Stravinsky's greatness as one of the most individualistic and original musical creators of all times, but also the breadth and depth, the stylistic flexibility inherent in the twelve-tone concept, allowing composers of talent to develop within it a completely personal and individualistic musical language.[74] This in turn gives the lie to the endless accusations that the twelve-tone technique is perforce narrowing, confining, and an inherent deterrent to musical creativity.

Like his great friend and artistic contemporary and collaborator, Pablo Picasso, whose career can also be divided into at least three stylistic periods, Stravinsky wrote masterful, completely original music in all the three styles he adopted during his lifetime.

* * * * *

The painful episode alluded to earlier occurred on the third day of our 1956 trip. Its memory has haunted me hundreds of times, and every time I think of it I cringe in an uncontrollable spasm, my hands flying involuntarily to my face, trying to hide my shame. We had just enjoyed a marvelous dinner in the great spacious dining room of our favorite hotel in Holland, the Kurhaus in Scheveningen. Edwin had been the perfect little gentleman, the food had been superb, our two waiters (who remembered us from before—always a nice feeling) had treated us like royalty. It was just one of those simple, contented, serendipitous experiences that made you feel good. When we got back to our room—I was holding Edwin in my arms—and as Margie unlocked the door, I, in a fit of unrestrained exuberance, tossed Edwin up in the air. I can hear the heavy thud now, as his little head hit the upper frame of the door. (In starting to write that sentence my hands flew involuntarily to my forehead, my eyes closing, my head bowed.) I realized instantly that I could have killed Edwin had I thrown him a little bit higher. What saved him was that in this wonderful, stately, venerable hotel, the doors were (as was fashionable in the late nineteenth century) taller by at least a foot or two than was common in newer buildings.

We were both hysterical, as Edwin screamed and cried—unabatedly. The concierge called a house doctor, who came immediately and—oh my God, what a relief—confirmed that there was nothing broken, and that there didn't even appear to have been an actual concussion.

The sound of that thud on my boy's little head will never leave me. In some deep way I will never recover from this frightful incident.

Premonition

I'm standing in front of a great orchestra, having just been introduced to it and welcomed by the orchestra's manager. Sporadic, not particularly enthusiastic applause follows—understandably—I'm a newcomer, an unknown quantity. In thirty seconds the hands on the clock in front of me will be in their appropriate position, the bigger one facing due west, the smaller directly due south. It will be nine thirty a.m., and the clock will at that moment tell me that I may begin rehearsing.

In these last seconds I am still thinking as to what kernels of musical wisdom I might impart to the ladies and gentlemen sitting in front of me. The rather portly, friendly looking man sitting at my immediate right in the first chair smiles at me—encouragingly. The night before an old friend from the Met, now sitting to my left in the assistant concertmaster chair, had told me: "Just do what you feel, and don't worry. Show us what you feel, and we'll do the rest." It was good, calming advice.

A gentle breeze wafted across the stage, and I thought I heard the distant rumble of a train. Yep, it was the train they had told me about, which during the concert would clatter by exactly on schedule at 8:31 p.m. I thought: Hmm, probably just when the music will be at its softest . . . oh, well!

A nod from the personnel manager told me it was nine thirty. I thought for a few seconds about exactly what kind of a gentle, inviting, *pianissimo* downbeat I needed to give, and how I might have to say something to the players by way of a correction for a certain upcoming passage that is often interpreted with the wrong rhythmic feeling. But, oh no; quite the contrary. The most heavenly, beautiful, warm *pianissimo* sound flowed out of the cello and bass section, so that the hair on my neck immediately stood on end. As I struggled to regain consciousness, my brain said to itself: Schuller, just shut up; say nothing, just let them play. By the ninth measure I had enough presence of mind to turn to the violins and violas for their *pianissimo* entrance, certain now that they would not disappoint me. And, of course, they didn't. And—how wonderful—they played the murmuring three-four rhythms in bar nine and ten exactly right.[75]

And the clarinet and oboe entered in the thirteenth bar with the most beautifully blended unison I had ever heard, by which point I realized that I would have very little to say to these fine musicians, that, in fact, it would be wise to stop worrying about what *they* might or might not do correctly, to concentrate instead on whether *I* was doing the right thing, and just ride along with the flow of the music.

It was heavenly. I felt that we were—all of us on that stage—wafted along on the serene sounds of this music. It went on, from one blissful moment to the next, coming to rest some twenty-five minutes later on an exquisitely soft, saturate E-major chord. My friend had been right. "Just show us what you feel. We'll do the rest." I am not sure who led whom, whether I led the orchestra or whether the orchestra—and the music—was leading me. Perhaps it was both, in a quiet, secret communion. That rehearsal was a revelatory experience, almost mystical in its effect on me.

The concert went even better than the rehearsal, if such a thing was possible. And oh—by the way—the train came by exactly at 8:31 p.m.—and of course, at a very quiet moment in the music. It was a very long train, and took almost twenty seconds to pass by.

*　*　*　*　*

Unquestionably, 1956 and 1957 stand out in retrospect as by far the most important seminal years in my early life and career as a composer. For in that two-year period a trio of events took place that clearly put me on the map as a composer of some consequence, both nationally and internationally: (1) the New York Philharmonic performances of *two* of my works in one season, (2) the European premiere of my first String Quartet at the Darmstadt Festival to wide international acclaim, and (3) the first performance of my *Brass Symphony* in Europe at the 1957 Salzburg Festival. I owe both the New York and Salzburg performances to Dimitri Mitropoulos, who not only programmed the work on one of his Salzburg concerts with the Vienna Philharmonic, but also invited me to come to Salzburg—at his expense—to be present at this for me most prestigious occasion.

Mitropoulos was much liked by the Vienna Philharmonic Orchestra musicians, a matter worth mentioning for two reasons. As one of the world's oldest and most preeminent orchestras,[76] and extremely prideful of its long association with so many of the world's most celebrated conductors, it is, with its self-governing management, inordinately possessive about who is allowed to conduct the orchestra. (You can't buy or bribe your way into the Vienna Philharmonic, or hire it for a recording date.) Second, only a conductor whom the orchestra loved and respected could get away with programming a contemporary work—not generally the Vienna Philharmonic's forte, let alone by an unknown, non-European, non-Austrian composer—and a piece that would take an exceptional amount of rehearsal time and, worse yet, require the hire of an extra half-dozen musicians, while at the same time *not using* more than seventy of its roster of players in the piece—a matter of not inconsequential financial implications.

Mitropoulos installed me, with his selfless generosity, not in some moderately priced simple pension, but in the luxurious Königshof, Salzburg's finest four-star hotel, where he also was staying. The first of that week's rehearsals was devoted entirely to my *Brass Symphony* and went reasonably well, considering that the Vienna Philharmonic rarely played any really modern contemporary music, and certainly not in the atonal or highly chromatic style of the Second Viennese School. In fact, I was quite impressed with how well and with what considerable agility the six trumpets, with their Viennese rotary-valve instruments, and the horns on their single F horns, negotiated their very difficult, challenging parts. I was quite relieved because one never knows how orchestra musicians who have no choice or say in what they are required to play will react, or how seriously they will take their task. I say that not only because of my lifelong involvements with orchestra musicians—I know them as a distinctive breed extremely well—but also because I had come to the rehearsal about thirty minutes early to greet and meet my four horn colleagues. One of them said to me, in his nearly incomprehensible Viennese dialect: "Na ja, da hamm se wieder mal 'was zusammen engeschrieben! (roughly: Well, you certainly scribbled together some stuff there)," delivered in a somewhat deprecating tone of voice and with a sardonic smile, as if really wishing to say "shit" instead of "stuff." (On the other hand, his caustic remark at least indicated that he had looked at his part, and possibly even practiced it.)

But one thing that really surprised me—alas disappointingly—was that certain muted horn passages were played incorrectly. My notation calls for the use of mutes, but the entire section played those passages "hand-stopped," a type of muting that produces a very distinctive sound, completely different from what is produced by using a metal or fibre mute inserted into the bell of the horn.

After the rehearsal I told Mitropoulos that he should please ask the horns to use mutes, instead of hand-stopping. (He had also wondered about that.) When he did so in the next rehearsal, to my astonishment, Gottfried von Freiberg rose to his full height—although portly and not very tall, he suddenly looked very imposing—and with an annoyed expression on his face and a rather adversarial, almost threatening don't-mess-with-me tone of voice, lectured Mitropoulos to the effect that "we Vienna horns DO NOT use mutes; we have *never* used mutes, and I doubt that we ever will. We don't even *own* mutes."

Whew! With that, Freiberg sat down with an unmistakably determined gesture, not without a side-glance at me that said: "So there! Take that!" His three colleagues smiled approvingly.

There was a stunned silence in the room. Mitropoulos turned to me with a deeply injured, confused look, completely intimidated[77] by Freiberg's defiant rhetoric. I knew that Mitropoulos, cowed into a pained silence, would not counter Freiberg. Almost any other conductor would have immediately told him, and in no uncertain terms: "What do you mean, you don't use mutes? If you don't own mutes, then get some! This is ridiculous. You have mutes by the next rehearsal, or else!" Mitropoulos just could not bring himself to say anything like that. He would just fall—collapse—into an agonized silence.[78]

The last part of the rehearsal didn't go very well; Mitropoulos was so distraught that he really wasn't able to function fully. Realizing how upset he was—maybe even with himself, for being unable to fight back—I told him after the rehearsal not to worry about the problem anymore, that I would take care of it. I would talk to the horn players, my professional colleagues; as such, they must have some degree of respect for me. I would resolve the standoff. Dimitri gave me a baleful look.

To tell the truth I wasn't all that sure myself. Frankly, I had never—never—heard of a group of horn players—*anywhere*—that didn't use mutes, didn't *want* to use mutes, didn't even *own* mutes. It was incomprehensible to me that high-level professional musicians would totally disregard what very great composers such as Wagner, Strauss, and Debussy (to mention just three) had written and required in their music. Later that day, I sought out Freiberg. We met at a café near where he lived when in Salzburg, the Goldene Krone (Golden Crown). The discussion was friendly and calm. It went something like this, as best as I can remember. I started by expressing my total disbelief that he and his horn section never used mutes. Incredulous, I said: "That *can't* be! You mean to tell me, that in all the years with Furtwängler—and Strauss and Walter and Clemens Krauss, and all those other famous conductors—you never used mutes in Wagner at the opera?"[79]

"No. Never," was his terse, unyielding reply.

"I don't believe you. That can't be."

"Well, it's true. Believe me or not."

"I bet you Stiegler [Freiberg's predecessor in the first three decades of the century] used mutes."

"I don't think so."

I wasn't getting anywhere. "Well, listen," I said, getting sort of desperate, "if I get you four mutes, just for my piece, would you please use them—*for me*, as a horn player colleague and friend?" I added, with an inviting smile: "I'll buy the rich Vienna Philharmonic a set of beautiful mutes, this afternoon, in the music store here."

"Don't bother," he countered smugly. "The music store here doesn't sell any mutes, doesn't carry any."

I couldn't believe my ears. "Well, then"—adamant—"I'll go to Munich and buy some mutes there. I *know* they have them."

He just smiled enigmatically.

"We'll see. I'll get you yet," was all I could bring myself to say.

Under the circumstances, I thought it was a reasonably amicable meeting. When I left him, he was still quaffing his big stein of Munich Löwenbräu beer.

But I really wasn't all that confident. Freiberg was unyielding; he taunted me in his peculiar manner, content to continue this little game, which he undoubtedly felt he would win in the end. It was a bizarre situation.

Then suddenly, I had a bright idea. I had just learned that the Berlin Philharmonic had arrived in Salzburg two days earlier. Everyone was talking about it because it was the first time ever that the Berliners were invited to appear at the Salzburg Festival. Even Furtwängler, music director of both orchestras, Berlin and Vienna, had never succeeded in bringing the BPO to Salzburg. I knew that if the Berlin horn section wasn't going to need their mutes for their first concert, my friend Martin Ziller would let me borrow their set. I called Martin, and told him what was going on. "I'm not surprised," was his immediate reaction. "No, we're not using our mutes in this concert. You can have them. But make sure we get them back."

And so it came to pass that the Vienna Philharmonic horns used mutes *for the first time*. Freiberg and company finally relented, but only after a private meeting between the horn section and Mitropoulos, a meeting called by the Vienna Philharmonic's orchestra committee and attended by two of its members, with Mitropoulos pleading as only he could. The committee apologized to me and Dimitri, saying that this whole episode was turning into "ein unangebrachtes und unerwünchtes cause célèbre." I'll never forget those words: "an uncalled for and unwelcome *cause célèbre*."

After all that tzimmes, the performances came off remarkably well. Mitropoulos, as usual conducting from memory, motivated and inspired the players with this amazing combination of intensity and sensitivity that characterized his art at its best. In one particular respect it was the most interesting and unusual sounding performance of this much-performed piece that I have ever heard. The Vienna brass got a deep, rich, slightly dark sound—I called it "blood red" in a letter to Margie—that gave the piece a certain weight and gravity. Part of that was Mitropoulos's influence; he always seemed to get a rich, full, weighted-down sound, whatever or wherever he conducted. But it was also, I realized, the particular type of instruments the Viennese played (the instruments' bores and mouthpieces), as well as their unique conception of a saturate sound. It was quite amazing; I just loved it. It enriched the piece.

I saw Freiberg after the concert. "Na, sint's jetzt zufrieden mit uns? (Well, are you satisfied with us now?)"

"Of course," I said—"and more."

The whole group was pretty jubilant backstage—and I'm sure quite relieved that it went so well. They were pleased with themselves, deservedly so.

It was a big critical success, and also with the audience, although I believe more because of the sheer novelty of the piece and the virtuoso playing of the ensemble than for any real understanding or appreciation of the work. Almost all the reviews, even the most favorable, revealed a certain bewilderment.

I was totally surprised and deeply touched by how many of my friends came to Salzburg from all over specifically to hear my work and to be in attendance at my big European debut: Horst Lippman, Lothar Faber, Albert Mangelsdorff, Ronnie Ross (all the way from England),

Joachim Behrendt, Franz Ortner, Hugo Burghauser (vacationing in Bad Gastein), Rolf Lieber-mann, and so many more. And it was a thrill to receive the heartfelt congratulations of three of the most prominent European composers attending the festival: Gottfried von Einem,[80] Werner Egk, and Boris Blacher, all colleagues, whose music I admired greatly.

It was also during that week in Salzburg that I met Alfred Schlee, the director of publica-tions at Universal Edition in Vienna. I had just seen him a few weeks earlier in Darmstadt, where he heard the European premiere of my first String Quartet. Now he had come espe-cially to Salzburg to hear my *Brass Symphony*. Very impressed and fulsome in his praise, he told me how beautiful he thought my String Quartet had been at Darmstadt, and that now, with the success "here in Salzburg of your *Brass Symphony*, we would like to have you in our catalogue, along with Schönberg, Berg, and Webern—and Stockhausen and Boulez. How does that appeal to you?"

I was, of course, flattered and impressed. But I had to tell him that the *Brass Symphony* was already committed to an American publisher, Broude Brothers in New York. He was quite dis-appointed. But after some further discussions I did sign a contract with Schlee for my String Quartet. And it was the beginning of a long, warm relationship with him and Universal Edi-tion, although they never became my main publisher. Schlee kept trying to sign me up with an exclusive contract, but eventually, as several other publishers, especially Schott, also fought over my music in the ensuing years, it was Associated Music Publishers in New York (most recently merged with G. Schirmer) that eventually became, in 1960, my main publisher.[81]

In Salzburg I was also approached by Heinrich Strobel, in this case not about publishing but about the possibility of writing a work for his Southwest German Radio Orchestra in Baden-Baden, with its great conductor Hans Rosbaud. That led eventually to a commission from the Südwestfunk and, in 1960, the performance in Donaueschingen of *Contrasts* for solo woodwind quintet and orchestra.

Looking back on those years, it is quite clear to me that all the good things that began to come my way as a composer were incubated in places like Salzburg and Darmstadt and Donaueschingen, as a result of performances there.

I suppose the most famous person I met in Salzburg was Herbert von Karajan. I had never even thought about meeting him, first of all because it never occurred to me that someone that high in the pantheon of world celebrities—with his five palatial houses scattered through-out Europe, his three or four Jaguars and BMWs, his several airplanes and yachts—would ever want or deign to meet a young, unknown American composer. Nor was I a particular admirer of Karajan's conducting—his penchant for doing pieces such as Beethoven's *Eroica* with six horns and four trumpets (!) was not exactly to my musical tastes—and I wasn't espe-cially enthralled with his Nazi associations and his unceremonious feuding with Furtwängler. Beyond all that, I have never been a celebrity chaser. And I was sure he would never be inter-ested in my music, as I knew that he was not much interested in *any* contemporary music. So what would be the point of meeting with him?

It was Karajan who, as artistic director of the Salzburg Festival, had invited Mitropoulos to conduct several concerts. I have no idea what Dimitri's feelings about Karajan were; I never asked him. But for whatever reason (I'm sure he only meant well), Dimitri thought I should meet with Karajan. He really pressed me on this, and since my admiration and respect for Dimitri was such that I would do anything for him, I acceded to his suggestion. An appointment was arranged for a fifteen-minute audience with Karajan right after one of his Berlin Philharmonic rehearsals. (I feel compelled to mention that I was disinvited from attending his rehearsal).

I don't remember very much about the meeting, except that we spoke German and that he was quite friendly—in his austere way. He mentioned that Mitropoulos had told him that I was "such a good horn player" and that I was one of his "most highly regarded young composers—"Er denkt sehr viel von Ihnen (He thinks very highly of you)." Which then, near the end of the meeting, led to the question du jour: "Tell me one modern American piece or composer I should do."

I wasn't prepared for that, but after five seconds' thought, I said: "Well, I would suggest Charles Ives's *Unanswered Question*. Do you know it?"

"I've heard of it. No, I don't really know it. Is it really good?"

"Oh yes, sir. It's a marvelous piece: short, very original, very prophetic for its time—from 1906."[82]

He thanked me in typical gracious Viennese. The meeting was over. "Sorry, I must go now"—in English.

Through von Einem I met Günther Rennert, considered at that time the most gifted, most outstanding stage director in the German-speaking opera world. I had already seen several of his productions (in Vienna, Munich, and Berlin), including my favorite, Rennert's incredible staging of von Einem's *The Trial*. I would never have anticipated that Rennert would some day be staging my first opera, *The Visitation*, in its premiere in Hamburg.

I wanted to take a few side trips in the immediate environs of Salzburg: for example, to the little village of Oberndorf, where in 1818 Franz Gruber composed and first performed *Silent Night, Holy Night* on Christmas Eve in St. Nicholas Church; or to Berchtesgaden, just a few miles across the border in Germany; or to the nearby Königssee, widely considered to be the most beautiful lake in Germany, vying in grandeur with those of Switzerland and northern Italy (it is five miles long and only three-quarters of a mile wide; the surrounding six-thousand-foot mountains rise almost perpendicularly from the water.) But ultimately I was prevented from undertaking any of those excursions[83] by my crowded schedule of rehearsals and meetings and performances, which I felt I had to go to (including seeing the first presentation in Europe of Eugene O'Neill's *A Touch of the Poet*).

But I did manage to squeeze in one short excursion, and that was an afternoon Kaffeeklatch meeting (featuring a great Sacher torte) with Hugo Burghauser, in his hotel Kaiserhof in Bad Gastein, one of the three most famous, most popular spa resorts in Austria. Gastein was only a short thirty-mile ride by bus from Salzburg[84]—and what a beautiful scenic ride it was, along the Salzach River, with many spectacular glimpses of the Gross Glockner, Austria's highest mountain (at 12,457 feet).

The visits to Darmstadt and Salzburg were the primary goals of that 1957 vacation and sight-seeing trip, unfortunately without Margie, who had to stay home to take care of little Edwin, still only two-and-a-half years old.

If I were to reduce all of my varied experiences and adventures (apart from Darmstadt and Salzburg) in Berlin, Frankfurt, Cologne, Munich, Paris, Nice, and Copenhagen to the three things that remain most vividly in my memory, it would represent a rich mixture of interests: A marvelous one-man show in Munich, at the famous Pinakothek, of some twenty recent paintings by Fritz Winter, one of the two German artists I admired most (the other is Hans Hartung) and who represented the ideal fusion to me of abstraction and expressionism viewed through a romantic lens.[85] My purchase in Berlin of Universal Edition's recently republished full score of *Wozzeck*, arguably the most exemplarily engraved musical score I know of. It is in itself a work of art—and it cost only fourteen dollars. A private demonstration in Cologne by Anton Springer, the inventor of a mechanism, the first one ever, that could speed up or slow down magnetic tape *without* changing the pitch level of the music, something that all of us who had been working with tape ever since 1948 had dreamt of many times.[86] It was Springer's first version of his invention and it was not yet perfected. There were a few more wrinkles to be straightened out. While the tempo of the music could be maintained and controlled, the vibrato on an instrument or a voice would unfortunately slow down as the tape speed decelerated; and there's nothing as unpleasant as an unnaturally slow vibrato, especially when it is mechanically produced or altered. Second, although the tempo at which the music seemed to be performed was correct, the sound spectrum was negatively affected, resulting in an artificial and unnatural sound, an intolerable listening experience. In parting, Springer told me that he expected to rectify all the remaining problems within a year or so. But Springer was a bit too optimistic. It wasn't until the early eighties that his invention was finally developed to the point where it could be applied practically and at a high professional level.

As the decade of the 1950s drew to a close, my life and career reached a distinctive watershed. It was in many ways the end of an era for me, and as such provides the perfect breakpoint to bring to a close the first half of this narrative.

While some things in my life ended—more or less—other things began. Within a very few years (1963) I was to abandon the one primary activity in which I had made my living, and happily so, for over twenty years: horn playing. When I left the Met in 1959, I continued playing for another three to four years as a freelancer, mostly in New York's recording studios, whether with jazz or pop or classical music. The last time I played the horn was at the Ojai Festival in California, performing the Mozart Quintet for Horn and Strings—a nice way to go.

By 1960 I had became established as one of the country's major composers, to such an extent that composing became my primary career and primary means of making a living. I had also become centrally active in the New York jazz scene—as a horn player, as an arranger and composer, as a conductor (a new thing in jazz), and, most significantly, as the inventor, the apostle of Third Stream—for which I was both heralded and vilified.[87] There were a few more important jazz or Third Stream recordings to come—with John Lewis and the Modern Jazz Quartet, with Dizzy Gillespie and J. J. Johnson. But many of my jazz-related activities soon came to a temporary halt, or to put it another way, modulated from performing and recording the music to writing about it—as in my jazz history, *Early Jazz*, and, some years later, *The Swing Era*.

As these particular endeavors diminished somewhat in my life, other career pursuits were added. In the second phase of my life I moved more proactively into education—teaching at Yale University, assuming the presidency of the New England Conservatory of Music, becoming head of the composition department at Tanglewood, and, later, artistic director of the Berkshire Music Center. Most important, I moved into a full-time career as a conductor. One of my first high-level guest conducting engagements was with the Chicago Symphony Orchestra, no less.

There soon followed two more full-time careers: the first, as a music publisher, founding Margun Music and Gunmar Music, publishing both jazz and modern classical music; the second, a bit later, founding, as an adjunct to the publishing companies, GM Records, which also produced contemporary jazz and classical music. I was devoted almost entirely to little known or unknown composers and performers, so my record and publishing endeavors were inherently incapable of being financially profitable, viable businesses. They were entirely subsidized by myself and were never conceived to be moneymaking ventures. I often called them my charitable institutions.

POSTLUDE

Who I Am—Now

WELL, TO BEGIN WITH, I'm a heck of a lot older—eighty-five, to be exact—and luckily still in very good health. In any case, I feel very young, more or less just as I felt when I was twenty-two. I am also fortunate that I love work, and love working hard. No, I'm not a workaholic. I just enjoy my work, and it consumes virtually my entire life. It may sound funny, but I wouldn't know what to do if it weren't for my work. In fact, the word "work" is hardly in my vocabulary, at least in the sense that most people use the word, as something onerous or awful, as something to constantly complain about. My work has been my life, and it has been largely a fulfilling joy—a fair share of unpleasant experiences notwithstanding.

I can't think of a single day in my life in which, upon getting up, I didn't know what I was going to do that day, what exciting things I was going to undertake and perhaps even accomplish. I have tried to fill every day with useful work, to contribute in some significant way to society, to humanity, to the world—if that doesn't sound too pretentious. How and how much we artists do or realistically contribute to humankind, to the common good—especially in a currently far too materialistic world—is an open question. All I can say for myself is that I at least have tried very hard to use my all too brief time on this planet as fruitfully as possible, as productively as I could imagine.

I take things very seriously. I always have, even as a young boy. By my philosophy of life, life is much too short to be unserious. This has nothing to do with not having fun, with not enjoying life. Serious does not mean unhappy. I have often been considered to be too serious. Even as a kid in school, whether in elementary school in New York or Germany, or later at St. Thomas, I was always teased for being "too serious." I was considered weird. But such people don't know how much fun I've had in my life. In fact part of being serious is having fun. I was *very serious* about enjoying life and having fun—whatever kind of fun one wants to imagine.

I am an Epicurean, not only in matters of food and drink, but also in the whole range of human pleasures, from the intellectual to the sensual. Among these enjoyments I still very much relish my daily preprandial martini (or Gibson, with cocktail onions), a delicious habit I have indulged in for over sixty years—and it hasn't hurt me yet.

I am at heart a rebel, or if not exactly a rebel in the full rebellious, revolutionary sense, at least highly independent. That makes me, if not exactly antiauthoritarian, constantly wary of authority, especially of regimes that threaten freedom and democracy.

I am very lonely. My wife died nineteen years ago. Being alone, in the deepest sense of those two words, is incredibly difficult. The void left by her disappearance from my life is at times not only unbearable but also incomprehensible. I mean in the sense and feeling of the word "unthinkable": *it can't be*, that *she simply cannot have died!* Or in Dickens's wonderful phrase (in *Bleak House*): "It is not to be thought of."

I am not afraid of dying, except, I suppose, in the case of a very long and very painful death. The only thing about the prospect of dying that upsets me—that I grieve over—is that I will never again hear all that beautiful music that I have come to know and love, and that I am ready to die for. But then some people tell me that I will, in fact, hear all that music—and more—in the afterlife.

While I would like to keep in touch with all my many, many friends and colleagues—hundreds (if not thousands) of them—I just can't; there just isn't enough time. I've always wished for a twenty-eight-hour day. (Come to think of it, I think I've actually lived a few of those.) I think it is so, so important—as Garrison Keillor says every morning on National Public Radio—to "keep in touch." It seems that our modern, congested, convoluted, technology- and gadget-driven world doesn't permit that any more.

In the meantime, I still live a very full life, almost always a full eighteen- to nineteen-hour day devoted to my work, my many loves. As the poet Edna St. Vincent Millay put it so unpoetically, but truthfully, "My candle burns at both ends"—although I suspect that her declaration is subject to at least three different parallel interpretations.

And I love language—and languages. I *love* words. What would we do without words, and the special intelligence they have given humankind? How would we keep in touch?

And, as you have learned, I like writing long books and long sentences!

NOTES

Chapter One

1. It is, I believe, more than casual coincidence that one of the movements of my 1959 *Seven Studies on Themes of Paul Klee*, considered by many my magnum opus, was inspired by Klee's masterful *Pastorale* (1927). I do not recall consciously relating this picture to my Webatuck experience, but it has to be more than random happenstance that the visual ingredients in both Klee's picture and that 1947 pastoral tableau are virtually identical: in Klee's vertical picture a narrow strip of blue sky extends horizontally across the top; below it a green-tinted celebration of the miraculous diversity of nature, captured in countless tiny stem figures of trees, branches, bushes, lined up in seven horizontal rows. (There is however, no Marjorie in Klee's picture.)

2. I'm sure my father, opera and particularly Wagner lover extraordinaire, associated his Webatuck knoll with the rocky heights of *Siegfried*'s act 3 finale—except there was no sleeping Brünnhilde, and no spear carrying Wotan to guard the scene.

3. My birth certificate, however, gives 321 E. Fifteenth Street as my actual birthplace (which was at that time the address of the New York Infirmary for Indigent Women and Children). I have never been able to resolve the discrepancy between these two bits of information.

4. Purcell died one day earlier, on November 21, 1695.

5. Forty-one years later my opera *The Visitation*, based loosely on Kafka's *The Trial*, was premiered at the Hamburg State Opera—to a tumultuous twenty-minute standing ovation.

6. Back home, my maternal grandfather's business flourished in those pre–World War I years, both in Germany and in Belgium, thriving on the industrial expansionism that Kaiser Wilhelm pushed; the steel industry obviously benefitted from what turned out to be Germany's heedless, arrogant unilateral preparation for war.

7. The only string opening at the time was in the viola section, an instrument my father had played for many years, including one whole season in 1919–20 as principal violist for Furtwängler when that eminent conductor was music director in Mannheim. As the New York Philharmonic's chief conductor, Josef Stransky, started to put the audition repertory on the stand for my father to read, he quietly (but I assume rather cockily) told Stransky that he didn't need any music; he would play the entire audition by heart, whatever he would be asked for. Some fifteen minutes later my father had landed the job.

8. Schuller is a non-Jewish German name, while Schuler is a Yiddish-Russian name, derived from both the German word *Schule* (school) and the Jewish word *Schul* (synagogue). As a child in Germany at my school, I suffered innumerable verbal indignities when some of the kids called me "Schnuller" (and other perversions of my name), which in German is the name for the rubber nipple on the bottle that babies drink from. That one hurt a lot.

9. In the last of those fights—I think he was ten and I was thirteen—Edgar was furiously flailing away at me, both fists flying, his tongue clenched hard between his teeth. As the older one I decided not to hit back, but to simply hold my right arm chest high to protect myself from his blows, which weren't that strong in any case. But at one point he charged at me in a wild rage and fury, and his face collided full force with my outstretched arm, at the impact nearly biting completely through his tongue. Half of it hung limply from his mouth, bleeding profusely. I was horrified, and felt terrible for days on end, even though in a way he had done it to himself. Edgar's tongue was stitched together, of course, and the upshot was that we never fought each other again, at least physically. We learned to settle our silly little boyish disputes in different, more coolheaded ways.

10. In one dream, which did recur night after night for many weeks in the wake of the Lindbergh kidnapping in 1932, I remember being abducted by faceless bad men, but no other details remain. I also recall having the common childhood chase nightmare in which we try to escape our pursuers, our legs

leaden with weight, as if trying to run in three feet of water; but I do not recall any specific details. The most recurring nightmare in my adult life has me arriving very late to an orchestra rehearsal or concert, held back by unseen, unknown forces, constantly encountering implacable obstacles, and at the last moment unable to even find my horn! But no other details survive.

11. His stand partner was Winthrop Sargeant, later a major critic, musicologist, and writer on jazz. My father was advanced to the first stand of the second violins a few years later, probably around 1928 or 1929.

12. Forty years later, when I moved to Boston, I realized that the stone building blocks I had played with as a child were miniature replicas of the massive yet beautifully decorative architectural style of Henry Hobson Richardson (1838–86), arguably (along with Sullivan) the most famous American nineteenth-century architect, active initially in Chicago and later primarily in Boston. There I instantly recognized Richardson's solid distinctive Romanesque style, in varied brownish colorations, whether it was his masterful Trinity Church on Copley Square, or the handsome churchlike Metropolitan Waterworks building in Brookline, or the fashionable townhouses (comparable to New York's brownstones) along Beacon Street.

13. Karl May's stories were to German kids what Zane Grey's and Max Brand's Westerns were to Americans. May's books were hugely popular in Germany, especially *Winnetou* (1893) and *Old Shatterhand* (1894). What is truly remarkable about May's work is that he never visited America or any of the other exotic places (North Africa, East Asia) in which he placed his novels. Incredibly, he wrote almost all his books in prison (spending many, many years in jail for a series of petty crimes). His writings are filled with an astonishing array of fascinating detail, conceived almost wholly out of his own vivid imagination, although, I would guess, with occasional doses of Fenimore Cooper and Mark Twain thrown in.

14. I had become fascinated with skiing when my mother took me and my brother to the 1932 Olympic Winter Games in Lake Placid, New York. I remember being especially excited by watching the ski jumping competitions when more than half the jumpers crashed in sometimes terrible falls. While my mother and I were horrified at the sight of so many skiers crashing in smash landings, yet were unable to turn our eyes away, my little four-year-old brother thought the falling skiers were funny, and greeted each fall with jubilant excitement. Ski jumping in 1932, with the primitive ski equipment of the day, was still a very young sport. My days in Lake Placid were spoiled, however, by what turned out to be the coldest winter in twenty years. I was constantly frozen, crying my eyes out, which, of course, annoyed the hell out of my mother, who persistently and mercilessly beat the dickens out of me.

15. A German legend, which we young students learned in our history classes, has it that Barbarossa never really died, but is sleeping beside a huge table in a cave in the Kyffhäuser Mountains. When his red beard grows completely around the table, so the legend goes, he will arise and conquer Germany's enemies—a story that Hitler's military exploited propagandistically for their warmongering purposes, especially with young people in schools.

16. Much of this reading in Burgstädt has stayed with me all my life, and has occasionally motivated me to use such materials in my work as a composer. In 1970 I composed a one-act, thirteen-scene opera on *The Fisherman and His Wife* tale, with a beautiful libretto created by my friend John Updike, for Sarah Caldwell's Boston Opera Company.

17. Over the years my Burgstädt relatives—lately Ilse's children Ruth and Günter—sent us Stollen *every* Christmas, after the war years as well as during the darkest days of the Communist German Democratic Republic (DDR), while in return my parents, and later Margie and I, sent them a constant stream of "care packages" containing butter, coffee, and other items impossible or hard to get in the DDR. The present baker in Burgstädt is as good as any of his predecessors; he gets the texture and consistency of the cake just right: not too dry, not too moist, not too sweet, just the right amount of raisins and lemon zest, and a rich *Zuckerguss* made of molten butter and sugar brushed over the whole fifteen-inch length of the cake. Yummy-yummy!

18. *Schrebergärten* are colonies of small gardens, rentable (very cheaply) from a city or town, and usually located on the outskirts of town. They are extremely popular in Germany. I have never been in any German city or town that didn't have hundreds of *Schrebergärten*. Both of my grandmothers had one, where they grew flowers to decorate their homes, and vegetables for their kitchen.

19. Oddly enough, given the deteriorating political situation in Gebesee, my parents had enrolled Edgar at the school in September. My mother, off on another one of her brief mountain climbing trips to Grainau and the Bavarian Alps, dropped Edgar off in Burgstädt, and those relatives brought him to Gebesee in mid-September. My eye accident abruptly cut short his stay in school (after only two-and-a-half months); he returned home to New York with me and my mother.

Chapter Two

1. My mother had taken a similar but even more ingenious route to learning English soon after her arrival in this country by regularly doing the crossword puzzles in the *New York Times*. Within a year or two she had amassed not only a very serviceable vocabulary but also correct English grammar and fluent sentence structuring. With her fine mind and excellent ear she also eventually retained only the slightest German accent.

2. Little did I guess that some twenty-two years later I would be playing first horn for several months in Radio City's fine symphony orchestra, four or five shows a day, between the film showings.

3. I was thirteen when I discovered Messiaen, actually through Grover Oberle, at that time Dr. Noble's assistant and most advanced organ student. Dr. Noble turned over several recitals each year to Oberle, who, still in his late twenties, featured quite a lot of modern organ music in his concerts. Messiaen's music, mind you, was virtually unknown in America at that time. By 1938–39 he had composed only eight works for organ, *L'Ascension* and *La Nativité du Seigneur* among them. Hearing these pieces, while deeply involved in turning pages and following the music, were transformative experiences for me. I was thus all the more astonished, and dismayed, when, telling my father excitedly about this great French composer named Messiaen, in my mind a "messiah of music" who spoke a remarkably new and important chromatic language, he admitted he had never even heard of him. Still more shocking, neither had any of my musical acquaintances: teachers, fellow students, music colleagues. It wasn't until 1946 that New Yorkers (other than organists) became aware of Messiaen. That was when Stokowski premiered the French master's *Hymn* for orchestra with the New York Philharmonic. In the intervening years I proudly preened myself among my musical friends because I knew the music of someone they didn't know!

4. If I remember correctly, it was Grover Oberle who played a wonderful *Symphonie pour orgue* by Maleingreau (1887–1956). I have never met *anyone*, except one organist about fifteen years ago, who even knew that composer's name, let alone any of his fine music. Maleingreau, known as a great Bach interpreter, became famous among organists in 1922 for playing Bach's *entire* organ oeuvre in a single prolonged series of recitals.

5. I have, for example, never been able to get through conducting the last twenty bars of *Sea Drift* without tears in my eyes, without sobbing, almost unable to breathe and conduct. I am overwhelmed by the sheer beauty and poignancy of that music, and of Whitman's poetry. That piece has been with me all my life, since age fourteen, and my discovery of it through Beecham's recording—and Hull's *Modern Harmony*—constitutes one of the most profoundly moving musical experiences of my early life.

6. I found out later that my father owned only three jazz records, and they weren't even jazz, but rather corny mid-1920s hotel dance band stuff of which I remember only one name, George Olsen.

7. This Cotton Club was a new jazz venue on Broadway, a predecessor of the Hurricane and Zanzibar clubs, and not the famous Cotton Club of the 1920s at Lenox Avenue and 142 Street in Harlem.

8. I found out many years later, when I had become much more familiar with Ellington's music and with jazz in general, that what I assumed in my excitement to be two bass clarinets was really one bass clarinet played by Harry Carney and Barney Bigard playing in the lowest register of his B-flat clarinet.

9. The horns made by Alexander Brothers of Mainz, Germany were considered to be one of the three really good horns made in the first half of the twentieth century. The other two makes were Schmidt and Kruspe. All American hornists played one or another of those three German makes.

10. It is a remarkable fact that we humans can direct our minds, our brains, to any place on our body, whether our right thigh or our left shoulder, or wherever. The mind travels instantaneously to the selected spot, almost as if it were physically there.

11. Errol Flynn was often the main protagonist in the erotic literature of the day. His notorious behavior in Hollywood with underage teens, fully detailed and freely expanded upon by the tabloids (such as the *Police Gazette*), eventually led to his arrest in 1938. Flynn continued to be the butt of thousands of jokes, mostly dirty, for years to come. Samuel Goldwyn offered one of the best of these, to wit: "When God made Flynn, He gave him a brain—and a penis—and just enough blood to run one at a time."

12. André Mathieu was a Canadian who, as far as I know, seems not to have pursued much of a career either as a pianist or a composer. I never heard a word about him until about a year ago when I read that he had died and that his Piano Concerto, the very piece with which he won that Young People's Concerts prize, had lately been recorded, and that—now—Mathieu was being celebrated as one of Canada's greatest and unduly neglected composers. A very strange case!

13. The late Allen Sapp was for many years a major figure in America in a variety of important positions as a composer, teacher, and administrator.

14. The late Luise Vosgerchian, a fine pianist, was for many decades a beloved teacher and coach on the faculty of Harvard University.

15. Dika Newlin became a much-respected author for her books on Mahler, Bruckner, Schönberg, and the Second Viennese School.

16. Mario di Bonaventura was later active as a conductor, teacher, and for many years head of publications at American Music Publishers.

17. In the thirties and forties very few recordings were issued each month; one would wait with bated breath for the new recording *that year* by, say, Koussevitzky and the Boston Symphony or Stokowski and the Philadelphia Orchestra, or a new release by the New York Philharmonic. These were often long agonizing waiting periods for me.

18. The other two movements of *Nocturnes*, "Nuages" and "Fêtes," were well represented in record catalogues, and I assume that "Sirènes" remained unrecorded for a long time because it required, in addition to a full orchestra, a sixteen-voice women's chorus. That is also the reason why "Sirènes" appears rarely on concert programs, while its two sister movements are considered regular fare.

19. If any reader is inclined to doubt the veracity of what I am reporting here, I invite them to find the two recordings in question—they have been reissued on both LP and CD. Recordings don't lie.

20. It has been a general consensus among musicians in the know that the cello and bass sections of the Berlin Philharmonic have consistently been, ever since Arthur Nikisch's days (1895–1922), the two most outstanding sections of that orchestra and the foundation and sonoric hallmark of the Berlin Philharmonic's legendary sound.

21. Nowadays eastern Long Island is the home of several dozen vineyards, the old potato and vegetable farms having all but disappeared. But it is also hopelessly overcrowded with constantly expanding townships, shopping malls, junk food joints, endless miles of car dealerships—all the accoutrements and symbols of our blighted modern urban civilization.

22. It was customary in Germany for apprentices, in whatever trade, to take a year off, just traveling, hiking, or biking; "wandering" around before settling down to the full-time practice of their chosen profession.

23. The Seventh Symphony was composed during the long siege of Leningrad by the Germans during the disastrously bitter cold winter of 1941–42. The three major conductors of the time in America—Stokowski, Koussevitzky, and Toscanini—had all vied vigorously for the right to premiere the work in the United States. After strenuous negotiations between the Russians and the three American rivals, the combined financial power and clout of the NBC Corporation and its affiliate, RCA Victor, prevailed, and Toscanini was given the premiere, on radio, with his NBC Symphony Orchestra. We were allies with the Soviets at that point in the war, and the concert, sponsored officially by the Russian War Relief Fund, turned out to be a sensational public success.

24. I played with Toscanini and the NBC Symphony Orchestra many times later in my fifteen years at the Met, when the maestro, fond of regularly programming various Wagner excerpts with his orchestra (which required eight instead of the usual four horns), would hire us horn players from the Met, knowing that we knew this opera repertory like the back of our hand. And I can verify that Toscanini, certainly one of the great conductors of that era (although perhaps not quite the unique godlike figure that the NBC Corporation and RCA Victor in their promotions made him out to be), would often seek and demand

from his players a degree of perfection—what he heard in his mind in some idealized way—that orchestras of that time perhaps could not attain. At least Toscanini seemed to think so.

25. We tend to remember where we were and what we were doing on certain indelibly memorable days. The three such occasions in my life are the Pearl Harbor bombing (and Roosevelt's subsequent declaration of war), John Kennedy's assassination in 1963—on my birthday—and, of course, the Boston Red Sox 2004 win in the World's Series.

26. WNYC's liberal programming policy was abruptly curtailed in 1942 when Mayor LaGuardia, after he and the station had received a number of irate letters from listeners who objected to the station's programming of Schönberg's *Pierrot lunaire*, officially prohibited any further performances of that work on WNYC. It had been recorded by Columbia under Schönberg's supervision just the year before. The ban on *Pierrot lunaire* held for several years until the mayor left office. It should be added that this was a very rare and exceptional example of official censorship.

27. Gladys Swarthout, who had a wonderfully rich, velvety mezzo-soprano voice, was for some twenty years one of America's reigning divas, very popular at both the Met and Chicago Lyric Opera, as well as on radio. She was featured regularly on concert music programs such as the Firestone, Telephone, Ford, Carnation, and Prudential Hours. I single her out because, one Monday evening in 1941 on the Firestone Hour, her vocal artistry really gripped me, moved me to tears. It was Swarthout's rendition of the so-called Card Aria from the third act of Bizet's *Carmen*, one of that opera's most inspired crowning moments. I went into one of my not-so-infrequent musical and emotional tailspins, playing the aria over and over and over again for several days, humming the voice part, savoring in slow motion Bizet's profoundly moving, poignantly tragic harmonies. It was as if I had been narcotized. Once again my parents were worried about my mental health.

28. Andre Kostelanetz was born in St. Petersburg, studied at the Academy of Music there, and immigrated to the United States in 1922. Working at first as a coach and accompanist for opera singers, by 1932 he had entered radioland, and pioneered on CBS the presentation of classical music and "serious" treatments of American popular music. Between that year and 1940 Kostelanetz directed and arranged for dozens of musical shows, all on CBS, culminating ultimately in the Coca-Cola Hour. In the late 1970s Kostelanetz became artistic director and conductor of the New York Philharmonic's very special and wonderful Promenade Concerts.

29. To offer just one trenchant example, my parents often made trips back to the old country in the summer, especially in the thirties while I was in Germany. My father, who was quite a penny pincher, did not want to pay rent during those months for an empty apartment, and would decide that the current apartment would be given up, all furniture stored in a warehouse, and in the fall a new apartment would be occupied. Well enough, as a pragmatic cost-saving idea. The trouble was that my poor mother always had to do all the packing, wrapping, and organizing for the moves—and of course *un*packing at the other end—while my father hardly ever gave a hand to help her because he was afraid of injuring his violinist fingers and because he was, unlike my mother, a very impractical and unhandy fellow and probably wouldn't have been much help anyway.

Chapter Three

1. The baby in the crib, I found out later, was Tonina, Dorati's daughter, whom not too many years later I saw again as a beautiful young lady, and who subsequently had a brief career in Europe as an opera stage director.

2. This ballet was originally choreographed by Michel Fokine for the Ballets Russes, and was more or less taken over by Dorati and Anton Dolin and renamed *Bluebeard* (based on the legend of Bluebeard and his many wives). Another ballet using Offenbach's wonderfully danceable music, adapted and arranged by Dorati, was *Helen of Troy*.

3. Since my rudimentary experiences at St. Thomas with this side of sexual behavior, I had never been similarly approached, and was still rather naïve about the realities of that world. Falling into the ballet's homosexual "den of iniquity" at a still very tender age, I took Joe's warnings very much to heart. He

enlightened me that, as the newest and youngest addition to the company, I was considered—in the common parlance of the day—"fresh meat," and, being slim and handsome, very desirous fodder.

Once Richard Reed realized that I was not available to satiate his libidinous needs, he and I became close (platonic) friends. I quickly learned that he was enormously intelligent, wonderfully educated, and literate in all the arts. We spent many a happy (for me vastly informative) hour together, roaming through the worlds of literature, music, painting, sculpture, and architecture.

4. Arthur eventually felt terrible for having cost me my job. He himself received a kind of comeuppance when he was demoted to third horn for the Ballet Theatre's New York season, although I don't think that had anything to do with the joke-telling episode. A very fine horn player named Forrest Standley took over as first horn. I went to one of the performances of *Romeo and Juliet* in New York, where Standley played those precious horn solos so beautifully. One of the outstanding but perhaps not widely or fully appreciated horn players of the time, Standley was for many years first horn in Pittsburgh—with Fritz Reiner—and a tougher assignment is not imaginable.

5. Generally speaking, the vast majority of symphony musicians still look down upon the whole field of opera, and on opera orchestra musicians in particular, as a lesser breed. Erich Leinsdorf many years ago proffered this explanation: since opera orchestras are submerged in a pit and not seen in full glory on a concert stage, they are thus deemed to be a lesser class of musician. Moreover, symphony musicians point to the (in their minds, denigrating) fact that opera orchestras play a limited repertory per season, even in major opera houses, amounting annually to some twenty to thirty standard operas, while symphony orchestras have to handle a different program every week—which amounts to some one hundred compositions, both familiar and unfamiliar, in a thirty-week season. (The seasons of most major orchestras are now more like forty-six to fifty weeks a year.) To me neither rationalization holds much water, and does an injustice to the many fine opera orchestras around the world.

6. Considerably smaller than Carnegie Hall, Town Hall was the favored home of solo recitalists, chamber ensembles, and chamber orchestras, as well as a great variety of lecture series. I remember how a lecture series by Richard Halliburton on the "Seven Wonders of the Ancient World," given over a period of six months, fired my imagination. Only the pyramids still existed; the other six wonders (the Hanging Gardens of Babylon, the Temple of Artemis at Ephesus, the gold and ivory statute of Zeus in Olympia, Greece, the Mausoleum at Halicarnassus, the Colossus of Rhodes, the Lighthouse of Alexandria) were rendered by drawings, and they kindled a deep and growing longing in me to travel the world, even to the ends of the world, if necessary, to see all its wonders.

7. Leonard Liebling, *Musical Courier*, October 1, 1944.

8. The two schools merged in the mid-1950s and later were both absorbed by the University of Cincinnati School of Music. The College of Music, one of the oldest conservatory-type music schools in the United States, had for decades prior to my arrival in Cincinnati enjoyed a stellar national reputation, along with Oberlin and the New England Conservatory. Part of its illustrious status was attributable to the outstanding directorship of Bertha Baur, longtime president of the college, and to the very popular weekly nationwide broadcasts heard on most stations of the CBS network for six years, from 1934 to 1940. My colleagues on the college faculty were, apart from the Heermann brothers, Olga Conus (wife of Leo Conus, friend and important interpreter of Scriabin, Rachmaninov, and Medtner), Sigmund Effron (later longtime concertmaster of the Cincinnati Symphony), Jack Kirstein (cellist and, later, member of the remarkable LaSalle String Quartet), Felix Labunski, expatriate Polish composer, and the venerable Albino Gorno, who was renowned for having been the accompanist for the world-famous nineteenth-century diva Adelina Patti.

9. Wohlgemuth's beautiful playing can be heard to best advantage on the Cincinnati Symphony's 1944 recording of Stravinsky's *Song of the Nightingale* Suite, especially in the melancholy Fisherman's Song, heard at the end of the Suite in the trumpet. Although our Cincinnati recording has not been available for many years—a crying shame, because it is in so many ways the best performance of that work ever recorded (even outdoing Reiner's fine recording with the Chicago Symphony)—it is worth searching for, as it represents Goossens and the orchestra's talent at their very best.

10. What is it with tuba players that they have a grip like a vise? Don Butterfield, a fine tuba player in New York who did a lot of jazz playing in the fifties through the nineties, would crush your hand with one handshake, leaving you grimacing with pain for about an hour as you limped away, while he seemed completely oblivious of the fact that he had just rendered you immobilized.

11. This passage has always been subject to very varied interpretations; for example, whether to play it in the first movement's basic tempo or slower, whether to play it as an introductory passage, or simply as the actual firm, straight-ahead opening of the concerto, etc.

12. Mme Leonard was a German Lieder and oratorio singer, who as a protégé of Bruno Walter had achieved some success and fame in Germany in the pre-Hilter era, but had emigrated to the United States in the thirties.

13. Inviting a young lady to listen to recordings in some privacy was the musical corollary in those days to the much-used old saw, "would you like to come to my place to see my etchings?"

14. Her father's family has been traced back more than 250 years to Cornvanaghan near Cookstown in Northern Ireland. It's a fascinating family history. Her grandfather, born in 1843, one of twelve children, experienced the hard times of the Irish plague and the Great Famine years of the 1850s. In 1865 he and two of his brothers left for America, and after a brief stay in New York he headed west to seek his fortune first in Indianapolis, then Terre Haute. There he met and married Jennie Perlee Osborne (Margie's grandmother), who was a descendent of Abraham Pierson, whose son Abraham was one of the eight ministers who founded Yale University in 1701. (One of the university's buildings is named after him.) On the paternal grandmother's side, two ancestors stand out. One, Margie's great aunt, was married to William McGuffey, the creator of the *McGuffey Reader*, which every American child in the last half of the nineteenth century *had* to read. The other ancestor, her grandmother's great-great-great grandfather was a close friend of William Penn, and came to America from England with him, settling in what became Pennsylvania. Margie's mother was born in Anaconda, Montana, in the heart of Montana's copper mining country.

15. The German born Elizabeth Schumann (1888–1952) was one of the reigning sopranos of the first half of the twentieth century in Europe (Vienna, Munich, Hamburg) and in America on countless tours as a Lieder recitalist (one, in 1921, with Richard Strauss as her accompanist). She was a longtime teacher at the famed Curtis Institute in Philadelphia. I met Elizabeth Schumann briefly in 1950 when my parents, who knew her quite well, invited her for an afternoon Kaffeklatsch. Margie happened not to be with me—probably a good thing—and I had neither the presence of mind nor the nerve to ask Mme Schumann whether she remembered a seventeen-year-old soprano from North Dakota singing "Caro nome" for her.

16. This bit of ill luck may have been one of the early instances of a jinx that has haunted me all my life, despite—I hasten to add—my generally enormous good fortune in my life and my career. The jinx has manifested itself more or less daily (especially in recent decades) in a thousand and one minor unpleasantnesses and casual mishaps. Most prominent among these: anytime I approach or touch some appliance or electronic equipment, it is bound to malfunction in some mysterious way. Like Murphy's Law, if it can go wrong, with Gunther it surely will. Many readers and many of my personal acquaintances will quickly suggest that it's not a jinx, that it's just my ineptitude in technical, mechanical matters, or they will say, oh, that happens to all of us. Sometimes I even agree with the former assessment. On the other hand, there is something eerily consistent in the way that little things go wrong with me *all the time* and have for many, many years. It really makes one wonder what is afoot: chance, fate, some arbitrary law of nature? Everyone in my family and in my close circle of acquaintances, including all the staff and secretaries who have worked for me over the years, have initially all laughed bemusedly, indulgently, at my claim that I am somehow especially jinxed. But as they continued to work or live in close proximity to me, they have all come to admit that there is, in my case, some bad-luck spell at work—in addition to my natural ineptitudes.

17. In later years Laverne Gustafson and Nell Foster both enjoyed distinguished careers in music, Gussie as a pianist, coach, and accompanist in New York, and eventually as the first woman conductor on Broadway; Nell as an opera singer, stage director, vocal coach, married to Lee Shaenen, a conductor both at the City Opera in New York and the Lyric Opera in Chicago.

18. That concert in 1940 in Fargo has entered the annals of jazz history as one of the legendary Ellington band performances, not because it necessarily displayed the orchestra at its best—although it was plenty exciting—but because a young Ellington fan, Jack Towers, had brought his personal recording equipment to the ballroom (mind you, in 1940 owning your own recording equipment was an absolute rarity), with which he recorded the entire evening. That recording was commercially issued many years

later and became a huge best seller. In 1944 Towers' recording had not yet been made available, so that even I did not yet have the recording of that evening in Fargo. Otherwise I would surely have played it for Margie.

19. It is easily forgotten these days, when all Mahler symphonies are recorded in multiple versions and interpretations, and performed as much as Beethoven, Brahms, and Tchaikovsky symphonies, that in the days of my youth most of Mahler's symphonies were not played at all in America. The only two conductors who programmed Mahler symphonies (primarily the First and Second) were Bruno Walter and Dimitri Mitropoulos. Leonard Bernstein, who is too often (and erroneously) credited with introducing Mahler's music to Americans, did not conduct any of the nine symphonies until the 1960s, by which time all of Mahler's works had began to be performed quite frequently, almost routinely, by not only Walter and Mitropoulos but also Maurice Abravanel and Eugene Ormandy. In Europe the regular performance of Mahler's music goes back to 1919, when Willem Mengelberg produced an entire Mahler festival (in which he performed all of his symphonies and *Das Lied*), and also, of course, to Bruno Walter in the 1930s.

20. I was so overwhelmed by the power and beauty of Mahler's Ninth Symphony that while still at St. Thomas's, composing Episcopal anthems and church services, I once unabashedly stole whole chunks of the first movement and grafted them almost note for note onto some New Testament text. As preposterous as this sounds, it was an urge I simply could not resist, to vicariously, re-creatively experience that music—and thereby get it out of my system.

21. I don't know, at my advanced age, whether necking is still practiced. It was considered in those earlier times the standard first step toward a more amorous relationship. It certainly was considered the outer limit of permissible public behavior, so different from today. It was usually practiced in cars, especially in rumble seats, and especially at outdoor drive-in movie theatres.

22. Busse was an extraordinarily popular trumpet player and bandleader, famous for his sweet, vibratoy, overly sentimental style. With his big hit tune *Hot Lips* (in the late thirties) he became the bobby-soxers national heartthrob.

23. It was on that occasion that I first met Rogers and his young student Jack Beeson. I visited with Rogers many more times in Rochester, where he was a most respected member of the composition faculty of the Eastman School of Music. Jack Beeson, a major opera composer (the opera *Lizzie Borden*) and longtime chairman of the music department of Columbia University, is a dear friend and most respected colleague.

24. The City Opera's first season was divided into three miniseasons of a few weeks each, during which only two or three operas were presented. The three operas (actually four) I played were *La Bohéme*, *La Traviata*, and *Cav* and *Pag*.

25. To cite just two comparisons, the year that Halász started the city opera in 1944, the Met offered no new productions at all, and its only less familiar opera was Rimsky-Korsakov's *The Golden Cockerel*. The rest consisted of the twenty-five standard operas, mostly with decor and staging that hadn't changed in a decade or more. In 1946 the Met managed to present its first opera in fifteen years by an American-born composer, Bernard Rogers's *The Warrior*, the previous incumbent having been Deems Taylor's *Peter Ibbetson* in 1931.

26. It's not that I found these transposed horn parts a serious hindrance to my performance; I never had any problems with transposition, even as a beginner student. I heard and played transposed horn parts in their real-sounding pitch, in effect ignoring the transposition. It was a method I tried to inculcate in all my students once I started teaching at the Manhattan School of Music in 1950. From my earliest composing days I wrote horn parts in F (but the score in actual pitch). The question of using transposition or not interested me from a syntactical and notational point of view. The transpositions in Brahms, in Wagner (even in the wildly chromatic *Tristan*), and decades later, in Strauss, are not only logical and inspiring, but in the case of *Cavalleria* and *Pagliacci*, their horn transpositions are oddly incompatible with the prevailing tonalities.

27. In Shakespeare's *Midsummer Night's Dream*, Queen Mab, a noble fairy, produces beautiful dreams in her subjects.

28. Film producers and directors in the forties and fifties were certainly aware of the deeply affecting impact that pieces such as Rachmaninov's Second Symphony or Second Piano Concerto, when

used as background music, could have on audiences in the telling of a love story. Perhaps the most outstanding early use of such underscoring occurs in David Lean's superb 1945 romantic drama *Brief Encounter*, in which some of the most haunting and passionate passages in Rachmaninov's Second Piano Concerto run like a thread throughout the film, always in the background, but gently, sensually supporting and embracing the story line, subliminally stirring the emotions of the viewer. The music's effect, floating, as it were, behind the scene, was all the more potent by being kept in the background, nicely contrasting Rachmaninov's passionate music with the superlatively understated acting of Trevor Howard and Celia Johnson.

29. As many times as I played *La Bohème*—over two hundred times at least—or heard it, I don't recall *ever* being left unmoved by its most passionate passages. When the music surges at you, like a gigantic wave, torrid and pulsating, topped by one of Puccini's most sublime melodies, e.g.,

, there is no way you can remain unaffected. *Con anima* (with animated emotion) indeed. Is it in fact possible to sing and play this passage without emotion? I doubt it.

30. Originally station manager of Cincinatti's powerhouse radio station WLW, Fred Smith had become famous in the 1930s as the creator (in collaboration with *Time* magazine) of *The March of Time*, which ran syndicated on radio from 1931 to mid-1945. Smith was appointed president of the college in the late 1930s, where he instituted the first program in an American college in careers on radio (later expanded to television).

31. Some readers will smile bemusedly at my florid verbosity. That's alright. They should remember that I was insanely in love and at the time incredibly lonely. And under such conditions one may say all kinds of curious but perhaps intrinsically beautiful things.

32. In that year the Philharmonic initiated a new series of summer concerts on Sunday afternoons in Carnegie Hall, in addition to the regular Lewisohn Stadium concerts, partly to be able to continue the widely heard CBS-sponsored weekly Sunday afternoon broadcasts of the regular season. I recall my father being very happy with the extra money these concerts paid, although also complaining about the even more backbreaking schedule.

33. Unfortunately, Pennsylvania Station was torn down in 1961. It was one of the great architectural treasures of New York City. Its demolition was a gratuitous, unwarranted undertaking, prompted by a series of political and business machinations by some uncultured real estate developers and some city politicians. Thank God, thirty years later, Grand Central Station did not suffer the same fate.

34. Pouny is the lone survivor of the four girls. Now separated from Milan, she lives in Florida and summers in Lake Placid. At age eighty she still plays the horn professionally, in a local orchestra—amazing. We are close friends and see each other several times a year.

35. Margie didn't mention that fateful audition with Schumann two years earlier. I think she had repressed all memory of that unpleasant experience, or perhaps just thought it was no longer relevant. Likewise, I did not refer to the matter.

36. Margie Ann is the big artistic talent in the whole Black-Schlossman clan. She is a very talented painter and a violinist (she plays in the Fargo Symphony Orchestra) who has in recent years also helped financially and otherwise in the founding of the Plaines Art Museum in Fargo. But probably she is closest to my heart because she was, four years after her Aunt Margie first saw her in Oceanside, the flower girl at our wedding in 1948.

37. Schlee and I became great friends and mutual admirers. He was one of the first to publish my music—with Universal Edition—and we kept very much in touch until the end of his life, over the decades sharing many incredible meals in his favorite culinary haunts in Vienna and Zurich.

38. Despite the fact that neither Berg nor Webern were Jewish, their music was nonetheless banished by the Nazis and forbidden to be performed. But since Webern was a Nazi sympathizer (despite the fact that the authorities despised Webern's music and considered it degenerate), they left him alone, letting him work and compose, although in complete isolation in a kind of house arrest. Berg was more severely treated. He was officially declared a noncitizen of Austria, just about the cruelest psychophysiological devastation that can be inflicted on a human being, in effect extermination just short of outright murder. Despite personal and financial deprivations near the end of his life—he didn't even have enough money

to visit his dentist to take care of persistent toothaches—Berg continued composing to the very day he died. He finished his Violin Concerto four months before his death on Christmas Eve, 1935.

39. I found out some years later that what I had assumed to be a horn was in fact an alto saxophone. It so happened that the Cleveland saxophonist played with almost no vibrato, *very* unusual in those days, when classical saxophone playing was totally dominated by the French school (headed by Marcel Mule), using a very pronounced vibrato. On the other hand, while horn players generally did *not* use a vibrato in those days—the lone exception to my knowledge was Weldon Wilber—it turned out that Rudi Puletz, principal horn in Cleveland at the time of the Berg recording, *did* play with a very subtle expressive vibrato. I didn't know that, and since I had never heard any saxophonist play with such a big, warm, hornlike sound—without vibrato—I just put all those occasionally prominent solo passages in the horn.

40. "Bernstein" is the German word for amber.

41. Stravinsky wrote: , which is almost

always played as if Stravinsky had written: .

If setting music in specific meters is to have any musical, audible meaning, then downbeats have to be felt and played with the subtlest kind of emphasis, of weight, of pulse—not anything like an accent—just as one would, in reading a classical poem, make a subtle inflection or differentiation between an iambic and or anapest meter. Lennie was extremely well read, and used to speak often in his famous young people's concerts about the relationship of poetry and music in terms of phrasing and inflection.

42. It is difficult nowadays to realize that Berlioz's music, except for one or two of his overtures and a few *Damnation of Faust* excerpts (such as the "Rakoczy March"), was rarely played in those days. His music was considered too strange, even weird, in its unusual harmonies and orchestration, its oddly shaped melodic lines. It didn't seem to fit into the conventional German or Russian symphonic mainstream. The real assessment, appreciation, and wider acceptance of Berlioz's music in America did not occur until after World War II, a development led primarily by Charles Munch and Beecham, and later Colin Davis.

43. Upon hearing this remarkably inventive and haunting succession of alternating Cs and Bs all week, I realized where Strauss, an avid admirer of Berlioz, received his inspiration for the ending of *Also sprach Zarathustra*, with its insistently, also gradually vanishing, alternating chords of C major (trombones) and B major (flutes/piccolos)—in Strauss's case not two octaves apart, but four (and finally) five octaves apart. Perhaps "borrowed" might be a better term than "inspired."

44. Heifetz came to Cincinnati in 1944 to play with us in what turned out to be only the second performance of Louis Gruenberg's Violin Concerto, which Heifetz had commissioned and then recorded with Pierre Monteux and the San Francisco Symphony Orchestra. After a huge flash success, with every important orchestra in the country lining up for a performance of the work, it was never played again, even by Heifetz, and has had to my knowledge only one performance since the 1940s.

Gruenberg had a considerable reputation not only as the composer of the very well-received opera *Emperor Jones*, based on Eugene O'Neill's great play and produced at the Metropolitan, but also as a successful Hollywood film composer, and a composer who became very involved with jazz in the 1920s. I believe it is high time that his Violin Concerto be revived.

45. There have been at least a dozen *Rosenkavalier* Suites fashioned from Strauss's opera by a host of conductor-arrangers, but in my opinion Dorati's, which was the first, is still the best.

46. In 1956 Goossens was arrested by immigration authorities in Sydney, Australia, for possession of fetishistic pornographic paraphernalia. Goossens claimed that it was his "misfortune" that he "allowed himself to be used to bring prohibited matter" into the country, and "that threats of a really dangerous nature were responsible for compelling my action." Blackmail threats? If so, why, and prompted by what? Strangely, the authorities never fully pursued or prosecuted the case. The commissioner of police determined "to take no further action" against Goossens on the ground that the available evidence "did not disclose any criminal offence with which he could be charged." Goossens resigned within three days as music director of the Sydney Symphony Orchestra. Rumors immediately began to circulate that Goossens had been framed, even that his estranged wife had informed Australian immigration that Sir

Eugene was attempting to bring prohibited materials into the country. The press, of course, did its best to exploit the situation by writing about "Black Mass sex orgies," "devil worship ceremonies in Sydney," and attempts of blackmail on alleged "cult members." Goossens was professionally disgraced, and the fact that he had brought the Sydney Symphony Orchestra back to international status was quickly forgotten in the wake of this debacle. When I visited Goossens in London in 1962, just a few months before his death, I barely recognized him. He was a broken man, a shattered spirit. See Carole Rosen, *The Goossens: A Musical Century* (Boston: Northeastern University Press, 1993).

47. Mary Leighton, *Cincinnati Enquirer*, April 7, 1945.

48. Unfortunately that issue of *Modern Music*, a first-rate quarterly devoted exclusively to contemporary music, supported and edited by Minna Lederman, was its last. I had been a subscriber to *Modern Music* since 1940, and had also acquired most of its back issues going back to the 1920s (it had been founded in 1923). It was a valuable fount of information for all of us young composers, containing not only highly intelligent and mostly ideologically unbiased reviews and accounts but also excellent technical analyses of new works and performances—in Europe and in America.

49. That was the first time I heard the entire opera, having previously only played excerpts from it and known its most popular songs ("Summertime," "I Got Plenty of Nothin,'" etc.). I recall being particularly impressed by the opera's richly chromatic harmonic language, especially in the many dramatic sequences, interludes, and transition episodes, which were never included in the excerpts generally played in pop concerts, not even in Robert Russell Bennett's *Porgy and Bess: A Symphonic Picture* (1942), which was played a lot in the early 1940s.

50. I immediately started collecting Raeburn recordings, such as the 1945 *March of the Boyds* and *Tonsilectomy*, and Dizzy Gillespie's *Night in Tunisia*. It was thus that I became aware of the remarkably advanced compositions and arrangements of Eddie Finkel and George Handy, and of the fact that Raeburn's band was another one of those—like Herman's, Eckstine's, and Gillespie's—in which so many of the young protoboppers found a welcoming home, such as Shelly Manne, Oscar Pettiford, Benny Harris, Hal McKusick, Al Cohn, and Serge Chaloff, to name just a few.

Interlude

1. Unbeknownst to me, Alec Wilder and Eddie Sauter had made tentative inroads on behalf of woodwinds on jazz recordings as early as 1940, with the orchestras of Red Norvo and Mildred Bailey. But these efforts were disregarded by jazz critics and writers as irrelevant exceptions.

2. It was composed originally for a great French film (René Clair's *The Italian Straw Hat*), and despite its lighthearted title is one of Ibert's very best pieces.

3. My Cello Concerto finally received its world premiere on July 20, 2001, at the Brevard Music Center in North Carolina, played beautifully by the talented Chilean-American cellist Andres Diaz, with myself conducting. A second performance followed eight years later in Boston, played by Richard Pittman's New England Philharmonic with Jan Müller-Szeraws as soloist.

4. However the summer's programs may have been chosen, one element that surely helped to reduce rehearsal time was that many pieces were played several times during the eight-week season. Works such as Beethoven's Fifth, Tchaikovsky's Fifth and Sixth Symphonies, Stravinsky's *Firebird* Suite, César Franck's Symphony, Strauss's *Don Juan*—and, oddly enough, Delius's *Walk to the Paradise Garden* and several other favorite "war horses"—were played three or four, or even five times, needless to say without any extra rehearsal. Even relatively obscure or new pieces (such as some of Haydn's symphonies or Kabalevsky's *Colas Breugnon* Overture) were recycled every few weeks.

5. I had come to admire Puletz's beautifully lyrical playing on several Cleveland Symphony recordings, but especially on the difficult first horn part in Alban Berg's Violin Concerto.

6. It was also a good practical habit, for not only were most conductors impressed that a player would know the music that well, but many were quite flattered that one was paying that much attention to *them*, to what *they* were doing. The reader may have observed, especially on television, that most musicians generally do not look at the conductor, except occasionally out of the corners of their eyes, and then only when absolutely necessary, as at a tempo change.

7. Paradoxically, most orchestral musicians, but especially woodwind and brass players, play staring at the printed page as if they had never seen the music before, even, amazingly, in solo repertoire, with which they must surely be *very* familiar, simply by dint of having practiced and studied and played it innumerable times.

8. One of my father's most impressive and always entertaining talents was to sit down at any piano and play from memory huge chunks of not only operas (by Strauss, Puccini, Wagner, and Schreker) but also the marvelous operettas produced in Germany and Vienna around the time of World War I, music that he got to know and love in his younger years, playing it constantly in the dozen or so different spa and theatre orchestras he worked with.

9. I must admit that when conducting Beethoven's Fifth from memory, as so many conductors do, it *is* possible to get mixed up at the very end of the piece. Beethoven ends the symphony with not the usual three or four final chords, but with *twenty-nine* (!) measures of C-major chords. A split-second's hesitation or distraction in one's concentration—or a moment of overconfidence (Well, that's almost finished; job well done!)—and you could easily wonder which measure you're actually on.

10. Sixty-two years letter I have no recollection of such a letter; on the other hand, I cannot dispute that I may have written her on that final day. The sad fact is that, while virtually all of Margie's letters to me—nearly two thousand—and those she wrote to her parents have survived and are in my possession, many of my letters to her have disappeared. I have no idea what happened to them. Fortunately, as is inevitable in any longtime mutual correspondence, her letters often refer to something I had previously written, from which one can deduce at least what the subject matter would have been. Often those references are tantalizingly unspecific, unrevealing of what was actually under discussion.

11. Romain Rolland's *Jean Christophe* (1904–12), much read in the thirties and forties by romantically inclined young people, is a gigantuan novel in several volumes about a musical genius—with an undeniable (and intended) resemblance to Beethoven.

12. Over the years I used to regularly read Ransom's poetry in various poetry magazines, as well as the *Kenyon Review*, and had the great pleasure of meeting him several times in meetings of the Academy of Arts and Letters, to which I was elected in 1967.

13. Now quite unremembered except by a few elderly modern dance afficionados, *The Green Table*, the 1932 masterpiece of choreographer-dancer Kurt Jooss, was a biting satire on arrogant, ruthless statesmen who plunge nations into war by secret negotiations and devious backroom machinations. The entire action takes place around a large green table during an international conference. Sounds familiar?

14. In using the word "concept," I wish to deemphasize such words as "method," "technique," "system," "manner," "mode," and "fashion," which, although perfectly good words, are unfortunately all too prone to various, mostly disparaging, interpretations. Method, which implies an orderly, logical arranging of the music—nothing wrong with that—has been often semantically reinterpreted to imply a dry, academic, cerebral approach. Technique, another perfectly good word, since it signifies the accomplishment of a desired goal, has been even more misused, mainly to condemn something as "merely" technical, devoid of expression and emotion. System has also been roundly misapplied, inferring some formulaic, "mathematical" orderliness. Mode and manner have been used to imply a degree of traditional or individual superficiality. Perhaps "way" would be the most neutral, generic term, but I've never seen it used in reference to twelve-tone music. (I guess it isn't opinionated enough.)

15. Why it was called a "jazz opera" is unfathomable, unless it was because one of the opera's protagonists was identified as a "black jazz musician" who played the violin (!), and because of the occasional use in the orchestra of a banjo—nothing else. It also contains a brief episode, a sort of aria, that is called a "blues," which, however, doesn't sound like a blues at all and is certainly not based on the traditional blues changes. *Jonny spielt auf* was a sensational success at its premiere in Leipzig in 1927, and was performed over the next two years in over a hundred cities and translated into eighteen languages. But by 1930 it was dropped from opera schedules, not to be heard again until well after World War II, in Austria. Suffering from an incredibly convoluted and silly libretto (written by Krenek himself), jazz opera or not, it is nonetheless a fascinating late-1920s period piece, couched in Krenek's rather acerbic early atonal style. I conducted the work in 1976 in a concert performance at the New England Conservatory, the first rendition (I believe) of the work in the United States since its American premiere at the Metropolitan in 1929.

16. Most readers will not realize how very divided the world of contemporary music was in the 1930s and 1940s, literally into two warring camps whose nominal leaders were Stravinsky and Schönberg. Young composers like myself coming onto the scene at that time were expected to join one side or the other. I and others like me—Leon Kirchner, Arthur Berger, George Perle, Donald Martino, come to mind—thought that was pretty silly, since Stravinsky and Schönberg were both great composers, and much could be learned from both of them and from both idioms.

Some of my composer enemies consider me a rabid Schönberg partisan. But anyone who *really* knows my music will readily hear in it the vestigal influences of both admired masters, in a more or less equivalent balance.

Chapter Four

1. One needs to remember that there was really no other purely American music around in those years, not even country music, which was just beginning to come in on radio in the 1930s, mainly on Nashville's *Grand Ole Opry* program. All the music that populates the American musical landscape nowadays, all offsprings and derivitives in one way or another of jazz—rock and roll, hip hop, disco, rap—didn't exist yet in the 1930s and 1940s.

2. This was reconfirmed for me many times over the years but especially by a most reliable witness, the trumpeter Joe Wilder. One day, many years later, at a recording date in New York, Joe had just come from a gig with Stewart, and was telling us that he couldn't believe what he had seen and heard: "That guy plays *everything* with the same finger and practically all on the same valve. He doesn't even *need* three valves. It's like he can play any note on any valve. Unbelievable!"

3. In late 1941 Raglin replaced the ailing Jimmy Blanton (who died of tuberculosis in 1942), staying with Ellington until November 1945, and then again briefly in 1947, along with Oscar Pettiford, when Ellington employed two bassists simultaneously. I don't know which bass player first used two fingers in jazz solos—now a commonplace, players use even three or four fingers—but it may have been Raglin, a technique he possibly carried over from his guitar playing days as a young man.

4. In the late 1930s Ellington's manager, Irving Mills, who was also a music publisher, printed several folios of simplified piano arrangements of Duke's most popular songs.

5. One of Ellington's most frequently applied bits of flattery to any attractive (or even not so attractive) lady, delivered with a ducal smile, was: "You make that dress look so pretty." Perhaps the ultimate in beguiling encomiums to the female gender used by Ellington in his later years all over the world in big-audience concerts began with the word "we"—he would always use the royal "we"—"We would like to dedicate our next number to the most beautiful lady in the house. There are many beautiful ladies here tonight, and we want to dedicate this number to *the* most beautiful lady. We know that she knows that we know who she is."

6. As far as I know, Ellington never played at the Cotton Club in Cincinnati. I was told repeatedly by blacks—musicians as well as others—that the people who frequented the Cotton Club didn't care for Duke's music, thought it was too sophisticated, too highbrow, preferring the more basic dance music of Basie or Lunceford—information that puzzled me and kind of upset me.

7. Brown didn't get around to leaving Ellington for a few more years (in 1951), and then returned to the orchestra in 1960, staying on until his retirement in 1970.

8. All the dates given here are confirmed in the extensive Ellington band itineraries and diaries that have been collected and published since Ellington's death by various Ellington historians and aficionados such as Willie E. Timner, Joe Igo, Sjef Hoefsmit, and even more recently by Ken Vail.

9. Although Mondays were always the free day in the week, that particular week our regular Tuesday morning rehearsal was postponed to Wednesday afternoon, we all assumed because it was an all-Tchaikovsky program that week, music that was thrice familiar to all of us, and therefore the number of rehearsals could be reduced to three, rather than the usual four or five. But then I heard—on the q.t. from Billy Knox, one of our violinists and the orchestra's renowned cutup and promulgator of all orchestra-related scuttlebut—that Goossens was actually in New York on those two days, in high-level meetings with Arthur Judson (his manager) reportedly in preliminary discussions about leaving the

Cincinnati Symphony in order to take over the musical directorship of the Sydney Symphony Orchestra (in Australia)—a position he did in fact assume in 1947.

This is another striking example of fate intervening on my behalf, in this case by allowing one of the most momentous, deeply affecting encounters in my young life to occur. Think about it: if Goossens had not been obliged to go to New York for those two days in crucial career-impacting meetings with his manager, and if the scheduled program that week had involved music unfamiliar to the orchestra rather than a program of popular Tchaikovsky bits, Goossens would have been rehearsing us for the full five rehearsals, and the Cleveland visit with Ellington and his band would—could—never have happened.

10. Tom Whaley really deserves more than a footnote. Little does the world of music know how important Tom was to the Ellington organization. He toiled for decades behind the scenes, unseen, unheard, unappreciated by the public, as Ellington's copyist, sometime arranger, rehearsal coordinator, and general factotum. I loved the man and admired him greatly. He was so humble, self-effacing, so unremittingly devoted to Ellington, always eager to help and serve the cause of good music. I am very proud to have known him.

11. In the early days of the controversy over whether jazz could somehow be equated qualitatively with classical music, the word "serious" constantly played a vociferous but also confusing role in the endless debates published in the modern music magazines and literary journals. Classical music was called "serious," which implied that jazz and popular music were unserious, that a great improvised solo by Charlie Parker wasn't serious music.

12. I am proud that Snooky Young entered my life when I was eighteen, and that in addition to various encounters with him in Los Angeles, especially when he played for some years in Doc Severinson's Tonight Show Band, I had the privilege of hiring him to play one of the two lead trumpet parts in the 1989 posthumous premiere of Charles Mingus's monumental nineteen-movement masterpiece, *Epitaph*, knowing that Snooky was Mingus's favorite lead trumpet. My relationship to Snooky, which spanned over fifty years (from 1943 to the present), is like two beautiful bookends in my life.

13. W. C. Handy's *Memphis Blues* is often credited as being the first blues to be published. Actually Matthews's *Baby Seals Blues* came out in 1912, a few weeks *before* Handy's.

14. Some readers may not realize that back then, while one could purchase scores of the great classical masterpieces (a tradition going back to the very early nineteenth century), one could not buy scores of jazz compositions. And even many, many decades later, publication of jazz music in a printed score-and-parts form is still very limited. More often than not, whatever purchasable jazz publications exist nowadays are the result of somebody transcribing the work from recordings.

To my knowledge, the first engraved, printed, full scores of jazz compositions were published in 1946 by Stan Kenton, including works by two of his star composer-arrangers: Ray Wetzel's *Intermission Riff* and Pete Rugolo's *Artistry in Rhythm, Artistry in Percussion*, and *Safranski*. Such publications were unheard of at the time, a real breakthrough. I know of no other published jazz scores after that for at least a decade, and then only sporadically. Certainly no works by Duke Ellington were available, nor were any compositions or arrangements by orchestras as important as Count Basie's or Jimmie Lunceford's or Sy Oliver's scores for Tommy Dorsey, or Eddie Sauter's for Benny Goodman. What was available was an occasional stock arrangement such as the Woody Herman Band's *Apple Honey*. But such publications consisted of a set of parts—no score—and of simplified, dumbed-down, commercialized versions.

While the publication of jazz music is more common today, it still is not considered as important, let alone necessary, as it is in classical music. There, it is understood that works of any quality or significance will sooner or later be published or made available for purchase in some form that permits performance and study of the work.

15. I tackled *Dusk* several times more, most recently for inclusion in my book *The Swing Era*; and after an eight-hour struggle with just one particular eight-bar phrase (the bridge of the second chorus), I think I may have finally gotten it right. But I'm still not 100 percent sure; verification has been impossible since Ellington's original score is lost and only three or four of the parts from which the band played and recorded the piece have survived.

16. The Basie band generally featured a lot of improvised solos, but the Cincinnati Symphony had, of course, no jazz soloists, certainly not on trumpet, trombone, or saxophone. Even if I had thought I could occasionally approximate a Harry "Sweets" Edison or Lester Young solo, I couldn't possibly have covered

all the solos in a given Basie number. Thus I had to limit myself mostly to the pieces' ensemble sections, the "heads" (jazz lingo for the initial statement of the composition) and a few short ensemble choruses taken from *Doggin' Around, Rockin' the Blues, Every Tub, Swinging the Blues, Jumpin' at the Woodside*. The result was a collage of some of the most familiar and swingingest moments in the early Basie band's book. Unfortunately, the score and parts of my *Tribute to Basie*, as well as some of the other arrangements I made at the time, have disappeared and, I assume, are irretrievably lost.

17. There were certainly no scores, and if there were parts they would have been rather sketchy affairs with—*maybe*—the ensemble chorus parts written out, along with the tune's chordal changes, on which the musicians would improvise. Familiar changes such as *I Got Rhythm* or blues changes weren't ever written out; it would simply say "blues" or "rhythm." Even if a Basie piece had been published, it would have been in a simplified stock variety that would have been of little use to me, since I was determined to present the music in as authentic a re-creation as possible, that is, the way they actually played it. Head arrangements obviously represent a quite different creative process than that of the compositions and fully notated arrangements of, say, the Ellington, Dorsey, or Goodman orchestras, where an arranger single-handedly created a specific arrangement, with, of course, spaces left for solo improvisations.

18. Symphony orchestras didn't have saxophone sections in those days, and I was afraid to use the strings, worried about their stiff and unswinging playing. Also, Lawson and the management would have regarded the hiring of four or five saxophones for just one piece an unwarranted expense.

19. Indeed, my arrangements of Ellington and Basie constituted the first time that the Cincinnati Symphony had played any music by black or jazz composers, with a single exception: Goossens had programmed over the years several William Grant Still works.

Chapter Five

1. Czech-born Allers (1905–95), although unfortunately typecast as a "mere" conductor of operettas and musicals, was actually a very intelligent, expert conductor who was ideally suited to do full justice to Grieg's beautiful music.

2. Paula, who had a most beautiful soprano voice with gorgeous high notes, but was musically somewhat limited, had a ten-year career at the Met singing minor parts such as one of the three youths in *Magic Flute*, Marguerite in *Faust*, Frasquita in *Carmen*, the backstage Forest Bird in Wagner's *Siegfried*, never advancing to any major roles. Perhaps her most prominent part was one of the two whores in Britten's *Peter Grimes*, a role that she sang quite well and to which she was also well suited due to her very ample, well-exposed bosom—very popular with the men in the orchestra.

I could never for the life of me figure out how Paula learned her parts. In my coaching her sometimes (in Cincinnati) I found out that most of the time she could not tell a third in a chord from the tonic—that is, even in the simplest tonal music, not some horrendously difficult modern stuff. But what saved her was that, as with many singers, once she had finally learned a part, it was there forever—indelibly.

After three seasons at the Met, Paula had a very successful multiyear tenure at the Stuttgart Opera as well as engagements at the Bayreuth Festival.

3. The New York Philharmonic's regular schedule per week in the 1940s and 1950s, for example, consisted of only four rehearsals and four performances, the last three a repeat of the first concert.

4. This account, probably the first time it has been published and accurately detailed, will, I hope, explain why there has occasionally been some confusion as to my actual position in the Met's orchestra, and why I sometimes allowed it to be said that I was first horn at the Met for fifteen years, rather than going into a lengthy, convoluted explanation that would have caused most people's eyes to glaze over, in a matter that was not of crucial importance or interest to anyone in the first place.

5. Although the third horn sits between the second and fourth horn, it plays the second highest part, notes directly below the first horn. If this seems a bit odd to the lay reader, who might easily ask why the third horn player doesn't play the *third* highest part in a four-horn section, it *is* odd. But there is a historical reason for this arrangement. In the baroque and early classical era orchestras usually had only two horns, one high, one low. When composers in the late eighteenth century began to write for four horns,

they thought of the two additional horns as a second pair, that is, as another pair of high and low horns. Thus the third horn was thought of as a high horn player, almost equal to the first.

Brahms, who was in some ways a very progressive, innovative composer, but in other respects quite conservative and conventional, clung throughout his entire life to the old notion of a four-person horn section divided into two equivalent pairs—the only composer, by the way, to do so, to the very end of his life in 1897. Brahms's traditional approach to horn writing is especially noticeable in his First Symphony and the two piano concertos. In the C Minor Symphony's first movement the exposition is essentially in the tonic key, but the lyrical "second subject" part lies a minor third higher (in E-flat major). When the exposition is recapitulated near the end of the movement, Brahms, knowing that he *has* to end in the tonic key, modulates the "second subject" down to C minor. Since Brahms always held that the first pair of horns had to be in the tonic key, and the second pair (third and fourth horn) in the other prevailing key (in this case E flat), it was inevitable that the third horn ended up with the higher lying, brighter part, and the first horn with the dark, lower one. That was the only way Brahms could get all the notes he wanted and needed. I've known more than one first horn who never forgave Brahms for giving the more prominent, higher lying horn parts to the third horn.

6. We had two violinists in the Met orchestra during my time who could play even the longest five-hour operas by heart. Ludwig Wittels and Josef Geringer, both for many years in the Vienna State Opera Orchestra, would at the beginning of, say, a long opera such as *Meistersinger* (or *Tristan* or *Götterdämmerung*) ceremoniously close the book and play the whole opera from memory!

7. Edwin Franko Goldman, with whose famous concert band I played for many years in the 1950s, a fine trumpet player in his younger days, was one of the earliest American-born musicians to join the Met orchestra, in 1895.

8. It was probably the Japanese composer and conductor Hidemaro Konoye (1898–1973) who revived the tradition of Gagaku. Konoye had studied in Germany in the 1920s and early 1930s, and upon his return to Japan had become head of the Imperial Academy of Music in Tokyo. There he began to propagate the idea of making his country's remarkable thousand-year-old musical tradition available to a larger audience than merely the Emperor of Japan and a few high-placed court officials. Konoye also transcribed *Etenraku* for modern symphony orchestra and published it in full score. By pure chance I found a copy of that score at Patelson's in New York sometime in the late 1940s. Stokowski recorded it in the 1930s with the Philadelphia Orchestra.

9. Miyako closed in 2007.

10. Unfortunately, the 1946–47 Donahue band was only sporadically recorded, and even then these mostly pop song vocals were hardly representative of what the band really played in clubs like the Aquarium. Actually, its best recordings by far were made for the so-called V-discs, but they were available solely to armed services radio stations, never to the general public, and are now no longer easy to find, except among hard-core record collectors.

11. I have over the years asked many a basically well-informed jazz aficionado about the Rey band, and always received blank stares or some annoyed deprecating gesture, seemingly resentful of the very question.

12. The one difference between the Wilson orchestra and the other three bands is that they did not survive, whereas Gerald Wilson and his orchestra are not only still around are very successfully so. Wilson, now eighty-eight, is still going strong, arranging and composing brilliantly, innovatively. He has kept his orchestra intact for over sixty years. Its most recent recording has just been issued; it is a real winner.

13. Her feelings are so touchingly expressed in her diary, and so characteristic. She chastised *herself*: "How did this happen to me, and why? How can I manage this?" She exclaimed: "Why does God make some people love others whom they can never have, because of the feeling not being mutual, especially such a good, kind, loveable person as Paul is." "I would never want to hurt him," she told me. Can you imagine how much more that made me love Margie, beyond what I already felt for her?

14. With the awesome dominance of Hollywood films worldwide it is easy to be left with the impression that there is no other film industry or film history worth knowing about. There are at least thirty countries in Europe, South America, and Asia that have either since the very beginning of cinema (in the mid-1890s) or at various periods in the last hundred-plus years, contributed significantly to the development of film as an art form and as high-level entertainment. The average American, alas, sees the movies

only as entertainment, a night out for some fun, not as a medium that can be informative, thought provoking, and educational.

Aside from the United States, France, Italy, England, Sweden, and Germany have been among the most prolific and artistically creative film producing countries. Italy, for example, developed the grand tradition of historic costume epics in the 1910s, with casts of thousands and unimaginably opulent scenic spectacles, which in turn profoundly influenced major American directors such as Cecil B. DeMille and D. W. Griffith, and for years Hollywood Westerns in general. Small countries such as Denmark and Sweden had "golden ages" of film making—silent films then—around the time of World War I, while others, such as Czechoslovakia, Iceland, Greece, Venezuela—just to pick a few at random—made their mark in creative film making at various later times. What is common to almost all of these foreign cinemas, from whatever era and whatever country, is their intellectual integrity, their mature outlook on life, and their sense of realism. They assume that their audiences are intelligent, mature, and would like to be enlightened as well as entertained.

15. The film program did not, alas, show the early French film *The Assassination of the Duke de Guise* (1908), for which the great French composer Camille Saint-Saens had written presumably the first film score, not, of course, imprinted on film—sound films did not appear until nearly twenty years later—but played live in an orchestra pit. Oh, how I would have loved to have seen and heard that, even if Saint Saens' score had been played at MOMA on the piano.

16. Fortunately *Greed* was recently restored to some of its initial grandeur. Though nearly two-thirds of Von Strohheim's original footage of ten hours was cut (and much of it then destroyed), Rick Schmidlin painstakingly and lovingly retrieved whatever original film footage had survived, and filled in many of the remaining gaps with still photos made during the original production.

17. This was a photographic process—years before there was something called Xerox—that was quite expensive: forty cents a page for a negative, eighty cents for a positive, a lot of money in those days. Twelve pages, say, of a Gabrieli *Canzona* for brass and strings would cost me $4.80, just for the negative, on which the notes and staves were white on a black background. I accumulated lots and lots of those negatives, unable or unwilling to spend twice as much for the positives. But by this method I acquired a lot of music, many rare printed scores that I still have to this day. In this way, too, along with the things I could buy in music stores such as Patelson's, across the street from Carnegie Hall on Fifty-Sixth Street, I had built an immense library of music by the time I was in my early twenties, all of which I studied, digested, learned from, and in later years often performed or conducted.

18. My sixty-year-old recollection was pleasantly confirmed when I recently heard a recording of that ancient WQXR broadcast that had been taken off the air in 1946, quite by chance and unbeknownst to me, by Robert Levin's father, and now given to me by Robert, a Harvard professor, a remarkable fortepianist and an outstanding Mozart and Bach scholar, famous for his new 1989 edition of Mozart's *Requiem*, and (less known) a most knowledgeable jazz aficionado.

19. "New Friends Give Masters' Works; Guilet String Quartet and Other Musicians Play Brahms, Schubert," *New York Times*, January 28, 1946.

There are many interpretive and re-creative questions, problems, and issues in regard to the Brahms Horn Trio, including the first movement's opening main theme, which to my knowledge has never been played correctly. That happens to be a fairly subtle and complex interpretive problem, and not one that it would be appropriate to examine in detail in this memoir. Some of these issues are quite obvious, such as ensemble balance and insuring that the horn, an inherently louder, more projecting instrument than a violin (at least the modern horn, not so the early nineteenth-century horn that Brahms wrote for), not overpower the violin. I have heard far too many performances of this work where precisely that occurs. Indeed, most of the time the Brahms Trio is played by orchestral players who, unfortunately, play the work as if it were an orchestral work instead of treating it as chamber music.

But those are only the most obvious problems. Of the many other realizational, re-creative problems, the one that fascinates me the most is the obligation (unfortunately, largely ignored) to differentiate in the horn part between the three levels of projection—or you might call it the horn's three differentiated ensemble functions: primary, when the horn has the leading voice; secondary, when the horn plays accompanimentally to the violin or piano, or blending in harmony with them; and tertiary, when the horn is given only subordinate harmony-filling notes, while the violin or piano have primary material. These three levels or strands must be controlled not only dynamically but also sonorically, timbrally. This seems to be something most hornists do not know or care about. And, in truth, this important functional—and thus interpretational—factor is evidently not all that obvious, judging by how often it is ignored. A given passage may start out as a primary or secondary melodic voice, suddenly dip down to a purely tertiary harmonic accompanimental level, and then return quickly to a higher level—what on paper, in notation, may all look alike, all in one line, as if in a single unvaried phrase.

Maybe it takes a composer to discern such important functional distinctions. But I would like to think that any reasonably intelligent player would immediately hear such role differentiations. Whatever virtue my (our) Brahms Horn Trio performance in 1946 may have had, I am very proud of the fact that I made such distinctions scrupulously, audibly clear.

20. I published a number of Steuermann's works years later when I created my publishing company, Margun Music—most notably his superb *Suite For Piano*.

21. Gussie and Neil stayed together for some fifty years, until her death in 1999. All through the years we kept hearing that Neil beat her terribly. After Margie and I had moved to Boston we lost touch with Gussie. I never saw her again until a few months before her death, when she was not well. She looked very weak and pale from Parkinson's disease.

22. In our largely prudish, hypocritical culture many people, including (in my experience) most women, variously restrained and inhibited by background or religious training, tend to regard men's sexual drives either as inherently excessive or sinful, akin to the (allegedly) baser instincts of mere animals. They believe that men should be able to exorcise such urges. I don't know—and I don't believe anybody *really* knows, unequivocally—whether women and men are intrinsically created as equally sexed, or whether religions and various social customs have over the millennia created an inherent imparity in this respect between male and female. But what I do know with absolute certainty is that the urges and drives of normally sexed males are affected and determined in varying degrees by testosterone levels and men's hormonal diathesis. While sexual intercourse relieves these accumulated urges, the sexual tensions normally reassert themselves rather quickly. They *always* do; they are *not* seasonal, as with most animals.

23. I feel the need to point out that in those days Boston had dozens of jazz clubs and dance emporia. Alas, now the jazz scene in Boston is reduced to a mere handful of places.

24. Not quite on the same qualitative level, but very interesting to me as a horn player, was my discovery of tons of horn ensemble music—in first editions yet—by a composer I had never heard of: Louis Dauprat. Neither had any of my horn player colleagues. It turned out that Dauprat was the leading horn virtuoso in France at the beginning of the nineteenth century. When Napoleon reorganized the Paris Conservatoire in 1800, he appointed Dauprat *Profeseur du Cor*. I had almost all of Dauprat's horn ensemble music (trios, quartets, sextets) photostatted (again only in negative), and on the rest of the tour spent untold hours copying out the individual parts from the scores. Years later, we used these same parts when I scheduled a few of Dauprat's sextets for performance at Tanglewood in chamber music concerts with my young protégé and friend Rick Todd brilliantly playing the extremely high C-alto parts.

25. Henry Eichheim (1870–1942) was a very talented but now quite forgotten composer whose music interested and fascinated me very much. Eichheim was a rarity among American composers of the early part of the twentieth century in that he was passionately interested in the music of the Far East, especially China and Japan, but also Burma and Java. He amassed over the years on his tours an immense collection of Oriental instruments, whose sounds he amply incorporated in his compositions. Stokowski, always with a yen for the exotic in music, performed and recorded some of Eichheim's music in the 1930s, most notably his 1921 *Oriental Impressions*.

26. Walden Pond looms large in Thoreau's voluminous writings, since that is where he elaborated his philosophy of passive resistance and his creed of the superiority of individual conscience over political majority, cogently expressed in his masterful *Walden, or Life in the Woods* (1854) and the controversial *Civil Disobedience* (1849).

27. During the 1920s and ensuing decades the Walker Art Center acquired much more contemporary art. That is where I first saw Franz Marc's famous *The Large Blue Horses* and works by Georgia O'Keefe, Stuart Davis, and Lyonel Feininger. In my annual visits with the Met in Minneapolis and in later years I always made it a point to visit the Walker, seeing wonderful works by Noguchi, Mirô, Kandinsky, Arp,

and Marin, and still later, Rauschenberg, Stella, Motherwell, and Ellsworth Kelly. In the 1970s and 1980s, when Martin Friedman became director of the Walker, I was several times invited to conduct concerts of contemporary music there, in collaboration with my violinist friend and colleague, Young Nam Kim.

28. It was only many years later, in 1958, that I finally heard the recordings of the Trent band, still unavailable and more or less forgotten. My friend John Hammond had a few of Trent's 78s (such as *Clementine* and *After You've Gone*), which he had bought in his youth, in 1928. I subsequently wrote many pages of praise on Trent's orchestra in volume 1 of my jazz history, *Early Jazz*.

29. Among the several unusual traits I possess, one of the more interesting ones—quite inexplicable—is that I have as long as I can remember approached every person as if we were brothers, had known each other forever. There never was a feeling on my part that I first had to get to know somebody.

30. One of my best friends in the Met's cello section was Dave Greenbaum, a remarkable musician and a technical wizard on the cello. He had played in Tommy Dorsey's string section in 1944, and was the only string player in the Met orchestra who had any interest in jazz. Amazingly, like me, Dave regarded it as an important, serious music. He was the first bebop cellist I ever met. He wanted me to write a jazz piece for him. One day on tour he showed me all kinds of effects that I had never heard before on a cello. I wasn't surprised to hear him play "slap" cello, an already well-established technique on the string bass. But some unusual chordal effects and timbrally special harmonics, which Dave admitted he had borrowed from Django Reinhardt, did surprise me. But he really startled me when I heard him play two scales simultaneously *in contrary motion*—on *one* string! I couldn't believe my ears; I thought it must be some magician's trick.

Actually, it was based on some very fundamental acoustic realities, related to Pythagorean theories of mathematical ratios. The explanation Dave gave me begins with the basic acoustic principle that any string, on a cello or a viola, or a guitar, or whatever, can be divided into two equivalent halves by placing your left-hand finger exactly on the middle of the string—let's say the D string on a cello. And if you now bow (or pluck) that string between the stopped note and *the bridge*, you will produce a D an octave higher than the open string. If you bow (or pluck) the string between the stopped note and *the nut* (the upper end of the fingerboard), you will still produce a D an octave higher than the open string, because in this case both sides of the stop are of equal length. But if you now move your finger up, say, a whole step, stopping the string at E, then the lower part of the string is now longer, and will therefore sound a lower pitch, namely, C. This can be continued on upward (or downward), creating two inverse scales, one going up, one going down. If in addition—and this is what Dave Greenbaum demonstrated for me on his cello—you now bow between the middle of the string and the bridge, stopping the notes with your left-hand third finger, and *simultaneously* pluck the string (with the left-hand thumb), you will produce two scales at once on the cello, one going up, the other going down.

31. In my diary I wrote: "Some of it not an entirely satisfying experience." Also, since my manuscript notebook shows that the next thing I wrote was the first of a set of jazz compositions for brass sextet and rhythm section, it could well be that the beckoning call of all the great jazz I was hearing on the road lured me away from the unusual preclassical rigors of the cello piece—to the more inviting spontaneity of jazz. I put the *Duo Concertante* temporarily aside, telling Silberstein that I would finish the piece in New York during the summer—which I did some weeks later. But I also told him that I wasn't entirely happy with the third movement yet; it had been too much of a struggle. In the end I never gave him the piece. By the time I finished it Silberstein had left the Met and New York. I never saw him again.

32. The performance took place under the aegis of Kenneth Radnofsky's ingenious commissioning scheme that he invented more than a decade ago, whereby x number of instrumentalists are approached to contribute a relatively small sum of money, the collected total of which is passed on to the chosen composer as the commission fee. The contributing performers are then presented with the composition as a "gift," with the understanding that each of them will on or near a certain scheduled date have the privilege of "premiering" the work locally, in their city or community. On one occasion, a thus-commissioned work was "premiered" 113 times, more or less simultaneously in a span of one week, in places ranging from Hong Kong to Frankfurt and a hundred cities in between.

Chapter Six

1. Cleveland-born Bill de Arango was one of the leading vanguard of modern bop guitarists, in the wake of Charlie Christian's earlier breakthrough innovations with the electric guitar. De Arango recorded prolifically in New York in the mid-1940s with everyone from Ben Wester, Eddie "Lockjaw" Davis, and Slam Stewart to Dizzy Gillespie, Charlie Parker, and Sarah Vaughan. In 1948 he left New York, playing locally in his hometown, Cleveland, for many years, but never involved with any recordings (with one exception in 1954). I am very proud of the fact that I brought Bill, as feisty and as innovative as ever, out of semiretirement in 1995 to record him on a CD called *Anything Went* for my recording company, GM Recordings.

2. Along with some of the outrageous liberties Stokowski took with Tchaikovsky's music in that recording session, I have to admit that he—and we—also produced some ravishingly beautiful moments, extraordinarily colorful, sensuous sounds, and some incredibly powerful climaxes. How he achieved this with his simple, almost bland baton technique remains a mystery to me and many of my colleagues who, like me, worked with Stokowski and experienced his magical sonic transformations in the different orchestras he conducted after his departure from Philadelphia.

3. One of my diary entries mentions a "fearful letter" from Margie, "her mother's near-hysteria" and "her father's impossible attitudes." Three days later, in a very long fourteen-dollar phone call (a lot of money in those days), Margie spent most of the time shouting into the phone, obviously affected by her struggles with her father and the related struggle for supremacy in her life between her parents and myself.

4. William Schlossman fit well into the Black family. He was a businessman and a very good one, and incidentally someone I could immediately relate to, as he had a much more modern and open-minded mentality than his father-in-law, and, to boot, was one of the most talented punsters I ever met—a new terrific pun every few minutes—gifted with a most wonderful sense of humor.

5. I like to distinguish between arrangement and transcription, the former implying a rather loose or free rearranging of the original material, whereas transcription connotes a stricter one-to-one translation, an as close as possible adherence to the original.

6. Wind instruments can actually produce two notes at a time, certain instruments even three or four, by way of a very special technique (called multiphonics), but only in an extremely limited fashion in respect to speed of execution, dynamic and intonational control, in other words, particularly inapplicable in lively fast-moving music.

7. It is ironic that the horn, with its unusual four-octave-plus range, had to be utilized in all its registers, from flutelike high notes to bass notes below the range of the bassoon, in order to adhere as much as possible to Ravel's precise pitches and chordal structures.

8. I had often enough observed this phenomenon and learned quite a bit about it over the years, especially in transcribing Duke Ellington and other jazz recordings in my Cincinnati days. There particularly I found, to my amazement, that I seemed at times to be hearing pitches that couldn't have been played by anyone in the orchestra. I learned that these were sympathetic vibrations that under certain conditions resonated along with the actual pitches played. I began to understand that Ellington, either intuitively or consciously—it being a phenomenon particularly audible on the piano and thus one that Ellington must have observed quite often—had learned to use this subtle acoustic effect regularly in his orchestrations and ensemble voice leadings.

9. Discographies, detailed listings of performing personnel on the recordings of jazz orchestras and small groups were, ironically, first compiled and published not in America but in France. (There are none, alas, in classical music.)

10. John L. Holmes, *Conductors on Record* (Westport, CT: Greenwood Press, 1982), 124.

11. Mimi and Rudolfo separate, and she dies in the fourth act.

12. In the 1990s, half a century after I made the James transcriptions, I performed them with the Smithsonian Jazz Masterworks Orchestra, to the utter delight of the audience—but still with puzzled resistance from some of the musicians in the orchestra. Old biases die very slowly, sometimes never.

13. George and I frequently worked together years later, both in Tanglewood and in Boston. He was an indefatigable organizer of chamber music concerts, especially concerts devoted to contemporary

music. He exuded an extraordinary enthusiasm for his work and for life that was truly infectious and irresistable. I see his son, Lee, quite often nowadays, as we are both members of the Harvard Musical Association.

14. Tragically, Pulis's career was relatively short, lasting only some ten years and ending under a cloud of severe alcoholism.

15. Nola Studios, now a faint memory in New York's musical history, was to musicians of my generation, especially jazz musicians, truly legendary. Occupying the entire third floor of a block-long building on Broadway in midtown Manhattan, Nola's was a swarm of some thirty or forty large and small rehearsal studios, where every big band and traveling orchestra could be found rehearsing at some time or other. Indeed, one could go there almost any time of day or night and find some famous group rehearsing some new arrangements or preparing for a Carnegie or Town Hall concert or a Broadway show. And the beauty of it was that you could usually listen in on such rehearsals. I hung around a lot at Nola's over the years and heard many of the big bands there, from Ellington, Gillespie, and Herman to Shep Fields, Charlie Ventura, and Boyd Raeburn. It was an incredibly busy and exciting place for a young aspiring musician with a healthy appetite for all kinds of music. In addition, Nola's had three good recording studios with state-of-the-art recording equipment. Tommy Nola Sr. and Jr. became good friends, and I was for years one of their best steady customers. I spent a lot of money there, rehearsing and making private recordings.

16. After much to-and-fro among various Mozart scholars and aficionados (Waldersee, Einstein, Flothuis, Jahn, Berke), and a more exacting respectful study of the original Imbault publication and the original manuscript in Mozart's own hand, the ultimate consensus regarding the K. 487 duets is that McGinnis & Marx's 1947 edition did indeed correctly identify these pieces as being for two horns, and not for two basset horns—and certainly not for two violins, as was originally thought.

17. Graettinger's first version of his atonal masterpiece, *City of Glass*, was composed in late 1947. Its expanded large orchestra version dates from 1951.

18. *Jumpin'* finally saw the light of day in 1988, when my son, George, discovered the score and parts somewhere in my basement. The piece was then performed and recorded by George and Matt Dariau's Orange Then Blue orchestra. I remember being very happy with the recording. But it was otherwise a very sad day because one of my great heroes, Gil Evans, had died the day before.

19. An indication of how far ahead Verdi was in the use of a tone cluster we can see in his notation, as shown in the above example. In the twentieth century, and after Cowell's use of the cluster in his youthful piano pieces, clusters have always been written as , that is, vertically stacked rather than horizontally tied. It should be noted that Charles Ives also used tone clusters as early as 1904. But again Verdi could not have heard those pieces, nor is it likely that Ives, who probably did hear *Otello* played at the Met, would have heard a performance that included that organ tone cluster. I say that because I now know through my research that most of the time Verdi's tone cluster is simply omitted, to a large extent because most venues in which *Otello* is played don't have an organ.

20. In the fifteen years I played at the Met I never heard the final three bars *after* the tenor's high B flat at the end of Verdi's "Celeste Aida." Nor did I ever hear, not even in the pit, the gently heartwarming, dying-away music Puccini composed at the end of *La Bohème*'s act 1, after the singers' final backstage high C—another fifteen seconds of sublime music.

21. The bass passage is an extended one and very difficult technically; it moves progressively into the very highest bass register and into some very strange keys (A-flat minor, E-flat minor, for example). I don't think that many (or any) bass sections in the world in those years could play this passage flawlessly. Our bass section at the time was okay, but not one of the best in New York. The passage was often slightly out of tune. So Busch eventually had it doubled by three or four cellos—something I knew had been done in many operas houses in Europe—also in Busch's Dresden years.

22. In those days the Met still used Rimsky-Korsakov's reorchestration. But by the time I left the Met in 1959 we had played an "authentic" but slightly edited revision of Moussorgsky's original score, made by the composer Karel Rathaus. Another adaptation by Dimitri Shostakovich was instituted by Leindorf in 1960.

23. I must add that over the years my feelings about Stiedry fluctuated between great admiration and deep loathing. Nonetheless, by the time I left the Met in 1959, he and I had arrived at a high degree of mutual esteem. After he retired from conducting he spent his final years in Zurich, Switzerland. As I frequently conducted the Tonhalle Orchestra there, I visited him and his wife, Erika, quite often. I also think that, underneath it all, our friendship was cemented by the knowledge that we both respected Schönberg as a composer and a great teacher. Stiedry had studied with Schönberg in Berlin in the 1920s, and Stiedry knew that I was neither ignorant of nor averse to Schönberg's music. Also, on one of those Zurich visits Stiedry showed me his orchestration of Bach's *Musical Offering*, which looked very good, though it was never performed as far as I know. He called it his "little lost orphan." Another point of interest for me in regard to Stiedry was that his actress wife, Erika Wagner Stiedry, was the reciter in the first recording of Schönberg's *Pierrot lunaire*, made in New York in 1940.

24. In one notation in my diary I called Szell "last year's anti-musical horror." (I tended to use rather strong language in my diaries.)

25. Garris came to a sudden tragic end when he was murdered on the Met's 1949 tour in the railroad yards of Atlanta, where our two trains had been sided for the night. Nowadays he is not even mentioned in music encyclopedias. Sic transit gloria!

26. I nonetheless retained a certain affection for Emil Cooper, simply because he had conducted many of the earliest performances of Scriabin's *Poem of Ecstasy* in Russia and in Paris—as my readers must surely know by now, one of my most favorite turn-of-the-century composers.

27. I, on the other hand, thought well enough of the music to copy some of its best parts into my manuscript notebooks, and later, when I began my conducting career, I programmed the orchestral Prelude to *The Warrior* several times in my guest conducting engagements, a lovely piece of contemplative music, ideal for opening a concert.

28. I feel so lucky to have had the privilege of playing *Rosenkavalier* some seventy times, under a host of fine conductors, notably Busch, Kempe, Stiedry, Reiner, and Max Rudolf. The latter's *Rosenkavalier* was particularly outstanding: calm, assured, elegant, and authentically Viennese.

29. It was also the first time I heard what I called the phenomenal playing of Sol Schoenbach, the orchestra's new principal bassoonist, who many years later became one of my close faculty associates both at Tanglewood and in the 1990s at my Sandpoint (Idaho) Festival. The orchestra, under Ormandy, also delivered a stunningly virtuosic performance of Ravel's very demanding and colorful *La Valse*. As good as it was, I had by that time begun to resent Columbia Records' marketing hype that Ormandy was the creator of the Philadelphia Orchestra's famous sumptuous sound—it was incessantly sold as "the Philadelphia Sound"—when, in fact, it was Stokowski who had fashioned the particular luxurious sound, starting already in the late 1920s. Ormandy simply inherited that sound and was smart enough, unlike Riccardo Muti decades later, not to try and change it.

30. I remember from my youth that two of the most common received wisdoms in music were: (1) the definition of a voice teacher is someone who manages to ruin your voice, and (2) there are about five thousand voice teachers in New York City, many of them with studios in the Carnegie Hall building, but only three know what they're doing. Though a bit on the cynical side, both adages unfortunately contain a lot of truth.

31. My son George, unbeknownst to me, discovered these ancient acetate discs a few years ago in my basement, cleaned them up, transferred them to a CD, and presented them to me as a gift for a recent birthday.

32. I am at heart a very neat person; I hate messes and messy rooms. I especially hate stacked dirty dishes, and have, ever since Margie's death nineteen years ago, washed the dishes every night and left the kitchen absolutely spotless. On the other hand, because I have lived—and still live—a kind of driven, hectic life, relentlessly catapulting from one project to another, from one composition instantly to another, valiantly juggling my six simultaneous musical careers, my twenty-room house in Boston is a god-awful mess. It's more like a warehouse than a home. Most people who visit me—after I have apologized for all the mess—wishing to put a benign face on it, will counter with, Oh no, that's alright, it looks *well lived in*. Except for my kitchen, which is like a calming sanctuary in an otherwise overwhelming chaos, there isn't a flat surface—a chair, a table, a bureau, a bed, a sofa, a floor, even a staircase—that is not covered with papers, compositions, stacks of books, recordings, piles of accumulated mail, files of one kind or other, and works in progress. I basically abhor that, but the peripatetic pace of my life has rarely permitted me

to clean up and organize this utter clutter. Luckily, I can more or less find anything I'm looking for; there is a certain weird order to this disorder.

33. After a most distinguished career as the premier freelance harpist in New York, Gloria died from a sudden unexpected bout with cancer in 2005.

34. It wasn't until seven years later when Margie and I saw *The Despoiled* again in Toledo, on our first trip to Europe, that she noticed what we had previously completely overlooked, namely, the ominous, premonitory sight of a carpenter in a yellowish-ochre surcoat preparing the wooden cross of the crucifixion and the hole for the nail that was to pierce Christ's foot. Wow!

35. Fortunately Cecil had a secure faculty position at the Manhattan School of Music, where he taught trumpet, and led and coached brass ensembles for many years, indeed until his death in the late 1980s. When I joined the MSM faculty in 1950, teaching horn there for fourteen years, Cecil and I frequently collaborated very successfully on various brass-related projects. Still later, when I had already moved to Boston as president of the New England Conservatory, Cecil produced a stunningly excellent performance with his student ensemble of my *Symphony for Brass and Percussion,* by that time a legendarily challenging virtuosic work for sixteen brass instruments.

36. Votipka, one of the enduring stalwarts on the Met's soloist roster, sang the role for some twenty-five years, always in perfect character and style.

37. In June 1947 the Met orchestra and Rudolf also recorded Ravel's Left Hand Piano Concerto with, of all people, the work's original commissioner-instigator, Paul Wittgenstein. I don't remember much about the occasion, except that, once again, Rudolf officiated with his usual exemplary skill and aplomb, and that I was thrilled to play in the recording, since that work had become already in my early teen years one of my favorite—and most influential—Ravel creations.

38. Alan had what one would surely have to call an interesting and varied life and career. In World War II he was a B-29 bombardier for three years, flying several hundred missions. After he left the Met in 1962 he moved to Provo, Utah, becoming that town's chief of police for some fifteen years.

39. One of Rudolf Bing's most important achievements during his twelve-year reign was, in fact, the establishment and maintenance of ensemble casting, very much in the tradition of European opera houses.

40. It happens that this passage is one of only two in all of Wagner's operas—the other is in the second act of *The Flying Dutchman*—that lies badly, awkwardly, and is quite unidiomatic. I say this in the context that Wagner was one of the three or four supreme, virtually perfect composers for the horn (The others, in my opinion, are Strauss, Mahler, and Stravinsky). This uncomfortable six-bar passage in the first act of *Meistersinger* lies a little too high—it is really a clarinet part—and is very rangy. It has to be played

very lightly.  . It is also one of those

exposed horn passages that, if you play it cleanly, no one in the audience will ever notice it, but if you should miss even one note, everyone will hear it, and emit an audible gasp. The grace notes in mm. 4 and 9 are not much help, nor are the leaping fourths and fifths scattered throughout the passage. Moreover, it has to be played lightly, not loud (which would make it easier), blending with the inherently softer clarinet and the tenor (about forty feet away on stage). Playing this solo feels like teetering on a tightrope.

In the final measure, correct transpositional sequencing would have required Wagner to write a high F sharp (cue-sized in the music example), which, however, he did not quite dare to do, that note being considered out of the range of the horn in his time. (Nowadays nearly every high school kid knocks off high F sharps and Gs with nonchalant ease.) Knowing that the F sharp was in the clarinet and tenor parts, I decided one day to include it in my playing of the passage, much to the delight of my brass playing colleagues. I repeated that stunt in almost all subsequent performances. (As far as I could tell, no conductor ever seemed to be aware of my having added a note.)

41. Mezzrow (1899–1972) was a fantastic character and spellbinding raconteur, a passionate devotee of jazz—real jazz—although a rather questionably talented clarinetist. He was a close friend of Louis Armstrong and Bessie Smith, and a whole cast of other New Orleans and Chicago greats. I was fascinated by Mezzrow's utterly realistic, vivid, and honest portrayal of life in the world of jazz, especially how black musicians dealt with segregation and racial injustice in the twenties and thirties and still managed to produce so much truly great new music that quickly conquered the world.

42. When I mentioned to my father that I was reading a terrific book on jazz by a guy named Winthrop Sargeant, the music critic of the *New Yorker*, he responded with a surprised smile: "My God, that guy was my stand partner in the Philharmonic around 1927. He was quite a good player; he had very good rhythm." A few moments later he added: "And you know what? He was crazy about Bruckner's symphonies." That surprised me. We both knew that Bruckner's music (along with Mahler's) was roundly ignored or rejected in America back then, and on those exceptional occasions when one of his symphonies was programmed (by Bruno Walter, for example), it was pretty much ridiculed by both the public and critics. Was Sargeant's love for Bruckner's music really a lone voice in the wilderness in those early years?

Sargeant's greatest moment of notoriety occurred on one occasion when, as music critic for the *New Yorker*, he left a concert early, in the second half of which the Tchaikovsky Fifth Symphony was, unbeknownst to him, substituted for the originally scheduled Sixth Symphony. Sargeant's review, in which he lavishly praised Toscanini's interpretation of the Sixth Symphony, would have embarrassed most every other critic. But not Sargeant. With supreme cockiness he simply announced in the following week's *New Yorker* that "had Toscanini and the NBC Symphony performed the Sixth Symphony, my review would still have been accurate and justified." One has to admire such chutzpah!

43. Tibbett, originally trained as a Shakespearean actor, had been a Met stalwart ever since the midtwenties. His sensational, previously unmatched success in 1925 as Ford (in Verdi's *Falstaff*) was followed by a career that encompassed not only some forty standard roles, but also lead roles in Krenek's *Jonny spielt auf*, Deems Taylor's *Peter Ibbetson*, Louis Gruenberg's *Emperor Jones*, and Howard Hanson's *Merry Mount*. He finally retired from the Met in 1950.

44. I also admired Melchior for his wonderfully dry, Danish, Victor Borge-like sense of humor, and for his penchant to not take himself too seriously. Unlike many of the Met's snobbish *artistes*, who considered it below their dignity to mingle with us mere musicians, Melchior loved hanging out with us in the orchestra, and enjoyed telling us some of his very funny and often obliquely corny jokes. Knowing that he was the world's only true *Heldentenor*, he could easily have been one of those arrogant, pretentious opera divos, of whom I saw my fair share in my years at the Met. Hearsay had it that it was Melchior's wife, Kleinchen (German for small and petite), who wore the pants in the family, and kept the big man, almost twice her size, humble and under control.

Chapter Seven

1. Even so, I consider myself blessed to have played *Parsifal* about forty-five times during my Met tenure, the horn parts being among the most beautiful and lyrically expressive in the entire horn repertory.

2. It seemed like such a big trip to us then, as if to some remote land. Now that I have lived in Boston for more than forty years, going to Cambridge is like a stroll around the block.

3. I have yet to meet one Bostonian who has visited the Glass Museum. If they only knew what they are missing!

4. Scollay Square, with its boisterous bars, cheap hotels, honky-tonks, pool parlors, and various other assorted entertainments, located only a few blocks from the harbor and the navy yard, was a paradise for thousands of sailors during and after the war. It was razed in the 1950s—the result of Beacon Hill and Boston blue-blood prudery plus the prospect of millions of dollars of profit and graft—and replaced by a cluster of fairly ugly, monolithic government buildings now called Government Center. But to many elderly Bostonians it is still a kind of sacred ground where they sowed some of their youthful oats.

5. When I became president of the New England Conservatory twenty years later, many of the elderly gents on my board of trustees, mostly Harvard graduates and generous supporters of the arts and fine music, often reminisced quite unabashedly about cutting classes once a week to spend an afternoon at the Old Howard.

6. This was during James Michael Curley's last tenure (out of four discrete terms) as mayor of Boston—the first was way back in 1914–18. Curley, an extraordinarily colorful character, was the most popular mayor in Boston's entire history, and also its most corrupt, rightly comparable to Boss Tweed and Jimmy Walker of Tammany Hall fame in New York.

7. The Old Howard and Casino were visited not by a bunch of grungy, old lecherous men in cheap raincoats, their faces haggard, but by the finest citizens of the Commonwealth, albeit under cover of darkness, as well as by lots of couples. I must say that what many of those dancers did, especially the featured acts, their teasingly slow acts of disrobing, was a fairly sophisticated performance art, certainly compared to the much more primitive, mindless topless dancing and so-called table dancing of today.

8. In the busy mid-to-late forties I was not very successful in keeping a diary with absolute consistency; sometimes month-long periods remain blank. Worse yet, I lost my diary from 1950 on tour with the Met, inadvertently leaving it in the King Cotton Hotel in Memphis.

9. Karin Dayas, an outstanding pianist, renowned in Cincinnati for her brilliant annual recitals and her forceful, vibrantly virtuosic style of playing, was the Martha Argerich of her day (although not as famous). Karin had been a student of the legendary Karl Friedberg, himself a student of Clara Schumann.

10. In those years Fountain Square was bounded on all four sides by streets. Two of these are now long gone, having been replaced by a large plaza and huge skyscraper bank buildings.

11. Having by this time forsaken his Trio and already embarked on a solo singing career, Cole quickly became one of the most popular male singers, easily rivaling even Crosby and Sinatra. But those of us who knew the early Nat Cole, and remember him primarily from his Trio days, lament that he more or less gave up the piano. For he must be counted as among the top five jazz pianists and stylists of the first two jazz decades.

12. Of the many fine recordings Lena Horne has made in her long career, none is more outstanding than her collaboration on *Frankie and Johnny* (a very rare recording) with composer-arranger Phil Moore, whose challenging quasi-symphonic treatment of that old perennial is a minor masterpiece. Both Moore and the recording were unfortunately seriously underrated and ignored.

13. I actually had a rather high opinion of D'Artega—that was the only name he went by—not as a conductor but as an arranger, and as a composer of some very fetching, well-made popular songs, particularly *In the Blue of Evening*, a big hit in the early 1940s in a wonderful Tommy Dorsey-Sy Oliver-Frank Sinatra collaboration.

14. Sticking piano keys were the bane of pianists in outdoor concerts, especially when they took place in venues near the ocean (such as New London or Jones Beach), where the ocean moisture wreaked havoc with pianos.

15. In my diary I called it "my beloved" Honegger Symphony. In those years I heard a lot of Honegger's music and became extremely fond of it, indeed to the point that some of his works became quite influential in my progress as a composer. Not only did the Philharmonic play (and premiere) a number of his works, but Ernest Ansermet, a close friend of Honegger, also performed a whole series of Honegger's compositions in his several years of guest conducting the NBC symphony. I also heard his music quite often in the French films Margie and I were constantly seeing, Honegger being at the time one of the most sought after composers by French filmmakers. I was mightily impressed by everything I heard form the pen of this remarkable composer.

16. Hugh Ross was already a well-known and much-respected name to me, not only for his work in New York as the leading choral conductor, but also for his involvement in one of my favorite recording projects, a three-record album (six 78 sides, of course) of eight marvelous pieces by Villa Lobos, recorded in Rio de Janeiro in the late 1930s, conducted by Hugh Ross under the overall artistic directorship of Burle Marx.

17. Herseth was for decades arguably the most admired and renowned brass player in the United States. As principal trumpet of the Chicago Symphony for an incredible fifty years, his flawless performances exemplify one of the most distinguished American orchestral careers of the last half century. I

take pride in the fact that I spotted his enormous talent immediately that first time at Tanglewood, and that, when in later years I conducted the Chicago Symphony, I had the privilege of working with Bud Herseth (as he is known to his colleagues), gaining his collegial respect and learning from his occasional constructive criticisms.

18. As we left that afternoon concert, intending to hitchhike to the Lenox train station, an elderly couple offered to take us in their chauffeur-driven car. I wish I could remember what make of car it was, for it was the most luxurious dream vehicle either of us had ever seen or heard of. Our hosts were obviously millionaires, patrons of the Boston Symphony. Their enormous, roomy car was air conditioned, had automatic window cleaners, plush folding seats, a small bar, new gadgets and devices—what we now call "extras"—that only very wealthy folks could afford. I remember how touched we were by our hosts' friendliness and interest in who we were, evidently impressed that we were musicians and that I was already a member of the Metropolitan Opera Orchestra.

19. The aria was written for a smaller bass and required a different tuning of the four strings than generally in use on modern basses. Never mind, it was for a bass! I immediately searched for a recording of "Per questa bella mano," but found none. It was one of Mozart's least known works, and had never been recorded at that time. The first recording came along only in 1948, although even then in an abridged form.

20. While there are now tons of good, demanding, even important music for bass in all categories (concertos, chamber music, solo pieces, etc.), in the 1940s and 1950s there was hardly any interesting literature for solo bass: a few nineteenth-century concertos by Dragonetti and Bottesini, and three or four short pieces and a concerto by Serge Koussevitzky.

21. The only passage I knew of that was even remotely similar to that Schönberg ending was the soft four-part divisi D-flat chord at the end of the slow movement of Dvořák's "New World" Symphony, also at that time a very novel and unheard of way to end a symphonic movement.

22. The reason for that should be fairly obvious. A leap of an octave, say, from C to C^1 on the A string of a cello will cover a distance of nine or ten inches, while on a violin the same intervallic jump might encompass only three or four inches. But on a bass that interval will require a millisecond leap of almost a foot and a half. The large size of a bass combined with the great length of its strings, about three-and-a-half feet (compared to about half that length on a violin), is the reason, although at first thought seemingly paradoxical, why good intonation is significantly harder to achieve on a bass than on any other string instrument.

Truly precise intonation is tricky on a bass because the space on the lower half of a bass string, within which a given note is to be found, is two inches long (but about half that length on the upper half of the string). One would think that such an amount of space, of leeway, would make it easier to pinpoint the note, but the exact opposite is the case. At the lower and upper ends of that space you will still get the note, but it will be slightly out of tune, thus not really good enough. And that means that you have to find the precise center of that space. On a violin, by comparison, the exact place, the node point where the note is to be found, is in a tiny short space, less than a quarter of an inch, which—ironically—makes it easier to find the note with intonational precision.

The fact that Serge Koussevitzky, the orchestra's conductor, was himself a renowned bass virtuoso in his younger years in Russia, and had also made some famous solo bass recordings, more or less guaranteed that his orchestra would have one of the world's finest bass sections.

23. When, in my advanced age, I assess my work as a composer it is clear to me that my creative achievements are not of the very highest order that characterizes the work of the greatest composers of our Western tradition, those two-dozen composers who reside in the composers' pantheon. My work is not quite of that class; my innovative breakthroughs lie at a slightly lesser level. They are, as in the case of the Bass Quartet, of enduring importance and considerable influence, but either technically or in the domain of individual ideas (as compared to large concepts); in other words, not of a language-changing or language-advancing nature. I have been able to occasionally accomplish something important and strikingly new, but it does not constitute the truly grand, visionary, life-changing creativity that defines the highest achievements in human cultural history.

24. Indeed, bassists who perform bass concertos always do so in scordatura, where the four strings are tuned one tone higher, thereby achieving slightly better projection of the sound.

25. Fred was one of my most admired heroes in music, a man of inviolable artistic and professional integrity, a truly gentle man, sensitive, generous, and giving, whose students adored and revered him. Although he was a first-rate player who could easily have been principal bass of the New York Philharmonic—and many of us thought he *should* have been—he was, with his innate modesty, content to remain during his forty years with the orchestra on the inside first stand of the section. I know this was in part so that he could pursue his many other cultural interests, have more time to concentrate on his teaching career, which included producing an immense amount of study material and superb transcriptions for bass, all in the interest of expanding bass players' musical horizons. Zimmerman was also a major art collector, specializing in the works of Klee, Kandinsky, Malevich, Schiele, and Beckmann. He was himself a wonderfully gifted painter, having studied with George Grosz in his youth. I have several of his beautiful, witty, and, occasionally, Klee-like pictures. It is, incidentally, a clear indication of the high esteem in which Fred was held as a teacher that Charles Mingus, himself a fantastically gifted bass player, revered Zimmerman, and often took lessons with him in order, as Charles put it, to "clean up my arco playing."

26. When I was in my early teens (the late 1930s, twenty years before the Zimmerman era), and just getting to be serious about becoming a musician, I remember my father often making fun of the Philharmonic's bass section, especially of their rendering of the famous bass (and cello) passage in the Trio of Beethoven's Fifth Symphony Scherzo. He said that when they played that run of fast eighth notes, it sounded like someone moving heavy furniture across a floor. Others said it sounded like a bunch of grunting gorillas—which was probably unfair to gorillas.

By the time I started playing regularly with the Philharmonic in the forties and fifties, you could actually make out the twelve pitches in those fast runs in Beethoven's Fifth Symphony, partly because the players had mostly switched to steel strings, but also because they just played with better intonation, cleaner articulation, and in a less lumbering fashion.

27. Although we all entreated Fred to take the lead part, he insisted on giving that honor to his star student.

28. Proof of that, if proof were still needed, can be heard on a CD issued on the GM Recordings label, which was recorded in a studio in the Bronx on April 28, two days after the premiere performance, along with my transcription for four basses of the extraordinary D Major *Sarabande* from Bach's Sixth Cello Suite.

29. Margie, growing up in North Dakota, certainly had not done much climbing—there weren't any hills or mountains to see, let alone climb—except for two summers as a teenager at Cheley Camp in Colorado, just outside Estes Park. Although most of the summer was spent riding horses, swimming, and other sports, she did climb Long's Peak (14,255 feet). But that was about eight years before our Mount Marcy ascent. Her riding companions in Colorado were Carlos Kleiber and his sister, whom the camp kids nicknamed Peaches and Cream. The Kleiber children spent the war years in America, while their father, Erich Kleiber, was working at the famous Teatro Colon in Buenos Aires, Argentina.

30. I never met Orson Welles, although I felt very privileged to sit not far from him and quietly observe him smoking his morning cigar and reading his newspaper at breakfast on many a day when we both, in the 1970s, happened to stay regularly at London's ritzy Carlton Tower Hotel. He seemed very lonely; he was always alone. I also think, despite all his bravura and grandeur, he was a very shy man.

31. Thornhill came from a classical background, and in the 1920s had studied at the Cincinnati Conservatory and the Curtis Institute of Music. He had a beautiful touch on the piano, and I admired his playing for its imaginative use of dynamics and tonal shadings.

32. It wasn't long before I realized that this was a quality to be found in a lot of late nineteenth-century French music, from Saint-Saens and César Frank to Fauré and Debussy, also in Délibes's ballet music (*Sylvia* and *Coppélia*).

33. As a horn player, I was quite amazed—and impressed—by finding in *Manon* a long, extended, and most beautiful horn solo that was written in the horn transposition of *G flat*. Why amazed and impressed? Because it is the *only* instance of a G-flat horn transposition that I know of.

34. My younger readers will not know or remember how heavy 78 albums were!

35. Svanholm had one particularly unfortunate habit: he expectorated rather sizeable gobs of saliva when singing forte, especially on certain very heavy German consonants. When he sometimes moved to the front of the stage very near the footlights, an arching spray of spittle would descend upon our poor bassoonists, clarinetists, and the last stand of cellists sitting in the pit right under the stage apron.

36. Years later I would occasionally hear recordings Ralf made in the thirties, when his voice was full and rich, solidly placed—but he was still no Melchior.

37. I should add that Munch's revelatory performances with the Philharmonic were countered by some disappointing concerts conducted by Bruno Walter. Given my early admiration for Walter, going back to my acquisition many years before of his seminal recordings of Mahler's *Lied von der Erde* and his Ninth Symphony, it was disconcerting, to say the least, to hear his rather messy, disjointed performances now of *Das Lied* and Beethoven's Fourth Symphony.

38. As it turned out, because of delays on my part in finishing the piece, Roland did not get to premiere *Symphonic Study* in Cincinnati until the spring of 1949.

39. I had a tendency in my younger years to make decisions on impulse, rather than by rational, thoughtful deliberation. It has always been an inherent part of my nature, a characteristic probably inherited from my mother and part of an innate proclivity for the constant search, the continual exploration of new ideas—the urge to try everything the imagination could conjure up. There clearly are risks in such an approach to life and career, but on the other hand a more cautious, prudent approach can lead to missing many important opportunities, capsulated in the old bromide, nothing ventured, nothing gained.

40. The Trio is one of my orphan offspring. Although it was nicely published by AMP/Schirmer some years later, it doesn't get all that many performances. But there is a fine recording of it on the CRI label, played beautifully by three Baltimore musicians (James Ostryniec, oboe; Noah Chaves, viola; and David Bakkegard, horn).

41. My father and Mitropoulos had become rather friendly over the years, in large part because Mitropoulos greatly admired my father's work as a very intelligent, vastly experienced, and most cooperative orchestral player—sitting there right under his nose. From time to time my father had told Mitropoulos of young Gunther's progress as a horn player and as a composer.

42. "Green room" is the term for the conductor's or soloist's room in concert halls, where visitors gather after a concert to greet and congratulate the artists.

43. Many years later I found an encyclopedia with a one-paragraph entry for Pittaluga: he was born in 1906 in Spain and was quite prolific, composing, among other things, several evening-long ballets. What really amazed me was that still later, in the seventies, I discovered that Pittaluga had been head of the film library between 1941 and 1945 at—of all places—the Museum of Modern Art. I never heard of him there and then because in those years I was not yet attending MOMA regularly. Still, an amazing coincidence.

44. Jean Wiener (1896–1982), a much neglected and forgotten French composer, is of great interest to me, not only because of the excellent film and theatre music he composed in the 1920s and 1930s, but also because, along with Ernest Ansermet, he was among the very first in France to discover and admire American ragtime and jazz. Wiener's music and career have fascinated me ever since my teen years, when I began to come across his name quite often, not only as a film composer but also as part of the 1920s modernist movement in Paris known as les Six, which was headquartered in the legendary Parisian cabaret, le Boeuf sur le toit.

In 1920 Wiener formed a piano duo with Clement Doucet, and in the next twenty years gave over two thousand concerts, featuring four-hand transcriptions for two pianos of works by his colleagues and contemporaries, as well as dozens of specially arranged early jazz compositions. Later Wiener organized concerts of new music in Paris (frequently first performances in France) of major composers such as Stravinsky, Schönberg, Berg, Webern, and DeFalla. Indeed, he was primarily responsible for introducing the music of the Second Viennese School to French audiences. It was in one of Wiener's concerts that Darius Milhaud conducted the French premiere of Schönberg's *Pierrot lunaire*. Wiener's first piano concerto, *Concerto Franco-Américain*, was written in a Gershwinesque style that anticipates Gershwin's Piano Concerto in F by about three years.

I haven't yet figured out why his star faded so quickly after the 1950s, above all in his native France.

45. Believe it or not, earlier that same day we also saw a stage version of *Volpone*, with José Ferrer and John Caradine, which, however, we felt was too slapstick laden to do justice to Voltaire's witty, bitingly serious satire.

46. I always equated Sokoloff's versatile talent in films with the Met's De Paolis's in opera. I could never get enough of either of them. I first discovered Sokoloff in some early German films such as Pabst's *The Love of Jeanne Ney* (1927) and the 1931 *Three Penny Opera*, then again later in fine Hollywood films such as *For Whom the Bell Tolls* and *While the City Sleeps*.

47. Ironically, virtually as I write these words, *Partisan Review*, after a valiant attempt to survive through vastly changing times, published its final issue in 2003.

48. My earliest foray into purchasing something artistic and creative goes back to my Ballet Theatre days, when, on tour in Canada, I bought several exquisite small sculptures of animals native to the arctic regions—polar bears, seals, reindeer—sculpted by unknown Eskimos out of grey soapstone.

49. Incidentally, it was also in Palestine that Joe first came to know the composer Stefan Wolpe, who in his New York days was very much sought after as a teacher by many jazz musicians such as Johnny Carisi, Joe Bushkin, Eddie Sauter, and George Russell. Joe's other great artist friends were Lyonel and Lux Feininger, and John Marin.

50. Nat Pierce had a somewhat erratic, checkered career. When he couldn't keep his band together for lack of work, he freelanced, for most of his life playing and arranging for a host of great jazz names— Basie, Herman, Earl Hines, singers such as Ella Fitzgerald and Anita O'Day. Nat Pierce has got to be one of the most unsung first-rate jazz musicians of the last sixty years.

51. De Vries also played flute in the world premiere of Schönberg's *Pierrot lunaire* in 1912, along with Steuermann and Kolisch.

52. It has both fascinated and puzzled me why and how it is that Chicago produces the most consistently superior architecture. Is there some clandestine artistic committee that advises and controls what is built in downtown Chicago, or—more crucially—what is not built? Is it the ghosts of Louis Sullivan and Frank Lloyd Wright? Is it something in the water? Once in a while, a clichéd or banal design creeps in, but that is an unusually rare occurrence. For over half a century I have always looked forward to visiting Chicago, if only to see what striking new edifice has been added to the city's vibrant skyline. I undertook several other photographic pilgrimages in those years, most notably in Denver, just months before that city tore down all its historic nineteenth-century buildings.

53. Wright's ultimate architectural masterpiece, Falling Water, near Pittsburgh, is undoubtedly the most perfect and ingenious example of that concept.

54. Bradley (1912–89) rivaled Dorsey in ballad playing, maybe not quite as warmly and expressively, but certainly in elegance of style, in dexterity and range. He and his drummer sidekick, Ray McKinley, had several big hits in the early 1940s with a series of boogie-woogie style numbers. But my favorites were several beautifully arranged and performed easy-swing pieces such as *Celery Stalks at Midnight*, *It's Square but It Rocks*, and his big hit *Beat Me, Daddy, Eight to the Bar*.

55. Bradley was not the only jazz musician to turn away from jazz in the late 1940s. Most notably, the great Mel Powell, for many years Benny Goodman's stellar pianist and arranger (composer of the big Goodman hit *Mission to Moscow*), broke away from jazz in 1949, and studied composition with Paul Hindemith at Yale. One of the finest American twelve-tone composers, Powell (1923–98) spent his postjazz career as dean of the California Institute of Art and composer in residence.

56. Contractors in music had nothing to do with erecting buildings. They were the musicians—often ex-instrumentalists—who hired you, especially in the relatively lucrative freelance field. In New York there were hundreds of contractors, most of them offering piddling little jobs, parades, bar mitzvahs, weddings, occasional Saturday night gigs, one-night-stand club dates, and the like. But there were also a dozen or so major contractors in New York who had control over the best, most lucrative, and most steady-paying work. Each specialized in a particular area; usually they stayed out of one another's territory. Some had the Broadway shows buttoned down, others the opera and ballet field; a few specialized in radio work, still others had recording session jobs under their sway; and finally, there were contractors who dominated the hotel job scene.

Top contractors such as Stonzek, Shoobe, Held, Fabbroni, Glickman, and Charlap were both feared and revered. As a freelancer your livelihood depended on them. You had better not cross them, or even turn them down for jobs. They expected loyalty from you. There were also lots of rumors of kickbacks and lavish present giving at Christmas or New Year's.

57. Charles Eames (1907–78), a great American designer, filmmaker, and inventor, created chairs in the midforties designed to better fit the contours of the human body. I met Charles years later in 1962 at the Seattle World's Fair, where we were both involved with different film projects.

58. I met Mike Glass soon after I had returned to New York from my two-year Cincinnati stint. We found ourselves frequently in the same horn section in various park and pop concerts, where I discovered

him to be a most intelligent, tasteful player with a beautiful, blooming tone. I had already admired his playing in some of Gil Evans's fabulous 1940s arrangements, when Mike was briefly first horn in the Claude Thornhill orchestra. Mike lived in the Alvin Hotel, right near Carnegie Hall, and he and I spent many a late hour after concerts together at the legendary Carnegie Delicatessen next door.

59. I didn't hear Parker live most of that year because he was rarely in New York. He was in California, seriously and increasingly involved with drugs (heroin), which often affected his playing quite negatively, as can be heard on the recordings of that year, especially *Relaxing at Camarillo*.

60. It is truly fascinating that Monk was able to fashion a uniquely personal keyboard style and technique with a touch on the piano that by any conventional standards would be considered hopelessly clumsy and wrong. It took a long time for listeners and the critics—and even most of Monk's fellow boppers—to comprehend that what seemed just ponderous or inept or weird was actually consummate music of real substance, of striking ideas—a whole new sound world.

61. Tadd Dameron and Fats Navarro have never been given their full due, in part because their careers were rather short lived. Tadd's talents as a pianist were too scantily documented on recordings. I have a feeling that most critics and audiences did not know what an excellent pianist and accompanist he was. I admired him so much because he always experimented with unorthodox harmonizations and chordal structures. I particularly remember a thrilling, wonderfully chromatic and sinuous piano solo in an *All the Things You Are* performance from that summer, which I dearly wish had been recorded.

Fats Navarro's career was even shorter than Dameron's, lasting only nine years. He died at age twenty-six in 1950 from tuberculosis. Fats played with many different bands and small groups; and despite the brevity of his career, he made a considerable number of recordings, some thirty sessions in all, and almost always of spectacular quality. Unfortunately many of them do not feature him enough as a soloist. He is best heard on the Blue Note label with Dameron's Sextet and his own combo in the last years of his life. He seems never to have been accorded the acclaim given to Gillespie, even by his brass-playing colleagues. Of the many attributes I admired most in Navarro's playing, it was the relaxed, cool fluency and speed of his eighth-note runs—faster even than Dizzy's—but rendered with a tonal voluptuousness that I don't think I ever encountered in any other trumpet player.

62. Unfortunately Navarro was not present, and as far as I know he never played with the Dameron Sextet again.

63. They were the stellar section of Stan Getz, Zoot Sims, Herbie Steward, and Serge Chaloff. Even when their names were announced, this didn't at first mean much to me because all four were relative newcomers (at least by name) and still in their early twenties: Getz was the youngest of the group (twenty-one), but had already been playing for four years with bands such as Stan Kenton, Benny Goodman, and Jimmy Dorsey. (Getz made his first recording at age seventeen, with Jack Teagarden's orchestra.)

64. Some research passed on to me by Tony Agostinelli (the world's super connoisseur on anything relating to Stan Kenton), revealed that Parker "Parky" Groat was not a figment of my imagination, but a highly respected first-call trombonist in the Detroit area. Groat replaced Milt Bernhart for a few months in late 1948, and returned to Detroit when Kenton disbanded in mid-December 1948.

65. I was fortunate to meet Wyschnegradsky several times in the 1970s, when I conducted quite a lot in Paris.

66. Eduard Tubin (1905–82) remained completely unknown (at least in this country) for many years until the late 1980s, when there suddenly appeared a plethora of Tubin recordings, including all of his eight symphonies, an opera, a ballet, and four of his concertos including the one for double bass.

67. Nell Tangeman (1917–85) was, along with Jennie Tourel, my most admired mezzo-soprano singer. She had an amazing career, and was, until Jan DeGaetani and Bethany Beardslee came along, one of the very few singers devoted to the most challenging new music of the time. I found out later that Nell's *Das Lied von der Erde* performance in Cincinnati in 1945 had been her debut appearance. In her distinguished but all too brief career she sang, in either world or American premieres, many of the most important works in the vocal or opera repertory: Messiaen's *Poèmes pour Mi*, the role of Mother Goose in Stravinsky's *The Rake's Progress* in its 1951 Venice premiere, and many works by Copland and Bernstein, to name but a few.

68. The phrase "Lovest Thou for Beauty" became our life's credo.

69. It is difficult to psychologically analyze an orchestra's collective behavior or its inevitably up-and-down qualitative standards. There are too many variables that play into an orchestra's total history. But I offer a probable scenario: the Philharmonic was in a somewhat demoralized state at the time, rebounding from the despotic regime of Artur Rodzinski—and his sudden departure—a reaction that eventually turned into a rebellion against conductors in general.

70. It would have been more accurate to call such pieces little known or unknown. After all, most of those "contemporary" pieces, as, for example, by Schönberg, Webern, and Mahler, were written in 1906 and 1909—hardly contemporary.

71. Since the Metropolitan Opera's management had given the orchestra notice and we were on strike, I was suddenly free to attend rehearsals at the Philharmonic, which in the Mitropoulos weeks I did almost religiously, enabling me, among other things, to closely observe the behavior of the orchestra.

72. Was Mitropoulos, raised in a Greek Orthodox monastery and a follower of St. Francis, intimidated by the tough guys in the orchestra? I'm certain it was the case. Mitropoulos was never one to fight back when attacked.

73. By "radical" I mean that this process, particularly in this specific Schönberg work, eliminates two major elements (or tools) of musical construction: melody and rhythm, leaving only harmony and timbre (tone color).

74. To cite just one of the dovetailing examples, imagine having to subtly transfer a *pp* D flat (around middle C), as part of a larger chord, from a second trumpet to a clarinet sitting fifteen feet away, and from there to the first stand of violas, another twenty or so feet away, and you can then envision what a challenge it is to have 516 such connections correctly realized, meaning perfectly balanced and smoothly connected.

75. Prausnitz was at the time conductor of the Juilliard orchestra. He did quite a lot of contemporary music, including that of the Second Viennese School. Later (in the 1960s) Prausnitz became conductor of the orchestra at the New England Conservatory, where, when I became president of that school in 1967, he remained for some years on the faculty. Perhaps Prausnitz's biggest claim to fame rests in his audaciously programming and performing with considerable success Karlheinz Stockhausen's *Gruppen* at the Conservatory, a work that I consider one of the composer's true masterpieces, and which makes the most extraordinary demands on a student orchestra. *Gruppen* requires among other things three conductors. Prausnitz's coconductors were Diamantis Diamantopoulos and Jacques Monod.)

76. Leibowitz was a most perceptive and insightful conductor, and I count his recordings of all nine Beethoven symphonies, utterly ignored and far too little known, as among the very best performances of those great works. (Leibowitz and I were to collaborate a few years later on a very important pioneering recording project with Dial Records.)

77. The owners, Elaine and Manny Levenson, started their small record company in the late forties as the EMS label, which specialized in recordings of previously unrecorded music, which they sold in their shop. They also put out a monthly listing of new recordings and reviews, including very insightful critiques of contemporary music. The Levensons were responsible for my first recording as a conductor and producer, and for quite some years I became one of the repertory advisors for their record company. The store (and the label) eventually perished in the middle of the LP era, unable to keep financially afloat in competition with the big chains like Sam Goody and Tower Records, which came into the field in the fifties and sixties.

78. Bosley Crowther, *New York Times*, September 14, 1948.

79. Slavik was an extraordinarily talented violinist who, by all accounts, was virtually the equal (and only rival) of Paganini. At age sixteen he became concertmaster of the Imperial Court Orchestra of Vienna, the forerunner of the Vienna Philharmonic. Slavik's works for violin are technical and harmonically daring tours de force. He must also have had an extraordinary ear, for it is reported that when he heard Paganini play his famous *La Campanella* in a concert in Vienna, he subsequently wrote the whole piece down from memory and played it for Paganini the next day. Paganini, not easily impressed, was astounded.

I remember hearing one of Slavik's violin concertos, recorded in Czechoslovakia after the war, on WQXR fairly often in the late 1940s. Schubert wrote his *Grand Fantasia* Sonata Op. 159 for Slavik. Amazingly, there are presently no recordings available of Slavik's works.

80. Initially my bassists were Ernie Gruen of the Met orchestra, and then Ed Gordon, when he came to New York from Rochester. Eventually, when Janet was hired by WMCA, where a fine jazz pianist named Ellis Larkins was on staff, I made her some trio arrangements for harp, piano (doubling on celesta), and bass.

81. However, at the insistent urgings of some of my friends at the radio stations (who were making good money) and Clara Silver, Steuermann's new wife (who worked for Carl Fisher, a big music publisher), I did have a very brief encounter with commercialism. I invented a new composer named Alex Sheeler—my middle name is Alexander, and many of my friends knew me only as Alex—who was going to conquer the world, or at least the high school music market, by composing catchy marches, innocuous light classics, and simplistically bland horn solo pieces. Margie thought I had gone nuts. She was right. The dalliance with commercialism lasted less than two weeks; I simply had no stomach for it.

82. I think I was the first person to do this kind of retuning of single strings. The advantage is that by tuning, say, an F below middle C a half tone higher, you get a G flat; this enables you to finger a simple octave (f^1 and f) but sound a major seventh interval (F and G flat). Similarly, if you want a tritone, say, G and D flat, tune the (middle) D string down to D flat, in which case when you play a fifth you get a tritone G-D flat. Major sevenths and their inversions, minor seconds, and tritones are the most common intervals in modern chromatic music, and are, because of the harp's inherent technical/structural limitations, more difficult to produce—in some cases impossible—especially when such intervals appear continuously or in rapid succession.

The disadvantage of this scordatura (which you may have to work around) is that in the first instance you lose the lower string's F flat, and in the second instance you lose the D string's D sharp. But, oddly enough, if you pedal that retuned D string down to its flat position you actually get C^1—which in some harmonic circumstances might come in very handy. In the end, this technique, depending on *which* strings and *how many* strings you retune—and which way, up or down—is a fascinating mixture of minuses and pluses. I found it to be mostly an advantage, and it enabled me to write many a "modern" chromatic or bitonal chords for Janet that would otherwise have been completely unattainable.

Excited with my new discovery and the results it produced, I decided to try to make some transcriptions for harp of middle to late Scriabin pieces, such as Op. 65. But I was soon forced to give it up; Scriabin's highly chromatic, tritonally rich music is literally unplayable on a harp, both vertically (harmonically) and horizontally (melodically), because of the aforementioned structural pedaling limitations.

83. It is interesting in retrospect that four of my early close female friends were harpists: Gloria Agostini, Linda Iacobucci, and, later in New York, Janet Putnam and Margaret Ross. I learned already in my midteen years that composing for the harp was not like composing for the piano, primarily through my study of three sources: Carlos Salzedo's harp studies, the Berlioz and Rimsky-Korsakov treatises on orchestration, and especially the works of Ravel and Debussy, both of whom wrote superbly for the harp. But these lady friends provided me over the years with an even closer, detailed, hands-on knowledge of what constitutes truly idiomatic harp writing.

A mistake many composers make, especially when writing in a modern chromatic or atonal language, is to write for the harp as if it were a piano. But there is something called pedals on a harp—seven of them—which, compared to the eighty-eight keys on a piano (allowing one to play any note or notes that the ten fingers can reach), will definitely limit the chords and harmonies one can play at any given time on a harp. The harp is thus an anachronism among orchestral instruments in that it is the only one that is not fully chromatic and has not yet entered even the twentieth century, let alone the twenty-first. One of the arrangements I made for Linda in Cincinnati, *Body and Soul*, is only a mildly chromatic piece of music; yet my fifty-eight-measure four-minute arrangement required—so Linda told me—157 pedal changes!

84. That little trip was a fulfillment of a long-held desire to see Whitman's birthplace. Whitman became one of my literary heroes at St. Thomas, along with Emerson, especially when I discovered *Leaves of Grass* and Frederick Delius's *Sea Drift* (one of my favorite musical masterpieces, based on one of the long poems in *Leaves of Grass*). In my teens, I drove dozens of times directly past Whitman's birthplace on Route 110 on the way to my parent's summer home in Rocky Point.

85. Luigi was not only a great clarinetist. As I learned on those visits to his home in Freeport, there seemed to be nothing that he couldn't do, build, or fix. He had built his motorized fishing

launch himself, likewise most of his house, which had a spacious porch right over the water. And to boot he was a fantastic cook.

86. Gussie stayed with Neil all of her life as a partner or wife—I don't know which. He must have gradually changed and mellowed, for when I finally met him again many, many years later, after Gussie's death, he was very friendly and calm.

87. Leon was one of three black singers, the only three blacks in the entire cast. They were all, by stereotypical predetermination, assigned the role of Pullman porters.

88. I was also very enthusiastic about having Lazzari, my longtime favorite (from Cincinnati days), sing the role of Sparafucile (in *Rigoletto)*, and to have Antonicelli conduct the opera.

89. Dorothy Kirsten was endowed with a beautiful voice, but I'm afraid that having started as a dancer in small ingénue roles on Broadway in the mid-1930s, she never lost some her show business habits in her many years at the Met.

90. It is not that I agreed with all of his tenets, but he expressed his ideas and beliefs so intelligently and, in his sincerity, so convincingly, that I had no choice but to respect him and the content of his message.

91. All her life this perfectionist zeal drove her to extraordinary lengths to achieve her desired goals, whether it was just an evening dinner, preparations for a big party, washing dishes, cleaning house, preparing for Christmas, or whatever. I must add that this was not some neurotic compulsion of hers, but rather a deep and healthy sense of neatness and correctness that she, I'm sure, inherited from her mother.

92. Her doctors were absolutely correct in their advice. In the ensuing years, my wife was to have more problems giving birth; she had two miscarriages and both of our children had to be delivered by cesarean section. How did they know? In all probability they saved her life.

93. The 78 discs John referred to were four sides recorded in August 1947: *Milestones, Little Willie Leaps, Half Nelson,* and *Sippin' at Bells,* on which John was the pianist, in the company not only of Miles, but also Charlie Parker, bassist Nelson Boyd, and the twenty-two-year-old Max Roach.

94. There was a game I and a Met colleague, the violinist Oscar Weizner (Austrian-born but raised in America, a very bright and well-educated fellow), played almost every day. It consisted of tracing any event that either of us had recently experienced back through a series of imagined accidental interconnections to some distant point in the past. Most evenings we ended up at the Bible's Genesis.

95. I regard the massive intrusion of commercialism over the last four decades into Christmas and other holidays a gross perversion of the meaning and spirit of what should be essentially commemorative days—the original etymology and meaning of the word holiday being, of course, "holy day."

Chapter Eight

1. In former times, say at least thirty years ago, audiences at classical concerts considered enthusiastic applause (while sitting down) a sufficient expression of their praise. In more recent times, classical audiences have taken to instantaneous standing ovations, perhaps influenced by the exuberant behavior of rock and pop audiences, for whom even mere standing ovations are totally inadequate, and only en masse jumping up and down, hooting and howling will suffice. What's next? Are audiences now going to levitate as the next stage of approbatory behavior, vaulting into the air in dancers leaps? (Since people now regularly fly through the air in films—along with cars—maybe that doesn't seem so far-fetched.)

2. Is it mere chance that Strauss's next opera, *Elektra,* starts with the same key, C minor, in a similar rhythmic figure, but this time as more of an outcry?

3. Patelson's, a music store directly opposite Carnegie Hall's stage door on Fifty-Sixth Street, was the musicians' mecca for getting anything in the way of sheet music that was commercially available. But they also had on hand an enormous collection of secondhand scores and parts, very often acquired from famous conductors, musicians, and singers. Both Patelson brothers became my best friends; and I became one of their best customers. I owe a lot to Patelson's for being able to acquire a very large personal library at a very early age.

4. Krafft-Ebing (1840–1902), a German neuropsychiatrist, was an early pioneer in the study of a wide range of dysfunctional or aberrational behaviors, including sadomasochism, hemicramia, and sexual psychopathology.

5. Stokowski had the same ability to transform an orchestra—any orchestra—only with an entirely different, and in his case more sumptuous, sonic result.

6. The Met orchestra became completely Reinerized in the first half of the 1948–49 season. Reiner was given five big, important operas: *Rosenkavalier, Meistersinger, Salomé, Figaro,* and *Don Giovanni,* the heart and soul of that season's repertory—probably much to the dismay of Fritz Stiedry. (The two Fritzes were no friends to begin with, Reiner being the much more successful and famous of the two, even in Germany in the 1920s.)

7. Once, in the early sixties, while Reiner was watching one of Bernstein's Young People's Concerts telecasts, seeing Lennie gyrate wildly on the podium, he indignantly exclaimed: "Well, I didn't teach him *that!*"

8. One reason for Reiner's immobility and extremely economical baton technique came to light some time later, when he confided to us that, a few years earlier, he had experienced what he called two minor heart infarctions, as a result of which his doctors admonished him to significantly reduce his conducting activities. Reiner told us that instead of following the doctors' advice he decided that henceforth everything he had previously conducted in four, he would now conduct in two (in *alla breve*), and what he had conducted in two, he would now do in one.

Believe it or not, he did spring that second option on us one night—without warning, mind you—in the Prelude to *Meistersinger,* by conducting the beginning in *one*! It is normally conducted in four, but Reiner had sometimes done it in two with us, to which the orchestra, having played the *Meistersinger* Overture hundreds of times, adjusted without any problem. It gave that music a wonderful lift and flow that the often stodgy, ponderous interpretations by most conductors of the time. But doing it in ONE? Wow. That was another matter. Had he warned us of his intention, we surely would have taken it in stride, knowing that he loved to play these kinds of testing games, generally accompanied with a taunting grin. But this time we almost all had heart failure. Yet miraculously, we played the first few bars on automatic pilot, as it were, realizing by the third measure what he was up to, quickly recovering and going right along with his game. Anyway, what choice did we have? About ten bars in he saluted us—the whole orchestra—with his standard (although rarely seen) gesture of approbation, which was very similar to an army private's salute to a lieutenant or general.

9. The custom in opera of sitting while conducting is undoubtedly due to the fact that almost all operas are considerably longer than any symphony concert (not to mention Wagner operas, some of which last up to five hours).

10. In his review of *Salomé* in the *Times,* Olin Downes had pointed out that Strauss's opera had experienced an at best checkered history in New York since its American premiere in 1907. That history began with only a single performance; all further performances were canceled by order of J. Pierpont Morgan and the directors of the Met, which had the effect of keeping *Salomé* out of the Met's repertory for twenty-seven years! (The opera was also banned in Vienna, London, Boston, and Philadelphia.)

Only three Metropolitan Opera stagings of *Salomé* preceded our 1949 revival: the first in 1934, with Bodanzky conducting and a Salomé (Göta Ljungberg) whose rendition was unanimously called "ridiculous" by the New York press; the second in 1937 with Panizza and Majorie Lawrence; the third in the two seasons (1942–44) before my arrival at the Met, with Szell and Lily Djanel.

11. Nearly forty years later, much wiser and much more concerned about this subject and other related matters that have plagued the orchestra world for years, I delivered myself of a major speech (at Tanglewood), widely reported and reprinted in the music press—also occasionally misprinted, truncated, inaccurately excerpted—which became very controversial and made me a whole new set of friends and enemies.

12. The 1948 *Gramophone Shop Encyclopedia of Recorded Music* listed only *fourteen* (!) works by Mahler, including five of his songs, and only five of his nine symphonies (almost all conducted by Bruno Walter— not Leonard Bernstein). *Das klagende Lied* was not recorded until the 1980s, and the first concert performance in America took place only in 1970 with the New Haven Symphony, conducted by Frank Brieff.

How little Mahler was appreciated in those earlier times is evidenced by the fact that the 2,089-page *McMillan Encyclopedia of Music and Musicians* of 1938, the major American music encyclopedia of the time, offered only some paltry 260 words on Mahler, and never mentioned *Das klagende Lied.* Thirty-seven years later, the 1975 *International Encyclopedia of Music and Musicians* entry on Mahler had grown to over three double-column pages, while the article on Mahler in the latest *Grove* now contains over *twenty-six* pages of double columns.

13. Ross Russell founded Dial Records in 1946, and he was one of the first to record Charlie Parker extensively, mostly partnered with Dizzy Gillespie. In the late 1940s Ross branched out into contemporary classical music, producing the first recordings of certain important works by Schönberg, Berg, Webern, and Bartók. He was also active as a writer on jazz.

14. I was too inexperienced at the time in my own jazz playing efforts to realize that in improvising, to a large extent you hear the notes you're about to play in your inner ear just split seconds before you actually play them. You are therefore, by some fascinating mysterious process, much less likely to miss notes than when playing a written part, as, say, in a difficult Strauss, Wagner, or Beethoven passage. You are, after all, choosing the notes yourself, not playing someone else's. The two approaches to playing each start at a different point, but through diligent practice and preparation one can arrive ultimately at the same level of ease and spontaneous-sounding execution.

15. Other pioneer jazz horn players who studied with me at MSM were David Amram, Ed London, Robert Northern (Brother Ah), and Bob Swisshelm.

16. The trumpet is a much more simply constructed instrument than the horn, and thus inherently easier to master than the more complex, mechanically somewhat compromised, horn, especially the double horn. (When I first heard Julius at Minton's that night, he was playing a single horn, a more manageable, tamable, lighter instrument. All of us symphony players used the heavier, harder-to-control double horn.)

17. Julius made some very fine recordings, especially with his own group, The Jazz Modes. He also made one very nice recording (on the Philips label) with an eleven-piece orchestra, which included five horns—Julius, myself, Bob Northern, Buffington, and Barrows—as well as tuba and flute. But perhaps his finest outing on disc occurred in some sessions recorded in 1960 in Yugoslavia (on the Radio Beograd label) with Jerome Richardson and John Lewis's future brother-in-law, pianist Davor Kajfes.

18. There are composers who always revise and retouch their works. Pierre Boulez is one such composer in our time; almost everything he has composed has been revised, in some cases several times. He has also called each performance of a revised work a new premiere.

19. Melchior's career at the Met ended in 1950, having begun in 1926. He had intended to continue for at least one more year but left the Met when he got into a major quarrel with Bing, the new general manager.

20. I did find the same qualities in Joe Williams's voice.

21. Svanholm used to arrive at the high C after an almost octave-long scoop.

22. *Sfogare* in Italian means to unbosom or unburden oneself. Most Italian tenors, alas, take that to mean sing loud and *excessivo*.

23. In successive years Bing brought to the Met many exceptional artists: the incomparable Viennese-born Hilde Güden; the wonderful Mildred Miller, soon to become one of my very good friends; Güden's equally impeccable artist colleague, Lisa Della Casa—what a team they made in *Arabella* in 1956; the baritone Teddy Uppman, one of the most intelligent singers I ever met; Rosalind Elias, another dear friend and versatile musician. Add to that Bing's courageous decision to engage Marian Anderson—although by then in vocal decline—finally breaking the color line at the Met; Nicolai Gedda, a very intelligent, eloquent and stylistically wide-ranging tenor; Martina Arroyo, a supreme though somewhat underappreciated artist; the wonderful Swedish soprano Elisabeth Söderstrom; Christa Ludwig; Jon Vickers; Leontyne Price; Giorgio Tozzi; Franco Corelli; the wonderfully intelligent lyric-dramatic tenor, John Alexander (with whom I had the privilege of working as a conductor many years later in Beethoven's *Fidelio*); and—above all—one of the three or four greatest artists in opera, Maria Callas. The list could go on to include, among others, Elizabeth Schwarzkopf and Luciano Pavarotti—after my time at the Met. It is an extraordinary Who's Who of opera history.

24. One reason I ended up playing Wagner's *Ring Cycle* for the next ten years was that in two of the four *Ring* operas there is something called the "Siegfried Call," one of the two or three most famous horn solos in the entire horn repertory. It is played on stage, not in the orchestra pit, unaccompanied, and is thus one of the more feared or at least most respected horn solos. Anyone who plays it is treated like a soloist, and paid extra money. Richard Moore was very interested in that extra money and insisted, as my

senior, that he would always be assigned to play the Call. And so it was agreed. As a result I had the (to my mind) greater privilege of playing those nearly twenty hours of great operatic music in virtually every one of my next ten years at the Met. (Dick always played the Siegfried Call very well; his outgoing, heroic style was ideally suited to it.)

25. Hotter also managed, unlike many German and Austrian singers, musicians, and conductors, to stay more or less out of Hitler's and the Nazi's grip, although he must have found ways of cooperating with the Nazi cultural authorities, as he was constantly and successfully employed during that entire period, often selected for some of the choicest operatic assignments.

26. Hotter brought the same dramatic, vocal interpretive skills to the role of Jochanaan in *Salomé*.

27. In this early opera, Wagner, for some reason, treated the horn section as if they were second violins, who generally (along with the violas) supply the underlying harmonic accompaniment, either in sustained half notes or in endless rhythmic figures, such as etc., with the result that there just aren't any rests. Three-and-a-half hours of pounding out such rhythmic accompaniments, especially for the higher-lying first horn, is a serious endurance test, since the human lips were not made to take such physical punishment. Wagner learned this lesson, and abandoned this approach after *Dutchman*.

28. It led among other things to his hiring me for quite a number of symphonic recording dates, including Bach's first *Brandenburg Concertos*.

29. Music publications—scores and parts—almost always have some engraving and printing errors. There are simply too many notes in a set of score and parts of a one-and-a-half-hour opera like *Salomé* for there not to be some errors. Page 313 of the *Salomé* score (an average page, picked at random) contains 410 notes, that is, 410 engraved imprints. There are 352 pages in the score. That comes to almost 150,000 printed notes. A complete set of some forty parts would contain another similar amount, and that does not include rests, instrumental nomenclatures, dynamics, and many other notational details. That makes altogether about six million notational imprints. Actually, it's surprising to me that in a huge opera such as Wagner's *Meistersinger*, for example, there are as few mistakes as there are.

30. Although I never took a poll of how the Met orchestra musicians spent their off hours, it was clear to me that on the overnight train trips the orchestra split into three separate, almost evenly divided coteries: one third, all-night card players and gamblers, another third, the all-night boozers, and the last third, those who dutifully went to bed right away. (You could mostly tell who the latter were, because they always wore earplugs, and you'd see them at early breakfast in the dining car.)

31. My father, an ardent Wagnerian, often joked with visitors to the hospital that he had always hoped to end up in Valhalla; here his wish had already come true!

32. During the rehearsals we started hearing rumors that Stravinsky wasn't particularly enthralled with Reiner's conducting and interpretation. The rumors turned out to be fact. But Stravinsky's lack of enthusiasm for Reiner's conducting must be seen in the context of Stravinsky's lifelong, vehement aversion to almost *all* the reigning conductors of the day, and his outspoken disapproval of their interpretations of his music. It was interesting to see how Stravinsky's very personal approach to conducting on the recording quickly—and subtly—crept into our live performances under Reiner's direction.

33. Güden was also a superb Sophie in *Rosenkavalier*, a very special Gilda in *Rigoletto* (because she didn't use that role for exhibiting vocal pyrotechnics, but rather to portray Gilda as an innocent, shy, and essentially tragic heroine), a fascinating Mimi in *La Bohème*, and the perfect Zdenka in *Arabella*, to name just four of her signature roles.

34. It is unfortunate that the Met's recording of *Rake's Progress*—the work's first recording—was taken out of the Columbia catalogue when, a few years later, Stravinsky made a second recording in England with a very good but different cast. I have to assume that the powers that be at Columbia decided that it was commercially unwise to have two recordings of the work competing with each other. The Met's recording of *Rake's Progress* was reissued—finally—in 2007.

35. I was fortunate to also record "Per pieta" with Eleanor Steber and Bruno Walter conducting on a Columbia LP consisting entirely of Mozart arias.

36. The word "tuning" has two meanings, one referring to what is done with an instrument, particularly a keyboard instrument (piano, organ), before it is played upon—as in the phrase "to tune the piano."

The other more general usage refers to what musicians do in adjusting pitches in order to play in tune, presumably on every note they play.

37. I am referring to the third scene in act 2, in which Hagen summons his vassals with powerful blasts on his *Stierhorn* and stentorian cries of *Hoi-ho!* The music is remarkable not only for its sustained *fortissimo* level—five minutes is a long time for a composer to stay at one single dynamic level—but also for Wagner's continual ingenious use of augmented triads and tritones, presumably to musically depict the evil, lawless Hagen.

38. In opera houses such as the Vienna State Opera, and in most of the German opera houses, they don't have an assistant first horn. Their tradition is to employ two first horns. One plays the first two acts, the other the third act. In that case, I know from experience, such players just leave out certain things in that scene, figuring that nobody in the audience, probably not even the conductor, will miss those notes and really know the difference.

39. George Lang switched "from the fiddle to the kitchen," as the jacket on his fascinating memoir, *Nobody Knows the Truffles I've Seen*, proclaims. Written in an entertaining, breezy style, generously sprinkled with typical Hungarian *comédie noire*, it is a remarkable account of a life that more or less began in a forced-labor camp in Hungary, but in America led to major stints as master chef at new York's Four Seasons Restaurant and the Waldorf Astoria, and eventually to inventing a new profession called "restaurant consultant." Along the way, he also brought one of New York's great culinary citadels, the Café des Artistes, back to life.

40. Babai was, like most gypsy violinists, self-taught, one of those inexplicably natural talents who couldn't read music and just improvised with all kinds of fanciful ornamentations on the traditional czardases, verbunks, and horas. He had no idea how he did what he did on a fiddle. One clear indication of how unique and astounding Babai's playing was is the fact that, whenever major violinists such as Heifetz or Milstein or Francescatti were in town, they would without fail pilgrimage to Czardas to listen in wonderment to this musical phenomenon.

41. I don't remember why Janos wanted to record the fearsome Kodály Cello Sonata *twice* in relatively short succession, for two different record labels. I can only recall that one of them was for Period Records, a company that flourished briefly in the late 1940s and early 1950s, and was headed by Peter Bartók, one of Béla Bartók's sons. I believe Period either went bankrupt or its assets were taken over by some other record company. That's how I first came to meet Peter and kept up intermittent contact with him over the next few decades. I also wondered how in the world anybody in 1915 could have played that astonishingly technically daunting and challenging work. One third of the piece is written in the violin's range! I knew many fine cellists in my younger years, but the vast majority thought the Kodály was too difficult, too much work, too hard to learn.

42. Starker and Varga, almost the same age, both big cello talents and students together at the Budapest Academy, had quite naturally become rivals over the years, although in a friendly, civil sort of way. Now one was ensconced as principal cellist at the Met, the other in an identical position at the Philharmonic. Would this quiet rivalry either positively or negatively affect Laçi's decision? As it turned out, it did neither, certainly not in any direct way. Laçi was—and is—a very wise, rational, philosophical person who just doesn't let such matters as personal or professional rivalries, even when instigated by others, get his goat.

43. Giorgio Ghedini (1892–1965), a now mostly unremembered composer, was in the early twentieth century highly regarded for his many excellent editions and orchestral transcriptions of works of Gabrieli, Monteverdi, and Bach, as well as a whole series of concertos for string instruments.

44. I have not held a grudge against Starker, and we have remained good friends through the years. Recently when I gave a concert at Indiana University, Jançi and his wife, Baba, hosted a lavish dinner party in my honor—she is a phenomenal *chef de cuisine*—and among other *spécialités de la maison*, broke out some of his most precious after-dinner liqueurs and spirits. Jançi proudly showed me his huge trilingual library and music collection, with all kinds of valuable first editions and facsimile manuscripts. A great, happy time was had by all. And I know he admires me as a first-rate musician and a great conductor, and wonders why I am not invited to conduct concerts and teach the students at Indiana University in Bloomington about orchestral playing. I also know, despite the anomalous cello *Fantasy* contretemps over fifty years ago, that our personal and professional friendship, not to mention my honorary Hungarian status, endures to this day, and will never be abrogated. Ours is a friendship that is based on a high

degree of abiding mutual respect and the notion that such a relationship ought to allow for disagreement on certain issues.

Neither of us has ever mentioned the *Fantasy* episode to the other, and he has, by the way, true to his word, never played the piece and—so I have been told—never allowed anyone to study the piece with him.

45. A famous work by Schubert, written for a long-obsolete instrument called *Arpeggione*, transcribed variously for viola or cello—a very difficult piece on the cello, with quite a few treacherous passages. In this instance, the performance was going to be in a concerto format, as transcribed by Ghedini.

46. It made me often think about what I had read about the Berlin street and cabaret scene in the 1920s, and about Kurt Weill and Bertolt Brecht's *Die Dreigroschenoper* (*The Threepenny Opera*) and *Rise and Fall of the City of Mahagonny*. Those two guys—geniuses both—must certainly have intimately observed and savored Berlin's notorious nightlife.

47. Montreal was in those days considered the northern tip of the underworld organized crime (read mafia) axis that stretched from Montreal via New York to Florida, with strong links as well to Chicago and Las Vegas. (I'm not making this up; it was all well documented and common knowledge.)

48. It is one thing to consider a harmonic progression or some transitional passage simplistic or crude or amateurish. It is another thing to consider it wrong. But that's what the critics and Mussorgsky's colleagues thought. Which is what led Rimsky-Korsakov to not only "correct" or "improve" hundreds of supposed blunders, but to also recompose entire sections and—even more invasive—add numerous sequences that weren't Mussorgsky's at all; they were pure Rimsky-Korsakov. All of this was well intended. Rimsky-Korsakov merely wanted to be helpful to his colleague—the Russian composers of that time were a very tight-knit group of friends—but he (and the others) did not see and hear what became clear decades later: most of Mussorgsky's compositional unorthodoxies were really the remarkably innovative, modern, virtually clairvoyant visions and explorations of a genius.

I'm sure that Mussorgsky's contemporaries also looked disparagingly at his composing because he led an amazingly chaotic, disorganized, unstable life, plagued by numerous nervous crises, repeated bouts of severe depression, alcoholism, and delirium tremens, all resulting in a pathological inability to finish pieces and an incurable need to flit from one work to another, constantly leaving pieces unfinished.

49. Leinsdorf had joined the Met's conducting staff at age twenty-five in 1937, after having been active in Europe as an assistant to both Toscanini and Bruno Walter, remaining at the Met for five seasons. Upon his return over a decade later, Leinsdorf became in my opinion the de facto music director of the Met, even though he had no such official title. (It was Bing's ironclad policy to *never* offer any conductor the Met's musical directorship, even though Szell, Reiner, and Stiedry all hoped—and more or less expected—to be offered such a position. Bing had to be the all-controlling boss.) Our careers became very fruitfully intertwined through the next twenty years.

50. It is hard to believe that Monteux, in addition to presiding over the legendary 1913 world premiere of Stravinsky's *Rite of Spring*, had also conducted the premieres of *Petroushka* and *Le Rossignol*, Debussy's *Jeux*, and Ravel's *Daphnis et Chloé*, all for Diaghilev's Ballets Russes.

51. At the time RCA Victor had just recently released Monteux's recording of *Sacre* with the Boston Symphony, which clearly was the finest recording of that work to that time, even superior to Stravinsky's 1940 recording with the New York Philharmonic.

52. I've never been impressed with what audiences and critics call charisma; it usually means some kind of ostentation or extrovert overconducting.

53. I feel the same way. When I conduct I know the work very well, though perhaps not every one of its thousands of notes from absolute total memory. (I doubt that any conductor, even someone like Mitropoulos or Ozawa, could ever claim that.) But I love it when, during a performance, I glance intermittently at the score; it is always such a beautiful sight. Because, in fact, every page of a score, especially in what is called a "French score," is different from any other page in its own distinctive layout and design, its own diagrammatic picture of a brief moment in the varied continuity and narrative of a piece of music.

54. *Scheinheilig* signifies being both hypocritical and self-righteous.

55. This is explainable by the fact that among fifteen musicians, playing six different types of instruments, all with varying articulative (speaking) capacities, there are bound to be minutely varying reaction spans. Only the very clearest conductor's direction and tremendous concentration on the part of the players will achieve the desired clean result.

56. I should point out that Louis Krasner, who spent much time in Vienna in the 1930s, engaged, among other things, in his famous undertaking of commissioning a violin concerto from Alban Berg, and visiting often with his brother-in-law, Felix Galimir, leader of the legendary Galimir Quartet, confirmed in great detail everything Burghauser told me.

57. Toscanini's NBC Symphony had just been disbanded by its parent broadcasting company when Toscanini retired in April 1954. It continued for some years as a cooperative orchestra under a new name: Symphony of the Air. Inevitably, its personnel changed over the years with ever less original NBC Symphony players. On the *Swan Lake* date it was only the string section that consisted primarily of former NBC Symphony players: Max Hollander, Samuel Anteck (who was also one of Toscanini's biographers), violist Manny Vardi, cellists Alan Shulman, Harry Shapiro, Benar Heifetz, bassist Philip Sklar. On the other hand, the woodwinds and brass included mostly the crème de la crème of New York's studio musicians: flutists Julie Baker and Paul Renzi, oboist Robert Bloom, clarinetist Bernard Portnoy, the wild genius bassoonist Eli Carmen, hornist Tony Miranda, me on second horn, a wonderful trumpeter and admired friend, Ray Crisara, along with Jimmy Burke (who played all of Tchaikovsky's prominent cornet parts), and my old friend John Clark, tubaist Joe Novotny, and Gloria Agostini, my harpist friend.

Most of these fine musicians are now forgotten. But I mention them—and will continue to cite many outstanding musicians I worked with over the years—to call attention in my small way to the important contribution thousands of musicians made to our American musical culture. I also do so because, in my reading of hundreds of famous musicians' biographies and autobiographies (opera singers, conductors, other musical celebrities), I have yet to read one that pays any tribute to the *musicians*, the workhorses of our music industry, without whose great talents and crucial supportive work the sanctified celebrities could never have achieved their successes and fame—a shameful lapse in my view.

58. "Espiègle" is a short, frothy piano piece by Tchaikovsky, arranged in the late 1890s for orchestra by Ricardo Drigo, an Italian composer living and working in St. Petersburg. It was often included in *Swan Lake* performances as an encore dance number.

59. Isn't there a kind of irony in the fact that this particular recording was issued under a label named Quintessence? I direct the reader to an absolutely invaluable bio-bibliography by John L. Holmes called *Conductors on Record* (Greenwood Press, 1982), an encyclopedic compendium offering concise life histories and recording listings of nearly two thousand conductors. It contains an excellent account of Stokowski's career and in several paragraphs also deals with Stokowski's idiosyncratic, narcissistic, eccentric podium behavior.

60. Coloratura is a vocal style developed in Italy that features high-speed elaborate embellishments and runs, a virtuosic technique that relatively few singers manage successfully.

61. Many prominent opera figures have testified to the same effect. George London, for example, confirmed that in his first encounters with Callas he found her to be a fanatical worker, an absolute stickler for detail, a consummate pro.

62. With Callas a *portamento* was never a technical exigency in order to *get* to a note, known in the trade as the all too common "scoop." With Callas it was always used with great discretion and good taste, strictly to serve a musical expressive purpose. (In my definition—and obviously hers too—a *portamento* must be executed in such a way that it is subtly softer than the two notes it connects.)

63. I can't remember much about the three years I played with that short-lived opera company, except that the orchestra consisted mostly of some Met and New York City Opera personnel, along with good players from various regional opera companies such as Philadelphia, Cincinnati, and Chicago. The casts were generally of quite a high level, featuring singers such as Stella, tenors Armand Tokatyan and Raoul Jobin, basses Nicholas Moscona, and the like. I think the Puerto Rico Opera Festival was an offshoot of the famous Casals Festival.

64. I will proudly assent to having played a major role in bringing ragtime back, but I must add in the interest of full disclosure that at least two other individuals contributed just as importantly to the revival of ragtime: Joshua Rifkin and Vera Lawrence; the former by making some wildly popular recordings of Joplin's music in the late 1960s, the latter by succeeding, after rejections by seventeen major publishers, in getting the complete works of Scott Joplin published by the New York Public Library.

65. Cleva had come to America in 1921 to become assistant chorus master at the Met. After some years as a conductor with various regional opera companies in the 1930s, he returned to the Met in 1950, and worked there until his retirement in 1971.

66. I am convinced that Fausto thought of himself as a second Toscanini, which he wasn't quite. He lacked some of the maestro's fiery energy and intensity, but, like Toscanini, he *really* knew the music, inside and out.

67. Kurt Baum was clearly the one Met singer whom most of us absolutely loathed, both as a singer and as a person. He was significantly more conceited and swaggering than tenors by nature already tend to be. The management felt that Baum was very useful to have around in an opera house because he had an absolutely surefire dramatic tenor voice. He could always be relied upon to belt out a ringing high C that would shake the rafters in the old Met and guarantee a hysterical response from the audience. But that was about the limit of his talent, if that term even applies to what was more vocal calisthenics than artistry. Thank God, Baum was limited mostly to very few roles, Manrico in *Trovatore* and Don José in *Carmen* being the only major roles he was given at the Met, and even then only when someone like Del Monaco or Richard Tucker was not available. An awful, corny actor, Baum would strut and prance around on the stage like the proverbial cock of the roost.

One night Baum really got his comeuppance when, as Manrico, at the end of "Di quella pira" as the final high C drew near, he strode heroically forward, right *onto* the footlights at the very front of the stage (where singers were never to tread), his sword outstretched like a giant phallus, getting ready once again to belt out the big "money note." But this time he decided to go a bit further for his audience. He hit the high C like a clarion trumpet that could be heard out on Broadway and held onto the note well beyond the end of the aria. He was still hanging on to that high C—all alone; we had stopped playing—when the Met's famous golden curtain came down on top of Baum's head, pulling his toupee off and leaving him out there alone, bald-headed, in front of the curtain, with the silliest grin on his face. It was worthy of a Marx Brother's movie. There was great jubilation in the orchestra pit that night.

68. Jacques Offenbach (1819–80) was a true Franco-German, born and raised in Cologne, Germany, but active much of his adult life at the Opéra Comique in Paris. In the course of his career he composed some ninety operas and operettas, all extremely successful.

69. Barber, who in 1948 had written one of his most beautiful, most perfectly realized compositions, *Knoxville: Summer of 1915*, for Eleanor Steber, conceived the leading role of Vanessa for her. The excellent cast also included Rosalind Elias, Nicolai Gedda, and the fine lyric baritone, Giorgio Tozzi.

70. The two men knew each other well since 1927, when Böhm was for four years the chief conductor of the Municipal Opera in Darmstadt. It is amazing how many of Bing's old Darmstadt friends ended up at the Met. Or perhaps it isn't so amazing when you consider the old maxim: It's not what you know, but *who* you know!

71. The Met recently released a recording of a *Don Giovanni* broadcast of February 14, 1959, with Böhm and a superb cast headed by London, Corena, Steber, Della Casa, Valetti, and Uppman. If one wants to get an idea of how very good the Met's performances could be, this is a recording to hear. I also think that Böhm's near-perfect Berlin Philharmonic Mozart Symphony recordings may just be the best ever made of those works.

72. It has irked me for many decades that, although Karajan and Böhm—the two most ardent Hitler sympathizers and among the first German musicians to join the Nazi Party—had in their politically expedient career moves constantly curried favor with Hitler, they were nevertheless quickly and miraculously denazified after the war. Furtwängler, on the other hand, was for many years unjustifiably vilified by much of the music world, although he in fact never joined the Nazi Party, and indeed, as much as possible, quietly fought against Hitler for years, in the process managing to keep many Jewish musicians in his orchestra and to help others escape from Germany. Of the many books written about Furtwängler and his relationship to the Nazi regime, the best, most balanced, most thoroughly researched is *Kraftprobe: Wilhelm Furtwängler im Dritten Reich*, by Fred K. Prieberg (translated by Christoper Dolan and published by Northeastern University Press in 1994 as *Trial of Strength: Wilhelm Furtwängler in the Third Reich*).

73. Over the many years of my career as a guest conductor I have been in hundreds of music director's offices or studies, both in Europe and in the United States, and I have never been in one where I did

not see huge stacks of scores that had been sent to the resident conductor for his consideration. I could sometimes tell that most of them had never been looked at.

74. The opening night performance of *Ballo* that season (1954–55) was an important historic occasion: Marian Anderson's debut as Ulrica (the Negro fortune teller). She was the first black artist to be hired by the Met, which in turn opened the doors for many other African-American artists. It was also that year that Bing engaged Robert McFerrin to sing the role of Amonasro, the Ethiopian king in *Aida*.

75. Although Mitropoulos lived extremely humbly in a few simple rooms in the Great Northern Hotel on Fifty-Seventh Street, just down the street from Carnegie Hall, one of the very few indulgences and personal pleasures he permitted himself was fine dining in the best, most exclusive restaurants in the world. I had never even heard of most of these places. On the other hand, you might also just as easily see him in some hole-in-the-wall, greasy spoon sandwich shop, eagerly downing the most ordinary grub.

76. Mitropoulos grew up in the famous monasteries of Mount Athos, where he came under the spiritual influence of two of his uncles, both highly regarded leading prelates, and where for several years he was torn between conflicting desires of pursuing the life of a musician or the life of a monk.

77. Max Rudolf (1902–95), born in Frankfurt, Germany, built a distinguished career not only in his home country (in Darmstadt and Freiburg) but as well in Italy and Czechoslovakia (Prague), and most impressively in Sweden (Göteborg and Stockholm)—all this before emigrating to the United States in 1940. After his twelve years at the Met as Rudolf Bing's artistic administrator and conductor of all the different Met repertories (German, Italian, French, and contemporary), he became music director of the Cincinnati Symphony, and eventually head of the opera department at Philadelphia's prestigious Curtis Institute. He is also the author of one of the finest books on the art and craft of conducting, *The Grammar of Conducting*. I feel very privileged to have been asked by Max Rudolf's son William to pay tribute to Max in the preface of a very fine book on the conductor: *Max Rudolf: A Musical Life, Writings and Letters*.

78. Max Rudolf, "A Question of Musical Allegiance" (commencement address, Curtis Institute of Music, Philadelphia, PA, May 14, 1981); published in the *Journal of the Conductors Guild* 18, no. 2 (Summer/Fall 1997): 99–104.

79. That occasion must surely have been the first time that nonreading improvising musicians performed with a symphony orchestra, which came to be commonplace a hundred years later with jazz-related works such as my Concertino for Jazz Quartet and Orchestra (in this instance with the Modern Jazz Quartet as the soloist group).

I am also proud of the fact that in 1997 I published in a full set (score and parts) the first authentic urtext edition of Gottschalk's *Night in the Tropics*, also known as *Symphonie Romantique*, based on original manuscripts and the voluminous research by Fred Starr for his biography of Gottschalk, *Bamboula*. (Previous publications and editions of *Night in the Tropics* were simplified, partially sanitized versions—rearrangements actually—of the work.)

80. It is ironic that seven years later, when I was presented with the 1966 Mark M. Horblit Award by the Boston Symphony Orchestra, that same Leinsdorf who fought me tooth and nail for over a year to try to prevent me from leaving the Met Orchestra, now, as the BSO's music director, was able to say in the public presentation at Tanglewood that he had always supported my departure from the Met, so that "Mr. Schuller could devote more time to composing," and that "I wished him well and prayed for his success." Short memory!

81. Around that time it had become widely known that Bing was said to be suffering from Alzheimer's disease, that he had earlier taken up with some lady friend, whom he eventually married, but that a year later the marriage was annulled amid various strange lawsuits, while Bing was declared mentally incompetent. One also learned that he had been seen at the Met at Lincoln Center, alone, in the standing-room-only section, and that the famous Sir Rudolf Bing became involved in a series of very bizarre incidents over the course of many years. He died penniless at age ninety-five in 1997. Sic transit gloria!

Chapter Nine

1. When I list jazz and classical music as two musical mainstreams I want to remind the reader that between sixty and seventy years ago those two species of music characterized our entire American musical

landscape. It was one or the other of those two genres that virtually everyone enjoyed and listened to on the radio and on recordings. The nation's airwaves were permeated with those two musical streams. A genre such as, say, country music, or what was eventually called "Nashville," occupied at the time only a very small part of the overall musical scene. (Even in that genre, groups such as the Bob Wills Texas Playboys and the Light Crust Doughboys were significantly influenced and inspired by jazz.) The enormous stylistic diversity of musical expressions we have nowadays in the United States and in the world, especially in the popular field—what with rock, hip-hop, rap, country rock, many subsets of country music, and all manner of ethnic or vernacular musics (Latino, Cajun, Zydeco, etc.)—was unknown in those earlier days. (Have a look at the sixty constantly expanding categories of music listed as eligible for the Grammys.) The sad thing is that the two genres that flourished more than half a century ago are now almost in the category of endangered species, both of them appealing to only about 3 percent of our population.

2. The title *Birth of the Cool* was eventually given to the entire set of recordings produced in three sessions over a period of one-and-a-half years when the twelve titles were issued on LP in the midfifties. Originally, six of the recordings were issued on ten-inch 78s, but had almost no impact. They were underappreciated and more or less ignored by both the critics and the public. I believe that, aside from the passage of time, during which the Nonet's sound and idiom (evolving primarily out of the stylings of the Claude Thornhill Orchestra) had become more familiar and more assimilated, the main reason for the Nonet recordings' sudden "overnight" success when reissued on LP lies in the brilliance of that title, *Birth of the Cool*, and the high-powered marketing that accompanied the reissue.

It is amazing that, after a great deal of diligent research, inquiry, and speculation over the last half century regarding the Davis Nonet recordings, there is still a considerable amount of confusion, contradictory information, and dubious assumptions. I don't think that I can clarify any of those issues; in fact, I might only add to the confusion. For example, regarding the title *Birth of the Cool*, my memory tells me very clearly that sometime in 1959, when I was living in Queens, in Rego Park, I met by the most curious of coincidences in the hallway leading to my apartment a man whom I had never seen before, coming out of his apartment. As we passed each other, he suddenly turned around and said: "Say! Aren't you Gunther Schuller?" I said: "Yes." "Well, I am. . . . I work for Capitol Records." (Here is where my memory begins to get shaky; I can neither remember what name he gave me, nor the position he said he held at Capitol.) "You were on the *Birth of the Cool* recordings, weren't you?," he continued. "Yes," I said, in considerable puzzlement. As we continued chatting, astonished at the idea of two people living in the same apartment building who both knew about a little-known jazz recording made nearly a decade earlier, he suddenly announced: "Well, you know, I was the one who thought up that title, *Birth of the Cool*."

Would I—could I—make up a story like that? The answer is—no.

3. A good idea of how difficult this Coda was back then in 1948 and 1950—and still is even now, more than half a century later—can be gained from two sources: (1) the 1998 CD release of live performances recorded at the Royal Roost in 1948, which includes two attempts at playing *Moon Dreams*; and (2) a very recent re-creation of *Moon Dreams* (recorded in 2005) by Joe Lovano's Nonet, with some of the very best musicians and myself conducting. Although markedly better performed than on the 1950 *Birth of the Cool* recording, it still displays some degree of strain, of tension, of rhythmic and intonation unease, even after extensive rehearsing and a lot of editing from different takes in order to achieve the best possible performance for the Blue Note recording.

The 1948 Royal Roost live performances of *Moon Dreams* (issued retrospectively on the aforementioned CD release in 1998) rather clearly show the difficulties in the questionable intonation, the considerable lack of understanding or feeling for the atonal harmonies, the rhythmic raggedness, some players clearly getting lost at times. The second of the Roost performances was the worst of the two. (At times I have wished that those Roost performances had never been included in that 1998 CD, although I understand from another point of view that it is important—and historically interesting—to trace through definitive documentation what a struggle it is sometimes for difficult new music (like this *Moon Dreams*) to be played properly, or that a great work of art must sometimes wait decades to be fully realized and appreciated.

4. A&R, short for "Artist and Repertoire," is the title for record company executives who choose and sign up artists and supervise and produce recording sessions. As famous and as celebrated as the *Birth of*

the Cool recordings are, it is strange that there is still, even at this late date and after a great deal of investigative inquiry by a veritable army of jazz record collectors and researchers, no exact knowledge as to who was supervising the 1950 recording session. Some say it was Pete Rugolo, who is said to have been in New York at the time, but really wasn't. Others insist it was Walter Rivers, who worked in New York's Capitol offices. I seem to remember that it was Lee Gillette, but I do not claim absolute certainty.

5. I don't know from what take or takes the issued recording was produced, but I feel it must have been mostly our last take, or it might have been cobbled together from several takes.

6. I have programmed *Moon Dreams* many times over the years in my jazz repertory concerts, and have always had to conduct that Coda. It hasn't really gotten all that much easier since 1950. It can, of course, be done without a conductor, but that would require a lot more rehearsal time, the one thing in the music business there is never enough of.

7. One may wonder why Gil Evans, *Moon Dreams*' creator, did not conduct us through the piece. The fact is that Gil, having gone to visit his sick mother, wasn't even at the session.

8. Mitch Miller, of "Sing Along" fame on TV, was in his earlier life a fine oboist (principal of the CBS Symphony as well as Andre Kostelanetz's broadcast orchestra) and, starting in 1949, the jazz and pop producer for Columbia Records. As such he organized and supervised any number of Sinatra recording sessions. In 1949 he was the prime initiator of the famous *Charlie Parker with Strings* recordings (for the Clef label), where, by the way, he made sure that the arrangements (by his close friend Jimmy Carroll) would prominently feature his own oboe playing, as the only nonstring player on the recording. Another close friend from his days at the Eastman School of Music was the great horn player John Barrows, a relationship that prompted Mitch to add horn sections whenever possible to jazz and pop recording dates; mind you, at a time when the horn was still considered an outsider to jazz. Barrows must have been unavailable for that Sinatra session—Mitch would surely have preferred to hire him—and, as it turned out, Barrows had recommended me.

9. Had I not been tied down at the Metropolitan Opera with a contractual commitment of ten to twelve services per week, I could easily have played on many more recordings.

10. Ironically, parts in actual pitch, i.e., "in C," in which all string parts, flute parts, and most orchestral instruments are notated, turn out to be a transposition for horn players—one of the more annoying ones to boot, so they feel. That's really weird.

11. The other players: Stan Freeman (harpsichord), Mundell Lowe (guitar), Frank Carroll (bass), and Terry Snyder (Drums).

12. John told me often that he owed everything good and important in his upbringing to his two grandmothers, both of his parents having died when he was still very young. I met these two remarkable matriarchs only once, when they came to New York on a brief visit. They were indeed high-grade, handsome, impressive personalities, of the finest imaginable human stock.

13. Let me remind the reader that improvisation is an act of composing, of creating. Jazz musicians who improvise *have* to be creative by definition, have to be composers. Classical musicians do not, and, with rare exceptions, are not.

14. There have been occasional instrumental duets in jazz, as, for example, for two saxophones, or for trumpet and saxophone, or two trumpets. But in most cases those were typically two independent solo improvisations, which *happened* to occur simultaneously—quite a different matter. Also, one shouldn't confuse duets (or duos) with a well-known, long-established tradition in jazz, the so-called battles—not only the battles of the bands, but the battles between, say, two trumpeters or two saxophonists. Those battles were rarely two people playing together, simultaneously, in a duet; rather, they were playing alternating solos in constant back and forth exchanges.

15. Percy had the same perpetual ingratiating smile the last time I saw him, at the 2004 Newport Jazz Festival, a few months before his death.

16. An equally heartfelt compliment was provoked years later by one of my compositions—a huge four-movement symphony for a very large wind ensemble called *In Praise of Winds*—when, after a terrific performance at Florida State University in Tallahassee conducted by James Croft, his fourteen year-old daughter was overheard to tell her dad: "You know, that piece really kicks major ass!"

17. There are already too many conflicting definitions of the term "classical." Thus I rather regret that many black intellectuals and writers on jazz have applied the term to American jazz, as in "our American

classical music." Let jazz just be itself: jazz. It doesn't need the imprimatur of associating with the classical tradition.

18. I find it amusing, in retrospect, to read nowadays all kinds of laudatory commentary about Third Stream—not only its basic concept, but also the music associated with it—by (in some cases) the very same writers and critics who railed against it in the 1960s.

19. They were already quite prevalent as a separate genre in symphony pop concerts and so-called symphonic jazz arrangements or Broadway show tunes, as pioneered most notably by Andre Kostelanetz, Morton Gould, and David Rose in the 1940s.

20. Gigi Gryce unfortunately gave up playing, disappeared from the music scene for many years (partly due to ill health), and then spent the rest of his life teaching music at a high school in the Bronx. I heard later that he had in the meantime composed three symphonies. I wonder whether they were ever performed, and what happened to his many classical and jazz compositions.

21. The transformation and expansion of rhythm and time that Parker singlehandedly developed was to take the standard 4/4 beat of the swing era (1930–45) and double it in pulse and feeling to what metrically and notationally would be called 8/8. But, as if that wasn't dramatic enough, Parker pushed even further in his own playing to another doubling of the tempo and feeling, i.e., to 16/16. In other words, in the 8/8 feeling, the eighth note—not the quarter note—was now the beat, the pulse; and what was between and inside the beats was even more finely sliced and diced. The same with 16/16. In some of his amazing, sharply articulated sixteenth note runs, every note is its own measure, with the full potential of exploring its micro subdivisions. It was Parker's dazzling technique, the lightning speed of his creative mind, that made this particular technical, expressive, stylistic breakthrough possible.

22. I am obviously paraphrasing a conversation that took place fifty-five years ago, and that I couldn't possibly remember verbatim at this late date. I vouch for the authenticity of my account in its essence, because what transpired was so completely surprising to me, so obviously of great import and interest, that it was indelibly imprinted in my memory—at least in its main features.

23. Had he lived a few years longer, his frustrations would surely have been assuaged, for by 1960 all kinds of important breakthroughs had been initiated and achieved, what with the innovations of the likes of Ornette Coleman, Eric Dolphy, Charles Mingus, Cecil Taylor, and—perhaps—even Third Stream.

24. Davis's performance at Newport in 1955 was deemed a comeback because after his early work for some five years as a sideman with various leaders (Charlie Parker, J. J. Johnson, and the Benny Carter, Tadd Dameron, and Billy Eckstine orchestras), and as a leader on the *Birth of the Cool* recordings, he had gone into a decline between 1950 and 1954, due in part to a serious heroin addiction; he appeared in public only intermittently and often with inferior players. Davis's sudden success at Newport in 1955 enabled him to establish his famous quintet with John Coltrane, Paul Chambers, Philly Joe Jones, and Red Garland.

25. John Wilson, *New York Times*, November 21, 1955.

26. The recording also included many striking compositions (such as *Lydian M-1*) based on Russell's *Lydian Chromatic Concept of Tonal Organization*, a theoretical tract first published in 1953.

27. In jazz lingo chords and chord progressions are called "changes," while accompanying is simply shortened to "comping."

28. The situation in the 1940s and 1950s in reality was that many of the younger classical composers were writing in an atonal or twelve-tone or at least highly chromatic language, the breakthrough into atonality, led by Stravinsky and Schönberg, having occurred way back around 1910. Mine was, in other words, a language and technique in wide use for already thirty, forty years; while even the stylistically most advanced players in jazz (with a few rare exceptions such as Cecil Taylor) were basically situated in the late nineteenth-century tonal language, the harmonic language of Ravel and Debussy.

29. Such disguisement as described above is no longer necessary; today there are plenty of players who can function well and improvise readily in any style or harmonic language. The various mergings and overlappings of jazz and classical in their most modern expressions, which began to develop half a century ago (although not necessarily pursued by everyone), became in due course a widely accepted creative option.

30. One of Bill Evan's most poignantly beautiful compositions, *Peace Piece*, is clearly modeled on Frederic Chopin's extraordinary *Berceuse* in D Flat, Op. 57.

31. I am not an expert on Bill Evans's drug addiction in its later stages, but I believe it is common knowledge that, as with many famous jazz musicians of the period (Miles Davis, Sonny Rollins, Jackie McLean, Chet Baker, Lucky Thompson), Bill learned to control his addiction enough to function fully and to perform at a very high professional, creative level.

32. John Lewis was still my main pianist colleague and collaborator. I sometimes thought of involving Cecil Taylor in some of my concerts and recordings; I was very impressed by his first recording in 1956 and its amazing breakthrough improvisations and compositions, which clearly revealed that Cecil was well acquainted with and influenced not only by Duke Ellington and Thelonious Monk but also Igor Stravinsky and Béla Bartók. But then I realized that Cecil was already too individualistic, too much his own man, his own highly original stylist self, to be able—or to want—to perform in some other composer's conceptions. (I also fantasized occasionally about working with Lennie Tristano and Oscar Peterson, but those dreams never became reality.)

33. Miles never had a strong or easy high register, and knowing his limitations in the upper range he rarely ventured beyond a high (concert) C. Nor was there any need for him to do so. The kind of lyric, introspective, sometimes brooding style that he espoused simply didn't call for the spectacular pyrotechnics and *ultissimo* displays for which a Dizzy Gillespie or some of the famous lead trumpeters of the day such as Ernie Royal, Al Killian, or Maynard Ferguson were so famous.

34. I am not claiming that John and I were the only ones to talk to Miles about these matters; I simply don't know. I do know that there were others who were aware of and concerned about Miles's technical problems. One heard talk like that once in a while among colleagues, more in sympathy than as criticism. I also recall and still have in my files a review by John Wilson in which he refers to a stylistic conversion that Miles had undergone in the late 1950s. Wilson speaks of Miles's earlier "fuzzy tone and hesitant presentation," that his tone and style had become "thin and wearing as a steady diet." He mentions a "new Miles Davis" whose playing is "noteworthy for being well-formed, clean edged and deeply imbued with a true jazz feeling." (John Wilson, "Miles Davis's New Group Cuts Deeper into Rock at the Fillmore," *New York Times*, June 19, 1970.)

35. Both Dizzy and Miles spent half a lifetime trying to find the perfect harmon mute. (Surprisingly, they were not manufactured with any great quality or timbral consistency back then.) Miles found his harmon sometime around 1958/1959. That led to *Kinda Blue* and to that very personal, moving poignancy that remained the expressive Miles hallmark for years.

36. Liner notes for Columbia LP CL941, *Music for Brass*, 1957.

37. Brandeis's Creative Arts Festival was originally the brainchild of Adolph Ullman, one of the school's early and most influential trustees. It was with his counsel and assistance that Brandeis University created a School of Creative Arts and subsequently sponsored an annual Creative Arts Festival, the first one held in 1952. Adolph Ullman died shortly before the 1957 festival.

38. Aaron was represented in the festival with an all-Copland concert. He had by that time already invited me several times to lecture at Tanglewood on jazz and its reciprocal relationship with contemporary classical music, a subject that interested him greatly, since he had been one of the first composers to write jazz-influenced concert music as early as the mid-1920s.

39. It is not that I specifically asked for this notation to be considered, nor did anyone else involved in the commissioning project. Improvising on an initially stated theme or motive has always been a great rarity in jazz, but it has come into serious consideration in more recent times.

40. Shapero's title is a play on the Italian composer's name: *monte* = mount (or mountain), *verdi* = green. And much of the thematic-melodic content of the piece is based on melodic lines, which two tenors sing in Monteverdi's original work.

41. I conducted *All Set* many times over the years, and also heard other performers tackle it. It wasn't until the 1990s that I finally was able to generate a performance that really swung. That wasn't so much because of me as it was the lucky circumstance of having available in that concert eight musicians who could really translate Babbitt's jagged, angular, widely leaping lines and unfamiliar atonal harmonies combined with complex rhythms into a relaxed jazz feeling, i.e., into swing. I could conduct with all the swing feeling in the world, but if the musicians were unable to play Babbitt's lines with the basic traditional jazz inflections, with the feeling of spontaneity inherent in jazz, then the piece could in no way become jazz. (Let's remember that a conductor's baton doesn't make a sound.)

The first performance of *All Set* I conducted in which a trumpet player was able to render the part with complete swing and authentic jazz feeling took place in the 1970s. That trumpet player was Doc Severinsen. He may have sweat bullets that night, but he did it!

42. Ross Parmenter, the *New York Times*, review of June 11, 1957.

43. Many years later, in the 1980s, I published *All About Rosie* in my publishing company, Margun Music, in a beautifully engraved edition, in full score and parts. In it I included Bill's solo, which I transcribed from the recording, for all the world to see, to admire, to study and learn from.

44. George Avakian, *Miles Davis and Gil Evans: The Complete Columbia Studio Recordings*, 1966 CD Reissue of the Miles Davis and Gil Evans collaboration, 32.

45. Gil also used such transitional bridges a year later in the *Porgy and Bess* Suite, but not as consistently and in a different manner. Whereas in *Miles Ahead* each of the nine bridging passages is different, each with newly composed material, in *Porgy* Gil used a single four-note phrase in varying instrumentations, but occurring only between movements two and three (in the trombones), and in the middle and at the end of movement nine (in the woodwinds, horns, and brass).

46. There are mighty few instances in the whole history of music where one composer takes an opera and arranges or recomposes it so resplendently that the ensuing offspring proves to be a transcendent enrichment of the parent work, or at least an equally wondrous parallel composition. It is more common that such endeavors demean the original, or, at best, raise the question of whether the undertaking was really worth the effort. In classical music I can think of only one composer capable of achieving such high creative results as to exceed in quality—or at least equal—the original, and that would be Ferrucio Busoni, as for example in his transcriptions of Liszt's *La Campanella* and of any number of works by Johann Sebastian Bach. In this connection, I think I am right in observing that neither Busoni nor Gil Evans was as great a composer as they were recomposers, transcribers, arrangers.

47. There is no intent to place blame here. Everyone involved had good reasons and the best intentions in how various technical, logistic decisions were made. It's just that certain pragmatic priorities took precedence over others that would have assured a better musical result.

48. Though a stereophonic (i.e., two-channel) recording, it was in a sense a precursor of the later developed multitrack, multichannel recording processes.

49. It has been one of my more astonishing discoveries over a long lifetime that many, many musicians, classical or jazz, who play with excellent rhythm and beautifully nuanced expression, suddenly become crude time beaters when they start conducting, their hands waving stiffly in the air, with little sense of steady pacing, and lacking any meaningful gestural expressions.

50. I am not suggesting that Gil wrote a solo trumpet part that was impractical or unidiomatic. Not at all. There are trumpet players who are blessed with the gift of long endurance, who can play the entire part with comparative ease. (But how many of those can play it with Miles's soulfulness and rich, warm sound?)

51. One can already hear in Gil's earliest work as arranger for the Claude Thornhill Orchestra his penchant for giving special consideration to the often-underappreciated lyric, expressive capabilities of brass instruments. It is the kind of thing that almost every other composer-arranger in the world, classical or jazz, would normally write for string instruments, which have a natural capacity for playing sustained, long lyric lines, where the endurance factor doesn't even came into play. But if you don't have access to string instruments, as was the case with all three Davis-Evans collaborations, and if you have an irresistible predilection for slow, expansive tempos (which Gil certainly had), then you have to involve the brass. Gil used this effect often, and about as ingeniously as it can be done, but those sections were some of the very hardest in the entire *Porgy* Suite.

52. I can think of many such passages in the standard classical repertory, where, however, invariably they appear as scored for strings, for whom this type of tremolando effect is very natural and easy to execute. And you don't have to deal with breathing problems. It is a sign of Gil's genial talents that he had the vision—and the courage—to consign such a quintessential string passage to wind instruments; it is also a compliment to us for rendering this exhausting passage so effectively.

53. We three horns rotated our parts around. I recall particularly enjoying playing first on *Summertime*, *Gone-Gone-Gone*, and *There's a Boat Dat's Leaving*.

54. Years earlier I had come to learn that Miles had a bad habit of losing music, which led in the case of some of the *Birth of the Cool* pieces to the recopying of some of the individual parts at least three times.

It also prompted me at the end of that October 1950 Birdland date to take some of the parts for *Moon Dreams* and *Boplicity* home with me, enabling me to perform those pieces frequently in my jazz repertory concerts without having to transcribe them from the recordings.

55. Occasional sporadic performances of some of these transcriptions began to take place, although usually of only two or three movements, never the whole work. Moreover, from what I heard on tape or CD of a few performances, the transcriptions were often quite inaccurate, evidently based more on random assumptions and the transcriber's own inclinations than on what was actually played on the recording. Generally, the resultant performances were, whether by intention or by default, inaccurate renditions, rather free and stylistically remote reinterpretations of the work. One of the more notorious of these attempts at reviving the music took place at the Montreux Jazz Festival a year or so before Miles's death with his participation as soloist; it was not considered very successful.

56. It is one of the strangest cases in the annals of copyright history that for years no one knew or could find out who the rightful copyright owner was—or even if there was one. I don't even know now whether someone has emerged to claim the rights.

57. *Odds against Tomorrow* presents a rather grim tale of a bungled bank robbery attempt, which in turn escalates into fierce racial conflicts when the two protagonists—a racist ex-con and a black nightclub singer—trying to escape the police, chase each other into an oil refinery where they meet their end in the fiery explosions they themselves set off in a gunfight. When found by the police, they have both burned to a crisp—of the same color.

58. Linc notes for United Artists LP UAL4061, *Odds against Tomorrow*, 1959.

59. There were only a few: Ellington's score for Otto Preminger's 1959 *Anatomy of a Murder*, Johnny Mandel's terrific score for Robert Wise's *I Want to Live*, and Louis Malle's 1957 *Ascenseur pour l'échafaud* (with Miles Davis) come to mind.

60. The best way to hear John's music for *Odds* is to hear it on the magnificently recorded United Artists LP—for which the descriptive words "a remarkably pregnant sound," in all four Webster definitions, come easily to mind.

61. In January and February 1960 I helped record two albums of John's music, as hornist on the *Golden Striker* album and as conductor on *Exposure*.

62. A clear indication of how hectic things could get for me and how the two main interests of my life would collide is when I had to wear both of my musical hats within a few hours. On January 15, 1960, I was conducting John Lewis's *Exposure* on an afternoon record date at A&R Studios, and three hours later I was witnessing the world premiere of my *Spectra* with the New York Philharmonic in Carnegie Hall. On February 14, I was again at Carnegie Hall for the New York premiere of my *Seven Studies on Themes of Paul Klee* by the Minneapolis Symphony, and the next morning at ten a.m. tooting my horn in John Lewis's *Piazza Navona* and other pieces from his *Golden Striker* Suite.

63. For me, recording sessions, especially those in jazz, were much more than another gig, or a chance to make some extra money. They were exciting musical events, and they also served an important social function. That's where I first met many of the great musicians with whom I was privileged to work over the years, and who, in many cases, became lifelong friends. I'll mention just a few (in no particular order): Benny Golson, Clark Terry, Leo Wright, Urbie Green, Richard Davis, Britt Woodman, Nick Travis, Doc Severinsen, Louis Mucci, Herb Pomeroy, Harvey Phillips, Mel Lewis, Bernie Leighton, Ed Shaughnessy, Bob Brookmeyer, Ralph Burns, Charlie Persip—and the list could go on for half a page. Alas, when I stopped playing the horn in 1963 and my conducting went much more in the direction of classical concerts—let's face it, conducting does *not* play a central role in jazz performance—I lost contact with that whole exciting recording scene. I miss it terribly.

64. This was all the more surprising to me since I was quite sure that Ran had little specific knowledge of the harmonic-stylistic breakthroughs in the first decade of the twentieth century, as exemplified by Stravinsky's *Rite of Spring* or Schönberg's freely atonal works. But I found out that while Ran had not encountered those specific works, he had been deeply impressed by Prokofiev's *Scythian Suite* and certain pieces by Debussy and Ravel, just as a listener. Yet, as I got to know him and his playing better, I could not help but feel that whatever sounds and harmonies and musical ideas he had picked up from early twentieth-century music, it was indirectly, through some strange intuitive, osmotic process. He also told me that he had become involved with black gospel music in his hometown of Hartford.

65. Ran's playing was so different from what, for example, Cecil Taylor was doing at the time. By the midfifties Cecil had gone completely over into free atonality; there was no harmonic-linguistic mixing or shading.

66. In the midsixties Jeanne Lee emigrated to Europe, living and working very successfully in Germany and Holland. She generally partnered with Günter Hampel, a triple-threat flutist, vibraphonist, and bass clarinetist, who was very prominent in the German jazz avant-garde.

67. The name Edwin was chosen mainly in memory of Marjorie's brother Edwin (Ned), and also as an agnate connection to my brother's name, Edgar, and the constant appearance for at least four prior generations of the name Edward in my father's genealogy, either as a first or middle name.

68. The *Saturday Review of Literature*, founded in 1924, but long since departed, was at the time one of the nation's half-dozen most respected and widely read serious journals; it covered a broad range of subjects and intellectual interests, from literature, the arts, science, and philosophy to morals and ethics. Its contributors and authors were a veritable *Who's Who* of the twentieth century's wisest and most original minds. I was amazed and thrilled to find myself suddenly in such august company.

69. It was on one of Elwood's programs that I first heard the remarkable protojazz music of James Reese Europe, on recordings from 1914. Europe was a very gifted black composer-conductor whose music I championed extensively with my ragtime ensemble in the 1970s and 1980s.

70. WBAI, part of the Pacifica network of FM radio stations, was in effect a forerunner of National Public Radio; it had extensive programming of classical music and jazz, programs on art, literature, and cinema, outspoken political commentaries—in general, what was in those days still proudly called educational or public service radio. WBAI was fearless in tackling highly controversial subjects and became quickly known as *the* radical station in New York.

71. It wasn't long before Nat ran out of shelf space for his vastly expanding LP collection. The never-ending flow of recordings began to take over, room by room, the entire floor space of his spacious West Twelfth Street apartment. My most vivid memory of many visits to Nat's place is facing this vast array of row upon row of vertically stacked LPs, and how precarious it was to negotiate one's way through this veritable ocean of recordings. Although Nat had devised an ingenious design of walkways by which one might reach most of his collection, these paths were of necessity so narrow that there was just *barely* enough room for two feet side by side.

72. It was a result of John Hammond's generosity in lending me from time to time some of his most precious 78 recordings that I was able to finally hear the music of the remarkable Texas-based Alphonso Trent orchestra from the late 1920s, and to do a whole one-hour program on Trent. After Marshall's death his library of books and records became the nucleus of what is now undoubtedly the biggest jazz record collection in the country, housed in the Institute of Jazz Studies founded by Stearns at Rutgers University in Newark, New Jersey.

73. This led to some *very* interesting and revealing juxtapositions of contemporaneously composed works, as for example when I reached the years 1908 and 1909, both incredibly rich, productive years in music. I spent six or seven weeks on just those two years, there was so much great music written then, and so much of it was also available on recordings. As for interesting, striking juxtapositions, at one point for the year 1908 I played and discussed side by side Webern's *Passacaglia* Op. 1 and Ravel's *Gaspard de la nuit*, Webern being considerably more advanced than Ravel, even though only eight years younger than Ravel. Some of the juxtapositions for the year 1909 were even more dramatic; I was able to program Rachmaninov's *Isle of the Dead* alongside Schönberg's atonal opera *Erwartung* and Mahler's Ninth Symphony, which lay stylistically somewhere between the two.

74. Compare that with today, when the standard classics exist in dozens, sometimes hundreds, of recorded versions, and an immense amount of modern music—certainly of the first half of the twentieth century, the period I was dealing with—is now generously available.

75. The woodwind quintet, at the time still more or less nonexistent as a standardized performing group, began to develop rather impressively after World War II, flourishing as a parallel counterpart to the two-hundred-year-old string quartet. In 1950 in the United States there couldn't have been more than three or four standing woodwind quintets, part-time for sure, whereas there are now in this country alone two hundred woodwinds quintets, more or less permanently engaged, with several hundred

recordings (LP and CD) to their credit—all a far cry from the time when Joe Marx and I founded our Metropolitan Quintet in 1947.

I remember standing at the stage door of Carnegie Hall chatting with Rainier De Intinis, second horn of the New York Philharmonic, when the question of woodwind quintets came up. I'll never forget, after a ten-minute argumentative discussion about the validity and practicality of the woodwind quintet, his deathless pronouncement: "Believe me, Gunther; there's no future in the woodwind quintet." Yeah, sure!

76. Many, many bandleaders in the early history of jazz did this all the time, although occasionally allowing the actual composer, or sometimes even the arranger, to be listed as a co–copyright owner.

77. It is understandable then that Buster's music had over a period of time taken on a slight rock and roll tinge, as the performances we ultimately recorded also show. One could argue that I was a decade too late to present Buster Smith in his earlier, personal artistic style.

78. Willis James was a highly respected folklorist and head of the music department at the Spelman-Morehouse Colleges in Atlanta, Georgia.

79. The resultant series of LP albums, recorded over a period of three years beginning in 1956, were made in the congenial acoustics of the Berkshire Music Barn. Along with the MJQ they featured guest artists such as Jimmy Giuffre, Jim Hall, Sonny Rollins, and Bob Brookmeyer.

80. For all of Marshall's many virtues and talents as a jazz historian, there was one aspect of his presence in Lenox that many of us found somewhat irritating. He had developed the habit at dinnertime of selecting someone to interview, whether on the faculty or a famous visiting guest (say, Freddie Hubbard or Artie Shaw), to pick their brains as eventual fodder for his voluminous writings on the history of jazz. You never knew when Marshall, having finished *his* dinner early, would descend upon you—regardless of whether you were still eating or not, or in the middle of a conversation with your family—and start asking you a series of questions on subjects that, as a nonmusician English professor, perplexed him. Most of us tolerated these intrusions, either out of respect for his stature in the field or because there was something endearing in his pleading manner and the persistence with which he pursued his goal. I have to think that he gathered an enormous amount of priceless information from the remarkable reservoir of talent gathered at the School of Jazz.

81. Ornette's legendary engagement at the Five Spot in 1959 didn't occur until after his stint at the Lenox school; he played at the Five Spot for five weeks to packed houses, constantly drawing in even classical celebrities such as Leonard Bernstein, Morton Gould, and Lukas Foss.

82. One of the things that always amazed me about Ornette's playing is that when he played some wild, convoluted *fortissimo* run or figure—the kind that with some other players would sound edgy, harsh, and aggressive—it remained basically gentle and lyrical. There was always something tender and warm, like a shining inner light deep inside. One could hear the same kind of thing in Charlie Parker's playing—when he was in full control.

83. John Wilson, "Music: A Third Stream of Sound," *New York Times*, May 17, 1960.

84. John Wilson, now alas a forgotten figure in the arts—well, one of the arts anyway: jazz—combined as quite no one else did the highest journalistic standards of impartial reporting with remarkable knowledge and balanced judgment. That he was able to exercise his talents on the staff of a leading newspaper such as the *Times* always seemed to me a kind of "minor miracle"—to use his own phrase. Wilson was a quiet, modest, unassuming man; his coverage of New York's jazz scene in those halcyon days had a most important, though I suspect even then not fully appreciated, role in the city's cultural life.

85. The program consisted of "Little Blue Devil" (a movement from my 1959 *Seven Studies on Themes of Paul Klee*, in a reduced orchestration I made especially for the occasion); *Variants on a Theme of Thelonious Monk* (that theme being *Criss Cross*); *Conversations* for string quartet and a jazz quartet of vibraphone, piano, bass, and drums; *Abstraction*, a twelve-tone piece written expressly for Ornette Coleman as soloist, backed by an ensemble of string quartet, two basses, guitar, and drums—as the most complex and advanced piece on the program we played it twice, once before the intermission, once after; *Transformation*, for an MJQ-type of quartet, five winds, and harp, in which Bill Evans was the main soloist; *Variants on a Theme of John Lewis* (*Django*) for string quartet—one variation featuring an extended viola solo (probably a first in jazz)—two basses, guitar, two flutes (one, Eric Dolphy, doubling on alto sax), vibraphone, and drums; and finally, "Progression in Tempo," a reduced instrumentation of the last movement of my *Concertino for Jazz Quartet and Orchestra*.

86. John Wilson, "Music: A Third Stream of Sound," *New York Times*, May 17, 1960; Whitney Balliett, *New Yorker*, May 28 1960. Whitney Balliett wrote about jazz subjects in the *New Yorker* for more than twenty years, consistently contributing some of the most insightful, broad-gauged, and eloquent commentary—Balliett is also a fine poet—on the jazz scene, both past and current, that many of us have ever read. I don't think that anyone ever equaled his astounding ability to create through words and verbal imagery the uncanny effect for the reader of actually hearing the music. He was also the prime initiator and advisor for what is arguably the finest jazz program ever produced on television, "The Sound of Jazz," broadcast live in 1957 on CBS.

87. I cite these favorable comments not as an exercise in self-congratulation, but rather to provide a reminder of how professional critics can write such totally divergent and oppositional evaluations of the same artistic event. It ought to make one wonder whether they were actually at the same concert.

88. Mingus played cello as well as bass and loved the instrument. Sometime in the forties he struck up a close friendship with the cellist Jackson Wiley (also conductor of the Springfield Symphony Orchestra in Ohio), and wrote the solo cello part for Wiley.

89. This statement may sound exaggerated, unless one realizes that real jazz, truly creative jazz, of whatever style or vintage, was never featured all that much on the three television networks. What often passed for jazz—by Lawrence Welk or some innocuous hotel dance band—was really a kind of watered down, easy-listening music, especially once rock and roll and rhythm and blues began to compete for the average American's attention. And the jazz that one *could* hear and see with some regularity in the first ten years of television was gradually reduced to a minimum and eventually dropped altogether. By the midsixties jazz—and, by the way, classical music—had disappeared entirely from the networks' offerings. It is a depressing fact that in the last forty years no jazz—no Ellington, no Parker, no Miles Davis, no Coltrane, no MJQ—has been heard or seen on network television. That has been left to public television and cable.

90. That "near perfect" caveat is necessary in the interest of full disclosure, to indicate that the one blemish on the program was Roy Eldridge's playing. In his solos he floundered around, missing and cracking far too many notes—that can happen, one can have a bad day—but worse, he was in one of his show-off grandstanding moods, squeezing out endless passages of high notes—what he called his "whistling notes"—that usually contribute nothing meaningful to an improvised solo. (Up in that highest altissimo register you cannot play melodic lines or create worthwhile phrase shapes; all you can do is squeeze out some high notes and hang on for dear life.)

One can hear the *Sound of Jazz* on LP and see the entire show on DVD.

91. Nat and Whitney had devised an ingenious format for the program that would allow an unusually large number of musicians (thirty-two in all) to be presented in a limited amount of time (one hour). The basic idea was to couple a standard fifteen-piece band with a more or less equal number of guest soloists, the orchestra available as needed to accompany the soloists, the soloists split up selectively into various-sized smaller groups and in different stylistic contexts. Thus, in the six separate segments of the show, Coleman Hawkins, for example, ended up playing with both the Basie band and Red Allen's septet, as well as with Billie Holiday's group; and Pee Wee Russell played not only with Allen but also with the Jimmy Giuffre Trio. The beauty of this design was that it solved the problem of how to accommodate in one relatively short program such a large number and diversity of musicians, and the size and variety of instrumental groups could range all the way from the power of a big band to the intimacy of a quiet little trio.

92. The rehearsals were primarily for the camera crew to line up their shots and different positions; they were not for the musicians. One does not rehearse improvisations.

93. Young had not been well for several years; he had been drinking to excess, eating little, in and out of hospitals, all of which resulted in prolonged bouts of depression.

94. Gunther Schuller, *The Swing Era* (New York: Oxford Univesity Press, 1991), 561.

Chapter Ten

1. Peggy Glanville-Hicks, *New York Herald Tribune*, November 29, 1954.

2. In that regard I believe that there are two types of composers—substitute, if you wish, painters, writers, choreographers, filmmakers—typified most clearly by Mozart and Beethoven. Mozart composed

with an extraordinary ease and fluency. By the time he wrote out his music it was fully conceived in all its details and required no further revising or editing. His manuscripts, with only rare exceptions, are free of revisions or corrections. I believe that this Mozartean type is always composing, always creating—subconsciously, subliminally—and at a certain point the composition is simply ready to be written down, to be notated, just as a baker knows at a certain point that the bread is ready to come out of the oven. The opposite type is exemplified by Beethoven. Much of the time he had to first put things down on paper, then study, revise, and rework it, until he too was satisfied. Beethoven's voluminous sketchbooks are a testimony to how laborious and prolonged this process could be, stretching occasionally over years. And yet even then, if we look, for instance, at the manuscript of his Fifth Symphony, which he wrote out in full score, presumably when he was satisfied that the piece was ready for performance, he still made quite a few last-minute revisions, some of them crucial to the final result. In many of Beethoven's manuscripts the margins of score pages are filled with rewritings, both minor and major—the kind of thing you almost never see in a Mozart manuscript. The two differing creative processes do not in themselves determine the greatness of the ultimate product or lack thereof. It is simply that certain extraordinarily talented composers write their music very quickly, while others, equally gifted, compose at a more measured pace.

3. As it turned out, the *Symphony for Brass and Percussion* was the first work composed for large brass ensemble in almost 350 years, specifically since the days of Giovanni Gabrieli and his magnificent compositions for antiphonal brass choirs written for St. Mark's Cathedral in Venice.

4. Among the selected players I remember particularly the trumpeters Ralph Kessler (my friend from *Annie Get Your Gun*), Arthur Statter (principal trumpet of the New York City Opera), and my Met colleague Harry Peers, and among the horns, Dick Moore and Silvio Coscia, John Clark, and Bill Barber (from the Claude Thornhill Orchestra and the Miles Davis *Birth of the Cool* nonet.) ISCM was a European-founded organization that had several branches in the United States, the main one in New York.

5. Jay Harrison, *New York Herald Tribune*, November 2, 1956.

6. While I greatly admired much of Hindemith's work and in particular his brilliant writing for brass instruments, his style and musical language were so far removed from mine that such a correlation as Harrison tried to make, with the further imputation that my Symphony was influenced by some of Hindemith's compositions, is simply not tenable. Besides, I very much resented Hindemith's attacks in his writings on twelve-tone and Schönberg.

7. John Rockwell, *New York Times*, November 23, 1981. Several other critics, knowing of my involvement with jazz and Third Stream, also assumed that my *Brass Symphony* must be jazz, and then praised it for that, or, alternatively, denounced the work for not being jazzy enough. Sometimes you just can't win.

8. Robert Sabin, *Musical America* (June 1955).

9. Carter Harman, *New York Times*, April 2, 1951.

10. Carl Apone, *Pittsburgh Press*, December 24, 1981.

11. Christopher Norris, *Music and Musicians*, November 21, 1973; Alvin Lowery, *Brass World*, September 1, 1974.

12. My sudden acquaintance with the *Corsair* Overture—a work that, like so many of his remarkably original compositions, was hardly ever performed in those days—also triggered my making an arrangement of it for band (or wind ensemble). This occurred in 1951 at the instigation of Ray Dvorak, director of bands at the University of Wisconsin, Madison, whom I had first met when I was working there with Rudolf Kolisch and the Pro Arte Quartet. Dvorak premiered the arrangement in Madison in 1953. It was my first venture into the concert band field, to be followed over the years by many more works in that genre.

13. Bill Barber also played the all-important tuba part in the first two New York performances of my *Symphony for Brass and Percussion*, as well as on the 1956 Columbia recording.

14. Young composers nowadays have it much easier than my generation half a century ago. In those days there was no music reproducing technology available by which you could record ad hoc a performance of your music, unless you were quite wealthy and could acquire very expensive, complex-to-operate and cumbersomely heavy professional disc cutting equipment, the kind that usually only record companies and radio stations could afford to own. When I was teaching composition at Tanglewood in the 1960s and 1970s, I used to marvel that, after the invention of magnetic tape and cassettes, every young composer, even nineteen- and twenty-year-olds, seemed to have already a dozen of their pieces available on cassette. Ten to fifteen years earlier we could enjoy no such luxury.

15. We had all heard rumors of Barzin's haughty, arrogant behavior at auditions for music director positions with various orchestras (including the New York Philharmonic), as a result of which—so the rumors went—he never attained any of them. Barzin certainly didn't allow himself such immature behavior with the seasoned professionals of the New York City Ballet Orchestra.

16. Nearly fifty years later I pulled off a similar stunt by assembling another handpicked orchestra: the best New York players from the Philharmonic, the Met, the Orpheus Chamber Orchestra, Broadway shows, various high-level chamber groups, including string quartets (normally, famous quartet players *never* take recording dates), and some of the most seasoned freelancers. But this time it was for a commercial recording date of six three-hour sessions of Beethoven's Fifth and Brahms's First Symphony. That recording was made for my own label, GM Recordings, and cost me over $150,000.

17. Eight years later I wrote an even more ambitious piece for my instrument, this time for sixteen horns, in the configuration of one solo horn with three accompanying horn quintets. That work was premiered in 1960 and beautifully recorded in 1961 by the Los Angeles Horn Club, with the incomparable Vincent de Rosa as the lead player.

18. Our mutual friend, Victor Aitay, was the first to play the orchestral version of the *Recitative and Rondo*, with the Chicago Symphony, Seiji Ozawa conducting.

19. Ernest Bour was born in Strasbourg, France, and for most of his career was the conductor of all three orchestras in that city. In 1964 he succeeded Hans Rosbaud as music director of the Southwest German Radio Orchestra in Baden-Baden, Germany.

20. Darmstadt attracted every important critic, music publisher, and radio station program director from every country in Europe. It was thus a place where an unknown composer could be discovered by the shakers and makers in the new music business.

21. David Drew, *Score* 10 (December 1954).

22. David Drew soon became not only a dear and much admired friend but also one of England's most influential, most important critics and writers on music, serving for many years as music critic of *The New Statesman*, then editor of publications at Boosey & Hawkes. His writings in the 1957 symposium *European Music in the Twentieth Century*, and on Stravinsky, Messiaen, and Kurt Weill, are widely regarded as among the most perceptive on those subjects. Drew also commissioned me to reorchestrate Kurt Weill's opera *The Royal Palace* (from a printed piano score), the orchestra score and parts having been destroyed by the Nazis.

23. One of them, Hugo Distler, committed suicide in 1942, unable to cope with the increasing bouts of spiritual depression caused by the ordeals of life in wartime Berlin and the constantly intensifying harassments of the Nazi authorities. Others such as Erwin Schulhoff and Viktor Ullmann perished in Hitler's concentration camps.

24. I conducted the first (and to my knowledge only) performance of *Zeitmasse* in the United States so far, with my Metropolitan Quintet. I was able to conduct that piece—not play the horn—because Stockhausen had used the English horn in *Zeitmasse* instead of a horn.

25. A few months later I heard from Milton Babbitt that a few of his Princeton mathematician colleagues, who had been sent some of the formulas and equations Stockhausen had presented in those lectures, stated that they were variously wrong; in plainer words, they were "pretty lousy mathematics."

26. I must add that during my first visit to Darmstadt in 1954 Gigi and I had almost immediately taken to each other, becoming the best of friends, mutually admiring colleagues, as close as brothers. I loved his music of that period, with its ardency of expression, its innate Italian lyricism—this despite all the rhythmic and textural complexity in his music. I thought of him as a twelve-tone Verdi.

27. I had several times told him about Elliot Carter's most recent work, particularly his First String Quartet and his brand new Orchestra Variations (1955), and about Milton Babbitt's exciting work in serialism and combinatoriality—neither of whom he reacted to with any particular interest.

28. When I say "Wagnerian" I am thinking of a number of demands Stockhausen made of the music world. Among the earliest of these were his repeated requests of the city of Cologne and the West German Radio (his employer) in 1956 and 1957—even of the German federal government—to build him a concert hall on the other side of the Rhine, in Neuss (a suburb of Cologne)—his Bayreuth—that could house his new three-orchestra work *Gruppen* and other supersized ensembles that he was already dreaming of composing.

29. Now retired from the Berlin Philharmonic, Wolfgang is today a much sought after, dedicated, and beloved teacher at Berlin's famed Hochschule, still bristling with youthful energy and enthusiasm for his work and for music. I love him.

30. The Donaueschingen Festival is the oldest music festival in the world devoted exclusively to contemporary music. Founded by Prince Max Egon von Fürstenberg in 1913 as the Society for the Friends of Music, it gave its first contemporary music concerts in 1921, right on the Fürstenberg estate. A quick idea of how adventurous its programming was from the outset can be gained from the fact that its very first concert started with a String Quartet by the Czech quarter-tone composer, Alois Hába. (The twenty-five-year-old Paul Hindemith was the festival's artistic director.) The name Donaueschingen is derived from the place: this little town at the eastern edge of the Black Forest is the cite of the Danube's spring, *Donau* being the German name of that mighty river, while *Eschingen* is medieval German for "coming out" or "exiting."

31. Strobel (1898–1970) was one of the most cultivated, artistically sophisticated persons —extraordinarily knowledgeable in *all* the arts—I have ever met, and I am proud to have known him as a friend. Margie and I were fortunate to team up with Strobel and his wife several times on our various European travels, especially in Italy (Venice and Florence) and France (Colmar, Strasbourg, and Reims.) We benefitted so much from Strobel's deep familiarity with all manner of cultural and artistic monuments and sights-to-see. He was the kind of person who knew, say, in Venice, the whereabouts of *every* significant, not-to-be-missed artistic and historic creation, be it a cathedral, church, museum, palace, painting, or famous statue. He would elaborate in amazing detail on the sight's historic importance and artistic uniqueness.

Strobel was also a major gourmet, who introduced us to half a dozen of the most famous, legendary restaurants in Alsace-Lorraine, especially Aux Armes de France in the medieval town of Riquewhir and L'Auberge de L'Ille in Illhäusern—restaurants that we never failed to revisit on our many trips to Europe. Strobel had gotten to know this region of France very well during his seven-year (1939 to 1946) exile from Germany. (Although not Jewish, his work as a music critic and editor of journals devoted primarily to modern music made him very much *persona non grata* in Hitler's Germany.) During his years of exile he managed to savor every artistic, epicurean, gastronomic attraction that Alsace-Lorraine had to offer: its legendary vineyards (going back to Roman times); its numerous Gothic cathedrals, churches, and cloisters; its many perfectly preserved medieval villages, like Riquewhir, perched precariously on a thousand-foot cone-shaped hill; not to mention Strasbourg's famous foie gras. How fortunate we were to be the beneficiaries of his extensive cultural adventures and explorations.

32. That was my first encounter with Nono's music. At the time I had barely heard of him. I had read only a tiny bit about him in a *Melos* article about the up-and-coming European composers like Boulez, Stockhausen, Nono, and Berio. I could not have anticipated that one year later Nono would become one of my closest composer friends.

33. Darmstadt didn't get around to getting involved with jazz until a decade or so later. That is not to be confused with the Darmstadt Institute for Jazz, a very worthy organization not related to the Darmstadt Summer Course Festival.

34. I met Rolf Liebermann at that time, and was surprised to find that he was amazingly well informed about the work that John Lewis and I were beginning to do in New York. Over a long dinner he pretty well picked my brain clean about the latest developments in avant-garde jazz. It is a matter of history that ten years later Rolf commissioned me to write a jazz opera for his Hamburg State Opera, which eventually premiered there in 1966.

35. German men, I had often observed, always wore very conservative, stiff-looking, button-down suits, typically in a dullish brown or grey, and cut in a certain unvaried formal way, never anything casual. It made them appear always to be in some kind of uniform. Bodies were held straight up and erect, seemingly incapable of any flexibility or relaxation. (Fortunately this all changed after the 1950s, once Germany's famous postwar economic boom occurred, and Italian and French couture invaded Central Europe.

36. Lothar and I became great friends. He retired from the orchestra in the 1980s (after some forty years), and died in 2005. At that first meeting with Lothar in September 1953, I could never have anticipated that Mitropoulos would be, just a few years later, beginning in 1956, conducting several of my works with the Cologne Orchestra, and that after Dimitri's death I would be commissioned by the

Cologne Radio Orchestra to write an *In Memoriam* piece for Mitropoulos, with Lothar as soloist, a work called *Threnos*—in effect a concerto for solo oboe and orchestra.

37. By way of contrast, Margie greatly admired Fritz's wife, Ingrid, and after our first visit with the Straubs—of only two or three days—Margie, always the generous giver of presents, presented Ingrid with a beautiful, elegant bra of the latest American fashion as a good-bye present, to which Ingrid responded with not one, not two, but three thank-you letters.

38. Probably Straub got the idea from Serge Koussevitzky's famous enterprise in the early 1900s of sailing up and down the Volga River, conducting orchestral concerts in the towns along the way.

39. Little did I know that a dozen years later I would be writing an opera based on the same Kafka material, except translated into an American racially contentious setting, for the famed Hamburg State Opera, commissioned by Rolf Liebermann and stage directed by none other than Günther Rennert.

40. It is a well-known phenomenon that occasionally in dress rehearsals the most inspired, the most resolved, the most relaxed performance takes place that is never matched in the actual concert.

41. For you jazzers, I think that this pizzicato bass passage is the first "walking bass" line in the history of music—the Symphony was composed in 1828.

42. Furtwängler had often featured the young Boris Blacher's works in performances and on recordings, even as far back as the 1930s.

43. I mentioned earlier that the Schubert rehearsal that morning offered several of those truly transcendent musical experiences we encounter every once in a while. If readers inferred that therefore the evening's concert performance did not come up to the same lofty level, they have inferred correctly. I know that to be the case from two sources: one was Martin Ziller, who, when I met him a day or two later, told me that the concert somehow lacked the relaxed ease of the rehearsal, "that sublime magic" as he put it, "that you heard that morning, and that we all felt. It just wasn't there in the evening." The other testifying source is the recording made of that September 15, 1953, concert, issued some thirty years later, where one can hear in the undeniably grand sweep of the whole performance an occasional untidyness in ensemble and a certain roughness, as contrasted with the inspired elegance of the rehearsal's rendition. Balances are a bit askew at times, although maybe I should ascribe that to the way the concert was originally recorded. The timpani and trombones are, for example, seriously overrecorded, while the strings (violins/violas and cellos/basses) are underrepresented.

I must mention that there are a number of famous musical artists—Furtwängler, Celibidache, Mitropoulos, Callas, to name just a few—who are victims of certain record company's practices of posthumously issuing unauthorized live performances that rarely come up to the high standards of commercial, officially approved recordings.

44. In the late 1940s and throughout the 1950s three million refugees fled to West Berlin from all parts of East Germany. In that same period, before the 1961 erection of the Berlin Wall and the fearsome Checkpoint Charlie divide of the two Berlins, travel for East Germans, especially Communist Party members, was still relatively unencumbered. But eventually the leaders of the DDR (*Deutsche Demokratische Republik*) became so alarmed by the greatly increased flow of East Germans fleeing to the West that much more restrictive travel limits were instituted, both for their own citizens and for foreigners. Once the wall went up, the authorities really cracked down on any and all travel. My relatives in Burgstädt, for example, were no longer allowed to cross over to West Berlin, which now meant that if westerners wanted to visit in the DDR, they would now have to brave the harassing searches and chicaneries of the East German border guards, whose mandate was to make the border crossing as unpleasant and as terrifying an experience as possible. (On one of our crossings to East Berlin in 1966, my wife was detained in isolation on some phony pretext for *five hours*, while my children and I could not, for that entire time, find out what had happened to her.)

45. Schmitz's many monographs, most prominently among them his *Prinzipien der Aufführungs-praxis alter Musik* (*Principals of Performance Practices in Older Music*), quickly became standard works on baroque ornamentation techniques. He was one of the first to write intelligently about the variables and differences in baroque embellishment concepts in Germany, France, and Italy, and in different periods during the baroque century (roughly 1650–1750). Even more important, he was one of the first to argue against the excessive nineteenth-century romanticization of Bach's and Handel's works.

46. The designation *Deutsche Demokratische Republik* (German Democratic Republic) is a pathetic misnomer for a government that was anything but democratic or based on republicanism. It was dictatorially controlled by the Soviet Union.

47. It is ironic that the same year (1989) the Berlin Wall came down, Chinese armored vehicles, five thousand miles away from Berlin, broke up the antigovernment demonstrations in Tiananmen, where freedom-fighter students tried to defy the oncoming tanks. I remember that Saturday evening not only for that historic event in China's and the world's recent history, but also as the evening on which I was privileged to bring to life, with the help of thirty-one terrific musicians, Charles Mingus's masterful *Epitaph*, at New York's Lincoln Center.

48. The huge eighteen-foot Roland statue (erected in 1412) celebrates the hero of the twelfth-century epic poem, *The Song of Roland*. It is one of the sights that every German feels bound to see sometime in his or her life. Roland, the son of Charlemagne, the most revered hero of very early German history, gave his life after all his companions had been killed in a tremendous battle defending the empire against an army of one hundred thousand Saracens (Moslems).

49. The two extra changes of train that day were particularly annoying, since in both cases the connecting trains arrived and departed not on the same platform but on tracks two or three platforms apart. This meant that we had to run down some stairs and through a tunnel to get to the other platform. With each of us lugging suitcases around, that was not an especially pleasant experience, knowing also that in the case of a tight connection a German train is bound to leave on time! (Again, German thoroughness.)

50. In my youth all horns played in America were made in Germany, either by Alexander in Mainz or by Schmidt and Kruspe in two small towns near the Czech border, not far from where my father was born. Alexander was the most popular of the German horns; the company had been founded in Mozart's time, in the late 1780s. The Conn and Yamaha horns came in very strong just around the time that I stopped playing horn, in the early 1960s.

51. Yes, Margie was still plugging away at the horn, off and on. She told me she'd practice a lot more if she had her own instrument, rather than having to borrow mine when I happened not to need it—which was a fairly rare occasion. (I became the school's horn teacher in 1950, replacing my teacher Robert Schulze upon his retirement.)

52. It could have been the model for the Met's second act *Meistersinger* scenery depicting a street scene in fifteenth-century Nürnberg with houses in the north Bavarian *Fachwerk* style.

53. We all know that Mozart wrote mountains of extraordinarily beautiful and perfectly constructed music. But it is doubly amazing that even music that he wrote under duress, as is the case with the music he was required to compose every week while in the employ of Archbishop Colleredo, whom he hated, is still so absolutely sublime.

54. But I didn't hear any alphorns as we toured Switzerland, as Brahms did in 1874, prompting him to send Clara Schumann a (now famous) postcard with a notation of the tranquil horn call he heard, off in the distance, and later interpolated in the last movement of his First Symphony.

55. I must add that a really fine player can vary and change his tone, if willing and if talented enough. The differing demands of different musical and stylistic situations can be easily met on the horn, in fact more easily than on most other instruments. But alas, there are far too many horn players who have—and play with—only one sound, what I call the store-bought sound, regardless of what music or style or performance tradition they are involved with. And it isn't a matter of the *type* of instrument. It is rather a matter of the ear, of the mindset, as quite a few players have ably demonstrated over the years. I am thinking of someone like Dale Clevinger, principal horn of the Chicago Symphony for over forty years, who can change the size and timbre of his tone in all the colors of the rainbow at will.

I most humbly include myself in that elite company of players. It was one of my great pleasures as a horn player to subtly vary the tone and even the size of the tone between, say, French opera literature (as in Debussy or Massenet) and, on the other hand, Strauss and Wagner. In Mozart I used still another lighter sound, akin to the old, late eighteenth-century hand horns—all without changing horns or mouthpieces.

56. There is a rationalization for such a flurry of mistakes to occur, an effect I have had occasion to observe many times in my experiences as an orchestral player and conductor. Every once in a while one or two unexpected mishaps will suddenly trigger a whole chain reaction of further accidents. I have never

heard any logical explanation for this phenomenon, except that it is perhaps parapsychologically or tele-pathetically induced, and that, typically, it spreads quickly like a virus.

57. Heurigen is a very young wine, the first to appear shortly after the grape harvesting, and is very popular in and unique to Austria.

58. On the bus ride to Granada the next day on the coastal road south we saw full confirmation that there was a German invasion in progress, for all directional signs, seaside shops, and booths were without exception in German. Even the streets were temporarily renamed in German. (The Germans were the first after the war to discover that Spain was the best tourist buy in Europe.)

59. I have often conjectured that my love of turquoise, aquamarine, and the whole range of blue-greens (my favorite colors) goes back to my first impressions of that El Greco painting.

60. The Edinburgh Festival had been created in 1947 at the instigation of Rudolf Bing (three years before he came to the Met as general manager), initially to find an additional outlet for the Glyhde-bourne Opera Festival, of which he had been the artistic director in the prewar years.

61. Loch Linnhe is the longest and widest loch in Scotland. Linked by the Caledonian Canal to Loch Ness, it bisects central Scotland, and provides the only fully navigable, direct through-passage from the Atlantic Ocean to the North Sea.

62. The reader may remember that it was Barbirolli who, when I was ten, had recommended that I join the St. Thomas Choir School, which, as it turned out, was the beginning of my musical career.

63. Everybody in New York seemed to know that I was willing to find and buy good instruments in Europe and bring them back to America, at no extra charge beyond the actual cost of the instrument. That year I had requests, in addition to the horns, to find a contrabassoon for Ralph Lorr, which I did at the Heckel Factory, and in Mainz, a bass clarinet for Sidney Keil, and—even more esoteric—a contrabass valve trombone. This was for Louis Counihan, our great Met bass trombonist, so that he could play the parts that Verdi wrote for that particular instrument in some of his operas—*Otello*, for example—in authentic sound and style. I found such an instrument, still fairly common at the time in Italian municipal bands, in Flor-ence. It had at its upper extension an elaborately florid, decorative, fearsome looking dragon's head.

64. I never did write the Savonarola opera, partly because other more practical composition proj-ects and paying commissions left no time to work on it—one doesn't knock off an opera in a couple of months—and partly because, when I once mentioned my Savanarola plan to Mitropoulos, he burst out: "Oh, no! Don't do *that*!" He was so adamantly negative about the idea—although he never mentioned why—that it really intimidated me.

65. Thirty years later I received the same treatment by the same orchestra; the arrogant, hateful behavior was once again not only directed at me but also at Girolamo Arrigo's fine *Tre occasioni*, which I was to premiere.

66. It was on the same concert that I first heard the remarkable music of Andrzej Panufnik, his *Noc-turne* for orchestra, which the orchestra seemed to like; at least they tolerated it and, paradoxically, played it rather well.

67. I am convinced that Rothenburg is the most photographed place in Germany, and that more post-cards are sent from there than from any other German town or village its size.

68. Freifrau translates into Free Lady (or Dame, as such nobility or honored persons are called in England), a title given to former royalty living now as private persons. Gebsattel was also the name of her castle. The one night we stayed there she kindly gave us pointers on especially worthwhile things to see in the Habsburg castles, and regaled us for several hours with stories about some of her most illustrious ancient ancestors and relatives.

69. I must not fail to mention that our delightful two-week vacation in Franconia was bounteously enlivened by our discovery of the region's excellent white wines, dry and wonderfully tart—virtually unknown in the United States.

70. Stravinsky had several times in previous works used altered or limited string sections, most nota-bly in the *Symphony of Psalms* of 1930 (only cellos and basses), also in his Concerto for Piano and Wind Instruments (only basses), and, of course, in the *Symphonies of Wind Instruments* (no strings at all).

71. Robert Craft writes in one of his books on Stravinsky that when he and the composer were in Greece in 1956 and came to visit the famous crossroads where Oedipus murdered his father, the road on which they were approaching the site happened to be under repair. Suddenly, dynamite explosions

directly ahead sent huge piles of rocks and earth tumbling down on the road, the power of the detonation nearly sending their car into the ditch aside the road. Stravinsky, only half in jest, interpreted this as the belated, unforgiving anger of the ancient Greeks for his setting *Oedipus Rex* in Latin rather than Greek.

72. Composers usually write their dedications in words in their native language above the title of the work or on the title page.

73. By contrast, quite a number of composers influenced by Stravinsky's stylistic conversion, most notably Aaron Copland, experimented with the twelve-tone technique but abandoned such efforts after one or two attempts. Copland's *Connotations* is probably the best example of his brief excursion into twelve-tone land. But it turned out to be a delimited encounter, as he quickly returned to the relatively safer ground of tonally based neoclassicism.

74. One has only to listen, albeit with open ears, to the works of any number of twelve-tone composers, past and present—Schönberg, Berg, Webern, Stravinsky, Perle, Kirchner, Schuller, Babbitt—to hear how they evolved entirely different personal, original styles quite distinguishable aurally from one other.

75. In many performances, both on recordings and live, this was not always the case. The composer had

written: [musical notation, *pp*], but many string sections

were used to playing the same passage with a 6/8 feeling, i.e.,

[musical notation]

76. The Vienna Philharmonic was founded in 1842, the same year the New York Philharmonic was created.

77. I have previously spoken of Mitropoulos's inability to respond in any effective manner to such verbal assaults, given his unassuming, humble, near-masochistic nature. The sad reality is that the type of verbal volley that Freiberg shot back at Dimitri in that rehearsal could never have happened with any other conductor I can think of. But it happened rather frequently with Dimitri.

78. During Mitropoulos's last two or three years as music director of the New York Philharmonic, I witnessed such skirmishes quite often, particularly one acrimonious attack by Harold Gomberg, principal oboist of the orchestra, that was extremely upsetting to Mitropoulos, especially since he had considered Gomberg his friend and supporter.

79. Wagner was one of the most meticulous notators of horn mutings ever, clearly and most effectively distinguishing between hand-stopping (marked "+" over the note) and *gedämpft* (muted). 80. Von Einem was also chairman of the Artistic Advisory Board of the Salzburg Festival.

81. However, a few years later, Schlee and UE did get my *Seven Studies on Themes of Paul Klee*, my most successful and most popular, most often played work.

82. Karajan did eventually perform *Unanswered Question* and even recorded it in the early 1980s.

83. More than two decades later, my wife and I were finally able to visit all those places and more in a two-week spree covering the entire region of northwestern Austria (Salzburg) and southeastern Bavaria.

84. Gastein was so close to Salzburg that after spending a little too much time with Burghauser—he had so many fascinating tales to tell about the whole Nazi history in Austria, the many shenanigans going on in the Vienna Philharmonic, the backstage intrigues at the Opera—I was able to take a taxi back to Salzburg on time to see the O'Neill play.

85. Fritz Winter (1905–76) studied with Klee and Kandinsky at the Bauhaus in Dessau, already a very high recommendation. The Nazis condemned his work as decadent, forbidding him to paint. He served in the German army, and was a Russian prisoner until 1949.

86. It was a commonplace in tape editing to have, for example, a note-perfect performance, except that the tempo was too slow or too fast; or a brief insert had to be spliced into a longer take, yet the insert's tempo didn't quite match. Adjusting the tempo mechanically solved the problem. The two alternatives were to leave the blemish of a wrong tempo in and hope that no one would notice it, *or*—completely impractical—to hire the conductor and orchestra back for another session to correct the problem.

87. If Jelly Roll Morton could call himself the inventor of jazz—the "Edison of Jazz"—I think I can rightly call myself the inventor and apostle of Third Stream.

INDEX

Simultaneously the memoir of a famed composer, conductor, and music educator, and an important historical sourcebook on the American musical scene during the twentieth century and into the twenty-first, the autobiography of Gunther Schuller chronicles the first thirty-five years of this multifaceted and expansive figure's life and work.

Schuller began composing music at an early age and joined the Cincinnati Symphony as its principal French horn player at seventeen. Since then he has written for many major orchestras and his work has earned him a MacArthur Foundation "genius" grant and the Pulitzer Prize in 1994 for his large-scale orchestral piece *Of Reminiscences and Reflections*. Perhaps most famously, Schuller contributed to a new stylistic blend between progressive factions of jazz and classical music, for which he coined the term "Third Stream," and collaborated with John Lewis, the Modern Jazz Quartet, and others in the development of this style.

In this exquisitely detailed reflection on his early influences, experiences of good fortune, and powers of curiosity, as well as firsthand recounting of critical cultural and social moments and major movers of the jazz world, Schuller here beautifully and honestly narrates a life lived beyond limits.

Gunther Schuller has been on the faculties of the Manhattan School of Music and Yale University; he was, for many years, head of contemporary music activities (succeeding Aaron Copland) and director of the Tanglewood Music Center, and served as president of the New England Conservatory. He is the author of *The Swing Era: The Development of Jazz, 1930–1945*; *Early Jazz: Its Roots and Musical Development*; *The Compleat Conductor*, and many other books.

Joan Shelley Rubin is professor of history at the University of Rochester. She is the author of *The Making of Middlebrow Culture* and *Songs of Ourselves: The Uses of Poetry in America*, and coeditor of *A History of the Book in America, Volume V: The Enduring Book*. She is currently writing a set of essays about cultural mediation in postwar America, of which her introduction to this book is one.

"Gunther Schuller's monumental memoir instantly becomes an essential document of twentieth-century music, in all its forms. Time and again Schuller has been witness to the making of history, and more than once he has made it himself. No future account of the period will be able to ignore this book."

—Alex Ross, *The New Yorker*

"Schuller's memoir is a revelatory document, a chronicle of a passionate life in music, rich in factual detail. As the narrative evolves we are immersed in a rich cultural world of music and musicians from all stylistic persuasions as well as references to art, literature, philosophy, and romance. What a life he has led . . . and continues to lead."

—Yehudi Wyner, Pulitzer Prize–winning
composer, pianist, conductor

"With laser-sharp ear, a sensitive, fertile, creative mind, endless energy, and a generous, humane soul, Schuller, a true Renaissance man, who during his lifetime (so far!) mastered seven musical careers, shares this first installment of his riveting memoir.

Rich with critical understandings and vivid testimonies, ranging from witty to determined to intriguing, this is a must-read-book for musicians, scholars, and music lovers.

Allow me to harvest just one example from Schuller's myriad chronicles that hold deep value: as we look back at music history, in roughly one hundred years, those who study and continue the cross-fertilization between jazz and classical music will find here a treasure-trove of essential insights.

Bravissimo Maestro Schuller!"

—Augusta Read-Thomas, composer, University Professor,
University of Chicago

"One of the world's great musical explorers guides us to some of the most interesting corners of American music history. Schuller gives a back-stage look not only at his emergence as a composer but also such history-making events as the 1949 Fritz Reiner–led *Salome* at the Metropolitan with Ljuba Welitsch and recording sessions in the '50s with Miles Davis, John Lewis, and Ornette Coleman."

—Travis Rivers, senior music correspondent,
Spokesman-Review, Spokane, Washington